DATABASE SYSTEMS

The Complete Book

Second Edition

Hector Garcia-Molina
Jeffrey D. Ullman
Jennifer Widom

PEARSON

Authorized adaptation from the United States edition, entitled *Database Systems: The Complete Book, Second Edition,* ISBN 9780131873254, by Hector Garcia-Molina, Jeffrey D. Ullman and Jennifer Widom, published by Pearson Education Inc.© 2009, Pearson Education Inc.

Indian Subcontinent Version

ISBN: 978-93-325-1867-4

First Impression, 2014
Fifth Impression, 2016
Sixth Impression

Published by Pearson India Education Services Pvt Ltd, CIN: U72200TN2005PTC057128, formerly known as TutorVista Global Pvt Ltd, licensee of Pearson Education in South Asia.

Head Office: 7th Floor, Knowledge Boulevard, A-8(A), Sector 62, Noida 201 309, UP, India. Registered Office: 4th floor, Software Block, Elnet Software City, TS-140,Block 2 and 9, Rajiv Gandhi Salai, Taramani, Chennai 600 113, Tamil Nadu, India. Fax: 080-30461003, Phone: 080-30461060, www.pearson.co.in, Email: companysecretary.india@pearson.com

Printed in India by India Binding House..

Table of Contents

The Worlds of Database Systems

Databases today are essential to every business. Whenever you visit a major Web site — Google, Yahoo!, Amazon.com, or thousands of smaller sites that provide information — there is a database behind the scenes serving up the information you request. Corporations maintain all their important records in databases. Databases are likewise found at the core of many scientific investigations. They represent the data gathered by astronomers, by investigators of the human genome, and by biochemists exploring properties of proteins, among many other scientific activities.

The power of databases comes from a body of knowledge and technology that has developed over several decades and is embodied in specialized software called a *database management system*, or *DBMS*, or more colloquially a "database system." A DBMS is a powerful tool for creating and managing large amounts of data efficiently and allowing it to persist over long periods of time, safely. These systems are among the most complex types of software available.

1 The Evolution of Database Systems

What is a database? In essence a database is nothing more than a collection of information that exists over a long period of time, often many years. In common parlance, the term *database* refers to a collection of data that is managed by a DBMS. The DBMS is expected to:

1. Allow users to create new databases and specify their *schemas* (logical structure of the data), using a specialized *data-definition language*.

From Chapter 1 of *Database Systems*, Second Edition. Hector Garcia-Molina, Jeffrey D. Ullman, Jennifer Widom.

2. Give users the ability to *query* the data (a "query" is database lingo for a question about the data) and modify the data, using an appropriate language, often called a *query language* or *data-manipulation language*.

3. Support the storage of very large amounts of data — many terabytes or more — over a long period of time, allowing efficient access to the data for queries and database modifications.

4. Enable *durability*, the recovery of the database in the face of failures, errors of many kinds, or intentional misuse.

5. Control access to data from many users at once, without allowing unexpected interactions among users (called *isolation*) and without actions on the data to be performed partially but not completely (called *atomicity*).

1.1 Early Database Management Systems

The first commercial database management systems appeared in the late 1960's. These systems evolved from file systems, which provide some of item (3) above; file systems store data over a long period of time, and they allow the storage of large amounts of data. However, file systems do not generally guarantee that data cannot be lost if it is not backed up, and they don't support efficient access to data items whose location in a particular file is not known.

Further, file systems do not directly support item (2), a query language for the data in files. Their support for (1) — a schema for the data — is limited to the creation of directory structures for files. Item (4) is not always supported by file systems; you can lose data that has not been backed up. Finally, file systems do not satisfy (5). While they allow concurrent access to files by several users or processes, a file system generally will not prevent situations such as two users modifying the same file at about the same time, so the changes made by one user fail to appear in the file.

The first important applications of DBMS's were ones where data was composed of many small items, and many queries or modifications were made. Examples of these applications are:

1. Banking systems: maintaining accounts and making sure that system failures do not cause money to disappear.

2. Airline reservation systems: these, like banking systems, require assurance that data will not be lost, and they must accept very large volumes of small actions by customers.

3. Corporate record keeping: employment and tax records, inventories, sales records, and a great variety of other types of information, much of it critical.

The early DBMS's required the programmer to visualize data much as it was stored. These database systems used several different data models for describing the structure of the information in a database, chief among them the "hierarchical" or tree-based model and the graph-based "network" model. The latter was standardized in the late 1960's through a report of CODASYL (Committee on Data Systems and Languages).[1]

A problem with these early models and systems was that they did not support high-level query languages. For example, the CODASYL query language had statements that allowed the user to jump from data element to data element, through a graph of pointers among these elements. There was considerable effort needed to write such programs, even for very simple queries.

1.2 Relational Database Systems

Following a famous paper written by Ted Codd in 1970,[2] database systems changed significantly. Codd proposed that database systems should present the user with a view of data organized as tables called *relations*. Behind the scenes, there might be a complex data structure that allowed rapid response to a variety of queries. But, unlike the programmers for earlier database systems, the programmer of a relational system would not be concerned with the storage structure. Queries could be expressed in a very high-level language, which greatly increased the efficiency of database programmers. SQL ("Structured Query Language") is the most important query language based on the relational model.

By 1990, relational database systems were the norm. Yet the database field continues to evolve, and new issues and approaches to the management of data surface regularly. Object-oriented features have infilrated the relational model. Some of the largest databases are organized rather differently from those using relational methodology. In the balance of this section, we shall consider some of the modern trends in database systems.

1.3 Smaller and Smaller Systems

Originally, DBMS's were large, expensive software systems running on large computers. The size was necessary, because to store a gigabyte of data required a large computer system. Today, hundreds of gigabytes fit on a single disk, and it is quite feasible to run a DBMS on a personal computer. Thus, database systems based on the relational model have become available for even very small machines, and they are beginning to appear as a common tool for computer applications, much as spreadsheets and word processors did before them.

Another important trend is the use of documents, often tagged using XML (eXtensible Modeling Language). Large collections of small documents can

---

[1] *CODASYL Data Base Task Group April 1971 Report*, ACM, New York.

[2] Codd, E. F., "A relational model for large shared data banks," *Comm. ACM*, **13**:6, pp. 377–387, 1970.

serve as a database, and the methods of querying and manipulating them are different from those used in relational systems.

1.4 Bigger and Bigger Systems

On the other hand, a gigabyte is not that much data any more. Corporate databases routinely store terabytes (10^{12} bytes). Yet there are many databases that store petabytes (10^{15} bytes) of data and serve it all to users. Some important examples:

1. Google holds petabytes of data gleaned from its crawl of the Web. This data is not held in a traditional DBMS, but in specialized structures optimized for search-engine queries.

2. Satellites send down petabytes of information for storage in specialized systems.

3. A picture is actually worth way more than a thousand words. You can store 1000 words in five or six thousand bytes. Storing a picture typically takes much more space. Repositories such as Flickr store millions of pictures and support search of those pictures. Even a database like Amazon's has millions of pictures of products to serve.

4. And if still pictures consume space, movies consume much more. An hour of video requires at least a gigabyte. Sites such as YouTube hold hundreds of thousands, or millions, of movies and make them available easily.

5. Peer-to-peer file-sharing systems use large networks of conventional computers to store and distribute data of various kinds. Although each node in the network may only store a few hundred gigabytes, together the database they embody is enormous.

1.5 Information Integration

To a great extent, the old problem of building and maintaining databases has become one of *information integration*: joining the information contained in many related databases into a whole. For example, a large company has many divisions. Each division may have built its own database of products or employee records independently of other divisions. Perhaps some of these divisions used to be independent companies, which naturally had their own way of doing things. These divisions may use different DBMS's and different structures for information. They may use different terms to mean the same thing or the same term to mean different things. To make matters worse, the existence of legacy applications using each of these databases makes it almost impossible to scrap them, ever.

As a result, it has become necessary with increasing frequency to build structures on top of existing databases, with the goal of integrating the information distributed among them. One popular approach is the creation of *data warehouses*, where information from many legacy databases is copied periodically, with the appropriate translation, to a central database. Another approach is the implementation of a mediator, or "middleware," whose function is to support an integrated model of the data of the various databases, while translating between this model and the actual models used by each database.

2 Overview of a Database Management System

In Fig. 1 we see an outline of a complete DBMS. Single boxes represent system components, while double boxes represent in-memory data structures. The solid lines indicate control and data flow, while dashed lines indicate data flow only. Since the diagram is complicated, we shall consider the details in several stages. First, at the top, we suggest that there are two distinct sources of commands to the DBMS:

1. Conventional users and application programs that ask for data or modify data.

2. A *database administrator*: a person or persons responsible for the structure or *schema* of the database.

2.1 Data-Definition Language Commands

The second kind of command is the simpler to process, and we show its trail beginning at the upper right side of Fig. 1. For example, the database administrator, or *DBA*, for a university registrar's database might decide that there should be a table or relation with columns for a student, a course the student has taken, and a grade for that student in that course. The DBA might also decide that the only allowable grades are A, B, C, D, and F. This structure and constraint information is all part of the schema of the database. It is shown in Fig. 1 as entered by the DBA, who needs special authority to execute schema-altering commands, since these can have profound effects on the database. These schema-altering data-definition language (DDL) commands are parsed by a DDL processor and passed to the execution engine, which then goes through the index/file/record manager to alter the *metadata*, that is, the schema information for the database.

2.2 Overview of Query Processing

The great majority of interactions with the DBMS follow the path on the left side of Fig. 1. A user or an application program initiates some action, using the data-manipulation language (DML). This command does not affect the schema of the database, but may affect the content of the database (if the

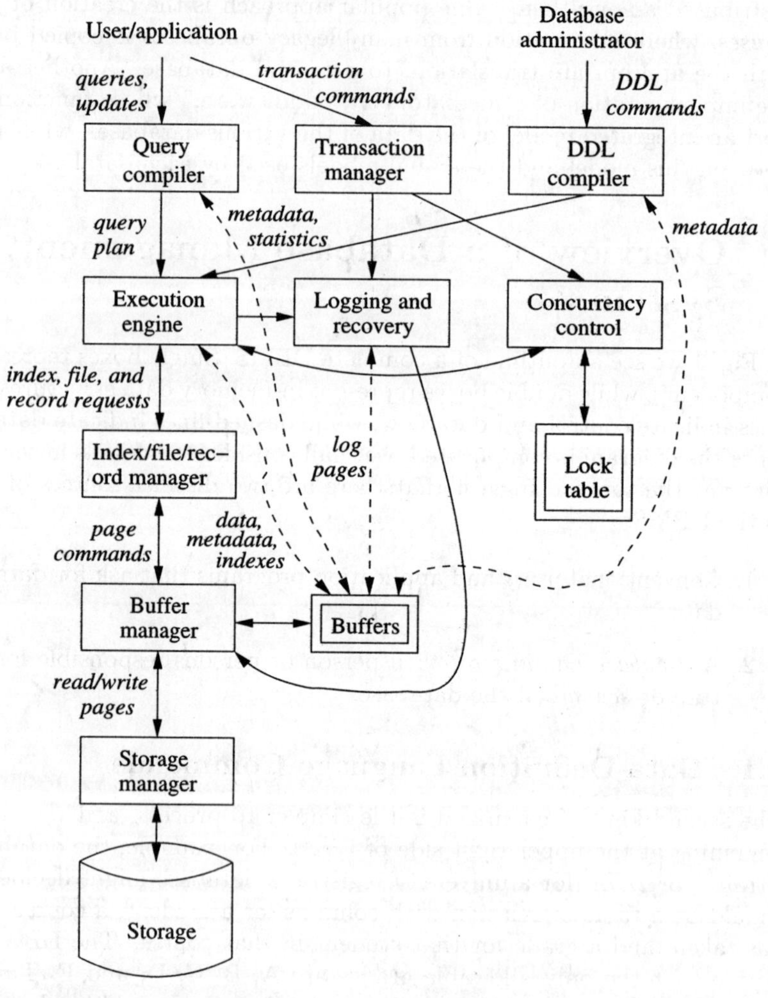

Figure 1: Database management system components

action is a modification command) or will extract data from the database (if the action is a query). DML statements are handled by two separate subsystems, as follows.

Answering the Query

The query is parsed and optimized by a *query compiler*. The resulting *query plan*, or sequence of actions the DBMS will perform to answer the query, is passed to the *execution engine*. The execution engine issues a sequence of requests for small pieces of data, typically records or tuples of a relation, to a resource manager that knows about *data files* (holding relations), the format and size of records in those files, and *index files*, which help find elements of data files quickly.

The requests for data are passed to the *buffer manager*. The buffer manager's task is to bring appropriate portions of the data from secondary storage (disk) where it is kept permanently, to the main-memory buffers. Normally, the page or "disk block" is the unit of transfer between buffers and disk.

The buffer manager communicates with a storage manager to get data from disk. The storage manager might involve operating-system commands, but more typically, the DBMS issues commands directly to the disk controller.

Transaction Processing

Queries and other DML actions are grouped into *transactions*, which are units that must be executed atomically and in isolation from one another. Any query or modification action can be a transaction by itself. In addition, the execution of transactions must be *durable*, meaning that the effect of any completed transaction must be preserved even if the system fails in some way right after completion of the transaction. We divide the transaction processor into two major parts:

1. A *concurrency-control manager*, or *scheduler*, responsible for assuring atomicity and isolation of transactions, and

2. A *logging and recovery manager*, responsible for the durability of transactions.

2.3 Storage and Buffer Management

The data of a database normally resides in secondary storage; in today's computer systems "secondary storage" generally means magnetic disk. However, to perform any useful operation on data, that data must be in main memory. It is the job of the *storage manager* to control the placement of data on disk and its movement between disk and main memory.

In a simple database system, the storage manager might be nothing more than the file system of the underlying operating system. However, for efficiency purposes, DBMS's normally control storage on the disk directly, at least under some circumstances. The *storage manager* keeps track of the location of files on the disk and obtains the block or blocks containing a file on request from the buffer manager.

The *buffer manager* is responsible for partitioning the available main memory into *buffers*, which are page-sized regions into which disk blocks can be transferred. Thus, all DBMS components that need information from the disk will interact with the buffers and the buffer manager, either directly or through the execution engine. The kinds of information that various components may need include:

1. *Data*: the contents of the database itself.

2. *Metadata*: the database schema that describes the structure of, and constraints on, the database.

3. *Log Records*: information about recent changes to the database; these support durability of the database.

4. *Statistics*: information gathered and stored by the DBMS about data properties such as the sizes of, and values in, various relations or other components of the database.

5. *Indexes*: data structures that support efficient access to the data.

2.4 Transaction Processing

It is normal to group one or more database operations into a *transaction*, which is a unit of work that must be executed atomically and in apparent isolation from other transactions. In addition, a DBMS offers the guarantee of durability: that the work of a completed transaction will never be lost. The *transaction manager* therefore accepts *transaction commands* from an application, which tell the transaction manager when transactions begin and end, as well as information about the expectations of the application (some may not wish to require atomicity, for example). The transaction processor performs the following tasks:

1. *Logging*: In order to assure durability, every change in the database is logged separately on disk. The *log manager* follows one of several policies designed to assure that no matter when a system failure or "crash" occurs, a *recovery manager* will be able to examine the log of changes and restore the database to some consistent state. The log manager initially writes the log in buffers and negotiates with the buffer manager to make sure that buffers are written to disk (where data can survive a crash) at appropriate times.

2. *Concurrency control*: Transactions must appear to execute in isolation. But in most systems, there will in truth be many transactions executing

The ACID Properties of Transactions

Properly implemented transactions are commonly said to meet the "ACID test," where:

- "A" stands for "atomicity," the all-or-nothing execution of transactions.
- "I" stands for "isolation," the fact that each transaction must appear to be executed as if no other transaction is executing at the same time.
- "D" stands for "durability," the condition that the effect on the database of a transaction must never be lost, once the transaction has completed.

The remaining letter, "C," stands for "consistency." That is, all databases have consistency constraints, or expectations about relationships among data elements (e.g., account balances may not be negative after a transaction finishes). Transactions are expected to preserve the consistency of the database.

at once. Thus, the scheduler (concurrency-control manager) must assure that the individual actions of multiple transactions are executed in such an order that the net effect is the same as if the transactions had in fact executed in their entirety, one-at-a-time. A typical scheduler does its work by maintaining *locks* on certain pieces of the database. These locks prevent two transactions from accessing the same piece of data in ways that interact badly. Locks are generally stored in a main-memory *lock table*, as suggested by Fig. 1. The scheduler affects the execution of queries and other database operations by forbidding the execution engine from accessing locked parts of the database.

3. *Deadlock resolution*: As transactions compete for resources through the locks that the scheduler grants, they can get into a situation where none can proceed because each needs something another transaction has. The transaction manager has the responsibility to intervene and cancel ("rollback" or "abort") one or more transactions to let the others proceed.

2.5 The Query Processor

The portion of the DBMS that most affects the performance that the user sees is the *query processor*. In Fig. 1 the query processor is represented by two components:

1. The *query compiler*, which translates the query into an internal form called a *query plan*. The latter is a sequence of operations to be performed on the data. Often the operations in a query plan are implementations of "relational algebra" operations. The query compiler consists of three major units:

   (a) A *query parser*, which builds a tree structure from the textual form of the query.

   (b) A *query preprocessor*, which performs semantic checks on the query (e.g., making sure all relations mentioned by the query actually exist), and performing some tree transformations to turn the parse tree into a tree of algebraic operators representing the initial query plan.

   (c) A *query optimizer*, which transforms the initial query plan into the best available sequence of operations on the actual data.

   The query compiler uses metadata and statistics about the data to decide which sequence of operations is likely to be the fastest. For example, the existence of an *index*, which is a specialized data structure that facilitates access to data, given values for one or more components of that data, can make one plan much faster than another.

2. The *execution engine*, which has the responsibility for executing each of the steps in the chosen query plan. The execution engine interacts with most of the other components of the DBMS, either directly or through the buffers. It must get the data from the database into buffers in order to manipulate that data. It needs to interact with the scheduler to avoid accessing data that is locked, and with the log manager to make sure that all database changes are properly logged.

3 References

Today, on-line searchable bibliographies cover essentially all recent papers concerning database systems. Thus, we shall not try to be exhaustive in our citations, but rather shall mention only the papers of historical importance and major secondary sources or useful surveys. A searchable index of database research papers was constructed by Michael Ley [5], and has recently been expanded to include references from many fields. Alf-Christian Achilles maintains a searchable directory of many indexes relevant to the database field [3].

While many prototype implementations of database systems contributed to the technology of the field, two of the most widely known are the System R project at IBM Almaden Research Center [4] and the INGRES project at Berkeley [7]. Each was an early relational system and helped establish this type of system as the dominant database technology. Many of the research papers that shaped the database field are found in [6].

The 2003 "Lowell report" [1] is the most recent in a series of reports on database-system research and directions. It also has references to earlier reports of this type.

You can find more about the theory of database systems than is covered here from [2] and [8].

1. S. Abiteboul et al., "The Lowell database research self-assessment," *Comm. ACM* **48**:5 (2005), pp. 111–118. `http://research.microsoft.com/~gray/lowell/LowellDatabaseResearchSelfAssessment.htm`

2. S. Abiteboul, R. Hull, and V. Vianu, *Foundations of Databases*, Addison-Wesley, Reading, MA, 1995.

3. `http://liinwww.ira.uka.de/bibliography/Database` .

4. M. M. Astrahan et al., "System R: a relational approach to database management," *ACM Trans. on Database Systems* **1**:2, pp. 97–137, 1976.

5. `http://www.informatik.uni-trier.de/~ley/db/index.html` . A mirror site is found at `http://www.acm.org/sigmod/dblp/db/index.html` .

6. M. Stonebraker and J. M. Hellerstein (eds.), *Readings in Database Systems*, Morgan-Kaufmann, San Francisco, 1998.

7. M. Stonebraker, E. Wong, P. Kreps, and G. Held, "The design and implementation of INGRES," *ACM Trans. on Database Systems* **1**:3, pp. 189–222, 1976.

8. J. D. Ullman, *Principles of Database and Knowledge-Base Systems, Volumes I and II*, Computer Science Press, New York, 1988, 1989.

The Relational Model of Data

This chapter introduces the most important model of data: the two-dimensional table, or "relation." We begin with an overview of data models in general. We give the basic terminology for relations and show how the model can be used to represent typical forms of data. We then introduce a portion of the language SQL — that part used to declare relations and their structure. The chapter closes with an introduction to relational algebra. We see how this notation serves as both a query language — the aspect of a data model that enables us to ask questions about the data — and as a constraint language — the aspect of a data model that lets us restrict the data in the database in various ways.

1 An Overview of Data Models

The notion of a "data model" is one of the most fundamental in the study of database systems. In this brief summary of the concept, we define some basic terminology and mention the most important data models.

1.1 What is a Data Model?

A *data model* is a notation for describing data or information. The description generally consists of three parts:

1. *Structure of the data.* You may be familiar with tools in programming languages such as C or Java for describing the structure of the data used by a program: arrays and structures ("structs") or objects, for example. The data structures used to implement data in the computer are sometimes referred to, in discussions of database systems, as a *physical data model*, although in fact they are far removed from the gates and electrons that truly serve as the physical implementation of the data. In the database

world, data models are at a somewhat higher level than data structures, and are sometimes referred to as a *conceptual model* to emphasize the difference in level. We shall see examples shortly.

2. *Operations on the data.* In programming languages, operations on the data are generally anything that can be programmed. In database data models, there is usually a limited set of operations that can be performed. We are generally allowed to perform a limited set of *queries* (operations that retrieve information) and *modifications* (operations that change the database). This limitation is not a weakness, but a strength. By limiting operations, it is possible for programmers to describe database operations at a very high level, yet have the database management system implement the operations efficiently. In comparison, it is generally impossible to optimize programs in conventional languages like C, to the extent that an inefficient algorithm (e.g., bubblesort) is replaced by a more efficient one (e.g., quicksort).

3. *Constraints on the data.* Database data models usually have a way to describe limitations on what the data can be. These constraints can range from the simple (e.g., "a day of the week is an integer between 1 and 7" or "a movie has at most one title") to some very complex limitations.

1.2 Important Data Models

Today, the two data models of preeminent importance for database systems are:

1. The relational model, including object-relational extensions.

2. The semistructured-data model, including XML and related standards.

The first, which is present in all commercial database management systems, is the subject of this chapter. The semistructured model, of which XML is the primary manifestation, is an added feature of most relational DBMS's, and appears in a number of other contexts as well.

1.3 The Relational Model in Brief

The relational model is based on tables, of which Fig. 1 is an example. We shall discuss this model beginning in Section 2. This relation, or table, describes movies: their title, the year in which they were made, their length in minutes, and the genre of the movie. We show three particular movies, but you should imagine that there are many more rows to this table — one row for each movie ever made, perhaps.

The structure portion of the relational model might appear to resemble an array of structs in C, where the column headers are the field names, and each

title	*year*	*length*	*genre*
Gone With the Wind	1939	231	drama
Star Wars	1977	124	sciFi
Wayne's World	1992	95	comedy

Figure 1: An example relation

of the rows represent the values of one struct in the array. However, it must be emphasized that this physical implementation is only one possible way the table could be implemented in physical data structures. In fact, it is not the normal way to represent relations, and a large portion of the study of database systems addresses the right ways to implement such tables. Much of the distinction comes from the scale of relations — they are not normally implemented as main-memory structures, and their proper physical implementation must take into account the need to access relations of very large size that are resident on disk.

The operations normally associated with the relational model form the "relational algebra," which we discuss beginning in Section 4. These operations are table-oriented. As an example, we can ask for all those rows of a relation that have a certain value in a certain column. For example, we can ask of the table in Fig. 1 for all the rows where the genre is "comedy."

The constraint portion of the relational data model will be touched upon briefly in Section 5. However, as a brief sample of what kinds of constraints are generally used, we could decide that there is a fixed list of genres for movies, and that the last column of every row must have a value that is on this list. Or we might decide (incorrectly, it turns out) that there could never be two movies with the same title, and constrain the table so that no two rows could have the same string in the first component.

1.4 The Semistructured Model in Brief

Semistructured data resembles trees or graphs, rather than tables or arrays. The principal manifestation of this viewpoint today is XML, a way to represent data by hierarchically nested tagged elements. The tags, similar to those used in HTML, define the role played by different pieces of data, much as the column headers do in the relational model. For example, the same data as in Fig. 1 might appear in an XML "document" as in Fig. 2.

The operations on semistructured data usually involve following paths in the implied tree from an element to one or more of its nested subelements, then to subelements nested within those, and so on. For example, starting at the outer `<Movies>` element (the entire document in Fig. 2), we might move to each of its nested `<Movie>` elements, each delimited by the tag `<Movie>` and matching `</Movie>` tag, and from each `<Movie>` element to its nested `<Genre>` element, to see which movies belong to the "comedy" genre.

```
<Movies>
    <Movie title="Gone With the Wind">
        <Year>1939</Year>
        <Length>231</Length>
        <Genre>drama</Genre>
    </Movie>
    <Movie title="Star Wars">
        <Year>1977</Year>
        <Length>124</Length>
        <Genre>sciFi</Genre>
    </Movie>
    <Movie title="Wayne's World">
        <Year>1992</Year>
        <Length>95</Length>
        <Genre>comedy</Genre>
    </Movie>
</Movies>
```

Figure 2: Movie data as XML

Constraints on the structure of data in this model often involve the data type of values associated with a tag. For instance, are the values associated with the `<Length>` tag integers or can they be arbitrary character strings? Other constraints determine which tags can appear nested within which other tags. For example, must each `<Movie>` element have a `<Length>` element nested within it? What other tags, besides those shown in Fig. 2 might be used within a `<Movie>` element? Can there be more than one genre for a movie?

1.5 Other Data Models

There are many other models that are, or have been, associated with DBMS's. A modern trend is to add object-oriented features to the relational model. There are two effects of object-orientation on relations:

1. Values can have structure, rather than being elementary types such as integer or strings, as they were in Fig. 1.

2. Relations can have associated methods.

In a sense, these extensions, called the *object-relational* model, are analogous to the way structs in C were extended to objects in C++.

There are even database models of the purely object-oriented kind. In these, the relation is no longer the principal data-structuring concept, but becomes only one option among many structures.

There are several other models that were used in some of the earlier DBMS's, but that have now fallen out of use. The *hierarchical model* was, like semistructured data, a tree-oriented model. Its drawback was that unlike more modern models, it really operated at the physical level, which made it impossible for programmers to write code at a conveniently high level. Another such model was the *network model*, which was a graph-oriented, physical-level model. In truth, both the hierarchical model and today's semistructured models, allow full graph structures, and do not limit us strictly to trees. However, the generality of graphs was built directly into the network model, rather than favoring trees as these other models do.

1.6 Comparison of Modeling Approaches

Even from our brief example, it appears that semistructured models have more flexibility than relations. This difference becomes even more apparent when we discuss, as we shall, how full graph structures are embedded into tree-like, semistructured models. Nevertheless, the relational model is still preferred in DBMS's, and we should understand why. A brief argument follows.

Because databases are large, efficiency of access to data and efficiency of modifications to that data are of great importance. Also very important is ease of use — the productivity of programmers who use the data. Surprisingly, both goals can be achieved with a model, particularly the relational model, that:

1. Provides a simple, limited approach to structuring data, yet is reasonably versatile, so anything can be modeled.

2. Provides a limited, yet useful, collection of operations on data.

Together, these limitations turn into features. They allow us to implement languages, such as SQL, that enable the programmer to express their wishes at a very high level. A few lines of SQL can do the work of thousands of lines of C, or hundreds of lines of the code that had to be written to access data under earlier models such as network or hierarchical. Yet the short SQL programs, because they use a strongly limited sets of operations, can be optimized to run as fast, or faster than the code written in alternative languages.

2 Basics of the Relational Model

The relational model gives us a single way to represent data: as a two-dimensional table called a *relation*. Figure 1, which we copy here as Fig. 3, is an example of a relation, which we shall call `Movies`. The rows each represent a movie, and the columns each represent a property of movies. In this section, we shall introduce the most important terminology regarding relations, and illustrate them with the Movies relation.

title	*year*	*length*	*genre*
Gone With the Wind	1939	231	drama
Star Wars	1977	124	sciFi
Wayne's World	1992	95	comedy

Figure 3: The relation Movies

2.1 Attributes

The columns of a relation are named by *attributes*; in Fig. 3 the attributes are title, year, length, and genre. Attributes appear at the tops of the columns. Usually, an attribute describes the meaning of entries in the column below. For instance, the column with attribute length holds the length, in minutes, of each movie.

2.2 Schemas

The name of a relation and the set of attributes for a relation is called the *schema* for that relation. We show the schema for the relation with the relation name followed by a parenthesized list of its attributes. Thus, the schema for relation Movies of Fig. 3 is

```
Movies(title, year, length, genre)
```

The attributes in a relation schema are a set, not a list. However, in order to talk about relations we often must specify a "standard" order for the attributes. Thus, whenever we introduce a relation schema with a list of attributes, as above, we shall take this ordering to be the standard order whenever we display the relation or any of its rows.

In the relational model, a database consists of one or more relations. The set of schemas for the relations of a database is called a *relational database schema*, or just a *database schema*.

2.3 Tuples

The rows of a relation, other than the header row containing the attribute names, are called *tuples*. A tuple has one *component* for each attribute of the relation. For instance, the first of the three tuples in Fig. 3 has the four components Gone With the Wind, 1939, 231, and drama for attributes title, year, length, and genre, respectively. When we wish to write a tuple

Conventions for Relations and Attributes

We shall generally follow the convention that relation names begin with a capital letter, and attribute names begin with a lower-case letter. However, later we shall talk of relations in the abstract, where the names of attributes do not matter. In that case, we shall use single capital letters for both relations and attributes, e.g., $R(A, B, C)$ for a generic relation with three attributes.

in isolation, not as part of a relation, we normally use commas to separate components, and we use parentheses to surround the tuple. For example,

(`Gone With the Wind`, 1939, 231, `drama`)

is the first tuple of Fig. 3. Notice that when a tuple appears in isolation, the attributes do not appear, so some indication of the relation to which the tuple belongs must be given. We shall always use the order in which the attributes were listed in the relation schema.

2.4 Domains

The relational model requires that each component of each tuple be atomic; that is, it must be of some elementary type such as integer or string. It is not permitted for a value to be a record structure, set, list, array, or any other type that reasonably can have its values broken into smaller components.

It is further assumed that associated with each attribute of a relation is a *domain*, that is, a particular elementary type. The components of any tuple of the relation must have, in each component, a value that belongs to the domain of the corresponding column. For example, tuples of the `Movies` relation of Fig. 3 must have a first component that is a string, second and third components that are integers, and a fourth component whose value is a string.

It is possible to include the domain, or data type, for each attribute in a relation schema. We shall do so by appending a colon and a type after attributes. For example, we could represent the schema for the `Movies` relation as:

```
Movies(title:string, year:integer, length:integer, genre:string)
```

2.5 Equivalent Representations of a Relation

Relations are sets of tuples, not lists of tuples. Thus the order in which the tuples of a relation are presented is immaterial. For example, we can list the three tuples of Fig. 3 in any of their six possible orders, and the relation is "the same" as Fig. 3.

Moreover, we can reorder the attributes of the relation as we choose, without changing the relation. However, when we reorder the relation schema, we must be careful to remember that the attributes are column headers. Thus, when we change the order of the attributes, we also change the order of their columns. When the columns move, the components of tuples change their order as well. The result is that each tuple has its components permuted in the same way as the attributes are permuted.

For example, Fig. 4 shows one of the many relations that could be obtained from Fig. 3 by permuting rows and columns. These two relations are considered "the same." More precisely, these two tables are different presentations of the same relation.

year	*genre*	*title*	*length*
1977	sciFi	Star Wars	124
1992	comedy	Wayne's World	95
1939	drama	Gone With the Wind	231

Figure 4: Another presentation of the relation `Movies`

2.6 Relation Instances

A relation about movies is not static; rather, relations change over time. We expect to insert tuples for new movies, as these appear. We also expect changes to existing tuples if we get revised or corrected information about a movie, and perhaps deletion of tuples for movies that are expelled from the database for some reason.

It is less common for the schema of a relation to change. However, there are situations where we might want to add or delete attributes. Schema changes, while possible in commercial database systems, can be very expensive, because each of perhaps millions of tuples needs to be rewritten to add or delete components. Also, if we add an attribute, it may be difficult or even impossible to generate appropriate values for the new component in the existing tuples.

We shall call a set of tuples for a given relation an *instance* of that relation. For example, the three tuples shown in Fig. 3 form an instance of relation `Movies`. Presumably, the relation `Movies` has changed over time and will continue to change over time. For instance, in 1990, `Movies` did not contain the tuple for `Wayne's World`. However, a conventional database system maintains only one version of any relation: the set of tuples that are in the relation "now." This instance of the relation is called the *current instance*.[1]

[1]Databases that maintain historical versions of data as it existed in past times are called *temporal databases*.

2.7 Keys of Relations

There are many constraints on relations that the relational model allows us to place on database schemas. One kind of constraint is so fundamental that we shall introduce it here: *key* constraints. A set of attributes forms a *key* for a relation if we do not allow two tuples in a relation instance to have the same values in all the attributes of the key.

Example 1: We can declare that the relation `Movies` has a key consisting of the two attributes `title` and `year`. That is, we don't believe there could ever be two movies that had both the same title and the same year. Notice that `title` by itself does not form a key, since sometimes "remakes" of a movie appear. For example, there are three movies named *King Kong*, each made in a different year. It should also be obvious that `year` by itself is not a key, since there are usually many movies made in the same year. □

We indicate the attribute or attributes that form a key for a relation by underlining the key attribute(s). For instance, the `Movies` relation could have its schema written as:

Movies(<u>title</u>, <u>year</u>, length, genre)

Remember that the statement that a set of attributes forms a key for a relation is a statement about all possible instances of the relation, not a statement about a single instance. For example, looking only at the tiny relation of Fig. 3, we might imagine that `genre` by itself forms a key, since we do not see two tuples that agree on the value of their `genre` components. However, we can easily imagine that if the relation instance contained more movies, there would be many dramas, many comedies, and so on. Thus, there would be distinct tuples that agreed on the `genre` component. As a consequence, it would be incorrect to assert that `genre` is a key for the relation `Movies`.

While we might be sure that `title` and `year` can serve as a key for `Movies`, many real-world databases use artificial keys, doubting that it is safe to make any assumption about the values of attributes outside their control. For example, companies generally assign employee ID's to all employees, and these ID's are carefully chosen to be unique numbers. One purpose of these ID's is to make sure that in the company database each employee can be distinguished from all others, even if there are several employees with the same name. Thus, the employee-ID attribute can serve as a key for a relation about employees.

In US corporations, it is normal for every employee to have a Social-Security number. If the database has an attribute that is the Social-Security number, then this attribute can also serve as a key for employees. Note that there is nothing wrong with there being several choices of key, as there would be for employees having both employee ID's and Social-Security numbers.

The idea of creating an attribute whose purpose is to serve as a key is quite widespread. In addition to employee ID's, we find student ID's to distinguish students in a university. We find drivers' license numbers and automobile registration numbers to distinguish drivers and automobiles, respectively. You undoubtedly can find more examples of attributes created for the primary purpose of serving as keys.

```
Movies(
    title:string,
    year:integer,
    length:integer,
    genre:string,
    studioName:string,
    producerC#:integer
)
MovieStar(
    name:string,
    address:string,
    gender:char,
    birthdate:date
)
StarsIn(
    movieTitle:string,
    movieYear:integer,
    starName:string
)
MovieExec(
    name:string,
    address:string,
    cert#:integer,
    netWorth:integer
)
Studio(
    name:string,
    address:string,
    presC#:integer
)
```

Figure 5: Example database schema about movies

2.8 An Example Database Schema

We shall close this section with an example of a complete database schema. The topic is movies, and it builds on the relation Movies that has appeared so far in examples. The database schema is shown in Fig. 5. Here are the things we need to know to understand the intention of this schema.

`Movies`

This relation is an extension of the example relation we have been discussing so far. Remember that its key is `title` and `year` together. We have added two new attributes; `studioName` tells us the studio that owns the movie, and `producerC#` is an integer that represents the producer of the movie in a way that we shall discuss when we talk about the relation `MovieExec` below.

`MovieStar`

This relation tells us something about stars. The key is `name`, the name of the movie star. It is not usual to assume names of persons are unique and therefore suitable as a key. However, movie stars are different; one would never take a name that some other movie star had used. Thus, we shall use the convenient fiction that movie-star names are unique. A more conventional approach would be to invent a serial number of some sort, like social-security numbers, so that we could assign each individual a unique number and use that attribute as the key. We take that approach for movie executives, as we shall see. Another interesting point about the `MovieStar` relation is that we see two new data types. The gender can be a single character, M or F. Also, birthdate is of type "date," which might be a character string of a special form.

`StarsIn`

This relation connects movies to the stars of that movie, and likewise connects a star to the movies in which they appeared. Notice that movies are represented by the key for `Movies` — the title and year — although we have chosen different attribute names to emphasize that attributes `movieTitle` and `movieYear` represent the movie. Likewise, stars are represented by the key for `MovieStar`, with the attribute called `starName`. Finally, notice that all three attributes are necessary to form a key. It is perfectly reasonable to suppose that relation `StarsIn` could have two distinct tuples that agree in any two of the three attributes. For instance, a star might appear in two movies in one year, giving rise to two tuples that agreed in `movieYear` and `starName`, but disagreed in `movieTitle`.

`MovieExec`

This relation tells us about movie executives. It contains their name, address, and networth as data about the executive. However, for a key we have invented "certificate numbers" for all movie executives, including producers (as appear in the relation `Movies`) and studio presidents (as appear in the relation `Studio`, below). These are integers; a different one is assigned to each executive.

acctNo	*type*	*balance*
12345	savings	12000
23456	checking	1000
34567	savings	25

The relation Accounts

firstName	*lastName*	*idNo*	*account*
Robbie	Banks	901-222	12345
Lena	Hand	805-333	12345
Lena	Hand	805-333	23456

The relation Customers

Figure 6: Two relations of a banking database

Studio

This relation tells about movie studios. We rely on no two studios having the same name, and therefore use name as the key. The other attributes are the address of the studio and the certificate number for the president of the studio. We assume that the studio president is surely a movie executive and therefore appears in MovieExec.

2.9 Exercises for Section 2

Exercise 2.1: In Fig. 6 are instances of two relations that might constitute part of a banking database. Indicate the following:

a) The attributes of each relation.

b) The tuples of each relation.

c) The components of one tuple from each relation.

d) The relation schema for each relation.

e) The database schema.

f) A suitable domain for each attribute.

g) Another equivalent way to present each relation.

Exercise 2.2: In Section 2.7 we suggested that there are many examples of attributes that are created for the purpose of serving as keys of relations. Give some additional examples.

!! **Exercise 2.3:** How many different ways (considering orders of tuples and attributes) are there to represent a relation instance if that instance has:

a) Three attributes and three tuples, like the relation `Accounts` of Fig. 6?

b) Four attributes and five tuples?

c) n attributes and m tuples?

3 Defining a Relation Schema in SQL

SQL (pronounced "sequel") is the principal language used to describe and manipulate relational databases. There is a current standard for SQL, called SQL-99. Most commercial database management systems implement something similar, but not identical to, the standard. There are two aspects to SQL:

1. The *Data-Definition* sublanguage for declaring database schemas and
2. The *Data-Manipulation* sublanguage for *querying* (asking questions about) databases and for modifying the database.

The distinction between these two sublanguages is found in most languages; e.g., C or Java have portions that declare data and other portions that are executable code. These correspond to data-definition and data-manipulation, respectively.

In this section we shall begin a discussion of the data-definition portion of SQL.

3.1 Relations in SQL

SQL makes a distinction between three kinds of relations:

1. Stored relations, which are called *tables.* These are the kind of relation we deal with ordinarily — a relation that exists in the database and that can be modified by changing its tuples, as well as queried.
2. *Views,* which are relations defined by a computation. These relations are not stored, but are constructed, in whole or in part, when needed.

3. Temporary tables, which are constructed by the SQL language processor when it performs its job of executing queries and data modifications. These relations are then thrown away and not stored.

In this section, we shall learn how to declare tables. We do not treat the declaration and definition of views here, and temporary tables are never declared. The SQL `CREATE TABLE` statement declares the schema for a stored relation. It gives a name for the table, its attributes, and their data types. It also allows us to declare a key, or even several keys, for a relation. There are many other features to the `CREATE TABLE` statement, including many forms of constraints that can be declared, and the declaration of *indexes* (data structures that speed up many operations on the table) but we shall leave those for the appropriate time.

3.2 Data Types

To begin, let us introduce the primitive data types that are supported by SQL systems. All attributes must have a data type.

1. Character strings of fixed or varying length. The type `CHAR(n)` denotes a fixed-length string of up to n characters. `VARCHAR(n)` also denotes a string of up to n characters. The difference is implementation-dependent; typically `CHAR` implies that short strings are padded to make n characters, while `VARCHAR` implies that an endmarker or string-length is used. SQL permits reasonable coercions between values of character-string types. Normally, a string is padded by trailing blanks if it becomes the value of a component that is a fixed-length string of greater length. For example, the string `'foo'`,[2] if it became the value of a component for an attribute of type `CHAR(5)`, would assume the value `'foo  '` (with two blanks following the second `o`).

2. Bit strings of fixed or varying length. These strings are analogous to fixed and varying-length character strings, but their values are strings of bits rather than characters. The type `BIT(n)` denotes bit strings of length n, while `BIT VARYING(n)` denotes bit strings of length up to n.

3. The type `BOOLEAN` denotes an attribute whose value is logical. The possible values of such an attribute are `TRUE`, `FALSE`, and — although it would surprise George Boole — `UNKNOWN`.

4. The type `INT` or `INTEGER` (these names are synonyms) denotes typical integer values. The type `SHORTINT` also denotes integers, but the number of bits permitted may be less, depending on the implementation (as with the types `int` and `short int` in C).

[2] Notice that in SQL, strings are surrounded by single-quotes, not double-quotes as in many other programming languages.

Dates and Times in SQL

Different SQL implementations may provide many different representations for dates and times, but the following is the SQL standard representation. A date value is the keyword `DATE` followed by a quoted string of a special form. For example, `DATE '1948-05-14'` follows the required form. The first four characters are digits representing the year. Then come a hyphen and two digits representing the month. Finally there is another hyphen and two digits representing the day. Note that single-digit months and days are padded with a leading 0.

A time value is the keyword `TIME` and a quoted string. This string has two digits for the hour, on the military (24-hour) clock. Then come a colon, two digits for the minute, another colon, and two digits for the second. If fractions of a second are desired, we may continue with a decimal point and as many significant digits as we like. For instance, `TIME '15:00:02.5'` represents the time at which all students will have left a class that ends at 3 PM: two and a half seconds past three o'clock.

5. Floating-point numbers can be represented in a variety of ways. We may use the type `FLOAT` or `REAL` (these are synonyms) for typical floating-point numbers. A higher precision can be obtained with the type `DOUBLE PRECISION`; again the distinction between these types is as in C. SQL also has types that are real numbers with a fixed decimal point. For example, `DECIMAL(n,d)` allows values that consist of n decimal digits, with the decimal point assumed to be d positions from the right. Thus, 0123.45 is a possible value of type `DECIMAL(6,2)`. `NUMERIC` is almost a synonym for `DECIMAL`, although there are possible implementation-dependent differences.

6. Dates and times can be represented by the data types `DATE` and `TIME`, respectively (see the box on "Dates and Times in SQL"). These values are essentially character strings of a special form. We may, in fact, coerce dates and times to string types, and we may do the reverse if the string "makes sense" as a date or time.

3.3 Simple Table Declarations

The simplest form of declaration of a relation schema consists of the keywords `CREATE TABLE` followed by the name of the relation and a parenthesized, comma-separated list of the attribute names and their types.

Example 2: The relation `Movies` with the schema given in Fig. 5 can be declared as in Fig. 7. The title is declared as a string of (up to) 100 characters.

```
CREATE TABLE Movies (
    title        CHAR(100),
    year         INT,
    length       INT,
    genre        CHAR(10),
    studioName   CHAR(30),
    producerC#   INT
);
```

Figure 7: SQL declaration of the table Movies

The year and length attributes are each integers, and the genre is a string of (up to) 10 characters. The decision to allow up to 100 characters for a title is arbitrary, but we don't want to limit the lengths of titles too strongly, or long titles would be truncated to fit. We have assumed that 10 characters are enough to represent a genre of movie; again, that is an arbitrary choice, one we could regret if we had a genre with a long name. Likewise, we have chosen 30 characters as sufficient for the studio name. The certificate number for the producer of the movie is another integer. □

Example 3: Figure 8 is a SQL declaration of the relation MovieStar from Fig. 5. It illustrates some new options for data types. The name of this table is MovieStar, and it has four attributes. The first two attributes, name and address, have each been declared to be character strings. However, with the name, we have made the decision to use a fixed-length string of 30 characters, padding a name out with blanks at the end if necessary and truncating a name to 30 characters if it is longer. In contrast, we have declared addresses to be variable-length character strings of up to 255 characters.[3] It is not clear that these two choices are the best possible, but we use them to illustrate the two major kinds of string data types.

```
CREATE TABLE MovieStar (
    name       CHAR(30),
    address    VARCHAR(255),
    gender     CHAR(1),
    birthdate  DATE
);
```

Figure 8: Declaring the relation schema for the MovieStar relation

[3]The number 255 is not the result of some weird notion of what typical addresses look like. A single byte can store integers between 0 and 255, so it is possible to represent a varying-length character string of up to 255 bytes by a single byte for the count of characters plus the bytes to store the string itself. Commercial systems generally support longer varying-length strings, however.

The gender attribute has values that are a single letter, M or F. Thus, we can safely use a single character as the type of this attribute. Finally, the birthdate attribute naturally deserves the data type DATE. □

3.4 Modifying Relation Schemas

We now know how to declare a table. But what if we need to change the schema of the table after it has been in use for a long time and has many tuples in its current instance? We can remove the entire table, including all of its current tuples, or we could change the schema by adding or deleting attributes.

We can delete a relation *R* by the SQL statement:

```
DROP TABLE R;
```

Relation *R* is no longer part of the database schema, and we can no longer access any of its tuples.

More frequently than we would drop a relation that is part of a long-lived database, we may need to modify the schema of an existing relation. These modifications are done by a statement that begins with the keywords ALTER TABLE and the name of the relation. We then have several options, the most important of which are

1. ADD followed by an attribute name and its data type.

2. DROP followed by an attribute name.

Example 4: Thus, for instance, we could modify the MovieStar relation by adding an attribute phone with:

```
ALTER TABLE MovieStar ADD phone CHAR(16);
```

As a result, the MovieStar schema now has five attributes: the four mentioned in Fig. 8 and the attribute phone, which is a fixed-length string of 16 bytes. In the actual relation, tuples would all have components for phone, but we know of no phone numbers to put there. Thus, the value of each of these components is set to the special *null value*, NULL. In Section 3.5, we shall see how it is possible to choose another "default" value to be used instead of NULL for unknown values.

As another example, the ALTER TABLE statement:

```
ALTER TABLE MovieStar DROP birthdate;
```

deletes the birthdate attribute. As a result, the schema for MovieStar no longer has that attribute, and all tuples of the current MovieStar instance have the component for birthdate deleted. □

3.5 Default Values

When we create or modify tuples, we sometimes do not have values for all components. For instance, we mentioned in Example 4 that when we add a column to a relation schema, the existing tuples do not have a known value, and it was suggested that `NULL` could be used in place of a "real" value. However, there are times when we would prefer to use another choice of *default* value, the value that appears in a column if no other value is known.

In general, any place we declare an attribute and its data type, we may add the keyword `DEFAULT` and an appropriate value. That value is either `NULL` or a constant. Certain other values that are provided by the system, such as the current time, may also be options.

Example 5: Let us consider Example 3. We might wish to use the character `?` as the default for an unknown `gender`, and we might also wish to use the earliest possible date, `DATE '0000-00-00'` for an unknown `birthdate`. We could replace the declarations of `gender` and `birthdate` in Fig. 8 by:

```
gender CHAR(1) DEFAULT '?',
birthdate DATE DEFAULT DATE '0000-00-00'
```

As another example, we could have declared the default value for new attribute `phone` to be `'unlisted'` when we added this attribute in Example 4. In that case,

```
ALTER TABLE MovieStar ADD phone CHAR(16) DEFAULT 'unlisted';
```

would be the appropriate `ALTER TABLE` statement. □

3.6 Declaring Keys

There are two ways to declare an attribute or set of attributes to be a key in the `CREATE TABLE` statement that defines a stored relation.

1. We may declare one attribute to be a key when that attribute is listed in the relation schema.

2. We may add to the list of items declared in the schema (which so far have only been attributes) an additional declaration that says a particular attribute or set of attributes forms the key.

If the key consists of more than one attribute, we have to use method (2). If the key is a single attribute, either method may be used.

There are two declarations that may be used to indicate keyness:

a) `PRIMARY KEY`, or

b) `UNIQUE`.

The effect of declaring a set of attributes S to be a key for relation R either using `PRIMARY KEY` or `UNIQUE` is the following:

- Two tuples in R cannot agree on all of the attributes in set S, unless one of them is `NULL`. Any attempt to insert or update a tuple that violates this rule causes the DBMS to reject the action that caused the violation.

In addition, if `PRIMARY KEY` is used, then attributes in S are not allowed to have `NULL` as a value for their components. Again, any attempt to violate this rule is rejected by the system. `NULL` is permitted if the set S is declared `UNIQUE`, however. A DBMS may make other distinctions between the two terms, if it wishes.

Example 6: Let us reconsider the schema for relation `MovieStar`. Since no star would use the name of another star, we shall assume that `name` by itself forms a key for this relation. Thus, we can add this fact to the line declaring `name`. Figure 9 is a revision of Fig. 8 that reflects this change. We could also substitute `UNIQUE` for `PRIMARY KEY` in this declaration. If we did so, then two or more tuples could have `NULL` as the value of `name`, but there could be no other duplicate values for this attribute.

```
CREATE TABLE MovieStar (
    name CHAR(30) PRIMARY KEY,
    address VARCHAR(255),
    gender CHAR(1),
    birthdate DATE
);
```

Figure 9: Making `name` the key

Alternatively, we can use a separate definition of the key. The resulting schema declaration would look like Fig. 10. Again, `UNIQUE` could replace `PRIMARY KEY`. □

```
CREATE TABLE MovieStar (
    name CHAR(30),
    address VARCHAR(255),
    gender CHAR(1),
    birthdate DATE,
    PRIMARY KEY (name)
);
```

Figure 10: A separate declaration of the key

Example 7: In Example 6, the form of either Fig. 9 or Fig. 10 is acceptable, because the key is a single attribute. However, in a situation where the key has more than one attribute, we must use the style of Fig. 10. For instance, the relation `Movie`, whose key is the pair of attributes `title` and `year`, must be declared as in Fig. 11. However, as usual, `UNIQUE` is an option to replace `PRIMARY KEY`. □

```
CREATE TABLE Movies (
    title        CHAR(100),
    year         INT,
    length       INT,
    genre        CHAR(10),
    studioName   CHAR(30),
    producerC#   INT,
    PRIMARY KEY (title, year)
);
```

Figure 11: Making `title` and `year` be the key of `Movies`

3.7 Exercises for Section 3

Exercise 3.1: In this exercise we introduce one of our running examples of a relational database schema. The database schema consists of four relations, whose schemas are:

```
Product(maker, model, type)
PC(model, speed, ram, hd, price)
Laptop(model, speed, ram, hd, screen, price)
Printer(model, color, type, price)
```

The `Product` relation gives the manufacturer, model number and type (PC, laptop, or printer) of various products. We assume for convenience that model numbers are unique over all manufacturers and product types; that assumption is not realistic, and a real database would include a code for the manufacturer as part of the model number. The `PC` relation gives for each model number that is a PC the speed (of the processor, in gigahertz), the amount of RAM (in megabytes), the size of the hard disk (in gigabytes), and the price. The `Laptop` relation is similar, except that the screen size (in inches) is also included. The `Printer` relation records for each printer model whether the printer produces color output (true, if so), the process type (laser or ink-jet, typically), and the price.

Write the following declarations:

a) A suitable schema for relation `Product`.

b) A suitable schema for relation `PC`.

c) A suitable schema for relation `Laptop`.

d) A suitable schema for relation `Printer`.

e) An alteration to your `Printer` schema from (d) to delete the attribute `color`.

f) An alteration to your `Laptop` schema from (c) to add the attribute `od` (optical-disk type, e.g., cd or dvd). Let the default value for this attribute be `'none'` if the laptop does not have an optical disk.

Exercise 3.2: This exercise introduces another running example, concerning World War II capital ships. It involves the following relations:

```
Classes(class, type, country, numGuns, bore, displacement)
Ships(name, class, launched)
Battles(name, date)
Outcomes(ship, battle, result)
```

Ships are built in "classes" from the same design, and the class is usually named for the first ship of that class. The relation `Classes` records the name of the class, the type (`'bb'` for battleship or `'bc'` for battlecruiser), the country that built the ship, the number of main guns, the bore (diameter of the gun barrel, in inches) of the main guns, and the displacement (weight, in tons). Relation `Ships` records the name of the ship, the name of its class, and the year in which the ship was launched. Relation `Battles` gives the name and date of battles involving these ships, and relation `Outcomes` gives the result (sunk, damaged, or ok) for each ship in each battle.

Write the following declarations:

a) A suitable schema for relation `Classes`.

b) A suitable schema for relation `Ships`.

c) A suitable schema for relation `Battles`.

d) A suitable schema for relation `Outcomes`.

e) An alteration to your `Classes` relation from (a) to delete the attribute `bore`.

f) An alteration to your `Ships` relation from (b) to include the attribute `yard` giving the shipyard where the ship was built.

4 An Algebraic Query Language

In this section, we introduce the data-manipulation aspect of the relational model. Recall that a data model is not just structure; it needs a way to query the data and to modify the data. To begin our study of operations on relations, we shall learn about a special algebra, called *relational algebra*, that consists of some simple but powerful ways to construct new relations from given relations. When the given relations are stored data, then the constructed relations can be answers to queries about this data.

Relational algebra is not used today as a query language in commercial DBMS's, although some of the early prototypes did use this algebra directly. Rather, the "real" query language, SQL, incorporates relational algebra at its center, and many SQL programs are really "syntactically sugared" expressions of relational algebra. Further, when a DBMS processes queries, the first thing that happens to a SQL query is that it gets translated into relational algebra or a very similar internal representation. Thus, there are several good reasons to start out learning this algebra.

4.1 Why Do We Need a Special Query Language?

Before introducing the operations of relational algebra, one should ask why, or whether, we need a new kind of programming languages for databases. Won't conventional languages like C or Java suffice to ask and answer any computable question about relations? After all, we can represent a tuple of a relation by a struct (in C) or an object (in Java), and we can represent relations by arrays of these elements.

The surprising answer is that relational algebra is useful because it is *less* powerful than C or Java. That is, there are computations one can perform in any conventional language that one cannot perform in relational algebra. An example is: determine whether the number of tuples in a relation is even or odd. By limiting what we can say or do in our query language, we get two huge rewards — ease of programming and the ability of the compiler to produce highly optimized code — that we discussed in Section 1.6.

4.2 What is an Algebra?

An algebra, in general, consists of operators and atomic operands. For instance, in the algebra of arithmetic, the atomic operands are variables like x and constants like 15. The operators are the usual arithmetic ones: addition, subtraction, multiplication, and division. Any algebra allows us to build *expressions* by applying operators to atomic operands and/or other expressions of the algebra. Usually, parentheses are needed to group operators and their operands. For instance, in arithmetic we have expressions such as $(x + y) * z$ or $((x + 7)/(y - 3)) + x$.

Relational algebra is another example of an algebra. Its atomic operands are:

1. Variables that stand for relations.
2. Constants, which are finite relations.

We shall next see the operators of relational algebra.

4.3 Overview of Relational Algebra

The operations of the traditional relational algebra fall into four broad classes:

a) The usual set operations — union, intersection, and difference — applied to relations.

b) Operations that remove parts of a relation: "selection" eliminates some rows (tuples), and "projection" eliminates some columns.

c) Operations that combine the tuples of two relations, including "Cartesian product," which pairs the tuples of two relations in all possible ways, and various kinds of "join" operations, which selectively pair tuples from two relations.

d) An operation called "renaming" that does not affect the tuples of a relation, but changes the relation schema, i.e., the names of the attributes and/or the name of the relation itself.

We generally shall refer to expressions of relational algebra as *queries*.

4.4 Set Operations on Relations

The three most common operations on sets are union, intersection, and difference. We assume the reader is familiar with these operations, which are defined as follows on arbitrary sets R and S:

- $R \cup S$, the *union* of R and S, is the set of elements that are in R or S or both. An element appears only once in the union even if it is present in both R and S.

- $R \cap S$, the *intersection* of R and S, is the set of elements that are in both R and S.

- $R - S$, the *difference* of R and S, is the set of elements that are in R but not in S. Note that $R - S$ is different from $S - R$; the latter is the set of elements that are in S but not in R.

When we apply these operations to relations, we need to put some conditions on R and S:

1. R and S must have schemas with identical sets of attributes, and the types (domains) for each attribute must be the same in R and S.

2. Before we compute the set-theoretic union, intersection, or difference of sets of tuples, the columns of R and S must be ordered so that the order of attributes is the same for both relations.

Sometimes we would like to take the union, intersection, or difference of relations that have the same number of attributes, with corresponding domains, but that use different names for their attributes. If so, we may use the renaming operator to be discussed in Section 4.11 to change the schema of one or both relations and give them the same set of attributes.

name	*address*	*gender*	*birthdate*
`Carrie Fisher`	`123 Maple St., Hollywood`	`F`	`9/9/99`
`Mark Hamill`	`456 Oak Rd., Brentwood`	`M`	`8/8/88`

Relation R

name	*address*	*gender*	*birthdate*
`Carrie Fisher`	`123 Maple St., Hollywood`	`F`	`9/9/99`
`Harrison Ford`	`789 Palm Dr., Beverly Hills`	`M`	`7/7/77`

Relation S

Figure 12: Two relations

Example 8 : Suppose we have the two relations R and S, whose schemas are both that of relation `MovieStar` Section 2.8. Current instances of R and S are shown in Fig. 12. Then the union $R \cup S$ is

name	*address*	*gender*	*birthdate*
`Carrie Fisher`	`123 Maple St., Hollywood`	`F`	`9/9/99`
`Mark Hamill`	`456 Oak Rd., Brentwood`	`M`	`8/8/88`
`Harrison Ford`	`789 Palm Dr., Beverly Hills`	`M`	`7/7/77`

Note that the two tuples for Carrie Fisher from the two relations appear only once in the result.

The intersection $R \cap S$ is

name	*address*	*gender*	*birthdate*
`Carrie Fisher`	`123 Maple St., Hollywood`	`F`	`9/9/99`

Now, only the Carrie Fisher tuple appears, because only it is in both relations.

The difference $R - S$ is

name	*address*	*gender*	*birthdate*
Mark Hamill	456 Oak Rd., Brentwood	M	8/8/88

That is, the Fisher and Hamill tuples appear in R and thus are candidates for $R - S$. However, the Fisher tuple also appears in S and so is not in $R - S$. □

4.5 Projection

The *projection* operator is used to produce from a relation R a new relation that has only some of R's columns. The value of expression $\pi_{A_1,A_2,\ldots,A_n}(R)$ is a relation that has only the columns for attributes $A_1, A_2, \ldots, A_n$ of R. The schema for the resulting value is the set of attributes $\{A_1, A_2, \ldots, A_n\}$, which we conventionally show in the order listed.

title	*year*	*length*	*genre*	*studioName*	*producerC#*
Star Wars	1977	124	sciFi	Fox	12345
Galaxy Quest	1999	104	comedy	DreamWorks	67890
Wayne's World	1992	95	comedy	Paramount	99999

Figure 13: The relation Movies

Example 9: Consider the relation Movies with the relation schema described in Section 2.8. An instance of this relation is shown in Fig. 13. We can project this relation onto the first three attributes with the expression:

$$\pi_{title,year,length}(\texttt{Movies})$$

The resulting relation is

title	*year*	*length*
Star Wars	1977	124
Galaxy Quest	1999	104
Wayne's World	1992	95

As another example, we can project onto the attribute genre with the expression $\pi_{genre}(\texttt{Movies})$. The result is the single-column relation

genre
sciFi
comedy

Notice that there are only two tuples in the resulting relation, since the last two tuples of Fig. 13 have the same value in their component for attribute genre, and in the relational algebra of sets, duplicate tuples are always eliminated. □

> **A Note About Data Quality :-)**
>
> While we have endeavored to make example data as accurate as possible, we have used bogus values for addresses and other personal information about movie stars, in order to protect the privacy of members of the acting profession, many of whom are shy individuals who shun publicity.

4.6 Selection

The *selection* operator, applied to a relation R, produces a new relation with a subset of R's tuples. The tuples in the resulting relation are those that satisfy some condition C that involves the attributes of R. We denote this operation $\sigma_C(R)$. The schema for the resulting relation is the same as R's schema, and we conventionally show the attributes in the same order as we use for R.

C is a conditional expression of the type with which we are familiar from conventional programming languages; for example, conditional expressions follow the keyword `if` in programming languages such as C or Java. The only difference is that the operands in condition C are either constants or attributes of R. We apply C to each tuple t of R by substituting, for each attribute A appearing in condition C, the component of t for attribute A. If after substituting for each attribute of C the condition C is true, then t is one of the tuples that appear in the result of $\sigma_C(R)$; otherwise t is not in the result.

Example 10: Let the relation `Movies` be as in Fig. 13. Then the value of expression $\sigma_{length \geq 100}$(`Movies`) is

title	*year*	*length*	*genre*	*studioName*	*producerC#*
Star Wars	1977	124	sciFi	Fox	12345
Galaxy Quest	1999	104	comedy	DreamWorks	67890

The first tuple satisfies the condition $length \geq 100$ because when we substitute for *length* the value 124 found in the component of the first tuple for attribute `length`, the condition becomes $124 \geq 100$. The latter condition is true, so we accept the first tuple. The same argument explains why the second tuple of Fig. 13 is in the result.

The third tuple has a `length` component 95. Thus, when we substitute for *length* we get the condition $95 \geq 100$, which is false. Hence the last tuple of Fig. 13 is not in the result. □

Example 11: Suppose we want the set of tuples in the relation `Movies` that represent Fox movies at least 100 minutes long. We can get these tuples with a more complicated condition, involving the AND of two subconditions. The expression is

$$\sigma_{length \geq 100 \text{ AND } studioName = \text{'Fox'}}(\texttt{Movies})$$

The tuple

title	*year*	*length*	*genre*	*studioName*	*producerC#*
Star Wars	1977	124	sciFi	Fox	12345

is the only one in the resulting relation. □

4.7 Cartesian Product

The *Cartesian product* (or *cross-product*, or just *product*) of two sets R and S is the set of pairs that can be formed by choosing the first element of the pair to be any element of R and the second any element of S. This product is denoted $R \times S$. When R and S are relations, the product is essentially the same. However, since the members of R and S are tuples, usually consisting of more than one component, the result of pairing a tuple from R with a tuple from S is a longer tuple, with one component for each of the components of the constituent tuples. By convention, the components from R (the left operand) precede the components from S in the attribute order for the result.

The relation schema for the resulting relation is the union of the schemas for R and S. However, if R and S should happen to have some attributes in common, then we need to invent new names for at least one of each pair of identical attributes. To disambiguate an attribute A that is in the schemas of both R and S, we use $R.A$ for the attribute from R and $S.A$ for the attribute from S.

Example 12: For conciseness, let us use an abstract example that illustrates the product operation. Let relations R and S have the schemas and tuples shown in Fig. 14(a) and (b). Then the product $R \times S$ consists of the six tuples shown in Fig. 14(c). Note how we have paired each of the two tuples of R with each of the three tuples of S. Since B is an attribute of both schemas, we have used $R.B$ and $S.B$ in the schema for $R \times S$. The other attributes are unambiguous, and their names appear in the resulting schema unchanged. □

4.8 Natural Joins

More often than we want to take the product of two relations, we find a need to *join* them by pairing only those tuples that match in some way. The simplest sort of match is the *natural join* of two relations R and S, denoted $R \bowtie S$, in which we pair only those tuples from R and S that agree in whatever attributes are common to the schemas of R and S. More precisely, let $A_1, A_2, \ldots, A_n$ be all the attributes that are in both the schema of R and the schema of S. Then a tuple r from R and a tuple s from S are successfully paired if and only if r and s agree on each of the attributes $A_1, A_2, \ldots, A_n$.

If the tuples r and s are successfully paired in the join $R \bowtie S$, then the result of the pairing is a tuple, called the *joined tuple*, with one component for each of the attributes in the union of the schemas of R and S. The joined tuple

A	B
1	2
3	4

(a) Relation R

B	C	D
2	5	6
4	7	8
9	10	11

(b) Relation S

A	$R.B$	$S.B$	C	D
1	2	2	5	6
1	2	4	7	8
1	2	9	10	11
3	4	2	5	6
3	4	4	7	8
3	4	9	10	11

(c) Result $R \times S$

Figure 14: Two relations and their Cartesian product

agrees with tuple r in each attribute in the schema of R, and it agrees with s in each attribute in the schema of S. Since r and s are successfully paired, the joined tuple is able to agree with both these tuples on the attributes they have in common. The construction of the joined tuple is suggested by Fig. 15. However, the order of the attributes need not be that convenient; the attributes of R and S can appear in any order.

Example 13: The natural join of the relations R and S from Fig. 14(a) and (b) is

A	B	C	D
1	2	5	6
3	4	7	8

The only attribute common to R and S is B. Thus, to pair successfully, tuples need only to agree in their B components. If so, the resulting tuple has components for attributes A (from R), B (from either R or S), C (from S), and D (from S).

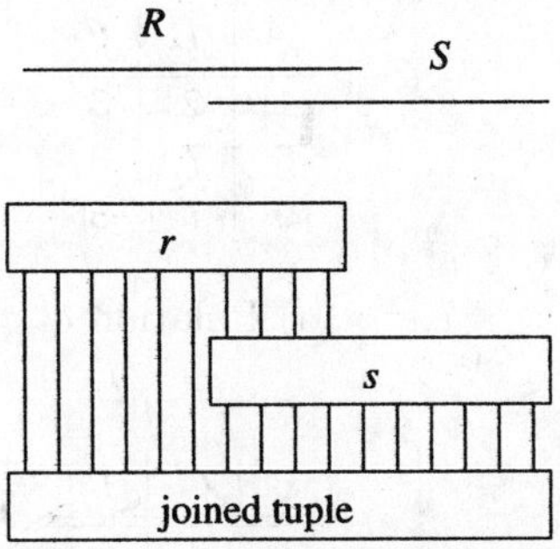

Figure 15: Joining tuples

In this example, the first tuple of R successfully pairs with only the first tuple of S; they share the value 2 on their common attribute B. This pairing yields the first tuple of the result: $(1, 2, 5, 6)$. The second tuple of R pairs successfully only with the second tuple of S, and the pairing yields $(3, 4, 7, 8)$. Note that the third tuple of S does not pair with any tuple of R and thus has no effect on the result of $R \bowtie S$. A tuple that fails to pair with any tuple of the other relation in a join is said to be a *dangling tuple*. □

Example 14: The previous example does not illustrate all the possibilities inherent in the natural join operator. For example, no tuple paired successfully with more than one tuple, and there was only one attribute in common to the two relation schemas. In Fig. 16 we see two other relations, U and V, that share two attributes between their schemas: B and C. We also show an instance in which one tuple joins with several tuples.

For tuples to pair successfully, they must agree in both the B and C components. Thus, the first tuple of U joins with the first two tuples of V, while the second and third tuples of U join with the third tuple of V. The result of these four pairings is shown in Fig. 16(c). □

4.9 Theta-Joins

The natural join forces us to pair tuples using one specific condition. While this way, equating shared attributes, is the most common basis on which relations are joined, it is sometimes desirable to pair tuples from two relations on some other basis. For that purpose, we have a related notation called the *theta-join*. Historically, the "theta" refers to an arbitrary condition, which we shall represent by C rather than θ.

The notation for a theta-join of relations R and S based on condition C is $R \bowtie_C S$. The result of this operation is constructed as follows:

1. Take the product of R and S.

2. Select from the product only those tuples that satisfy the condition C.

A	B	C
1	2	3
6	7	8
9	7	8

(a) Relation U

B	C	D
2	3	4
2	3	5
7	8	10

(b) Relation V

A	B	C	D
1	2	3	4
1	2	3	5
6	7	8	10
9	7	8	10

(c) Result $U \bowtie V$

Figure 16: Natural join of relations

As with the product operation, the schema for the result is the union of the schemas of R and S, with "R." or "S." prefixed to attributes if necessary to indicate from which schema the attribute came.

Example 15: Consider the operation $U \bowtie_{A<D} V$, where U and V are the relations from Fig. 16(a) and (b). We must consider all nine pairs of tuples, one from each relation, and see whether the A component from the U-tuple is less than the D component of the V-tuple. The first tuple of U, with an A component of 1, successfully pairs with each of the tuples from V. However, the second and third tuples from U, with A components of 6 and 9, respectively, pair successfully with only the last tuple of V. Thus, the result has only five tuples, constructed from the five successful pairings. This relation is shown in Fig. 17. □

Notice that the schema for the result in Fig. 17 consists of all six attributes, with U and V prefixed to their respective occurrences of attributes B and C to distinguish them. Thus, the theta-join contrasts with natural join, since in the latter common attributes are merged into one copy. Of course it makes sense to do so in the case of the natural join, since tuples don't pair unless they agree in

A	$U.B$	$U.C$	$V.B$	$V.C$	D
1	2	3	2	3	4
1	2	3	2	3	5
1	2	3	7	8	10
6	7	8	7	8	10
9	7	8	7	8	10

Figure 17: Result of $U \bowtie_{A<D} V$

their common attributes. In the case of a theta-join, there is no guarantee that compared attributes will agree in the result, since they may not be compared with $=$.

Example 16: Here is a theta-join on the same relations U and V that has a more complex condition:

$$U \bowtie_{A<D \texttt{ AND } U.B \neq V.B} V$$

That is, we require for successful pairing not only that the A component of the U-tuple be less than the D component of the V-tuple, but that the two tuples disagree on their respective B components. The tuple

A	$U.B$	$U.C$	$V.B$	$V.C$	D
1	2	3	7	8	10

is the only one to satisfy both conditions, so this relation is the result of the theta-join above. □

4.10 Combining Operations to Form Queries

If all we could do was to write single operations on one or two relations as queries, then relational algebra would not be nearly as useful as it is. However, relational algebra, like all algebras, allows us to form expressions of arbitrary complexity by applying operations to the result of other operations.

One can construct expressions of relational algebra by applying operators to subexpressions, using parentheses when necessary to indicate grouping of operands. It is also possible to represent expressions as expression trees; the latter often are easier for us to read, although they are less convenient as a machine-readable notation.

Example 17: Suppose we want to know, from our running `Movies` relation, "What are the titles and years of movies made by Fox that are at least 100 minutes long?" One way to compute the answer to this query is:

1. Select those `Movies` tuples that have *length* ≥ 100.

2. Select those `Movies` tuples that have $studioName =$ `'Fox'`.

3. Compute the intersection of (1) and (2).

4. Project the relation from (3) onto attributes `title` and `year`.

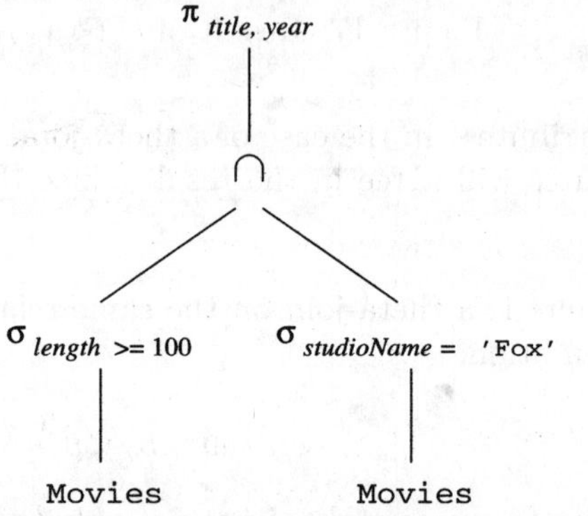

Figure 18: Expression tree for a relational algebra expression

In Fig. 18 we see the above steps represented as an expression tree. Expression trees are evaluated bottom-up by applying the operator at an interior node to the arguments, which are the results of its children. By proceeding bottom-up, we know that the arguments will be available when we need them. The two selection nodes correspond to steps (1) and (2). The intersection node corresponds to step (3), and the projection node is step (4).

Alternatively, we could represent the same expression in a conventional, linear notation, with parentheses. The formula

$$\pi_{title,year}\Big(\sigma_{length\geq 100}(\texttt{Movies}) \cap \sigma_{studioName=\texttt{'Fox'}}(\texttt{Movies})\Big)$$

represents the same expression.

Incidentally, there is often more than one relational algebra expression that represents the same computation. For instance, the above query could also be written by replacing the intersection by logical `AND` within a single selection operation. That is,

$$\pi_{title,year}\Big(\sigma_{length\geq 100 \texttt{ AND } studioName=\texttt{'Fox'}}(\texttt{Movies})\Big)$$

is an equivalent form of the query. □

Equivalent Expressions and Query Optimization

All database systems have a query-answering system, and many of them are based on a language that is similar in expressive power to relational algebra. Thus, the query asked by a user may have many *equivalent expressions* (expressions that produce the same answer whenever they are given the same relations as operands), and some of these may be much more quickly evaluated. An important job of the query "optimizer" is to replace one expression of relational algebra by an equivalent expression that is more efficiently evaluated.

4.11 Naming and Renaming

In order to control the names of the attributes used for relations that are constructed by applying relational-algebra operations, it is often convenient to use an operator that explicitly renames relations. We shall use the operator $\rho_{S(A_1,A_2,\ldots,A_n)}(R)$ to rename a relation R. The resulting relation has exactly the same tuples as R, but the name of the relation is S. Moreover, the attributes of the result relation S are named $A_1, A_2, \ldots, A_n$, in order from the left. If we only want to change the name of the relation to S and leave the attributes as they are in R, we can just say $\rho_S(R)$.

Example 18: In Example 12 we took the product of two relations R and S from Fig. 14(a) and (b) and used the convention that when an attribute appears in both operands, it is renamed by prefixing the relation name to it. Suppose, however, that we do not wish to call the two versions of B by names $R.B$ and $S.B$; rather we want to continue to use the name B for the attribute that comes from R, and we want to use X as the name of the attribute B coming from S. We can rename the attributes of S so the first is called X. The result of the expression $\rho_{S(X,C,D)}(S)$ is a relation named S that looks just like the relation S from Fig. 14, but its first column has attribute X instead of B.

A	B	X	C	D
1	2	2	5	6
1	2	4	7	8
1	2	9	10	11
3	4	2	5	6
3	4	4	7	8
3	4	9	10	11

Figure 19: $R \times \rho_{S(X,C,D)}(S)$

When we take the product of R with this new relation, there is no conflict of names among the attributes, so no further renaming is done. That is, the result of the expression $R \times \rho_{S(X,C,D)}(S)$ is the relation $R \times S$ from Fig. 14(c), except that the five columns are labeled A, B, X, C, and D, from the left. This relation is shown in Fig. 19.

As an alternative, we could take the product without renaming, as we did in Example 12, and then rename the result. The expression

$$\rho_{RS(A,B,X,C,D)}(R \times S)$$

yields the same relation as in Fig. 19, with the same set of attributes. But this relation has a name, RS, while the result relation in Fig. 19 has no name. □

4.12 Relationships Among Operations

Some of the operations that we have described in Section 4 can be expressed in terms of other relational-algebra operations. For example, intersection can be expressed in terms of set difference:

$$R \cap S = R - (R - S)$$

That is, if R and S are any two relations with the same schema, the intersection of R and S can be computed by first subtracting S from R to form a relation T consisting of all those tuples in R but not S. We then subtract T from R, leaving only those tuples of R that are also in S.

The two forms of join are also expressible in terms of other operations. Theta-join can be expressed by product and selection:

$$R \bowtie_C S = \sigma_C(R \times S)$$

The natural join of R and S can be expressed by starting with the product $R \times S$. We then apply the selection operator with a condition C of the form

$$R.A_1 = S.A_1 \texttt{ AND } R.A_2 = S.A_2 \texttt{ AND} \cdots \texttt{AND } R.A_n = S.A_n$$

where $A_1, A_2, \ldots, A_n$ are all the attributes appearing in the schemas of both R and S. Finally, we must project out one copy of each of the equated attributes. Let L be the list of attributes in the schema of R followed by those attributes in the schema of S that are not also in the schema of R. Then

$$R \bowtie S = \pi_L\Big(\sigma_C(R \times S)\Big)$$

Example 19: The natural join of the relations U and V from Fig. 16 can be written in terms of product, selection, and projection as:

$$\pi_{A,U.B,U.C,D}\Big(\sigma_{U.B=V.B \texttt{ AND } U.C=V.C}(U \times V)\Big)$$

That is, we take the product $U \times V$. Then we select for equality between each pair of attributes with the same name — B and C in this example. Finally, we project onto all the attributes except one of the B's and one of the C's; we have chosen to eliminate the attributes of V whose names also appear in the schema of U.

For another example, the theta-join of Example 16 can be written

$$\sigma_{A<D \texttt{ AND } U.B \neq V.B}(U \times V)$$

That is, we take the product of the relations U and V and then apply the condition that appeared in the theta-join. □

The rewriting rules mentioned in this section are the only "redundancies" among the operations that we have introduced. The six remaining operations — union, difference, selection, projection, product, and renaming — form an independent set, none of which can be written in terms of the other five.

4.13 A Linear Notation for Algebraic Expressions

In Section 4.10 we used an expression tree to represent a complex expression of relational algebra. An alternative is to invent names for the temporary relations that correspond to the interior nodes of the tree and write a sequence of assignments that create a value for each. The order of the assignments is flexible, as long as the children of a node N have had their values created before we attempt to create the value for N itself.

The notation we shall use for assignment statements is:

1. A relation name and parenthesized list of attributes for that relation. The name `Answer` will be used conventionally for the result of the final step; i.e., the name of the relation at the root of the expression tree.

2. The assignment symbol `:=`.

3. Any algebraic expression on the right. We can choose to use only one operator per assignment, in which case each interior node of the tree gets its own assignment statement. However, it is also permissible to combine several algebraic operations in one right side, if it is convenient to do so.

Example 20: Consider the tree of Fig. 18. One possible sequence of assignments to evaluate this expression is:

R(t,y,l,i,s,p) := $\sigma_{length \geq 100}$(Movies)
S(t,y,l,i,s,p) := $\sigma_{studioName=\texttt{'Fox'}}$(Movies)
T(t,y,l,i,s,p) := R $\cap$ S
Answer(title, year) := $\pi_{t,y}$(T)

The first step computes the relation of the interior node labeled $\sigma_{length \geq 100}$ in Fig. 18, and the second step computes the node labeled $\sigma_{studioName='Fox'}$. Notice that we get renaming "for free," since we can use any attributes and relation name we wish for the left side of an assignment. The last two steps compute the intersection and the projection in the obvious way.

It is also permissible to combine some of the steps. For instance, we could combine the last two steps and write:

$$\texttt{R(t,y,l,i,s,p)} := \sigma_{length \geq 100}(\texttt{Movies})$$
$$\texttt{S(t,y,l,i,s,p)} := \sigma_{studioName='Fox'}(\texttt{Movies})$$
$$\texttt{Answer(title, year)} := \pi_{t,y}(\texttt{R} \cap \texttt{S})$$

We could even substitute for R and S in the last line and write the entire expression in one line. □

4.14 Exercises for Section 4

Exercise 4.1: This exercise builds upon the products schema of Exercise 3.1. Recall that the database schema consists of four relations, whose schemas are:

```
Product(maker, model, type)
PC(model, speed, ram, hd, price)
Laptop(model, speed, ram, hd, screen, price)
Printer(model, color, type, price)
```

Some sample data for the relation `Product` is shown in Fig. 20. Sample data for the other three relations is shown in Fig. 21. Manufacturers and model numbers have been "sanitized," but the data is typical of products on sale at the beginning of 2007.

Write expressions of relational algebra to answer the following queries. You may use the linear notation of Section 4.13 if you wish. For the data of Figs. 20 and 21, show the result of your query. However, your answer should work for arbitrary data, not just the data of these figures.

a) What PC models have a speed of at least 3.00?

b) Which manufacturers make laptops with a hard disk of at least 100GB?

c) Find the model number and price of all products (of any type) made by manufacturer B.

d) Find the model numbers of all color laser printers.

e) Find those manufacturers that sell Laptops, but not PC's.

! f) Find those hard-disk sizes that occur in two or more PC's.

maker	*model*	*type*
A	1001	pc
A	1002	pc
A	1003	pc
A	2004	laptop
A	2005	laptop
A	2006	laptop
B	1004	pc
B	1005	pc
B	1006	pc
B	2007	laptop
C	1007	pc
D	1008	pc
D	1009	pc
D	1010	pc
D	3004	printer
D	3005	printer
E	1011	pc
E	1012	pc
E	1013	pc
E	2001	laptop
E	2002	laptop
E	2003	laptop
E	3001	printer
E	3002	printer
E	3003	printer
F	2008	laptop
F	2009	laptop
G	2010	laptop
H	3006	printer
H	3007	printer

Figure 20: Sample data for Product

model	*speed*	*ram*	*hd*	*price*
1001	2.66	1024	250	2114
1002	2.10	512	250	995
1003	1.42	512	80	478
1004	2.80	1024	250	649
1005	3.20	512	250	630
1006	3.20	1024	320	1049
1007	2.20	1024	200	510
1008	2.20	2048	250	770
1009	2.00	1024	250	650
1010	2.80	2048	300	770
1011	1.86	2048	160	959
1012	2.80	1024	160	649
1013	3.06	512	80	529

(a) Sample data for relation PC

model	*speed*	*ram*	*hd*	*screen*	*price*
2001	2.00	2048	240	20.1	3673
2002	1.73	1024	80	17.0	949
2003	1.80	512	60	15.4	549
2004	2.00	512	60	13.3	1150
2005	2.16	1024	120	17.0	2500
2006	2.00	2048	80	15.4	1700
2007	1.83	1024	120	13.3	1429
2008	1.60	1024	100	15.4	900
2009	1.60	512	80	14.1	680
2010	2.00	2048	160	15.4	2300

(b) Sample data for relation Laptop

model	*color*	*type*	*price*
3001	true	ink-jet	99
3002	false	laser	239
3003	true	laser	899
3004	true	ink-jet	120
3005	false	laser	120
3006	true	ink-jet	100
3007	true	laser	200

(c) Sample data for relation Printer

Figure 21: Sample data for relations of Exercise 4.1

! g) Find those pairs of PC models that have both the same speed and RAM. A pair should be listed only once; e.g., list (i, j) but not (j, i).

!! h) Find those manufacturers of at least two different computers (PC's or laptops) with speeds of at least 2.80.

!! i) Find the manufacturer(s) of the computer (PC or laptop) with the highest available speed.

!! j) Find the manufacturers of PC's with at least three different speeds.

!! k) Find the manufacturers who sell exactly three different models of PC.

Exercise 4.2: Draw expression trees for each of your expressions of Exercise 4.1.

Exercise 4.3: This exercise builds upon Exercise 3.2 concerning World War II capital ships. Recall it involves the following relations:

```
Classes(class, type, country, numGuns, bore, displacement)
Ships(name, class, launched)
Battles(name, date)
Outcomes(ship, battle, result)
```

Figures 22 and 23 give some sample data for these four relations.[4] Note that, unlike the data for Exercise 4.1, there are some "dangling tuples" in this data, e.g., ships mentioned in `Outcomes` that are not mentioned in `Ships`.

Write expressions of relational algebra to answer the following queries. You may use the linear notation of Section 4.13 if you wish. For the data of Figs. 22 and 23, show the result of your query. However, your answer should work for arbitrary data, not just the data of these figures.

a) Give the class names and countries of the classes that carried guns of at least 16-inch bore.

b) Find the ships launched prior to 1921.

c) Find the ships sunk in the battle of the Denmark Strait.

d) The treaty of Washington in 1921 prohibited capital ships heavier than 35,000 tons. List the ships that violated the treaty of Washington.

e) List the name, displacement, and number of guns of the ships engaged in the battle of Guadalcanal.

f) List all the capital ships mentioned in the database. (Remember that all these ships may not appear in the `Ships` relation.)

[4]Source: J. N. Westwood, *Fighting Ships of World War II*, Follett Publishing, Chicago, 1975 and R. C. Stern, *US Battleships in Action*, Squadron/Signal Publications, Carrollton, TX, 1980.

class	*type*	*country*	*numGuns*	*bore*	*displacement*
Bismarck	bb	Germany	8	15	42000
Iowa	bb	USA	9	16	46000
Kongo	bc	Japan	8	14	32000
North Carolina	bb	USA	9	16	37000
Renown	bc	Gt. Britain	6	15	32000
Revenge	bb	Gt. Britain	8	15	29000
Tennessee	bb	USA	12	14	32000
Yamato	bb	Japan	9	18	65000

(a) Sample data for relation Classes

name	*date*
Denmark Strait	5/24-27/41
Guadalcanal	11/15/42
North Cape	12/26/43
Surigao Strait	10/25/44

(b) Sample data for relation Battles

ship	*battle*	*result*
Arizona	Pearl Harbor	sunk
Bismarck	Denmark Strait	sunk
California	Surigao Strait	ok
Duke of York	North Cape	ok
Fuso	Surigao Strait	sunk
Hood	Denmark Strait	sunk
King George V	Denmark Strait	ok
Kirishima	Guadalcanal	sunk
Prince of Wales	Denmark Strait	damaged
Rodney	Denmark Strait	ok
Scharnhorst	North Cape	sunk
South Dakota	Guadalcanal	damaged
Tennessee	Surigao Strait	ok
Washington	Guadalcanal	ok
West Virginia	Surigao Strait	ok
Yamashiro	Surigao Strait	sunk

(c) Sample data for relation Outcomes

Figure 22: Data for Exercise 4.3

name	*class*	*launched*
California	Tennessee	1921
Haruna	Kongo	1915
Hiei	Kongo	1914
Iowa	Iowa	1943
Kirishima	Kongo	1915
Kongo	Kongo	1913
Missouri	Iowa	1944
Musashi	Yamato	1942
New Jersey	Iowa	1943
North Carolina	North Carolina	1941
Ramillies	Revenge	1917
Renown	Renown	1916
Repulse	Renown	1916
Resolution	Revenge	1916
Revenge	Revenge	1916
Royal Oak	Revenge	1916
Royal Sovereign	Revenge	1916
Tennessee	Tennessee	1920
Washington	North Carolina	1941
Wisconsin	Iowa	1944
Yamato	Yamato	1941

Figure 23: Sample data for relation Ships

! g) Find the classes that had only one ship as a member of that class.

! h) Find those countries that had both battleships and battlecruisers.

! i) Find those ships that "lived to fight another day"; they were damaged in one battle, but later fought in another.

Exercise 4.4: Draw expression trees for each of your expressions of Exercise 4.3.

Exercise 4.5: What is the difference between the natural join $R \bowtie S$ and the theta-join $R \bowtie_C S$ where the condition C is that $R.A = S.A$ for each attribute A appearing in the schemas of both R and S?

! **Exercise 4.6:** An operator on relations is said to be *monotone* if whenever we add a tuple to one of its arguments, the result contains all the tuples that it contained before adding the tuple, plus perhaps more tuples. Which of the operators described in this section are monotone? For each, either explain why it is monotone or give an example showing it is not.

! **Exercise 4.7:** Suppose relations R and S have n tuples and m tuples, respectively. Give the minimum and maximum numbers of tuples that the results of the following expressions can have.

a) $R \cup S$.

b) $R \bowtie S$.

c) $\sigma_C(R) \times S$, for some condition C.

d) $\pi_L(R) - S$, for some list of attributes L.

! **Exercise 4.8:** The *semijoin* of relations R and S, written $R \ltimes S$, is the set of tuples t in R such that there is at least one tuple in S that agrees with t in all attributes that R and S have in common. Give three different expressions of relational algebra that are equivalent to $R \ltimes S$.

! **Exercise 4.9:** The *antisemijoin* $R \overline{\ltimes} S$ is the set of tuples t in R that do *not* agree with any tuple of S in the attributes common to R and S. Give an expression of relational algebra equivalent to $R \overline{\ltimes} S$.

!! **Exercise 4.10:** Let R be a relation with schema

$$(A_1, A_2, \ldots, A_n, B_1, B_2, \ldots, B_m)$$

and let S be a relation with schema $(B_1, B_2, \ldots, B_m)$; that is, the attributes of S are a subset of the attributes of R. The *quotient* of R and S, denoted $R \div S$, is the set of tuples t over attributes $A_1, A_2, \ldots, A_n$ (i.e., the attributes of R that are not attributes of S) such that for every tuple s in S, the tuple ts, consisting of the components of t for $A_1, A_2, \ldots, A_n$ and the components of s for $B_1, B_2, \ldots, B_m$, is a member of R. Give an expression of relational algebra, using the operators we have defined previously in this section, that is equivalent to $R \div S$.

5 Constraints on Relations

We now take up the third important aspect of a data model: the ability to restrict the data that may be stored in a database. So far, we have seen only one kind of constraint, the requirement that an attribute or attributes form a key (Section 3.6). These and many other kinds of constraints can be expressed in relational algebra. In this section, we show how to express both key constraints and "referential-integrity" constraints; the latter require that a value appearing in one column of one relation also appear in some other column of the same or a different relation.

5.1 Relational Algebra as a Constraint Language

There are two ways in which we can use expressions of relational algebra to express constraints.

1. If R is an expression of relational algebra, then $R = \emptyset$ is a constraint that says "The value of R must be empty," or equivalently "There are no tuples in the result of R."

2. If R and S are expressions of relational algebra, then $R \subseteq S$ is a constraint that says "Every tuple in the result of R must also be in the result of S." Of course the result of S may contain additional tuples not produced by R.

These ways of expressing constraints are actually equivalent in what they can express, but sometimes one or the other is clearer or more succinct. That is, the constraint $R \subseteq S$ could just as well have been written $R - S = \emptyset$. To see why, notice that if every tuple in R is also in S, then surely $R - S$ is empty. Conversely, if $R - S$ contains no tuples, then every tuple in R must be in S (or else it would be in $R - S$).

On the other hand, a constraint of the first form, $R = \emptyset$, could just as well have been written $R \subseteq \emptyset$. Technically, $\emptyset$ is not an expression of relational algebra, but since there are expressions that evaluate to $\emptyset$, such as $R - R$, there is no harm in using $\emptyset$ as a relational-algebra expression.

In the following sections, we shall see how to express significant constraints in one of these two styles. It is the first style — equal-to-the-emptyset — that is most commonly used in SQL programming. However, as shown above, we are free to think in terms of set-containment if we wish and later convert our constraint to the equal-to-the-emptyset style.

5.2 Referential Integrity Constraints

A common kind of constraint, called a *referential integrity constraint*, asserts that a value appearing in one context also appears in another, related context. For example, in our movies database, should we see a `StarsIn` tuple that has person p in the `starName` component, we would expect that p appears as the name of some star in the `MovieStar` relation. If not, then we would question whether the listed "star" really was a star.

In general, if we have any value v as the component in attribute A of some tuple in one relation R, then because of our design intentions we may expect that v will appear in a particular component (say for attribute B) of some tuple of another relation S. We can express this integrity constraint in relational algebra as $\pi_A(R) \subseteq \pi_B(S)$, or equivalently, $\pi_A(R) - \pi_B(S) = \emptyset$.

Example 21 : Consider the two relations from our running movie database:

```
Movies(title, year, length, genre, studioName, producerC#)
MovieExec(name, address, cert#, netWorth)
```

We might reasonably assume that the producer of every movie would have to appear in the `MovieExec` relation. If not, there is something wrong, and we would at least want a system implementing a relational database to inform us that we had a movie with a producer of which the database had no knowledge.

To be more precise, the `producerC#` component of each `Movies` tuple must also appear in the `cert#` component of some `MovieExec` tuple. Since executives are uniquely identified by their certificate numbers, we would thus be assured that the movie's producer is found among the movie executives. We can express this constraint by the set-containment

$$\pi_{producerC\#}(\texttt{Movies}) \subseteq \pi_{cert\#}(\texttt{MovieExec})$$

The value of the expression on the left is the set of all certificate numbers appearing in `producerC#` components of `Movies` tuples. Likewise, the expression on the right's value is the set of all certificates in the `cert#` component of `MovieExec` tuples. Our constraint says that every certificate in the former set must also be in the latter set. □

Example 22: We can similarly express a referential integrity constraint where the "value" involved is represented by more than one attribute. For instance, we may want to assert that any movie mentioned in the relation

```
StarsIn(movieTitle, movieYear, starName)
```

also appears in the relation

```
Movies(title, year, length, genre, studioName, producerC#)
```

Movies are represented in both relations by title-year pairs, because we agreed that one of these attributes alone was not sufficient to identify a movie. The constraint

$$\pi_{movieTitle,\ movieYear}(\texttt{StarsIn}) \subseteq \pi_{title,\ year}(\texttt{Movies})$$

expresses this referential integrity constraint by comparing the title-year pairs produced by projecting both relations onto the appropriate lists of components. □

5.3 Key Constraints

The same constraint notation allows us to express far more than referential integrity. Here, we shall see how we can express algebraically the constraint that a certain attribute or set of attributes is a key for a relation.

Example 23: Recall that `name` is the key for relation

```
MovieStar(name, address, gender, birthdate)
```

That is, no two tuples agree on the `name` component. We shall express algebraically one of several implications of this constraint: that if two tuples agree on `name`, then they must also agree on `address`. Note that in fact these "two" tuples, which agree on the key `name`, must be the same tuple and therefore certainly agree in all attributes.

The idea is that if we construct all pairs of `MovieStar` tuples (t_1, t_2), we must not find a pair that agree in the `name` component and disagree in the `address` component. To construct the pairs we use a Cartesian product, and to search for pairs that violate the condition we use a selection. We then assert the constraint by equating the result to $\emptyset$.

To begin, since we are taking the product of a relation with itself, we need to rename at least one copy, in order to have names for the attributes of the product. For succinctness, let us use two new names, `MS1` and `MS2`, to refer to the `MovieStar` relation. Then the requirement can be expressed by the algebraic constraint:

$$\sigma_{MS1.name=MS2.name \texttt{ AND } MS1.address \neq MS2.address}(\texttt{MS1} \times \texttt{MS2}) = \emptyset$$

In the above, `MS1` in the product `MS1` × `MS2` is shorthand for the renaming:

$$\rho_{MS1(name,address,gender,birthdate)}(\texttt{MovieStar})$$

and `MS2` is a similar renaming of `MovieStar`. □

5.4 Additional Constraint Examples

There are many other kinds of constraints that we can express in relational algebra and that are useful for restricting database contents. A large family of constraints involve the permitted values in a context. For example, the fact that each attribute has a type constrains the values of that attribute. Often the constraint is quite straightforward, such as "integers only" or "character strings of length up to 30." Other times we want the values that may appear in an attribute to be restricted to a small enumerated set of values. Other times, there are complex limitations on the values that may appear. We shall give two examples, one of a simple *domain constraint* for an attribute, and the second a more complicated restriction.

Example 24: Suppose we wish to specify that the only legal values for the `gender` attribute of `MovieStar` are `'F'` and `'M'`. We can express this constraint algebraically by:

$$\sigma_{gender \neq \texttt{'F'} \texttt{ AND } gender \neq \texttt{'M'}}(\texttt{MovieStar}) = \emptyset$$

That is, the set of tuples in `MovieStar` whose `gender` component is equal to neither `'F'` nor `'M'` is empty. □

Example 25: Suppose we wish to require that one must have a net worth of at least \$10,000,000 to be the president of a movie studio. We can express this constraint algebraically as follows. First, we need to theta-join the two relations

```
MovieExec(name, address, cert#, netWorth)
Studio(name, address, presC#)
```

using the condition that `presC#` from `Studio` and `cert#` from `MovieExec` are equal. That join combines pairs of tuples consisting of a studio and an executive, such that the executive is the president of the studio. If we select from this relation those tuples where the net worth is less than ten million, we have a set that, according to our constraint, must be empty. Thus, we may express the constraint as:

$$\sigma_{netWorth<10000000}(\texttt{Studio} \bowtie_{presC\#=cert\#} \texttt{MovieExec}) = \emptyset$$

An alternative way to express the same constraint is to compare the set of certificates that represent studio presidents with the set of certificates that represent executives with a net worth of at least \$10,000,000; the former must be a subset of the latter. The containment

$$\pi_{presC\#}(\texttt{Studio}) \subseteq \pi_{cert\#}\Big(\sigma_{netWorth\geq 10000000}(\texttt{MovieExec})\Big)$$

expresses the above idea. □

5.5 Exercises for Section 5

Exercise 5.1: Express the following constraints about the relations of Exercise 3.1, reproduced here:

```
Product(maker, model, type)
PC(model, speed, ram, hd, price)
Laptop(model, speed, ram, hd, screen, price)
Printer(model, color, type, price)
```

You may write your constraints either as containments or by equating an expression to the empty set. For the data of Exercise 4.1, indicate any violations to your constraints.

a) A PC with a processor speed less than 2.00 must not sell for more than \$500.

b) A laptop with a screen size less than 15.4 inches must have at least a 100 gigabyte hard disk or sell for less than \$1000.

! c) No manufacturer of PC's may also make laptops.

!! d) A manufacturer of a PC must also make a laptop with at least as great a processor speed.

! e) If a laptop has a larger main memory than a PC, then the laptop must also have a higher price than the PC.

Exercise 5.2: Express the following constraints in relational algebra. The constraints are based on the relations of Exercise 3.2:

```
Classes(class, type, country, numGuns, bore, displacement)
Ships(name, class, launched)
Battles(name, date)
Outcomes(ship, battle, result)
```

You may write your constraints either as containments or by equating an expression to the empty set. For the data of Exercise 4.3, indicate any violations to your constraints.

a) No class of ships may have guns with larger than 16-inch bore.

b) If a class of ships has more than 9 guns, then their bore must be no larger than 14 inches.

! c) No class may have more than 2 ships.

! d) No country may have both battleships and battlecruisers.

!! e) No ship with more than 9 guns may be in a battle with a ship having fewer than 9 guns that was sunk.

! **Exercise 5.3:** Suppose R and S are two relations. Let C be the referential integrity constraint that says: whenever R has a tuple with some values $v_1, v_2, \ldots, v_n$ in particular attributes $A_1, A_2, \ldots, A_n$, there must be a tuple of S that has the same values $v_1, v_2, \ldots, v_n$ in particular attributes $B_1, B_2, \ldots, B_n$. Show how to express constraint C in relational algebra.

! **Exercise 5.4:** Another algebraic way to express a constraint is $E_1 = E_2$, where both E_1 and E_2 are relational-algebra expressions. Can this form of constraint express more than the two forms we discussed in this section?

6 Summary

✦ *Data Models*: A data model is a notation for describing the structure of the data in a database, along with the constraints on that data. The data model also normally provides a notation for describing operations on that data: queries and data modifications.

- *Relational Model*: Relations are tables representing information. Columns are headed by attributes; each attribute has an associated domain, or data type. Rows are called tuples, and a tuple has one component for each attribute of the relation.

- *Schemas*: A relation name, together with the attributes of that relation and their types, form the relation schema. A collection of relation schemas forms a database schema. Particular data for a relation or collection of relations is called an instance of that relation schema or database schema.

- *Keys*: An important type of constraint on relations is the assertion that an attribute or set of attributes forms a key for the relation. No two tuples of a relation can agree on all attributes of the key, although they can agree on some of the key attributes.

- *Semistructured Data Model*: In this model, data is organized in a tree or graph structure. XML is an important example of a semistructured data model.

- *SQL*: The language SQL is the principal query language for relational database systems. The current standard is called SQL-99. Commercial systems generally vary from this standard but adhere to much of it.

- *Data Definition*: SQL has statements to declare elements of a database schema. The `CREATE TABLE` statement allows us to declare the schema for stored relations (called tables), specifying the attributes, their types, default values, and keys.

- *Altering Schemas*: We can change parts of the database schema with an `ALTER` statement. These changes include adding and removing attributes from relation schemas and changing the default value associated with an attribute. We may also use a `DROP` statement to completely eliminate relations or other schema elements.

- *Relational Algebra*: This algebra underlies most query languages for the relational model. Its principal operators are union, intersection, difference, selection, projection, Cartesian product, natural join, theta-join, and renaming.

- *Selection and Projection*: The selection operator produces a result consisting of all tuples of the argument relation that satisfy the selection condition. Projection removes undesired columns from the argument relation to produce the result.

- *Joins*: We join two relations by comparing tuples, one from each relation. In a natural join, we splice together those pairs of tuples that agree on all attributes common to the two relations. In a theta-join, pairs of tuples are concatenated if they meet a selection condition associated with the theta-join.

✦ *Constraints in Relational Algebra*: Many common kinds of constraints can be expressed as the containment of one relational algebra expression in another, or as the equality of a relational algebra expression to the empty set.

7 References

The classic paper by Codd on the relational model is [1]. This paper introduces relational algebra, as well. The use of relational algebra to describe constraints is from [2].

The semistructured data model is from [3]. XML is a standard developed by the World-Wide-Web Consortium. The home page for information about XML is [4].

1. E. F. Codd, "A relational model for large shared data banks," *Comm. ACM* **13**:6, pp. 377–387, 1970.

2. J.-M. Nicolas, "Logic for improving integrity checking in relational databases," *Acta Informatica* **18**:3, pp. 227–253, 1982.

3. Y. Papakonstantinou, H. Garcia-Molina, and J. Widom, "Object exchange across heterogeneous information sources," *IEEE Intl. Conf. on Data Engineering*, pp. 251–260, March 1995.

4. World-Wide-Web Consortium, `http://www.w3.org/XML/`

Design Theory for Relational Databases

There are many ways we could go about designing a relational database schema for an application. There are several high-level notations for describing the structure of data and the ways in which these high-level designs can be converted into relations. We can also examine the requirements for a database and define relations directly, without going through a high-level intermediate stage. Whatever approach we use, it is common for an initial relational schema to have room for improvement, especially by eliminating redundancy. Often, the problems with a schema involve trying to combine too much into one relation.

Fortunately, there is a well developed theory for relational databases: "dependencies," their implications for what makes a good relational database schema, and what we can do about a schema if it has flaws. In this chapter, we first identify the problems that are caused in some relation schemas by the presence of certain dependencies; these problems are referred to as "anomalies."

Our discussion starts with "functional dependencies," a generalization of the idea of a key for a relation. We then use the notion of functional dependencies to define normal forms for relation schemas. The impact of this theory, called "normalization," is that we decompose relations into two or more relations when that will remove anomalies. Next, we introduce "multivalued dependencies," which intuitively represent a condition where one or more attributes of a relation are independent from one or more other attributes. These dependencies also lead to normal forms and decomposition of relations to eliminate redundancy.

1 Functional Dependencies

There is a design theory for relations that lets us examine a design carefully and make improvements based on a few simple principles. The theory begins by

From Chapter 3 of *Database Systems*, Second Edition. Hector Garcia-Molina, Jeffrey D. Ullman, Jennifer Widom.

having us state the constraints that apply to the relation. The most common constraint is the "functional dependency," a statement of a type that generalizes the idea of a key for a relation. Later in this chapter, we shall see how this theory gives us simple tools to improve our designs by the process of "decomposition" of relations: the replacement of one relation by several, whose sets of attributes together include all the attributes of the original.

1.1 Definition of Functional Dependency

A *functional dependency* (FD) on a relation R is a statement of the form "If two tuples of R agree on all of the attributes $A_1, A_2, \ldots, A_n$ (i.e., the tuples have the same values in their respective components for each of these attributes), then they must also agree on all of another list of attributes $B_1, B_2, \ldots, B_m$. We write this FD formally as $A_1A_2 \cdots A_n \rightarrow B_1B_2 \cdots B_m$ and say that

"$A_1, A_2, \ldots, A_n$ functionally determine $B_1, B_2, \ldots, B_m$"

Figure 1 suggests what this FD tells us about any two tuples t and u in the relation R. However, the A's and B's can be anywhere; it is not necessary for the A's and B's to appear consecutively or for the A's to precede the B's.

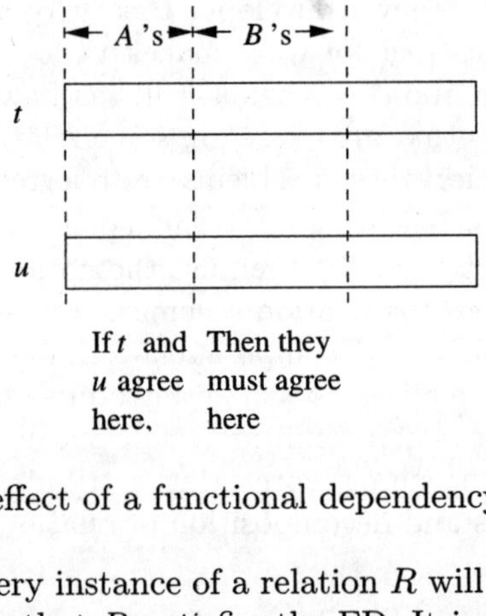

Figure 1: The effect of a functional dependency on two tuples.

If we can be sure every instance of a relation R will be one in which a given FD is true, then we say that R *satisfies* the FD. It is important to remember that when we say that R satisfies an FD f, we are asserting a constraint on R, not just saying something about one particular instance of R.

It is common for the right side of an FD to be a single attribute. In fact, we shall see that the one functional dependency $A_1A_2 \cdots A_n \rightarrow B_1B_2 \cdots B_m$ is equivalent to the set of FD's:

$$A_1A_2 \cdots A_n \rightarrow B_1$$
$$A_1A_2 \cdots A_n \rightarrow B_2$$
$$\ldots$$
$$A_1A_2 \cdots A_n \rightarrow B_m$$

title	*year*	*length*	*genre*	*studioName*	*starName*
Star Wars	1977	124	SciFi	Fox	Carrie Fisher
Star Wars	1977	124	SciFi	Fox	Mark Hamill
Star Wars	1977	124	SciFi	Fox	Harrison Ford
Gone With the Wind	1939	231	drama	MGM	Vivien Leigh
Wayne's World	1992	95	comedy	Paramount	Dana Carvey
Wayne's World	1992	95	comedy	Paramount	Mike Meyers

Figure 2: An instance of the relation `Movies1(title, year, length, genre, studioName, starName)`

Example 1: Let us consider the relation

`Movies1(title, year, length, genre, studioName, starName)`

an instance of which is shown in Fig. 2. While related to our running `Movies` relation, it has additional attributes, which is why we call it "`Movies1`" instead of "`Movies`." Notice that this relation tries to "do too much." It holds information that in our running database schema was attributed to three different relations: `Movies`, `Studio`, and `StarsIn`. As we shall see, the schema for `Movies1` is not a good design. But to see what is wrong with the design, we must first determine the functional dependencies that hold for the relation. We claim that the following FD holds:

`title year` → `length genre studioName`

Informally, this FD says that if two tuples have the same value in their `title` components, and they also have the same value in their `year` components, then these two tuples must also have the same values in their `length` components, the same values in their `genre` components, and the same values in their `studioName` components. This assertion makes sense, since we believe that it is not possible for there to be two movies released in the same year with the same title (although there could be movies of the same title released in different years). Thus, we expect that given a title and year, there is a unique movie. Therefore, there is a unique length for the movie, a unique genre, and a unique studio.

On the other hand, we observe that the statement

`title year` → `starName`

is false; it is not a functional dependency. Given a movie, it is entirely possible that there is more than one star for the movie listed in our database. Notice that even had we been lazy and only listed one star for *Star Wars* and one star for *Wayne's World* (just as we only listed one of the many stars for *Gone With the Wind*), this FD would not suddenly become true for the relation `Movies1`.

The reason is that the FD says something about all possible instances of the relation, not about one of its instances. The fact that we *could* have an instance with multiple stars for a movie rules out the possibility that title and year functionally determine starName. □

1.2 Keys of Relations

We say a set of one or more attributes $\{A_1, A_2, \ldots, A_n\}$ is a *key* for a relation R if:

1. Those attributes functionally determine all other attributes of the relation. That is, it is impossible for two distinct tuples of R to agree on all of $A_1, A_2, \ldots, A_n$.

2. No proper subset of $\{A_1, A_2, \ldots, A_n\}$ functionally determines all other attributes of R; i.e., a key must be *minimal.*

When a key consists of a single attribute A, we often say that A (rather than $\{A\}$) is a key.

Example 2: Attributes {`title`, `year`, `starName`} form a key for the relation `Movies1` of Fig. 2. First, we must show that they functionally determine all the other attributes. That is, suppose two tuples agree on these three attributes: `title`, `year`, and `starName`. Because they agree on `title` and `year`, they must agree on the other attributes — `length`, `genre`, and `studioName` — as we discussed in Example 1. Thus, two different tuples cannot agree on all of `title`, `year`, and `starName`; they would in fact be the same tuple.

Now, we must argue that no proper subset of {`title`, `year`, `starName`} functionally determines all other attributes. To see why, begin by observing that `title` and `year` do not determine `starName`, because many movies have more than one star. Thus, {`title`, `year`} is not a key.

{`year`, `starName`} is not a key because we could have a star in two movies in the same year; therefore

$$\texttt{year starName} \rightarrow \texttt{title}$$

is not an FD. Also, we claim that {`title`, `starName`} is not a key, because two movies with the same title, made in different years, occasionally have a star in common.[1] □

Sometimes a relation has more than one key. If so, it is common to designate one of the keys as the *primary key.* In commercial database systems, the choice of primary key can influence some implementation issues such as how the relation is stored on disk. However, the theory of FD's gives no special role to "primary keys."

[1]Since we asserted in an earlier book that there were no known examples of this phenomenon, several people have shown us we were wrong. It's an interesting challenge to discover stars that appeared in two versions of the same movie.

What Is "Functional" About Functional Dependencies?

$A_1A_2 \cdots A_n \rightarrow B$ is called a "functional" dependency because in principle there is a function that takes a list of values, one for each of attributes $A_1, A_2, \ldots, A_n$ and produces a unique value (or no value at all) for B. For instance, in the `Movies1` relation, we can imagine a function that takes a string like `"Star Wars"` and an integer like 1977 and produces the unique value of `length`, namely 124, that appears in the relation `Movies1`. However, this function is not the usual sort of function that we meet in mathematics, because there is no way to compute it from first principles. That is, we cannot perform some operations on strings like `"Star Wars"` and integers like 1977 and come up with the correct length. Rather, the function is only computed by lookup in the relation. We look for a tuple with the given `title` and `year` values and see what value that tuple has for `length`.

1.3 Superkeys

A set of attributes that contains a key is called a *superkey*, short for "superset of a key." Thus, every key is a superkey. However, some superkeys are not (minimal) keys. Note that every superkey satisfies the first condition of a key: it functionally determines all other attributes of the relation. However, a superkey need not satisfy the second condition: minimality.

Example 3: In the relation of Example 2, there are many superkeys. Not only is the key

`{title, year, starName}`

a superkey, but any superset of this set of attributes, such as

`{title, year, starName, length, studioName}`

is a superkey. □

1.4 Exercises for Section 1

Exercise 1.1: Consider a relation about people in the United States, including their name, Social Security number, street address, city, state, ZIP code, area code, and phone number (7 digits). What FD's would you expect to hold? What are the keys for the relation? To answer this question, you need to know something about the way these numbers are assigned. For instance, can an area

Other Key Terminology

In some books and articles one finds different terminology regarding keys. One can find the term "key" used the way we have used the term "superkey," that is, a set of attributes that functionally determine all the attributes, with no requirement of minimality. These sources typically use the term "candidate key" for a key that is minimal — that is, a "key" in the sense we use the term.

code straddle two states? Can a ZIP code straddle two area codes? Can two people have the same Social Security number? Can they have the same address or phone number?

Exercise 1.2: Consider a relation representing the present position of molecules in a closed container. The attributes are an ID for the molecule, the x, y, and z coordinates of the molecule, and its velocity in the x, y, and z dimensions. What FD's would you expect to hold? What are the keys?

!! **Exercise 1.3:** Suppose R is a relation with attributes $A_1, A_2, \ldots, A_n$. As a function of n, tell how many superkeys R has, if:

a) The only key is A_1.

b) The only keys are A_1 and A_2.

c) The only keys are $\{A_1, A_2\}$ and $\{A_3, A_4\}$.

d) The only keys are $\{A_1, A_2\}$ and $\{A_1, A_3\}$.

2 Rules About Functional Dependencies

In this section, we shall learn how to *reason* about FD's. That is, suppose we are told of a set of FD's that a relation satisfies. Often, we can deduce that the relation must satisfy certain other FD's. This ability to discover additional FD's is essential when we discuss the design of good relation schemas in Section 3.

2.1 Reasoning About Functional Dependencies

Let us begin with a motivating example that will show us how we can infer a functional dependency from other given FD's.

Example 4: If we are told that a relation $R(A, B, C)$ satisfies the FD's $A \to B$ and $B \to C$, then we can deduce that R also satisfies the FD $A \to C$. How does that reasoning go? To prove that $A \to C$, we must consider two tuples of R that agree on A and prove they also agree on C.

Let the tuples agreeing on attribute A be (a, b_1, c_1) and (a, b_2, c_2). Since R satisfies $A \to B$, and these tuples agree on A, they must also agree on B. That is, $b_1 = b_2$, and the tuples are really (a, b, c_1) and (a, b, c_2), where b is both b_1 and b_2. Similarly, since R satisfies $B \to C$, and the tuples agree on B, they agree on C. Thus, $c_1 = c_2$; i.e., the tuples *do* agree on C. We have proved that any two tuples of R that agree on A also agree on C, and that is the FD $A \to C$. $\square$

FD's often can be presented in several different ways, without changing the set of legal instances of the relation. We say:

- Two sets of FD's S and T are *equivalent* if the set of relation instances satisfying S is exactly the same as the set of relation instances satisfying T.

- More generally, a set of FD's S *follows* from a set of FD's T if every relation instance that satisfies all the FD's in T also satisfies all the FD's in S.

Note then that two sets of FD's S and T are equivalent if and only if S follows from T, and T follows from S.

In this section we shall see several useful rules about FD's. In general, these rules let us replace one set of FD's by an equivalent set, or to add to a set of FD's others that follow from the original set. An example is the *transitive rule* that lets us follow chains of FD's, as in Example 4. We shall also give an algorithm for answering the general question of whether one FD follows from one or more other FD's.

2.2 The Splitting/Combining Rule

Recall that in Section 1.1 we commented that the FD:

$$A_1A_2 \cdots A_n \to B_1B_2 \cdots B_m$$

was equivalent to the set of FD's:

$$A_1A_2 \cdots A_n \to B_1, \quad A_1A_2 \cdots A_n \to B_2, \ldots, A_1A_2 \cdots A_n \to B_m$$

That is, we may split attributes on the right side so that only one attribute appears on the right of each FD. Likewise, we can replace a collection of FD's having a common left side by a single FD with the same left side and all the right sides combined into one set of attributes. In either event, the new set of FD's is equivalent to the old. The equivalence noted above can be used in two ways.

- We can replace an FD $A_1A_2 \cdots A_n \to B_1B_2 \cdots B_m$ by a set of FD's $A_1A_2 \cdots A_n \to B_i$ for $i = 1, 2, \ldots, m$. This transformation we call the *splitting rule.*

- We can replace a set of FD's $A_1A_2 \cdots A_n \rightarrow B_i$ for $i = 1, 2, \ldots, m$ by the single FD $A_1A_2 \cdots A_n \rightarrow B_1B_2 \cdots B_m$. We call this transformation the *combining rule.*

Example 5: In Example 1 the set of FD's:

```
title year → length
title year → genre
title year → studioName
```

is equivalent to the single FD:

```
title year → length genre studioName
```

that we asserted there. □

The reason the splitting and combining rules are true should be obvious. Suppose we have two tuples that agree in $A_1, A_2, \ldots, A_n$. As a single FD, we would assert "then the tuples must agree in all of $B_1, B_2, \ldots, B_m$." As individual FD's, we assert "then the tuples agree in B_1, and they agree in B_2, and,..., and they agree in B_m." These two conclusions say exactly the same thing.

One might imagine that splitting could be applied to the left sides of FD's as well as to right sides. However, there is no splitting rule for left sides, as the following example shows.

Example 6: Consider one of the FD's such as:

```
title year → length
```

for the relation `Movies1` in Example 1. If we try to split the left side into

```
title → length
year → length
```

then we get two false FD's. That is, `title` does not functionally determine `length`, since there can be several movies with the same title (e.g., *King Kong*) but of different lengths. Similarly, `year` does not functionally determine `length`, because there are certainly movies of different lengths made in any one year. □

2.3 Trivial Functional Dependencies

A constraint of any kind on a relation is said to be *trivial* if it holds for every instance of the relation, regardless of what other constraints are assumed. When the constraints are FD's, it is easy to tell whether an FD is trivial. They are the FD's $A_1A_2 \cdots A_n \rightarrow B_1B_2 \cdots B_m$ such that

$$\{B_1, B_2, \ldots, B_m\} \subseteq \{A_1, A_2, \ldots, A_n\}$$

That is, a trivial FD has a right side that is a subset of its left side. For example, title year → title

is a trivial FD, as is

title → title

Every trivial FD holds in every relation, since it says that "two tuples that agree in all of $A_1, A_2, \ldots, A_n$ agree in a subset of them." Thus, we may assume any trivial FD, without having to justify it on the basis of what FD's are asserted for the relation.

There is an intermediate situation in which some, but not all, of the attributes on the right side of an FD are also on the left. This FD is not trivial, but it can be simplifed by removing from the right side of an FD those attributes that appear on the left. That is:

- The FD $A_1A_2 \cdots A_n \rightarrow B_1B_2 \cdots B_m$ is equivalent to

$$A_1A_2 \cdots A_n \rightarrow C_1C_2 \cdots C_k$$

where the C's are all those B's that are not also A's.

We call this rule, illustrated in Fig. 3, the *trivial-dependency rule.*

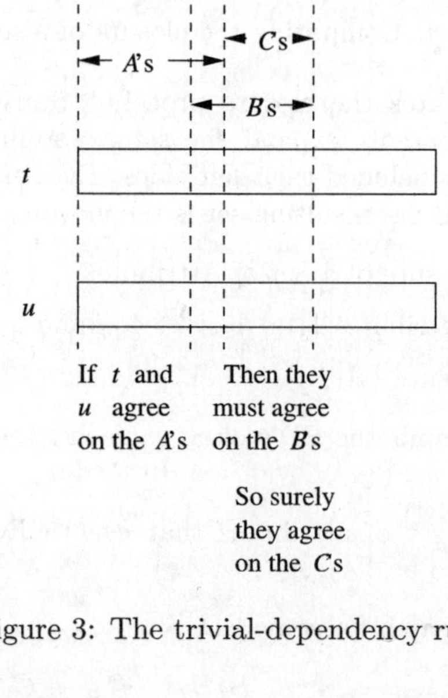

Figure 3: The trivial-dependency rule

2.4 Computing the Closure of Attributes

Before proceeding to other rules, we shall give a general principle from which all true rules follow. Suppose $\{A_1, A_2, \ldots, A_n\}$ is a set of attributes and S

is a set of FD's. The *closure* of $\{A_1, A_2, \ldots, A_n\}$ under the FD's in S is the set of attributes B such that every relation that satisfies all the FD's in set S also satisfies $A_1A_2 \cdots A_n \to B$. That is, $A_1A_2 \cdots A_n \to B$ follows from the FD's of S. We denote the closure of a set of attributes $A_1A_2 \cdots A_n$ by $\{A_1, A_2, \ldots, A_n\}^+$. Note that $A_1, A_2, \ldots, A_n$ are always in $\{A_1, A_2, \ldots, A_n\}^+$ because the FD $A_1A_2 \cdots A_n \to A_i$ is trivial when i is one of $1, 2, \ldots, n$.

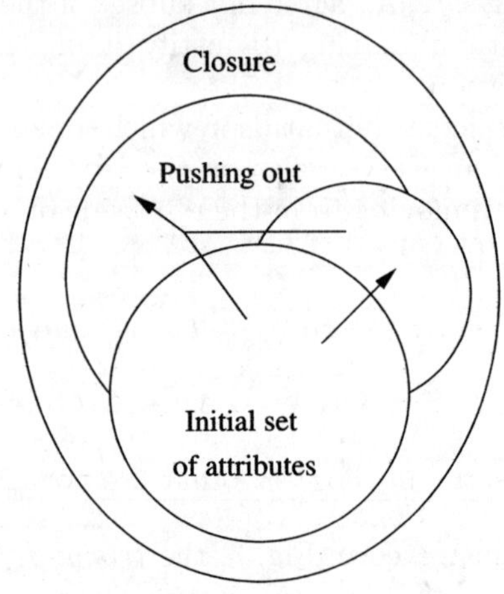

Figure 4: Computing the closure of a set of attributes

Figure 4 illustrates the closure process. Starting with the given set of attributes, we repeatedly expand the set by adding the right sides of FD's as soon as we have included their left sides. Eventually, we cannot expand the set any further, and the resulting set is the closure. More precisely:

Algorithm 7: Closure of a Set of Attributes.

INPUT: A set of attributes $\{A_1, A_2, \ldots, A_n\}$ and a set of FD's S.

OUTPUT: The closure $\{A_1, A_2, \ldots, A_n\}^+$.

1. If necessary, split the FD's of S, so each FD in S has a single attribute on the right.

2. Let X be a set of attributes that eventually will become the closure. Initialize X to be $\{A_1, A_2, \ldots, A_n\}$.

3. Repeatedly search for some FD

$$B_1B_2 \cdots B_m \to C$$

such that all of $B_1, B_2, \ldots, B_m$ are in the set of attributes X, but C is not. Add C to the set X and repeat the search. Since X can only grow, and the number of attributes of any relation schema must be finite, eventually nothing more can be added to X, and this step ends.

4. The set X, after no more attributes can be added to it, is the correct value of $\{A_1, A_2, \ldots, A_n\}^+$.

□

Example 8: Let us consider a relation with attributes A, B, C, D, E, and F. Suppose that this relation has the FD's $AB \to C$, $BC \to AD$, $D \to E$, and $CF \to B$. What is the closure of $\{A, B\}$, that is, $\{A, B\}^+$?

First, split $BC \to AD$ into $BC \to A$ and $BC \to D$. Then, start with $X = \{A, B\}$. First, notice that both attributes on the left side of FD $AB \to C$ are in X, so we may add the attribute C, which is on the right side of that FD. Thus, after one iteration of Step 3, X becomes $\{A, B, C\}$.

Next, we see that the left sides of $BC \to A$ and $BC \to D$ are now contained in X, so we may add to X the attributes A and D. A is already there, but D is not, so X next becomes $\{A, B, C, D\}$. At this point, we may use the FD $D \to E$ to add E to X, which is now $\{A, B, C, D, E\}$. No more changes to X are possible. In particular, the FD $CF \to B$ can not be used, because its left side never becomes contained in X. Thus, $\{A, B\}^+ = \{A, B, C, D, E\}$. □

By computing the closure of any set of attributes, we can test whether any given FD $A_1A_2 \cdots A_n \to B$ follows from a set of FD's S. First compute $\{A_1, A_2, \ldots, A_n\}^+$ using the set of FD's S. If B is in $\{A_1, A_2, \ldots, A_n\}^+$, then $A_1A_2 \cdots A_n \to B$ does follow from S, and if B is not in $\{A_1, A_2, \ldots, A_n\}^+$, then this FD does not follow from S. More generally, $A_1A_2 \cdots A_n \to B_1B_2 \cdots B_m$ follows from set of FD's S if and only if all of $B_1, B_2, \ldots, B_m$ are in

$$\{A_1, A_2, \ldots, A_n\}^+$$

Example 9: Consider the relation and FD's of Example 8. Suppose we wish to test whether $AB \to D$ follows from these FD's. We compute $\{A, B\}^+$, which is $\{A, B, C, D, E\}$, as we saw in that example. Since D is a member of the closure, we conclude that $AB \to D$ does follow.

On the other hand, consider the FD $D \to A$. To test whether this FD follows from the given FD's, first compute $\{D\}^+$. To do so, we start with $X = \{D\}$. We can use the FD $D \to E$ to add E to the set X. However, then we are stuck. We cannot find any other FD whose left side is contained in $X = \{D, E\}$, so $\{D\}^+ = \{D, E\}$. Since A is not a member of $\{D, E\}$, we conclude that $D \to A$ does not follow. □

2.5 Why the Closure Algorithm Works

In this section, we shall show why Algorithm 7 correctly decides whether or not an FD $A_1A_2 \cdots A_n \to B$ follows from a given set of FD's S. There are two parts to the proof:

1. We must prove that Algorithm 7 does not claim too much. That is, we must show that if $A_1A_2 \cdots A_n \to B$ is asserted by the closure test (i.e.,

B is in $\{A_1, A_2, \ldots, A_n\}^+$), then $A_1A_2 \cdots A_n \rightarrow B$ holds in any relation that satisfies all the FD's in S.

2. We must prove that Algorithm 7 does not fail to discover a FD that truly follows from the set of FD's S.

Why the Closure Algorithm Claims only True FD's

We can prove by induction on the number of times that we apply the growing operation of Step 3 that for every attribute D in X, the FD $A_1A_2 \cdots A_n \rightarrow D$ holds. That is, every relation R satisfying all of the FD's in S also satisfies $A_1A_2 \cdots A_n \rightarrow D$.

BASIS: The basis case is when there are zero steps. Then D must be one of $A_1, A_2, \ldots, A_n$, and surely $A_1A_2 \cdots A_n \rightarrow D$ holds in any relation, because it is a trivial FD.

INDUCTION: For the induction, suppose D was added when we used the FD $B_1B_2 \cdots B_m \rightarrow D$ of S. We know by the inductive hypothesis that R satisfies $A_1A_2 \cdots A_n \rightarrow B_1B_2 \cdots B_m$. Now, suppose two tuples of R agree on all of $A_1, A_2, \ldots, A_n$. Then since R satisfies $A_1A_2 \cdots A_n \rightarrow B_1B_2 \cdots B_m$, the two tuples must agree on all of $B_1, B_2, \ldots, B_m$. Since R satisfies $B_1B_2 \cdots B_m \rightarrow D$, we also know these two tuples agree on D. Thus, R satisfies $A_1A_2 \cdots A_n \rightarrow D$.

Why the Closure Algorithm Discovers All True FD's

Suppose $A_1A_2 \cdots A_n \rightarrow B$ were an FD that Algorithm 7 says does not follow from set S. That is, the closure of $\{A_1, A_2, \ldots, A_n\}$ using set of FD's S does not include B. We must show that FD $A_1A_2 \cdots A_n \rightarrow B$ really doesn't follow from S. That is, we must show that there is at least one relation instance that satisfies all the FD's in S, and yet does not satisfy $A_1A_2 \cdots A_n \rightarrow B$.

This instance I is actually quite simple to construct; it is shown in Fig. 5. I has only two tuples: t and s. The two tuples agree in all the attributes of $\{A_1, A_2, \ldots, A_n\}^+$, and they disagree in all the other attributes. We must show first that I satisfies all the FD's of S, and then that it does not satisfy $A_1A_2 \cdots A_n \rightarrow B$.

	$\{A_1, A_2, \ldots, A_n\}^+$	Other Attributes
t:	1 1 1 ⋯ 1 1	0 0 0 ⋯ 0 0
s:	1 1 1 ⋯ 1 1	1 1 1 ⋯ 1 1

Figure 5: An instance I satisfying S but not $A_1A_2 \cdots A_n \rightarrow B$

Suppose there were some FD $C_1C_2 \cdots C_k \rightarrow D$ in set S (after splitting right sides) that instance I does not satisfy. Since I has only two tuples, t and s, those must be the two tuples that violate $C_1C_2 \cdots C_k \rightarrow D$. That is, t and s agree in all the attributes of $\{C_1, C_2, \ldots, C_k\}$, yet disagree on D. If we examine Fig. 5 we see that all of $C_1, C_2, \ldots, C_k$ must be among the attributes of $\{A_1, A_2, \ldots, A_n\}^+$, because those are the only attributes on which t and s agree. Likewise, D must be among the other attributes, because only on those attributes do t and s disagree.

But then we did not compute the closure correctly. $C_1C_2 \cdots C_k \rightarrow D$ should have been applied when X was $\{A_1, A_2, \ldots, A_n\}$ to add D to X. We conclude that $C_1C_2 \cdots C_k \rightarrow D$ cannot exist; i.e., instance I satisfies S.

Second, we must show that I does not satisfy $A_1A_2 \cdots A_n \rightarrow B$. However, this part is easy. Surely, $A_1, A_2, \ldots, A_n$ are among the attributes on which t and s agree. Also, we know that B is not in $\{A_1, A_2, \ldots, A_n\}^+$, so B is one of the attributes on which t and s disagree. Thus, I does not satisfy $A_1A_2 \cdots A_n \rightarrow B$. We conclude that Algorithm 7 asserts neither too few nor too many FD's; it asserts exactly those FD's that do follow from S.

2.6 The Transitive Rule

The transitive rule lets us cascade two FD's, and generalizes the observation of Example 4.

- If $A_1A_2 \cdots A_n \rightarrow B_1B_2 \cdots B_m$ and $B_1B_2 \cdots B_m \rightarrow C_1C_2 \cdots C_k$ hold in relation R, then $A_1A_2 \cdots A_n \rightarrow C_1C_2 \cdots C_k$ also holds in R.

If some of the C's are among the A's, we may eliminate them from the right side by the trivial-dependencies rule.

To see why the transitive rule holds, apply the test of Section 2.4. To test whether $A_1A_2 \cdots A_n \rightarrow C_1C_2 \cdots C_k$ holds, we need to compute the closure $\{A_1, A_2, \ldots, A_n\}^+$ with respect to the two given FD's.

The FD $A_1A_2 \cdots A_n \rightarrow B_1B_2 \cdots B_m$ tells us that all of $B_1, B_2, \ldots, B_m$ are in $\{A_1, A_2, \ldots, A_n\}^+$. Then, we can use the FD $B_1B_2 \cdots B_m \rightarrow C_1C_2 \cdots C_k$ to add $C_1, C_2, \ldots, C_k$ to $\{A_1, A_2, \ldots, A_n\}^+$. Since all the C's are in

$$\{A_1, A_2, \ldots, A_n\}^+$$

we conclude that $A_1A_2 \cdots A_n \rightarrow C_1C_2 \cdots C_k$ holds for any relation that satisfies both $A_1A_2 \cdots A_n \rightarrow B_1B_2 \cdots B_m$ and $B_1B_2 \cdots B_m \rightarrow C_1C_2 \cdots C_k$.

Example 10: Here is another version of the `Movies` relation that includes both the studio of the movie and some information about that studio.

title	*year*	*length*	*genre*	*studioName*	*studioAddr*
`Star Wars`	1977	124	`sciFi`	`Fox`	`Hollywood`
`Eight Below`	2005	120	`drama`	`Disney`	`Buena Vista`
`Wayne's World`	1992	95	`comedy`	`Paramount`	`Hollywood`

Two of the FD's that we might reasonably claim to hold are:

$$\texttt{title year} \rightarrow \texttt{studioName}$$
$$\texttt{studioName} \rightarrow \texttt{studioAddr}$$

> **Closures and Keys**
>
> Notice that $\{A_1, A_2, \ldots, A_n\}^+$ is the set of all attributes of a relation if and only if $A_1, A_2, \ldots, A_n$ is a superkey for the relation. For only then does $A_1, A_2, \ldots, A_n$ functionally determine all the other attributes. We can test if $A_1, A_2, \ldots, A_n$ is a key for a relation by checking first that $\{A_1, A_2, \ldots, A_n\}^+$ is all attributes, and then checking that, for no set X formed by removing one attribute from $\{A_1, A_2, \ldots, A_n\}$, is X^+ the set of all attributes.

The first is justified because there can be only one movie with a given title and year, and there is only one studio that owns a given movie. The second is justified because studios have unique addresses.

The transitive rule allows us to combine the two FD's above to get a new FD:

$$\texttt{title year} \rightarrow \texttt{studioAddr}$$

This FD says that a title and year (i.e., a movie) determines an address — the address of the studio owning the movie. □

2.7 Closing Sets of Functional Dependencies

Sometimes we have a choice of which FD's we use to represent the full set of FD's for a relation. If we are given a set of FD's S (such as the FD's that hold in a given relation), then any set of FD's equivalent to S is said to be a *basis* for S. To avoid some of the explosion of possible bases, we shall limit ourselves to considering only bases whose FD's have singleton right sides. If we have any basis, we can apply the splitting rule to make the right sides be singletons. A *minimal basis* for a relation is a basis B that satisfies three conditions:

1. All the FD's in B have singleton right sides.

2. If any FD is removed from B, the result is no longer a basis.

3. If for any FD in B we remove one or more attributes from the left side of F, the result is no longer a basis.

Notice that no trivial FD can be in a minimal basis, because it could be removed by rule (2).

Example 11: Consider a relation $R(A, B, C)$ such that each attribute functionally determines the other two attributes. The full set of derived FD's thus includes six FD's with one attribute on the left and one on the right; $A \rightarrow B$, $A \rightarrow C$, $B \rightarrow A$, $B \rightarrow C$, $C \rightarrow A$, and $C \rightarrow B$. It also includes the three

A Complete Set of Inference Rules

If we want to know whether one FD follows from some given FD's, the closure computation of Section 2.4 will always serve. However, it is interesting to know that there is a set of rules, called *Armstrong's axioms*, from which it is possible to derive any FD that follows from a given set. These axioms are:

1. *Reflexivity.* If $\{B_1, B_2, \ldots, B_m\} \subseteq \{A_1, A_2, \ldots, A_n\}$, then $A_1A_2\cdots A_n \rightarrow B_1B_2\cdots B_m$. These are what we have called trivial FD's.

2. *Augmentation.* If $A_1A_2\cdots A_n \rightarrow B_1B_2\cdots B_m$, then

$$A_1A_2\cdots A_nC_1C_2\cdots C_k \rightarrow B_1B_2\cdots B_mC_1C_2\cdots C_k$$

for any set of attributes $C_1, C_2, \ldots, C_k$. Since some of the C's may also be A's or B's or both, we should eliminate from the left side duplicate attributes and do the same for the right side.

3. *Transitivity.* If

$$A_1A_2\cdots A_n \rightarrow B_1B_2\cdots B_m \text{ and } B_1B_2\cdots B_m \rightarrow C_1C_2\cdots C_k$$

then $A_1A_2\cdots A_n \rightarrow C_1C_2\cdots C_k$.

nontrivial FD's with two attributes on the left: $AB \rightarrow C$, $AC \rightarrow B$, and $BC \rightarrow A$. There are also FD's with more than one attribute on the right, such as $A \rightarrow BC$, and trivial FD's such as $A \rightarrow A$.

Relation R and its FD's have several minimal bases. One is

$$\{A \rightarrow B,\ B \rightarrow A,\ B \rightarrow C,\ C \rightarrow B\}$$

Another is $\{A \rightarrow B,\ B \rightarrow C,\ C \rightarrow A\}$. There are several other minimal bases for R, and we leave their discovery as an exercise. □

2.8 Projecting Functional Dependencies

When we study design of relation schemas, we shall also have need to answer the following question about FD's. Suppose we have a relation R with set of FD's S, and we project R by computing $R_1 = \pi_L(R)$, for some list of attributes R. What FD's hold in R_1?

The answer is obtained in principle by computing the *projection of functional dependencies* S, which is all FD's that:

a) Follow from S, and

b) Involve only attributes of R_1.

Since there may be a large number of such FD's, and many of them may be redundant (i.e., they follow from other such FD's), we are free to simplify that set of FD's if we wish. However, in general, the calculation of the FD's for R_1 is exponential in the number of attributes of R_1. The simple algorithm is summarized below.

Algorithm 12: Projecting a Set of Functional Dependencies.

INPUT: A relation R and a second relation R_1 computed by the projection $R_1 = \pi_L(R)$. Also, a set of FD's S that hold in R.

OUTPUT: The set of FD's that hold in R_1.

METHOD:

1. Let T be the eventual output set of FD's. Initially, T is empty.

2. For each set of attributes X that is a subset of the attributes of R_1, compute X^+. This computation is performed with respect to the set of FD's S, and may involve attributes that are in the schema of R but not R_1. Add to T all nontrivial FD's $X \to A$ such that A is both in X^+ and an attribute of R_1.

3. Now, T is a basis for the FD's that hold in R_1, but may not be a minimal basis. We may construct a minimal basis by modifying T as follows:

   (a) If there is an FD F in T that follows from the other FD's in T, remove F from T.

   (b) Let $Y \to B$ be an FD in T, with at least two attributes in Y, and let Z be Y with one of its attributes removed. If $Z \to B$ follows from the FD's in T (including $Y \to B$), then replace $Y \to B$ by $Z \to B$.

   (c) Repeat the above steps in all possible ways until no more changes to T can be made.

□

Example 13: Suppose $R(A, B, C, D)$ has FD's $A \to B$, $B \to C$, and $C \to D$. Suppose also that we wish to project out the attribute B, leaving a relation $R_1(A, C, D)$. In principle, to find the FD's for R_1, we need to take the closure of all eight subsets of $\{A, C, D\}$, using the full set of FD's, including those involving B. However, there are some obvious simplifications we can make.

- Closing the empty set and the set of all attributes cannot yield a nontrivial FD.

- If we already know that the closure of some set X is all attributes, then we cannot discover any new FD's by closing supersets of X.

Thus, we may start with the closures of the singleton sets, and then move on to the doubleton sets if necessary. For each closure of a set X, we add the FD $X \rightarrow E$ for each attribute E that is in X^+ and in the schema of R_1, but not in X.

First, $\{A\}^+ = \{A, B, C, D\}$. Thus, $A \rightarrow C$ and $A \rightarrow D$ hold in R_1. Note that $A \rightarrow B$ is true in R, but makes no sense in R_1 because B is not an attribute of R_1.

Next, we consider $\{C\}^+ = \{C, D\}$, from which we get the additional FD $C \rightarrow D$ for R_1. Since $\{D\}^+ = \{D\}$, we can add no more FD's, and are done with the singletons.

Since $\{A\}^+$ includes all attributes of R_1, there is no point in considering any superset of $\{A\}$. The reason is that whatever FD we could discover, for instance $AC \rightarrow D$, follows from an FD with only A on the left side: $A \rightarrow D$ in this case. Thus, the only doubleton whose closure we need to take is $\{C, D\}^+ = \{C, D\}$. This observation allows us to add nothing. We are done with the closures, and the FD's we have discovered are $A \rightarrow C$, $A \rightarrow D$, and $C \rightarrow D$.

If we wish, we can observe that $A \rightarrow D$ follows from the other two by transitivity. Therefore a simpler, equivalent set of FD's for R_1 is $A \rightarrow C$ and $C \rightarrow D$. This set is, in fact, a minimal basis for the FD's of R_1. □

2.9 Exercises for Section 2

Exercise 2.1: Consider a relation with schema $R(A, B, C, D)$ and FD's $AB \rightarrow C$, $C \rightarrow D$, and $D \rightarrow A$.

a) What are all the nontrivial FD's that follow from the given FD's? You should restrict yourself to FD's with single attributes on the right side.

b) What are all the keys of R?

c) What are all the superkeys for R that are not keys?

Exercise 2.2: Repeat Exercise 2.1 for the following schemas and sets of FD's:

i) $S(A, B, C, D)$ with FD's $A \rightarrow B$, $B \rightarrow C$, and $B \rightarrow D$.

ii) $T(A, B, C, D)$ with FD's $AB \rightarrow C$, $BC \rightarrow D$, $CD \rightarrow A$, and $AD \rightarrow B$.

iii) $U(A, B, C, D)$ with FD's $A \rightarrow B$, $B \rightarrow C$, $C \rightarrow D$, and $D \rightarrow A$.

Exercise 2.3: Show that the following rules hold, by using the closure test of Section 2.4.

a) *Augmenting left sides.* If $A_1 A_2 \cdots A_n \rightarrow B$ is an FD, and C is another attribute, then $A_1 A_2 \cdots A_n C \rightarrow B$ follows.

b) *Full augmentation.* If $A_1A_2 \cdots A_n \rightarrow B$ is an FD, and C is another attribute, then $A_1A_2 \cdots A_nC \rightarrow BC$ follows. Note: from this rule, the "augmentation" rule mentioned in the box of Section 2.7 on "A Complete Set of Inference Rules" can easily be proved.

c) *Pseudotransitivity.* Suppose FD's $A_1A_2 \cdots A_n \rightarrow B_1B_2 \cdots B_m$ and

$$C_1C_2 \cdots C_k \rightarrow D$$

hold, and the B's are each among the C's. Then

$$A_1A_2 \cdots A_nE_1E_2 \cdots E_j \rightarrow D$$

holds, where the E's are all those of the C's that are not found among the B's.

d) *Addition.* If FD's $A_1A_2 \cdots A_n \rightarrow B_1B_2 \cdots B_m$ and

$$C_1C_2 \cdots C_k \rightarrow D_1D_2 \cdots D_j$$

hold, then FD $A_1A_2 \cdots A_nC_1C_2 \cdots C_k \rightarrow B_1B_2 \cdots B_mD_1D_2 \cdots D_j$ also holds. In the above, we should remove one copy of any attribute that appears among both the A's and C's or among both the B's and D's.

! **Exercise 2.4:** Show that each of the following are *not* valid rules about FD's by giving example relations that satisfy the given FD's (following the "if") but not the FD that allegedly follows (after the "then").

a) If $A \rightarrow B$ then $B \rightarrow A$.

b) If $AB \rightarrow C$ and $A \rightarrow C$, then $B \rightarrow C$.

c) If $AB \rightarrow C$, then $A \rightarrow C$ or $B \rightarrow C$.

! **Exercise 2.5:** Show that if a relation has no attribute that is functionally determined by all the other attributes, then the relation has no nontrivial FD's at all.

! **Exercise 2.6:** Let X and Y be sets of attributes. Show that if $X \subseteq Y$, then $X^+ \subseteq Y^+$, where the closures are taken with respect to the same set of FD's.

! **Exercise 2.7:** Prove that $(X^+)^+ = X^+$.

!! **Exercise 2.8:** We say a set of attributes X is *closed* (with respect to a given set of FD's) if $X^+ = X$. Consider a relation with schema $R(A, B, C, D)$ and an unknown set of FD's. If we are told which sets of attributes are closed, we can discover the FD's. What are the FD's if:

a) All sets of the four attributes are closed.

b) The only closed sets are $\emptyset$ and $\{A, B, C, D\}$.

c) The closed sets are $\emptyset$, {A,B}, and $\{A, B, C, D\}$.

! **Exercise 2.9:** Find all the minimal bases for the FD's and relation of Example 11.

! **Exercise 2.10:** Suppose we have relation $R(A, B, C, D, E)$, with some set of FD's, and we wish to project those FD's onto relation $S(A, B, C)$. Give the FD's that hold in S if the FD's for R are:

a) $AB \to DE$, $C \to E$, $D \to C$, and $E \to A$.

b) $A \to D$, $BD \to E$, $AC \to E$, and $DE \to B$.

c) $AB \to D$, $AC \to E$, $BC \to D$, $D \to A$, and $E \to B$.

d) $A \to B$, $B \to C$, $C \to D$, $D \to E$, and $E \to A$.

In each case, it is sufficient to give a minimal basis for the full set of FD's of S.

!! **Exercise 2.11:** Show that if an FD F follows from some given FD's, then we can prove F from the given FD's using Armstrong's axioms (defined in the box "A Complete Set of Inference Rules" in Section 2.7). *Hint*: Examine Algorithm 7 and show how each step of that algorithm can be mimicked by inferring some FD's by Armstrong's axioms.

3 Design of Relational Database Schemas

Careless selection of a relational database schema can lead to redundancy and related anomalies. For instance, consider the relation in Fig. 2, which we reproduce here as Fig. 6. Notice that the length and genre for *Star Wars* and *Wayne's World* are each repeated, once for each star of the movie. The repetition of this information is redundant. It also introduces the potential for several kinds of errors, as we shall see.

In this section, we shall tackle the problem of design of good relation schemas in the following stages:

1. We first explore in more detail the problems that arise when our schema is poorly designed.

2. Then, we introduce the idea of "decomposition," breaking a relation schema (set of attributes) into two smaller schemas.

3. Next, we introduce "Boyce-Codd normal form," or "BCNF," a condition on a relation schema that eliminates these problems.

4. These points are tied together when we explain how to assure the BCNF condition by decomposing relation schemas.

title	*year*	*length*	*genre*	*studioName*	*starName*
Star Wars	1977	124	SciFi	Fox	Carrie Fisher
Star Wars	1977	124	SciFi	Fox	Mark Hamill
Star Wars	1977	124	SciFi	Fox	Harrison Ford
Gone With the Wind	1939	231	drama	MGM	Vivien Leigh
Wayne's World	1992	95	comedy	Paramount	Dana Carvey
Wayne's World	1992	95	comedy	Paramount	Mike Meyers

Figure 6: The relation Movies1 exhibiting anomalies

3.1 Anomalies

Problems such as redundancy that occur when we try to cram too much into a single relation are called *anomalies.* The principal kinds of anomalies that we encounter are:

1. *Redundancy.* Information may be repeated unnecessarily in several tuples. Examples are the length and genre for movies in Fig. 6.

2. *Update Anomalies.* We may change information in one tuple but leave the same information unchanged in another. For example, if we found that *Star Wars* is really 125 minutes long, we might carelessly change the length in the first tuple of Fig. 6 but not in the second or third tuples. You might argue that one should never be so careless, but it is possible to redesign relation Movies1 so that the risk of such mistakes does not exist.

3. *Deletion Anomalies.* If a set of values becomes empty, we may lose other information as a side effect. For example, should we delete Vivien Leigh from the set of stars of *Gone With the Wind,* then we have no more stars for that movie in the database. The last tuple for *Gone With the Wind* in the relation Movies1 would disappear, and with it information that it is 231 minutes long and a drama.

3.2 Decomposing Relations

The accepted way to eliminate these anomalies is to *decompose* relations. Decomposition of R involves splitting the attributes of R to make the schemas of two new relations. After describing the decomposition process, we shall show how to pick a decomposition that eliminates anomalies.

Given a relation $R(A_1, A_2, \ldots, A_n)$, we may *decompose* R into two relations $S(B_1, B_2, \ldots, B_m)$ and $T(C_1, C_2, \ldots, C_k)$ such that:

1. $\{A_1, A_2, \ldots, A_n\} = \{B_1, B_2, \ldots, B_m\} \cup \{C_1, C_2, \ldots, C_k\}$.

2. $S = \pi_{B_1, B_2, \ldots, B_m}(R)$.

3. $T = \pi_{C_1, C_2, \ldots, C_k}(R)$.

Example 14: Let us decompose the `Movies1` relation of Fig. 6. Our choice, whose merit will be seen in Section 3.3, is to use:

1. A relation called `Movies2`, whose schema is all the attributes except for `starName`.

2. A relation called `Movies3`, whose schema consists of the attributes `title`, `year`, and `starName`.

The projection of `Movies1` onto these two new schemas is shown in Fig, 7. □

title	*year*	*length*	*genre*	*studioName*
Star Wars	1977	124	sciFi	Fox
Gone With the Wind	1939	231	drama	MGM
Wayne's World	1992	95	comedy	Paramount

(b) The relation `Movies2`.

title	*year*	*starName*
Star Wars	1977	Carrie Fisher
Star Wars	1977	Mark Hamill
Star Wars	1977	Harrison Ford
Gone With the Wind	1939	Vivien Leigh
Wayne's World	1992	Dana Carvey
Wayne's World	1992	Mike Meyers

(b) The relation `Movies3`.

Figure 7: Projections of relation `Movies1`

Notice how this decomposition eliminates the anomalies we mentioned in Section 3.1. The redundancy has been eliminated; for example, the length of each film appears only once, in relation `Movies2`. The risk of an update anomaly is gone. For instance, since we only have to change the length of *Star Wars* in one tuple of `Movies2`, we cannot wind up with two different lengths for that movie.

Finally, the risk of a deletion anomaly is gone. If we delete all the stars for *Gone With the Wind*, say, that deletion makes the movie disappear from `Movies3`. But all the other information about the movie can still be found in `Movies2`.

It might appear that `Movies3` still has redundancy, since the title and year of a movie can appear several times. However, these two attributes form a key for movies, and there is no more succinct way to represent a movie. Moreover, `Movies3` does not offer an opportunity for an update anomaly. For instance, one might suppose that if we changed to 2008 the year in the Carrie Fisher tuple, but not the other two tuples for *Star Wars*, then there would be an update anomaly. However, there is nothing in our assumed FD's that prevents there being a different movie named *Star Wars* in 2008, and Carrie Fisher may star in that one as well. Thus, we do not want to prevent changing the year in one *Star Wars* tuple, nor is such a change necessarily incorrect.

3.3 Boyce-Codd Normal Form

The goal of decomposition is to replace a relation by several that do not exhibit anomalies. There is, it turns out, a simple condition under which the anomalies discussed above can be guaranteed not to exist. This condition is called *Boyce-Codd normal form*, or *BCNF*.

- A relation R is in BCNF if and only if: whenever there is a nontrivial FD $A_1A_2 \cdots A_n \rightarrow B_1B_2 \cdots B_m$ for R, it is the case that $\{A_1, A_2, \ldots, A_n\}$ is a superkey for R.

That is, the left side of every nontrivial FD must be a superkey. Recall that a superkey need not be minimal. Thus, an equivalent statement of the BCNF condition is that the left side of every nontrivial FD must contain a key.

Example 15: Relation `Movies1`, as in Fig. 6, is not in BCNF. To see why, we first need to determine what sets of attributes are keys. We argued in Example 2 why {`title`, `year`, `starName`} is a key. Thus, any set of attributes containing these three is a superkey. The same arguments we followed in Example 2 can be used to explain why no set of attributes that does not include all three of `title`, `year`, and `starName` could be a superkey. Thus, we assert that {`title`, `year`, `starName`} is the only key for `Movies1`.

However, consider the FD

`title year` $\rightarrow$ `length genre studioName`

which holds in `Movies1` according to our discussion in Example 2.

Unfortunately, the left side of the above FD is not a superkey. In particular, we know that `title` and `year` do not functionally determine the sixth attribute, `starName`. Thus, the existence of this FD violates the BCNF condition and tells us `Movies1` is not in BCNF. □

Example 16: On the other hand, `Movies2` of Fig. 7 is in BCNF. Since

`title year` $\rightarrow$ `length genre studioName`

holds in this relation, and we have argued that neither `title` nor `year` by itself functionally determines any of the other attributes, the only key for `Movies2` is {`title`, `year`}. Moreover, the only nontrivial FD's must have at least `title` and `year` on the left side, and therefore their left sides must be superkeys. Thus, `Movies2` is in BCNF. □

Example 17: We claim that any two-attribute relation is in BCNF. We need to examine the possible nontrivial FD's with a single attribute on the right. There are not too many cases to consider, so let us consider them in turn. In what follows, suppose that the attributes are A and B.

1. There are no nontrivial FD's. Then surely the BCNF condition must hold, because only a nontrivial FD can violate this condition. Incidentally, note that $\{A, B\}$ is the only key in this case.

2. $A \rightarrow B$ holds, but $B \rightarrow A$ does not hold. In this case, A is the only key, and each nontrivial FD contains A on the left (in fact the left can only be A). Thus there is no violation of the BCNF condition.

3. $B \rightarrow A$ holds, but $A \rightarrow B$ does not hold. This case is symmetric to case (2).

4. Both $A \rightarrow B$ and $B \rightarrow A$ hold. Then both A and B are keys. Surely any FD has at least one of these on the left, so there can be no BCNF violation.

It is worth noticing from case (4) above that there may be more than one key for a relation. Further, the BCNF condition only requires that *some* key be contained in the left side of any nontrivial FD, not that all keys are contained in the left side. Also observe that a relation with two attributes, each functionally determining the other, is not completely implausible. For example, a company may assign its employees unique employee ID's and also record their Social Security numbers. A relation with attributes `empID` and `ssNo` would have each attribute functionally determining the other. Put another way, each attribute is a key, since we don't expect to find two tuples that agree on either attribute. □

3.4 Decomposition into BCNF

By repeatedly choosing suitable decompositions, we can break any relation schema into a collection of subsets of its attributes with the following important properties:

1. These subsets are the schemas of relations in BCNF.

2. The data in the original relation is represented faithfully by the data in the relations that are the result of the decomposition, in a sense to be made precise in Section 4.1. Roughly, we need to be able to reconstruct the original relation instance exactly from the decomposed relation instances.

Example 17 suggests that perhaps all we have to do is break a relation schema into two-attribute subsets, and the result is surely in BCNF. However, such an arbitrary decomposition will not satisfy condition (2), as we shall see in Section 4.1. In fact, we must be more careful and use the violating FD's to guide our decomposition.

The decomposition strategy we shall follow is to look for a nontrivial FD $A_1A_2 \cdots A_n \rightarrow B_1B_2 \cdots B_m$ that violates BCNF; i.e., $\{A_1, A_2, \ldots, A_n\}$ is not a superkey. We shall add to the right side as many attributes as are functionally determined by $\{A_1, A_2, \ldots, A_n\}$. This step is not mandatory, but it often reduces the total amount of work done, and we shall include it in our algorithm. Figure 8 illustrates how the attributes are broken into two overlapping relation schemas. One is all the attributes involved in the violating FD, and the other is the left side of the FD plus all the attributes *not* involved in the FD, i.e., all the attributes except those B's that are not A's.

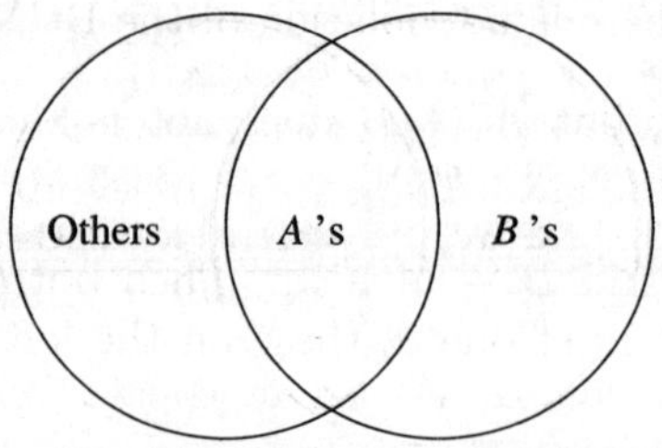

Figure 8: Relation schema decomposition based on a BCNF violation

Example 18: Consider our running example, the `Movies1` relation of Fig. 6. We saw in Example 15 that

`title year` $\rightarrow$ `length genre studioName`

is a BCNF violation. In this case, the right side already includes all the attributes functionally determined by `title` and `year`, so we shall use this BCNF violation to decompose `Movies1` into:

1. The schema {`title`, `year`, `length`, `genre`, `studioName`} consisting of all the attributes on either side of the FD.

2. The schema {`title`, `year`, `starName`} consisting of the left side of the FD plus all attributes of `Movies1` that do not appear in either side of the FD (only `starName`, in this case).

Notice that these schemas are the ones selected for relations `Movies2` and `Movies3` in Example 14. We observed in Example 16 that `Movies2` is in BCNF. `Movies3` is also in BCNF; it has no nontrivial FD's. □

In Example 18, one judicious application of the decomposition rule is enough to produce a collection of relations that are in BCNF. In general, that is not the case, as the next example shows.

Example 19: Consider a relation with schema

{`title`, `year`, `studioName`, `president`, `presAddr`}

That is, each tuple of this relation tells about a movie, its studio, the president of the studio, and the address of the president of the studio. Three FD's that we would assume in this relation are

`title year` → `studioName`
`studioName` → `president`
`president` → `presAddr`

By closing sets of these five attributes, we discover that {`title`, `year`} is the only key for this relation. Thus the last two FD's above violate BCNF. Suppose we choose to decompose starting with

`studioName` → `president`

First, we add to the right side of this functional dependency any other attributes in the closure of `studioName`. That closure includes `presAddr`, so our final choice of FD for the decomposition is:

`studioName` → `president presAddr`

The decomposition based on this FD yields the following two relation schemas.

{`title`, `year`, `studioName`}
{`studioName`, `president`, `presAddr`}

If we use Algorithm 12 to project FD's, we determine that the FD's for the first relation has a basis:

`title year` → `studioName`

while the second has:

`studioName` → `president`
`president` → `presAddr`

The sole key for the first relation is {`title`, `year`}, and it is therefore in BCNF. However, the second has {`studioName`} for its only key but also has the FD:

`president` → `presAddr`

which is a BCNF violation. Thus, we must decompose again, this time using the above FD. The resulting three relation schemas, all in BCNF, are:

{title, year, studioName}
{studioName, president}
{president, presAddr}

□

In general, we must keep applying the decomposition rule as many times as needed, until all our relations are in BCNF. We can be sure of ultimate success, because every time we apply the decomposition rule to a relation R, the two resulting schemas each have fewer attributes than that of R. As we saw in Example 17, when we get down to two attributes, the relation is sure to be in BCNF; often relations with larger sets of attributes are also in BCNF. The strategy is summarized below.

Algorithm 20: BCNF Decomposition Algorithm.

INPUT: A relation R_0 with a set of functional dependencies S_0.

OUTPUT: A decomposition of R_0 into a collection of relations, all of which are in BCNF.

METHOD: The following steps can be applied recursively to any relation R and set of FD's S. Initially, apply them with $R = R_0$ and $S = S_0$.

1. Check whether R is in BCNF. If so, nothing more needs to be done. Return $\{R\}$ as the answer.

2. If there are BCNF violations, let one be $X \rightarrow Y$. Use Algorithm 7 to compute X^+. Choose $R_1 = X^+$ as one relation schema and let R_2 have attributes X and those attributes of R that are not in X^+.

3. Use Algorithm 12 to compute the sets of FD's for R_1 and R_2; let these be S_1 and S_2, respectively.

4. Recursively decompose R_1 and R_2 using this algorithm. Return the union of the results of these decompositions.

□

3.5 Exercises for Section 3

Exercise 3.1: For each of the following relation schemas and sets of FD's:

a) $R(A, B, C, D)$ with FD's $AB \rightarrow C$, $C \rightarrow D$, and $D \rightarrow A$.

b) $R(A, B, C, D)$ with FD's $B \rightarrow C$ and $B \rightarrow D$.

c) $R(A, B, C, D)$ with FD's $AB \rightarrow C$, $BC \rightarrow D$, $CD \rightarrow A$, and $AD \rightarrow B$.

d) $R(A, B, C, D)$ with FD's $A \rightarrow B$, $B \rightarrow C$, $C \rightarrow D$, and $D \rightarrow A$.

e) $R(A, B, C, D, E)$ with FD's $AB \rightarrow C$, $DE \rightarrow C$, and $B \rightarrow D$.

f) $R(A, B, C, D, E)$ with FD's $AB \rightarrow C$, $C \rightarrow D$, $D \rightarrow B$, and $D \rightarrow E$.

do the following:

i) Indicate all the BCNF violations. Do not forget to consider FD's that are not in the given set, but follow from them. However, it is not necessary to give violations that have more than one attribute on the right side.

ii) Decompose the relations, as necessary, into collections of relations that are in BCNF.

Exercise 3.2: We mentioned in Section 3.4 that we would exercise our option to expand the right side of an FD that is a BCNF violation if possible. Consider a relation R whose schema is the set of attributes $\{A, B, C, D\}$ with FD's $A \rightarrow B$ and $A \rightarrow C$. Either is a BCNF violation, because the only key for R is $\{A, D\}$. Suppose we begin by decomposing R according to $A \rightarrow B$. Do we ultimately get the same result as if we first expand the BCNF violation to $A \rightarrow BC$? Why or why not?

! **Exercise 3.3:** Let R be as in Exercise 3.2, but let the FD's be $A \rightarrow B$ and $B \rightarrow C$. Again compare decomposing using $A \rightarrow B$ first against decomposing by $A \rightarrow BC$ first.

! **Exercise 3.4:** Suppose we have a relation schema $R(A, B, C)$ with FD $A \rightarrow B$. Suppose also that we decide to decompose this schema into $S(A, B)$ and $T(B, C)$. Give an example of an instance of relation R whose projection onto S and T and subsequent rejoining as in Section 4.1 does not yield the same relation instance. That is, $\pi_{A,B}(R) \bowtie \pi_{B,C}(R) \neq R$.

4 Decomposition: The Good, Bad, and Ugly

So far, we observed that before we decompose a relation schema into BCNF, it can exhibit anomalies; after we decompose, the resulting relations do not exhibit anomalies. That's the "good." But decomposition can also have some bad, if not downright ugly, consequences. In this section, we shall consider three distinct properties we would like a decomposition to have.

1. *Elimination of Anomalies* by decomposition as in Section 3.

2. *Recoverability of Information.* Can we recover the original relation from the tuples in its decomposition?

3. *Preservation of Dependencies.* If we check the projected FD's in the relations of the decomposition, can we can be sure that when we reconstruct the original relation from the decomposition by joining, the result will satisfy the original FD's?

It turns out that the BCNF decomposition of Algorithm 20 gives us (1) and (2), but does not necessarily give us all three. In Section 5 we shall see another way to pick a decomposition that gives us (2) and (3) but does not necessarily give us (1). In fact, there is no way to get all three at once.

4.1 Recovering Information from a Decomposition

Since we learned that every two-attribute relation is in BCNF, why did we have to go through the trouble of Algorithm 20? Why not just take any relation R and decompose it into relations, each of whose schemas is a pair of R's attributes? The answer is that the data in the decomposed relations, even if their tuples were each the projection of a relation instance of R, might not allow us to join the relations of the decomposition and get the instance of R back. If we do get R back, then we say the decomposition has a *lossless join*.

However, if we decompose using Algorithm 20, where all decompositions are motivated by a BCNF-violating FD, then the projections of the original tuples can be joined again to produce all and only the original tuples. We shall consider why here. Then, in Section 4.2 we shall give an algorithm called the "chase," for testing whether the projection of a relation onto any decomposition allows us to recover the relation by rejoining.

To simplify the situation, consider a relation $R(A, B, C)$ and an FD $B \to C$ that is a BCNF violation. The decomposition based on the FD $B \to C$ separates the attributes into relations $R_1(A, B)$ and $R_2(B, C)$.

Let t be a tuple of R. We may write $t = (a, b, c)$, where a, b, and c are the components of t for attributes A, B, and C, respectively. Tuple t projects as (a, b) in $R_1(A, B) = \pi_{A,B}(R)$ and as (b, c) in $R_2(B, C) = \pi_{B,C}(R)$. When we compute the natural join $R_1 \bowtie R_2$, these two projected tuples join, because they agree on the common B component (they both have b there). They give us $t = (a, b, c)$, the tuple we started with, in the join. That is, regardless of what tuple t we started with, we can always join its projections to get t back.

However, getting back those tuples we started with is not enough to assure that the original relation R is truly represented by the decomposition. Consider what happens if there are two tuples of R, say $t = (a, b, c)$ and $v = (d, b, e)$. When we project t onto $R_1(A, B)$ we get $u = (a, b)$, and when we project v onto $R_2(B, C)$ we get $w = (b, e)$. These tuples also match in the natural join, and the resulting tuple is $x = (a, b, e)$. Is it possible that x is a bogus tuple? That is, could (a, b, e) not be a tuple of R?

Since we assume the FD $B \to C$ for relation R, the answer is "no." Recall that this FD says any two tuples of R that agree in their B components must also agree in their C components. Since t and v agree in their B components, they also agree on their C components. That means $c = e$; i.e., the two values we supposed were different are really the same. Thus, tuple (a, b, e) of R is really (a, b, c); that is, $x = t$.

Since t is in R, it must be that x is in R. Put another way, as long as FD $B \to C$ holds, the joining of two projected tuples cannot produce a bogus tuple. Rather, every tuple produced by the natural join is guaranteed to be a tuple of R.

This argument works in general. We assumed A, B, and C were each single attributes, but the same argument would apply if they were any sets of attributes X, Y and Z. That is, if $Y \rightarrow Z$ holds in R, whose attributes are $X \cup Y \cup Z$, then $R = \pi_{X \cup Y}(R) \bowtie \pi_{Y \cup Z}(R)$.

We may conclude:

- If we decompose a relation according to Algorithm 20, then the original relation can be recovered exactly by the natural join.

To see why, we argued above that at any one step of the recursive decomposition, a relation is equal to the join of its projections onto the two components. If those components are decomposed further, they can also be recovered by the natural join from their decomposed relations. Thus, an easy induction on the number of binary decomposition steps says that the original relation is always the natural join of whatever relations it is decomposed into. We can also prove that the natural join is associative and commutative, so the order in which we perform the natural join of the decomposition components does not matter.

The FD $Y \rightarrow Z$, or its symmetric FD $Y \rightarrow X$, is essential. Without one of these FD's, we might not be able to recover the original relation. Here is an example.

Example 21: Suppose we have the relation $R(A, B, C)$ as above, but neither of the FD's $B \rightarrow A$ nor $B \rightarrow C$ holds. Then R might consist of the two tuples

A	B	C
1	2	3
4	2	5

The projections of R onto the relations with schemas $\{A, B\}$ and $\{B, C\}$ are $R_1 = \pi_{AB}(R) =$

A	B
1	2
4	2

and $R_2 = \pi_{BC}(R) =$

B	C
2	3
2	5

respectively. Since all four tuples share the same B-value, 2, each tuple of one relation joins with both tuples of the other relation. When we try to reconstruct R by the natural join of the projected relations, we get $R_3 = R_1 \bowtie R_2 =$

Is Join the Only Way to Recover?

We have assumed that the only possible way we could reconstruct a relation from its projections is to use the natural join. However, might there be some other algorithm to reconstruct the original relation that would work even in cases where the natural join fails? There is in fact no such other way. In Example 21, the relations R and R_3 are different instances, yet have exactly the same projections onto $\{A, B\}$ and $\{B, C\}$, namely the instances we called R_1 and R_2, respectively. Thus, given R_1 and R_2, no algorithm whatsoever can tell whether the original instance was R or R_3.

Moreover, this example is not unusual. Given any decomposition of a relation with attributes $X \cup Y \cup Z$ into relations with schemas $X \cup Y$ and $Y \cup Z$, where neither $Y \rightarrow X$ nor $Y \rightarrow Z$ holds, we can construct an example similar to Example 21 where the original instance cannot be determined from its projections.

A	B	C
1	2	3
1	2	5
4	2	3
4	2	5

That is, we get "too much"; we get two bogus tuples, $(1, 2, 5)$ and $(4, 2, 3)$, that were not in the original relation R. □

4.2 The Chase Test for Lossless Join

In Section 4.1 we argued why a particular decomposition, that of $R(A, B, C)$ into $\{A, B\}$ and $\{B, C\}$, with a particular FD, $B \rightarrow C$, had a lossless join. Now, consider a more general situation. We have decomposed relation R into relations with sets of attributes $S_1, S_2, \ldots, S_k$. We have a given set of FD's F that hold in R. Is it true that if we project R onto the relations of the decomposition, then we can recover R by taking the natural join of all these relations? That is, is it true that $\pi_{S_1}(R) \bowtie \pi_{S_2}(R) \bowtie \cdots \bowtie \pi_{S_k}(R) = R$? Three important things to remember are:

- The natural join is associative and commutative. It does not matter in what order we join the projections; we shall get the same relation as a result. In particular, the result is the set of tuples t such that for all $i = 1, 2, \ldots, k$, t projected onto the set of attributes S_i is a tuple in $\pi_{S_i}(R)$.

- Any tuple t in R is surely in $\pi_{S_1}(R) \bowtie \pi_{S_2}(R) \bowtie \cdots \bowtie \pi_{S_k}(R)$. The reason is that the projection of t onto S_i is surely in $\pi_{S_i}(R)$ for each i, and therefore by our first point above, t is in the result of the join.

- As a consequence, $\pi_{S_1}(R) \bowtie \pi_{S_2}(R) \bowtie \cdots \bowtie \pi_{S_k}(R) = R$ when the FD's in F hold for R if and only if every tuple in the join is also in R. That is, the membership test is all we need to verify that the decomposition has a lossless join.

The *chase* test for a lossless join is just an organized way to see whether a tuple t in $\pi_{S_1}(R) \bowtie \pi_{S_2}(R) \bowtie \cdots \bowtie \pi_{S_k}(R)$ can be proved, using the FD's in F, also to be a tuple in R. If t is in the join, then there must be tuples in R, say $t_1, t_2, \ldots, t_k$, such that t is the join of the projections of each t_i onto the set of attributes S_i, for $i = 1, 2, \ldots, k$. We therefore know that t_i agrees with t on the attributes of S_i, but t_i has unknown values in its components not in S_i.

We draw a picture of what we know, called a *tableau*. Assuming R has attributes $A, B, \ldots$ we use $a, b, \ldots$ for the components of t. For t_i, we use the same letter as t in the components that are in S_i, but we subscript the letter with i if the component is not in i. In that way, t_i will agree with t for the attributes of S_i, but have a unique value — one that can appear nowhere else in the tableau — for other attributes.

Example 22: Suppose we have relation $R(A, B, C, D)$, which we have decomposed into relations with sets of attributes $S_1 = \{A, D\}$, $S_2 = \{A, C\}$, and $S_3 = \{B, C, D\}$. Then the tableau for this decomposition is shown in Fig. 9.

A	B	C	D
a	b_1	c_1	d
a	b_2	c	d_2
a_3	b	c	d

Figure 9: Tableau for the decomposition of R into $\{A, D\}$, $\{A, C\}$, and $\{B, C, D\}$

The first row corresponds to set of attributes A and D. Notice that the components for attributes A and D are the unsubscripted letters a and d. However, for the other attributes, b and c, we add the subscript 1 to indicate that they are arbitrary values. This choice makes sense, since the tuple (a, b_1, c_1, d) represents a tuple of R that contributes to $t = (a, b, c, d)$ by being projected onto $\{A, D\}$ and then joined with other tuples. Since the B- and C-components of this tuple are projected out, we know nothing yet about what values the tuple had for those attributes.

Similarly, the second row has the unsubscripted letters in attributes A and C, while the subscript 2 is used for the other attributes. The last row has the unsubscripted letters in components for $\{B, C, D\}$ and subscript 3 on a. Since each row uses its own number as a subscript, the only symbols that can appear more than once are the unsubscripted letters. □

Remember that our goal is to use the given set of FD's F to prove that t is really in R. In order to do so, we "chase" the tableau by applying the FD's in F to equate symbols in the tableau whenever we can. If we discover that one of the rows is actually the same as t (that is, the row becomes all unsubscripted symbols), then we have proved that any tuple t in the join of the projections was actually a tuple of R.

To avoid confusion, when equating two symbols, if one of them is unsubscripted, make the other be the same. However, if we equate two symbols, both with their own subscript, then you can change either to be the other. However, remember that when equating symbols, you must change all occurrences of one to be the other, not just some of the occurences.

Example 23: Let us continue with the decomposition of Example 22, and suppose the given FD's are $A \to B$, $B \to C$, and $CD \to A$. Start with the tableau of Fig. 9. Since the first two rows agree in their A-components, the FD $A \to B$ tells us they must also agree in their B-components. That is, $b_1 = b_2$. We can replace either one with the other, since they are both subscripted. Let us replace b_2 by b_1. Then the resulting tableau is:

A	B	C	D
a	b_1	c_1	d
a	b_1	c	d_2
a_3	b	c	d

Now, we see that the first two rows have equal B-values, and so we may use the FD $B \to C$ to deduce that their C-components, c_1 and c, are the same. Since c is unsubscripted, we replace c_1 by c, leaving:

A	B	C	D
a	b_1	c	d
a	b_1	c	d_2
a_3	b	c	d

Next, we observe that the first and third rows agree in both columns C and D. Thus, we may apply the FD $CD \to A$ to deduce that these rows also have the same A-value; that is, $a = a_3$. We replace a_3 by a, giving us:

A	B	C	D
a	b_1	c	d
a	b_1	c	d_2
a	b	c	d

At this point, we see that the last row has become equal to t, that is, (a, b, c, d). We have proved that if R satisfies the FD's $A \rightarrow B$, $B \rightarrow C$, and $CD \rightarrow A$, then whenever we project onto $\{A, D\}$, $\{A, C\}$, and $\{B, C, D\}$ and rejoin, what we get must have been in R. In particular, what we get is the same as the tuple of R that we projected onto $\{B, C, D\}$. □

4.3 Why the Chase Works

There are two issues to address:

1. When the chase results in a row that matches the tuple t (i.e., the tableau is shown to have a row with all unsubscripted variables), why must the join be lossless?

2. When, after applying FD's whenever we can, we still find no row of all unsubscripted variables, why must the join not be lossless?

Question (1) is easy to answer. The chase process itself is a proof that one of the projected tuples from R must in fact be the tuple t that is produced by the join. We also know that every tuple in R is sure to come back if we project and join. Thus, the chase has proved that the result of projection and join is exactly R.

For the second question, suppose that we eventually derive a tableau without an unsubscripted row, and that this tableau does not allow us to apply any of the FD's to equate any symbols. Then think of the tableau as an instance of the relation R. It obviously satisfies the given FD's, because none can be applied to equate symbols. We know that the ith row has unsubscripted symbols in the attributes of S_i, the ith relation of the decomposition. Thus, when we project this relation onto the S_i's and take the natural join, we get the tuple with all unsubscripted variables. This tuple is not in R, so we conclude that the join is not lossless.

Example 24: Consider the relation $R(A, B, C, D)$ with the FD $B \rightarrow AD$ and the proposed decomposition $\{A, B\}$, $\{B, C\}$, and $\{C, D\}$. Here is the initial tableau:

A	B	C	D
a	b	c_1	d_1
a_2	b	c	d_2
a_3	b_3	c	d

When we apply the lone FD, we deduce that $a = a_2$ and $d_1 = d_2$. Thus, the final tableau is:

A	B	C	D
a	b	c_1	d_1
a	b	c	d_1
a_3	b_3	c	d

No more changes can be made because of the given FD's, and there is no row that is fully unsubscripted. Thus, this decomposition does not have a lossless join. We can verify that fact by treating the above tableau as a relation with three tuples. When we project onto $\{A, B\}$, we get $\{(a, b)\}$, $(a_3, b_3)\}$. The projection onto $\{B, C\}$ is $\{(b, c_1),\ (b, c),\ (b_3, c)\}$, and the projection onto $\{C, D\}$ is $(c_1, d_1),\ (c, d_1),\ (c, d)\}$. If we join the first two projections, we get $\{(a, b, c_1),\ (a, b, c),\ (a_3, b_3, c)\}$. Joining this relation with the third projection gives $\{(a, b, c_1, d_1),\ (a, b, c, d_1),\ (a, b, c, d),\ (a_3, b_3, c, d_1),\ (a_3, b_3, c, d)\}$. Notice that this join has two more tuples than R, and in particular it has the tuple (a, b, c, d), as it must. □

4.4 Dependency Preservation

We mentioned that it is not possible, in some cases, to decompose a relation into BCNF relations that have both the lossless-join and dependency-preservation properties. Below is an example where we need to make a tradeoff between preserving dependencies and BNCF.

Example 25: Suppose we have a relation `Bookings` with attributes:

1. `title`, the name of a movie.
2. `theater`, the name of a theater where the movie is being shown.
3. `city`, the city where the theater is located.

The intent behind a tuple (m, t, c) is that the movie with title m is currently being shown at theater t in city c.

We might reasonably assert the following FD's:

```
theater → city
title city → theater
```

The first says that a theater is located in one city. The second is not obvious but is based on the common practice of not booking a movie into two theaters in the same city. We shall assert this FD if only for the sake of the example.

Let us first find the keys. No single attribute is a key. For example, `title` is not a key because a movie can play in several theaters at once and in several cities at once.[2] Also, `theater` is not a key, because although `theater` functionally determines `city`, there are multiscreen theaters that show many movies at once. Thus, `theater` does not determine `title`. Finally, `city` is not a key because cities usually have more than one theater and more than one movie playing.

[2]In this example we assume that there are not two "current" movies with the same title, even though we have previously recognized that there could be two movies with the same title made in different years.

On the other hand, two of the three sets of two attributes are keys. Clearly {`title`, `city`} is a key because of the given FD that says these attributes functionally determine `theater`.

It is also true that {`theater`, `title`} is a key, because its closure includes `city` due to the given FD `theater` → `city`. The remaining pair of attributes, `city` and `theater`, do not functionally determine `title`, because of multiscreen theaters, and are therefore not a key. We conclude that the only two keys are

{`title`, `city`}
{`theater`, `title`}

Now we immediately see a BCNF violation. We were given functional dependency `theater` → `city`, but its left side, `theater`, is not a superkey. We are therefore tempted to decompose, using this BCNF-violating FD, into the two relation schemas:

{`theater`, `city`}
{`theater`, `title`}

There is a problem with this decomposition, concerning the FD

`title city`→`theater`

There could be current relations for the decomposed schemas that satisfy the FD `theater` → `city` (which can be checked in the relation {`theater`, `city`}) but that, when joined, yield a relation not satisfying `title city`→`theater`. For instance, the two relations

theater	*city*
Guild	Menlo Park
Park	Menlo Park

and

theater	*title*
Guild	Antz
Park	Antz

are permissible according to the FD's that apply to each of the above relations, but when we join them we get two tuples

theater	*city*	*title*
Guild	Menlo Park	Antz
Park	Menlo Park	Antz

that violate the FD `title city` → `theater`. □

4.5 Exercises for Section 4

Exercise 4.1: Let $R(A, B, C, D, E)$ be decomposed into relations with the following three sets of attributes: $\{A, B, C\}$, $\{B, C, D\}$, and $\{A, C, E\}$. For each of the following sets of FD's, use the chase test to tell whether the decomposition of R is lossless. For those that are not lossless, give an example of an instance of R that returns more than R when projected onto the decomposed relations and rejoined.

a) $B \rightarrow E$ and $CE \rightarrow A$.

b) $AC \rightarrow E$ and $BC \rightarrow D$.

c) $A \rightarrow D$, $D \rightarrow E$, and $B \rightarrow D$.

d) $A \rightarrow D$, $CD \rightarrow E$, and $E \rightarrow D$.

! **Exercise 4.2:** For each of the sets of FD's in Exercise 4.1, are dependencies preserved by the decomposition?

5 Third Normal Form

The solution to the problem illustrated by Example 25 is to relax our BCNF requirement slightly, in order to allow the occasional relation schema that cannot be decomposed into BCNF relations without our losing the ability to check the FD's. This relaxed condition is called "third normal form." In this section we shall give the requirements for third normal form, and then show how to do a decomposition in a manner quite different from Algorithm 20, in order to obtain relations in third normal form that have both the lossless-join and dependency-preservation properties.

5.1 Definition of Third Normal Form

A relation R is in *third normal form* (3NF) if:

- Whenever $A_1A_2 \cdots A_n \rightarrow B_1B_2 \cdots B_m$ is a nontrivial FD, either

$$\{A_1, A_2, \ldots, A_n\}$$

  is a superkey, or those of $B_1, B_2, \ldots, B_m$ that are not among the A's, are each a member of some key (not necessarily the same key).

An attribute that is a member of some key is often said to be *prime*. Thus, the 3NF condition can be stated as "for each nontrivial FD, either the left side is a superkey, or the right side consists of prime attributes only."

Note that the difference between this 3NF condition and the BCNF condition is the clause "is a member of some key (i.e., prime)." This clause "excuses" an FD like `theater` $\rightarrow$ `city` in Example 25, because the right side, `city`, is prime.

Other Normal Forms

If there is a "third normal form," what happened to the first two "normal forms"? They indeed were defined, but today there is little use for them. *First normal form* is simply the condition that every component of every tuple is an atomic value. *Second normal form* is a less restrictive verison of 3NF. There is also a "fourth normal form" that we shall meet in Section 6.

5.2 The Synthesis Algorithm for 3NF Schemas

We can now explain and justify how we decompose a relation R into a set of relations such that:

a) The relations of the decomposition are all in 3NF.

b) The decomposition has a lossless join.

c) The decomposition has the dependency-preservation property.

Algorithm 26: Synthesis of Third-Normal-Form Relations With a Lossless Join and Dependency Preservation.

INPUT: A relation R and a set F of functional dependencies that hold for R.

OUTPUT: A decomposition of R into a collection of relations, each of which is in 3NF. The decomposition has the lossless-join and dependency-preservation properties.

METHOD: Perform the following steps:

1. Find a minimal basis for F, say G.

2. For each functional dependency $X \rightarrow A$ in G, use XA as the schema of one of the relations in the decomposition.

3. If none of the relation schemas from Step 2 is a superkey for R, add another relation whose schema is a key for R.

□

Example 27: Consider the relation $R(A, B, C, D, E)$ with FD's $AB \rightarrow C$, $C \rightarrow B$, and $A \rightarrow D$. To start, notice that the given FD's are their own minimal basis. To check, we need to do a bit of work. First, we need to verify that we cannot eliminate any of the given dependencies. That is, we show, using Algorithm 7, that no two of the FD's imply the third. For example, we must take the closure of $\{A, B\}$, the left side of the first FD, using only the second and third FD's, $C \to B$ and $A \to D$. This closure includes D but not C, so we conclude that the first FD $AB \to C$ is not implied by the second and third FD's. We get a similar conclusion if we try to drop the second or third FD.

We must also verify that we cannot eliminate any attributes from a left side. In this simple case, the only possibility is that we could eliminate A or B from the first FD. For example, if we eliminate A, we would be left with $B \to C$. We must show that $B \to C$ is not implied by the three original FD's, $AB \to C$, $C \to B$, and $A \to D$. With these FD's, the closure of $\{B\}$ is just B, so $B \to C$ does not follow. A similar conclusion is drawn if we try to drop B from $AB \to C$. Thus, we have our minimal basis.

We start the 3NF synthesis by taking the attributes of each FD as a relation schema. That is, we get relations $S_1(A,B,C)$, $S_2(B,C)$, and $S_3(A,D)$. It is never necessary to use a relation whose schema is a proper subset of another relation's schema, so we can drop S_2.

We must also consider whether we need to add a relation whose schema is a key. In this example, R has two keys: $\{A,B,E\}$ and $\{A,C,E\}$, as you can verify. Neither of these keys is a subset of the schemas chosen so far. Thus, we must add one of them, say $S_4(A,B,E)$. The final decomposition of R is thus $S_1(A,B,C)$, $S_3(A,D)$, and $S_4(A,B,E)$. □

5.3 Why the 3NF Synthesis Algorithm Works

We need to show three things: that the lossless-join and dependency-preservation properties hold, and that all the relations of the decomposition are in 3NF.

1. *Lossless Join.* Start with a relation of the decomposition whose set of attributes K is a superkey. Consider the sequence of FD's that are used in Algorithm 7 to expand K to become K^+. Since K is a superkey, we know K^+ is all the attributes. The same sequence of FD applications on the tableau cause the subscripted symbols in the row corresponding to K to be equated to unsubscripted symbols in the same order as the attributes were added to the closure. Thus, the chase test concludes that the decomposition is lossless.

2. *Dependency Preservation.* Each FD of the minimal basis has all its attributes in some relation of the decomposition. Thus, each dependency can be checked in the decomposed relations.

3. *Third Normal Form.* If we have to add a relation whose schema is a key, then this relation is surely in 3NF. The reason is that all attributes of this relation are prime, and thus no violation of 3NF could be present in this relation. For the relations whose schemas are derived from the FD's of a minimal basis, the proof that they are in 3NF is beyond the scope of this book. The argument involves showing that a 3NF violation implies that the basis is not minimal.

5.4 Exercises for Section 5

Exercise 5.1: For each of the relation schemas and sets of FD's of Exercise 3.1:

i) Indicate all the 3NF violations.

ii) Decompose the relations, as necessary, into collections of relations that are in 3NF.

Exercise 5.2: Consider the relation `Courses` (C, T, H, R, S, G), whose attributes may be thought of informally as course, teacher, hour, room, student, and grade. Let the set of FD's for `Courses` be $C \to T$, $HR \to C$, $HT \to R$, $HS \to R$, and $CS \to G$. Intuitively, the first says that a course has a unique teacher, and the second says that only one course can meet in a given room at a given hour. The third says that a teacher can be in only one room at a given hour, and the fourth says the same about students. The last says that students get only one grade in a course.

a) What are all the keys for `Courses`?

b) Verify that the given FD's are their own minimal basis.

c) Use the 3NF synthesis algorithm to find a lossless-join, dependency-preserving decomposition of R into 3NF relations. Are any of the relations not in BCNF?

Exercise 5.3: Consider a relation `Stocks`(B, O, I, S, Q, D), whose attributes may be thought of informally as broker, office (of the broker), investor, stock, quantity (of the stock owned by the investor), and dividend (of the stock). Let the set of FD's for `Stocks` be $S \to D$, $I \to B$, $IS \to Q$, and $B \to O$. Repeat Exercise 5.2 for the relation `Stocks`.

Exercise 5.4: Verify, using the chase, that the decomposition of Example 27 has a lossless join.

!! **Exercise 5.5:** Suppose we modified Algorithm 20 (BNCF decomposition) so that instead of decomposing a relation R whenever R was not in BCNF, we only decomposed R if it was not in 3NF. Provide a counterexample to show that this modified algorithm would not necessarily produce a 3NF decomposition with dependency preservation.

6 Multivalued Dependencies

A "multivalued dependency" is an assertion that two attributes or sets of attributes are independent of one another. This condition is, as we shall see, a generalization of the notion of a functional dependency, in the sense that every FD implies the corresponding multivalued dependency. However, there are some situations involving independence of attribute sets that cannot be explained as FD's. In this section we shall explore the cause of multivalued dependencies and see how they can be used in database schema design.

6.1 Attribute Independence and Its Consequent Redundancy

There are occasional situations where we design a relation schema and find it is in BCNF, yet the relation has a kind of redundancy that is not related to FD's. The most common source of redundancy in BCNF schemas is an attempt to put two or more set-valued properties of the key into a single relation.

Example 28: In this example, we shall suppose that stars may have several addresses, which we break into street and city components. The set of addresses is one of the set-valued properties this relation will store. The second set-valued property of stars that we shall put into this relation is the set of titles and years of movies in which the star appeared. Then Fig. 10 is a typical instance of this relation.

name	*street*	*city*	*title*	*year*
C. Fisher	123 Maple St.	Hollywood	Star Wars	1977
C. Fisher	5 Locust Ln.	Malibu	Star Wars	1977
C. Fisher	123 Maple St.	Hollywood	Empire Strikes Back	1980
C. Fisher	5 Locust Ln.	Malibu	Empire Strikes Back	1980
C. Fisher	123 Maple St.	Hollywood	Return of the Jedi	1983
C. Fisher	5 Locust Ln.	Malibu	Return of the Jedi	1983

Figure 10: Sets of addresses independent from movies

We focus in Fig. 10 on Carrie Fisher's two hypothetical addresses and her three best-known movies. There is no reason to associate an address with one movie and not another. Thus, the only way to express the fact that addresses and movies are independent properties of stars is to have each address appear with each movie. But when we repeat address and movie facts in all combinations, there is obvious redundancy. For instance, Fig. 10 repeats each of Carrie Fisher's addresses three times (once for each of her movies) and each movie twice (once for each address).

Yet there is no BCNF violation in the relation suggested by Fig. 10. There are, in fact, no nontrivial FD's at all. For example, attribute `city` is not functionally determined by the other four attributes. There might be a star with two homes that had the same street address in different cities. Then there would be two tuples that agreed in all attributes but `city` and disagreed in `city`. Thus,

$$\texttt{name street title year} \rightarrow \texttt{city}$$

is not an FD for our relation. We leave it to the reader to check that none of the five attributes is functionally determined by the other four. Since there are no nontrivial FD's, it follows that all five attributes form the only key and that there are no BCNF violations. □

6.2 Definition of Multivalued Dependencies

A *multivalued dependency* (abbreviated MVD) is a statement about some relation R that when you fix the values for one set of attributes, then the values in certain other attributes are independent of the values of all the other attributes in the relation. More precisely, we say the MVD

$$A_1A_2 \cdots A_n \twoheadrightarrow B_1B_2 \cdots B_m$$

holds for a relation R if when we restrict ourselves to the tuples of R that have particular values for each of the attributes among the A's, then the set of values we find among the B's is independent of the set of values we find among the attributes of R that are not among the A's or B's. Still more precisely, we say this MVD holds if

> For each pair of tuples t and u of relation R that agree on all the A's, we can find in R some tuple v that agrees:
>
> 1. With both t and u on the A's,
> 2. With t on the B's, and
> 3. With u on all attributes of R that are not among the A's or B's.

Note that we can use this rule with t and u interchanged, to infer the existence of a fourth tuple w that agrees with u on the B's and with t on the other attributes. As a consequence, for any fixed values of the A's, the associated values of the B's and the other attributes appear in all possible combinations in different tuples. Figure 11 suggests how v relates to t and u when an MVD holds. However, the A's and B's to not have to appear consecutively.

In general, we may assume that the A's and B's (left side and right side) of an MVD are disjoint. However, as with FD's, it is permissible to add some of the A's to the right side if we wish.

Example 29: In Example 28 we encountered an MVD that in our notation is expressed:

$$\texttt{name} \twoheadrightarrow \texttt{street city}$$

That is, for each star's name, the set of addresses appears in conjunction with each of the star's movies. For an example of how the formal definition of this MVD applies, consider the first and fourth tuples from Fig. 10:

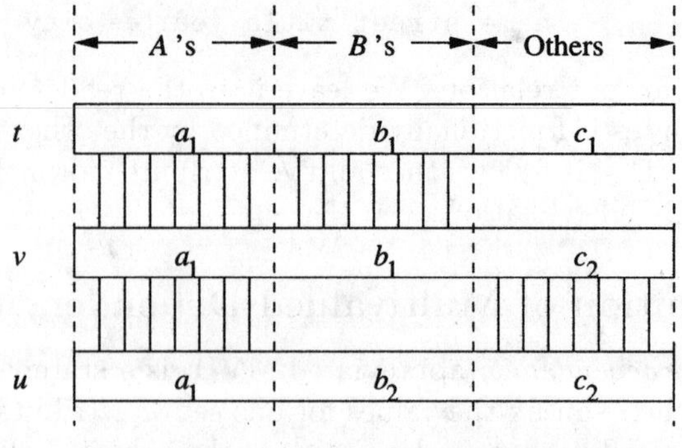

Figure 11: A multivalued dependency guarantees that v exists

name	*street*	*city*	*title*	*year*
C. Fisher	123 Maple St.	Hollywood	Star Wars	1977
C. Fisher	5 Locust Ln.	Malibu	Empire Strikes Back	1980

If we let the first tuple be t and the second be u, then the MVD asserts that we must also find in R the tuple that has name `C. Fisher`, a street and city that agree with the first tuple, and other attributes (`title` and `year`) that agree with the second tuple. There is indeed such a tuple; it is the third tuple of Fig. 10.

Similarly, we could let t be the second tuple above and u be the first. Then the MVD tells us that there is a tuple of R that agrees with the second in attributes `name`, `street`, and `city` and with the first in `name`, `title`, and `year`. This tuple also exists; it is the second tuple of Fig. 10. □

6.3 Reasoning About Multivalued Dependencies

There are a number of rules about MVD's that are similar to the rules we learned for FD's in Section 2. For example, MVD's obey

- *Trivial MVD's.* The MVD

$$A_1A_2\cdots A_n \twoheadrightarrow B_1B_2\cdots B_m$$

  holds in any relation if $\{B_1, B_2, \ldots, B_m\} \subseteq \{A_1, A_2, \ldots, A_n\}$.

- The *transitive rule*, which says that if $A_1A_2\cdots A_n \twoheadrightarrow B_1B_2\cdots B_m$ and $B_1B_2\cdots B_m \twoheadrightarrow C_1C_2\cdots C_k$ hold for some relation, then so does

$$A_1A_2\cdots A_n \twoheadrightarrow C_1C_2\cdots C_k$$

  Any C's that are also A's must be deleted from the right side.

On the other hand, MVD's do not obey the splitting part of the splitting/combining rule, as the following example shows.

Example 30: Consider again Fig. 10, where we observed the MVD:

$$\texttt{name} \twoheadrightarrow \texttt{street city}$$

If the splitting rule applied to MVD's, we would expect

$$\texttt{name} \twoheadrightarrow \texttt{street}$$

also to be true. This MVD says that each star's street addresses are independent of the other attributes, including `city`. However, that statement is false. Consider, for instance, the first two tuples of Fig. 10. The hypothetical MVD would allow us to infer that the tuples with the streets interchanged:

name	*street*	*city*	*title*	*year*
C. Fisher	5 Locust Ln.	Hollywood	Star Wars	1977
C. Fisher	123 Maple St.	Malibu	Star Wars	1977

were in the relation. But these are not true tuples, because, for instance, the home on 5 Locust Ln. is in Malibu, not Hollywood. □

However, there are several new rules dealing with MVD's that we can learn.

- *FD Promotion.* Every FD is an MVD. That is, if

$$A_1A_2 \cdots A_n \rightarrow B_1B_2 \cdots B_m$$

then $A_1A_2 \cdots A_n \twoheadrightarrow B_1B_2 \cdots B_m$.

To see why, suppose R is some relation for which the FD

$$A_1A_2 \cdots A_n \rightarrow B_1B_2 \cdots B_m$$

holds, and suppose t and u are tuples of R that agree on the A's. To show that the MVD $A_1A_2 \cdots A_n \twoheadrightarrow B_1B_2 \cdots B_m$ holds, we have to show that R also contains a tuple v that agrees with t and u on the A's, with t on the B's, and with u on all other attributes. But v can be u. Surely u agrees with t and u on the A's, because we started by assuming that these two tuples agree on the A's. The FD $A_1A_2 \cdots A_n \rightarrow B_1B_2 \cdots B_m$ assures us that u agrees with t on the B's. And of course u agrees with itself on the other attributes. Thus, whenever an FD holds, the corresponding MVD holds.

- *Complementation Rule.* If $A_1A_2 \cdots A_n \twoheadrightarrow B_1B_2 \cdots B_m$ is an MVD for relation R, then R also satisfies $A_1A_2 \cdots A_n \twoheadrightarrow C_1C_2 \cdots C_k$, where the C's are all attributes of R not among the A's and B's.

That is, swapping the B's between two tuples that agree in the A's has the same effect as swapping the C's.

Example 31: Again consider the relation of Fig. 10, for which we asserted the MVD:

$$\texttt{name} \twoheadrightarrow \texttt{street city}$$

The complementation rule says that

$$\texttt{name} \twoheadrightarrow \texttt{title year}$$

must also hold in this relation, because `title` and `year` are the attributes not mentioned in the first MVD. The second MVD intuitively means that each star has a set of movies starred in, which are independent of the star's addresses. □

An MVD whose right side is a subset of the left side is trivial — it holds in every relation. However, an interesting consequence of the complementation rule is that there are some other MVD's that are trivial, but that look distinctly nontrivial.

- *More Trivial MVD's.* If all the attributes of relation R are

$$\{A_1, A_2, \ldots, A_n, B_1, B_2, \ldots, B_m\}$$

then $A_1A_2 \cdots A_n \twoheadrightarrow B_1B_2 \cdots B_m$ holds in R.

To see why these additional trivial MVD's hold, notice that if we take two tuples that agree in $A_1, A_2, \ldots, A_n$ and swap their components in attributes $B_1, B_2, \ldots, B_m$, we get the same two tuples back, although in the opposite order.

6.4 Fourth Normal Form

The redundancy that we found in Section 6.1 to be caused by MVD's can be eliminated if we use these dependencies for decomposition. In this section we shall introduce a new normal form, called "fourth normal form." In this normal form, all nontrivial MVD's are eliminated, as are all FD's that violate BCNF. As a result, the decomposed relations have neither the redundancy from FD's that we discussed in Section 3.1 nor the redundancy from MVD's that we discussed in Section 6.1.

The "fourth normal form" condition is essentially the BCNF condition, but applied to MVD's instead of FD's. Formally:

- A relation R is in *fourth normal form* (4NF) if whenever

$$A_1A_2 \cdots A_n \twoheadrightarrow B_1B_2 \cdots B_m$$

is a nontrivial MVD, $\{A_1, A_2, \ldots, A_n\}$ is a superkey.

That is, if a relation is in 4NF, then every nontrivial MVD is really an FD with a superkey on the left. Note that the notions of keys and superkeys depend on FD's only; adding MVD's does not change the definition of "key."

Example 32: The relation of Fig. 10 violates the 4NF condition. For example,

$$\texttt{name} \twoheadrightarrow \texttt{street city}$$

is a nontrivial MVD, yet `name` by itself is not a superkey. In fact, the only key for this relation is all the attributes. □

Fourth normal form is truly a generalization of BCNF. Recall from Section 6.3 that every FD is also an MVD. Thus, every BCNF violation is also a 4NF violation. Put another way, every relation that is in 4NF is therefore in BCNF.

However, there are some relations that are in BCNF but not 4NF. Figure 10 is a good example. The only key for this relation is all five attributes, and there are no nontrivial FD's. Thus it is surely in BCNF. However, as we observed in Example 32, it is not in 4NF.

6.5 Decomposition into Fourth Normal Form

The 4NF decomposition algorithm is quite analogous to the BCNF decomposition algorithm.

Algorithm 33: Decomposition into Fourth Normal Form.

INPUT: A relation R_0 with a set of functional and multivalued dependencies S_0.

OUTPUT: A decomposition of R_0 into relations all of which are in 4NF. The decomposition has the lossless-join property.

METHOD: Do the following steps, with $R = R_0$ and $S = S_0$:

1. Find a 4NF violation in R, say $A_1A_2 \cdots A_n \twoheadrightarrow B_1B_2 \cdots B_m$, where

$$\{A_1, A_2, \ldots, A_n\}$$

is not a superkey. Note this MVD could be a true MVD in S, or it could be derived from the corresponding FD $A_1A_2 \cdots A_n \rightarrow B_1B_2 \cdots B_m$ in S, since every FD is an MVD. If there is none, return; R by itself is a suitable decomposition.

2. If there is such a 4NF violation, break the schema for the relation R that has the 4NF violation into two schemas:

   (a) R_1, whose schema is A's and the B's.

   (b) R_2, whose schema is the A's and all attributes of R that are not among the A's or B's.

3. Find the FD's and MVD's that hold in R_1 and R_2 (Section 7 explains how to do this task in general, but often this "projection" of dependencies is straightforward). Recursively decompose R_1 and R_2 with respect to their projected dependencies.

□

Example 34: Let us continue Example 32. We observed that

`name` $\twoheadrightarrow$ `street city`

was a 4NF violation. The decomposition rule above tells us to replace the five-attribute schema by one schema that has only the three attributes in the above MVD and another schema that consists of the left side, `name`, plus the attributes that do not appear in the MVD. These attributes are `title` and `year`, so the following two schemas

{`name, street, city`}
{`name, title, year`}

are the result of the decomposition. In each schema there are no nontrivial multivalued (or functional) dependencies, so they are in 4NF. Note that in the relation with schema {`name, street, city`}, the MVD:

`name` $\twoheadrightarrow$ `street city`

is trivial since it involves all attributes. Likewise, in the relation with schema {`name, title, year`}, the MVD:

`name` $\twoheadrightarrow$ `title year`

is trivial. Should one or both schemas of the decomposition not be in 4NF, we would have had to decompose the non-4NF schema(s). □

As for the BCNF decomposition, each decomposition step leaves us with schemas that have strictly fewer attributes than we started with, so eventually we get to schemas that need not be decomposed further; that is, they are in 4NF. Moreover, the argument justifying the decomposition that we gave in Section 4.1 carries over to MVD's as well. When we decompose a relation because of an MVD $A_1A_2\cdots A_n \twoheadrightarrow B_1B_2\cdots B_m$, this dependency is enough to justify the claim that we can reconstruct the original relation from the relations of the decomposition.

We shall, in Section 7, give an algorithm by which we can verify that the MVD used to justify a 4NF decomposition also proves that the decomposition has a lossless join. Also in that section, we shall show how it is possible, although time-consuming, to perform the projection of MVD's onto the decomposed relations. This projection is required if we are to decide whether or not further decomposition is necessary.

6.6 Relationships Among Normal Forms

As we have mentioned, 4NF implies BCNF, which in turn implies 3NF. Thus, the sets of relation schemas (including dependencies) satisfying the three normal forms are related as in Fig. 12. That is, if a relation with certain dependencies is in 4NF, it is also in BCNF and 3NF. Also, if a relation with certain dependencies is in BCNF, then it is in 3NF.

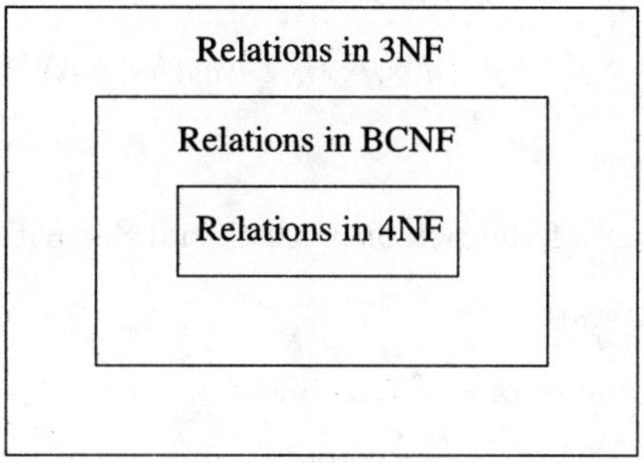

Figure 12: 4NF implies BCNF implies 3NF

Another way to compare the normal forms is by the guarantees they make about the set of relations that result from a decomposition into that normal form. These observations are summarized in the table of Fig. 13. That is, BCNF (and therefore 4NF) eliminates the redundancy and other anomalies that are caused by FD's, while only 4NF eliminates the additional redundancy that is caused by the presence of MVD's that are not FD's. Often, 3NF is enough to eliminate this redundancy, but there are examples where it is not. BCNF does not guarantee preservation of FD's, and none of the normal forms guarantee preservation of MVD's, although in typical cases the dependencies are preserved.

Property	3NF	BCNF	4NF
Eliminates redundancy due to FD's	No	Yes	Yes
Eliminates redundancy due to MVD's	No	No	Yes
Preserves FD's	Yes	No	No
Preserves MVD's	No	No	No

Figure 13: Properties of normal forms and their decompositions

6.7 Exercises for Section 6

Exercise 6.1: Suppose we have a relation $R(A, B, C)$ with an MVD $A \twoheadrightarrow B$.

If we know that the tuples (a, b_1, c_1), (a, b_2, c_2), and (a, b_3, c_3) are in the current instance of R, what other tuples do we know must also be in R?

Exercise 6.2: Suppose we have a relation in which we want to record for each person their name, Social Security number, and birthdate. Also, for each child of the person, the name, Social Security number, and birthdate of the child, and for each automobile the person owns, its serial number and make. To be more precise, this relation has all tuples

$$(n, s, b, cn, cs, cb, as, am)$$

such that

1. n is the name of the person with Social Security number s.
2. b is n's birthdate.
3. cn is the name of one of n's children.
4. cs is cn's Social Security number.
5. cb is cn's birthdate.
6. as is the serial number of one of n's automobiles.
7. am is the make of the automobile with serial number as.

For this relation:

a) Tell the functional and multivalued dependencies we would expect to hold.

b) Suggest a decomposition of the relation into 4NF.

Exercise 6.3: For each of the following relation schemas and dependencies

a) $R(A, B, C, D)$ with MVD's $A \twoheadrightarrow B$ and $A \twoheadrightarrow C$.

b) $R(A, B, C, D)$ with MVD's $A \twoheadrightarrow B$ and $B \twoheadrightarrow CD$.

c) $R(A, B, C, D)$ with MVD $AB \twoheadrightarrow C$ and FD $B \rightarrow D$.

d) $R(A, B, C, D, E)$ with MVD's $A \twoheadrightarrow B$ and $AB \twoheadrightarrow C$ and FD's $A \rightarrow D$ and $AB \rightarrow E$.

do the following:

i) Find all the 4NF violations.

ii) Decompose the relations into a collection of relation schemas in 4NF.

Exercise 6.4: Give informal arguments why we would not expect any of the five attributes in Example 28 to be functionally determined by the other four.

7 An Algorithm for Discovering MVD's

Reasoning about MVD's, or combinations of MVD's and FD's, is rather more difficult than reasoning about FD's alone. For FD's, we have Algorithm 7 to decide whether or not an FD follows from some given FD's. In this section, we shall first show that the closure algorithm is really the same as the chase algorithm we studied in Section 4.2. The ideas behind the chase can be extended to incorporate MVD's as well as FD's. Once we have that tool in place, we can solve all the problems we need to solve about MVD's and FD's, such as finding whether an MVD follows from given dependencies or projecting MVD's and FD's onto the relations of a decomposition.

7.1 The Closure and the Chase

In Section 2.4 we saw how to take a set of attributes X and compute its closure X^+ of all attributes that functionally depend on X. In that manner, we can test whether an FD $X \rightarrow Y$ follows from a given set of FD's F, by closing X with respect to F and seeing whether $Y \subseteq X^+$. We could see the closure as a variant of the chase, in which the starting tableau and the goal condition are different from what we used in Section 4.2.

Suppose we start with a tableau that consists of two rows. These rows agree in the attributes of X and disagree in all other attributes. If we apply the FD's in F to chase this tableau, we shall equate the symbols in exactly those columns that are in $X^+ - X$. Thus, a chase-based test for whether $X \rightarrow Y$ follows from F can be summarized as:

1. Start with a tableau having two rows that agree only on X.
2. Chase the tableau using the FD's of F.
3. If the final tableau agrees in all columns of Y, then $X \rightarrow Y$ holds; otherwise it does not.

Example 35: Let us repeat Example 8, where we had a relation

$$R(A, B, C, D, E, F)$$

with FD's $AB \rightarrow C$, $BC \rightarrow AD$, $D \rightarrow E$, and $CF \rightarrow B$. We want to test whether $AB \rightarrow D$ holds. Start with the tableau:

A	B	C	D	E	F
a	b	c_1	d_1	e_1	f_1
a	b	c_2	d_2	e_2	f_2

We can apply $AB \rightarrow C$ to infer $c_1 = c_2$; say both become c_1. The resulting tableau is:

A	B	C	D	E	F
a	b	c_1	d_1	e_1	f_1
a	b	c_1	d_2	e_2	f_2

Next, apply $BC \rightarrow AD$ to infer that $d_1 = d_2$, and apply $D \rightarrow E$ to infer $e_1 = e_2$. At this point, the tableau is:

A	B	C	D	E	F
a	b	c_1	d_1	e_1	f_1
a	b	c_1	d_1	e_1	f_2

and we can go no further. Since the two tuples now agree in the D column, we know that $AB \rightarrow D$ does follow from the given FD's. □

7.2 Extending the Chase to MVD's

The method of inferring an FD using the chase can be applied to infer MVD's as well. When we try to infer an FD, we are asking whether we can conclude that two possibly unequal values must indeed be the same. When we apply an FD $X \rightarrow Y$, we search for pairs of rows in the tableau that agree on all the columns of X, and we force the symbols in each column of Y to be equal.

However, MVD's do not tell us to conclude symbols are equal. Rather, $X \twoheadrightarrow Y$ tells us that if we find two rows of the tableau that agree in X, then we can form two new tuples by swapping all their components in the attributes of Y; the resulting two tuples must also be in the relation, and therefore in the tableau. Likewise, if we want to infer some MVD $X \twoheadrightarrow Y$ from given FD's and MVD's, we start with a tableau consisting of two tuples that agree in X and disagree in all attributes not in the set X. We apply the given FD's to equate symbols, and we apply the given MVD's to swap the values in certain attributes between two existing rows of the tableau in order to add new rows to the tableau. If we ever discover that one of the original tuples, with its components for Y replaced by those of the other original tuple, is in the tableau, then we have inferred the MVD.

There is a point of caution to be observed in this more complex chase process. Since symbols may get equated and replaced by other symbols, we may not recognize that we have created one of the desired tuples, because some of the original symbols may be replaced by others. The simplest way to avoid a problem is to define the target tuple initially, and never change its symbols. That is, let the target row be one with an unsubscripted letter in each component. Let the two initial rows of the tableau for the test of $X \twoheadrightarrow Y$ have the unsubscripted letters in X. Let the first row also have unsubscripted letters in Y, and let the second row have the unsubscripted letters in all attributes not in X or Y. Fill in the other positions of the two rows with new symbols that each occur only once. When we equate subscripted and unsubscripted symbols, always replace a subscripted one by the unsubscripted one, as we did in Section 4.2. Then, when applying the chase, we have only to ask whether the all-unsubscripted-letters row ever appears in the tableau.

Example 36: Suppose we have a relation $R(A, B, C, D)$ with given dependencies $A \rightarrow B$ and $B \twoheadrightarrow C$. We wish to prove that $A \twoheadrightarrow C$ holds in R. Start with the two-row tableau that represents $A \twoheadrightarrow C$:

A	B	C	D
a	b_1	c	d_1
a	b	c_2	d

Notice that our target row is (a, b, c, d). Both rows of the tableau have the unsubscripted letter in the column for A. The first row has the unsubscripted letter in C, and the second row has unsubscripted letters in the remaining columns.

We first apply the FD $A \rightarrow B$ to infer that $b = b_1$. We must therefore replace the subscripted b_1 by the unsubscripted b. The tableau becomes:

A	B	C	D
a	b	c	d_1
a	b	c_2	d

Next, we apply the MVD $B \twoheadrightarrow C$, since the two rows now agree in the B column. We swap the C columns to get two more rows which we add to the tableau, which becomes:

A	B	C	D
a	b	c	d_1
a	b	c_2	d
a	b	c_2	d_1
a	b	c	d

We have now a row with all unsubscripted symbols, which proves that $A \twoheadrightarrow C$ holds in relation R. Notice how the tableau manipulations really give a proof that $A \twoheadrightarrow C$ holds. This proof is: "Given two tuples of R that agree in A, they must also agree in B because $A \rightarrow B$. Since they agree in B, we can swap their C components by $B \twoheadrightarrow C$, and the resulting tuples will be in R. Thus, if two tuples of R agree in A, the tuples that result when we swap their C's are also in R; i.e., $A \twoheadrightarrow C$." □

Example 37: There is a surprising rule for FD's and MVD's that says whenever there is an MVD $X \twoheadrightarrow Y$, and any FD whose right side is a (not necessarily proper) subset of Y, say Z, then $X \rightarrow Z$. We shall use the chase process to prove a simple example of this rule. Let us be given relation $R(A, B, C, D)$ with MVD $A \twoheadrightarrow BC$ and FD $D \rightarrow C$. We claim that $A \rightarrow C$.

Since we are trying to prove an FD, we don't have to worry about a target tuple of unsubscripted letters. We can start with any two tuples that agree in A and disagree in every other column. such as:

A	B	C	D
a	b_1	c_1	d_1
a	b_2	c_2	d_2

Our goal is to prove that $c_1 = c_2$.

The only thing we can do to start is to apply the MVD $A \twoheadrightarrow BC$, since the two rows agree on A, but no other columns. When we swap the B and C columns of these two rows, we get two new rows to add:

A	B	C	D
a	b_1	c_1	d_1
a	b_2	c_2	d_2
a	b_2	c_2	d_1
a	b_1	c_1	d_2

Now, we have pairs of rows that agree in D, so we can apply the FD $D \rightarrow C$. For instance, the first and third rows have the same D-value d_1, so we can apply the FD and conclude $c_1 = c_2$. That is our goal, so we have proved $A \rightarrow C$. The new tableau is:

A	B	C	D
a	b_1	c_1	d_1
a	b_2	c_1	d_2
a	b_2	c_1	d_1
a	b_1	c_1	d_2

It happens that no further changes are possible, using the given dependencies. However, that doesn't matter, since we already proved what we need. □

7.3 Why the Chase Works for MVD's

The arguments are essentially the same as we have given before. Each step of the chase, whether it equates symbols or generates new rows, is a true observation about tuples of the given relation R that is justified by the FD or MVD that we apply in that step. Thus, a positive conclusion of the chase is always a proof that the concluded FD or MVD holds in R.

When the chase ends in failure — the goal row (for an MVD) or the desired equality of symbols (for an FD) is not produced — then the final tableau is a counterexample. It satisfies the given dependencies, or else we would not be finished making changes. However, it does not satisfy the dependency we were trying to prove.

There is one other issue that did not come up when we performed the chase using only FD's. Since the chase with MVD's adds rows to the tableau, how do we know we ever terminate the chase? Could we keep adding rows forever, never reaching our goal, but not sure that after a few more steps we would achieve that goal? Fortunately, that cannot happen. The reason is that we never create any new symbols. We start out with at most two symbols in each of k columns, and all rows we create will have one of these two symbols in its component for that column. Thus, we cannot ever have more than 2^k rows in our tableau, if k is the number of columns. The chase with MVD's can take exponential time, but it cannot run forever.

7.4 Projecting MVD's

Recall that our reason for wanting to infer MVD's was to perform a cascade of decompositions leading to 4NF relations. To do that task, we need to be able to project the given dependencies onto the schemas of the two relations that we get in the first step of the decomposition. Only then can we know whether they are in 4NF or need to be decomposed further.

In the worst case, we have to test every possible FD and MVD for each of the decomposed relations. The chase test is applied on the full set of attributes of the original relation. However, the goal for an MVD is to produce a row of the tableau that has unsubscripted letters in all the attributes of one of the relations of the decomposition; that row may have any letters in the other attributes. The goal for an FD is the same: equality of the symbols in a given column.

Example 38: Suppose we have a relation $R(A, B, C, D, E)$ that we decompose, and let one of the relations of the decomposition be $S(A, B, C)$. Suppose that the MVD $A \twoheadrightarrow CD$ holds in R. Does this MVD imply any dependency in S? We claim that $A \twoheadrightarrow C$ holds in S, as does $A \twoheadrightarrow B$ (by the complementation rule). Let us verify that $A \twoheadrightarrow C$ holds in S. We start with the tableau:

A	B	C	D	E
a	b_1	c	d_1	e_1
a	b	c_2	d	e

Use the MVD of R, $A \twoheadrightarrow CD$ to swap the C and D components of these two rows to get two new rows:

A	B	C	D	E
a	b_1	c	d_1	e_1
a	b	c_2	d	e
a	b_1	c_2	d	e_1
a	b	c	d_1	e

Notice that the last row has unsubscripted symbols in all the attributes of S, that is, A, B, and C. That is enough to conclude that $A \twoheadrightarrow C$ holds in S. □

Often, our search for FD's and MVD's in the projected relations does not have to be completely exhaustive. Here are some simplifications.

1. It is surely not necessary to check the trivial FD's and MVD's.

2. For FD's, we can restrict ourselves to looking for FD's with a singleton right side, because of the combining rule for FD's.

3. An FD or MVD whose left side does not contain the left side of any given dependency surely cannot hold, since there is no way for its chase test to get started. That is, the two rows with which you start the test are unchanged by the given dependencies.

7.5 Exercises for Section 7

Exercise 7.1: Use the chase test to tell whether each of the following dependencies hold in a relation $R(A, B, C, D, E)$ with the dependencies $A \twoheadrightarrow BC$, $B \rightarrow D$, and $C \twoheadrightarrow E$.

a) $A \rightarrow D$.

b) $A \twoheadrightarrow D$.

c) $A \rightarrow E$.

d) $A \twoheadrightarrow E$.

! **Exercise 7.2:** If we project the relation R of Exercise 7.1 onto $S(A, C, E)$, what nontrivial FD's and MVD's hold in S?

! **Exercise 7.3:** Show the following rules for MVD's. In each case, you can set up the proof as a chase test, but you must think a little more generally than in the examples, since the set of attributes are arbitrary sets X, Y, Z, and the other unnamed attributes of the relation in which these dependencies hold.

a) The *Union Rule.* If X, Y, and Z are sets of attributes, $X \twoheadrightarrow Y$, and $X \twoheadrightarrow Z$, then $X \twoheadrightarrow (Y \cup Z)$.

b) The *Intersection Rule.* If X, Y, and Z are sets of attributes, $X \twoheadrightarrow Y$, and $X \twoheadrightarrow Z$, then $X \twoheadrightarrow (Y \cap Z)$.

c) The *Difference Rule.* If X, Y, and Z are sets of attributes, $X \twoheadrightarrow Y$, and $X \twoheadrightarrow Z$, then $X \twoheadrightarrow (Y - Z)$.

d) *Removing attributes shared by left and right side.* If $X \twoheadrightarrow Y$ holds, then $X \twoheadrightarrow (Y - X)$ holds.

! **Exercise 7.4:** Give counterexample relations to show why the following rules for MVD's do *not* hold. *Hint*: apply the chase test and see what happens.

a) If $A \twoheadrightarrow BC$, then $A \twoheadrightarrow B$.

b) If $A \twoheadrightarrow B$, then $A \rightarrow B$.

c) If $AB \twoheadrightarrow C$, then $A \twoheadrightarrow C$.

8 Summary

- ✦ *Functional Dependencies*: A functional dependency is a statement that two tuples of a relation that agree on some particular set of attributes must also agree on some other particular set of attributes.

- ✦ *Keys of a Relation*: A superkey for a relation is a set of attributes that functionally determines all the attributes of the relation. A key is a superkey, no proper subset of which is also a superkey.

- ✦ *Reasoning About Functional Dependencies*: There are many rules that let us infer that one FD $X \rightarrow A$ holds in any relation instance that satisfies some other given set of FD's. To verify that $X \rightarrow A$ holds, compute the closure of X, using the given FD's to expand X until it includes A.

- ✦ *Minimal Basis for a set of FD's*: For any set of FD's, there is at least one minimal basis, which is a set of FD's equivalent to the original (each set implies the other set), with singleton right sides, no FD that can be eliminated while preserving equivalence, and no attribute in a left side that can be eliminated while preserving equivalence.

- ✦ *Boyce-Codd Normal Form*: A relation is in BCNF if the only nontrivial FD's say that some superkey functionally determines one or more of the other attributes. A major benefit of BCNF is that it eliminates redundancy caused by the existence of FD's.

- ✦ *Lossless-Join Decomposition*: A useful property of a decomposition is that the original relation can be recovered exactly by taking the natural join of the relations in the decomposition. Any decomposition gives us back at least the tuples with which we start, but a carelessly chosen decomposition can give tuples in the join that were not in the original relation.

- ✦ *Dependency-Preserving Decomposition*: Another desirable property of a decomposition is that we can check all the functional dependencies that hold in the original relation by checking FD's in the decomposed relations.

- ✦ *Third Normal Form*: Sometimes decomposition into BCNF can lose the dependency-preservation property. A relaxed form of BCNF, called 3NF, allows an FD $X \rightarrow A$ even if X is not a superkey, provided A is a member of some key. 3NF does not guarantee to eliminate all redundancy due to FD's, but often does so.

- ✦ *The Chase*: We can test whether a decomposition has the lossless-join property by setting up a tableau — a set of rows that represent tuples of the original relation. We chase a tableau by applying the given functional dependencies to infer that certain pairs of symbols must be the same. The decomposition is lossless with respect to a given set of FD's if and only if the chase leads to a row identical to the tuple whose membership in the join of the projected relations we assumed.

- ✦ *Synthesis Algorithm for 3NF*: If we take a minimal basis for a given set of FD's, turn each of these FD's into a relation, and add a key for the relation, if necessary, the result is a decomposition into 3NF that has the lossless-join and dependency-preservation properties.

- ✦ *Multivalued Dependencies*: A multivalued dependency is a statement that two sets of attributes in a relation have sets of values that appear in all possible combinations.

- ✦ *Fourth Normal Form*: MVD's can also cause redundancy in a relation. 4NF is like BCNF, but also forbids nontrivial MVD's whose left side is not a superkey. It is possible to decompose a relation into 4NF without losing information.

- ✦ *Reasoning About MVD's*: We can infer MVD's and FD's from a given set of MVD's and FD's by a chase process. We start with a two-row tableau that represent the dependency we are trying to prove. FD's are applied by equating symbols, and MVD's are applied by adding rows to the tableau that have the appropriate components interchanged.

9 References

Third normal form was described in [6]. This paper introduces the idea of functional dependencies, as well as the basic relational concept. Boyce-Codd normal form is in a later paper [7].

Multivalued dependencies and fourth normal form were defined by Fagin in [9]. However, the idea of multivalued dependencies also appears independently in [8] and [11].

Armstrong was the first to study rules for inferring FD's [2]. The rules for FD's that we have covered here (including what we call "Armstrong's axioms") and rules for inferring MVD's as well, come from [3].

The technique for testing an FD by computing the closure for a set of attributes is from [4], as is the fact that a minimal basis provides a 3NF decomposition. The fact that this decomposition provides the lossless-join and dependency-preservation propoerties is from [5].

The tableau test for the lossless-join property and the chase are from [1]. More information and the history of the idea is found in [10].

1. A. V. Aho, C. Beeri, and J. D. Ullman, "The theory of joins in relational databases," *ACM Transactions on Database Systems* **4**:3, pp. 297-314, 1979.

2. W. W. Armstrong, "Dependency structures of database relationships," *Proceedings of the 1974 IFIP Congress*, pp. 580–583.

3. C. Beeri, R. Fagin, and J. H. Howard, "A complete axiomatization for functional and multivalued dependencies," *ACM SIGMOD Intl. Conf. on Management of Data*, pp. 47–61, 1977.

4. P. A. Bernstein, "Synthesizing third normal form relations from functional dependencies," *ACM Transactions on Database Systems* **1**:4, pp. 277–298, 1976.

5. J. Biskup, U. Dayal, and P. A. Bernstein, "Synthesizing independent database schemas," *ACM SIGMOD Intl. Conf. on Management of Data*, pp. 143–152, 1979.

6. E. F. Codd, "A relational model for large shared data banks," *Comm. ACM* **13**:6, pp. 377–387, 1970.

7. E. F. Codd, "Further normalization of the data base relational model," in *Database Systems* (R. Rustin, ed.), Prentice-Hall, Englewood Cliffs, NJ, 1972.

8. C. Delobel, "Normalization and hierarchical dependencies in the relational data model," *ACM Transactions on Database Systems* **3**:3, pp. 201–222, 1978.

9. R. Fagin, "Multivalued dependencies and a new normal form for relational databases," *ACM Transactions on Database Systems* **2**:3, pp. 262–278, 1977.

10. J. D. Ullman, *Principles of Database and Knowledge-Base Systems, Volume I*, Computer Science Press, New York, 1988.

11. C. Zaniolo and M. A. Melkanoff, "On the design of relational database schemata," *ACM Transactions on Database Systems* **6**:1, pp. 1–47, 1981.

High-Level Database Models

Let us consider the process whereby a new database, such as our movie database, is created. Figure 1 suggests the process. We begin with a design phase, in which we address and answer questions about what information will be stored, how information elements will be related to one another, what constraints such as keys or referential integrity may be assumed, and so on. This phase may last for a long time, while options are evaluated and opinions are reconciled. We show this phase in Fig. 1 as the conversion of ideas to a high-level design.

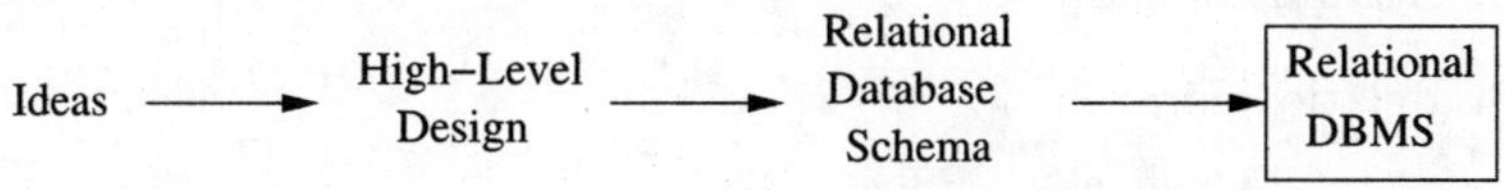

Figure 1: The database modeling and implementation process

Since the great majority of commercial database systems use the relational model, we might suppose that the design phase should use this model too. However, in practice it is often easier to start with a higher-level model and then convert the design to the relational model. The primary reason for doing so is that the relational model has only one concept — the relation — rather than several complementary concepts that more closely model real-world situations. Simplicity of concepts in the relational model is a great strength of the model, especially when it comes to efficient implementation of database operations. Yet that strength becomes a weakness when we do a preliminary design, which is why it often is helpful to begin by using a high-level design model.

There are several options for the notation in which the design is expressed. The first, and oldest, method is the "entity-relationship diagram," and here is where we shall start in Section 1. A more recent trend is the use of UML ("Unified Modeling Language"), a notation that was originally designed for describing object-oriented software projects, but which has been adapted to describe database schemas as well. We shall see this model in Section 7. Finally, in Section 9, we shall consider ODL ("Object Description Language"), which was created to describe databases as collections of classes and their objects.

The next phase shown in Fig. 1 is the conversion of our high-level design to a relational design. This phase occurs only when we are confident of the high-level design. Whichever of the high-level models we use, there is a fairly mechanical way of converting the high-level design into a relational database schema, which then runs on a conventional DBMS. Sections 5 and 6 discuss conversion of E/R diagrams to relational database schemas. Section 8 does the same for UML, and Section 10 serves for ODL.

1 The Entity/Relationship Model

In the *entity-relationship model* (or *E/R model*). the structure of data is represented graphically, as an "entity-relationship diagram," using three principal element types:

1. Entity sets,
2. Attributes, and
3. Relationships.

We shall cover each in turn.

1.1 Entity Sets

An *entity* is an abstract object of some sort, and a collection of similar entities forms an *entity set.* An entity in some ways resembles an "object" in the sense of object-oriented programming. Likewise, an entity set bears some resemblance to a class of objects. However, the E/R model is a static concept, involving the structure of data and not the operations on data. Thus, one would not expect to find methods associated with an entity set as one would with a class.

Example 1 : Let us consider the design of our running movie-database example. Each movie is an entity, and the set of all movies constitutes an entity set. Likewise, the stars are entities, and the set of stars is an entity set. A studio is another kind of entity, and the set of studios is a third entity set that will appear in our examples. □

1.2 Attributes

Entity sets have associated *attributes*, which are properties of the entities in that set. For instance, the entity set *Movies* might be given attributes such as *title* and *length.* It should not surprise you if the attributes for the entity

E/R Model Variations

In some versions of the E/R model, the type of an attribute can be either:

1. A primitive type, as in the version presented here.

2. A "struct," as in C, or tuple with a fixed number of primitive components.

3. A set of values of one type: either primitive or a "struct" type.

For example, the type of an attribute in such a model could be a set of pairs, each pair consisting of an integer and a string.

set *Movies* resemble the attributes of the relation `Movies` in our example. It is common for entity sets to be implemented as relations, although not every relation in our final relational design will come from an entity set.

In our version of the E/R model, we shall assume that attributes are of primitive types, such as strings, integers, or reals. There are other variations of this model in which attributes can have some limited structure; see the box on "E/R Model Variations."

1.3 Relationships

Relationships are connections among two or more entity sets. For instance, if *Movies* and *Stars* are two entity sets, we could have a relationship *Stars-in* that connects movies and stars. The intent is that a movie entity m is related to a star entity s by the relationship *Stars-in* if s appears in movie m. While binary relationships, those between two entity sets, are by far the most common type of relationship, the E/R model allows relationships to involve any number of entity sets. We shall defer discussion of these multiway relationships until Section 1.7.

1.4 Entity-Relationship Diagrams

An *E/R diagram* is a graph representing entity sets, attributes, and relationships. Elements of each of these kinds are represented by nodes of the graph, and we use a special shape of node to indicate the kind, as follows:

- Entity sets are represented by rectangles.
- Attributes are represented by ovals.
- Relationships are represented by diamonds.

Edges connect an entity set to its attributes and also connect a relationship to its entity sets.

Example 2: In Fig. 2 is an E/R diagram that represents a simple database about movies. The entity sets are *Movies*, *Stars*, and *Studios*.

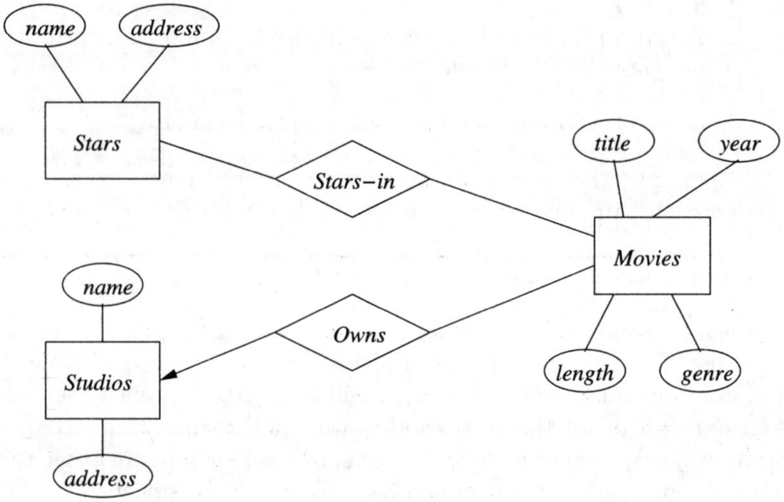

Figure 2: An entity-relationship diagram for the movie database

The *Movies* entity set has four of our usual attributes: *title*, *year*, *length*, and *genre*. The other two entity sets *Stars* and *Studios* happen to have the same two attributes: *name* and *address*, each with an obvious meaning. We also see two relationships in the diagram:

1. *Stars-in* is a relationship connecting each movie to the stars of that movie. This relationship consequently also connects stars to the movies in which they appeared.

2. *Owns* connects each movie to the studio that owns the movie. The arrow pointing to entity set *Studios* in Fig. 2 indicates that each movie is owned by at most one studio. We shall discuss uniqueness constraints such as this one in Section 1.6.

□

1.5 Instances of an E/R Diagram

E/R diagrams are a notation for describing schemas of databases. We may imagine that a database described by an E/R diagram contains particular data, an "instance" of the database. Since the database is not implemented in the E/R model, only designed, the instance never exists in the sense that a relation's instances exist in a DBMS. However, it is often useful to visualize the database being designed as if it existed.

For each entity set, the database instance will have a particular finite set of entities. Each of these entities has particular values for each attribute. A relationship R that connects n entity sets $E_1, E_2, \ldots, E_n$ may be imagined to have an "instance" that consists of a finite set of tuples $(e_1, e_2, \ldots, e_n)$, where each e_i is chosen from the entities that are in the current instance of entity set E_i. We regard each of these tuples as "connected" by relationship R.

This set of tuples is called the *relationship set* for R. It is often helpful to visualize a relationship set as a table or relation. However, the "tuples" of a relationship set are not really tuples of a relation, since their components are entities rather than primitive types such as strings or integers. The columns of the table are headed by the names of the entity sets involved in the relationship, and each list of connected entities occupies one row of the table. As we shall see, however, when we convert relationships to relations, the resulting relation is not the same as the relationship set.

Example 3: An instance of the *Stars-in* relationship could be visualized as a table with pairs such as:

Movies	*Stars*
Basic Instinct	Sharon Stone
Total Recall	Arnold Schwarzenegger
Total Recall	Sharon Stone

The members of the relationship set are the rows of the table. For instance, (Basic Instinct, Sharon Stone) is a tuple in the relationship set for the current instance of relationship *Stars-in*. □

1.6 Multiplicity of Binary E/R Relationships

In general, a binary relationship can connect any member of one of its entity sets to any number of members of the other entity set. However, it is common for there to be a restriction on the "multiplicity" of a relationship. Suppose R is a relationship connecting entity sets E and F. Then:

- If each member of E can be connected by R to at most one member of F, then we say that R is *many-one* from E to F. Note that in a many-one relationship from E to F, each entity in F can be connected to many members of E. Similarly, if instead a member of F can be connected by R to at most one member of E, then we say R is many-one from F to E (or equivalently, one-many from E to F).

- If R is both many-one from E to F and many-one from F to E, then we say that R is *one-one*. In a one-one relationship an entity of either entity set can be connected to at most one entity of the other set.

- If R is neither many-one from E to F or from F to E, then we say R is *many-many.*

As we mentioned in Example 2, arrows can be used to indicate the multiplicity of a relationship in an E/R diagram. If a relationship is many-one from entity set E to entity set F, then we place an arrow entering F. The arrow indicates that each entity in set E is related to at most one entity in set F. Unless there is also an arrow on the edge to E, an entity in F may be related to many entities in E.

Example 4: A one-one relationship between entity sets E and F is represented by arrows pointing to both E and F. For instance, Fig. 3 shows two entity sets, *Studios* and *Presidents*, and the relationship *Runs* between them (attributes are omitted). We assume that a president can run only one studio and a studio has only one president, so this relationship is one-one, as indicated by the two arrows, one entering each entity set.

Figure 3: A one-one relationship

Remember that the arrow means "at most one"; it does not guarantee existence of an entity of the set pointed to. Thus, in Fig. 3, we would expect that a "president" is surely associated with some studio; how could they be a "president" otherwise? However, a studio might not have a president at some particular time, so the arrow from *Runs* to *Presidents* truly means "at most one" and not "exactly one." We shall discuss the distinction further in Section 3.3. □

1.7 Multiway Relationships

The E/R model makes it convenient to define relationships involving more than two entity sets. In practice, ternary (three-way) or higher-degree relationships are rare, but they occasionally are necessary to reflect the true state of affairs. A multiway relationship in an E/R diagram is represented by lines from the relationship diamond to each of the involved entity sets.

Example 5: In Fig. 4 is a relationship *Contracts* that involves a studio, a star, and a movie. This relationship represents that a studio has contracted with a particular star to act in a particular movie. In general, the value of an E/R relationship can be thought of as a relationship set of tuples whose components are the entities participating in the relationship, as we discussed in Section 1.5. Thus, relationship *Contracts* can be described by triples of the form (studio, star, movie).

Implications Among Relationship Types

We should be aware that a many-one relationship is a special case of a many-many relationship, and a one-one relationship is a special case of a many-one relationship. Thus, any useful property of many-one relationships holds for one-one relationships too. For example, a data structure for representing many-one relationships will work for one-one relationships, although it might not be suitable for many-many relationships.

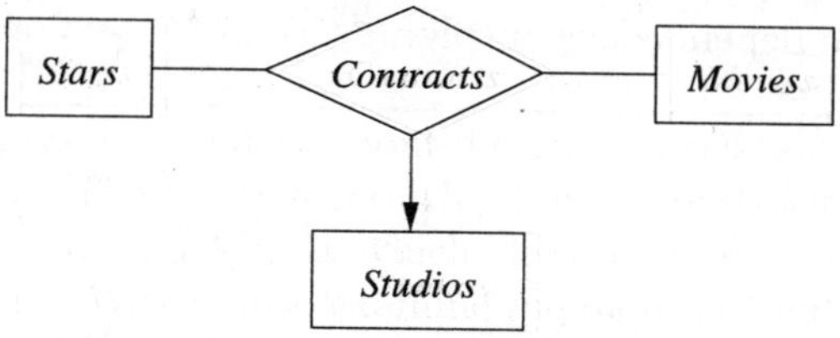

Figure 4: A three-way relationship

In multiway relationships, an arrow pointing to an entity set E means that if we select one entity from each of the other entity sets in the relationship, those entities are related to at most one entity in E. (Note that this rule generalizes the notation used for many-one, binary relationships.) Informally, we may think of a functional dependency with E on the right and all the other entity sets of the relationship on the left.

In Fig. 4 we have an arrow pointing to entity set *Studios*, indicating that for a particular star and movie, there is only one studio with which the star has contracted for that movie. However, there are no arrows pointing to entity sets *Stars* or *Movies*. A studio may contract with several stars for a movie, and a star may contract with one studio for more than one movie. □

1.8 Roles in Relationships

It is possible that one entity set appears two or more times in a single relationship. If so, we draw as many lines from the relationship to the entity set as the entity set appears in the relationship. Each line to the entity set represents a different *role* that the entity set plays in the relationship. We therefore label the edges between the entity set and relationship by names, which we call "roles."

Example 6: In Fig. 5 is a relationship *Sequel-of* between the entity set *Movies* and itself. Each relationship is between two movies, one of which is the sequel of the other. To differentiate the two movies in a relationship, one line is labeled by the role *Original* and one by the role *Sequel*, indicating the original movie

Limits on Arrow Notation in Multiway Relationships

There are not enough choices of arrow or no-arrow on the lines attached to a relationship with three or more participants. Thus, we cannot describe every possible situation with arrows. For instance, in Fig. 4, the studio is really a function of the movie alone, not the star and movie jointly, since only one studio produces a movie. However, our notation does not distinguish this situation from the case of a three-way relationship where the entity set pointed to by the arrow is truly a function of both other entity sets. To handle all possible situations, we would have to give a set of functional dependencies involving the entity sets of the relationship.

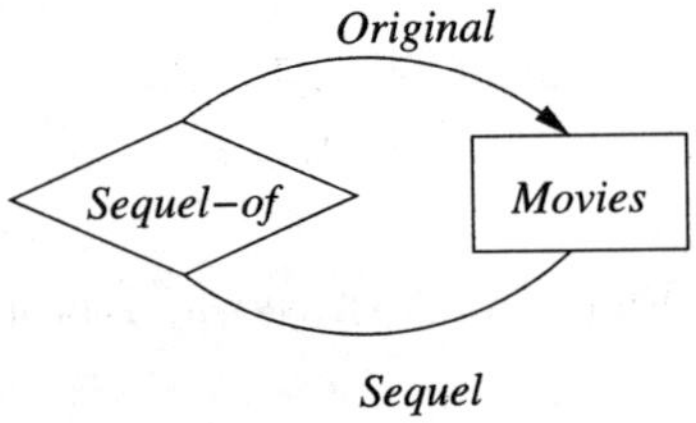

Figure 5: A relationship with roles

and its sequel, respectively. We assume that a movie may have many sequels, but for each sequel there is only one original movie. Thus, the relationship is many-one from *Sequel* movies to *Original* movies, as indicated by the arrow in the E/R diagram of Fig. 5. □

Example 7: As a final example that includes both a multiway relationship and an entity set with multiple roles, in Fig. 6 is a more complex version of the *Contracts* relationship introduced earlier in Example 5. Now, relationship *Contracts* involves two studios, a star, and a movie. The intent is that one studio, having a certain star under contract (in general, not for a particular movie), may further contract with a second studio to allow that star to act in a particular movie. Thus, the relationship is described by 4-tuples of the form (studio1, studio2, star, movie), meaning that studio2 contracts with studio1 for the use of studio1's star by studio2 for the movie.

We see in Fig. 6 arrows pointing to *Studios* in both of its roles, as "owner" of the star and as producer of the movie. However, there are not arrows pointing to *Stars* or *Movies*. The rationale is as follows. Given a star, a movie, and a studio producing the movie, there can be only one studio that "owns" the star. (We assume a star is under contract to exactly one studio.) Similarly, only one studio produces a given movie, so given a star, a movie, and the star's studio, we can determine a unique producing studio. Note that in both

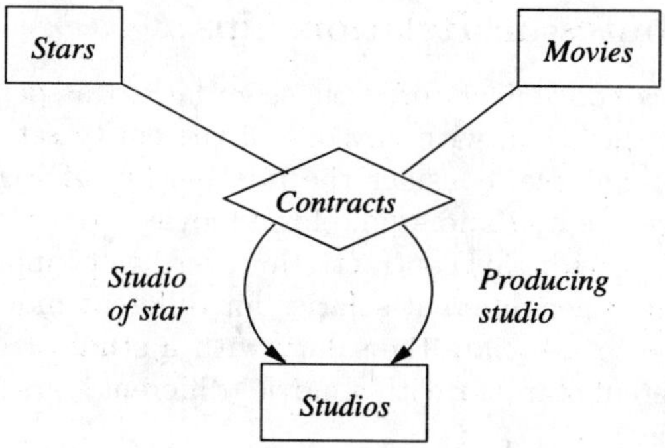

Figure 6: A four-way relationship

cases we actually needed only one of the other entities to determine the unique entity—for example, we need only know the movie to determine the unique producing studio—but this fact does not change the multiplicity specification for the multiway relationship.

There are no arrows pointing to *Stars* or *Movies*. Given a star, the star's studio, and a producing studio, there could be several different contracts allowing the star to act in several movies. Thus, the other three components in a relationship 4-tuple do not necessarily determine a unique movie. Similarly, a producing studio might contract with some other studio to use more than one of their stars in one movie. Thus, a star is not determined by the three other components of the relationship. □

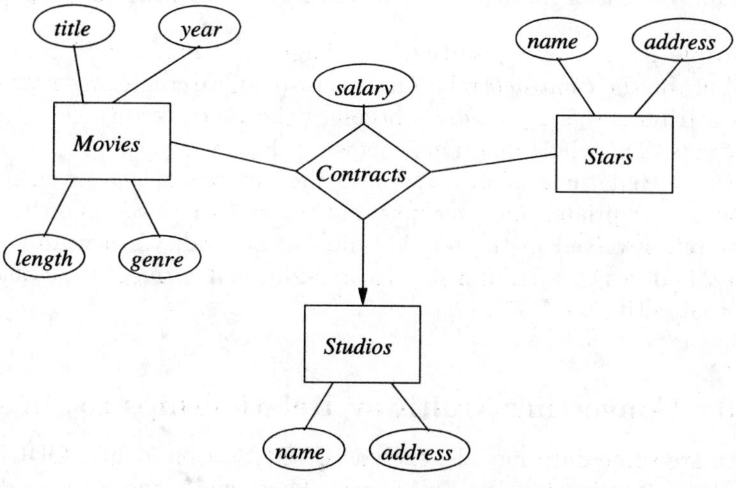

Figure 7: A relationship with an attribute

1.9 Attributes on Relationships

Sometimes it is convenient, or even essential, to associate attributes with a relationship, rather than with any one of the entity sets that the relationship connects. For example, consider the relationship of Fig. 4, which represents contracts between a star and studio for a movie.[1] We might wish to record the salary associated with this contract. However, we cannot associate it with the star; a star might get different salaries for different movies. Similarly, it does not make sense to associate the salary with a studio (they may pay different salaries to different stars) or with a movie (different stars in a movie may receive different salaries).

However, we can associate a unique salary with the (star, movie, studio) triple in the relationship set for the *Contracts* relationship. In Fig. 7 we see Fig. 4 fleshed out with attributes. The relationship has attribute *salary*, while the entity sets have the same attributes that we showed for them in Fig. 2.

In general, we may place one or more attributes on any relationship. The values of these attributes are functionally determined by the entire tuple in the relationship set for that relation. In some cases, the attributes can be determined by a subset of the entity sets involved in the relation, but presumably not by any single entity set (or it would make more sense to place the attribute on that entity set). For instance, in Fig. 7, the salary is really determined by the movie and star entities, since the studio entity is itself determined by the movie entity.

It is never necessary to place attributes on relationships. We can instead invent a new entity set, whose entities have the attributes ascribed to the relationship. If we then include this entity set in the relationship, we can omit the attributes on the relationship itself. However, attributes on a relationship are a useful convention, which we shall continue to use where appropriate.

Example 8: Let us revise the E/R diagram of Fig. 7, which has the salary attribute on the *Contracts* relationship. Instead, we create an entity set *Salaries*, with attribute *salary*. *Salaries* becomes the fourth entity set of relationship *Contracts*. The whole diagram is shown in Fig. 8.

Notice that there is an arrow into the *Salaries* entity set in Fig. 8. That arrow is appropriate, since we know that the salary is determined by all the other entity sets involved in the relationship. In general, when we do a conversion from attributes on a relationship to an additional entity set, we place an arrow into that entity set. □

1.10 Converting Multiway Relationships to Binary

There are some data models, such as UML (Section 7) and ODL (Section 9), that limit relationships to be binary. Thus, while the E/R model does not

[1] Here, we have reverted to the earlier notion of three-way contracts in Example 5, not the four-way relationship of Example 7.

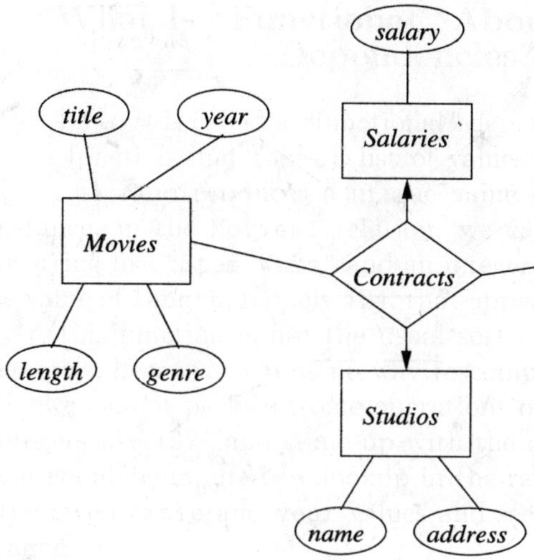

Figure 8: Moving the attribute to an entity set

require binary relationships, it is useful to observe that any relationship connecting more than two entity sets can be converted to a collection of binary, many-one relationships. To do so, introduce a new entity set whose entities we may think of as tuples of the relationship set for the multiway relationship. We call this entity set a *connecting* entity set. We then introduce many-one relationships from the connecting entity set to each of the entity sets that provide components of tuples in the original, multiway relationship. If an entity set plays more than one role, then it is the target of one relationship for each role.

Example 9: The four-way *Contracts* relationship in Fig. 6 can be replaced by an entity set that we may also call *Contracts.* As seen in Fig. 9, it participates in four relationships. If the relationship set for the relationship *Contracts* has a 4-tuple (studio1, studio2, star, movie) then the entity set *Contracts* has an entity *e*. This entity is linked by relationship *Star-of* to the entity *star* in entity set *Stars.* It is linked by relationship *Movie-of* to the entity *movie* in *Movies.* It is linked to entities *studio1* and *studio2* of *Studios* by relationships *Studio-of-star* and *Producing-studio*, respectively.

Note that we have assumed there are no attributes of entity set *Contracts*, although the other entity sets in Fig. 9 have unseen attributes. However, it is possible to add attributes, such as the date of signing, to entity set *Contracts.* □

1.11 Subclasses in the E/R Model

Often, an entity set contains certain entities that have special properties not associated with all members of the set. If so, we find it useful to define certain

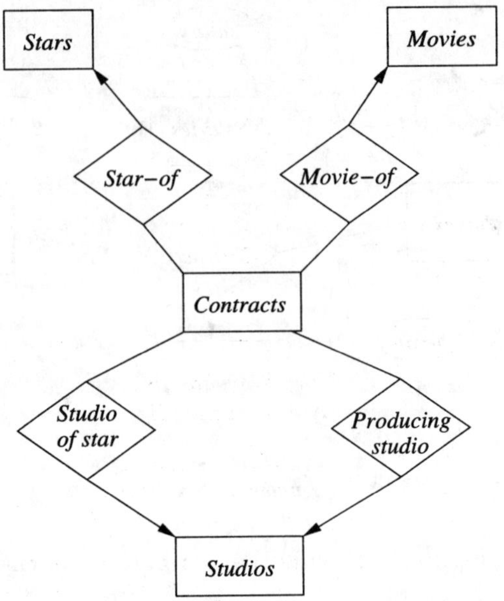

Figure 9: Replacing a multiway relationship by an entity set and binary relationships

special-case entity sets, or *subclasses*, each with its own special attributes and/or relationships. We connect an entity set to its subclasses using a relationship called *isa* (i.e., "an A is a B" expresses an "isa" relationship from entity set A to entity set B).

An isa relationship is a special kind of relationship, and to emphasize that it is unlike other relationships, we use a special notation: a triangle. One side of the triangle is attached to the subclass, and the opposite point is connected to the superclass. Every isa relationship is one-one, although we shall not draw the two arrows that are associated with other one-one relationships.

Example 10: Among the special kinds of movies we might store in our example database are cartoons and murder mysteries. For each of these special movie types, we could define a subclass of the entity set *Movies*. For instance, let us postulate two subclasses: *Cartoons* and *Murder-Mysteries*. A cartoon has, in addition to the attributes and relationships of *Movies*, an additional relationship called *Voices* that gives us a set of stars who speak, but do not appear in the movie. Movies that are not cartoons do not have such stars. Murder-mysteries have an additional attribute *weapon*. The connections among the three entity sets *Movies*, *Cartoons*, and *Murder-Mysteries* is shown in Fig. 10. □

While, in principle, a collection of entity sets connected by *isa* relationships could have any structure, we shall limit isa-structures to trees, in which there

Parallel Relationships Can Be Different

Figure 9 illustrates a subtle point about relationships. There are two different relationships, *Studio-of-Star* and *Producing-Studio*, that each connect entity sets *Contracts* and *Studios*. We should not presume that these relationships therefore have the same relationship sets. In fact, in this case, it is unlikely that both relationships would ever relate the same contract to the same studios, since a studio would then be contracting with itself.

More generally, there is nothing wrong with an E/R diagram having several relationships that connect the same entity sets. In the database, the instances of these relationships will normally be different, reflecting the different meanings of the relationships.

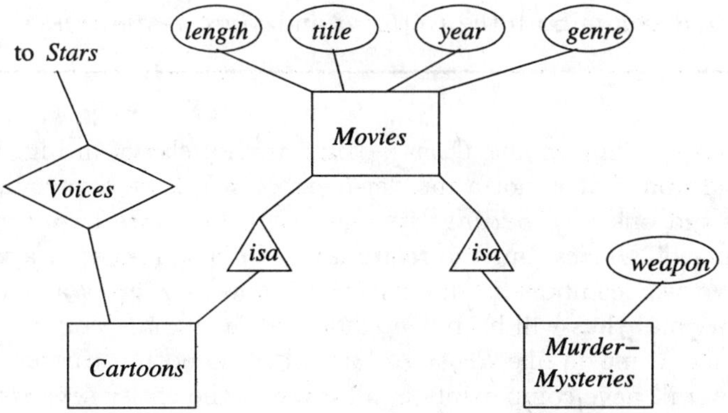

Figure 10: Isa relationships in an E/R diagram

is one *root* entity set (e.g., *Movies* in Fig. 10) that is the most general, with progressively more specialized entity sets extending below the root in a tree.

Suppose we have a tree of entity sets, connected by *isa* relationships. A single entity consists of *components* from one or more of these entity sets, as long as those components are in a subtree including the root. That is, if an entity e has a component c in entity set E, and the parent of E in the tree is F, then entity e also has a component d in F. Further, c and d must be paired in the relationship set for the *isa* relationship from E to F. The entity e has whatever attributes any of its components has, and it participates in whatever relationships any of its components participate in.

Example 11: The typical movie, being neither a cartoon nor a murder-mystery, will have a component only in the root entity set *Movies* in Fig. 10. These entities have only the four attributes of *Movies* (and the two relationships

The E/R View of Subclasses

There is a significant resemblance between "isa" in the E/R model and subclasses in object-oriented languages. In a sense, "isa" relates a subclass to its superclass. However, there is also a fundamental difference between the conventional E/R view and the object-oriented approach: entities are allowed to have representatives in a tree of entity sets, while objects are assumed to exist in exactly one class or subclass.

The difference becomes apparent when we consider how the movie *Roger Rabbit* was handled in Example 11. In an object-oriented approach, we would need for this movie a fourth entity set, "cartoon-murder-mystery," which inherited all the attributes and relationships of *Movies*, *Cartoons*, and *Murder-Mysteries*. However, in the E/R model, the effect of this fourth subclass is obtained by putting components of the movie *Roger Rabbit* in both the *Cartoons* and *Murder-Mysteries* entity sets.

of *Movies* — *Stars-in* and *Owns* — that are not shown in Fig. 10).

A cartoon that is not a murder-mystery will have two components, one in *Movies* and one in *Cartoons*. Its entity will therefore have not only the four attributes of *Movies*, but the relationship *Voices*. Likewise, a murder-mystery will have two components for its entity, one in *Movies* and one in *Murder-Mysteries* and thus will have five attributes, including *weapon*.

Finally, a movie like *Roger Rabbit*, which is both a cartoon and a murder-mystery, will have components in all three of the entity sets *Movies*, *Cartoons*, and *Murder-Mysteries*. The three components are connected into one entity by the *isa* relationships. Together, these components give the *Roger Rabbit* entity all four attributes of *Movies* plus the attribute *weapon* of entity set *Murder-Mysteries* and the relationship *Voices* of entity set *Cartoons*. □

1.12 Exercises for Section 1

Exercise 1.1: Design a database for a bank, including information about customers and their accounts. Information about a customer includes their name, address, phone, and Social Security number. Accounts have numbers, types (e.g., savings, checking) and balances. Also record the customer(s) who own an account. Draw the E/R diagram for this database. Be sure to include arrows where appropriate, to indicate the multiplicity of a relationship.

Exercise 1.2: Modify your solution to Exercise 1.1 as follows:

a) Change your diagram so an account can have only one customer.

b) Further change your diagram so a customer can have only one account.

! c) Change your original diagram of Exercise 1.1 so that a customer can have a set of addresses (which are street-city-state triples) and a set of phones. Remember that we do not allow attributes to have nonprimitive types, such as sets, in the E/R model.

! d) Further modify your diagram so that customers can have a set of addresses, and at each address there is a set of phones.

Exercise 1.3: Give an E/R diagram for a database recording information about teams, players, and their fans, including:

1. For each team, its name, its players, its team captain (one of its players), and the colors of its uniform.

2. For each player, his/her name.

3. For each fan, his/her name, favorite teams, favorite players, and favorite color.

Remember that a set of colors is not a suitable attribute type for teams. How can you get around this restriction?

Exercise 1.4: Suppose we wish to add to the schema of Exercise 1.3 a relationship *Led-by* among two players and a team. The intention is that this relationship set consists of triples (player1, player2, team) such that player 1 played on the team at a time when some other player 2 was the team captain.

a) Draw the modification to the E/R diagram.

b) Replace your ternary relationship with a new entity set and binary relationships.

! c) Are your new binary relationships the same as any of the previously existing relationships? Note that we assume the two players are different, i.e., the team captain is not self-led.

Exercise 1.5: Modify Exercise 1.3 to record for each player the history of teams on which they have played, including the start date and ending date (if they were traded) for each such team.

! **Exercise 1.6:** Design a genealogy database with one entity set: *People*. The information to record about persons includes their name (an attribute), their mother, father, and children.

! **Exercise 1.7:** Modify your "people" database design of Exercise 1.6 to include the following special types of people:

1. Females.

2. Males.
3. People who are parents.

You may wish to distinguish certain other kinds of people as well, so relationships connect appropriate subclasses of people.

Exercise 1.8 : An alternative way to represent the information of Exercise 1.6 is to have a ternary relationship *Family* with the intent that in the relationship set for *Family*, triple (person, mother, father) is a person, their mother, and their father; all three are in the *People* entity set, of course.

a) Draw this diagram, placing arrows on edges where appropriate.

b) Replace the ternary relationship *Family* by an entity set and binary relationships. Again place arrows to indicate the multiplicity of relationships.

Exercise 1.9 : Design a database suitable for a university registrar. This database should include information about students, departments, professors, courses, which students are enrolled in which courses, which professors are teaching which courses, student grades, TA's for a course (TA's are students), which courses a department offers, and any other information you deem appropriate. Note that this question is more free-form than the questions above, and you need to make some decisions about multiplicities of relationships, appropriate types, and even what information needs to be represented.

! **Exercise 1.10 :** Informally, we can say that two E/R diagrams "have the same information" if, given a real-world situation, the instances of these two diagrams that reflect this situation can be computed from one another. Consider the E/R diagram of Fig. 6. This four-way relationship can be decomposed into a three-way relationship and a binary relationship by taking advantage of the fact that for each movie, there is a unique studio that produces that movie. Give an E/R diagram without a four-way relationship that has the same information as Fig. 6.

2 Design Principles

We have yet to learn many of the details of the E/R model, but we have enough to begin study of the crucial issue of what constitutes a good design and what should be avoided. In this section, we offer some useful design principles.

2.1 Faithfulness

First and foremost, the design should be faithful to the specifications of the application. That is, entity sets and their attributes should reflect reality. You can't attach an attribute *number-of-cylinders* to *Stars*, although that attribute would make sense for an entity set *Automobiles*. Whatever relationships are asserted should make sense given what we know about the part of the real world being modeled.

Example 12: If we define a relationship *Stars-in* between *Stars* and *Movies*, it should be a many-many relationship. The reason is that an observation of the real world tells us that stars can appear in more than one movie, and movies can have more than one star. It is incorrect to declare the relationship *Stars-in* to be many-one in either direction or to be one-one. □

Example 13: On the other hand, sometimes it is less obvious what the real world requires us to do in our E/R design. Consider, for instance, entity sets *Courses* and *Instructors*, with a relationship *Teaches* between them. Is *Teaches* many-one from *Courses* to *Instructors*? The answer lies in the policy and intentions of the organization creating the database. It is possible that the school has a policy that there can be only one instructor for any course. Even if several instructors may "team-teach" a course, the school may require that exactly one of them be listed in the database as the instructor responsible for the course. In either of these cases, we would make *Teaches* a many-one relationship from *Courses* to *Instructors*.

Alternatively, the school may use teams of instructors regularly and wish its database to allow several instructors to be associated with a course. Or, the intent of the *Teaches* relationship may not be to reflect the current teacher of a course, but rather those who have ever taught the course, or those who are capable of teaching the course; we cannot tell simply from the name of the relationship. In either of these cases, it would be proper to make *Teaches* be many-many. □

2.2 Avoiding Redundancy

We should be careful to say everything once only. Problems regarding redundancy and anomalies are typical of problems that can arise in E/R designs. However, in the E/R model, there are several new mechanisms whereby redundancy and other anomalies can arise.

For instance, we have used a relationship *Owns* between movies and studios. We might also choose to have an attribute *studioName* of entity set *Movies*. While there is nothing illegal about doing so, it is dangerous for several reasons.

1. Doing so leads to repetition of a fact, with the result that extra space is required to represent the data, once we convert the E/R design to a relational (or other type of) concrete implementation.

2. There is an update-anomaly potential, since we might change the relationship but not the attribute, or vice-versa.

We shall say more about avoiding anomalies in Sections 2.4 and 2.5.

2.3 Simplicity Counts

Avoid introducing more elements into your design than is absolutely necessary.

Example 14: Suppose that instead of a relationship between *Movies* and *Studios* we postulated the existence of "movie-holdings," the ownership of a single movie. We might then create another entity set *Holdings.* A one-one relationship *Represents* could be established between each movie and the unique holding that represents the movie. A many-one relationship from *Holdings* to *Studios* completes the picture shown in Fig. 11.

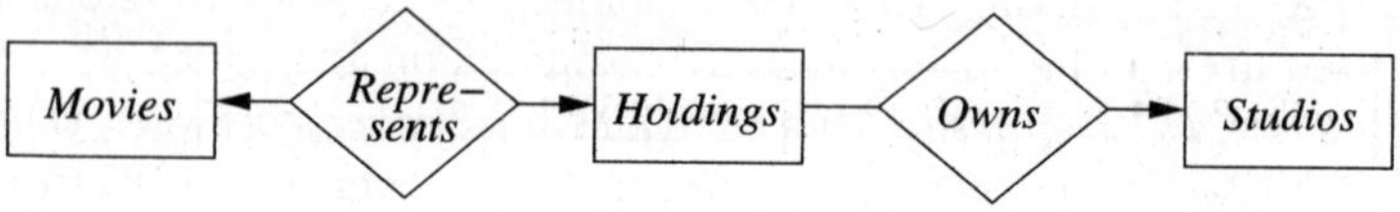

Figure 11: A poor design with an unnecessary entity set

Technically, the structure of Fig. 11 truly represents the real world, since it is possible to go from a movie to its unique owning studio via *Holdings.* However, *Holdings* serves no useful purpose, and we are better off without it. It makes programs that use the movie-studio relationship more complicated, wastes space, and encourages errors. □

2.4 Choosing the Right Relationships

Entity sets can be connected in various ways by relationships. However, adding to our design every possible relationship is not often a good idea. Doing so can lead to redundancy, update anomalies, and deletion anomalies, where the connected pairs or sets of entities for one relationship can be deduced from one or more other relationships. We shall illustrate the problem and what to do about it with two examples. In the first example, several relationships could represent the same information; in the second, one relationship could be deduced from several others.

Example 15: Let us review Fig. 7, where we connected movies, stars, and studios with a three-way relationship *Contracts.* We omitted from that figure the two binary relationships *Stars-in* and *Owns* from Fig. 2. Do we also need these relationships, between *Movies* and *Stars*, and between *Movies* and *Studios*, respectively? The answer is: "we don't know; it depends on our assumptions regarding the three relationships in question."

It might be possible to deduce the relationship *Stars-in* from *Contracts.* If a star can appear in a movie only if there is a contract involving that star, that movie, and the owning studio for the movie, then there truly is no need for relationship *Stars-in.* We could figure out all the star-movie pairs by looking at the star-movie-studio triples in the relationship set for *Contracts* and taking only the star and movie components, i.e., projecting *Contracts* onto *Stars-in.*

However, if a star can work on a movie without there being a contract — or what is more likely, without there being a contract that we know about in our database — then there could be star-movie pairs in *Stars-in* that are not part of star-movie-studio triples in *Contracts*. In that case, we need to retain the *Stars-in* relationship.

A similar observation applies to relationship *Owns*. If for every movie, there is at least one contract involving that movie, its owning studio, and some star for that movie, then we can dispense with *Owns*. However, if there is the possibility that a studio owns a movie, yet has no stars under contract for that movie, or no such contract is known to our database, then we must retain *Owns*.

In summary, we cannot tell you whether a given relationship will be redundant. You must find out from those who wish the database implemented what to expect. Only then can you make a rational decision about whether or not to include relationships such as *Stars-in* or *Owns*. □

Example 16 : Now, consider Fig. 2 again. In this diagram, there is no relationship between stars and studios. Yet we can use the two relationships *Stars-in* and *Owns* to build a connection by the process of composing those two relationships. That is, a star is connected to some movies by *Stars-in*, and those movies are connected to studios by *Owns*. Thus, we could say that a star is connected to the studios that own movies in which the star has appeared.

Would it make sense to have a relationship *Works-for*, as suggested in Fig. 12, between *Stars* and *Studios* too? Again, we cannot tell without knowing more. First, what would the meaning of this relationship be? If it is to mean "the star appeared in at least one movie of this studio," then probably there is no good reason to include it in the diagram. We could deduce this information from *Stars-in* and *Owns* instead.

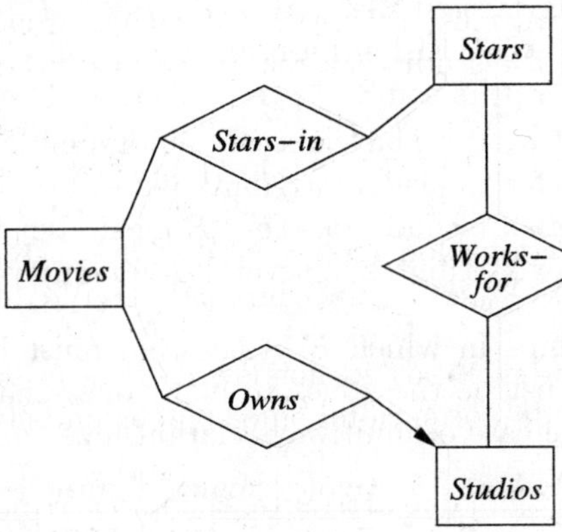

Figure 12: Adding a relationship between *Stars* and *Studios*

However, perhaps we have other information about stars working for studios that is not implied by the connection through a movie. In that case, a relationship connecting stars directly to studios might be useful and would not be redundant. Alternatively, we might use a relationship between stars and studios to mean something entirely different. For example, it might represent the fact that the star is under contract to the studio, in a manner unrelated to any movie. As we suggested in Example 7, it is possible for a star to be under contract to one studio and yet work on a movie owned by another studio. In this case, the information found in the new *Works-for* relation would be independent of the *Stars-in* and *Owns* relationships, and would surely be nonredundant. □

2.5 Picking the Right Kind of Element

Sometimes we have options regarding the type of design element used to represent a real-world concept. Many of these choices are between using attributes and using entity set/relationship combinations. In general, an attribute is simpler to implement than either an entity set or a relationship. However, making everything an attribute will usually get us into trouble.

Example 17: Let us consider a specific problem. In Fig. 2, were we wise to make studios an entity set? Should we instead have made the name and address of the studio be attributes of movies and eliminated the *Studio* entity set? One problem with doing so is that we repeat the address of the studio for each movie. We can also have an update anomaly if we change the address for one movie but not another with the same studio, and we can have a deletion anomaly if we delete the last movie owned by a given studio.

On the other hand, if we did not record addresses of studios, then there is no harm in making the studio name an attribute of movies. We have no anomalies in this case. Saying the name of a studio for each movie is not true redundancy, since we must represent the owner of each movie somehow, and saying the name of the studio is a reasonable way to do so. □

We can abstract what we have observed in Example 17 to give the conditions under which we prefer to use an attribute instead of an entity set. Suppose E is an entity set. Here are conditions that E must obey in order for us to replace E by an attribute or attributes of several other entity sets.

1. All relationships in which E is involved must have arrows entering E. That is, E must be the "one" in many-one relationships, or its generalization for the case of multiway relationships.

2. If E has more than one attribute, then no attribute depends on the other attributes, the way *address* depends on *name* for *Studios*. That is, the only key for E is all its attributes.

3. No relationship involves E more than once.

If these conditions are met, then we can replace entity set E as follows:

a) If there is a many-one relationship R from some entity set F to E, then remove R and make the attributes of E be attributes of F, suitably renamed if they conflict with attribute names for F. In effect, each F-entity takes, as attributes, the name of the unique, related E-entity.[2] For instance, *Movies* entities could take their studio name as an attribute, should we dispense with studio addresses.

b) If there is a multiway relationship R with an arrow to E, make the attributes of E be attributes of R and delete the arc from R to E. An example of this transformation is replacing Fig. 8, where there is an entity set *Salaries* with a number as its lone attribute, by its original diagram in Fig. 7.

Example 18: Let us consider a point where there is a tradeoff between using a multiway relationship and using a connecting entity set with several binary relationships. We saw a four-way relationship *Contracts* among a star, a movie, and two studios in Fig. 6. In Fig. 9, we mechanically converted it to an entity set *Contracts*. Does it matter which we choose?

As the problem was stated, either is appropriate. However, should we change the problem just slightly, then we are almost forced to choose a connecting entity set. Let us suppose that contracts involve one star, one movie, but any set of studios. This situation is more complex than the one in Fig. 6, where we had two studios playing two roles. In this case, we can have any number of studios involved, perhaps one to do production, one for special effects, one for distribution, and so on. Thus, we cannot assign roles for studios.

It appears that a relationship set for the relationship *Contracts* must contain triples of the form (star, movie, set-of-studios), and the relationship *Contracts* itself involves not only the usual *Stars* and *Movies* entity sets, but a new entity set whose entities are *sets of* studios. While this approach is possible, it seems unnatural to think of sets of studios as basic entities, and we do not recommend it.

A better approach is to think of contracts as an entity set. As in Fig. 9, a contract entity connects a star, a movie and a set of studios, but now there must be no limit on the number of studios. Thus, the relationship between contracts and studios is many-many, rather than many-one as it would be if contracts were a true "connecting" entity set. Figure 13 sketches the E/R diagram. Note that a contract is related to a single star and to a single movie, but to any number of studios. □

2.6 Exercises for Section 2

Exercise 2.1: In Fig. 14 is an E/R diagram for a bank database involving customers and accounts. Since customers may have several accounts, and

[2]In a situation where an F-entity is not related to any E-entity, the new attributes of F would be given special "null" values to indicate the absence of a related E-entity. A similar arrangement would be used for the new attributes of R in case (b).

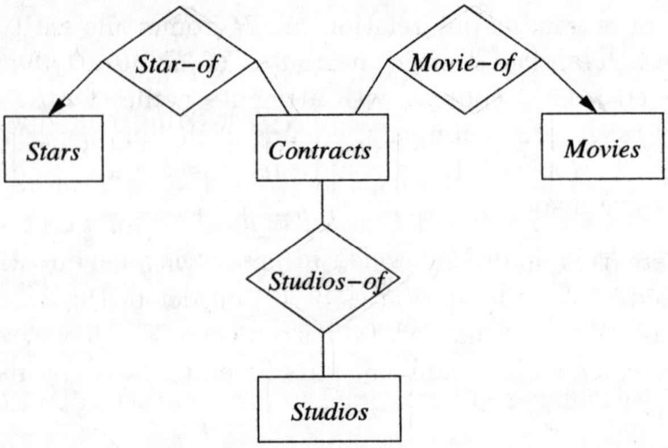

Figure 13: Contracts connecting a star, a movie, and a set of studios

accounts may be held jointly by several customers, we associate with each customer an "account set," and accounts are members of one or more account sets. Assuming the meaning of the various relationships and attributes are as expected given their names, criticize the design. What design rules are violated? Why? What modifications would you suggest?

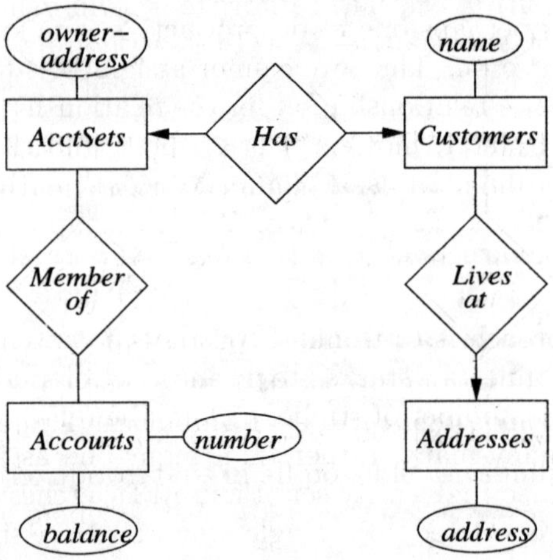

Figure 14: A poor design for a bank database

Exercise 2.2: Under what circumstances (regarding the unseen attributes of *Studios* and *Presidents*) would you recommend combining the two entity sets and relationship in Fig. 3 into a single entity set and attributes?

Exercise 2.3: Suppose we delete the attribute *address* from *Studios* in Fig. 7. Show how we could then replace an entity set by an attribute. Where would that attribute appear?

Exercise 2.4: Give choices of attributes for the following entity sets in Fig. 13 that will allow the entity set to be replaced by an attribute:

a) *Stars.*

b) *Movies.*

! c) *Studios.*

!! **Exercise 2.5:** In this and following exercises we shall consider two design options in the E/R model for describing births. At a birth, there is one baby (twins would be represented by two births), one mother, any number of nurses, and any number of doctors. Suppose, therefore, that we have entity sets *Babies*, *Mothers*, *Nurses*, and *Doctors*. Suppose we also use a relationship *Births*, which connects these four entity sets, as suggested in Fig. 15. Note that a tuple of the relationship set for *Births* has the form (baby, mother, nurse, doctor). If there is more than one nurse and/or doctor attending a birth, then there will be several tuples with the same baby and mother, one for each combination of nurse and doctor.

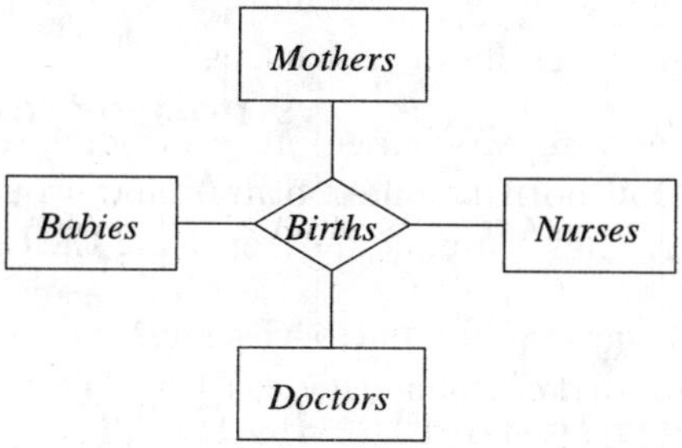

Figure 15: Representing births by a multiway relationship

There are certain assumptions that we might wish to incorporate into our design. For each, tell how to add arrows or other elements to the E/R diagram in order to express the assumption.

a) For every baby, there is a unique mother.

b) For every combination of a baby, nurse, and doctor, there is a unique mother.

c) For every combination of a baby and a mother there is a unique doctor.

! **Exercise 2.6:** Another approach to the problem of Exercise 2.5 is to connect the four entity sets *Babies*, *Mothers*, *Nurses*, and *Doctors* by an entity set

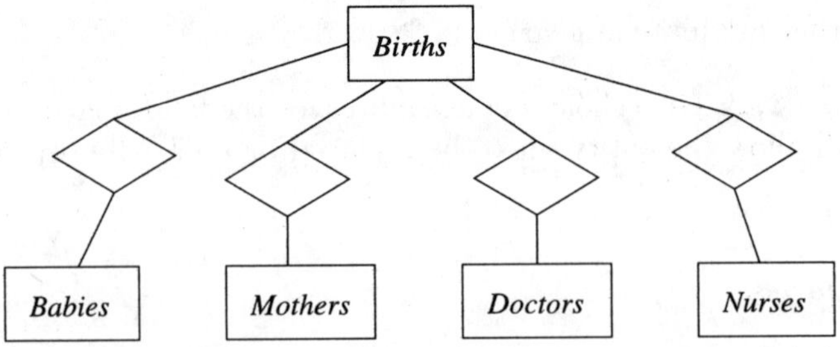

Figure 16: Representing births by an entity set

Births, with four relationships, one between *Births* and each of the other entity sets, as suggested in Fig. 16. Use arrows (indicating that certain of these relationships are many-one) to represent the following conditions:

a) Every baby is the result of a unique birth, and every birth is of a unique baby.

b) In addition to (a), every baby has a unique mother.

c) In addition to (a) and (b), for every birth there is a unique doctor.

In each case, what design flaws do you see?

!! **Exercise 2.7:** Suppose we change our viewpoint to allow a birth to involve more than one baby born to one mother. How would you represent the fact that every baby still has a unique mother using the approaches of Exercises 2.5 and 2.6?

3 Constraints in the E/R Model

The E/R model has several ways to express the common kinds of constraints on the data that will populate the database being designed. Like the relational model, there is a way to express the idea that an attribute or attributes are a key for an entity set. We have already seen how an arrow connecting a relationship to an entity set serves as a "functional dependency." There is also a way to express a referential-integrity constraint, where an entity in one set is required to have an entity in another set to which it is related.

3.1 Keys in the E/R Model

A *key* for an entity set E is a set K of one or more attributes such that, given any two distinct entities e_1 and e_2 in E, e_1 and e_2 cannot have identical values for each of the attributes in the key K. If K consists of more than one attribute, then it is possible for e_1 and e_2 to agree in some of these attributes, but never in all attributes. Some important points to remember are:

- Every entity set must have a key, although in some cases — isa-hierarchies and "weak" entity sets (see Section 4), the key actually belongs to another entity set.

- There can be more than one possible key for an entity set. However, it is customary to pick one key as the "primary key," and to act as if that were the only key.

- When an entity set is involved in an isa-hierarchy, we require that the root entity set have all the attributes needed for a key, and that the key for each entity is found from its component in the root entity set, regardless of how many entity sets in the hierarchy have components for the entity.

In our running movies example, we have used *title* and *year* as the key for *Movies*, counting on the observation that it is unlikely that two movies with the same title would be released in one year. We also decided that it was safe to use *name* as a key for *MovieStar*, believing that no real star would ever want to use the name of another star.

3.2 Representing Keys in the E/R Model

In our E/R-diagram notation, we underline the attributes belonging to a key for an entity set. For example, Fig. 17 reproduces our E/R diagram for movies, stars, and studios from Fig. 2, but with key attributes underlined. Attribute *name* is the key for *Stars*. Likewise, *Studios* has a key consisting of only its own attribute *name*.

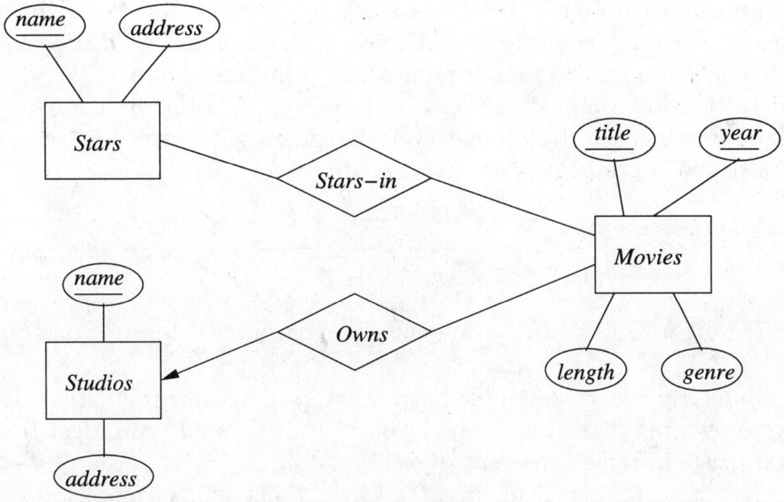

Figure 17: E/R diagram; keys are indicated by underlines

The attributes *title* and *year* together form the key for *Movies.* Note that when several attributes are underlined, as in Fig. 17, then they are each members of the key. There is no notation for representing the situation where there are several keys for an entity set; we underline only the primary key. You should also be aware that in some unusual situations, the attributes forming the key for an entity set do not all belong to the entity set itself. We shall defer this matter, called "weak entity sets," until Section 4.

3.3 Referential Integrity

You may recall a discussion of referential-integrity constraints. These constraints say that a value appearing in one context must also appear in another. For example, let us consider the many-one relationship *Owns* from *Movies* to *Studios* in Fig. 2. The many-one requirement simply says that no movie can be owned by more than one studio. It does *not* say that a movie must surely be owned by a studio, or that the owning studio must be present in the *Studios* entity set, as stored in our database. An appropriate referential integrity constraint on relationship *Owns* is that for each movie, the owning studio (the entity "referenced" by the relationship for this movie) must exist in our database.

The arrow notation in E/R diagrams is able to indicate whether a relationship is expected to support referential integrity in one or more directions. Suppose R is a relationship from entity set E to entity set F. A rounded arrowhead pointing to F indicates not only that the relationship is many-one from E to F, but that the entity of set F related to a given entity of set E is required to exist. The same idea applies when R is a relationship among more than two entity sets.

Example 19: Figure 18 shows some appropriate referential integrity constraints among the entity sets *Movies*, *Studios*, and *Presidents.* These entity sets and relationships were first introduced in Figs. 2 and 3. We see a rounded arrow entering *Studios* from relationship *Owns.* That arrow expresses the referential integrity constraint that every movie must be owned by one studio, and this studio is present in the *Studios* entity set.

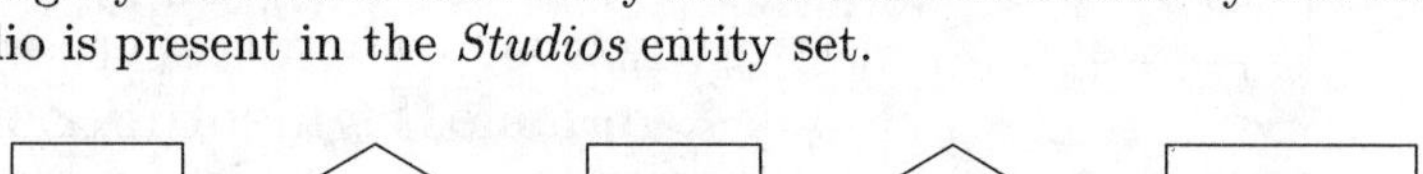

Figure 18: E/R diagram showing referential integrity constraints

Similarly, we see a rounded arrow entering *Studios* from *Runs.* That arrow expresses the referential integrity constraint that every president runs a studio that exists in the *Studios* entity set.

Note that the arrow to *Presidents* from *Runs* remains a pointed arrow. That choice reflects a reasonable assumption about the relationship between studios and their presidents. If a studio ceases to exist, its president can no longer be called a president, so we would expect the president of the studio to be deleted from the entity set *Presidents*. Hence there is a rounded arrow to *Studios*. On the other hand, if a president were fired or resigned, the studio would continue to exist. Thus, we place an ordinary, pointed arrow to *Presidents*, indicating that each studio has at most one president, but might have no president at some time. □

3.4 Degree Constraints

In the E/R model, we can attach a bounding number to the edges that connect a relationship to an entity set, indicating limits on the number of entities that can be connected to any one entity of the related entity set. For example, we could choose to place a constraint on the degree of a relationship, such as that a movie entity cannot be connected by relationship *Stars-in* to more than 10 star entities.

Figure 19: Representing a constraint on the number of stars per movie

Figure 19 shows how we can represent this constraint. As another example, we can think of the arrow as a synonym for the constraint "≤ 1," and we can think of the rounded arrow of Fig. 18 as standing for the constraint "$= 1$."

3.5 Exercises for Section 3

Exercise 3.1: For your E/R diagrams of:

a) Exercise 1.1.

b) Exercise 1.3.

c) Exercise 1.6.

(*i*) Select and specify keys, and (*ii*) Indicate appropriate referential integrity constraints.

! Exercise 3.2: We may think of relationships in the E/R model as having keys, just as entity sets do. Let R be a relationship among the entity sets $E_1, E_2, \ldots, E_n$. Then a *key* for R is a set K of attributes chosen from the attributes of $E_1, E_2, \ldots, E_n$ such that if $(e_1, e_2, \ldots, e_n)$ and $(f_1, f_2, \ldots, f_n)$ are two different tuples in the relationship set for R, then it is not possible that these tuples agree in all the attributes of K. Now, suppose $n = 2$; that is, R is a binary relationship. Also, for each i, let K_i be a set of attributes that is a key for entity set E_i. In terms of E_1 and E_2, give a smallest possible key for R under the assumption that:

a) R is many-many.

b) R is many-one from E_1 to E_2.

c) R is many-one from E_2 to E_1.

d) R is one-one.

!! **Exercise 3.3:** Consider again the problem of Exercise 3.2, but with n allowed to be any number, not just 2. Using only the information about which arcs from R to the E_i's have arrows, show how to find a smallest possible key K for R in terms of the K_i's.

4 Weak Entity Sets

It is possible for an entity set's key to be composed of attributes, some or all of which belong to another entity set. Such an entity set is called a *weak entity set.*

4.1 Causes of Weak Entity Sets

There are two principal reasons we need weak entity sets. First, sometimes entity sets fall into a hierarchy based on classifications unrelated to the "isa hierarchy" of Section 1.11. If entities of set E are subunits of entities in set F, then it is possible that the names of E-entities are not unique until we take into account the name of the F-entity to which the E entity is subordinate. Several examples will illustrate the problem.

Example 20: A movie studio might have several film crews. The crews might be designated by a given studio as crew 1, crew 2, and so on. However, other studios might use the same designations for crews, so the attribute *number* is not a key for crews. Rather, to name a crew uniquely, we need to give both the name of the studio to which it belongs and the number of the crew. The situation is suggested by Fig. 20. The double-rectangle indicates a weak entity set, and the double-diamond indicates a many-one relationship that helps provide the key for the weak entity set. The notation will be explained further in Section 4.3. The key for weak entity set *Crews* is its own *number* attribute and the *name* attribute of the unique studio to which the crew is related by the many-one *Unit-of* relationship. □

Example 21: A species is designated by its genus and species names. For example, humans are of the species *Homo sapiens*; *Homo* is the genus name and *sapiens* the species name. In general, a genus consists of several species, each of which has a name beginning with the genus name and continuing with the species name. Unfortunately, species names, by themselves, are not unique.

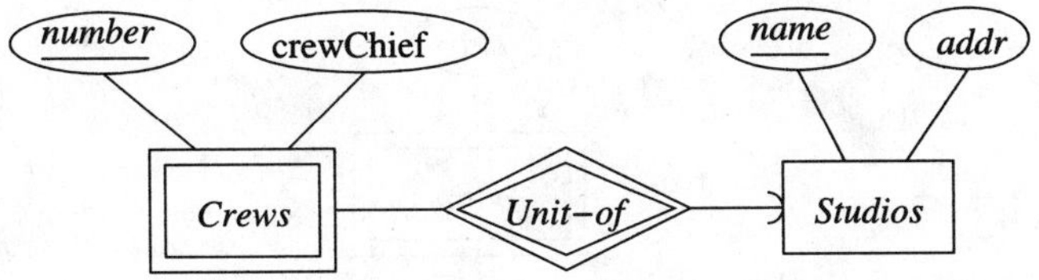

Figure 20: A weak entity set for crews, and its connections

Two or more genera may have species with the same species name. Thus, to designate a species uniquely we need both the species name and the name of the genus to which the species is related by the *Belongs-to* relationship, as suggested in Fig. 21. *Species* is a weak entity set whose key comes partially from its genus. □

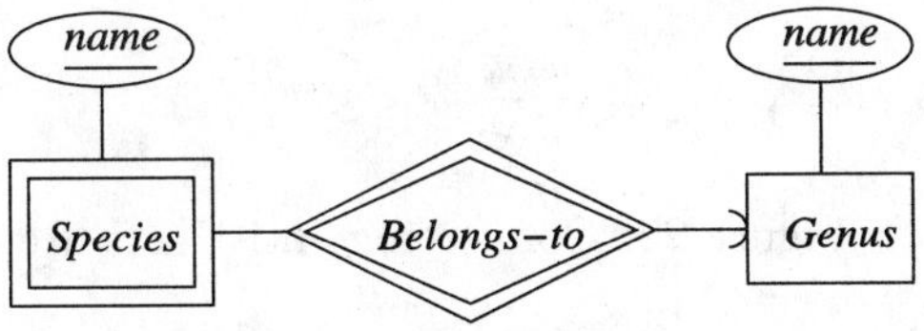

Figure 21: Another weak entity set, for species

The second common source of weak entity sets is the connecting entity sets that we introduced in Section 1.10 as a way to eliminate a multiway relationship.[3] These entity sets often have no attributes of their own. Their key is formed from the attributes that are the key attributes for the entity sets they connect.

Example 22 : In Fig. 22 we see a connecting entity set *Contracts* that replaces the ternary relationship *Contracts* of Example 5. *Contracts* has an attribute *salary*, but this attribute does not contribute to the key. Rather, the key for a contract consists of the name of the studio and the star involved, plus the title and year of the movie involved. □

4.2 Requirements for Weak Entity Sets

We cannot obtain key attributes for a weak entity set indiscriminately. Rather, if E is a weak entity set then its key consists of:

1. Zero or more of its own attributes, and

[3]Remember that there is no particular requirement in the E/R model that multiway relationships be eliminated, although this requirement exists in some other database design models.

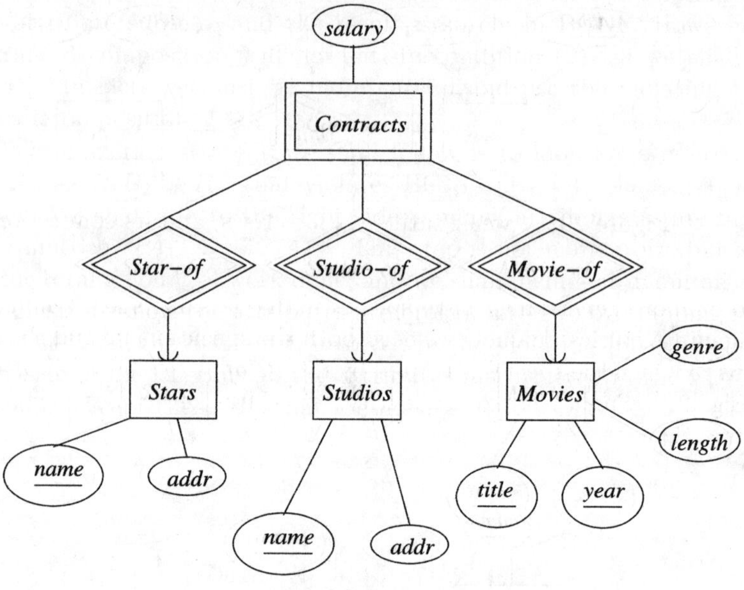

Figure 22: Connecting entity sets are weak

2. Key attributes from entity sets that are reached by certain many-one relationships from E to other entity sets. These many-one relationships are called *supporting relationships* for E, and the entity sets reached from E are *supporting entity sets.*

In order for R, a many-one relationship from E to some entity set F, to be a supporting relationship for E, the following conditions must be obeyed:

a) R must be a binary, many-one relationship[4] from E to F.

b) R must have referential integrity from E to F. That is, for every E-entity, there must be exactly one existing F-entity related to it by R. Put another way, a rounded arrow from R to F must be justified.

c) The attributes that F supplies for the key of E must be key attributes of F.

d) However, if F is itself weak, then some or all of the key attributes of F supplied to E will be key attributes of one or more entity sets G to which F is connected by a supporting relationship. Recursively, if G is weak, some key attributes of G will be supplied from elsewhere, and so on.

[4]Remember that a one-one relationship is a special case of a many-one relationship. When we say a relationship must be many-one, we always include one-one relationships as well.

e) If there are several different supporting relationships from E to the same entity set F, then each relationship is used to supply a copy of the key attributes of F to help form the key of E. Note that an entity e from E may be related to different entities in F through different supporting relationships from E. Thus, the keys of several different entities from F may appear in the key values identifying a particular entity e from E.

The intuitive reason why these conditions are needed is as follows. Consider an entity in a weak entity set, say a crew in Example 20. Each crew is unique, abstractly. In principle we can tell one crew from another, even if they have the same number but belong to different studios. It is only the data about crews that makes it hard to distinguish crews, because the number alone is not sufficient. The only way we can associate additional information with a crew is if there is some deterministic process leading to additional values that make the designation of a crew unique. But the only unique values associated with an abstract crew entity are:

1. Values of attributes of the *Crews* entity set, and

2. Values obtained by following a relationship from a crew entity to a unique entity of some other entity set, where that other entity has a unique associated value of some kind. That is, the relationship followed must be many-one to the other entity set F, and the associated value must be part of a key for F.

4.3 Weak Entity Set Notation

We shall adopt the following conventions to indicate that an entity set is weak and to declare its key attributes.

1. If an entity set is weak, it will be shown as a rectangle with a double border. Examples of this convention are *Crews* in Fig. 20 and *Contracts* in Fig. 22.

2. Its supporting many-one relationships will be shown as diamonds with a double border. Examples of this convention are *Unit-of* in Fig. 20 and all three relationships in Fig. 22.

3. If an entity set supplies any attributes for its own key, then those attributes will be underlined. An example is in Fig. 20, where the number of a crew participates in its own key, although it is not the complete key for *Crews*.

We can summarize these conventions with the following rule:

- Whenever we use an entity set E with a double border, it is weak. The key for E is whatever attributes of E are underlined plus the key attributes of those entity sets to which E is connected by many-one relationships with a double border.

We should remember that the double-diamond is used only for supporting relationships. It is possible for there to be many-one relationships from a weak entity set that are not supporting relationships, and therefore do not get a double diamond.

Example 23: In Fig. 22, the relationship *Studio-of* need not be a supporting relationship for *Contracts*. The reason is that each movie has a unique owning studio, determined by the (not shown) many-one relationship from *Movies* to *Studios*. Thus, if we are told the name of a star and a movie, there is at most one contract with any studio for the work of that star in that movie. In terms of our notation, it would be appropriate to use an ordinary single diamond, rather than the double diamond, for *Studio-of* in Fig. 22. □

4.4 Exercises for Section 4

Exercise 4.1: One way to represent students and the grades they get in courses is to use entity sets corresponding to students, to courses, and to "enrollments." Enrollment entities form a "connecting" entity set between students and courses and can be used to represent not only the fact that a student is taking a certain course, but the grade of the student in the course. Draw an E/R diagram for this situation, indicating weak entity sets and the keys for the entity sets. Is the grade part of the key for enrollments?

Exercise 4.2: Modify your solution to Exercise 4.1 so that we can record grades of the student for each of several assignments within a course. Again, indicate weak entity sets and keys.

Exercise 4.3: For your E/R diagrams of Exercise 2.6(a)–(c), indicate weak entity sets, supporting relationships, and keys.

Exercise 4.4: Draw E/R diagrams for the following situations involving weak entity sets. In each case indicate keys for entity sets.

a) Entity sets *Courses* and *Departments*. A course is given by a unique department, but its only attribute is its number. Different departments can offer courses with the same number. Each department has a unique name.

! b) Entity sets *Leagues*, *Teams*, and *Players*. League names are unique. No league has two teams with the same name. No team has two players with the same number. However, there can be players with the same number on different teams, and there can be teams with the same name in different leagues.

5 From E/R Diagrams to Relational Designs

To a first approximation, converting an E/R design to a relational database schema is straightforward:

- Turn each entity set into a relation with the same set of attributes, and
- Replace a relationship by a relation whose attributes are the keys for the connected entity sets.

While these two rules cover much of the ground, there are also several special situations that we need to deal with, including:

1. Weak entity sets cannot be translated straightforwardly to relations.
2. "Isa" relationships and subclasses require careful treatment.
3. Sometimes, we do well to combine two relations, especially the relation for an entity set E and the relation that comes from a many-one relationship from E to some other entity set.

5.1 From Entity Sets to Relations

Let us first consider entity sets that are not weak. We shall take up the modifications needed to accommodate weak entity sets in Section 5.4. For each non-weak entity set, we shall create a relation of the same name and with the same set of attributes. This relation will not have any indication of the relationships in which the entity set participates; we'll handle relationships with separate relations, as discussed in Section 5.2.

Example 24: Consider the three entity sets *Movies*, *Stars* and *Studios* from Fig. 17, which we reproduce here as Fig. 23. The attributes for the *Movies* entity set are *title*, *year*, *length*, and *genre*.

Next, consider the entity set *Stars* from Fig. 23. There are two attributes, *name* and *address*. Thus, we would expect the corresponding `Stars` relation to have schema `Stars(name, address)` and for

name	*address*
`Carrie Fisher`	`123 Maple St., Hollywood`
`Mark Hamill`	`456 Oak Rd., Brentwood`
`Harrison Ford`	`789 Palm Dr., Beverly Hills`

to be a typical instance. □

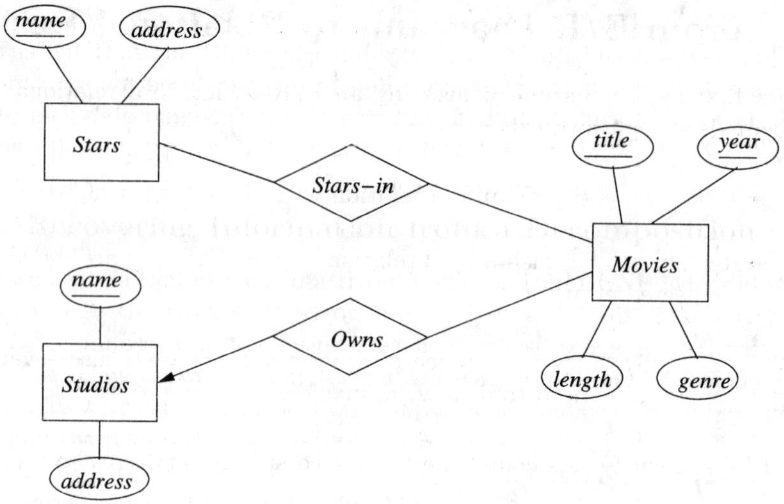

Figure 23: E/R diagram for the movie database

5.2 From E/R Relationships to Relations

Relationships in the E/R model are also represented by relations. The relation for a given relationship R has the following attributes:

1. For each entity set involved in relationship R, we take its key attribute or attributes as part of the schema of the relation for R.

2. If the relationship has attributes, then these are also attributes of relation R.

If one entity set is involved several times in a relationship, in different roles, then its key attributes each appear as many times as there are roles. We must rename the attributes to avoid name duplication. More generally, should the same attribute name appear twice or more among the attributes of R itself and the keys of the entity sets involved in relationship R, then we need to rename to avoid duplication.

Example 25: Consider the relationship *Owns* of Fig. 23. This relationship connects entity sets *Movies* and *Studios*. Thus, for the schema of relation `Owns` we use the key for *Movies*, which is *title* and *year*, and the key of *Studios*, which is *name*. That is, the schema for relation `Owns` is:

```
Owns(title, year, studioName)
```

A sample instance of this relation is:

title	*year*	*studioName*
Star Wars	1977	Fox
Gone With the Wind	1939	MGM
Wayne's World	1992	Paramount

We have chosen the attribute `studioName` for clarity; it corresponds to the attribute *name* of *Studios*. □

title	*year*	*starName*
Star Wars	1977	Carrie Fisher
Star Wars	1977	Mark Hamill
Star Wars	1977	Harrison Ford
Gone With the Wind	1939	Vivien Leigh
Wayne's World	1992	Dana Carvey
Wayne's World	1992	Mike Meyers

Figure 24: A relation for relationship *Stars-In*

Example 26: Similarly, the relationship *Stars-In* of Fig. 23 can be transformed into a relation with the attributes `title` and `year` (the key for *Movies*) and attribute `starName`, which is the key for entity set *Stars*. Figure 24 shows a sample relation `Stars-In`. □

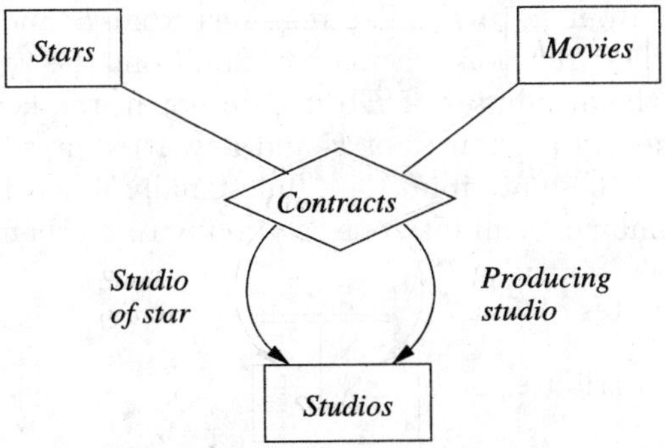

Figure 25: The relationship *Contracts*

Example 27: Multiway relationships are also easy to convert to relations. Consider the four-way relationship *Contracts* of Fig. 6, reproduced here as Fig. 25, involving a star, a movie, and two studios — the first holding the star's contract and the second contracting for that star's services in that movie. We represent this relationship by a relation `Contracts` whose schema consists of the attributes from the keys of the following four entity sets:

1. The key `starName` for the star.

2. The key consisting of attributes `title` and `year` for the movie.

3. The key `studioOfStar` indicating the name of the first studio; recall we assume the studio name is a key for the entity set `Studios`.

4. The key `producingStudio` indicating the name of the studio that will produce the movie using that star.

That is, the relation schema is:

```
Contracts(starName, title, year, studioOfStar, producingStudio)
```

Notice that we have been inventive in choosing attribute names for our relation schema, avoiding "name" for any attribute, since it would be unobvious whether that referred to a star's name or studio's name, and in the latter case, which studio role. Also, were there attributes attached to entity set *Contracts*, such as *salary*, these attributes would be added to the schema of relation `Contracts`. □

5.3 Combining Relations

Sometimes, the relations that we get from converting entity sets and relationships to relations are not the best possible choice of relations for the given data. One common situation occurs when there is an entity set E with a many-one relationship R from E to F. The relations from E and R will each have the key for E in their relation schema. In addition, the relation for E will have in its schema the attributes of E that are not in the key, and the relation for R will have the key attributes of F and any attributes of R itself. Because R is many-one, all these attributes are functionally determined by the key for E, and we can combine them into one relation with a schema consisting of:

1. All attributes of E.

2. The key attributes of F.

3. Any attributes belonging to relationship R.

For an entity e of E that is not related to any entity of F, the attributes of types (2) and (3) will have null values in the tuple for e.

Example 28: In our running movie example, *Owns* is a many-one relationship from *Movies* to *Studios*, which we converted to a relation in Example 25. The relation obtained from entity set *Movies* was discussed in Example 24. We can combine these relations by taking all their attributes and forming one relation schema. If we do, the relation looks like that in Fig. 26. □

title	*year*	*length*	*genre*	*studioName*
Star Wars	1977	124	sciFi	Fox
Gone With the Wind	1939	239	drama	MGM
Wayne's World	1992	95	comedy	Paramount

Figure 26: Combining relation Movies with relation Owns

Whether or not we choose to combine relations in this manner is a matter of judgement. However, there are some advantages to having all the attributes that are dependent on the key of entity set E together in one relation, even if there are a number of many-one relationships from E to other entity sets. For example, it is often more efficient to answer queries involving attributes of one relation than to answer queries involving attributes of several relations. In fact, some design systems based on the E/R model combine these relations automatically.

On the other hand, one might wonder if it made sense to combine the relation for E with the relation of a relationship R that involved E but was not many-one from E to some other entity set. Doing so is risky, because it often leads to redundancy, as the next example shows.

Example 29: To get a sense of what can go wrong, suppose we combined the relation of Fig. 26 with the relation that we get for the many-many relationship *Stars-in*; recall this relation was suggested by Fig. 24. Then the combined relation would look like Fig. 27. This relation has anomalies that we need to remove by the process of normalization. □

title	*year*	*length*	*genre*	*studioName*	*starName*
Star Wars	1977	124	SciFi	Fox	Carrie Fisher
Star Wars	1977	124	SciFi	Fox	Mark Hamill
Star Wars	1977	124	SciFi	Fox	Harrison Ford
Gone With the Wind	1939	231	drama	MGM	Vivien Leigh
Wayne's World	1992	95	comedy	Paramount	Dana Carvey
Wayne's World	1992	95	comedy	Paramount	Mike Meyers

Figure 27: The relation Movies with star information

5.4 Handling Weak Entity Sets

When a weak entity set appears in an E/R diagram, we need to do three things differently.

1. The relation for the weak entity set W itself must include not only the attributes of W but also the key attributes of the supporting entity sets.

The supporting entity sets are easily recognized because they are reached by supporting (double-diamond) relationships from W.

2. The relation for any relationship in which the weak entity set W appears must use as a key for W all of its key attributes, including those of other entity sets that contribute to W's key.

3. However, a supporting relationship R, from the weak entity set W to a supporting entity set, need not be converted to a relation at all. The justification is that, as discussed in Section 5.3, the attributes of many-one relationship R's relation will either *be* attributes of the relation for W, or (in the case of attributes on R) can be added to the schema for W's relation.

Of course, when introducing additional attributes to build the key of a weak entity set, we must be careful not to use the same name twice. If necessary, we rename some or all of these attributes.

Example 30: Let us consider the weak entity set *Crews* from Fig. 20, which we reproduce here as Fig. 28. From this diagram we get three relations, whose schemas are:

```
Studios(name, addr)
Crews(number, studioName, crewChief)
Unit-of(number, studioName, name)
```

The first relation, `Studios`, is constructed in a straightforward manner from the entity set of the same name. The second, `Crews`, comes from the weak entity set *Crews*. The attributes of this relation are the key attributes of *Crews* and the one nonkey attribute of *Crews*, which is *crewChief*. We have chosen `studioName` as the attribute in relation `Crews` that corresponds to the attribute *name* in the entity set *Studios*.

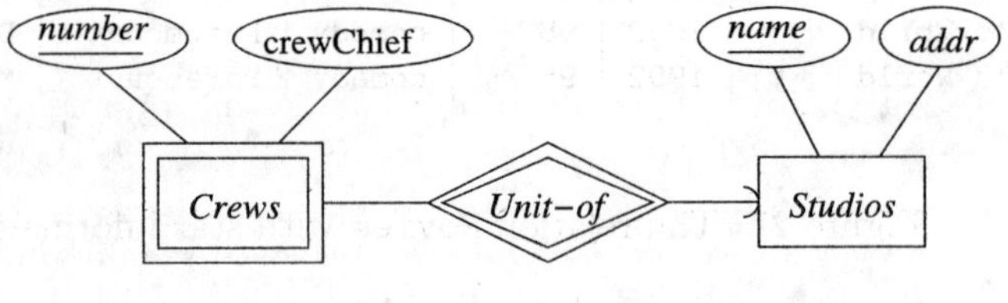

Figure 28: The crews example of a weak entity set

The third relation, `Unit-of`, comes from the relationship of the same name. As always, we represent an E/R relationship in the relational model by a relation whose schema has the key attributes of the related entity sets. In this case, `Unit-of` has attributes `number` and `studioName`, the key for weak entity set *Crews*, and attribute `name`, the key for entity set *Studios*. However, notice that since *Unit-of* is a many-one relationship, the studio `studioName` is surely the same as the studio `name`.

For instance, suppose Disney crew #3 is one of the crews of the Disney studio. Then the relationship set for E/R relationship *Unit-of* includes the pair

(Disney-crew-#3, Disney)

This pair gives rise to the tuple

(3, Disney, Disney)

for the relation `Unit-of`.

Notice that, as must be the case, the components of this tuple for attributes `studioName` and `name` are identical. As a consequence, we can "merge" the attributes `studioName` and `name` of `Unit-of`, giving us the simpler schema:

```
Unit-of(number, name)
```

However, now we can dispense with the relation `Unit-of` altogether, since its attributes are now a subset of the attributes of relation `Crews`. □

The phenomenon observed in Example 30 — that a supporting relationship needs no relation — is universal for weak entity sets. The following is a modified rule for converting to relations entity sets that are weak.

- If W is a weak entity set, construct for W a relation whose schema consists of:

  1. All attributes of W.
  2. All attributes of supporting relationships for W.
  3. For each supporting relationship for W, say a many-one relationship from W to entity set E, all the *key* attributes of E.

  Rename attributes, if necessary, to avoid name conflicts.

- Do *not* construct a relation for any supporting relationship for W.

5.5 Exercises for Section 5

Exercise 5.1: Convert the E/R diagram of Fig. 29 to a relational database schema.

! Exercise 5.2: There is another E/R diagram that could describe the weak entity set *Bookings* in Fig. 29. Notice that a booking can be identified uniquely by the flight number, day of the flight, the row, and the seat; the customer is not then necessary to help identify the booking.

Relations With Subset Schemas

You might imagine from Example 30 that whenever one relation R has a set of attributes that is a subset of the attributes of another relation S, we can eliminate R. That is not exactly true. R might hold information that doesn't appear in S because the additional attributes of S do not allow us to extend a tuple from R to S.

For instance, the Internal Revenue Service tries to maintain a relation `People(name, ss#)` of potential taxpayers and their social-security numbers, even if the person had no income and did not file a tax return. They might also maintain a relation `TaxPayers(name, ss#, amount)` indicating the amount of tax paid by each person who filed a return in the current year. The schema of `People` is a subset of the schema of `TaxPayers`, yet there may be value in remembering the social-security number of those who are mentioned in `People` but not in `Taxpayers`.

In fact, even identical sets of attributes may have different semantics, so it is not possible to merge their tuples. An example would be two relations `Stars(name, addr)` and `Studios(name, addr)`. Although the schemas look alike, we cannot turn star tuples into studio tuples, or vice-versa.

On the other hand, when the two relations come from the weak-entity-set construction, then there can be no such additional value to the relation with the smaller set of attributes. The reason is that the tuples of the relation that comes from the supporting relationship correspond one-for-one with the tuples of the relation that comes from the weak entity set. Thus, we routinely eliminate the former relation.

a) Revise the diagram of Fig. 29 to reflect this new viewpoint.

b) Convert your diagram from (a) into relations. Do you get the same database schema as in Exercise 5.1?

Exercise 5.3: The E/R diagram of Fig. 30 represents ships. Ships are said to be *sisters* if they were designed from the same plans. Convert this diagram to a relational database schema.

Exercise 5.4: Convert the following E/R diagrams to relational database schemas.

a) Figure 22.

b) Your answer to Exercise 4.1.

c) Your answer to Exercise 4.4(a).

d) Your answer to Exercise 4.4(b).

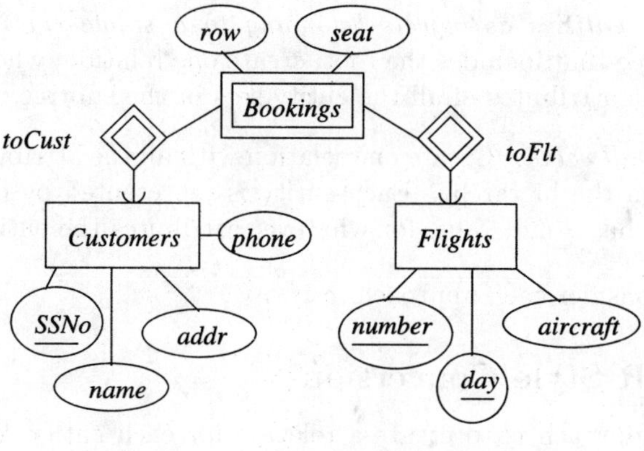

Figure 29: An E/R diagram about airlines

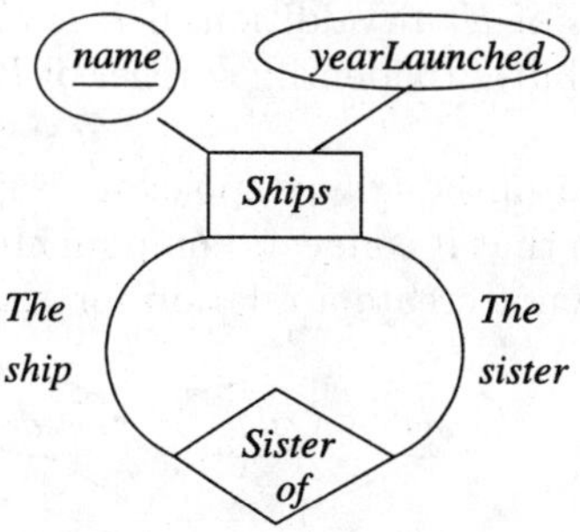

Figure 30: An E/R diagram about sister ships

6 Converting Subclass Structures to Relations

When we have an isa-hierarchy of entity sets, we are presented with several choices of strategy for conversion to relations. Recall we assume that:

- There is a root entity set for the hierarchy,
- This entity set has a key that serves to identify every entity represented by the hierarchy, and
- A given entity may have *components* that belong to the entity sets of any subtree of the hierarchy, as long as that subtree includes the root.

The principal conversion strategies are:

1. *Follow the E/R viewpoint.* For each entity set E in the hierarchy, create a relation that includes the key attributes from the root and any attributes belonging to E.

2. *Treat entities as objects belonging to a single class.* For each possible subtree that includes the root, create one relation, whose schema includes all the attributes of all the entity sets in the subtree.

3. *Use null values.* Create one relation with all the attributes of all the entity sets in the hierarchy. Each entity is represented by one tuple, and that tuple has a null value for whatever attributes the entity does not have.

We shall consider each approach in turn.

6.1 E/R-Style Conversion

Our first approach is to create a relation for each entity set, as usual. If the entity set E is not the root of the hierarchy, then the relation for E will include the key attributes at the root, to identify the entity represented by each tuple, plus all the attributes of E. In addition, if E is involved in a relationship, then we use these key attributes to identify entities of E in the relation corresponding to that relationship.

Note, however, that although we spoke of "isa" as a relationship, it is unlike other relationships, in that it connects components of a single entity, not distinct entities. Thus, we do not create a relation for "isa."

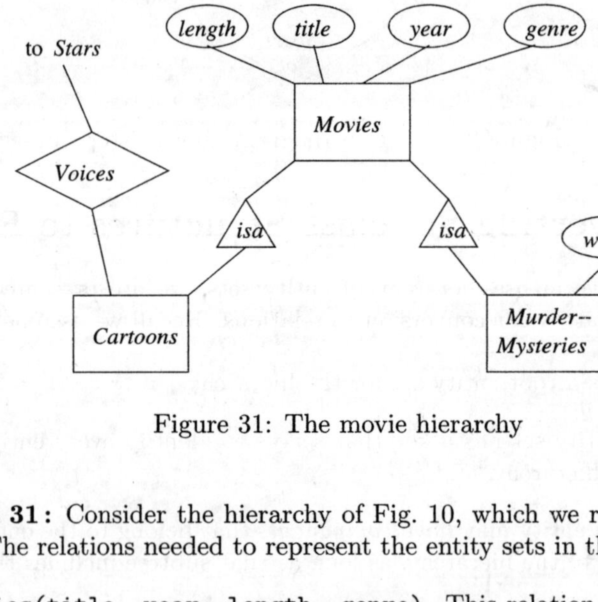

Figure 31: The movie hierarchy

Example 31: Consider the hierarchy of Fig. 10, which we reproduce here as Fig. 31. The relations needed to represent the entity sets in this hierarchy are:

1. `Movies(title, year, length, genre)`. This relation was discussed in Example 24, and every movie is represented by a tuple here.

2. `MurderMysteries(title, year, weapon)`. The first two attributes are the key for all movies, and the last is the lone attribute for the corresponding entity set. Those movies that are murder mysteries have a tuple here as well as in `Movies`.

3. `Cartoons(title, year)`. This relation is the set of cartoons. It has no attributes other than the key for movies, since the extra information about cartoons is contained in the relationship *Voices*. Movies that are cartoons have a tuple here as well as in `Movies`.

Note that the fourth kind of movie — those that are both cartoons and murder mysteries — have tuples in all three relations.

In addition, we shall need the relation `Voices(title, year, starName)` that corresponds to the relationship *Voices* between *Stars* and *Cartoons*. The last attribute is the key for *Stars* and the first two form the key for *Cartoons*.

For instance, the movie *Roger Rabbit* would have tuples in all four relations. Its basic information would be in `Movies`, the murder weapon would appear in `MurderMysteries`, and the stars that provided voices for the movie would appear in `Voices`.

Notice that the relation `Cartoons` has a schema that is a subset of the schema for the relation `Voices`. In many situations, we would be content to eliminate a relation such as `Cartoons`, since it appears not to contain any information beyond what is in `Voices`. However, there may be silent cartoons in our database. Those cartoons would have no voices, and we would therefore lose information should we eliminate relation `Cartoons`. □

6.2 An Object-Oriented Approach

An alternative strategy for converting isa-hierarchies to relations is to enumerate all the possible subtrees of the hierarchy. For each, create one relation that represents entities having components in exactly those subtrees. The schema for this relation has all the attributes of any entity set in the subtree. We refer to this approach as "object-oriented," since it is motivated by the assumption that entities are "objects" that belong to one and only one class.

Example 32: Consider the hierarchy of Fig. 31. There are four possible subtrees including the root:

1. *Movies* alone.

2. *Movies* and *Cartoons* only.

3. *Movies* and *Murder-Mysteries* only.

4. All three entity sets.

We must construct relations for all four "classes." Since only Murder-Mysteries contributes an attribute that is unique to its entities, there is actually some repetition, and these four relations are:

```
Movies(title, year, length, genre)
MoviesC(title, year, length, genre)
MoviesMM(title, year, length, genre, weapon)
MoviesCMM(title, year, length, genre, weapon)
```

If *Cartoons* had attributes unique to that entity set, then all four relations would have different sets of attributes. As that is not the case here, we could combine `Movies` with `MoviesC` (i.e., create one relation for non-murder-mysteries) and combine `MoviesMM` with `MoviesCMM` (i.e., create one relation for all murder mysteries), although doing so loses some information — which movies are cartoons.

We also need to consider how to handle the relationship *Voices* from *Cartoons* to *Stars*. If *Voices* were many-one from *Cartoons*, then we could add a `voice` attribute to `MoviesC` and `MoviesCMM`, which would represent the *Voices* relationship and would have the side-effect of making all four relations different. However, *Voices* is many-many, so we need to create a separate relation for this relationship. As always, its schema has the key attributes from the entity sets connected; in this case

```
Voices(title, year, starName)
```

would be an appropriate schema.

One might consider whether it was necessary to create two such relations, one connecting cartoons that are not murder mysteries to their voices, and the other for cartoons that *are* murder mysteries. However, there does not appear to be any benefit to doing so in this case. □

6.3 Using Null Values to Combine Relations

There is one more approach to representing information about a hierarchy of entity sets. If we are allowed to use `NULL` (the null value as in SQL) as a value in tuples, we can handle a hierarchy of entity sets with a single relation. This relation has all the attributes belonging to any entity set of the hierarchy. An entity is then represented by a single tuple. This tuple has `NULL` in each attribute that is not defined for that entity.

Example 33: If we applied this approach to the diagram of Fig. 31, we would create a single relation whose schema is:

```
Movie(title, year, length, genre, weapon)
```

Those movies that are not murder mysteries would have `NULL` in the `weapon` component of their tuple. It would also be necessary to have a relation `Voices` to connect those movies that are cartoons to the stars performing the voices, as in Example 32. □

6.4 Comparison of Approaches

Each of the three approaches, which we shall refer to as "straight-E/R," "object-oriented," and "nulls," respectively, have advantages and disadvantages. Here is a list of the principal issues.

1. It can be expensive to answer queries involving several relations, so we would prefer to find all the attributes we needed to answer a query in one relation. The nulls approach uses only one relation for all the attributes, so it has an advantage in this regard. The other two approaches have advantages for different kinds of queries. For instance:

   (a) A query like "what films of 2008 were longer than 150 minutes?" can be answered directly from the relation `Movies` in the straight-E/R approach of Example 31. However, in the object-oriented approach of Example 32, we need to examine `Movies`, `MoviesC`, `MoviesMM`, and `MoviesCMM`, since a long movie may be in any of these four relations.

   (b) On the other hand, a query like "what weapons were used in cartoons of over 150 minutes in length?" gives us trouble in the straight-E/R approach. We must access `Movies` to find those movies of over 150 minutes. We must access `Cartoons` to verify that a movie is a cartoon, and we must access `MurderMysteries` to find the murder weapon. In the object-oriented approach, we have only to access the relation `MoviesCMM`, where all the information we need will be found.

2. We would like not to use too many relations. Here again, the nulls method shines, since it requires only one relation. However, there is a difference between the other two methods, since in the straight-E/R approach, we use only one relation per entity set in the hierarchy. In the object-oriented approach, if we have a root and n children ($n + 1$ entity sets in all), then there are 2^n different classes of entities, and we need that many relations.

3. We would like to minimize space and avoid repeating information. Since the object-oriented method uses only one tuple per entity, and that tuple has components for only those attributes that make sense for the entity, this approach offers the minimum possible space usage. The nulls approach also has only one tuple per entity, but these tuples are "long"; i.e., they have components for all attributes, whether or not they are appropriate for a given entity. If there are many entity sets in the hierarchy, and there are many attributes among those entity sets, then a large fraction of the space could be wasted in the nulls approach. The straight-E/R method has several tuples for each entity, but only the key attributes are repeated. Thus, this method could use either more or less space than the nulls method.

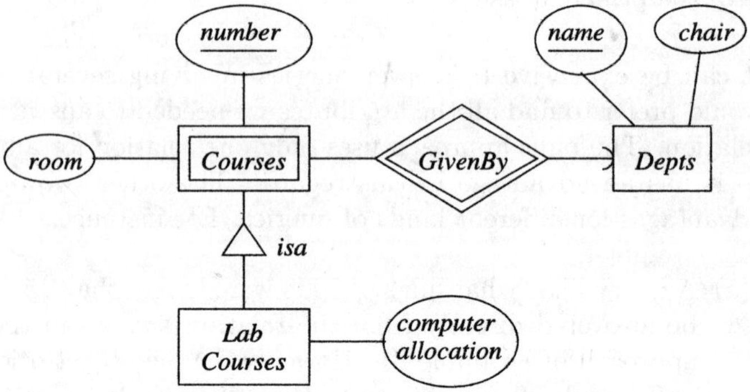

Figure 32: E/R diagram for Exercise 6.1

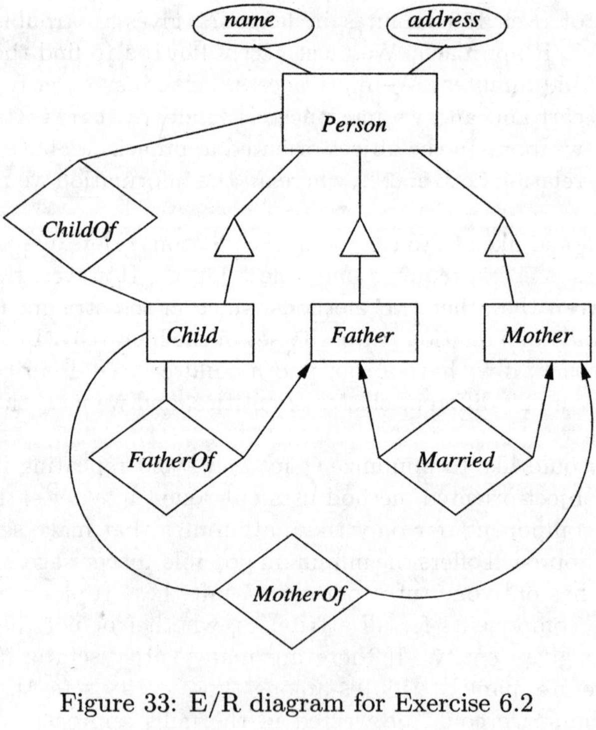

Figure 33: E/R diagram for Exercise 6.2

6.5 Exercises for Section 6

Exercise 6.1: Convert the E/R diagram of Fig. 32 to a relational database schema, using each of the following approaches:

a) The straight-E/R method.

b) The object-oriented method.

c) The nulls method.

! **Exercise 6.2:** Convert the E/R diagram of Fig. 33 to a relational database schema, using:

a) The straight-E/R method.

b) The object-oriented method.

c) The nulls method.

Exercise 6.3: Convert your E/R design from Exercise 1.7 to a relational database schema, using:

a) The straight-E/R method.

b) The object-oriented method.

c) The nulls method.

! **Exercise 6.4:** Suppose that we have an isa-hierarchy involving e entity sets. Each entity set has a attributes, and k of those at the root form the key for all these entity sets. Give formulas for (i) the minimum and maximum number of relations used, and (ii) the minimum and maximum number of components that the tuple(s) for a single entity have all together, when the method of conversion to relations is:

a) The straight-E/R method.

b) The object-oriented method.

c) The nulls method.

7 Unified Modeling Language

UML (*Unified Modeling Language*) was developed originally as a graphical notation for describing software designs in an object-oriented style. It has been extended, with some modifications, to be a popular notation for describing database designs, and it is this portion of UML that we shall study here. UML offers much the same capabilities as the E/R model, with the exception of multiway relationships. UML also offers the ability to treat entity sets as true classes, with methods as well as data. Figure 34 summarizes the common concepts, with different terminology, used by E/R and UML.

UML	E/R Model
Class	Entity set
Association	Binary relationship
Association Class	Attributes on a relationship
Subclass	Isa hierarchy
Aggregation	Many-one relationship
Composition	Many-one relationship with referential integrity

Figure 34: Comparison between UML and E/R terminology

7.1 UML Classes

A class in UML is similar to an entity set in the E/R model. The notation for a class is rather different, however. Figure 35 shows the class that corresponds to the E/R entity set *Movies* from our running example of this chapter.

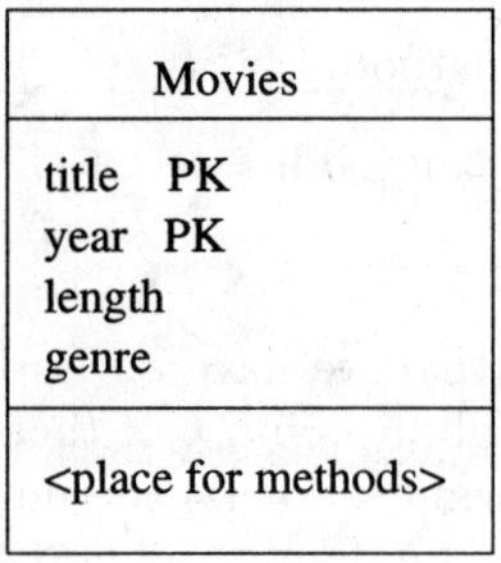

Figure 35: The *Movies* class in UML

The box for a class is divided into three parts. At the top is the name of the class. The middle has the attributes, which are like instance variables of a class. In our *Movies* class, we use the attributes *title, year, length*, and *genre.*

The bottom portion is for methods. Neither the E/R model nor the relational model provides methods. However, they are an important concept, and one that actually appears in modern relational systems, called "object-relational" DBMS's.

Example 34: We might have added an instance method *lengthInHours*(). The UML specification doesn't tell anything more about a method than the types of any arguments and the type of its return-value. Perhaps this method returns *length*/60.0, but we cannot know from the design. □

In this section, we shall not use methods in our design. Thus, in the future, UML class boxes will have only two sections, for the class name and the attributes.

7.2 Keys for UML classes

As for entity sets, we can declare one key for a UML class. To do so, we follow each attribute in the key by the letters PK, standing for "primary key." There is no convenient way to stipulate that several attributes or sets of attributes are each keys.

Example 35: In Fig. 35, we have made our standard assumption that *title* and *year* together form the key for *Movies.* Notice that PK appears on the lines for these attributes and not for the others. □

7.3 Associations

A binary relationship between classes is called an *association.* There is no analog of multiway relationships in UML. Rather, a multiway relationship has to be broken into binary relationships, which as we suggested in Section 1.10, can always be done. The interpretation of an association is exactly what we described for relationships in Section 1.5 on relationship sets. The association is a set of pairs of objects, one from each of the classes it connects.

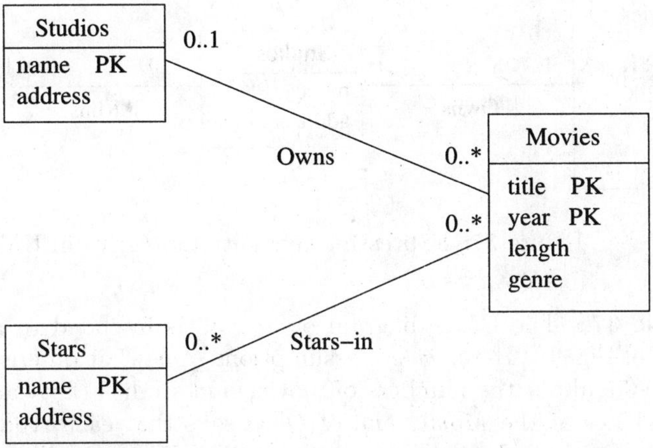

Figure 36: Movies, stars, and studios in UML

We draw a UML association between two classes simply by drawing a line between them, and giving the line a name. Usually, we'll place the name below the line. For example, Fig. 36 is the UML analog of the E/R diagram of Fig. 17. There are two associations, *Stars-in* and *Owns*; the first connects *Movies* with *Stars* and the second connects *Movies* with *Studios.*

Every association has constraints on the number of objects from each of its classes that can be connected to an object of the other class. We indicate these constraints by a label of the form $m..n$ at each end. The meaning of this label is that each object at the other end is connected to at least m and at most n objects at this end. In addition:

- A $*$ in place of n, as in $m..*$, stands for "infinity." That is, there is no upper limit.
- A $*$ alone, in place of $m..n$, stands for the range $0..*$, that is, no constraint at all on the number of objects.
- If there is no label at all at an end of an association edge, then the label is taken to be 1..1, i.e., "exactly one."

Example 36: In Fig. 36 we see $0..*$ at the *Movies* end of both associations. That says that a star appears in zero or more movies, and a studio owns zero or more movies; i.e., there is no constraint for either. There is also a $0..*$ at the *Stars* end of association *Stars-in*, telling us that a movie has any number of stars. However, the label on the *Studios* end of association *Owns* is 0..1, which means either 0 or 1 studio. That is, a given movie can either be owned by one studio, or not be owned by any studio in the database. Notice that this constraint is exactly what is said by the pointed arrow entering *Studios* in the E/R diagram of Fig. 17. □

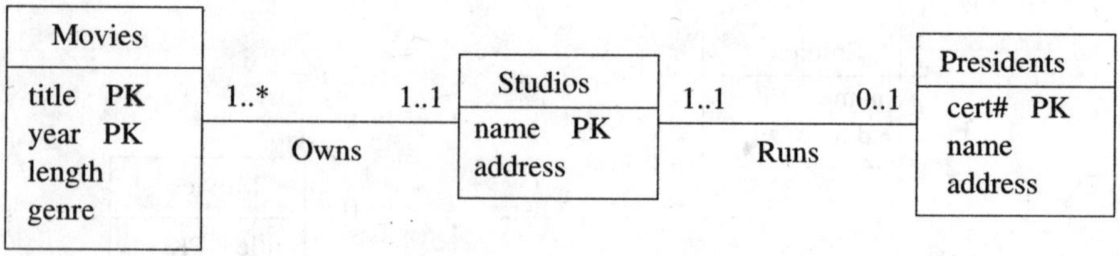

Figure 37: Expressing referential integrity in UML

Example 37: The UML diagram of Fig. 37 is intended to mirror the E/R diagram of Fig. 18. Here, we see assumptions somewhat different from those in Example 36, about the numbers of movies and studios that can be associated. The label $1..*$ at the *Movies* end of *Owns* says that each studio must own at least one movie (or else it isn't really a studio). There is still no upper limit on how many movies a studio can own.

At the *Studios* end of *Owns*, we see the label 1..1. That label says that a movie must be owned by one studio and only one studio. It is not possible for a movie not to be owned by any studio, as was possible in Fig. 36. The label 1..1 says exactly what the rounded arrow in E/R diagrams says.

We also see the association *Runs* between studios and presidents. At the *Studios* end we see label 1..1. That is, a president must be the president of one and only one studio. That label reflects the same constraint as the rounded arrow from *Presidents* to *Studios* in Fig. 18. At the other end of association *Runs* is the label 0..1. That label says that a studio can have at most one president, but it could not have a president at some time. This constraint is exactly the constraint of a pointed arrow. □

7.4 Self-Associations

An association can have both ends at the same class; such an association is called a *self-association*. To distinguish the two roles played by one class in a self-association, we give the association two names, one for each end.

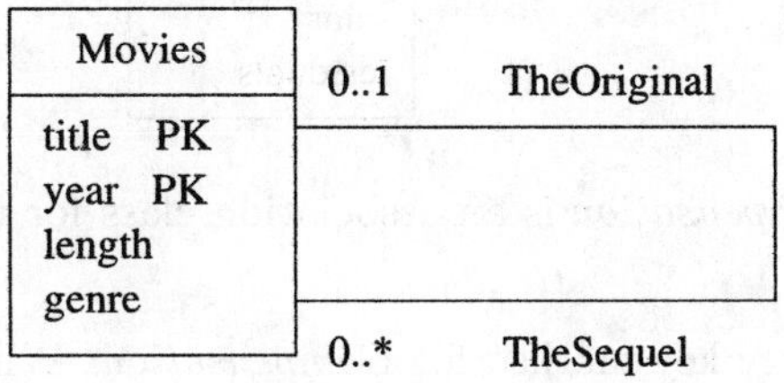

Figure 38: A self-association representing sequels of movies

Example 38: Figure 38 represents the relationship "sequel-of" on movies. We see one association with each end at the class *Movies*. The end with role *TheOriginal* points to the original movie, and it has label 0..1. That is, for a movie to be a sequel, there has to be exactly one movie that was the original. However, some movies are not sequels of any movie. The other role, *TheSequel* has label 0..∗. The reasoning is that an original can have any number of sequels. Note we take the point of view that there is an original movie for any sequence of sequels, and a sequel is a sequel of the original, not of the previous movie in the sequence. For instance, *Rocky II* through *Rocky V* are sequels of *Rocky*. We do not assume *Rocky IV* is a sequel of *Rocky III*, and so on. □

7.5 Association Classes

We can attach attributes to an association in much the way we did in the E/R model, in Section 1.9.[5] In UML, we create a new class, called an *association class*, and attach it to the middle of the association. The association class has its own name, but its attributes may be thought of as attributes of the association to which it attaches.

Example 39: Suppose we want to add to the association *Stars-in* between *Movies* and *Stars* some information about the compensation the star received for the movie. This information is not associated with the movie (different stars get different salaries) nor with the star (stars can get different salaries for different movies). Thus, we must attach this information with the association itself. That is, every movie-star pair has its own salary information.

Figure 39 shows the association *Stars-in* with an association class called *Compensation*. This class has two attributes, *salary* and *residuals*. Notice that

[5]However, the example there in Fig. 7 will not carry over directly, because the relationship there is 3-way.

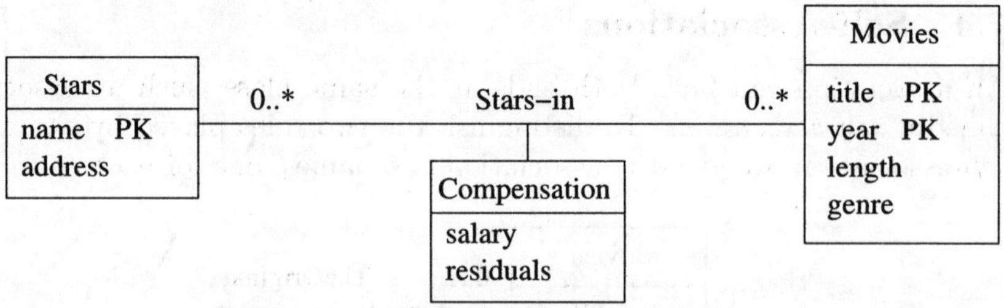

Figure 39: *Compensation* is an association class for the association *Stars-in*

there is no primary key marked for *Compensation.* When we convert a diagram such as Fig. 39 to relations, the attributes of *Compensation* will attach to tuples created for movie-star pairs, as was described for relationships in Section 5.2. □

7.6 Subclasses in UML

Any UML class can have a hierarchy of subclasses below it. The primary key comes from the root of the hierarchy, just as with E/R hierarchies. UML permits a class C to have four different kinds of subclasses below it, depending on our choices of answer to two questions:

1. *Complete versus Partial.* Is every object in the class C a member of some subclass? If so, the subclasses are *complete*; otherwise they are *partial* or *incomplete.*

2. *Disjoint versus Overlapping.* Are the subclasses *disjoint* (an object cannot be in two of the subclasses)? If an object can be in two or more of the subclasses, then the subclasses are said to be *overlapping.*

Note that these decisions are taken at each level of a hierarchy, and the decisions may be made independently at each point.

There are several interesting relationships between the classification of UML subclasses given above, the standard notion of subclasses in object-oriented systems, and the E/R notion of subclasses.

- In a typical object-oriented system, subclasses are disjoint. That is, no object can be in two classes. Of course they inherit properties from their parent class, so in a sense, an object also "belongs" in the parent class. However, the object may not also be in a sibling class.

- The E/R model automatically allows overlapping subclasses.

- Both the E/R model and object-oriented systems allow either complete or partial subclasses. That is, there is no requirement that a member of the superclass be in any subclass.

Subclasses are represented by rectangles, like any class. We assume a subclass inherits the properties (attributes and associations) from its superclass. However, any additional attributes belonging to the subclass are shown in the box for that subclass, and the subclass may have its own, additional, associations to other classes. To represent the class/subclass relationship in UML diagrams, we use a triangular, open arrow pointing to the superclass. The subclasses are usually connected by a horizontal line, feeding into the arrow.

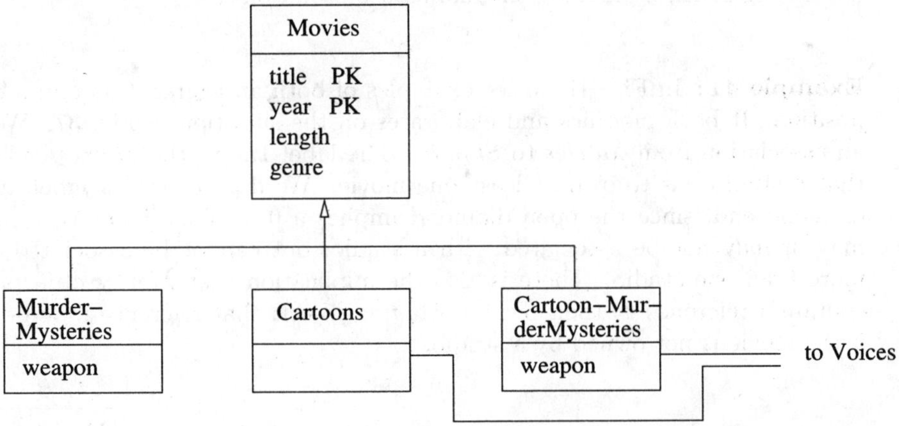

Figure 40: Cartoons and murder mysteries as disjoint subclasses of movies

Example 40: Figure 40 shows a UML variant of the subclass example from Section 1.11. However, unlike the E/R subclasses, which are of necessity overlapping, we have chosen here to make the subclasses disjoint. They are partial, of course, since many movies are neither cartoons nor murder mysteries.

Because the subclasses were chosen disjoint, there must be a third subclass for movies like *Roger Rabbit* that are both cartoons and murder mysteries. Notice that both the classes *MurderMysteries* and *Cartoon-MurderMysteries* have additional attribute *weapon*, while the two subclasses *MurderMysteries* and *Cartoon-Murder Mysteries* have associations with the unseen class *Voices*. □

7.7 Aggregations and Compositions

There are two special notations for many-one associations whose implications are rather subtle. In one sense, they reflect the object-oriented style of programming, where it is common for one class to have references to other classes among its attributes. In another sense, these special notations are really stipulations about how the diagram should be converted to relations; we discuss this aspect of the matter in Section 8.3.

An *aggregation* is a line between two classes that ends in an open diamond at one end. The implication of the diamond is that the label at that end must be 0..1, i.e., the aggregation is a many-one association from the class at the opposite end to the class at the diamond end. Although the aggregation is an association, we do not need to name it, since in practice that name will never be used in a relational implementation.

A *composition* is similar to an association, but the label at the diamond end must be 1..1. That is, every object at the opposite end from the diamond must be connected to exactly one object at the diamond end. Compositions are distinguished by making the diamond be solid black.

Example 41: In Fig. 41 we see examples of both an aggregation and a composition. It both modifies and elaborates on the situation of Fig. 37. We see an association from *Movies* to *Studios*. The label 1..* at the *Movies* end says that a studio has to own at least one movie. We do not need a label at the diamond end, since the open diamond implies a 0..1 label. That is, a movie may or may not be associated with a studio, but cannot be associated with more than one studio. There is also the implication that *Movies* objects will contain a reference to their owning *Studios* object; that reference may be null if the movie is not owned by a studio.

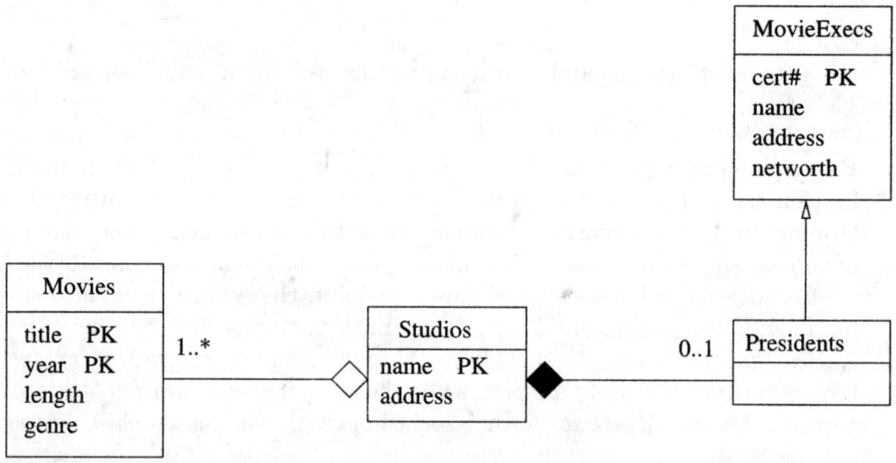

Figure 41: An aggregation from *Movies* to *Studios* and a composition from *Presidents* to *Studios*

At the right, we see the class *MovieExecs* with a subclass *Presidents*. There is a composition from *Presidents* to *Studios*. meaning that every president is the president of exactly one studio. A label 1..1 at the *Studios* end is implied by the solid diamond. The implication of the composition is that *Presidents* objects will contain a reference to a *Studios* object, and that this reference cannot be null. □

7.8 Exercises for Section 7

Exercise 7.1: Draw a UML diagram for the problem of Exercise 1.1.

Exercise 7.2: Modify your diagram from Exercise 7.1 in accordance with the requirements of Exercise 1.2.

Exercise 7.3: Repeat Exercise 1.3 using UML.

Exercise 7.4: Repeat Exercise 1.6 using UML.

Exercise 7.5: Repeat Exercise 1.7 using UML. Are your subclasses disjoint or overlapping? Are they complete or partial?

Exercise 7.6: Repeat Exercise 1.9 using UML.

Exercise 7.7: Convert the E/R diagram of Fig. 30 to a UML diagram.

! **Exercise 7.8:** How would you represent the 3-way relationship of *Contracts* among movies, stars, and studios (see Fig. 4) in UML?

! **Exercise 7.9:** Repeat Exercise 2.5 using UML.

Exercise 7.10: Usually, when we constrain associations with a label of the form $m..n$, we find that m and n are each either 0, 1, or $*$. Give some examples of associations where it would make sense for at least one of m and n to be something different.

8 From UML Diagrams to Relations

Many of the ideas needed to turn E/R diagrams into relations work for UML diagrams as well. We shall therefore briefly review the important techniques, dwelling only on points where the two modeling methods diverge.

8.1 UML-to-Relations Basics

Here is an outline of the points that should be familiar from our discussion in Section 5:

- *Classes to Relations.* For each class, create a relation whose name is the name of the class, and whose attributes are the attributes of the class.
- *Associations to Relations.* For each association, create a relation with the name of that association. The attributes of the relation are the key attributes of the two connected classes. If there is a coincidence of attributes between the two classes, rename them appropriately. If there is an association class attached to the association, include the attributes of the association class among the attributes of the relation.

Example 42: Consider the UML diagram of Fig. 36. For the three classes we create relations:

```
Movies(title, year, length genre)
Stars(name, address)
Studios(name, address)
```

For the two associations, we create relations

```
Stars-In(movieTitle, movieYear, starName)
Owns(movieTitle, movieYear, studioName)
```

Note that we have taken some liberties with the names of attributes, for clarity of intention, even though we were not required to do so.

For another example, consider the UML diagram of Fig. 39, which shows an association class. The relations for the classes *Movies* and *Stars* would be the same as above. However, for the association, we would have a relation

```
Stars-In(movieTitle, movieYear, starName, salary, residuals)
```

That is, we add to the key attributes of the associated classes, the two attributes of the association class *Compensation.* Note that there is no relation created for *Compensation* itself. □

8.2 From UML Subclasses to Relations

The three options we enumerated in Section 6 apply to UML subclass hierarchies as well. Recall these options are "E/R style" (relations for each subclass have only the key attributes and attributes of that subclass), "object-oriented" (each entity is represented in the relation for only one subclass), and "use nulls" (one relation for all subclasses). However, if we have information about whether subclasses are disjoint or overlapping, and complete or partial, then we may find one or another method more appropriate. Here are some considerations:

1. If a hierarchy is disjoint at every level, then an object-oriented representation is suggested. We do not have to consider each possible tree of subclasses when forming relations, since we know that each object can belong to only one class and its ancestors in the hierarchy. Thus, there is no possibility of an exponentially exploding number of relations being created.

2. If the hierarchy is both complete and disjoint at every level, then the task is even simpler. If we use the object-oriented approach, then we have only to construct relations for the classes at the leaves of the hierarchy.

3. If the hierarchy is large and overlapping at some or all levels, then the E/R approach is indicated. We are likely to need so many relations that the relational database schema becomes unwieldy.

8.3 From Aggregations and Compositions to Relations

Aggregations and compositions are really types of many-one associations. Thus, one approach to their representation in a relational database schema is to convert them as we do for any association in Section 8.1. Since these elements are not necessarily named in the UML diagram, we need to invent a name for the corresponding relation.

However, there is a hidden assumption that this implementation of aggregations and compositions is undesirable. Recall from Section 5.3 that when we have an entity set E and a many-one relationship R from E to another entity set F, we have the option — some would say the obligation — to combine the relation for E with the relation for R. That is, the one relation constructed from E and R has all the attributes of E plus the key attributes of F.

We suggest that aggregations and compositions be treated routinely in this manner. Construct no relation for the aggregation or composition. Rather, add to the relation for the class at the nondiamond end the key attribute(s) of the class at the diamond end. In the case of an aggregation (but not a composition), it is possible that these attributes can be null.

Example 43: Consider the UML diagram of Fig. 41. Since there is a small hierarchy, we need to decide how *MovieExecs* and *Presidents* will be translated. Let us adopt the E/R approach, so the `Presidents` relation has only the `cert#` attribute from *MovieExecs.*

The aggregation from *Movies* to *Studios* is represented by putting the key *name* for *Studios* among the attributes for the relation `Movies`. The composition from *Presidents* to *Studios* is represented by adding the key for *Studios* to the relation `Presidents` as well. No relations are constructed for the aggregation or the composition. The following are all the relations we construct from this UML diagram.

```
MovieExecs(cert#, name, address, netWorth)
Presidents(cert#, studioName)
Movies(title, year, length, genre, studioName)
Studios(name, address)
```

As before, we take some liberties with names of attributes to make our intentions clear. □

8.4 The UML Analog of Weak Entity Sets

We have not mentioned a UML notation that corresponds to the double-border notation for weak entity sets in the E/R model. There is a sense in which none is needed. The reason is that UML, unlike E/R, draws on the tradition of object-oriented systems, which takes the point of view that each object has its own *object-identity.* That is, we can distinguish two objects, even if they have the same values for each of their attributes and other properties. That object-identity is typically viewed as a reference or pointer to the object.

In UML, we can take the point of view that the objects belonging to a class likewise have object-identity. Thus, even if the stated attributes for a class do not serve to identify a unique object of the class, we can create a new attribute that serves as a key for the corresponding relation and represents the object-identity of the object.

However, it is also possible, in UML, to use a composition as we used supporting relationships for weak entity sets in the E/R model. This composition goes from the "weak" class (the class whose attributes do not provide its key) to the "supporting" class. If there are several "supporting" classes, then several compositions can be used. We shall use a special notation for a *supporting* composition: a small box attached to the *weak* class with "PK" in it will serve as the anchor for the supporting composition. The implication is that the key attribute(s) for the *supporting* class at the other end of the composition is part of the key of the weak class, along with any of the attributes of the weak class that are marked "PK." As with weak entity sets, there can be several supporting compositions and classes, and those supporting classes could themselves be weak, in which case the rule just described is applied recursively.

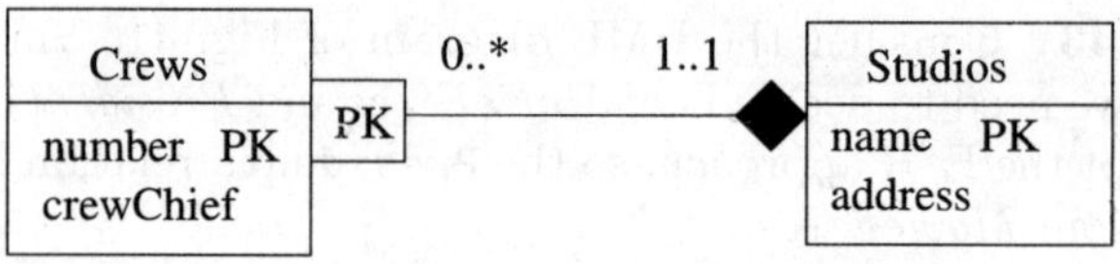

Figure 42: Weak class *Crews* supported by a composition and the class *Studios*

Example 44: Figure 42 shows the analog of the weak entity set *Crews* of Example 20. There is a composition from *Crews* to *Studios* anchored by a box labeled "PK" to indicate that this composition provides part of the key for *Crews*. □

We convert weak structures such as Fig. 42 to relations exactly as we did in Section 5.4. There is a relation for class *Studios* as usual. There is no relation for the composition, again as usual. The relation for class *Crews* includes not only its own attribute *number*, but the key for the class at the end of the composition, which is *Studios*.

Example 45: The relations for Example 44 are thus:

```
Studios(name, address)
Crews(number, crewChief, studioName)
```

As before, we renamed the attribute *name* of *Studios* in the `Crews` relation, for clarity. □

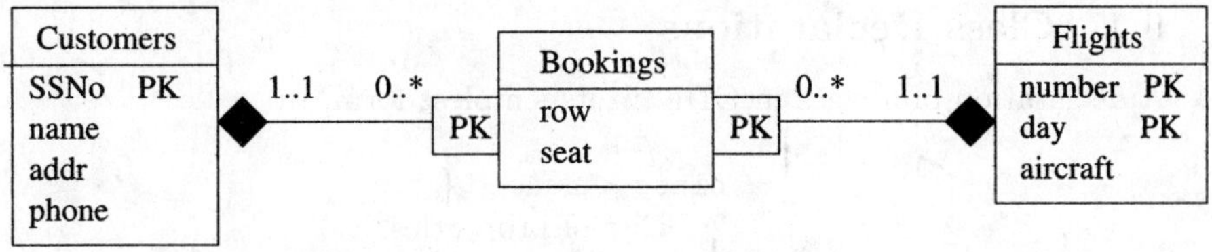

Figure 43: A UML diagram analogous to the E/R diagram of Fig. 29

8.5 Exercises for Section 8

Exercise 8.1: Convert the UML diagram of Fig. 43 to relations.

Exercise 8.2: Convert the following UML diagrams to relations:

a) Figure 37.

b) Figure 40.

c) Your solution to Exercise 7.1.

d) Your solution to Exercise 7.3.

e) Your solution to Exercise 7.4.

f) Your solution to Exercise 7.6.

! **Exercise 8.3:** How many relations do we create, using the object-oriented approach, if we have a three-level hierarchy with three subclasses of each class at the first and second levels, and that hierarchy is:

a) Disjoint and complete at each level.

b) Disjoint but not complete at each level.

c) Neither disjoint nor complete.

9 Object Definition Language

ODL (*Object Definition Language*) is a text-based language for specifying the structure of databases in object-oriented terms. Like UML, the class is the central concept in ODL. Classes in ODL have a name, attributes, and methods, just as UML classes do. Relationships, which are analogous to UML's associations, are not an independent concept in ODL, but are embedded within classes as an additional family of properties.

9.1 Class Declarations

A declaration of a class in ODL, in its simplest form, is:

```
class <name> {
    <list of properties>
};
```

That is, the keyword `class` is followed by the name of the class and a bracketed list of properties. A property can be an attribute, a relationship, or a method.

9.2 Attributes in ODL

The simplest kind of property is the *attribute*. In ODL, attributes need not be of simple types, such as integers and strings. ODL has a type system, described in Section 9.6, that allows us to form structured types and collection types (e.g., sets). For example, an attribute `address` might have a structured type with fields for the street, city, and zip code. An attribute `phones` might have a set of strings as its type, and even more complex types are possible. An attribute is represented in the declaration for its class by the keyword `attribute`, the type of the attribute, and the name of the attribute.

```
1)  class Movie {
2)      attribute string title;
3)      attribute integer year;
4)      attribute integer length;
5)      attribute enum Genres
                {drama, comedy, sciFi, teen} genre;
    };
```

Figure 44: An ODL declaration of the class `Movie`

Example 46: In Fig. 44 is an ODL declaration of the class of movies. It is not a complete declaration; we shall add more to it later. Line (1) declares `Movie` to be a class. Following line (1) are the declarations of four attributes that all `Movie` objects will have.

Lines (2), (3), and (4) declare three attributes, `title`, `year`, and `length`. The first of these is of character-string type, and the other two are integers. Line (5) declares attribute `genre` to be of enumerated type. The name of the enumeration (list of symbolic constants) is `Genres`, and the four values the attribute `genre` is allowed to take are `drama`, `comedy`, `sciFi`, and `teen`. An enumeration must have a name, which can be used to refer to the same type anywhere. □

Why Name Enumerations and Structures?

The enumeration-name `Genres` in Fig. 44 appears to play no role. However, by giving this set of symbolic constants a name, we can refer to it elsewhere, including in the declaration of other classes. In some other class, the *scoped name* `Movie::Genres` can be used to refer to the definition of the enumerated type of this name within the class `Movie`.

Example 47: In Example 46, all the attributes have primitive types. Here is an example with a complex type. We can define the class `Star` by

```
1)  class Star {
2)     attribute string name;
3)     attribute Struct Addr
           {string street, string city} address;
    };
```

Line (2) specifies an attribute `name` (of the star) that is a string. Line (3) specifies another attribute `address`. This attribute has a type that is a *record structure*. The name of this structure is `Addr`, and the type consists of two fields: `street` and `city`. Both fields are strings. In general, one can define record structure types in ODL by the keyword `Struct` and curly braces around the list of field names and their types. Like enumerations, structure types must have a name, which can be used elsewhere to refer to the same structure type. □

9.3 Relationships in ODL

An ODL relationship is declared inside a class declaration, by the keyword `relationship`, a type, and the name of the relationship. The type of a relationship describes what a single object of the class is connected to by the relationship. Typically, this type is either another class (if the relationship is many-one) or a collection type (if the relationship is one-many or many-many). We shall show complex types by example, until the full type system is described in Section 9.6.

Example 48: Suppose we want to add to the declaration of the `Movie` class from Example 46 a property that is a set of stars. More precisely, we want each `Movie` object to connect the set of `Star` objects that are its stars. The best way to represent this connection between the `Movie` and `Star` classes is with a *relationship*. We may represent this relationship by a line:

```
relationship Set<Star> stars;
```

in the declaration of class Movie. It says that in each object of class Movie there is a set of references to Star objects. The set of references is called stars. □

9.4 Inverse Relationships

Just as we might like to access the stars of a given movie, we might like to know the movies in which a given star acted. To get this information into Star objects, we can add the line

```
relationship Set<Movie> starredIn;
```

to the declaration of class Star in Example 47. However, this line and a similar declaration for Movie omits a very important aspect of the relationship between movies and stars. We expect that if a star S is in the stars set for movie M, then movie M is in the starredIn set for star S. We indicate this connection between the relationships stars and starredIn by placing in each of their declarations the keyword inverse and the name of the other relationship. If the other relationship is in some other class, as it usually is, then we refer to that relationship by its scoped name — the name of its class, followed by a double colon (::) and the name of the relationship.

Example 49: To define the relationship starredIn of class Star to be the inverse of the relationship stars in class Movie, we revise the declarations of these classes, as shown in Fig. 45 (which also contains a definition of class Studio to be discussed later). Line (6) shows the declaration of relationship stars of movies, and says that its inverse is Star::starredIn. Since relationship starredIn is defined in another class, its scoped name must be used.

Similarly, relationship starredIn is declared in line (11). Its inverse is declared by that line to be stars of class Movie, as it must be, because inverses always are linked in pairs. □

As a general rule, if a relationship R for class C associates with object x of class C with objects $y_1, y_2, \ldots, y_n$ of class D, then the inverse relationship of R associates with each of the y_i's the object x (perhaps along with other objects).

9.5 Multiplicity of Relationships

Like the binary relationships of the E/R model, a pair of inverse relationships in ODL can be classified as either many-many, many-one in either direction, or one-one. The type declarations for the pair of relationships tells us which.

1. If we have a many-many relationship between classes C and D, then in class C the type of the relationship is Set<D>, and in class D the type is Set<C>.[6]

[6]Actually, the Set could be replaced by another "collection type," such as list or bag, as discussed in Section 9.6. We shall assume all collections are sets in our exposition of relationships, however.

```
1)  class Movie {
2)     attribute string title;
3)     attribute integer year;
4)     attribute integer length;
5)     attribute enum Genres
              {drama, comedy, sciFi, teen} genre;
6)     relationship Set<Star> stars
                    inverse Star::starredIn;
7)     relationship Studio ownedBy
                    inverse Studio::owns;
    };

8)  class Star {
9)     attribute string name;
10)    attribute Struct Addr
           {string street, string city} address;
11)    relationship Set<Movie> starredIn
                    inverse Movie::stars;
    };

12) class Studio {
13)    attribute string name;
14)    attribute Star::Addr address;
15)    relationship Set<Movie> owns
                    inverse Movie::ownedBy;
    };
```

Figure 45: Some ODL classes and their relationships

2. If the relationship is many-one from C to D, then the type of the relationship in C is just D, while the type of the relationship in D is `Set<`C`>`.

3. If the relationship is many-one from D to C, then the roles of C and D are reversed in (2) above.

4. If the relationship is one-one, then the type of the relationship in C is just D, and in D it is just C.

Note that, as in the E/R model, we allow a many-one or one-one relationship to include the case where for some objects the "one" is actually "none." For instance, a many-one relationship from C to D might have a "null" value of the relationship in some of the C objects. Of course, since a D object could be associated with any set of C objects, it is also permissible for that set to be empty for some D objects.

Example 50: In Fig. 45 we have the declaration of three classes, `Movie`, `Star`, and `Studio`. The first two of these have already been introduced in Examples 46 and 47. We also discussed the relationship pair `stars` and `starredIn`. Since each of their types uses `Set`, we see that this pair represents a many-many relationship between `Star` and `Movie`.

`Studio` objects have attributes `name` and `address`; these appear in lines (13) and (14). We have used the same type for addresses of studios as we defined in class `Star` for addresses of stars.

In line (7) we see a relationship `ownedBy` from movies to studios, and the inverse of this relationship is `owns` on line (15). Since the type of `ownedBy` is `Studio`, while the type of `owns` is Set<Movie>, we see that this pair of inverse relationships is many-one from `Movie` to `Studio`. □

9.6 Types in ODL

ODL offers the database designer a type system similar to that found in C or other conventional programming languages. A type system is built from a basis of types that are defined by themselves and certain recursive rules whereby complex types are built from simpler types. In ODL, the basis consists of:

1. *Primitive types*: integer, float, character, character string, boolean, and *enumerations*. The latter are lists of symbolic names, such as `drama` in line (5) of Fig. 45.

2. *Class names*, such as `Movie`, or `Star`, which represent types that are actually structures, with components for each of the attributes and relationships of that class.

These types are combined into structured types using the following *type constructors*:

1. *Set*. If T is any type, then Set<T> denotes the type whose values are finite sets of elements of type T. Examples using the set type-constructor occur in lines (6), (11), and (15) of Fig. 45.

2. *Bag*. If T is any type, then Bag<T> denotes the type whose values are finite bags or *multisets* of elements of type T.

3. *List*. If T is any type, then List<T> denotes the type whose values are finite lists of zero or more elements of type T.

4. *Array*. If T is a type and i is an integer, then Array<T,i> denotes the type whose elements are arrays of i elements of type T. For example, Array<char,10> denotes character strings of length 10.

5. *Dictionary*. If T and S are types, then Dictionary<T,S> denotes a type whose values are finite sets of pairs. Each pair consists of a value of the *key type* T and a value of the *range type* S. The dictionary may not contain two pairs with the same key value.

Sets, Bags, and Lists

To understand the distinction between sets, bags, and lists, remember that a set has unordered elements, and only one occurrence of each element. A bag allows more than one occurrence of an element, but the elements and their occurrences are unordered. A list allows more than one occurrence of an element, but the occurrences are ordered. Thus, $\{1,2,1\}$ and $\{2,1,1\}$ are the same bag, but $(1,2,1)$ and $(2,1,1)$ are not the same list.

6. *Structures.* If $T_1, T_2, \ldots, T_n$ are types, and $F_1, F_2, \ldots, F_n$ are names of fields, then

$$\texttt{Struct N \{}T_1\ F_1,\ T_2\ F_2, \ldots,\ T_n\ F_n\texttt{\}}$$

denotes the type named N whose elements are structures with n fields. The ith field is named F_i and has type T_i. For example, line (10) of Fig. 45 showed a structure type named `Addr`, with two fields. Both fields are of type `string` and have names `street` and `city`, respectively.

The first five types — set, bag, list, array, and dictionary — are called *collection types.* There are different rules about which types may be associated with attributes and which with relationships.

- The type of a relationship is either a class type or a single use of a collection type constructor applied to a class type.
- The type of an attribute is built starting with a primitive type or types.[7] We may then apply the structure and collection type constructors as we wish, as many times as we wish.

Example 51: Some of the possible types of attributes are:

1. `integer`.
2. `Struct N {string field1, integer field2}`.
3. `List<real>`.
4. `Array<Struct N {string field1, integer field2}, 10>`.

[7]Class types may also be used, which makes the attribute behave like a "one-way" relationship. We shall not consider such attributes here.

Example (1) is a primitive type, (2) is a structure of primitive types, (3) a collection of a primitive type, and (4) a collection of structures built from primitive types.

Now, suppose the class names `Movie` and `Star` are available primitive types. Then we may construct relationship types such as `Movie` or `Bag<Star>`. However, the following are illegal as relationship types:

1. `Struct N {Movie field1, Star field2}`. Relationship types cannot involve structures.

2. `Set<integer>`. Relationship types cannot involve primitive types.

3. `Set<Array<Star, 10>>`. Relationship types cannot involve two applications of collection types.

□

9.7 Subclasses in ODL

We can declare one class C to be a subclass of another class D. To do so, follow the name C in its declaration with the keyword `extends` and the name D. Then, class C inherits all the properties of D, and may have additional properties of its own.

Example 52: Recall Example 10, where we declared cartoons to be a subclass of movies, with the additional property of a relationship from a cartoon to a set of stars that are its "voices." We can create a subclass `Cartoon` for Movie with the ODL declaration:

```
class Cartoon extends Movie {
    relationship Set<Star> voices;
};
```

Also in that example, we defined a class of murder mysteries with additional attribute `weapon`.

```
class MurderMystery extends Movie {
    attribute string weapon;
};
```

is a suitable declaration of this subclass. □

Sometimes, as in the case of a movie like "Roger Rabbit," we need a class that is a subclass of two or more other classes at the same time. In ODL, we may follow the keyword `extends` by several classes, separated by colons.[8] Thus, we may declare a fourth class by:

[8]Technically, the second and subsequent names must be "interfaces," rather than classes. Roughly, an *interface* in ODL is a class definition without an associated set of objects.

```
class CartoonMurderMystery
    extends MurderMystery : Cartoon;
```

Note that when there is multiple inheritance, there is the potential for a class to inherit two properties with the same name. The way such conflicts are resolved is implementation-dependent.

9.8 Declaring Keys in ODL

The declaration of a key or keys for a class is optional. The reason is that ODL, being object-oriented, assumes that all objects have an object-identity, as discussed in connection with UML in Section 8.4.

In ODL we may declare one or more attributes to be a key for a class by using the keyword `key` or `keys` (it doesn't matter which) followed by the attribute or attributes forming keys. If there is more than one attribute in a key, the list of attributes must be surrounded by parentheses. The key declaration itself appears inside parentheses, following the name of the class itself in the first line of its declaration.

Example 53: To declare that the set of two attributes `title` and `year` form a key for class `Movie`, we could begin its declaration:

```
class Movie (key (title, year)) {
```

We could have used `keys` in place of `key`, even though only one key is declared. □

It is possible that several sets of attributes are keys. If so, then following the word `key(s)` we may place several keys separated by commas. A key that consists of more than one attribute must have parentheses around the list of its attributes, so we can disambiguate a key of several attributes from several keys of one attribute each.

The ODL standard also allows properties other than attributes to appear in keys. There is no fundamental problem with a method or relationship being declared a key or part of a key, since keys are advisory statements that the DBMS can take advantage of or not, as it wishes. For instance, one could declare a method to be a key, meaning that on distinct objects of the class the method is guaranteed to return distinct values.

When we allow many-one relationships to appear in key declarations, we can get an effect similar to that of weak entity sets in the E/R model. We can declare that the object O_1 referred to by an object O_2 on the "many" side of the relationship, perhaps together with other properties of O_2 that are included in the key, is unique for different objects O_2. However, we should remember that there is no requirement that classes have keys; we are never obliged to handle, in some special way, classes that lack attributes of their own to form a key, as we did for weak entity sets.

Example 54: Let us review the example of a weak entity set *Crews* in Fig. 20. Recall that we hypothesized that crews were identified by their number, and the studio for which they worked, although two studios might have crews with the same number. We might declare the class `Crew` as in Fig. 46. Note that we should modify the declaration of `Studio` to include the relationship `crewsOf` that is an inverse to the relationship `unitOf` in `Crew`; we omit this change.

```
class Crew (key (number, unitOf)) {
    attribute integer number;
    attribute string crewChief;
    relationship Studio unitOf
        inverse Studio::crewsOf;
};
```

Figure 46: A ODL declaration for crews

What this key declaration asserts is that there cannot be two crews that both have the same value for the `number` attribute and are related to the same studio by `unitOf`. Notice how this assertion resembles the implication of the E/R diagram in Fig. 20, which is that the number of a crew and the name of the related studio (i.e., the key for studios) uniquely determine a crew entity. □

9.9 Exercises for Section 9

Exercise 9.1: In Exercise 1.1 was the informal description of a bank database. Render this design in ODL, including keys as appropriate.

Exercise 9.2: Modify your design of Exercise 9.1 in the ways enumerated in Exercise 1.2. Describe the changes; do not write a complete, new schema.

Exercise 9.3: Render the teams-players-fans database of Exercise 1.3 in ODL, including keys, as appropriate. Why does the complication about sets of team colors, which was mentioned in the original exercise, not present a problem in ODL?

! **Exercise 9.4:** Suppose we wish to keep a genealogy. We shall have one class, `Person`. The information we wish to record about persons includes their name (an attribute) and the following relationships: mother, father, and children. Give an ODL design for the `Person` class. Be sure to indicate the inverses of the relationships that, like `mother`, `father`, and `children`, are also relationships from `Person` to itself. Is the inverse of the `mother` relationship the `children` relationship? Why or why not? Describe each of the relationships and their inverses as sets of pairs.

! **Exercise 9.5:** Let us add to the design of Exercise 9.4 the attribute `education`. The value of this attribute is intended to be a collection of the degrees obtained by each person, including the name of the degree (e.g., B.S.), the school, and the date. This collection of structs could be a set, bag, list, or array. Describe the consequences of each of these four choices. What information could be gained or lost by making each choice? Is the information lost likely to be important in practice?

Exercise 9.6: In Exercise 4.4 we saw two examples of situations where weak entity sets were essential. Render these databases in ODL, including declarations for suitable keys.

Exercise 9.7: Give an ODL design for the registrar's database described in Exercise 1.9.

!! **Exercise 9.8:** Under what circumstances is a relationship its own inverse? *Hint*: Think about the relationship as a set of pairs, as discussed in Section 9.4.

10 From ODL Designs to Relational Designs

ODL was actually intended as the data-definition part of a language standard for object-oriented DBMS's, analogous to the SQL `CREATE TABLE` statement. Indeed, there have been some attempts to implement such a system. However, it is also possible to see ODL as a text-based, high-level design notation, from which we eventually derive a relational database schema. Thus, in this section we shall consider how to convert ODL designs into relational designs.

Much of the process is similar to that we discussed for E/R diagrams in Section 5 and for UML in Section 8. Classes become relations, and relationships become relations that connect the key attributes of the classes involved in the relationship. Yet some new problems arise for ODL, including:

1. Entity sets must have keys, but there is no such guarantee for ODL classes.

2. While attributes in E/R, UML, and the relational model are of primitive type, there is no such constraint for ODL attributes.

10.1 From ODL Classes to Relations

As a starting point, let us assume that our goal is to have one relation for each class and for that relation to have one attribute for each property. We shall see many ways in which this approach must be modified, but for the moment, let us consider the simplest possible case, where we can indeed convert classes to relations and properties to attributes. The restrictions we assume are:

1. All properties of the class are attributes (not relationships or methods).

2. The types of the attributes are primitive (not structures or sets).

In this case, the ODL class looks almost like an entity set or a UML class. Although there might be no key for the ODL class, ODL assumes object-identity. We can create an artificial attribute to represent the object-identity and serve as a key for the relation; this issue was introduced for UML in Section 8.4.

Example 55: Figure 47 is an ODL description of movie executives. No key is listed, and we do not assume that `name` uniquely determines a movie executive (unlike stars, who will make sure their chosen name is unique).

```
class MovieExec {
    attribute string name;
    attribute string address;
    attribute integer netWorth;
};
```

Figure 47: The class `MovieExec`

We create a relation with the same name as the class. The relation has four attributes, one for each attribute of the class, and one for the object-identity:

```
MovieExecs(cert#, name, address, netWorth)
```

We use `cert#` as the key attribute, representing the object-identity. □

10.2 Complex Attributes in Classes

Even when a class' properties are all attributes we may have some difficulty converting the class to a relation. The reason is that attributes in ODL can have complex types such as structures, sets, bags, or lists. On the other hand, a fundamental principle of the relational model is that a relation's attributes have a primitive type, such as numbers and strings. Thus, we must find some way to represent complex attribute types as relations.

Record structures whose fields are themselves primitive are the easiest to handle. We simply expand the structure definition, making one attribute of the relation for each field of the structure.

Example 56: In Fig. 48 is a declaration for class `Star`, with only attributes as properties. The attribute `name` is of primitive type, but attribute `address` is a structure with two fields, `street` and `city`. We represent this class by the relation:

```
Star(name, street, city)
```

The key is `name`, and the attributes `street` and `city` represent the structure `address`. □

```
class Star (key name) {
   attribute string name;
   attribute Struct Addr
       {string street, string city} address;
};
```

Figure 48: Class with a structured attribute

10.3 Representing Set-Valued Attributes

However, record structures are not the most complex kind of attribute that can appear in ODL class definitions. Values can also be built using type constructors `Set`, `Bag`, `List`, `Array`, and `Dictionary` from Section 9.6. Each presents its own problems when migrating to the relational model. We shall only discuss the `Set` constructor, which is the most common, in detail.

One approach to representing a set of values for an attribute A is to make one tuple for each value. That tuple includes the appropriate values for all the other attributes besides A. This approach works, although it is likely to produce unnormalized relations, as we shall see in the next example.

```
class Star (key name) {
   attribute string name;
   attribute Set<
           Struct Addr {string street, string city}
       > address;
   attribute Date birthdate;
};
```

Figure 49: Stars with a set of addresses and a birthdate

Example 57: Figure 49 shows a new definition of the class `Star`, in which we have allowed stars to have a set of addresses and also added a nonkey, primitive attribute `birthdate`. The `birthdate` attribute can be an attribute of the `Star` relation, whose schema now becomes:

```
Star(name, street, city, birthdate)
```

Unfortunately, this relation exhibits anomalies. If Carrie Fisher has two addresses, say a home and a beach house, then she is represented by two tuples in the relation `Star`. If Harrison Ford has an empty set of addresses, then he does not appear at all in `Star`. A typical set of tuples for `Star` is shown in Fig. 50.

Although `name` is a key for the class `Star`, our need to have several tuples for one star to represent all their addresses means that `name` is *not* a key for

name	*street*	*city*	*birthdate*
Carrie Fisher	123 Maple St.	Hollywood	9/9/99
Carrie Fisher	5 Locust Ln.	Malibu	9/9/99
Mark Hamill	456 Oak Rd.	Brentwood	8/8/88

Figure 50: Adding birthdates

the relation Star. In fact, the key for that relation is {name, street, city}. Thus, the functional dependency

$$\texttt{name} \rightarrow \texttt{birthdate}$$

is a BCNF violation and the multivalued dependency

$$\texttt{name} \twoheadrightarrow \texttt{street city}$$

is a 4NF violation as well. □

There are several options regarding how to handle set-valued attributes that appear in a class declaration along with other attributes, set-valued or not. One approach is to separate out each set-valued attribute as if it were a many-many relationship between the objects of the class and the values that appear in the sets.

An alternative approach is to place all attributes, set-valued or not, in the schema for the relation, then use normalization techniques to eliminate the resulting BCNF and 4NF violations. Notice that any set-valued attribute in conjunction with any single-valued attribute leads to a BNCF violation, as in Example 57. Two set-valued attributes in the same class declaration will lead to a 4NF violation, even if there are no single-valued attributes.

10.4 Representing Other Type Constructors

Besides record structures and sets, an ODL class definition could use Bag, List, Array, or Dictionary to construct values. To represent a bag (multiset), in which a single object can be a member of the bag n times, we cannot simply introduce into a relation n identical tuples.[9] Instead, we could add to the relation schema another attribute count representing the number of times that

[9]To be precise, we cannot introduce identical tuples into relations of an abstract relational model. However, SQL-based relational DBMS's *do* allow duplicate tuples; i.e., relations are bags rather than sets in SQL. If queries are likely to ask for tuple counts, we advise using a scheme such as that described here, even if your DBMS allows duplicate tuples.

each element is a member of the bag. For instance, suppose that `address` in Fig. 49 were a bag instead of a set. We could say that 123 Maple St., Hollywood is Carrie Fisher's address twice and 5 Locust Ln., Malibu is her address 3 times (whatever that may mean) by

name	*street*	*city*	*count*
Carrie Fisher	123 Maple St.	Hollywood	2
Carrie Fisher	5 Locust Ln.	Malibu	3

A list of addresses could be represented by a new attribute `position`, indicating the position in the list. For instance, we could show Carrie Fisher's addresses as a list, with Hollywood first, by:

name	*street*	*city*	*position*
Carrie Fisher	123 Maple St.	Hollywood	1
Carrie Fisher	5 Locust Ln.	Malibu	2

A fixed-length array of addresses could be represented by attributes for each position in the array. For instance, if `address` were to be an array of two street-city structures, we could represent `Star` objects as:

name	*street1*	*city1*	*street2*	*city2*
Carrie Fisher	123 Maple St.	Hollywood	5 Locust Ln.	Malibu

Finally, a dictionary could be represented as a set, but with attributes for both the key-value and range-value components of the pairs that are members of the dictionary. For instance, suppose that instead of star's addresses, we really wanted to keep, for each star, a dictionary giving the mortgage holder for each of their homes. Then the dictionary would have address as the key value and bank name as the range value. A hypothetical rendering of the Carrie-Fisher object with a dictionary attribute is:

name	*street*	*city*	*mortgage-holder*
Carrie Fisher	123 Maple St.	Hollywood	Bank of Burbank
Carrie Fisher	5 Locust Ln.	Malibu	Torrance Trust

Of course attribute types in ODL may involve more than one type constructor. If a type is any collection type besides dictionary applied to a structure (e.g., a set of structs), then we may apply the techniques from Sections 10.3 or 10.4 as if the struct were an atomic value, and then replace the single attribute representing the atomic value by several attributes, one for each field of the struct. This strategy was used in the examples above, where the address is a struct. The case of a dictionary applied to structs is similar and left as an exercise.

There are many reasons to limit the complexity of attribute types to an optional struct followed by an optional collection type. We mentioned in Section 1.1 that some versions of the E/R model allow exactly this much generality in the types of attributes, although we restricted ourselves to attributes of primitive type in the E/R model. We recommend that, if you are going to use an ODL design for the purpose of eventual translation to a relational database schema, you similarly limit yourself. We take up in the exercises some options for dealing with more complex types as attributes.

10.5 Representing ODL Relationships

Usually, an ODL class definition will contain relationships to other ODL classes. As in the E/R model, we can create for each relationship a new relation that connects the keys of the two related classes. However, in ODL, relationships come in inverse pairs, and we must create only one relation for each pair.

When a relationship is many-one, we have an option to combine it with the relation that is constructed for the class on the "many" side. Doing so has the effect of combining two relations that have a common key, as we discussed in Section 5.3. It therefore does not cause a BCNF violation and is a legitimate and commonly followed option.

10.6 Exercises for Section 10

Exercise 10.1: Convert your ODL designs from the following exercises to relational database schemas.

a) Exercise 9.1.

b) Exercise 9.2 (include all four of the modifications specified by that exercise).

c) Exercise 9.3.

d) Exercise 9.4.

e) Exercise 9.5.

! **Exercise 10.2:** Consider an attribute of type `Dictionary` with key and range types both structs of primitive types. Show how to convert a class with an attribute of this type to a relation.

Exercise 10.3: We mentioned that when attributes are of a type more complex than a collection of structs, it becomes tricky to convert them to relations; in particular, it becomes necessary to create some intermediate concepts and relations for them. The following sequence of questions will examine increasingly more complex types and how to represent them as relations.

a) A *card* can be represented as a struct with fields `rank` $(2, 3, \ldots, 10$, Jack, Queen, King, and Ace) and `suit` (Clubs, Diamonds, Hearts, and Spades). Give a suitable definition of a structured type `Card`. This definition should be independent of any class declarations but available to them all.

b) A *hand* is a set of cards. The number of cards may vary. Give a declaration of a class `Hand` whose objects are hands. That is, this class declaration has an attribute `theHand`, whose type is a hand.

! c) Convert your class declaration `Hand` from (b) to a relation schema.

d) A *poker hand* is a set of five cards. Repeat (b) and (c) for poker hands.

! e) A *deal* is a set of pairs, each pair consisting of the name of a player and a hand for that player. Declare a class `Deal`, whose objects are deals. That is, this class declaration has an attribute `theDeal`, whose type is a deal.

f) Repeat (e), but restrict hands of a deal to be hands of exactly five cards.

g) Repeat (e), using a dictionary for a deal. You may assume the names of players in a deal are unique.

!! h) Convert your class declaration from (e) to a relational database schema.

! i) Suppose we defined deals to be sets of sets of cards, with no player associated with each hand (set of cards). It is proposed that we represent such deals by a relation schema `Deals(dealID, card)`, meaning that the card was a member of one of the hands in the deal with the given ID. What, if anything, is wrong with this representation? How would you fix the problem?

Exercise 10.4: Suppose we have a class C defined by

```
class C (key a) {
    attribute string a;
    attribute T b;
};
```

where T is some type. Give the relation schema for the relation derived from C and indicate its key attributes if T is:

a) `Set<Struct S {string f, string g}>`

! b) `Bag<Struct S {string f, string g}>`

! c) `List<Struct S {string f, string }>`

! d) `Dictionary<Struct K {string f, string g}, Struct R {string i, string j}>`

11 Summary

- *The Entity-Relationship Model*: In the E/R model we describe entity sets, relationships among entity sets, and attributes of entity sets and relationships. Members of entity sets are called entities.

- *Entity-Relationship Diagrams*: We use rectangles, diamonds, and ovals to draw entity sets, relationships, and attributes, respectively.

- *Multiplicity of Relationships*: Binary relationships can be one-one, many-one, or many-many. In a one-one relationship, an entity of either set can be associated with at most one entity of the other set. In a many-one relationship, each entity of the "many" side is associated with at most one entity of the other side. Many-many relationships place no restriction.

- *Good Design*: Designing databases effectively requires that we represent the real world faithfully, that we select appropriate elements (e.g., relationships, attributes), and that we avoid redundancy — saying the same thing twice or saying something in an indirect or overly complex manner.

- *Subclasses*: The E/R model uses a special relationship *isa* to represent the fact that one entity set is a special case of another. Entity sets may be connected in a hierarchy with each child node a special case of its parent. Entities may have components belonging to any subtree of the hierarchy, as long as the subtree includes the root.

- *Weak Entity Sets*: These require attributes of some supporting entity set(s) to identify their own entities. A special notation involving diamonds and rectangles with double borders is used to distinguish weak entity sets.

- *Converting Entity Sets to Relations*: The relation for an entity set has one attribute for each attribute of the entity set. An exception is a weak entity set E, whose relation must also have attributes for the key attributes of its supporting entity sets.

- *Converting Relationships to Relations*: The relation for an E/R relationship has attributes corresponding to the key attributes of each entity set that participates in the relationship. However, if a relationship is a supporting relationship for some weak entity set, it is not necessary to produce a relation for that relationship.

- *Converting Isa Hierarchies to Relations*: One approach is to create a relation for each entity set with the key attributes of the hierarchy's root plus the attributes of the entity set itself. A second approach is to create a relation for each possible subset of the entity sets in the hierarchy, and create for each entity one tuple; that tuple is in the relation for exactly the set of entity sets to which the entity belongs. A third approach is to create only one relation and to use null values for those attributes that do not apply to the entity represented by a given tuple.

- *Unified Modeling Language*: In UML, we describe classes and associations between classes. Classes are analogous to E/R entity sets, and associations are like binary E/R relationships. Special kinds of many-one associations, called aggregations and compositions, are used and have implications as to how they are translated to relations.

- *UML Subclass Hierarchies*: UML permits classes to have subclasses, with inheritance from the superclass. The subclasses of a class can be complete or partial, and they can be disjoint or overlapping.

- *Converting UML Diagrams to Relations*: The methods are similar to those used for the E/R model. Classes become relations and associations become relations connecting the keys of the associated classes. Aggregations and compositions are combined with the relation constructed from the class at the "many" end.

- *Object Definition Language*: This language is a notation for formally describing the schemas of databases in an object-oriented style. One defines classes, which may have three kinds of properties: attributes, methods, and relationships.

- *ODL Relationships*: A relationship in ODL must be binary. It is represented, in the two classes it connects, by names that are declared to be inverses of one another. Relationships can be many-many, many-one, or one-one, depending on whether the types of the pair are declared to be a single object or a set of objects.

- *The ODL Type System*: ODL allows types to be constructed, beginning with class names and atomic types such as integer, by applying any of the following type constructors: structure formation, set-of, bag-of, list-of, array-of, and dictionary-of.

- *Keys in ODL*: Keys are optional in ODL. We can declare one or more keys, but because objects have an object-ID that is not one of its properties, a system implementing ODL can tell the difference between objects, even if they have identical values for all properties.

- *Converting ODL Classes to Relations*: The method is the same as for E/R or UML, except if the class has attributes of complex type. If that happens the resulting relation may be unnormalized and will have to be decomposed. It may also be necessary to create a new attribute to represent the object-identity of objects and serve as a key.

- *Converting ODL Relationships to Relations*: The method is the same as for E/R relationships, except that we must first pair ODL relationships and their inverses, and create only one relation for the pair.

12 References

The original paper on the Entity-Relationship model is [5]. Two books on the subject of E/R design are [2] and [7].

The manual defining ODL is [4]. One can also find more about the history of object-oriented database systems from [1], [3], and [6].

1. F. Bancilhon, C. Delobel, and P. Kanellakis, *Building an Object-Oriented Database System*, Morgan-Kaufmann, San Francisco, 1992.

2. Carlo Batini, S. Ceri, S. B. Navathe, and Carol Batini, *Conceptual Database Design: an Entity/Relationship Approach*, Addison-Wesley, Boston MA, 1991.

3. R. G. G. Cattell, *Object Data Management*, Addison-Wesley, Reading, MA, 1994.

4. R. G. G. Cattell (ed.), *The Object Database Standard: ODMG–99*, Morgan-Kaufmann, San Francisco, 1999.

5. P. P. Chen, "The entity-relationship model: toward a unified view of data," *ACM Trans. on Database Systems* **1**:1, pp. 9–36, 1976.

6. W. Kim (ed.), *Modern Database Systems: The Object Model, Interoperability, and Beyond*, ACM Press, New York, 1994.

7. B. Thalheim, "Fundamentals of Entity-Relationship Modeling," Springer-Verlag, Berlin, 2000.

Algebraic and Logical Query Languages

We start in this discussion with two abstract programming languages, one algebraic and the other logic-based. In this chapter, we extend set-based algebra to bags, which better reflect the way the relational model is implemented in practice. We also extend the algebra so it can handle several more operations than were described previously; for example, we need to do aggregations (e.g., averages) of columns of a relation.

We close the chapter with another form of query language, based on logic. This language, called "Datalog," allows us to express queries by describing the desired results, rather than by giving an algorithm to compute the results, as relational algebra requires.

1 Relational Operations on Bags

In this section, we shall consider relations that are bags (multisets) rather than sets. That is, we shall allow the same tuple to appear more than once in a relation. When relations are bags, there are changes that need to be made to the definition of some relational operations, as we shall see. First, let us look at a simple example of a relation that is a bag but not a set.

Example 1: The relation in Fig. 1 is a bag of tuples. In it, the tuple $(1, 2)$ appears three times and the tuple $(3, 4)$ appears once. If Fig. 1 were a set-valued relation, we would have to eliminate two occurrences of the tuple $(1, 2)$. In a bag-valued relation, we *do* allow multiple occurrences of the same tuple, but like sets, the order of tuples does not matter. □

A	B
1	2
3	4
1	2
1	2

Figure 1: A bag

1.1 Why Bags?

As we mentioned, commercial DBMS's implement relations that are bags, rather than sets. An important motivation for relations as bags is that some relational operations are considerably more efficient if we use the bag model. For example:

1. To take the union of two relations as bags, we simply copy one relation and add to the copy all the tuples of the other relation. There is no need to eliminate duplicate copies of a tuple that happens to be in both relations.

2. When we project relation as sets, we need to compare each projected tuple with all the other projected tuples, to make sure that each projection appears only once. However, if we can accept a bag as the result, then we simply project each tuple and add it to the result; no comparison with other projected tuples is necessary.

A	B	C
1	2	5
3	4	6
1	2	7
1	2	8

Figure 2: Bag for Example 2

Example 2: The bag of Fig. 1 could be the result of projecting the relation shown in Fig. 2 onto attributes A and B, provided we allow the result to be a bag and do not eliminate the duplicate occurrences of $(1, 2)$. Had we used the ordinary projection operator of relational algebra, and therefore eliminated duplicates, the result would be only:

A	B
1	2
3	4

Note that the bag result, although larger, can be computed more quickly, since there is no need to compare each tuple $(1,2)$ or $(3,4)$ with previously generated tuples. □

Another motivation for relations as bags is that there are some situations where the expected answer can only be obtained if we use bags, at least temporarily. Here is an example.

Example 3: Suppose we want to take the average of the A-components of a set-valued relation such as Fig. 2. We could not use the set model to think of the relation projected onto attribute A. As a set, the average value of A is 2, because there are only two values of A — 1 and 3 — in Fig. 2, and their average is 2. However, if we treat the A-column in Fig. 2 as a bag $\{1,3,1,1\}$, we get the correct average of A, which is 1.5, among the four tuples of Fig. 2. □

1.2 Union, Intersection, and Difference of Bags

These three operations have new definitions for bags. Suppose that R and S are bags, and that tuple t appears n times in R and m times in S. Note that either n or m (or both) can be 0. Then:

- In the bag union $R \cup S$, tuple t appears $n+m$ times.
- In the bag intersection $R \cap S$, tuple t appears $\min(n,m)$ times.
- In the bag difference $R - S$, tuple t appears $\max(0, n-m)$ times. That is, if tuple t appears in R more times than it appears in S, then t appears in $R - S$ the number of times it appears in R, minus the number of times it appears in S. However, if t appears at least as many times in S as it appears in R, then t does not appear at all in $R - S$. Intuitively, occurrences of t in S each "cancel" one occurrence in R.

Example 4: Let R be the relation of Fig. 1, that is, a bag in which tuple $(1,2)$ appears three times and $(3,4)$ appears once. Let S be the bag

A	B
1	2
3	4
3	4
5	6

Then the bag union $R \cup S$ is the bag in which $(1,2)$ appears four times (three times for its occurrences in R and once for its occurrence in S); $(3,4)$ appears three times, and $(5,6)$ appears once.

The bag intersection $R \cap S$ is the bag

A	B
1	2
3	4

with one occurrence each of (1, 2) and (3, 4). That is, (1, 2) appears three times in R and once in S, and $\min(3, 1) = 1$, so (1, 2) appears once in $R \cap S$. Similarly, (3, 4) appears $\min(1, 2) = 1$ time in $R \cap S$. Tuple (5, 6), which appears once in S but zero times in R appears $\min(0, 1) = 0$ times in $R \cap S$. In this case, the result happens to be a set, but any set is also a bag.

The bag difference $R - S$ is the bag

A	B
1	2
1	2

To see why, notice that (1, 2) appears three times in R and once in S, so in $R - S$ it appears $\max(0, 3 - 1) = 2$ times. Tuple (3, 4) appears once in R and twice in S, so in $R - S$ it appears $\max(0, 1 - 2) = 0$ times. No other tuple appears in R, so there can be no other tuples in $R - S$.

As another example, the bag difference $S - R$ is the bag

A	B
3	4
5	6

Tuple (3, 4) appears once because that is the number of times it appears in S minus the number of times it appears in R. Tuple (5, 6) appears once in $S - R$ for the same reason. □

1.3 Projection of Bags

We have already illustrated the projection of bags. As we saw in Example 2, each tuple is processed independently during the projection. If R is the bag of Fig. 2 and we compute the bag-projection $\pi_{A,B}(R)$, then we get the bag of Fig. 1.

If the elimination of one or more attributes during the projection causes the same tuple to be created from several tuples, these duplicate tuples are not eliminated from the result of a bag-projection. Thus, the three tuples (1, 2, 5), (1, 2, 7), and (1, 2, 8) of the relation R from Fig. 2 each gave rise to the same tuple (1, 2) after projection onto attributes A and B. In the bag result, there are three occurrences of tuple (1, 2), while in the set-projection, this tuple appears only once.

Bag Operations on Sets

Imagine we have two sets R and S. Every set may be thought of as a bag; the bag just happens to have at most one occurrence of any tuple. Suppose we intersect $R \cap S$, but we think of R and S as bags and use the bag intersection rule. Then we get the same result as we would get if we thought of R and S as sets. That is, thinking of R and S as bags, a tuple t is in $R \cap S$ the minimum of the number of times it is in R and S. Since R and S are sets, t can be in each only 0 or 1 times. Whether we use the bag or set intersection rules, we find that t can appear at most once in $R \cap S$, and it appears once exactly when it is in both R and S. Similarly, if we use the bag difference rule to compute $R - S$ or $S - R$ we get exactly the same result as if we used the set rule.

However, union behaves differently, depending on whether we think of R and S as sets or bags. If we use the bag rule to compute $R \cup S$, then the result may not be a set, even if R and S are sets. In particular, if tuple t appears in both R and S, then t appears twice in $R \cup S$ if we use the bag rule for union. But if we use the set rule then t appears only once in $R \cup S$.

1.4 Selection on Bags

To apply a selection to a bag, we apply the selection condition to each tuple independently. As always with bags, we do not eliminate duplicate tuples in the result.

Example 5: If R is the bag

A	B	C
1	2	5
3	4	6
1	2	7
1	2	7

then the result of the bag-selection $\sigma_{C \geq 6}(R)$ is

A	B	C
3	4	6
1	2	7
1	2	7

That is, all but the first tuple meets the selection condition. The last two tuples, which are duplicates in R, are each included in the result. □

Algebraic Laws for Bags

An algebraic law is an equivalence between two expressions of relational algebra whose arguments are variables standing for relations. The equivalence asserts that no matter what relations we substitute for these variables, the two expressions define the same relation. An example of a well-known law is the commutative law for union: $R \cup S = S \cup R$. This law happens to hold whether we regard relation-variables R and S as standing for sets or bags. However, there are a number of other laws that hold when relational algebra is applied to sets but that do not hold when relations are interpreted as bags. A simple example of such a law is the distributive law of set difference over union, $(R \cup S) - T = (R - T) \cup (S - T)$. This law holds for sets but not for bags. To see why it fails for bags, suppose R, S, and T each have one copy of tuple t. Then the expression on the left has one t, while the expression on the right has none. As sets, neither would have t. Some exploration of algebraic laws for bags appears in Exercises 1.1 and 1.2.

1.5 Product of Bags

The rule for the Cartesian product of bags is the expected one. Each tuple of one relation is paired with each tuple of the other, regardless of whether it is a duplicate or not. As a result, if a tuple r appears in a relation R m times, and tuple s appears n times in relation S, then in the product $R \times S$, the tuple rs will appear mn times.

Example 6: Let R and S be the bags shown in Fig. 3. Then the product $R \times S$ consists of six tuples, as shown in Fig. 3(c). Note that the usual convention regarding attribute names that we developed for set-relations applies equally well to bags. Thus, the attribute B, which belongs to both relations R and S, appears twice in the product, each time prefixed by one of the relation names. □

1.6 Joins of Bags

Joining bags presents no surprises. We compare each tuple of one relation with each tuple of the other, decide whether or not this pair of tuples joins successfully, and if so we put the resulting tuple in the answer. When constructing the answer, we do not eliminate duplicate tuples.

Example 7: The natural join $R \bowtie S$ of the relations R and S seen in Fig. 3 is

A	B
1	2
1	2

(a) The relation R

B	C
2	3
4	5
4	5

(b) The relation S

A	R.B	S.B	C
1	2	2	3
1	2	2	3
1	2	4	5
1	2	4	5
1	2	4	5
1	2	4	5

(c) The product $R \times S$

Figure 3: Computing the product of bags

A	B	C
1	2	3
1	2	3

That is, tuple $(1,2)$ of R joins with $(2,3)$ of S. Since there are two copies of $(1,2)$ in R and one copy of $(2,3)$ in S, there are two pairs of tuples that join to give the tuple $(1,2,3)$. No other tuples from R and S join successfully.

As another example on the same relations R and S, the theta-join

$$R \bowtie_{R.B<S.B} S$$

produces the bag

A	R.B	S.B	C
1	2	4	5
1	2	4	5
1	2	4	5
1	2	4	5

The computation of the join is as follows. Tuple $(1, 2)$ from R and $(4, 5)$ from S meet the join condition. Since each appears twice in its relation, the number of times the joined tuple appears in the result is 2×2 or 4. The other possible join of tuples — $(1, 2)$ from R with $(2, 3)$ from S — fails to meet the join condition, so this combination does not appear in the result. □

1.7 Exercises for Section 1

! **Exercise 1.1:** Certain algebraic laws for relations as sets also hold for relations as bags. Explain why each of the laws below hold for bags as well as sets.

a) The associative law for union: $(R \cup S) \cup T = R \cup (S \cup T)$.

b) The associative law for intersection: $(R \cap S) \cap T = R \cap (S \cap T)$.

c) The associative law for natural join: $(R \bowtie S) \bowtie T = R \bowtie (S \bowtie T)$.

d) The commutative law for union: $(R \cup S) = (S \cup R)$.

e) The commutative law for intersection: $(R \cap S) = (S \cap R)$.

f) The commutative law for natural join: $(R \bowtie S) = (S \bowtie R)$.

g) $\pi_L(R \cup S) = \pi_L(R) \cup \pi_L(S)$. Here, L is an arbitrary list of attributes.

h) The distributive law of union over intersection:

$$R \cup (S \cap T) = (R \cup S) \cap (R \cup T)$$

i) $\sigma_{C \text{ AND } D}(R) = \sigma_C(R) \cap \sigma_D(R)$. Here, C and D are arbitrary conditions about the tuples of R.

!! **Exercise 1.2:** The following algebraic laws hold for sets but not for bags. Explain why they hold for sets and give counterexamples to show that they do not hold for bags.

a) $(R \cap S) - T = R \cap (S - T)$.

b) The distributive law of intersection over union:

$$R \cap (S \cup T) = (R \cap S) \cup (R \cap T)$$

c) $\sigma_{C \text{ OR } D}(R) = \sigma_C(R) \cup \sigma_D(R)$. Here, C and D are arbitrary conditions about the tuples of R.

2 Extended Operators of Relational Algebra

To classical relational algebra Section 1 introduced the modifications necessary to treat relations as bags of tuples rather than sets. These ideas serve as a foundation for most of modern query languages. However, languages such as SQL have several other operations that have proved quite important in applications. Thus, a full treatment of relational operations must include a number of other operators, which we introduce in this section. The additions:

1. The *duplicate-elimination operator* δ turns a bag into a set by eliminating all but one copy of each tuple.

2. *Aggregation operators*, such as sums or averages, are not operations of relational algebra, but are used by the grouping operator (described next). Aggregation operators apply to attributes (columns) of a relation; e.g., the sum of a column produces the one number that is the sum of all the values in that column.

3. *Grouping* of tuples according to their value in one or more attributes has the effect of partitioning the tuples of a relation into "groups." Aggregation can then be applied to columns within each group, giving us the ability to express a number of queries that are impossible to express in the classical relational algebra. The *grouping operator* γ is an operator that combines the effect of grouping and aggregation.

4. *Extended projection* gives additional power to the operator π. In addition to projecting out some columns, in its generalized form π can perform computations involving the columns of its argument relation to produce new columns.

5. The *sorting operator* τ turns a relation into a list of tuples, sorted according to one or more attributes. This operator should be used judiciously, because some relational-algebra operators do not make sense on lists. We can, however, apply selections or projections to lists and expect the order of elements on the list to be preserved in the output.

6. The *outerjoin* operator is a variant of the join that avoids losing dangling tuples. In the result of the outerjoin, dangling tuples are "padded" with the null value, so the dangling tuples can be represented in the output.

2.1 Duplicate Elimination

Sometimes, we need an operator that converts a bag to a set. For that purpose, we use $\delta(R)$ to return the set consisting of one copy of every tuple that appears one or more times in relation R.

Example 8: If R is the relation

A	B
1	2
3	4
1	2
1	2

from Fig. 1, then $\delta(R)$ is

A	B
1	2
3	4

Note that the tuple $(1, 2)$, which appeared three times in R, appears only once in $\delta(R)$. □

2.2 Aggregation Operators

There are several operators that apply to sets or bags of numbers or strings. These operators are used to summarize or "aggregate" the values in one column of a relation, and thus are referred to as *aggregation* operators. The standard operators of this type are:

1. `SUM` produces the sum of a column with numerical values.

2. `AVG` produces the average of a column with numerical values.

3. `MIN` and `MAX`, applied to a column with numerical values, produces the smallest or largest value, respectively. When applied to a column with character-string values, they produce the lexicographically (alphabetically) first or last value, respectively.

4. `COUNT` produces the number of (not necessarily distinct) values in a column. Equivalently, `COUNT` applied to any attribute of a relation produces the number of tuples of that relation, including duplicates.

Example 9: Consider the relation

A	*B*
1	2
3	4
1	2
1	2

Some examples of aggregations on the attributes of this relation are:

1. `SUM(B)` $= 2 + 4 + 2 + 2 = 10$.
2. `AVG(A)` $= (1 + 3 + 1 + 1)/4 = 1.5$.
3. `MIN(A)` $= 1$.
4. `MAX(B)` $= 4$.
5. `COUNT(A)` $= 4$.

□

2.3 Grouping

Often we do not want simply the average or some other aggregation of an entire column. Rather, we need to consider the tuples of a relation in groups, corresponding to the value of one or more other columns, and we aggregate only within each group. As an example, suppose we wanted to compute the total number of minutes of movies produced by each studio, i.e., a relation such as:

studioName	*sumOfLengths*
Disney	12345
MGM	54321
...	...

Starting with the relation

```
Movies(title, year, length, genre, studioName, producerC#)
```

we must group the tuples according to their value for attribute `studioName`. We must then sum the `length` column within each group. That is, we imagine that the tuples of `Movies` are grouped as suggested in Fig. 4, and we apply the aggregation `SUM(length)` to each group independently.

studioName	
Disney	
Disney	
Disney	
MGM	
MGM	
∘	
∘	
∘	

Figure 4: A relation with imaginary division into groups

2.4 The Grouping Operator

We shall now introduce an operator that allows us to group a relation and/or aggregate some columns. If there is grouping, then the aggregation is within groups.

The subscript used with the γ operator is a list L of elements, each of which is either:

a) An attribute of the relation R to which the γ is applied; this attribute is one of the attributes by which R will be grouped. This element is said to be a *grouping attribute.*

b) An aggregation operator applied to an attribute of the relation. To provide a name for the attribute corresponding to this aggregation in the result, an arrow and new name are appended to the aggregation. The underlying attribute is said to be an *aggregated attribute.*

The relation returned by the expression $\gamma_L(R)$ is constructed as follows:

1. Partition the tuples of R into *groups.* Each group consists of all tuples having one particular assignment of values to the grouping attributes in the list L. If there are no grouping attributes, the entire relation R is one group.

2. For each group, produce one tuple consisting of:

   i. The grouping attributes' values for that group and

   ii. The aggregations, over all tuples of that group, for the aggregated attributes on list L.

Example 10: Suppose we have the relation

```
StarsIn(title, year, starName)
```

δ is a Special Case of γ

Technically, the δ operator is redundant. If $R(A_1, A_2, \ldots, A_n)$ is a relation, then $\delta(R)$ is equivalent to $\gamma_{A_1,A_2,\ldots,A_n}(R)$. That is, to eliminate duplicates, we group on all the attributes of the relation and do no aggregation. Then each group corresponds to a tuple that is found one or more times in R. Since the result of γ contains exactly one tuple from each group, the effect of this "grouping" is to eliminate duplicates. However, because δ is such a common and important operator, we shall continue to consider it separately when we study algebraic laws and algorithms for implementing the operators.

One can also see γ as an extension of the projection operator on sets. That is, $\gamma_{A_1,A_2,\ldots,A_n}(R)$ is also the same as $\pi_{A_1,A_2,\ldots,A_n}(R)$, if R is a set. However, if R is a bag, then γ eliminates duplicates while π does not.

and we wish to find, for each star who has appeared in at least three movies, the earliest year in which they appeared. The first step is to group, using `starName` as a grouping attribute. We clearly must compute for each group the `MIN(year)` aggregate. However, in order to decide which groups satisfy the condition that the star appears in at least three movies, we must also compute the `COUNT(title)` aggregate for each group.

We begin with the grouping expression

$$\gamma_{starName,\ \mathtt{MIN}(year)\rightarrow minYear,\ \mathtt{COUNT}(title)\rightarrow ctTitle}(\mathtt{StarsIn})$$

The first two columns of the result of this expression are needed for the query result. The third column is an auxiliary attribute, which we have named `ctTitle`; it is needed to determine whether a star has appeared in at least three movies. That is, we continue the algebraic expression for the query by selecting for `ctTitle >= 3` and then projecting onto the first two columns. An expression tree for the query is shown in Fig. 5. □

2.5 Extending the Projection Operator

Let us reconsider the projection operator $\pi_L(R)$. In the classical relational algebra, L is a list of (some of the) attributes of R. We extend the projection operator to allow it to compute with components of tuples as well as choose components. In *extended projection*, also denoted $\pi_L(R)$, projection lists can have the following kinds of elements:

1. A single attribute of R.

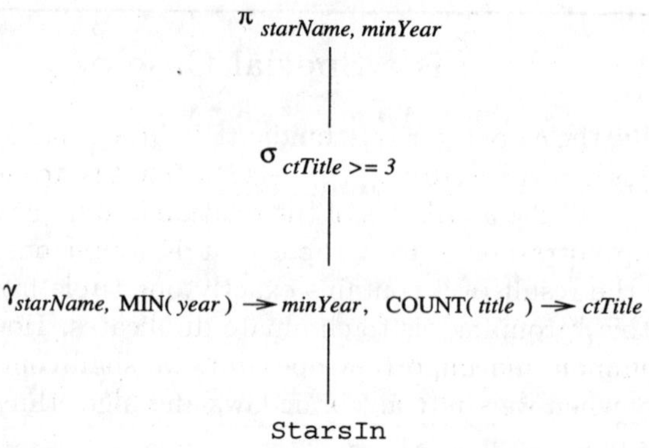

Figure 5: Algebraic expression tree for the query of Example 10

2. An expression $x \to y$, where x and y are names for attributes. The element $x \to y$ in the list L asks that we take the attribute x of R and *rename* it y; i.e., the name of this attribute in the schema of the result relation is y.

3. An expression $E \to z$, where E is an expression involving attributes of R, constants, arithmetic operators, and string operators, and z is a new name for the attribute that results from the calculation implied by E. For example, $a+b \to x$ as a list element represents the sum of the attributes a and b, renamed x. Element $c \,||\, d \to e$ means concatenate the presumably string-valued attributes c and d and call the result e.

The result of the projection is computed by considering each tuple of R in turn. We evaluate the list L by substituting the tuple's components for the corresponding attributes mentioned in L and applying any operators indicated by L to these values. The result is a relation whose schema is the names of the attributes on list L, with whatever renaming the list specifies. Each tuple of R yields one tuple of the result. Duplicate tuples in R surely yield duplicate tuples in the result, but the result can have duplicates even if R does not.

Example 11: Let R be the relation

A	B	C
0	1	2
0	1	2
3	4	5

Then the result of $\pi_{A,B+C\to X}(R)$ is

A	X
0	3
0	3
3	9

The result's schema has two attributes. One is A, the first attribute of R, not renamed. The second is the sum of the second and third attributes of R, with the name X.

For another example, $\pi_{B-A\rightarrow X, C-B\rightarrow Y}(R)$ is

X	Y
1	1
1	1
1	1

Notice that the calculation required by this projection list happens to turn different tuples $(0, 1, 2)$ and $(3, 4, 5)$ into the same tuple $(1, 1)$. Thus, the latter tuple appears three times in the result. □

2.6 The Sorting Operator

There are several contexts in which we want to sort the tuples of a relation by one or more of its attributes. Often, when querying data, one wants the result relation to be sorted. For instance, in a query about all the movies in which Sean Connery appeared, we might wish to have the list sorted by title, so we could more easily find whether a certain movie was on the list. We shall also see when we study query optimization how execution of queries by the DBMS is often made more efficient if we sort the relations first.

The expression $\tau_L(R)$, where R is a relation and L a list of some of R's attributes, is the relation R, but with the tuples of R sorted in the order indicated by L. If L is the list $A_1, A_2, \ldots, A_n$, then the tuples of R are sorted first by their value of attribute A_1. Ties are broken according to the value of A_2; tuples that agree on both A_1 and A_2 are ordered according to their value of A_3, and so on. Ties that remain after attribute A_n is considered may be ordered arbitrarily.

Example 12: If R is a relation with schema $R(A, B, C)$, then $\tau_{C,B}(R)$ orders the tuples of R by their value of C, and tuples with the same C-value are ordered by their B value. Tuples that agree on both B and C may be ordered arbitrarily. □

If we apply another operator such as join to the sorted result of a τ, the sorted order usually becomes meaningless, and the elements on the list should be treated as a bag, not a list. However, bag projections can be made to preserve the order. Also, a selection on a list drops out the tuples that do not satisfy the condition of the selection, but the remaining tuples can be made to appear in their original sorted order.

2.7 Outerjoins

A property of the join operator is that it is possible for certain tuples to be "dangling"; that is, they fail to match any tuple of the other relation in the common attributes. Dangling tuples do not have any trace in the result of the join, so the join may not represent the data of the original relations completely. In cases where this behavior is undesirable, a variation on the join, called "outerjoin," has been proposed and appears in various commercial systems.

We shall consider the "natural" case first, where the join is on equated values of all attributes in common to the two relations. The *outerjoin* $R \overset{\circ}{\bowtie} S$ is formed by starting with $R \bowtie S$, and adding any dangling tuples from R or S. The added tuples must be padded with a special *null* symbol, $\perp$, in all the attributes that they do not possess but that appear in the join result. Note that $\perp$ is written NULL in SQL.

A	B	C
1	2	3
4	5	6
7	8	9

(a) Relation U

B	C	D
2	3	10
2	3	11
6	7	12

(b) Relation V

A	B	C	D
1	2	3	10
1	2	3	11
4	5	6	$\perp$
7	8	9	$\perp$
$\perp$	6	7	12

(c) Result $U \overset{\circ}{\bowtie} V$

Figure 6: Outerjoin of relations

Example 13: In Fig. 6(a) and (b) we see two relations U and V. Tuple $(1, 2, 3)$ of U joins with both $(2, 3, 10)$ and $(2, 3, 11)$ of V, so these three tuples are not dangling. However, the other three tuples — $(4, 5, 6)$ and $(7, 8, 9)$ of U and $(6, 7, 12)$ of V — are dangling. That is, for none of these three tuples is there a tuple of the other relation that agrees with it on both the B and C components. Thus, in $U \overset{\circ}{\bowtie} V$, seen in Fig. 6(c), the three dangling tuples are padded with

$\perp$ in the attributes that they do not have: attribute D for the tuples of U and attribute A for the tuple of V. □

There are many variants of the basic (natural) outerjoin idea. The *left outerjoin* $R \overset{\circ}{\bowtie}_L S$ is like the outerjoin, but only dangling tuples of the left argument R are padded with $\perp$ and added to the result. The *right outerjoin* $R \overset{\circ}{\bowtie}_R S$ is like the outerjoin, but only the dangling tuples of the right argument S are padded with $\perp$ and added to the result.

Example 14: If U and V are as in Fig. 6, then $U \overset{\circ}{\bowtie}_L V$ is:

A	B	C	D
1	2	3	10
1	2	3	11
4	5	6	$\perp$
7	8	9	$\perp$

and $U \overset{\circ}{\bowtie}_R V$ is:

A	B	C	D
1	2	3	10
1	2	3	11
$\perp$	6	7	12

□

In addition, all three natural outerjoin operators have theta-join analogs, where first a theta-join is taken and then those tuples that failed to join with any tuple of the other relation, when the condition of the theta-join was applied, are padded with $\perp$ and added to the result. We use $\overset{\circ}{\bowtie}_C$ to denote a theta-outerjoin with condition C. This operator can also be modified with L or R to indicate left- or right-outerjoin.

Example 15: Let U and V be the relations of Fig. 6, and consider

$$U \overset{\circ}{\bowtie}_{A>V.C} V$$

Tuples $(4, 5, 6)$ and $(7, 8, 9)$ of U each satisfy the condition with both of the tuples $(2, 3, 10)$ and $(2, 3, 11)$ of V. Thus, none of these four tuples are dangling in this theta-join. However, the two other tuples — $(1, 2, 3)$ of U and $(6, 7, 12)$ of V — are dangling. They thus appear, padded, in the result shown in Fig. 7. □

A	$U.B$	$U.C$	$V.B$	$V.C$	D
4	5	6	2	3	10
4	5	6	2	3	11
7	8	9	2	3	10
7	8	9	2	3	11
1	2	3	⊥	⊥	⊥
⊥	⊥	⊥	6	7	12

Figure 7: Result of a theta-outerjoin

2.8 Exercises for Section 2

Exercise 2.1: Here are two relations:

$R(A, B)$: $\{(0,1),\ (2,3),\ (0,1),\ (2,4),\ (3,4)\}$

$S(B, C)$: $\{(0,1),\ (2,4),\ (2,5),\ (3,4),\ (0,2),\ (3,4)\}$

Compute the following: a) $\pi_{A+B,A^2,B^2}(R)$; b) $\pi_{B+1,C-1}(S)$; c) $\tau_{B,A}(R)$; d) $\tau_{B,C}(S)$; e) $\delta(R)$; f) $\delta(S)$; g) $\gamma_{A,\ \mathtt{SUM}(B)}(R)$; h) $\gamma_{B,\mathtt{AVG}(C)}(S)$; ! i) $\gamma_A(R)$; ! j) $\gamma_{A,\mathtt{MAX}(C)}(R \bowtie S)$; k) $R \overset{\circ}{\bowtie}_L S$; l) $R \overset{\circ}{\bowtie}_R S$; m) $R \overset{\circ}{\bowtie} S$; n) $R \overset{\circ}{\bowtie}_{R.B<S.B} S$.

! **Exercise 2.2:** A unary operator f is said to be *idempotent* if for all relations R, $f(f(R)) = f(R)$. That is, applying f more than once is the same as applying it once. Which of the following operators are idempotent? Either explain why or give a counterexample.

a) δ; b) π_L; c) σ_C; d) γ_L; e) τ.

! **Exercise 2.3:** One thing that can be done with an extended projection is to duplicate columns. For example, if $R(A, B)$ is a relation, then $\pi_{A,A}(R)$ produces the tuple (a, a) for every tuple (a, b) in R. Can this operation be done using only the classical operations of relation algebra? Explain your reasoning.

3 A Logic for Relations

As an alternative to abstract query languages based on algebra, one can use a form of logic to express queries. The logical query language *Datalog* ("database logic") consists of if-then rules. Each of these rules expresses the idea that from certain combinations of tuples in certain relations, we may infer that some other tuple must be in some other relation, or in the answer to a query.

3.1 Predicates and Atoms

Relations are represented in Datalog by *predicates.* Each predicate takes a fixed number of arguments, and a predicate followed by its arguments is called an *atom.* The syntax of atoms is just like that of function calls in conventional programming languages; for example $P(x_1, x_2, \ldots, x_n)$ is an atom consisting of the predicate P with arguments $x_1, x_2, \ldots, x_n$.

In essence, a predicate is the name of a function that returns a boolean value. If R is a relation with n attributes in some fixed order, then we shall also use R as the name of a predicate corresponding to this relation. The atom $R(a_1, a_2, \ldots, a_n)$ has value `TRUE` if $(a_1, a_2, \ldots, a_n)$ is a tuple of R; the atom has value `FALSE` otherwise.

Notice that a relation defined by a predicate can be assumed to be a set. In Section 3.6, we shall discuss how it is possible to extend Datalog to bags. However, outside that section, you should assume in connection with Datalog that relations are sets.

Example 16: Let R be the relation

A	B
1	2
3	4

Then $R(1,2)$ is true and so is $R(3,4)$. However, for any other combination of values x and y, $R(x,y)$ is false. □

A predicate can take variables as well as constants as arguments. If an atom has variables for one or more of its arguments, then it is a boolean-valued function that takes values for these variables and returns `TRUE` or `FALSE`.

Example 17: If R is the predicate from Example 16, then $R(x,y)$ is the function that tells, for any x and y, whether the tuple (x,y) is in relation R. For the particular instance of R mentioned in Example 16, $R(x,y)$ returns `TRUE` when either

1. $x = 1$ and $y = 2$, or

2. $x = 3$ and $y = 4$

and returns `FALSE` otherwise. As another example, the atom $R(1,z)$ returns `TRUE` if $z = 2$ and returns `FALSE` otherwise. □

3.2 Arithmetic Atoms

There is another kind of atom that is important in Datalog: an *arithmetic atom.* This kind of atom is a comparison between two arithmetic expressions, for example $x < y$ or $x + 1 \geq y + 4 \times z$. For contrast, we shall call the atoms introduced in Section 3.1 *relational atoms*; both kinds are "atoms."

Note that arithmetic and relational atoms each take as arguments the values of any variables that appear in the atom, and they return a boolean value. In effect, arithmetic comparisons like $<$ or $\geq$ are like the names of relations that contain all the true pairs. Thus, we can visualize the relation "$<$" as containing all the tuples, such as $(1, 2)$ or $(-1.5, 65.4)$, whose first component is less than their second component. Remember, however, that database relations are always finite, and usually change from time to time. In contrast, arithmetic-comparison relations such as $<$ are both infinite and unchanging.

3.3 Datalog Rules and Queries

Operations similar to those of relational algebra are described in Datalog by *rules*, which consist of

1. A relational atom called the *head*, followed by

2. The symbol $\leftarrow$, which we often read "if," followed by

3. A *body* consisting of one or more atoms, called *subgoals*, which may be either relational or arithmetic. Subgoals are connected by `AND`, and any subgoal may optionally be preceded by the logical operator `NOT`.

Example 18: The Datalog rule

```
LongMovie(t,y) ← Movies(t,y,l,g,s,p) AND l ≥ 100
```

defines the set of "long" movies, those at least 100 minutes long. It refers to our standard relation `Movies` with schema

```
Movies(title, year, length, genre, studioName, producerC#)
```

The head of the rule is the atom *LongMovie*(t, y). The body of the rule consists of two subgoals:

1. The first subgoal has predicate *Movies* and six arguments, corresponding to the six attributes of the `Movies` relation. Each of these arguments has a different variable: t for the `title` component, y for the `year` component, l for the `length` component, and so on. We can see this subgoal as saying: "Let (t, y, l, g, s, p) be a tuple in the current instance of relation `Movies`." More precisely, *Movies*(t, y, l, g, s, p) is true whenever the six variables have values that are the six components of some one `Movies` tuple.

2. The second subgoal, $l \geq 100$, is true whenever the length component of a `Movies` tuple is at least 100.

The rule as a whole can be thought of as saying: *LongMovie*(t, y) is true whenever we can find a tuple in `Movies` with:

a) t and y as the first two components (for `title` and `year`),

Anonymous Variables

Frequently, Datalog rules have some variables that appear only once. The names used for these variables are irrelevant. Only when a variable appears more than once do we care about its name, so we can see it is the same variable in its second and subsequent appearances. Thus, we shall allow the common convention that an underscore, _, as an argument of an atom, stands for a variable that appears only there. Multiple occurrences of _ stand for different variables, never the same variable. For instance, the rule of Example 18 could be written

$$\texttt{LongMovie(t,y)} \leftarrow \texttt{Movies(t,y,l,\_,\_,\_)} \texttt{ AND l} \geq \texttt{100}$$

The three variables g, s, and p that appear only once have each been replaced by underscores. We cannot replace any of the other variables, since each appears twice in the rule.

b) A third component l (for `length`) that is at least 100, and

c) Any values in components 4 through 6.

Notice that this rule is thus equivalent to the "assignment statement" in relational algebra:

$$\texttt{LongMovie} := \pi_{title,year}\big(\sigma_{length \geq 100}(\texttt{Movies})\big)$$

whose right side is a relational-algebra expression. □

A *query* in Datalog is a collection of one or more rules. If there is only one relation that appears in the rule heads, then the value of this relation is taken to be the answer to the query. Thus, in Example 18, `LongMovie` is the answer to the query. If there is more than one relation among the rule heads, then one of these relations is the answer to the query, while the others assist in the definition of the answer. When there are several predicates defined by a collection of rules, we shall usually assume that the query result is named `Answer`.

3.4 Meaning of Datalog Rules

Example 18 gave us a hint of the meaning of a Datalog rule. More precisely, imagine the variables of the rule ranging over all possible values. Whenever these variables have values that together make all the subgoals true, then we see what the value of the head is for those variables, and we add the resulting tuple to the relation whose predicate is in the head.

For instance, we can imagine the six variables of Example 18 ranging over all possible values. The only combinations of values that can make all the subgoals true are when the values of (t, y, l, g, s, p) in that order form a tuple of `Movies`. Moreover, since the $l \geq 100$ subgoal must also be true, this tuple must be one where l, the value of the `length` component, is at least 100. When we find such a combination of values, we put the tuple (t, y) in the head's relation `LongMovie`.

There are, however, restrictions that we must place on the way variables are used in rules, so that the result of a rule is a finite relation and so that rules with arithmetic subgoals or with *negated* subgoals (those with `NOT` in front of them) make intuitive sense. This condition, which we call the *safety* condition, is:

- Every variable that appears anywhere in the rule must appear in some nonnegated, relational subgoal of the body.

In particular, any variable that appears in the head, in a negated relational subgoal, or in any arithmetic subgoal, must also appear in a nonnegated, relational subgoal of the body.

Example 19: Consider the rule

```
LongMovie(t,y) ← Movies(t,y,l,_,_,_) AND l ≥ 100
```

from Example 18. The first subgoal is a nonnegated, relational subgoal, and it contains all the variables that appear anywhere in the rule, including the anonymous ones represented by underscores. In particular, the two variables t and y that appear in the head also appear in the first subgoal of the body. Likewise, variable l appears in an arithmetic subgoal, but it also appears in the first subgoal. Thus, the rule is safe. □

Example 20: The following rule has three safety violations:

```
P(x,y) ← Q(x,z) AND NOT R(w,x,z) AND x<y
```

1. The variable y appears in the head but not in any nonnegated, relational subgoal of the body. Notice that y's appearance in the arithmetic subgoal $x < y$ does not help to limit the possible values of y to a finite set. As soon as we find values a, b, and c for w, x, and z respectively that satisfy the first two subgoals, we are forced to add the infinite number of tuples (b, d) such that $d > b$ to the relation for the head predicate P.

2. Variable w appears in a negated, relational subgoal but not in a nonnegated, relational subgoal.

3. Variable y appears in an arithmetic subgoal, but not in a nonnegated, relational subgoal.

Thus, it is not a safe rule and cannot be used in Datalog. □

There is another way to define the meaning of rules. Instead of considering all of the possible assignments of values to variables, we consider the sets of tuples in the relations corresponding to each of the nonnegated, relational subgoals. If some assignment of tuples for each nonnegated, relational subgoal is *consistent*, in the sense that it assigns the same value to each occurrence of any one variable, then consider the resulting assignment of values to all the variables of the rule. Notice that because the rule is safe, every variable is assigned a value.

For each consistent assignment, we consider the negated, relational subgoals and the arithmetic subgoals, to see if the assignment of values to variables makes them all true. Remember that a negated subgoal is true if its atom is false. If all the subgoals are true, then we see what tuple the head becomes under this assignment of values to variables. This tuple is added to the relation whose predicate is the head.

Example 21: Consider the Datalog rule

```
P(x,y) ← Q(x,z) AND R(z,y) AND NOT Q(x,y)
```

Let relation Q contain the two tuples $(1,2)$ and $(1,3)$. Let relation R contain tuples $(2,3)$ and $(3,1)$. There are two nonnegated, relational subgoals, $Q(x,z)$ and $R(z,y)$, so we must consider all combinations of assignments of tuples from relations Q and R, respectively, to these subgoals. The table of Fig. 8 considers all four combinations.

	Tuple for `Q(x,z)`	Tuple for `R(z,y)`	Consistent Assignment?	`NOT Q(x,y)` True?	Resulting Head
1)	$(1,2)$	$(2,3)$	Yes	No	—
2)	$(1,2)$	$(3,1)$	No; $z = 2,3$	Irrelevant	—
3)	$(1,3)$	$(2,3)$	No; $z = 3,2$	Irrelevant	—
4)	$(1,3)$	$(3,1)$	Yes	Yes	$P(1,1)$

Figure 8: All possible assignments of tuples to $Q(x,z)$ and $R(z,y)$

The second and third options in Fig. 8 are not consistent. Each assigns two different values to the variable z. Thus, we do not consider these tuple-assignments further.

The first option, where subgoal $Q(x,z)$ is assigned the tuple $(1,2)$ and subgoal $R(z,y)$ is assigned tuple $(2,3)$, yields a consistent assignment, with x, y, and z given the values 1, 3, and 2, respectively. We thus proceed to the test of the other subgoals, those that are not nonnegated, relational subgoals. There is only one: `NOT Q(x,y)`. For this assignment of values to the variables, this subgoal becomes `NOT Q(1,3)`. Since $(1,3)$ is a tuple of Q, this subgoal is false, and no head tuple is produced for the tuple-assignment (1).

The final option is (4). Here, the assignment is consistent; x, y, and z are assigned the values 1, 1, and 3, respectively. The subgoal `NOT Q(x,y)` takes on the value `NOT Q(1,1)`. Since $(1,1)$ is not a tuple of Q, this subgoal is true. We thus evaluate the head $P(x,y)$ for this assignment of values to variables and find it is $P(1,1)$. Thus the tuple $(1,1)$ is in the relation P. Since we have exhausted all tuple-assignments, this is the only tuple in P. □

3.5 Extensional and Intensional Predicates

It is useful to make the distinction between

- *Extensional* predicates, which are predicates whose relations are stored in a database, and
- *Intensional* predicates, whose relations are computed by applying one or more Datalog rules.

The difference is the same as that between the operands of a relational-algebra expression, which are "extensional" (i.e., defined by their *extension*, which is another name for the "current instance of a relation") and the relations computed by a relational-algebra expression, either as the final result or as an intermediate result corresponding to some subexpression; these relations are "intensional" (i.e., defined by the programmer's "intent").

When talking of Datalog rules, we shall refer to the relation corresponding to a predicate as "intensional" or "extensional," if the predicate is intensional or extensional, respectively. We shall also use the abbreviation *IDB* for "intensional database" to refer to either an intensional predicate or its corresponding relation. Similarly, we use abbreviation *EDB*, standing for "extensional database," for extensional predicates or relations.

Thus, in Example 18, `Movies` is an EDB relation, defined by its extension. The predicate *Movies* is likewise an EDB predicate. Relation and predicate `LongMovie` are both intensional.

An EDB predicate can never appear in the head of a rule, although it can appear in the body of a rule. IDB predicates can appear in either the head or the body of rules, or both. It is also common to construct a single relation by using several rules with the same IDB predicate in the head. We shall see an illustration of this idea in Example 24, regarding the union of two relations.

By using a series of intensional predicates, we can build progressively more complicated functions of the EDB relations. The process is similar to the building of relational-algebra expressions using several operators.

3.6 Datalog Rules Applied to Bags

Datalog is inherently a logic of sets. However, as long as there are no negated, relational subgoals, the ideas for evaluating Datalog rules when relations are sets apply to bags as well. When relations are bags, it is conceptually simpler to use the second approach for evaluating Datalog rules that we gave in Section 3.4. Recall this technique involves looking at each of the nonnegated, relational subgoals and substituting for it all tuples of the relation for the predicate of that subgoal. If a selection of tuples for each subgoal gives a consistent value to each variable, and the arithmetic subgoals all become true,[1] then we see what the head becomes with this assignment of values to variables. The resulting tuple is put in the head relation.

Since we are now dealing with bags, we do not eliminate duplicates from the head. Moreover, as we consider all combinations of tuples for the subgoals, a tuple appearing n times in the relation for a subgoal gets considered n times as the tuple for that subgoal, each time in conjunction with all combinations of tuples for the other subgoals.

Example 22: Consider the rule

```
H(x,z) ← R(x,y) AND S(y,z)
```

where relation $R(A, B)$ has the tuples:

A	B
1	2
1	2

and $S(B, C)$ has tuples:

B	C
2	3
4	5
4	5

The only time we get a consistent assignment of tuples to the subgoals (i.e., an assignment where the value of y from each subgoal is the same) is when the first subgoal is assigned one of the tuples $(1, 2)$ from R and the second subgoal is assigned tuple $(2, 3)$ from S. Since $(1, 2)$ appears twice in R, and $(2, 3)$ appears once in S, there will be two assignments of tuples that give the variable assignments $x = 1$, $y = 2$, and $z = 3$. The tuple of the head, which is (x, z), is for each of these assignments $(1, 3)$. Thus the tuple $(1, 3)$ appears twice in the head relation H, and no other tuple appears there. That is, the relation

1	3
1	3

[1]Note that there must not be any negated relational subgoals in the rule. There is not a clearly defined meaning of arbitrary Datalog rules with negated, relational subgoals under the bag model.

is the head relation defined by this rule. More generally, had tuple $(1, 2)$ appeared n times in R and tuple $(2, 3)$ appeared m times in S, then tuple $(1, 3)$ would appear nm times in H. □

If a relation is defined by several rules, then the result is the bag-union of whatever tuples are produced by each rule.

Example 23: Consider a relation H defined by the two rules

```
H(x,y) ← S(x,y) AND x>1
H(x,y) ← S(x,y) AND y<5
```

where relation $S(B, C)$ is as in Example 22; that is, $S = \{(2, 3),\ (4, 5),\ (4, 5)\}$. The first rule puts each of the three tuples of S into H, since they each have a first component greater than 1. The second rule puts only the tuple $(2, 3)$ into H, since $(4, 5)$ does not satisfy the condition $y < 5$. Thus, the resulting relation H has two copies of the tuple $(2, 3)$ and two copies of the tuple $(4, 5)$. □

3.7 Exercises for Section 3

!! **Exercise 3.1:** The requirement we gave for safety of Datalog rules is sufficient to guarantee that the head predicate has a finite relation if the predicates of the relational subgoals have finite relations. However, this requirement is too strong. Give an example of a Datalog rule that violates the condition, yet whatever finite relations we assign to the relational predicates, the head relation will be finite.

4 Relational Algebra and Datalog

Each of the relational-algebra operators can be mimicked by one or several Datalog rules. In this section we shall consider each operator in turn. We shall then consider how to combine Datalog rules to mimic complex algebraic expressions. It is also true that any single safe Datalog rule can be expressed in relational algebra, although we shall not prove that fact here. However, Datalog queries are more powerful than relational algebra when several rules are allowed to interact; they can express recursions that are not expressable in the algebra (see Example 35).

4.1 Boolean Operations

The boolean operations of relational algebra — union, intersection, and set difference — can each be expressed simply in Datalog. Here are the three techniques needed. We assume R and S are relations with the same number of attributes, n. We shall describe the needed rules using `Answer` as the name of the head predicate in all cases. However, we can use anything we wish for the name of the result, and in fact it is important to choose different predicates for the results of different operations.

- To take the union $R \cup S$, use two rules and n distinct variables

$$a_1, a_2, \ldots, a_n$$

  One rule has $R(a_1, a_2, \ldots, a_n)$ as the lone subgoal and the other has $S(a_1, a_2, \ldots, a_n)$ alone. Both rules have the head $Answer(a_1, a_2, \ldots, a_n)$. As a result, each tuple from R and each tuple of S is put into the answer relation.

- To take the intersection $R \cap S$, use a rule with body

$$R(a_1, a_2, \ldots, a_n) \texttt{ AND } S(a_1, a_2, \ldots, a_n)$$

  and head $Answer(a_1, a_2, \ldots, a_n)$. Then, a tuple is in the answer relation if and only if it is in both R and S.

- To take the difference $R - S$, use a rule with body

$$R(a_1, a_2, \ldots, a_n) \texttt{ AND NOT } S(a_1, a_2, \ldots, a_n)$$

  and head $Answer(a_1, a_2, \ldots, a_n)$. Then, a tuple is in the answer relation if and only if it is in R but not in S.

Example 24: Let the schemas for the two relations be $R(A, B, C)$ and $S(A, B, C)$. To avoid confusion, we use different predicates for the various results, rather than calling them all `Answer`.

To take the union $R \cup S$ we use the two rules:

```
1. U(x,y,z) ← R(x,y,z)
2. U(x,y,z) ← S(x,y,z)
```

Rule (1) says that every tuple in R is a tuple in the IDB relation U. Rule (2) similarly says that every tuple in S is in U.

To compute $R \cap S$, we use the rule

```
I(a,b,c) ← R(a,b,c) AND S(a,b,c)
```

Finally, the rule

```
D(a,b,c) ← R(a,b,c) AND NOT S(a,b,c)
```

computes the difference $R - S$. □

Variables Are Local to a Rule

Notice that the names we choose for variables in a rule are arbitrary and have no connection to the variables used in any other rule. The reason there is no connection is that each rule is evaluated alone and contributes tuples to its head's relation independent of other rules. Thus, for instance, we could replace the second rule of Example 24 by

```
U(a,b,c) ← S(a,b,c)
```

while leaving the first rule unchanged, and the two rules would still compute the union of R and S. Note, however, that when substituting one variable u for another variable v within a rule, we must substitute u for all occurrences of v within the rule. Moreover, the substituting variable u that we choose must not be a variable that already appears in the rule.

4.2 Projection

To compute a projection of a relation R, we use one rule with a single subgoal with predicate R. The arguments of this subgoal are distinct variables, one for each attribute of the relation. The head has an atom with arguments that are the variables corresponding to the attributes in the projection list, in the desired order.

Example 25: Suppose we want to project the relation

```
Movies(title, year, length, genre, studioName, producerC#)
```

onto its first three attributes — `title`, `year`, and `length`. The rule

```
P(t,y,l) ← Movies(t,y,l,g,s,p)
```

serves, defining a relation called P to be the result of the projection. □

4.3 Selection

Selections can be somewhat more difficult to express in Datalog. The simple case is when the selection condition is the `AND` of one or more arithmetic comparisons. In that case, we create a rule with

1. One relational subgoal for the relation upon which we are performing the selection. This atom has distinct variables for each component, one for each attribute of the relation.

2. For each comparison in the selection condition, an arithmetic subgoal that is identical to this comparison. However, while in the selection condition an attribute name was used, in the arithmetic subgoal we use the corresponding variable, following the correspondence established by the relational subgoal.

Example 26: The selection

$$\sigma_{length \geq 100 \texttt{ AND } studioName = \texttt{'Fox'}}(\texttt{Movies})$$

can be written as a Datalog rule

$$\texttt{S(t,y,l,g,s,p)} \leftarrow \texttt{Movies(t,y,l,g,s,p) AND l} \geq \texttt{100 AND s = 'Fox'}$$

The result is the relation S. Note that l and s are the variables corresponding to attributes `length` and `studioName` in the standard order we have used for the attributes of `Movies`. □

Now, let us consider selections that involve the `OR` of conditions. We cannot necessarily replace such selections by single Datalog rules. However, selection for the `OR` of two conditions is equivalent to selecting for each condition separately and then taking the union of the results. Thus, the `OR` of n conditions can be expressed by n rules, each of which defines the same head predicate. The ith rule performs the selection for the ith of the n conditions.

Example 27: Let us modify the selection of Example 26 by replacing the `AND` by an `OR` to get the selection:

$$\sigma_{length \geq 100 \texttt{ OR } studioName = \texttt{'Fox'}}(\texttt{Movies})$$

That is, find all those movies that are either long or by Fox. We can write two rules, one for each of the two conditions:

1. $\texttt{S(t,y,l,g,s,p)} \leftarrow \texttt{Movies(t,y,l,g,s,p) AND l} \geq \texttt{100}$
2. $\texttt{S(t,y,l,g,s,p)} \leftarrow \texttt{Movies(t,y,l,g,s,p) AND s = 'Fox'}$

Rule (1) produces movies at least 100 minutes long, and rule (2) produces movies by Fox. □

Even more complex selection conditions can be formed by several applications, in any order, of the logical operators `AND`, `OR`, and `NOT`. However, there is a widely known technique, which we shall not present here, for rearranging any such logical expression into "disjunctive normal form," where the expression is the disjunction (`OR`) of "conjuncts." A *conjunct*, in turn, is the `AND` of "literals," and a *literal* is either a comparison or a negated comparison.[2]

---

[2] See, e.g., A. V. Aho and J. D. Ullman, *Foundations of Computer Science*, Computer Science Press, New York, 1992.

We can represent any literal by a subgoal, perhaps with a NOT in front of it. If the subgoal is arithmetic, the NOT can be incorporated into the comparison operator. For example, NOT $x \geq 100$ can be written as $x < 100$. Then, any conjunct can be represented by a single Datalog rule, with one subgoal for each comparison. Finally, every disjunctive-normal-form expression can be written by several Datalog rules, one rule for each conjunct. These rules take the union, or OR, of the results from each of the conjuncts.

Example 28: We gave a simple instance of this algorithm in Example 27. A more difficult example can be formed by negating the condition of that example. We then have the expression:

$$\sigma_{\texttt{NOT}\ (length \geq 100\ \texttt{OR}\ studioName=\texttt{'Fox'})}(\texttt{Movies})$$

That is, find all those movies that are neither long nor by Fox.

Here, a NOT is applied to an expression that is itself not a simple comparison. Thus, we must push the NOT down the expression, using one form of *DeMorgan's laws*, which says that the negation of an OR is the AND of the negations. That is, the selection can be rewritten:

$$\sigma_{(\texttt{NOT}\ (length \geq 100))\ \texttt{AND}\ (\texttt{NOT}\ (studioName=\texttt{'Fox'}))}(\texttt{Movies})$$

Now, we can take the NOT's inside the comparisons to get the expression:

$$\sigma_{length < 100\ \texttt{AND}\ studioName \neq \texttt{'Fox'}}(\texttt{Movies})$$

This expression can be converted into the Datalog rule

$$\texttt{S(t,y,l,g,s,p)} \leftarrow \texttt{Movies(t,y,l,g,s,p) AND l} < \texttt{100 AND s} \neq \texttt{'Fox'}$$

□

Example 29: Let us consider a similar example where we have the negation of an AND in the selection. Now, we use the second form of DeMorgan's law, which says that the negation of an AND is the OR of the negations. We begin with the algebraic expression

$$\sigma_{\texttt{NOT}\ (length \geq 100\ \texttt{AND}\ studioName=\texttt{'Fox'})}(\texttt{Movies})$$

That is, find all those movies that are not both long and by Fox.

We apply DeMorgan's law to push the NOT below the AND, to get:

$$\sigma_{(\texttt{NOT}\ (length \geq 100))\ \texttt{OR}\ (\texttt{NOT}\ (studioName=\texttt{'Fox'}))}(\texttt{Movies})$$

Again we take the NOT's inside the comparisons to get:

$$\sigma_{length < 100\ \texttt{OR}\ studioName \neq \texttt{'Fox'}}(\texttt{Movies})$$

Finally, we write two rules, one for each part of the OR. The resulting Datalog rules are:

1. $\texttt{S(t,y,l,g,s,p)} \leftarrow \texttt{Movies(t,y,l,g,s,p) AND l} < \texttt{100}$
2. $\texttt{S(t,y,l,g,s,p)} \leftarrow \texttt{Movies(t,y,l,g,s,p) AND s} \neq \texttt{'Fox'}$

□

4.4 Product

The product of two relations $R \times S$ can be expressed by a single Datalog rule. This rule has two subgoals, one for R and one for S. Each of these subgoals has distinct variables, one for each attribute of R or S. The IDB predicate in the head has as arguments all the variables that appear in either subgoal, with the variables appearing in the R-subgoal listed before those of the S-subgoal.

Example 30: Let us consider the two three-attribute relations R and S from Example 24. The rule

```
P(a,b,c,x,y,z) ← R(a,b,c) AND S(x,y,z)
```

defines P to be $R \times S$. We have arbitrarily used variables at the beginning of the alphabet for the arguments of R and variables at the end of the alphabet for S. These variables all appear in the rule head. □

4.5 Joins

We can take the natural join of two relations by a Datalog rule that looks much like the rule for a product. The difference is that if we want $R \bowtie S$, then we must use the same variable for attributes of R and S that have the same name and must use different variables otherwise. For instance, we can use the attribute names themselves as the variables. The head is an IDB predicate that has each variable appearing once.

Example 31: Consider relations with schemas $R(A, B)$ and $S(B, C, D)$. Their natural join may be defined by the rule

```
J(a,b,c,d) ← R(a,b) AND S(b,c,d)
```

Notice how the variables used in the subgoals correspond in an obvious way to the attributes of the relations R and S. □

We also can convert theta-joins to Datalog. A theta-join can be expressed as a product followed by a selection. If the selection condition is a conjunct, that is, the AND of comparisons, then we may simply start with the Datalog rule for the product and add additional, arithmetic subgoals, one for each of the comparisons.

Example 32: Consider the relations $U(A, B, C)$ and $V(B, C, D)$ and the theta-join:

$$U \bowtie_{A<D \text{ AND } U.B \neq V.B} V$$

We can construct the Datalog rule

```
J(a,ub,uc,vb,vc,d)  ←  U(a,ub,uc) AND V(vb,vc,d) AND
                        a < d AND ub ≠ vb
```

to perform the same operation. We have used *ub* as the variable corresponding to attribute B of U, and similarly used *vb*, *uc*, and *vc*, although any six distinct variables for the six attributes of the two relations would be fine. The first two subgoals introduce the two relations, and the second two subgoals enforce the two comparisons that appear in the condition of the theta-join. □

If the condition of the theta-join is not a conjunction, then we convert it to disjunctive normal form, as discussed in Section 4.3. We then create one rule for each conjunct. In this rule, we begin with the subgoals for the product and then add subgoals for each literal in the conjunct. The heads of all the rules are identical and have one argument for each attribute of the two relations being theta-joined.

Example 33: In this example, we shall make a simple modification to the algebraic expression of Example 32. The AND will be replaced by an OR. There are no negations in this expression, so it is already in disjunctive normal form. There are two conjuncts, each with a single literal. The expression is:

$$U \bowtie_{A<D \texttt{ OR } U.B \neq V.B} V$$

Using the same variable-naming scheme as in Example 32, we obtain the two rules

1. J(a,ub,uc,vb,vc,d) ← U(a,ub,uc) AND V(vb,vc,d) AND a < d
2. J(a,ub,uc,vb,vc,d) ← U(a,ub,uc) AND V(vb,vc,d) AND ub ≠ vb

Each rule has subgoals for the two relations involved plus a subgoal for one of the two conditions $A < D$ or $U.B \neq V.B$. □

4.6 Simulating Multiple Operations with Datalog

Datalog rules are not only capable of mimicking a single operation of relational algebra. We can in fact mimic any algebraic expression. The trick is to look at the expression tree for the relational-algebra expression and create one IDB predicate for each interior node of the tree. The rule or rules for each IDB predicate is whatever we need to apply the operator at the corresponding node of the tree. Those operands of the tree that are extensional (i.e., they are relations of the database) are represented by the corresponding predicate. Operands that are themselves interior nodes are represented by the corresponding IDB predicate. The result of the algebraic expression is the relation for the predicate associated with the root of the expression tree.

Example 34: Consider the algebraic expression

$$\pi_{title,year}\Big(\sigma_{length\geq 100}(\texttt{Movies}) \cap \sigma_{studioName=\texttt{'Fox'}}(\texttt{Movies})\Big)$$

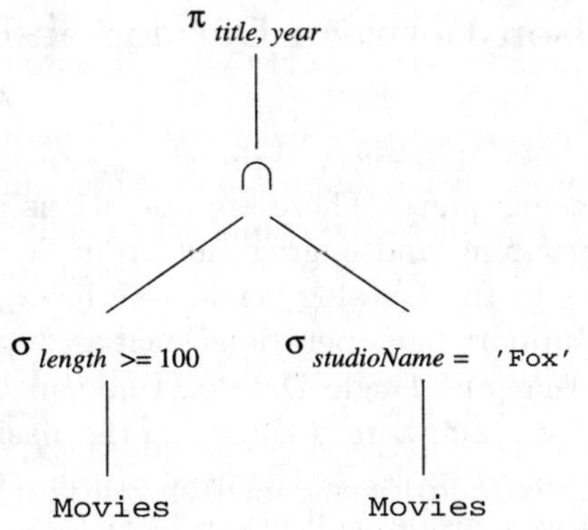

Figure 9: Expression tree

```
1. W(t,y,l,g,s,p) ← Movies(t,y,l,g,s,p) AND l ≥ 100
2. X(t,y,l,g,s,p) ← Movies(t,y,l,g,s,p) AND s = 'Fox'
3. Y(t,y,l,g,s,p) ← W(t,y,l,g,s,p) AND X(t,y,l,g,s,p)
4. Answer(t,y) ← Y(t,y,l,g,s,p)
```

Figure 10: Datalog rules to perform several algebraic operations

Fig. 9 has four interior nodes, so we need to create four IDB predicates. Each of these predicates has a single Datalog rule, and we summarize all the rules in Fig. 10.

The lowest two interior nodes perform simple selections on the EDB relation `Movies`, so we can create the IDB predicates W and X to represent these selections. Rules (1) and (2) of Fig. 10 describe these selections. For example, rule (1) defines W to be those tuples of `Movies` that have a length at least 100.

Then rule (3) defines predicate Y to be the intersection of W and X, using the form of rule we learned for an intersection in Section 4.1. Finally, rule (4) defines the answer to be the projection of Y onto the `title` and `year` attributes. We here use the technique for simulating a projection that we learned in Section 4.2.

Note that, because Y is defined by a single rule, we can substitute for the Y subgoal in rule (4) of Fig. 10, replacing it with the body of rule (3). Then, we can substitute for the W and X subgoals, using the bodies of rules (1) and (2). Since the `Movies` subgoal appears in both of these bodies, we can eliminate one copy. As a result, the single rule

```
Answer(t,y) ← Movies(t,y,l,g,s,p) AND l ≥ 100 AND s = 'Fox'
```

suffices. □

4.7 Comparison Between Datalog and Relational Algebra

We see from Section 4.6 that every expression in basic relational algebra can be expressed as a Datalog query. There are operations in the extended relational algebra, such as grouping and aggregation from Section 2, that have no corresponding features in the Datalog version we have presented here. Likewise, Datalog does not support bag operations such as duplicate elimination.

It is also true that any single Datalog rule can be expressed in relational algebra. That is, we can write a query in the basic relational algebra that produces the same set of tuples as the head of that rule produces.

However, when we consider collections of Datalog rules, the situation changes. Datalog rules can express recursion, which relational algebra can not. The reason is that IDB predicates can also be used in the bodies of rules, and the tuples we discover for the heads of rules can thus feed back to rule bodies and help produce more tuples for the heads. We shall not discuss here any of the complexities that arise, especially when the rules have negated subgoals. However, the following example will illustrate recursive Datalog.

Example 35: Suppose we have a relation `Edge(X,Y)` that says there is a directed edge (arc) from node X to node Y. We can express the transitive closure of the edge relation, that is, the relation `Path(X,Y)` meaning that there is a path of length 1 or more from node X to node Y, as follows:

1. `Path(X,Y)` $\leftarrow$ `Edge(X,Y)`
2. `Path(X,Y)` $\leftarrow$ `Edge(X,Z) AND Path(Z,Y)`

Rule (1) says that every edge is a path. Rule (2) says that if there is an edge from node X to some node Z and a path from Z to Y, then there is also a path from X to Y. If we apply Rule (1) and then Rule (2), we get the paths of length 2. If we take the *Path* facts we get from this application and use them in another application of Rule (2), we get paths of length 3. Feeding those *Path* facts back again gives us paths of length 4, and so on. Eventually, we discover all possible path facts, and on one round we get no new facts. At that point, we can stop. If we haven't discovered the fact $Path(a, b)$, then there really is no path in the graph from node a to node b. □

4.8 Exercises for Section 4

Exercise 4.1: Let $R(a, b, c)$, $S(a, b, c)$, and $T(a, b, c)$ be three relations. Write one or more Datalog rules that define the result of each of the following expressions of relational algebra:

a) $R \cup S$.

b) $R \cap S$.

c) $R - S$.

d) $(R \cup S) - T$.

! e) $(R - S) \cap (R - T)$.

f) $\pi_{a,b}(R)$.

! g) $\pi_{a,b}(R) \cap \rho_{U(a,b)}\big(\pi_{b,c}(S)\big)$.

Exercise 4.2: Let $R(x, y, z)$ be a relation. Write one or more Datalog rules that define $\sigma_C(R)$, where C stands for each of the following conditions:

a) $x = y$.

b) $x < y$ AND $y < z$.

c) $x < y$ OR $y < z$.

d) NOT $(x < y$ OR $x > y)$.

! e) NOT $\big((x < y$ OR $x > y)$ AND $y < z\big)$.

! f) NOT $\big((x < y$ OR $x < z)$ AND $y < z\big)$.

Exercise 4.3: Let $R(a, b, c)$, $S(b, c, d)$, and $T(d, e)$ be three relations. Write single Datalog rules for each of the natural joins:

a) $R \bowtie S$.

b) $S \bowtie T$.

c) $(R \bowtie S) \bowtie T$. (*Note*: since the natural join is associative and commutative, the order of the join of these three relations is irrelevant.)

Exercise 4.4: Let $R(x, y, z)$ and $S(x, y, z)$ be two relations. Write one or more Datalog rules to define each of the theta-joins $R \bowtie_C S$, where C is one of the conditions of Exercise 4.2. For each of these conditions, interpret each arithmetic comparison as comparing an attribute of R on the left with an attribute of S on the right. For instance, $x < y$ stands for $R.x < S.y$.

! **Exercise 4.5:** It is also possible to convert Datalog rules into equivalent relational-algebra expressions. While we have not discussed the method of doing so in general, it is possible to work out many simple examples. For each of the Datalog rules below, write an expression of relational algebra that defines the same relation as the head of the rule.

a) `P(x,y) ← Q(x,z) AND R(z,y)`

b) `P(x,y) ← Q(x,z) AND Q(z,y)`

c) `P(x,y) ← Q(x,z) AND R(z,y) AND x < y`

5 Summary

- ✦ *Relations as Bags*: In commercial database systems, relations are actually bags, in which the same tuple is allowed to appear several times. The operations of relational algebra on sets can be extended to bags, but there are some algebraic laws that fail to hold.

- ✦ *Extensions to Relational Algebra*: To match the capabilities of SQL, some operators not present in the core relational algebra are needed. Sorting of a relation is an example, as is an extended projection, where computation on columns of a relation is supported. Grouping, aggregation, and outerjoins are also needed.

- ✦ *Grouping and Aggregation*: Aggregations summarize a column of a relation. Typical aggregation operators are sum, average, count, minimum, and maximum. The grouping operator allows us to partition the tuples of a relation according to their value(s) in one or more attributes before computing aggregation(s) for each group.

- ✦ *Outerjoins*: The outerjoin of two relations starts with a join of those relations. Then, dangling tuples (those that failed to join with any tuple) from either relation are padded with null values for the attributes belonging only to the other relation, and the padded tuples are included in the result.

- ✦ *Datalog*: This form of logic allows us to write queries in the relational model. In Datalog, one writes rules in which a head predicate or relation is defined in terms of a body, consisting of subgoals.

- ✦ *Atoms*: The head and subgoals are each atoms, and an atom consists of an (optionally negated) predicate applied to some number of arguments. Predicates may represent either relations or arithmetic comparisons such as $<$.

- ✦ *IDB and EDB Predicates*: Some predicates correspond to stored relations, and are called EDB (extensional database) predicates or relations. Other predicates, called IDB (intensional database), are defined by the rules. EDB predicates may not appear in rule heads.

- ✦ *Safe Rules*: Datalog rules must be safe, meaning that every variable in the rule appears in some nonnegated, relational subgoal of the body. Safe rules guarantee that if the EDB relations are finite, then the IDB relations will be finite.

- ✦ *Relational Algebra and Datalog*: All queries that can be expressed in core relational algebra can also be expressed in Datalog. If the rules are safe and nonrecursive, then they define exactly the same set of queries as core relational algebra.

6 References

The relational algebra comes from [2]. The extended operator γ is from [5].

Codd also introduced two forms of first-order logic called *tuple relational calculus* and *domain relational calculus* in one of his early papers on the relational model [3]. These forms of logic are equivalent in expressive power to relational algebra, a fact proved in [3].

Datalog, looking more like logical rules, was inspired by the programming language Prolog. The book [4] originated much of the development of logic as a query language, while [1] placed the ideas in the context of database systems.

More on Datalog and relational calculus can be found in [6] and [7].

1. F. Bancilhon, and R. Ramakrishnan, "An amateur's introduction to recursive query-processing strategies," *ACM SIGMOD Intl. Conf. on Management of Data*, pp. 16–52, 1986.

2. E. F. Codd, "A relational model for large shared data banks," *Comm. ACM* **13**:6, pp. 377–387, 1970.

3. E. F. Codd, "Relational completeness of database sublanguages," in *Database Systems* (R. Rustin, ed.), Prentice Hall, Englewood Cliffs, NJ, 1972.

4. H. Gallaire and J. Minker, *Logic and Databases*, Plenum Press, New York, 1978.

5. A. Gupta, V. Harinarayan, and D. Quass, "Generalized projections: a powerful approach to aggregation," *Intl. Conf. on Very Large Databases*, pp. 358–369, 1995.

6. M. Liu, "Deductive database languages: problems and solutions," *Computing Surveys* **31**:1 (March, 1999), pp. 27–62.

7. J. D. Ullman, *Principles of Database and Knowledge-Base Systems, Volumes I and II*, Computer Science Press, New York, 1988, 1989.

The Database Language SQL

The most commonly used relational DBMS's query and modify the database through a language called SQL (sometimes pronounced "sequel"). SQL stands for "Structured Query Language." The portion of SQL that supports queries has capabilities very close to that of relational algebra. However, SQL also includes statements for modifying the database (e.g., inserting and deleting tuples from relations) and for declaring a database schema. Thus, SQL serves as both a data-manipulation language and as a data-definition language. SQL also standardizes many other database commands.

There are many different dialects of SQL. First, there are three major standards. There is ANSI (American National Standards Institute) SQL and an updated standard adopted in 1992, called SQL-92 or SQL2. The most recent SQL-99 (previously referred to as SQL3) standard extends SQL2 with object-relational features and a number of other new capabilities. There is also a collection of extensions to SQL-99, collectively called SQL:2003. Then, there are versions of SQL produced by the principal DBMS vendors. These all include the capabilities of the original ANSI standard. They also conform to a large extent to the more recent SQL2, although each has its variations and extensions beyond SQL2, including some, but not all, of the features in the SQL-99 and SQL:2003 standards.

This chapter introduces the basics of SQL: the query language and database modification statements. We also introduce the notion of a "transaction," the basic unit of work for database systems. This study, although simplifed, will give you a sense of how database operations can interact and some of the resulting pitfalls.

The intent of this chapter is to provide the reader with a sense of what SQL is about, more at the level of a "tutorial" than a "manual." Thus, we focus on the most commonly used features only, and we try to use code that not only conforms to the standard, but to the usage of commercial DBMS's. The references mention places where more of the details of the language and its dialects can be found.

1 Simple Queries in SQL

Perhaps the simplest form of query in SQL asks for those tuples of some one relation that satisfy a condition. Such a query is analogous to a selection in relational algebra. This simple query, like almost all SQL queries, uses the three keywords, SELECT, FROM, and WHERE that characterize SQL.

```
Movies(title, year, length, genre, studioName, producerC#)
StarsIn(movieTitle, movieYear, starName)
MovieStar(name, address, gender, birthdate)
MovieExec(name, address, cert#, netWorth)
Studio(name, address, presC#)
```

Figure 1: Example database schema

Example 1: In this and subsequent examples, we shall use the movie database schema shown in Fig. 1.

As our first query, let us ask about the relation

```
Movies(title, year, length, genre, studioName, producerC#)
```

for all movies produced by Disney Studios in 1990. In SQL, we say

```
SELECT *
FROM Movies
WHERE studioName = 'Disney' AND year = 1990;
```

This query exhibits the characteristic select-from-where form of most SQL queries.

How SQL is Used

In this chapter, we assume a *generic query interface*, where we type SQL queries or other statements and have them execute. In practice, the generic interface is used rarely. Rather, there are large programs, written in a conventional language such as C or Java (called the *host language*). These programs issue SQL statements to a database, using a special library for the host language. Data is moved from host-language variables to the SQL statements, and the results of those statements are moved from the database to host-language variables.

- The `FROM` clause gives the relation or relations to which the query refers. In our example, the query is about the relation `Movies`.

- The `WHERE` clause is a condition, much like a selection-condition in relational algebra. Tuples must satisfy the condition in order to match the query. Here, the condition is that the `studioName` attribute of the tuple has the value `'Disney'` and the `year` attribute of the tuple has the value 1990. All tuples meeting both stipulations satisfy the condition; other tuples do not.

- The `SELECT` clause tells which attributes of the tuples matching the condition are produced as part of the answer. The `*` in this example indicates that the entire tuple is produced. The result of the query is the relation consisting of all tuples produced by this process.

One way to interpret this query is to consider each tuple of the relation mentioned in the `FROM` clause. The condition in the `WHERE` clause is applied to the tuple. More precisely, any attributes mentioned in the `WHERE` clause are replaced by the value in the tuple's component for that attribute. The condition is then evaluated, and if true, the components appearing in the `SELECT` clause are produced as one tuple of the answer. Thus, the result of the query is the `Movies` tuples for those movies produced by Disney in 1990, for example, *Pretty Woman.*

In detail, when the SQL query processor encounters the `Movies` tuple

title	*year*	*length*	*genre*	*studioName*	*producerC#*
Pretty Woman	1990	119	romance	Disney	999

(here, 999 is the imaginary certificate number for the producer of the movie), the value `'Disney'` is substituted for attribute `studioName` and value 1990 is substituted for attribute `year` in the condition of the `WHERE` clause, because these are the values for those attributes in the tuple in question. The `WHERE` clause thus becomes

A Trick for Reading and Writing Queries

It is generally easist to examine a select-from-where query by first looking at the FROM clause, to learn which relations are involved in the query. Then, move to the WHERE clause, to learn what it is about tuples that is important to the query. Finally, look at the SELECT clause to see what the output is. The same order — from, then where, then select — is often useful when writing queries of your own, as well.

```
WHERE 'Disney' = 'Disney' AND 1990 = 1990
```

Since this condition is evidently true, the tuple for *Pretty Woman* passes the test of the WHERE clause and the tuple becomes part of the result of the query. □

1.1 Projection in SQL

We can, if we wish, eliminate some of the components of the chosen tuples; that is, we can project the relation produced by a SQL query onto some of its attributes. In place of the * of the SELECT clause, we may list some of the attributes of the relation mentioned in the FROM clause. The result will be projected onto the attributes listed.[1]

Example 2: Suppose we wish to modify the query of Example 1 to produce only the movie title and length. We may write

```
SELECT title, length
FROM Movies
WHERE studioName = 'Disney' AND year = 1990;
```

The result is a table with two columns, headed title and length. The tuples in this table are pairs, each consisting of a movie title and its length, such that the movie was produced by Disney in 1990. For instance, the relation schema and one of its tuples looks like:

title	*length*
Pretty Woman	119
...	...

□

[1]Thus, the keyword SELECT in SQL actually corresponds most closely to the projection operator of relational algebra, while the selection operator of the algebra corresponds to the WHERE clause of SQL queries.

Sometimes, we wish to produce a relation with column headers different from the attributes of the relation mentioned in the FROM clause. We may follow the name of the attribute by the keyword AS and an *alias*, which becomes the header in the result relation. Keyword AS is optional. That is, an alias can immediately follow what it stands for, without any intervening punctuation.

Example 3: We can modify Example 2 to produce a relation with attributes name and duration in place of title and length as follows.

```
SELECT title AS name, length AS duration
FROM Movies
WHERE studioName = 'Disney' AND year = 1990;
```

The result is the same set of tuples as in Example 2, but with the columns headed by attributes name and duration. For example,

name	*duration*
Pretty Woman	119
...	...

could be the first tuple in the result. □

Another option in the SELECT clause is to use an expression in place of an attribute. Put another way, the SELECT list can function like the lists in an extended projection. We shall see in Section 4 that the SELECT list can also include aggregates as in the γ operator.

Example 4: Suppose we want output as in Example 3, but with the length in hours. We might replace the SELECT clause of that example with

```
SELECT title AS name, length*0.016667 AS lengthInHours
```

Then the same movies would be produced, but lengths would be calculated in hours and the second column would be headed by attribute lengthInHours, as:

name	*lengthInHours*
Pretty Woman	1.98334
...	...

□

Example 5: We can even allow a constant as an expression in the SELECT clause. It might seem pointless to do so, but one application is to put some useful words into the output that SQL displays. The following query:

Case Insensitivity

SQL is *case insensitive*, meaning that it treats upper- and lower-case letters as the same letter. For example, although we have chosen to write keywords like `FROM` in capitals, it is equally proper to write this keyword as `From` or `from`, or even `FrOm`. Names of attributes, relations, aliases, and so on are similarly case insensitive. Only inside quotes does SQL make a distinction between upper- and lower-case letters. Thus, `'FROM'` and `'from'` are different character strings. Of course, neither is the keyword `FROM`.

```
SELECT title, length*0.016667 AS length, 'hrs.' AS inHours
FROM Movies
WHERE studioName = 'Disney' AND year = 1990;
```

produces tuples such as

title	*length*	*inHours*
Pretty Woman	1.98334	hrs.
...	...	...

We have arranged that the third column is called `inHours`, which fits with the column header `length` in the second column. Every tuple in the answer will have the constant `hrs.` in the third column, which gives the illusion of being the units attached to the value in the second column. □

1.2 Selection in SQL

The selection operator of relational algebra, and much more, is available through the `WHERE` clause of SQL. The expressions that may follow `WHERE` include conditional expressions like those found in common languages such as C or Java.

We may build expressions by comparing values using the six common comparison operators: `=`, `<>`, `<`, `>`, `<=`, and `>=`. The last four operators are as in C, but `<>` is the SQL symbol for "not equal to" (`!=` in C), and `=` in SQL is equality (`==` in C).

The values that may be compared include constants and attributes of the relations mentioned after `FROM`. We may also apply the usual arithmetic operators, $+$, $*$, and so on, to numeric values before we compare them. For instance, $(\texttt{year} - 1930) * (\texttt{year} - 1930) < 100$ is true for those years within 9 of 1930. We may apply the concatenation operator `||` to strings; for example `'foo' || 'bar'` has value `'foobar'`.

An example comparison is

```
studioName = 'Disney'
```

SQL Queries and Relational Algebra

The simple SQL queries that we have seen so far all have the form:

```
SELECT L
FROM R
WHERE C
```

in which L is a list of expressions, R is a relation, and C is a condition. The meaning of any such expression is the same as that of the relational-algebra expression

$$\pi_L\big(\sigma_C(R)\big)$$

That is, we start with the relation in the `FROM` clause, apply to each tuple whatever condition is indicated in the `WHERE` clause, and then project onto the list of attributes and/or expressions in the `SELECT` clause.

in Example 1. The attribute `studioName` of the relation `Movies` is tested for equality against the constant `'Disney'`. This constant is string-valued; strings in SQL are denoted by surrounding them with single quotes. Numeric constants, integers and reals, are also allowed, and SQL uses the common notations for reals such as `-12.34` or `1.23E45`.

The result of a comparison is a boolean value: either `TRUE` or `FALSE`.[2] Boolean values may be combined by the logical operators `AND`, `OR`, and `NOT`, with their expected meanings. For instance, we saw in Example 1 how two conditions could be combined by `AND`. The `WHERE` clause of this example evaluates to true if and only if both comparisons are satisfied; that is, the studio name is `'Disney'` and the year is 1990. Here is an example of a query with a complex `WHERE` clause.

Example 6 : Consider the query

```
SELECT title
FROM Movies
WHERE (year > 1970 OR length < 90) AND studioName = 'MGM';
```

This query asks for the titles of movies made by MGM Studios that either were made after 1970 or were less than 90 minutes long. Notice that comparisons can be grouped using parentheses. The parentheses are needed here because the precedence of logical operators in SQL is the same as in most other languages: `AND` takes precedence over `OR`, and `NOT` takes precedence over both. □

[2] Well there's a bit more to boolean values; see Section 1.7.

Representing Bit Strings

A string of bits is represented by `B` followed by a quoted string of 0's and 1's. Thus, `B'011'` represents the string of three bits, the first of which is 0 and the other two of which are 1. Hexadecimal notation may also be used, where an `X` is followed by a quoted string of hexadecimal digits (0 through 9, and *a* through *f*, with the latter representing "digits" 10 through 15). For instance, `X'7ff'` represents a string of twelve bits, a 0 followed by eleven 1's. Note that each hexadecimal digit represents four bits, and leading 0's are not suppressed.

1.3 Comparison of Strings

Two strings are equal if they are the same sequence of characters. Strings can be stored as fixed-length strings, using `CHAR`, or variable-length strings, using `VARCHAR`. When comparing strings with different declarations, only the actual strings are compared; SQL ignores any "pad" characters that must be present in the database in order to give a string its required length.

When we compare strings by one of the "less than" operators, such as `<` or `>=`, we are asking whether one precedes the other in lexicographic order (i.e., in dictionary order, or alphabetically). That is, if $a_1a_2\cdots a_n$ and $b_1b_2\cdots b_m$ are two strings, then the first is "less than" the second if either $a_1 < b_1$, or if $a_1 = b_1$ and $a_2 < b_2$, or if $a_1 = b_1$, $a_2 = b_2$, and $a_3 < b_3$, and so on. We also say $a_1a_2\cdots a_n < b_1b_2\cdots b_m$ if $n < m$ and $a_1a_2\cdots a_n = b_1b_2\cdots b_n$; that is, the first string is a proper prefix of the second. For instance, `'fodder'` $<$ `'foo'`, because the first two characters of each string are the same, `fo`, and the third character of `fodder` precedes the third character of `foo`. Also, `'bar'` $<$ `'bargain'` because the former is a proper prefix of the latter.

1.4 Pattern Matching in SQL

SQL also provides the capability to compare strings on the basis of a simple pattern match. An alternative form of comparison expression is

```
s LIKE p
```

where s is a string and p is a *pattern*, that is, a string with the optional use of the two special characters `%` and `_`. Ordinary characters in p match only themselves in s. But `%` in p can match any sequence of 0 or more characters in s, and `_` in p matches any one character in s. The value of this expression is true if and only if string s matches pattern p. Similarly, s `NOT LIKE` p is true if and only if string s does not match pattern p.

Example 7: We remember a movie "Star something," and we remember that the something has four letters. What could this movie be? We can retrieve all such names with the query:

```
SELECT title
FROM Movies
WHERE title LIKE 'Star ____';
```

This query asks if the title attribute of a movie has a value that is nine characters long, the first five characters being `Star` and a blank. The last four characters may be anything, since any sequence of four characters matches the four _ symbols. The result of the query is the set of complete matching titles, such as *Star Wars* and *Star Trek.* □

Example 8: Let us search for all movies with a possessive ('s) in their titles. The desired query is

```
SELECT title
FROM Movies
WHERE title LIKE '%''s%';
```

To understand this pattern, we must first observe that the apostrophe, being the character that surrounds strings in SQL, cannot also represent itself. The convention taken by SQL is that two consecutive apostrophes in a string represent a single apostrophe and do not end the string. Thus, `''s` in a pattern is matched by a single apostrophe followed by an `s`.

The two `%` characters on either side of the `'s` match any strings whatsoever. Thus, any title with `'s` as a substring will match the pattern, and the answer to this query will include films such as *Logan's Run* or *Alice's Restaurant.* □

1.5 Dates and Times

Implementations of SQL generally support dates and times as special data types. These values are often representable in a variety of formats such as `05/14/1948` or `14 May 1948`. Here we shall describe only the SQL standard notation, which is very specific about format.

A *date* constant is represented by the keyword `DATE` followed by a quoted string of a special form. For example, `DATE '1948-05-14'` follows the required form. The first four characters are digits representing the year. Then come a hyphen and two digits representing the month. Note that, as in our example, a one-digit month is padded with a leading 0. Finally there is another hyphen and two digits representing the day. As with months, we pad the day with a leading 0 if that is necessary to make a two-digit number.

A *time* constant is represented similarly by the keyword `TIME` and a quoted string. This string has two digits for the hour, on the military (24-hour)

Escape Characters in LIKE expressions

What if the pattern we wish to use in a LIKE expression involves the characters % or _? Instead of having a particular character used as the escape character (e.g., the backslash in most UNIX commands), SQL allows us to specify any one character we like as the escape character for a single pattern. We do so by following the pattern by the keyword ESCAPE and the chosen escape character, in quotes. A character % or _ preceded by the escape character in the pattern is interpreted literally as that character, not as a symbol for any sequence of characters or any one character, respectively. For example,

```
s LIKE 'x%%x%' ESCAPE 'x'
```

makes x the escape character in the pattern x%%x%. The sequence x% is taken to be a single %. This pattern matches any string that begins and ends with the character %. Note that only the middle % has its "any string" interpretation.

clock. Then come a colon, two digits for the minute, another colon, and two digits for the second. If fractions of a second are desired, we may continue with a decimal point and as many significant digits as we like. For instance, TIME '15:00:02.5' represents the time at which all students will have left a class that ends at 3 PM: two and a half seconds past three o'clock.

Alternatively, time can be expressed as the number of hours and minutes ahead of (indicated by a plus sign) or behind (indicated by a minus sign) Greenwich Mean Time (GMT). For instance, TIME '12:00:00-8:00' represents noon in Pacific Standard Time, which is eight hours behind GMT.

To combine dates and times we use a value of type TIMESTAMP. These values consist of the keyword TIMESTAMP, a date value, a space, and a time value. Thus, TIMESTAMP '1948-05-14 12:00:00' represents noon on May 14, 1948.

We can compare dates or times using the same comparison operators we use for numbers or strings. That is, $<$ on dates means that the first date is earlier than the second; $<$ on times means that the first is earlier (within the same day) than the second.

1.6 Null Values and Comparisons Involving NULL

SQL allows attributes to have a special value NULL, which is called the *null value*. There are many different interpretations that can be put on null values. Here are some of the most common:

1. *Value unknown*: that is, "I know there is some value that belongs here but I don't know what it is." An unknown birthdate is an example.

2. *Value inapplicable*: "There is no value that makes sense here." For example, if we had a `spouse` attribute for the `MovieStar` relation, then an unmarried star might have `NULL` for that attribute, not because we don't know the spouse's name, but because there is none.

3. *Value withheld*: "We are not entitled to know the value that belongs here." For instance, an unlisted phone number might appear as `NULL` in the component for a `phone` attribute.

The use of the outerjoin operator of relational algebra produces null values in some components of tuples; SQL allows outerjoins and also produces `NULL`'s when a query involves outerjoins; see Section 3.8. There are other ways SQL produces `NULL`'s as well. For example, certain insertions of tuples create null values, as we shall see in Section 5.1.

In `WHERE` clauses, we must be prepared for the possibility that a component of some tuple we are examining will be `NULL`. There are two important rules to remember when we operate upon a `NULL` value.

1. When we operate on a `NULL` and any value, including another `NULL`, using an arithmetic operator like $\times$ or $+$, the result is `NULL`.

2. When we compare a `NULL` value and any value, including another `NULL`, using a comparison operator like `=` or `>`, the result is `UNKNOWN`. The value `UNKNOWN` is another truth-value, like `TRUE` and `FALSE`; we shall discuss how to manipulate truth-value `UNKNOWN` shortly.

However, we must remember that, although `NULL` is a value that can appear in tuples, it is *not* a constant. Thus, while the above rules apply when we try to operate on an expression whose value is `NULL`, we cannot use `NULL` explicitly as an operand.

Example 9: Let x have the value `NULL`. Then the value of $x + 3$ is also `NULL`. However, `NULL` $+ 3$ is not a legal SQL expression. Similarly, the value of $x = 3$ is `UNKNOWN`, because we cannot tell if the value of x, which is `NULL`, equals the value 3. However, the comparison `NULL` $= 3$ is not correct SQL. □

The correct way to ask if x has the value `NULL` is with the expression `x IS NULL`. This expression has the value `TRUE` if x has the value `NULL` and it has value `FALSE` otherwise. Similarly, `x IS NOT NULL` has the value `TRUE` unless the value of x is `NULL`.

1.7 The Truth-Value `UNKNOWN`

In Section 1.2 we assumed that the result of a comparison was either `TRUE` or `FALSE`, and these truth-values were combined in the obvious way using the logical operators `AND`, `OR`, and `NOT`. We have just seen that when `NULL` values

Pitfalls Regarding Nulls

It is tempting to assume that NULL in SQL can always be taken to mean "a value that we don't know but that surely exists." However, there are several ways that intuition is violated. For instance, suppose x is a component of some tuple, and the domain for that component is the integers. We might reason that $0 * x$ surely has the value 0, since no matter what integer x is, its product with 0 is 0. However, if x has the value NULL, rule (1) of Section 1.6 applies; the product of 0 and NULL is NULL. Similarly, we might reason that $x - x$ has the value 0, since whatever integer x is, its difference with itself is 0. However, again the rule about operations on nulls applies, and the result is NULL.

occur, comparisons can yield a third truth-value: UNKNOWN. We must now learn how the logical operators behave on combinations of all three truth-values.

The rule is easy to remember if we think of TRUE as 1 (i.e., fully true), FALSE as 0 (i.e., not at all true), and UNKNOWN as 1/2 (i.e., somewhere between true and false). Then:

1. The AND of two truth-values is the minimum of those values. That is, x AND y is FALSE if either x or y is FALSE; it is UNKNOWN if neither is FALSE but at least one is UNKNOWN, and it is TRUE only when both x and y are TRUE.

2. The OR of two truth-values is the maximum of those values. That is, x OR y is TRUE if either x or y is TRUE; it is UNKNOWN if neither is TRUE but at least one is UNKNOWN, and it is FALSE only when both are FALSE.

3. The negation of truth-value v is $1 - v$. That is, NOT x has the value TRUE when x is FALSE, the value FALSE when x is TRUE, and the value UNKNOWN when x has value UNKNOWN.

In Fig. 2 is a summary of the result of applying the three logical operators to the nine different combinations of truth-values for operands x and y. The value of the last operator, NOT, depends only on x.

SQL conditions, as appear in WHERE clauses of select-from-where statements, apply to each tuple in some relation, and for each tuple, one of the three truth values, TRUE, FALSE, or UNKNOWN is produced. However, only the tuples for which the condition has the value TRUE become part of the answer; tuples with either UNKNOWN or FALSE as value are excluded from the answer. That situation leads to another surprising behavior similar to that discussed in the box on "Pitfalls Regarding Nulls," as the next example illustrates.

Example 10: Suppose we ask about our running-example relation

x	y	x AND y	x OR y	NOT x
TRUE	TRUE	TRUE	TRUE	FALSE
TRUE	UNKNOWN	UNKNOWN	TRUE	FALSE
TRUE	FALSE	FALSE	TRUE	FALSE
UNKNOWN	TRUE	UNKNOWN	TRUE	UNKNOWN
UNKNOWN	UNKNOWN	UNKNOWN	UNKNOWN	UNKNOWN
UNKNOWN	FALSE	FALSE	UNKNOWN	UNKNOWN
FALSE	TRUE	FALSE	TRUE	TRUE
FALSE	UNKNOWN	FALSE	UNKNOWN	TRUE
FALSE	FALSE	FALSE	FALSE	TRUE

Figure 2: Truth table for three-valued logic

```
Movies(title, year, length, genre, studioName, producerC#)
```

the following query:

```
SELECT *
FROM Movies
WHERE length <= 120 OR length > 120;
```

Intuitively, we would expect to get a copy of the `Movies` relation, since each movie has a length that is either 120 or less or that is greater than 120.

However, suppose there are `Movies` tuples with `NULL` in the `length` component. Then both comparisons `length <= 120` and `length > 120` evaluate to `UNKNOWN`. The `OR` of two `UNKNOWN`'s is `UNKNOWN`, by Fig. 2. Thus, for any tuple with a `NULL` in the `length` component, the `WHERE` clause evaluates to `UNKNOWN`. Such a tuple is *not* returned as part of the answer to the query. As a result, the true meaning of the query is "find all the `Movies` tuples with non-`NULL` lengths." □

1.8 Ordering the Output

We may ask that the tuples produced by a query be presented in sorted order. The order may be based on the value of any attribute, with ties broken by the value of a second attribute, remaining ties broken by a third, and so on, as in the τ operation. To get output in sorted order, we may add to the select-from-where statement a clause:

```
ORDER BY <list of attributes>
```

The order is by default ascending, but we can get the output highest-first by appending the keyword `DESC` (for "descending") to an attribute. Similarly, we can specify ascending order with the keyword `ASC`, but that word is unnecessary.

The `ORDER BY` clause follows the `WHERE` clause and any other clauses (i.e., the optional `GROUP BY` and `HAVING` clauses, which are introduced in Section 4).

The ordering is performed on the result of the FROM, WHERE, and other clauses, just before we apply the SELECT clause. The tuples of this result are then sorted by the attributes in the list of the ORDER BY clause, and then passed to the SELECT clause for processing in the normal manner.

Example 11: The following is a rewrite of our original query of Example 1, asking for the Disney movies of 1990 from the relation

```
Movies(title, year, length, genre, studioName, producerC#)
```

To get the movies listed by length, shortest first, and among movies of equal length, alphabetically, we can say:

```
SELECT *
FROM Movies
WHERE studioName = 'Disney' AND year = 1990
ORDER BY length, title;
```

A subtlety of ordering is that all the attributes of Movies are available at the time of sorting, even if they are not part of the SELECT clause. Thus, we could replace SELECT * by SELECT producerC#, and the query would still be legal. □

An additional option in ordering is that the list following ORDER BY can include expressions, just as the SELECT clause can. For instance, we can order the tuples of a relation $R(A, B)$ by the sum of the two components of the tuples, highest first, with:

```
SELECT *
FROM R
ORDER BY A+B DESC;
```

1.9 Exercises for Section 1

Exercise 1.1: If a query has a SELECT clause

```
SELECT A B
```

how do we know whether A and B are two different attributes or B is an alias of A?

Exercise 1.2: Write the following queries, based on our running movie database example

```
Movies(title, year, length, genre, studioName, producerC#)
StarsIn(movieTitle, movieYear, starName)
MovieStar(name, address, gender, birthdate)
MovieExec(name, address, cert#, netWorth)
Studio(name, address, presC#)
```

in SQL.

a) Find the address of MGM studios.

b) Find Sandra Bullock's birthdate.

c) Find all the stars that appeared either in a movie made in 1980 or a movie with "Love" in the title.

d) Find all executives worth at least $10,000,000.

e) Find all the stars who either are male or live in Malibu (have string `Malibu` as a part of their address).

Exercise 1.3: Let a and b be integer-valued attributes that may be `NULL` in some tuples. For each of the following conditions (as may appear in a `WHERE` clause), describe exactly the set of (a, b) tuples that satisfy the condition, including the case where a and/or b is `NULL`.

a) `a = 10 OR b = 20`

b) `a = 10 AND b = 20`

c) `a < 10 OR a >= 10`

! d) `a = b`

! e) `a <= b`

! **Exercise 1.4:** In Example 10 we discussed the query

```
SELECT *
FROM Movies
WHERE length <= 120 OR length > 120;
```

which behaves unintuitively when the length of a movie is `NULL`. Find a simpler, equivalent query, one with a single condition in the `WHERE` clause (no `AND` or `OR` of conditions).

2 Queries Involving More Than One Relation

Much of the power of relational algebra comes from its ability to combine two or more relations through joins, products, unions, intersections, and differences. We get all of these operations in SQL. The set-theoretic operations — union, intersection, and difference — appear directly in SQL, as we shall learn in Section 2.5. First, we shall learn how the select-from-where statement of SQL allows us to perform products and joins.

2.1 Products and Joins in SQL

SQL has a simple way to couple relations in one query: list each relation in the `FROM` clause. Then, the `SELECT` and `WHERE` clauses can refer to the attributes of any of the relations in the `FROM` clause.

Example 12: Suppose we want to know the name of the producer of *Star Wars.* To answer this question we need the following two relations from our running example:

```
Movies(title, year, length, genre, studioName, producerC#)
MovieExec(name, address, cert#, netWorth)
```

The producer certificate number is given in the `Movies` relation, so we can do a simple query on `Movies` to get this number. We could then do a second query on the relation `MovieExec` to find the name of the person with that certificate number.

However, we can phrase both these steps as one query about the pair of relations `Movies` and `MovieExec` as follows:

```
SELECT name
FROM Movies, MovieExec
WHERE title = 'Star Wars' AND producerC# = cert#;
```

This query asks us to consider all pairs of tuples, one from `Movies` and the other from `MovieExec`. The conditions on this pair are stated in the `WHERE` clause:

1. The `title` component of the tuple from `Movies` must have value `'Star Wars'`.

2. The `producerC#` attribute of the `Movies` tuple must be the same certificate number as the `cert#` attribute in the `MovieExec` tuple. That is, these two tuples must refer to the same producer.

Whenever we find a pair of tuples satisfying both conditions, we produce the `name` attribute of the tuple from `MovieExec` as part of the answer. If the data is what we expect, the only time both conditions will be met is when the tuple from `Movies` is for *Star Wars*, and the tuple from `MovieExec` is for George Lucas. Then and only then will the title be correct and the certificate numbers agree. Thus, `George Lucas` should be the only value produced. This process is suggested in Fig. 3. We take up in more detail how to interpret multirelation queries in Section 2.4. □

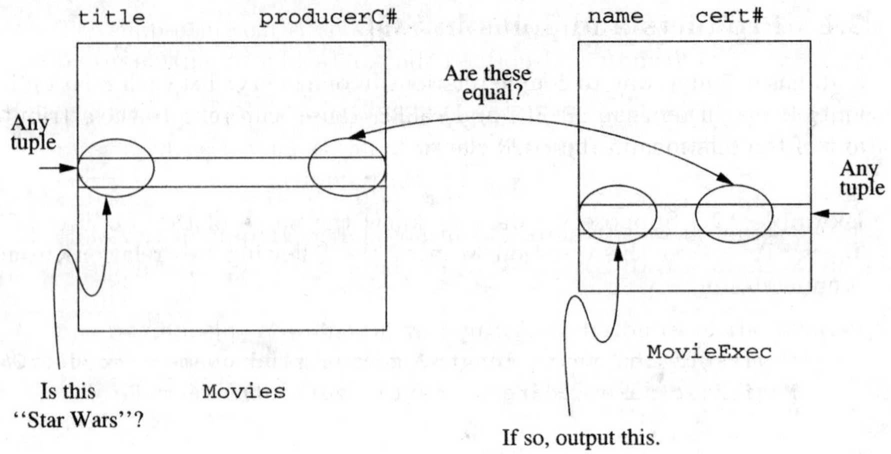

Figure 3: The query of Example 12 asks us to pair every tuple of `Movies` with every tuple of `MovieExec` and test two conditions

2.2 Disambiguating Attributes

Sometimes we ask a query involving several relations, and among these relations are two or more attributes with the same name. If so, we need a way to indicate which of these attributes is meant by a use of their shared name. SQL solves this problem by allowing us to place a relation name and a dot in front of an attribute. Thus $R.A$ refers to the attribute A of relation R.

Example 13 : The two relations

```
MovieStar(name, address, gender, birthdate)
MovieExec(name, address, cert#, netWorth)
```

each have attributes `name` and `address`. Suppose we wish to find pairs consisting of a star and an executive with the same address. The following query does the job.

```
SELECT MovieStar.name, MovieExec.name
FROM MovieStar, MovieExec
WHERE MovieStar.address = MovieExec.address;
```

In this query, we look for a pair of tuples, one from `MovieStar` and the other from `MovieExec`, such that their address components agree. The `WHERE` clause enforces the requirement that the `address` attributes from each of the two tuples agree. Then, for each matching pair of tuples, we extract the two `name` attributes, first from the `MovieStar` tuple and then from the other. The result would be a set of pairs such as

MovieStar.name	*MovieExec.name*
Jane Fonda	Ted Turner
...	...

□

The relation name, followed by a dot, is permissible even in situations where there is no ambiguity. For instance, we are free to write the query of Example 12 as

```
SELECT MovieExec.name
FROM Movies, MovieExec
WHERE Movie.title = 'Star Wars'
      AND Movie.producerC# = MovieExec.cert#;
```

Alternatively, we may use relation names and dots in front of any subset of the attributes in this query.

2.3 Tuple Variables

Disambiguating attributes by prefixing the relation name works as long as the query involves combining several different relations. However, sometimes we need to ask a query that involves two or more tuples from the same relation. We may list a relation R as many times as we need to in the `FROM` clause, but we need a way to refer to each occurrence of R. SQL allows us to define, for each occurrence of R in the `FROM` clause, an "alias" which we shall refer to as a *tuple variable.* Each use of R in the `FROM` clause is followed by the (optional) keyword `AS` and the name of the tuple variable; we shall generally omit the `AS` in this context.

In the `SELECT` and `WHERE` clauses, we can disambiguate attributes of R by preceding them by the appropriate tuple variable and a dot. Thus, the tuple variable serves as another name for relation R and can be used in its place when we wish.

Example 14: While Example 13 asked for a star and an executive sharing an address, we might similarly want to know about two stars who share an address. The query is essentially the same, but now we must think of two tuples chosen from relation `MovieStar`, rather than tuples from each of `MovieStar` and `MovieExec`. Using tuple variables as aliases for two uses of `MovieStar`, we can write the query as

```
SELECT Star1.name, Star2.name
FROM MovieStar Star1, MovieStar Star2
WHERE Star1.address = Star2.address
      AND Star1.name < Star2.name;
```

Tuple Variables and Relation Names

Technically, references to attributes in SELECT and WHERE clauses are *always* to a tuple variable. However, if a relation appears only once in the FROM clause, then we can use the relation name as its own tuple variable. Thus, we can see a relation name R in the FROM clause as shorthand for R AS R. Furthermore, as we have seen, when an attribute belongs unambiguously to one relation, the relation name (tuple variable) may be omitted.

We see in the FROM clause the declaration of two tuple variables, `Star1` and `Star2`; each is an alias for relation `MovieStar`. The tuple variables are used in the SELECT clause to refer to the `name` components of the two tuples. These aliases are also used in the WHERE clause to say that the two `MovieStar` tuples represented by `Star1` and `Star2` have the same value in their `address` components.

The second condition in the WHERE clause, `Star1.name < Star2.name`, says that the name of the first star precedes the name of the second star alphabetically. If this condition were omitted, then tuple variables `Star1` and `Star2` could both refer to the same tuple. We would find that the two tuple variables referred to tuples whose `address` components are equal, of course, and thus produce each star name paired with itself.[3] The second condition also forces us to produce each pair of stars with a common address only once, in alphabetical order. If we used `<>` (not-equal) as the comparison operator, then we would produce pairs of married stars twice, like

Star1.name	*Star2.name*
Paul Newman	Joanne Woodward
Joanne Woodward	Paul Newman
...	...

□

2.4 Interpreting Multirelation Queries

There are several ways to define the meaning of the select-from-where expressions that we have just covered. All are *equivalent*, in the sense that they each give the same answer for each query applied to the same relation instances. We shall consider each in turn.

[3] A similar problem occurs in Example 13 when the same individual is both a star and an executive. We could solve that problem by requiring that the two names be unequal.

Nested Loops

The semantics that we have implicitly used in examples so far is that of tuple variables. Recall that a tuple variable ranges over all tuples of the corresponding relation. A relation name that is not aliased is also a tuple variable ranging over the relation itself, as we mentioned in the box on "Tuple Variables and Relation Names." If there are several tuple variables, we may imagine nested loops, one for each tuple variable, in which the variables each range over the tuples of their respective relations. For each assignment of tuples to the tuple variables, we decide whether the WHERE clause is true. If so, we produce a tuple consisting of the values of the expressions following SELECT; note that each term is given a value by the current assignment of tuples to tuple variables. This query-answering algorithm is suggested by Fig. 4.

```
LET the tuple variables in the from-clause range over
        relations R1, R2, ..., Rn;
FOR each tuple t1 in relation R1 DO
    FOR each tuple t2 in relation R2 DO
        ...
            FOR each tuple tn in relation Rn DO
                IF the where-clause is satisfied when the values
                from t1, t2, ..., tn are substituted for all
                attribute references THEN
                    evaluate the expressions of the select-clause
                    according to t1, t2, ..., tn and produce the
                    tuple of values that results.
```

Figure 4: Answering a simple SQL query

Parallel Assignment

There is an equivalent definition in which we do not explicitly create nested loops ranging over the tuple variables. Rather, we consider in arbitrary order, or in parallel, all possible assignments of tuples from the appropriate relations to the tuple variables. For each such assignment, we consider whether the WHERE clause becomes true. Each assignment that produces a true WHERE clause contributes a tuple to the answer; that tuple is constructed from the attributes of the SELECT clause, evaluated according to that assignment.

Conversion to Relational Algebra

A third approach is to relate the SQL query to relational algebra. We start with the tuple variables in the FROM clause and take the Cartesian product of their relations. If two tuple variables refer to the same relation, then this relation appears twice in the product, and we rename its attributes so all attributes have

An Unintuitive Consequence of SQL Semantics

Suppose R, S, and T are unary (one-component) relations, each having attribute A alone, and we wish to find those elements that are in R and also in either S or T (or both). That is, we want to compute $R \cap (S \cup T)$. We might expect the following SQL query would do the job.

```
SELECT R.A
FROM R, S, T
WHERE R.A = S.A OR R.A = T.A;
```

However, consider the situation in which T is empty. Since then $R.A = T.A$ can never be satisfied, we might expect the query to produce exactly $R \cap S$, based on our intuition about how "OR" operates. Yet whichever of the three equivalent definitions of Section 2.4 one prefers, we find that the result is empty, regardless of how many elements R and S have in common. If we use the nested-loop semantics of Figure 4, then we see that the loop for tuple variable T iterates 0 times, since there are no tuples in the relation for the tuple variable to range over. Thus, the if-statement inside the for-loops never executes, and nothing can be produced. Similarly, if we look for assignments of tuples to the tuple variables, there is no way to assign a tuple to T, so no assignments exist. Finally, if we use the Cartesian-product approach, we start with $R \times S \times T$, which is empty because T is empty.

unique names. Similarly, attributes of the same name from different relations are renamed to avoid ambiguity.

Having created the product, we apply a selection operator to it by converting the `WHERE` clause to a selection condition in the obvious way. That is, each attribute reference in the `WHERE` clause is replaced by the attribute of the product to which it corresponds. Finally, we create from the `SELECT` clause a list of expressions for a final (extended) projection operation. As we did for the `WHERE` clause, we interpret each attribute reference in the `SELECT` clause as the corresponding attribute in the product of relations.

Example 15: Let us convert the query of Example 14 to relational algebra. First, there are two tuple variables in the `FROM` clause, both referring to relation `MovieStar`. Thus, our expression (without the necessary renaming) begins:

$$\texttt{MovieStar} \times \texttt{MovieStar}$$

The resulting relation has eight attributes, the first four correspond to attributes `name`, `address`, `gender`, and `birthdate` from the first copy of relation `MovieStar`, and the second four correspond to the same attributes from the other copy of

MovieStar. We could create names for these attributes with a dot and the aliasing tuple variable — e.g., Star1.gender — but for succinctness, let us invent new symbols and call the attributes simply $A_1, A_2, \ldots, A_8$. Thus, A_1 corresponds to Star1.name, A_5 corresponds to Star2.name, and so on.

Under this naming strategy for attributes, the selection condition obtained from the WHERE clause is $A_2 = A_6$ and $A_1 < A_5$. The projection list is A_1, A_5. Thus,

$$\pi_{A_1,A_5}\Big(\sigma_{A_2=A_6 \texttt{ AND } A_1<A_5}\big(\rho_{M(A_1,A_2,A_3,A_4)}(\texttt{MovieStar}) \times \rho_{N(A_5,A_6,A_7,A_8)}(\texttt{MovieStar})\big)\Big)$$

renders the entire query in relational algebra. □

2.5 Union, Intersection, and Difference of Queries

Sometimes we wish to combine relations using the set operations of relational algebra: union, intersection, and difference. SQL provides corresponding operators that apply to the results of queries, provided those queries produce relations with the same list of attributes and attribute types. The keywords used are UNION, INTERSECT, and EXCEPT for $\cup$, $\cap$, and $-$, respectively. Words like UNION are used between two queries, and those queries must be parenthesized.

Example 16 : Suppose we wanted the names and addresses of all female movie stars who are also movie executives with a net worth over $10,000,000. Using the following two relations:

```
MovieStar(name, address, gender, birthdate)
MovieExec(name, address, cert#, netWorth)
```

we can write the query as in Fig. 5. Lines (1) through (3) produce a relation whose schema is (name, address) and whose tuples are the names and addresses of all female movie stars.

```
1)  (SELECT name, address
2)   FROM MovieStar
3)   WHERE gender = 'F')
4)        INTERSECT
5)  (SELECT name, address
6)   FROM MovieExec
7)   WHERE netWorth > 10000000);
```

Figure 5: Intersecting female movie stars with rich executives

Similarly, lines (5) through (7) produce the set of "rich" executives, those with net worth over $10,000,000. This query also yields a relation whose schema

Readable SQL Queries

Generally, one writes SQL queries so that each important keyword like FROM or WHERE starts a new line. This style offers the reader visual clues to the structure of the query. However, when a query or subquery is short, we shall sometimes write it out on a single line, as we did in Example 17. That style, keeping a complete query compact, also offers good readability.

has the attributes name and address only. Since the two schemas are the same, we can intersect them, and we do so with the operator of line (4). □

Example 17: In a similar vein, we could take the difference of two sets of persons, each selected from a relation. The query

```
(SELECT name, address FROM MovieStar)
    EXCEPT
(SELECT name, address FROM MovieExec);
```

gives the names and addresses of movie stars who are not also movie executives, regardless of gender or net worth. □

In the two examples above, the attributes of the relations whose intersection or difference we took were conveniently the same. However, if necessary to get a common set of attributes, we can rename attributes as in Example 3.

Example 18: Suppose we wanted all the titles and years of movies that appeared in either the Movies or StarsIn relation of our running example:

```
Movies(title, year, length, genre, studioName, producerC#)
StarsIn(movieTitle, movieYear, starName)
```

Ideally, these sets of movies would be the same, but in practice it is common for relations to diverge; for instance we might have movies with no listed stars or a StarsIn tuple that mentions a movie not found in the Movies relation.[4] Thus, we might write

```
(SELECT title, year FROM Movie)
    UNION
(SELECT movieTitle AS title, movieYear AS year FROM StarsIn);
```

The result would be all movies mentioned in either relation, with title and year as the attributes of the resulting relation. □

[4]There are ways to prevent this divergence; they are not covered here.

2.6 Exercises for Section 2

Exercise 2.1: Using the database schema of our running movie example

```
Movies(title, year, length, genre, studioName, producerC#)
StarsIn(movieTitle, movieYear, starName)
MovieStar(name, address, gender, birthdate)
MovieExec(name, address, cert#, netWorth)
Studio(name, address, presC#)
```

write the following queries in SQL.

a) Who were the male stars in *Titanic*?

b) Which stars appeared in movies produced by MGM in 1995?

c) Who is the president of MGM studios?

! d) Which movies are longer than *Gone With the Wind*?

! e) Which executives are worth more than Merv Griffin?

! Exercise 2.2: A general form of relational-algebra query is

$$\pi_L\Big(\sigma_C(R_1 \times R_2 \times \cdots \times R_n)\Big)$$

Here, L is an arbitrary list of attributes, and C is an arbitrary condition. The list of relations $R_1, R_2, \ldots, R_n$ may include the same relation repeated several times, in which case appropriate renaming may be assumed applied to the R_i's. Show how to express any query of this form in SQL.

! Exercise 2.3: Another general form of relational-algebra query is

$$\pi_L\Big(\sigma_C(R_1 \bowtie R_2 \bowtie \cdots \bowtie R_n)\Big)$$

The same assumptions as in Exercise 2.2 apply here; the only difference is that the natural join is used instead of the product. Show how to express any query of this form in SQL.

3 Subqueries

In SQL, one query can be used in various ways to help in the evaluation of another. A query that is part of another is called a *subquery.* Subqueries can have subqueries, and so on, down as many levels as we wish. We already saw one example of the use of subqueries; in Section 2.5 we built a union, intersection, or difference query by connecting two subqueries to form the whole query. There are a number of other ways that subqueries can be used:

1. Subqueries can return a single constant, and this constant can be compared with another value in a WHERE clause.

2. Subqueries can return relations that can be used in various ways in WHERE clauses.

3. Subqueries can appear in FROM clauses, followed by a tuple variable that represents the tuples in the result of the subquery.

3.1 Subqueries that Produce Scalar Values

An atomic value that can appear as one component of a tuple is referred to as a *scalar*. A select-from-where expression can produce a relation with any number of attributes in its schema, and there can be any number of tuples in the relation. However, often we are only interested in values of a single attribute. Furthermore, sometimes we can deduce from information about keys, or from other information, that there will be only a single value produced for that attribute.

If so, we can use this select-from-where expression, surrounded by parentheses, as if it were a constant. In particular, it may appear in a WHERE clause any place we would expect to find a constant or an attribute representing a component of a tuple. For instance, we may compare the result of such a subquery to a constant or attribute.

Example 19: Let us recall Example 12, where we asked for the producer of *Star Wars.* We had to query the two relations

```
Movies(title, year, length, genre, studioName, producerC#)
MovieExec(name, address, cert#, netWorth)
```

because only the former has movie title information and only the latter has producer names. The information is linked by "certificate numbers." These numbers uniquely identify producers. The query we developed is:

```
SELECT name
FROM Movies, MovieExec
WHERE title = 'Star Wars' AND producerC# = cert#;
```

There is another way to look at this query. We need the Movies relation only to get the certificate number for the producer of *Star Wars.* Once we have it, we can query the relation MovieExec to find the name of the person with this certificate. The first problem, getting the certificate number, can be written as a subquery, and the result, which we expect will be a single value, can be used in the "main" query to achieve the same effect as the query above. This query is shown in Fig. 6.

Lines (4) through (6) of Fig. 6 are the subquery. Looking only at this simple query by itself, we see that the result will be a unary relation with attribute

```
1) SELECT name
2) FROM MovieExec
3) WHERE cert# =
4)      (SELECT producerC#
5)       FROM Movies
6)       WHERE title = 'Star Wars'
        );
```

Figure 6: Finding the producer of *Star Wars* by using a nested subquery

producerC#, and we expect to find only one tuple in this relation. The tuple will look like (12345), that is, a single component with some integer, perhaps 12345 or whatever George Lucas' certificate number is. If zero tuples or more than one tuple is produced by the subquery of lines (4) through (6), it is a run-time error.

Having executed this subquery, we can then execute lines (1) through (3) of Fig. 6, as if the value 12345 replaced the entire subquery. That is, the "main" query is executed as if it were

```
SELECT name
FROM MovieExec
WHERE cert# = 12345;
```

The result of this query should be George Lucas. □

3.2 Conditions Involving Relations

There are a number of SQL operators that we can apply to a relation R and produce a boolean result. However, the relation R must be expressed as a subquery. As a trick, if we want to apply these operators to a stored table Foo, we can use the subquery (SELECT * FROM Foo). The same trick works for union, intersection, and difference of relations. Notice that those operators, introduced in Section 2.5 are applied to two subqueries.

Some of the operators below — IN, ALL, and ANY — will be explained first in their simple form where a scalar value s is involved. In this situation, the subquery R is required to produce a one-column relation. Here are the definitions of the operators:

1. EXISTS R is a condition that is true if and only if R is not empty.

2. s IN R is true if and only if s is equal to one of the values in R. Likewise, s NOT IN R is true if and only if s is equal to no value in R. Here, we assume R is a unary relation. We shall discuss extensions to the IN and NOT IN operators where R has more than one attribute in its schema and s is a tuple in Section 3.3.

3. s > ALL R is true if and only if s is greater than every value in unary relation R. Similarly, the > operator could be replaced by any of the other five comparison operators, with the analogous meaning: s stands in the stated relationship to every tuple in R. For instance, s <> ALL R is the same as s NOT IN R.

4. s > ANY R is true if and only if s is greater than at least one value in unary relation R. Similarly, any of the other five comparisons could be used in place of >, with the meaning that s stands in the stated relationship to at least one tuple of R. For instance, s = ANY R is the same as s IN R.

The EXISTS, ALL, and ANY operators can be negated by putting NOT in front of the entire expression, just like any other boolean-valued expression. Thus, NOT EXISTS R is true if and only if R is empty. NOT s >= ALL R is true if and only if s is not the maximum value in R, and NOT s > ANY R is true if and only if s is the minimum value in R. We shall see several examples of the use of these operators shortly.

3.3 Conditions Involving Tuples

A tuple in SQL is represented by a parenthesized list of scalar values. Examples are (123, 'foo') and (name, address, networth). The first of these has constants as components; the second has attributes as components. Mixing of constants and attributes is permitted.

If a tuple t has the same number of components as a relation R, then it makes sense to compare t and R in expressions of the type listed in Section 3.2. Examples are t IN R or t <> ANY R. The latter comparison means that there is some tuple in R other than t. Note that when comparing a tuple with members of a relation R, we must compare components using the assumed standard order for the attributes of R.

```
SELECT name
FROM MovieExec
WHERE cert# IN
     (SELECT producerC#
      FROM Movies
      WHERE (title, year) IN
           (SELECT movieTitle, movieYear
            FROM StarsIn
            WHERE starName = 'Harrison Ford'
           )
     );
```

Figure 7: Finding the producers of Harrison Ford's movies

Example 20: In Fig. 7 is a SQL query on the three relations

```
Movies(title, year, length, genre, studioName, producerC#)
StarsIn(movieTitle, movieYear, starName)
MovieExec(name, address, cert#, netWorth)
```

asking for all the producers of movies in which Harrison Ford stars. It consists of a "main" query, a query nested within that, and a third query nested within the second.

We should analyze any query with subqueries from the inside out. Thus, let us start with the innermost nested subquery: lines (7) through (9). This query examines the tuples of the relation `StarsIn` and finds all those tuples whose `starName` component is `'Harrison Ford'`. The titles and years of those movies are returned by this subquery. Recall that title and year, not title alone, is the key for movies, so we need to produce tuples with both attributes to identify a movie uniquely. Thus, we would expect the value produced by lines (7) through (9) to look something like Fig. 8.

title	*year*
Star Wars	1977
Raiders of the Lost Ark	1981
The Fugitive	1993
...	...

Figure 8: Title-year pairs returned by inner subquery

Now, consider the middle subquery, lines (4) through (6). It searches the `Movies` relation for tuples whose title and year are in the relation suggested by Fig. 8. For each tuple found, the producer's certificate number is returned, so the result of the middle subquery is the set of certificates of the producers of Harrison Ford's movies.

Finally, consider the "main" query of lines (1) through (3). It examines the tuples of the `MovieExec` relation to find those whose `cert#` component is one of the certificates in the set returned by the middle subquery. For each of these tuples, the name of the producer is returned, giving us the set of producers of Harrison Ford's movies, as desired. □

Incidentally, the nested query of Fig. 7 can, like many nested queries, be written as a single select-from-where expression with relations in the `FROM` clause for each of the relations mentioned in the main query or a subquery. The `IN` relationships are replaced by equalities in the `WHERE` clause. For instance, the query of Fig. 9 is essentially that of Fig. 7. There is a difference regarding the way duplicate occurrences of a producer — e.g., George Lucas — are handled, as we shall discuss in Section 4.1.

```
SELECT name
FROM MovieExec, Movies, StarsIn
WHERE cert# = producerC# AND
      title = movieTitle AND
      year = movieYear AND
      starName = 'Harrison Ford';
```

Figure 9: Ford's producers without nested subqueries

3.4 Correlated Subqueries

The simplest subqueries can be evaluated once and for all, and the result used in a higher-level query. A more complicated use of nested subqueries requires the subquery to be evaluated many times, once for each assignment of a value to some term in the subquery that comes from a tuple variable outside the subquery. A subquery of this type is called a *correlated* subquery. Let us begin our study with an example.

Example 21: We shall find the titles that have been used for two or more movies. We start with an outer query that looks at all tuples in the relation

```
Movies(title, year, length, genre, studioName, producerC#)
```

For each such tuple, we ask in a subquery whether there is a movie with the same title and a greater year. The entire query is shown in Fig. 10.

As with other nested queries, let us begin at the innermost subquery, lines (4) through (6). If `Old.title` in line (6) were replaced by a constant string such as `'King Kong'`, we would understand it quite easily as a query asking for the year or years in which movies titled *King Kong* were made. The present subquery differs little. The only problem is that we don't know what value `Old.title` has. However, as we range over `Movies` tuples of the outer query of lines (1) through (3), each tuple provides a value of `Old.title`. We then execute the query of lines (4) through (6) with this value for `Old.title` to decide the truth of the `WHERE` clause that extends from lines (3) through (6).

```
1)  SELECT title
2)  FROM Movies Old
3)  WHERE year < ANY
4)      (SELECT year
5)       FROM Movies
6)       WHERE title = Old.title
        );
```

Figure 10: Finding movie titles that appear more than once

The condition of line (3) is true if any movie with the same title as `Old.title` has a later year than the movie in the tuple that is the current value of tuple variable `Old`. This condition is true unless the year in the tuple `Old` is the last year in which a movie of that title was made. Consequently, lines (1) through (3) produce a title one fewer times than there are movies with that title. A movie made twice will be listed once, a movie made three times will be listed twice, and so on.[5] □

When writing a correlated query it is important that we be aware of the *scoping rules* for names. In general, an attribute in a subquery belongs to one of the tuple variables in that subquery's `FROM` clause if some tuple variable's relation has that attribute in its schema. If not, we look at the immediately surrounding subquery, then to the one surrounding that, and so on. Thus, `year` on line (4) and `title` on line (6) of Fig. 10 refer to the attributes of the tuple variable that ranges over all the tuples of the copy of relation `Movies` introduced on line (5) — that is, the copy of the `Movies` relation addressed by the subquery of lines (4) through (6).

However, we can arrange for an attribute to belong to another tuple variable if we prefix it by that tuple variable and a dot. That is why we introduced the alias `Old` for the `Movies` relation of the outer query, and why we refer to `Old.title` in line (6). Note that if the two relations in the `FROM` clauses of lines (2) and (5) were different, we would not need an alias. Rather, in the subquery we could refer directly to attributes of a relation mentioned in line (2).

3.5 Subqueries in FROM Clauses

Another use for subqueries is as relations in a `FROM` clause. In a `FROM` list, instead of a stored relation, we may use a parenthesized subquery. Since we don't have a name for the result of this subquery, we must give it a tuple-variable alias. We then refer to tuples in the result of the subquery as we would tuples in any relation that appears in the `FROM` list.

Example 22: Let us reconsider the problem of Example 20, where we wrote a query that finds the producers of Harrison Ford's movies. Suppose we had a relation that gave the certificates of the producers of those movies. It would then be a simple matter to look up the names of those producers in the relation `MovieExec`. Figure 11 is such a query.

Lines (2) through (7) are the `FROM` clause of the outer query. In addition to the relation `MovieExec`, it has a subquery. That subquery joins `Movies` and `StarsIn` on lines (3) through (5), adds the condition that the star is Harrison Ford on line (6), and returns the set of producers of the movies at line (2). This set is given the alias `Prod` on line (7).

[5] This example is the first occasion on which we've been reminded that relations in SQL are bags, not sets. There are several ways that duplicates may crop up in SQL relations. We shall discuss the matter in detail in Section 4.

```
1)  SELECT name
2)  FROM MovieExec, (SELECT producerC#
3)                   FROM Movies, StarsIn
4)                   WHERE title = movieTitle AND
5)                         year = movieYear AND
6)                         starName = 'Harrison Ford'
7)                  ) Prod
8)  WHERE cert# = Prod.producerC#;
```

Figure 11: Finding the producers of Ford's movies using a subquery in the FROM clause

At line (8), the relations MovieExec and the subquery aliased Prod are joined with the requirement that the certificate numbers be the same. The names of the producers from MovieExec that have certificates in the set aliased by Prod is returned at line (1). □

3.6 SQL Join Expressions

We can construct relations by a number of variations on the join operator applied to two relations. These variants include products, natural joins, theta-joins, and outerjoins. The result can stand as a query by itself. Alternatively, all these expressions, since they produce relations, may be used as subqueries in the FROM clause of a select-from-where expression. These expressions are principally shorthands for more complex select-from-where queries (see Exercise 3.7).

The simplest form of join expression is a *cross join*; that term is a synonym for what we called a Cartesian product or just "product". For instance, if we want the product of the two relations

```
Movies(title, year, length, genre, studioName, producerC#)
StarsIn(movieTitle, movieYear, starName)
```

we can say

```
Movies CROSS JOIN StarsIn;
```

and the result will be a nine-column relation with all the attributes of Movies and StarsIn. Every pair consisting of one tuple of Movies and one tuple of StarsIn will be a tuple of the resulting relation.

The attributes in the product relation can be called $R.A$, where R is one of the two joined relations and A is one of its attributes. If only one of the relations has an attribute named A, then the R and dot can be dropped, as usual. In this instance, since Movies and StarsIn have no common attributes, the nine attribute names suffice in the product.

However, the product by itself is rarely a useful operation. A more conventional theta-join is obtained with the keyword ON. We put JOIN between two relation names R and S and follow them by ON and a condition. The meaning of JOIN...ON is that the product of $R \times S$ is followed by a selection for whatever condition follows ON.

Example 23: Suppose we want to join the relations

```
Movies(title, year, length, genre, studioName, producerC#)
StarsIn(movieTitle, movieYear, starName)
```

with the condition that the only tuples to be joined are those that refer to the same movie. That is, the titles and years from both relations must be the same. We can ask this query by

```
Movies JOIN StarsIn ON
        title = movieTitle AND year = movieYear;
```

The result is again a nine-column relation with the obvious attribute names. However, now a tuple from Movies and one from StarsIn combine to form a tuple of the result only if the two tuples agree on both the title and year. As a result, two of the columns are redundant, because every tuple of the result will have the same value in both the title and movieTitle components and will have the same value in both year and movieYear.

If we are concerned with the fact that the join above has two redundant components, we can use the whole expression as a subquery in a FROM clause and use a SELECT clause to remove the undesired attributes. Thus, we could write

```
SELECT title, year, length, genre, studioName,
        producerC#, starName
FROM Movies JOIN StarsIn ON
        title = movieTitle AND year = movieYear;
```

to get a seven-column relation which is the Movies relation's tuples, each extended in all possible ways with a star of that movie. □

3.7 Natural Joins

A natural join differs from a theta-join in that:

1. The join condition is that all pairs of attributes from the two relations having a common name are equated, and there are no other conditions.

2. One of each pair of equated attributes is projected out.

The SQL natural join behaves exactly this way. Keywords NATURAL JOIN appear between the relations to express the $\bowtie$ operator.

Example 24: Suppose we want to compute the natural join of the relations

```
MovieStar(name, address, gender, birthdate)
MovieExec(name, address, cert#, netWorth)
```

The result will be a relation whose schema includes attributes `name` and `address` plus all the attributes that appear in one or the other of the two relations. A tuple of the result will represent an individual who is both a star and an executive and will have all the information pertinent to either: a name, address, gender, birthdate, certificate number, and net worth. The expression

```
MovieStar NATURAL JOIN MovieExec;
```

succinctly describes the desired relation. □

3.8 Outerjoins

The outerjoin operator is a way to augment the result of a join by the dangling tuples, padded with null values. In SQL, we can specify an outerjoin; `NULL` is used as the null value.

Example 25: Suppose we wish to take the outerjoin of the two relations

```
MovieStar(name, address, gender, birthdate)
MovieExec(name, address, cert#, netWorth)
```

SQL refers to the standard outerjoin, which pads dangling tuples from both of its arguments, as a *full* outerjoin. The syntax is unsurprising:

```
MovieStar NATURAL FULL OUTER JOIN MovieExec;
```

The result of this operation is a relation with the same six-attribute schema as Example 24. The tuples of this relation are of three kinds. Those representing individuals who are both stars and executives have tuples with all six attributes non-`NULL`. These are the tuples that are also in the result of Example 24.

The second kind of tuple is one for an individual who is a star but not an executive. These tuples have values for attributes `name`, `address`, `gender`, and `birthdate` taken from their tuple in `MovieStar`, while the attributes belonging only to `MovieExec`, namely `cert#` and `netWorth`, have `NULL` values.

The third kind of tuple is for an executive who is not also a star. These tuples have values for the attributes of `MovieExec` taken from their `MovieExec` tuple and `NULL`'s in the attributes `gender` and `birthdate` that come only from `MovieStar`. For instance, the three tuples of the result relation shown in Fig. 12 correspond to the three types of individuals, respectively. □

All the variations on the outerjoin are also available in SQL. If we want a left- or right-outerjoin, we add the appropriate word `LEFT` or `RIGHT` in place of `FULL`. For instance,

```
MovieStar NATURAL LEFT OUTER JOIN MovieExec;
```

name	*address*	*gender*	*birthdate*	*cert#*	*networth*
Mary Tyler Moore	Maple St.	'F'	9/9/99	12345	$100···
Tom Hanks	Cherry Ln.	'M'	8/8/88	NULL	NULL
George Lucas	Oak Rd.	NULL	NULL	23456	$200···

Figure 12: Three tuples in the outerjoin of MovieStar and MovieExec

would yield the first two tuples of Fig. 12 but not the third. Similarly,

```
MovieStar NATURAL RIGHT OUTER JOIN MovieExec;
```

would yield the first and third tuples of Fig. 12 but not the second.

Next, suppose we want a theta-outerjoin instead of a natural outerjoin. Instead of using the keyword NATURAL, we may follow the join by ON and a condition that matching tuples must obey. If we also specify FULL OUTER JOIN, then after matching tuples from the two joined relations, we pad dangling tuples of either relation with NULL's and include the padded tuples in the result.

Example 26: Let us reconsider Example 23, where we joined the relations Movies and StarsIn using the conditions that the title and movieTitle attributes of the two relations agree and that the year and movieYear attributes of the two relations agree. If we modify that example to call for a full outerjoin:

```
Movies FULL OUTER JOIN StarsIn ON
    title = movieTitle AND year = movieYear;
```

then we shall get not only tuples for movies that have at least one star mentioned in StarsIn, but we shall get tuples for movies with no listed stars, padded with NULL's in attributes movieTitle, movieYear, and starName. Likewise, for stars not appearing in any movie listed in relation Movies we get a tuple with NULL's in the six attributes of Movies. □

The keyword FULL can be replaced by either LEFT or RIGHT in outerjoins of the type suggested by Example 26. For instance,

```
Movies LEFT OUTER JOIN StarsIn ON
    title = movieTitle AND year = movieYear;
```

gives us the Movies tuples with at least one listed star and NULL-padded Movies tuples without a listed star, but will not include stars without a listed movie. Conversely,

```
Movies RIGHT OUTER JOIN StarsIn ON
    title = movieTitle AND year = movieYear;
```

will omit the tuples for movies without a listed star but will include tuples for stars not in any listed movies, padded with NULL's.

3.9 Exercises for Section 3

! **Exercise 3.1:** Write the query of Fig. 10 without any subqueries.

! **Exercise 3.2:** Consider expression $\pi_L(R_1 \bowtie R_2 \bowtie \cdots \bowtie R_n)$ of relational algebra, where L is a list of attributes all of which belong to R_1. Show that this expression can be written in SQL using subqueries only. More precisely, write an equivalent SQL expression where no FROM clause has more than one relation in its list.

! **Exercise 3.3:** Write the following queries without using the intersection or difference operators:

a) The intersection query of Fig. 5.

b) The difference query of Example 17.

!! **Exercise 3.4:** We have noticed that certain operators of SQL are redundant, in the sense that they always can be replaced by other operators. For example, we saw that s IN R can be replaced by s = ANY R. Show that EXISTS and NOT EXISTS are redundant by explaining how to replace any expression of the form EXISTS R or NOT EXISTS R by an expression that does not involve EXISTS (except perhaps in the expression R itself). *Hint*: Remember that it is permissible to have a constant in the SELECT clause.

Exercise 3.5: For these relations from our running movie database schema

```
StarsIn(movieTitle, movieYear, starName)
MovieStar(name, address, gender, birthdate)
MovieExec(name, address, cert#, netWorth)
Studio(name, address, presC#)
```

describe the tuples that would appear in the following SQL expressions:

a) `Studio CROSS JOIN MovieExec;`

b) `StarsIn NATURAL FULL OUTER JOIN MovieStar;`

c) `StarsIn FULL OUTER JOIN MovieStar ON name = starName;`

! **Exercise 3.6:** Using the database schema

```
Product(maker, model, type)
PC(model, speed, ram, hd, rd, price)
Laptop(model, speed, ram, hd, screen, price)
Printer(model, color, type, price)
```

write a SQL query that will produce information about all products — PC's, laptops, and printers — including their manufacturer if available, and whatever information about that product is relevant (i.e., found in the relation for that type of product).

! **Exercise 3.7:** The join operators (other than outerjoin) we learned in this section are redundant, in the sense that they can always be replaced by select-from-where expressions. Explain how to write expressions of the following forms using select-from-where:

a) `R CROSS JOIN S;`

b) `R NATURAL JOIN S;`

c) `R JOIN S ON` C;, where C is a SQL condition.

4 Full-Relation Operations

In this section we shall study some operations that act on relations as a whole, rather than on tuples individually or in small numbers (as do joins of several relations, for instance). First, we deal with the fact that SQL uses relations that are bags rather than sets, and a tuple can appear more than once in a relation. We shall see how to force the result of an operation to be a set in Section 4.1, and in Section 4.2 we shall see that it is also possible to prevent the elimination of duplicates in circumstances where SQL systems would normally eliminate them.

Then, we discuss how SQL supports the grouping and aggregation operator γ. SQL has aggregation operators and a `GROUP-BY` clause. There is also a "`HAVING`" clause that allows selection of certain groups in a way that depends on the group as a whole, rather than on individual tuples.

4.1 Eliminating Duplicates

As mentioned in Section 3.4, SQL's notion of relations differs from the abstract notion of relations. A relation, being a set, cannot have more than one copy of any given tuple. When a SQL query creates a new relation, the SQL system does not ordinarily eliminate duplicates. Thus, the SQL response to a query may list the same tuple several times.

Recall from Section 2.4 that one of several equivalent definitions of the meaning of a SQL select-from-where query is that we begin with the Cartesian product of the relations referred to in the `FROM` clause. Each tuple of the product is tested by the condition in the `WHERE` clause, and the ones that pass the test are given to the output for projection according to the `SELECT` clause. This projection may cause the same tuple to result from different tuples of the product, and if so, each copy of the resulting tuple is printed in its turn. Further, since there is nothing wrong with a SQL relation having duplicates, the relations from which the Cartesian product is formed may have duplicates, and each identical copy is paired with the tuples from the other relations, yielding a proliferation of duplicates in the product.

If we do not wish duplicates in the result, then we may follow the keyword `SELECT` by the keyword `DISTINCT`. That word tells SQL to produce only one copy of any tuple and is the SQL analog of applying the δ operator to the result of the query.

Example 27: Let us reconsider the query of Fig. 9, where we asked for the producers of Harrison Ford's movies using no subqueries. As written, George Lucas will appear many times in the output. If we want only to see each producer once, we may change line (1) of the query to

```
1)  SELECT DISTINCT name
```

Then, the list of producers will have duplicate occurrences of names eliminated before printing.

Incidentally, the query of Fig. 7, where we used subqueries, does not necessarily suffer from the problem of duplicate answers. True, the subquery at line (4) of Fig. 7 will produce the certificate number of George Lucas several times. However, in the "main" query of line (1), we examine each tuple of `MovieExec` once. Presumably, there is only one tuple for George Lucas in that relation, and if so, it is only this tuple that satisfies the `WHERE` clause of line (3). Thus, George Lucas is printed only once. □

4.2 Duplicates in Unions, Intersections, and Differences

Unlike the `SELECT` statement, which preserves duplicates as a default and only eliminates them when instructed to by the `DISTINCT` keyword, the union, intersection, and difference operations, which we introduced in Section 2.5, normally eliminate duplicates. That is, bags are converted to sets, and the set version of the operation is applied. In order to prevent the elimination of duplicates, we must follow the operator `UNION`, `INTERSECT`, or `EXCEPT` by the keyword `ALL`. If we do, then we get the bag semantics of these operators.

Example 28: Consider again the union expression from Example 18, but now add the keyword `ALL`, as:

The Cost of Duplicate Elimination

One might be tempted to place DISTINCT after every SELECT, on the theory that it is harmless. In fact, it is very expensive to eliminate duplicates from a relation. The relation must be sorted or partitioned so that identical tuples appear next to each other. Only by grouping the tuples in this way can we determine whether or not a given tuple should be eliminated. The time it takes to sort the relation so that duplicates may be eliminated is often greater than the time it takes to execute the query itself. Thus, duplicate elimination should be used judiciously if we want our queries to run fast.

```
(SELECT title, year FROM Movies)
    UNION ALL
(SELECT movieTitle AS title, movieYear AS year FROM StarsIn);
```

Now, a title and year will appear as many times in the result as it appears in each of the relations Movies and StarsIn put together. For instance, if a movie appeared once in the Movies relation and there were three stars for that movie listed in StarsIn (so the movie appeared in three different tuples of StarsIn), then that movie's title and year would appear four times in the result of the union. □

As for union, the operators INTERSECT ALL and EXCEPT ALL are intersection and difference of bags. Thus, if R and S are relations, then the result of expression

$$R \texttt{ INTERSECT ALL } S$$

is the relation in which the number of times a tuple t appears is the minimum of the number of times it appears in R and the number of times it appears in S.

The result of expression

$$R \texttt{ EXCEPT ALL } S$$

has tuple t as many times as the difference of the number of times it appears in R minus the number of times it appears in S, provided the difference is positive.

4.3 Grouping and Aggregation in SQL

You may remember the grouping-and-aggregation operator γ. Recall that this operator allows us to partition the tuples of a relation into "groups," based on the values of tuples in one or more attributes. We are then able to aggregate certain other columns of the relation by applying "aggregation" operators to those columns. If there are groups, then the aggregation is done separately for each group. SQL provides all the capability of the γ operator through the use of aggregation operators in SELECT clauses and a special GROUP BY clause.

4.4 Aggregation Operators

SQL uses the five aggregation operators SUM, AVG, MIN, MAX, and COUNT. These operators are used by applying them to a scalar-valued expression, typically a column name, in a SELECT clause. One exception is the expression COUNT(*), which counts all the tuples in the relation that is constructed from the FROM clause and WHERE clause of the query.

In addition, we have the option of eliminating duplicates from the column before applying the aggregation operator by using the keyword DISTINCT. That is, an expression such as COUNT(DISTINCT x) counts the number of distinct values in column x. We could use any of the other operators in place of COUNT here, but expressions such as SUM(DISTINCT x) rarely make sense, since it asks us to sum the different values in column x.

Example 29: The following query finds the average net worth of all movie executives:

```
SELECT AVG(netWorth)
FROM MovieExec;
```

Note that there is no WHERE clause at all, so the keyword WHERE is properly omitted. This query examines the netWorth column of the relation

```
MovieExec(name, address, cert#, netWorth)
```

sums the values found there, one value for each tuple (even if the tuple is a duplicate of some other tuple), and divides the sum by the number of tuples. If there are no duplicate tuples, then this query gives the average net worth as we expect. If there were duplicate tuples, then a movie executive whose tuple appeared n times would have his or her net worth counted n times in the average. □

Example 30: The following query:

```
SELECT COUNT(*)
FROM StarsIn;
```

counts the number of tuples in the StarsIn relation. The similar query:

```
SELECT COUNT(starName)
FROM StarsIn;
```

counts the number of values in the `starName` column of the relation. Since duplicate values are not eliminated when we project onto the `starName` column in SQL, this count should be the same as the count produced by the query with `COUNT(*)`.

If we want to be certain that we do not count duplicate values more than once, we can use the keyword `DISTINCT` before the aggregated attribute, as:

```
SELECT COUNT(DISTINCT starName)
FROM StarsIn;
```

Now, each star is counted once, no matter in how many movies they appeared. □

4.5 Grouping

To group tuples, we use a `GROUP BY` clause, following the `WHERE` clause. The keywords `GROUP BY` are followed by a list of *grouping* attributes. In the simplest situation, there is only one relation reference in the `FROM` clause, and this relation has its tuples grouped according to their values in the grouping attributes. Whatever aggregation operators are used in the `SELECT` clause are applied only within groups.

Example 31: The problem of finding, from the relation

```
Movies(title, year, length, genre, studioName, producerC#)
```

the sum of the lengths of all movies for each studio is expressed by

```
SELECT studioName, SUM(length)
FROM Movies
GROUP BY studioName;
```

We may imagine that the tuples of relation `Movies` are reorganized and grouped so that all the tuples for Disney studios are together, all those for MGM are together, and so on. The sums of the length components of all the tuples in each group are calculated, and for each group, the studio name is printed along with that sum. □

Observe in Example 31 how the `SELECT` clause has two kinds of terms. These are the only terms that may appear when there is an aggregation in the `SELECT` clause.

1. Aggregations, where an aggregate operator is applied to an attribute or expression involving attributes. As mentioned, these terms are evaluated on a per-group basis.

2. Attributes, such as studioName in this example, that appear in the GROUP BY clause. In a SELECT clause that has aggregations, only those attributes that are mentioned in the GROUP BY clause may appear unaggregated in the SELECT clause.

While queries involving GROUP BY generally have both grouping attributes and aggregations in the SELECT clause, it is technically not necessary to have both. For example, we could write

```
SELECT studioName
FROM Movies
GROUP BY studioName;
```

This query would group the tuples of Movies according to their studio name and then print the studio name for each group, no matter how many tuples there are with a given studio name. Thus, the above query has the same effect as

```
SELECT DISTINCT studioName
FROM Movies;
```

It is also possible to use a GROUP BY clause in a query about several relations. Such a query is interpreted by the following sequence of steps:

1. Evaluate the relation R expressed by the FROM and WHERE clauses. That is, relation R is the Cartesian product of the relations mentioned in the FROM clause, to which the selection of the WHERE clause is applied.

2. Group the tuples of R according to the attributes in the GROUP BY clause.

3. Produce as a result the attributes and aggregations of the SELECT clause, as if the query were about a stored relation R.

Example 32: Suppose we wish to print a table listing each producer's total length of film produced. We need to get information from the two relations

```
Movies(title, year, length, genre, studioName, producerC#)
MovieExec(name, address, cert#, netWorth)
```

so we begin by taking their theta-join, equating the certificate numbers from the two relations. That step gives us a relation in which each MovieExec tuple is paired with the Movies tuples for all the movies of that producer. Note that an executive who is not a producer will not be paired with any movies, and therefore will not appear in the relation. Now, we can group the selected tuples of this relation according to the name of the producer. Finally, we sum the lengths of the movies in each group. The query is shown in Fig. 13. □

```
SELECT name, SUM(length)
FROM MovieExec, Movies
WHERE producerC# = cert#
GROUP BY name;
```

Figure 13: Computing the length of movies for each producer

4.6 Grouping, Aggregation, and Nulls

When tuples have nulls, there are a few rules we must remember:

- The value NULL is ignored in any aggregation. It does not contribute to a sum, average, or count of an attribute, nor can it be the minimum or maximum in its column. For example, COUNT(*) is always a count of the number of tuples in a relation, but COUNT(A) is the number of tuples with non-NULL values for attribute A.

- On the other hand, NULL is treated as an ordinary value when forming groups. That is, we can have a group in which one or more of the grouping attributes are assigned the value NULL.

- When we perform any aggregation except count over an empty bag of values, the result is NULL. The count of an empty bag is 0.

Example 33: Suppose we have a relation $R(A, B)$ with one tuple, both of whose components are NULL:

A	B
NULL	NULL

Then the result of:

```
SELECT A, COUNT(B)
FROM R
GROUP BY A;
```

is the one tuple (NULL, 0). The reason is that when we group by A, we find only a group for value NULL. This group has one tuple, and its B-value is NULL. We thus count the bag of values {NULL}. Since the count of a bag of values does not count the NULL's, this count is 0.

On the other hand, the result of:

```
SELECT A, SUM(B)
FROM R
GROUP BY A;
```

> **Order of Clauses in SQL Queries**
>
> We have now met all six clauses that can appear in a SQL "select-from-where" query: `SELECT`, `FROM`, `WHERE`, `GROUP BY`, `HAVING`, and `ORDER BY`. Only the `SELECT` and `FROM` clauses are required. Whichever additional clauses appear must be in the order listed above.

is the one tuple (`NULL,NULL`). The reason is as follows. The group for value `NULL` has one tuple, the only tuple in R. However, when we try to sum the B-values for this group, we only find `NULL`, and `NULL` does not contribute to a sum. Thus, we are summing an empty bag of values, and this sum is defined to be `NULL`. □

4.7 HAVING Clauses

Suppose that we did not wish to include all of the producers in our table of Example 32. We could restrict the tuples prior to grouping in a way that would make undesired groups empty. For instance, if we only wanted the total length of movies for producers with a net worth of more than $10,000,000, we could change the third line of Fig. 13 to

```
WHERE producerC# = cert# AND networth > 10000000
```

However, sometimes we want to choose our groups based on some aggregate property of the group itself. Then we follow the `GROUP BY` clause with a `HAVING` clause. The latter clause consists of the keyword `HAVING` followed by a condition about the group.

Example 34: Suppose we want to print the total film length for only those producers who made at least one film prior to 1930. We may append to Fig. 13 the clause

```
HAVING MIN(year) < 1930
```

The resulting query, shown in Fig. 14, would remove from the grouped relation all those groups in which every tuple had a `year` component 1930 or higher. □

There are several rules we must remember about `HAVING` clauses:

- An aggregation in a `HAVING` clause applies only to the tuples of the group being tested.

- Any attribute of relations in the `FROM` clause may be aggregated in the `HAVING` clause, but only those attributes that are in the `GROUP BY` list may appear unaggregated in the `HAVING` clause (the same rule as for the `SELECT` clause).

```
SELECT name, SUM(length)
FROM MovieExec, Movies
WHERE producerC# = cert#
GROUP BY name
HAVING MIN(year) < 1930;
```

Figure 14: Computing the total length of film for early producers

4.8 Exercises for Section 4

! **Exercise 4.1:** For each of your answers to Exercise 3.1, determine whether or not the result of your query can have duplicates. If so, rewrite the query to eliminate duplicates. If not, write a query without subqueries that has the same, duplicate-free answer.

! **Exercise 4.2:** In Example 27, we mentioned that different versions of the query "find the producers of Harrison Ford's movies" can have different answers as bags, even though they yield the same set of answers. Consider the version of the query in Example 22, where we used a subquery in the FROM clause. Does this version produce duplicates, and if so, why?

Exercise 4.3: You may recall an example of the query: "find, for each star who has appeared in at least three movies, the earliest year in which they appeared." We wrote this query as a γ operation. Write it in SQL.

! **Exercise 4.4:** The γ operator of extended relational algebra does not have a feature that corresponds to the `HAVING` clause of SQL. Is it possible to mimic a SQL query with a `HAVING` clause in relational algebra? If so, how would we do it in general?

5 Database Modifications

To this point, we have focused on the normal SQL query form: the select-from-where statement. There are a number of other statement forms that do not return a result, but rather change the state of the database. In this section, we shall focus on three types of statements that allow us to

1. Insert tuples into a relation.

2. Delete certain tuples from a relation.

3. Update values of certain components of certain existing tuples.

We refer to these three types of operations collectively as *modifications.*

5.1 Insertion

The basic form of insertion statement is:

$$\texttt{INSERT INTO } R(A_1, \ldots, A_n) \texttt{ VALUES } (v_1, \ldots, v_n);$$

A tuple is created using the value v_i for attribute A_i, for $i = 1, 2, \ldots, n$. If the list of attributes does not include all attributes of the relation R, then the tuple created has default values for all missing attributes.

Example 35: Suppose we wish to add Sydney Greenstreet to the list of stars of *The Maltese Falcon.* We say:

```
1) INSERT INTO StarsIn(movieTitle, movieYear, starName)
2) VALUES('The Maltese Falcon', 1942, 'Sydney Greenstreet');
```

The effect of executing this statement is that a tuple with the three components on line (2) is inserted into the relation `StarsIn`. Since all attributes of `StarsIn` are mentioned on line (1), there is no need to add default components. The values on line (2) are matched with the attributes on line (1) in the order given, so `'The Maltese Falcon'` becomes the value of the component for attribute `movieTitle`, and so on. □

If, as in Example 35, we provide values for all attributes of the relation, then we may omit the list of attributes that follows the relation name. That is, we could just say:

```
INSERT INTO StarsIn
VALUES('The Maltese Falcon', 1942, 'Sydney Greenstreet');
```

However, if we take this option, we must be sure that the order of the values is the same as the standard order of attributes for the relation.

- If you are not sure of the declared order for the attributes, it is best to list them in the INSERT clause in the order you choose for their values in the VALUES clause.

The simple INSERT described above only puts one tuple into a relation. Instead of using explicit values for one tuple, we can compute a set of tuples to be inserted, using a subquery. This subquery replaces the keyword VALUES and the tuple expression in the INSERT statement form described above.

Example 36: Suppose we want to add to the relation

```
Studio(name, address, presC#)
```

all movie studios that are mentioned in the relation

```
Movies(title, year, length, genre, studioName, producerC#)
```

but do not appear in Studio. Since there is no way to determine an address or a president for such a studio, we shall have to be content with value NULL for attributes address and presC# in the inserted Studio tuples. A way to make this insertion is shown in Fig. 15.

```
1)  INSERT INTO Studio(name)
2)       SELECT DISTINCT studioName
3)       FROM Movies
4)       WHERE studioName NOT IN
5)            (SELECT name
6)             FROM Studio);
```

Figure 15: Adding new studios

Like most SQL statements with nesting, Fig. 15 is easiest to examine from the inside out. Lines (5) and (6) generate all the studio names in the relation Studio. Thus, line (4) tests that a studio name from the Movies relation is none of these studios.

Now, we see that lines (2) through (6) produce the set of studio names found in Movies but not in Studio. The use of DISTINCT on line (2) assures that each studio will appear only once in this set, no matter how many movies it owns. Finally, line (1) inserts each of these studios, with NULL for the attributes address and presC#, into relation Studio. □

5.2 Deletion

The form of a deletion is

DELETE FROM *R* WHERE <condition>;

The Timing of Insertions

The SQL standard requires that the query be evaluated completely before any tuples are inserted. For example, in Fig. 15, the query of lines (2) through (6) must be evaluated prior to executing the insertion of line (1). Thus, there is no possibility that new tuples added to `Studio` at line (1) will affect the condition on line (4).

In this particular example, it does not matter whether or not insertions are delayed until the query is completely evaluated. However, suppose `DISTINCT` were removed from line (2) of Fig. 15. If we evaluate the query of lines (2) through (6) before doing any insertion, then a new studio name appearing in several `Movies` tuples would appear several times in the result of this query and therefore would be inserted several times into relation `Studio`. However, if the DBMS inserted new studios into `Studio` as soon as we found them during the evaluation of the query of lines (2) through (6), something that would be incorrect according to the standard, then the same new studio would not be inserted twice. Rather, as soon as the new studio was inserted once, its name would no longer satisfy the condition of lines (4) through (6), and it would not appear a second time in the result of the query of lines (2) through (6).

The effect of executing this statement is that every tuple satisfying the condition will be deleted from relation R.

Example 37: We can delete from relation

```
StarsIn(movieTitle, movieYear, starName)
```

the fact that Sydney Greenstreet was a star in *The Maltese Falcon* by the SQL statement:

```
DELETE FROM StarsIn
WHERE movieTitle = 'The Maltese Falcon' AND
      movieYear = 1942 AND
      starName = 'Sydney Greenstreet';
```

Notice that unlike the insertion statement of Example 35, we cannot simply specify a tuple to be deleted. Rather, we must describe the tuple exactly by a `WHERE` clause. □

Example 38: Here is another example of a deletion. This time, we delete from relation

```
MovieExec(name, address, cert#, netWorth)
```

several tuples at once by using a condition that can be satisfied by more than one tuple. The statement

```
DELETE FROM MovieExec
WHERE netWorth < 10000000;
```

deletes all movie executives whose net worth is low — less than ten million dollars. □

5.3 Updates

While we might think of both insertions and deletions of tuples as "updates" to the database, an *update* in SQL is a very specific kind of change to the database: one or more tuples that already exist in the database have some of their components changed. The general form of an update statement is:

`UPDATE` *R* `SET` <new-value assignments> `WHERE` <condition>`;`

Each new-value assignment is an attribute, an equal sign, and an expression. If there is more than one assignment, they are separated by commas. The effect of this statement is to find all the tuples in *R* that satisfy the condition. Each of these tuples is then changed by having the expressions in the assignments evaluated and assigned to the components of the tuple for the corresponding attributes of *R*.

Example 39: Let us modify the relation

```
MovieExec(name, address, cert#, netWorth)
```

by attaching the title `Pres.` in front of the name of every movie executive who is the president of a studio. The condition the desired tuples satisfy is that their certificate numbers appear in the `presC#` component of some tuple in the `Studio` relation. We express this update as:

```
1)  UPDATE MovieExec
2)  SET name = 'Pres. ' || name
3)  WHERE cert# IN (SELECT presC# FROM Studio);
```

Line (3) tests whether the certificate number from the `MovieExec` tuple is one of those that appear as a president's certificate number in `Studio`.

Line (2) performs the update on the selected tuples. Recall that the operator `||` denotes concatenation of strings, so the expression following the `=` sign in line (2) places the characters `Pres.` and a blank in front of the old value of the `name` component of this tuple. The new string becomes the value of the `name` component of this tuple; the effect is that `'Pres. '` has been prepended to the old value of `name`. □

6 Transactions in SQL

To this point, our model of operations on the database has been that of one user querying or modifying the database. Thus, operations on the database are executed one at a time, and the database state left by one operation is the state upon which the next operation acts. Moreover, we imagine that operations are carried out in their entirety ("atomically"). That is, we assumed it is impossible for the hardware or software to fail in the middle of a modification, leaving the database in a state that cannot be explained as the result of the operations performed on it.

Real life is often considerably more complicated. We shall first consider what can happen to leave the database in a state that doesn't reflect the operations performed on it, and then we shall consider the tools SQL gives the user to assure that these problems do not occur.

6.1 Serializability

In applications like Web services, banking, or airline reservations, hundreds of operations per second may be performed on the database. The operations initiate at any of thousands or millions of sites, such as desktop computers or automatic teller machines. It is entirely possible that we could have two operations affecting the same bank account or flight, and for those operations to overlap in time. If so, they might interact in strange ways.

Here is an example of what could go wrong if the DBMS were completely unconstrained as to the order in which it operated upon the database. This example involves a database interacting with people, and it is intended to illustrate why it is important to control the sequences in which interacting events can occur. However, a DBMS would not control events that were so "large" that they involved waiting for a user to make a choice. The event sequences controlled by the DBMS involve only the execution of SQL statements.

Example 40: The typical airline gives customers a Web interface where they can choose a seat for their flight. This interface shows a map of available seats, and the data for this map is obtained from the airline's database. There might be a relation such as:

```
Flights(fltNo, fltDate, seatNo, seatStatus)
```

upon which we can issue the query:

```
SELECT seatNo
FROM Flights
WHERE fltNo = 123 AND fltDate = DATE '2008-12-25'
    AND seatStatus = 'available';
```

The flight number and date are example data, which would in fact be obtained from previous interactions with the customer.

When the customer clicks on an empty seat, say 22A, that seat is reserved for them. The database is modified by an update-statement, such as:

```
UPDATE Flights
SET seatStatus = 'occupied'
WHERE fltNo = 123 AND fltDate = DATE '2008-12-25'
    AND seatNo = '22A';
```

However, this customer may not be the only one reserving a seat on flight 123 on Dec. 25, 2008 and this exact moment. Another customer may have asked for the seat map at the same time, in which case they also see seat 22A empty. Should they also choose seat 22A, they too believe they have reserved 22A. The timing of these events is as suggested by Fig. 16. □

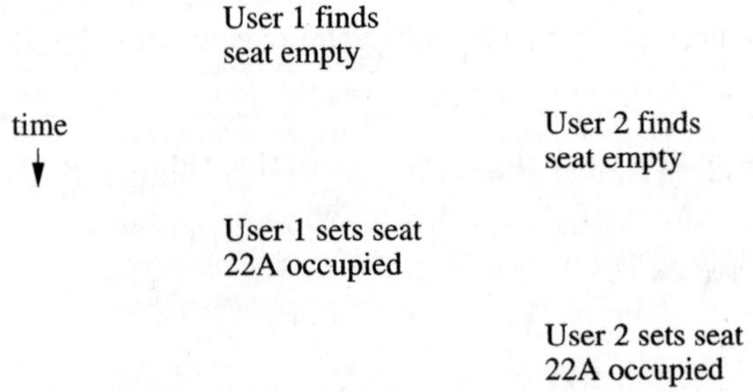

Figure 16: Two customers trying to book the same seat simultaneously

As we see from Example 40, it is conceivable that two operations could each be performed correctly, and yet the global result not be correct: both customers believe they have been granted seat 22A. The problem is solved in SQL by the notion of a "transaction," which is informally a group of operations that need to be performed together. Suppose that in Example 40, the query

> **Assuring Serializable Behavior**
>
> In practice it is often impossible to require that operations run serially; there are just too many of them, and some parallelism is required. Thus, DBMS's adopt a mechanism for assuring serializable behavior; even if the execution is not serial, the result looks to users as if operations were executed serially.
>
> One common approach is for the DBMS to *lock* elements of the database so that two functions cannot access them at the same time. There is an extensive technology of how to implement locks in a DBMS. For example, if the transaction of Example 40 were written to lock other transactions out of the `Flights` relation, then transactions that did not access `Flights` could run in parallel with the seat-selection transaction, but no other invocation of the seat-selection operation could run in parallel.

and update shown would be grouped into one transaction.[6] SQL then allows the programmer to state that a certain transaction must be *serializable* with respect to other transactions. That is, these transactions must behave as if they were run *serially* — one at a time, with no overlap.

Clearly, if the two invocations of the seat-selection operation are run serially (or serializably), then the error we saw cannot occur. One customer's invocation occurs first. This customer sees seat 22A is empty, and books it. The other customer's invocation then begins and is not given 22A as a choice, because it is already occupied. It may matter to the customers who gets the seat, but to the database all that is important is that a seat is assigned only once.

6.2 Atomicity

In addition to nonserialized behavior that can occur if two or more database operations are performed about the same time, it is possible for a single operation to put the database in an unacceptable state if there is a hardware or software "crash" while the operation is executing. Here is another example suggesting what might occur. As in Example 40, we should remember that real database systems do not allow this sort of error to occur in properly designed application programs.

Example 41: Let us picture another common sort of database: a bank's account records. We can represent the situation by a relation

[6]However, it would be extremely unwise to group into a single transaction operations that involved a user, or even a computer that was not owned by the airline, such as a travel agent's computer. Another mechanism must be used to deal with event sequences that include operations outside the database.

```
Accounts(acctNo, balance)
```

Consider the operation of transferring $100 from the account numbered 123 to the account 456. We might first check whether there is at least $100 in account 123, and if so, we execute the following two steps:

1. Add $100 to account 456 by the SQL update statement:

```
UPDATE Accounts
SET balance = balance + 100
WHERE acctNo = 456;
```

2. Subtract $100 from account 123 by the SQL update statement:

```
UPDATE Accounts
SET balance = balance - 100
WHERE acctNo = 123;
```

Now, consider what happens if there is a failure after Step (1) but before Step (2). Perhaps the computer fails, or the network connecting the database to the processor that is actually performing the transfer fails. Then the database is left in a state where money has been transferred into the second account, but the money has not been taken out of the first account. The bank has in effect given away the amount of money that was to be transferred. □

The problem illustrated by Example 41 is that certain combinations of database operations, like the two updates of that example, need to be done *atomically*; that is, either they are both done or neither is done. For example, a simple solution is to have all changes to the database done in a local workspace, and only after all work is done do we *commit* the changes to the database, whereupon all changes become part of the database and visible to other operations.

6.3 Transactions

The solution to the problems of serialization and atomicity posed in Sections 6.1 and 6.2 is to group database operations into *transactions.* A transaction is a collection of one or more operations on the database that must be executed atomically; that is, either all operations are performed or none are. In addition, SQL requires that, as a default, transactions are executed in a serializable manner. A DBMS may allow the user to specify a less stringent constraint on the interleaving of operations from two or more transactions. We shall discuss these modifications to the serializability condition in later sections.

When using the *generic SQL interface* (the facility wherein one types queries and other SQL statements), each statement is a transaction by itself. However,

How the Database Changes During Transactions

Different systems may do different things to implement transactions. It is possible that as a transaction executes, it makes changes to the database. If the transaction aborts, then (unless the programmer took precautions) it is possible that these changes were seen by some other transaction. The most common solution is for the database system to lock the changed items until `COMMIT` or `ROLLBACK` is chosen, thus preventing other transactions from seeing the tentative change. Locks or an equivalent would surely be used if the user wants the transactions to run in a serializable fashion.

However, as we shall see starting in Section 6.4, SQL offers us several options regarding the treatment of tentative database changes. It is possible that the changed data is not locked and becomes visible even though a subsequent rollback makes the change disappear. It is up to the author of a transaction to decide whether it is safe for that transaction to see tentative changes of other transactions.

SQL allows the programmer to group several statements into a single transaction. The SQL command `START TRANSACTION` is used to mark the beginning of a transaction. There are two ways to end a transaction:

1. The SQL statement `COMMIT` causes the transaction to end successfully. Whatever changes to the database were caused by the SQL statement or statements since the current transaction began are installed permanently in the database (i.e., they are *committed*). Before the `COMMIT` statement is executed, changes are tentative and may or may not be visible to other transactions.

2. The SQL statement `ROLLBACK` causes the transaction to *abort*, or terminate unsuccessfully. Any changes made in response to the SQL statements of the transaction are undone (i.e., they are *rolled back*), so they never permanently appear in the database.

Example 42: Suppose we want the transfer operation of Example 41 to be a single transaction. We execute `BEGIN TRANSACTION` before accessing the database. If we find that there are insufficient funds to make the transfer, then we would execute the `ROLLBACK` command. However, if there are sufficient funds, then we execute the two update statements and then execute `COMMIT`. □

6.4 Read-Only Transactions

Examples 40 and 41 each involved a transaction that read and then (possibly) wrote some data into the database. This sort of transaction is prone to

> **Application- Versus System-Generated Rollbacks**
>
> In our discussion of transactions, we have presumed that the decision whether a transaction is committed or rolled back is made as part of the application issuing the transaction. That is, as in Examples 44 and 42, a transaction may perform a number of database operations, then decide whether to make any changes permanent by issuing `COMMIT`, or to return to the original state by issuing `ROLLBACK`. However, the system may also perform transaction rollbacks, to ensure that transactions are executed atomically and conform to their specified isolation level in the presence of other concurrent transactions or system crashes. Typically, if the system aborts a transaction then a special error code or exception is generated. If an application wishes to guarantee that its transactions are executed successfully, it must catch such conditions and reissue the transaction in question.

serialization problems. Thus we saw in Example 40 what could happen if two executions of the function tried to book the same seat at the same time, and we saw in Example 41 what could happen if there was a crash in the middle of a funds transfer. However, when a transaction only reads data and does not write data, we have more freedom to let the transaction execute in parallel with other transactions.

Example 43: Suppose we wrote a program that read data from the `Flights` relation of Example 40 to determine whether a certain seat was available. We could execute many invocations of this program at once, without risk of permanent harm to the database. The worst that could happen is that while we were reading the availability of a certain seat, that seat was being booked or was being released by the execution of some other program. Thus, we might get the answer "available" or "occupied," depending on microscopic differences in the time at which we executed the query, but the answer would make sense at some time. □

If we tell the SQL execution system that our current transaction is *read-only*, that is, it will never change the database, then it is quite possible that the SQL system will be able to take advantage of that knowledge. Generally it will be possible for many read-only transactions accessing the same data to run in parallel, while they would not be allowed to run in parallel with a transaction that wrote the same data.

We tell the SQL system that the next transaction is read-only by:

```
SET TRANSACTION READ ONLY;
```

This statement must be executed before the transaction begins. We can also inform SQL that the coming transaction may write data by the statement

```
SET TRANSACTION READ WRITE;
```

However, this option is the default.

6.5 Dirty Reads

Dirty data is a common term for data written by a transaction that has not yet committed. A *dirty read* is a read of dirty data written by another transaction. The risk in reading dirty data is that the transaction that wrote it may eventually abort. If so, then the dirty data will be removed from the database, and the world is supposed to behave as if that data never existed. If some other transaction has read the dirty data, then that transaction might commit or take some other action that reflects its knowledge of the dirty data.

Sometimes the dirty read matters, and sometimes it doesn't. Other times it matters little enough that it makes sense to risk an occasional dirty read and thus avoid:

1. The time-consuming work by the DBMS that is needed to prevent dirty reads, and
2. The loss of parallelism that results from waiting until there is no possibility of a dirty read.

Here are some examples of what might happen when dirty reads are allowed.

Example 44: Let us reconsider the account transfer of Example 41. However, suppose that transfers are implemented by a program P that executes the following sequence of steps:

1. Add money to account 2.
2. Test if account 1 has enough money.
   (a) If there is not enough money, remove the money from account 2 and end.[7]
   (b) If there is enough money, subtract the money from account 1 and end.

If program P is executed serializably, then it doesn't matter that we have put money temporarily into account 2. No one will see that money, and it gets removed if the transfer can't be made.

However, suppose dirty reads are possible. Imagine there are three accounts: $A1$, $A2$, and $A3$, with \$100, \$200, and \$300, respectively. Suppose transaction

[7] You should be aware that the program P is trying to perform functions that would more typically be done by the DBMS. In particular, when P decides, as it has done at this step, that it must not complete the transaction, it would issue a rollback (abort) command to the DBMS and have the DBMS reverse the effects of this execution of P.

T_1 executes program P to transfer \$150 from $A1$ to $A2$. At roughly the same time, transaction T_2 runs program P to transfer \$250 from $A2$ to $A3$. Here is a possible sequence of events:

1. T_2 executes Step (1) and adds \$250 to $A3$, which now has \$550.

2. T_1 executes Step (1) and adds \$150 to $A2$, which now has \$350.

3. T_2 executes the test of Step (2) and finds that $A2$ has enough funds (\$350) to allow the transfer of \$250 from $A2$ to $A3$.

4. T_1 executes the test of Step (2) and finds that $A1$ does not have enough funds (\$100) to allow the transfer of \$150 from $A1$ to $A2$.

5. T_2 executes Step (2b). It subtracts \$250 from $A2$, which now has \$100, and ends.

6. T_1 executes Step (2a). It subtracts \$150 from $A2$, which now has −\$50, and ends.

The total amount of money has not changed; there is still \$600 among the three accounts. But because T_2 read dirty data at the third of the six steps above, we have not protected against an account going negative, which supposedly was the purpose of testing the first account to see if it had adequate funds. □

Example 45: Let us imagine a variation on the seat-choosing function of Example 40. In the new approach:

1. We find an available seat and reserve it by setting `seatStatus` to `'occ-upied'` for that seat. If there is none, end.

2. We ask the customer for approval of the seat. If so, we commit. If not, we release the seat by setting `seatStatus` to `'available'` and repeat Step (1) to get another seat.

If two transactions are executing this algorithm at about the same time, one might reserve a seat S, which later is rejected by the customer. If the second transaction executes Step (1) at a time when seat S is marked occupied, the customer for that transaction is not given the option to take seat S.

As in Example 44, the problem is that a dirty read has occurred. The second transaction saw a tuple (with S marked occupied) that was written by the first transaction and later modified by the first transaction. □

How important is the fact that a read was dirty? In Example 44 it was very important; it caused an account to go negative despite apparent safeguards against that happening. In Example 45, the problem does not look too serious. Indeed, the second traveler might not get their favorite seat, or might even be told that no seats existed. However, in the latter case, running the transaction again will almost certainly reveal the availability of seat S. It might well make sense to implement this seat-choosing function in a way that allowed dirty reads, in order to speed up the average processing time for booking requests.

SQL allows us to specify that dirty reads are acceptable for a given transaction. We use the `SET TRANSACTION` statement that we discussed in Section 6.4. The appropriate form for a transaction like that described in Example 45 is:

```
1)  SET TRANSACTION READ WRITE
2)      ISOLATION LEVEL READ UNCOMMITTED;
```

The statement above does two things:

1. Line (1) declares that the transaction may write data.

2. Line (2) declares that the transaction may run with the "isolation level" *read-uncommitted.* That is, the transaction is allowed to read dirty data. We shall discuss the four isolation levels in Section 6.6. So far, we have seen two of them: serializable and read-uncommitted.

Note that if the transaction is not read-only (i.e., it may modify the database), and we specify isolation level `READ UNCOMMITTED`, then we must also specify `READ WRITE`. Recall from Section 6.4 that the default assumption is that transactions are read-write. However, SQL makes an exception for the case where dirty reads are allowed. Then, the default assumption is that the transaction is read-only, because read-write transactions with dirty reads entail significant risks, as we saw. If we want a read-write transaction to run with read-uncommitted as the isolation level, then we need to specify `READ WRITE` explicitly, as above.

6.6 Other Isolation Levels

SQL provides a total of four *isolation levels.* Two of them we have already seen: serializable and read-uncommitted (dirty reads allowed). The other two are *read-committed* and *repeatable-read.* They can be specified for a given transaction by

```
SET TRANSACTION ISOLATION LEVEL READ COMMITTED;
```

or

```
SET TRANSACTION ISOLATION LEVEL REPEATABLE READ;
```

respectively. For each, the default is that transactions are read-write, so we can add `READ ONLY` to either statement, if appropriate. Incidentally, we also have the option of specifying

```
SET TRANSACTION ISOLATION LEVEL SERIALIZABLE;
```

Interactions Among Transactions Running at Different Isolation Levels

A subtle point is that the isolation level of a transaction affects only what data *that* transaction may see; it does not affect what any other transaction sees. As a case in point, if a transaction T is running at level serializable, then the execution of T must appear as if all other transactions run either entirely before or entirely after T. However, if some of those transactions are running at another isolation level, then *they* may see the data written by T as T writes it. They may even see dirty data from T if they are running at isolation level read-uncommitted, and T aborts.

However, that is the SQL default and need not be stated explicitly.

The read-committed isolation level, as its name implies, forbids the reading of dirty (uncommitted) data. However, it does allow a transaction running at this isolation level to issue the same query several times and get different answers, as long as the answers reflect data that has been written by transactions that already committed.

Example 46: Let us reconsider the seat-choosing program of Example 45, but suppose we declare it to run with isolation level read-committed. Then when it searches for a seat at Step (1), it will not see seats as booked if some other transaction is reserving them but not committed.[8] However, if the traveler rejects seats, and one execution of the function queries for available seats many times, it may see a different set of available seats each time it queries, as other transactions successfully book seats or cancel seats in parallel with our transaction. □

Now, let us consider isolation level repeatable-read. The term is something of a misnomer, since the same query issued more than once is not quite guaranteed to get the same answer. Under repeatable-read isolation, if a tuple is retrieved the first time, then we can be sure that the identical tuple will be retrieved again if the query is repeated. However, it is also possible that a second or subsequent execution of the same query will retrieve *phantom* tuples. The latter are tuples that result from insertions into the database while our transaction is executing.

Example 47: Let us continue with the seat-choosing problem of Examples 45 and 46. If we execute this function under isolation level repeatable-read, then

[8] What actually happens may seem mysterious, since we have not addressed the algorithms for enforcing the various isolation levels. Possibly, should two transactions both see a seat as available and try to book it, one will be forced by the system to roll back in order to break the deadlock (see the box on "Application- Versus System-Generated Rollbacks" in Section 6.3).

a seat that is available on the first query at Step (1) will remain available at subsequent queries.

However, suppose some new tuples enter the relation `Flights`. For example, the airline may have switched the flight to a larger plane, creating some new tuples that weren't there before. Then under repeatable-read isolation, a subsequent query for available seats may also retrieve the new seats. □

Figure 17 summarizes the differences between the four SQL isolation levels.

Isolation Level	Dirty Reads	Nonrepeatable Reads	Phantoms
Read Uncommitted	Allowed	Allowed	Allowed
Read Committed	Not Allowed	Allowed	Allowed
Repeatable Read	Not Allowed	Not Allowed	Allowed
Serializable	Not Allowed	Not Allowed	Not Allowed

Figure 17: Properties of SQL isolation levels

6.7 Exercises for Section 6

Exercise 6.1: This and the next exercises involve certain programs that operate on the two relations

```
Product(maker, model, type)
PC(model, speed, ram, hd, price)
```

from our running PC exercise. Sketch the following programs, including SQL statements and work done in a conventional language. Do not forget to issue `BEGIN TRANSACTION`, `COMMIT`, and `ROLLBACK` statements at the proper times and to tell the system your transactions are read-only if they are.

a) Given a speed and amount of RAM (as arguments of the function), look up the PC's with that speed and RAM, printing the model number and price of each.

b) Given a model number, delete the tuple for that model from both `PC` and `Product`.

c) Given a model number, decrease the price of that model PC by $100.

d) Given a maker, model number, processor speed, RAM size, hard-disk size, and price, check that there is no product with that model. If there is such a model, print an error message for the user. If no such model existed in the database, enter the information about that model into the `PC` and `Product` tables.

! **Exercise 6.2:** For each of the programs of Exercise 6.1, discuss the atomicity problems, if any, that could occur should the system crash in the middle of an execution of the program.

! **Exercise 6.3:** Suppose we execute as a transaction T one of the four programs of Exercise 6.1, while other transactions that are executions of the same or a different one of the four programs may also be executing at about the same time. What behaviors of transaction T may be observed if all the transactions run with isolation level `READ UNCOMMITTED` that would not be possible if they all ran with isolation level `SERIALIZABLE`? Consider separately the case that T is any of the programs (a) through (d) of Exercise 6.1.

!! **Exercise 6.4:** Suppose we have a transaction T that is a function which runs "forever," and at each hour checks whether there is a PC that has a speed of 3.5 or more and sells for under $1000. If it finds one, it prints the information and terminates. During this time, other transactions that are executions of one of the four programs described in Exercise 6.1 may run. For each of the four isolation levels — serializable, repeatable read, read committed, and read uncommitted — tell what the effect on T of running at this isolation level is.

7 Summary

✦ *SQL*: The language SQL is the principal query language for relational database systems. The most recent full standard is called SQL-99 or SQL3. Commercial systems generally vary from this standard.

✦ *Select-From-Where Queries*: The most common form of SQL query has the form select-from-where. It allows us to take the product of several relations (the `FROM` clause), apply a condition to the tuples of the result (the `WHERE` clause), and produce desired components (the `SELECT` clause).

✦ *Subqueries*: Select-from-where queries can also be used as subqueries within a `WHERE` clause or `FROM` clause of another query. The operators `EXISTS`, `IN`, `ALL`, and `ANY` may be used to express boolean-valued conditions about the relations that are the result of a subquery in a `WHERE` clause.

✦ *Set Operations on Relations*: We can take the union, intersection, or difference of relations by connecting the relations, or connecting queries defining the relations, with the keywords `UNION`, `INTERSECT`, and `EXCEPT`, respectively.

✦ *Join Expressions*: SQL has operators such as `NATURAL JOIN` that may be applied to relations, either as queries by themselves or to define relations in a `FROM` clause.

- *Null Values*: SQL provides a special value NULL that appears in components of tuples for which no concrete value is available. The arithmetic and logic of NULL is unusual. Comparison of any value to NULL, even another NULL, gives the truth value UNKNOWN. That truth value, in turn, behaves in boolean-valued expressions as if it were halfway between TRUE and FALSE.

- *Outerjoins*: SQL provides an OUTER JOIN operator that joins relations but also includes in the result dangling tuples from one or both relations; the dangling tuples are padded with NULL's in the resulting relation.

- *The Bag Model of Relations*: SQL actually regards relations as bags of tuples, not sets of tuples. We can force elimination of duplicate tuples with the keyword DISTINCT, while keyword ALL allows the result to be a bag in certain circumstances where bags are not the default.

- *Aggregations*: The values appearing in one column of a relation can be summarized (aggregated) by using one of the keywords SUM, AVG (average value), MIN, MAX, or COUNT. Tuples can be partitioned prior to aggregation with the keywords GROUP BY. Certain groups can be eliminated with a clause introduced by the keyword HAVING.

- *Modification Statements*: SQL allows us to change the tuples in a relation. We may INSERT (add new tuples), DELETE (remove tuples), or UPDATE (change some of the existing tuples), by writing SQL statements using one of these three keywords.

- *Transactions*: SQL allows the programmer to group SQL statements into transactions, which may be committed or rolled back (aborted). Transactions may be rolled back by the application in order to undo changes, or by the system in order to guarantee atomicity and isolation.

- *Isolation Levels*: SQL defines four isolation levels called, from most stringent to least stringent: "serializable" (the transaction must appear to run either completely before or completely after each other transaction), "repeatable-read" (every tuple read in response to a query will reappear if the query is repeated), "read-committed" (only tuples written by transactions that have already committed may be seen by this transaction), and "read-uncommitted" (no constraint on what the transaction may see).

8 References

Many books on SQL programming are available. Some popular ones are [3], [5], and [7]. [6] is an early exposition of the SQL-99 standard.

SQL was first defined in [4]. It was implemented as part of System R [1], one of the first generation of relational database prototypes.

There is a discussion of problems with this standard in the area of transactions and cursors in [2].

1. M. M. Astrahan et al., "System R: a relational approach to data management," *ACM Transactions on Database Systems* **1**:2, pp. 97–137, 1976.

2. H. Berenson, P. A. Bernstein, J. N. Gray, J. Melton, E. O'Neil, and P. O'Neil, "A critique of ANSI SQL isolation levels," *Proceedings of ACM SIGMOD Intl. Conf. on Management of Data*, pp. 1–10, 1995.

3. J. Celko, *SQL for Smarties*, Morgan-Kaufmann, San Francisco, 2005.

4. D. D. Chamberlin et al., "SEQUEL 2: a unified approach to data definition, manipulation, and control," *IBM Journal of Research and Development* **20**:6, pp. 560–575, 1976.

5. C. J. Date and H. Darwen, *A Guide to the SQL Standard*, Addison-Wesley, Reading, MA, 1997.

6. P. Gulutzan and T. Pelzer, *SQL-99 Complete, Really*, R&D Books, Lawrence, KA, 1999.

7. J. Melton and A. R. Simon, *Understanding the New SQL: A Complete Guide*, Morgan-Kaufmann, San Francisco, 2006.

Constraints and Triggers

In this chapter we shall cover those aspects of SQL that let us create "active" elements. An *active* element is an expression or statement that we write once and store in the database, expecting the element to execute at appropriate times. The time of action might be when a certain event occurs, such as an insertion into a particular relation, or it might be whenever the database changes so that a certain boolean-valued condition becomes true.

One of the serious problems faced by writers of applications that update the database is that the new information could be wrong in a variety of ways. For example, there are often typographical or transcription errors in manually entered data. We could write application programs in such a way that every insertion, deletion, and update command has associated with it the checks necessary to assure correctness. However, it is better to store these checks in the database, and have the DBMS administer the checks. In this way, we can be sure a check will not be forgotten, and we can avoid duplication of work.

SQL provides a variety of techniques for expressing *integrity constraints* as part of the database schema. In this chapter we shall study the principal methods. We have already seen key constraints, where an attribute or set of attributes is declared to be a key for a relation. SQL supports a form of referential integrity, called a "foreign-key constraint," the requirement that a value in an attribute or attributes of one relation must also appear as a value in an attribute or attributes of another relation. SQL also allows constraints on attributes, constraints on tuples, and interrelation constraints called "assertions." Finally, we discuss "triggers," which are a form of active element that is called into play on certain specified events, such as insertion into a specific relation.

1 Keys and Foreign Keys

SQL allows us to define an attribute or attributes to be a key for a relation with the keywords `PRIMARY KEY` or `UNIQUE`. SQL also uses the term "key" in connection with certain referential-integrity constraints. These constraints, called

From Chapter 7 of *Database Systems*, Second Edition. Hector Garcia-Molina, Jeffrey D. Ullman, Jennifer Widom.

"foreign-key constraints," assert that a value appearing in one relation must also appear in the primary-key component(s) of another relation.

1.1 Declaring Foreign-Key Constraints

A foreign key constraint is an assertion that values for certain attributes must make sense. You may recall that we considered how to express in relational algebra the constraint that the producer "certificate number" for each movie was also the certificate number of some executive in the `MovieExec` relation.

In SQL we may declare an attribute or attributes of one relation to be a *foreign key*, referencing some attribute(s) of a second relation (possibly the same relation). The implication of this declaration is twofold:

1. The referenced attribute(s) of the second relation must be declared `UNIQUE` or the `PRIMARY KEY` for their relation. Otherwise, we cannot make the foreign-key declaration.

2. Values of the foreign key appearing in the first relation must also appear in the referenced attributes of some tuple. More precisely, let there be a foreign-key F that references set of attributes G of some relation. Suppose a tuple t of the first relation has non-`NULL` values in all the attributes of F; call the list of t's values in these attributes $t[F]$. Then in the referenced relation there must be some tuple s that agrees with $t[F]$ on the attributes G. That is, $s[G] = t[F]$.

As for primary keys, we have two ways to declare a foreign key.

a) If the foreign key is a single attribute we may follow its name and type by a declaration that it "references" some attribute (which must be a key — primary or unique) of some table. The form of the declaration is

`REFERENCES` <table>(<attribute>)

b) Alternatively, we may append to the list of attributes in a `CREATE TABLE` statement one or more declarations stating that a set of attributes is a foreign key. We then give the table and its attributes (which must be a key) to which the foreign key refers. The form of this declaration is:

`FOREIGN KEY` (<attributes>) `REFERENCES` <table>(<attributes>)

Example 1: Suppose we wish to declare the relation

```
Studio(name, address, presC#)
```

whose primary key is `name` and which has a foreign key `presC#` that references `cert#` of relation

```
MovieExec(name, address, cert#, netWorth)
```

We may declare `presC#` directly to reference `cert#` as follows:

```
CREATE TABLE Studio (
    name CHAR(30) PRIMARY KEY,
    address VARCHAR(255),
    presC# INT REFERENCES MovieExec(cert#)
);
```

An alternative form is to add the foreign key declaration separately, as

```
CREATE TABLE Studio (
    name CHAR(30) PRIMARY KEY,
    address VARCHAR(255),
    presC# INT,
    FOREIGN KEY (presC#) REFERENCES MovieExec(cert#)
);
```

Notice that the referenced attribute, `cert#` in `MovieExec`, is a key of that relation, as it must be. The meaning of either of these two foreign key declarations is that whenever a value appears in the `presC#` component of a `Studio` tuple, that value must also appear in the `cert#` component of some `MovieExec` tuple. The one exception is that, should a particular `Studio` tuple have `NULL` as the value of its `presC#` component, there is no requirement that `NULL` appear as the value of a `cert#` component (but note that `cert#` is a primary key and therefore cannot have `NULL`'s anyway). □

1.2 Maintaining Referential Integrity

The schema designer may choose from among three alternatives to enforce a foreign-key constraint. We can learn the general idea by exploring Example 1, where it is required that a `presC#` value in relation `Studio` also be a `cert#` value in `MovieExec`. The following actions will be prevented by the DBMS (i.e., a run-time exception or error will be generated).

a) We try to insert a new `Studio` tuple whose `presC#` value is not `NULL` and is not the `cert#` component of any `MovieExec` tuple.

b) We try to update a `Studio` tuple to change the `presC#` component to a non-`NULL` value that is not the `cert#` component of any `MovieExec` tuple.

c) We try to delete a `MovieExec` tuple, and its `cert#` component, which is not `NULL`, appears as the `presC#` component of one or more `Studio` tuples.

d) We try to update a MovieExec tuple in a way that changes the cert# value, and the old cert# is the value of presC# of some movie studio.

For the first two modifications, where the change is to the relation where the foreign-key constraint is declared, there is no alternative; the system has to reject the violating modification. However, for changes to the referenced relation, of which the last two modifications are examples, the designer can choose among three options:

1. *The Default Policy: Reject Violating Modifications.* SQL has a default policy that any modification violating the referential integrity constraint is rejected.

2. *The Cascade Policy.* Under this policy, changes to the referenced attribute(s) are mimicked at the foreign key. For example, under the cascade policy, when we delete the MovieExec tuple for the president of a studio, then to maintain referential integrity the system will delete the referencing tuple(s) from Studio. If we update the cert# for some movie executive from c_1 to c_2, and there was some Studio tuple with c_1 as the value of its presC# component, then the system will also update this presC# component to have value c_2.

3. *The Set-Null Policy.* Here, when a modification to the referenced relation affects a foreign-key value, the latter is changed to NULL. For instance, if we delete from MoveExec the tuple for a president of a studio, the system would change the presC# value for that studio to NULL. If we updated that president's certificate number in MovieExec, we would again set presC# to NULL in Studio.

These options may be chosen for deletes and updates, independently, and they are stated with the declaration of the foreign key. We declare them with ON DELETE or ON UPDATE followed by our choice of SET NULL or CASCADE.

Example 2: Let us see how we might modify the declaration of

```
Studio(name, address, presC#)
```

in Example 1 to specify the handling of deletes and updates in the

```
MovieExec(name, address, cert#, netWorth)
```

relation. Figure 1 takes the first of the CREATE TABLE statements in that example and expands it with ON DELETE and ON UPDATE clauses. Line (5) says that when we delete a MovieExec tuple, we set the presC# of any studio of which he or she was the president to NULL. Line (6) says that if we update the cert# component of a MovieExec tuple, then any tuples in Studio with the same value in the presC# component are changed similarly.

```
CREATE TABLE Studio (
    name CHAR(30) PRIMARY KEY,
    address VARCHAR(255),
    presC# INT REFERENCES MovieExec(cert#)
        ON DELETE SET NULL
        ON UPDATE CASCADE
);
```

Figure 1: Choosing policies to preserve referential integrity

Dangling Tuples and Modification Policies

A tuple with a foreign key value that does not appear in the referenced relation is said to be a *dangling tuple*. Recall that a tuple which fails to participate in a join is also called "dangling." The two ideas are closely related. If a tuple's foreign-key value is missing from the referenced relation, then the tuple will not participate in a join of its relation with the referenced relation, if the join is on equality of the foreign key and the key it references (called a *foreign-key join*). The dangling tuples are exactly the tuples that violate referential integrity for this foreign-key constraint.

Note that in this example, the set-null policy makes more sense for deletes, while the cascade policy seems preferable for updates. We would expect that if, for instance, a studio president retires, the studio will exist with a "null" president for a while. However, an update to the certificate number of a studio president is most likely a clerical change. The person continues to exist and to be the president of the studio, so we would like the `presC#` attribute in `Studio` to follow the change. □

1.3 Deferred Checking of Constraints

Let us assume the situation of Example 1, where `presC#` in `Studio` is a foreign key referencing `cert#` of `MovieExec`. Arnold Schwarzenegger retires as Governor of California and decides to found a movie studio, called La Vista Studios, of which he will naturally be the president. If we execute the insertion:

```
INSERT INTO Studio
VALUES('La Vista', 'New York', 23456);
```

we are in trouble. The reason is that there is no tuple of `MovieExec` with certificate number 23456 (the presumed newly issued certificate for Arnold Schwarzenegger), so there is an obvious violation of the foreign-key constraint.

One possible fix is first to insert the tuple for La Vista without a president's certificate, as:

```
INSERT INTO Studio(name, address)
VALUES('La Vista', 'New York');
```

This change avoids the constraint violation, because the La-Vista tuple is inserted with NULL as the value of presC#, and NULL in a foreign key does not require that we check for the existence of any value in the referenced column. However, we must insert a tuple for Arnold Schwarzenegger into MovieExec, with his correct certificate number before we can apply an update statement such as

```
UPDATE Studio
SET presC# = 23456
WHERE name = 'La Vista';
```

If we do not fix MovieExec first, then this update statement will also violate the foreign-key constraint.

Of course, inserting Arnold Schwarzenegger and his certificate number into MovieExec before inserting La Vista into Studio will surely protect against a foreign-key violation in this case. However, there are cases of *circular constraints* that cannot be fixed by judiciously ordering the database modification steps we take.

Example 3: If movie executives were limited to studio presidents, then we might want to declare cert# to be a foreign key referencing Studio(presC#); we would first have to declare presC# to be UNIQUE, but that declaration makes sense if you assume a person cannot be the president of two studios at the same time.

Now, it is impossible to insert new studios with new presidents. We can't insert a tuple with a new value of presC# into Studio, because that tuple would violate the foreign-key constraint from presC# to MovieExec(cert#). We can't insert a tuple with a new value of cert# into MovieExec, because that would violate the foreign-key constraint from cert# to Studio(presC#). □

The problem of Example 3 can be solved as follows.

1. First, we must group the two insertions (one into Studio and the other into MovieExec) into a single transaction.

2. Then, we need a way to tell the DBMS not to check the constraints until after the whole transaction has finished its actions and is about to commit.

To inform the DBMS about point (2), the declaration of any constraint — key, foreign-key, or other constraint types we shall meet later in this chapter — may be followed by one of DEFERRABLE or NOT DEFERRABLE. The latter is the default, and means that every time a database modification statement is executed, the constraint is checked immediately afterwards, if the modification could violate the foreign-key constraint. However, if we declare a constraint to be `DEFERRABLE`, then we have the option of having it wait until a transaction is complete before checking the constraint.

We follow the keyword `DEFERRABLE` by either `INITIALLY DEFERRED` or `INITIALLY IMMEDIATE`. In the former case, checking will be deferred to just before each transaction commits. In the latter case, the check will be made immediately after each statement.

Example 4: Figure 2 shows the declaration of `Studio` modified to allow the checking of its foreign-key constraint to be deferred until the end of each transaction. We have also declared `presC#` to be `UNIQUE`, in order that it may be referenced by other relations' foreign-key constraints.

```
CREATE TABLE Studio (
    name CHAR(30) PRIMARY KEY,
    address VARCHAR(255),
    presC# INT UNIQUE
        REFERENCES MovieExec(cert#)
        DEFERRABLE INITIALLY DEFERRED
);
```

Figure 2: Making `presC#` unique and deferring the checking of its foreign-key constraint

If we made a similar declaration for the hypothetical foreign-key constraint from `MovieExec(cert#)` to `Studio(presC#)` mentioned in Example 3, then we could write transactions that inserted two tuples, one into each relation, and the two foreign-key constraints would not be checked until after both insertions had been done. Then, if we insert both a new studio and its new president, and use the same certificate number in each tuple, we would avoid violation of any constraint. □

There are two additional points about deferring constraints that we should bear in mind:

- Constraints of any type can be given names. We shall discuss how to do so in Section 3.1.
- If a constraint has a name, say `MyConstraint`, then we can change a deferrable constraint from immediate to deferred by the SQL statement

  ```
  SET CONSTRAINT MyConstraint DEFERRED;
  ```

  and we can reverse the process by replacing `DEFERRED` in the above to `IMMEDIATE`.

1.4 Exercises for Section 1

Exercise 1.1: Our running example movie database has keys defined for all its relations.

```
Movies(title, year, length, genre, studioName, producerC#)
StarsIn(movieTitle, movieYear, starName)
MovieStar(name, address, gender, birthdate)
MovieExec(name, address, cert#, netWorth)
Studio(name, address, presC#)
```

Declare the following referential integrity constraints for the movie database as in Exercise 1.1.

a) The producer of a movie must be someone mentioned in `MovieExec`. Modifications to `MovieExec` that violate this constraint are rejected.

b) Repeat (a), but violations result in the `producerC#` in `Movie` being set to `NULL`.

c) Repeat (a), but violations result in the deletion or update of the offending `Movie` tuple.

d) A movie that appears in `StarsIn` must also appear in `Movie`. Handle violations by rejecting the modification.

e) A star appearing in `StarsIn` must also appear in `MovieStar`. Handle violations by deleting violating tuples.

! **Exercise 1.2:** We would like to declare the constraint that every movie in the relation `Movie` must appear with at least one star in `StarsIn`. Can we do so with a foreign-key constraint? Why or why not?

2 Constraints on Attributes and Tuples

Within a SQL CREATE TABLE statement, we can declare two kinds of constraints:

1. A constraint on a single attribute.

2. A constraint on a tuple as a whole.

In Section 2.1 we shall introduce a simple type of constraint on an attribute's value: the constraint that the attribute not have a NULL value. Then in Section 2.2 we cover the principal form of constraints of type (1): *attribute-based* CHECK *constraints.* The second type, the tuple-based constraints, are covered in Section 2.3.

There are other, more general kinds of constraints that we shall meet in Sections 4 and 5. These constraints can be used to restrict changes to whole relations or even several relations, as well as to constrain the value of a single attribute or tuple.

2.1 Not-Null Constraints

One simple constraint to associate with an attribute is NOT NULL. The effect is to disallow tuples in which this attribute is NULL. The constraint is declared by the keywords NOT NULL following the declaration of the attribute in a CREATE TABLE statement.

Example 5: Suppose relation Studio required presC# not to be NULL, perhaps by changing line (4) of Fig. 1 to:

```
4)      presC# INT REFERENCES MovieExec(cert#) NOT NULL
```

This change has several consequences. For instance:

- We could not insert a tuple into Studio by specifying only the name and address, because the inserted tuple would have NULL in the presC# component.

- We could not use the set-null policy in situations like line (5) of Fig. 1, which tells the system to fix foreign-key violations by making presC# be NULL.

□

2.2 Attribute-Based CHECK Constraints

More complex constraints can be attached to an attribute declaration by the keyword CHECK and a parenthesized condition that must hold for every value of this attribute. In practice, an attribute-based CHECK constraint is likely to be a simple limit on values, such as an enumeration of legal values or an arithmetic inequality. However, in principle the condition can be anything that could follow WHERE in a SQL query. This condition may refer to the attribute being constrained, by using the name of that attribute in its expression. However, if the condition refers to any other relations or attributes of relations, then the relation must be introduced in the FROM clause of a subquery (even if the relation referred to is the one to which the checked attribute belongs).

An attribute-based CHECK constraint is checked whenever any tuple gets a new value for this attribute. The new value could be introduced by an update for the tuple, or it could be part of an inserted tuple. In the case of an update, the constraint is checked on the new value, not the old value. If the constraint is violated by the new value, then the modification is rejected.

It is important to understand that an attribute-based CHECK constraint is not checked if the database modification does not change the attribute with which the constraint is associated. This limitation can result in the constraint becoming violated, if other values involved in the constraint do change. First, let us consider a simple example of an attribute-based check. Then we shall see a constraint that involves a subquery, and also see the consequence of the fact that the constraint is only checked when its attribute is modified.

Example 6: Suppose we want to require that certificate numbers be at least six digits. We could modify line (4) of Fig. 1, a declaration of the schema for relation

```
Studio(name, address, presC#)
```

to be

```
4)     presC# INT REFERENCES MovieExec(cert#)
                  CHECK (presC# >= 100000)
```

For another example, the attribute gender of relation

```
MovieStar(name, address, gender, birthdate)
```

was declared to be of data type `CHAR(1)` — that is, a single character. However, we really expect that the only characters that will appear there are `'F'` and `'M'`. The following enforces the rule:

```
4) gender CHAR(1) CHECK (gender IN ('F', 'M')),
```

Note that the expression `('F' 'M')` describes a one-component relation with two tuples. The constraint says that the value of any `gender` component must be in this set. □

Example 7: We might suppose that we could simulate a referential integrity constraint by an attribute-based `CHECK` constraint that requires the existence of the referred-to value. The following is an *erroneous* attempt to simulate the requirement that the `presC#` value in a

```
Studio(name, address, presC#)
```

tuple must appear in the `cert#` component of some

```
MovieExec(name, address, cert#, netWorth)
```

tuple. Suppose line (4) of Fig. 1 were replaced by

```
4)      presC# INT CHECK
            (presC# IN (SELECT cert# FROM MovieExec))
```

This statement is a legal attribute-based `CHECK` constraint, but let us look at its effect. Modifications to `Studio` that introduce a `presC#` that is not also a `cert#` of `MovieExec` will be rejected. That is almost what the similar foreign-key constraint would do, except that the attribute-based check will also reject a `NULL` value for `presC#` if there is no `NULL` value for `cert#`. But far more importantly, if we change the `MovieExec` relation, say by deleting the tuple for the president of a studio, this change is invisible to the above `CHECK` constraint. Thus, the deletion is permitted, even though the attribute-based `CHECK` constraint on `presC#` is now violated. □

2.3 Tuple-Based `CHECK` Constraints

To declare a constraint on the tuples of a single table R, we may add to the list of attributes and key or foreign-key declarations, in R's `CREATE TABLE` statement, the keyword `CHECK` followed by a parenthesized condition. This condition can be anything that could appear in a `WHERE` clause. It is interpreted as a condition about a tuple in the table R, and the attributes of R may be referred to by name in this expression. However, as for attribute-based `CHECK` constraints, the condition may also mention, in subqueries, other relations or other tuples of the same relation R.

Limited Constraint Checking: Bug or Feature?

One might wonder why attribute- and tuple-based checks are allowed to be violated if they refer to other relations or other tuples of the same relation. The reason is that such constraints can be implemented much more efficiently than more general constraints can. With attribute- or tuple-based checks, we only have to evaluate that constraint for the tuple(s) that are inserted or updated. On the other hand, assertions must be evaluated every time any one of the relations they mention is changed. The careful database designer will use attribute- and tuple-based checks only when there is no possibility that they will be violated, and will use another mechanism, such as assertions (Section 4) or triggers (Section 5) otherwise.

The condition of a tuple-based `CHECK` constraint is checked every time a tuple is inserted into R and every time a tuple of R is updated. The condition is evaluated for the new or updated tuple. If the condition is false for that tuple, then the constraint is violated and the insertion or update statement that caused the violation is rejected. However, if the condition mentions some other relation in a subquery, and a change to that relation causes the condition to become false for some tuple of R, the check does not inhibit this change. That is, like an attribute-based `CHECK`, a tuple-based `CHECK` is invisible to other relations. In fact, even a deletion from R can cause the condition to become false, if R is mentioned in a subquery.

On the other hand, if a tuple-based check does not have subqueries, then we can rely on its always holding. Here is an example of a tuple-based `CHECK` constraint that involves several attributes of one tuple, but no subqueries.

Example 8: You may recall when we declared the schema of table `MovieStar`. Figure 3 repeats the `CREATE TABLE` statement with the addition of a primary-key declaration and one other constraint, which is one of several possible "consistency conditions" that we might wish to check. This constraint says that if the star's gender is male, then his name must not begin with `'Ms.'`.

In line (2), `name` is declared the primary key for the relation. Then line (6) declares a constraint. The condition of this constraint is true for every female movie star and for every star whose name does not begin with `'Ms.'`. The only tuples for which it is *not* true are those where the gender is male and the name *does* begin with `'Ms.'`. Those are exactly the tuples we wish to exclude from `MovieStar`. □

```
CREATE TABLE MovieStar (
    name CHAR(30) PRIMARY KEY,
    address VARCHAR(255),
    gender CHAR(1),
    birthdate DATE,
    CHECK (gender = 'F' OR name NOT LIKE 'Ms.%')
);
```

Figure 3: A constraint on the table MovieStar

> **Writing Constraints Correctly**
>
> Many constraints are like Example 8, where we want to forbid tuples that satisfy two or more conditions. The expression that should follow the check is the `OR` of the negations, or opposites, of each condition; this transformation is one of "DeMorgan's laws": the negation of the `AND` of terms is the `OR` of the negations of the same terms. Thus, in Example 8 the first condition was that the star is male, and we used `gender = 'F'` as a suitable negation (although perhaps `gender <> 'M'` would be the more normal way to phrase the negation). The second condition is that the `name` begins with `'Ms.'`, and for this negation we used the `NOT LIKE` comparison. This comparison negates the condition itself, which would be `name LIKE 'Ms.%'` in SQL.

2.4 Comparison of Tuple- and Attribute-Based Constraints

If a constraint on a tuple involves more than one attribute of that tuple, then it must be written as a tuple-based constraint. However, if the constraint involves only one attribute of the tuple, then it can be written as either a tuple- or attribute-based constraint. In either case, we do not count attributes mentioned in subqueries, so even a attribute-based constraint can mention other attributes of the same relation in subqueries.

When only one attribute of the tuple is involved (not counting subqueries), then the condition checked is the same, regardless of whether a tuple- or attribute-based constraint is written. However, the tuple-based constraint will be checked more frequently than the attribute-based constraint — whenever any attribute of the tuple changes, rather than only when the attribute mentioned in the constraint changes.

2.5 Exercises for Section 2

Exercise 2.1: Write the following constraints for attributes of the relation

```
Movies(title, year, length, genre, studioName, producerC#)
```

a) The year cannot be before 1915.

b) The length cannot be less than 60 nor more than 250.

c) The studio name can only be Disney, Fox, MGM, or Paramount.

Exercise 2.2: Write the following constraints as tuple-based CHECK constraints on one of the relations of our running movies example:

```
Movies(title, year, length, genre, studioName, producerC#)
StarsIn(movieTitle, movieYear, starName)
MovieStar(name, address, gender, birthdate)
MovieExec(name, address, cert#, netWorth)
Studio(name, address, presC#)
```

If the constraint actually involves two relations, then you should put constraints in both relations so that whichever relation changes, the constraint will be checked on insertions and updates. Assume no deletions; it is not always possible to maintain tuple-based constraints in the face of deletions.

a) A star may not appear in a movie made before they were born.

! b) No two studios may have the same address.

! c) A name that appears in MovieStar must not also appear in MovieExec.

! d) A studio name that appears in Studio must also appear in at least one Movies tuple.

!! e) If a producer of a movie is also the president of a studio, then they must be the president of the studio that made the movie.

Exercise 2.3: Write the following as tuple-based `CHECK` constraints about our "PC" schema.

a) A PC with a processor speed less than 2.0 must not sell for more than $600.

b) A laptop with a screen size less than 15 inches must have at least a 40 gigabyte hard disk or sell for less than $1000.

Exercise 2.4: Write the following as tuple-based `CHECK` constraints about our "battleships" schema:

```
Classes(class, type, country, numGuns, bore, displacement)
Ships(name, class, launched)
Battles(name, date)
Outcomes(ship, battle, result)
```

a) No class of ships may have guns with larger than a 16-inch bore.

b) If a class of ships has more than 9 guns, then their bore must be no larger than 14 inches.

! c) No ship can be in battle before it is launched.

! **Exercise 2.5:** In Examples 6 and 8, we introduced constraints on the `gender` attribute of`MovieStar`. What restrictions, if any, do each of these constraints enforce if the value of `gender` is `NULL`?

3 Modification of Constraints

It is possible to add, modify, or delete constraints at any time. The way to express such modifications depends on whether the constraint involved is associated with an attribute, a table, or (as in Section 4) a database schema.

3.1 Giving Names to Constraints

In order to modify or delete an existing constraint, it is necessary that the constraint have a name. To do so, we precede the constraint by the keyword `CONSTRAINT` and a name for the constraint.

Example 9: We could write a line to name the constraint that says attribute `name` is a primary key, as

```
2)      name CHAR(30) CONSTRAINT NameIsKey PRIMARY KEY,
```

Similarly, we could name the attribute-based CHECK constraint that appeared in Example 6 by:

```
4) gender CHAR(1) CONSTRAINT NoAndro
                  CHECK (gender IN ('F', 'M')),
```

Finally, the following constraint:

```
6)      CONSTRAINT RightTitle
            CHECK (gender = 'F' OR name NOT LIKE 'Ms.%');
```

is a rewriting of the tuple-based CHECK constraint in line (6) of Fig. 3 to give that constraint a name. □

3.2 Altering Constraints on Tables

We mentioned in Section 1.3 that we can switch the checking of a constraint from immediate to deferred or vice-versa with a SET CONSTRAINT statement. Other changes to constraints are effected with an ALTER TABLE statement.

ALTER TABLE statements can affect constraints in several ways. You may drop a constraint with keyword DROP and the name of the constraint to be dropped. You may also add a constraint with the keyword ADD, followed by the constraint to be added. Note, however, that the added constraint must be of a kind that can be associated with tuples, such as tuple-based constraints, key, or foreign-key constraints. Also note that you cannot add a constraint to a table unless it holds at that time for every tuple in the table.

Example 10: Let us see how we would drop and add the constraints of Example 9 on relation MovieStar. The following sequence of three statements drops them:

```
ALTER TABLE MovieStar DROP CONSTRAINT NameIsKey;
ALTER TABLE MovieStar DROP CONSTRAINT NoAndro;
ALTER TABLE MovieStar DROP CONSTRAINT RightTitle;
```

Should we wish to reinstate these constraints, we would alter the schema for relation MovieStar by adding the same constraints, for example:

```
ALTER TABLE MovieStar ADD CONSTRAINT NameIsKey
    PRIMARY KEY (name);
ALTER TABLE MovieStar ADD CONSTRAINT NoAndro
    CHECK (gender IN ('F', 'M'));
ALTER TABLE MovieStar ADD CONSTRAINT RightTitle
    CHECK (gender = 'F' OR name NOT LIKE 'Ms.%');
```

> **Name Your Constraints**
>
> Remember, it is a good idea to give each of your constraints a name, even if you do not believe you will ever need to refer to it. Once the constraint is created without a name, it is too late to give it one later, should you wish to alter it. However, should you be faced with a situation of having to alter a nameless constraint, you will find that your DBMS probably has a way for you to query it for a list of all your constraints, and that it has given your unnamed constraint an internal name of its own, which you may use to refer to the constraint.

These constraints are now tuple-based, rather than attribute-based checks. We cannot bring them back as attribute-based constraints.

The name is optional for these reintroduced constraints. However, we cannot rely on SQL remembering the dropped constraints. Thus, when we add a former constraint we need to write the constraint again; we cannot refer to it by its former name. □

3.3 Exercises for Section 3

Exercise 3.1: Show how to alter your relation schemas for the movie example:

```
Movie(title, year, length, genre, studioName, producerC#)
StarsIn(movieTitle, movieYear, starName)
MovieStar(name, address, gender, birthdate)
MovieExec(name, address, cert#, netWorth)
Studio(name, address, presC#)
```

in the following ways.

a) Make `title` and `year` the key for `Movie`.

b) Require the referential integrity constraint that the producer of every movie appear in `MovieExec`.

c) Require that no movie length be less than 60 nor greater than 250.

! d) Require that no name appear as both a movie star and movie executive (this constraint need not be maintained in the face of deletions).

! e) Require that no two studios have the same address.

Exercise 3.2: Show how to alter the schemas of the "battleships" database:

```
Classes(class, type, country, numGuns, bore, displacement)
Ships(name, class, launched)
Battles(name, date)
Outcomes(ship, battle, result)
```

to have the following tuple-based constraints.

a) `Class` and `country` form a key for relation `Classes`.

b) Require the referential integrity constraint that every battle appearing in `Outcomes` also appears in `Battles`.

c) Require the referential integrity constraint that every ship appearing in `Outcomes` appears in `Ships`.

d) Require that no ship has more than 14 guns.

! e) Disallow a ship being in battle before it is launched.

4 Assertions

The most powerful forms of active elements in SQL are not associated with particular tuples or components of tuples. These elements, called "triggers" and "assertions," are part of the database schema, on a par with tables.

- An assertion is a boolean-valued SQL expression that must be true at all times.
- A trigger is a series of actions that are associated with certain events, such as insertions into a particular relation, and that are performed whenever these events arise.

Assertions are easier for the programmer to use, since they merely require the programmer to state what must be true. However, triggers are the feature DBMS's typically provide as general-purpose, active elements. The reason is that it is very hard to implement assertions efficiently. The DBMS must deduce whether any given database modification could affect the truth of an assertion. Triggers, on the other hand, tell exactly when the DBMS needs to deal with them.

4.1 Creating Assertions

The SQL standard proposes a simple form of *assertion* that allows us to enforce any condition (expression that can follow `WHERE`). Like other schema elements, we declare an assertion with a `CREATE` statement. The form of an assertion is:

```
CREATE ASSERTION <assertion-name> CHECK (<condition>)
```

The condition in an assertion must be true when the assertion is created and must remain true; any database modification that causes it to become false will be rejected.[1] Recall that the other types of CHECK constraints we have covered can be violated under certain conditions, if they involve subqueries.

4.2 Using Assertions

There is a difference between the way we write tuple-based CHECK constraints and the way we write assertions. Tuple-based checks can refer directly to the attributes of that relation in whose declaration they appear. An assertion has no such privilege. Any attributes referred to in the condition must be introduced in the assertion, typically by mentioning their relation in a select-from-where expression.

Since the condition must have a boolean value, it is necessary to combine results in some way to make a single true/false choice. For example, we might write the condition as an expression producing a relation, to which NOT EXISTS is applied; that is, the constraint is that this relation is always empty. Alternatively, we might apply an aggregation operator like SUM to a column of a relation and compare it to a constant. For instance, this way we could require that a sum always be less than some limiting value.

Example 11 : Suppose we wish to require that no one can become the president of a studio unless their net worth is at least $10,000,000. We declare an assertion to the effect that the set of movie studios with presidents having a net worth less than $10,000,000 is empty. This assertion involves the two relations

```
MovieExec(name, address, cert#, netWorth)
Studio(name, address, presC#)
```

The assertion is shown in Fig. 4. □

```
CREATE ASSERTION RichPres CHECK
    (NOT EXISTS
        (SELECT Studio.name
         FROM Studio, MovieExec
         WHERE presC# = cert# AND netWorth < 10000000
        )
    );
```

Figure 4: Assertion guaranteeing rich studio presidents

[1] However, remember from Section 1.3 that it is possible to defer the checking of a constraint until just before its transaction commits. If we do so with an assertion, it may briefly become false until the end of a transaction.

Example 12: Here is another example of an assertion. It involves the relation

```
Movies(title, year, length, genre, studioName, producerC#)
```

and says the total length of all movies by a given studio shall not exceed 10,000 minutes.

```
CREATE ASSERTION SumLength CHECK (10000 >= ALL
    (SELECT SUM(length) FROM Movies GROUP BY studioName)
);
```

As this constraint involves only the relation `Movies`, it seemingly could have been expressed as a tuple-based `CHECK` constraint in the schema for `Movies` rather than as an assertion. That is, we could add to the definition of table `Movies` the tuple-based `CHECK` constraint

```
CHECK (10000 >= ALL
    (SELECT SUM(length) FROM Movies GROUP BY studioName));
```

Notice that in principle this condition applies to every tuple of table `Movies`. However, it does not mention any attributes of the tuple explicitly, and all the work is done in the subquery.

Also observe that if implemented as a tuple-based constraint, the check would not be made on deletion of a tuple from the relation `Movies`. In this example, that difference causes no harm, since if the constraint was satisfied before the deletion, then it is surely satisfied after the deletion. However, if the constraint were a lower bound on total length, rather than an upper bound as in this example, then we could find the constraint violated had we written it as a tuple-based check rather than an assertion. □

As a final point, it is possible to drop an assertion. The statement to do so follows the pattern for any database schema element:

`DROP ASSERTION` <assertion name>

4.3 Exercises for Section 4

Exercise 4.1: Write the following assertions. The database schema is from the "PC" example:

```
Product(maker, model, type)
PC(model, speed, ram, hd, price)
Laptop(model, speed, ram, hd, screen, price)
Printer(model, color, type, price)
```

a) No manufacturer of PC's may also make laptops.

Comparison of Constraints

The following table lists the principal differences among attribute-based checks, tuple-based checks, and assertions.

Type of Constraint	Where Declared	When Activated	Guaranteed to Hold?
Attribute-based `CHECK`	With attribute	On insertion to relation or attribute update	Not if subqueries
Tuple-based `CHECK`	Element of relation schema	On insertion to relation or tuple update	Not if subqueries
Assertion	Element of database schema	On any change to any mentioned relation	Yes

b) A manufacturer of a PC must also make a laptop with at least as great a processor speed.

c) If a laptop has a larger main memory than a PC, then the laptop must also have a higher price than the PC.

d) If the relation `Product` mentions a model and its type, then this model must appear in the relation appropriate to that type.

Exercise 4.2: Write the following as assertions. The database schema is from the battleships example.

```
Classes(class, type, country, numGuns, bore, displacement)
Ships(name, class, launched)
Battles(name, date)
Outcomes(ship, battle, result)
```

a) No class may have more than 2 ships.

! b) No country may have both battleships and battlecruisers.

! c) No ship with more than 9 guns may be in a battle with a ship having fewer than 9 guns that was sunk.

! d) No ship may be launched before the ship that bears the name of the first ship's class.

! e) For every class, there is a ship with the name of that class.

! **Exercise 4.3:** The assertion of Exercise 11 can be written as two tuple-based constraints. Show how to do so.

5 Triggers

Triggers, sometimes called *event-condition-action rules* or *ECA rules*, differ from the kinds of constraints discussed previously in three ways.

1. Triggers are only awakened when certain *events*, specified by the database programmer, occur. The sorts of events allowed are usually insert, delete, or update to a particular relation. Another kind of event allowed in many SQL systems is a transaction end.

2. Once awakened by its triggering event, the trigger tests a *condition*. If the condition does not hold, then nothing else associated with the trigger happens in response to this event.

3. If the condition of the trigger is satisfied, the *action* associated with the trigger is performed by the DBMS. A possible action is to modify the effects of the event in some way, even aborting the transaction of which the event is part. However, the action could be any sequence of database operations, including operations not connected in any way to the triggering event.

5.1 Triggers in SQL

The SQL trigger statement gives the user a number of different options in the event, condition, and action parts. Here are the principal features.

1. The check of the trigger's condition and the action of the trigger may be executed either on the *state of the database* (i.e., the current instances of all the relations) that exists before the triggering event is itself executed or on the state that exists after the triggering event is executed.

2. The condition and action can refer to both old and/or new values of tuples that were updated in the triggering event.

3. It is possible to define update events that are limited to a particular attribute or set of attributes.

4. The programmer has an option of specifying that the trigger executes either:

   (a) Once for each modified tuple (a *row-level trigger*), or

   (b) Once for all the tuples that are changed in one SQL statement (a *statement-level trigger*; remember that one SQL modification statement can affect many tuples).

Before giving the details of the syntax for triggers, let us consider an example that will illustrate the most important syntactic as well as semantic points. Notice in the example trigger, Fig. 5, the key elements and the order in which they appear:

a) The `CREATE TRIGGER` statement (line 1).

b) A clause indicating the triggering event and telling whether the trigger uses the database state before or after the triggering event (line 2).

c) A `REFERENCING` clause to allow the condition and action of the trigger to refer to the tuple being modified (lines 3 through 5). In the case of an update, such as this one, this clause allows us to give names to the tuple both before and after the change.

d) A clause telling whether the trigger executes once for each modified row or once for all the modifications made by one SQL statement (line 6).

e) The condition, which uses the keyword `WHEN` and a boolean expression (line 7).

f) The action, consisting of one or more SQL statements (lines 8 through 10).

Each of these elements has options, which we shall discuss after working through the example.

Example 13: In Fig. 13 is a SQL trigger that applies to the

```
MovieExec(name, address, cert#, netWorth)
```

table. It is triggered by updates to the `netWorth` attribute. The effect of this trigger is to foil any attempt to lower the net worth of a movie executive.

```
 1)  CREATE TRIGGER NetWorthTrigger
 2)  AFTER UPDATE OF netWorth ON MovieExec
 3)  REFERENCING
 4)      OLD ROW AS OldTuple,
 5)      NEW ROW AS NewTuple
 6)  FOR EACH ROW
 7)  WHEN (OldTuple.netWorth > NewTuple.netWorth)
 8)      UPDATE MovieExec
 9)      SET netWorth = OldTuple.netWorth
10)      WHERE cert# = NewTuple.cert#;
```

Figure 5: A SQL trigger

Line (1) introduces the declaration with the keywords CREATE TRIGGER and the name of the trigger. Line (2) then gives the triggering event, namely the update of the netWorth attribute of the MovieExec relation. Lines (3) through (5) set up a way for the condition and action portions of this trigger to talk about both the old tuple (the tuple before the update) and the new tuple (the tuple after the update). These tuples will be referred to as OldTuple and NewTuple, according to the declarations in lines (4) and (5), respectively. In the condition and action, these names can be used as if they were tuple variables declared in the FROM clause of an ordinary SQL query.

Line (6), the phrase FOR EACH ROW, expresses the requirement that this trigger is executed once for each updated tuple. Line (7) is the condition part of the trigger. It says that we only perform the action when the new net worth is lower than the old net worth; i.e., the net worth of an executive has shrunk.

Lines (8) through (10) form the action portion. This action is an ordinary SQL update statement that has the effect of restoring the net worth of the executive to what it was before the update. Note that in principle, every tuple of MovieExec is considered for update, but the WHERE-clause of line (10) guarantees that only the updated tuple (the one with the proper cert#) will be affected. □

5.2 The Options for Trigger Design

Of course Example 13 illustrates only some of the features of SQL triggers. In the points that follow, we shall outline the options that are offered by triggers and how to express these options.

- Line (2) of Fig. 5 says that the condition test and action of the rule are executed on the database state that exists after the triggering event, as indicated by the keyword AFTER. We may replace AFTER by BEFORE, in which case the WHEN condition is tested on the database state that exists before the triggering event is executed. If the condition is true, then the action of the trigger is executed on that state. Finally, the event that awakened the trigger is executed, regardless of whether the condition is still true.

- Besides UPDATE, other possible triggering events are INSERT and DELETE. The OF netWorth clause in line (2) of Fig. 5 is optional for UPDATE events, and if present defines the event to be only an update of the attribute(s) listed after the keyword OF. An OF clause is not permitted for INSERT or DELETE events; these events make sense for entire tuples only.

- The WHEN clause is optional. If it is missing, then the action is executed whenever the trigger is awakened. If present, then the action is executed only if the condition following WHEN is true.

- While we showed a single SQL statement as an action, there can be any number of such statements, separated by semicolons and surrounded by BEGIN...END.

- When the triggering event of a row-level trigger is an update, then there will be old and new tuples, which are the tuple before the update and after, respectively. We give these tuples names by the OLD ROW AS and NEW ROW AS clauses seen in lines (4) and (5). If the triggering event is an insertion, then we may use a NEW ROW AS clause to give a name for the inserted tuple, and OLD ROW AS is disallowed. Conversely, on a deletion OLD ROW AS is used to name the deleted tuple and NEW ROW AS is disallowed.

- If we omit the FOR EACH ROW on line (6) or replace it by the default FOR EACH STATEMENT, then a row-level trigger such as Fig. 5 becomes a statement-level trigger. A statement-level trigger is executed once whenever a statement of the appropriate type is executed, no matter how many rows — zero, one, or many — it actually affects. For instance, if we update an entire table with a SQL update statement, a statement-level update trigger would execute only once, while a row-level trigger would execute once for each tuple to which an update was applied.

- In a statement-level trigger, we cannot refer to old and new tuples directly, as we did in lines (4) and (5). However, any trigger — whether row- or statement-level — can refer to the relation of *old tuples* (deleted tuples or old versions of updated tuples) and the relation of *new tuples* (inserted tuples or new versions of updated tuples), using declarations such as OLD TABLE AS OldStuff and NEW TABLE AS NewStuff.

Example 14: Suppose we want to prevent the average net worth of movie executives from dropping below $500,000. This constraint could be violated by an insertion, a deletion, or an update to the netWorth column of

```
MovieExec(name, address, cert#, netWorth)
```

The subtle point is that we might, in one statement insert, delete, or change many tuples of MovieExec. During the modification, the average net worth might temporarily dip below $500,000 and then rise above it by the time all the modifications are made. We only want to reject the entire set of modifications if the net worth is below $500,000 at the end of the statement.

It is necessary to write one trigger for each of these three events: insert, delete, and update of relation MovieExec. Figure 6 shows the trigger for the update event. The triggers for the insertion and deletion of tuples are similar.

Lines (3) through (5) declare that NewStuff and OldStuff are the names of relations containing the new tuples and old tuples that are involved in the database operation that awakened our trigger. Note that one database statement can modify many tuples of a relation, and if such a statement executes, there can be many tuples in NewStuff and OldStuff.

```
1)  CREATE TRIGGER AvgNetWorthTrigger
2)  AFTER UPDATE OF netWorth ON MovieExec
3)  REFERENCING
4)      OLD TABLE AS OldStuff,
5)      NEW TABLE AS NewStuff
6)  FOR EACH STATEMENT
7)  WHEN (500000 > (SELECT AVG(netWorth) FROM MovieExec))
8)  BEGIN
9)      DELETE FROM MovieExec
10)     WHERE (name, address, cert#, netWorth) IN NewStuff;
11)     INSERT INTO MovieExec
12)         (SELECT * FROM OldStuff);
13) END;
```

Figure 6: Constraining the average net worth

If the operation is an update, then tables NewStuff and OldStuff are the new and old versions of the updated tuples, respectively. If an analogous trigger were written for deletions, then the deleted tuples would be in OldStuff, and there would be no declaration of a relation name like NewStuff for NEW TABLE in this trigger. Likewise, in the analogous trigger for insertions, the new tuples would be in NewStuff, and there would be no declaration of OldStuff.

Line (6) tells us that this trigger is executed once for a statement, regardless of how many tuples are modified. Line (7) is the condition. This condition is satisfied if the average net worth *after* the update is less than $500,000.

The action of lines (8) through (13) consists of two statements that restore the old relation MovieExec if the condition of the WHEN clause is satisfied; i.e., the new average net worth is too low. Lines (9) and (10) remove all the new tuples, i.e., the updated versions of the tuples, while lines (11) and (12) restore the tuples as they were before the update. □

Example 15: An important use of BEFORE triggers is to fix up the inserted tuples in some way before they are inserted. Suppose that we want to insert movie tuples into

`Movies(title, year, length, genre, studioName, producerC#)`

but sometimes, we will not know the year of the movie. Since year is part of the primary key, we cannot have NULL for this attribute. However, we could make sure that year is not NULL with a trigger and replace NULL by some suitable value, perhaps one that we compute in a complex way. In Fig. 7 is a trigger that takes the simple expedient of replacing NULL by 1915 (something that could be handled by a default value, but which will serve as an example).

Line (2) says that the condition and action execute before the insertion event. In the referencing-clause of lines (3) through (5), we define names for

```
1) CREATE TRIGGER FixYearTrigger
2) BEFORE INSERT ON Movies
3) REFERENCING
4)     NEW ROW AS NewRow
5)     NEW TABLE AS NewStuff
6) FOR EACH ROW
7) WHEN NewRow.year IS NULL
8) UPDATE NewStuff SET year = 1915;
```

Figure 7: Fixing NULL's in inserted tuples

both the new row being inserted and a table consisting of only that row. Even though the trigger executes once for each inserted tuple [because line (6) declares this trigger to be row-level], the condition of line (7) needs to be able to refer to an attribute of the inserted row, while the action of line (8) needs to refer to a table in order to describe an update. □

5.3 Exercises for Section 5

Exercise 5.1: Write the triggers analogous to Fig. 6 for the insertion and deletion events on MovieExec.

Exercise 5.2: Write the following as triggers. In each case, disallow or undo the modification if it does not satisfy the stated constraint. The database schema is from the "PC" example:

```
Product(maker, model, type)
PC(model, speed, ram, hd, price)
Laptop(model, speed, ram, hd, screen, price)
Printer(model, color, type, price)
```

a) When updating the price of a PC, check that there is no lower priced PC with the same speed.

b) When inserting a new printer, check that the model number exists in Product.

! c) When making any modification to the Laptop relation, check that the average price of laptops for each manufacturer is at least $1500.

! d) When updating the RAM or hard disk of any PC, check that the updated PC has at least 100 times as much hard disk as RAM.

! e) When inserting a new PC, laptop, or printer, make sure that the model number did not previously appear in any of PC, Laptop, or Printer.

Exercise 5.3: Write the following as triggers. In each case, disallow or undo the modification if it does not satisfy the stated constraint. The database schema is from the battleships example.

```
Classes(class, type, country, numGuns, bore, displacement)
Ships(name, class, launched)
Battles(name, date)
Outcomes(ship, battle, result)
```

a) When a new class is inserted into `Classes`, also insert a ship with the name of that class and a `NULL` launch date.

b) When a new class is inserted with a displacement greater than 35,000 tons, allow the insertion, but change the displacement to 35,000.

! c) If a tuple is inserted into `Outcomes`, check that the ship and battle are listed in `Ships` and `Battles`, respectively, and if not, insert tuples into one or both of these relations, with `NULL` components where necessary.

! d) When there is an insertion into `Ships` or an update of the `class` attribute of `Ships`, check that no country has more than 20 ships.

!! e) Check, under all circumstances that could cause a violation, that no ship fought in a battle that was at a later date than another battle in which that ship was sunk.

! **Exercise 5.4:** Write the following as triggers. In each case, disallow or undo the modification if it does not satisfy the stated constraint. The problems are based on our running movie example:

```
Movies(title, year, length, genre, studioName, producerC#)
StarsIn(movieTitle, movieYear, starName)
MovieStar(name, address, gender, birthdate)
MovieExec(name, address, cert#, netWorth)
Studio(name, address, presC#)
```

You may assume that the desired condition holds before any change to the database is attempted. Also, prefer to modify the database, even if it means inserting tuples with `NULL` or default values, rather than rejecting the attempted modification.

a) Assure that at all times, any star appearing in `StarsIn` also appears in `MovieStar`.

b) Assure that at all times every movie executive appears as either a studio president, a producer of a movie, or both.

c) Assure that every movie has at least one male and one female star.

d) Assure that the number of movies made by any studio in any year is no more than 100.

e) Assure that the average length of all movies made in any year is no more than 120.

6 Summary

✦ *Referential-Integrity Constraints*: We can declare that a value appearing in some attribute or set of attributes must also appear in the corresponding attribute(s) of some tuple of the same or another relation. To do so, we use a `REFERENCES` or `FOREIGN KEY` declaration in the relation schema.

✦ *Attribute-Based Check Constraints*: We can place a constraint on the value of an attribute by adding the keyword `CHECK` and the condition to be checked after the declaration of that attribute in its relation schema.

✦ *Tuple-Based Check Constraints*: We can place a constraint on the tuples of a relation by adding the keyword `CHECK` and the condition to be checked to the declaration of the relation itself.

✦ *Modifying Constraints*: A tuple-based check can be added or deleted with an `ALTER` statement for the appropriate table.

✦ *Assertions*: We can declare an assertion as an element of a database schema. The declaration gives a condition to be checked. This condition may involve one or more relations of the database schema, and may involve the relation as a whole, e.g., with aggregation, as well as conditions about individual tuples.

✦ *Invoking the Checks*: Assertions are checked whenever there is a change to one of the relations involved. Attribute- and tuple-based checks are only checked when the attribute or relation to which they apply changes by insertion or update. Thus, the latter constraints can be violated if they have subqueries.

✦ *Triggers*: The SQL standard includes triggers that specify certain events (e.g., insertion, deletion, or update to a particular relation) that awaken them. Once awakened, a condition can be checked, and if true, a specified sequence of actions (SQL statements such as queries and database modifications) will be executed.

7 References

References [5] and [4] survey all aspects of active elements in database systems. [1] discusses recent thinking regarding active elements in SQL-99 and future standards. References [2] and [3] discuss HiPAC, an early prototype system that offered active database elements.

1. R. J. Cochrane, H. Pirahesh, and N. Mattos, "Integrating triggers and declarative constraints in SQL database systems," *Intl. Conf. on Very Large Databases*, pp. 567–579, 1996.

2. U. Dayal et al., "The HiPAC project: combining active databases and timing constraints," *SIGMOD Record* **17**:1, pp. 51–70, 1988.

3. D. R. McCarthy and U. Dayal, "The architecture of an active database management system," *Proc. ACM SIGMOD Intl. Conf. on Management of Data*, pp. 215–224, 1989.

4. N. W. Paton and O. Diaz, "Active database systems," *Computing Surveys* **31**:1 (March, 1999), pp. 63–103.

5. J. Widom and S. Ceri, *Active Database Systems*, Morgan-Kaufmann, San Francisco, 1996.

Views and Indexes

We begin this chapter by introducing virtual views, which are relations that are defined by a query over other relations. Virtual views are not stored in the database, but can be queried as if they existed. The query processor will replace the view by its definition in order to execute the query.

Views can also be materialized, in the sense that they are constructed periodically from the database and stored there. The existence of these materialized views can speed up the execution of queries. A very important specialized type of "materialized view" is the index, a stored data structure whose sole purpose is to speed up the access to specified tuples of one of the stored relations. We introduce indexes here and consider the principal issues in selecting the right indexes for a stored table.

1 Virtual Views

Relations that are defined with a `CREATE TABLE` statement actually exist in the database. That is, a SQL system stores tables in some physical organization. They are persistent, in the sense that they can be expected to exist indefinitely and not to change unless they are explicitly told to change by a SQL modification statement.

There is another class of SQL relations, called (*virtual*) *views*, that do not exist physically. Rather, they are defined by an expression much like a query. Views, in turn, can be queried as if they existed physically, and in some cases, we can even modify views.

1.1 Declaring Views

The simplest form of view definition is:

`CREATE VIEW` <view-name> `AS` <view-definition>;

The view definition is a SQL query.

Relations, Tables, and Views

SQL programmers tend to use the term "table" instead of "relation." The reason is that it is important to make a distinction between stored relations, which are "tables," and virtual relations, which are "views." Now that we know the distinction between a table and a view, we shall use "relation" only where either a table or view could be used. When we want to emphasize that a relation is stored, rather than a view, we shall sometimes use the term "base relation" or "base table."

There is also a third kind of relation, one that is neither a view nor stored permanently. These relations are temporary results, as might be constructed for some subquery. Temporaries will also be referred to as "relations" subsequently.

Example 1: Suppose we want to have a view that is a part of the

```
Movies(title, year, length, genre, studioName, producerC#)
```

relation, specifically, the titles and years of the movies made by Paramount Studios. We can define this view by

```
1)  CREATE VIEW ParamountMovies AS
2)      SELECT title, year
3)      FROM Movies
4)      WHERE studioName = 'Paramount';
```

First, the name of the view is `ParamountMovies`, as we see from line (1). The attributes of the view are those listed in line (2), namely `title` and `year`. The definition of the view is the query of lines (2) through (4). □

Example 2: Let us consider a more complicated query used to define a view. Our goal is a relation `MovieProd` with movie titles and the names of their producers. The query defining the view involves two relations:

```
Movies(title, year, length, genre, studioName, producerC#)
MovieExec(name, address, cert#, netWorth)
```

The following view definition

```
CREATE VIEW MovieProd AS
    SELECT title, name
    FROM Movies, MovieExec
    WHERE producerC# = cert#;
```

joins the two relations and requires that the certificate numbers match. It then extracts the movie title and producer name from pairs of tuples that agree on the certificates. □

1.2 Querying Views

A view may be queried exactly as if it were a stored table. We mention its name in a FROM clause and rely on the DBMS to produce the needed tuples by operating on the relations used to define the virtual view.

Example 3: We may query the view ParamountMovies just as if it were a stored table, for instance:

```
SELECT title
FROM ParamountMovies
WHERE year = 1979;
```

finds the movies made by Paramount in 1979. □

Example 4: It is also possible to write queries involving both views and base tables. An example is:

```
SELECT DISTINCT starName
FROM ParamountMovies, StarsIn
WHERE title = movieTitle AND year = movieYear;
```

This query asks for the name of all stars of movies made by Paramount. □

The simplest way to interpret what a query involving virtual views means is to replace each view in a FROM clause by a subquery that is identical to the view definition. That subquery is followed by a tuple variable, so we can refer to its tuples. For instance, the query of Example 4 can be thought of as the query of Fig. 1.

```
SELECT DISTINCT starName
FROM (SELECT title, year
      FROM Movies
      WHERE studioName = 'Paramount'
     ) Pm, StarsIn
WHERE Pm.title = movieTitle AND Pm.year = movieYear;
```

Figure 1: Interpreting the use of a virtual view as a subquery

1.3 Renaming Attributes

Sometimes, we might prefer to give a view's attributes names of our own choosing, rather than use the names that come out of the query defining the view. We may specify the attributes of the view by listing them, surrounded by parentheses, after the name of the view in the CREATE VIEW statement. For instance, we could rewrite the view definition of Example 2 as:

```
CREATE VIEW MovieProd(movieTitle, prodName) AS
    SELECT title, name
    FROM Movies, MovieExec
    WHERE producerC# = cert#;
```

The view is the same, but its columns are headed by attributes `movieTitle` and `prodName` instead of `title` and `name`.

1.4 Exercises for Section 1

Exercise 1.1: From the following base tables of our running example

```
MovieStar(name, address, gender, birthdate)
MovieExec(name, address, cert#, netWorth)
Studio(name, address, presC#)
```

Construct the following views:

a) A view `RichExec` giving the name, address, certificate number and net worth of all executives with a net worth of at least $10,000,000.

b) A view `StudioPres` giving the name, address, and certificate number of all executives who are studio presidents.

c) A view `ExecutiveStar` giving the name, address, gender, birth date, certificate number, and net worth of all individuals who are both executives and stars.

Exercise 1.2: Write each of the queries below, using one or more of the views from Exercise 1.1 and no base tables.

a) Find the names of females who are both stars and executives.

b) Find the names of those executives who are both studio presidents and worth at least $10,000,000.

! c) Find the names of studio presidents who are also stars and are worth at least $50,000,000.

2 Modifying Views

In limited circumstances it is possible to execute an insertion, deletion, or update to a view. At first, this idea makes no sense at all, since the view does not exist the way a base table (stored relation) does. What could it mean, say, to insert a new tuple into a view? Where would the tuple go, and how would the database system remember that it was supposed to be in the view?

For many views, the answer is simply "you can't do that." However, for sufficiently simple views, called *updatable views*, it is possible to translate the modification of the view into an equivalent modification on a base table, and the modification can be done to the base table instead. In addition, "instead-of" triggers can be used to turn a view modification into modifications of base tables. In that way, the programmer can force whatever interpretation of a view modification is desired.

2.1 View Removal

An extreme modification of a view is to delete it altogether. This modification may be done whether or not the view is updatable. A typical `DROP` statement is

```
DROP VIEW ParamountMovies;
```

Note that this statement deletes the definition of the view, so we may no longer make queries or issue modification commands involving this view. However dropping the view does not affect any tuples of the underlying relation `Movies`. In contrast,

```
DROP TABLE Movies
```

would not only make the `Movies` table go away. It would also make the view `ParamountMovies` unusable, since a query that used it would indirectly refer to the nonexistent relation `Movies`.

2.2 Updatable Views

SQL provides a formal definition of when modifications to a view are permitted. The SQL rules are complex, but roughly, they permit modifications on views that are defined by selecting (using `SELECT`, not `SELECT DISTINCT`) some attributes from one relation R (which may itself be an updatable view). Two important technical points:

- The `WHERE` clause must not involve R in a subquery.
- The `FROM` clause can only consist of one occurrence of R and no other relation.
- The list in the `SELECT` clause must include enough attributes that for every tuple inserted into the view, we can fill the other attributes out with `NULL` values or the proper default. For example, it is not permitted to project out an attribute that is declared `NOT NULL` and has no default.

An insertion on the view can be applied directly to the underlying relation R. The only nuance is that we need to specify that the attributes in the `SELECT` clause of the view are the only ones for which values are supplied.

Example 5: Suppose we insert into view ParamountMovies of Example 1 a tuple like:

```
INSERT INTO ParamountMovies
VALUES('Star Trek', 1979);
```

View ParamountMovies meets the SQL updatability conditions, since the view asks only for some components of some tuples of one base table:

```
Movies(title, year, length, genre, studioName, producerC#)
```

The insertion on ParamountMovies is executed as if it were the same insertion on Movies:

```
INSERT INTO Movies(title, year)
VALUES('Star Trek', 1979);
```

Notice that the attributes title and year had to be specified in this insertion, since we cannot provide values for other attributes of Movies.

The tuple inserted into Movies has values 'Star Trek' for title, 1979 for year, and NULL for the other four attributes. Curiously, the inserted tuple, since it has NULL as the value of attribute studioName, will not meet the selection condition for the view ParamountMovies, and thus, the inserted tuple has no effect on the view. For instance, the query of Example 3 would not retrieve the tuple ('Star Trek', 1979).

To fix this apparent anomaly, we could add studioName to the SELECT clause of the view, as:

```
CREATE VIEW ParamountMovies AS
    SELECT studioName, title, year
    FROM Movies
    WHERE studioName = 'Paramount';
```

Then, we could insert the *Star-Trek* tuple into the view by:

```
INSERT INTO ParamountMovies
VALUES('Paramount', 'Star Trek', 1979);
```

This insertion has the same effect on Movies as:

```
INSERT INTO Movies(studioName, title, year)
VALUES('Paramount', 'Star Trek', 1979);
```

Notice that the resulting tuple, although it has NULL in the attributes not mentioned, does yield the appropriate tuple for the view ParamountMovies. □

We may also delete from an updatable view. The deletion, like the insertion, is passed through to the underlying relation R. However, to make sure that only tuples that can be seen in the view are deleted, we add (using AND) the condition of the WHERE clause in the view to the WHERE clause of the deletion.

Example 6: Suppose we wish to delete from the updatable ParamountMovies view all movies with "Trek" in their titles. We may issue the deletion statement

```
DELETE FROM ParamountMovies
WHERE title LIKE '%Trek%';
```

This deletion is translated into an equivalent deletion on the Movies base table; the only difference is that the condition defining the view ParamountMovies is added to the conditions of the WHERE clause.

```
DELETE FROM Movies
WHERE title LIKE '%Trek%' AND studioName = 'Paramount';
```

is the resulting delete statement. □

Similarly, an update on an updatable view is passed through to the underlying relation. The view update thus has the effect of updating all tuples of the underlying relation that give rise in the view to updated view tuples.

Example 7: The view update

```
UPDATE ParamountMovies
SET year = 1979
WHERE title = 'Star Trek the Movie';
```

is equivalent to the base-table update

```
UPDATE Movies
SET year = 1979
WHERE title = 'Star Trek the Movie' AND
    studioName = 'Paramount';
```

□

2.3 Instead-Of Triggers on Views

When a trigger is defined on a view, we can use INSTEAD OF in place of BEFORE or AFTER. If we do so, then when an event awakens the trigger, the action of the trigger is done instead of the event itself. That is, an instead-of trigger intercepts attempts to modify the view and in its place performs whatever action the database designer deems appropriate. The following is a typical example.

Why Some Views Are Not Updatable

Consider the view `MovieProd` of Example 2, which relates movie titles and producers' names. This view is not updatable according to the SQL definition, because there are two relations in the `FROM` clause: `Movies` and `MovieExec`. Suppose we tried to insert a tuple like

```
('Greatest Show on Earth', 'Cecil B. DeMille')
```

We would have to insert tuples into both `Movies` and `MovieExec`. We could use the default value for attributes like `length` or `address`, but what could be done for the two equated attributes `producerC#` and `cert#` that both represent the unknown certificate number of DeMille? We could use `NULL` for both of these. However, when joining relations with `NULL`'s, SQL does not recognize two `NULL` values as equal. Thus, `'Greatest Show on Earth'` would not be connected with `'Cecil B. DeMille'` in the `MovieProd` view, and our insertion would not have been done correctly.

Example 8: Let us recall the definition of the view of all movies owned by Paramount:

```
CREATE VIEW ParamountMovies AS
    SELECT title, year
    FROM Movies
    WHERE studioName = 'Paramount';
```

from Example 1. As we discussed in Example 5, this view is updatable, but it has the unexpected flaw that when you insert a tuple into `ParamountMovies`, the system cannot deduce that the `studioName` attribute is surely Paramount, so `studioName` is `NULL` in the inserted `Movies` tuple.

A better result can be obtained if we create an instead-of trigger on this view, as shown in Fig. 2. Much of the trigger is unsurprising. We see the keyword `INSTEAD OF` on line (2), establishing that an attempt to insert into `ParamountMovies` will never take place.

Rather, lines (5) and (6) is the action that replaces the attempted insertion. There is an insertion into `Movies`, and it specifies the three attributes that we know about. Attributes `title` and `year` come from the tuple we tried to insert into the view; we refer to these values by the tuple variable `NewRow` that was declared in line (3) to represent the tuple we are trying to insert. The value of attribute `studioName` is the constant `'Paramount'`. This value is not part of the inserted view tuple. Rather, we assume it is the correct studio for the inserted movie, because the insertion came through the view `ParamountMovies`. □

```
CREATE TRIGGER ParamountInsert
INSTEAD OF INSERT ON ParamountMovies
REFERENCING NEW ROW AS NewRow
FOR EACH ROW
INSERT INTO Movies(title, year, studioName)
VALUES(NewRow.title, NewRow.year, 'Paramount');
```

Figure 2: Trigger to replace an insertion on a view by an insertion on the underlying base table

2.4 Exercises for Section 2

Exercise 2.1: Which of the views of Exercise 1.1 are updatable?

Exercise 2.2: Suppose we create the view:

```
CREATE VIEW DisneyComedies AS
    SELECT title, year, length FROM Movies
    WHERE studioName = 'Disney' AND genre = 'comedy';
```

a) Is this view updatable?

b) Write an instead-of trigger to handle an insertion into this view.

c) Write an instead-of trigger to handle an update of the length for a movie (given by title and year) in this view.

Exercise 2.3: Using the base tables

```
Product(maker, model, type)
PC(model, speed, ram, hd, price)
```

suppose we create the view:

```
CREATE VIEW NewPC AS
SELECT maker, model, speed, ram, hd, price
FROM Product, PC
WHERE Product.model = PC.model AND type = 'pc';
```

Notice that we have made a check for consistency: that the model number not only appears in the PC relation, but the type attribute of Product indicates that the product is a PC.

a) Is this view updatable?

b) Write an instead-of trigger to handle an insertion into this view.

c) Write an instead-of trigger to handle an update of the price.

d) Write an instead-of trigger to handle a deletion of a specified tuple from this view.

3 Indexes in SQL

An *index* on an attribute A of a relation is a data structure that makes it efficient to find those tuples that have a fixed value for attribute A. We could think of the index as a binary search tree of (key, value) pairs, in which a key a (one of the values that attribute A may have) is associated with a "value" that is the set of locations of the tuples that have a in the component for attribute A. Such an index may help with queries in which the attribute A is compared with a constant, for instance $A = 3$, or even $A \leq 3$. Note that the key for the index can be any attribute or set of attributes, and need not be the key for the relation on which the index is built. We shall refer to the attributes of the index as the *index key* when a distinction needs to be made.

The technology of implementing indexes on large relations is of central importance in the implementation of DBMS's. The most important data structure used by a typical DBMS is the "B-tree," which is a generalization of a balanced binary tree. We shall take up B-trees when we talk about DBMS implementation, but for the moment, thinking of indexes as binary search trees will suffice.

3.1 Motivation for Indexes

When relations are very large, it becomes expensive to scan all the tuples of a relation to find those (perhaps very few) tuples that match a given condition. For example, consider the first query we examined:

```
SELECT *
FROM Movies
WHERE studioName = 'Disney' AND year = 1990;
```

There might be 10,000 `Movies` tuples, of which only 200 were made in 1990.

The naive way to implement this query is to get all 10,000 tuples and test the condition of the `WHERE` clause on each. It would be much more efficient if we had some way of getting only the 200 tuples from the year 1990 and testing each of them to see if the studio was Disney. It would be even more efficient if we could obtain directly only the 10 or so tuples that satisfied both the conditions of the `WHERE` clause — that the studio is Disney and the year is 1990; see the discussion of "multiattribute indexes," in Section 3.2.

Indexes may also be useful in queries that involve a join. The following example illustrates the point.

Example 9: Recall the query

```
SELECT name
FROM Movies, MovieExec
WHERE title = 'Star Wars' AND producerC# = cert#;
```

that asks for the name of the producer of *Star Wars.* If there is an index on `title` of `Movies`, then we can use this index to get the tuple for *Star Wars.* From this tuple, we can extract the `producerC#` to get the certificate of the producer.

Now, suppose that there is also an index on `cert#` of `MovieExec`. Then we can use the `producerC#` with this index to find the tuple of `MovieExec` for the producer of *Star Wars.* From this tuple, we can extract the producer's name. Notice that with these two indexes, we look at only the two tuples, one from each relation, that are needed to answer the query. Without indexes, we have to look at every tuple of the two relations. □

3.2 Declaring Indexes

Although the creation of indexes is not part of any SQL standard up to and including SQL-99, most commercial systems have a way for the database designer to say that the system should create an index on a certain attribute for a certain relation. The following syntax is typical. Suppose we want to have an index on attribute `year` for the relation `Movies`. Then we say:

```
CREATE INDEX YearIndex ON Movies(year);
```

The result will be that an index whose name is `YearIndex` will be created on attribute `year` of the relation `Movies`. Henceforth, SQL queries that specify a year may be executed by the SQL query processor in such a way that only those tuples of `Movies` with the specified year are ever examined; there is a resulting decrease in the time needed to answer the query.

Often, a DBMS allows us to build a single index on multiple attributes. This type of index takes values for several attributes and efficiently finds the tuples with the given values for these attributes.

Example 10: Since `title` and `year` form a key for `Movies`, we might expect it to be common that values for both these attributes will be specified, or neither will. The following is a typical declaration of an index on these two attributes:

```
CREATE INDEX KeyIndex ON Movies(title, year);
```

Since (`title`, `year`) is a key, if follows that when we are given a title and year, we know the index will find only one tuple, and that will be the desired tuple. In contrast, if the query specifies both the title and year, but only `YearIndex` is available, then the best the system can do is retrieve all the movies of that year and check through them for the given title.

If, as is often the case, the key for the multiattribute index is really the concatenation of the attributes in some order, then we can even use this index to find all the tuples with a given value in the first of the attributes. Thus, part of the design of a multiattribute index is the choice of the order in which the attributes are listed. For instance, if we were more likely to specify a title than a year for a movie, then we would prefer to order the attributes as above; if a year were more likely to be specified, then we would ask for an index on `(year, title)`. □

If we wish to delete the index, we simply use its name in a statement like:

```
DROP INDEX YearIndex;
```

3.3 Exercises for Section 3

Exercise 3.1: For our running movies example:

```
Movies(title, year, length, genre, studioName, producerC#)
StarsIn(movieTitle, movieYear, starName)
MovieExec(name, address, cert#, netWorth)
Studio(name, address, presC#)
```

Declare indexes on the following attributes or combination of attributes:

a) `studioName`.

b) `address` of `MovieExec`.

c) `genre` and `length`.

4 Selection of Indexes

Choosing which indexes to create requires the database designer to analyze a trade-off. In practice, this choice is one of the principal factors that influence whether a database design gives acceptable performance. Two important factors to consider are:

- The existence of an index on an attribute may speed up greatly the execution of those queries in which a value, or range of values, is specified for that attribute, and may speed up joins involving that attribute as well.

- On the other hand, every index built for one or more attributes of some relation makes insertions, deletions, and updates to that relation more complex and time-consuming.

4.1 A Simple Cost Model

To understand how to choose indexes for a database, we first need to know where the time is spent answering a query. The details of how relations are stored will be taken up when we consider DBMS implementation. But for the moment, let us state that the tuples of a relation are normally distributed among many pages of a disk.[1] One page, which is typically several thousand bytes at least, will hold many tuples.

To examine even one tuple requires that the whole page be brought into main memory. On the other hand, it costs little more time to examine all the tuples on a page than to examine only one. There is a great time saving if the page you want is already in main memory, but for simplicity we shall assume that never to be the case, and every page we need must be retrieved from the disk.

4.2 Some Useful Indexes

Often, the most useful index we can put on a relation is an index on its key. There are two reasons:

1. Queries in which a value for the key is specified are common. Thus, an index on the key will get used frequently.

2. Since there is at most one tuple with a given key value, the index returns either nothing or one location for a tuple. Thus, at most one page must be retrieved to get that tuple into main memory (although there may be other pages that need to be retrieved to use the index itself).

The following example shows the power of key indexes, even in a query that involves a join.

Example 11 : You may recall that we suggested an exhaustive pairing of tuples of `Movies` and `MovieExec` to compute a join. Implementing the join this way requires us to read each of the pages holding tuples of `Movies` and each of the pages holding tuples of `MovieExec` at least once. In fact, since these pages may be too numerous to fit in main memory at the same time, we may have to read each page from disk many times. With the right indexes, the whole query might be done with as few as two page reads.

An index on the key `title` and `year` for `Movies` would help us find the one `Movies` tuple for *Star Wars* quickly. Only one page — the page containing that tuple — would be read from disk. Then, after finding the producer-certificate number in that tuple, an index on the key `cert#` for `MovieExec` would help us quickly find the one tuple for the producer in the `MovieExec` relation. Again, only one page with `MovieExec` tuples would be read from disk, although we might need to read a small number of other pages to use the `cert#` index. □

When the index is not on a key, it may or may not be able to improve the time spent retrieving from disk the tuples needed to answer a query. There are two situations in which an index can be effective, even if it is not on a key.

[1] Pages are usually referred to as "blocks" in discussion of databases, but if you are familiar with a paged-memory system from operating systems you should think of the disk as divided into pages.

1. If the attribute is almost a key; that is, relatively few tuples have a given value for that attribute. Even if each of the tuples with a given value is on a different page, we shall not have to retrieve many pages from disk.

2. If the tuples are "clustered" on that attribute. We *cluster* a relation on an attribute by grouping the tuples with a common value for that attribute onto as few pages as possible. Then, even if there are many tuples, we shall not have to retrieve nearly as many pages as there are tuples.

Example 12: As an example of an index of the first kind, suppose `Movies` had an index on `title` rather than `title` and `year`. Since `title` by itself is not a key for the relation, there would be titles such as *King Kong*, where several tuples matched the index key `title`. If we compared use of the index on `title` with what happens in Example 11, we would find that a search for movies with title *King Kong* would produce three tuples (because there are three movies with that title, from years 1933, 1976, and 2005). It is possible that these tuples are on three different pages, so all three pages would be brought into main memory, roughly tripling the amount of time this step takes. However, since the relation `Movies` probably is spread over many more than three pages, there is still a considerable time saving in using the index.

At the next step, we need to get the three `producerC#` values from these three tuples, and find in the relation `MovieExec` the producers of these three movies. We can use the index on `cert#` to find the three relevant tuples of `MovieExec`. Possibly they are on three different pages, but we still spend less time than we would if we had to bring the entire `MovieExec` relation into main memory. □

Example 13: Now, suppose the only index we have on `Movies` is one on `year`, and we want to answer the query:

```
SELECT *
FROM Movies
WHERE year = 1990;
```

First, suppose the tuples of `Movies` are not clustered by year; say they are stored alphabetically by title. Then this query gains little from the index on `year`. If there are, say, 100 movies per page, there is a good chance that any given page has at least one movie made in 1990. Thus, a large fraction of the pages used to hold the relation `Movies` will have to be brought to main memory.

However, suppose the tuples of `Movies` are clustered on `year`. Then we could use the index on `year` to find only the small number of pages that contained tuples with `year` = 1990. In this case, the `year` index will be of great help. In comparison, an index on the combination of `title` and `year` would be of little help, no matter what attribute or attributes we used to cluster `Movies`. □

4.3 Calculating the Best Indexes to Create

It might seem that the more indexes we create, the more likely it is that an index useful for a given query will be available. However, if modifications are the most frequent action, then we should be very conservative about creating indexes. Each modification on a relation R forces us to change any index on one or more of the modified attributes of R. Thus, we must read and write not only the pages of R that are modified, but also read and write certain pages that hold the index. But even when modifications are the dominant form of database action, it may be an efficiency gain to create an index on a frequently used attribute. In fact, since some modification commands involve querying the database (e.g., an `INSERT` with a select-from-where subquery or a `DELETE` with a condition) one must be very careful how one estimates the relative frequency of modifications and queries.

Remember that the typical relation is stored over many disk blocks (pages), and the principal cost of a query or modification is often the number of pages that need to be brought to main memory. Thus, indexes that let us find a tuple without examining the entire relation can save a lot of time. However, the indexes themselves have to be stored, at least partially, on disk, so accessing and modifying the indexes themselves cost disk accesses. In fact, modification, since it requires one disk access to read a page and another disk access to write the changed page, is about twice as expensive as accessing the index or the data in a query.

To calculate the new value of an index, we need to make assumptions about which queries and modifications are most likely to be performed on the database. Sometimes, we have a history of queries that we can use to get good information, on the assumption that the future will be like the past. In other cases, we may know that the database supports a particular application or applications, and we can see in the code for those applications all the SQL queries and modifications that they will ever do. In either situation, we are able to list what we expect are the most common query and modification forms. These forms can have variables in place of constants, but should otherwise look like real SQL statements. Here is a simple example of the process, and of the calculations that we need to make.

Example 14: Let us consider the relation

```
StarsIn(movieTitle, movieYear, starName)
```

Suppose that there are three database operations that we sometimes perform on this relation:

Q_1: We look for the title and year of movies in which a given star appeared. That is, we execute a query of the form:

```
SELECT movieTitle, movieYear
FROM StarsIn
WHERE starName = s;
```

for some constant s.

Q_2: We look for the stars that appeared in a given movie. That is, we execute a query of the form:

```
SELECT starName
FROM StarsIn
WHERE movieTitle = t AND movieYear = y;
```

for constants t and y.

I: We insert a new tuple into `StarsIn`. That is, we execute an insertion of the form:

```
INSERT INTO StarsIn VALUES(t, y, s);
```

for constants t, y, and s.

Let us make the following assumptions about the data:

1. `StarsIn` occupies 10 pages, so if we need to examine the entire relation the cost is 10.

2. On the average, a star has appeared in 3 movies and a movie has 3 stars.

3. Since the tuples for a given star or a given movie are likely to be spread over the 10 pages of `StarsIn`, even if we have an index on `starName` or on the combination of `movieTitle` and `movieYear`, it will take 3 disk accesses to find the (average of) 3 tuples for a star or movie. If we have no index on the star or movie, respectively, then 10 disk accesses are required.

4. One disk access is needed to read a page of the index every time we use that index to locate tuples with a given value for the indexed attribute(s). If an index page must be modified (in the case of an insertion), then another disk access is needed to write back the modified page.

5. Likewise, in the case of an insertion, one disk access is needed to read a page on which the new tuple will be placed, and another disk access is needed to write back this page. We assume that, even without an index, we can find some page on which an additional tuple will fit, without scanning the entire relation.

Figure 3 gives the costs of each of the three operations; Q_1 (query given a star), Q_2 (query given a movie), and I (insertion). If there is no index, then we must scan the entire relation for Q_1 or Q_2 (cost 10),[2] while an insertion requires

[2]There is a subtle point that we shall ignore here. In many situations, it is possible to store a relation on disk using consecutive pages or tracks. In that case, the cost of retrieving the entire relation may be significantly less than retrieving the same number of pages chosen randomly.

Action	No Index	Star Index	Movie Index	Both Indexes
Q_1	10	4	10	4
Q_2	10	10	4	4
I	2	4	4	6
Average	$2 + 8p_1 + 8p_2$	$4 + 6p_2$	$4 + 6p_1$	$6 - 2p_1 - 2p_2$

Figure 3: Costs associated with the three actions, as a function of which indexes are selected

merely that we access a page with free space and rewrite it with the new tuple (cost of 2, since we assume that page can be found without an index). These observations explain the column labeled "No Index."

If there is an index on stars only, then Q_2 still requires a scan of the entire relation (cost 10). However, Q_1 can be answered by accessing one index page to find the three tuples for a given star and then making three more accesses to find those tuples. Insertion I requires that we read and write both a page for the index and a page for the data, for a total of 4 disk accesses.

The case where there is an index on movies only is symmetric to the case for stars only. Finally, if there are indexes on both stars and movies, then it takes 4 disk accesses to answer either Q_1 or Q_2. However, insertion I requires that we read and write two index pages as well as a data page, for a total of 6 disk accesses. That observation explains the last column in Fig. 3.

The final row in Fig. 3 gives the average cost of an action, on the assumption that the fraction of the time we do Q_1 is p_1 and the fraction of the time we do Q_2 is p_2; therefore, the fraction of the time we do I is $1 - p_1 - p_2$.

Depending on p_1 and p_2, any of the four choices of index/no index can yield the best average cost for the three actions. For example, if $p_1 = p_2 = 0.1$, then the expression $2+8p_1+8p_2$ is the smallest, so we would prefer not to create any indexes. That is, if we are doing mostly insertion, and very few queries, then we don't want an index. On the other hand, if $p_1 = p_2 = 0.4$, then the formula $6 - 2p_1 - 2p_2$ turns out to be the smallest, so we would prefer indexes on both `starName` and on the (`movieTitle, movieYear`) combination. Intuitively, if we are doing a lot of queries, and the number of queries specifying movies and stars are roughly equally frequent, then both indexes are desired.

If we have $p_1 = 0.5$ and $p_2 = 0.1$, then an index on stars only gives the best average value, because $4 + 6p_2$ is the formula with the smallest value. Likewise, $p_1 = 0.1$ and $p_2 = 0.5$ tells us to create an index on only movies. The intuition is that if only one type of query is frequent, create only the index that helps that type of query. □

4.4 Automatic Selection of Indexes to Create

"Tuning" a database is a process that includes not only index selection, but the choice of many different parameters. We have not yet discussed much about physical implementation of databases, but some examples of tuning issues are the amount of main memory to allocate to various processes and the rate at which backups and checkpoints are made (to facilitate recovery from a crash). There are a number of tools that have been designed to take the responsibility from the database designer and have the system tune itself, or at least advise the designer on good choices.

We shall mention some of these projects in the bibliographic notes for this chapter. However, here is an outline of how the index-selection portion of tuning advisors work.

1. The first step is to establish the query workload. Since a DBMS normally logs all operations anyway, we may be able to examine the log and find a set of representative queries and database modifications for the database at hand. Or it is possible that we know, from the application programs that use the database, what the typical queries will be.

2. The designer may be offered the opportunity to specify some constraints, e.g., indexes that must, or must not, be chosen.

3. The tuning advisor generates a set of possible *candidate* indexes, and evaluates each one. Typical queries are given to the query optimizer of the DBMS. The query optimizer has the ability to estimate the running times of these queries under the assumption that one particular set of indexes is available.

4. The index set resulting in the lowest cost for the given workload is suggested to the designer, or it is automatically created.

A subtle issue arises when we consider possible indexes in step (3). The existence of previously chosen indexes may influence how much *benefit* (improvement in average execution time of the query mix) another index offers. A "greedy" approach to choosing indexes has proven effective.

a) Initially, with no indexes selected, evaluate the benefit of each of the candidate indexes. If at least one provides positive benefit (i.e., it reduces the average execution time of queries), then choose that index.

b) Then, reevaluate the benefit of each of the remaining candidate indexes, assuming that the previously selected index is also available. Again, choose the index that provides the greatest benefit, assuming that benefit is positive.

c) In general, repeat the evaluation of candidate indexes under the assumption that all previously selected indexes are available. Pick the index with maximum benefit, until no more positive benefits can be obtained.

4.5 Exercises for Section 4

Exercise 4.1: Suppose that the relation `StarsIn` discussed in Example 14 required 100 pages rather than 10, but all other assumptions of that example continued to hold. Give formulas in terms of p_1 and p_2 to measure the cost of queries Q_1 and Q_2 and insertion I, under the four combinations of index/no index discussed there.

! **Exercise 4.2:** In this problem, we consider indexes for the relation

```
Ships(name, class, launched)
```

from our running battleships exercise. Assume:

i. `name` is the key.

ii. The relation `Ships` is stored over 50 pages.

iii. The relation is clustered on `class` so we expect that only one disk access is needed to find the ships of a given class.

iv. On average, there are 5 ships of a class, and 25 ships launched in any given year.

v. With probability p_1 the operation on this relation is a query of the form `SELECT * FROM Ships WHERE name =` n.

vi. With probability p_2 the operation on this relation is a query of the form `SELECT * FROM Ships WHERE class =` c.

vii. With probability p_3 the operation on this relation is a query of the form `SELECT * FROM Ships WHERE launched =` y.

viii. With probability $1 - p_1 - p_2 - p_3$ the operation on this relation is an insertion of a new tuple into `Ships`.

You can also make the assumptions about accessing indexes and finding empty space for insertions that were made in Example 14.

Consider the creation of indexes on `name`, `class`, and `launched`. For each combination of indexes, estimate the average cost of an operation. As a function of p_1, p_2, and p_3, what is the best choice of indexes?

5 Materialized Views

A view describes how a new relation can be constructed from base tables by executing a query on those tables. Until now, we have thought of views only as logical descriptions of relations. However, if a view is used frequently enough, it may even be efficient to *materialize* it; that is, to maintain its value at all times. As with maintaining indexes, there is a cost involved in maintaining a materialized view, since we must recompute parts of the materialized view each time one of the underlying base tables changes.

5.1 Maintaining a Materialized View

In principle, the DBMS needs to recompute a materialized view every time one of its base tables changes in any way. For simple views, it is possible to limit the number of times we need to consider changing the materialized view, and it is possible to limit the amount of work we do when we must maintain the view. We shall take up an example of a join view, and see that there are a number of opportunities to simplify our work.

Example 15: Suppose we frequently want to find the name of the producer of a given movie. We might find it advantageous to materialize a view:

```
CREATE MATERIALIZED VIEW MovieProd AS
    SELECT title, year, name
    FROM Movies, MovieExec
    WHERE producerC# = cert#
```

To start, the DBMS does not have to consider the effect on `MovieProd` of an update on any attribute of `Movies` or `MovieExec` that is not mentioned in the query that defines the materialized view. Surely any modification to a relation that is neither `Movies` nor `MovieExec` can be ignored as well. However, there are a number of other simplifications that enable us to handle other modifications to `Movies` or `MovieExec` more efficiently than a re-execution of the query that defines the materialized view.

1. Suppose we insert a new movie into `Movies`, say `title = 'Kill Bill'`, `year` = 2003, and `producerC#` = 23456. Then we only need to look up `cert#` = 23456 in `MovieExec`. Since `cert#` is the key for `MovieExec`, there can be at most one name returned by the query

   ```
   SELECT name FROM MovieExec
   WHERE cert# = 23456;
   ```

   As this query returns `name = 'Quentin Tarantino'`, the DBMS can insert the proper tuple into `MovieProd` by:

   ```
   INSERT INTO MovieProd
   VALUES('Kill Bill', 2003, 'Quentin Tarantino');
   ```

   Note that, since `MovieProd` is materialized, it is stored like any base table, and this operation makes sense; it does not have to be reinterpreted by an instead-of trigger or any other mechanism.

2. Suppose we delete a movie from `Movies`, say the movie with `title = 'Dumb & Dumber'` and `year` = 1994. The DBMS has only to delete this one movie from `MovieProd` by:

```
DELETE FROM MovieProd
WHERE title = 'Dumb & Dumber' AND year = 1994;
```

3. Suppose we insert a tuple into MovieExec, and that tuple has cert# = 34567 and name = 'Max Bialystock'. Then the DBMS may have to insert into MovieProd some movies that were not there because their producer was previously unknown. The operation is:

```
INSERT INTO MovieProd
    SELECT title, year, 'Max Bialystock'
    FROM Movies
    WHERE producerC# = 34567;
```

4. Suppose we delete the tuple with cert# = 45678 from MovieExec. Then the DBMS must delete from MovieProd all movies that have producerC# = 45678, because there now can be no matching tuple in MovieExec for their underlying Movies tuple. Thus, the DBMS executes:

```
DELETE FROM MovieProd
WHERE (title, year) IN
    (SELECT title, year FROM Movies
     WHERE producerC# = 45678);
```

Notice that it is not sufficient to look up the name corresponding to 45678 in MovieExec and delete all movies from MovieProd that have that producer name. The reason is that, because name is not a key for MovieExec, there could be two producers with the same name.

We leave as an exercise the consideration of how updates to Movies that involve title or year are handled, and how updates to MovieExec involving cert# are handled. □

The most important thing to take away from Example 15 is that all the changes to the materialized view are *incremental*. That is, we never have to reconstruct the whole view from scratch. Rather, insertions, deletions, and updates to a base table can be implemented in a join view such as MovieProd by a small number of queries to the base tables followed by modification statements on the materialized view. Moreover, these modifications do not affect all the tuples of the view, but only those that have at least one attribute with a particular constant.

It is not possible to find rules such as those in Example 15 for any materialized view we could construct; some are just too complicated. However, many common types of materialized view *do* allow the view to be maintained incrementally. We shall explore another common type of materialized view — aggregation views — in the exercises.

5.2 Periodic Maintenance of Materialized Views

There is another setting in which we may use materialized views, yet not have to worry about the cost or complexity of maintaining them up-to-date as the underlying base tables change. For example, a department store may use its database to record its current inventory; this data changes with every sale. The same database may be used by analysts to study buyer patterns and to predict when the store is going to need to restock an item.

The analysts' queries may be answered more efficiently if they can query materialized views, especially views that aggregate data (e.g., sum the inventories of different sizes of shirt after grouping by style). But the database is updated with each sale, so modifications are far more frequent than queries. When modifications dominate, it is costly to have materialized views, or even indexes, on the data.

What is usually done is to create materialized views, but not to try to keep them up-to-date as the base tables change. Rather, the materialized views are reconstructed periodically (typically each night), when other activity in the database is low. The materialized views are only used by analysts, and their data might be out of date by as much as 24 hours. However, in normal situations, the rate at which an item is bought by customers changes slowly. Thus, the data will be "good enough" for the analysts to predict items that are selling well and those that are selling poorly. Of course if Brad Pitt is seen wearing a Hawaiian shirt one morning, and every cool guy has to buy one by that evening, the analysts will not notice they are out of Hawaiian shirts until the next morning, but the risk of that sort of occurrence is low.

5.3 Rewriting Queries to Use Materialized Views

A materialized view can be referred to in the FROM clause of a query, just as a virtual view can (Section 1.2). However, because a materialized view is stored in the database, it is possible to rewrite a query to use a materialized view, even if that view was not mentioned in the query as written. Such a rewriting may enable the query to execute much faster, because the hard parts of the query, e.g., joining of relations, may have been carried out already when the materialized view was constructed.

However,we must be very careful to check that the query can be rewritten to use a materialized view. A complete set of rules that will let us use materialized views of any kind is beyond the scope of this book. However, we shall offer a relatively simple rule that applies to the view of Example 15 and similar views.

Suppose we have a materialized view V defined by a query of the form:

SELECT L_V
FROM R_V
WHERE C_V

where L_V is a list of attributes, R_V is a list of relations, and C_V is a condition. Similarly, suppose we have a query Q of the same form:

SELECT L_Q
FROM R_Q
WHERE C_Q

Here are the conditions under which we can replace part of the query Q by the view V.

1. The relations in list R_V all appear in the list R_Q.

2. The condition C_Q is equivalent to C_V AND C for some condition C. As a special case, C_Q could be equivalent to C_V, in which case the "AND C" is unnecessary.

3. If C is needed, then the attributes of relations on list R_V that C mentions are attributes on the list L_V.

4. Attributes on the list L_Q that come from relations on the list R_V are also on the list L_V.

If all these conditions are met, then we can rewrite Q to use V, as follows:

a) Replace the list R_Q by V and the relations that are on list R_Q but not on R_V.

b) Replace C_Q by C. If C is not needed (i.e., $C_V = C_Q$), then there is no WHERE clause.

Example 16 : Suppose we have the materialized view MovieProd from Example 15. This view is defined by the query V:

```
SELECT title, year, name
FROM Movies, MovieExec
WHERE producerC# = cert#
```

Suppose also that we need to answer the query Q that asks for the names of the stars of movies produced by Max Bialystock. For this query we need the relations:

```
Movies(title, year, length, genre, studioName, producerC#)
StarsIn(movieTitle, movieYear, starName)
MovieExec(name, address, cert#, netWorth)
```

The query Q can be written:

```
SELECT starName
FROM StarsIn, Movies, MovieExec
WHERE movieTitle = title AND movieYear = year AND
      producerC# = cert# AND name = 'Max Bialystock';
```

Let us compare the view definition V with the query Q, to see that they meet the conditions listed above.

1. The relations in the FROM clause of V are all in the FROM clause of Q.

2. The condition from Q can be written as the condition from V AND C, where C =

```
movieTitle = title AND movieYear = year AND
    name = 'Max Bialystock'
```

3. The attributes of C that come from relations of V (Movies and MovieExec) are title, year, and name. These attributes all appear in the SELECT clause of V.

4. No attribute from the SELECT list of Q is from a relation that appears in the FROM list of V.

We may thus use V in Q, yielding the rewritten query:

```
SELECT starName
FROM StarsIn, MovieProd
WHERE movieTitle = title AND movieYear = year AND
    name = 'Max Bialystock';
```

That is, we replaced Movies and MovieExec in the FROM clause by the materialized view MovieProd. We also removed the condition of the view from the WHERE clause, leaving only the condition C. Since the rewritten query involves the join of only two relations, rather than three, we expect the rewritten query to execute in less time than the original. □

5.4 Automatic Creation of Materialized Views

The ideas that were discussed in Section 4.4 for indexes can apply as well to materialized views. We first need to establish or approximate the query workload. An automated materialized-view-selection advisor needs to generate candidate views. This task can be far more difficult than generating candidate indexes. In the case of indexes, there is only one possibile index for each attribute of each relation. We could also consider indexes on small sets of attributes of a relation, but even if we do, generating all the candidate indexes is straightforward. However, with materialized views, any query could in principle define a view, so there is no limit on what views we need to consider.

The process can be limited if we remember that there is no point in creating a materialized view that does not help for at least one query of our expected workload. For example, suppose some or all of the queries in our workload have the form considered in Section 5.3. Then we can use the analysis of that section to find the views that can help a given query. We can limit ourselves to candidate materialized views that:

1. Have a list of relations in the FROM clause that is a subset of those in the FROM clause of at least one query of the workload.

2. Have a WHERE clause that is the AND of conditions that each appear in at least one query.

3. Have a list of attributes in the SELECT clause that is sufficient to be used in at least one query.

To evaluate the benefit of a materialized view, let the query optimizer estimate the running times of the queries, both with and without the materialized view. Of course, the optimizer must be designed to take advantage of materialized views; all modern optimizers know how to exploit indexes, but not all can exploit materialized views. Section 5.3 was an example of the reasoning that would be necessary for a query optimizer to perform, if it were to take advantage of such views.

There is another issue that comes up when we consider automatic choice of materialized views, but that did not surface for indexes. An index on a relation is generally smaller than the relation itself, and all indexes on one relation take roughly the same amount of space. However, materialized views can vary radically in size, and some — those involving joins — can be very much larger than the relation or relations on which they are built. Thus, we may need to rethink the definition of the "benefit" of a materialized view. For example, we might want to define the benefit to be the improvement in average running time of the query workload divided by the amount of space the view occupies.

5.5 Exercises for Section 5

Exercise 5.1: Complete Example 15 by considering updates to either of the base tables.

! **Exercise 5.2:** Suppose the view NewPC of Exercise 2.3 were a materialized view. What modifications to the base tables Product and PC would require a modification of the materialized view? How would you implement those modifications incrementally?

! **Exercise 5.3:** This exercise explores materialized views that are based on aggregation of data. Suppose we build a materialized view on the base tables

```
Classes(class, type, country, numGuns, bore, displacement)
Ships(name, class, launched)
```

from our running battleships exercise, as follows:

```
CREATE MATERIALIZED VIEW ShipStats AS
    SELECT country, AVG(displacement), COUNT(*)
    FROM Classes, Ships
    WHERE Classes.class = Ships.class
    GROUP BY country;
```

What modifications to the base tables `Classes` and `Ships` would require a modification of the materialized view? How would you implement those modifications incrementally?

! **Exercise 5.4:** In Section 5.3 we gave conditions under which a materialized view of simple form could be used in the execution of a query of similar form. For the view of Example 15, describe all the queries of that form, for which this view could be used.

6 Summary

- *Virtual Views*: A virtual view is a definition of how one relation (the view) may be constructed logically from tables stored in the database or other views. Views may be queried as if they were stored relations. The query processor modifies queries about a view so the query is instead about the base tables that are used to define the view.

- *Updatable Views*: Some virtual views on a single relation are updatable, meaning that we can insert into, delete from, and update the view as if it were a stored table. These operations are translated into equivalent modifications to the base table over which the view is defined.

- *Instead-Of Triggers*: SQL allows a special type of trigger to apply to a virtual view. When a modification to the view is called for, the instead-of trigger turns the modification into operations on base tables that are specified in the trigger.

- *Indexes*: While not part of the SQL standard, commercial SQL systems allow the declaration of indexes on attributes; these indexes speed up certain queries or modifications that involve specification of a value, or range of values, for the indexed attribute(s).

- *Choosing Indexes*: While indexes speed up queries, they slow down database modifications, since the indexes on the modified relation must also be modified. Thus, the choice of indexes is a complex problem, depending on the actual mix of queries and modifications performed on the database.

- *Automatic Index Selection*: Some DBMS's offer tools that choose indexes for a database automatically. They examine the typical queries and modifications performed on the database and evaluate the cost trade-offs for different indexes that might be created.

- *Materialized Views*: Instead of treating a view as a query on base tables, we can use the query as a definition of an additional stored relation, whose value is a function of the values of the base tables.

- *Maintaining Materialized Views*: As the base tables change, we must make the corresponding changes to any materialized view whose value is affected by the change. For many common kinds of materialized views, it is possible to make the changes to the view incrementally, without recomputing the entire view.

- *Rewriting Queries to Use Materialized Views*: The conditions under which a query can be rewritten to use a materialized view are complex. However, if the query optimizer can perform such rewritings, then an automatic design tool can consider the improvement in performance that results from creating materialized views and can select views to materialize, automatically.

7 References

The technology behind materialized views is surveyed in [2] and [7]. Reference [3] introduces the greedy algorithm for selecting materialized views.

Two projects for automatically tuning databases are AutoAdmin at Microsoft and SMART at IBM. Current information on AutoAdmin can be found on-line at [8]. A description of the technology behind this system is in [1].

A survey of the SMART project is in [4]. The index-selection aspect of the project is described in [6].

Reference [5] surveys index selection, materialized views, automatic tuning, and related subjects covered in this chapter.

1. S. Agrawal, S. Chaudhuri, and V. R. Narasayya, "Automated selection of materialized views and indexes in SQL databases," *Intl. Conf. on Very Large Databases*, pp. 496–505, 2000.

2. A. Gupta and I. S. Mumick, *Materialized Views: Techniques, Implementations, and Applications*, MIT Press, Cambridge MA, 1999.

3. V. Harinarayan, A. Rajaraman, and J. D. Ullman, "Implementing data cubes efficiently," *Proc. ACM SIGMOD Intl. Conf. on Management of Data* (1996), pp. 205–216.

4. S. S. Lightstone, G. Lohman, and S. Zilio, "Toward autonomic computing with DB2 universal database," *SIGMOD Record* **31**:3, pp. 55–61, 2002.

5. S. S. Lightstone, T. Teorey, and T. Nadeau, *Physical Database Design*, Morgan-Kaufmann, San Francisco, 2007.

6. G. Lohman, G. Valentin, D. Zilio, M. Zuliani, and A. Skelley, "DB2 Advisor: an optimizer smart enough to recommend its own indexes," *Proc. Sixteenth IEEE Conf. on Data Engineering*, pp. 101–110, 2000.

7. D. Lomet and J. Widom (eds.), Special issue on materialized views and data warehouses, *IEEE Data Engineering Bulletin* **18**:2 (1995).

8. Microsoft on-line description of the AutoAdmin project.

`http://research.microsoft.com/dmx/autoadmin/`

SQL in a Server Environment

We now turn to the question of how SQL fits into a complete programming environment. The typical server environment is introduced in Section 1. Section 2 introduces the SQL terminology for client-server computing and connecting to a database.

Then, we turn to how programming is really done, when SQL must be used to access a database as part of a typical application. In Section 3 we see how to embed SQL in programs that are written in an ordinary programming language, such as C. A critical issue is how we move data between SQL relations and the variables of the surrounding, or "host," language. Section 4 considers another way to combine SQL with general-purpose programming: persistent stored modules, which are pieces of code stored as part of a database schema and executable on command from the user.

A third programming approach is a "call-level interface," where we program in some conventional language and use a library of functions to access the database. In Section 5 we discuss the SQL-standard library called SQL/CLI, for making calls from C programs. Then, in Section 6 we meet Java's JDBC (database connectivity), which is an alternative call-level interface. Finally, another popular call-level interface, PHP, is covered in Section 7.

1 The Three-Tier Architecture

Databases are used in many different settings, including small, standalone databases. For example, a scientist may run a copy of MySQL or Microsoft Access on a laboratory computer to store experimental data. However, there is a very common architecture for large database installations; this architecture motivates the discussion of the entire chapter. The architecture is called *three-tier* or *three-layer*, because it distinguishes three different, interacting functions:

1. *Web Servers.* These are processes that connect clients to the database system, usually over the Internet or possibly a local connection.

2. *Application Servers.* These processes perform the "business logic," whatever it is the system is intended to do.

3. *Database Servers.* These processes run the DBMS and perform queries and modifications at the request of the application servers.

The processes may all run on the same processor in a small system, but it is common to dedicate a large number of processors to each of the tiers. Figure 1 suggests how a large database installation would be organized.

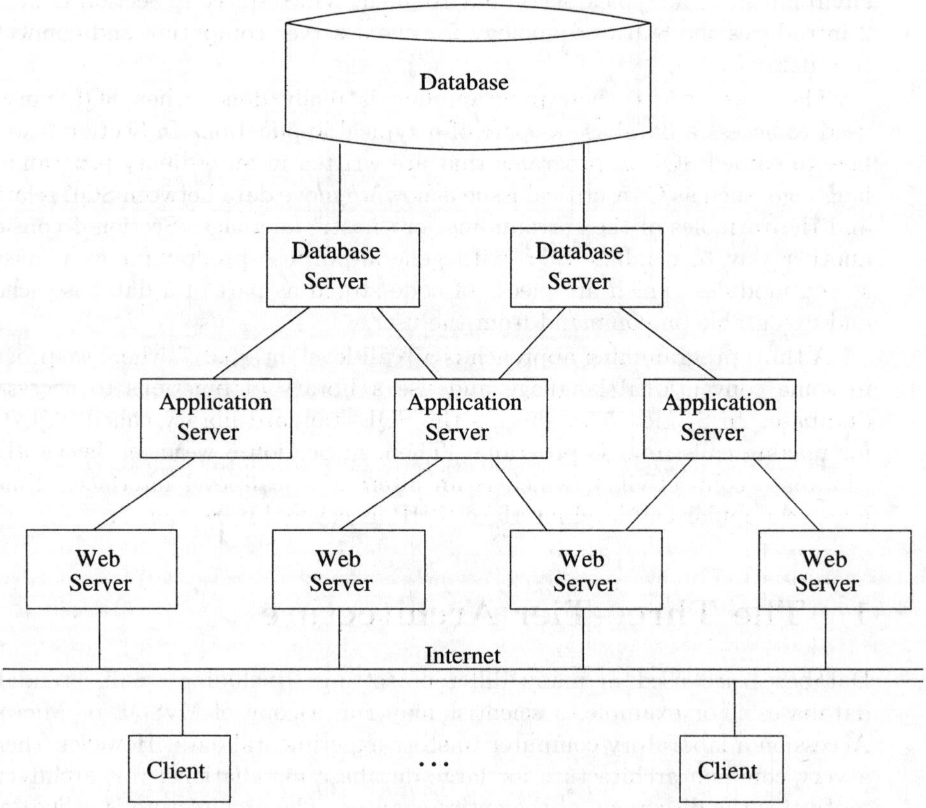

Figure 1: The Three-Tier Architecture

1.1 The Web-Server Tier

The web-server processes manage the interactions with the user. When a user makes contact, perhaps by opening a URL, a web server, typically running

Apache/Tomcat, responds to the request. The user then becomes a *client* of this web-server process. Typically, the client's actions are performed by the web-browser, e.g., managing of the filling of forms, which are then posted to the web server.

As an example, let us consider a site such as Amazon.com. A user (customer) opens a connection to the Amazon database system by entering the URL `www.amazon.com` into their browser. The Amazon web-server presents a "home page" to the user, which includes forms, menus, and buttons enabling the user to express what it is they want to do. For example, the user may set a menu to `Books` and enter into a form the title of the book they are interested in. The client web-browser transmits this information to the Amazon web-server, and that web-server must negotiate with the next tier — the application tier — to fulfill the client's request.

1.2 The Application Tier

The job of the application tier is to turn data, from the database, into a response to the request that it receives from the web-server. Each web-server process can invoke one or more application-tier processes to handle the request; these processes can be on one machine or many, and they may be on the same or different machines from the web-server processes.

The actions performed by the application tier are often referred to as the *business logic* of the organization operating the database. That is, one designs the application tier by reasoning out what the response to a request by the potential customer should be, and then implementing that strategy.

In the case of our example of a book at Amazon.com, this response would be the elements of the page that Amazon displays about a book. That data includes the title, author, price, and several other pieces of information about the book. It also includes links to more information, such as reviews, alternative sellers of the book, and similar books.

In a simple system, the application tier may issue database queries directly to the database tier, and assemble the results of those queries, perhaps in an HTML page. In a more complex system, there can be several subtiers to the application tier, and each may have its own processes. A common architecture is to have a subtier that supports "objects." These objects can contain data such as the title and price of a book in a "book object." Data for this object is obtained by a database query. The object may also have methods that can be invoked by the application-tier processes, and these methods may in turn cause additional queries to be issued to the database when and if they are invoked.

Another subtier may be present to support *database integration.* That is, there may be several quite independent databases that support operations, and it may not be possible to issue queries involving data from more than one database at a time. The results of queries to different sources may need to be combined at the integration subtier. To make integration more complex, the databases may not be compatable in a number of important ways. We shall examine the technology of information integration elsewhere. However, for the moment, consider the following hypothetical example.

Example 1: The Amazon database containing information about a book may have a price in dollars. But the customer is in Europe, and their account information is in another database, located in Europe, with billing information in Euros. The integration subtier needs to know that there is a difference in currencies, when it gets a price from the books database and uses that price to enter data into a bill that is displayed to the customer. □

1.3 The Database Tier

Like the other tiers, there can be many processes in the database tier, and the processes can be distributed over many machines, or all be together on one. The database tier executes queries that are requested from the application tier, and may also provide some buffering of data. For example, a query that produces many tuples may be fed one-at-a-time to the requesting process of the application tier.

Since creating connections to the database takes significant time, we normally keep a large number of connections open and allow application processes to share these connections. Each application process must return the connection to the state in which it was found, to avoid unexpected interactions between application processes.

The balance of this chapter is about how we implement a database tier. Especially, we need to learn:

1. How do we enable a database to interact with "ordinary" programs that are written in a conventional language such as C or Java?

2. How do we deal with the differences in data-types supported by SQL and conventional languages? In particular, relations are the results of queries, and these are not directly supported by conventional languages.

3. How do we manage connections to a database when these connections are shared between many short-lived processes?

2 The SQL Environment

In this section we shall take the broadest possible view of a DBMS and the databases and programs it supports. We shall see how databases are defined and organized into clusters, catalogs, and schemas. We shall also see how programs are linked with the data they need to manipulate. Many of the details depend on the particular implementation, so we shall concentrate on the general ideas that are contained in the SQL standard. Sections 5, 6, and 7 illustrate how these high-level concepts appear in a "call-level interface," which requires the programmer to make explicit connections to databases.

2.1 Environments

A *SQL environment* is the framework under which data may exist and SQL operations on data may be executed. In practice, we should think of a SQL environment as a DBMS running at some installation. For example, ABC company buys a license for the Megatron 2010 DBMS to run on a collection of ABC's machines. The system running on these machines constitutes a SQL environment.

All the database elements we have discussed — tables, views, triggers, and so on — are defined within a SQL environment. These elements are organized into a hierarchy of structures, each of which plays a distinct role in the organization. The structures defined by the SQL standard are indicated in Fig. 2.

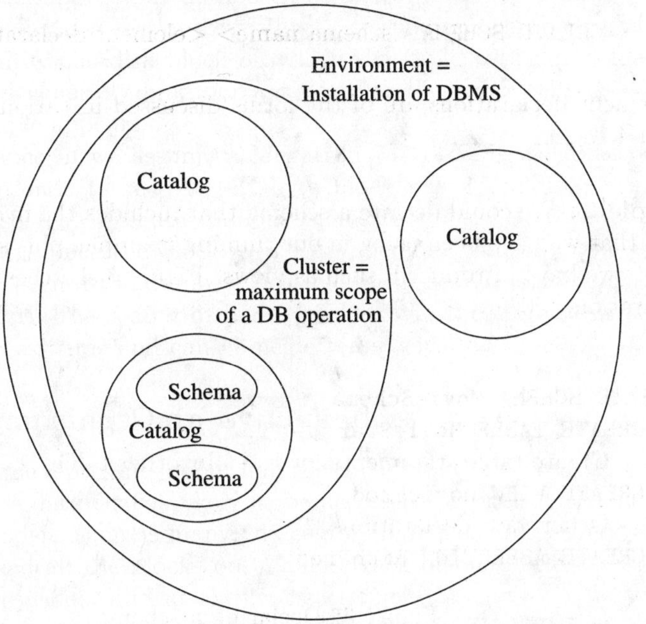

Figure 2: Organization of database elements within the environment

Briefly, the organization consists of the following structures:

1. *Schemas.* These are collections of tables, views, assertions, triggers, and some other types of information (see the box on "More Schema Elements" in Section 2.2). Schemas are the basic units of organization, close to what we might think of as a "database," but in fact somewhat less than a database as we shall see in point (3) below.

2. *Catalogs.* These are collections of schemas. They are the basic unit for supporting unique, accessible terminology. Each catalog has one or more schemas; the names of schemas within a catalog must be unique, and

each catalog contains a special schema called INFORMATION_SCHEMA that contains information about all the schemas in the catalog.

3. *Clusters.* These are collections of catalogs. Each user has an associated cluster: the set of all catalogs accessible to the user. A cluster is the maximum scope over which a query can be issued, so in a sense, a cluster is "the database" as seen by a particular user.

2.2 Schemas

The simplest form of schema declaration is:

```
CREATE SCHEMA <schema name> <element declarations>
```

The element declarations are of the forms discussed in various places, such as Section 4.1.

Example 2 : We could declare a schema that includes the five relations about movies that we have been using in our running example, plus some of the other elements we have introduced, such as views. Figure 3 sketches the form of such a declaration. □

```
CREATE SCHEMA MovieSchema
    CREATE TABLE MovieStar
        Create-table statements for the four other tables
    CREATE VIEW MovieProd
        Other view declarations
    CREATE ASSERTION RichPres
```

Figure 3: Declaring a schema

It is not necessary to declare the schema all at once. One can modify or add to the "current" schema using the appropriate CREATE, DROP, or ALTER statement, e.g., CREATE TABLE followed by the declaration of a new table for the schema. We change the "current" schema with a SET SCHEMA statement. For example,

```
SET SCHEMA MovieSchema;
```

makes the schema described in Fig. 3 the current schema. Then, any declarations of schema elements are added to that schema, and any DROP or ALTER statements refer to elements already in that schema.

More Schema Elements

Some schema elements that we have not already mentioned, but that occasionally are useful are:

- *Domains*: These are sets of values or simple data types. They are little used today, because object-relational DBMS's provide more powerful type-creation mechanisms.

- *Character sets*: These are sets of symbols and methods for encoding them. ASCII and Unicode are common options.

- *Collations*: A collation specifies which characters are "less than" which others. For example, we might use the ordering implied by the ASCII code, or we might treat lower-case and capital letters the same and not compare anything that isn't a letter.

- *Grant statements*: These concern who has access to schema elements.

- *Stored Procedures*: These are executable code; see Section 4.

2.3 Catalogs

Just as schema elements like tables are created within a schema, schemas are created and modified within a catalog. In principle, we would expect the process of creating and populating catalogs to be analogous to the process of creating and populating schemas. Unfortunately, SQL does not define a standard way to do so, such as a statement

`CREATE CATALOG` <catalog name>

followed by a list of schemas belonging to that catalog and the declarations of those schemas.

However, SQL does stipulate a statement

`SET CATALOG` <catalog name>

This statement allows us to set the "current" catalog, so new schemas will go into that catalog and schema modifications will refer to schemas in that catalog should there be a name ambiguity.

2.4 Clients and Servers in the SQL Environment

A SQL environment is more than a collection of catalogs and schemas. It contains elements whose purpose is to support operations on the database or

> **Complete Names for Schema Elements**
>
> Formally, the name for a schema element such as a table is its catalog name, its schema name, and its own name, connected by dots in that order. Thus, the table `Movies` in the schema `MovieSchema` in the catalog `MovieCatalog` can be referred to as
>
> `MovieCatalog.MovieSchema.Movies`
>
> If the catalog is the default or current catalog, then we can omit that component of the name. If the schema is also the default or current schema, then that part too can be omitted, and we are left with the element's own name, as is usual. However, we have the option to use the full name if we need to access something outside the current schema or catalog.

databases represented by those catalogs and schemas. According to the SQL standard, within a SQL environment are two special kinds of processes: SQL clients and SQL servers.

In terms of Fig. 1, a "SQL server" plays the role what we called a "database server there. A "SQL client" is like the application servers from that figure. The SQL standard does not define processes analogous to what we called "Web servers" or "clients" in Fig. 1.

2.5 Connections

If we wish to run some program involving SQL at a host where a SQL client exists, then we may open a connection between the client and server by executing a SQL statement

```
CONNECT TO <server name> AS <connection name>
    AUTHORIZATION <name and password>
```

The server name is something that depends on the installation. The word `DEFAULT` can substitute for a name and will connect the user to whatever SQL server the installation treats as the "default server." We have shown an authorization clause followed by the user's name and password. The latter is the typical method by which a user would be identified to the server, although other strings following `AUTHORIZATION` might be used.

The connection name can be used to refer to the connection later on. The reason we might have to refer to the connection is that SQL allows several connections to be opened by the user, but only one can be active at any time. To switch among connections, we can make `conn1` become the active connection by the statement:

```
SET CONNECTION conn1;
```

Whatever connection was currently active becomes *dormant* until it is reactivated with another `SET CONNECTION` statement that mentions it explicitly.

We also use the name when we drop the connection. We can drop connection `conn1` by

```
DISCONNECT conn1;
```

Now, `conn1` is terminated; it is not dormant and cannot be reactivated.

However, if we shall never need to refer to the connection being created, then `AS` and the connection name may be omitted from the `CONNECT TO` statement. It is also permitted to skip the connection statements altogether. If we simply execute SQL statements at a host with a SQL client, then a default connection will be established on our behalf.

2.6 Sessions

The SQL operations that are performed while a connection is active form a *session*. The session lasts as long as the connection that created it. For example, when a connection is made dormant, its session also becomes dormant, and reactivation of the connection by a `SET CONNECTION` statement also makes the session active. Thus, we have shown the session and connection as two aspects of the link between client and server in Fig. 4.

Each session has a current catalog and a current schema within that catalog. These may be set with statements `SET SCHEMA` and `SET CATALOG`, as discussed in Sections 2.2 and 2.3. There is also an authorized user for every session.

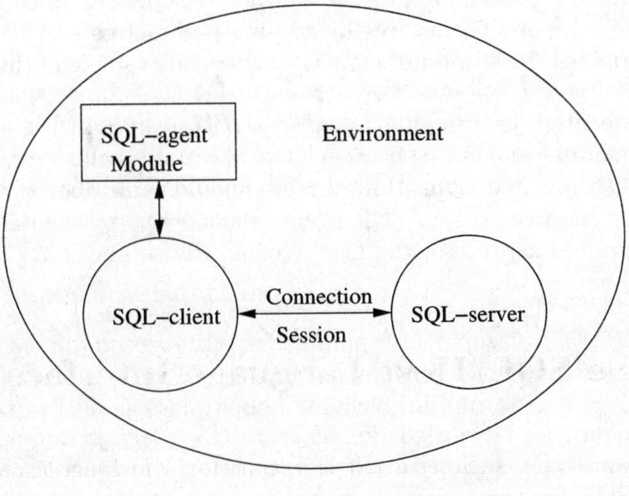

Figure 4: The SQL client-server interactions

The Languages of the SQL Standard

Implementations conforming to the SQL standard are required to support at least one of the following seven host languages: ADA, C, Cobol, Fortran, M (formerly called Mumps, and used primarily in the medical community), Pascal, and PL/I. We shall use C in our examples.

2.7 Modules

A *module* is the SQL term for an application program. The SQL standard suggests that there are three kinds of modules, but insists only that a SQL implementation offer the user at least one of these types.

1. *Generic SQL Interface.* The user may type SQL statements that are executed by a SQL server. In this mode, each query or other statement is a module by itself. It is this mode that we imagined for most of our examples in this book, although in practice it is rarely used.

2. *Embedded SQL.* This style will be discussed in Section 3. Typically, a preprocessor turns the embedded SQL statements into suitable function or procedure calls to the SQL system. The compiled host-language program, including these function calls, is a module.

3. *True Modules.* The most general style of modules envisioned by SQL is a collection of stored functions or procedures, some of which are host-language code and some of which are SQL statements. They communicate among themselves by passing parameters and perhaps via shared variables. PSM modules (Section 4) are an example of this type of module.

An execution of a module is called a *SQL agent.* In Fig. 4 we have shown both a module and an SQL agent, as one unit, calling upon a SQL client to establish a connection. However, we should remember that the distinction between a module and an SQL agent is analogous to the distinction between a program and a process; the first is code, the second is an execution of that code.

3 The SQL/Host-Language Interface

To this point, we have used the *generic SQL interface* in our examples. That is, we have assumed there is a SQL interpreter, which accepts and executes the sorts of SQL queries and commands that we have learned. Although provided as an option by almost all DBMS's, this mode of operation is actually rare. In real systems, such as those described in Section 1, there is a program in some conventional *host* language such as C, but some of the steps in this program are actually SQL statements.

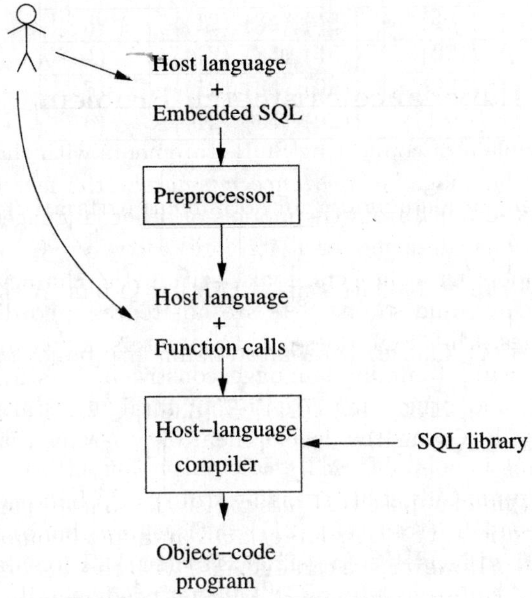

Figure 5: Processing programs with SQL statements embedded

A sketch of a typical programming system that involves SQL statements is in Fig. 5. There, we see the programmer writing programs in a host language, but with some special "embedded" SQL statements. There are two ways this embedding could take place.

1. *Call-Level Interface.* A library is provided, and the embedding of SQL in the host language is really calls to functions or methods in this library. SQL statements are usually string arguments of these methods. This approach, often referred to as a call-level interface or CLI, is discussed in Section 5 and is represented by the curved arrow in Fig. 5 from the user directly to the host language.

2. *Directly Embedded SQL.* The entire host-language program, with embedded SQL statements, is sent to a preprocessor, which changes the embedded SQL statements into something that makes sense in the host language. Typically, the SQL statements are replaced by calls to library functions or methods, so the difference between a CLI and direct embedding of SQL is more a matter of "look and feel" than of substance. The preprocessed host-language program is then compiled in the usual manner and operates on the database through execution of the library calls.

In this section, we shall learn the SQL standard for direct embedding in a host language — C in particular. We are also introduced to a number of concepts, such as cursors, that appear in all, or almost all, systems for embedding SQL.

3.1 The Impedance Mismatch Problem

The basic problem of connecting SQL statements with those of a conventional programming language is *impedance mismatch*: the fact that the data model of SQL differs so much from the models of other languages. As we know, SQL uses the relational data model at its core. However, C and similar languages use a data model with integers, reals, arithmetic, characters, pointers, record structures, arrays, and so on. Sets are not represented directly in C or these other languages, while SQL does not use pointers, loops and branches, or many other common programming-language constructs. As a result, passing data between SQL and other languages is not straightforward, and a mechanism must be devised to allow the development of programs that use both SQL and another language.

One might first suppose that it is preferable to use a single language. Either do all computation in SQL or forget SQL and do all computation in a conventional language. However, we can dispense with the idea of omitting SQL when there are database operations involved. SQL systems greatly aid the programmer in writing database operations that can be executed efficiently, yet that can be expressed at a very high level. SQL takes from the programmer's shoulders the need to understand how data is organized in storage or how to exploit that storage structure to operate efficiently on the database.

On the other hand, there are many important things that SQL cannot do at all. For example, one cannot write a SQL query to compute n factorial, something that is an easy exercise in C or similar languages.[1] As another example, SQL cannot format its output directly into a convenient form such as a graphic. Thus, real database programming requires both SQL and a host language.

3.2 Connecting SQL to the Host Language

When we wish to use a SQL statement within a host-language program, we warn the preprocessor that SQL code is coming with the keywords `EXEC SQL` in front of the statement. We transfer information between the database, which is accessed only by SQL statements, and the host-language program through *shared variables*, which are allowed to appear in both host-language statements

[1]We should be careful here. There are extensions to the basic SQL language, such as recursive SQL or SQL/PSM discussed in Section 4, that do offer "Turing completeness" — the ability to compute anything that can be computed in any other programming language. However, these extensions were never intended for general-purpose calculation, and we do not regard them as general-purpose languages.

and SQL statements. Shared variables are prefixed by a colon within a SQL statement, but they appear without the colon in host-language statements.

A special variable, called SQLSTATE in the SQL standard, serves to connect the host-language program with the SQL execution system. The type of SQLSTATE is an array of five characters. Each time a function of the SQL library is called, a code is put in the variable SQLSTATE that indicates any problems found during that call. The SQL standard also specifies a large number of five-character codes and their meanings.

For example, '00000' (five zeroes) indicates that no error condition occurred, and '02000' indicates that a tuple requested as part of the answer to a SQL query could not be found. The latter code is very important, since it allows us to create a loop in the host-language program that examines tuples from some relation one-at-a-time and to break the loop after the last tuple has been examined.

3.3 The DECLARE Section

To declare shared variables, we place their declarations between two embedded SQL statements:

```
EXEC SQL BEGIN DECLARE SECTION;
    ...
EXEC SQL END DECLARE SECTION;
```

What appears between them is called the *declare section*. The form of variable declarations in the declare section is whatever the host language requires. It only makes sense to declare variables to have types that both the host language and SQL can deal with, such as integers, reals, and character strings or arrays.

Example 3: The following statements might appear in a C function that updates the Studio relation:

```
EXEC SQL BEGIN DECLARE SECTION;
    char studioName[50], studioAddr[256];
    char SQLSTATE[6];
EXEC SQL END DECLARE SECTION;
```

The first and last statements are the required beginning and end of the declare section. In the middle is a statement declaring two shared variables, studioName and studioAddr. These are both character arrays and, as we shall see, they can be used to hold a name and address of a studio that are made into a tuple and inserted into the Studio relation. The third statement declares SQLSTATE to be a six-character array.[2] □

[2]We shall use six characters for the five-character value of SQLSTATE because in programs to follow we want to use the C function strcmp to test whether SQLSTATE has a certain value. Since strcmp expects strings to be terminated by '\0', we need a sixth character for this endmarker. The sixth character must be set initially to '\0', but we shall not show this assignment in programs to follow.

3.4 Using Shared Variables

A shared variable can be used in SQL statements in places where we expect or allow a constant. Recall that shared variables are preceded by a colon when so used. Here is an example in which we use the variables of Example 3 as components of a tuple to be inserted into relation `Studio`.

Example 4: In Fig. 6 is a sketch of a C function `getStudio` that prompts the user for the name and address of a studio, reads the responses, and inserts the appropriate tuple into `Studio`. Lines (1) through (4) are the declarations from Example 3. We omit the C code that prints requests and scans entered text to fill the two arrays `studioName` and `studioAddr`.

```
    void getStudio() {

1)      EXEC SQL BEGIN DECLARE SECTION;
2)          char studioName[50], studioAddr[256];
3)          char SQLSTATE[6];
4)      EXEC SQL END DECLARE SECTION;

        /* print request that studio name and address
           be entered and read response into variables
           studioName and studioAddr */

5)      EXEC SQL INSERT INTO Studio(name, address)
6)              VALUES (:studioName, :studioAddr);
    }
```

Figure 6: Using shared variables to insert a new studio

Then, in lines (5) and (6) is an embedded SQL `INSERT` statement. This statement is preceded by the keywords `EXEC SQL` to indicate that it is indeed an embedded SQL statement rather than ungrammatical C code. The values inserted by lines (5) and (6) are not explicit constants, as they were in all previous examples; rather, the values appearing in line (6) are shared variables whose current values become components of the inserted tuple. □

Any SQL statement that does not return a result (i.e., is not a query) can be embedded in a host-language program by preceding it with `EXEC SQL`. Examples of embeddable SQL statements include insert-, delete-, and update-statements and those statements that create, modify, or drop schema elements such as tables and views.

However, select-from-where queries are not embeddable directly into a host language, because of the "impedance mismatch." Queries produce bags of tuples as a result, while none of the major host languages support a set or bag data type directly. Thus, embedded SQL must use one of two mechanisms for connecting the result of queries with a host-language program:

1. *Single-Row* SELECT *Statements.* A query that produces a single tuple can have that tuple stored in shared variables, one variable for each component of the tuple.

2. *Cursors.* Queries producing more than one tuple can be executed if we declare a *cursor* for the query. The cursor ranges over all tuples in the answer relation, and each tuple in turn can be fetched into shared variables and processed by the host-language program.

We shall consider each of these mechanisms in turn.

3.5 Single-Row Select Statements

The form of a single-row select is the same as an ordinary select-from-where statement, except that following the `SELECT` clause is the keyword `INTO` and a list of shared variables. These shared variables each are preceded by a colon, as is the case for all shared variables within a SQL statement. If the result of the query is a single tuple, this tuple's components become the values of these variables. If the result is either no tuple or more than one tuple, then no assignment to the shared variables is made, and an appropriate error code is written in the variable `SQLSTATE`.

Example 5 : We shall write a C function to read the name of a studio and print the net worth of the studio's president. A sketch of this function is shown in Fig. 7. It begins with a declare section, lines (1) through (5), for the variables we shall need. Next, C statements that we do not show explicitly obtain a studio name from the standard input.

Lines (6) through (9) are the single-row select statement. It is quite similar to queries we have already seen. The two differences are that the value of variable `studioName` is used in place of a constant string in the condition of line (9), and there is an `INTO` clause at line (7) that tells us where to put the result of the query. In this case, we expect a single tuple, and tuples have only one component, that for attribute `netWorth`. The value of this one component of one tuple is placed in the shared variable `presNetWorth`. □

3.6 Cursors

The most versatile way to connect SQL queries to a host language is with a cursor that runs through the tuples of a relation. This relation can be a stored table, or it can be something that is generated by a query. To create and use a cursor, we need the following statements:

1. A cursor declaration, whose simplest form is:

```
void printNetWorth() {
        EXEC SQL BEGIN DECLARE SECTION;
            char studioName[50];
            int presNetWorth;
            char SQLSTATE[6];
        EXEC SQL END DECLARE SECTION;

        /* print request that studio name be entered.
           read response into studioName */

        EXEC SQL SELECT netWorth
                INTO :presNetWorth
                FROM Studio, MovieExec
                WHERE presC# = cert# AND
                      Studio.name = :studioName;

        /* check that SQLSTATE has all 0's and if so, print
           the value of presNetWorth */
}
```

Figure 7: A single-row select embedded in a C function

EXEC SQL DECLARE <cursor name> CURSOR FOR <query>

The query can be either an ordinary select-from-where query or a relation name. The cursor *ranges* over the tuples of the relation produced by the query.

2. A statement EXEC SQL OPEN, followed by the cursor name. This statement initializes the cursor to a position where it is ready to retrieve the first tuple of the relation over which the cursor ranges.

3. One or more uses of a *fetch statement.* The purpose of a fetch statement is to get the next tuple of the relation over which the cursor ranges. The fetch statement has the form:

   EXEC SQL FETCH FROM <cursor name> INTO <list of variables>

   There is one variable in the list for each attribute of the tuple's relation. If there is a tuple available to be fetched, these variables are assigned the values of the corresponding components from that tuple. If the tuples have been exhausted, then no tuple is returned, and the value of SQLSTATE is set to '02000', a code that means "no tuple found."

4. The statement EXEC SQL CLOSE followed by the name of the cursor. This statement closes the cursor, which now no longer ranges over tuples of the relation. It can, however, be reinitialized by another OPEN statement, in which case it ranges anew over the tuples of this relation.

Example 6: Suppose we wish to determine the number of movie executives whose net worths fall into a sequence of bands of exponentially growing size, each band corresponding to a number of digits in the net worth. We shall design a query that retrieves the netWorth field of all the MovieExec tuples into a shared variable called worth. A cursor called execCursor will range over all these one-component tuples. Each time a tuple is fetched, we compute the number of digits in the integer worth and increment the appropriate element of an array counts.

The C function worthRanges begins in line (1) of Fig. 8. Line (2) declares some variables used only by the C function, not by the embedded SQL. The array counts holds the counts of executives in the various bands, digits counts the number of digits in a net worth, and i is an index ranging over the elements of array counts.

Lines (3) through (6) are a SQL declare section in which shared variable worth and the usual SQLSTATE are declared. Lines (7) and (8) declare execCursor to be a cursor that ranges over the values produced by the query on line (8). This query simply asks for the netWorth components of all the tuples in MovieExec. This cursor is then opened at line (9). Line (10) completes the initialization by zeroing the elements of array counts.

The main work is done by the loop of lines (11) through (16). At line (12) a tuple is fetched into shared variable worth. Since tuples produced by the query of line (8) have only one component, we need only one shared variable, although in general there would be as many variables as there are components of the retrieved tuples. Line (13) tests whether the fetch has been successful. Here, we use a macro NO_MORE_TUPLES, defined by

```
#define NO_MORE_TUPLES !(strcmp(SQLSTATE,"02000"))
```

Recall that "02000" is the SQLSTATE code that means no tuple was found. If there are no more tuples, we break out of the loop and go to line (17).

If a tuple has been fetched, then at line (14) we initialize the number of digits in the net worth to 1. Line (15) is a loop that repeatedly divides the net worth by 10 and increments digits by 1. When the net worth reaches 0 after division by 10, digits holds the correct number of digits in the value of worth that was originally retrieved. Finally, line (16) increments the appropriate element of the array counts by 1. We assume that the number of digits is no more than 14. However, should there be a net worth with 15 or more digits, line (16) will not increment any element of the counts array, since there is no appropriate range; i.e., enormous net worths are thrown away and do not affect the statistics.

Line (17) begins the wrap-up of the function. The cursor is closed, and lines (18) and (19) print the values in the counts array. □

```
void worthRanges() {

    int i, digits, counts[15];
    EXEC SQL BEGIN DECLARE SECTION;
        int worth;
        char SQLSTATE[6];
    EXEC SQL END DECLARE SECTION;
    EXEC SQL DECLARE execCursor CURSOR FOR
        SELECT netWorth FROM MovieExec;

    EXEC SQL OPEN execCursor;
    for(i=1; i<15; i++) counts[i] = 0;
    while(1) {
        EXEC SQL FETCH FROM execCursor INTO :worth;
        if(NO_MORE_TUPLES) break;
        digits = 1;
        while((worth /= 10) > 0) digits++;
        if(digits <= 14) counts[digits]++;
    }
    EXEC SQL CLOSE execCursor;
    for(i=0; i<15; i++)
        printf("digits = %d: number of execs = %d\n",
            i, counts[i]);
}
```

Figure 8: Grouping executive net worths into exponential bands

3.7 Modifications by Cursor

When a cursor ranges over the tuples of a base table (i.e., a relation that is stored in the database), then one can not only read the current tuple, but one can update or delete the current tuple. The `WHERE` clause may only be `WHERE CURRENT OF` followed by the name of the cursor. Of course it is possible for the host-language program reading the tuple to apply whatever condition it likes to the tuple before deciding whether or not to delete or update it.

Example 7 : In Fig. 9 we see a C function that looks at each tuple of `MovieExec` and decides either to delete the tuple or to double the net worth. In lines (3) and (4) we declare variables that correspond to the four attributes of `MovieExec`, as well as the necessary `SQLSTATE`. Then, at line (6), `execCursor` is declared to range over the stored relation `MovieExec` itself.

Lines (8) through (14) are the loop, in which the cursor `execCursor` refers to each tuple of `MovieExec`, in turn. Line (9) fetches the current tuple into

```
1)  void changeWorth() {

2)      EXEC SQL BEGIN DECLARE SECTION;
3)          int certNo, worth;
4)          char execName[31], execAddr[256], SQLSTATE[6];
5)      EXEC SQL END DECLARE SECTION;
6)      EXEC SQL DECLARE execCursor CURSOR FOR MovieExec;

7)      EXEC SQL OPEN execCursor;
8)      while(1) {
9)          EXEC SQL FETCH FROM execCursor INTO :execName,
                :execAddr, :certNo, :worth;
10)         if(NO_MORE_TUPLES) break;
11)         if (worth < 1000)
12)             EXEC SQL DELETE FROM MovieExec
                             WHERE CURRENT OF execCursor;
13)         else
14)             EXEC SQL UPDATE MovieExec
                            SET netWorth = 2 * netWorth
                            WHERE CURRENT OF execCursor;
        }
15)     EXEC SQL CLOSE execCursor;
    }
```

Figure 9: Modifying executive net worths

the four variables used for this purpose; note that only `worth` is actually used. Line (10) tests whether we have exhausted the tuples of `MovieExec`. We have again used the macro `NO_MORE_TUPLES` for the condition that variable `SQLSTATE` has the "no more tuples" code `"02000"`.

In the test of line (11) we ask if the net worth is under \$1000. If so, the tuple is deleted by the `DELETE` statement of line (12). Note that the `WHERE` clause refers to the cursor, so the current tuple of `MovieExec`, the one we just fetched, is deleted from `MovieExec`. If the net worth is at least \$1000, then at line (14), the net worth in the same tuple is doubled, instead. □

3.8 Protecting Against Concurrent Updates

Suppose that as we examine the net worths of movie executives using the function `worthRanges` of Fig. 8, some other process is modifying the underlying `MovieExec` relation. What should we do about this possibility? Perhaps nothing. We might be happy with approximate statistics, and we don't care whether or not we count an executive who was in the process of being deleted, for example. Then, we simply accept what tuples we get through the cursor.

However, we may not wish to allow concurrent changes to affect the tuples we see through this cursor. Rather, we may insist on the statistics being taken on the relation as it exists at some point in time. In terms of the transactions, we want the code that runs the cursor through the relation to be serializable with any other operations on the relation. To obtain this guarantee, we may declare the cursor *insensitive* to concurrent changes.

Example 8: We could modify lines (7) and (8) of Fig. 8 to be:

```
7)      EXEC SQL DECLARE execCursor INSENSITIVE CURSOR FOR
8)          SELECT netWorth FROM MovieExec;
```

If execCursor is so declared, then the SQL system will guarantee that changes to relation MovieExec made between one opening and closing of execCursor will not affect the set of tuples fetched. □

There are certain cursors ranging over a relation R about which we may say with certainty that they will not change R. Such a cursor can run simultaneously with an insensitive cursor for R, without risk of changing the relation R that the insensitive cursor sees. If we declare a cursor FOR READ ONLY, then the database system can be sure that the underlying relation will not be modified because of access to the relation through this cursor.

Example 9: We could append after line (8) of worthRanges in Fig. 8 a line

```
FOR READ ONLY;
```

If so, then any attempt to execute a modification through cursor execCursor would cause an error. □

3.9 Dynamic SQL

Our model of SQL embedded in a host language has been that of specific SQL queries and commands within a host-language program. An alternative style of embedded SQL has the statements themselves be computed by the host language. Such statements are not known at compile time, and thus cannot be handled by a SQL preprocessor or a host-language compiler.

An example of such a situation is a program that prompts the user for an SQL query, reads the query, and then executes that query. The generic interface for ad-hoc SQL queries is an example of just such a program. If queries are read and executed at run-time, there is nothing that can be done at compile-time. The query has to be parsed and a suitable way to execute the query found by the SQL system, immediately after the query is read.

The host-language program must instruct the SQL system to take the character string just read, to turn it into an executable SQL statement, and finally to execute that statement. There are two *dynamic SQL* statements that perform these two steps.

1. EXEC SQL PREPARE V FROM <expression>, where V is a SQL variable. The expression can be any host-language expression whose value is a string; this string is treated as a SQL statement. Presumably, the SQL statement is parsed and a good way to execute it is found by the SQL system, but the statement is not executed. Rather, the plan for executing the SQL statement becomes the value of V.

2. EXEC SQL EXECUTE V. This statement causes the SQL statement denoted by variable V to be executed.

Both steps can be combined into one, with the statement:

EXEC SQL EXECUTE IMMEDIATE <expression>

The disadvantage of combining these two parts is seen if we prepare a statement once and then execute it many times. With EXECUTE IMMEDIATE the cost of preparing the statement is paid each time the statement is executed, rather than paid only once, when we prepare it.

Example 10: In Fig. 10 is a sketch of a C program that reads text from standard input into a variable query, prepares it, and executes it. The SQL variable SQLquery holds the prepared query. Since the query is only executed once, the line:

```
EXEC SQL EXECUTE IMMEDIATE :query;
```

could replace lines (6) and (7) of Fig. 10. □

```
1)  void readQuery() {

2)      EXEC SQL BEGIN DECLARE SECTION;
3)          char *query;
4)      EXEC SQL END DECLARE SECTION;

5)      /* prompt user for a query, allocate space (e.g.,
           use malloc) and make shared variable :query point
           to the first character of the query */
6)      EXEC SQL PREPARE SQLquery FROM :query;
7)      EXEC SQL EXECUTE SQLquery;
    }
```

Figure 10: Preparing and executing a dynamic SQL query

3.10 Exercises for Section 3

Exercise 3.1: Write the following embedded SQL queries, based on the database schema

```
Product(maker, model, type)
PC(model, speed, ram, hd, price)
Laptop(model, speed, ram, hd, screen, price)
Printer(model, color, type, price)
```

You may use any host language with which you are familiar, and details of host-language programming may be replaced by clear comments if you wish.

a) Ask the user for a price and find the PC whose price is closest to the desired price. Print the maker, model number, and speed of the PC.

b) Ask the user for minimum values of the speed, RAM, hard-disk size, and screen size that they will accept. Find all the laptops that satisfy these requirements. Print their specifications (all attributes of `Laptop`) and their manufacturer.

! c) Ask the user for a manufacturer. Print the specifications of all products by that manufacturer. That is, print the model number, product-type, and all the attributes of whichever relation is appropriate for that type.

!! d) Ask the user for a "budget" (total price of a PC and printer), and a minimum speed of the PC. Find the cheapest "system" (PC plus printer) that is within the budget and minimum speed, but make the printer a color printer if possible. Print the model numbers for the chosen system.

e) Ask the user for a manufacturer, model number, speed, RAM, hard-disk size, and price of a new PC. Check that there is no PC with that model number. Print a warning if so, and otherwise insert the information into tables `Product` and `PC`.

Exercise 3.2: Write the following embedded SQL queries, based on the database schema

```
Classes(class, type, country, numGuns, bore, displacement)
Ships(name, class, launched)
Battles(name, date)
Outcomes(ship, battle, result)
```

a) The firepower of a ship is roughly proportional to the number of guns times the cube of the bore of the guns. Find the class with the largest firepower.

! b) Ask the user for the name of a battle. Find the countries of the ships involved in the battle. Print the country with the most ships sunk and the country with the most ships damaged.

c) Ask the user for the name of a class and the other information required for a tuple of table `Classes`. Then ask for a list of the names of the ships of that class and their dates launched. However, the user need not give the first name, which will be the name of the class. Insert the information gathered into `Classes` and `Ships`.

! d) Examine the `Battles`, `Outcomes`, and `Ships` relations for ships that were in battle before they were launched. Prompt the user when there is an error found, offering the option to change the date of launch or the date of the battle. Make whichever change is requested.

4 Stored Procedures

In this section, we introduce you to *Persistent, Stored Modules* (SQL/PSM, or just PSM). PSM is part of the latest revision to the SQL standard, called SQL:2003. It allows us to write procedures in a simple, general-purpose language and to store them in the database, as part of the schema. We can then use these procedures in SQL queries and other statements to perform computations that cannot be done with SQL alone. Each commercial DBMS offers its own extension of PSM. In this book, we shall describe the SQL/PSM standard, which captures the major ideas of these facilities, and which should help you understand the language associated with any particular system. References to PSM extensions provided with several major commercial systems are in the bibliographic notes.

4.1 Creating PSM Functions and Procedures

In PSM, you define *modules*, which are collections of function and procedure definitions, temporary relation declarations, and several other optional declarations. The major elements of a procedure declaration are:

```
CREATE PROCEDURE <name> (<parameters>)
    <local declarations>
    <procedure body>;
```

This form should be familiar from a number of programming languages; it consists of a procedure name, a parenthesized list of parameters, some optional local-variable declarations, and the executable body of code that defines the procedure. A function is defined in almost the same way, except that the keyword `FUNCTION` is used, and there is a return-value type that must be specified. That is, the elements of a function definition are:

```
CREATE FUNCTION <name> (<parameters>) RETURNS <type>
    <local declarations>
    <function body>;
```

The parameters of a PSM procedure are mode-name-type triples. That is, the parameter name is not only followed by its declared type, as usual in programming languages, but it is preceded by a "mode," which is either `IN`, `OUT`, or `INOUT`. These three keywords indicate that the parameter is input-only, output-only, or both input and output, respectively. `IN` is the default, and can be omitted.

Function parameters, on the other hand, may only be of mode `IN`. That is, PSM forbids side-effects in functions, so the only way to obtain information from a function is through its return-value. We shall not specify the `IN` mode for function parameters, although we do so in procedure definitions.

Example 11: While we have not yet learned the variety of statements that can appear in procedure and function bodies, one kind should not surprise us: an SQL statement. The limitation on these statements is the same as for embedded SQL, as we introduced in Section 3.4: only single-row-select statements and cursor-based accesses are permitted as queries. In Fig. 11 is a PSM procedure that takes two addresses — an old address and a new address — as parameters and replaces the old address by the new everywhere it appears in `MovieStar`.

```
1)  CREATE PROCEDURE Move(
2)      IN oldAddr VARCHAR(255),
3)      IN newAddr VARCHAR(255)
    )
4)  UPDATE MovieStar
5)  SET address = newAddr
6)  WHERE address = oldAddr;
```

Figure 11: A procedure to change addresses

Line (1) introduces the procedure and its name, `Move`. Lines (2) and (3) declare two input parameters, both of whose types are `VARCHAR(255)`. Lines (4) through (6) are a conventional `UPDATE` statement. However, notice that the parameter names can be used as if they were constants. Unlike host-language variables, which require a colon prefix when used in SQL (see Section 3.2), parameters and other local variables of PSM procedures and functions require no colon. □

4.2 Some Simple Statement Forms in PSM

Let us begin with a potpourri of statement forms that are easy to master.

1. *The call-statement*: The form of a procedure call is:

   `CALL` <procedure name> `(`<argument list>`);`

   That is, the keyword `CALL` is followed by the name of the procedure and a parenthesized list of arguments, as in most any language. This call can, however, be made from a variety of places:

   i. From a host-language program, in which it might appear as

   ```
   EXEC SQL CALL Foo(:x, 3);
   ```

   for instance.

   ii. As a statement of another PSM function or procedure.

   iii. As a SQL command issued to the generic SQL interface. For example, we can issue a statement such as

   ```
   CALL Foo(1, 3);
   ```

   to such an interface, and have stored procedure `Foo` executed with its two parameters set equal to 1 and 3, respectively.

   Note that it is not permitted to call a function. You invoke functions in PSM as you do in C: use the function name and suitable arguments as part of an expression.

2. *The return-statement*: Its form is

   `RETURN` <expression>`;`

   This statement can only appear in a function. It evaluates the expression and sets the return-value of the function equal to that result. However, at variance with common programming languages, the return-statement of PSM does *not* terminate the function. Rather, control continues with the following statement, and it is possible that the return-value will be changed before the function completes.

3. *Declarations of local variables*: The statement form

   `DECLARE` <name> <type>`;`

   declares a variable with the given name to have the given type. This variable is local, and its value is not preserved by the DBMS after a running of the function or procedure. Declarations must precede executable statements in the function or procedure body.

4. *Assignment Statements*: The form of an assignment is:

SET <variable> = <expression>;

Except for the introductory keyword `SET`, assignment in PSM is quite like assignment in other languages. The expression on the right of the equal-sign is evaluated, and its value becomes the value of the variable on the left. `NULL` is a permissible expression. The expression may even be a query, as long as it returns a single value.

5. *Statement groups*: We can form a list of statements ended by semicolons and surrounded by keywords `BEGIN` and `END`. This construct is treated as a single statement and can appear anywhere a single statement can. In particular, since a procedure or function body is expected to be a single statement, we can put any sequence of statements in the body by surrounding them by `BEGIN...END`.

6. *Statement labels*: We label a statement by prefixing it with a name (the label) and a colon.

4.3 Branching Statements

For our first complex PSM statement type, let us consider the if-statement. The form is only a little strange; it differs from C or similar languages in that:

1. The statement ends with keywords `END IF`.

2. If-statements nested within the else-clause are introduced with the single word `ELSEIF`.

Thus, the general form of an if-statement is as suggested by Fig. 12. The condition is any boolean-valued expression, as can appear in the `WHERE` clause of SQL statements. Each statement list consists of statements ended by semicolons, but does not need a surrounding `BEGIN...END`. The final `ELSE` and its statement(s) are optional; i.e., `IF...THEN...END IF` alone or with `ELSEIF`'s is acceptable.

Example 12: Let us write a function to take a year y and a studio s, and return a boolean that is `TRUE` if and only if studio s produced at least one comedy in year y or did not produce any movies at all in that year. The code appears in Fig. 13.

Line (1) introduces the function and includes its arguments. We do not need to specify a mode for the arguments, since that can only be `IN` for a function. Lines (2) and (3) test for the case where there are no movies at all by studio s in year y, in which case we set the return-value to `TRUE` at line (4). Note that line (4) does not cause the function to return. Technically, it is the flow of control dictated by the if-statements that causes control to jump from line (4) to line (9), where the function completes and returns.

```
IF <condition> /tt THEN
    <statement list>
ELSEIF <condition> /tt THEN
    <statement list>
ELSEIF
        ...
ELSE
    <statement list>
END IF;
```

Figure 12: The form of an if-statement

```
1)  CREATE FUNCTION BandW(y INT, s CHAR(15)) RETURNS BOOLEAN

2)  IF NOT EXISTS(
3)      SELECT * FROM Movies WHERE year = y AND
            studioName = s)
4)  THEN RETURN TRUE;
5)  ELSEIF 1 <=
6)      (SELECT COUNT(*) FROM Movies WHERE year = y AND
            studioName = s AND genre = 'comedy')
7)  THEN RETURN TRUE;
8)  ELSE RETURN FALSE;
9)  END IF;
```

Figure 13: If there are any movies at all, then at least one has to be a comedy

If studio *s* made movies in year *y*, then lines (5) and (6) test if at least one of them was a comedy. If so, the return-value is again set to true, this time at line (7). In the remaining case, studio *s* made movies but only in color, so we set the return-value to `FALSE` at line (8). □

4.4 Queries in PSM

There are several ways that select-from-where queries are used in PSM.

1. Subqueries can be used in conditions, or in general, any place a subquery is legal in SQL. We saw two examples of subqueries in lines (3) and (6) of Fig. 13, for instance.

2. Queries that return a single value can be used as the right sides of assignment statements.

3. A single-row select statement is a legal statement in PSM. Recall this statement has an `INTO` clause that specifies variables into which the com-

ponents of the single returned tuple are placed. These variables could be local variables or parameters of a PSM procedure. The general form was discussed in the context of embedded SQL in Section 3.5.

4. We can declare and use a cursor, essentially as it was described in Section 3.6 for embedded SQL. The declaration of the cursor, OPEN, FETCH, and CLOSE statements are all as described there, with the exceptions that:

   (a) No EXEC SQL appears in the statements, and

   (b) The variables do not use a colon prefix.

```
CREATE PROCEDURE SomeProc(IN studioName CHAR(15))

DECLARE presNetWorth INTEGER;

SELECT netWorth
INTO presNetWorth
FROM Studio, MovieExec
WHERE presC# = cert# AND Studio.name = studioName;
    ...
```

Figure 14: A single-row select in PSM

Example 13: In Fig. 14 is the single-row select of Fig. 7, redone for PSM and placed in the context of a hypothetical procedure definition. Note that, because the single-row select returns a one-component tuple, we could also get the same effect from an assignment statement, as:

```
SET presNetWorth = (SELECT netWorth
    FROM Studio, MovieExec
    WHERE presC# = cert# AND Studio.name = studioName);
```

We shall defer examples of cursor use until we learn the PSM loop statements in the next section. □

4.5 Loops in PSM

The basic loop construct in PSM is:

```
LOOP
    <statement list>
END LOOP;
```

One often labels the LOOP statement, so it is possible to break out of the loop, using a statement:

```
LEAVE <loop label>;
```

In the common case that the loop involves the fetching of tuples via a cursor, we often wish to leave the loop when there are no more tuples. It is useful to declare a *condition* name for the SQLSTATE value that indicates no tuple found ('02000', recall); we do so with:

```
DECLARE Not_Found CONDITION FOR SQLSTATE '02000';
```

More generally, we can declare a condition with any desired name corresponding to any SQLSTATE value by

```
DECLARE <name> CONDITION FOR SQLSTATE <value>;
```

We are now ready to take up an example that ties together cursor operations and loops in PSM.

Example 14: Figure 15 shows a PSM procedure that takes a studio name *s* as an input argument and produces in output arguments mean and variance the mean and variance of the lengths of all the movies owned by studio *s*. Lines (1) through (4) declare the procedure and its parameters.

Lines (5) through (8) are local declarations. We define Not_Found to be the name of the condition that means a FETCH failed to return a tuple at line (5). Then, at line (6), the cursor MovieCursor is defined to return the set of the lengths of the movies by studio *s*. Lines (7) and (8) declare two local variables that we'll need. Integer newLength holds the result of a FETCH, while movieCount counts the number of movies by studio *s*. We need movieCount so that, at the end, we can convert a sum of lengths into an average (mean) of lengths and a sum of squares of the lengths into a variance.

The rest of the lines are the body of the procedure. We shall use mean and variance as temporary variables, as well as for "returning" the results at the end. In the major loop, mean actually holds the sum of the lengths, and variance actually holds the sum of the squares of the lengths. Thus, lines (9) through (11) initialize these variables and the count of the movies to 0. Line (12) opens the cursor, and lines (13) through (19) form the loop labeled movieLoop.

Line (14) performs a fetch, and at line (15) we check that another tuple was found. If not, we leave the loop. Lines (16) through (18) accumulate values; we add 1 to movieCount, add the length to mean (which, recall, is really computing the sum of lengths), and we add the square of the length to variance.

When all movies by studio *s* have been seen, we leave the loop, and control passes to line (20). At that line, we turn mean into its correct value by dividing the sum of lengths by the count of movies. At line (21), we make variance truly hold the variance by dividing the sum of squares of the lengths by the number of movies and subtracting the square of the mean. See Exercise 4.4 for a discussion of why this calculation is correct. Line (22) closes the cursor, and we are done. □

```
1)  CREATE PROCEDURE MeanVar(
2)      IN s CHAR(15),
3)      OUT mean REAL,
4)      OUT variance REAL
    )
5)  DECLARE Not_Found CONDITION FOR SQLSTATE '02000';
6)  DECLARE MovieCursor CURSOR FOR
        SELECT length FROM Movies WHERE studioName = s;
7)  DECLARE newLength INTEGER;
8)  DECLARE movieCount INTEGER;

    BEGIN
9)      SET mean = 0.0;
10)     SET variance = 0.0;
11)     SET movieCount = 0;
12)     OPEN MovieCursor;
13)     movieLoop: LOOP
14)         FETCH FROM MovieCursor INTO newLength;
15)         IF Not_Found THEN LEAVE movieLoop END IF;
16)         SET movieCount = movieCount + 1;
17)         SET mean = mean + newLength;
18)         SET variance = variance + newLength * newLength;
19)     END LOOP;
20)     SET mean = mean/movieCount;
21)     SET variance = variance/movieCount - mean * mean;
22)     CLOSE MovieCursor;
    END;
```

Figure 15: Computing the mean and variance of lengths of movies by one studio

4.6 For-Loops

There is also in PSM a for-loop construct, but it is used only to iterate over a cursor. The form of the statement is shown in Fig. 16. This statement not only declares a cursor, but it handles for us a number of "grubby details": the opening and closing of the cursor, the fetching, and the checking whether there are no more tuples to be fetched. However, since we are not fetching tuples for ourselves, we can not specify the variable(s) into which component(s) of a tuple are placed. Thus, the names used for the attributes in the result of the query are also treated by PSM as local variables of the same type.

Example 15: Let us redo the procedure of Fig. 15 using a for-loop. The code is shown in Fig. 17. Many things have not changed. The declaration of the procedure in lines (1) through (4) of Fig. 17 are the same, as is the declaration

Other Loop Constructs

PSM also allows while- and repeat-loops, which have the expected meaning, as in C. That is, we can create a loop of the form

```
WHILE <condition> DO
    <statement list>
END WHILE;
```

or a loop of the form

```
REPEAT
    <statement list>
UNTIL <condition>
END REPEAT;
```

Incidentally, if we label these loops, or the loop formed by a loop-statement or for-statement, then we can place the label as well after the **END LOOP** or other ender. The advantage of doing so is that it makes clearer where each loop ends, and it allows the PSM compiler to catch some syntactic errors involving the omission of an END.

```
FOR <loop name> AS <cursor name> CURSOR FOR
    <query>
DO
    <statement list>
END FOR;
```

Figure 16: The PSM for-statement

of local variable `movieCount` at line (5).

However, we no longer need to declare a cursor in the declaration portion of the procedure, and we do not need to define the condition **Not_Found**. Lines (6) through (8) initialize the variables, as before. Then, in line (9) we see the for-loop, which also defines the cursor `MovieCursor`. Lines (11) through (13) are the body of the loop. Notice that in lines (12) and (13), we refer to the length retrieved via the cursor by the attribute name `length`, rather than by the local variable name `newLength`, which does not exist in this version of the procedure. Lines (15) and (16) compute the correct values for the output variables, exactly as in the earlier version of this procedure. □

```
CREATE PROCEDURE MeanVar(
     IN s CHAR(15),
     OUT mean REAL,
     OUT variance REAL
)
DECLARE movieCount INTEGER;

BEGIN
     SET mean = 0.0;
     SET variance = 0.0;
     SET movieCount = 0;
     FOR movieLoop AS MovieCursor CURSOR FOR
          SELECT length FROM Movies WHERE studioName = s;
     DO
          SET movieCount = movieCount + 1;
          SET mean = mean + length;
          SET variance = variance + length * length;
     END FOR;
     SET mean = mean/movieCount;
     SET variance = variance/movieCount - mean * mean;
END;
```

Figure 17: Computing the mean and variance of lengths using a for-loop

4.7 Exceptions in PSM

A SQL system indicates error conditions by setting a nonzero sequence of digits in the five-character string `SQLSTATE`. We have seen one example of these codes: `'02000'` for "no tuple found." For another example, `'21000'` indicates that a single-row select has returned more than one row.

PSM allows us to declare a piece of code, called an *exception handler*, that is invoked whenever one of a list of these error codes appears in `SQLSTATE` during the execution of a statement or list of statements. Each exception handler is associated with a block of code, delineated by `BEGIN...END`. The handler appears within this block, and it applies only to statements within the block.

The components of the handler are:

1. A list of exception conditions that invoke the handler when raised.

2. Code to be executed when one of the associated exceptions is raised.

3. An indication of where to go after the handler has finished its work.

The form of a handler declaration is:

`DECLARE` <where to go next> `HANDLER FOR` <condition list>
<statement>

Why Do We Need Names in For-Loops?

Notice that `movieLoop` and `MovieCursor`, although declared at line (9) of Fig. 17, are never used in that procedure. Nonetheless, we have to invent names, both for the for-loop itself and for the cursor over which it iterates. The reason is that the PSM interpreter will translate the for-loop into a conventional loop, much like the code of Fig. 15, and in this code, there is a need for both names.

The choices for "where to go" are:

a) `CONTINUE`, which means that after executing the statement in the handler declaration, we execute the statement after the one that raised the exception.

b) `EXIT`, which means that after executing the handler's statement, control leaves the `BEGIN...END` block in which the handler is declared. The statement after this block is executed next.

c) `UNDO`, which is the same as `EXIT`, except that any changes to the database or local variables that were made by the statements of the block executed so far are undone. That is, the block is a transaction, which is aborted by the exception.

The "condition list" is a comma-separated list of conditions, which are either declared conditions, like `Not_Found` in line (5) of Fig. 15, or expressions of the form `SQLSTATE` and a five-character string.

Example 16: Let us write a PSM function that takes a movie title as argument and returns the year of the movie. If there is no movie of that title or more than one movie of that title, then `NULL` must be returned. The code is shown in Fig. 18.

Lines (2) and (3) declare symbolic conditions; we do not have to make these definitions, and could as well have used the SQL states for which they stand in line (4). Lines (4), (5), and (6) are a block, in which we first declare a handler for the two conditions in which either zero tuples are returned, or more than one tuple is returned. The action of the handler, on line (5), is simply to set the return-value to `NULL`.

Line (6) is the statement that does the work of the function `GetYear`. It is a `SELECT` statement that is expected to return exactly one integer, since that is what the function `GetYear` returns. If there is exactly one movie with title t (the input parameter of the function), then this value will be returned. However, if an exception is raised at line (6), either because there is no movie with title t or several movies with that title, then the handler is invoked, and `NULL` instead

```
1)  CREATE FUNCTION GetYear(t VARCHAR(255)) RETURNS INTEGER

2)  DECLARE Not_Found CONDITION FOR SQLSTATE '02000';
3)  DECLARE Too_Many CONDITION FOR SQLSTATE '21000';

    BEGIN
4)      DECLARE EXIT HANDLER FOR Not_Found, Too_Many
5)          RETURN NULL;
6)      RETURN (SELECT year FROM Movies WHERE title = t);
    END;
```

Figure 18: Handling exceptions in which a single-row select returns other than one tuple

becomes the return-value. Also, since the handler is an EXIT handler, control next passes to the point after the END. Since that point is the end of the function, GetYear returns at that time, with the return-value NULL. □

4.8 Using PSM Functions and Procedures

As we mentioned in Section 4.2, we can call a PSM procedure anywhere SQL statements can appear, e.g., as embedded SQL, from PSM code itself, or from SQL issued to the generic interface. We invoke a procedure by preceding it by the keyword CALL. In addition, a PSM function can be used as part of an expression, e.g., in a WHERE clause. Here is an example of how a function can be used within an expression.

Example 17: Suppose that our schema includes a module with the function GetYear of Fig. 18. Imagine that we are sitting at the generic interface, and we want to enter the fact that Denzel Washington was a star of *Remember the Titans*. However, we forget the year in which that movie was made. As long as there was only one movie of that name, and it is in the Movies relation, we don't have to look it up in a preliminary query. Rather, we can issue to the generic SQL interface the following insertion:

```
INSERT INTO StarsIn(movieTitle, movieYear, starName)
VALUES('Remember the Titans', GetYear('Remember the Titans'),
    'Denzel Washington');
```

Since GetYear returns NULL if there is not a unique movie by the name of *Remember the Titans*, it is possible that this insertion will have NULL in the middle component. □

4.9 Exercises for Section 4

Exercise 4.1: Using our running movie database:

```
Movies(title, year, length, genre, studioName, producerC#)
StarsIn(movieTitle, movieYear, starName)
MovieStar(name, address, gender, birthdate)
MovieExec(name, address, cert#, netWorth)
Studio(name, address, presC#)
```

write PSM procedures or functions to perform the following tasks:

a) Given the name of a movie studio, produce the net worth of its president.

b) Given a name and address, return 1 if the person is a movie star but not an executive, 2 if the person is an executive but not a star, 3 if both, and 4 if neither.

! c) Given a studio name, assign to output parameters the titles of the two longest movies by that studio. Assign NULL to one or both parameters if there is no such movie (e.g., if there is only one movie by a studio, there is no "second-longest").

! d) Given a star name, find the earliest (lowest year) movie of more than 120 minutes length in which they appeared. If there is no such movie, return the year 0.

e) Given an address, find the name of the unique star with that address if there is exactly one, and return NULL if there is none or more than one.

f) Given the name of a star, delete them from MovieStar and delete all their movies from StarsIn and Movies.

Exercise 4.2: Write the following PSM functions or procedures, based on the database schema

```
Product(maker, model, type)
PC(model, speed, ram, hd, price)
Laptop(model, speed, ram, hd, screen, price)
Printer(model, color, type, price)
```

a) Take a price as argument and return the model number of the PC whose price is closest.

b) Take a maker and model as arguments, and return the price of whatever type of product that model is.

! c) Take model, speed, ram, hard-disk, and price information as arguments, and insert this information into the relation PC. However, if there is already a PC with that model number (tell by assuming that violation of a key constraint on insertion will raise an exception with SQLSTATE equal to '23000'), then keep adding 1 to the model number until you find a model number that is not already a PC model number.

! d) Given a price, produce the number of PC's, the number of laptops, and the number of printers selling for more than that price.

Exercise 4.3: Write the following PSM functions or procedures, based on the database schema

```
Classes(class, type, country, numGuns, bore, displacement)
Ships(name, class, launched)
Battles(name, date)
Outcomes(ship, battle, result)
```

a) The firepower of a ship is roughly proportional to the number of guns times the cube of the bore. Given a class, find its firepower.

! b) Given the name of a battle, produce the two countries whose ships were involved in the battle. If there are more or fewer than two countries involved, produce `NULL` for both countries.

c) Take as arguments a new class name, type, country, number of guns, bore, and displacement. Add this information to `Classes` and also add the ship with the class name to `Ships`.

! d) Given a ship name, determine if the ship was in a battle with a date before the ship was launched. If so, set the date of the battle and the date the ship was launched to 0.

! **Exercise 4.4:** In Fig. 15, we used a tricky formula for computing the variance of a sequence of numbers $x_1, x_2, \ldots, x_n$. Recall that the variance is the average square of the deviation of these numbers from their mean. That is, the variance is $\left(\sum_{i=1}^{n}(x_i - \overline{x})^2\right)/n$, where the mean $\overline{x}$ is $\left(\sum_{i=1}^{n} x_i\right)/n$. Prove that the formula for the variance used in Fig. 15, which is

$$\Big(\sum_{i=1}^{n}(x_i)^2\Big)/n - \Big(\big(\sum_{i=1}^{n} x_i\big)/n\Big)^2$$

yields the same value.

5 Using a Call-Level Interface

When using a *call-level interface* (CLI), we write ordinary host-language code, and we use a library of functions that allow us to connect to and access a database, passing SQL statements to that database. The differences between this approach and embedded SQL programming are, in one sense, cosmetic, since the preprocessor replaces embedded SQL by calls to library functions much like the functions in the standard SQL/CLI.

We shall give three examples of call-level interfaces. In this section, we cover the standard SQL/CLI, which is an adaptation of ODBC (Open Database Connectivity). We cover JDBC, which is a collection of classes that support database access from Java programs. Then, we explore PHP, which is a way to embed database access in Web pages described by HTML.

5.1 Introduction to SQL/CLI

A program written in C and using SQL/CLI (hereafter, just CLI) will include the header file `sqlcli.h`, from which it gets a large number of functions, type definitions, structures, and symbolic constants. The program is then able to create and deal with four kinds of records (structs, in C):

1. *Environments.* A record of this type is created by the application (client) program in preparation for one or more connections to the database server.

2. *Connections.* One of these records is created to connect the application program to the database. Each connection exists within some environment.

3. *Statements.* An application program can create one or more statement records. Each holds information about a single SQL statement, including an implied cursor if the statement is a query. At different times, the same CLI statement can represent different SQL statements. Every CLI statement exists within some connection.

4. *Descriptions.* These records hold information about either tuples or parameters. The application program or the database server, as appropriate, sets components of description records to indicate the names and types of attributes and/or their values. Each statement has several of these created implicitly, and the user can create more if needed. In our presentation of CLI, description records will generally be invisible.

Each of these records is represented in the application program by a *handle*, which is a pointer to the record. The header file `sqlcli.h` provides types for the handles of environments, connections, statements, and descriptions: `SQLHENV`, `SQLHDBC`, `SQLHSTMT`, and `SQLHDESC`, respectively, although we may think of them as pointers or integers. We shall use these types and also some other defined types with obvious interpretations, such as `SQL_CHAR` and `SQL_INTEGER`, that are provided in `sqlcli.h`.

We shall not go into detail about how descriptions are set and used. However, (handles for) the other three types of records are created by the use of a function

`SQLAllocHandle(`*hType, hIn, hOut*`)`

Here, the three arguments are:

1. *hType* is the type of handle desired. Use SQL_HANDLE_ENV for a new environment, SQL_HANDLE_DBC for a new connection, or SQL_HANDLE_STMT for a new statement.

2. *hIn* is the handle of the higher-level element in which the newly allocated element lives. This parameter is SQL_NULL_HANDLE if you want an environment; the latter name is a defined constant telling SQLAllocHandle that there is no relevant value here. If you want a connection handle, then *hIn* is the handle of the environment within which the connection will exist, and if you want a statement handle, then *hIn* is the handle of the connection within which the statement will exist.

3. *hOut* is the address of the handle that is created by SQLAllocHandle.

SQLAllocHandle also returns a value of type SQLRETURN (an integer). This value is 0 if no errors occurred, and there are certain nonzero values returned in the case of errors.

Example 18: Let us see how the function worthRanges of Fig. 8, which we used as an example of embedded SQL, would begin in CLI. Recall this function examines all the tuples of MovieExec and breaks their net worths into ranges. The initial steps are shown in Fig. 19.

```
 1)  #include sqlcli.h
 2)  SQLHENV myEnv;
 3)  SQLHDBC myCon;
 4)  SQLHSTMT execStat;
 5)  SQLRETURN errorCode1, errorCode2, errorCode3;

 6)  errorCode1 = SQLAllocHandle(SQL_HANDLE_ENV,
         SQL_NULL_HANDLE, &myEnv);
 7)  if(!errorCode1) {
 8)      errorCode2 = SQLAllocHandle(SQL_HANDLE_DBC,
             myEnv, &myCon);
 9)  if(!errorCode2)
10)      errorCode3 = SQLAllocHandle(SQL_HANDLE_STMT,
             myCon, &execStat); }
```

Figure 19: Declaring and creating an environment, a connection, and a statement

Lines (2) through (4) declare handles for an environment, connection, and statement, respectively; their names are myEnv, myCon, and execStat, respectively. We plan that execStat will represent the SQL statement

```
SELECT netWorth FROM MovieExec;
```

much as did the cursor `execCursor` in Fig. 8, but as yet there is no SQL statement associated with `execStat`. Line (5) declares three variables into which function calls can place their response and indicate an error. A value of 0 indicates no error occurred in the call.

Line (6) calls `SQLAllocHandle`, asking for an environment handle (the first argument), providing a null handle in the second argument (because none is needed when we are requesting an environment handle), and providing the address of `myEnv` as the third argument; the generated handle will be placed there. If line (6) is successful, lines (7) and (8) use the environment handle to get a connection handle in `myCon`. Assuming that call is also successful, lines (9) and (10) get a statement handle for `execStat`. □

5.2 Processing Statements

At the end of Fig. 19, a statement record whose handle is `execStat`, has been created. However, there is as yet no SQL statement with which that record is associated. The process of associating and executing SQL statements with statement handles is analogous to the dynamic SQL described in Section 3.9. There, we associated the text of a SQL statement with what we called a "SQL variable," using `PREPARE`, and then executed it using `EXECUTE`.

The situation in CLI is quite analogous, if we think of the "SQL variable" as a statement handle. There is a function

`SQLPrepare(`*sh, st, sl*`)`

that takes:

1. A statement handle *sh*,
2. A pointer to a SQL statement *st*, and
3. A length *sl* for the character string pointed to by *st*. If we don't know the length, a defined constant `SQL_NTS` tells `SQLPrepare` to figure it out from the string itself. Presumably, the string is a "null-terminated string," and it is sufficient for `SQLPrepare` to scan it until encountering the endmarker `'\0'`.

The effect of this function is to arrange that the statement referred to by the handle *sh* now represents the particular SQL statement *st*.

Another function

`SQLExecute(`*sh*`)`

causes the statement to which handle *sh* refers to be executed. For many forms of SQL statement, such as insertions or deletions, the effect of executing this statement on the database is obvious. Less obvious is what happens when the SQL statement referred to by *sh* is a query. As we shall see in Section 5.3, there is an implicit cursor for this statement that is part of the statement record itself. The statement is in principle executed, so we can imagine that all the answer tuples are sitting somewhere, ready to be accessed. We can fetch tuples one at a time, using the implicit cursor, much as we did with real cursors in Sections 3 and 4.

Example 19: Let us continue with the function `worthRanges` that we began in Fig. 19. The following two function calls associate the query

```
SELECT netWorth FROM MovieExec;
```

with the statement referred to by handle `execStat`:

```
11)  SQLPrepare(execStat, "SELECT netWorth FROM MovieExec",
         SQL_NTS);
12)  SQLExecute(execStat);
```

These lines could appear right after line (10) of Fig. 19. Remember that `SQL_NTS` tells `SQLPrepare` to determine the length of the null-terminated string to which its second argument refers. □

As with dynamic SQL, the prepare and execute steps can be combined into one if we use the function `SQLExecDirect`. An example that combines lines (11) and (12) above is:

```
SQLExecDirect(execStat, "SELECT netWorth FROM MovieExec",
    SQL_NTS);
```

5.3 Fetching Data From a Query Result

The function that corresponds to a `FETCH` command in embedded SQL or PSM is

`SQLFetch(`*sh*`)`

where *sh* is a statement handle. We presume the statement referred to by *sh* has been executed already, or the fetch will cause an error. `SQLFetch`, like all CLI functions, returns a value of type `SQLRETURN` that indicates either success or an error. The return value `SQL_NO_DATA` tells us tuples were left in the query result. As in our previous examples of fetching, this value will be used to get us out of a loop in which we repeatedly fetch new tuples from the result.

However, if we follow the `SQLExecute` of Example 19 by one or more `SQLFetch` calls, where does the tuple appear? The answer is that its components go into one of the description records associated with the statement whose handle appears in the `SQLFetch` call. We can extract the same component at each fetch by binding the component to a host-language variable, before we begin fetching. The function that does this job is:

`SQLBindCol`(*sh, colNo, colType, pVar, varSize, varInfo*)

The meanings of these six arguments are:

1. *sh* is the handle of the statement involved.

2. *colNo* is the number of the component (within the tuple) whose value we obtain.

3. *colType* is a code for the type of the variable into which the value of the component is to be placed. Examples of codes provided by `sqlcli.h` are `SQL_CHAR` for character arrays and strings, and `SQL_INTEGER` for integers.

4. *pVar* is a pointer to the variable into which the value is to be placed.

5. *varSize* is the length in bytes of the value of the variable pointed to by *pVar*.

6. *varInfo* is a pointer to an integer that can be used by `SQLBindCol` to provide additional information about the value produced.

Example 20: Let us redo the entire function `worthRanges` from Fig. 8, using CLI calls instead of embedded SQL. We begin as in Fig. 19, but for the sake of succinctness, we skip all error checking except for the test whether `SQLFetch` indicates that no more tuples are present. The code is shown in Fig. 20.

Line (3) declares the same local variables that the embedded-SQL version of the function uses, and lines (4) through (7) declare additional local variables using the types provided in `sqlcli.h`; these are variables that involve SQL in some way. Lines (4) through (6) are as in Fig. 19. New are the declarations on line (7) of `worth` (which corresponds to the shared variable of that name in Fig. 8) and `worthInfo`, which is required by `SQLBindCol`, but not used.

Lines (8) through (10) allocate the needed handles, as in Fig. 19, and lines (11) and (12) prepare and execute the SQL statement, as discussed in Example 19. In line (13), we see the binding of the first (and only) column of the result of this query to the variable `worth`. The first argument is the handle for the statement involved, and the second argument is the column involved, 1 in this case. The third argument is the type of the column, and the fourth argument is a pointer to the place where the value will be placed: the variable `worth`. The fifth argument is the size of that variable, and the final argument points to `worthInfo`, a place for `SQLBindCol` to put additional information (which we do not use here).

The balance of the function resembles closely lines (11) through (19) of Fig. 8. The while-loop begins at line (14) of Fig. 20. Notice that we fetch a tuple and check that we are not out of tuples, all within the condition of the while-loop, on line (14). If there is a tuple, then in lines (15) through (17) we determine the number of digits the integer (which is bound to `worth`) has and increment the appropriate count. After the loop finishes, i.e., all tuples returned

```
1)  #include sqlcli.h
2)  void worthRanges() {

3)      int i, digits, counts[15];
4)      SQLHENV myEnv;
5)      SQLHDBC myCon;
6)      SQLHSTMT execStat;
7)      SQLINTEGER worth, worthInfo;

8)      SQLAllocHandle(SQL_HANDLE_ENV,
            SQL_NULL_HANDLE, &myEnv);
9)      SQLAllocHandle(SQL_HANDLE_DBC, myEnv, &myCon);
10)     SQLAllocHandle(SQL_HANDLE_STMT, myCon, &execStat);
11)     SQLPrepare(execStat,
            "SELECT netWorth FROM MovieExec", SQL_NTS);
12)     SQLExecute(execStat);
13)     SQLBindCol(execStat, 1, SQL_INTEGER, &worth,
            sizeof(worth), &worthInfo);
14)     while(SQLFetch(execStat) != SQL_NO_DATA) {
15)         digits = 1;
16)         while((worth /= 10) > 0) digits++;
17)         if(digits <= 14) counts[digits]++;
        }
18)     for(i=0; i<15; i++)
19)         printf("digits = %d: number of execs = %d\n",
                i, counts[i]);
    }
```

Figure 20: Grouping executive net worths: CLI version

by the statement execution of line (12) have been examined, the resulting counts are printed out at lines (18) and (19). □

5.4 Passing Parameters to Queries

Embedded SQL gives us the ability to execute a SQL statement, part of which consists of values determined by the current contents of shared variables. There is a similar capability in CLI, but it is rather more complicated. The steps needed are:

1. Use `SQLPrepare` to prepare a statement in which some portions, called *parameters*, are replaced by a question-mark. The ith question-mark represents the ith parameter.

Extracting Components with SQLGetData

An alternative to binding a program variable to an output of a query's result relation is to fetch tuples without any binding and then transfer components to program variables as needed. The function to use is `SQLGetData`, and it takes the same arguments as `SQLBindCol`. However, it only copies data once, and it must be used after each fetch in order to have the same effect as initially binding the column to a variable.

2. Use function `SQLBindParameter` to bind values to the places where the question-marks are found. This function has ten arguments, of which we shall explain only the essentials.

3. Execute the query with these bindings, by calling `SQLExecute`. Note that if we change the values of one or more parameters, we need to call `SQLExecute` again.

The following example will illustrate the process, as well as indicate the important arguments needed by `SQLBindParameter`.

Example 21: Let us reconsider the embedded SQL code of Fig. 6, where we obtained values for two variables `studioName` and `studioAddr` and used them as the components of a tuple, which we inserted into `Studio`. Figure 21 sketches how this process would work in CLI. It assumes that we have a statement handle `myStat` to use for the insertion statement.

```
    /* get values for studioName and studioAddr */

1)  SQLPrepare(myStat,
        "INSERT INTO Studio(name, address) VALUES(?, ?)",
        SQL_NTS);
2)  SQLBindParameter(myStat, 1,..., studioName,...);
3)  SQLBindParameter(myStat, 2,..., studioAddr,...);
4)  SQLExecute(myStat);
```

Figure 21: Inserting a new studio by binding parameters to values

The code begins with steps (not shown) to give `studioName` and `studioAddr` values. Line (1) shows statement `myStat` being prepared to be an insertion statement with two parameters (the question-marks) in the `VALUE` clause. Then, lines (2) and (3) bind the first and second question-marks, to the current contents of `studioName` and `studioAddr`, respectively. Finally, line (4) executes the insertion. If the entire sequence of steps in Fig. 21, including the unseen work to obtain new values for `studioName` and `studioAddr`, are placed in a loop, then each time around the loop, a new tuple, with a new name and address for a studio, is inserted into `Studio`. □

5.5 Exercises for Section 5

Exercise 5.1: Repeat the problems of Exercise 3.1, but write the code in C with CLI calls.

Exercise 5.2: Repeat the problems of Exercise 3.2, but write the code in C with CLI calls.

6 JDBC

Java Database Connectivity, or JDBC, is a facility similar to CLI for allowing Java programs to access SQL databases. The concepts resemble those of CLI, although Java's object-oriented flavor is evident in JDBC.

6.1 Introduction to JDBC

The first steps we must take to use JDBC are:

1. include the line:

   ```
   import java.sql.*;
   ```

   to make the JDBC classes available to your Java program.

2. Load a "driver" for the database system we shall use. The driver we need depends on which DBMS is available to us, but we load the needed driver with the statement:

   ```
   Class.forName(<driver name>);
   ```

   For example, to get the driver for a MySQL database, execute:

   ```
   Class.forName("com.mysql.jdbc.Driver");
   ```

   The effect is that a class called `DriverManager` is available. This class is analogous in many ways to the environment whose handle we get as the first step in using CLI.

3. Establish a connection to the database. A variable of class Connection is created if we apply the method `getConnection` to `DriverManager`.

The Java statement to establish a connection looks like:

```
Connection myCon = DriverManager.getConnection(<URL>,
        <user name>, <password>);
```

That is, the method `getConnection` takes as arguments the URL for the database to which you wish to connect, your user name, and your password. It returns an object of class Connection, which we have chosen to call `myCon`.

Example 22: Each DBMS has its own way of specifying the URL in the `getConnection` method. For instance, if you want to connect to a MySQL database, the form of the URL is

```
jdbc:mysql://<host name>/<database name>
```

□

A JDBC Connection object is quite analogous to a CLI connection, and it serves the same purpose. By applying the appropriate methods to a Connection like `myCon`, we can create statement objects, place SQL statements "in" those objects, bind values to SQL statement parameters, execute the SQL statements, and examine results a tuple at a time.

6.2 Creating Statements in JDBC

There are two methods we can apply to a Connection object in order to create statements:

1. `createStatement()` returns a Statement object. This object has no associated SQL statement yet, so method `createStatement()` may be thought of as analogous to the CLI call to `SQLAllocHandle` that takes a connection handle and returns a statement handle.

2. `prepareStatement(`Q`)`, where Q is a SQL query passed as a string argument, returns a PreparedStatement object. Thus, we may draw an analogy between executing `prepareStatement(`Q`)` in JDBC with the two CLI steps in which we get a statement handle with `SQLAllocHandle` and then apply `SQLPrepare` to that handle and the query Q.

There are four different methods that execute SQL statements. Like the methods above, they differ in whether or not they take a SQL statement as an argument. However, these methods also distinguish between SQL statements that are queries and other statements, which are collectively called "updates." Note that the SQL `UPDATE` statement is only one small example of what JDBC terms an "update." The latter include all modification statements, such as inserts, and all schema-related statements such as `CREATE TABLE`. The four "execute" methods are:

a) `executeQuery(`Q`)` takes a statement Q, which must be a query, and is applied to a Statement object. This method returns a ResultSet object, which is the set (bag, to be precise) of tuples produced by the query Q. We shall see how to access these tuples in Section 6.3.

b) `executeQuery()` is applied to a PreparedStatement object. Since a prepared statement already has an associated query, there is no argument. This method also returns a ResultSet object.

c) `executeUpdate(`U`)` takes a nonquery statement U and, when applied to a Statement object, executes U. The effect is felt on the database only; no ResultSet object is returned.

d) `executeUpdate()`, with no argument, is applied to a PreparedStatement object. In that case, the SQL statement associated with the prepared statement is executed. This SQL statement must not be a query, of course.

Example 23 : Suppose we have a Connection object `myCon`, and we wish to execute the query

```
SELECT netWorth FROM MovieExec;
```

One way to do so is to create a Statement object `execStat`, and then use it to execute the query directly.

```
Statement execStat = myCon.createStatement();
ResultSet worths = execStat.executeQuery(
    "SELECT netWorth FROM MovieExec");
```

The result of the query is a ResultSet object, which we have named `worths`. We'll see in Section 6.3 how to extract the tuples from `worths` and process them.

An alternative is to prepare the query immediately and later execute it. This approach would be preferable should we want to execute the same query repeatedly. Then, it makes sense to prepare it once and execute it many times, rather than having the DBMS prepare the same query many times. The JDBC steps needed to follow this approach are:

```
PreparedStatement execStat = myCon.prepareStatement(
    "SELECT netWorth FROM MovieExec");
ResultSet worths = execStat.executeQuery();
```

The result of executing the query is again a ResultSet object, which we have called `worths`. □

Example 24: If we want to execute a parameterless nonquery, we can perform analogous steps in both styles. There is no result set, however. For instance, suppose we want to insert into `StarsIn` the fact that Denzel Washington starred in *Remember the Titans* in the year 2000. We may create and use a statement `starStat` in either of the following ways:

```
Statement starStat = myCon.createStatement();
starStat.executeUpdate("INSERT INTO StarsIn VALUES(" +
    "'Remember the Titans', 2000, 'Denzel Washington')");
```

or

```
PreparedStatement starStat = myCon.prepareStatement(
    "INSERT INTO StarsIn VALUES('Remember the Titans'," +
    "2000, 'Denzel Washington')");
starStat.executeUpdate();
```

Notice that each of these sequences of Java statements takes advantage of the fact that + is the Java operator that concatenates strings. Thus, we are able to extend SQL statements over several lines of Java, as needed. □

6.3 Cursor Operations in JDBC

When we execute a query and obtain a result-set object, we may, in effect, run a cursor through the tuples of the result set. To do so, the `ResultSet` class provides the following useful methods:

1. `next()`, when applied to a ResultSet object, causes an implicit cursor to move to the next tuple (to the first tuple the first time it is applied). This method returns `FALSE` if there is no next tuple.

2. `getString(`*i*`)`, `getInt(`*i*`)`, `getFloat(`*i*`)`, and analogous methods for the other types that SQL values can take, each return the *i*th component of the tuple currently indicated by the cursor. The method appropriate to the type of the *i*th component must be used.

Example 25: Having obtained the result set `worths` as in Example 23, we may access its tuples one at a time. Recall that these tuples have only one component, of type integer. The form of the loop is:

```
while(worths.next()) {
    int worth = worths.getInt(1);
    /* process this net worth */
};
```

□

6.4 Parameter Passing

As in CLI, we can use a question-mark in place of a portion of a query, and then bind values to those *parameters.* To do so in JDBC, we need to create a prepared statement, and we need to apply to that PreparedStatement object methods such as `setString(`i`, `v`)` or `setInt(`i`, `v`)` that bind the value v, which must be of the appropriate type for the method, to the ith parameter in the query.

Example 26: Let us mimic the CLI code in Example 21, where we prepared a statement to insert a new studio into relation `Studio`, with parameters for the name and address of that studio. The Java code to prepare this statement, set its parameters, and execute it is shown in Fig. 22. We continue to assume that connection object `myCon` is available to us.

```
1)  PreparedStatement studioStat = myCon.prepareStatement(
2)      "INSERT INTO Studio(name, address) VALUES(?, ?)");
    /* get values for variables studioName and studioAddr
       from the user */
3)  studioStat.setString(1, studioName);
4)  studioStat.setString(2, studioAddr);
5)  studioStat.executeUpdate();
```

Figure 22: Setting and using parameters in JDBC

In lines (1) and (2), we create and prepare the insertion statement. It has parameters for each of the values to be inserted. After line (2), we could begin a loop in which we repeatedly ask the user for a studio name and address, and place these strings in the variables `studioName` and `studioAddr`. This assignment is not shown, but represented by a comment. Lines (3) and (4) set the first and second parameters to the strings that are the current values of `studioName` and `studioAddr`, respectively. Finally, at line (5), we execute the insertion statement with the current values of its parameters. After line (5), we could go around the loop again, beginning with the steps represented by the comment. □

6.5 Exercises for Section 6

Exercise 6.1: Repeat Exercise 3.1, but write the code in Java using JDBC.

Exercise 6.2: Repeat Exercise 3.2, but write the code in Java using JDBC.

7 PHP

PHP is a scripting language for helping to create HTML Web pages. It provides support for database operations through an available library, much as JDBC

> **What Does PHP Stand For?**
>
> Originally, PHP was an acronym for "Personal Home Page." More recently, it is said to be the recursive acronym "PHP: Hypertext Preprocessor" in the spirit of other recursive acronyms such as GNU (= "GNU is Not Unix").

does. In this section we shall give a brief overview of PHP and show how database operations are performed in this language.

7.1 PHP Basics

All PHP code is intended to exist inside HTML text. A browser will recognize that text is PHP code by placing it inside a special tag, which looks like:

```
<?php
    PHP code goes here
?>
```

Many aspects of PHP, such as assignment statements, branches, and loops, will be familiar to the C or Java programmer, and we shall not cover them explicitly. However, there are some interesting features of PHP of which we should be aware.

Variables

Variables are untyped and need not be declared. All variable names begin with $.

Often, a variable will be declared to be a member of a "class," in which case certain *functions* (analogous to methods in Java) may be applied to that variable. The function-application operator is `->`, comparable to the dot in Java or C++.

Strings

String values in PHP can be surrounded by either single or double quotes, but there is an important difference. Strings surrounded by single quotes are treated literally, just like SQL strings. However, when a string has double quotes around it, any variable names within the string are replaced by their values.

Example 27: In the following code:

```
$foo = 'bar';
$x = 'Step up to the $foo';
```

the value of $x is `Step up to the $foo`. However, if the following code is executed instead:

```
$foo = "bar";
$x = "Step up to the $foo";
```

the value of $x is `Step up to the bar`. It doesn't matter whether `bar` has single or double quotes, since it contains no dollar-signs and therefore no variables. However, the variable `$foo` is replaced only when surrounded by double quotes, as in the second example. □

Concatenation of strings is denoted by a dot. Thus,

```
$y = "$foo" . 'bar';
```

gives $y the value `barbar`.

7.2 Arrays

PHP has ordinary arrays (called *numeric*), which are indexed $0, 1, \ldots$. It also has arrays that are really mappings, called *associative arrays*. The indexes (*keys*) of an associative array can be any strings, and the array associates a single value with each key. Both kinds of arrays use the conventional square brackets for indexing, but for associative arrays, an array element is represented by:

<key> => <value>

Example 28: The following line:

```
$a = array(30,20,10,0);
```

sets `$a` to be a numeric array of length four, with `$a[0]` equal to 30, `$a[1]` equal to 20, and so on. □

Example 29: The following line:

```
$seasons = array('spring' => 'warm', 'summer' => 'hot',
                 'fall' => 'warm', 'winter' => 'cold');
```

makes `$seasons` be an array of length four, but it is an associative array. For instance, `$seasons['summer']` has the value `'hot'`. □

7.3 The PEAR DB Library

PHP has a collection of libraries called PEAR (PHP Extension and Application Repository). One of these libraries, DB, has generic functions that are analogous to the methods of JDBC. We tell the function `DB::connect` which vendor's DBMS we wish to access, but none of the other functions of DB need to know about which DBMS we are using. Note that the double colon in `DB::connect` is PHP's way of saying "the function `connect` in the DB library." We make the DB library available to our PHP program with the statement:

```
include(DB.php);
```

7.4 Creating a Database Connection Using DB

The form of an invocation of the `connect` function is:

```
$myCon = DB::connect(<vendor>://<user name>:<password>
                  <host name>/<database name>);
```

The components of this call are like those in the analogous JDBC statement that creates a connection (see Section 6.1). The one exception is the vendor, which is a code used by the DB library. For example, `mysqli` is the code for recent versions of the MySQL database.

After executing this statement, the variable `$myCon` is a connection. Like all PHP variables, `$myCon` can change its type. But as long as it is a connection, we may apply to it a number of useful functions that enable us to manipulate the database to which the connection was made. For example, we can disconnect from the database by

```
$myCon->disconnect();
```

Remember that `->` is the PHP way of applying a function to an "object."

7.5 Executing SQL Statements

All SQL statements are referred to as "queries" and are executed by the function `query`, which takes the statement as an argument and is applied to the connection variable.

Example 30: Let us duplicate the insertion statement of Example 24, where we inserted Denzel Washington and *Remember the Titans* into the `StarsIn` table. Assuming that `$myCon` has connected to our movie database, We can simply say:

```
$result = $myCon->query("INSERT INTO StarsIn VALUES(" .
    "'Denzel Washington', 2000, 'Remember the Titans')");
```

Note that the dot concatenates the two strings that form the query. We only broke the query into two strings because it was necessary to break it over two lines.

The variable `$result` will hold an error code if the insert-statement failed to execute. If the "query" were really a SQL query, then `$result` is a cursor to the tuples of the result (see Section 7.6). □

PHP allows SQL to have parameters, denoted by question-marks, as we shall discuss in Section 7.7. However, the ability to expand variables in doubly quoted strings gives us another easy way to execute SQL statements that depend on user input. In particular, since PHP is used within Web pages, there are built-in ways to exploit HTML's capabilities.

We often get information from a user of a Web page by showing them a form and having their answers "posted." PHP provides an associative array called `$_POST` with all the information provided by the user. Its keys are the names of the form elements, and the associated values are what the user has entered into the form.

Example 31: Suppose we ask the user to fill out a form whose elements are `title`, `year`, and `starName`. These three values will form a tuple that we may insert into the table `StarsIn`. The statement:

```
$result = $myCon->query("INSERT INTO StarsIn VALUES(
    $_POST['title'], $_POST['year'], $_POST['starName'])");
```

will obtain the posted values for these three form elements. Since the query argument is a double-quoted string, PHP evaluates terms like `$_POST['title']` and replaces them by their values. □

7.6 Cursor Operations in PHP

When the `query` function gets a true query as argument, it returns a result object, that is, a list of tuples. Each tuple is a numeric array, indexed by integers starting at 0. The essential function that we can apply to a result object is `fetchRow()`, which returns the next row, or 0 (false) if there is no next row.

```
$worths = $myCon->query("SELECT netWorth FROM MovieExec");
while ($tuple = $worths->fetchRow()) {
    $worth = $tuple[0];
        // process this value of $worth
}
```

Figure 23: Finding and processing net worths in PHP

Example 32: In Fig. 23 is PHP code that is the equivalent of the JDBC in Examples 23 and 25. It assumes that connection `$myCon` is available, as before.

Line (1) passes the query to the connection `$myCon`, and the result object is assigned to the variable `$worths`. We then enter a loop, in which we repeatedly get a tuple from the result and assign this tuple to the variable `$tuple`, which technically becomes an array of length 1, with only a component for the column `netWorth`. As in C, the value returned by `fetchRow()` becomes the value of the condition in the while-statement. Thus, if no tuple is found, this value, 0, terminates the loop. At line (3), the value of the tuple's first (and only) component is extracted and assigned to the variable `$worth`. We do not show the processing of this value. □

7.7 Dynamic SQL in PHP

As in JDBC, PHP allows a SQL query to contain question-marks. These question-marks are placeholders for values that can be filled in later, during the execution of the statement. The process of doing so is as follows.

We may apply `prepare` and `execute` functions to a connection; these functions are analogous to similarly named functions discussed in Section 3.9 and elsewhere. Function `prepare` takes a SQL statement as argument and returns a prepared version of that statement. Function `execute` takes two arguments: the prepared statement and an array of values to substitute for the question-marks in the statement. If there is only one question-mark, a simple variable, rather than an array, suffices.

Example 33: Let us again look at the problem of Example 26, where we prepared to insert many name-address pairs into relation `Studio`. To begin, we prepare the query, with parameters, by:

```
$prepQuery = $myCon->prepare("INSERT INTO Studio(name, " .
                    "address) VALUES(?,?)");
```

Now, `$prepQuery` is a "prepared query." We can use it as an argument to `execute` along with an array of two values, a studio name and address. For example, we could perform the following statements:

```
$args = array('MGM', 'Los Angeles');
$result = $myCon->execute($prepQuery, $args);
```

The advantage of this arrangement is the same as for all implementations of dynamic SQL. If we insert many different tuples this way, we only have to prepare the insertion statement once and can execute it many times. □

7.8 Exercises for Section 7

Exercise 7.1: Repeat Exercise 3.1, but write the code using PHP.

Exercise 7.2: Repeat Exercise 3.2, but write the code using PHP.

! **Exercise 7.3:** In Example 31 we exploited the feature of PHP that strings in double-quotes have variables expanded. How essential is this feature? Could we have done something analogous in JDBC? If so, how?

8 Summary

✦ *Three-Tier Architectures*: Large database installations that support large-scale user interactions over the Web commonly use three tiers of processes: web servers, application servers, and database servers. There can be many processes active at each tier, and these processes can be at one processor or distributed over many processors.

✦ *Client-Server Systems in the SQL Standard*: The standard talks of SQL clients connecting to SQL servers, creating a connection (link between the two processes) and a session (sequence of operations). The code executed during the session comes from a module, and the execution of the module is called a SQL agent.

✦ *The Database Environment*: An installation using a SQL DBMS creates a SQL environment. Within the environment, database elements such as relations are grouped into (database) schemas, catalogs, and clusters. A catalog is a collection of schemas, and a cluster is the largest collection of elements that one user may see.

✦ *Impedance Mismatch*: The data model of SQL is quite different from the data models of conventional host languages. Thus, information passes between SQL and the host language through shared variables that can represent components of tuples in the SQL portion of the program.

✦ *Embedded SQL*: Instead of using a generic query interface to express SQL queries and modifications, it is often more effective to write programs that embed SQL queries in a conventional host language. A preprocessor converts the embedded SQL statements into suitable function calls of the host language.

✦ *Cursors*: A cursor is a SQL variable that indicates one of the tuples of a relation. Connection between the host language and SQL is facilitated by having the cursor range over each tuple of the relation, while the components of the current tuple are retrieved into shared variables and processed using the host language.

- ✦ *Dynamic SQL*: Instead of embedding particular SQL statements in a host-language program, the host program may create character strings that are interpreted by the SQL system as SQL statements and executed.

- ✦ *Persistent Stored Modules*: We may create collections of procedures and functions as part of a database schema. These are written in a special language that has all the familiar control primitives, as well as SQL statements.

- *The Call-Level Interface*: There is a standard library of functions, called SQL/CLI or ODBC, that can be linked into any C program. These functions give capabilities similar to embedded SQL, but without the need for a preprocessor.

- ✦ *JDBC*: Java Database Connectivity is a collection of Java classes analogous to CLI for connecting Java programs to a database.

- ✦ *PHP*: Another popular system for implementing a call-level interface is PHP. This language is found embedded in HTML pages and enables these pages to interact with a database.

9 References

The PSM standard is [4], and [5] is a comprehensive book on the subject. Oracle's version of PSM is called PL/SQL; a summary can be found in [2]. SQL Server has a version called Transact-SQL [6]. IBM's version is SQL PL [1].

[3] is a popular reference on JDBC. [7] is one on PHP, which was originally developed by one of the book's authors, R. Lerdorf.

1. D. Bradstock et al., *DB2 SQL Procedure Language for Linux, Unix, and Windows*, IBM Press, 2005.

2. Y.-M. Chang et al., "Using Oracle PL/SQL"
   `http://infolab.stanford.edu/~ullman/fcdb/oracle/or-plsql.html`

3. M. Fisher, J. Ellis, and J. Bruce, *JDBC API Tutorial and Reference*, Prentice-Hall, Upper Saddle River, NJ, 2003.

4. ISO/IEC Report 9075-4, 2003.

5. J. Melton, *Understanding SQL's Stored Procedures: A Complete Guide to SQL/PSM*, Morgan-Kaufmann, San Francisco, 1998.

6. Microsoft Corp., "Transact-SQL Reference"
   `http://msdn2.microsoft.com/en-us/library/ms189826.aspx`

7. K. Tatroe, R. Lerdorf, and P. MacIntyre, *Programming PHP*, O'Reilly Media, Cambridge, MA, 2006.

References

Advanced Topics in Relational Databases

This chapter introduces additional topics that are of interest to the database programmer. We begin with a section on the SQL standard for authorization of access to database elements. Next, we see the SQL extension that allows for recursive programming in SQL — queries that use their own results. Then, we look at the object-relational model, and how it is implemented in the SQL standard.

The remainder of the chapter concerns "OLAP," or on-line analytic processing. OLAP refers to complex queries of a nature that causes them to take significant time to execute. Because they are so expensive, some special technology has developed to handle them efficiently. One important direction is an implementation of relations, called the "data cube," that is rather different from the conventional bag-of-tuples approach of SQL.

1 Security and User Authorization in SQL

SQL postulates the existence of *authorization ID's*, which are essentially user names. SQL also has a special authorization ID called `PUBLIC`, which includes any user. Authorization ID's may be granted privileges, much as they would be in the file system environment maintained by an operating system. For example, a UNIX system generally controls three kinds of privileges: read, write, and execute. That list of privileges makes sense, because the protected objects of a UNIX system are files, and these three operations characterize well the things one typically does with files. However, databases are much more complex than file systems, and the kinds of privileges used in SQL are correspondingly more complex.

In this section, we shall first learn what privileges SQL allows on database elements. We shall then see how privileges may be acquired by users (by authorization ID's, that is). Finally, we shall see how privileges may be taken away.

1.1 Privileges

SQL defines nine types of privileges: SELECT, INSERT, DELETE, UPDATE, REFERENCES, USAGE, TRIGGER, EXECUTE, and UNDER. The first four of these apply to a relation, which may be either a base table or a view. As their names imply, they give the holder of the privilege the right to query (select from) the relation, insert into the relation, delete from the relation, and update tuples of the relation, respectively.

A SQL statement cannot be executed without the privileges appropriate to that statement; e.g., a select-from-where statement requires the SELECT privilege on every table it accesses. We shall see how the module can get those privileges shortly. SELECT, INSERT, and UPDATE may also have an associated list of attributes, for instance, SELECT(name, addr). If so, then only those attributes may be seen in a selection, specified in an insertion, or changed in an update, respectively. Note that, when granted, privileges such as these will be associated with a particular relation, so it will be clear at that time to what relation attributes name and addr belong.

The REFERENCES privilege on a relation is the right to refer to that relation in an integrity constraint. These constraints may take many forms, such as assertions, attribute- or tuple-based checks, or referential integrity constraints. The REFERENCES privilege may also have an attached list of attributes, in which case only those attributes may be referenced in a constraint. A constraint cannot be created unless the owner of the schema in which the constraint appears has the REFERENCES privilege on all data involved in the constraint.

USAGE is a privilege that applies to several kinds of schema elements other than relations and assertions: it is the right to use that element in one's own declarations. The TRIGGER privilege on a relation is the right to define triggers on that relation. EXECUTE is the right to execute a piece of code, such as a PSM procedure or function. Finally, UNDER is the right to create subtypes of a given type. The matter of types appears in Section 4.

Example 1: Let us consider what privileges are needed to execute the insertion statement of Fig. 1. First, it is an insertion into the relation Studio, so we require an INSERT privilege on Studio. However, since the insertion specifies only the component for attribute name, it is acceptable to have either the privilege INSERT or the privilege INSERT(name) on relation Studio. The latter privilege allows us to insert Studio tuples that specify only the name component and leave other components to take their default value or NULL, which is what Fig. 1 does.

However, notice that the insertion statement of Fig. 1 involves two subqueries, starting at lines (2) and (5). To carry out these selections we require

Triggers and Privileges

It is a bit subtle how privileges are handled for triggers. First, if you have the TRIGGER privilege for a relation, you can attempt to create any trigger you like on that relation. However, since the condition and action portions of the trigger are likely to query and/or modify portions of the database, the trigger creator must have the necessary privileges for those actions. When someone performs an activity that awakens the trigger, they do not need the privileges that the trigger condition and action require; the trigger is executed under the privileges of its creator.

```
INSERT INTO Studio(name)
     SELECT DISTINCT studioName
     FROM Movies
     WHERE studioName NOT IN
          (SELECT name
           FROM Studio);
```

Figure 1: Adding new studios

the privileges needed for the subqueries. Thus, we need the `SELECT` privilege on both relations involved in `FROM` clauses: `Movies` and `Studio`. Note that just because we have the `INSERT` privilege on `Studio` doesn't mean we have the `SELECT` privilege on `Studio`, or vice versa. Since it is only particular attributes of `Movies` and `Studio` that get selected, it is sufficient to have the privilege `SELECT(studioName)` on `Movies` and the privilege `SELECT(name)` on `Studio`, or privileges that include these attributes within a list of attributes. □

1.2 Creating Privileges

There are two aspects to the awarding of privileges: how they are created initially, and how they are passed from user to user. We shall discuss initialization here and the transmission of privileges in Section 1.4.

First, SQL elements such as schemas or modules have an owner. The owner of something has all privileges associated with that thing. There are three points at which ownership is established in SQL.

1. When a schema is created, it and all the tables and other schema elements in it are owned by the user who created it. This user thus has all possible privileges on elements of the schema.

2. When a session is initiated by a `CONNECT` statement, there is an opportunity to indicate the user with an `AUTHORIZATION` clause. For instance,

the connection statement

```
CONNECT TO Starfleet-sql-server AS conn1
    AUTHORIZATION kirk;
```

would create a connection called `conn1` to a database server whose name is `Starfleet-sql-server`, on behalf of user `kirk`. Presumably, the SQL implementation would verify that the user name is valid, for example by asking for a password. It is also possible to include the password in the `AUTHORIZATION` clause. That approach is somewhat insecure, since passwords are then visible to someone looking over Kirk's shoulder.

3. When a module is created, there is an option to give it an owner by using an `AUTHORIZATION` clause. For instance, a clause

```
AUTHORIZATION picard;
```

in a module-creation statement would make user `picard` the owner of the module. It is also acceptable to specify no owner for a module, in which case the module is publicly executable, but the privileges necessary for executing any operations in the module must come from some other source, such as the user associated with the connection and session during which the module is executed.

1.3 The Privilege-Checking Process

As we saw above, each module, schema, and session has an associated user; in SQL terms, there is an associated authorization ID for each. Any SQL operation has two parties:

1. The database elements upon which the operation is performed and

2. The agent that causes the operation.

The privileges available to the agent derive from a particular authorization ID called the *current authorization ID.* That ID is either

a) The module authorization ID, if the module that the agent is executing has an authorization ID, or

b) The session authorization ID if not.

We may execute the SQL operation only if the current authorization ID possesses all the privileges needed to carry out the operation on the database elements involved.

Example 2: To see the mechanics of checking privileges, let us reconsider Example 1. We might suppose that the referenced tables — `Movies` and `Studio` — are part of a schema called `MovieSchema`, which was created by and is owned by user `janeway`. At this point, user `janeway` has all privileges on these tables and any other elements of the schema `MovieSchema`. She may choose to grant some privileges to others by the mechanism to be described in Section 1.4, but let us assume none have been granted yet. There are several ways that the insertion of Example 1 can be executed.

1. The insertion could be executed as part of a module created by user `janeway` and containing an `AUTHORIZATION janeway` clause. The module authorization ID, if there is one, always becomes the current authorization ID. Then, the module and its SQL insertion statement have exactly the same privileges user `janeway` has, which includes all privileges on the tables `Movies` and `Studio`.

2. The insertion could be part of a module that has no owner. User `janeway` opens a connection with an `AUTHORIZATION janeway` clause in the `CONNECT` statement. Now, `janeway` is again the current authorization ID, so the insertion statement has all the privileges needed.

3. User `janeway` grants all privileges on tables `Movies` and `Studio` to user `archer`, or perhaps to the special user `PUBLIC`, which stands for "all users." Suppose the insertion statement is in a module with the clause

    ```
    AUTHORIZATION archer
    ```

    Since the current authorization ID is now `archer`, and this user has the needed privileges, the insertion is again permitted.

4. As in (3), suppose user `janeway` has given user `archer` the needed privileges. Also, suppose the insertion statement is in a module without an owner; it is executed in a session whose authorization ID was set by an `AUTHORIZATION archer` clause. The current authorization ID is thus `archer`, and that ID has the needed privileges.

□

There are several principles that are illustrated by Example 2. We shall summarize them below.

- The needed privileges are always available if the data is owned by the same user as the user whose ID is the current authorization ID. Scenarios (1) and (2) above illustrate this point.

- The needed privileges are available if the user whose ID is the current authorization ID has been granted those privileges by the owner of the data, or if the privileges have been granted to user `PUBLIC`. Scenarios (3) and (4) illustrate this point.

- Executing a module owned by the owner of the data, or by someone who has been granted privileges on the data, makes the needed privileges available. Of course, one needs the EXECUTE privilege on the module itself. Scenarios (1) and (3) illustrate this point.

- Executing a publicly available module during a session whose authorization ID is that of a user with the needed privileges is another way to execute the operation legally. Scenarios (2) and (4) illustrate this point.

1.4 Granting Privileges

So far, the only way we have seen to have privileges on a database element is to be the creator and owner of that element. SQL provides a GRANT statement to allow one user to give a privilege to another. The first user retains the privilege granted, as well; thus GRANT can be thought of as "copy a privilege."

There is one important difference between granting privileges and copying. Each privilege has an associated *grant option.* That is, one user may have a privilege like SELECT on table Movies "with grant option," while a second user may have the same privilege, but without the grant option. Then the first user may grant the privilege SELECT on Movies to a third user, and moreover that grant may be with or without the grant option. However, the second user, who does not have the grant option, may not grant the privilege SELECT on Movies to anyone else. If the third user got the privilege with the grant option, then that user may grant the privilege to a fourth user, again with or without the grant option, and so on.

A *grant statement* has the form:

GRANT <privilege list> ON <database element> TO <user list>

possibly followed by WITH GRANT OPTION.

The database element is typically a relation, either a base table or a view. If it is another kind of element, the name of the element is preceded by the type of that element, e.g., ASSERTION. The privilege list is a list of one or more privileges, e.g., SELECT or INSERT(name). Optionally, the keywords ALL PRIVILEGES may appear here, as a shorthand for all the privileges that the grantor may legally grant on the database element in question.

In order to execute this grant statement legally, the user executing it must possess the privileges granted, and these privileges must be held with the grant option. However, the grantor may hold a more general privilege (with the grant option) than the privilege granted. For instance, the privilege INSERT(name) on table Studio might be granted, while the grantor holds the more general privilege INSERT on Studio, with grant option.

Example 3: User janeway, who is the owner of the MovieSchema schema that contains tables

```
Movies(title, year, length, genre, studioName, producerC#)
Studio(name, address, presC#)
```

grants the INSERT and SELECT privileges on table Studio and privilege SELECT on Movies to users kirk and picard. Moreover, she includes the grant option with these privileges. The grant statements are:

```
GRANT SELECT, INSERT ON Studio TO kirk, picard
    WITH GRANT OPTION;
GRANT SELECT ON Movies TO kirk, picard
    WITH GRANT OPTION;
```

Now, picard grants to user sisko the same privileges, but without the grant option. The statements executed by picard are:

```
GRANT SELECT, INSERT ON Studio TO sisko;
GRANT SELECT ON Movies TO sisko;
```

Also, kirk grants to sisko the minimal privileges needed for the insertion of Fig. 1, namely SELECT and INSERT(name) on Studio and SELECT on Movies. The statements are:

```
GRANT SELECT, INSERT(name) ON Studio TO sisko;
GRANT SELECT ON Movies TO sisko;
```

Note that sisko has received the SELECT privilege on Movies and Studio from two different users. He has also received the INSERT(name) privilege on Studio twice: directly from kirk and via the generalized privilege INSERT from picard. □

1.5 Grant Diagrams

Because of the complex web of grants and overlapping privileges that may result from a sequence of grants, it is useful to represent grants by a graph called a *grant diagram.* A SQL system maintains a representation of this diagram to keep track of both privileges and their origins (in case a privilege is revoked; see Section 1.6).

The nodes of a grant diagram correspond to a user and a privilege. Note that the ability to do something (e.g., SELECT on relation R) with the grant option and the same ability without the grant option are different privileges. These two different privileges, even if they belong to the same user, must be represented by two different nodes. Likewise, a user may hold two privileges, one of which is strictly more general than the other (e.g., SELECT on R and SELECT on $R(A)$. These two privileges are also represented by two different nodes.

If user U grants privilege P to user V, and this grant was based on the fact that U holds privilege Q (Q could be P with the grant option, or it could be some generalization of P, again with the grant option), then we draw an arc from the node for U/Q to the node for V/P. As we shall see, privileges may be lost when arcs of this graph are deleted. That is why we use separate nodes for a pair of privileges, one of which includes the other, such as a privilege with and without the grant option. If the more powerful privilege is lost, the less powerful one might still be retained.

Example 4: Figure 2 shows the grant diagram that results from the sequence of grant statements of Example 3. We use the convention that a * after a user-privilege combination indicates that the privilege includes the grant option. Also, ** after a user-privilege combination indicates that the privilege derives from ownership of the database element in question and was not due to a grant of the privilege from elsewhere. This distinction will prove important when we discuss revoking privileges in Section 1.6. A doubly starred privilege automatically includes the grant option. □

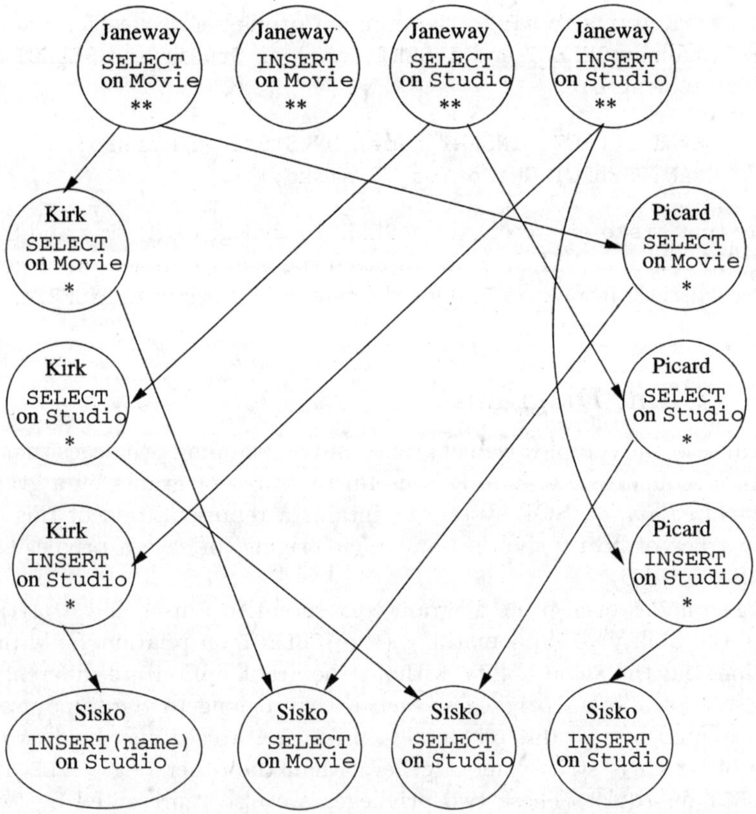

Figure 2: A grant diagram

1.6 Revoking Privileges

A granted privilege can be revoked at any time. The revoking of privileges may be required to *cascade*, in the sense that revoking a privilege with the grant option that has been passed on to other users may require those privileges to be revoked too. The simple form of a *revoke statement* begins:

REVOKE <privilege list> ON <database element> FROM <user list>

The statement ends with one of the following:

1. CASCADE. If chosen, then when the specified privileges are revoked, we also revoke any privileges that were granted *only* because of the revoked privileges. More precisely, if user U has revoked privilege P from user V, based on privilege Q belonging to U, then we delete the arc in the grant diagram from U/Q to V/P. Now, any node that is not accessible from some ownership node (doubly starred node) is also deleted.

2. RESTRICT. In this case, the revoke statement cannot be executed if the cascading rule described in the previous item would result in the revoking of any privileges due to the revoked privileges having been passed on to others.

It is permissible to replace REVOKE by REVOKE GRANT OPTION FOR, in which case the core privileges themselves remain, but the option to grant them to others is removed. We may have to modify a node, redirect arcs, or create a new node to reflect the changes for the affected users. This form of REVOKE also must be followed by either CASCADE or RESTRICT.

Example 5: Continuing with Example 3, suppose that janeway revokes the privileges she granted to picard with the statements:

```
REVOKE SELECT, INSERT ON Studio FROM picard CASCADE;
REVOKE SELECT ON Movies FROM picard CASCADE;
```

We delete the arcs of Fig. 2 from these janeway privileges to the corresponding picard privileges. Since CASCADE was stipulated, we also have to see if there are any privileges that are not reachable in the graph from a doubly starred (ownership-based) privilege. Examining Fig. 2, we see that picard's privileges are no longer reachable from a doubly starred node (they might have been, had there been another path to a picard node). Also, sisko's privilege to INSERT into Studio is no longer reachable. We thus delete not only picard's privileges from the grant diagram, but we delete sisko's INSERT privilege.

Note that we do not delete sisko's SELECT privileges on Movies and Studio or his INSERT(name) privilege on Studio, because these are all reachable from janeway's ownership-based privileges via kirk's privileges. The resulting grant diagram is shown in Fig. 3. □

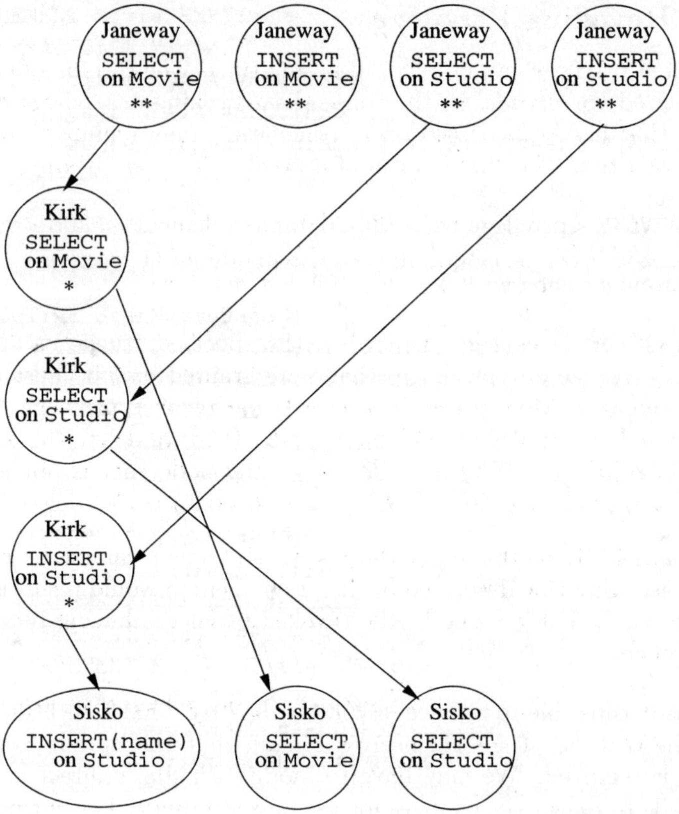

Figure 3: Grant diagram after revocation of picard's privileges

Example 6: There are a few subtleties that we shall illustrate with abstract examples. First, when we revoke a general privilege p, we do not also revoke a privilege that is a special case of p. For instance, consider the following sequence of steps, whereby user U, the owner of relation R, grants the INSERT privilege on relation R to user V, and also grants the INSERT(A) privilege on the same relation.

Step	By	Action
1	U	GRANT INSERT ON R TO V
2	U	GRANT INSERT(A) ON R TO V
3	U	REVOKE INSERT ON R FROM V RESTRICT

When U revokes INSERT from V, the INSERT(A) privilege remains. The grant diagrams after steps (2) and (3) are shown in Fig. 4.

Notice that after step (2) there are two separate nodes for the two similar but distinct privileges that user V has. Also observe that the RESTRICT option in step (3) does not prevent the revocation, because V had not granted the

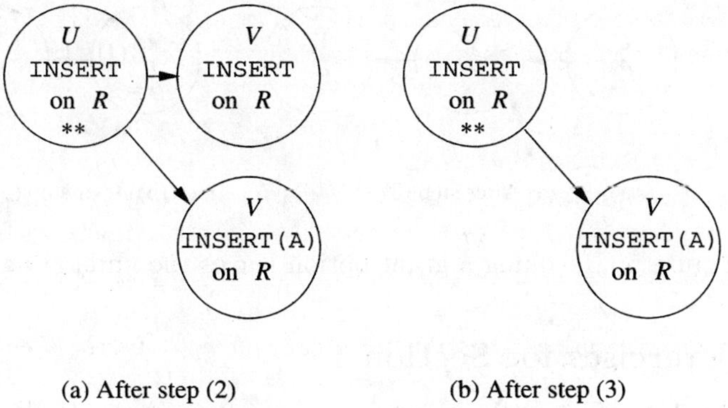

Figure 4: Revoking a general privilege leaves a more specific privilege

option to any other user. In fact, V could not have granted either privilege, because V obtained them without grant option. □

Example 7: Now, let us consider a similar example where U grants V a privilege $p*$ that includes the grant option and then revokes only the grant option. Assume the grant by U was based on its privilege $q*$. In this case, we must replace the arc from the $U/q*$ node to $V/p*$ by an arc from $U/q*$ to V/p, i.e., the same privilege without the grant option. If there was no such node V/p, it must be created. In normal circumstances, the node $V/p*$ becomes unreachable, and any grants of p made by V will also be unreachable. However, it may be that V was granted $p*$ by some other user besides U, in which case the $V/p*$ node remains accessible.

Here is a typical sequence of steps:

Step	By	Action
1	U	GRANT p TO V WITH GRANT OPTION
2	V	GRANT p TO W
3	U	REVOKE GRANT OPTION FOR p FROM V CASCADE

In step (1), U grants the privilege p to V with the grant option. In step (2), V uses the grant option to grant p to W. The diagram is then as shown in Fig. 5(a).

Then in step (3), U revokes the grant option for privilege p from V, but does not revoke the privilege itself. Since there is no node V/p, we create one. The arc from $U/p**$ to $V/P*$ is removed and replaced by one from $U/p**$ to V/p.

Now, the nodes $V/p*$ and W/p are not reachable from any ** node. Thus, these nodes are deleted from the diagram. The resulting grant diagram is shown in Fig. 5(b). □

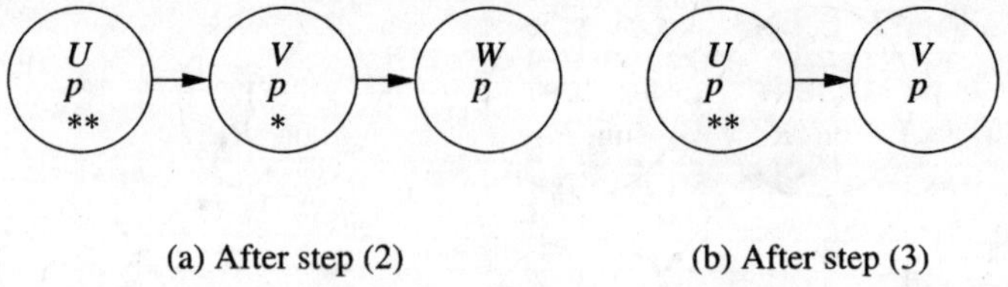

Figure 5: Revoking a grant option leaves the underlying privilege

1.7 Exercises for Section 1

Exercise 1.1: Show the grant diagrams after steps (4) through (6) of the sequence of actions listed in Fig. 6. Assume A is the owner of the relation to which privilege p refers.

Step	By	Action
1	A	GRANT p TO B WITH GRANT OPTION
2	A	GRANT p TO C
3	B	GRANT p TO D WITH GRANT OPTION
4	D	GRANT p TO B, C, E WITH GRANT OPTION
5	B	REVOKE p FROM D CASCADE
6	A	REVOKE p FROM C CASCADE

Figure 6: Sequence of actions for Exercise 1.1

Exercise 1.2: Show the grant diagrams after steps (5) and (6) of the sequence of actions listed in Fig. 7. Assume A is the owner of the relation to which privilege p refers.

Step	By	Action
1	A	GRANT p TO B, E WITH GRANT OPTION
2	B	GRANT p TO C WITH GRANT OPTION
3	C	GRANT p TO D WITH GRANT OPTION
4	E	GRANT p TO C
5	E	GRANT p TO D WITH GRANT OPTION
6	A	REVOKE GRANT OPTION FOR p FROM B CASCADE

Figure 7: Sequence of actions for Exercise 1.2

! **Exercise 1.3:** Show the final grant diagram after the following steps, assuming A is the owner of the relation to which privilege p refers.

Step	By	Action
1	A	GRANT p TO B WITH GRANT OPTION
2	B	GRANT p TO B WITH GRANT OPTION
3	A	REVOKE p FROM B CASCADE

2 Recursion in SQL

The SQL-99 standard includes provision for recursive definitions of queries. Although this feature is not part of the "core" SQL-99 standard that every DBMS is expected to implement, at least one major system — IBM's DB2 — does implement the SQL-99 proposal, which we describe in this section.

2.1 Defining Recursive Relations in SQL

The `WITH` statement in SQL allows us to define temporary relations, recursive or not. To define a recursive relation, the relation can be used within the `WITH` statement itself. A simple form of the `WITH` statement is:

WITH *R* AS <definition of *R*> <query involving *R*>

That is, one defines a temporary relation named R, and then uses R in some query. The temporary relation is not available outside the query that is part of the `WITH` statement.

More generally, one can define several relations after the `WITH`, separating their definitions by commas. Any of these definitions may be recursive. Several defined relations may be mutually recursive; that is, each may be defined in terms of some of the other relations, optionally including itself. However, any relation that is involved in a recursion must be preceded by the keyword `RECURSIVE`. Thus, a more general form of `WITH` statement is shown in Fig. 8.

Example 8: Many examples of the use of recursion can be found in a study of paths in a graph. Figure 9 shows a graph representing some flights of two

WITH
    [RECURSIVE] R_1 AS <definition of R_1>,
    [RECURSIVE] R_2 AS <definition of R_2>,
    ...
    [RECURSIVE] R_n AS <definition of R_n>
<query involving $R_1, R_2, \ldots, R_n$ >

Figure 8: Form of a WITH statement defining several temporary relations

hypothetical airlines — *Untried Airlines* (UA), and *Arcane Airlines* (AA) — among the cities San Francisco, Denver, Dallas, Chicago, and New York. The data of the graph can be represented by a relation

```
Flights(airline, frm, to, departs, arrives)
```

and the particular tuples in this table are shown in Fig. 9.

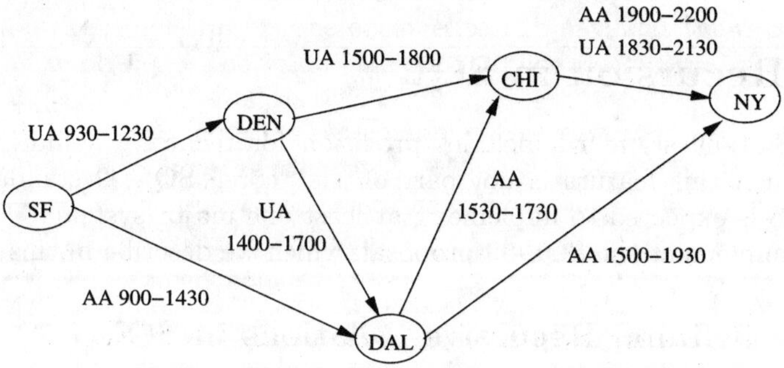

Figure 9: A map of some airline flights

airline	*from*	*to*	*departs*	*arrives*
UA	SF	DEN	930	1230
AA	SF	DAL	900	1430
UA	DEN	CHI	1500	1800
UA	DEN	DAL	1400	1700
AA	DAL	CHI	1530	1730
AA	DAL	NY	1500	1930
AA	CHI	NY	1900	2200
UA	CHI	NY	1830	2130

Figure 10: Tuples in the relation Flights

The simplest recursive question we can ask is "For what pairs of cities (x, y) is it possible to get from city x to city y by taking one or more flights?" Before writing this query in recursive SQL, it is useful to express the recursion in Datalog notation. Since many concepts involving recursion are easier to express in Datalog than in SQL, you may wish to review the terminology before proceeding. The following two Datalog rules describe a relation `Reaches(x,y)` that contains exactly these pairs of cities.

1. `Reaches(x,y)` ← `Flights(a,x,y,d,r)`
2. `Reaches(x,y)` ← `Reaches(x,z) AND Reaches(z,y)`

The first rule says that `Reaches` contains those pairs of cities for which there is a direct flight from the first to the second; the airline a, departure time d, and arrival time r are arbitrary in this rule. The second rule says that if you can reach from city x to city z and you can reach from z to city y, then you can reach from x to y.

Evaluating a recursive relation requires that we apply the Datalog rules repeatedly, starting by assuming there are no tuples in `Reaches`. We begin by using Rule (1) to get the following pairs in `Reaches`: (`SF`, `DEN`), (`SF`, `DAL`), (`DEN`, `CHI`), (`DEN`, `DAL`), (`DAL`, `CHI`), (`DAL`, `NY`), and (`CHI`, `NY`). These are the seven pairs represented by arcs in Fig. 9.

In the next round, we apply the recursive Rule (2) to put together pairs of arcs such that the head of one is the tail of the next. That gives us the additional pairs (`SF`, `CHI`), (`DEN`, `NY`), and (`SF`, `NY`). The third round combines all one- and two-arc pairs together to form paths of length up to four arcs. In this particular diagram, we get no new pairs. The relation `Reaches` thus consists of the ten pairs (x, y) such that y is reachable from x in the diagram of Fig. 9. Because of the way we drew the diagram, these pairs happen to be exactly those (x, y) such that y is to the right of x in Fig. 9.

From the two Datalog rules for `Reaches` in Example 8, we can develop a SQL query that produces the relation `Reaches`. This SQL query places the Datalog rules for `Reaches` in a `WITH` statement, and follows it by a query. In our example, the desired result was the entire `Reaches` relation, but we could also ask some query about `Reaches`, for instance the set of cities reachable from Denver.

```
1)  WITH RECURSIVE Reaches(frm, to) AS
2)          (SELECT frm, to FROM Flights)
3)      UNION
4)          (SELECT R1.frm, R2.to
5)           FROM Reaches R1, Reaches R2
6)           WHERE R1.to = R2.frm)
7)  SELECT * FROM Reaches;
```

Figure 11: Recursive SQL query for pairs of reachable cities

Figure 11 shows how to express `Reaches` as a SQL query. Line (1) introduces the definition of `Reaches`, while the actual definition of this relation is in

> **Mutual Recursion**
>
> There is a graph-theoretic way to check whether two relations or predicates are mutually recursive. Construct a *dependency graph* whose nodes correspond to the relations (or predicates if we are using Datalog rules). Draw an arc from relation A to relation B if the definition of B depends directly on the definition of A. That is, if Datalog is being used, then A appears in the body of a rule with B at the head. In SQL, A would appear in a `FROM` clause, somewhere in the definition of B, possibly in a subquery. If there is a cycle involving nodes R and S, then R and S are *mutually recursive.* The most common case will be a loop from R to R, indicating that R depends recursively upon itself.

lines (2) through (6).

That definition is a union of two queries, corresponding to the two Datalog rules by which `Reaches` was defined. Line (2) is the first term of the union and corresponds to the first, or basis rule. It says that for every tuple in the `Flights` relation, the second and third components (the `frm` and `to` components) are a tuple in `Reaches`.

Lines (4) through (6) correspond to Rule (2), the recursive rule, in the definition of `Reaches`. The two `Reaches` subgoals in Rule (2) are represented in the `FROM` clause by two aliases `R1` and `R2` for `Reaches`. The first component of `R1` corresponds to x in Rule (2), and the second component of `R2` corresponds to y. Variable z is represented by both the second component of `R1` and the first component of `R2`; note that these components are equated in line (6).

Finally, line (7) describes the relation produced by the entire query. It is a copy of the `Reaches` relation. As an alternative, we could replace line (7) by a more complex query. For instance,

```
7)  SELECT to FROM Reaches WHERE frm = 'DEN';
```

would produce all those cities reachable from Denver. □

2.2 Problematic Expressions in Recursive SQL

The SQL standard for recursion does not allow an arbitrary collection of mutually recursive relations to be written in a `WITH` clause. There is a small matter that the standard requires only that *linear* recursion be supported. A linear recursion, in Datalog terms, is one in which no rule has more than one subgoal that is mutually recursive with the head. Notice that Rule (2) in Example 8 has two subgoals with predicate `Reaches` that are mutually recursive with the head (a predicate is always mutually recursive with itself; see the box on Mutual

Recursion). Thus, technically, a DBMS might refuse to execute Fig. 11 and yet conform to the standard.[1]

But there is a more important restriction on SQL recursions, one that, if violated leads to recursions that cannot be executed by the query processor in any meaningful way. To be a legal SQL recursion, the definition of a recursive relation R may involve only the use of a mutually recursive relation S (including R itself) if that use is "monotone" in S. A use of S is *monotone* if adding an arbitrary tuple to S might add one or more tuples to R, or it might leave R unchanged, but it can never cause any tuple to be deleted from R. The following example suggests what can happen if the monotonicity requirement is not respected.

Example 9: Suppose relation R is a unary (one-attribute) relation, and its only tuple is (0). R is used as an EDB relation in the following Datalog rules:

1. `P(x)` ← `R(x) AND NOT Q(x)`
2. `Q(x)` ← `R(x) AND NOT P(x)`

Informally, the two rules tell us that an element x in R is either in P or in Q but not both. Notice that P and Q are mutually recursive.

If we start out, assuming that both P and Q are empty, and apply the rules once, we find that $P = \{(0)\}$ and $Q = \{(0)\}$; that is, (0) is in both IDB relations. On the next round, we apply the rules to the new values for P and Q again, and we find that now both are empty. This cycle repeats as long as we like, but we never converge to a solution.

In fact, there are two "solutions" to the Datalog rules:

a) $P = \{(0)\}$ $\quad Q = \emptyset$
b) $P = \emptyset$ $\quad Q = \{(0)\}$

However, there is no reason to assume one over the other, and the simple iteration we suggested as a way to compute recursive relations never converges to either. Thus, we cannot answer a simple question such as "Is $P(0)$ true?"

The problem is not restricted to Datalog. The two Datalog rules of this example can be expressed in recursive SQL. Figure 12 shows one way of doing so. This SQL does not adhere to the standard, and no DBMS should execute it. □

The problem in Example 9 is that the definitions of P and Q in Fig. 12 are not monotone. Look at the definition of P in lines (2) through (5) for instance. P depends on Q, with which it is mutually recursive, but adding a tuple to Q can delete a tuple from P. Notice that if $R = \{(0)\}$ and Q is empty, then $P = \{(0)\}$. But if we add (0) to Q, then we delete (0) from P. Thus, the definition of P is not monotone in Q, and the SQL code of Fig. 12 does not meet the standard.

[1] Note, however, that we can replace either one of the uses of `Reaches` in line (5) of Fig. 11 by `Flights`, and thus make the recursion linear. Nonlinear recursions can frequently — although not always — be made linear in this fashion.

```
WITH
        RECURSIVE P(x) AS
                (SELECT * FROM R)
            EXCEPT
                (SELECT * FROM Q),

        RECURSIVE Q(x) AS
                (SELECT * FROM R)
            EXCEPT
                (SELECT * FROM P)

SELECT * FROM P;
```

Figure 12: Query with nonmonotonic behavior, illegal in SQL

Example 10: Aggregation can also lead to nonmonotonicity. Suppose we have unary (one-attribute) relations P and Q defined by the following two conditions:

1. P is the union of Q and an EDB relation R.

2. Q has one tuple that is the sum of the members of P.

We can express these conditions by a WITH statement, although this statement violates the monotonicity requirement of SQL. The query shown in Fig. 13 asks for the value of P.

```
WITH
        RECURSIVE P(x) AS
                (SELECT * FROM R)
            UNION
                (SELECT * FROM Q),

        RECURSIVE Q(x) AS
            SELECT SUM(x) FROM P

SELECT * FROM P;
```

Figure 13: Nonmonotone query involving aggregation, illegal in SQL

Suppose that R consists of the tuples (12) and (34), and initially P and Q are both empty. Figure 14 summarizes the values computed in the first six rounds. Note that both relations are computed, in one round, from the values of the relations at the previous round. Thus, P is computed in the first round

Round	P	Q
1)	$\{(12), (34)\}$	{NULL}
2)	$\{(12), (34),$ NULL$\}$	$\{(46)\}$
3)	$\{(12), (34), (46)\}$	$\{(46)\}$
4)	$\{(12), (34), (46)\}$	$\{(92)\}$
5)	$\{(12), (34), (92)\}$	$\{(92)\}$
6)	$\{(12), (34), (92)\}$	$\{(138)\}$

Figure 14: Iterative calculation for a nonmonotone aggregation

to be the same as R, and Q is {NULL}, since the old, empty value of P is used in line (7).

At the second round, the union of lines (3) through (5) is the set

$$R \cup \{\texttt{NULL}\} = \{(12),\ (34),\ \texttt{NULL}\}$$

so that set becomes the new value of P. The old value of P was $\{(12),\ (34)\}$, so on the second round $Q = \{(46)\}$. That is, 46 is the sum of 12 and 34.

At the third round, we get $P = \{(12), (34), (46)\}$ at lines (2) through (5). Using the old value of P, $\{(12), (34), \texttt{NULL}\}$, Q is defined by lines (6) and (7) to be $\{(46)\}$ again. Remember that NULL is ignored in a sum.

At the fourth round, P has the same value, $\{(12), (34), (46)\}$, but Q gets the value $\{(92)\}$, since 12+34+46=92. Notice that Q has lost the tuple (46), although it gained the tuple (92). That is, adding the tuple (46) to P has caused a tuple (by coincidence the same tuple) to be deleted from Q. That behavior is the nonmonotonicity that SQL prohibits in recursive definitions, confirming that the query of Fig. 13 is illegal. In general, at the $2i$th round, P will consist of the tuples (12), (34), and $(46i - 46)$, while Q consists only of the tuple $(46i)$. □

2.3 Exercises for Section 2

Exercise 2.1: The relation

```
Flights(airline, frm, to, departs, arrives)
```

from Example 8 has arrival- and departure-time information that we did not consider. Suppose we are interested not only in whether it is possible to reach one city from another, but whether the journey has reasonable connections. That is, when using more than one flight, each flight must arrive at least an hour before the next flight departs. You may assume that no journey takes place over more than one day, so it is not necessary to worry about arrival close to midnight followed by a departure early in the morning.

a) Write this recursion in Datalog.

b) Write the recursion in SQL.

! **Exercise 2.2:** In Example 8 we used `frm` as an attribute name. Why did we not use the more obvious name `from`?

Exercise 2.3: Suppose we have a relation

```
SequelOf(movie, sequel)
```

that gives the immediate sequels of a movie, of which there can be more than one. We want to define a recursive relation `FollowOn` whose pairs (x, y) are movies such that y was either a sequel of x, a sequel of a sequel, or so on.

a) Write the definition of `FollowOn` as recursive Datalog rules.

b) Write the definition of `FollowOn` as a SQL recursion.

c) Write a recursive SQL query that returns the set of pairs (x, y) such that movie y is a follow-on to movie x, but is not a sequel of x.

d) Write a recursive SQL query that returns the set of pairs (x, y) meaning that y is a follow-on of x, but is neither a sequel nor a sequel of a sequel.

! e) Write a recursive SQL query that returns the set of movies x that have at least two follow-ons. Note that both could be sequels, rather than one being a sequel and the other a sequel of a sequel.

! f) Write a recursive SQL query that returns the set of pairs (x, y) such that movie y is a follow-on of x but y has at most one follow-on.

Exercise 2.4: Suppose we have a relation

```
Rel(class, rclass, mult)
```

that describes how one ODL class is related to other classes. Specifically, this relation has tuple (c, d, m) if there is a relation from class c to class d. This relation is multivalued if $m =$ `'multi'` and it is single-valued if $m =$ `'single'`. It is possible to view `Rel` as defining a graph whose nodes are classes and in which there is an arc from c to d labeled m if and only if (c, d, m) is a tuple of `Rel`. Write a recursive SQL query that produces the set of pairs (c, d) such that:

a) There is a path from class c to class d in the graph described above.

b) There is a path from c to d along which every arc is labeled `single`.

! c) There is a path from c to d along which at least one arc is labeled `multi`.

d) There is a path from c to d but no path along which all arcs are labeled `single`.

! e) There is a path from c to d along which arc labels alternate `single` and `multi`.

f) There are paths from c to d and from d to c along which every arc is labeled `single`.

3 The Object-Relational Model

The relational model and the object-oriented model typified by ODL are two important points in a spectrum of options that could underlie a DBMS. For an extended period, the relational model was dominant in the commercial DBMS world. Object-oriented DBMS's made limited inroads during the 1990's, but never succeeded in winning significant market share from the vendors of relational DBMS's. Rather, the vendors of relational systems have moved to incorporate many of the ideas found in ODL or other object-oriented-database proposals. As a result, many DBMS products that used to be called "relational" are now called "object-relational."

This section extends the abstract relational model to incorporate several important object-relational ideas. It is followed by sections that cover object-relational extensions of SQL. We introduce the concept of object-relations in Section 3.1, then discuss one of its earliest embodiments — nested relations — in Section 3.2. ODL-like references for object-relations are discussed in Section 3.3, and in Section 3.4 we compare the object-relational model with the pure object-oriented approach.

3.1 From Relations to Object-Relations

While the relation remains the fundamental concept, the relational model has been extended to the *object-relational model* by incorporation of features such as:

1. *Structured types for attributes.* Instead of allowing only atomic types for attributes, object-relational systems support a type system like ODL's: types built from atomic types and type constructors for structs, sets, and bags, for instance. Especially important is a type that is a bag of structs, which is essentially a relation. That is, a value of one component of a tuple can be an entire relation, called a "nested relation."

2. *Methods.* These are similar to methods in ODL or any object-oriented programming system.

3. *Identifiers for tuples.* In object-relational systems, tuples play the role of objects. It therefore becomes useful in some situations for each tuple to have a unique ID that distinguishes it from other tuples, even from tuples that have the same values in all components. This ID, like the object-identifier assumed in ODL, is generally invisible to the user, although

there are even some circumstances where users can see the identifier for a tuple in an object-relational system.

4. *References.* While the pure relational model has no notion of references or pointers to tuples, object-relational systems can use these references in various ways.

In the next sections, we shall elaborate upon and illustrate each of these additional capabilities of object-relational systems.

3.2 Nested Relations

In the *nested-relational model*, we allow attributes of relations to have a type that is not atomic; in particular, a type can be a relation schema. As a result, there is a convenient, recursive definition of the types of attributes and the types (schemas) of relations:

BASIS: An atomic type (integer, real, string, etc.) can be the type of an attribute.

INDUCTION: A relation's type can be any *schema* consisting of names for one or more attributes, and any legal type for each attribute. In addition, a schema also can be the type of any attribute.

In what follows, we shall generally omit atomic types where they do not matter. An attribute that is a schema will be represented by the attribute name and a parenthesized list of the attributes of its schema. Since those attributes may themselves have structure, parentheses can be nested to any depth.

Example 11: Let us design a nested-relation schema for stars that incorporates within the relation an attribute `movies`, which will be a relation representing all the movies in which the star has appeared. The relation schema for attribute `movies` will include the title, year, and length of the movie. The relation schema for the relation `Stars` will include the name, address, and birthdate, as well as the information found in `movies`. Additionally, the `address` attribute will have a relation type with attributes `street` and `city`. We can record in this relation several addresses for the star. The schema for `Stars` can be written:

```
Stars(name, address(street, city), birthdate,
    movies(title, year, length))
```

An example of a possible relation for nested relation `Stars` is shown in Fig. 15. We see in this relation two tuples, one for Carrie Fisher and one for Mark Hamill. The values of components are abbreviated to conserve space, and the dashed lines separating tuples are only for convenience and have no notational significance.

<table>
<tr><th>name</th><th>address</th><th>birthdate</th><th>movies</th></tr>
<tr><td>Fisher</td><td><table><tr><th>street</th><th>city</th></tr><tr><td>Maple</td><td>H'wood</td></tr><tr><td>Locust</td><td>Malibu</td></tr></table></td><td>9/9/99</td><td><table><tr><th>title</th><th>year</th><th>length</th></tr><tr><td>Star Wars</td><td>1977</td><td>124</td></tr><tr><td>Empire</td><td>1980</td><td>127</td></tr><tr><td>Return</td><td>1983</td><td>133</td></tr></table></td></tr>
<tr><td>Hamill</td><td><table><tr><th>street</th><th>city</th></tr><tr><td>Oak</td><td>B'wood</td></tr></table></td><td>8/8/88</td><td><table><tr><th>title</th><th>year</th><th>length</th></tr><tr><td>Star Wars</td><td>1977</td><td>124</td></tr><tr><td>Empire</td><td>1980</td><td>127</td></tr><tr><td>Return</td><td>1983</td><td>133</td></tr></table></td></tr>
</table>

Figure 15: A nested relation for stars and their movies

In the Carrie Fisher tuple, we see her name, an atomic value, followed by a relation for the value of the address component. That relation has two attributes, `street` and `city`, and there are two tuples, corresponding to her two houses. Next comes the birthdate, another atomic value. Finally, there is a component for the `movies` attribute; this attribute has a relation schema as its type, with components for the title, year, and length of a movie. The relation for the `movies` component of the Carrie Fisher tuple has tuples for her three best-known movies.

The second tuple, for Mark Hamill, has the same components. His relation for `address` has only one tuple, because in our imaginary data, he has only one house. His relation for `movies` looks just like Carrie Fisher's because their best-known movies happen, by coincidence, to be the same. Note that these two relations are two different tuple-components. These components happen to be identical, just like two components that happened to have the same integer value, e.g., 124. □

3.3 References

The fact that movies like *Star Wars* will appear in several relations that are values of the `movies` attribute in the nested relation `Stars` is a cause of redundancy. In effect, the schema of Example 11 has the nested-relation analog of not being in BCNF. However, decomposing this `Stars` relation will not eliminate the redundancy. Rather, we need to arrange that among all the tuples of all the `movies` relations, a movie appears only once.

To cure the problem, object-relations need the ability for one tuple t to refer to another tuple s, rather than incorporating s directly in t. We thus add to our model an additional inductive rule: the type of an attribute also can be a reference to a tuple with a given schema or a set of references to tuples with a given schema.

If an attribute A has a type that is a reference to a single tuple with a relation schema named R, we show the attribute A in a schema as $A(*R)$. Notice that this situation is analogous to an ODL relationship A whose type is R; i.e., it connects to a single object of type R. Similarly, if an attribute A has a type that is a set of references to tuples of schema R, then A will be shown in a schema as $A(\{*R\})$. This situation resembles an ODL relationship A that has type `Set`<R>.

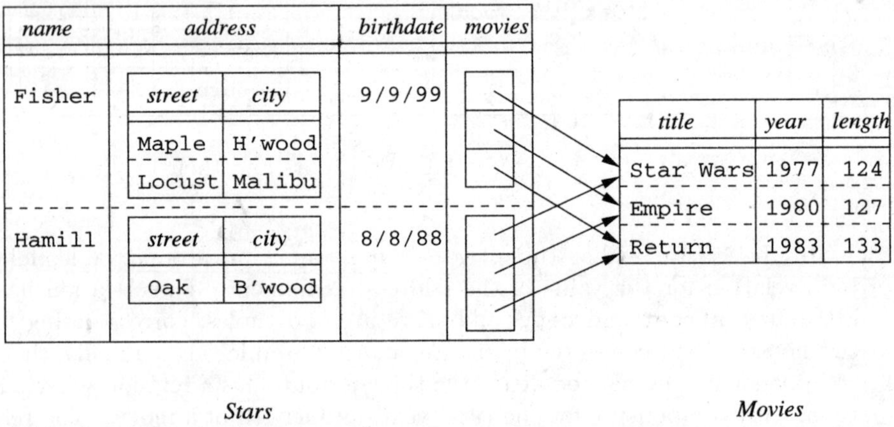

Figure 16: Sets of references as the value of an attribute

Example 12: An appropriate way to fix the redundancy in Fig. 15 is to use two relations, one for stars and one for movies. In this example only, we shall use a relation called `Movies` that is an ordinary relation with the same schema as the attribute `movies` in Example 11. A new relation `Stars` has a schema similar to the nested relation `Stars` of that example, but the movies attribute will have a type that is a set of references to `Movies` tuples. The schemas of the two relations are thus:

```
Movies(title, year, length)
Stars(name, address(street, city), birthdate,
    movies({*Movies}))
```

The data of Fig. 15, converted to this new schema, is shown in Fig. 16. Notice that, because each movie has only one tuple, although it can have many references, we have eliminated the redundancy inherent in the schema of Example 11. □

3.4 Object-Oriented Versus Object-Relational

The object-oriented data model, as typified by ODL, and the object-relational model discussed here, are remarkably similar. Some of the salient points of comparison follow.

Objects and Tuples

An object's value is really a struct with components for its attributes and relationships. It is not specified in the ODL standard how relationships are to be represented, but we may assume that an object is connected to related objects by some collection of references. A tuple is likewise a struct, but in the conventional relational model, it has components for only the attributes. Relationships would be represented by tuples in another relation. However the object-relational model, by allowing sets of references to be a component of tuples, also allows relationships to be incorporated directly into the tuples that represent an "object" or entity.

Methods

We did not discuss the use of methods as part of an object-relational schema. However, in practice, the SQL-99 standard and all implementations of object-relational ideas allow the same ability as ODL to declare and define methods associated with any class or type.

Type Systems

The type systems of the object-oriented and object-relational models are quite similar. Each is based on atomic types and construction of new types by struct- and collection-type-constructors. The choice of collection types may vary, but all variants include at least sets and bags. Moreover, the set (or bag) of structs type plays a special role in both models. It is the type of classes in ODL, and the type of relations in the object-relational model.

References and Object-ID's

A pure object-oriented model uses object-ID's that are completely hidden from the user, and thus cannot be seen or queried. The object-relational model allows references to be part of a type, and thus it is possible under some circumstances for the user to see their values and even remember them for future use. You may regard this situation as anything from a serious bug to a stroke of genius, depending on your point of view, but in practice it appears to make little difference.

Backwards Compatibility

With little difference in essential features of the two models, it is interesting to consider why object-relational systems have dominated the pure object-oriented systems in the marketplace. The reason, we believe, is as follows. As relational DBMS's evolved into object-relational DBMS's, the vendors were careful to maintain backwards compatibility. That is, newer versions of the system would still run the old code and accept the same schemas, should the user not care to adopt any of the object-oriented features. On the other hand, migration to a pure object-oriented DBMS would require the installations to rewrite and reorganize extensively. Thus, whatever competitive advantage could be argued for object-oriented database systems was insufficient to motivate many to make the switch.

3.5 Exercises for Section 3

Exercise 3.1: Using the notation developed for nested relations and relations with references, give one or more relation schemas that represent the following information. In each case, you may exercise some discretion regarding what attributes of a relation are included, but try to keep close to the attributes found in our running movie example. Also, indicate whether your schemas exhibit redundancy, and if so, what could be done to avoid it.

a) Movies, with the usual attributes plus all their stars and the usual information about the stars.

! b) Studios, all the movies made by that studio, and all the stars of each movie, including all the usual attributes of studios, movies, and stars.

c) Movies with their studio, their stars, and all the usual attributes of these.

4 User-Defined Types in SQL

We now turn to the way SQL-99 incorporates many of the object-oriented features that we saw in Section 3. The central extension that turns the relational model into the object-relational model in SQL is the *user-defined type*, or UDT. We find UDT's used in two distinct ways:

1. A UDT can be the type of a table.

2. A UDT can be the type of an attribute belonging to some table.

4.1 Defining Types in SQL

The SQL-99 standard allows the programmer to define UDT's in several ways. The simplest is as a renaming of an existing type.

CREATE TYPE *T* AS <primitive type>;

renames a primitive type such as `INTEGER`. Its purpose is to prevent errors caused by accidental coercions among values that logically should not be compared or interchanged, even though they have the same primitive data type. An example should make the purpose clear.

Example 13: In our running movies example, there are several attributes of type `INTEGER`. These include `length` of `Movies`, `cert#` of `MovieExec`, and `presC#` of `Studio`. It makes sense to compare a value of `cert#` with a value of `presC#`, and we could even take a value from one of these two attributes and store it in a tuple as the value of the other attribute. However, It would not make sense to compare a movie length with the certificate number of a movie executive, or to take a `length` value from a `Movies` tuple and store it in the `cert#` attribute of a `MovieExec` tuple.

If we create types:

```
CREATE TYPE CertType AS INTEGER;
CREATE TYPE LengthType AS INTEGER;
```

then we can declare `cert#` and `presC#` to be of type `CertType` instead of `INTEGER` in their respective relation declarations, and we can declare `length` to be of type `LengthType` in the `Movies` declaration. In that case, an object-relational DBMS will intercept attempts to compare values of one type with the other, or to use a value of one type in place of the other. □

A more powerful form of UDT declaration in SQL is similar to a class declaration in ODL, with some distinctions. First, key declarations for a relation with a user-defined type are part of the table definition, not the type definition; that is, many SQL relations can be declared to have the same UDT but different keys and other constraints. Second, in SQL we do not treat relationships as properties. A relationship can be represented by a separate relation or through references, which are covered in Section 4.5. This form of UDT definition is:

CREATE TYPE *T* AS (<attribute declarations>);

Example 14: Figure 17 shows two UDT's, `AddressType` and `StarType`. A tuple of type `AddressType` has two components, whose attributes are `street` and `city`. The types of these components are character strings of length 50 and 20, respectively. A tuple of type `StarType` also has two components. The first is attribute `name`, whose type is a 30-character string, and the second is `address`, whose type is itself a UDT `AddressType`, that is, a tuple with `street` and `city` components. □

```
CREATE TYPE AddressType AS (
    street  CHAR(50),
    city    CHAR(20)
);

CREATE TYPE StarType AS (
    name     CHAR(30),
    address AddressType
);
```

Figure 17: Two type definitions

4.2 Method Declarations in UDT's

The declaration of a method resembles the way a function in PSM is introduced. There is no analog of PSM procedures as methods. That is, every method returns a value of some type. While function declarations and definitions in PSM are combined, a method needs both a declaration, which follows the parenthesized list of attributes in the `CREATE TYPE` statement, and a separate definition, in a `CREATE METHOD` statement. The actual code for the method need not be PSM, although it could be. For example, the method body could be Java with JDBC used to access the database.

A method declaration looks like a PSM function declaration, with the keyword `METHOD` replacing `CREATE FUNCTION`. However, SQL methods typically have no arguments; they are applied to rows, just as ODL methods are applied to objects. In the definition of the method, `SELF` refers to this tuple, if necessary.

Example 15: Let us extend the definition of the type `AddressType` of Fig. 17 with a method `houseNumber` that extracts from the `street` component the portion devoted to the house address. For instance, if the `street` component were '123 Maple St.', then houseNumber should return '123'. Exactly how houseNumber works is not visible in its declaration; the details are left for the definition. The revised type definition is thus shown in Fig. 18.

```
CREATE TYPE AddressType AS (
    street  CHAR(50),
    city    CHAR(20)
    )
    METHOD houseNumber() RETURNS CHAR(10);
```

Figure 18: Adding a method declaration to a UDT

We see the keyword METHOD, followed by the name of the method and a parenthesized list of its arguments and their types. In this case, there are no arguments, but the parentheses are still needed. Had there been arguments, they would have appeared, followed by their types, such as (a INT, b CHAR(5)). □

4.3 Method Definitions

Separately, we need to define the method. A simple form of method definition is:

```
CREATE METHOD <method name, arguments, and return type>
    FOR <UDT name>
        <method body>
```

That is, the UDT for which the method is defined is indicated in a FOR clause. The method definition need not be contiguous to, or part of, the definition of the type to which it belongs.

Example 16: For instance, we could define the method houseNumber from Example 15 as in Fig. 19. We have omitted the body of the method because accomplishing the intended separation of the string string as intended is non-trivial, even if a general-purpose host language is used. □

```
CREATE METHOD houseNumber() RETURNS CHAR(10)
FOR AddressType
BEGIN
    ...
END;
```

Figure 19: Defining a method

4.4 Declaring Relations with a UDT

Having declared a type, we may declare one or more relations whose tuples are of that type. The attribute declarations are omitted from the parenthesized list of elements, and replaced by a clause with `OF` and the name of the UDT. That is, the alternative form of a `CREATE TABLE` statement, using a UDT, is:

```
CREATE TABLE <table name> OF <UDT name>
             (<list of elements>);
```

The parenthesized list of elements can include keys, foreign keys, and tuple-based constraints. Note that all these elements are declared for a particular table, not for the UDT. Thus, there can be several tables with the same UDT as their row type, and these tables can have different constraints, and even different keys. If there are no constraints or key declarations desired for the table, then the parentheses are not needed.

Example 17: We could declare `MovieStar` to be a relation whose tuples are of type `StarType` by

```
CREATE TABLE MovieStar OF StarType (
    PRIMARY KEY (name)
);
```

As a result, table `MovieStar` has two attributes, `name` and `address`. The first attribute, `name`, is an ordinary character string, but the second, `address`, has a type that is itself a UDT, namely the type `AddressType`. Attribute `name` is a key for this relation, so it is not possible to have two tuples with the same name. □

4.5 References

The effect of object identity in object-oriented languages is obtained in SQL through the notion of a *reference*. A table may have a *reference column* that serves as the "identity" for its tuples. This column could be the primary key of the table, if there is one, or it could be a column whose values are generated and maintained unique by the DBMS, for example. We shall defer to Section 4.6 the matter of defining reference columns until we first see how reference types are used.

To refer to the tuples of a table with a reference column, an attribute may have as its type a reference to another type. If T is a UDT, then `REF`(T) is the type of a reference to a tuple of type T. Further, the reference may be given a *scope*, which is the name of the relation whose tuples are referred to. Thus, an attribute A whose values are references to tuples in relation R, where R is a table whose type is the UDT T, would be declared by:

```
CREATE TYPE StarType AS (
    name      CHAR(30),
    address   AddressType,
    bestMovie REF(MovieType) SCOPE Movies
);
```

Figure 20: Adding a best movie reference to `StarType`

A REF(T) SCOPE R

If no scope is specified, the reference can go to any relation of type T.

Example 18: Let us record in `MovieStar` the best movie for each star. Assume that we have declared an appropriate relation `Movies`, and that the type of this relation is the UDT `MovieType`; we shall define both `MovieType` and `Movies` later, in Fig. 21. Figure 20 is a new definition of `StarType` that includes an attribute `bestMovies` that is a reference to a movie. Now, if relation `MovieStar` is defined to have the UDT of Fig. 20, then each star tuple will have a component that refers to a `Movies` tuple — the star's best movie. □

4.6 Creating Object ID's for Tables

In order to refer to rows of a table, such as `Movies` in Example 18, that table needs to have an "object-ID" for its tuples. Such a table is said to be *referenceable.* In a `CREATE TABLE` statement where the type of the table is a UDT (as in Section 4.4), we may include an element of the form:

REF IS <attribute name> <how generated>

The attribute name is a name given to the column that will serve as the object-ID for tuples. The "how generated" clause can be:

1. `SYSTEM GENERATED`, meaning that the DBMS is responsible for maintaining a unique value in this column of each tuple, or

2. `DERIVED`, meaning that the DBMS will use the primary key of the relation to produce unique values for this column.

Example 19: Figure 21 shows how the UDT `MovieType` and relation `Movies` could be declared so that `Movies` is referenceable. The UDT is declared in lines (1) through (4). Then the relation `Movies` is defined to have this type in lines (5) through (7). Notice that we have declared `title` and `year`, together, to be the key for relation `Movies` in line (7).

We see in line (6) that the name of the "identity" column for `Movies` is `movieID`. This attribute, which automatically becomes a fourth attribute of

```
1)  CREATE TYPE MovieType AS (
2)      title   CHAR(30),
3)      year    INTEGER,
4)      genre   CHAR(10)
    );

5)  CREATE TABLE Movies OF MovieType (
6)      REF IS movieID SYSTEM GENERATED,
7)      PRIMARY KEY (title, year)
    );
```

Figure 21: Creating a referenceable table

Movies, along with title, year, and genre, may be used in queries like any other attribute of Movies.

Line (6) also says that the DBMS is responsible for generating the value of movieID each time a new tuple is inserted into Movies. Had we replaced SYSTEM GENERATED by DERIVED, then new tuples would get their value of movieID by some calculation, performed by the system, on the values of the primary-key attributes title and year taken from the new tuple. □

Example 20: Now, let us see how to represent the many-many relationship between movies and stars using references. Previously, we represented this relationship by a relation like StarsIn that contains tuples with the keys of Movies and MovieStar. As an alternative, we may define StarsIn to have references to tuples from these two relations.

First, we need to redefine MovieStar so it is a referenceable table, thusly:

```
CREATE TABLE MovieStar OF StarType (
    REF IS starID SYSTEM GENERATED,
    PRIMARY KEY (name)
);
```

Then, we may declare the relation StarsIn to have two attributes, which are references, one to a movie tuple and one to a star tuple. Here is a direct definition of this relation:

```
CREATE TABLE StarsIn (
    star    REF(StarType) SCOPE MovieStar,
    movie   REF(MovieType) SCOPE Movies
);
```

Optionally, we could have defined a UDT as above, and then declared StarsIn to be a table of that type. □

4.7 Exercises for Section 4

Exercise 4.1: Write type declarations for the following types:

a) `NameType`, with components for first, middle, and last names and a title.

b) `PersonType`, with a name of the person and references to the persons that are their mother and father. You must use the type from part (a) in your declaration.

c) `MarriageType`, with the date of the marriage and references to the husband and wife.

5 Operations on Object-Relational Data

All appropriate SQL operations from previous chapters apply to tables that are declared with a UDT or that have attributes whose type is a UDT. There are also some entirely new operations we can use, such as reference-following. However, some familiar operations, especially those that access or modify columns whose type is a UDT, involve new syntax.

5.1 Following References

Suppose x is a value of type `REF(`T`)`. Then x refers to some tuple t of type T. We can obtain tuple t itself, or components of t, by two means:

1. Operator -> has essentially the same meaning as this operator does in C. That is, if x is a reference to a tuple t, and a is an attribute of t, then `x->a` is the value of the attribute a in tuple t.

2. The DEREF operator applies to a reference and produces the tuple referenced.

Example 21: Let us use the relation `StarsIn` from Example 20 to find the movies in which Brad Pitt starred. Recall that the schema is

```
StarsIn(star, movie)
```

where `star` and `movie` are references to tuples of `MovieStar` and `Movies`, respectively. A possible query is:

```
1)  SELECT DEREF(movie)
2)  FROM StarsIn
3)  WHERE star->name = 'Brad Pitt';
```

In line (3), the expression `star->name` produces the value of the `name` component of the `MovieStar` tuple referred to by the `star` component of any given `StarsIn` tuple. Thus, the WHERE clause identifies those `StarsIn` tuples whose `star` components are references to the Brad-Pitt `MovieStar` tuple. Line (1) then produces the movie tuple referred to by the `movie` component of those tuples. All three attributes — `title`, `year`, and `genre` — will appear in the printed result.

Note that we could have replaced line (1) by:

```
1)  SELECT  movie
```

However, had we done so, we would have gotten a list of system-generated gibberish that serves as the internal unique identifiers for certain movie tuples. We would not see the information in the referenced tuples. □

5.2 Accessing Components of Tuples with a UDT

When we define a relation to have a UDT, the tuples must be thought of as single objects, rather than lists with components corresponding to the attributes of the UDT. As a case in point, consider the relation `Movies` declared in Fig. 21. This relation has UDT `MovieType`, which has three attributes: `title`, `year`, and `genre`. However, a tuple t in `Movies` has only *one* component, not three. That component is the object itself.

If we "drill down" into the object, we can extract the values of the three attributes in the type `MovieType`, as well as use any methods defined for that type. However, we have to access these attributes properly, since they are not attributes of the tuple itself. Rather, every UDT has an implicitly defined *observer method* for each attribute of that UDT. The name of the observer method for an attribute x is $x()$. We apply this method as we would any other method for this UDT; we attach it with a dot to an expression that evaluates to an object of this type. Thus, if t is a variable whose value is of type T, and x is an attribute of T, then $t.x()$ is the value of x in the tuple (object) denoted by t.

Example 22: Let us find, from the relation `Movies` of Fig. 21 the year(s) of movies with title *King Kong*. Here is one way to do so:

```
SELECT m.year()
FROM Movies m
WHERE m.title() = 'King Kong';
```

Even though the tuple variable m would appear not to be needed here, we need a variable whose value is an object of type `MovieType` — the UDT for relation `Movies`. The condition of the `WHERE` clause compares the constant `'King Kong'` to the value of `m.title()`, the observer method for attribute `title` applied to a `MovieType` object m. Similarly, the value in the `SELECT` clause is expressed `m.year()`; this expression applies the observer method for `year` to the object m. □

In practice, object-relational DBMS's do not use method syntax to extract an attribute from an object. Rather, the parentheses are dropped, and we shall do so in what follows. For instance, the query of Example 22 will be written:

```
SELECT m.year
FROM Movies m
WHERE m.title = 'King Kong';
```

The tuple variable m is still necessary, however.

The dot operator can be used to apply methods as well as to find attribute values within objects. These methods should have the parentheses attached, even if they take no arguments.

Example 23: Suppose relation `MovieStar` has been declared to have UDT `StarType`, which we should recall from Example 14 has an attribute `address` of type `AddressType`. That type, in turn, has a method `houseNumber()`, which extracts the house number from an object of type `AddressType` (see Example 15). Then the query

```
SELECT MAX(s.address.houseNumber())
FROM MovieStar s
```

extracts the address component from a `StarType` object s, then applies the `houseNumber()` method to that `AddressType` object. The result returned is the largest house number of any movie star. □

5.3 Generator and Mutator Functions

In order to create data that conforms to a UDT, or to change components of objects with a UDT, we can use two kinds of methods that are created automatically, along with the observer methods, whenever a UDT is defined. These are:

1. A *generator method.* This method has the name of the type and no argument. It may be invoked without being applied to any object. That is, if T is a UDT, then $T()$ returns an object of type T, with no values in its various components.

2. *Mutator methods.* For each attribute x of UDT T, there is a mutator method $x(v)$. When applied to an object of type T, it changes the x attribute of that object to have value v. Notice that the mutator and observer method for an attribute each have the name of the attribute, but differ in that the mutator has an argument.

Example 24: We shall write a PSM procedure that takes as arguments a street, a city, and a name, and inserts into the relation `MovieStar` (of type `StarType` according to Example 17) an object constructed from these values, using calls to the proper generator and mutator functions. Recall from Example 14 that objects of `StarType` have a `name` component that is a character string, but an `address` component that is itself an object of type `AddressType`. The procedure `InsertStar` is shown in Fig. 22.

```
 1)  CREATE PROCEDURE InsertStar(
 2)      IN s CHAR(50),
 3)      IN c CHAR(20),
 4)      IN n CHAR(30)
     )
 5)  DECLARE newAddr AddressType;
 6)  DECLARE newStar StarType;

     BEGIN
 7)      SET newAddr = AddressType();
 8)      SET newStar = StarType();
 9)      newAddr.street(s);
10)      newAddr.city(c);
11)      newStar.name(n);
12)      newStar.address(newAddr);
13)      INSERT INTO MovieStar VALUES(newStar);
     END;
```

Figure 22: Creating and storing a `StarType` object

Lines (2) through (4) introduce the arguments s, c, and n, which will provide values for a street, city, and star name, respectively. Lines (5) and (6) declare two local variables. Each is of one of the UDT's involved in the type for objects that exist in the relation `MovieStar`. At lines (7) and (8) we create empty objects of each of these two types.

Lines (9) and (10) put real values in the object `newAddr`; these values are taken from the procedure arguments that provide a street and a city. Line (11) similarly installs the argument n as the value of the `name` component in the object `newStar`. Then line (12) takes the entire `newAddr` object and makes it the value of the `address` component in `newStar`. Finally, line (13) inserts the constructed object into relation `MovieStar`. Notice that, as always, a relation that has a UDT as its type has but a single component, even if that component has several attributes, such as `name` and `address` in this example.

To insert a star into `MovieStar`, we can call procedure `InsertStar`.

```
CALL InsertStar('345 Spruce St.', 'Glendale', 'Gwyneth Paltrow');
```

is an example. □

It is much simpler to insert objects into a relation with a UDT if your DBMS provides a generator function that takes values for the attributes of the UDT and returns a suitable object. For example, if we have functions `AddressType(s,c)` and `StarType(n,a)` that return objects of the indicated types, then we can make the insertion at the end of Example 24 with an `INSERT` statement of a familiar form:

```
INSERT INTO MovieStar VALUES(
    StarType('Gwyneth Paltrow',
        AddressType('345 Spruce St.', 'Glendale')));
```

5.4 Ordering Relationships on UDT's

Objects that are of some UDT are inherently abstract, in the sense that there is no way to compare two objects of the same UDT, either to test whether they are "equal" or whether one is less than another. Even two objects that have all components identical will not be considered equal unless we tell the system to regard them as equal. Similarly, there is no obvious way to sort the tuples of a relation that has a UDT unless we define a function that tells which of two objects of that UDT precedes the other.

Yet there are many SQL operations that require either an equality test or both an equality and a "less than" test. For instance, we cannot eliminate duplicates if we can't tell whether two tuples are equal. We cannot group by an attribute whose type is a UDT unless there is an equality test for that UDT. We cannot use an `ORDER BY` clause or a comparison like $<$ in a `WHERE` clause unless we can compare two elements.

To specify an ordering or comparison, SQL allows us to issue a CREATE ORDERING statement for any UDT. There are a number of forms this statement may take, and we shall only consider the two simplest options:

1. The statement

   ```
   CREATE ORDERING FOR T EQUALS ONLY BY STATE;
   ```

   says that two members of UDT T are considered equal if all of their corresponding components are equal. There is no $<$ defined on objects of UDT T.

2. The following statement

   ```
   CREATE ORDERING FOR T
   ORDERING FULL BY RELATIVE WITH F;
   ```

   says that any of the six comparisons (<, <=, >, >=, =, and <>) may be performed on objects of UDT T. To tell how objects x_1 and x_2 compare, we apply the function F to these objects. This function must be written so that $F(x_1, x_2) < 0$ whenever we want to conclude that $x_1 < x_2$; $F(x_1, x_2) = 0$ means that $x_1 = x_2$, and $F(x_1, x_2) > 0$ means that $x_1 > x_2$. If we replace "ORDERING FULL" with "EQUALS ONLY," then $F(x_1, x_2) = 0$ indicates that $x_1 = x_2$, while any other value of $F(x_1, x_2)$ means that $x_1 \neq x_2$. Comparison by $<$ is impossible in this case.

Example 25: Let us consider a possible ordering on the UDT StarType from Example 14. If we want only an equality on objects of this UDT, we could declare:

```
CREATE ORDERING FOR StarType EQUALS ONLY BY STATE;
```

That statement says that two objects of StarType are equal if and only if their names are equal as character strings, and their addresses are equal as objects of UDT AddressType.

The problem is that, unless we define an ordering for AddressType, an object of that type is not even equal to itself. Thus, we also need to create at least an equality test for AddressType. A simple way to do so is to declare that two AddressType objects are equal if and only if their streets and cities are each equal as strings. We could do so by:

```
CREATE ORDERING FOR AddressType EQUALS ONLY BY STATE;
```

Alternatively, we could define a complete ordering of AddressType objects. One reasonable ordering is to order addresses first by cities, alphabetically, and among addresses in the same city, by street address, alphabetically. To do so, we have to define a function, say AddrLEG, that takes two AddressType arguments and returns a negative, zero, or positive value to indicate that the first is less than, equal to, or greater than the second. We declare:

```
CREATE ORDERING FOR AddressType
ORDERING FULL BY RELATIVE WITH AddrLEG;
```

The function `AddrLEG` is shown in Fig. 23. Notice that if we reach line (7), it must be that the two `city` components are the same, so we compare the `street` components. Likewise, if we reach line (9), the only remaining possibility is that the cities are the same and the first street precedes the second alphabetically. □

```
1)  CREATE FUNCTION AddrLEG(
2)       x1 AddressType,
3)       x2 AddressType
4)  ) RETURNS INTEGER

5)  IF x1.city() < x2.city() THEN RETURN(-1)
6)  ELSEIF x1.city() > x2.city() THEN RETURN(1)
7)  ELSEIF x1.street() < x2.street() THEN RETURN(-1)
8)  ELSEIF x1.street() = x2.street() THEN RETURN(0)
9)  ELSE RETURN(1)
    END IF;
```

Figure 23: A comparison function for address objects

In practice, commercial DBMS's each have their own way of allowing the user to define comparisons for a UDT. In addition to the two approaches mentioned above, some of the capabilities offered are:

a) *Strict Object Equality.* Two objects are equal if and only if they are the same object.

b) *Method-Defined Equality.* A function is applied to two objects and returns true or false, depending on whether or not the two objects should be considered equal.

c) *Method-Defined Mapping.* A function is applied to one object and returns a real number. Objects are compared by comparing the real numbers returned.

5.5 Exercises for Section 5

Exercise 5.1: Use the `StarsIn` relation of Example 20 and the `Movies` and `MovieStar` relations accessible through `StarsIn` to write the following queries:

a) Find the names of the stars of *Dogma*.

! b) Find the titles and years of all movies in which at least one star lives in Malibu.

c) Find all the movies (objects of type `MovieType`) that starred Melanie Griffith.

! d) Find the movies (title and year) with at least five stars.

Exercise 5.2: Assuming the function `AddrLEG` of Fig. 23 is available, write a suitable function to compare objects of type `StarType`, and declare your function to be the basis of the ordering of `StarType` objects.

! **Exercise 5.3:** Write a procedure to take a star name as argument and delete from `StarsIn` and `MovieStar` all tuples involving that star.

6 On-Line Analytic Processing

An important application of databases is examination of data for patterns or trends. This activity, called *OLAP* (standing for *On-Line Analytic Processing* and pronounced "oh-lap"), generally involves highly complex queries that use one or more aggregations. These queries are often termed *OLAP queries* or *decision-support queries.* Some examples will be given in Section 6.2. A typical example is for a company to search for those of its products that have markedly increasing or decreasing overall sales.

Decision-support queries typically examine very large amounts of data, even if the query results are small. In contrast, common database operations, such as bank deposits or airline reservations, each touch only a tiny portion of the database; the latter type of operation is often referred to as *OLTP* (*On-Line Transaction Processing*, spoken "oh-ell-tee-pee").

A recent trend in DBMS's is to provide specialized support for OLAP queries. For example, systems often support a "data cube" in some way. We shall discuss the architecture of these systems in Section 7.

6.1 OLAP and Data Warehouses

It is common for OLAP applications to take place in a separate copy of the master database, called a *data warehouse*. Data from many separate databases may be integrated into the warehouse. In a common scenario, the warehouse is only updated overnight, while the analysts work on a frozen copy during the day. The warehouse data thus gets out of date by as much as 24 hours, which limits the timeliness of its answers to OLAP queries, but the delay is tolerable in many decision-support applications.

There are several reasons why data warehouses play an important role in OLAP applications. First, the warehouse may be necessary to organize and centralize data in a way that supports OLAP queries; the data may initially be scattered across many different databases. But often more important is the fact that OLAP queries, being complex and touching much of the data, take too much time to be executed in a transaction-processing system with high throughput requirements. Trying to run a long transaction that needed to touch much of the database serializably with other transactions would stall ordinary OLTP operations more than could be tolerated. For instance, recording new sales as they occur might not be permitted if there were a concurrent OLAP query computing average sales.

6.2 OLAP Applications

A common OLAP application uses a warehouse of sales data. Major store chains will accumulate terabytes of information representing every sale of every item at every store. Queries that aggregate sales into groups and identify significant groups can be of great use to the company in predicting future problems and opportunities.

Example 26: Suppose the Aardvark Automobile Co. builds a data warehouse to analyze sales of its cars. The schema for the warehouse might be:

```
Sales(serialNo, date, dealer, price)
Autos(serialNo, model, color)
Dealers(name, city, state, phone)
```

A typical decision-support query might examine sales on or after April 1, 2006 to see how the recent average price per vehicle varies by state. Such a query is shown in Fig. 24.

```
SELECT state, AVG(price)
FROM Sales, Dealers
WHERE Sales.dealer = Dealers.name AND
      date >= '2006-01-04'
GROUP BY state;
```

Figure 24: Find average sales price by state

Notice how the query of Fig. 24 touches much of the data of the database, as it classifies every recent `Sales` fact by the state of the dealer that sold it. In contrast, a typical OLTP query such as "find the price at which the auto with serial number 123 was sold," would touch only a single tuple of the data, provided there was an index on serial number. □

For another OLAP example, consider a credit-card company trying to decide whether applicants for a card are likely to be credit-worthy. The company creates a warehouse of all its current customers and their payment history. OLAP queries search for factors, such as age, income, home-ownership, and zip-code, that might help predict whether customers will pay their bills on time. Similarly, hospitals may use a warehouse of patient data — their admissions, tests administered, outcomes, diagnoses, treatments, and so on — to analyze for risks and select the best modes of treatment.

6.3 A Multidimensional View of OLAP Data

In typical OLAP applications there is a central relation or collection of data, called the *fact table.* A fact table represents events or objects of interest, such as sales in Example 26. Often, it helps to think of the objects in the fact table as arranged in a multidimensional space, or "cube." Figure 25 suggests three-dimensional data, represented by points within the cube; we have called the dimensions car, dealer, and date, to correspond to our earlier example of automobile sales. Thus, in Fig. 25 we could think of each point as a sale of a single automobile, while the dimensions represent properties of that sale.

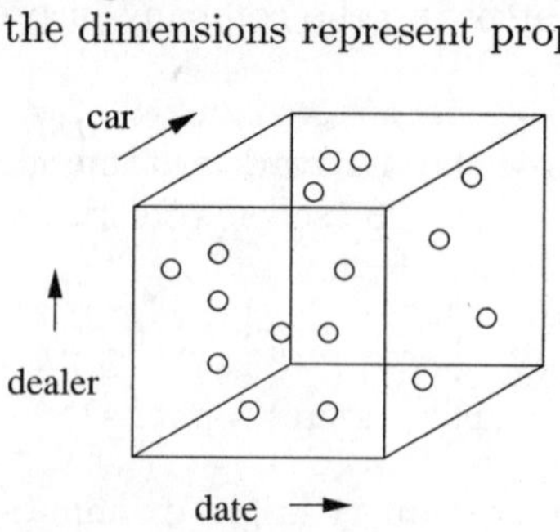

Figure 25: Data organized in a multidimensional space

A data space such as Fig. 25 will be referred to informally as a "data cube," or more precisely as a *raw-data cube* when we want to distinguish it from the more complex "data cube" of Section 7. The latter, which we shall refer to as a *formal* data cube when a distinction from the raw-data cube is needed, differs from the raw-data cube in two ways:

1. It includes aggregations of the data in all subsets of dimensions, as well as the data itself.

2. Points in the formal data cube may represent an initial aggregation of points in the raw-data cube. For instance, instead of the "car" dimension representing each individual car (as we suggested for the raw-data cube), that dimension might be aggregated by model only. There are points of a formal data cube that represent the total sales of all cars of a given model by a given dealer on a given day.

The distinctions between the raw-data cube and the formal data cube are reflected in the two broad directions that have been taken by specialized systems that support cube-structured data for OLAP:

1. *ROLAP*, or *Relational OLAP*. In this approach, data may be stored in relations with a specialized structure called a "star schema," described in Section 6.4. One of these relations is the "fact table," which contains the *raw*, or unaggregated, data, and corresponds to what we called the raw-data cube. Other relations give information about the values along each dimension. The query language, index structures, and other capabilities of the system may be tailored to the assumption that data is organized this way.

2. *MOLAP*, or *Multidimensional OLAP*. Here, a specialized structure, the formal "data cube" mentioned above, is used to hold the data, including its aggregates. Nonrelational operators may be implemented by the system to support OLAP queries on data in this structure.

6.4 Star Schemas

A *star schema* consists of the schema for the fact table, which links to several other relations, called "dimension tables." The fact table is at the center of the "star," whose points are the dimension tables. A fact table normally has several attributes that represent *dimensions*, and one or more *dependent* attributes that represent properties of interest for the point as a whole. For instance, dimensions for sales data might include the date of the sale, the place (store) of the sale, the type of item sold, the method of payment (e.g., cash or a credit card), and so on. The dependent attribute(s) might be the sales price, the cost of the item, or the tax, for instance.

Example 27: The `Sales` relation from Example 26

```
Sales(serialNo, date, dealer, price)
```

is a fact table. The dimensions are:

1. `serialNo`, representing the automobile sold, i.e., the position of the point in the space of possible automobiles.

2. `date`, representing the day of the sale, i.e., the position of the event in the time dimension.

3. `dealer`, representing the position of the event in the space of possible dealers.

The one dependent attribute is `price`, which is what OLAP queries to this database will typically request in an aggregation. However, queries asking for a count, rather than sum or average price would also make sense, e.g., "list the total number of sales for each dealer in the month of May, 2006." □

Supplementing the fact table are *dimension tables* describing the values along each dimension. Typically, each dimension attribute of the fact table is a foreign key, referencing the key of the corresponding dimension table, as suggested by Fig. 26. The attributes of the dimension tables also describe the possible groupings that would make sense in a SQL `GROUP BY` query. An example should make the ideas clearer.

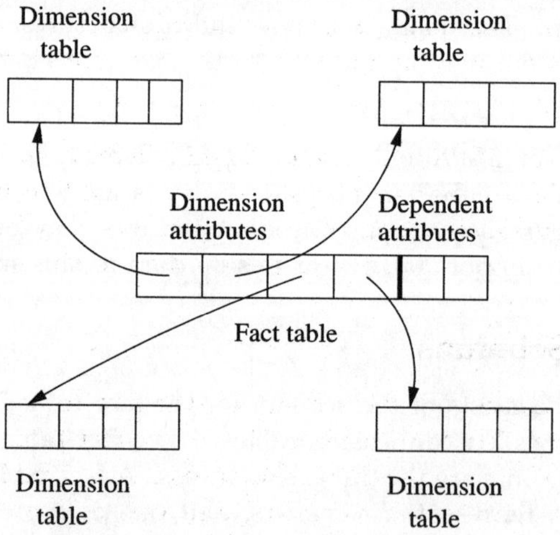

Figure 26: The dimension attributes in the fact table reference the keys of the dimension tables

Example 28: For the automobile data of Example 26, two of the three dimension tables might be:

```
Autos(serialNo, model, color)
Dealers(name, city, state, phone)
```

Attribute serialNo in the fact table Sales is a foreign key, referencing serialNo of dimension table Autos.[2] The attributes Autos.model and Autos.color give properties of a given auto. If we join the fact table Sales with the dimension table Autos, then the attributes model and color may be used for grouping sales in interesting ways. For instance, we can ask for a breakdown of sales by color, or a breakdown of sales of the Gobi model by month and dealer.

Similarly, attribute dealer of Sales is a foreign key, referencing name of the dimension table Dealers. If Sales and Dealers are joined, then we have additional options for grouping our data; e.g., we can ask for a breakdown of sales by state or by city, as well as by dealer.

One might wonder where the dimension table for time (the date attribute of Sales) is. Since time is a physical property, it does not make sense to store facts about time in a database, since we cannot change the answer to questions such as "in what year does the day July 5, 2007 appear?" However, since grouping by various time units, such as weeks, months, quarters, and years, is frequently desired by analysts, it helps to build into the database a notion of time, as if there were a time "dimension table" such as

```
Days(day, week, month, year)
```

A typical tuple of this imaginary "relation" would be $(5, 27, 7, 2007)$, representing July 5, 2007. The interpretation is that this day is the fifth day of the seventh month of the year 2007; it also happens to fall in the 27th full week of the year 2007. There is a certain amount of redundancy, since the week is calculable from the other three attributes. However, weeks are not exactly commensurate with months, so we cannot obtain a grouping by months from a grouping by weeks, or vice versa. Thus, it makes sense to imagine that both weeks and months are represented in this "dimension table." □

6.5 Slicing and Dicing

We can think of the points of the raw-data cube as partitioned along each dimension at some level of granularity. For example, in the time dimension, we might partition ("group by" in SQL terms) according to days, weeks, months, years, or not partition at all. For the cars dimension, we might partition by model, by color, by both model and color, or not partition. For dealers, we can partition by dealer, by city, by state, or not partition.

A choice of partition for each dimension "dices" the cube, as suggested by Fig. 27. The result is that the cube is divided into smaller cubes that represent groups of points whose statistics are aggregated by a query that performs this partitioning in its GROUP BY clause. Through the WHERE clause, a query also

[2]It happens that serialNo is also a key for the Sales relation, but there need not be an attribute that is both a key for the fact table and a foreign key for some dimension table.

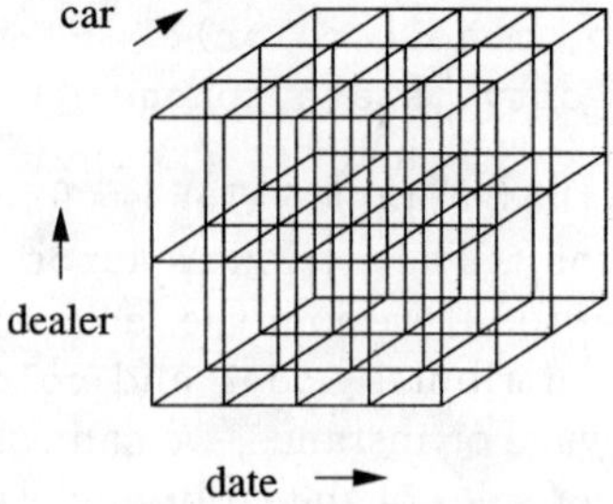

Figure 27: Dicing the cube by partitioning along each dimension

has the option of focusing on particular partitions along one or more dimensions (i.e., on a particular "slice" of the cube).

Example 29: Figure 28 suggests a query in which we ask for a slice in one dimension (the date), and dice in two other dimensions (car and dealer). The date is divided into four groups, perhaps the four years over which data has been accumulated. The shading in the diagram suggests that we are only interested in one of these years.

The cars are partitioned into three groups, perhaps sedans, SUV's, and convertibles, while the dealers are partitioned into two groups, perhaps the eastern and western regions. The result of the query is a table giving the total sales in six categories for the one year of interest. □

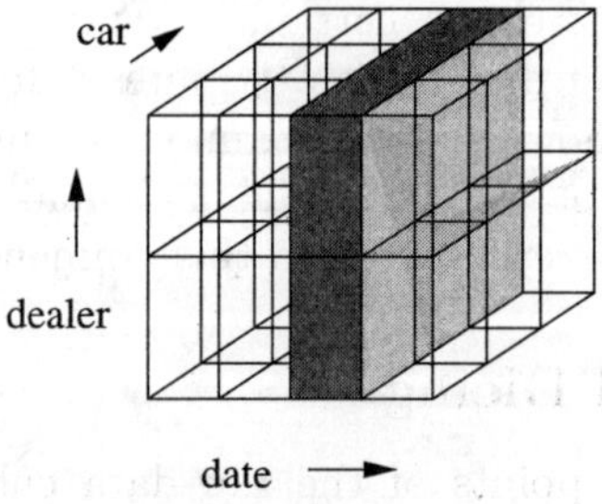

Figure 28: Selecting a slice of a diced cube

The general form of a so-called "slicing and dicing" query is thus:

```
SELECT <grouping attributes and aggregations>
FROM <fact table joined with some dimension tables>
WHERE <certain attributes are constant>
GROUP BY <grouping attributes>;
```

Example 30: Let us continue with our automobile example, but include the conceptual `Days` dimension table for time discussed in Example 28. If

Drill-Down and Roll-Up

Example 30 illustrates two common patterns in sequences of queries that slice-and-dice the data cube.

1. *Drill-down* is the process of partitioning more finely and/or focusing on specific values in certain dimensions. Each of the steps except the last in Example 30 is an instance of drill-down.

2. *Roll-up* is the process of partitioning more coarsely. The last step, where we grouped by years instead of months to eliminate the effect of randomness in the data, is an example of roll-up.

the Gobi isn't selling as well as we thought it would, we might try to find out which colors are not doing well. This query uses only the Autos dimension table and can be written in SQL as:

```
SELECT color, SUM(price)
FROM Sales NATURAL JOIN Autos
WHERE model = 'Gobi'
GROUP BY color;
```

This query dices by color and then slices by model, focusing on a particular model, the Gobi, and ignoring other data.

Suppose the query doesn't tell us much; each color produces about the same revenue. Since the query does not partition on time, we only see the total over all time for each color. We might suppose that the recent trend is for one or more colors to have weak sales. We may thus issue a revised query that also partitions time by month. This query is:

```
SELECT color, month, SUM(price)
FROM (Sales NATURAL JOIN Autos) JOIN Days ON date = day
WHERE model = 'Gobi'
GROUP BY color, month;
```

It is important to remember that the Days relation is not a conventional stored relation, although we may treat it as if it had the schema

```
Days(day, week, month, year)
```

The ability to use such a "relation" is one way that a system specialized to OLAP queries could differ from a conventional DBMS.

We might discover that red Gobis have not sold well recently. The next question we might ask is whether this problem exists at all dealers, or whether only some dealers have had low sales of red Gobis. Thus, we further focus the query by looking at only red Gobis, and we partition along the dealer dimension as well. This query is:

```
SELECT dealer, month, SUM(price)
FROM (Sales NATURAL JOIN Autos) JOIN Days ON date = day
WHERE model = 'Gobi' AND color = 'red'
GROUP BY month, dealer;
```

At this point, we find that the sales per month for red Gobis are so small that we cannot observe any trends easily. Thus, we decide that it was a mistake to partition by month. A better idea would be to partition only by years, and look at only the last two years (2006 and 2007, in this hypothetical example). The final query is shown in Fig. 29. □

```
SELECT dealer, year, SUM(price)
FROM (Sales NATURAL JOIN Autos) JOIN Days ON date = day
WHERE model = 'Gobi' AND
      color = 'red' AND
      (year = 2006 OR year = 2007)
GROUP BY year, dealer;
```

Figure 29: Final slicing-and-dicing query about red Gobi sales

6.6 Exercises for Section 6

Exercise 6.1: An on-line seller of computers wishes to maintain data about orders. Customers can order their PC with any of several processors, a selected amount of main memory, any of several disk units, and any of several CD or DVD readers. The fact table for such a database might be:

```
Orders(cust, date, proc, memory, hd, od, quant, price)
```

We should understand attribute `cust` to be an ID that is the foreign key for a dimension table about customers, and understand attributes `proc`, `hd` (hard disk), and `od` (optical disk: CD or DVD, typically) analogously. For example, an `hd` ID might be elaborated in a dimension table giving the manufacturer of the disk and several disk characteristics. The `memory` attribute is simply an integer: the number of megabytes of memory ordered. The `quant` attribute is the number of machines of this type ordered by this customer, and the `price` attribute is the total cost of each machine ordered.

a) Which are dimension attributes, and which are dependent attributes?

b) For some of the dimension attributes, a dimension table is likely to be needed. Suggest appropriate schemas for these dimension tables.

! **Exercise 6.2:** Suppose that we want to examine the data of Exercise 6.1 to find trends and thus predict which components the company should order more of. Describe a series of drill-down and roll-up queries that could lead to the conclusion that customers are beginning to prefer a DVD drive to a CD drive.

7 Data Cubes

In this section, we shall consider the "formal" data cube and special operations on data presented in this form. Recall from Section 6.3 that the formal data cube (just "data cube" in this section) precomputes all possible aggregates in a systematic way. Surprisingly, the amount of extra storage needed is often tolerable, and as long as the warehoused data does not change, there is no penalty incurred trying to keep all the aggregates up-to-date.

In the data cube, it is normal for there to be some aggregation of the raw data of the fact table before it is entered into the data-cube and its further aggregates computed. For instance, in our cars example, the dimension we thought of as a serial number in the star schema might be replaced by the model of the car. Then, each point of the data cube becomes a description of a model, a dealer and a date, together with the sum of the sales for that model, on that date, by that dealer. We shall continue to call the points of the (formal) data cube a "fact table," even though the interpretation of the points may be slightly different from fact tables in a star schema built from a raw-data cube.

7.1 The Cube Operator

Given a fact table F, we can define an augmented table CUBE(F) that adds an additional value, denoted $*$, to each dimension. The $*$ has the intuitive meaning "any," and it represents aggregation along the dimension in which it appears. Figure 30 suggests the process of adding a border to the cube in each dimension, to represent the $*$ value and the aggregated values that it implies. In this figure we see three dimensions, with the lightest shading representing aggregates in one dimension, darker shading for aggregates over two dimensions, and the darkest cube in the corner for aggregation over all three dimensions. Notice that if the number of values along each dimension is reasonably large, then the "border" represents only a small addition to the volume of the cube (i.e., the number of tuples in the fact table). In that case, the size of the stored data CUBE(F) is not much greater than the size of F itself.

A tuple of the table CUBE(F) that has $*$ in one or more dimensions will have for each dependent attribute the sum (or another aggregate function) of the values of that attribute in all the tuples that we can obtain by replacing

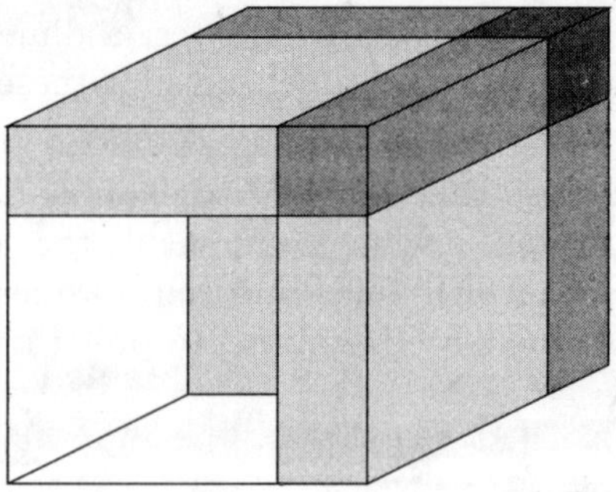

Figure 30: The cube operator augments a data cube with a border of aggregations in all combinations of dimensions

the *'s by real values. In effect, we build into the data the result of aggregating along any set of dimensions. Notice, however, that the CUBE operator does not support aggregation at intermediate levels of granularity based on values in the dimension tables. For instance, we may either leave data broken down by day (or whatever the finest granularity for time is), or we may aggregate time completely, but we cannot, with the CUBE operator alone, aggregate by weeks, months, or years.

Example 31: Let us reconsider the Aardvark database from Example 26 in the light of what the CUBE operator can give us. Recall the fact table from that example is

```
Sales(serialNo, date, dealer, price)
```

However, the dimension represented by `serialNo` is not well suited for the cube, since the serial number is a key for `Sales`. Thus, summing the price over all dates, or over all dealers, but keeping the serial number fixed has no effect; we would still get the "sum" for the one auto with that serial number. A more useful data cube would replace the serial number by the two attributes — model and color — to which the serial number connects `Sales` via the dimension table `Autos`. Notice that if we replace `serialNo` by `model` and `color`, then the cube no longer has a key among its dimensions. Thus, an entry of the cube would have the total sales price for all automobiles of a given model, with a given color, by a given dealer, on a given date.

There is another change that is useful for the data-cube implementation of the `Sales` fact table. Since the CUBE operator normally sums dependent variables, and we might want to get average prices for sales in some category, we need both the sum of the prices for each category of automobiles (a given model of a given color sold on a given day by a given dealer) and the total number of sales in that category. Thus, the relation `Sales` to which we apply the CUBE operator is

```
Sales(model, color, date, dealer, val, cnt)
```

The attribute `val` is intended to be the total price of all automobiles for the given model, color, date, and dealer, while `cnt` is the total number of automobiles in that category.

Now, let us consider the relation CUBE(`Sales`). A hypothetical tuple that would be in CUBE(`Sales`) is:

```
('Gobi', 'red', '2001-05-21', 'Friendly Fred', 45000, 2)
```

The interpretation is that on May 21, 2001, dealer Friendly Fred sold two red Gobis for a total of $45,000. In `Sales`, this tuple might appear as well, or there could be in `Sales` two tuples, each with a `cnt` of 1, whose `val`'s summed to 45,000.

The tuple

```
('Gobi', *, '2001-05-21', 'Friendly Fred', 152000, 7)
```

says that on May 21, 2001, Friendly Fred sold seven Gobis of all colors, for a total price of $152,000. Note that this tuple is in CUBE(`Sales`) but not in `Sales`.

Relation CUBE(`Sales`) also contains tuples that represent the aggregation over more than one attribute. For instance,

```
('Gobi', *, '2001-05-21', *, 2348000, 100)
```

says that on May 21, 2001, there were 100 Gobis sold by all the dealers, and the total price of those Gobis was $2,348,000.

```
('Gobi', *, *, *, 1339800000, 58000)
```

Says that over all time, dealers, and colors, 58,000 Gobis have been sold for a total price of $1,339,800,000. Lastly, the tuple

```
(*, *, *, *, 3521727000, 198000)
```

tells us that total sales of all Aardvark models in all colors, over all time at all dealers is 198,000 cars for a total price of $3,521,727,000. □

7.2 The Cube Operator in SQL

SQL gives us a way to apply the cube operator within queries. If we add the term `WITH CUBE` to a group-by clause, then we get not only the tuple for each group, but also the tuples that represent aggregation along one or more of the dimensions along which we have grouped. These tuples appear in the result with `NULL` where we have used*.

Example 32: We can construct a materialized view that is the data cube we called CUBE(Sales) in Example 31 by the following:

```
CREATE MATERIALIZED VIEW SalesCube AS
    SELECT model, color, date, dealer, SUM(val), SUM(cnt)
    FROM Sales
    GROUP BY model, color, date, dealer WITH CUBE;
```

The view SalesCube will then contain not only the tuples that are implied by the group-by operation, such as

```
('Gobi', 'red', '2001-05-21', 'Friendly Fred', 45000, 2)
```

but will also contain those tuples of CUBE(Sales) that are constructed by rolling up the dimensions listed in the GROUP BY. Some examples of such tuples would be:

```
('Gobi', NULL, '2001-05-21', 'Friendly Fred', 152000, 7)
('Gobi', NULL, '2001-05-21', NULL, 2348000, 100)
('Gobi', NULL, NULL, NULL, 1339800000, 58000)
(NULL, NULL, NULL, NULL, 3521727000, 198000)
```

Recall that NULL is used to indicate a rolled-up dimension, equivalent to the * we used in the abstract CUBE operator's result. □

A variant of the CUBE operator, called ROLLUP, produces the additional aggregated tuples only if they aggregate over a tail of the sequence of grouping attributes. We indicate this option by appending WITH ROLLUP to the group-by clause.

Example 33: We can get the part of the data cube for Sales that is constructed by the ROLLUP operator with:

```
CREATE MATERIALIZED VIEW SalesRollup AS
    SELECT model, color, date, dealer, SUM(val), SUM(cnt)
    FROM Sales
    GROUP BY model, color, date, dealer WITH ROLLUP;
```

The view SalesRollup will contain tuples

```
('Gobi', 'red', '2001-05-21', 'Friendly Fred', 45000, 2)
('Gobi', 'red', '2001-05-21', NULL, 3678000, 135)
('Gobi', 'red', NULL, NULL, 657100000, 34566)
('Gobi', NULL, NULL, NULL, 1339800000, 58000)
(NULL, NULL, NULL, NULL, 3521727000, 198000)
```

because these tuples represent aggregation along some dimension and all dimensions, if any, that follow it in the list of grouping attributes.

However, SalesRollup would not contain tuples such as

```
('Gobi', NULL, '2001-05-21', 'Friendly Fred', 152000, 7)
('Gobi', NULL, '2001-05-21', NULL, 2348000, 100)
```

These each have `NULL` in a dimension (`color` in both cases) but do not have `NULL` in one or more of the following dimension attributes. □

7.3 Exercises for Section 7

Exercise 7.1: What is the ratio of the size of CUBE(F) to the size of F if fact table F has the following characteristics?

a) F has ten dimension attributes, each with ten different values.

b) F has ten dimension attributes, each with two different values.

Exercise 7.2: Use the materialized view `SalesCube` from Example 32 to answer the following queries:

a) Find the total sales of blue cars for each dealer.

b) Find the total number of green Gobis sold by dealer "Smilin' Sally."

c) Find the average number of Gobis sold on each day of March, 2007 by each dealer.

! **Exercise 7.3:** What help, if any, would the rollup `SalesRollup` of Example 33 be for each of the queries of Exercise 7.2?

Exercise 7.4: In Exercise 6.1 we spoke of PC-order data organized as a fact table with dimension tables for attributes `cust`, `proc`, `memory`, `hd`, and `od`. That is, each tuple of the fact table `Orders` has an ID for each of these attributes, leading to information about the PC involved in the order. Write a SQL query that will produce the data cube for this fact table.

Exercise 7.5: Answer the following queries using the data cube from Exercise 7.4. If necessary, use dimension tables as well. You may invent suitable names and attributes for the dimension tables.

a) Find, for each processor speed, the total number of computers ordered in each month of the year 2007.

b) List for each type of hard disk (e.g., SCSI or IDE) and each processor type the number of computers ordered.

c) Find the average price of computers with 3.0 gigahertz processors for each month from Jan., 2005.

! **Exercise 7.6:** The cube tuples mentioned in Example 32 are not in the rollup of Example 33. Are there other rollups that would contain these tuples?

!! **Exercise 7.7:** If the fact table F to which we apply the CUBE operator is sparse (i.e., there are many fewer tuples in F than the product of the number of possible values along each dimension), then the ratio of the sizes of CUBE(F) and F can be very large. How large can it be?

8 Summary

✦ *Privileges*: For security purposes, SQL systems allow many different kinds of privileges to be managed for database elements. These privileges include the right to select (read), insert, delete, or update relations, the right to reference relations (refer to them in a constraint), and the right to create triggers.

✦ *Grant Diagrams*: Privileges may be granted by owners to other users or to the general user `PUBLIC`. If granted with the grant option, then these privileges may be passed on to others. Privileges may also be revoked. The grant diagram is a useful way to remember enough about the history of grants and revocations to keep track of who has what privilege and from whom they obtained those privileges.

✦ *SQL Recursive Queries*: In SQL, one can define a relation recursively — that is, in terms of itself. Or, several relations can be defined to be mutually recursive.

✦ *Monotonicity*: Negations and aggregations involved in a SQL recursion must be monotone — inserting tuples in one relation does not cause tuples to be deleted from any relation, including itself. Intuitively, a relation may not be defined, directly or indirectly, in terms of a negation or aggregation of itself.

✦ *The Object-Relational Model*: An alternative to pure object-oriented database models like ODL is to extend the relational model to include the major features of object-orientation. These extensions include nested relations, i.e., complex types for attributes of a relation, including relations as types. Other extensions include methods defined for these types, and the ability of one tuple to refer to another through a reference type.

✦ *User-Defined Types in SQL*: Object-relational capabilities of SQL are centered around the UDT, or user-defined type. These types may be declared by listing their attributes and other information, as in table declarations. In addition, methods may be declared for UDT's.

✦ *Relations With a UDT as Type*: Instead of declaring the attributes of a relation, we may declare that relation to have a UDT. If we do so, then its tuples have one component, and this component is an object of the UDT.

- *Reference Types*: A type of an attribute can be a reference to a UDT. Such attributes essentially are pointers to objects of that UDT.

- *Object Identity for UDT's*: When we create a relation whose type is a UDT, we declare an attribute to serve as the "object-ID" of each tuple. This component is a reference to the tuple itself. Unlike in object-oriented systems, this "OID" column may be accessed by the user, although it is rarely meaningful.

- *Accessing components of a UDT*: SQL provides observer and mutator functions for each attribute of a UDT. These functions, respectively, return and change the value of that attribute when applied to any object of that UDT.

- *Ordering Functions for UDT's*: In order to compare objects, or to use SQL operations such as `DISTINCT`, `GROUP BY`, or `ORDER BY`, it is necessary for the implementer of a UDT to provide a function that tells whether two objects are equal or whether one precedes the other.

- *OLAP*: On-line analytic processing involves complex queries that touch all or much of the data, at the same time. Often, a separate database, called a data warehouse, is constructed to run such queries while the actual database is used for short-term transactions (OLTP, or on-line transaction processing).

- *ROLAP and MOLAP*: It is frequently useful, for OLAP queries, to think of the data as residing in a multidimensional space, with dimensions corresponding to independent aspects of the data represented. Systems that support such a view of data take either a relational point of view (ROLAP, or relational-OLAP systems), or use the specialized data-cube model (MOLAP, or multidimensional-OLAP systems).

- *Star Schemas*: In a star schema, each data element (e.g., a sale of an item) is represented in one relation, called the fact table, while information helping to interpret the values along each dimension (e.g., what kind of product is item 1234?) is stored in a dimension table for each dimension.

- *The Cube Operator*: A specialized operator called cube pre-aggregates the fact table along all subsets of dimensions. It may add little to the space needed by the fact table, and greatly increases the speed with which many OLAP queries can be answered.

- *Data Cubes in SQL*: We can turn the result of a query into a data cube by appending `WITH CUBE` to a group-by clause. We can also construct a portion of the cube by using `WITH ROLLUP` there.

9 References

The ideas behind the SQL authorization mechanism originated in [4] and [1].

The source of the SQL-99 proposal for recursion is [2]. This proposal, and its monotonicity requirement, built on foundations developed over many years, involving recursion and negation in Datalog; see [5].

The cube operator was proposed in [3].

1. R. Fagin, "On an authorization mechanism," *ACM Transactions on Database Systems* **3**:3, pp. 310–319, 1978.

2. S. J. Finkelstein, N. Mattos, I. S. Mumick, and H. Pirahesh, "Expressing recursive queries in SQL," ISO WG3 report X3H2–96–075, March, 1996.

3. J. N. Gray, A. Bosworth, A. Layman, and H. Pirahesh, "Data cube: a relational aggregation operator generalizing group-by, cross-tab, and subtotals," *Proc. Intl. Conf. on Data Engineering* (1996), pp. 152–159.

4. P. P. Griffiths and B. W. Wade, "An authorization mechanism for a relational database system," *ACM Transactions on Database Systems* **1**:3, pp. 242–255, 1976.

5. J. D. Ullman, *Principles of Database and Knowledge-Base Systems, Volume I*, Computer Science Press, New York, 1988.

The Semistructured-Data Model

We now turn to a different kind of data model. This model, called "semistructured," is distinguished by the fact that the schema is implied by the data, rather than being declared separately from the data as is the case for the relational model and all the other models we studied up to this point. After a general discussion of semistructured data, we turn to the most important manifestation of this idea: XML. We shall cover ways to describe XML data, in effect enforcing a schema for this "schemaless" data. These methods include DTD's (Document Type Definitions) and the language XML Schema.

1 Semistructured Data

The *semistructured-data* model plays a special role in database systems:

1. It serves as a model suitable for *integration* of databases, that is, for describing the data contained in two or more databases that contain similar data with different schemas.
2. It serves as the underlying model for notations such as XML, to be taken up in Section 2, that are being used to share information on the Web.

In this section, we shall introduce the basic ideas behind "semistructured data" and how it can represent information more flexibly than the other models we have met previously.

1.1 Motivation for the Semistructured-Data Model

The models we have seen so far — E/R, UML, relational, ODL — each start with a schema. The schema is a rigid framework into which data is placed. This rigidity provides certain advantages. Especially, the relational model owes much of its success to the existence of efficient implementations. This efficiency comes from the fact that the data in a relational database must fit the schema, and the schema is known to the query processor. For instance, fixing the schema allows the data to be organized with data structures that support efficient answering of queries.

On the other hand, interest in the semistructured-data model is motivated primarily by its flexibility. In particular, semistructured data is "schemaless." More precisely, the data is *self-describing*; it carries information about what its schema is, and that schema can vary arbitrarily, both over time and within a single database.

One might naturally wonder whether there is an advantage to creating a database without a schema, where one could enter data at will, and attach to the data whatever schema information you felt was appropriate for that data. There are actually some small-scale information systems, such as Lotus Notes, that take the self-describing-data approach. This flexibility may make query processing harder, but it offers significant advantages to users. For example, we can maintain a database of movies in the semistructured model and add new attributes like "would I like to see this movie?" as we wish. The attributes do not need to have a value for all movies, or even for more than one movie. Likewise, we can add relationships like "homage to," without having to change the schema or even represent the relationship in more than one pair of movies.

1.2 Semistructured Data Representation

A database of *semistructured data* is a collection of *nodes*. Each node is either a *leaf* or *interior*. Leaf nodes have associated data; the type of this data can be any atomic type, such as numbers and strings. Interior nodes have one or more arcs out. Each arc has a *label*, which indicates how the node at the head of the arc relates to the node at the tail. One interior node, called the *root*, has no arcs entering and represents the entire database. Every node must be reachable from the root, although the graph structure is not necessarily a tree.

Example 1: Figure 1 is an example of a semistructured database about stars and movies. We see a node at the top labeled *Root*; this node is the entry point to the data and may be thought of as representing all the information in the database. The central objects or entities — stars and movies in this case — are represented by nodes that are children of the root.

We also see many leaf nodes. At the far left is a leaf labeled `Carrie Fisher`, and at the far right is a leaf labeled 1977, for instance. There are also many interior nodes. Three particular nodes we have labeled *cf*, *mh*, and *sw*, standing for "Carrie Fisher," "Mark Hamill," and "Star Wars," respectively. These labels are not part of the model, and we placed them on these nodes only so we would have a way of referring to the nodes, which otherwise would be nameless, in the text. We may think of node *sw*, for instance, as representing the concept "Star

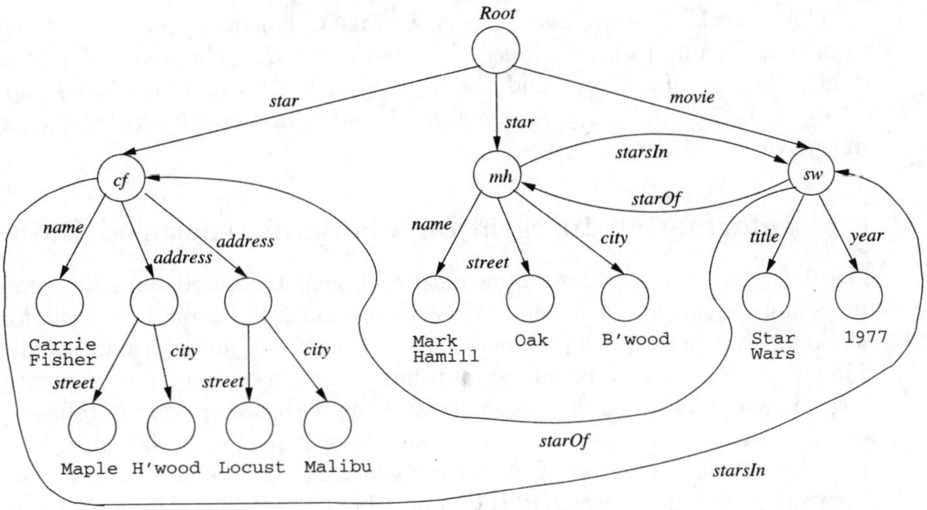

Figure 1: Semistructured data representing a movie and stars

Wars": the title and year of this movie, other information not shown, such as its length, and its stars, two of which are shown. □

A label L on the arc from node N to node M can play one of two roles:

1. It may be possible to think of N as representing an object or entity, while M represents one of its attributes. Then, L represents the name of the attribute.

2. We may be able to think of N and M as objects or entities and L as the name of a relationship from N to M.

Example 2: Consider Fig. 1 again. The node indicated by *cf* may be thought of as representing the `Star` object for Carrie Fisher. We see, leaving this node, an arc labeled *name*, which represents the attribute `name` and leads to a leaf node holding the correct name. We also see two arcs, each labeled *address.* These arcs lead to unnamed nodes which we may think of as representing two addresses of Carrie Fisher. There is no schema to tell us whether stars can have more than one address; we simply put two address nodes in the graph if we feel it is appropriate.

Notice in Fig. 1 how both nodes have out-arcs labeled *street* and *city.* Moreover, these arcs each lead to leaf nodes with the appropriate atomic values. We may think of *address* nodes as structs or objects with two fields, named *street* and *city.* However, in the semistructured model, it is entirely appropriate to add other components, e.g., zip, to some addresses, or to have one or both fields missing.

The other kind of arc also appears in Fig. 1. For instance, the node *cf* has an out-arc leading to the node *sw* and labeled *starsIn*. The node *mh* (for Mark Hamill) has a similar arc, and the node *sw* has arcs labeled *starOf* to both nodes *cf* and *mh*. These arcs represent the stars-in relationship between stars and movies. □

1.3 Information Integration Via Semistructured Data

The flexibility and self-describing nature of semistructured data has made it important in two applications. We shall discuss its use for data exchange in Section 2, but here we shall consider its use as a tool for information integration. As databases have proliferated, it has become a common requirement that data in two or more of them be accessible as if they were one database. For instance, companies may merge; each has its own personnel database, its own database of sales, inventory, product designs, and perhaps many other matters. If corresponding databases had the same schemas, then combining them would be simple; for instance, we could take the union of the tuples in two relations that had the same schema and played the same roles in the the two databases.

However, life is rarely that simple. Independently developed databases are unlikely to share a schema, even if they talk about the same things, such as personnel. For instance, one employee database may record spouse-name, another not. One may have a way to represent several addresses, phones, or emails for an employee, another database may allow only one of each. One may treat consultants as employees, another not. One database might be relational, another object-oriented.

To make matters more complex, databases tend over time to be used in so many different applications that it is impossible to turn them off and copy or translate their data into another database, even if we could figure out an efficient way to transform the data from one schema to another. This situation is often referred to as the *legacy-database problem*; once a database has been in existence for a while, it becomes impossible to disentangle it from the applications that grow up around it, so the database can never be decommissioned.

A possible solution to the legacy-database problem is suggested in Fig. 2. We show two legacy databases with an interface; there could be many legacy systems involved. The legacy systems are each unchanged, so they can support their usual applications.

For flexibility in integration, the interface supports semistructured data, and the user is allowed to query the interface using a query language that is suitable for such data. The semistructured data may be constructed by translating the data at the sources, using components called *wrappers* (or "adapters") that are each designed for the purpose of translating one source to semistructured data.

Alternatively, the semistructured data at the interface may not exist at all. Rather, the user queries the interface as if there were semistructured data, while the interface answers the query by posing queries to the sources, each referring to the schema found at that source.

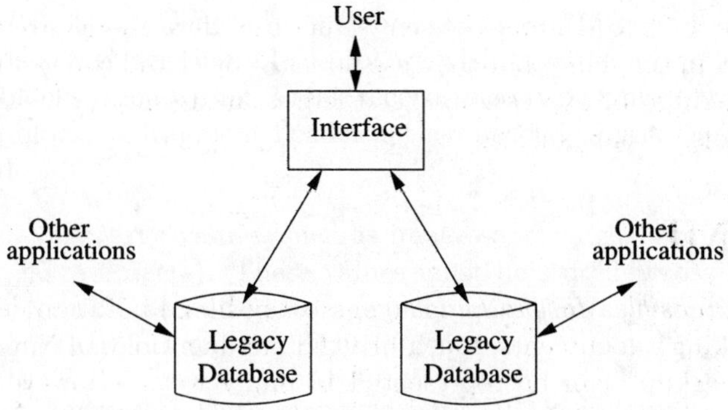

Figure 2: Integrating two legacy databases through an interface that supports semistructured data

Example 3: We can see in Fig. 1 a possible effect of information about stars being gathered from several sources. Notice that the address information for Carrie Fisher has an address concept, and the address is then broken into street and city. That situation corresponds roughly to data that had a nested-relation schema like `Stars(name, address(street, city))`.

On the other hand, the address information for Mark Hamill has no address concept at all, just street and city. This information may have come from a schema such as `Stars(name, street, city)` that can represent only one address for a star. Some of the other variations in schema that are not reflected in the tiny example of Fig. 1, but that could be present if movie information were obtained from several sources, include: optional film-type information, a director, a producer or producers, the owning studio, revenue, and information on where the movie is currently playing. □

1.4 Exercises for Section 1

Exercise 1.1: Since there is no schema to design in the semistructured-data model, we cannot ask you to design schemas to describe different situations. Rather, in the following exercises we shall ask you to suggest how particular data might be organized to reflect certain facts.

a) Add to Fig. 1 the facts that *Star Wars* was directed by George Lucas and produced by Gary Kurtz.

b) Add to Fig. 1 information about *Empire Strikes Back* and *Return of the Jedi*, including the facts that Carrie Fisher and Mark Hamill appeared in these movies.

c) Add to (b) information about the studio (Fox) for these movies and the address of the studio (Hollywood).

! **Exercise 1.2:** UML and the semistructured-data model are both "graphical" in nature, in the sense that they use nodes, labels, and connections among nodes as the medium of expression. Yet there is an essential difference between the two models. What is it?

2 XML

XML (*Extensible Markup Language*) is a tag-based notation designed originally for "marking" documents, much like the familiar HTML. Nowadays, data with XML "markup" can be represented in many ways. However, in this section we shall refer to XML data as represented in one or more documents. While HTML's tags talk about the presentation of the information contained in documents — for instance, which portion is to be displayed in italics or what the entries of a list are — XML tags are intended to talk about the meanings of pieces of the document.

In this section we shall introduce the rudiments of XML. We shall see that it captures, in a linear form, the same structure as do the graphs of semistructured data introduced in Section 1. In particular, tags can play the same role as the labels on the arcs of a semistructured-data graph.

2.1 Semantic Tags

Tags in XML are text surrounded by triangular brackets, i.e., `<...>`, as in HTML. Also as in HTML, tags generally come in matching pairs, with an *opening tag* like `<Foo>` and a matched *closing* tag that is the same word with a slash, like `</Foo>`. Between a matching pair `<Foo>` and `</Foo>`, there can be text, including text with nested HTML tags, and any number of other nested matching pairs of XML tags. A pair of matching tags and everything that comes between them is called an *element.*

A single tag, with no matched closing tag, is also permitted in XML. In this form, the tag has a slash before the right bracket, for example, `<Foo/>`. Such a tag cannot have any other elements or text nested within it. It can, however, have attributes (see Section 2.4).

2.2 XML With and Without a Schema

XML is designed to be used in two somewhat different modes:

1. *Well-formed* XML allows you to invent your own tags, much like the arc-labels in semistructured data. This mode corresponds quite closely to semistructured data, in that there is no predefined schema, and each document is free to use whatever tags the author of the document wishes. Of course the nesting rule for tags must be obeyed, or the document is not well-formed.

2. *Valid* XML involves a "DTD," or "Document Type Definition" (see Section 3) that specifies the allowable tags and gives a grammar for how they may be nested. This form of XML is intermediate between the strict-schema models such as the relational model, and the completely schemaless world of semistructured data. As we shall see in Section 3, DTD's generally allow more flexibility in the data than does a conventional schema; DTD's often allow optional fields or missing fields, for instance.

2.3 Well-Formed XML

The minimal requirement for well-formed XML is that the document begin with a declaration that it is XML, and that it have a *root element* that is the entire body of the text. Thus, a well-formed XML document would have an outer structure like:

```
<? xml version = "1.0" encoding = "utf-8" standalone = "yes" ?>
<SomeTag>
    ...
</SomeTag>
```

The first line indicates that the file is an XML document. The encoding UTF-8 (UTF = "Unicode Transformation Format") is a common choice of encoding for characters in documents, because it is compatible with ASCII and uses only one byte for the ASCII characters. The attribute `standalone = "yes"` indicates that there is no DTD for this document; i.e., it is well-formed XML. Notice that this initial declaration is delineated by special markers `<?...?>`. The root element for this document is labeled `<SomeTag>`.

Example 4: In Fig. 3 is an XML document that corresponds roughly to the data in Fig. 1. In particular, it corresponds to the tree-like portion of the semistructured data — the root and all the nodes and arcs except the "sideways" arcs among the nodes *cf*, *mh*, and *sw*. We shall see in Section 2.4 how those may be represented.

The root element is `StarMovieData`. Within this element, we see two elements, each beginning with the tag `<Star>` and ending with its matching

```
<? xml version = "1.0" encoding = "utf-8" standalone = "yes" ?>
<StarMovieData>
    <Star>
        <Name>Carrie Fisher</Name>
        <Address>
            <Street>123 Maple St.</Street>
            <City>Hollywood</City>
        </Address>
        <Address>
            <Street>5 Locust Ln.</Street>
            <City>Malibu</City>
        </Address>
    </Star>
    <Star>
        <Name>Mark Hamill</Name>
        <Street>456 Oak Rd.</Street>
        <City>Brentwood</City>
    </Star>
    <Movie>
        <Title>Star Wars</Title>
        <Year>1977</Year>
    </Movie>
</StarMovieData>
```

Figure 3: An XML document about stars and movies

</Star>. Within each element is a subelement giving the name of the star. One element, for Carrie Fisher, also has two subelements, each giving the address of one of her homes. These elements are each delineated by an <Address> opening tag and its matched closing tag. The element for Mark Hamill has only subelements for one street and one city, and does not use an <Address> tag to group these. This distinction appeared as well in Fig. 1. We also see one element with opening tag <Movie> and its matched closing tag. This element has subelements for the title and year of the movie.

Notice that the document of Fig. 3 does not represent the relationship "stars-in" between stars and movies. We could indicate the movies of a star by including, within the element devoted to that star, the titles and years of their movies. Figure 4 is an example of this representation. □

2.4 Attributes

As in HTML, an XML element can have *attributes* (name-value pairs) within its opening tag. An attribute is an alternative way to represent a leaf node of semistructured data. Attributes, like tags, can represent labeled arcs in

```
<Star>
    <Name>Mark Hamill</Name>
    <Street>Oak</Street>
    <City>Brentwood</City>
    <Movie>
        <Title>Star Wars</Title>
        <Year>1977</Year>
    </Movie>
    <Movie>
        <Title>Empire Strikes Back</Title>
        <Year>1980</Year>
    </Movie>
</Star>
```

Figure 4: Nesting movies within stars

a semistructured-data graph. Attributes can also be used to represent the "sideways" arcs as in Fig. 1.

Example 5: The *title* or *year* children of the movie node labeled *sw* could be represented directly in the <Movie> element, rather than being represented by nested elements. That is, we could replace the <Movie> element of Fig. 3 by:

```
<Movie year = 1977><Title>Star Wars</Title></Movie>
```

We could even make both child nodes be attributes by:

```
<Movie title = "Star Wars" year = 1977></Movie>
```

or even:

```
<Movie title = "Star Wars" year = 1977 />
```

Notice that here we use a single tag without a matched closing tag, as indicated by the slash at the end. □

2.5 Attributes That Connect Elements

An important use for attributes is to represent connections in a semistructured data graph that do not form a tree. We shall see in Section 3.4 how to declare certain attributes to be identifiers for their elements. We shall also see how to declare that other attributes are references to these element identifiers. For the moment, let us just see an example of how these attributes could be used.

Example 6: Figure 5 can be interpreted as an exact representation in XML of the semistructured data graph of Fig. 1. However, in order to make the interpretation, we need to have enough schema information that we know the attribute `starID` is an identifier for the element in which it appears. That is, `cf` is the identifier of the first `<Star>` element (for Carrie Fisher) and `mh` is the identifier of the second `<Star>` element (for Mark Hamill). Likewise, we must establish that the attribute `movieID` within a `<Movie>` tag is an identifier for that element. Thus, `sw` is an identifier for the lone `<Movie>` element in Fig. 5.

```
<? xml version = "1.0" encoding = "utf-8" standalone = "yes" ?>
<StarMovieData>
    <Star starID = "cf" starredIn = "sw">
        <Name>Carrie Fisher</Name>
        <Address>
            <Street>123 Maple St.</Street>
            <City>Hollywood</City>
        </Address>
        <Address>
            <Street>5 Locust Ln.</Street>
            <City>Malibu</City>
        </Address>
    </Star>
    <Star starID = "mh" starredIn = "sw">
        <Name>Mark Hamill</Name>
        <Street>456 Oak Rd.</Street>
        <City>Brentwood</City>
    </Star>
    <Movie movieID = "sw" starsOf = "cf", "mh">
        <Title>Star Wars</Title>
        <Year>1977</Year>
    </Movie>
</StarMovieData>
```

Figure 5: Adding stars-in information to our XML document

Moreover, the schema must also say that the attributes `starredIn` for `<Star>` elements and `starsOf` for `<Movie>` elements are references to one or more ID's. That is, the value `sw` for `starredIn` within each of the `<Movie>` elements says that both Carrie Fisher and Mark Hamill starred in *Star Wars*. Likewise, the list of ID's `cf` and `mh` that is the value of `starsOf` in the `<Movie>` element says that both these stars were stars of *Star Wars*. □

2.6 Namespaces

There are situations in which XML data involves tags that come from two or more different sources, and which may therefore have conflicting names. For example, we would not want to confuse an HTML tag used in text with an XML tag that represents the meaning of that text. In Section 4, we shall see how XML Schema requires tags from two separate vocabularies. To distinguish among different vocabularies for tags in the same document, we can use a *namespace* for a set of tags.

To say that an element's tag should be interpreted as part of a certain namespace, we can use the attribute `xmlns` in its opening tag. There is a special form used for this attribute:

`xmlns:`*name*=" *URI*"

Within the element having this attribute, *name* can modify any tag to say the tag belongs to this namespace. That is, we can create *qualified* names of the form *name*:*tag*, where *name* is the name of the namespace to which the tag *tag* belongs.

The URI (Universal Resource Identifier) is typically a URL referring to a document that describes the meaning of the tags in the namespace. This description need not be formal; it could be an informal article about expectations. It could even be nothing at all, and still serve the purpose of distinguishing different tags that had the same name.

Example 7: Suppose we want to say that in element `StarMovieData` of Fig. 5 certain tags belong to the namespace defined in the document `infolab.stanford.edu/movies`. We could choose a name such as `md` for the namespace by using the opening tag:

```
<md:StarMovieData xmlns:md=
    "http://infolab.stanford.edu/movies">
```

Our intent is that `StarMovieData` itself is part of this namespace, so it gets the prefix `md:`, as does its closing tag `/md:StarMovieData`. Inside this element, we have the option of asserting that the tags of subelements belong to this namespace by prefixing their opening and closing tags with `md:`. □

2.7 XML and Databases

Information encoded in XML is not always intended to be stored in a database. It has become common for computers to share data across the Internet by passing messages in the form of XML elements. These messages live for a very short time, although they may have been generated using data from one database and wind up being stored as tuples of a database at the receiving end. For example, the XML data in Fig. 5 might be turned into some tuples to insert into relations MovieStar and StarsIn of our running example movie database.

However, it is becoming increasingly common for XML to appear in roles traditionally reserved for relational databases. For example, we discussed in Section 1.3 how systems that integrate the data of an enterprise produce integrated views of many databases. XML is becoming an important option as the way to represent these views, as an alternative to views consisting of relations or classes of objects. The integrated views are then queried using one of specialized XML query languages.

When we store XML in a database, we must deal with the requirement that access to information must be efficient, especially for very large XML documents or very large collections of small documents.[1] A relational DBMS provides indexes and other tools for making access efficient. There are two approaches to storing XML to provide some efficiency:

1. Store the XML data in a parsed form, and provide a library of tools to navigate the data in that form. Two common standards are called SAX (Simple API for XML) and DOM (Document Object Model).

2. Represent the documents and their elements as relations, and use a conventional, relational DBMS to store them.

In order to represent XML documents as relations, we should start by giving each document and each element of those documents a unique ID. For the document, the ID could be its URL or path in a file system. A possible relational database schema is:

```
DocRoot(docID, rootElementID)
SubElement(parentID, childID, position)
ElementAttribute(elementID, name, value)
ElementValue(elementID, value)
```

This schema is suitable for documents that obey the restriction that each element either contains only text or contains only subelements. Accommodating elements with *mixed content* of text and subelements is left as an exercise.

The first relation, DocRoot relates document ID's to the ID's of their root element. The second relation, SubElement, connects an element (the "parent") to each of its immediate subelements ("children"). The third attribute of SubElement gives the position of the child among all the children of the parent.

The third relation, ElementAttribute relates elements to their attributes; each tuple gives the name and value of one of the attributes of an element. Finally, ElementValue relates those elements that have no subelements to the text, if any, that is contained in that element.

[1]Recall that XML data need not take the form of documents (i.e., a header with a root element) at all. For example, XML data could be a stream of elements without headers. However, we shall continue to speak of "documents" as XML data.

There is a small matter that values of attributes and elements can have different types, e.g., integers or strings, while relational attributes each have a unique type. We could treat the two attributes named `value` as always being strings, and interpret those strings that were integers or another type properly as we processed the data. Or we could split each of the last two relations into as many relations as there are different types of data.

2.8 Exercises for Section 2

Exercise 2.1: Repeat Exercise 1.1 using XML.

Exercise 2.2: Show that any relation can be represented by an XML document. *Hint*: Create an element for each tuple with a subelement for each component of that tuple.

! **Exercise 2.3:** How would you represent an empty element (one that had neither text nor subelements) in the database schema of Section 2.7?

! **Exercise 2.4:** In Section 2.7 we gave a database schema for representing documents that do not have *mixed content* — elements that contain a mixture of text (`#PCDATA`) and subelements. Show how to modify the schema when elements can have mixed content.

3 Document Type Definitions

For a computer to process XML documents automatically, it is helpful for there to be something like a schema for the documents. It is useful to know what kinds of elements can appear in a collection of documents and how elements can be nested. The description of the schema is given by a grammar-like set of rules, called a *document type definition*, or DTD. It is intended that companies or communities wishing to share data will each create a DTD that describes the form(s) of the data they share, thus establishing a shared view of the semantics of their elements. For instance, there could be a DTD for describing protein structures, a DTD for describing the purchase and sale of auto parts, and so on.

3.1 The Form of a DTD

The gross structure of a DTD is:

```
<!DOCTYPE root-tag [
        <!ELEMENT element-name (components)>
              more elements
]>
```

The opening *root-tag* and its matched closing tag surround a document that conforms to the rules of this DTD. Element declarations, introduced by !ELEMENT, give the tag used to surround the portion of the document that represents the element, and also give a parenthesized list of "components." The latter are elements that may or must appear in the element being described. The exact requirements on components are indicated in a manner we shall see shortly.

There are two important special cases of components:

1. (#PCDATA) ("parsed character data") after an element name means that element has a value that is text, and it has no elements nested within. Parsed character data may be thought of as HTML text. It can have formatting information within it, and the special characters like < must be escaped, by < and similar HTML codes. For instance,

   ```
   <!ELEMENT Title (#PCDATA)>
   ```

   says that between <Title> and </Title> tags a character string can appear. However, any nested tags are not part of the XML; they could be HTML, for instance.

2. The keyword EMPTY, with no parentheses, indicates that the element is one of those that has no matched closing tag. It has no subelements, nor does it have text as a value. For instance,

   ```
   <!ELEMENT Foo EMPTY>
   ```

   says that the only way the tag Foo can appear is as <Foo/>.

Example 8: In Fig. 6 we see a DTD for stars.[2] The DTD name and root element is Stars. The first element definition says that inside the matching pair of tags <Stars>...</Stars> we shall find zero or more Star elements, each representing a single star. It is the * in (Star*) that says "zero or more," i.e., "any number of."

The second element, Star, is declared to consist of three kinds of subelements: Name, Address, and Movies. They must appear in this order, and each must be present. However, the + following Address says "one or more"; that is, there can be any number of addresses listed for a star, but there must be at least one. The Name element is then defined to be parsed character data. The fourth element says that an address element consists of subelements for a street and a city, in that order.

Then, the Movies element is defined to have zero or more elements of type Movie within it; again, the * says "any number of." A Movie element is defined to consist of title and year elements, each of which are simple text. Figure 7 is an example of a document that conforms to the DTD of Fig. 6. □

```
<!DOCTYPE Stars [
    <!ELEMENT Stars (Star*)>
    <!ELEMENT Star (Name, Address+, Movies)>
    <!ELEMENT Name (#PCDATA)>
    <!ELEMENT Address (Street, City)>
    <!ELEMENT Street (#PCDATA)>
    <!ELEMENT City (#PCDATA)>
    <!ELEMENT Movies (Movie*)>
    <!ELEMENT Movie (Title, Year)>
    <!ELEMENT Title (#PCDATA)>
    <!ELEMENT Year (#PCDATA)>
]>
```

Figure 6: A DTD for movie stars

The components of an element E are generally other elements. They must appear between the tags $<E>$ and $</E>$ in the order listed. However, there are several operators that control the number of times elements appear.

1. A * following an element means that the element may occur any number of times, including zero times.

2. A + following an element means that the element may occur one or more times.

3. A ? following an element means that the element may occur either zero times or one time, but no more.

4. We can connect a list of options by the "or" symbol | to indicate that exactly one option appears. For example, if `<Movie>` elements had `<Genre>` subelements, we might declare these by

   ```
   <!ELEMENT Genre (Comedy|Drama|SciFi|Teen)>
   ```

   to indicate that each `<Genre>` element has one of these four subelements.

5. Parentheses can be used to group components. For example, if we declared addresses to have the form

   ```
   <!ELEMENT Address Street, (City|Zip)>
   ```

   then `<Address>` elements would each have a `<Street>` subelement followed by either a `<City>` or `<Zip>` subelement, but not both.

[2]Note that the stars-and-movies XML document of Fig. 3 is not intended to conform to this DTD.

```
<Stars>
    <Star>
        <Name>Carrie Fisher</Name>
        <Address>
            <Street>123 Maple St.</Street>
            <City>Hollywood</City>
        </Address>
        <Address>
            <Street>5 Locust Ln.</Street>
            <City>Malibu</City>
        </Address>
        <Movies>
            <Movie>
                <Title>Star Wars</Title>
                <Year>1977</Year>
            </Movie>
            <Movie>
                <Title>Empire Strikes Back</Title>
                <Year>1980</Year>
            </Movie>
            <Movie>
                <Title>Return of the Jedi</Title>
                <Year>1983</Year>
            </Movie>
        </Movies>
    </Star>
    <Star>
        <Name>Mark Hamill</Name>
        <Address>
            <Street>456 Oak Rd.<Street>
            <City>Brentwood</City>
        </Address>
        <Movies>
            <Movie>
                <Title>Star Wars</Title>
                <Year>1977</Year>
            </Movie>
            <Movie>
                <Title>Empire Strikes Back</Title>
                <Year>1980</Year>
            </Movie>
            <Movie>
                <Title>Return of the Jedi</Title>
                <Year>1983</Year>
            </Movie>
        </Movies>
    </Star>
</Stars>
```

Figure 7: Example of a document following the DTD of Fig. 6

3.2 Using a DTD

If a document is intended to conform to a certain DTD, we can either:

a) Include the DTD itself as a preamble to the document, or

b) In the opening line, refer to the DTD, which must be stored separately in the file system accessible to the application that is processing the document.

Example 9: Here is how we might introduce the document of Fig. 7 to assert that it is intended to conform to the DTD of Fig. 6.

```
<?xml version = "1.0" encoding = "utf-8" standalone = "no"?>
<!DOCTYPE Stars SYSTEM "star.dtd">
```

The attribute `standalone = "no"` says that a DTD is being used. Recall we set this attribute to `"yes"` when we did not wish to specify a DTD for the document. The location from which the DTD can be obtained is given in the `!DOCTYPE` clause, where the keyword `SYSTEM` followed by a file name gives this location. □

3.3 Attribute Lists

A DTD also lets us specify which attributes an element may have, and what the types of these attributes are. A declaration of the form

`<!ATTLIST` *element-name attribute-name type* `>`

says that the named attribute can be an attribute of the named element, and that the type of this attribute is the indicated type. Several attributes can be defined in one `ATTLIST` statement, but it is not necessary to do so, and the `ATTLIST` statements can appear in any position in the DTD.

The most common type for attributes is `CDATA`. This type is essentially character-string data with special characters like `<` escaped as in `#PCDATA`. Notice that `CDATA` does not take a pound sign as `#PCDATA` does. Another option is an enumerated type, which is a list of possible strings, surrounded by parentheses and separated by `|`'s. Following the data type there can be a keyword `#REQUIRED` or `#IMPLIED`, which means that the attribute must be present, or is optional, respectively.

Example 10: Instead of having the title and year be subelements of a `<Movie>` element, we could make these be attributes instead. Figure 8 shows possible attribute-list declarations. Notice that `Movie` is now an empty element. We have given it three attributes: `title`, `year`, and `genre`. The first two are `CDATA`, while the `genre` has values from an enumerated type. Note that in the document, the values, such as *comedy*, appear with quotes. Thus,

```
<Movie title = "Star Wars" year = "1977" genre = "sciFi" />
```

is a possible movie element in a document that conforms to this DTD. □

```
<!ELEMENT Movie EMPTY>
    <!ATTLIST Movie
        title CDATA #REQUIRED
        year CDATA #REQUIRED
        genre (comedy | drama | sciFi | teen) #IMPLIED
    >
```

Figure 8: Data about movies will appear as attributes

```
<!DOCTYPE StarMovieData [
    <!ELEMENT StarMovieData (Star*, Movie*)>
    <!ELEMENT Star (Name, Address+)>
        <!ATTLIST Star
            starId ID #REQUIRED
            starredIn IDREFS #IMPLIED
        >
    <!ELEMENT Name (#PCDATA)>
    <!ELEMENT Address (Street, City)>
    <!ELEMENT Street (#PCDATA)>
    <!ELEMENT City (#PCDATA)>
    <!ELEMENT Movie (Title, Year)>
        <!ATTLIST Movie
            movieId ID #REQUIRED
            starsOf IDREFS #IMPLIED
        >
    <!ELEMENT Title (#PCDATA)>
    <!ELEMENT Year (#PCDATA)>
]>
```

Figure 9: A DTD for stars and movies, using ID's and IDREF's

3.4 Identifiers and References

Recall from Section 2.5 that certain attributes can be used as identifiers for elements. In a DTD, we give these attributes the type ID. Other attributes have values that are references to these element ID's; these attributes may be declared to have type IDREF. The value of an IDREF attribute must also be the value of some ID attribute of some element, so the IDREF is in effect a pointer to the ID. An alternative is to give an attribute the type IDREFS. In that case, the value of the attribute is a string consisting of a list of ID's, separated by whitespace. The effect is that an IDREFS attribute links its element to a set of elements — the elements identified by the ID's on the list.

Example 11: Figure 9 shows a DTD in which stars and movies are given equal status, and the ID-IDREFS correspondence is used to describe the many-many relationship between movies and stars that was suggested in the semistructured data of Fig. 1. The structure differs from that of the DTD in Fig. 6, in that stars and movies have equal status; both are subelements of the root element. That is, the name of the root element for this DTD is `StarMovieData`, and its elements are a sequence of stars followed by a sequence of movies.

A star no longer has a set of movies as subelements, as was the case for the DTD of Fig. 6. Rather, its only subelements are a name and address, and in the beginning `<Star>` tag we shall find an attribute `starredIn` of type `IDREFS`, whose value is a list of ID's for the movies of the star.

```
<? xml version = "1.0" encoding = "utf-8" standalone = "yes" ?>
<StarMovieData>
    <Star starID = "cf" starredIn = "sw">
        <Name>Carrie Fisher</Name>
        <Address>
            <Street>123 Maple St.</Street>
            <City>Hollywood</City>
        </Address>
        <Address>
            <Street>5 Locust Ln.</Street>
            <City>Malibu</City>
        </Address>
    </Star>
    <Star starID = "mh" starredIn = "sw">
        <Name>Mark Hamill</Name>
        <Address>
            <Street>456 Oak Rd.</Street>
            <City>Brentwood</City>
        </Address>
    </Star>
    <Movie movieID = "sw" starsOf = "cf mh">
        <Title>Star Wars</Title>
        <Year>1977</Year>
    </Movie>
</StarMovieData>
```

Figure 10: Adding stars-in information to our XML document

A `<Star>` element also has an attribute `starId`. Since it is declared to be of type `ID`, the value of `starId` may be referenced by `<Movie>` elements to indicate the stars of the movie. That is, when we look at the attribute list for `Movie` in Fig. 9, we see that it has an attribute `movieId` of type `ID`; these are the ID's that will appear on lists that are the values of `starredIn` elements. Symmetrically, the attribute `starsOf` of `Movie` is an `IDREFS`, a list of ID's for stars. □

3.5 Exercises for Section 3

Exercise 3.1: Add to the document of Fig. 10 the following facts:

a) Carrie Fisher and Mark Hamill also starred in *The Empire Strikes Back* (1980) and *Return of the Jedi* (1983).

b) Harrison Ford also starred in *Star Wars*, in the two movies mentioned in (a), and the movie *Firewall* (2006).

c) Carrie Fisher also starred in *Hannah and Her Sisters* (1985).

d) Matt Damon starred in *The Bourne Identity* (2002).

! **Exercise 3.2:** Using your representation from Exercise 2.2, devise an algorithm that will take any relation schema (a relation name and a list of attribute names) and produce a DTD describing a document that represents that relation.

4 XML Schema

XML Schema is an alternative way to provide a schema for XML documents. It is more powerful than DTD's, giving the schema designer extra capabilities. For instance, XML Schema allows arbitrary restrictions on the number of occurrences of subelements. It allows us to declare types, such as integer or float, for simple elements, and it gives us the ability to declare keys and foreign keys.

4.1 The Form of an XML Schema

An XML Schema description of a schema is itself an XML document. It uses the namespace at the URL:

```
http://www.w3.org/2001/XMLSchema
```

that is provided by the World-Wide-Web Consortium. Each XML-Schema document thus has the form:

```
<? xml version = "1.0" encoding = "utf-8" ?>
<xs:schema xmlns:xs="http://www.w3.org/2001/XMLSchema">
  ...
</xs:schema>
```

The first line indicates XML, and uses the special brackets `<?` amd `?>`. The second line is the root tag for the document that is the schema. The attribute `xmlns` (XML namespace) makes the variable `xs` stand for the namespace for XML Schema that was mentioned above. It is this namespace that causes the tag `<xs:schema>` to be interpreted as `schema` in the namespace for XML Schema. As discussed in Section 2.6, qualifying each XML-Schema term we use with the prefix `xs:` will cause each such tag to be interpreted according to the rules for XML Schema. Between the opening `<xs:schema>` tag and its matched closing tag `</xs:schema>` will appear a schema. In what follows, we shall learn the most important tags from the XML-Schema namespace and what they mean.

4.2 Elements

An important component of schemas is the *element*, which is similar to an element definition in a DTD. In the discussion that follows, you should be alert to the fact that, because XML-Schema definitions are XML documents, these schemas are themselves composed of "elements." However, the elements of the schema itself, each of which has a tag that begins with `xs:`, are not the elements being defined by the schema.[3] The form of an element definition in XML Schema is:

```
<xs:element name = element name type = element type >
    constraints and/or structure information
</xs:element>
```

The element name is the chosen tag for these elements in the schema being defined. The type can be either a simple type or a complex type. Simple types include the common primitive types, such as `xs:integer`, `xs:string`, and `xs:boolean`. There can be no subelements for an element of a simple type.

Example 12: Here are title and year elements defined in XML Schema:

```
<xs:element name = "Title" type = "xs:string" />
<xs:element name = "Year" type = "xs:integer" />
```

[3]To further assist in the distinction between tags that are part of a schema definition and the tags of the schema being defined, we shall begin each of the latter with a capital letter.

Each of these `<xs:element>` elements is itself empty, so it can be closed by `/>` with no matched closing tag. The first defined element has name `Title` and is of string type. The second element is named `Year` and is of type integer. In documents (perhaps talking about movies) with `<Title>` and `<Year>` elements, these elements will not be empty, but rather will be followed by a string (the title) or integer (the year), and a matched closing tag, `</Title>` or `</Year>`, respectively. □

4.3 Complex Types

A *complex type* in XML Schema can have several forms, but the most common is a sequence of elements. These elements are required to occur in the sequence given, but the number of repetitions of each element can be controlled by attributes `minOccurs` and `maxOccurs`, that appear in the element definitions themselves. The meanings of these attributes are as expected; no fewer than `minOccurs` occurrences of each element may appear in the sequence, and no more than `maxOccurs` occurrences may appear. If there is more than one occurrence, they must all appear consecutively. The default, if one or both of these attributes are missing, is one occurrence. To say that there is no upper limit on occurrences, use the value `"unbounded"` for `maxOccurs`.

```
<xs:complexType name = type name >
    <xs:sequence>
        list of element definitions
    </xs:sequence>
</xs:complexType>
```

Figure 11: Defining a complex type that is a sequence of elements

The form of a definition for a complex-type that is a sequence of elements is shown in Fig. 11. The name for the complex type is optional, but is needed if we are going to use this complex type as the type of one or more elements of the schema being defined. An alternative is to place the complex-type definition between an opening `<xs:element>` tag and its matched closing tag, to make that complex type be the type of the element.

Example 13: Let us write a complete XML-Schema document that defines a very simple schema for movies. The root element for movie documents will be `<Movies>`, and the root will have zero or more `<Movie>` subelements. Each `<Movie>` element will have two subelements: a title and year, in that order. The XML-Schema document is shown in Fig. 12.

Lines (1) and (2) are a typical preamble to an XML-Schema definition. In lines (3) through (8), we define a complex type, whose name is `movieType`. This type consists of a sequence of two elements named `Title` and `Year`; they are the elements we saw in Example 12. The type definition itself does not create

```
 1)  <? xml version = "1.0" encoding = "utf-8" ?>
 2)  <xs:schema xmlns:xs = "http://www.w3.org/2001/XMLSchema">

 3)      <xs:complexType name = "movieType">
 4)          <xs:sequence>
 5)              <xs:element name = "Title" type = "xs:string" />
 6)              <xs:element name = "Year" type = "xs:integer" />
 7)          </xs:sequence>
 8)      </xs:complexType>

 9)      <xs:element name = "Movies">
10)          <xs:complexType>
11)              <xs:sequence>
12)                  <xs:element name = "Movie" type = "movieType"
                             minOccurs = "0" maxOccurs = "unbounded" />
13)              </xs:sequence>
14)          </xs:complexType>
15)      </xs:element>

16)  </xs:schema>
```

Figure 12: A schema for movies in XML Schema

any elements, but notice how the name movieType is used in line (12) to make this type be the type of Movie elements.

Lines (9) through (15) define the element Movies. Although we could have created a complex type for this element, as we did for Movie, we have chosen to include the type in the element definition itself. Thus, we put no type attribute in line (9). Rather, between the opening <xs:element> tag at line (9) and its matched closing tag at line (15) appears a complex-type definition for the element Movies. This complex type has no name, but it is defined at line (11) to be a sequence. In this case, the sequence has only one kind of element, Movie, as indicated by line (12). This element is defined to have type movieType — the complex type we defined at lines (3) through (8). It is also defined to have between zero and infinity occurrences. Thus, the schema of Fig. 12 says the same thing as the DTD we show in Fig. 13. □

There are several other ways we can construct a complex type.

- In place of xs:sequence we could use xs:all, which means that each of the elements between the opening <xs:all> tag and its matched closing tag must occur, in any order, exactly once each.

- Alternatively, we could replace xs:sequence by xs:choice. Then, exactly one of the elements found between the opening <xs:choice> tag and its

```
<!DOCTYPE Movies [
    <!ELEMENT Movies (Movie*)>
    <!ELEMENT Movie (Title, Year)>
    <!ELEMENT Title (#PCDATA)>
    <!ELEMENT Year (#PCDATA)>
]>
```

Figure 13: A DTD for movies

matched closing tag will appear.

The elements inside a sequence or choice can have `minOccurs` and `maxOccurs` attributes to govern how many times they can appear. In the case of a choice, only one of the elements can appear at all, but it can appear more than once if it has a value of `maxOccurs` greater than 1. The rules for `xs:all` are different. It is not permitted to have a `maxOccurs` value other than 1, but `minOccurs` can be either 0 or 1. In the former case, the element might not appear at all.

4.4 Attributes

A complex type can have attributes. That is, when we define a complex type T, we can include instances of element `<xs:attribute>`. When we use T as the type of an element E, then E can have (or must have) an instance of this attribute. The form of an attribute definition is:

`<xs:attribute name =` *attribute name* `type =` *type name*
other information about the attribute `/>`

The "other information" may include information such as a default value and usage (required or optional — the latter is the default).

Example 14: The notation

```
<xs:attribute name = "year" type = "xs:integer"
    default = "0" />
```

defines `year` to be an attribute of type integer. We do not know of what element `year` is an attribute; it depends where the above definition is placed. The default value of `year` is 0, meaning that if an element without a value for attribute `year` occurs in a document, then the value of `year` is taken to be 0.

As another instance:

```
<xs:attribute name = "year" type = "xs:integer"
    use = "required" />
```

is another definition of the attribute `year`. However, setting `use` to `required` means that any element of the type being defined must have a value for attribute `year`. □

Attribute definitions are placed within a complex-type definition. In the next example, we rework Example 13 by making the type `movieType` have attributes for the title and year, rather than subelements for that information.

```
 1)  <? xml version = "1.0" encoding = "utf-8" ?>
 2)  <xs:schema xmlns:xs = "http://www.w3.org/2001/XMLSchema">

 3)      <xs:complexType name = "movieType">
 4)          <xs:attribute name = "title" type = "xs:string"
                 use = "required" />
 5)          <xs:attribute name = "year" type = "xs:integer"
                 use = "required" />
 6)      </xs:complexType>

 7)      <xs:element name = "Movies">
 8)          <xs:complexType>
 9)              <xs:sequence>
10)                  <xs:element name = "Movie" type = "movieType"
                         minOccurs = "0" maxOccurs = "unbounded" />
11)              </xs:sequence>
12)          </xs:complexType>
13)      </xs:element>

14)  </xs:schema>
```

Figure 14: Using attributes in place of simple elements

Example 15: Figure 14 shows the revised XML Schema definition. At lines (4) and (5), the attributes `title` and `year` are defined to be required attributes for elements of type `movieType`. When element `Movie` is given that type at line (10), we know that every `<Movie>` element must have values for `title` and `year`. Figure 15 shows the DTD resembling Fig. 14. □

4.5 Restricted Simple Types

It is possible to create a restricted version of a simple type such as integer or string by limiting the values the type can take. These types can then be used as the type of an attribute or element. We shall consider two kinds of restrictions here:

```
<!DOCTYPE Movies [
    <!ELEMENT Movies (Movie*)>
    <!ELEMENT Movie EMPTY>
        <!ATTLIST Movie
            title CDATA #REQUIRED
            year  CDATA #REQUIRED
        >
]>
```

Figure 15: DTD equivalent for Fig. 14

1. Restricting numerical values by using `minInclusive` to state the lower bound, `maxInclusive` to state the upper bound.[4]

2. Restricting values to an enumerated type.

The form of a range restriction is shown in Fig. 16. The restriction has a base, which may be a primitive type (e.g., `xs:string`) or another simple type.

```
<xs:simpleType name = type name >
   <xs:restriction base = base type >
      upper and/or lower bounds
   </xs:restriction>
</xs:simpleType>
```

Figure 16: Form of a range restriction

Example 16: Suppose we want to restrict the year of a movie to be no earlier than 1915. Instead of using `xs:integer` as the type for element `Year` in line (6) of Fig. 12 or for the attribute `year` in line (5) of Fig. 14, we could define a new simple type as in Fig. 17. The type `movieYearType` would then be used in place of `xs:integer` in the two lines cited above. □

Our second way to restrict a simple type is to provide an enumeration of values. The form of a single enumerated value is:

```
<xs:enumeration value = some value />
```

A restriction can consist of any number of these values.

[4]The "inclusive" means that the range of values includes the given bound. An alternative is to replace `Inclusive` by `Exclusive`, meaning that the stated bounds are just outside the permitted range.

```
<xs:simpleType name = "movieYearType">
    <xs:restriction base = "xs:integer">
        <xs:minInclusive value = "1915" />
    </xs:restriction>
<xs:simpleType>
```

Figure 17: A type that restricts integer values to be 1915 or greater

Example 17: Let us design a simple type suitable for the genre of movies. In our running example, we have supposed that there are only four possible genres: comedy, drama, sciFi, and teen. Figure 18 shows how to define a type `genreType` that could serve as the type for an element or attribute representing our genres of movies. □

```
<xs:simpleType name = "genreType">
    <xs:restriction base = "xs:string">
        <xs:enumeration value = "comedy" />
        <xs:enumeration value = "drama" />
        <xs:enumeration value = "sciFi" />
        <xs:enumeration value = "teen" />
    </xs:restriction>
<xs:simpleType>
```

Figure 18: A enumerated type in XML Schema

4.6 Keys in XML Schema

An element can have a key declaration, which says that when we look at a certain class C of elements, values of one or more given *fields* within those elements are unique. The concept of "field" is actually quite general, but the most common case is for a field to be either a subelement or an attribute. The class C of elements is defined by a "selector." Like fields, selectors can be complex, but the most common case is a sequence of one or more element names, each a subelement of the one before it. In terms of a tree of semistructured data, the class is all those nodes reachable from a given node by following a particular sequence of arc labels.

Example 18: Suppose we want to say, about the semistructured data in Fig. 1, that among all the nodes we can reach from the root by following a *star* label, what we find following a further *name* label leads us to a unique value. Then the "selector" would be *star* and the "field" would be *name*. The implication of asserting this key is that within the root element shown, there cannot be two stars with the same name. If movies had names instead of titles, then the key assertion would not prevent a movie and a star from having the same name. Moreover, if there were actually many elements like the tree of Fig. 1 found in one document (e.g., each of the objects we called "Root" in that figure were actually a single movie and its stars), then different trees could have the same star name without violating the key constraint. □

The form of a key declaration is

```
<xs:key name = key name >
   <xs:selector xpath = path description >
   <xs:field xpath = path description >
</xs:key>
```

There can be more than one line with an `xs:field` element, in case several fields are needed to form the key. An alternative is to use the element `xs:unique` in place of `xs:key`. The difference is that if "key" is used, then the fields must exist for each element defined by the selector. However, if "unique" is used, then they might not exist, and the constraint is only that they are unique if they exist.

The selector path can be any sequence of elements, each of which is a subelement of the previous. The element names are separated by slashes. The field can be any subelement of the last element on the selector path, or it can be an attribute of that element. If it is an attribute, then it is preceded by the "at-sign." There are other options, and in fact, the selector and field can be any XPath expressions.

Example 19: In Fig. 19 we see an elaboration of Fig. 12. We have added the element `Genre` to the definition of `movieType`, in order to have a nonkey subelement for a movie. Lines (3) through (10) define `genreType` as in Example 17. The `Genre` subelement of `movieType` is added at line (15).

The definition of the `Movies` element has been changed in lines (24) through (28) by the addition of a key. The name of the key is `movieKey`; this name will be used if it is referenced by a foreign key, as we shall discuss in Section 4.7. Otherwise, the name is irrelevant. The selector path is just `Movie`, and there are two fields, `Title` and `Year`. The meaning of this key declaration is that, within any `Movies` element, among all its `Movie` subelements, no two can have both the same title and the same year, nor can any of these values be missing. Note that because of the way `movieType` was defined at lines (13) and (14), with no values for `minOccurs` or `maxOccurs` for `Title` or `Year`, the defaults, 1, apply, and there must be exactly one occurrence of each. □

4.7 Foreign Keys in XML Schema

We can also declare that an element has, perhaps deeply nested within it, a field or fields that serve as a reference to the key for some other element. This

```
 1)  <? xml version = "1.0" encoding = "utf-8" ?>
 2)  <xs:schema xmlns:xs = "http://www.w3.org/2001/XMLSchema">

 3)  <xs:simpleType name = "genreType">
 4)     <xs:restriction base = "xs:string">
 5)        <xs:enumeration value = "comedy" />
 6)        <xs:enumeration value = "drama" />
 7)        <xs:enumeration value = "sciFi" />
 8)        <xs:enumeration value = "teen" />
 9)     </xs:restriction>
10)  <xs:simpleType>

11)     <xs:complexType name = "movieType">
12)        <xs:sequence>
13)           <xs:element name = "Title" type = "xs:string" />
14)           <xs:element name = "Year" type = "xs:integer" />
15)           <xs:element name = "Genre" type = "genreType"
                 minOccurs = "0" maxOccurs = "1" />
16)        </xs:sequence>
17)     </xs:complexType>

18)     <xs:element name = "Movies">
19)        <xs:complexType>
20)           <xs:sequence>
21)              <xs:element name = "Movie" type = "movieType"
                     minOccurs = "0" maxOccurs = "unbounded" />
22)           </xs:sequence>
23)        </xs:complexType>
24)        <xs:key name = "movieKey">
25)           <xs:selector xpath = "Movie" />
26)           <xs:field xpath = "Title" />
27)           <xs:field xpath = "Year" />
28)        </xs:key>
29)     </xs:element>

30)  </xs:schema>
```

Figure 19: A schema for movies in XML Schema

capability is similar to what we get with ID's and IDREF's in a DTD (see Section 3.4). However, the latter are untyped references, while references in XML Schema are to particular types of elements. The form of a foreign-key definition in XML Schema is:

```
<xs:keyref name = foreign-key name refer = key name >
    <xs:selector xpath = path description >
    <xs:field xpath = path description >
</xs:keyref>
```

The schema element is `xs:keyref`. The foreign-key itself has a name, and it refers to the name of some key or unique value. The selector and field(s) are as for keys.

Example 20: Figure 20 shows the definition of an element `<Stars>`. We have used the style of XML Schema where each complex type is defined within the element that uses it. Thus, we see at lines (4) through (6) that a `<Stars>` element consists of one or more `<Star>` subelements.

At lines (7) through (11), we see that each `<Star>` element has three kinds of subelements. There is exactly one `<Name>` and one `<Address>` subelement, and any number of `<StarredIn>` subelements. In lines (12) through (15), we find that a `<StarredIn>` element has no subelements, but it does have two attributes, `title` and `year`.

Lines (22) through (26) define a foreign key. In line (22) we see that the name of this foreign-key constraint is `movieRef` and that it refers to the key `movieKey` that was defined in Fig. 19. Notice that this foreign key is defined within the `<Stars>` definition. The selector is `Star/StarredIn`. That is, it says we should look at every `<StarredIn>` subelement of every `<Star>` subelement of a `<Stars>` element. From that `<StarredIn>` element, we extract the two fields `title` and `year`. The `@` indicates that these are attributes rather than subelements. The assertion made by this foreign-key constraint is that any title-year pair we find in this way will appear in some `<Movie>` element as the pair of values for its subelements `<Title>` and `<Year>`. □

4.8 Exercises for Section 4

Exercise 4.1: Give an example of a document that conforms to the XML Schema definition of Fig. 12 and an example of one that has all the elements mentioned, but does not conform to the definition.

Exercise 4.2: Rewrite Fig. 12 so that there is a named complex type for `Movies`, but no named type for `Movie`.

Exercise 4.3: Write the XML Schema definitions of Figs. 19 and 20 as a DTD.

```
<? xml version = "1.0" encoding = "utf-8" ?>
<xs:schema xmlns:xs = "http://www.w3.org/2001/XMLSchema">

<xs:element name = "Stars">

    <xs:complexType>
        <xs:sequence>
            <xs:element name = "Star" minOccurs = "1"
                    maxOccurs = "unbounded">
                <xs:complexType>
                    <xs:sequence>
                        <xs:element name = "Name"
                            type = "xs;string" />
                        <xs:element name = "Address"
                            type = "xs:string" />
                        <xs:element name = "StarredIn"
                                minOccurs = "0"
                                maxOccurs = "unbounded">
                            <xs:complexType>
                                <xs:attribute name = "title"
                                    type = "xs:string" />
                                <xs:attribute name = "year"
                                    type = "xs:integer" />
                            </xs:complexType>
                        </xs:element>
                    </xs:sequence>
                </xs:complexType>
            </xs:element>
        </xs:sequence>
    </xs:complexType>

    <xs:keyref name = "movieRef" refers = "movieKey">
        <xs:selector xpath = "Star/StarredIn" />
        <xs:field  xpath = "@title" />
        <xs:field  xpath = "@year" />
    </xs:keyref>

</xs:element>
```

Figure 20: Stars with a foreign key

5 Summary

✦ *Semistructured Data*: In this model, data is represented by a graph. Nodes are like objects or values of attributes, and labeled arcs connect an object to both the values of its attributes and to other objects to which it is connected by a relationship.

✦ *XML*: The Extensible Markup Language is a World-Wide-Web Consortium standard that representes semistructured data linearly.

✦ *XML Elements*: Elements consist of an opening tag `<Foo>`, a matched closing tag `</Foo>`, and everything between them. What appears can be text, or it can be subelements, nested to any depth.

✦ *XML Attributes*: Tags can have attribute-value pairs within them. These attributes provide additional information about the element with which they are associated.

✦ *Document Type Definitions*: The DTD is a simple, grammatical form of defining elements and attributes of XML, thus providing a rudimentary schema for those XML documents that use the DTD. An element is defined to have a sequence of subelements, and these elements can be required to appear exactly once, at most once, at least once, or any number of times. An element can also be defined to have a list of required and/or optional attributes.

✦ *Identifiers and References in DTD's*: To represent graphs that are not trees, a DTD allows us to declare attributes of type `ID` and `IDREF(S)`. An element can thus be given an identifier, and that identifier can be referred to by other elements from which we would like to establish a link.

✦ *XML Schema*: This notation is another way to define a schema for certain XML documents. XML Schema definitions are themselves written in XML, using a set of tags in a namespace that is provided by the World-Wide-Web Consortium.

✦ *Simple Types in XML Schema*: The usual sorts of primitive types, such as integers and strings, are provided. Additional simple types can be defined by restricting a simple type, such as by providing a range for values or by giving an enumeration of permitted values.

✦ *Complex Types in XML Schema*: Structured types for elements may be defined to be sequences of elements, each with a minimum and maximum number of occurrences. Attributes of an element may also be defined in its complex type.

✦ *Keys and Foreign Keys in XML Schema*: A set of elements and/or attributes may be defined to have a unique value within the scope of some enclosing element. Other sets of elements and/or attributes may be defined to have a value that appears as a key within some other kind of element.

6 References

Semistructured data as a data model was first studied in [5] and [4]. LOREL, the prototypical query language for this model is described in [3]. Surveys of work on semistructured data include [1], [7], and the book [2].

XML is a standard developed by the World-Wide-Web Consortium. The home page for information about XML is [9]. References on DTD's and XML Schema are also found there. For XML parsers, the definition of DOM is in [8] and for SAX it is [6]. A useful place to go for quick tutorials on many of these subjects is [10].

1. S. Abiteboul, "Querying semi-structured data," *Proc. Intl. Conf. on Database Theory* (1997), Lecture Notes in Computer Science 1187 (F. Afrati and P. Kolaitis, eds.), Springer-Verlag, Berlin, pp. 1–18.

2. S. Abiteboul, D. Suciu, and P. Buneman, *Data on the Web: From Relations to Semistructured Data and XML*, Morgan-Kaufmann, San Francisco, 1999.

3. S. Abiteboul, D. Quass, J. McHugh, J. Widom, and J. L. Weiner, "The LOREL query language for semistructured data," In *J. Digital Libraries* **1**:1, 1997.

4. P. Buneman, S. B. Davidson, and D. Suciu, "Programming constructs for unstructured data," *Proceedings of the Fifth International Workshop on Database Programming Languages*, Gubbio, Italy, Sept., 1995.

5. Y. Papakonstantinou, H. Garcia-Molina, and J. Widom, "Object exchange across heterogeneous information sources," *IEEE Intl. Conf. on Data Engineering*, pp. 251–260, March 1995.

6. Sax Project, `http://www.saxproject.org/`

7. D. Suciu (ed.) Special issue on management of semistructured data, *SIGMOD Record* **26**:4 (1997).

8. World-Wide-Web Consortium, `http://www.w3.org/DOM/`

9. World-Wide-Web Consortium, `http://www.w3.org/XML/`

10. W3 Schools, `http://www.w3schools.com`

Programming Languages for XML

We now turn to programming languages for semistructured data. All the widely used languages of this type apply to XML data, and might be used for semistructured data represented in other ways as well. In this chapter, we shall study three such languages. The first, XPath, is a simple language for describing sets of similar paths in a graph of semistructured data. XQuery is an extension of XPath that adopts something of the style of SQL. It allows iterations over sets, subqueries, and many other features that will be familiar from the study of SQL.

The third topic of this chapter is XSLT. This language was developed originally as a transformation language, capable of restructuring XML documents or turning them into printable (HTML) documents. However, its expressive power is actually quite similar to that of XQuery, and it is capable of producing XML results. Thus, it can serve as a query language for XML.

1 XPath

In this section, we introduce XPath. We begin with a discussion of the data model used in the most recent version of XPath, called XPath 2.0; this model is used in XQuery as well. This model plays a role analogous to the "bag of tuples of primitive-type components" that is used in the relational model as the value of a relation.

In later sections, we learn about XPath path expressions and their meaning. In general, these expressions allow us to move from elements of a document to some or all of their subelements. Using "axes," we are also able to move within documents in a variety of ways, and to obtain the attributes of elements.

1.1 The XPath Data Model

As in the relational model, XPath assumes that all values — those it produces and those constructed in intermediate steps — have the same general "shape." In the relational model, this "shape" is a bag of tuples. Tuples in a given bag all have the same number of components, and the components each have a primitive type, e.g., integer or string. In XPath, the analogous "shape" is *sequence of items.* An *item* is either:

1. A value of primitive type: integer, real, boolean, or string, for example.
2. A *node.* There are many kinds of nodes, but in our introduction, we shall only talk about three kinds:
   (a) *Documents.* These are files containing an XML document, perhaps denoted by their local path name or a URL.
   (b) *Elements.* These are XML elements, including their opening tags, their matched closing tag if there is one, and everything in between (i.e., below them in the tree of semistructured data that an XML document represents).
   (c) *Attributes.* These are found inside opening tags.

The items in a sequence need not be all of the same type, although often they will be.

Example 1 : Figure 1 is a sequence of four items. The first is the integer 10; the second is a string, and the third is a real. These are all items of primitive type.

```
10

"ten"

10.0

<Number base = "8">
     <Digit>1</Digit>
     <Digit>2</Digit>
</Number>

@val="10"
```

Figure 1: A sequence of five items

The fourth item is a node, and this node's type is "element." Notice that the element has tag `Number` with an attribute and two subelements with tag `Digit`. The last item is an attribute node. □

1.2 Document Nodes

While the documents to which XPath is applied can come from various sources, it is common to apply XPath to documents that are files. We can make a document node from a file by applying the function:

doc(*file name*)

The named file should be an XML document. We can name a file either by giving its local name or a URL if it is remote. Thus, examples of document nodes include:

```
doc("movies.xml")
doc("/usr/sally/data/movies.xml")
doc("infolab.stanford.edu/~hector/movies.xml")
```

Every XPath query refers to a document. In many cases, this document will be apparent from the context. You may recall our discussion of XML-Schema keys. We used XPath expressions to denote the selector and field(s) for a key. In that context, the document was "whatever document the schema definition is being applied to."

1.3 Path Expressions

Typically, an XPath expression starts at the root of a document and gives a sequence of tags and slashes (/), say $/T_1/T_2/\cdots/T_n$. We evaluate this expression by starting with a sequence of items consisting of one node: the document. We then process each of $T_1, T_2, \ldots$ in turn. To process T_i, consider the sequence of items that results from processing the previous tags, if any. Examine those items, in order, and find for each all its subelements whose tag is T_i. Those items are appended to the output sequence, in the order in which they appear in the document.

As a special case, the root tag T_1 for the document is considered a "subelement" of the document node. Thus, the expression $/T_1$ produces a sequence of one item, which is an element node consisting of the entire contents of the document. The difference may appear subtle; before we applied the expression $/T_1$, we had a document node representing the file, and after applying $/T_1$ to that node we have an element node representing the text in the file.

Example 2: Suppose our document is a file containing the XML text of Fig. 2. The path expression `/StarMovieData` produces the sequence of one element. This element has tag `<StarMovieData>`, of course, and it consists of everything in Fig. 2 except for line (1).

Now, consider the path expression

```
/StarMovieData/Star/Name
```

```
1)  <? xml version="1.0" encoding="utf-8" standalone="yes" ?>
2)  <StarMovieData>
3)      <Star starID = "cf" starredIn = "sw">
4)          <Name>Carrie Fisher</Name>
5)          <Address>
6)              <Street>123 Maple St.</Street>
7)              <City>Hollywood</City>
8)          </Address>
9)          <Address>
10)             <Street>5 Locust Ln.</Street>
11)             <City>Malibu</City>
12)         </Address>
13)     </Star>
14)     <Star starID = "mh" starredIn = "sw">
15)         <Name>Mark Hamill</Name>
16)         <Street>456 Oak Rd.</Street>
17)         <City>Brentwood</City>
18)     </Star>
19)     <Movie movieID = "sw" starsOf = "cf", "mh">
20)         <Title>Star Wars</Title>
21)         <Year>1977</Year>
22)     </Movie>
23) </StarMovieData>
```

Figure 2: An XML document for applying path expressions

When we apply the `StarMovieData` tag to the sequence consisting of the document, we get the sequence consisting of the root element, as discussed above. Next, we apply to this sequence the tag `Star`. There are two subelements of the `StarMovieData` element that have tag `Star`. These are lines (3) through (12) for star Carrie Fisher and lines (14) through (18) for star Mark Hamill. Thus, the result of the path expression `/StarMovieData/Star` is the sequence of these two elements, in that order.

Finally, we apply to this sequence the tag `Name`. The first element has one `Name` subelement, at line (4). The second element also has one `Name` subelement, at line (15). Thus, the sequence

```
<Name>Carrie Fisher</Name>
<Name>Mark Hamill</Name>
```

is the result of applying the path expression `/StarMovieData/Star/Name` to the document of Fig. 2. □

1.4 Relative Path Expressions

In several contexts, we shall use XPath expressions that are *relative* to the current node or sequence of nodes.

- You may recall that we talked about selector and field values that were really XPath expressions relative to a node or sequence of nodes for which we were defining a key.

- In Example 2 we talked about applying the XPath expression `Star` to the element consisting of the entire document, or the expression `Name` to a sequence of `Star` elements.

Relative expressions do not start with a slash. Each such expression must be applied in some context, which will be clear from its use. The similarity to the way files and directories are designated in a UNIX file system is not accidental.

1.5 Attributes in Path Expressions

Path expressions allow us to find all the elements within a document that are reached from the root along a particular kind of path (a sequence of tags). Sometimes, we want to find not these elements but rather the values of an attribute of those elements. If so, we can end the path expression by an attribute name preceded by an at-sign. That is, the path-expression form is $/T_1/T_2/\cdots/T_n/\texttt{@}A$.

The result of this expression is computed by first applying the path expression $/T_1/T_2/\cdots/T_n$ to get a sequence of elements. We then look at the opening tag of each element, in turn, to find an attribute A. If there is one, then the value of that attribute is appended to the sequence that forms the result.

Example 3: The path expression

```
/StarMovieData/Star/@starID
```

applied to the document of Fig. 2 finds the two `Star` elements and looks into their opening tags at lines (3) and (14) to find the values of their `starID` attributes. Both elements have this attribute, so the result sequence is `"cf" "mh"`. □

1.6 Axes

So far, we have only navigated through semistructured-data graphs in two ways: from a node to its children or to an attribute. XPath in fact provides a large number of *axes*, which are modes of navigation. Two of these axes are *child* (the default axis) and *attribute*, for which `@` is really a shorthand. At each step in a path expression, we can prefix a tag or attribute name by an axis name and a double-colon. For example,

```
/StarMovieData/Star/@starID
```

is really shorthand for:

```
/child::StarMovieData/child::Star/attribute::starID
```

Some of the other axes are parent, ancestor (really a proper ancestor), descendant (a proper descendant), next-sibling (any sibling to the right), previous-sibling (any sibling to the left), self, and descendant-or-self. The latter has a shorthand `//` and takes us from a sequence of elements to those elements and all their subelements, at any level of nesting.

Example 4: It might look hard to find, in the document of Fig. 2, all the cities where stars live. The problem is that Mark Hamill's city is not nested within an `Address` element, so it is not reached along the same paths as Carrie Fisher's cities. However, the path expression

```
//City
```

finds all the `City` subelements, at any level of nesting, and returns them in the order in which they appear in the document. That is, the result of this path expression is the sequence:

```
<City>Hollywood</City>
<City>Malibu</City>
<City>Brentwood</City>
```

which we obtain from lines (7), (11), and (17), respectively.

We could also use the `//` axis within the path expression. For example, should the document contain city information that wasn't about stars (e.g., studios and their addresses), then we could restrict the paths that we consider to make sure that the city was a subelement of a `Star` element. For the given document, the path expression

```
/StarMovieData/Star//City
```

produces the same three `City` elements as a result. □

Some of the other axes have shorthands as well. For example, `..` stands for parent, and `.` for self. We have already seen `@` for attribute and `/` for child.

1.7 Context of Expressions

In order to understand the meaning of an axis like parent, we need to explore further the view of data in XPath. Results of expressions are sequences of elements or primitive values. However, XPath expressions and their results do not exist in isolation; if they did, it would not make sense to ask for the "parent" of an element. Rather, there is normally a context in which the expression is evaluated. In all our examples, there is a single document from which elements are extracted. If we think of an element in the result of some XPath expression as a reference to the element in the document, then it makes sense to apply axes like parent, ancestor, or next-sibling to the element in the sequence.

For example, keys in XML Schema are defined by a pair of XPath expressions. Key constraints apply to XML documents that obey the schema that includes the constraint. Each such document provides the context for the XPath expressions in the schema itself. Thus, it is permitted to use all the XPath axes in these expressions.

1.8 Wildcards

Instead of specifying a tag along every step of a path, we can use a `*` to say "any tag." Likewise, instead of specifying an attribute, `@*` says "any attribute."

Example 5: Consider the path expression

```
/StarMovieData/*/@*
```

applied to the document of Fig. 2. First, `/StarMovieData/*` takes us to every subelement of the root element. There are three: two stars and a movie. Thus, the result of this path expression is the sequence of elements in lines (3) through (13), (14) through (18), and (19) through (22).

However, the expression asks for the values of all the attributes of these elements. We therefore look for attributes among the outermost tags of each of these elements, and return their values in the order in which they appear in the document. Thus, the sequence

```
"cf" "sw" "mh" "sw" "sw" "cf" "mh"
```

is the result of the XPath query.

A subtle point is that the value of the `starsOf` attribute in line (19) is itself a sequence of items — strings `"cf"` and `"mh"`. XPath expands sequences that are part of other sequences, so all items are at the "top level," as we showed above. That is, a sequence of items is not itself an item. □

1.9 Conditions in Path Expressions

As we evaluate a path expression, we can restrict ourselves to follow only a subset of the paths whose tags match the tags in the expression. To do so, we follow a tag by a condition, surrounded by square brackets. This condition can be anything that has a boolean value. Values can be compared by comparison operators such as `=` or `>=`. "Not equal" is represented as in C, by `!=`. A compound condition can be constructed by connecting comparisons with operators `or` or `and`.

The values compared can be path expressions, in which case we are comparing the sequences returned by the expressions. Comparisons have an implied "there exists" sense; two sequences are related if any pair of items, one from each sequence, are related by the given comparison operator. An example should make this concept clear.

Example 6: The following path expression:

```
/StarMovieData/Star[//City = "Malibu"]/Name
```

returns the names of the movie stars who have at least one home in Malibu. To begin, the path expression `/StarMovieData/Star` returns a sequence of all the `Star` elements. For each of these elements, we need to evaluate the truth of the condition `//City = "Malibu"`. Here, `//City` is a path expression, but it, like any path expression in a condition, is evaluated relative to the element to which the condition is applied. That is, we interpret the expression assuming that the element were the entire document to which the path expression is applied.

We start with the element for Carrie Fisher, lines (3) through (13) of Fig. 2. The expression `//City` causes us to look for all subelements, nested zero or more levels deep, that have a `City` tag. There are two, at lines (7) and (11). The result of the path expression `//City` applied to the Carrie-Fisher element is thus the sequence:

```
<City>Hollywood</City>
<City>Malibu</City>
```

Each item in this sequence is compared with the value `"Malibu"`. An element whose type is a primitive value such as a string can be equated to that string, so the second item passes the test. As a result, the entire `Star` element of lines (3) through (13) satisfies the condition.

When we apply the condition to the second item, lines (14) through (18) for Mark Hamill, we find a `City` subelement, but its value does not match `"Malibu"` and this element fails the condition. Thus, only the Carrie-Fisher element is in the result of the path expression

```
/StarMovieData/Star[//City = "Malibu"]
```

We have still to finish the XPath query by applying to this sequence of one element the continuation of the path expression, `/Name`. At this stage, we search for a `Name` subelement of the Carrie-Fisher element and find it at line (4). Consequently, the query result is the sequence of one element, `<Name>Carrie Fisher</Name>`. □

Several other useful forms of condition are:

- An integer $[i]$ by itself is true only when applied the ith child of its parent.
- A tag $[T]$ by itself is true only for elements that have one or more subelements with tag T.

- Similarly, an attribute $[A]$ by itself is true only for elements that have a value for the attribute A.

Example 7: Figure 3 is a variant of our running movie example, in which we have grouped all the movies with a common title as one `Movie` element, with subelements that have tag `Version`. The title is an attribute of the movie, and the year is an attribute of the version. Versions have `Star` subelements. Consider the XPath query, applied to this document:

```
/Movies/Movie/Version[1]/@year
```

It asks for the year in which the first version of each movie was made, and the result is the sequence "1933" "1984".

```
 1)  <? xml version="1.0" encoding="utf-8" standalone="yes" ?>
 2)  <Movies>
 3)      <Movie title = "King Kong">
 4)          <Version year = "1933">
 5)              <Star>Fay Wray</Star>
 6)          </Version>
 7)          <Version year = "1976">
 8)              <Star>Jeff Bridges</Star>
 9)              <Star>Jessica Lange</Star>
10)          </Version>
11)          <Version year = "2005" />
12)      </Movie>
13)      <Movie title = "Footloose">
14)          <Version year = "1984">
15)              <Star>Kevin Bacon</Star>
16)              <Star>John Lithgow</Star>
17)              <Star>Sarah Jessica Parker</Star>
18)          </Version>
19)      </Movie>
20)  </Movies>
```

Figure 3: An XML document for applying path expressions

In more detail, there are four `Version` elements that match the path

```
/Movies/Movie/Version
```

These are at lines (4) through (6), (7) through (10), line (11), and lines (14) through (18), respectively. Of these, the first and last are the first children of their respective parents. The `year` attributes for these versions are 1933 and 1984, respectively. □

Example 8: The XPath query:

```
/Movies/Movie/Version[Star]
```

applied to the document of Fig. 3 returns three `Version` elements. The condition `[Star]` is interpreted as "has at least one `Star` subelement." That condition is true for the `Version` elements of lines (4) through (6), (7) through (10), and (14) through (18); it is false for the element of line (11). □

```
<Products>
    <Maker name = "A">
        <PC model = "1001" price = "2114">
            <Speed>2.66</Speed>
            <RAM>1024</RAM>
            <HardDisk>250</HardDisk>
        </PC>
        <PC model = "1002" price = "995">
            <Speed>2.10</Speed>
            <RAM>512</RAM>
            <HardDisk>250</HardDisk>
        </PC>
        <Laptop model = "2004" price = "1150">
            <Speed>2.00</Speed>
            <RAM>512</RAM>
            <HardDisk>60</HardDisk>
            <Screen>13.3</Screen>
        </Laptop>
        <Laptop model = "2005" price = "2500">
            <Speed>2.16</Speed>
            <RAM>1024</RAM>
            <HardDisk>120</HardDisk>
            <Screen>17.0</Screen>
        </Laptop>
    </Maker>
```

Figure 4: XML document with product data — beginning

1.10 Exercises for Section 1

Exercise 1.1: Figures 4 and 5 are the beginning and end, respectively, of an XML document that contains some of the data from our running products exercise. Write the following XPath queries. What is the result of each?

```
    <Maker name = "E">
        <PC model = "1011" price = "959">
            <Speed>1.86</Speed>
            <RAM>2048</RAM>
            <HardDisk>160</HardDisk>
        </PC>
        <PC model = "1012" price = "649">
            <Speed>2.80</Speed>
            <RAM>1024</RAM>
            <HardDisk>160</HardDisk>
        </PC>
        <Laptop model = "2001" price = "3673">
            <Speed>2.00</Speed>
            <RAM>2048</RAM>
            <HardDisk>240</HardDisk>
            <Screen>20.1</Screen>
        </Laptop>
        <Printer model = "3002" price = "239">
            <Color>false</Color>
            <Type>laser</Type>
        </Printer>
    <Maker name = "H">
        <Printer model = "3006" price = "100">
            <Color>true</Color>
            <Type>ink-jet</Type>
        </Printer>
        <Printer model = "3007" price = "200">
            <Color>true</Color>
            <Type>laser</Type>
        </Printer>
    </Maker>
</Products>
```

Figure 5: XML document with product data — end

a) Find the amount of RAM on each PC.

b) Find the price of each product of any kind.

c) Find all the printer elements.

! d) Find the makers of laser printers.

! e) Find the makers of PC's and/or laptops.

f) Find the model numbers of PC's with a hard disk of at least 200 gigabytes.

!! g) Find the makers of at least two PC's.

Exercise 1.2: The document of Fig. 6 contains data similar to that used in our running battleships exercise. In this document, data about ships is nested within their class element, and information about battles appears inside each ship element. Write the following queries in XPath. What is the result of each?

a) Find the names of all ships.

b) Find all the `Class` elements for classes with a displacement larger than 35000.

c) Find all the `Ship` elements for ships that were launched before 1917.

d) Find the names of the ships that were sunk.

! e) Find the years in which ships having the same name as their class were launched.

! f) Find the names of all ships that were in battles.

!! g) Find the `Ship` elements for all ships that fought in two or more battles.

2 XQuery

XQuery is an extension of XPath that has become a standard for high-level querying of databases containing data in XML form. This section will introduce some of the important capabilities of XQuery.

```
<Ships>
    <Class name = "Kongo" type = "bc" country = "Japan"
            numGuns = "8" bore = "14" displacement = "32000">
        <Ship name = "Kongo" launched = "1913" />
        <Ship name = "Hiei" launched = "1914" />
        <Ship name = "Kirishima" launched = "1915">
            <Battle outcome = "sunk">Guadalcanal</Battle>
        </Ship>
        <Ship name = "Haruna" launched = "1915" />
    </Class>
    <Class name = "North Carolina" type = "bb" country = "USA"
            numGuns = "9" bore = "16" displacement = "37000">
        <Ship name = "North Carolina" launched = "1941" />
        <Ship name = "Washington" launched = "1941">
            <Battle outcome = "ok">Guadalcanal</Battle>
        </Ship>
    </Class>
    <Class name = "Tennessee" type = "bb" country = "USA"
            numGuns = "12" bore = "14" displacement = "32000">
        <Ship name = "Tennessee" launched = "1920">
            <Battle outcome = "ok">Surigao Strait</Battle>
        </Ship>
        <Ship name = "California" launched = "1921">
            <Battle outcome = "ok">Surigao Strait</Battle>
    </Class>
    <Class name = "King George V" type = "bb"
            country = "Great Britain"
            numGuns = "10" bore = "14" displacement = "32000">
        <Ship name = "King George V" launched = "1940" />
        <Ship name = "Prince of Wales" launched = "1941">
            <Battle outcome = "damaged">Denmark Strait</Battle>
            <Battle outcome = "sunk">Malaya</Battle>
        </Ship>
        <Ship name = "Duke of York" launched = "1941">
            <Battle outcome = "ok">North Cape</Battle>
        </Ship>
        <Ship name = "Howe" launched = "1942" />
        <Ship name = "Anson" launched = "1942" />
    </Class>
</Ships>
```

Figure 6: XML document containing battleship data

Case Sensitivity of XQuery

XQuery is case sensitive. Thus, keywords such as `let` or `for` need to be written in lower case, just like keywords in C or Java.

2.1 XQuery Basics

XQuery uses the same model for values that we introduced for XPath in Section 1.1. That is, all values produced by XQuery expressions are sequences of items. Items are either primitive values or nodes of various types, including elements, attributes, and documents. Elements in a sequence are assumed to exist in the context of some document, as discussed in Section 1.7.

XQuery is a *functional language*, which implies that any XQuery expression can be used in any place that an expression is expected. This property is a very strong one. SQL, for example, allows subqueries in many places; but SQL does not permit, for example, any subquery to be any operand of any comparison in a where-clause. The functional property is a double-edged sword. It requires every operator of XQuery to make sense when applied to lists of more than one item, leading to some unexpected consequences.

To start, every XPath expression is an XQuery expression. There is, however, much more to XQuery, including FLWR (pronounced "flower") expressions, which are in some sense analogous to SQL select-from-where expressions.

2.2 FLWR Expressions

Beyond XPath expressions, the most important form of XQuery expression involves clauses of four types, called for-, let-, where-, and return- (FLWR) clauses.[1] We shall introduce each type of clause in turn. However, we should be aware that there are options in the order and occurrences of these clauses.

1. The query begins with zero or more for- and let-clauses. There can be more than one of each kind, and they can be interlaced in any order, e.g., for, for, let, for, let.

2. Then comes an optional where-clause.

3. Finally, there is exactly one return-clause.

Example 9: Perhaps the simplest FLWR expression is:

```
return <Greeting>Hello World</Greeting>
```

It examines no data, and produces a value that is a simple XML element. □

[1] There is also an order-by clause that we shall introduce in Section 2.10. For that reason, FLWR is a less common acronym for the principal form of XQuery query than is FLWOR.

Let Clauses

The simple form of a let-clause is:

`let` *variable* `:=` *expression*

The intent of this clause is that the expression is evaluated and assigned to the variable for the remainder of the FLWR expression. Variables in XQuery must begin with a dollar-sign. Notice that the assignment symbol is `:=`, not an equal sign (which is used, as in XPath, in comparisons). More generally, a comma-separated list of assignments to variables can appear where we have shown one.

Example 10: One use of let-clauses is to assign a variable to refer to one of the documents whose data is used by the query. For example, if we want to query a document in file `stars.xml`, we can start our query with:

```
let $stars := doc("stars.xml")
```

In what follows, the value of `$stars` is a single doc node. It can be used in front of an XPath expression, and that expression will apply to the XML document contained in the file `stars.xml`. □

For Clauses

The simple form of a for-clause is:

`for` *variable* `in` *expression*

The intent is that the expression is evaluated. The result of any expression is a sequence of items. The variable is assigned to each item, in turn, and what follows this for-clause in the query is executed once for each value of the variable. You will not be much deceived if you draw an analogy between an XQuery for-clause and a C for-statement. More generally, several variables may be set ranging over different sequences of items in one for-clause.

Example 11: We shall use the data suggested in Fig. 7 for a number of examples in this section. The data consists of two files, `stars.xml` in Fig. 7(a) and `movies.xml` in Fig. 7(b). Each of these files has data similar to what we used in Section 1, but the intent is that what is shown is just a small sample of the actual contents of these files.

Suppose we start a query:

```
let $movies := doc("movies.xml")
for $m in $movies/Movies/Movie
    ... something done with each Movie element
```

```
<? xml version="1.0" encoding="utf-8" standalone="yes" ?>
<Stars>
    <Star>
        <Name>Carrie Fisher</Name>
        <Address>
            <Street>123 Maple St.</Street>
            <City>Hollywood</City>
        </Address>
        <Address>
            <Street>5 Locust Ln.</Street>
            <City>Malibu</City>
        </Address>
    </Star>
        ... more stars
</Stars>
```

(a) Document stars.xml

```
<? xml version="1.0" encoding="utf-8" standalone="yes" ?>
<Movies>
    <Movie title = "King Kong">
        <Version year = "1933">
            <Star>Fay Wray</Star>
        </Version>
        <Version year = "1976">
            <Star>Jeff Bridges</Star>
            <Star>Jessica Lange</Star>
        </Version>
        <Version year = "2005" />
    </Movie>
    <Movie title = "Footloose">
        <Version year = "1984">
            <Star>Kevin Bacon</Star>
            <Star>John Lithgow</Star>
            <Star>Sarah Jessica Parker</Star>
        </Version>
    </Movie>
        ... more movies
</Movies>
```

(b) Document movies.xml

Figure 7: Data for XQuery examples

Boolean Values in XQuery

A comparision like `$x = 10` evaluates to true or false (strictly speaking, to one of the names `xs:true` or `xs:false` from the namespace for XML Schema). However, several other types of expressions can be interpreted as true or false, and so can serve as the value of a condition in a where-clause. The important coercions to remember are:

1. If the value is a sequence of items, then the empty sequence is interpreted as false and nonempty sequences as true.

2. Among numbers, 0 and NaN ("not a number," in essence an infinite number) are false, and other numbers are true.

3. Among strings, the empty string is false and other strings are true.

Notice that `$movies/Movies/Movie` is an XPath expression that tells us to start with the document in file `movies.xml`, then go to the root `Movies` element, and then form the sequence of all `Movie` subelements. The body of the "for-loop" will be executed first with `$m` equal to the element of lines (17) through (26) of Fig. 7, then with `$m` equal to the element of lines (27) through (33), and then with each of the remaining `Movie` elements in the document. □

The Where Clause

The form of a where-clause is:

`where` *condition*

This clause is applied to an item, and the *condition*, which is an expression, evaluates to true or false. If the value is true, then the return-clause is applied to the current values of any variables in the query. Otherwise, nothing is produced for the current values of variables.

The Return Clause

The form of this clause is:

`return` *expression*

The result of a FLWR expression, like that of any expression in XQuery, is a sequence of items. The sequence of items produced by the expression in the return-clause is appended to the sequence of items produced so far. Note that although there is only one return-clause, this clause may be executed many times inside "for-loops," so the result of the query may be constructed in stages. We should not think of the return-clause as a "return-statement," since it does not end processing of the query.

Example 12: Let us complete the query we started in Example 11 by asking for a list of all the star elements found among the versions of all movies. The query is:

```
let $movies := doc("movies.xml")
for $m in $movies/Movies/Movie
return $m/Version/Star
```

The first value of `$m` in the "for-loop" is the element of lines (17) through (26) of Fig. 7. From that `Movie` element, the XPath expression `/Version/Star` produces a sequence of the three `Star` elements at lines (19), (22), and (23). That sequence begins the result of the query.

```
<Star>Fay Wray</Star>
<Star>Jeff Bridges</Star>
<Star>Jessica Lange</Star>
<Star>Kevin Bacon</Star>
<Star>John Lithgow</Star>
<Star>Sarah Jessica Parker</Star>
    ...
```

Figure 8: Beginning of the result sequence for the query of Example 12

The next value of `$m` is the element of lines (27) through (33). Now, the result of the expression in the return-clause is the sequence of elements in lines (29), (30), and (31). Thus the beginning of the result sequence looks like that in Fig. 8. □

2.3 Replacement of Variables by Their Values

Let us consider a modification to the query of Example 12. Here, we want to produce not just a sequence of `<Star>` elements, but rather a sequence of `Movie` elements, each containing all the stars of movies with a given title, regardless of which version they starred in. The title will be an attribute of the `Movie` element.

Figure 9 shows an attempt that seems right, but in fact *is not correct.* The expression we return for each value of `$m` seems to be an opening `<Movie>` tag followed by the sequence of `Star` elements for that movie, and finally a closing `</Movie>` tag. The `<Movie>` tag has a `title` attribute that is a copy of the same attribute from the `Movie` element in file `movies.xml`. However, when we execute this program, what appears is:

Sequences of Sequences

We should remind the reader that sequences of items can have no internal structure. Thus, in Fig. 8, there is no separator between Jessica Lange and Kevin Bacon, or any grouping of the first three stars and the last three, even though these groups were produced by different executions of the return-clause.

```
let $movies := doc("movies.xml")
for $m in $movies/Movies/Movie
return <Movie title = $m/@title>$m/Version/Star</Movie>
```

Figure 9: Erroneous attempt to produce Movie elements

```
<Movie title = "$m/@title">$m/Version/Star</Movie>
<Movie title = "$m/@title">$m/Version/Star</Movie>
...
```

The problem is that, between tags, or as the value of an attribute, any text string is permissible. This return statement looks no different, to the XQuery processor, than the return of Example 9, where we really were producing text inside matching tags. In order to get text interpreted as XQuery expressions inside tags, we need to surround the text by curly braces.

```
let $movies := doc("movies.xml")
for $m in $movies/Movies/Movie
return <Movie title = {$m/@title}>{$m/Version/Star}</Movie>
```

Figure 10: Adding curly braces fixes the problem

The proper way to meet our goal is shown in Fig. 10. In this query, the expressions `$m/title` and `$m/Version/Star` inside the braces are properly interpreted as XPath expressions. The first is replaced by a text string, and the second is replaced by a sequence of `Star` elements, as intended.

Example 13 : This example not only further illustrates the use of curly braces to force interpretation of expressions, but also emphasizes how any XQuery expression can be used wherever an expression of any kind is permitted. Our goal is to duplicate the result of Example 12, where we got a sequence of `Star` elements, but to make the entire sequence of stars be within a `Stars` element. We cannot use the trick of Fig. 10 with `Stars` in place of `Star`, because that would place many `Stars` tags around separate groups of stars.

```
let $starSeq := (
    let $movies := doc("movies.xml")
    for $m in $movies/Movies/Movie
    return $m/Version/Star
)
return <Stars>{$starSeq}</Stars>
```

Figure 11: Putting tags around a sequence

Figure 11 does the job. We assign the sequence of `Star` elements that results from the query of Example 12 to a local variable `$starSeq`. We then return that sequence, surrounded by tags, being careful to enclose the variable in braces so it is evaluated and not treated literally. □

2.4 Joins in XQuery

We can join two or more documents in XQuery in much the same way as we join two or more relations in SQL. In each case we need variables, each of which ranges over elements of one of the documents or tuples of one of the relations, respectively. In SQL, we use a from-clause to introduce the needed tuple variables (which may just be the table name itself); in XQuery we use a for-clause.

However, we must be very careful how we do comparisons in a join. First, there is the matter of comparison operators such as = or < operating on sequences with the meaning of "there exist elements that compare" as discussed in Section 1.9. We shall take up this point again in Section 2.5. Additionally, equality of elements is by "element identity" (analogous to "object identity"). That is, an element is not equal to a different element, even if it looks the same, character-by-character. Fortunately, we usually do not want to compare elements, but really the primitive values such as strings and integers that appear as values of their attributes and subelements. The comparison operators work as expected on primitive values; < is "precedes in lexicographic order" for strings.

There is a built-in function `data(E)` that extracts the value of an element *E*. We can use this function to extract the text from an element that is a string with matching tags.

Example 14: Suppose we want to find the cities in which stars mentioned in the `movies.xml` file of Fig. 7(b) live. We need to consult the `stars.xml` file of Fig. 7(a) to get that information. Thus, we set up a variable ranging over the `Star` elements of `movies.xml` and another variable ranging over the `Star` elements of `stars.xml`. When the data in a `Star` element of `movies.xml` matches the data in the `Name` subelement of a `Star` element of `stars.xml`, then we have a match, and we extract the `City` element of the latter.

Figure 12 shows a solution. The let-clause introduces variables to stand for the two documents. As before, this shorthand is not necessary, and we could have used the document nodes themselves in the XPath expressions of the next two lines. The for-clause introduces a doubly nested loop. Variable `$s1` ranges over each `Star` element of `movies.xml` and `$s2` does the same for `stars.xml`.

```
let $movies := doc("movies.xml"),
    $stars  := doc("stars.xml")
for $s1 in $movies/Movies/Movie/Version/Star,
    $s2 in $stars/Stars/Star
where data($s1) = data($s2/Name)
return $s2/Address/City
```

Figure 12: Finding the cities of stars

The where-clause uses the built-in function `data` to extract the strings that are the values of the elements `$s1` and `$s2`. Finally, the return-clause produces a `City` element. □

2.5 XQuery Comparison Operators

We shall now consider another puzzle where things don't quite work as expected. Our goal is to find the stars in `stars.xml` of Fig. 7(a) that live at 123 Maple St., Malibu. Our first attempt is in Fig. 13.

```
let $stars := doc("stars.xml")
for $s in $stars/Stars/Star
where $s/Address/Street = "123 Maple St." and
      $s/Address/City = "Malibu"
return $s/Name
```

Figure 13: An erroneous attempt to find who lives at 123 Maple St., Malibu

In the where-clause, we compare `Street` elements and `City` elements with strings, but that works as expected, because an element whose value is a string is coerced to that string, and the comparison will succeed when expected. The problem is seen when `$s` takes the `Star` element of lines (3) through (13) of Fig. 7 as its value. Then, XPath expression `$s/Address/Street` produces the sequence of two elements of lines (6) and (10) as its value. Since the = operator returns true if any pair of items, one from each side, equate, the value of the first condition is true; line (6), after coercion, is equal to the string `"123 Maple St."`. Similarly, the second condition compares the list of two `City` elements of lines (7) and (11) with the string `"Malibu"`, and equality is found for line (11). As a result, the `Name` element for Carrie Fisher [line (4)] is returned.

But Carrie Fisher doesn't live at 123 Maple St., Malibu. She lives at 123 Maple St., Hollywood, and elsewhere in Malibu. The existential nature of comparisons has caused us to fail to notice that we were getting a street and city from different addresses.

XQuery provides a set of comparison operators that only compare sequences consisting of a single item, and fail if either operand is a sequence of more than one item. These operators are two-letter abbreviations for the comparisons: `eq`, `ne`, `lt`, `gt`, `le`, and `ge`. We could use `eq` in place of `=` to catch the case where we are actually comparing a string with several streets or cities. The revised query is shown in Fig. 14.

```
let $stars := doc("stars.xml")
for $s in $stars/Stars/Star
where $s/Address/Street eq "123 Maple St." and
      $s/Address/City eq "Malibu"
return $s/Name
```

Figure 14: A second erroneous attempt to find who lives at 123 Maple St., Malibu

This query does not allow the Carrie-Fisher element to pass the test of the where-clause, because the left sides of the `eq` operator are not single items, and therefore the comparison fails. Unfortunately, it will not report any star with two or more addresses, even if one of those addresses is 123 Maple St., Malibu. Writing a correct query is tricky, regardless of which version of the comparison operators we use, and we leave a correct query as an exercise.

2.6 Elimination of Duplicates

XQuery allows us to eliminate duplicates in sequences of any kind, by applying the built-in function `distinct-values`. There is a subtlely that must be noted, however. Strictly speaking, distinct-values applies to primitive types. It will strip the tags from an element that is a tagged text-string, but it won't put them back. Thus, the input to `distinct-values` can be a list of elements and the result a list of strings.

Example 15: Figure 11 gathered all the `Star` elements from all the movies and returned them as a sequence. However, a star that appeared in several movies would appear several times in the sequence. By applying `distinct-values` to the result of the subquery that becomes the value of variable `$starseq`, we can eliminate all but one copy of each `Star` element. The new query is shown in Fig. 15.

Notice, however, that what is produced is a list of the names of the stars surrounded by the `Stars` tags, as:

```
<Stars>"Fay Wray" "Jeff Bridges" ··· </Stars>
```

In comparison, the version in Fig. 11 produced

```
let $starSeq := distinct-values(
    let $movies := doc("movies.xml")
    for $m in $movies/Movies/Movie
    return $m/Version/Star
)
return <Stars>{$starSeq}</Stars>
```

Figure 15: Eliminating duplicate stars

```
<Stars><Star>Fay Wray</Star> <Star>Jeff Bridges</Star> ···
                    </Stars>
```

but might produce duplicates. □

2.7 Quantification in XQuery

There are expressions that say, in effect, "for all" and "there exists." Their forms, respectively, are:

`every` *variable* `in` *expression1* `satisfies` *expression2*
`some` *variable* `in` *expression1* `satisfies` *expression2*

Here, *expression1* produces a sequence of items, and the variable takes on each item, in turn, as its value. For each such value, *expression2* (which normally involves the variable) is evaluated, and should produce a boolean value.

In the "every" version, the result of the entire expression is false if some item produced by *expression1* makes *expression2* false; the result is true otherwise. In the "some" version, the result of the entire expression is true if some item produced by *expression1* makes *expression2* true; the result is false otherwise.

```
let $stars := doc("stars.xml")
for $s in $stars/Stars/Star
where every $c in $s/Address/City satisfies
    $c = "Hollywood"
return $s/Name
```

Figure 16: Finding the stars who only live in Hollywood

Example 16: Using the data in the file `stars.xml` of Fig. 7(a), we want to find those stars who live in Hollywood and nowhere else. That is, no matter how many addresses they have, they all have city Hollywood. Figure 16 shows how to write this query. Notice that `$s/Address/City` produces the sequence of City elements of the star $s. The where-clause is thus satisfied if and only if every element on that list is <City>Hollywood</City>.

Incidentally, we could change the "every" to "some" and find the stars that have at least one home in Hollywood. However, it is rarely necessary to use the "some" version, since most tests in XQuery are existentially quantified anyway. For instance,

```
let $stars := doc("stars.xml")
for $s in $stars/Stars/Star
where $s/Address/City = "Hollywood"
return $s/Name
```

produces the stars with a home in Hollywood, without using a "some" expression. Recall our discussion in Section 2.5 of how a comparision such as =, with a sequence of more than one item on either or both sides, is true if we can match any items from the two sides. □

2.8 Aggregations

XQuery provides built-in functions to compute the usual aggregations such as count, sum, or max. They take any sequence as argument; that is, they can be applied to the result of any XQuery expression.

```
let $movies := doc("movies.xml")
for $m in $movies/Movies/Movie
where count($m/Version) > 1
return $m
```

Figure 17: Finding the movies with multiple versions

Example 17: Let us examine the data in file movies.xml of Fig. 7(b) and produce those Movie elements that have more than one version. Figure 17 does the job. The XPath expression $m/Version produces the sequence of Version elements for the movie $m. The number of items in the sequence is counted. If that count exceeds 1, the where-clause is satisfied, and the movie element $m is appended to the result. □

2.9 Branching in XQuery Expressions

There is an if-then-else expression in XQuery of the form

if (*expression1*) then *expression2* else *expression3*

To evaluate this expression, first evaluate *expression1*; if it is true, evaluate *expression2*, which becomes the result of the whole expression. If *expression1* is false, the result of the whole expression is *expression3*.

This expression is not a statement — there are no statements in XQuery, only expressions. Thus, the analog in C is the `?:` expression, not the if-then-else statement. Like the expression in C, there is no way to omit the "else" part. However, we can use as *expression3* the empty sequence, which is denoted `()`. This choice makes the conditional expression produce the empty sequence when the test-condition is not satisfied.

Example 18: Our goal in this example is to produce each of the versions of *King Kong*, tagging the most recent version `Latest` and the earlier versions `Old`. In line (1), we set variable `$kk` to be the `Movie` element for `King Kong`. Notice that we have used an XPath condition in this line, to make sure that we produce only that one element. Of course, if there were several `Movie` elements that had the title `King Kong`, then all of them would be on the sequence of items that is the value of `$kk`, and the query would make no sense. However, we are assuming title is a key for movies in this structure, since we have explicitly grouped versions of movies with the same title.

```
1)  let $kk :=
          doc("movies.xml")/Movies/Movie[@title = "King Kong"]
2)  for $v in $kk/Version
3)  return
4)      if ($v/@year = max($kk/Version/@year))
5)      then <Latest>{$v}</Latest>
6)      else <Old>{$v}</Old>
```

Figure 18: Tagging the versions of *King Kong*

Line (2) causes `$v` to iterate over all versions of *King Kong*. For each such version, we return one of two elements. To tell which, we evaluate the condition of line (4). On the right of the equal-sign is the maximum year of any of the *King-Kong* versions, and on the left is the year of the version `$v`. If they are equal, then `$v` is the latest version, and we produce the element of line (5). If not, then `$v` is an old version, and we produce the element of line (6). □

2.10 Ordering the Result of a Query

It is possible to sort the results as part of a FLWR query, if we add an order-clause before the return-clause. In fact, the query form we have been concentrating on here is usually called FLWOR (but still pronounced "flower"), to acknowledge the optional presence of an order-clause. The form of this clause is:

`order` *list of expressions*

The sort is based on the value of the first expression, ties are broken by the value of the second expression, and so on. The default order is ascending, but the keyword `descending` following an expression reverses the order.

What happens when an order is present is analogous to what happens in SQL. Just before we reach the stage in query processing where the output is assembled (the SELECT clause in SQL; the return-clause in XQuery), the result of previous clauses is assembled and sorted. In the case of SQL, the intermediate result is a set of bindings of tuples to the tuple variables that range over each of the relations in the FROM clause. Specifically, it is all those bindings that pass the test of the WHERE clause.

In XQuery, we should think of the intermediate result as a sequence of bindings of variables to values. The variables are those defined in the for- and let-clauses that precede the order-clause, and the sequence consists of all those bindings that pass the test of the where-clause. These bindings are each used to evaluate the expressions in the order-clause, and the values of those expressions govern the position of the binding in the order of all the bindings. Once we have the order of bindings, we use them, in turn, to evaluate the expression in the return-clause.

Example 19: Let us consider all versions of all movies, order them by year, and produce a sequence of Movie elements with the title and year as attributes. The data comes from file movies.xml in Fig. 7(b), as usual. The query is shown in Fig. 19.

```
let $movies := doc("movies.xml")
for $m in $movies/Movies/Movie,
    $v in $m/Version
order $v/@year
return <Movie title = "{$m/@title}" year = "{$v/@year}" />
```

Figure 19: Construct the sequence of title-year pairs, ordered by year

When we reach the order-clause, bindings provide values for the three variables $movies, $m, and $v. The value doc("movies.xml) is bound to $movies in every one of these bindings. However, the values of $m and $v vary; for each pair consisting of a movie and a version of that movie, there will be one binding for the two variables. For instance, the first such binding associates with $m the element in lines (17) through (26) of Fig. 7(b) and associates with $v the element of lines (18) through (20).

The bindings are sorted according to the value of attribute year in the element to which $v is bound. There may be many movies with the same year, and the ordering does not specify how these are to be ordered. As a result, all we know is that the movie-version pairs with a given year will appear together in some order, and the groups for each year will be in the ascending order of year. If we wanted to specify a total ordering of the bindings, we could, for example, add a second term to the list in the order-clause, such as:

```
order $v/@year, $m/@title
```

to break ties alphabetically by title.

After sorting the bindings, each binding is passed to the return-clause, in the order chosen. By substituting for the variables in the return-clause, we produce from each binding a single `Movie` element. □

2.11 Exercises for Section 2

Exercise 2.1: Using the product data from Figs. 4 and 5, write the following in XQuery.

a) Find the `Printer` elements with a price less than 100.

b) Find the `Printer` elements with a price less than 100, and produce the sequence of these elements surrounded by a tag `<CheapPrinters>`.

! c) Find the names of the makers of both printers and laptops.

! d) Find the names of the makers that produce at least two PC's with a speed of 3.00 or more.

! e) Find the makers such that every PC they produce has a price no more than 1000.

!! f) Produce a sequence of elements of the form

`<Laptop><Model>`x`</Model><Maker>`y`</Maker></Laptop>`

where x is the model number and y is the name of the maker of the laptop.

Exercise 2.2: Using the battleships data of Fig. 6, write the following in XQuery.

a) Find the names of the classes that had at least 10 guns.

b) Find the names of the ships that had at least 10 guns.

c) Find the names of the ships that were sunk.

d) Find the names of the classes with at least 3 ships.

! e) Find the names of the classes such that no ship of that class was in a battle.

!! f) Find the names of the classes that had at least two ships launched in the same year.

!! g) Produce a sequence of items of the form

`<Battle name = `x`><Ship name = `y` />`$\cdots$`</Battle>`

where x is the name of a battle and y the name of a ship in the battle. There may be more than one `Ship` element in the sequence.

! Exercise 2.3: Solve the problem of Section 2.5; write a query that finds the star(s) living at a given address, even if they have several addresses, without finding stars that do not live at that address.

! Exercise 2.4: Do there exist expressions E and F such that the expression `every $x in` E `satisfies` F is true, but `some $x in` E `satisfies` F is false? Either give an example or explain why it is impossible.

3 Extensible Stylesheet Language

XSLT (Extensible Stylesheet Language for Transformations) is a standard of the World-Wide-Web Consortium. Its original purpose was to allow XML documents to be transformed into HTML or similar forms that allowed the document to be viewed or printed. However, in practice, XSLT is another query language for XML. Like XPath or XQuery, we can use XSLT to extract data from documents or turn one document form into another form.

3.1 XSLT Basics

Like XML Schema, XSLT specifications are XML documents; these specifications are usually called *stylesheets*. The tags used in XSLT are found in a namespace, which is `http://www.w3.org/1999/XSL/Transform`. Thus, at the highest level, a stylesheet looks like Fig. 20.

```
<? xml version = "1.0" encoding = "utf-8" ?>
<xsl:stylesheet xmlns:xsl =
        "http://www.w3.org/1999/XSL/Transform">
    ...
</xsl:stylesheet>
```

Figure 20: The form of an XSLT stylesheet

3.2 Templates

A stylesheet will have one or more *templates*. To apply a stylesheet to an XML document, we go down the list of templates until we find one that matches the root. As processing proceeds, we often need to find matching templates for elements nested within the document. If so, we again search the list of templates for a match according to matching rules that we shall learn in this section. The simplest form of a template tag is:

```
<xsl:template match = "XPath expression">
```

The XPath expression, which can be either rooted (beginning with a slash) or relative, describes the elements of an XML document to which this template is applied. If the expression is rooted, then the template is applied to every element of the document that matches the path. Relative expressions are applied when a template T has within it a tag `<xsl:apply-templates>`. In that case, we look among the children of the elements to which T is applied. In that way, we can traverse an XML document's tree in a depth-first manner, performing complicated transformations on the document.

The simplest content of a template is text, typically HTML. When a template matches a document, the text inside that document is produced as output. Within the text can be calls to apply templates to the children and/or obtain values from the document itself, e.g., from attributes of the current element.

```
 1)  <? xml version = "1.0" encoding = "utf-8" ?>
 2)  <xsl:stylesheet xmlns:xsl =
 3)          "http://www.w3.org/1999/XSL/Transform">
 4)      <xsl:template match = "/">
 5)          <HTML>
 6)              <BODY>
 7)                  <B>This is a document</b>
 8)              </body>
 9)          </html>
10)      </xsl:template>
11)  </xsl:stylesheet>
```

Figure 21: Printing output for any document

Example 20: In Fig. 21 is an exceedingly simple stylesheet. It applies to any document and produces the same HTML document, regardless of its input. This HTML document says "This is a document" in boldface.

Line (4) introduces the one template in the stylesheet. The value of the `match` attribute is `"/"`, which matches only the root. The body of the template, lines (5) through (9), is simple HTML. When these lines are produced as output, the resulting file can be treated as HTML and displayed by a browser or other HTML processor. □

3.3 Obtaining Values From XML Data

It is unusual that the document we produce does not depend in any way on the input to the transformation, as was the case in Example 20. The simplest way to extract data from the input is with the `value-of` tag. The form of this tag is:

```
<? xml version="1.0" encoding="utf-8" standalone="yes" ?>
<Movies>
    <Movie title = "King Kong">
        <Version year = "1933">
            <Star>Fay Wray</Star>
        </Version>
        <Version year = "1976">
            <Star>Jeff Bridges</Star>
            <Star>Jessica Lange</Star>
        </Version>
        <Version year = "2005" />
    </Movie>
    <Movie title = "Footloose">
        <Version year = "1984">
            <Star>Kevin Bacon</Star>
            <Star>John Lithgow</Star>
            <Star>Sarah Jessica Parker</Star>
        </Version>
    </Movie>
            ... more movies
</Movies>
```

Figure 22: The file `movies.xml`

```
<xsl:value-of select = "expression" />
```

The expression is an XPath expression that should produce a string as value. Other values, such as elements containing text, are coerced into strings in the obvious way.

Example 21: In Fig. 22 we reproduce the file `movies.xml` that was used in Section 2 as a running example. In this example of a stylesheet, we shall use `value-of` to obtain all the titles of movies and print them, one to a line. The stylesheet is shown in Fig. 23.

At line (4), we see that the template matches every `Movie` element, so we process them one at a time. Line (5) applies the `value-of` operation with an XPath expression `@title`. That is, we go to the `title` attribute of each `Movie` element and take the value of that attribute. This value is produced as output, and followed at line (6) by the HTML break tag, so the next movie title will be printed on the next line. □

3.4 Recursive Use of Templates

The most interesting and powerful transformations require recursive application of templates at various elements of the input. Having selected a template to

```
<? xml version = "1.0" encoding = "utf-8" ?>
<xsl:stylesheet xmlns:xsl =
        "http://www.w3.org/1999/XSL/Transform">
    <xsl:template match = "/Movies/Movie">
        <xsl:value-of select = "@title" />
        <BR/>
    </xsl:template>
</xsl:stylesheet>
```

Figure 23: Printing the titles of movies

apply to the root of the input document, we can ask that a template be applied to each of its subelements, by using the `apply-templates` tag. If we want to apply a certain template to only some subset of the subelements, e.g., those with a certain tag, we can use a `select` expression, as:

<xsl:apply-templates select = "*expression*" />

When we encounter such a tag within a template, we find the set of matching subelements of the current element (the element to which the template is being applied). For each subelement, we find the first template that matches and apply it to the subelement.

Example 22 : In this example, we shall use XSLT to transform an XML document into another XML document, rather than into an HTML document. Let us examine Fig. 24. There are four templates, and together they process movie data in the form of Fig. 22. The first template, lines (4) through (8), matches the root. It says to output the text `<Movies>` and then apply templates to the children of the root element. We could have specified that templates were to be applied only to children that are tagged `<Movie>`, but since we expect no other tags among the children, we did not specify:

```
6)          <xsl:apply-templates select = "Movie" />
```

Notice that after applying templates to the `<Movie>` children (which will result in the printing of many elements), we close the `<Movies>` element in the output with the appropriate closing tag at line (7). Also observe that we can tell the difference between tags that are output text, such as lines (5) and (7), from tags that are XSLT, because all XSLT tags must be from the `xsl` namespace.

Now, let us see what applying templates to the `<Movie>` elements does. The first (and only) template that matches these elements is the second, at lines (9) through (15). This template begins by outputting the text `<Movie title = "` at line (10). Then, line (11) obtains the title of the movie and emits it to the output. Line (12) finishes the quoted attribute value and the `<Movie>` tag in the output. Line (13) applies templates to all the children of the movie, which should be versions. Finally, line (14) emits the matching `</Movie>` ending tag.

```
1)  <? xml version = "1.0" encoding = "utf-8" ?>
2)  <xsl:stylesheet xmlns:xsl =
3)          "http://www.w3.org/1999/XSL/Transform">

4)      <xsl:template match = "/Movies">
5)          <Movies>
6)          <xsl:apply-templates />
7)          </Movies>
8)      </xsl:template>

9)      <xsl:template match = "Movie">
10)         <Movie title = "
11)         <xsl:value-of select = "@title" />
12)         ">
13)         <xsl:apply-templates />
14)         </Movie>
15)     </xsl:template>

16)     <xsl:template match = "Version">
17)         <xsl:apply-templates />
18)     </xsl:template>

19)     <xsl:template match = "Star">
20)         <Star name = "
21)         <xsl:value-of select = "." />
22)         " />
23)     </xsl:template>

24) </xsl:stylesheet>
```

Figure 24: Transforming the `movies.xml` file

When line (13) calls for templates to be applied to all the versions of a movie, the only matching template is that of lines (16) through (18), which does nothing but apply templates to the children of the version, which should be `<Star>` elements. Thus, what gets generated between each opening `<Movie>` tag and its matched closing tag is determined by the last template of lines (19) through (23). This template is applied to each `<Star>` element.

Star elements from the input are transformed in the output. Instead of the star's name being text, as it is in Fig. 22, the template starting at line (19) produces a `<Star>` element with the name as an attribute. Line (21) says to select the `<Star>` element itself (the dot represents the "self" axis as an XPath expression) as a value for the output. However, all output is text, so the tags of the element are not part of the output. That result is exactly what we want, since the value of the attribute `name` should be a string, not an element. The empty `<Star>` element is completed on line (22). For instance, given the input of Fig. 22, the output would be as shown in Fig. 25. □

```
<Movies>
    <Movie title = "King Kong">
        <Star name = "Fay Wray" />
        <Star name = "Jeff Bridges" />
        <Star name = "Jessica Lange" />
    </Movie>
    <Movie title = "Footloose">
        <Star name = "Kevin Bacon" />
        <Star name = "John Lithgow" />
        <Star name = "Sarah Jessica Parker" />
    </Movie>
            ... more movies
</Movies>
```

Figure 25: Output of the transform of Fig. 24

3.5 Iteration in XSLT

We can put a loop within a template that gives us freedom over the order in which we visit certain subelements of the element to which the template is being applied. The `for-each` tag creates the loop, with a form:

`<xsl:for-each select = "`*expression*`">`

The expression is an XPath expression whose value is a sequence of items. Whatever is between the opening `<for-each>` tag and its matched closing tag is executed for each item, in turn.

Example 23: In Fig. 26 is a copy of our document `stars.xml`; we wish to transform it to an HTML list of all the names of stars followed by an HTML list of all the cities in which stars live. Figure 27 has a template that does the job.

There is one template, which matches the root. The first thing that happens is at line (5), where the HTML tag `<OL>` is emitted to start an ordered list. Then, line (6) starts a loop, which iterates over each `<Star>` subelement. At lines (7) through (9), a list item with the name of that star is emitted. Line (11) ends the list of names and begins a list of cities. The second loop, lines (12) through (16), runs through each `<Address>` element and emits a list item for the city. Line (17) closes the second list. □

```
<? xml version="1.0" encoding="utf-8" standalone="yes" ?>
<Stars>
    <Star>
        <Name>Carrie Fisher</Name>
        <Address>
            <Street>123 Maple St.</Street>
            <City>Hollywood</City>
        </Address>
        <Address>
            <Street>5 Locust Ln.</Street>
            <City>Malibu</City>
        </Address>
    </Star>
            ... more stars
</Stars>
```

Figure 26: Document stars.xml

```
<? xml version = "1.0" encoding = "utf-8" ?>
<xsl:stylesheet xmlns:xsl =
        "http://www.w3.org/1999/XSL/Transform">
    <xsl:template match = "/">
        <OL>
        <xsl:for-each select = "Stars/Star" />
            <LI>
            <xsl:value-of select = "Name">
            </li>
        </xsl:for-each>
        </ol><P/><OL>
        <xsl:for-each select = "Stars/Star/Address" />
            <LI>
            <xsl:value-of select = "City">
            </li>
        </xsl:for-each>
        </ol>
    </xsl:template>
</xsl:stylesheet>
```

Figure 27: Printing names and cities of stars

3.6 Conditionals in XSLT

We can introduce branching into our templates by using an `if` tag. The form of this tag is:

```
<xsl:if test = "boolean expression">
```

Whatever appears between this tag and its matched closing tag is executed if and only if the boolean expression is true. There is no else-clause, but we can follow this expression by another `if` that has the opposite test condition should we wish.

```
1)    <? xml version = "1.0" encoding = "utf-8" ?>
2)    <xsl:stylesheet xmlns:xsl =
3)            "http://www.w3.org/1999/XSL/Transform">
4)        <xsl:template match = "/">
5)            <TABLE border = "5"><TR><TH>Stars</th></tr>
6)            <xsl:for-each select = "Stars/Star" />
7)                <xsl:if test = "Address/City = 'Hollywood'">
8)                    <TR><TD>
9)                    <xsl:value-of select = "Name" />
10)                   </td></tr>
11)               </xsl:if>
12)           </xsl:for-each>
13)           </table>
14)       </xsl:template>
15)   </xsl:stylesheet>
```

Figure 28: Finding the names of the stars who live in Hollywood

Example 24: Figure 28 is a stylesheet that prints a one-column table, with header “Stars.” There is one template, which matches the root. The first thing this template does is print the header row at line (5). The for-each loop of lines (6) through (12) iterates over each star. The conditional of line (7) tests whether the star has at least one home in Hollywood. Remember that the equal-sign represents a comparison is true if any item on the left equals any item on the right. That is what we want, since we asked whether any of the homes a star has is in Hollywood. Lines (8) through (10) print a row of the table. □

3.7 Exercises for Section 3

Exercise 3.1: Suppose our input XML document has the form of the product data of Figs. 4 and 5. Write XSLT stylesheets to produce each of the following documents.

a) An HTML file consisting of a header "Manufacturers" followed by an enumerated list of the names of all the makers of products listed in the input.

b) An HTML file consisting of a table with headers "Model" and "Price," with a row for each PC. That row should have the proper model and price for the PC.

! c) An HTML file consisting of a table whose headers are "Model," "Price," "Speed," and "Ram" for all Laptops, followed by another table with the same headers for PC's.

d) An XML file with root tag <PCs> and subelements having tag <PC>. This tag has attributes `model`, `price`, `speed`, and `ram`. In the output, there should be one <PC> element for each <PC> element of the input file, and the values of the attributes should be taken from the corresponding input element.

!! e) An XML file with root tag <Products> whose subelements are <Product> elements. Each <Product> element has attributes `type`, `maker`, `model`, and `price`, where the type is one of `"PC"`, `"Laptop"`, or `"Printer"`. There should be one <Product> element in the output for every PC, laptop, and printer in the input file, and the output values should be chosen appropriately from the input data.

! f) Repeat part (b), but make the output file a Latex file.

Exercise 3.2: Suppose our input XML document has the form of the product data of Fig. 6. Write XSLT stylesheets to produce each of the following documents.

a) An HTML file with a header for each class. Under each header is a table with column-headers "Name" and "Launched" with the appropriate entry for each ship of the class.

b) An HTML file with root tag <Losers> and subelements <Ship>, each of whose values is the name of one of the ships that were sunk.

! c) An XML file with root tag <Ships> and subelements <Ship> for each ship. These elements each should have attributes `name`, `class`, `country` and `numGuns` with the appropriate values taken from the input file.

! d) Repeat (c), but only list those ships that were in at least one battle.

e) An XML file identical to the input, except that <Battle> elements should be empty, with the outcome and name of the battle as two attributes.

4 Summary

- *XPath*: This language is a simple way to express many queries about XML data. You describe paths from the root of the document by sequences of tags. The path may end at an attribute rather than an element.

- *The XPath Data Model*: All XPath values are sequences of items. An item is either a primitive value or an element. An element is an opening XML tag, its matched closing tag, and everything in between.

- *Axes*: Instead of proceeding down the tree in a path, one can follow another axis, including jumps to any descendant, a parent, or a sibling.

- *XPath Conditions*: Any step in a path can be constrained by a condition, which is a boolean-valued expression. This expression appears in square brackets.

- *XQuery*: This language is a more advanced form of query language for XML documents. It uses the same data model as XPath. XQuery is a functional language.

- *FLWR Expressions*: Many queries in XQuery consist of let-, for-, where- and return-clauses. "Let" introduces temporary definitions of variables; "for" creates loops; "where" supplies conditions to be tested, and "return" defines the result of the query.

- *Comparison Operators in XQuery and XPath*: The conventional comparison operators such as < apply to sequences of items, and have a "there-exists" meaning. They are true if the stated relation holds between any pair of items, one from each of the lists. To be assured that single items are being compared, we can use letter codes for the operators, such as `lt` for "less than."

- *Other XQuery Expressions*: XQuery has many operations that resemble those in SQL. These operators include existential and universal quantification, aggregation, duplicate-elimination, and sorting of results.

- *XSLT*: This language is designed for transformations of XML documents, although it also can be used as a query language. A "program" in this language has the form of an XML document, with a special namespace that allows us to use tags to describe a transformation.

- *Templates*: The heart of XSLT is a template, which matches certain elements of the input document. The template describes output text, and can extract values from the input document for inclusion in the output. A template can also call for templates to be applied recursively to the children of an element.

✦ *XSLT Programming Constructs*: A template can also include XSLT constructs that behave like an iterative programming language. These constructs include for-loops and if-statements.

5 References

The World-Wide-Web Consortium site for the definition of XPath is [2]. The site for XQuery is [3], and for XSLT it is [4].

[1] is an introduction to the XQuery language. There are tutorials for XPath, XQuery, and XSLT at [5].

1. D. D. Chamberlin, "XQuery: an XML Query Language," *IBM Systems Journal* **41**:4 (2002), pp. 597–615. See also `www.research.ibm.com/journal/sj/414/chamberlin.pdf`

2. World-Wide-Web Consortium `http://www.w3.org/TR/xpath`

3. World-Wide-Web Consortium `http://www.w3.org/TR/xquery`

4. World-Wide-Web Consortium `http://www.w3.org/TR/xslt`

5. W3 Schools, `http://www.w3schools.com`

Secondary Storage Management

Database systems always involve secondary storage — the disks and other devices that store large amounts of data that persists over time. This chapter summarizes what we need to know about how a typical computer system manages storage. We review the memory hierarchy of devices with progressively slower access but larger capacity. We examine disks in particular and see how the speed of data access is affected by how we organize our data on the disk. We also study mechanisms for making disks more reliable.

Then, we turn to how data is represented. We discuss the way tuples of a relation or similar records or objects are stored. Efficiency, as always, is the key issue. We cover ways to find records quickly, and how to manage insertions and deletions of records, as well as records whose sizes grow and shrink.

1 The Memory Hierarchy

We begin this section by examining the memory hierarchy of a computer system. We then focus on disks, by far the most common device at the "secondary-storage" level of the hierarchy. We give the rough parameters that determine the speed of access and look at the transfer of data from disks to the lower levels of the memory hierarchy.

1.1 The Memory Hierarchy

A typical computer system has several different components in which data may be stored. These components have data capacities ranging over at least seven orders of magnitude and also have access speeds ranging over seven or more orders of magnitude. The cost per byte of these components also varies, but more slowly, with perhaps three orders of magnitude between the cheapest and

From Chapter 13 of *Database Systems*, Second Edition. Hector Garcia-Molina, Jeffrey D. Ullman, Jennifer Widom.

most expensive forms of storage. Not surprisingly, the devices with smallest capacity also offer the fastest access speed and have the highest cost per byte. A schematic of the memory hierarchy is shown in Fig. 1.

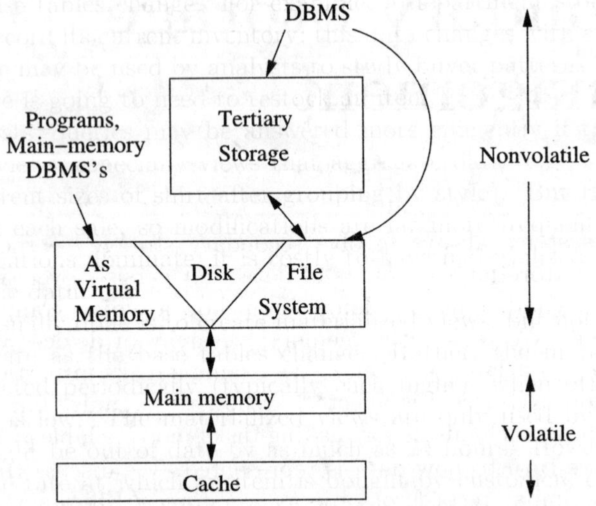

Figure 1: The memory hierarchy

Here are brief descriptions of the levels, from the lowest, or fastest-smallest level, up.

1. *Cache.* A typical machine has a megabyte or more of cache storage. *On-board cache* is found on the same chip as the microprocessor itself, and additional *level-2 cache* is found on another chip. Data and instructions are moved to cache from main memory when they are needed by the processor. Cached data can be accessed by the processor in a few nanoseconds.

2. *Main Memory.* In the center of the action is the computer's *main memory.* We may think of everything that happens in the computer — instruction executions and data manipulations — as working on information that is resident in main memory (although in practice, it is normal for what is used to migrate to the cache). A typical machine in 2008 is configured with about a gigabyte of main memory, although much larger main memories are possible. Typical times to move data from main memory to the processor or cache are in the 10–100 nanosecond range.

3. *Secondary Storage.* Secondary storage is typically magnetic disk, a device we shall consider in detail in Section 2. In 2008, single disk units have capacities of up to a terabyte, and one machine can have several disk units. The time to transfer a single byte between disk and main

Computer Quantities are Powers of 2

It is conventional to talk of sizes or capacities of computer components as if they were powers of 10: megabytes, gigabytes, and so on. In reality, since it is most efficient to design components such as memory chips to hold a number of bits that is a power of 2, all these numbers are really shorthands for nearby powers of 2. Since $2^{10} = 1024$ is very close to a thousand, we often maintain the fiction that $2^{10} = 1000$, and talk about 2^{10} with the prefix "kilo," 2^{20} as "mega," 2^{30} as "giga," 2^{40} as "tera," and 2^{50} as "peta," even though these prefixes in scientific parlance refer to 10^3, 10^6, 10^9, 10^{12} and 10^{15}, respectively. The discrepancy grows as we talk of larger numbers. A "gigabyte" is really 1.074×10^9 bytes.

We use the standard abbreviations for these numbers: K, M, G, T, and P for kilo, mega, giga, tera, and peta, respectively. Thus, 16Gb is sixteen gigabytes, or strictly speaking 2^{34} bytes. Since we sometimes want to talk about numbers that are the conventional powers of 10, we shall reserve for these the traditional numbers, without the prefixes "kilo," "mega," and so on. For example, "one million bytes" is 1,000,000 bytes, while "one megabyte" is 1,048,576 bytes.

A recent trend is to use "kilobyte," "megabyte," and so on for exact powers of ten, and to replace the third and fourth letters by "bi" to represent the similar powers of two. Thus, "kibibyte" is 1024 bytes, "mebibyte" is 1,048,576 bytes, and so on. We shall not use this convention.

memory is around 10 miliseconds. However, large numbers of bytes can be transferred at one time, so the matter of how fast data moves from and to disk is somewhat complex.

4. *Tertiary Storage.* As capacious as a collection of disk units can be, there are databases much larger than what can be stored on the disk(s) of a single machine, or even several machines. To serve such needs, *tertiary storage* devices have been developed to hold data volumes measured in terabytes. Tertiary storage is characterized by significantly higher read/write times than secondary storage, but also by much larger capacities and smaller cost per byte than is available from magnetic disks. Many tertiary devices involve robotic arms or conveyors that bring storage media such as magnetic tape or optical disks (e.g., DVD's) to a reading device. Retrieval takes seconds or minutes, but capacities in the petabyte range are possible.

1.2 Transfer of Data Between Levels

Normally, data moves between adjacent levels of the hierarchy. At the secondary and tertiary levels, accessing the desired data or finding the desired place to store data takes a great deal of time, so each level is organized to transfer large amounts of data to or from the level below, whenever any data at all is needed. Especially important for understanding the operation of a database system is the fact that the disk is organized into *disk blocks* (or just *blocks*, or as in operating systems, *pages*) of perhaps 4–64 kilobytes. Entire blocks are moved to or from a continuous section of main memory called a *buffer*. Thus, a key technique for speeding up database operations is to arrange data so that when one piece of a disk block is needed, it is likely that other data on the same block will also be needed at about the same time.

The same idea applies to other hierarchy levels. If we use tertiary storage, we try to arrange so that when we select a unit such as a DVD to read, we need much of what is on that DVD. At a lower level, movement between main memory and cache is by units of *cache lines*, typically 32 consecutive bytes. The hope is that entire cache lines will be used together. For example, if a cache line stores consecutive instructions of a program, we hope that when the first instruction is needed, the next few instructions will also be executed immediately thereafter.

1.3 Volatile and Nonvolatile Storage

An additional distinction among storage devices is whether they are *volatile* or *nonvolatile*. A volatile device "forgets" what is stored in it when the power goes off. A nonvolatile device, on the other hand, is expected to keep its contents intact even for long periods when the device is turned off or there is a power failure. The question of volatility is important, because one of the characteristic capabilities of a DBMS is the ability to retain its data even in the presence of errors such as power failures.

Magnetic and optical materials hold their data in the absence of power. Thus, essentially all secondary and tertiary storage devices are nonvolatile. On the other hand, main memory is generally volatile (although certain types of more expensive memory chips, such as flash memory, can hold their data after a power failure). A significant part of the complexity in a DBMS comes from the requirement that no change to the database can be considered final until it has migrated to nonvolatile, secondary storage.

1.4 Virtual Memory

Typical software executes in *virtual-memory*, an address space that is typically 32 bits; i.e., there are 2^{32} bytes, or 4 gigabytes, in a virtual memory. The operating system manages virtual memory, keeping some of it in main memory and the rest on disk. Transfer between memory and disk is in units of disk

Moore's Law

Gordon Moore observed many years ago that integrated circuits were improving in many ways, following an exponential curve that doubles about every 18 months. Some of these parameters that follow "Moore's law" are:

1. The number of instructions per second that can be executed for unit cost. Until about 2005, the improvement was achieved by making processor chips faster, while keeping the cost fixed. After that year, the improvement has been maintained by putting progressively more processors on a single, fixed-cost chip.

2. The number of memory bits that can be bought for unit cost and the number of bits that can be put on one chip.

3. The number of bytes per unit cost on a disk and the capacity of the largest disks.

On the other hand, there are some other important parameters that do not follow Moore's law; they grow slowly if at all. Among these slowly growing parameters are the speed of accessing data in main memory and the speed at which disks rotate. Because they grow slowly, "latency" becomes progressively larger. That is, the time to move data between levels of the memory hierarchy appears enormous today, and will only get worse.

blocks (pages). Virtual memory is an artifact of the operating system and its use of the machine's hardware, and it is not a level of the memory hierarchy.

The path in Fig. 1 involving virtual memory represents the treatment of conventional programs and applications. It does *not* represent the typical way data in a database is managed, since a DBMS manages the data itself. However, there is increasing interest in *main-memory database systems*, which do indeed manage their data through virtual memory, relying on the operating system to bring needed data into main memory through the paging mechanism. Main-memory database systems, like most applications, are most useful when the data is small enough to remain in main memory without being swapped out by the operating system.

1.5 Exercises for Section 1

Exercise 1.1: Suppose that in 2008 the typical computer has a processor chip with two processors ("cores") that each run at 3 gigahertz, has a disk of 250 gigabytes, and a main memory of 1 gigabyte. Assume that Moore's law (these factors double every 18 months) holds into the indefinite future.

a) When will petabyte disks be common?

b) When will terabyte main memories be common?

c) When will terahertz processor chips be common (i.e., the total number of cycles per second of all the cores on a chip will be approximately 10^{12}?

d) What will be a typical configuration (processor, disk, memory) in the year 2015?

! **Exercise 1.2:** Commander Data, the android from the 24th century on *Star Trek: The Next Generation* once proudly announced that his processor runs at "12 teraops." While an operation and a cycle may not be the same, let us suppose they are, and that Moore's law continues to hold for the next 300 years. If so, what would Data's true processor speed be?

2 Disks

The use of secondary storage is one of the important characteristics of a DBMS, and secondary storage is almost exclusively based on magnetic disks. Thus, to motivate many of the ideas used in DBMS implementation, we must examine the operation of disks in detail.

2.1 Mechanics of Disks

The two principal moving pieces of a disk drive are shown in Fig. 2; they are a *disk assembly* and a *head assembly.* The disk assembly consists of one or more circular *platters* that rotate around a central spindle. The upper and lower surfaces of the platters are covered with a thin layer of magnetic material, on which bits are stored. 0's and 1's are represented by different patterns in the magnetic material. A common diameter for disk platters is 3.5 inches, although disks with diameters from an inch to several feet have been built.

The disk is organized into *tracks*, which are concentric circles on a single platter. The tracks that are at a fixed radius from the center, among all the surfaces, form one *cylinder.* Tracks occupy most of a surface, except for the region closest to the spindle, as can be seen in the top view of Fig. 3. The density of data is much greater along a track than radially. In 2008, a typical disk has about 100,000 tracks per inch but stores about a million bits per inch along the tracks.

Tracks are organized into *sectors*, which are segments of the circle separated by *gaps* that are not magnetized to represent either 0's or 1's.[1] The sector is an indivisible unit, as far as reading and writing the disk is concerned. It is also indivisible as far as errors are concerned. Should a portion of the magnetic layer

[1]We show each track with the same number of sectors in Fig. 3. However, the number of sectors per track normally varies, with the outer tracks having more sectors than inner tracks.

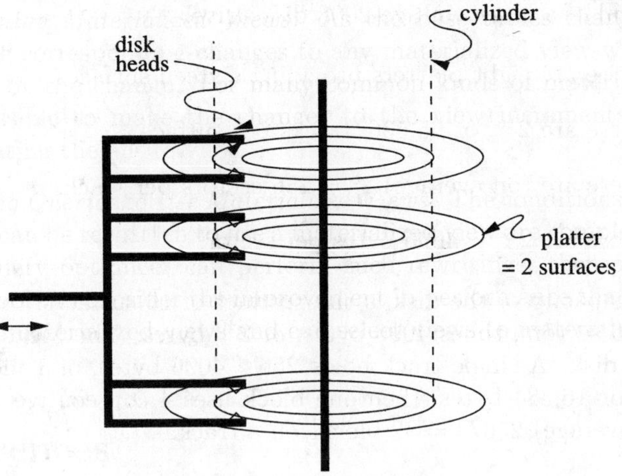

Figure 2: A typical disk

be corrupted in some way, so that it cannot store information, then the entire sector containing this portion cannot be used. Gaps often represent about 10% of the total track and are used to help identify the beginnings of sectors. As we mentioned in Section 1.2, blocks are logical units of data that are transferred between disk and main memory; blocks consist of one or more sectors.

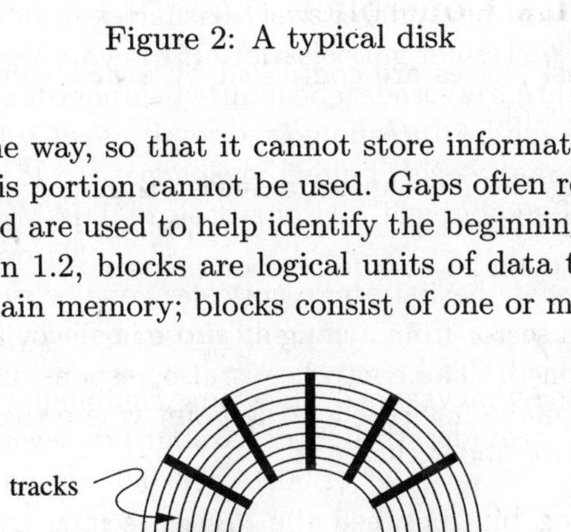

Figure 3: Top view of a disk surface

The second movable piece shown in Fig. 2, the head assembly, holds the *disk heads.* For each surface there is one head, riding extremely close to the surface but never touching it (or else a "head crash" occurs and the disk is destroyed). A head reads the magnetism passing under it, and can also alter the magnetism to write information on the disk. The heads are each attached to an arm, and the arms for all the surfaces move in and out together, being part of the rigid head assembly.

Example 1 : The *Megatron 747* disk has the following characteristics, which are typical of a large vintage-2008 disk drive.

- There are eight platters providing sixteen surfaces.
- There are 2^{16}, or 65,536, tracks per surface.
- There are (on average) $2^8 = 256$ sectors per track.
- There are $2^{12} = 4096$ bytes per sector.

The capacity of the disk is the product of 16 surfaces, times 65,536 tracks, times 256 sectors, times 4096 bytes, or 2^{40} bytes. The Megatron 747 is thus a terabyte disk. A single track holds 256×4096 bytes, or 1 megabyte. If blocks are 2^{14}, or 16,384 bytes, then one block uses 4 consecutive sectors, and there are (on average) $256/4 = 32$ blocks on a track. □

2.2 The Disk Controller

One or more disk drives are controlled by a *disk controller*, which is a small processor capable of:

1. Controlling the mechanical actuator that moves the head assembly, to position the heads at a particular radius, i.e., so that any track of one particular cylinder can be read or written.
2. Selecting a sector from among all those in the cylinder at which the heads are positioned. The controller is also responsible for knowing when the rotating spindle has reached the point where the desired sector is beginning to move under the head.
3. Transferring bits between the desired sector and the computer's main memory.
4. Possibly, buffering an entire track or more in local memory of the disk controller, hoping that many sectors of this track will be read soon, and additional accesses to the disk can be avoided.

Figure 4 shows a simple, single-processor computer. The processor communicates via a data bus with the main memory and the disk controller. A disk controller can control several disks; we show three disks in this example.

2.3 Disk Access Characteristics

Accessing (reading or writing) a block requires three steps, and each step has an associated delay.

1. The disk controller positions the head assembly at the cylinder containing the track on which the block is located. The time to do so is the *seek time*.

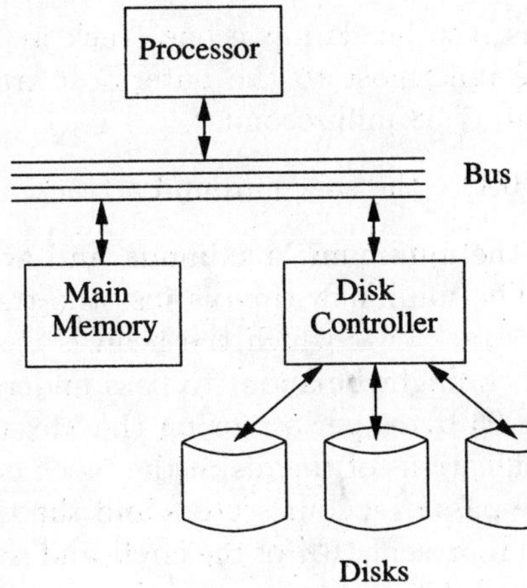

Figure 4: Schematic of a simple computer system

2. The disk controller waits while the first sector of the block moves under the head. This time is called the *rotational latency.*

3. All the sectors and the gaps between them pass under the head, while the disk controller reads or writes data in these sectors. This delay is called the *transfer time.*

The sum of the seek time, rotational latency, and transfer time is the *latency* of the disk.

The seek time for a typical disk depends on the distance the heads have to travel from where they are currently located. If they are already at the desired cylinder, the seek time is 0. However, it takes roughly a millisecond to start the disk heads moving, and perhaps 10 milliseconds to move them across all the tracks.

A typical disk rotates once in roughly 10 milliseconds. Thus, rotational latency ranges from 0 to 10 milliseconds, and the average is 5. Transfer times tend to be much smaller, since there are often many blocks on a track. Thus, transfer times are in the sub-millisecond range. When you add all three delays, the typical average latency is about 10 milliseconds, and the maximum latency about twice that.

Example 2: Let us examine the time it takes to read a 16,384-byte block from the Megatron 747 disk. First, we need to know some timing properties of the disk:

- The disk rotates at 7200 rpm; i.e., it makes one rotation in 8.33 milliseconds.

- To move the head assembly between cylinders takes one millisecond to start and stop, plus one additional millisecond for every 4000 cylinders traveled. Thus, the heads move one track in 1.00025 milliseconds and move from the innermost to the outermost track, a distance of 65,536 tracks, in about 17.38 milliseconds.

- Gaps occupy 10% of the space around a track.

Let us calculate the minimum, maximum, and average times to read that 16,384-byte block. The minimum time is just the transfer time. That is, the block might be on a track over which the head is positioned already, and the first sector of the block might be about to pass under the head.

Since there are 4096 bytes per sector on the Megatron 747 (see Example 1 for the physical specifications of the disk), the block occupies four sectors. The heads must therefore pass over four sectors and the three gaps between them. We assume that gaps represent 10% of the circle and sectors the remaining 90%. There are 256 gaps and 256 sectors around the circle. Since the gaps together cover 36 degrees of arc and sectors the remaining 324 degrees, the total degrees of arc covered by 3 gaps and 4 sectors is $36 \times 3/256 + 324 \times 4/256 = 5.48$ degrees. The transfer time is thus $(5.48/360) \times 0.00833 = .00013$ seconds. That is, 5.48/360 is the fraction of a rotation needed to read the entire block, and .00833 seconds is the amount of time for a 360-degree rotation.

Now, let us look at the maximum possible time to read the block. In the worst case, the heads are positioned at the innermost cylinder, and the block we want to read is on the outermost cylinder (or vice versa). Thus, the first thing the controller must do is move the heads. As we observed above, the time it takes to move the Megatron 747 heads across all cylinders is about 17.38 milliseconds. This quantity is the seek time for the read.

The worst thing that can happen when the heads arrive at the correct cylinder is that the beginning of the desired block has just passed under the head. Assuming we must read the block starting at the beginning, we have to wait essentially a full rotation, or 8.33 milliseconds, for the beginning of the block to reach the head again. Once that happens, we have only to wait an amount equal to the transfer time, 0.13 milliseconds, to read the entire block. Thus, the worst-case latency is $17.38 + 8.33 + 0.13 = 25.84$ milliseconds.

Last, let us compute the average latency. Two of the components of the latency are easy to compute: the transfer time is always 0.13 milliseconds, and the average rotational latency is the time to rotate the disk half way around, or 4.17 milliseconds. We might suppose that the average seek time is just the time to move across half the tracks. However, that is not quite right, since typically, the heads are initially somewhere near the middle and therefore will have to move less than half the distance, on average, to the desired cylinder. We leave it as an exercise to show that the average distance traveled is 1/3 of the way across the disk.

The time it takes the Megatron 747 to move 1/3 of the way across the disk is $1 + (65536/3)/4000 = 6.46$ milliseconds. Our estimate of the average latency is thus $6.46 + 4.17 + 0.13 = 10.76$ milliseconds; the three terms represent average seek time, average rotational latency, and transfer time, respectively. □

2.4 Exercises for Section 2

Exercise 2.1: The *Megatron 777* disk has the following characteristics:

1. There are ten surfaces, with 100,000 tracks each.

2. Tracks hold an average of 1000 sectors of 1024 bytes each.

3. 20% of each track is used for gaps.

4. The disk rotates at 10,000 rpm.

5. The time it takes the head to move n tracks is $1 + 0.0002n$ milliseconds.

Answer the following questions about the Megatron 777.

a) What is the capacity of the disk?

b) If tracks are located on the outer inch of a 3.5-inch-diameter surface, what is the average density of bits in the sectors of a track?

c) What is the maximum seek time?

d) What is the maximum rotational latency?

e) If a block is 65,546 bytes (i.e., 64 sectors), what is the transfer time of a block?

! f) What is the average seek time?

g) What is the average rotational latency?

! **Exercise 2.2:** Suppose the Megatron 747 disk head is at cylinder 8192, i.e., 1/8 of the way across the cylinders. Suppose that the next request is for a block on a random cylinder. Calculate the average time to read this block.

!! **Exercise 2.3:** Prove that if we move the head from a random cylinder to another random cylinder, the average distance we move is 1/3 of the way across the disk (neglecting edge effects due to the fact that the number of cylinders is finite).

!! **Exercise 2.4:** Exercise 2.3 assumes that we move from a random track to another random track. Suppose, however, that the number of sectors per track is proportional to the length (or radius) of the track, so the bit density is the same for all tracks. Suppose also that we need to move the head from a random *sector* to another random sector. Since the sectors tend to congregate at the outside of the disk, we might expect that the average head move would be less than 1/3 of the way across the tracks. Assuming that tracks occupy radii from 0.75 inches to 1.75 inches, calculate the average number of tracks the head travels when moving between two random sectors.

! **Exercise 2.5:** To modify a block on disk, we must read it into main memory, perform the modification, and write it back. Assume that the modification in main memory takes less time than it does for the disk to rotate, and that the disk controller postpones other requests for disk access until the block is ready to be written back to the disk. For the Megatron 747 disk, what is the time to modify a block?

3 Accelerating Access to Secondary Storage

Just because a disk takes an average of, say, 10 milliseconds to access a block, it does not follow that an application such as a database system will get the data it requests 10 milliseconds after the request is sent to the disk controller. If there is only one disk, the disk may be busy with another access for the same process or another process. In the worst case, a request for a disk access arrives more than once every 10 milliseconds, and these requests back up indefinitely. In that case, the *scheduling latency* becomes infinite.

There are several things we can do to decrease the average time a disk access takes, and thus improve the *throughput* (number of disk accesses per second that the system can accomodate). We begin this section by arguing that the "I/O model" is the right one for measuring the time database operations take. Then, we consider a number of techniques for speeding up typical database accesses to disk:

1. Place blocks that are accessed together on the same cylinder, so we can often avoid seek time, and possibly rotational latency as well.

2. Divide the data among several smaller disks rather than one large one. Having more head assemblies that can go after blocks independently can increase the number of block accesses per unit time.

3. "Mirror" a disk: making two or more copies of the data on different disks. In addition to saving the data in case one of the disks fails, this strategy, like dividing the data among several disks, lets us access several blocks at once.

4. Use a disk-scheduling algorithm, either in the operating system, in the DBMS, or in the disk controller, to select the order in which several requested blocks will be read or written.

5. Prefetch blocks to main memory in anticipation of their later use.

3.1 The I/O Model of Computation

Let us imagine a simple computer running a DBMS and trying to serve a number of users who are performing queries and database modifications. For the moment, assume our computer has one processor, one disk controller, and one disk. The database itself is much too large to fit in main memory. Key parts of the database may be buffered in main memory, but generally, each piece of the database that one of the users accesses will have to be retrieved initially from disk. The following rule, which defines the *I/O model of computation*, can thus be assumed.

> **Dominance of I/O cost**: The time taken to perform a disk access is much larger than the time likely to be used manipulating that data in main memory. Thus, the number of block accesses (*Disk I/O's*) is a good approximation to the time needed by the algorithm and should be minimized.

Example 3: Suppose our database has a relation R and a query asks for the tuple of R that has a certain key value k. It is quite desirable to have an index on R to identify the disk block on which the tuple with key value k appears. However it is generally unimportant whether the index tells us where on the block this tuple appears.

For instance, if we assume a Megatron 747 disk, it will take on the order of 11 milliseconds to read a 16K-byte block. In 11 milliseconds, a modern microprocessor can execute millions of instructions. However, searching for the key value k once the block is in main memory will only take thousands of instructions, even if the dumbest possible linear search is used. The additional time to perform the search in main memory will therefore be less than 1% of the block access time and can be neglected safely. □

3.2 Organizing Data by Cylinders

Since seek time represents about half the time it takes to access a block, it makes sense to store data that is likely to be accessed together, such as relations, on a single cylinder, or on as many adjacent cylinders as are needed. In fact, if we choose to read all the blocks on a single track or on a cylinder consecutively, then we can neglect all but the first seek time (to move to the cylinder) and the first rotational latency (to wait until the first of the blocks moves under the head). In that case, we can approach the theoretical transfer rate for moving data on or off the disk.

Example 4: Suppose relation R requires 1024 blocks of a Megatron 747 disk to hold its tuples. Suppose also that we need to access all the tuples of R; for example we may be doing a search without an index or computing a sum of the values of a particular attribute of R. If the blocks holding R are distributed around the disk at random, then we shall need an average latency (10.76 milliseconds — see Example 2) to access each, for a total of 11 seconds.

However, 1024 blocks are exactly one cylinder of the Megatron 747. We can access them all by performing one average seek (6.46 milliseconds), after which we can read the blocks in some order, one right after another. We can read all the blocks on a cylinder in 16 rotations of the disk, since there are 16 tracks.

Sixteen rotations take $16 \times 8.33 = 133$ milliseconds. The total time to access R is thus about 139 milliseconds, and we speed up the operation on R by a factor of about 80. □

3.3 Using Multiple Disks

We can often improve the performance of our system if we replace one disk, with many heads locked together, by several disks with their independent heads. The arrangement was suggested in Fig. 4, where we showed three disks connected to a single controller. As long as the disk controller, bus, and main memory can handle n times the data-transfer rate, then n disks will have approximately the performance of one disk that operates n times as fast.

Thus, using several disks can increase the ability of a database system to handle heavy loads of disk-access requests. However, as long as the system is not overloaded (when requests will queue up and are delayed for a long time or ignored), there is no change in how long it takes to perform any single block access. If we have several disks, then the technique known as *striping* (described in the next example) will speed up access to large database objects — those that occupy a large number of blocks.

Example 5: Suppose we have four Megatron 747 disks and want to access the relation R of Example 4 faster than the 139-millisecond time that was suggested for storing R on one cylinder of one disk. We can "stripe" R by dividing it among the four disks. The first disk can receive blocks $1, 5, 9, \ldots$ of R, the second disk holds blocks $2, 6, 10, \ldots$, the third holds blocks $3, 7, 11, \ldots$, and the last disk holds blocks $4, 8, 12, \ldots$, as suggested by Fig. 5. Let us contrive that on each of the disks, all the blocks of R are on four tracks of a single cylinder.

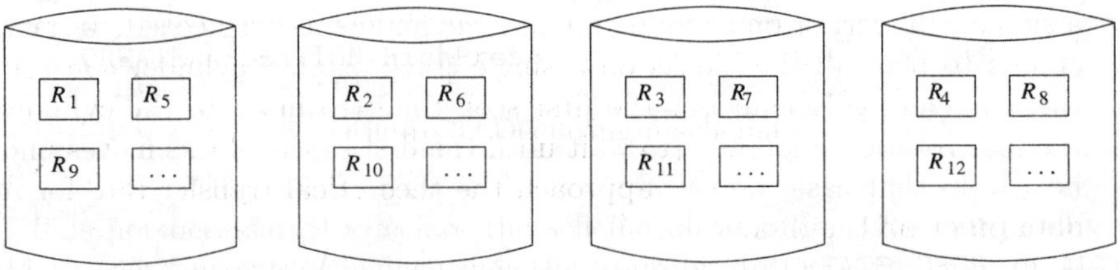

Figure 5: Striping a relation across four disks

Then to retrieve the 256 blocks of R on one of the disks requires an average seek time (6.46 milliseconds) plus four rotations of the disk, one rotation for each track. That is $6.46 + 4 \times 8.33 = 39.8$ milliseconds. Of course we have to wait for the last of the four disks to finish, and there is a high probability that one will take substantially more seek time than average. However, we should get a speedup in the time to access R by about a factor of three on the average, when there are four disks. □

3.4 Mirroring Disks

There are situations where it makes sense to have two or more disks hold identical copies of data. The disks are said to be *mirrors* of each other. One important motivation is that the data will survive a head crash by either disk, since it is still readable on a mirror of the disk that crashed. Systems designed to enhance reliability often use pairs of disks as mirrors of each other.

If we have n disks, each holding the same data, then the rate at which we can read blocks goes up by a factor of n, since the disk controller can assign a read request to any of the n disks. In fact, the speedup could be even greater than n, if a clever controller chooses to read a block from the disk whose head is currently closest to that block. Unfortunately, the writing of disk blocks does not speed up at all. The reason is that the new block must be written to each of the n disks.

3.5 Disk Scheduling and the Elevator Algorithm

Another effective way to improve the throughput of a disk system is to have the disk controller choose which of several requests to execute first. This approach cannot be used if accesses have to be made in a certain sequence, but if the requests are from independent processes, they can all benefit, on the average, from allowing the scheduler to choose among them judiciously.

A simple and effective way to schedule large numbers of block requests is known as the *elevator algorithm*. We think of the disk head as making sweeps across the disk, from innermost to outermost cylinder and then back again, just as an elevator makes vertical sweeps from the bottom to top of a building and back again. As heads pass a cylinder, they stop if there are one or more requests for blocks on that cylinder. All these blocks are read or written, as requested. The heads then proceed in the same direction they were traveling until the next cylinder with blocks to access is encountered. When the heads reach a position where there are no requests ahead of them in their direction of travel, they reverse direction.

Example 6: Suppose we are scheduling a Megatron 747 disk, which we recall has average seek, rotational latency, and transfer times of 6.46, 4.17, and 0.13, respectively (in this example, all times are in milliseconds). Suppose that at some time there are pending requests for block accesses at cylinders 8000, 24,000, and 56,000. The heads are located at cylinder 8000. In addition, there are three more requests for block accesses that come in at later times, as summarized in Fig. 6. For instance, the request for a block from cylinder 16,000 is made at time 10 milliseconds.

We shall assume that each block access incurs time 0.13 for transfer and 4.17 for average rotational latency, i.e., we need 4.3 milliseconds plus whatever the seek time is for each block access. The seek time can be calculated by the rule for the Megatron 747 given in Example 2: 1 plus the number of tracks divided by 4000. Let us see what happens if we schedule disk accesses using

Cylinder of request	First time available
8000	0
24000	0
56000	0
16000	10
64000	20
40000	30

Figure 6: Arrival times for four block-access requests

the elevator algorithm. The first request, at cylinder 8000, requires no seek, since the heads are already there. Thus, at time 4.3 the first access will be complete. The request for cylinder 16,000 has not arrived at this point, so we move the heads to cylinder 24,000, the next requested "stop" on our sweep to the highest-numbered tracks. The seek from cylinder 8000 to 24,000 takes 5 milliseconds, so we arrive at time 9.3 and complete the access in another 4.3. Thus, the second access is complete at time 13.6. By this time, the request for cylinder 16,000 has arrived, but we passed that cylinder at time 7.3 and will not come back to it until the next pass.

We thus move next to cylinder 56,000, taking time 9 to seek and 4.3 for rotation and transfer. The third access is thus complete at time 26.9. Now, the request for cylinder 64,000 has arrived, so we continue outward. We require 3 milliseconds for seek time, so this access is complete at time $26.9 + 3 + 4.3 = 34.2$.

At this time, the request for cylinder 40,000 has been made, so it and the request at cylinder 16,000 remain. We thus sweep inward, honoring these two requests. Figure 7 summarizes the times at which requests are honored.

Cylinder of request	Time completed
8000	4.3
24000	13.6
56000	26.9
64000	34.2
40000	45.5
16000	56.8

Figure 7: Finishing times for block accesses using the elevator algorithm

Let us compare the performance of the elevator algorithm with a more naive approach such as first-come-first-served. The first three requests are satisfied in exactly the same manner, assuming that the order of the first three requests was 8000, 24,000, and 56,000. However, at that point, we go to cylinder 16,000, because that was the fourth request to arrive. The seek time is 11 for this request, since we travel from cylinder 56,000 to 16,000, more than half way across the disk. The fifth request, at cylinder 64,000, requires a seek time of 13, and the last, at 40,000, uses seek time 7. Figure 8 summarizes the activity caused by first-come-first-served scheduling. The difference between the two algorithms — 14 milliseconds — may not appear significant, but recall that the number of requests in this simple example is small and the algorithms were assumed not to deviate until the fourth of the six requests. □

Cylinder of request	Time completed
8000	4.3
24000	13.6
56000	26.9
16000	42.2
64000	59.5
40000	70.8

Figure 8: Finishing times for block accesses using the first-come-first-served algorithm

3.6 Prefetching and Large-Scale Buffering

Our final suggestion for speeding up some secondary-memory algorithms is called *prefetching* or sometimes *double buffering*. In some applications we can predict the order in which blocks will be requested from disk. If so, then we can load them into main memory buffers before they are needed. One advantage to doing so is that we are thus better able to schedule the disk, such as by using the elevator algorithm, to reduce the average time needed to access a block. In the extreme case, where there are many access requests waiting at all times, we can make the seek time per request be very close to the minimum seek time, rather than the average seek time.

3.7 Exercises for Section 3

Exercise 3.1: Suppose we are scheduling I/O requests for a Megatron 747 disk, and the requests in Fig. 9 are made, with the head initially at track 32,000. At what time is each request serviced fully if:

a) We use the elevator algorithm (it is permissible to start moving in either direction at first).

b) We use first-come-first-served scheduling.

Cylinder of Request	First time available
8000	0
48000	1
4000	10
40000	20

Figure 9: Arrival times for four block-access requests

! **Exercise 3.2:** Suppose we use two Megatron 747 disks as mirrors of one another. However, instead of allowing reads of any block from either disk, we keep the head of the first disk in the inner half of the cylinders, and the head of the second disk in the outer half of the cylinders. Assuming read requests are on random tracks, and we never have to write:

a) What is the average rate at which this system can read blocks?

b) How does this rate compare with the average rate for mirrored Megatron 747 disks with no restriction?

c) What disadvantages do you foresee for this system?

! **Exercise 3.3:** Let us explore the relationship between the arrival rate of requests, the throughput of the elevator algorithm, and the average delay of requests. To simplify the problem, we shall make the following assumptions:

1. A pass of the elevator algorithm always proceeds from the innermost to outermost track, or vice-versa, even if there are no requests at the extreme cylinders.

2. When a pass starts, only those requests that are already pending will be honored, not requests that come in while the pass is in progress, even if the head passes their cylinder.[2]

3. There will never be two requests for blocks on the same cylinder waiting on one pass.

Let A be the interarrival rate, that is the time between requests for block accesses. Assume that the system is in steady state, that is, it has been accepting and answering requests for a long time. For a Megatron 747 disk, compute as a function of A:

[2]The purpose of this assumption is to avoid having to deal with the fact that a typical pass of the elevator algorithm goes fast at first, as there will be few waiting requests where the head has recently been, and slows down as it moves into an area of the disk where it has not recently been. The analysis of the way request density varies during a pass is an interesting exercise in its own right.

a) The average time taken to perform one pass.

b) The number of requests serviced on one pass.

c) The average time a request waits for service.

!! **Exercise 3.4:** In Example 5, we saw how dividing the data to be sorted among four disks could allow more than one block to be read at a time. Suppose our data is divided randomly among n disks, and requests for data are also random. Requests must be executed in the order in which they are received because there are dependencies among them that must be respected. What is the average throughput for such a system?

! **Exercise 3.5:** If we read k randomly chosen blocks from one cylinder, on the average how far around the cylinder must we go before we pass all of the blocks?

4 Disk Failures

In this section we shall consider the ways in which disks can fail and what can be done to mitigate these failures.

1. The most common form of failure is an *intermittent failure*, where an attempt to read or write a sector is unsuccessful, but with repeated tries we are able to read or write successfully.

2. A more serious form of failure is one in which a bit or bits are permanently corrupted, and it becomes impossible to read a sector correctly no matter how many times we try. This form of error is called *media decay*.

3. A related type of error is a *write failure*, where we attempt to write a sector, but we can neither write successfully nor can we retrieve the previously written sector. A possible cause is that there was a power outage during the writing of the sector.

4. The most serious form of disk failure is a *disk crash*, where the entire disk becomes unreadable, suddenly and permanently.

We shall discuss parity checks as a way to detect intermittent failures. We also discuss "stable storage," a technique for organizing a disk so that media decays or failed writes do not result in permanent loss. Finally, we examine techniques collectively known as "RAID" for coping with disk crashes.

4.1 Intermittent Failures

An intermittent failure occurs if we try to read a sector, but the correct content of that sector is not delivered to the disk controller. If the controller has a way to tell that the sector is good or bad (as we shall discuss in Section 4.2), then the controller can reissue the read request when bad data is read, until the sector is returned correctly, or some preset limit, like 100 tries, is reached.

Similarly, the controller may attempt to write a sector, but the contents of the sector are not what was intended. The only way to check that the write was correct is to let the disk go around again and read the sector. A straightforward way to perform the check is to read the sector and compare it with the sector we intended to write. However, instead of performing the complete comparison at the disk controller, it is simpler to read the sector and see if a good sector was read. If so, we assume the write was correct, and if the sector read is bad, then the write was apparently unsuccessful and must be repeated.

4.2 Checksums

How a reading operation can determine the good/bad status of a sector may appear mysterious at first. Yet the technique used in modern disk drives is quite simple: each sector has some additional bits, called the *checksum*, that are set depending on the values of the data bits stored in that sector. If, on reading, we find that the checksum is not proper for the data bits, then we know there is an error in reading. If the checkum is proper, there is still a small chance that the block was not read correctly, but by using many checksum bits we can make the probability of missing a bad read arbitrarily small.

A simple form of checksum is based on the *parity* of all the bits in the sector. If there is an odd number of 1's among a collection of bits, we say the bits have *odd* parity and add a parity bit that is 1. Similarly, if there is an even number of 1's among the bits, then we say the bits have *even* parity and add parity bit 0. As a result:

- The number of 1's among a collection of bits and their parity bit is always even.

When we write a sector, the disk controller can compute the parity bit and append it to the sequence of bits written in the sector. Thus, every sector will have even parity.

Example 7: If the sequence of bits in a sector were 01101000, then there is an odd number of 1's, so the parity bit is 1. If we follow this sequence by its parity bit we have 011010001. If the given sequence of bits were 11101110, we have an even number of 1's, and the parity bit is 0. The sequence followed by its parity bit is 111011100. Note that each of the nine-bit sequences constructed by adding a parity bit has even parity. □

Any one-bit error in reading or writing the bits and their parity bit results in a sequence of bits that has *odd parity*; i.e., the number of 1's is odd. It is easy for the disk controller to count the number of 1's and to determine the presence of an error if a sector has odd parity.

Of course, more than one bit of the sector may be corrupted. If so, the probability is 50% that the number of 1-bits will be even, and the error will not be detected. We can increase our chances of detecting errors if we keep several parity bits. For example, we could keep eight parity bits, one for the first bit of every byte, one for the second bit of every byte, and so on, up to the eighth and last bit of every byte. Then, on a massive error, the probability is 50% that any one parity bit will detect an error, and the chance that none of the eight do so is only one in 2^8, or 1/256. In general, if we use n independent bits as a checksum, then the chance of missing an error is only $1/2^n$. For instance, if we devote 4 bytes to a checksum, then there is only one chance in about four billion that the error will go undetected.

4.3 Stable Storage

While checksums will almost certainly detect the existence of a media failure or a failure to read or write correctly, it does not help us correct the error. Moreover, when writing we could find ourselves in a position where we overwrite the previous contents of a sector and yet cannot read the new contents correctly. That situation could be serious if, say, we were adding a small increment to an account balance and now have lost both the original balance and the new balance. If we could be assured that the contents of the sector contained either the new or old balance, then we would only have to determine whether the write was successful or not.

To deal with the problems above, we can implement a policy known as *stable storage* on a disk or on several disks. The general idea is that sectors are paired, and each pair represents one sector-contents X. We shall refer to the pair of sectors representing X as the "left" and "right" copies, X_L and X_R. We continue to assume that the copies are written with a sufficient number of parity-check bits so that we can rule out the possibility that a bad sector looks good when the parity checks are considered. Thus, we shall assume that if the read function returns a good value w for either X_L or X_R, then w is the true value of X. The stable-storage writing policy is:

1. Write the value of X into X_L. Check that the value has status "good"; i.e., the parity-check bits are correct in the written copy. If not, repeat the write. If after a set number of write attempts, we have not successfully written X into X_L, assume that there is a media failure in this sector. A fix-up such as substituting a spare sector for X_L must be adopted.

2. Repeat (1) for X_R.

The stable-storage reading policy is to alternate trying to read X_L and X_R, until a good value is returned. Only if no good value is returned after some large, prechosen number of tries, is X truly unreadable.

4.4 Error-Handling Capabilities of Stable Storage

The policies described in Section 4.3 are capable of compensating for several different kinds of errors. We shall outline them here.

1. *Media failures.* If, after storing X in sectors X_L and X_R, one of them undergoes a media failure and becomes permanently unreadable, we can always read X from the other. If both X_L and X_R have failed, then we cannot read X, but the probability of both failing is extremely small.

2. *Write failure.* Suppose that as we write X, there is a system failure — e.g., a power outage. It is possible that X will be lost in main memory, and also the copy of X being written at the time will be garbled. For example, half the sector may be written with part of the new value of X, while the other half remains as it was. When the system becomes available and we examine X_L and X_R, we are sure to be able to determine either the old or new value of X. The possible cases are:

   (a) The failure occurred as we were writing X_L. Then we shall find that the status of X_L is "bad." However, since we never got to write X_R, its status will be "good" (unless there is a coincident media failure at X_R, which is extremely unlikely). Thus, we can obtain the old value of X. We may also copy X_R into X_L to repair the damage to X_L.

   (b) The failure occurred after we wrote X_L. Then we expect that X_L will have status "good," and we may read the new value of X from X_L. Since X_R may or may not have the correct value of X, we should also copy X_L into X_R.

4.5 Recovery from Disk Crashes

The most serious mode of failure for disks is the "disk crash" or "head crash," where data is permanently destroyed. If the data was not backed up on another medium, such as a tape backup system, or on a mirror disk as we discussed in Section 3.4, then there is nothing we can do to recover the data. This situation represents a disaster for many DBMS applications, such as banking and other financial applications.

Several schemes have been developed to reduce the risk of data loss by disk crashes. They generally involve redundancy, extending the idea of parity checks from Section 4.2 or duplicated sectors, as in Section 4.3. The common term for this class of strategies is RAID, or *Redundant Arrays of Independent Disks.*

The rate at which disk crashes occur is generally measured by the *mean time to failure*, the time after which 50% of a population of disks can be expected to fail and be unrecoverable. For modern disks, the mean time to failure is about 10 years. We shall make the convenient assumption that if the mean time to failure is n years, then in any given year, $1/n$th of the surviving disks fail. In reality, there is a tendency for disks, like most electronic equipment, to fail early or fail late. That is, a small percentage have manufacturing defects that lead to their early demise, while those without such defects will survive for many years, until wear-and-tear causes a failure.

However, the mean time to a disk crash does not have to be the same as the mean time to data loss. The reason is that there are a number of schemes available for assuring that if one disk fails, there are others to help recover the data of the failed disk. In the remainder of this section, we shall study the most common schemes.

Each of these schemes starts with one or more disks that hold the data (we'll call these the *data disks*) and adding one or more disks that hold information that is completely determined by the contents of the data disks. The latter are called *redundant disks.* When there is a disk crash of either a data disk or a redundant disk, the other disks can be used to restore the failed disk, and there is no permanent information loss.

4.6 Mirroring as a Redundancy Technique

The simplest scheme is to mirror each disk, as discussed in Section 3.4. We shall call one of the disks the *data disk*, while the other is the *redundant disk*; which is which doesn't matter in this scheme. Mirroring, as a protection against data loss, is often referred to as *RAID level 1.* It gives a mean time to memory loss that is much greater than the mean time to disk failure, as the following example illustrates. Essentially, with mirroring and the other redundancy schemes we discuss, the only way data can be lost is if there is a second disk crash while the first crash is being repaired.

Example 8: Suppose each disk has a 10-year mean time to failure, which we shall take to mean that the probability of failure in any given year is 10%. If disks are mirrored, then when a disk fails, we have only to replace it with a good disk and copy the mirror disk to the new one. At the end, we have two disks that are mirrors of each other, and the system is restored to its former state.

The only thing that could go wrong is that during the copying the mirror disk fails. Now, both copies of at least part of the data have been lost, and there is no way to recover.

But how often will this sequence of events occur? Suppose that the process of replacing the failed disk takes 3 hours, which is 1/8 of a day, or 1/2920 of a year. Since we assume the average disk lasts 10 years, the probability that the mirror disk will fail during copying is $(1/10) \times (1/2920)$, or one in 29,200.

If one disk fails every 10 years, then one of the two disks will fail once in 5 years on the average. One in every 29,200 of these failures results in data loss. Put another way, the mean time to a failure involving data loss is $5 \times 29{,}200 = 146{,}000$ years. □

4.7 Parity Blocks

While mirroring disks is an effective way to reduce the probability of a disk crash involving data loss, it uses as many redundant disks as there are data disks. Another approach, often called *RAID level 4*, uses only one redundant disk, no matter how many data disks there are. We assume the disks are identical, so we can number the blocks on each disk from 1 to some number n. Of course, all the blocks on all the disks have the same number of bits; for instance, the 16,384-byte blocks of the Megatron 747 have $8 \times 16{,}384 = 131{,}072$ bits. In the redundant disk, the ith block consists of parity checks for the ith blocks of all the data disks. That is, the jth bits of all the ith blocks, including both the data disks and the redundant disk, must have an even number of 1's among them, and we always choose the bit of the redundant disk to make this condition true.

We saw in Example 7 how to force the condition to be true. In the redundant disk, we choose bit j to be 1 if an odd number of the data disks have 1 in that bit, and we choose bit j of the redundant disk to be 0 if there are an even number of 1's in that bit among the data disks. The term for this calculation is the *modulo-2 sum*. That is, the modulo-2 sum of bits is 0 if there are an even number of 1's among those bits, and 1 if there are an odd number of 1's.

Example 9: Suppose for sake of an extremely simple example that blocks consist of only one byte — eight bits. Let there be three data disks, called 1, 2, and 3, and one redundant disk, called disk 4. Focus on the first block of all these disks. If the data disks have in their first blocks the following bit sequences:

disk 1: 11110000
disk 2: 10101010
disk 3: 00111000

then the redundant disk will have in block 1 the parity check bits:

disk 4: 01100010

Notice how in each position, an even number of the four 8-bit sequences have 1's. There are two 1's in positions 1, 2, 4, 5, and 7, four 1's in position 3, and zero 1's in positions 6 and 8. □

Reading

Reading blocks from a data disk is no different from reading blocks from any disk. There is generally no reason to read from the redundant disk, but we could.

Writing

When we write a new block of a data disk, we need not only to change that block, but we need to change the corresponding block of the redundant disk so it continues to hold the parity checks for the corresponding blocks of all the data disks. A naive approach would read the corresponding blocks of the n data disks, take their modulo-2 sum, and rewrite the block of the redundant disk. That approach requires a write of the data block that is rewritten, the reading of the $n-1$ other data blocks, and a write of the block of the redundant disk. The total is thus $n+1$ disk I/O's.

A better approach is to look only at the old and new versions of the data block i being rewritten. If we take their modulo-2 sum, we know in which positions there is a change in the number of 1's among the blocks numbered i on all the disks. Since these changes are always by one, any even number of 1's changes to an odd number. If we change the same positions of the redundant block, then the number of 1's in each position becomes even again. We can perform these calculations using four disk I/O's:

1. Read the old value of the data block being changed.
2. Read the corresponding block of the redundant disk.
3. Write the new data block.
4. Recalculate and write the block of the redundant disk.

Example 10: Suppose the three first blocks of the data disks are as in Example 9:

disk 1: 11110000
disk 2: 10101010
disk 3: 00111000

Suppose also that the block on the second disk changes from 10101010 to 11001100. We take the modulo-2 sum of the old and new values of the block on disk 2, to get 01100110. That tells us we must change positions 2, 3, 6, and 7 of the first block of the redundant disk. We read that block: 01100010. We replace this block by a new block that we get by changing the appropriate positions; in effect we replace the redundant block by the modulo-2 sum of itself and 01100110, to get 00000100. Another way to express the new redundant block is that it is the modulo-2 sum of the old and new versions of the

The Algebra of Modulo-2 Sums

It may be helpful for understanding some of the tricks used with parity checks to know the algebraic rules involving the modulo-2 sum operation on bit vectors. We shall denote this operation $\oplus$. As an example, $1100 \oplus 1010 = 0110$. Here are some useful rules about $\oplus$:

- The *commutative law*: $x \oplus y = y \oplus x$.
- The *associative law*: $x \oplus (y \oplus z) = (x \oplus y) \oplus z$.
- The all-0 vector of the appropriate length, which we denote $\bar{0}$, is the *identity* for $\oplus$; that is, $x \oplus \bar{0} = \bar{0} \oplus x = x$.
- $\oplus$ is its own inverse: $x \oplus x = \bar{0}$. As a useful consequence, if $x \oplus y = z$, then we can "add" x to both sides and get $y = x \oplus z$.

block being rewritten and the old value of the redundant block. In our example, the first blocks of the four disks — three data disks and one redundant — have become:

disk 1: 11110000
disk 2: 11001100
disk 3: 00111000
disk 4: 00000100

after the write to the block on the second disk and the necessary recomputation of the redundant block. Notice that in the blocks above, each column continues to have an even number of 1's. □

Failure Recovery

Now, let us consider what we would do if one of the disks crashed. If it is the redundant disk, we swap in a new disk, and recompute the redundant blocks. If the failed disk is one of the data disks, then we need to swap in a good disk and recompute its data from the other disks. The rule for recomputing any missing data is actually simple, and doesn't depend on which disk, data or redundant, is failed. Since we know that the number of 1's among corresponding bits of all disks is even, it follows that:

- The bit in any position is the modulo-2 sum of all the bits in the corresponding positions of all the other disks.

If one doubts the above rule, one has only to consider the two cases. If the bit in question is 1, then the number of corresponding bits in the other disks that are 1 must be odd, so their modulo-2 sum is 1. If the bit in question is 0, then there are an even number of 1's among the corresponding bits of the other disks, and their modulo-2 sum is 0.

Example 11: Suppose that disk 2 fails. We need to recompute each block of the replacement disk. Following Example 9, let us see how to recompute the first block of the second disk. We are given the corresponding blocks of the first and third data disks and the redundant disk, so the situation looks like:

disk 1: 11110000
disk 2: ????????
disk 3: 00111000
disk 4: 01100010

If we take the modulo-2 sum of each column, we deduce that the missing block is 10101010, as was initially the case in Example 9. □

4.8 An Improvement: RAID 5

The RAID level 4 strategy described in Section 4.7 effectively preserves data unless there are two almost simultaneous disk crashes. However, it suffers from a bottleneck defect that we can see when we re-examine the process of writing a new data block. Whatever scheme we use for updating the disks, we need to read and write the redundant disk's block. If there are n data disks, then the number of disk writes to the redundant disk will be n times the average number of writes to any one data disk.

However, as we observed in Example 11, the rule for recovery is the same as for the data disks and redundant disks: take the modulo-2 sum of corresponding bits of the other disks. Thus, we do not have to treat one disk as the redundant disk and the others as data disks. Rather, we could treat each disk as the redundant disk for some of the blocks. This improvement is often called *RAID level 5.*

For instance, if there are $n+1$ disks numbered 0 through n, we could treat the ith cylinder of disk j as redundant if j is the remainder when i is divided by $n+1$.

Example 12: In our running example, $n = 3$ so there are 4 disks. The first disk, numbered 0, is redundant for its cylinders numbered 4, 8, 12, and so on, because these are the numbers that leave remainder 0 when divided by 4. The disk numbered 1 is redundant for blocks numbered 1, 5, 9, and so on; disk 2 is redundant for blocks 2, 6, 10, ..., and disk 3 is redundant for 3, 7, 11, ...

As a result, the reading and writing load for each disk is the same. If all blocks are equally likely to be written, then for one write, each disk has a 1/4 chance that the block is on that disk. If not, then it has a 1/3 chance that it will be the redundant disk for that block. Thus, each of the four disks is involved in $1/4 + (3/4) \times (1/3) = 1/2$ of the writes. □

4.9 Coping With Multiple Disk Crashes

There is a theory of error-correcting codes that allows us to deal with any number of disk crashes — data or redundant — if we use enough redundant disks. This strategy leads to the highest RAID "level," *RAID level 6*. We shall give only a simple example here, where two simultaneous crashes are correctable, and the strategy is based on the simplest error-correcting code, known as a *Hamming code*.

In our description we focus on a system with seven disks, numbered 1 through 7. The first four are data disks, and disks 5 through 7 are redundant. The relationship between data and redundant disks is summarized by the 3×7 matrix of 0's and 1's in Fig. 10. Notice that:

a) Every possible column of three 0's and 1's, except for the all-0 column, appears in the matrix of Fig. 10.

b) The columns for the redundant disks have a single 1.

c) The columns for the data disks each have at least two 1's.

	Data				|	Redundant		
Disk number	1	2	3	4	|	5	6	7
	1	1	1	0	|	1	0	0
	1	1	0	1	|	0	1	0
	1	0	1	1	|	0	0	1

Figure 10: Redundancy pattern for a system that can recover from two simultaneous disk crashes

The meaning of each of the three rows of 0's and 1's is that if we look at the corresponding bits from all seven disks, and restrict our attention to those disks that have 1 in that row, then the modulo-2 sum of these bits must be 0. Put another way, the disks with 1 in a given row of the matrix are treated as if they were the entire set of disks in a RAID level 4 scheme. Thus, we can compute the bits of one of the redundant disks by finding the row in which that disk has 1, and taking the modulo-2 sum of the corresponding bits of the other disks that have 1 in the same row.

For the matrix of Fig. 10, this rule implies:

1. The bits of disk 5 are the modulo-2 sum of the corresponding bits of disks 1, 2, and 3.

2. The bits of disk 6 are the modulo-2 sum of the corresponding bits of disks 1, 2, and 4.

3. The bits of disk 7 are the modulo-2 sum of the corresponding bits of disks 1, 3, and 4.

We shall see shortly that the particular choice of bits in this matrix gives us a simple rule by which we can recover from two simultaneous disk crashes.

Reading

We may read data from any data disk normally. The redundant disks can be ignored.

Writing

The idea is similar to the writing strategy outlined in Section 4.8, but now several redundant disks may be involved. To write a block of some data disk, we compute the modulo-2 sum of the new and old versions of that block. These bits are then added, in a modulo-2 sum, to the corresponding blocks of all those redundant disks that have 1 in a row in which the written disk also has 1.

Example 13: Let us again assume that blocks are only eight bits long, and focus on the first blocks of the seven disks involved in our RAID level 6 example. First, suppose the data and redundant first blocks are as given in Fig. 11. Notice that the block for disk 5 is the modulo-2 sum of the blocks for the first three disks, the sixth row is the modulo-2 sum of rows 1, 2, and 4, and the last row is the modulo-2 sum of rows 1, 3, and 4.

Disk	Contents
1)	11110000
2)	10101010
3)	00111000
4)	01000001
5)	01100010
6)	00011011
7)	10001001

Figure 11: First blocks of all disks

Suppose we rewrite the first block of disk 2 to be 00001111. If we sum this sequence of bits modulo-2 with the sequence 10101010 that is the old value of this block, we get 10100101. If we look at the column for disk 2 in Fig. 10, we find that this disk has 1's in the first two rows, but not the third. Since redundant disks 5 and 6 have 1 in rows 1 and 2, respectively, we must perform the sum modulo-2 operation on the current contents of their first blocks and the sequence 10100101 just calculated. That is, we flip the values of positions 1, 3, 6, and 8 of these two blocks. The resulting contents of the first blocks of all disks is shown in Fig. 12. Notice that the new contents continue to satisfy the constraints implied by Fig. 10: the modulo-2 sum of corresponding blocks that have 1 in a particular row of the matrix of Fig. 10 is still all 0's. □

Disk	Contents
1)	11110000
2)	00001111
3)	00111000
4)	01000001
5)	11000111
6)	10111110
7)	10001001

Figure 12: First blocks of all disks after rewriting disk 2 and changing the redundant disks

Failure Recovery

Now, let us see how the redundancy scheme outlined above can be used to correct up to two simultaneous disk crashes. Let the failed disks be a and b. Since all columns of the matrix of Fig. 10 are different, we must be able to find some row r in which the columns for a and b are different. Suppose that a has 0 in row r, while b has 1 there.

Then we can compute the correct b by taking the modulo-2 sum of corresponding bits from all the disks other than b that have 1 in row r. Note that a is not among these, so none of these disks have failed. Having recomputed b, we must recompute a, with all other disks available. Since every column of the matrix of Fig. 10 has a 1 in some row, we can use this row to recompute disk a by taking the modulo-2 sum of bits of those other disks with a 1 in this row.

Disk	Contents
1)	11110000
2)	????????
3)	00111000
4)	01000001
5)	????????
6)	10111110
7)	10001001

Figure 13: Situation after disks 2 and 5 fail

Example 14: Suppose that disks 2 and 5 fail at about the same time. Consulting the matrix of Fig. 10, we find that the columns for these two disks differ in row 2, where disk 2 has 1 but disk 5 has 0. We may thus reconstruct disk 2 by taking the modulo-2 sum of corresponding bits of disks 1, 4, and 6, the other three disks with 1 in row 2. Notice that none of these three disks has failed. For instance, following from the situation regarding the first blocks in Fig. 12, we would initially have the data of Fig. 13 available after disks 2 and 5 failed.

If we take the modulo-2 sum of the contents of the blocks of disks 1, 4, and 6, we find that the block for disk 2 is 00001111. This block is correct as can be verified from Fig. 12. The situation is now as in Fig. 14.

Disk	Contents
1)	11110000
2)	00001111
3)	00111000
4)	01000001
5)	????????
6)	10111110
7)	10001001

Figure 14: After recovering disk 2

Now, we see that disk 5's column in Fig. 10 has a 1 in the first row. We can therefore recompute disk 5 by taking the modulo-2 sum of corresponding bits from disks 1, 2, and 3, the other three disks that have 1 in the first row. For block 1, this sum is 11000111. Again, the correctness of this calculation can be confirmed by Fig. 12. □

4.10 Exercises for Section 4

Exercise 4.1: Compute the parity bit for the following bit sequences:

a) 00111011.

b) 00000000.

c) 10101101.

Exercise 4.2: We can have two parity bits associated with a string if we follow the string by one bit that is a parity bit for the odd positions and a second that is the parity bit for the even positions. For each of the strings in Exercise 4.1, find the two bits that serve in this way.

Additional Observations About RAID Level 6

1. We can combine the ideas of RAID levels 5 and 6, by varying the choice of redundant disks according to the block or cylinder number. Doing so will avoid bottlenecks when writing; the scheme described in Section 4.9 will cause bottlenecks at the redundant disks.

2. The scheme described in Section 4.9 is not restricted to four data disks. The number of disks can be one less than any power of 2, say $2^k - 1$. Of these disks, k are redundant, and the remaining $2^k - k - 1$ are data disks, so the redundancy grows roughly as the logarithm of the number of data disks. For any k, we can construct the matrix corresponding to Fig. 10 by writing all possible columns of k 0's and 1's, except the all-0's column. The columns with a single 1 correspond to the redundant disks, and the columns with more than one 1 are the data disks.

Exercise 4.3: Suppose we use mirrored disks as in Example 8, the failure rate is 4% per year, and it takes 8 hours to replace a disk. What is the mean time to a disk failure involving loss of data?

! **Exercise 4.4:** Suppose that a disk has probability F of failing in a given year, and it takes H hours to replace a disk.

a) If we use mirrored disks, what is the mean time to data loss, as a function of F and H?

b) If we use a RAID level 4 or 5 scheme, with N disks, what is the mean time to data loss?

!! **Exercise 4.5:** Suppose we use three disks as a mirrored group; i.e., all three hold identical data. If the yearly probability of failure for one disk is F, and it takes H hours to restore a disk, what is the mean time to data loss?

Exercise 4.6: Suppose we are using a RAID level 4 scheme with four data disks and one redundant disk. As in Example 9 assume blocks are a single byte. Give the block of the redundant disk if the corresponding blocks of the data disks are:

a) 01010110, 11000000, 00111011, and 11111011.

b) 11110000, 11111000, 00111111, and 00000001.

Error-Correcting Codes and RAID Level 6

There is a theory that guides our selection of a suitable matrix, like that of Fig. 10, to determine the content of redundant disks. A *code* of length n is a set of bit-vectors (called *code words*) of length n. The *Hamming distance* between two code words is the number of positions in which they differ, and the *minimum distance* of a code is the smallest Hamming distance of any two different code words.

If C is any code of length n, we can require that the corresponding bits on n disks have one of the sequences that are members of the code. As a very simple example, if we are using a disk and its mirror, then $n = 2$, and we can use the code $C = \{00, 11\}$. That is, the corresponding bits of the two disks must be the same. For another example, the matrix of Fig. 10 defines the code consisting of the 16 bit-vectors of length 7 that have arbitrary values for the first four bits and have the remaining three bits determined by the rules for the three redundant disks.

If the minimum distance of a code is d, then disks whose corresponding bits are required to be a vector in the code will be able to tolerate $d - 1$ simultaneous disk crashes. The reason is that, should we obscure $d - 1$ positions of a code word, and there were two different ways these positions could be filled in to make a code word, then the two code words would have to differ in at most the $d-1$ positions. Thus, the code could not have minimum distance d. As an example, the matrix of Fig. 10 actually defines the well-known *Hamming code*, which has minimum distance 3. Thus, it can handle two disk crashes.

Exercise 4.7: Using the same RAID level 4 scheme as in Exercise 4.6, suppose that data disk 1 has failed. Recover the block of that disk under the following circumstances:

a) The contents of disks 2 through 4 are 01010110, 11000000, and 00111011, while the redundant disk holds 11111011.

b) The contents of disks 2 through 4 are 11110000, 11111000, and 00111111, while the redundant disk holds 00000001.

Exercise 4.8: Suppose the block on the first disk in Exercise 4.6 is changed to 10101010. What changes to the corresponding blocks on the other disks must be made?

Exercise 4.9: Suppose we have the RAID level 6 scheme of Example 13, and the blocks of the four data disks are 00111100, 11000111, 01010101, and 10000100, respectively.

a) What are the corresponding blocks of the redundant disks?

b) If the third disk's block is rewritten to be 10000000, what steps must be taken to change other disks?

Exercise 4.10: Describe the steps taken to recover from the following failures using the RAID level 6 scheme with seven disks: (a) disks 1 and 7, (b) disks 1 and 4, (c) disks 3 and 6.

5 Arranging Data on Disk

We now turn to the matter of how disks are used store databases. A data element such as a tuple or object is represented by a *record*, which consists of consecutive bytes in some disk block. Collections such as relations are usually represented by placing the records that represent their data elements in one or more blocks. It is normal for a disk block to hold only elements of one relation, although there are organizations where blocks hold tuples of several relations. In this section, we shall cover the basic layout techniques for both records and blocks.

5.1 Fixed-Length Records

The simplest sort of record consists of fixed-length *fields*, one for each attribute of the represented tuple. Many machines allow more efficient reading and writing of main memory when data begins at an address that is a multiple of 4 or 8; some even require us to do so. Thus, it is common to begin all fields at a multiple of 4 or 8, as appropriate. Space not used by the previous field is wasted. Note that, even though records are kept in secondary, not main, memory, they are manipulated in main memory. Thus it is necessary to lay out the record so it can be moved to main memory and accessed efficiently there.

Often, the record begins with a *header*, a fixed-length region where information about the record itself is kept. For example, we may want to keep in the record:

1. A pointer to the schema for the data stored in the record. For example, a tuple's record could point to the schema for the relation to which the tuple belongs. This information helps us find the fields of the record.

2. The length of the record. This information helps us skip over records without consulting the schema.

3. Timestamps indicating the time the record was last modified, or last read. This information may be useful for implementing database transactions.

4. Pointers to the fields of the record. This information can substitute for schema information, and it will be seen to be important when we consider variable-length fields in Section 7.

```
CREATE TABLE MovieStar(
    name CHAR(30) PRIMARY KEY,
    address VARCHAR(255),
    gender CHAR(1),
    birthdate DATE
);
```

Figure 15: A SQL table declaration

Example 15: Figure 15 repeats our running MovieStar schema. Let us assume all fields must start at a byte that is a multiple of four. Tuples of this relation have a header and the following four fields:

1. The first field is for name, and this field requires 30 bytes. If we assume that all fields begin at a multiple of 4, then we allocate 32 bytes for the name.

2. The next attribute is address. A VARCHAR attribute requires a fixed-length segment of bytes, with one more byte than the maximum length (for the string's endmarker). Thus, we need 256 bytes for address.

3. Attribute gender is a single byte, holding either the character 'M' or 'F'. We allocate 4 bytes, so the next field can start at a multiple of 4.

4. Attribute birthdate is a SQL DATE value, which is a 10-byte string. We shall allocate 12 bytes to its field, to keep subsequent records in the block aligned at multiples of 4.

. The header of the record will hold:

a) A pointer to the record schema.

b) The record length.

c) A timestamp indicating when the record was created.

We shall assume each of these items is 4 bytes long. Figure 16 shows the layout of a record for a MovieStar tuple. The length of the record is 316 bytes. □

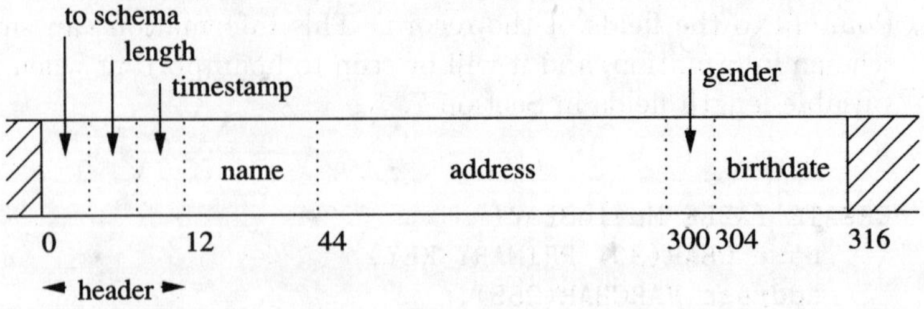

Figure 16: Layout of records for tuples of the `MovieStar` relation

5.2 Packing Fixed-Length Records into Blocks

Records representing tuples of a relation are stored in blocks of the disk and moved into main memory (along with their entire block) when we need to access or update them. The layout of a block that holds records is suggested in Fig. 17.

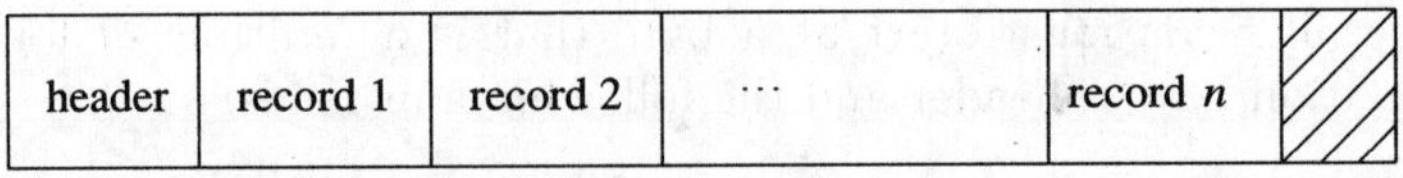

Figure 17: A typical block holding records

In addition to the records, there is a *block header* holding information such as:

1. Links to one or more other blocks that are part of a network of blocks for creating indexes to the tuples of a relation.

2. Information about the role played by this block in such a network.

3. Information about which relation the tuples of this block belong to.

4. A "directory" giving the offset of each record in the block.

5. Timestamp(s) indicating the time of the block's last modification and/or access.

By far the simplest case is when the block holds tuples from one relation, and the records for those tuples have a fixed format. In that case, following the header, we pack as many records as we can into the block and leave the remaining space unused.

Example 16: Suppose we are storing records with the layout developed in Example 15. These records are 316 bytes long. Suppose also that we use 4096-byte blocks. Of these bytes, say 12 will be used for a block header, leaving 4084 bytes for data. In this space we can fit twelve records of the given 316-byte format, and 292 bytes of each block are wasted space. □

5.3 Exercises for Section 5

Exercise 5.1: Suppose a record has the following fields in this order: A character string of length 15, an integer of 2 bytes, a SQL date, and a SQL time (no decimal point). How many bytes does the record take if:

a) Fields can start at any byte.

b) Fields must start at a byte that is a multiple of 4.

c) Fields must start at a byte that is a multiple of 8.

Exercise 5.2: Repeat Exercise 5.1 for the list of fields: a real of 8 bytes, a character string of length 17, a single byte, and a SQL date.

Exercise 5.3: Assume fields are as in Exercise 5.1, but records also have a record header consisting of two 4-byte pointers and a character. Calculate the record length for the three situations regarding field alignment (a) through (c) in Exercise 5.1.

Exercise 5.4: Repeat Exercise 5.2 if the records also include a header consisting of an 8-byte pointer, and ten 2-byte integers.

6 Representing Block and Record Addresses

When in main memory, the address of a block is the virtual-memory address of its first byte, and the address of a record within that block is the virtual-memory address of the first byte of that record. However, in secondary storage, the block is not part of the application's virtual-memory address space. Rather, a sequence of bytes describes the location of the block within the overall system of data accessible to the DBMS: the device ID for the disk, the cylinder number, and so on. A record can be identified by giving its block address and the offset of the first byte of the record within the block.

In this section, we shall begin with a discussion of address spaces, especially as they pertain to the common "client-server" architecture for DBMS's. We then discuss the options for representing addresses, and finally look at "pointer swizzling," the ways in which we can convert addresses in the data server's world to the world of the client application programs.

6.1 Addresses in Client-Server Systems

Commonly, a database system consists of a *server* process that provides data from secondary storage to one or more *client* processes that are applications using the data. The server and client processes may be on one machine, or the server and the various clients can be distributed over many machines.

The client application uses a conventional "virtual" address space, typically 32 bits, or about 4 billion different addresses. The operating system or DBMS decides which parts of the address space are currently located in main memory, and hardware maps the virtual address space to physical locations in main memory. We shall not think further of this virtual-to-physical translation, and shall think of the client address space as if it were main memory itself.

The server's data lives in a *database address space.* The addresses of this space refer to blocks, and possibly to offsets within the block. There are several ways that addresses in this address space can be represented:

1. *Physical Addresses.* These are byte strings that let us determine the place within the secondary storage system where the block or record can be found. One or more bytes of the physical address are used to indicate each of:

   (a) The host to which the storage is attached (if the database is stored across more than one machine),

   (b) An identifier for the disk or other device on which the block is located,

   (c) The number of the cylinder of the disk,

   (d) The number of the track within the cylinder,

   (e) The number of the block within the track, and

   (f) (In some cases) the offset of the beginning of the record within the block.

2. *Logical Addresses.* Each block or record has a "logical address," which is an arbitrary string of bytes of some fixed length. A *map table*, stored on disk in a known location, relates logical to physical addresses, as suggested in Fig. 18.

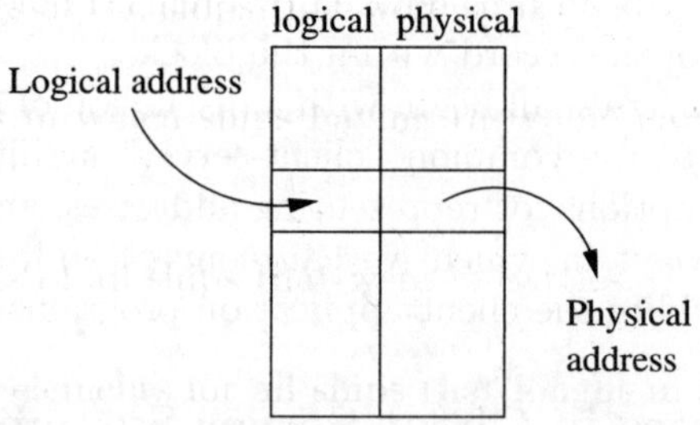

Figure 18: A map table translates logical to physical addresses

Notice that physical addresses are long. Eight bytes is about the minimum we could use if we incorporate all the listed elements, and some systems use many more bytes. For example, imagine a database of objects that is designed to last for 100 years. In the future, the database may grow to encompass one million machines, and each machine might be fast enough to create one object every nanosecond. This system would create around 2^{77} objects, which requires a minimum of ten bytes to represent addresses. Since we would probably prefer to reserve some bytes to represent the host, others to represent the storage unit, and so on, a rational address notation would use considerably more than 10 bytes for a system of this scale.

6.2 Logical and Structured Addresses

One might wonder what the purpose of logical addresses could be. All the information needed for a physical address is found in the map table, and following logical pointers to records requires consulting the map table and then going to the physical address. However, the level of indirection involved in the map table allows us considerable flexibility. For example, many data organizations require us to move records around, either within a block or from block to block. If we use a map table, then all pointers to the record refer to this map table, and all we have to do when we move or delete the record is to change the entry for that record in the table.

Many combinations of logical and physical addresses are possible as well, yielding *structured* address schemes. For instance, one could use a physical address for the block (but not the offset within the block), and add the key value for the record being referred to. Then, to find a record given this structured address, we use the physical part to reach the block containing that record, and we examine the records of the block to find the one with the proper key.

A similar, and very useful, combination of physical and logical addresses is to keep in each block an *offset table* that holds the offsets of the records within the block, as suggested in Fig. 19. Notice that the table grows from the front end of the block, while the records are placed starting at the end of the block. This strategy is useful when the records need not be of equal length. Then, we do not know in advance how many records the block will hold, and we do not have to allocate a fixed amount of the block header to the table initially.

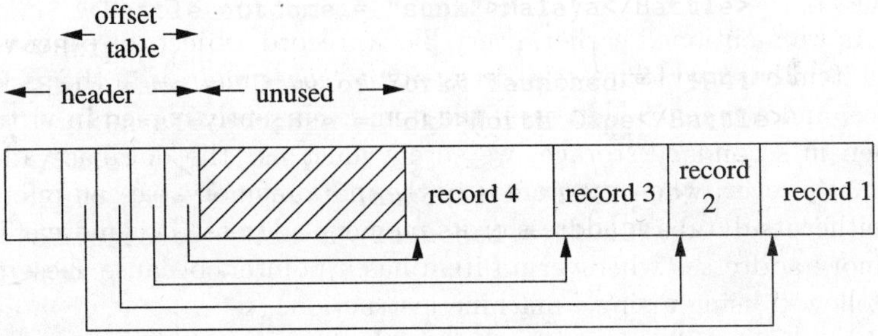

Figure 19: A block with a table of offsets telling us the position of each record within the block

The address of a record is now the physical address of its block plus the offset of the entry in the block's offset table for that record. This level of indirection within the block offers many of the advantages of logical addresses, without the need for a global map table.

- We can move the record around within the block, and all we have to do is change the record's entry in the offset table; pointers to the record will still be able to find it.

- We can even allow the record to move to another block, if the offset table entries are large enough to hold a *forwarding address* for the record, giving its new location.

- Finally, we have an option, should the record be deleted, of leaving in its offset-table entry a *tombstone*, a special value that indicates the record has been deleted. Prior to its deletion, pointers to this record may have been stored at various places in the database. After record deletion, following a pointer to this record leads to the tombstone, whereupon the pointer can either be replaced by a null pointer, or the data structure otherwise modified to reflect the deletion of the record. Had we not left the tombstone, the pointer might lead to some new record, with surprising, and erroneous, results.

6.3 Pointer Swizzling

Often, pointers or addresses are part of records. This situation is not typical for records that represent tuples of a relation, but it is common for tuples that represent objects. Also, modern object-relational database systems allow attributes of pointer type (called references), so even relational systems need the ability to represent pointers in tuples. Finally, index structures are composed of blocks that usually have pointers within them. Thus, we need to study the management of pointers as blocks are moved between main and secondary memory.

As we mentioned earlier, every block, record, object, or other referenceable data item has two forms of address: its *database address* in the server's address space, and a *memory address* if the item is currently copied in virtual memory. When in secondary storage, we surely must use the database address of the item. However, when the item is in the main memory, we can refer to the item by either its database address or its memory address. It is more efficient to put memory addresses wherever an item has a pointer, because these pointers can be followed using a single machine instruction.

In contrast, following a database address is much more time-consuming. We need a table that translates from all those database addresses that are currently in virtual memory to their current memory address. Such a *translation table* is suggested in Fig. 20. It may look like the map table of Fig. 18 that translates between logical and physical addresses. However:

a) Logical and physical addresses are both representations for the database address. In contrast, memory addresses in the translation table are for copies of the corresponding object in memory.

b) All addressable items in the database have entries in the map table, while only those items currently in memory are mentioned in the translation table.

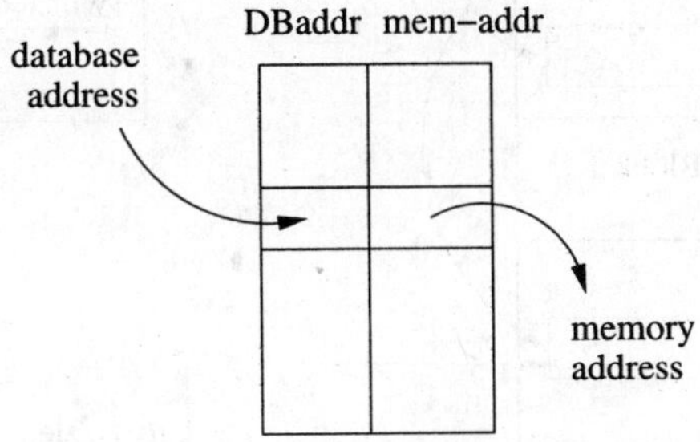

Figure 20: The translation table turns database addresses into their equivalents in memory

To avoid the cost of translating repeatedly from database addresses to memory addresses, several techniques have been developed that are collectively known as *pointer swizzling*. The general idea is that when we move a block from secondary to main memory, pointers within the block may be "swizzled," that is, translated from the database address space to the virtual address space. Thus, a pointer actually consists of:

1. A bit indicating whether the pointer is currently a database address or a (swizzled) memory address.

2. The database or memory pointer, as appropriate. The same space is used for whichever address form is present at the moment. Of course, not all the space may be used when the memory address is present, because it is typically shorter than the database address.

Example 17: Figure 21 shows a simple situation in which the Block 1 has a record with pointers to a second record on the same block and to a record on another block. The figure also shows what might happen when Block 1 is copied to memory. The first pointer, which points within Block 1, can be swizzled so it points directly to the memory address of the target record.

However, if Block 2 is not in memory at this time, then we cannot swizzle the second pointer; it must remain unswizzled, pointing to the database address of its target. Should Block 2 be brought to memory later, it becomes theoretically possible to swizzle the second pointer of Block 1. Depending on the swizzling strategy used, there may or may not be a list of such pointers that are in memory, referring to Block 2; if so, then we have the option of swizzling the pointer at that time. □

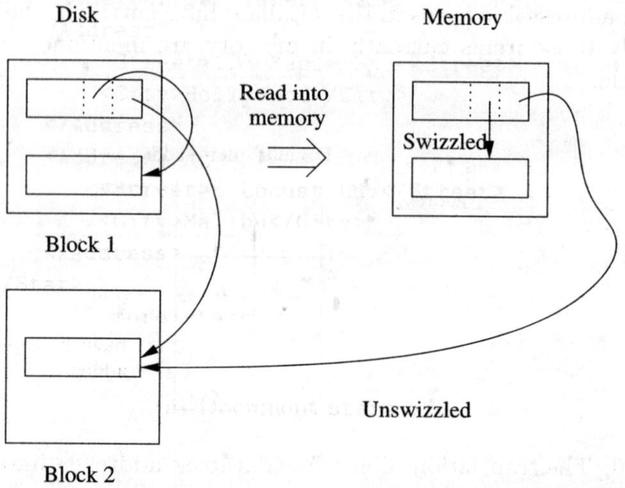

Figure 21: Structure of a pointer when swizzling is used

Automatic Swizzling

There are several strategies we can use to determine when to swizzle pointers. If we use *automatic swizzling*, then as soon as a block is brought into memory, we locate all its pointers and addresses and enter them into the translation table if they are not already there. These pointers include both the pointers *from* records in the block to elsewhere and the addresses of the block itself and/or its records, if these are addressable items. We need some mechanism to locate the pointers within the block. For example:

1. If the block holds records with a known schema, the schema will tell us where in the records the pointers are found.

2. If the block is used for an index structure, then the block will hold pointers at known locations.

3. We may keep within the block header a list of where the pointers are.

When we enter into the translation table the addresses for the block just moved into memory, and/or its records, we know where in memory the block has been buffered. We may thus create the translation-table entry for these database addresses straightforwardly. When we insert one of these database addresses A into the translation table, we may find it in the table already, because its block is currently in memory. In this case, we replace A in the block just moved to memory by the corresponding memory address, and we set the "swizzled" bit to true. On the other hand, if A is not yet in the translation table, then its block has not been copied into main memory. We therefore cannot swizzle this pointer and leave it in the block as a database pointer.

Suppose that during the use of this data, we follow a pointer P and we find that P is still unswizzled, i.e., in the form of a database pointer. We consult the translation table to see if database address P currently has a memory equivalent. If not, block B must be copied into a memory buffer. Once B is in memory, we can "swizzle" P by replacing its database form by the equivalent memory form.

Swizzling on Demand

Another approach is to leave all pointers unswizzled when the block is first brought into memory. We enter its address, and the addresses of its pointers, into the translation table, along with their memory equivalents. If we follow a pointer P that is inside some block of memory, we swizzle it, using the same strategy that we followed when we found an unswizzled pointer using automatic swizzling.

The difference between on-demand and automatic swizzling is that the latter tries to get all the pointers swizzled quickly and efficiently when the block is loaded into memory. The possible time saved by swizzling all of a block's pointers at one time must be weighed against the possibility that some swizzled pointers will never be followed. In that case, any time spent swizzling and unswizzling the pointer will be wasted.

An interesting option is to arrange that database pointers look like invalid memory addresses. If so, then we can allow the computer to follow any pointer as if it were in its memory form. If the pointer happens to be unswizzled, then the memory reference will cause a hardware trap. If the DBMS provides a function that is invoked by the trap, and this function "swizzles" the pointer in the manner described above, then we can follow swizzled pointers in single instructions, and only need to do something more time consuming when the pointer is unswizzled.

No Swizzling

Of course it is possible never to swizzle pointers. We still need the translation table, so the pointers may be followed in their unswizzled form. This approach does offer the advantage that records cannot be pinned in memory, as discussed in Section 6.5, and decisions about which form of pointer is present need not be made.

Programmer Control of Swizzling

In some applications, it may be known by the application programmer whether the pointers in a block are likely to be followed. This programmer may be able to specify explicitly that a block loaded into memory is to have its pointers swizzled, or the programmer may call for the pointers to be swizzled only as needed. For example, if a programmer knows that a block is likely to be accessed heavily, such as the root block of a B-tree, then the pointers would be swizzled. However, blocks that are loaded into memory, used once, and then likely dropped from memory, would not be swizzled.

6.4 Returning Blocks to Disk

When a block is moved from memory back to disk, any pointers within that block must be "unswizzled"; that is, their memory addresses must be replaced by the corresponding database addresses. The translation table can be used to associate addresses of the two types in either direction, so in principle it is possible to find, given a memory address, the database address to which the memory address is assigned.

However, we do not want each unswizzling operation to require a search of the entire translation table. While we have not discussed the implementation of this table, we might imagine that the table of Fig. 20 has appropriate indexes. If we think of the translation table as a relation, then the problem of finding the memory address associated with a database address x can be expressed as the query:

```
SELECT memAddr
FROM TranslationTable
WHERE dbAddr = x;
```

For instance, a hash table using the database address as the key might be appropriate for an index on the dbAddr attribute.

If we want to support the reverse query,

```
SELECT dbAddr
FROM TranslationTable
WHERE memAddr = y;
```

then we need to have an index on attribute memAddr as well. Section 6.5 talks about linked-list structures that in some circumstances can be used to go from a memory address to all main-memory pointers to that address.

6.5 Pinned Records and Blocks

A block in memory is said to be *pinned* if it cannot at the moment be written back to disk safely. A bit telling whether or not a block is pinned can be located in the header of the block. There are many reasons why a block could be pinned, including requirements of a recovery system. Pointer swizzling introduces an important reason why certain blocks must be pinned.

If a block B_1 has within it a swizzled pointer to some data item in block B_2, then we must be very careful about moving block B_2 back to disk and reusing its main-memory buffer. The reason is that, should we follow the pointer in B_1, it will lead us to the buffer, which no longer holds B_2; in effect, the pointer has become dangling. A block, like B_2, that is referred to by a swizzled pointer from somewhere else is therefore pinned.

When we write a block back to disk, we not only need to "unswizzle" any pointers in that block. We also need to make sure it is not pinned. If it is pinned, we must either unpin it, or let the block remain in memory, occupying space that could otherwise be used for some other block. To unpin a block that is pinned because of swizzled pointers from outside, we must "unswizzle" any pointers to it. Consequently, the translation table must record, for each database address whose data item is in memory, the places in memory where swizzled pointers to that item exist. Two possible approaches are:

1. Keep the list of references to a memory address as a linked list attached to the entry for that address in the translation table.

2. If memory addresses are significantly shorter than database addresses, we can create the linked list in the space used for the pointers themselves. That is, each space used for a database pointer is replaced by

   (a) The swizzled pointer, and

   (b) Another pointer that forms part of a linked list of all occurrences of this pointer.

Figure 22 suggests how two occurrences of a memory pointer y could be linked, starting at the entry in the translation table for database address x and its corresponding memory address y.

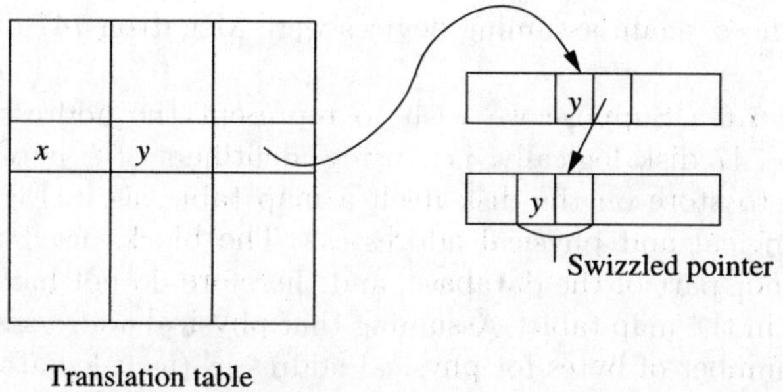

Figure 22: A linked list of occurrences of a swizzled pointer

6.6 Exercises for Section 6

Exercise 6.1: If we represent physical addresses for the Megatron 747 disk by allocating a separate byte or bytes to each of the cylinder, track within a cylinder, and block within a track, how many bytes do we need? Make a reasonable assumption about the maximum number of blocks on each track; recall that the Megatron 747 has a variable number of sectors/track.

Exercise 6.2: Repeat Exercise 6.1 for the Megatron 777 disk described in Exercise 2.1

Exercise 6.3: If we wish to represent record addresses as well as block addresses, we need additional bytes. Assuming we want addresses for a single Megatron 747 disk as in Exercise 6.1, how many bytes would we need for record addresses if we:

a) Included the number of the byte within a block as part of the physical address.

b) Used structured addresses for records. Assume that the stored records have a 4-byte integer as a key.

Exercise 6.4: Today, IP addresses have four bytes. Suppose that block addresses for a world-wide address system consist of an IP address for the host, a device number between 1 and 1000, and a block address on an individual device (assumed to be a Megatron 747 disk). How many bytes would block addresses require?

Exercise 6.5: In IP version 6, IP addresses are 16 bytes long. In addition, we may want to address not only blocks, but records, which may start at any byte of a block. However, devices will have their own IP address, so there will be no need to represent a device within a host, as we suggested was necessary in Exercise 6.4. How many bytes would be needed to represent addresses in these circumstances, again assuming devices were Megatron 747 disks?

! **Exercise 6.6:** Suppose we wish to represent the addresses of blocks on a Megatron 747 disk logically, i.e., using identifiers of k bytes for some k. We also need to store on the disk itself a map table, as in Fig. 18, consisting of pairs of logical and physical addresses. The blocks used for the map table itself are not part of the database, and therefore do not have their own logical addresses in the map table. Assuming that physical addresses use the minimum possible number of bytes for physical addresses (as calculated in Exercise 6.1), and logical addresses likewise use the minimum possible number of bytes for logical addresses, how many blocks of 4096 bytes does the map table for the disk occupy?

! **Exercise 6.7:** Suppose that we have 4096-byte blocks in which we store records of 100 bytes. The block header consists of an offset table, as in Fig. 19, using 2-byte pointers to records within the block. On an average day, two records per block are inserted, and one record is deleted. A deleted record must have its pointer replaced by a "tombstone," because there may be dangling pointers to it. For specificity, assume the deletion on any day always occurs before the insertions. If the block is initially empty, after how many days will there be no room to insert any more records?

Exercise 6.8: Suppose that if we swizzle all pointers automatically, we can perform the swizzling in half the time it would take to swizzle each one separately. If the probability that a pointer in main memory will be followed at least once is p, for what values of p is it more efficient to swizzle automatically than on demand?

! **Exercise 6.9:** Generalize Exercise 6.8 to include the possibility that we never swizzle pointers. Suppose that the important actions take the following times, in some arbitrary time units:

i. On-demand swizzling of a pointer: 30.

ii. Automatic swizzling of pointers: 20 per pointer.

iii. Following a swizzled pointer: 1.

iv. Following an unswizzled pointer: 10.

Suppose that in-memory pointers are either not followed (probability $1-p$) or are followed k times (probability p). For what values of k and p do no-swizzling, automatic-swizzling, and on-demand-swizzling each offer the best average performance?

7 Variable-Length Data and Records

Until now, we have made the simplifying assumptions that records have a fixed schema, and that the schema is a list of fixed-length fields. However, in practice, we also may wish to represent:

1. *Data items whose size varies.* For instance, in Fig. 15 we considered a `MovieStar` relation that had an address field of up to 255 bytes. While there might be some addresses that long, the vast majority of them will probably be 50 bytes or less. We could save more than half the space used for storing `MovieStar` tuples if we used only as much space as the actual address needed.

2. *Repeating fields.* If we try to represent a many-many relationship in a record representing an object, we shall have to store references to as many objects as are related to the given object.

3. *Variable-format records.* Sometimes we do not know in advance what the fields of a record will be, or how many occurrences of each field there will be. An important example is a record that represents an XML element, which might have no constraints at all, or might be allowed to have repeating subelements, optional attributes, and so on.

4. *Enormous fields.* Modern DBMS's support attributes whose values are very large. For instance, a movie record might have a field that is a 2-gigabyte MPEG encoding of the movie itself, as well as more mundane fields such as the title of the movie.

7.1 Records With Variable-Length Fields

If one or more fields of a record have variable length, then the record must contain enough information to let us find any field of the record. A simple but effective scheme is to put all fixed-length fields ahead of the variable-length fields. We then place in the record header:

1. The length of the record.

2. Pointers to (i.e., offsets of) the beginnings of all the variable-length fields other than the first (which we know must immediately follow the fixed-length fields).

Example 18: Suppose we have movie-star records with name, address, gender, and birthdate. We shall assume that the gender and birthdate are fixed-length fields, taking 4 and 12 bytes, respectively. However, both name and address will be represented by character strings of whatever length is appropriate. Figure 23 suggests what a typical movie-star record would look like. Note that no pointer to the beginning of the name is needed; that field begins right after the fixed-length portion of the record. □

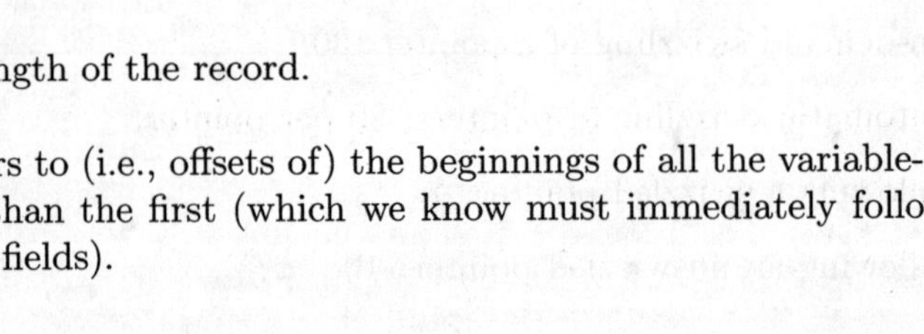

Figure 23: A `MovieStar` record with `name` and `address` implemented as variable-length character strings

Representing Null Values

Tuples often have fields that may be NULL. The record format of Fig. 23 offers a convenient way to represent NULL values. If a field such as address is null, then we put a null pointer in the place where the pointer to an address goes. Then, we need no space for an address, except the place for the pointer. This arrangement can save space on average, even if address is a fixed-length field but frequently has the value NULL.

7.2 Records With Repeating Fields

A similar situation occurs if a record contains a variable number of occurrences of a field F, but the field itself is of fixed length. It is sufficient to group all occurrences of field F together and put in the record header a pointer to the first. We can locate all the occurrences of the field F as follows. Let the number of bytes devoted to one instance of field F be L. We then add to the offset for the field F all integer multiples of L, starting at 0, then L, $2L$, $3L$, and so on. Eventually, we reach the offset of the field following F or the end of the record, whereupon we stop.

Example 19: Suppose we redesign our movie-star records to hold only the name and address (which are variable-length strings) and pointers to all the movies of the star. Figure 24 shows how this type of record could be represented. The header contains pointers to the beginning of the address field (we assume the name field always begins right after the header) and to the first of the movie pointers. The length of the record tells us how many movie pointers there are. □

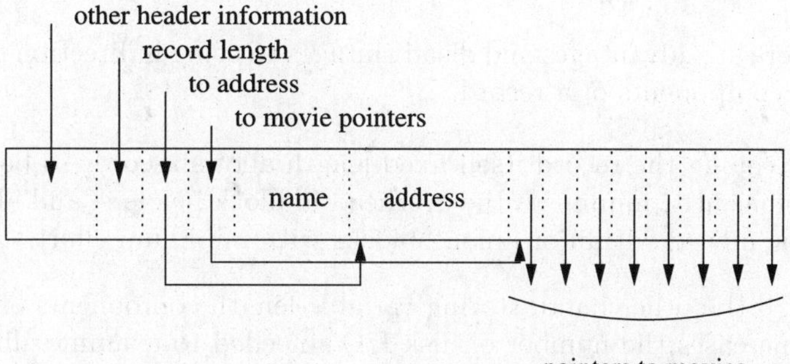

Figure 24: A record with a repeating group of references to movies

An alternative representation is to keep the record of fixed length, and put the variable-length portion — be it fields of variable length or fields that repeat an indefinite number of times — on a separate block. In the record itself we keep:

1. Pointers to the place where each repeating field begins, and
2. Either how many repetitions there are, or where the repetitions end.

Figure 25 shows the layout of a record for the problem of Example 19, but with the variable-length fields `name` and `address`, and the repeating field `starredIn` (a set of movie references) kept on a separate block or blocks.

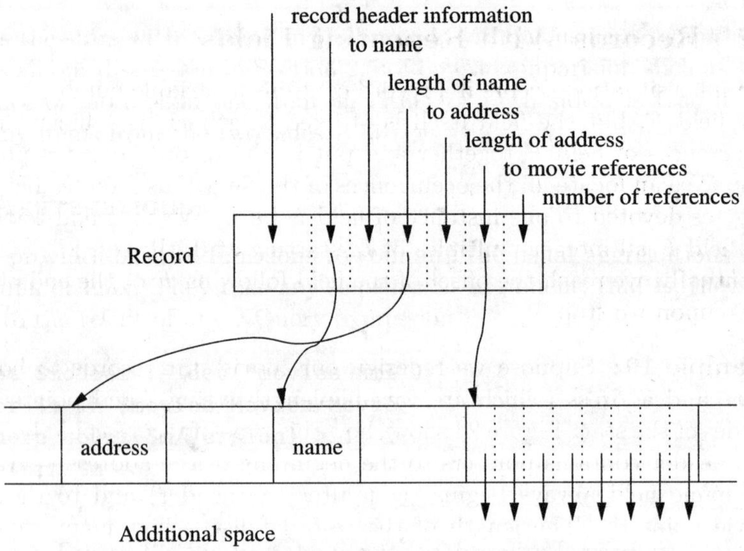

Figure 25: Storing variable-length fields separately from the record

There are advantages and disadvantages to using indirection for the variable-length components of a record:

- Keeping the record itself fixed-length allows records to be searched more efficiently, minimizes the overhead in block headers, and allows records to be moved within or among blocks with minimum effort.

- On the other hand, storing variable-length components on another block increases the number of disk I/O's needed to examine all components of a record.

A compromise strategy is to keep in the fixed-length portion of the record enough space for:

1. Some reasonable number of occurrences of the repeating fields,

2. A pointer to a place where additional occurrences could be found, and

3. A count of how many additional occurrences there are.

If there are fewer than this number, some of the space would be unused. If there are more than can fit in the fixed-length portion, then the pointer to additional space will be nonnull, and we can find the additional occurrences by following this pointer.

7.3 Variable-Format Records

An even more complex situation occurs when records do not have a fixed schema. We mentioned an example: records that represent XML elements. For another example, medical records may contain information about many tests, but there are thousands of possible tests, and each patient has results for relatively few of them. If the outcome of each test is an attribute, we would prefer that the record for each tuple hold only the attributes for which the outcome is nonnull.

The simplest representation of variable-format records is a sequence of *tagged fields*, each of which consists of the value of the field preceded by information about the role of this field, such as:

1. The attribute or field name,

2. The type of the field, if it is not apparent from the field name and some readily available schema information, and

3. The length of the field, if it is not apparent from the type.

Example 20: Suppose movie stars may have additional attributes such as movies directed, former spouses, restaurants owned, and a number of other known but unusual pieces of information. In Fig. 26 we see the beginning of a hypothetical movie-star record using tagged fields. We suppose that single-byte codes are used for the various possible field names and types. Appropriate codes are indicated on the figure, along with lengths for the two fields shown, both of which happen to be of type string. □

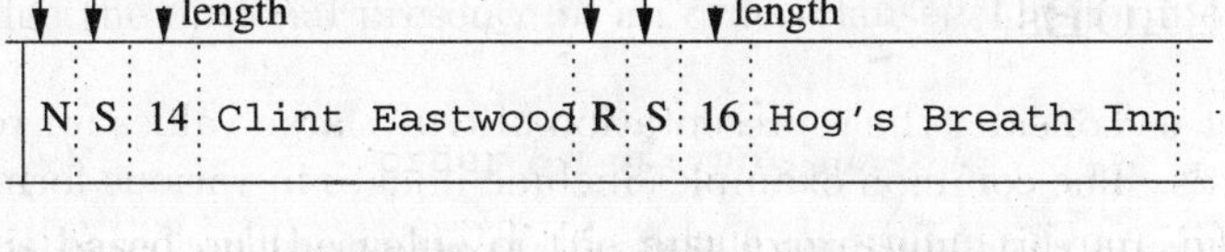

Figure 26: A record with tagged fields

7.4 Records That Do Not Fit in a Block

Today, DBMS's frequently are used to manage datatypes with large values; often values do not fit in one block. Typical examples are video or audio "clips." Often, these large values have a variable length, but even if the length is fixed for all values of the type, we need special techniques to represent values that are larger than blocks. In this section we shall consider a technique called "spanned records." The management of extremely large values (megabytes or gigabytes) is addressed in Section 7.5.

Spanned records also are useful in situations where records are smaller than blocks, but packing whole records into blocks wastes significant amounts of space. For instance, the wasted space in Example 16 was only 7%, but if records are just slightly larger than half a block, the wasted space can approach 50%. The reason is that then we can pack only one record per block.

The portion of a record that appears in one block is called a *record fragment.* A record with two or more fragments is called *spanned*, and records that do not cross a block boundary are *unspanned.*

If records can be spanned, then every record and record fragment requires some extra header information:

1. Each record or fragment header must contain a bit telling whether or not it is a fragment.

2. If it is a fragment, then it needs bits telling whether it is the first or last fragment for its record.

3. If there is a next and/or previous fragment for the same record, then the fragment needs pointers to these other fragments.

Example 21 : Figure 27 suggests how records that were about 60% of a block in size could be stored with three records for every two blocks. The header for record fragment $2a$ contains an indicator that it is a fragment, an indicator that it is the first fragment for its record, and a pointer to next fragment, $2b$. Similarly, the header for $2b$ indicates it is the last fragment for its record and holds a back-pointer to the previous fragment $2a$. □

7.5 BLOBs

Now, let us consider the representation of truly large values for records or fields of records. The common examples include images in various formats (e.g., GIF, or JPEG), movies in formats such as MPEG, or signals of all sorts: audio, radar, and so on. Such values are often called *binary, large objects*, or BLOBs. When a field has a BLOB as value, we must rethink at least two issues.

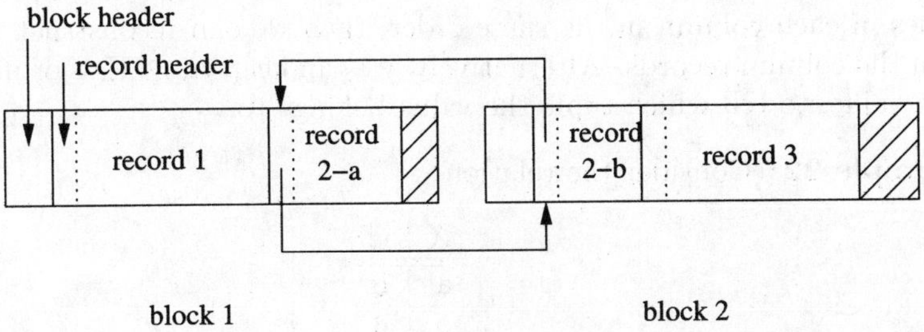

Figure 27: Storing spanned records across blocks

Storage of BLOBs

A BLOB must be stored on a sequence of blocks. Often we prefer that these blocks are allocated consecutively on a cylinder or cylinders of the disk, so the BLOB may be retrieved efficiently. However, it is also possible to store the BLOB on a linked list of blocks.

Moreover, it is possible that the BLOB needs to be retrieved so quickly (e.g., a movie that must be played in real time), that storing it on one disk does not allow us to retrieve it fast enough. Then, it is necessary to *stripe* the BLOB across several disks, that is, to alternate blocks of the BLOB among these disks. Thus, several blocks of the BLOB can be retrieved simultaneously, increasing the retrieval rate by a factor approximately equal to the number of disks involved in the striping.

Retrieval of BLOBs

Our assumption that when a client wants a record, the block containing the record is passed from the database server to the client in its entirety may not hold. We may want to pass only the "small" fields of the record, and allow the client to request blocks of the BLOB one at a time, independently of the rest of the record. For instance, if the BLOB is a 2-hour movie, and the client requests that the movie be played, the BLOB could be shipped several blocks at a time to the client, at just the rate necessary to play the movie.

In many applications, it is also important that the client be able to request interior portions of the BLOB without having to receive the entire BLOB. Examples would be a request to see the 45th minute of a movie, or the ending of an audio clip. If the DBMS is to support such operations, then it requires a suitable index structure, e.g., an index by seconds on a movie BLOB.

7.6 Column Stores

An alternative to storing tuples as records is to store each column as a record. Since an entire column of a relation may occupy far more than a single block, these records may span many blocks, much as long files do. If we keep the values in each column in the same order, then we can reconstruct the relation from the column records. Alternatively, we can keep tuple ID's or integers with each value, to tell which tuple the value belongs to.

Example 22: Consider the relation

X	Y
a	b
c	d
e	f

The column for X can be represented by the record (a, c, e) and the column for Y can be represented by the record (b, d, f). If we want to indicate the tuple to which each value belongs, then we can represent the two columns by the records $\big((1, a),\ (2, c),\ (3, e)\big)$ and $\big((1, b),\ (2, d),\ (3, f)\big)$, respectively. No matter how many tuples the relation above had, the columns would be represented by variable-length records of values or repeating groups of tuple ID's and values. □

If we store relations by columns, it is often possible to compress data, the the values all have a known type. For example, an attribute `gender` in a relation might have type `CHAR(1)`, but we would use four bytes in a tuple-based record, because it is more convenient to have all components of a tuple begin at word boundaries. However, if all we are storing is a sequence of `gender` values, then it would make sense to store the column by a sequence of bits. If we did so, we would compress the data by a factor of 32.

However, in order for column-based storage to make sense, it must be the case that most queries call for examination of all, or a large fraction of the values in each of several columns. "Analytic" queries are the common kind of queries with the desired characteristic. These "OLAP" queries may benefit from organizing the data by columns.

7.7 Exercises for Section 7

Exercise 7.1: A patient record consists of the following fixed-length fields: the patient's date of birth, social-security number, and patient ID, each 10 bytes long. It also has the following variable-length fields: name, address, and patient history. If pointers within a record require 4 bytes, and the record length is a 4-byte integer, how many bytes, exclusive of the space needed for the variable-length fields, are needed for the record? You may assume that no alignment of fields is required.

Exercise 7.2: Suppose records are as in Exercise 7.1, and the variable-length fields name, address, and history each have a length that is uniformly distributed. For the name, the range is 10–50 bytes; for address it is 20–80 bytes, and for history it is 0–1000 bytes. What is the average length of a patient record?

The Merits of Data Compression

One might think that with storage so cheap, there is little advantage to compressing data. However, storing data in fewer disk blocks enables us to read and write the data faster, since we use fewer disk I/O's. When we need to read entire columns, then storage by compressed columns can result in significant speedups. However, if we want to read or write only a single tuple, then column-based storage can lose. The reason is that in order to decompress and find the value for the one tuple we want, we need to read the entire column. In contrast, tuple-based storage allows us to read only the block containing the tuple. An even more extreme case is when the data is not only compressed, but encrypted.

In order to make access of single values efficient, we must both compress and encrypt on a block-by-block basis. The most efficient compression methods generally perform better when they are allowed to compress large amounts of data as a group, and they do not lend themselves to block-based decompression. However, in special cases such as the compression of a `gender` column discussed in Section 7.6, we can in fact do block-by-block compression that is as good as possible.

Exercise 7.3: Suppose that the patient records of Exercise 7.1 are augmented by an additional repeating field that represents cholesterol tests. Each cholesterol test requires 16 bytes for a date and an integer result of the test. Show the layout of patient records if:

a) The repeating tests are kept with the record itself.

b) The tests are stored on a separate block, with pointers to them in the record.

Exercise 7.4: Starting with the patient records of Exercise 7.1, suppose we add fields for tests and their results. Each test consists of a test name, a date, and a test result. Assume that each such test requires 40 bytes. Also, suppose that for each patient and each test a result is stored with probability p.

a) Assuming pointers and integers each require 4 bytes, what is the average number of bytes devoted to test results in a patient record, assuming that all test results are kept within the record itself, as a variable-length field?

b) Repeat (a), if test results are represented by pointers within the record to test-result fields kept elsewhere.

! c) Suppose we use a hybrid scheme, where room for k test results are kept within the record, and additional test results are found by following a pointer to another block (or chain of blocks) where those results are kept. As a function of p, what value of k minimizes the amount of storage used for test results?

!! d) The amount of space used by the repeating test-result fields is not the only issue. Let us suppose that the figure of merit we wish to minimize is the number of bytes used, plus a penalty of 10,000 if we have to store some results on another block (and therefore will require a disk I/O for many of the test-result accesses we need to do. Under this assumption, what is the best value of k as a function of p?

!! **Exercise 7.5:** Suppose blocks have 1000 bytes available for the storage of records, and we wish to store on them fixed-length records of length r, where $500 < r \leq 1000$. The value of r includes the record header, but a record fragment requires an additional 16 bytes for the fragment header. For what values of r can we improve space utilization by spanning records?

!! **Exercise 7.6:** An MPEG movie uses about one gigabyte per hour of play. If we carefully organized several movies on a Megatron 747 disk, how many could we deliver with only small delay (say 100 milliseconds) from one disk. Use the timing estimates of Example 2, but remember that you can choose how the movies are laid out on the disk.

8 Record Modifications

Insertions, deletions, and updates of records often create special problems. These problems are most severe when the records change their length, but they come up even when records and fields are all of fixed length.

8.1 Insertion

First, let us consider insertion of new records into a relation. If the records of a relation are kept in no particular order, we can just find a block with some empty space, or get a new block if there is none, and put the record there.

There is more of a problem when the tuples must be kept in some fixed order, such as sorted by their primary key. If we need to insert a new record, we first locate the appropriate block for that record. Suppose first that there is space in the block to put the new record. Since records must be kept in order, we may have to slide records around in the block to make space available at the proper point. If we need to slide records, then the block organization that we showed in Fig. 19, which we reproduce here as Fig. 28, is useful. Recall from our discussion in Section 6.2 that we may create an "offset table" in the header of each block, with pointers to the location of each record in the block. A pointer to a record from outside the block is a "structured address," that is, the block address and the location of the entry for the record in the offset table.

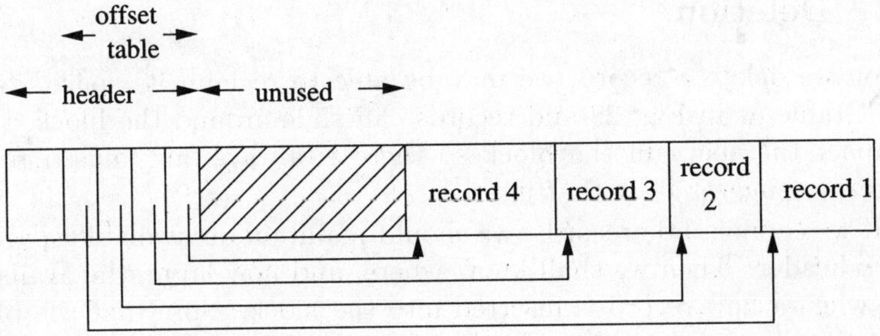

Figure 28: An offset table lets us slide records within a block to make room for new records

If we can find room for the inserted record in the block at hand, then we simply slide the records within the block and adjust the pointers in the offset table. The new record is inserted into the block, and a new pointer to the record is added to the offset table for the block. However, there may be no room in the block for the new record, in which case we have to find room outside the block. There are two major approaches to solving this problem, as well as combinations of these approaches.

1. *Find space on a "nearby" block.* For example, if block B_1 has no available space for a record that needs to be inserted in sorted order into that block, then look at the following block B_2 in the sorted order of the blocks. If there is room in B_2, move the highest record(s) of B_1 to B_2, leave forwarding addresses (recall Section 6.2) and slide the records around on both blocks.

2. *Create an overflow block.* In this scheme, each block B has in its header a place for a pointer to an *overflow* block where additional records that theoretically belong in B can be placed. The overflow block for B can point to a second overflow block, and so on. Figure 29 suggests the structure. We show the pointer for overflow blocks as a nub on the block, although it is in fact part of the block header.

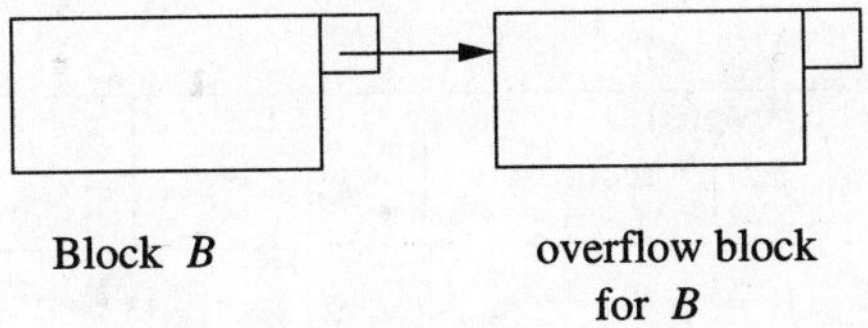

Figure 29: A block and its first overflow block

8.2 Deletion

When we delete a record, we may be able to reclaim its space. If we use an offset table as in Fig. 28 and records can slide around the block, then we can compact the space in the block so there is always one unused region in the center, as suggested by that figure.

If we cannot slide records, we should maintain an available-space list in the block header. Then we shall know where, and how large, the available regions are, when a new record is inserted into the block. Note that the block header normally does not need to hold the entire available space list. It is sufficient to put the list head in the block header, and use the available regions themselves to hold the links in the list, much as we did in Fig. 22.

There is one additional complication involved in deletion, which we must remember regardless of what scheme we use for reorganizing blocks. There may be pointers to the deleted record, and if so, we don't want these pointers to dangle or wind up pointing to a new record that is put in the place of the deleted record. The usual technique, which we pointed out in Section 6.2, is to place a *tombstone* in place of the record. This tombstone is permanent; it must exist until the entire database is reconstructed.

Where the tombstone is placed depends on the nature of record pointers. If pointers go to fixed locations from which the location of the record is found, then we put the tombstone in that fixed location. Here are two examples:

1. We suggested in Section 6.2 that if the offset-table scheme of Fig. 28 were used, then the tombstone could be a null pointer in the offset table, since pointers to the record were really pointers to the offset table entries.

2. If we are using a map table, as in Fig. 18, to translate logical record addresses to physical addresses, then the tombstone can be a null pointer in place of the physical address.

If we need to replace records by tombstones, we should place the bit that serves as a tombstone at the very beginning of the record. Then, only this bit must remain where the record used to begin, and subsequent bytes can be reused for another record, as suggested by Fig. 30.

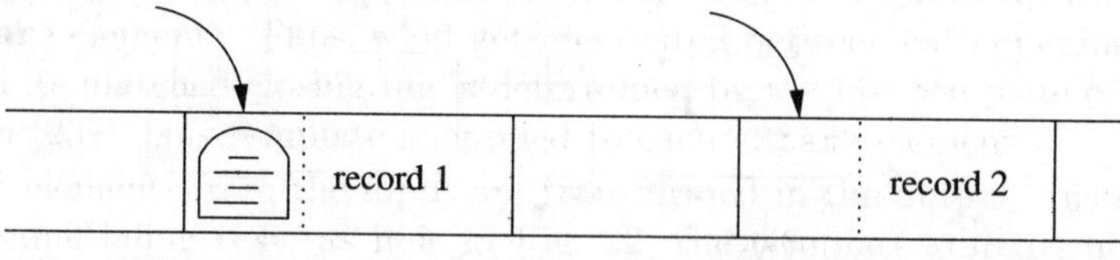

Figure 30: Record 1 can be replaced, but the tombstone remains; record 2 has no tombstone and can be seen when we follow a pointer to it

8.3 Update

When a fixed-length record is updated, there is no effect on the storage system, because we know it can occupy exactly the same space it did before the update. However, when a variable-length record is updated, we have all the problems associated with both insertion and deletion, except that it is never necessary to create a tombstone for the old version of the record.

If the updated record is longer than the old version, then we may need to create more space on its block. This process may involve sliding records or even the creation of an overflow block. If variable-length portions of the record are stored on another block, as in Fig. 25, then we may need to move elements around that block or create a new block for storing variable-length fields. Conversely, if the record shrinks because of the update, we have the same opportunities as with a deletion to recover or consolidate space.

8.4 Exercises for Section 8

Exercise 8.1 : Relational database systems have always preferred to use fixed-length tuples if possible. Give three reasons for this preference.

9 Summary

✦ *Memory Hierarchy*: A computer system uses storage components ranging over many orders of magnitude in speed, capacity, and cost per bit. From the smallest/most expensive to largest/cheapest, they are: cache, main memory, secondary memory (disk), and tertiary memory.

✦ *Disks/Secondary Storage*: Secondary storage devices are principally magnetic disks with multigigabyte capacities. Disk units have several circular platters of magnetic material, with concentric tracks to store bits. Platters rotate around a central spindle. The tracks at a given radius from the center of a platter form a cylinder.

✦ *Blocks and Sectors*: Tracks are divided into sectors, which are separated by unmagnetized gaps. Sectors are the unit of reading and writing from the disk. Blocks are logical units of storage used by an application such as a DBMS. Blocks typically consist of several sectors.

✦ *Disk Controller*: The disk controller is a processor that controls one or more disk units. It is responsible for moving the disk heads to the proper cylinder to read or write a requested track. It also may schedule competing requests for disk access and buffers the blocks to be read or written.

✦ *Disk Access Time*: The latency of a disk is the time between a request to read or write a block, and the time the access is completed. Latency is caused principally by three factors: the seek time to move the heads to the proper cylinder, the rotational latency during which the desired block rotates under the head, and the transfer time, while the block moves under the head and is read or written.

✦ *Speeding Up Disk Access*: There are several techniques for accessing disk blocks faster for some applications. They include dividing the data among several disks (striping), mirroring disks (maintaining several copies of the data, also to allow parallel access), and organizing data that will be accessed together by tracks or cylinders.

✦ *Elevator Algorithm*: We can also speed accesses by queueing access requests and handling them in an order that allows the heads to make one sweep across the disk. The heads stop to handle a request each time it reaches a cylinder containing one or more blocks with pending access requests.

✦ *Disk Failure Modes*: To avoid loss of data, systems must be able to handle errors. The principal types of disk failure are intermittent (a read or write error that will not reoccur if repeated), permanent (data on the disk is corrupted and cannot be properly read), and the disk crash, where the entire disk becomes unreadable.

✦ *Checksums*: By adding a parity check (extra bit to make the number of 1's in a bit string even), intermittent failures and permanent failures can be detected, although not corrected.

✦ *Stable Storage*: By making two copies of all data and being careful about the order in which those copies are written, a single disk can be used to protect against almost all permanent failures of a single sector.

✦ *RAID*: These schemes allow data to survive a disk crash. RAID level 4 adds a disk whose contents are a parity check on corresponding bits of all other disks, level 5 varies the disk holding the parity bit to avoid making the parity disk a writing bottleneck. Level 6 involves the use of error-correcting codes and may allow survival after several simultaneous disk crashes.

✦ *Records*: Records are composed of several fields plus a record header. The header contains information about the record, possibly including such matters as a timestamp, schema information, and a record length. If the record has varying-length fields, the header may also help locate those fields.

✦ *Blocks*: Records are generally stored within blocks. A block header, with information about that block, consumes some of the space in the block, with the remainder occupied by one or more records. To support insertions, deletions and modifications of records, we can put in the block header an offset table that has pointers to each of the records in the block.

- *Spanned Records*: Generally, a record exists within one block. However, if records are longer than blocks, or we wish to make use of leftover space within blocks, then we can break records into two or more fragments, one on each block. A fragment header is then needed to link the fragments of a record.

- *BLOBs*: Very large values, such as images and videos, are called BLOBs (binary, large objects). These values must be stored across many blocks and may require specialized storage techniques such as reserving a cylinder or striping the blocks of the BLOB.

- *Database Addresses*: Data managed by a DBMS is found among several storage devices, typically disks. To locate blocks and records in this storage system, we can use physical addresses, which are a description of the device number, cylinder, track, sector(s), and possibly byte within a sector. We can also use logical addresses, which are arbitrary character strings that are translated into physical addresses by a map table.

- *Pointer Swizzling*: When disk blocks are brought to main memory, the database addresses need to be translated to memory addresses, if pointers are to be followed. The translation is called swizzling, and can either be done automatically, when blocks are brought to memory, or on-demand, when a pointer is first followed.

- *Tombstones*: When a record is deleted, pointers to it will dangle. A tombstone in place of (part of) the deleted record warns the system that the record is no longer there.

- *Pinned Blocks*: For various reasons, including the fact that a block may contain swizzled pointers, it may be unacceptable to copy a block from memory back to its place on disk. Such a block is said to be pinned. If the pinning is due to swizzled pointers, then they must be unswizzled before returning the block to disk.

10 References

The RAID idea can be traced back to [8] on disk striping. The name and error-correcting capability is from [7]. The model of disk failures in Section 4 appears in unpublished work of Lampson and Sturgis [5].

There are several useful surveys of disk-related material. A study of RAID systems is in [2]. [10] surveys algorithms suitable for the secondary storage model (block model) of computation. [3] is an important study of how one optimizes a system involving processor, memory, and disk, to perform specific tasks.

References [4] and [11] have more information on record and block structures. [9] discusses column stores as an alternative to the conventional record structures. Tombstones as a technique for dealing with deletion is from [6]. [1] covers data representation issues, such as addresses and swizzling in the context of object-oriented DBMS's.

1. R. G. G. Cattell, *Object Data Management*, Addison-Wesley, Reading MA, 1994.

2. P. M. Chen et al., "RAID: high-performance, reliable secondary storage," *Computing Surveys* **26**:2 (1994), pp. 145–186.

3. J. N. Gray and F. Putzolo, "The five minute rule for trading memory for disk accesses and the 10 byte rule for trading memory for CPU time," *Proc. ACM SIGMOD Intl. Conf. on Management of Data*, pp. 395–398, 1987.

4. D. E. Knuth, *The Art of Computer Programming, Vol. I, Fundamental Algorithms, Third Edition*, Addison-Wesley, Reading MA, 1997.

5. B. Lampson and H. Sturgis, "Crash recovery in a distributed data storage system," Technical report, Xerox Palo Alto Research Center, 1976.

6. D. Lomet, "Scheme for invalidating free references," *IBM J. Research and Development* **19**:1 (1975), pp. 26–35.

7. D. A. Patterson, G. A. Gibson, and R. H. Katz, "A case for redundant arrays of inexpensive disks," *Proc. ACM SIGMOD Intl. Conf. on Management of Data*, pp. 109–116, 1988.

8. K. Salem and H. Garcia-Molina, "Disk striping," *Proc. Second Intl. Conf. on Data Engineering*, pp. 336–342, 1986.

9. M. Stonebraker et al., "C-Store: a column-oriented DBMS," *Proc. Thirty-first Intl. Conf. on Very Large Database Systems*" (2005).

10. J. S. Vitter, "External memory algorithms," *Proc. Seventeenth Annual ACM Symposium on Principles of Database Systems*, pp. 119–128, 1998.

11. G. Wiederhold, *File Organization for Database Design*, McGraw-Hill, New York, 1987.

Index Structures

It is not sufficient simply to scatter the records that represent tuples of a relation among various blocks. To see why, think how we would answer the simple query `SELECT * FROM R`. We would have to examine every block in the storage system to find the tuples of R. A better idea is to reserve some blocks, perhaps several whole cylinders, for R. Now, at least we can find the tuples of R without scanning the entire data store.

However, this organization offers little help for a query like

```
SELECT * FROM R WHERE a=10;
```

You may recall the importance of creating *indexes* to speed up queries that specify values for one or more attributes. As suggested in Fig. 1, an index is any data structure that takes the value of one or more fields and finds the records with that value "quickly." In particular, an index lets us find a record without having to look at more than a small fraction of all possible records. The field(s) on whose values the index is based is called the *search key*, or just "key" if the index is understood.

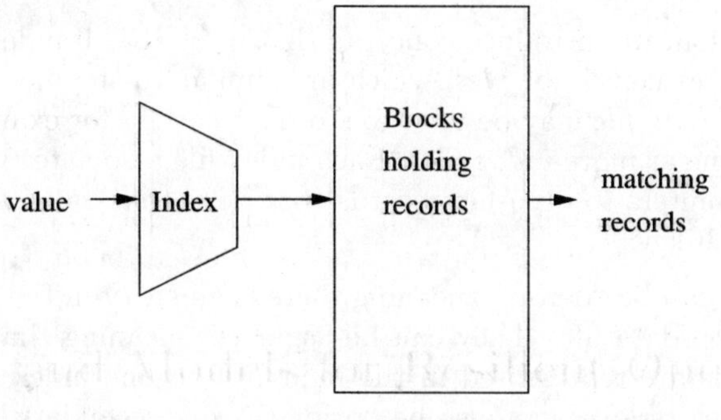

Figure 1: An index takes a value for some field(s) and finds records with the matching value

Different Kinds of "Keys"

There are many meanings of the term "key." It can be used to mean the primary key of a relation. We shall also speak of "sort keys," the attribute(s) on which a file of records is sorted. We just introduced "search keys," the attribute(s) for which we are given values and asked to search, through an index, for tuples with matching values. We try to use the appropriate adjective — "primary," "sort," or "search" — when the meaning of "key" is unclear. However, in many cases, the three kinds of keys are one and the same.

In this chapter, we shall introduce the most common form of index in database systems: the B-tree. We shall also discuss hash tables in secondary storage, which is another important index structure. Finally, we consider other index structures that are designed to handle multidimensional data. These structures support queries that specify values or ranges for several attributes at once.

1 Index-Structure Basics

In this section, we introduce concepts that apply to all index structures. Storage structures consist of *files*, which are similar to the files used by operating systems. A *data file* may be used to store a relation, for example. The data file may have one or more *index files*. Each index file associates values of the search key with pointers to data-file records that have that value for the attribute(s) of the search key.

Indexes can be "dense," meaning there is an entry in the index file for every record of the data file. They can be "sparse," meaning that only some of the data records are represented in the index, often one index entry per block of the data file. Indexes can also be "primary" or "secondary." A primary index determines the location of the records of the data file, while a secondary index does not. For example, it is common to create a primary index on the primary key of a relation and to create secondary indexes on some of the other attributes.

We conclude the section with a study of information retrieval from documents. The ideas of the section are combined to yield "inverted indexes," which enable efficient retrieval of documents that contain one or more given keywords. This technique is essential for answering search queries on the Web, for instance.

1.1 Sequential Files

A *sequential file* is created by sorting the tuples of a relation by their primary key. The tuples are then distributed among blocks, in this order.

Example 1: Fig 2 shows a sequential file on the right. We imagine that keys are integers; we show only the key field, and we make the atypical assumption that there is room for only two records in one block. For instance, the first block of the file holds the records with keys 10 and 20. In this and several other examples, we use integers that are sequential multiples of 10 as keys, although there is surely no requirement that keys form an arithmetic sequence. □

Although in Example 1 we supposed that records were packed as tightly as possible into blocks, it is common to leave some space initially in each block to accomodate new tuples that may be added to a relation. Alternatively, we may accomodate new tuples with overflow blocks.

1.2 Dense Indexes

If records are sorted, we can build on them a *dense index*, which is a sequence of blocks holding only the keys of the records and pointers to the records themselves. The index blocks of the dense index maintain these keys in the same sorted order as in the file itself. Since keys and pointers presumably take much less space than complete records, we expect to use many fewer blocks for the index than for the file itself. The index is especially advantageous when it, but not the data file, can fit in main memory. Then, by using the index, we can find any record given its search key, with only one disk I/O per lookup.

Example 2: Figure 2 suggests a dense index on a sorted file. The first index block contains pointers to the first four records (an atypically small number of pointers for one block), the second block has pointers to the next four, and so on. □

The dense index supports queries that ask for records with a given search-key value. Given key value K, we search the index blocks for K, and when we find it, we follow the associated pointer to the record with key K. It might appear that we need to examine every block of the index, or half the blocks of the index, on average, before we find K. However, there are several factors that make the index-based search more efficient than it seems.

1. The number of index blocks is usually small compared with the number of data blocks.

2. Since keys are sorted, we can use binary search to find K. If there are n blocks of the index, we only look at $\log_2 n$ of them.

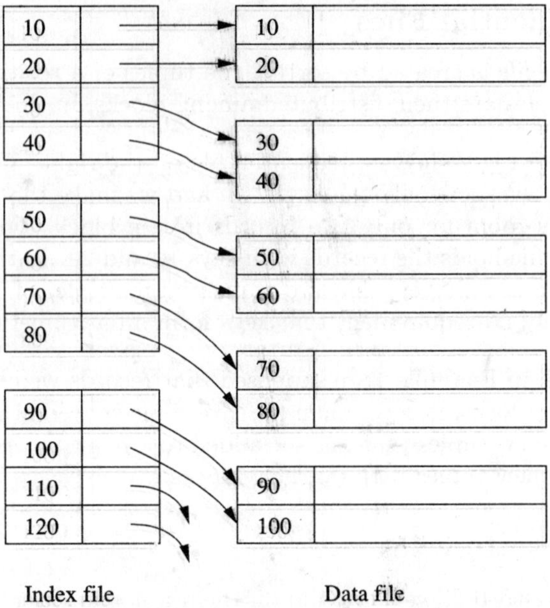

Figure 2: A dense index (left) on a sequential data file (right)

3. The index may be small enough to be kept permanently in main memory buffers. If so, the search for key K involves only main-memory accesses, and there are no expensive disk I/O's to be performed.

1.3 Sparse Indexes

A sparse index typically has only one key-pointer pair per block of the data file. It thus uses less space than a dense index, at the expense of somewhat more time to find a record given its key. You can only use a sparse index if the data file is sorted by the search key, while a dense index can be used for any search key. Figure 3 shows a sparse index with one key-pointer per data block. The keys are for the first records on each data block.

Example 3: As in Example 2, we assume that the data file is sorted, and keys are all the integers divisible by 10, up to some large number. We also continue to assume that four key-pointer pairs fit on an index block. Thus, the first sparse-index block has entries for the first keys on the first four blocks, which are 10, 30, 50, and 70. Continuing the assumed pattern of keys, the second index block has the first keys of the fifth through eighth blocks, which we assume are 90, 110, 130, and 150. We also show a third index block with first keys from the hypothetical ninth through twelfth data blocks. □

To find the record with search-key value K, we search the sparse index for the largest key less than or equal to K. Since the index file is sorted by key, a

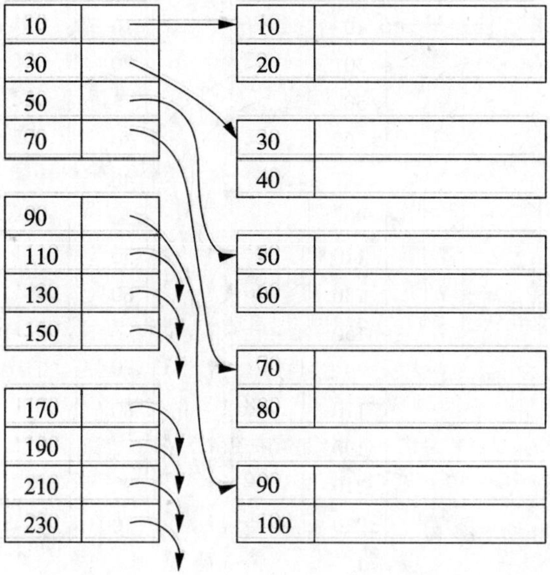

Figure 3: A sparse index on a sequential file

binary search can locate this entry. We follow the associated pointer to a data block. Now, we must search this block for the record with key K. Of course the block must have enough format information that the records and their contents can be identified.

1.4 Multiple Levels of Index

An index file can cover many blocks. Even if we use binary search to find the desired index entry, we still may need to do many disk I/O's to get to the record we want. By putting an index on the index, we can make the use of the first level of index more efficient.

Figure 4 extends Fig. 3 by adding a second index level (as before, we assume keys are every multiple of 10). The same idea would let us place a third-level index on the second level, and so on. However, this idea has its limits, and we prefer the B-tree structure described in Section 2 over building many levels of index.

In this example, the first-level index is sparse, although we could have chosen a dense index for the first level. However, the second and higher levels must be sparse. The reason is that a dense index on an index would have exactly as many key-pointer pairs as the first-level index, and therefore would take exactly as much space as the first-level index.

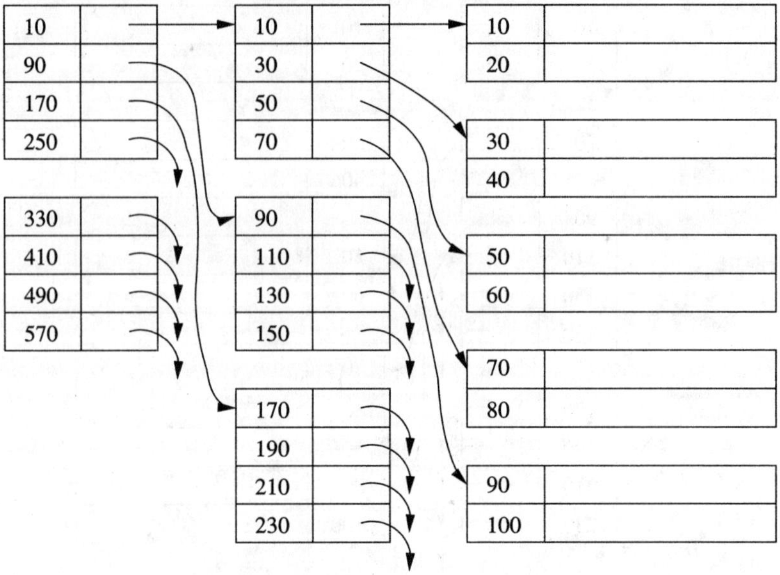

Figure 4: Adding a second level of sparse index

1.5 Secondary Indexes

A secondary index serves the purpose of any index: it is a data structure that facilitates finding records given a value for one or more fields. However, the secondary index is distinguished from the primary index in that a secondary index does not determine the placement of records in the data file. Rather, the secondary index tells us the current locations of records; that location may have been decided by a primary index on some other field. An important consequence of the distinction between primary and secondary indexes is that:

- Secondary indexes are always dense. It makes no sense to talk of a sparse, secondary index. Since the secondary index does not influence location, we could not use it to predict the location of any record whose key was not mentioned in the index file explicitly.

Example 4: Figure 5 shows a typical secondary index. The data file is shown with two records per block, as has been our standard for illustration. The records have only their search key shown; this attribute is integer valued, and as before we have taken the values to be multiples of 10. Notice that, unlike the data file in Fig. 2, here the data is not sorted by the search key.

However, the keys in the index file *are* sorted. The result is that the pointers in one index block can go to many different data blocks, instead of one or a few consecutive blocks. For example, to retrieve all the records with search key 20, we not only have to look at two index blocks, but we are sent by their pointers to three different data blocks. Thus, using a secondary index may result in

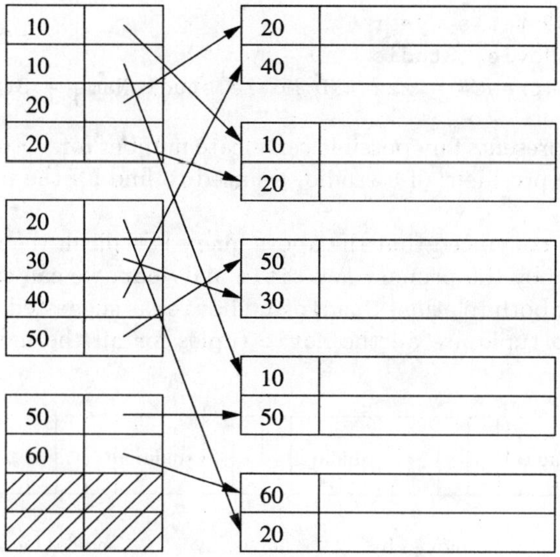

Figure 5: A secondary index

many more disk I/O's than if we get the same number of records via a primary index. However, there is no help for this problem; we cannot control the order of tuples in the data block, because they are presumably ordered according to some other attribute(s). □

1.6 Applications of Secondary Indexes

Besides supporting additional indexes on relations that are organized as sequential files, there are some data structures where secondary indexes are needed for even the primary key. One of these is the "heap" structure, where the records of the relation are kept in no particular order.

A second common structure needing secondary indexes is the *clustered file.* Suppose there are relations R and S, with a many-one relationship from the tuples of R to tuples of S. It may make sense to store each tuple of R with the tuple of S to which it is related, rather than according to the primary key of R. An example will illustrate why this organization makes good sense in special situations.

Example 5: Consider our standard movie and studio relations:

```
Movie(title, year, length, genre, studioName, producerC#)
Studio(name, address, presC#)
```

Suppose further that the most common form of query is:

```
SELECT title, year
FROM Movie, Studio
WHERE presC# = zzz AND Movie.studioName = Studio.name;
```

Here, *zzz* represents any possible certificate number for a studio president. That is, given the president of a studio, we need to find all the movies made by that studio.

If we are convinced that the above query is typical, then instead of ordering `Movie` tuples by the primary key `title` and `year`, we can create a *clustered file structure* for both relations `Studio` and `Movie`, as suggested by Fig. 6. Following each `Studio` tuple are all the `Movie` tuples for all the movies owned by that studio.

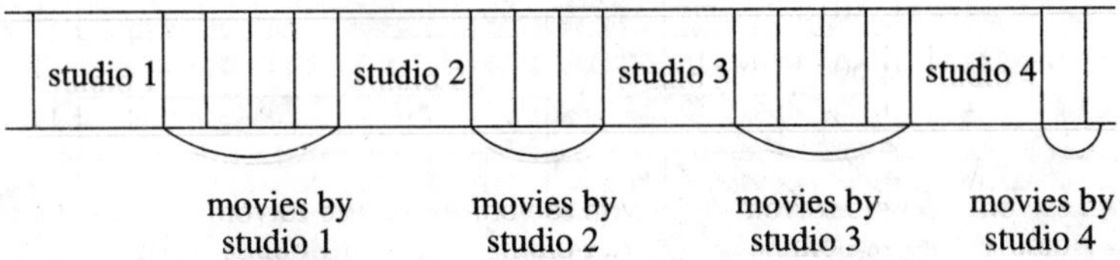

Figure 6: A clustered file with each studio clustered with the movies made by that studio

If we create an index for `Studio` with search key `presC#`, then whatever the value of *zzz* is, we can quickly find the tuple for the proper studio. Moreover, all the `Movie` tuples whose value of attribute `studioName` matches the value of `name` for that studio will follow the studio's tuple in the clustered file. As a result, we can find the movies for this studio by making almost as few disk I/O's as possible. The reason is that the desired `Movie` tuples are packed almost as densely as possible onto the following blocks. However, an index on any attribute(s) of `Movie` would have to be a secondary index. □

1.7 Indirection in Secondary Indexes

There is some wasted space, perhaps a significant amount of wastage, in the structure suggested by Fig. 5. If a search-key value appears n times in the data file, then the value is written n times in the index file. It would be better if we could write the key value once for all the pointers to data records with that value.

A convenient way to avoid repeating values is to use a level of indirection, called *buckets*, between the secondary index file and the data file. As shown in Fig. 7, there is one pair for each search key K. The pointer of this pair goes to a position in a "bucket file," which holds the "bucket" for K. Following this position, until the next position pointed to by the index, are pointers to all the records with search-key value K.

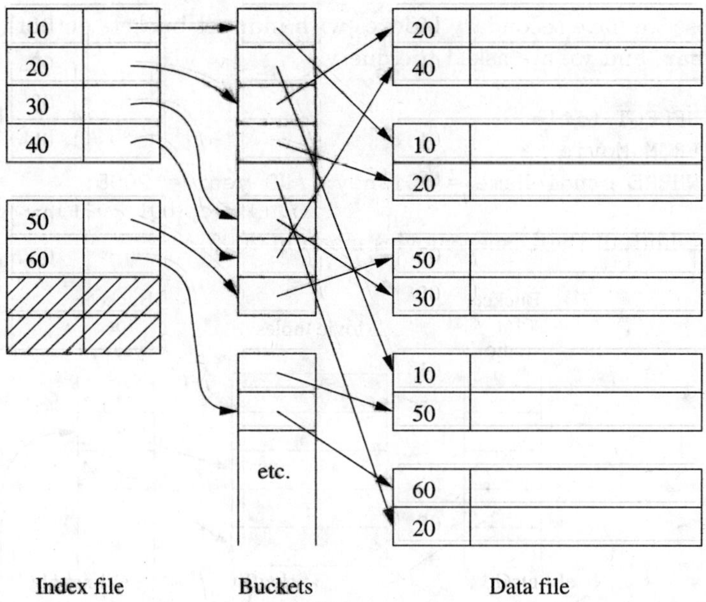

Figure 7: Saving space by using indirection in a secondary index

Example 6 : For instance, let us follow the pointer from search key 50 in the index file of Fig. 7 to the intermediate "bucket" file. This pointer happens to take us to the last pointer of one block of the bucket file. We search forward, to the first pointer of the next block. We stop at that point, because the next pointer of the index file, associated with search key 60, points to the next record in the bucket file. □

The scheme of Fig. 7 saves space as long as search-key values are larger than pointers, and the average key appears at least twice. However, even if not, there is an important advantage to using indirection with secondary indexes: often, we can use the pointers in the buckets to help answer queries without ever looking at most of the records in the data file. Specifically, when there are several conditions to a query, and each condition has a secondary index to help it, we can find the bucket pointers that satisfy all the conditions by intersecting sets of pointers in memory, and retrieving only the records pointed to by the surviving pointers. We thus save the I/O cost of retrieving records that satisfy some, but not all, of the conditions.[1]

Example 7 : Consider the usual `Movie` relation:

```
Movie(title, year, length, genre, studioName, producerC#)
```

[1]We also could use this pointer-intersection trick if we got the pointers directly from the index, rather than from buckets.

Suppose we have secondary indexes with indirect buckets on both `studioName` and `year`, and we are asked the query

```
SELECT title
FROM Movie
WHERE studioName = 'Disney' AND year = 2005;
```

that is, find all the Disney movies made in 2005.

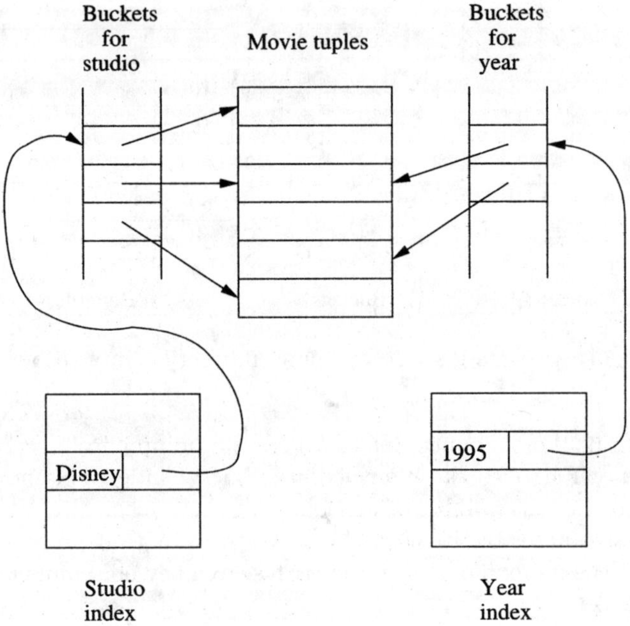

Figure 8: Intersecting buckets in main memory

Figure 8 shows how we can answer this query using the indexes. Using the index on `studioName`, we find the pointers to all records for Disney movies, but we do not yet bring any of those records from disk to memory. Instead, using the index on `year`, we find the pointers to all the movies of 2005. We then intersect the two sets of pointers, getting exactly the movies that were made by Disney in 2005. Finally, we retrieve from disk all data blocks holding one or more of these movies, thus retrieving the minimum possible number of blocks. □

1.8 Document Retrieval and Inverted Indexes

For many years, the information-retrieval community has dealt with the storage of documents and the efficient retrieval of documents with a given set of keywords. With the advent of the World-Wide Web and the feasibility of keeping all documents on-line, the retrieval of documents given keywords has become one of the largest database problems. While there are many kinds of queries that one can use to find relevant documents, the simplest and most common form can be seen in relational terms as follows:

- A document may be thought of as a tuple in a relation `Doc`. This relation has very many attributes, one corresponding to each possible word in a document. Each attribute is boolean — either the word is present in the document, or it is not. Thus, the relation schema may be thought of as

  ```
  Doc(hasCat, hasDog, ... )
  ```

  where `hasCat` is true if and only if the document has the word "cat" at least once.

- There is a secondary index on each of the attributes of `Doc`. However, we save the trouble of indexing those tuples for which the value of the attribute is `FALSE`; instead, the index leads us to only the documents for which the word is present. That is, the index has entries only for the search-key value `TRUE`.

- Instead of creating a separate index for each attribute (i.e., for each word), the indexes are combined into one, called an *inverted index*. This index uses indirect buckets for space efficiency, as was discussed in Section 1.7.

Example 8: An inverted index is illustrated in Fig. 9. In place of a data file of records is a collection of documents, each of which may be stored on one or more disk blocks. The inverted index itself consists of a set of word-pointer pairs; the words are in effect the search key for the index. The inverted index is kept in a sequence of blocks, just like any of the indexes discussed so far.

The pointers refer to positions in a "bucket" file. For instance, we have shown in Fig. 9 the word "cat" with a pointer to the bucket file. That pointer leads us to the beginning of a list of pointers to all the documents that contain the word "cat." We have shown some of these in the figure. Similarly, the word "dog" is shown leading to a list of pointers to all the documents with "dog." □

Pointers in the bucket file can be:

1. Pointers to the document itself.

2. Pointers to an occurrence of the word. In this case, the pointer might be a pair consisting of the first block for the document and an integer indicating the number of the word in the document.

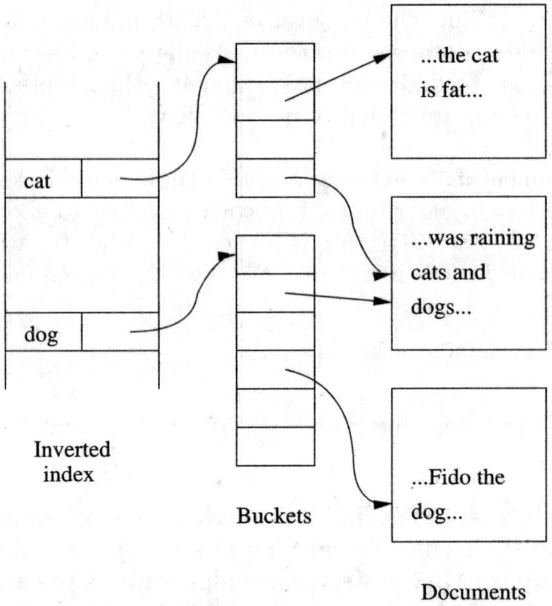

Figure 9: An inverted index on documents

When we use "buckets" of pointers to occurrences of each word, we may extend the idea to include in the bucket array some information about each occurrence. Now, the bucket file itself becomes a collection of records with important structure. Early uses of the idea distinguished occurrences of a word in the title of a document, the abstract, and the body of text. With the growth of documents on the Web, especially documents using HTML, XML, or another markup language, we can also indicate the markings associated with words. For instance, we can distinguish words appearing in titles, headers, tables, or anchors, as well as words appearing in different fonts or sizes.

Example 9: Figure 10 illustrates a bucket file that has been used to indicate occurrences of words in HTML documents. The first column indicates the type of occurrence, i.e., its marking, if any. The second and third columns are together the pointer to the occurrence. The third column indicates the document, and the second column gives the number of the word in the document.

We can use this data structure to answer various queries about documents without having to examine the documents in detail. For instance, suppose we want to find documents about dogs that compare them with cats. Without a deep understanding of the meaning of the text, we cannot answer this query precisely. However, we could get a good hint if we searched for documents that

a) Mention dogs in the title, and

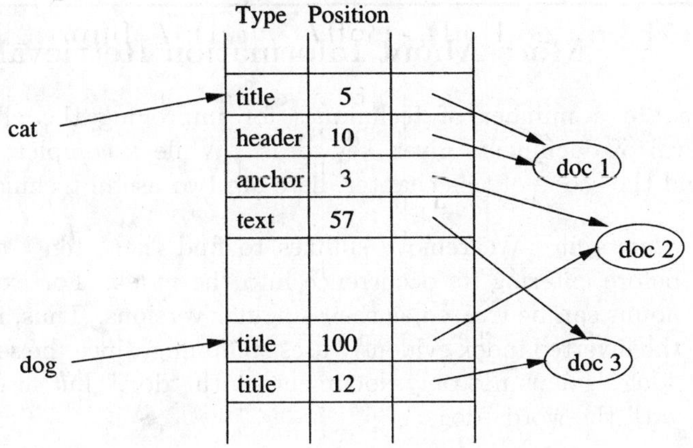

Figure 10: Storing more information in the inverted index

> **Insertion and Deletion From Buckets**
>
> We show buckets in figures such as Fig. 9 as compacted arrays of appropriate size. In practice, they are records with a single field (the pointer) and are stored in blocks like any other collection of records. Thus, when we insert or delete pointers, we may use any of the techniques seen so far, such as leaving extra space in blocks for expansion of the file, overflow blocks, and possibly moving records within or among blocks. In the latter case, we must be careful to change the pointer from the inverted index to the bucket file, as we move the records it points to.

b) Mention cats in an anchor — presumably a link to a document about cats.

We can answer this query by intersecting pointers. That is, we follow the pointer associated with "cat" to find the occurrences of this word. We select from the bucket file the pointers to documents associated with occurrences of "cat" where the type is "anchor." We then find the bucket entries for "dog" and select from them the document pointers associated with the type "title." If we intersect these two sets of pointers, we have the documents that meet the conditions: they mention "dog" in the title and "cat" in an anchor. □

1.9 Exercises for Section 1

Exercise 1.1: Suppose blocks hold either three records, or ten key-pointer pairs. As a function of n, the number of records, how many blocks do we need to hold a data file and: (a) A dense index (b) A sparse index?

More About Information Retrieval

There are a number of techniques for improving the effectiveness of retrieval of documents given keywords. While a complete treatment is beyond the scope of this chapter, here are two useful techniques:

1. *Stemming.* We remove suffixes to find the "stem" of each word, before entering its occurrence into the index. For example, plural nouns can be treated as their singular versions. Thus, in Example 8, the inverted index evidently uses stemming, since the search for word "dog" got us not only documents with "dog," but also a document with the word "dogs."

2. *Stop words.* The most common words, such as "the" or "and," are called *stop words* and often are excluded from the inverted index. The reason is that the several hundred most common words appear in too many documents to make them useful as a way to find documents about specific subjects. Eliminating stop words also reduces the size of the inverted index significantly.

Exercise 1.2: Repeat Exercise 1.1 if blocks can hold up to 30 records or 200 key-pointer pairs, but neither data- nor index-blocks are allowed to be more than 80% full.

! **Exercise 1.3:** Repeat Exercise 1.1 if we use as many levels of index as is appropriate, until the final level of index has only one block.

! **Exercise 1.4:** Consider a clustered file organization like Fig. 6, and suppose that ten records, either studio records or movie records, will fit on one block. Also assume that the number of movies per studio is uniformly distributed between 1 and m. As a function of m, what is the average number of disk I/O's needed to retrieve a studio and all its movies? What would the number be if movies were randomly distributed over a large number of blocks?

Exercise 1.5: Suppose that blocks can hold either three records, ten key-pointer pairs, or fifty pointers. Using the indirect-buckets scheme of Fig. 7:

a) If the average search-key value appears in 10 records, how many blocks do we need to hold 3000 records and its secondary index structure? How many blocks would be needed if we did *not* use buckets?

! b) If there are no constraints on the number of records that can have a given search-key value, what are the minimum and maximum number of blocks needed?

! **Exercise 1.6:** On the assumptions of Exercise 1.5(a), what is the average number of disk I/O's to find and retrieve the ten records with a given search-key value, both with and without the bucket structure? Assume nothing is in memory to begin, but it is possible to locate index or bucket blocks without incurring additional I/O's beyond what is needed to retrieve these blocks into memory.

Exercise 1.7: Suppose we have a repository of 1000 documents, and we wish to build an inverted index with 10,000 words. A block can hold ten word-pointer pairs or 50 pointers to either a document or a position within a document. The distribution of words is Zipfian; the number of occurrences of the ith most frequent word is $100000/\sqrt{i}$, for $i = 1, 2, \ldots, 10000$.

a) What is the averge number of words per document?

b) Suppose our inverted index only records for each word all the documents that have that word. What is the maximum number of blocks we could need to hold the inverted index?

c) Suppose our inverted index holds pointers to each occurrence of each word. How many blocks do we need to hold the inverted index?

d) Repeat (b) if the 400 most common words ("stop" words) are *not* included in the index.

e) Repeat (c) if the 400 most common words are not included in the index.

Exercise 1.8: If we use an augmented inverted index, such as in Fig. 10, we can perform a number of other kinds of searches. Suggest how this index could be used to find:

a) Documents in which "cat" and "dog" appeared within five positions of each other in the same type of element (e.g., title, text, or anchor).

b) Documents in which "dog" followed "cat" separated by exactly one position.

c) Documents in which "dog" and "cat" both appear in the title.

2 B-Trees

While one or two levels of index are often very helpful in speeding up queries, there is a more general structure that is commonly used in commercial systems. This family of data structures is called *B-trees*, and the particular variant that is most often used is known as a *B+ tree*. In essence:

- B-trees automatically maintain as many levels of index as is appropriate for the size of the file being indexed.
- B-trees manage the space on the blocks they use so that every block is between half used and completely full.

In the following discussion, we shall talk about "B-trees," but the details will all be for the B+ tree variant. Other types of B-tree are discussed in exercises.

2.1 The Structure of B-trees

A B-tree organizes its blocks into a tree that is *balanced*, meaning that all paths from the root to a leaf have the same length. Typically, there are three layers in a B-tree: the root, an intermediate layer, and leaves, but any number of layers is possible. To help visualize B-trees, you may wish to look ahead at Figs. 11 and 12, which show nodes of a B-tree, and Fig. 13, which shows an entire B-tree.

There is a parameter n associated with each B-tree index, and this parameter determines the layout of all blocks of the B-tree. Each block will have space for n search-key values and $n+1$ pointers. In a sense, a B-tree block is similar to the index blocks introduced in Section 1.2, except that the B-tree block has an extra pointer, along with n key-pointer pairs. We pick n to be as large as will allow $n+1$ pointers and n keys to fit in one block.

Example 10: Suppose our blocks are 4096 bytes. Also let keys be integers of 4 bytes and let pointers be 8 bytes. If there is no header information kept on the blocks, then we want to find the largest integer value of n such that $4n + 8(n+1) \leq 4096$. That value is $n = 340$. □

There are several important rules about what can appear in the blocks of a B-tree:

- The keys in leaf nodes are copies of keys from the data file. These keys are distributed among the leaves in sorted order, from left to right.
- At the root, there are at least two used pointers.[2] All pointers point to B-tree blocks at the level below.
- At a leaf, the last pointer points to the next leaf block to the right, i.e., to the block with the next higher keys. Among the other n pointers in a leaf block, at least $\lfloor (n+1)/2 \rfloor$ of these pointers are used and point to data records; unused pointers are null and do not point anywhere. The ith pointer, if it is used, points to a record with the ith key.

[2]Technically, there is a possibility that the entire B-tree has only one pointer because it is an index into a data file with only one record. In this case, the entire tree is a root block that is also a leaf, and this block has only one key and one pointer. We shall ignore this trivial case in the descriptions that follow.

- At an interior node, all $n + 1$ pointers can be used to point to B-tree blocks at the next lower level. At least $\lceil (n+1)/2 \rceil$ of them are actually used (but if the node is the root, then we require only that at least 2 be used, regardless of how large n is). If j pointers are used, then there will be $j - 1$ keys, say $K_1, K_2, \ldots, K_{j-1}$. The first pointer points to a part of the B-tree where some of the records with keys less than K_1 will be found. The second pointer goes to that part of the tree where all records with keys that are at least K_1, but less than K_2 will be found, and so on. Finally, the jth pointer gets us to the part of the B-tree where some of the records with keys greater than or equal to K_{j-1} are found. Note that some records with keys far below K_1 or far above K_{j-1} may not be reachable from this block at all, but will be reached via another block at the same level.

- All used pointers and their keys appear at the beginning of the block, with the exception of the $(n + 1)$st pointer in a leaf, which points to the next leaf.

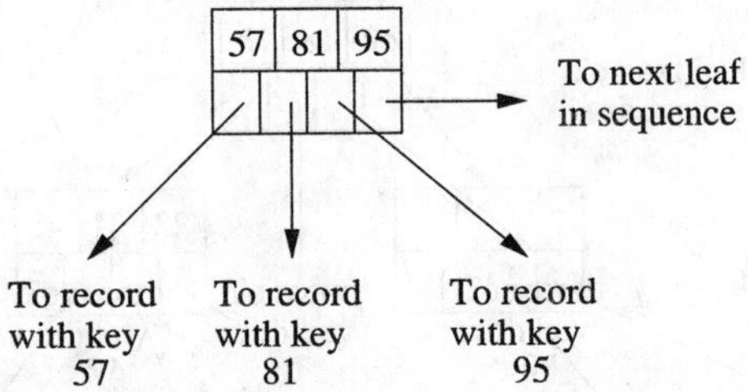

Figure 11: A typical leaf of a B-tree

Example 11: Our running example of B-trees will use $n = 3$. That is, blocks have room for three keys and four pointers, which are atypically small numbers. Keys are integers. Figure 11 shows a leaf that is completely used. There are three keys, 57, 81, and 95. The first three pointers go to records with these keys. The last pointer, as is always the case with leaves, points to the next leaf to the right in the order of keys; it would be null if this leaf were the last in sequence.

A leaf is not necessarily full, but in our example with $n = 3$, there must be at least two key-pointer pairs. That is, the key 95 in Fig. 11 might be missing, and if so, the third pointer would be null.

Figure 12 shows a typical interior node. There are three keys, 14, 52, and 78. There are also four pointers in this node. The first points to a part of the B-tree from which we can reach only records with keys less than 14 — the first of the keys. The second pointer leads to all records with keys between the first and second keys of the B-tree block; the third pointer is for those records

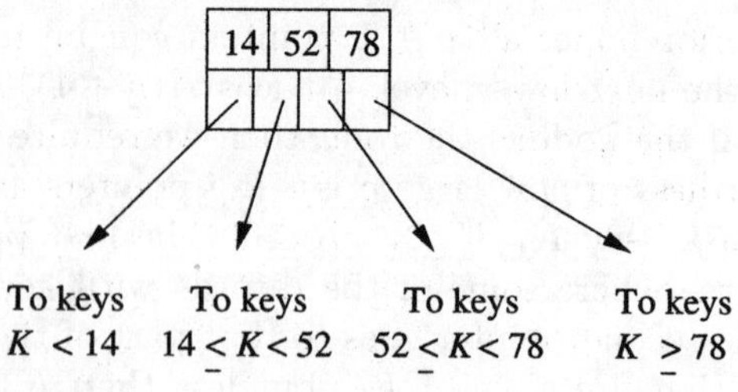

Figure 12: A typical interior node of a B-tree

between the second and third keys of the block, and the fourth pointer lets us reach some of the records with keys equal to or above the third key of the block.

As with our example leaf, it is not necessarily the case that all slots for keys and pointers are occupied. However, with $n = 3$, at least the first key and the first two pointers must be present in an interior node. □

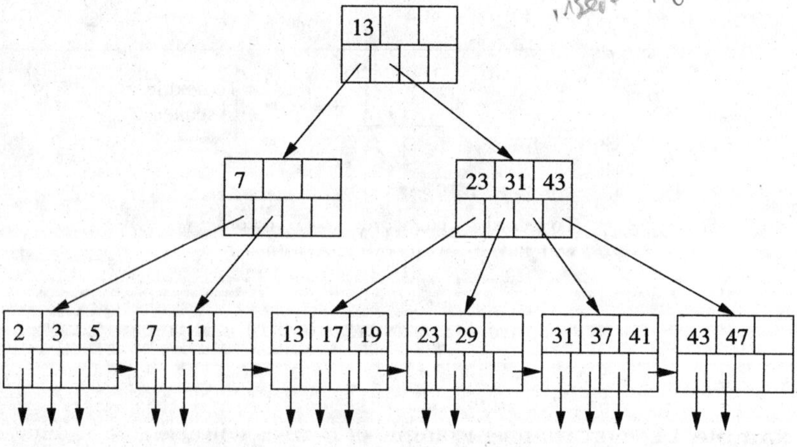

Figure 13: A B-tree

Example 12: Figure 13 shows an entire three-level B-tree, with $n = 3$, as in Example 11. We have assumed that the data file consists of records whose keys are all the primes from 2 to 47. Notice that at the leaves, each of these keys appears once, in order. All leaf blocks have two or three key-pointer pairs, plus a pointer to the next leaf in sequence. The keys are in sorted order as we look across the leaves from left to right.

The root has only two pointers, the minimum possible number, although it could have up to four. The one key at the root separates those keys reachable via the first pointer from those reachable via the second. That is, keys up to 12 could be found in the first subtree of the root, and keys 13 and up are in the second subtree.

If we look at the first child of the root, with key 7, we again find two pointers, one to keys less than 7 and the other to keys 7 and above. Note that the second pointer in this node gets us only to keys 7 and 11, not to *all* keys ≥ 7, such as 13.

Finally, the second child of the root has all four pointer slots in use. The first gets us to some of the keys less than 23, namely 13, 17, and 19. The second pointer gets us to all keys K such that $23 \leq K < 31$; the third pointer lets us reach all keys K such that $31 \leq K < 43$, and the fourth pointer gets us to some of the keys ≥ 43 (in this case, to all of them). □

2.2 Applications of B-trees

The B-tree is a powerful tool for building indexes. The sequence of pointers at the leaves of a B-tree can play the role of any of the pointer sequences coming out of an index file that we learned about in Section 1. Here are some examples:

1. The search key of the B-tree is the primary key for the data file, and the index is dense. That is, there is one key-pointer pair in a leaf for every record of the data file. The data file may or may not be sorted by primary key.

2. The data file is sorted by its primary key, and the B-tree is a sparse index with one key-pointer pair at a leaf for each block of the data file.

3. The data file is sorted by an attribute that is not a key, and this attribute is the search key for the B-tree. For each key value K that appears in the data file there is one key-pointer pair at a leaf. That pointer goes to the first of the records that have K as their sort-key value.

There are additional applications of B-tree variants that allow multiple occurrences of the search key[3] at the leaves. Figure 14 suggests what such a B-tree might look like.

If we do allow duplicate occurrences of a search key, then we need to change slightly the definition of what the keys at interior nodes mean, which we discussed in Section 2.1. Now, suppose there are keys $K_1, K_2, \ldots, K_n$ at an interior node. Then K_i will be the smallest new key that appears in the part of the subtree accessible from the $(i+1)$st pointer. By "new," we mean that there are no occurrences of K_i in the portion of the tree to the left of the $(i+1)$st subtree, but at least one occurrence of K_i in that subtree. Note that in some situations, there will be no such key, in which case K_i can be taken to be null. Its associated pointer is still necessary, as it points to a significant portion of the tree that happens to have only one key value within it.

[3]Remember that a "search key" is not necessarily a "key" in the sense of being unique.

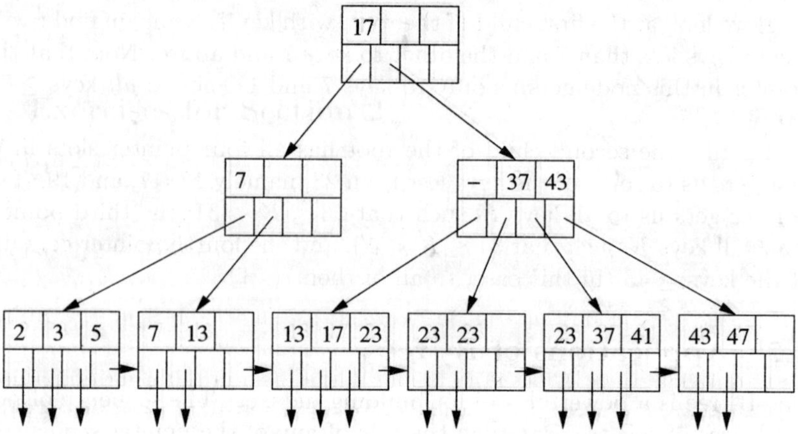

Figure 14: A B-tree with duplicate keys

Example 13 : Figure 14 shows a B-tree similar to Fig. 13, but with duplicate values. In particular, key 11 has been replaced by 13, and keys 19, 29, and 31 have all been replaced by 23. As a result, the key at the root is 17, not 13. The reason is that, although 13 is the lowest key in the second subtree of the root, it is not a *new* key for that subtree, since it also appears in the first subtree.

We also had to make some changes to the second child of the root. The second key is changed to 37, since that is the first new key of the third child (fifth leaf from the left). Most interestingly, the first key is now null. The reason is that the second child (fourth leaf) has no new keys at all. Put another way, if we were searching for any key and reached the second child of the root, we would never want to start at its second child. If we are searching for 23 or anything lower, we want to start at its first child, where we will either find what we are looking for (if it is 17), or find the first of what we are looking for (if it is 23). Note that:

- We would not reach the second child of the root searching for 13; we would be directed at the root to its first child instead.

- If we are looking for any key between 24 and 36, we are directed to the third leaf, but when we don't find even one occurrence of what we are looking for, we know not to search further right. For example, if there were a key 24 among the leaves, it would either be on the 4th leaf, in which case the null key in the second child of the root would be 24 instead, or it would be in the 5th leaf, in which case the key 37 at the second child of the root would be 24.

□

2.3 Lookup in B-Trees

We now revert to our original assumption that there are no duplicate keys at the leaves. We also suppose that the B-tree is a dense index, so every search-key value that appears in the data file will also appear at a leaf. These assumptions make the discussion of B-tree operations simpler, but is not essential for these operations. In particular, modifications for sparse indexes are similar to the changes we introduced in Section 1.3 for indexes on sequential files.

Suppose we have a B-tree index and we want to find a record with search-key value K. We search for K recursively, starting at the root and ending at a leaf. The search procedure is:

BASIS: If we are at a leaf, look among the keys there. If the ith key is K, then the ith pointer will take us to the desired record.

INDUCTION: If we are at an interior node with keys $K_1, K_2, \ldots, K_n$, follow the rules given in Section 2.1 to decide which of the children of this node should next be examined. That is, there is only one child that could lead to a leaf with key K. If $K < K_1$, then it is the first child, if $K_1 \leq K < K_2$, it is the second child, and so on. Recursively apply the search procedure at this child.

Example 14: Suppose we have the B-tree of Fig. 13, and we want to find a record with search key 40. We start at the root, where there is one key, 13. Since $13 \leq 40$, we follow the second pointer, which leads us to the second-level node with keys 23, 31, and 43.

At that node, we find $31 \leq 40 < 43$, so we follow the third pointer. We are thus led to the leaf with keys 31, 37, and 41. If there had been a record in the data file with key 40, we would have found key 40 at this leaf. Since we do not find 40, we conclude that there is no record with key 40 in the underlying data.

Note that had we been looking for a record with key 37, we would have taken exactly the same decisions, but when we got to the leaf we would find key 37. Since it is the second key in the leaf, we follow the second pointer, which will lead us to the data record with key 37. □

2.4 Range Queries

B-trees are useful not only for queries in which a single value of the search key is sought, but for queries in which a range of values are asked for. Typically, *range queries* have a term in the `WHERE`-clause that compares the search key with a value or values, using one of the comparison operators other than `=` or `<>`. Examples of range queries using a search-key attribute k are:

```
SELECT * FROM R     SELECT * FROM R
WHERE R.k > 40;     WHERE R.k >= 10 AND R.k <= 25;
```

If we want to find all keys in the range $[a, b]$ at the leaves of a B-tree, we do a lookup to find the key a. Whether or not it exists, we are led to a leaf where

a could be, and we search the leaf for keys that are a or greater. Each such key we find has an associated pointer to one of the records whose key is in the desired range. As long as we do not find a key greater than b in the current block, we follow the pointer to the next leaf and repeat our search for keys in the range $[a, b]$.

The above search algorithm also works if b is infinite; i.e., there is only a lower bound and no upper bound. In that case, we search all the leaves from the one that would hold key a to the end of the chain of leaves. If a is $-\infty$ (that is, there is an upper bound on the range but no lower bound), then the search for "minus infinity" as a search key will always take us to the first leaf. The search then proceeds as above, stopping only when we pass the key b.

Example 15: Suppose we have the B-tree of Fig. 13, and we are given the range $(10, 25)$ to search for. We look for key 10, which leads us to the second leaf. The first key is less than 10, but the second, 11, is at least 10. We follow its associated pointer to get the record with key 11.

Since there are no more keys in the second leaf, we follow the chain to the third leaf, where we find keys 13, 17, and 19. All are less than or equal to 25, so we follow their associated pointers and retrieve the records with these keys. Finally, we move to the fourth leaf, where we find key 23. But the next key of that leaf, 29, exceeds 25, so we are done with our search. Thus, we have retrieved the five records with keys 11 through 23. □

2.5 Insertion Into B-Trees

We see some of the advantages of B-trees over simpler multilevel indexes when we consider how to insert a new key into a B-tree. The corresponding record will be inserted into the file being indexed by the B-tree, using any of the methods discussed in Section 1; here we consider how the B-tree changes. The insertion is, in principle, recursive:

- We try to find a place for the new key in the appropriate leaf, and we put it there if there is room.

- If there is no room in the proper leaf, we split the leaf into two and divide the keys between the two new nodes, so each is half full or just over half full.

- The splitting of nodes at one level appears to the level above as if a new key-pointer pair needs to be inserted at that higher level. We may thus recursively apply this strategy to insert at the next level: if there is room, insert it; if not, split the parent node and continue up the tree.

- As an exception, if we try to insert into the root, and there is no room, then we split the root into two nodes and create a new root at the next higher level; the new root has the two nodes resulting from the split as its children. Recall that no matter how large n (the number of slots for keys at a node) is, it is always permissible for the root to have only one key and two children.

When we split a node and insert it into its parent, we need to be careful how the keys are managed. First, suppose N is a leaf whose capacity is n keys. Also suppose we are trying to insert an $(n+1)$st key and its associated pointer. We create a new node M, which will be the sibling of N, immediately to its right. The first $\lceil (n+1)/2 \rceil$ key-pointer pairs, in sorted order of the keys, remain with N, while the other key-pointer pairs move to M. Note that both nodes N and M are left with a sufficient number of key-pointer pairs — at least $\lfloor (n+1)/2 \rfloor$ pairs.

Now, suppose N is an interior node whose capacity is n keys and $n+1$ pointers, and N has just been assigned $n+2$ pointers because of a node splitting below. We do the following:

1. Create a new node M, which will be the sibling of N, immediately to its right.

2. Leave at N the first $\lceil (n+2)/2 \rceil$ pointers, in sorted order, and move to M the remaining $\lfloor (n+2)/2 \rfloor$ pointers.

3. The first $\lceil n/2 \rceil$ keys stay with N, while the last $\lfloor n/2 \rfloor$ keys move to M. Note that there is always one key in the middle left over; it goes with neither N nor M. The leftover key K indicates the smallest key reachable via the first of M's children. Although this key doesn't appear in N or M, it is associated with M, in the sense that it represents the smallest key reachable via M. Therefore K will be inserted into the parent of N and M to divide searches between those two nodes.

Example 16: Let us insert key 40 into the B-tree of Fig. 13. We find the proper leaf for the insertion by the lookup procedure of Section 2.3. As found in Example 14, the insertion goes into the fifth leaf. Since this leaf now has four key-pointer pairs — 31, 37, 40, and 41 — we need to split the leaf. Our first step is to create a new node and move the highest two keys, 40 and 41, along with their pointers, to that node. Figure 15 shows this split.

Notice that although we now show the nodes on four ranks to save space, there are still only three levels to the tree. The seven leaves are linked by their last pointers, which still form a chain from left to right.

We must now insert a pointer to the new leaf (the one with keys 40 and 41) into the node above it (the node with keys 23, 31, and 43). We must also associate with this pointer the key 40, which is the least key reachable through the new leaf. Unfortunately, the parent of the split node is already full; it has no room for another key or pointer. Thus, it too must be split.

We start with pointers to the last five leaves and the list of keys representing the least keys of the last four of these leaves. That is, we have pointers P_1, P_2, P_3, P_4, P_5 to the leaves whose least keys are 13, 23, 31, 40, and 43, and

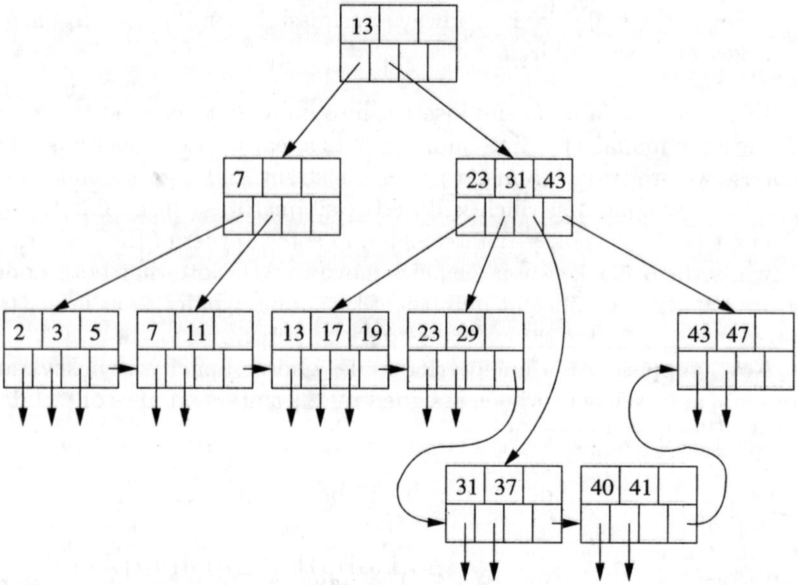

Figure 15: Beginning the insertion of key 40

we have the key sequence 23, 31, 40, 43 to separate these pointers. The first three pointers and first two keys remain with the split interior node, while the last two pointers and last key go to the new node. The remaining key, 40, represents the least key accessible via the new node.

Figure 16 shows the completion of the insert of key 40. The root now has three children; the last two are the split interior node. Notice that the key 40, which marks the lowest of the keys reachable via the second of the split nodes, has been installed in the root to separate the keys of the root's second and third children. □

2.6 Deletion From B-Trees

If we are to delete a record with a given key K, we must first locate that record and its key-pointer pair in a leaf of the B-tree. This part of the deletion process is essentially a lookup, as in Section 2.3. We then delete the record itself from the data file, and we delete the key-pointer pair from the B-tree.

If the B-tree node from which a deletion occurred still has at least the minimum number of keys and pointers, then there is nothing more to be done.[4] However, it is possible that the node was right at the minimum occupancy before the deletion, so after deletion the constraint on the number of keys is

[4]If the data record with the least key at a leaf is deleted, then we have the option of raising the appropriate key at one of the ancestors of that leaf, but there is no requirement that we do so; all searches will still go to the appropriate leaf.

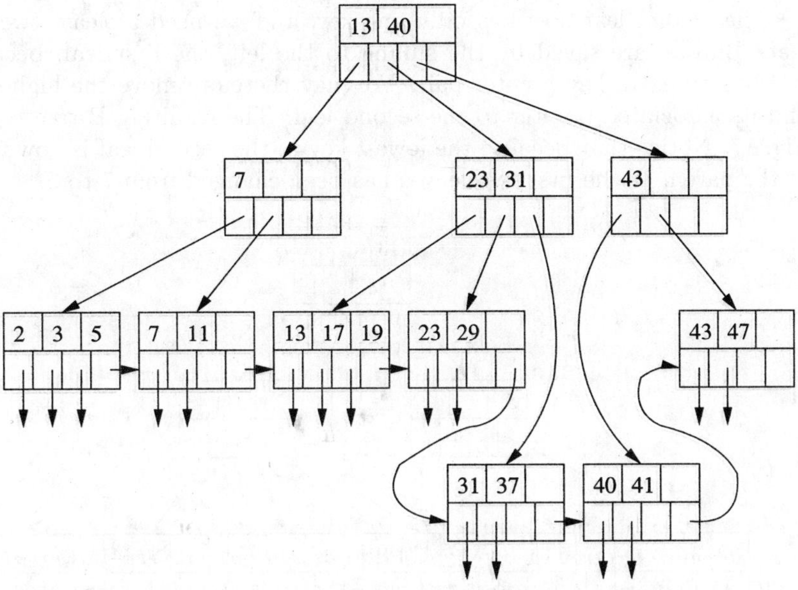

Figure 16: Completing the insertion of key 40

violated. We then need to do one of two things for a node N whose contents are subminimum; one case requires a recursive deletion up the tree:

1. If one of the adjacent siblings of node N has more than the minimum number of keys and pointers, then one key-pointer pair can be moved to N, keeping the order of keys intact. Possibly, the keys at the parent of N must be adjusted to reflect the new situation. For instance, if the right sibling of N, say node M, provides an extra key and pointer, then it must be the smallest key that is moved from M to N. At the parent of M and N, there is a key that represents the smallest key accessible via M; that key must be increased to reflect the new M.

2. The hard case is when neither adjacent sibling can be used to provide an extra key for N. However, in that case, we have two adjacent nodes, N and a sibling M; the latter has the minimum number of keys and the former has fewer than the minimum. Therefore, together they have no more keys and pointers than are allowed in a single node. We merge these two nodes, effectively deleting one of them. We need to adjust the keys at the parent, and then delete a key and pointer at the parent. If the parent is still full enough, then we are done. If not, then we recursively apply the deletion algorithm at the parent.

Example 17: Let us begin with the original B-tree of Fig. 13, before the insertion of key 40. Suppose we delete key 7. This key is found in the second leaf. We delete it, its associated pointer, and the record that pointer points to.

The second leaf now has only one key, and we need at least two in every leaf. But we are saved by the sibling to the left, the first leaf, because that leaf has an extra key-pointer pair. We may therefore move the highest key, 5, and its associated pointer to the second leaf. The resulting B-tree is shown in Fig. 17. Notice that because the lowest key in the second leaf is now 5, the key in the parent of the first two leaves has been changed from 7 to 5.

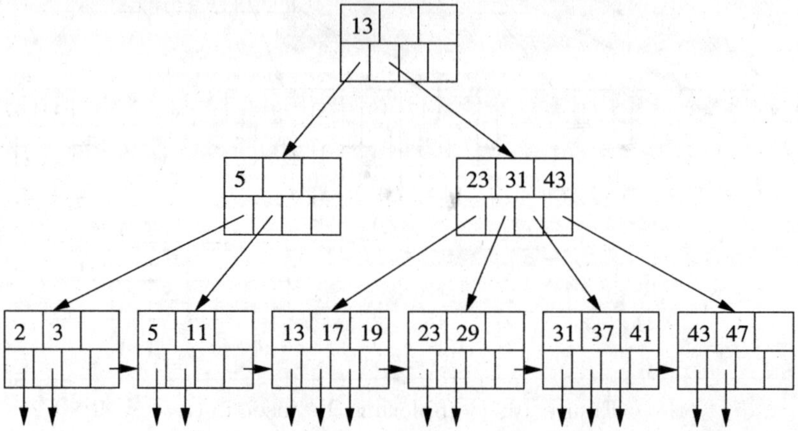

Figure 17: Deletion of key 7

Next, suppose we delete key 11. This deletion has the same effect on the second leaf; it again reduces the number of its keys below the minimum. This time, however, we cannot take a key from the first leaf, because the latter is down to the minimum number of keys. Additionally, there is no sibling to the right from which to take a key.[5] Thus, we need to merge the second leaf with a sibling, namely the first leaf.

The three remaining key-pointer pairs from the first two leaves fit in one leaf, so we move 5 to the first leaf and delete the second leaf. The pointers and keys in the parent are adjusted to reflect the new situation at its children; specifically, the two pointers are replaced by one (to the remaining leaf) and the key 5 is no longer relevant and is deleted. The situation is now as shown in Fig. 18.

The deletion of a leaf has adversely affected the parent, which is the left child of the root. That node, as we see in Fig. 18, now has no keys and only one pointer. Thus, we try to obtain an extra key and pointer from an adjacent sibling. This time we have the easy case, since the other child of the root can afford to give up its smallest key and a pointer.

The change is shown in Fig. 19. The pointer to the leaf with keys 13, 17,

[5]Notice that the leaf to the right, with keys 13, 17, and 19, is not a sibling, because it has a different parent. We could take a key from that node anyway, but then the algorithm for adjusting keys throughout the tree becomes more complex. We leave this enhancement as an exercise.

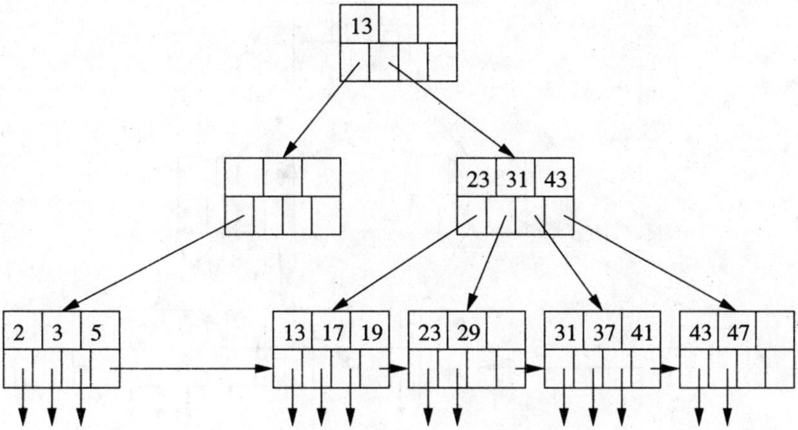

Figure 18: Beginning the deletion of key 11

and 19 has been moved from the second child of the root to the first child. We have also changed some keys at the interior nodes. The key 13, which used to reside at the root and represented the smallest key accessible via the pointer that was transferred, is now needed at the first child of the root. On the other hand, the key 23, which used to separate the first and second children of the second child of the root now represents the smallest key accessible from the second child of the root. It therefore is placed at the root itself. □

2.7 Efficiency of B-Trees

B-trees allow lookup, insertion, and deletion of records using very few disk I/O's per file operation. First, we should observe that if n, the number of keys per block, is reasonably large, then splitting and merging of blocks will be rare events. Further, when such an operation is needed, it almost always is limited to the leaves, so only two leaves and their parent are affected. Thus, we can essentially neglect the disk-I/O cost of B-tree reorganizations.

However, every search for the record(s) with a given search key requires us to go from the root down to a leaf, to find a pointer to the record. Since we are only reading B-tree blocks, the number of disk I/O's will be the number of levels the B-tree has, plus the one (for lookup) or two (for insert or delete) disk I/O's needed for manipulation of the record itself. We must thus ask: how many levels does a B-tree have? For the typical sizes of keys, pointers, and blocks, three levels are sufficient for all but the largest databases. Thus, we shall generally take 3 as the number of levels of a B-tree. The following example illustrates why.

Example 18: Recall our analysis in Example 10, where we determined that 340 key-pointer pairs could fit in one block for our example data. Suppose

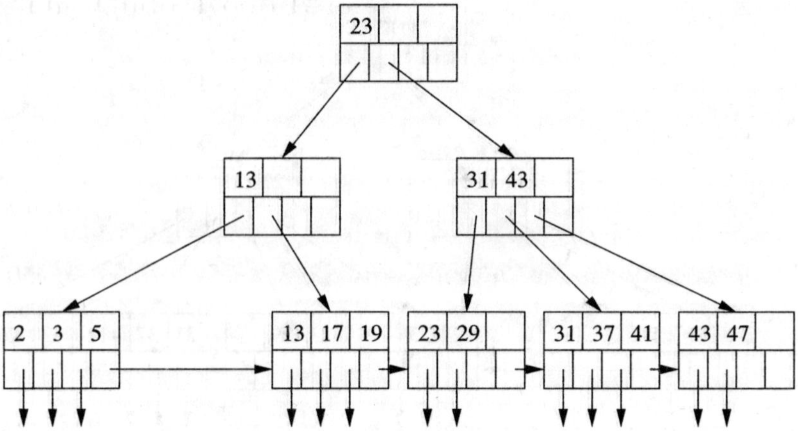

Figure 19: Completing the deletion of key 11

that the average block has an occupancy midway between the minimum and maximum, i.e., a typical block has 255 pointers. With a root, 255 children, and $255^2 = 65025$ leaves, we shall have among those leaves 255^3, or about 16.6 million pointers to records. That is, files with up to 16.6 million records can be accommodated by a 3-level B-tree. □

However, we can use even fewer than three disk I/O's per search through the B-tree. The root block of a B-tree is an excellent choice to keep permanently buffered in main memory. If so, then every search through a 3-level B-tree requires only two disk reads. In fact, under some circumstances it may make sense to keep second-level nodes of the B-tree buffered in main memory as well, reducing the B-tree search to a single disk I/O, plus whatever is necessary to manipulate the blocks of the data file itself.

2.8 Exercises for Section 2

Exercise 2.1: Suppose that blocks can hold either ten records or 99 keys and 100 pointers. Also assume that the average B-tree node is 70% full; i.e., it will have 69 keys and 70 pointers. We can use B-trees as part of several different structures. For each structure described below, determine (*i*) the total number of blocks needed for a 1,000,000-record file, and (*ii*) the average number of disk I/O's to retrieve a record given its search key. You may assume nothing is in memory initially, and the search key is the primary key for the records.

a) The data file is a sequential file, sorted on the search key, with 10 records per block. The B-tree is a dense index.

b) The same as (a), but the data file consists of records in no particular order, packed 10 to a block.

Should We Delete From B-Trees?

There are B-tree implementations that don't fix up deletions at all. If a leaf has too few keys and pointers, it is allowed to remain as it is. The rationale is that most files grow on balance, and while there might be an occasional deletion that makes a leaf become subminimum, the leaf will probably soon grow again and attain the minimum number of key-pointer pairs once again.

Further, if records have pointers from outside the B-tree index, then we need to replace the record by a "tombstone," and we don't want to delete its pointer from the B-tree anyway. In certain circumstances, when it can be guaranteed that all accesses to the deleted record will go through the B-tree, we can even leave the tombstone in place of the pointer to the record at a leaf of the B-tree. Then, space for the record can be reused.

c) The same as (a), but the B-tree is a sparse index.

! d) Instead of the B-tree leaves having pointers to data records, the B-tree leaves hold the records themselves. A block can hold ten records, but on average, a leaf block is 70% full; i.e., there are seven records per leaf block.

e) The data file is a sequential file, and the B-tree is a sparse index, but each primary block of the data file has one overflow block. On average, the primary block is full, and the overflow block is half full. However, records are in no particular order within a primary block and its overflow block.

Exercise 2.2: Repeat Exercise 2.1 in the case that the query is a range query that is matched by 1000 records.

Exercise 2.3: Suppose pointers are 4 bytes long, and keys are 12 bytes long. How many keys and pointers will a block of 16,384 bytes have?

Exercise 2.4: What are the minimum numbers of keys and pointers in B-tree (*i*) interior nodes and (*ii*) leaves, when:

a) $n = 10$; i.e., a block holds 10 keys and 11 pointers.

b) $n = 11$; i.e., a block holds 11 keys and 12 pointers.

Exercise 2.5: Execute the following operations on Fig. 13. Describe the changes for operations that modify the tree.

a) Lookup the record with key 41.

b) Lookup the record with key 40.

c) Lookup all records in the range 20 to 30.

d) Lookup all records with keys less than 30.

e) Lookup all records with keys greater than 30.

f) Insert a record with key 1.

g) Insert records with keys 14 through 16.

h) Delete the record with key 23.

i) Delete all the records with keys 23 and higher.

Exercise 2.6: When duplicate keys are allowed in a B-tree, there are some necessary modifications to the algorithms for lookup, insertion, and deletion that we described in this section. Give the changes for: (a) lookup (b) insertion (c) deletion.

! **Exercise 2.7:** In Example 17 we suggested that it would be possible to borrow keys from a nonsibling to the right (or left) if we used a more complicated algorithm for maintaining keys at interior nodes. Describe a suitable algorithm that rebalances by borrowing from adjacent nodes at a level, regardless of whether they are siblings of the node that has too many or too few key-pointer pairs.

! **Exercise 2.8:** If we use the 3-key, 4-pointer nodes of our examples in this section, how many different B-trees are there when the data file has the following numbers of records: (a) 6 (b) 10 **!!** (c) 15.

! **Exercise 2.9:** Suppose we have B-tree nodes with room for three keys and four pointers, as in the examples of this section. Suppose also that when we split a leaf, we divide the pointers 2 and 2, while when we split an interior node, the first 3 pointers go with the first (left) node, and the last 2 pointers go with the second (right) node. We start with a leaf containing pointers to records with keys 1, 2, and 3. We then add in order, records with keys 4, 5, 6, and so on. At the insertion of what key will the B-tree first reach four levels?

3 Hash Tables

There are a number of data structures involving a hash table that are useful as indexes. We assume the reader has seen the hash table used as a main-memory data structure. In such a structure there is a *hash function* h that takes a search key (the *hash key*) as an argument and computes from it an integer in the range 0 to $B-1$, where B is the number of *buckets*. A *bucket array*, which is an array indexed from 0 to $B-1$, holds the headers of B linked lists, one for each bucket of the array. If a record has search key K, then we store the record by linking it to the bucket list for the bucket numbered $h(K)$.

3.1 Secondary-Storage Hash Tables

A hash table that holds a very large number of records, so many that they must be kept mainly in secondary storage, differs from the main-memory version in small but important ways. First, the bucket array consists of blocks, rather than pointers to the headers of lists. Records that are hashed by the hash function h to a certain bucket are put in the block for that bucket. If a bucket has too many records, a chain of overflow blocks can be added to the bucket to hold more records.

We shall assume that the location of the first block for any bucket i can be found given i. For example, there might be a main-memory array of pointers to blocks, indexed by the bucket number. Another possibility is to put the first block for each bucket in fixed, consecutive disk locations, so we can compute the location of bucket i from the integer i.

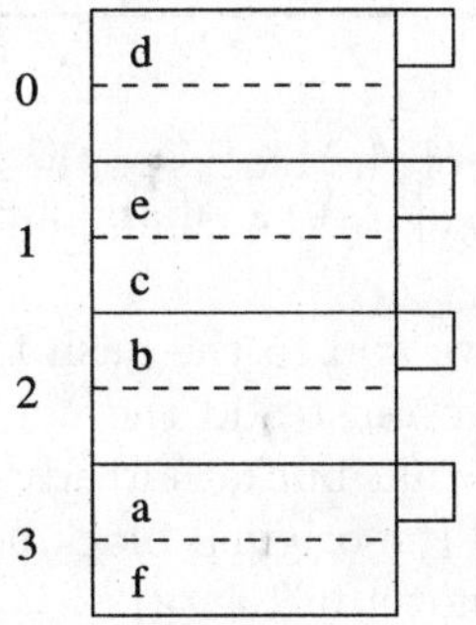

Figure 20: A hash table

Example 19: Figure 20 shows a hash table. To keep our illustrations manageable, we assume that a block can hold only two records, and that $B = 4$; i.e., the hash function h returns values from 0 to 3. We show certain records populating the hash table. Keys are letters a through f in Fig. 20. We assume that $h(d) = 0$, $h(c) = h(e) = 1$, $h(b) = 2$, and $h(a) = h(f) = 3$. Thus, the six records are distributed into blocks as shown. □

Note that we show each block in Fig. 20 with a "nub" at the right end. This nub represents additional information in the block's header. We shall use it to chain overflow blocks together, and starting in Section 3.5, we shall use it to keep other critical information about the block.

3.2 Insertion Into a Hash Table

When a new record with search key K must be inserted, we compute $h(K)$. If the bucket numbered $h(K)$ has space, then we insert the record into the block for this bucket, or into one of the overflow blocks on its chain if there is no room

> **Choice of Hash Function**
>
> The hash function should "hash" the key so the resulting integer is a seemingly random function of the key. Thus, buckets will tend to have equal numbers of records, which improves the average time to access a record, as we shall discuss in Section 3.4. Also, the hash function should be easy to compute, since we shall compute it many times.
>
> A common choice of hash function when keys are integers is to compute the remainder of K/B, where K is the key value and B is the number of buckets. Often, B is chosen to be a prime, although there are reasons to make B a power of 2, as we discuss starting in Section 3.5. For character-string search keys, we may treat each character as an integer, sum these integers, and take the remainder when the sum is divided by B.

in the first block. If none of the blocks of the chain for bucket $h(K)$ has room, we add a new overflow block to the chain and store the new record there.

Example 20: Suppose we add to the hash table of Fig. 20 a record with key g, and $h(g) = 1$. Then we must add the new record to the bucket numbered 1. However, the block for that bucket already has two records. Thus, we add a new block and chain it to the original block for bucket 1. The record with key g goes in that block, as shown in Fig. 21. □

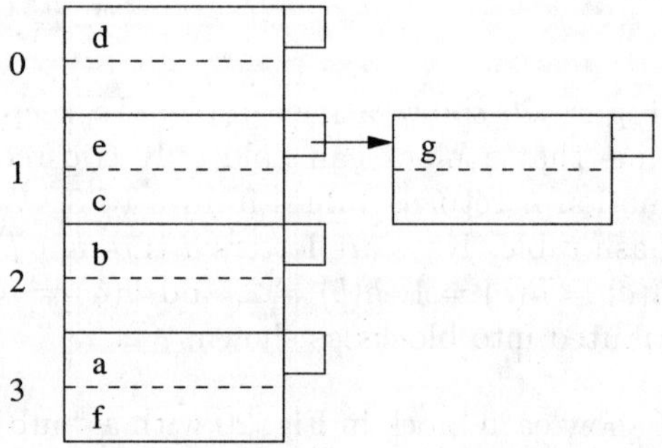

Figure 21: Adding an additional block to a hash-table bucket

3.3 Hash-Table Deletion

Deletion of the record (or records) with search key K follows the same pattern as insertion. We go to the bucket numbered $h(K)$ and search for records with that search key. Any that we find are deleted. If we are able to move records around among blocks, then after deletion we may optionally consolidate the blocks of a bucket into one fewer block.[6]

Example 21: Figure 22 shows the result of deleting the record with key c from the hash table of Fig. 21. Recall $h(c) = 1$, so we go to the bucket numbered 1 (i.e., the second bucket) and search all its blocks to find a record (or records if the search key were not the primary key) with key c. We find it in the first block of the chain for bucket 1. Since there is now room to move the record with key g from the second block of the chain to the first, we can do so and remove the second block.

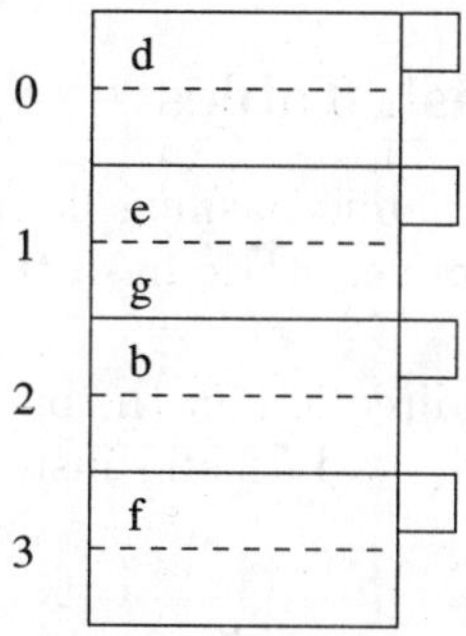

Figure 22: Result of deletions from a hash table

We also show the deletion of the record with key a. For this key, we found our way to bucket 3, deleted it, and "consolidated" the remaining record at the beginning of the block. □

3.4 Efficiency of Hash Table Indexes

Ideally, there are enough buckets that most of them fit on one block. If so, then the typical lookup takes only one disk I/O, and insertion or deletion from the file takes only two disk I/O's. That number is significantly better than straightforward sparse or dense indexes, or B-tree indexes (although hash tables do not support range queries as B-trees do; see Section 2.4).

However, if the file grows, then we shall eventually reach a situation where there are many blocks in the chain for a typical bucket. If so, then we need to search long lists of blocks, taking at least one disk I/O per block. Thus, there is a good reason to try to keep the number of blocks per bucket low.

The hash tables we have examined so far are called *static hash tables*, because B, the number of buckets, never changes. However, there are several kinds of *dynamic hash tables*, where B is allowed to vary so it approximates the number

[6] A risk of consolidating blocks of a chain whenever possible is that an oscillation, where we alternately insert and delete records from a bucket, will cause a block to be created or destroyed at each step.

of records divided by the number of records that can fit on a block; i.e., there is about one block per bucket. We shall discuss two such methods:

1. Extensible hashing in Section 3.5, and

2. Linear hashing in Section 3.7.

The first grows B by doubling it whenever it is deemed too small, and the second grows B by 1 each time statistics of the file suggest some growth is needed.

3.5 Extensible Hash Tables

Our first approach to dynamic hashing is called *extensible hash tables.* The major additions to the simpler static hash table structure are:

1. There is a level of indirection for the buckets. That is, an array of pointers to blocks represents the buckets, instead of the array holding the data blocks themselves.

2. The array of pointers can grow. Its length is always a power of 2, so in a growing step the number of buckets doubles.

3. However, there does not have to be a data block for each bucket; certain buckets can share a block if the total number of records in those buckets can fit in the block.

4. The hash function h computes for each key a sequence of k bits for some large k, say 32. However, the bucket numbers will at all times use some smaller number of bits, say i bits, from the beginning or end of this sequence. The bucket array will have 2^i entries when i is the number of bits used.

Example 22: Figure 23 shows a small extensible hash table. We suppose, for simplicity of the example, that $k = 4$; i.e., the hash function produces a sequence of only four bits. At the moment, only one of these bits is used, as indicated by $i = 1$ in the box above the bucket array. The bucket array therefore has only two entries, one for 0 and one for 1.

The bucket array entries point to two blocks. The first holds all the current records whose search keys hash to a bit sequence that begins with 0, and the second holds all those whose search keys hash to a sequence beginning with 1. For convenience, we show the keys of records as if they were the entire bit sequence to which the hash function converts them. Thus, the first block holds a record whose key hashes to 0001, and the second holds records whose keys hash to 1001 and 1100. □

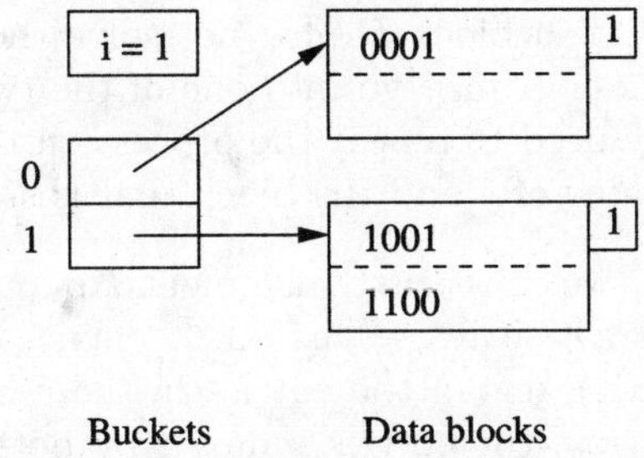

Figure 23: An extensible hash table

We should notice the number 1 appearing in the "nub" of each of the blocks in Fig. 23. This number, which would actually appear in the block header, indicates how many bits of the hash function's sequence is used to determine membership of records in this block. In the situation of Example 22, there is only one bit considered for all blocks and records, but as we shall see, the number of bits considered for various blocks can differ as the hash table grows. That is, the bucket array size is determined by the maximum number of bits we are now using, but some blocks may use fewer.

3.6 Insertion Into Extensible Hash Tables

Insertion into an extensible hash table begins like insertion into a static hash table. To insert a record with search key K, we compute $h(K)$, take the first i bits of this bit sequence, and go to the entry of the bucket array indexed by these i bits. Note that we can determine i because it is kept as part of the data structure.

We follow the pointer in this entry of the bucket array and arrive at a block B. If there is room to put the new record in block B, we do so and we are done. If there is no room, then there are two possibilities, depending on the number j, which indicates how many bits of the hash value are used to determine membership in block B (recall the value of j is found in the "nub" of each block in figures).

1. If $j < i$, then nothing needs to be done to the bucket array. We:

   (a) Split block B into two.

   (b) Distribute records in B to the two blocks, based on the value of their $(j+1)$st bit — records whose key has 0 in that bit stay in B and those with 1 there go to the new block.

   (c) Put $j+1$ in each block's "nub" (header) to indicate the number of bits used to determine membership.

   (d) Adjust the pointers in the bucket array so entries that formerly pointed to B now point either to B or the new block, depending on their $(j+1)$st bit.

Note that splitting block B may not solve the problem, since by chance all the records of B may go into one of the two blocks into which it was split. If so, we need to repeat the process on the overfull block, using the next higher value of j and the block that is still overfull.

2. If $j = i$, then we must first increment i by 1. We double the length of the bucket array, so it now has 2^{i+1} entries. Suppose w is a sequence of i bits indexing one of the entries in the previous bucket array. In the new bucket array, the entries indexed by both $w0$ and $w1$ (i.e., the two numbers derived from w by extending it with 0 or 1) each point to the same block that the w entry used to point to. That is, the two new entries share the block, and the block itself does not change. Membership in the block is still determined by whatever number of bits was previously used. Finally, we proceed to split block B as in case 1. Since i is now greater than j, that case applies.

Example 23: Suppose we insert into the table of Fig. 23 a record whose key hashes to the sequence 1010. Since the first bit is 1, this record belongs in the second block. However, that block is already full, so it needs to be split. We find that $j = i = 1$ in this case, so we first need to double the bucket array, as shown in Fig. 24. We have also set $i = 2$ in this figure.

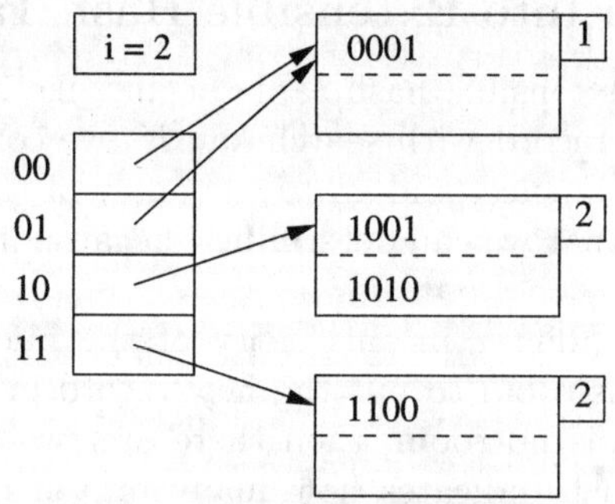

Figure 24: Now, two bits of the hash function are used

Notice that the two entries beginning with 0 each point to the block for records whose hashed keys begin with 0, and that block still has the integer 1 in its "nub" to indicate that only the first bit determines membership in the block. However, the block for records beginning with 1 needs to be split, so we partition its records into those beginning 10 and those beginning 11. A 2 in each of these blocks indicates that two bits are used to determine membership. Fortunately, the split is successful; since each of the two new blocks gets at least one record, we do not have to split recursively.

Now suppose we insert records whose keys hash to 0000 and 0111. These both go in the first block of Fig. 24, which then overflows. Since only one bit is used to determine membership in this block, while $i = 2$, we do not have to adjust the bucket array. We simply split the block, with 0000 and 0001 staying, and 0111 going to the new block. The entry for 01 in the bucket array is made to point to the new block. Again, we have been fortunate that the records did not all go in one of the new blocks, so we have no need to split recursively.

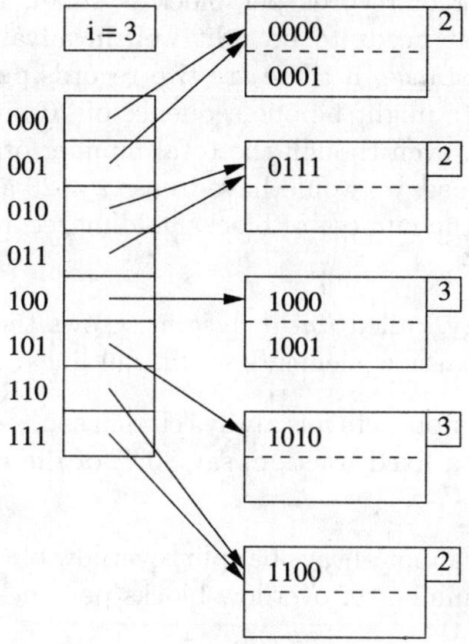

Figure 25: The hash table now uses three bits of the hash function

Now suppose a record whose key hashes to 1000 is inserted. The block for 10 overflows. Since it already uses two bits to determine membership, it is time to split the bucket array again and set $i = 3$. Figure 25 shows the data structure at this point. Notice that the block for 10 has been split into blocks for 100 and 101, while the other blocks continue to use only two bits to determine membership. □

3.7 Linear Hash Tables

Extensible hash tables have some important advantages. Most significant is the fact that when looking for a record, we never need to search more than one data block. We also have to examine an entry of the bucket array, but if the bucket array is small enough to be kept in main memory, then there is no disk I/O needed to access the bucket array. However, extensible hash tables also suffer from some defects:

1. When the bucket array needs to be doubled in size, there is a substantial amount of work to be done (when i is large). This work interrupts access to the data file, or makes certain insertions appear to take a long time.

2. When the bucket array is doubled in size, it may no longer fit in main memory, or may crowd out other data that we would like to hold in main memory. As a result, a system that was performing well might suddenly start using many more disk I/O's per operation.

3. If the number of records per block is small, then there is likely to be one block that needs to be split well in advance of the logical time to do so. For instance, if there are two records per block as in our running example, there might be one sequence of 20 bits that begins the keys of three records, even though the total number of records is much less than 2^{20}. In that case, we would have to use $i = 20$ and a million-bucket array, even though the number of blocks holding records was much smaller than a million.

Another strategy, called *linear hashing*, grows the number of buckets more slowly. The principal new elements we find in linear hashing are:

- The number of buckets n is always chosen so the average number of records per bucket is a fixed fraction, say 80%, of the number of records that fill one block.

- Since blocks cannot always be split, overflow blocks are permitted, although the average number of overflow blocks per bucket will be much less than 1.

- The number of bits used to number the entries of the bucket array is $\lceil \log_2 n \rceil$, where n is the current number of buckets. These bits are always taken from the *right* (low-order) end of the bit sequence that is produced by the hash function.

- Suppose i bits of the hash function are being used to number array entries, and a record with key K is intended for bucket $a_1 a_2 \cdots a_i$; that is, $a_1 a_2 \cdots a_i$ are the last i bits of $h(K)$. Then let $a_1 a_2 \cdots a_i$ be m, treated as an i-bit binary integer. If $m < n$, then the bucket numbered m exists, and we place the record in that bucket. If $n \leq m < 2^i$, then the bucket m does not yet exist, so we place the record in bucket $m - 2^{i-1}$, that is, the bucket we would get if we changed a_1 (which must be 1) to 0.

Example 24: Figure 26 shows a linear hash table with $n = 2$. We currently are using only one bit of the hash value to determine the buckets of records. Following the pattern established in Example 22, we assume the hash function h produces 4 bits, and we represent records by the value produced by h when applied to the search key of the record.

We see in Fig. 26 the two buckets, each consisting of one block. The buckets are numbered 0 and 1. All records whose hash value ends in 0 go in the first bucket, and those whose hash value ends in 1 go in the second.

Also part of the structure are the parameters i (the number of bits of the hash function that currently are used), n (the current number of buckets), and r

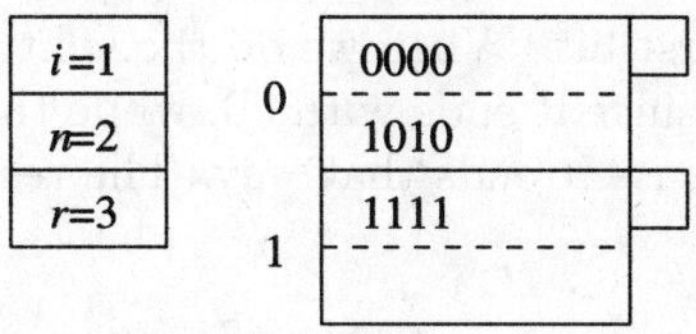

Figure 26: A linear hash table

(the current number of records in the hash table). The ratio r/n will be limited so that the typical bucket will need about one disk block. We shall adopt the policy of choosing n, the number of buckets, so that there are no more than $1.7n$ records in the file; i.e., $r \leq 1.7n$. That is, since blocks hold two records, the average occupancy of a bucket does not exceed 85% of the capacity of a block. □

3.8 Insertion Into Linear Hash Tables

When we insert a new record, we determine its bucket by the algorithm outlined in Section 3.7. We compute $h(K)$, where K is the key of the record, and we use the i bits at the end of bit sequence $h(K)$ as the bucket number, m. If $m < n$, we put the record in bucket m, and if $m \geq n$, we put the record in bucket $m - 2^{i-1}$. If there is no room in the designated bucket, then we create an overflow block, add it to the chain for that bucket, and put the record there.

Each time we insert, we compare the current number of records r with the threshold ratio of r/n, and if the ratio is too high, we add the next bucket to the table. Note that the bucket we add bears no relationship to the bucket into which the insertion occurs! If the binary representation of the number of the bucket we add is $1a_2 \cdots a_i$, then we split the bucket numbered $0a_2 \cdots a_i$, putting records into one or the other bucket, depending on their last i bits. Note that all these records will have hash values that end in $a_2 \cdots a_i$, and only the ith bit from the right end will vary.

The last important detail is what happens when n exceeds 2^i. Then, i is incremented by 1. Technically, all the bucket numbers get an additional 0 in front of their bit sequences, but there is no need to make any physical change, since these bit sequences, interpreted as integers, remain the same.

Example 25 : We shall continue with Example 24 and consider what happens when a record whose key hashes to 0101 is inserted. Since this bit sequence ends in 1, the record goes into the second bucket of Fig. 26. There is room for the record, so no overflow block is created.

However, since there are now 4 records in 2 buckets, we exceed the ratio 1.7, and we must therefore raise n to 3. Since $\lceil \log_2 3 \rceil = 2$, we should begin to think of buckets 0 and 1 as 00 and 01, but no change to the data structure is necessary. We add to the table the next bucket, which would have number 10. Then, we split the bucket 00, that bucket whose number differs from the added bucket only in the first bit. When we do the split, the record whose key hashes to 0000 stays in 00, since it ends with 00, while the record whose key hashes to 1010 goes to 10 because it ends that way. The resulting hash table is shown in Fig. 27.

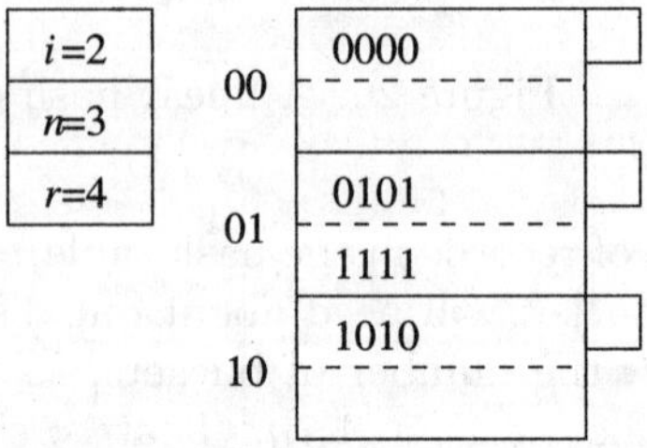

Figure 27: Adding a third bucket

Next, let us suppose we add a record whose search key hashes to 0001. The last two bits are 01, so we put it in this bucket, which currently exists. Unfortunately, the bucket's block is full, so we add an overflow block. The three records are distributed among the two blocks of the bucket; we chose to keep them in numerical order of their hashed keys, but order is not important. Since the ratio of records to buckets for the table as a whole is 5/3, and this ratio is less than 1.7, we do not create a new bucket. The result is seen in Fig. 28.

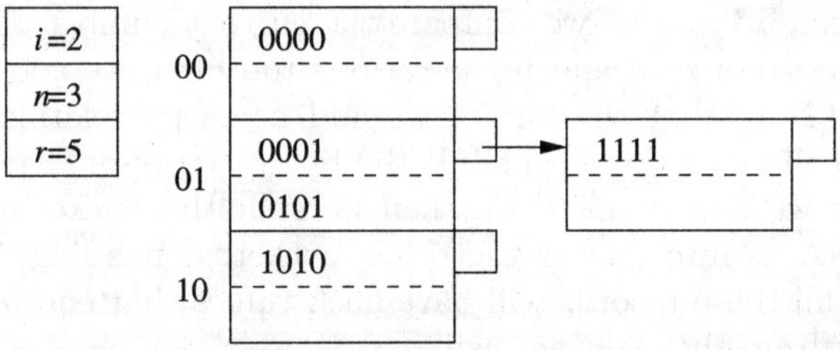

Figure 28: Overflow blocks are used if necessary

Finally, consider the insertion of a record whose search key hashes to 0111. The last two bits are 11, but bucket 11 does not yet exist. We therefore redirect this record to bucket 01, whose number differs by having a 0 in the first bit. The new record fits in the overflow block of this bucket.

However, the ratio of the number of records to buckets has exceeded 1.7, so we must create a new bucket, numbered 11. Coincidentally, this bucket is the one we wanted for the new record. We split the four records in bucket 01, with 0001 and 0101 remaining, and 0111 and 1111 going to the new bucket. Since bucket 01 now has only two records, we can delete the overflow block. The hash table is now as shown in Fig. 29.

Notice that the next time we insert a record into Fig. 29, we shall exceed

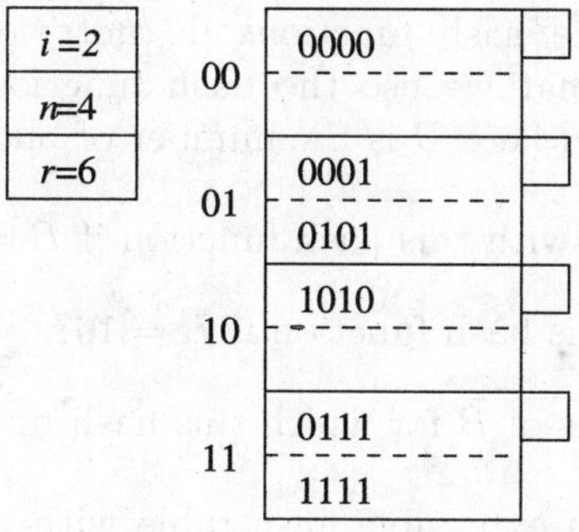

Figure 29: Adding a fourth bucket

the 1.7 ratio of records to buckets. Then, we shall raise n to 5 and i becomes 3. □

Lookup in a linear hash table follows the procedure we described for selecting the bucket in which an inserted record belongs. If the record we wish to look up is not in that bucket, it cannot be anywhere.

3.9 Exercises for Section 3

Exercise 3.1: Show what happens to the buckets in Fig. 20 if the following insertions and deletions occur:

i. Records g through j are inserted into buckets 0 through 3, respectively.

ii. Records a and b are deleted.

iii. Records k through n are inserted into buckets 0 through 3, respectively.

iv. Records c and d are deleted.

Exercise 3.2: We did not discuss how deletions can be carried out in a linear or extensible hash table. The mechanics of locating the record(s) to be deleted should be obvious. What method would you suggest for executing the deletion? In particular, what are the advantages and disadvantages of restructuring the table if its smaller size after deletion allows for compression of certain blocks?

! **Exercise 3.3:** The material of this section assumes that search keys are unique. However, only small modifications are needed to allow the techniques to work for search keys with duplicates. Describe the necessary changes to insertion, deletion, and lookup algorithms, and suggest the major problems that arise when there are duplicates in each of the following kinds of hash tables: (a) simple (b) linear (c) extensible.

! **Exercise 3.4:** Some hash functions do not work as well as theoretically possible. Suppose that we use the hash function on integer keys i defined by $h(i) = i^2 \bmod B$, where B is the number of buckets.

a) What is wrong with this hash function if $B = 10$?

b) How good is this hash function if $B = 16$?

c) Are there values of B for which this hash function is useful?

Exercise 3.5: In an extensible hash table with n records per block, what is the probability that an overflowing block will have to be handled recursively; i.e., all members of the block will go into the same one of the two blocks created in the split?

Exercise 3.6: Suppose keys are hashed to four-bit sequences, as in our examples of extensible and linear hashing in this section. However, also suppose that blocks can hold three records, rather than the two-record blocks of our examples. If we start with a hash table with two empty blocks (corresponding to 0 and 1), show the organization after we insert records with hashed keys:

a) $0000, 0001, \ldots, 1111$, and the method of hashing is extensible hashing.

b) $0000, 0001, \ldots, 1111$, and the method of hashing is linear hashing with a capacity threshold of 100%.

c) $1111, 1110, \ldots, 0000$, and the method of hashing is extensible hashing.

d) $1111, 1110, \ldots, 0000$, and the method of hashing is linear hashing with a capacity threshold of 75%.

Exercise 3.7: Suppose we use a linear or extensible hashing scheme, but there are pointers to records from outside. These pointers prevent us from moving records between blocks, as is sometimes required by these hashing methods. Suggest several ways that we could modify the structure to allow pointers from outside.

!! **Exercise 3.8:** A linear-hashing scheme with blocks that hold k records uses a threshold constant c, such that the current number of buckets n and the current number of records r are related by $r = ckn$. For instance, in Example 24 we used $k = 2$ and $c = 0.85$, so there were 1.7 records per bucket; i.e., $r = 1.7n$.

a) Suppose for convenience that each key occurs exactly its expected number of times.[7] As a function of c, k, and n, how many blocks, including overflow blocks, are needed for the structure?

[7]This assumption does not mean all buckets have the same number of records, because some buckets represent twice as many keys as others.

b) Keys will not generally distribute equally, but rather the number of records with a given key (or suffix of a key) will be *Poisson distributed.* That is, if λ is the expected number of records with a given key suffix, then the actual number of such records will be i with probability $e^{-\lambda}\lambda^i/i!$. Under this assumption, calculate the expected number of blocks used, as a function of c, k, and n.

! **Exercise 3.9:** Suppose we have a file of 1,000,000 records that we want to hash into a table with 1000 buckets. 100 records will fit in a block, and we wish to keep blocks as full as possible, but not allow two buckets to share a block. What are the minimum and maximum number of blocks that we could need to store this hash table?

4 Multidimensional Indexes

All the index structures discussed so far are *one dimensional*; that is, they assume a single search key, and they retrieve records that match a given search-key value. Although the search key may involve several attributes, the one-dimensional nature of indexes such as B-trees comes from the fact that values must be provided for all attributes of the search key, or the index is useless. So far in this chapter, we took advantage of a one-dimensional search-key space in several ways:

- Indexes on sequential files and B-trees both take advantage of having a single linear order for the keys.
- Hash tables require that the search key be completely known for any lookup. If a key consists of several fields, and even one is unknown, we cannot apply the hash function, but must instead search all the buckets.

In the balance of this chapter, we shall look at index structures that are suitable for multidimensional data. In these structures, any nonempty subset of the fields that form the dimensions can be given values, and some speedup will result.

4.1 Applications of Multidimensional Indexes

There are a number of applications that require us to view data as existing in a 2-dimensional space, or sometimes in higher dimensions. Some of these applications can be supported by conventional DBMS's, but there are also some specialized systems designed for multidimensional applications. One way in which these specialized systems distinguish themselves is by using data structures that support certain kinds of queries that are not common in SQL applications.

One important application of multidimensional indexes involves geographic data. A *geographic information system* stores objects in a (typically) two-dimensional space. The objects may be points or shapes. Often, these databases are maps, where the stored objects could represent houses, roads, bridges, pipelines, and many other physical objects. A suggestion of such a map is in Fig. 30.

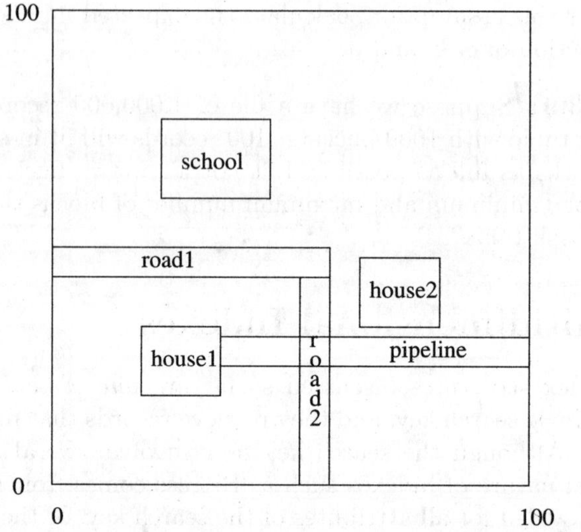

Figure 30: Some objects in 2-dimensional space

However, there are many other uses as well. For instance, an integrated-circuit design is a two-dimensional map of regions, often rectangles, composed of specific materials, called "layers." Likewise, we can think of the windows and icons on a screen as a collection of objects in two-dimensional space.

The queries asked of geographic information systems are not typical of SQL queries, although many can be expressed in SQL with some effort. Examples of these types of queries are:

1. *Partial match queries.* We specify values for one or more dimensions and look for all points matching those values in those dimensions.

2. *Range queries.* We give ranges for one or more of the dimensions, and we ask for the set of points within those ranges. If shapes are represented, then we may ask for the shapes that are partially or wholly within the range. These queries generalize the one-dimensional range queries that we considered in Section 2.4.

3. *Nearest-neighbor queries.* We ask for the closest point to a given point. For instance, if points represent cities, we might want to find the city of over 100,000 population closest to a given small city.

4. *Where-am-I queries.* We are given a point and we want to know in which shape, if any, the point is located. A familiar example is what happens

when you click your mouse, and the system determines which of the displayed elements you were clicking.

4.2 Executing Range Queries Using Conventional Indexes

Now, let us consider to what extent one-dimensional indexes help in answering range queries. Suppose for simplicity that there are two dimensions, x and y. We could put a secondary index on each of the dimensions, x and y. Using a B-tree for each would make it especially easy to get a range of values for each dimension.

Given ranges in both dimensions, we could begin by using the B-tree for x to get pointers to all of the records in the range for x. Next, we use the B-tree for y to get pointers to the records for all points whose y-coordinate is in the range for y. Then, we intersect these pointers, using the idea of Section 1.7. If the pointers fit in main memory, then the total number of disk I/O's is the number of leaf nodes of each B-tree that need to be examined, plus a few I/O's for finding our way down the B-trees (see Section 2.7). To this amount we must add the disk I/O's needed to retrieve all the matching records, however many they may be.

Example 26 : Let us consider a hypothetical set of 1,000,000 points distributed randomly in a space in which both the x- and y-coordinates range from 0 to 1000. Suppose that 100 point records fit on a block, and an average B-tree leaf has about 200 key-pointer pairs (recall that not all slots of a B-tree block are necessarily occupied, at any given time). We shall assume there are B-tree indexes on both x and y.

Imagine we are given the range query asking for points in the square of side 100 surrounding the center of the space, that is, $450 \le x \le 550$ and $450 \le y \le 550$. Using the B-tree for x, we can find pointers to all the records with x in the range; there should be about 100,000 pointers, and this number of pointers should fit in main memory. Similarly, we use the B-tree for y to get the pointers to all the records with y in the desired range; again there are about 100,000 of them. Approximately 10,000 pointers will be in the intersection of these two sets, and it is the records reached by the 10,000 pointers in the intersection that form our answer.

Now, let us estimate the number of disk I/O's needed to answer the range query. First, as we pointed out in Section 2.7, it is generally feasible to keep the root of any B-tree in main memory. Section 2.4 showed how to access the 100,000 pointers in either dimension by examining one intermediate-level node and all the leaves that contain the desired pointers. Since we assumed leaves have about 200 key-pointer pairs each, we shall have to look at about 500 leaf blocks in each of the B-trees. When we add in one intermediate node per B-tree, we have a total of 1002 disk I/O's.

Finally, we have to retrieve the blocks containing the 10,000 desired records.

If they are stored randomly, we must expect that they will be on almost 10,000 different blocks. Since the entire file of a million records is assumed stored over 10,000 blocks, packed 100 to a block, we essentially have to look at every block of the data file anyway. Thus, in this example at least, conventional indexes have been little if any help in answering the range query. Of course, if the range were smaller, then constructing the intersection of the two pointer sets would allow us to limit the search to a fraction of the blocks in the data file. □

4.3 Executing Nearest-Neighbor Queries Using Conventional Indexes

Almost any data structure we use will allow us to answer a nearest-neighbor query by picking a range in each dimension, asking the range query, and selecting the point closest to the target within that range. Unfortunately, there are two things that could go wrong:

1. There is no point within the selected range.
2. The closest point within the range might not be the closest point overall, as suggested by Fig. 31.

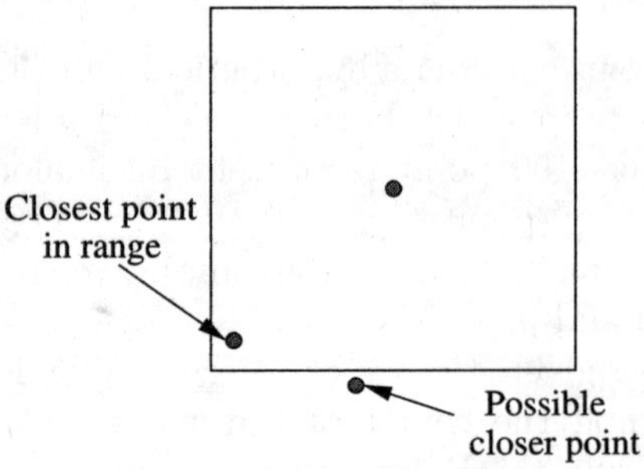

Figure 31: The point is in the range, but there could be a closer point outside the range

The general technique we shall use for answering nearest-neighbor queries is to begin by estimating a range in which the nearest point is likely to be found, and executing the corresponding range query. If no points are found within that range, we repeat with a larger range, until eventually we find at least one point. We then consider whether there is the possibility that a closer point exists, but that point is outside the range just used, as in Fig. 31. If so, we increase the range once more and retrieve all points in the larger range, to check.

4.4 Overview of Multidimensional Index Structures

Most data structures for supporting queries on multidimensional data fall into one of two categories:

1. Hash-table-like approaches.

2. Tree-like approaches.

For each of these structures, we give up something that we have in one-dimensional index structures. With the hash-based schemes — grid files and partitioned hash functions in Section 5 — we no longer have the advantage that the answer to our query is in exactly one bucket. However, each of these schemes limit our search to a subset of the buckets. With the tree-based schemes, we give up at least one of these important properties of B-trees:

1. The balance of the tree, where all leaves are at the same level.

2. The correspondence between tree nodes and disk blocks.

3. The speed with which modifications to the data may be performed.

As we shall see in Section 6, trees often will be deeper in some parts than in others; often the deep parts correspond to regions that have many points. We shall also see that it is common that the information corresponding to a tree node is considerably smaller than what fits in one block. It is thus necessary to group nodes into blocks in some useful way.

5 Hash Structures for Multidimensional Data

In this section we shall consider two data structures that generalize hash tables built using a single key. In each case, the bucket for a point is a function of all the attributes or dimensions. One scheme, called the "grid file," usually doesn't "hash" values along the dimensions, but rather partitions the dimensions by sorting the values along that dimension. The other, called "partitioned hashing," does "hash" the various dimensions, with each dimension contributing to the bucket number.

5.1 Grid Files

One of the simplest data structures that often outperforms single-dimension indexes for queries involving multidimensional data is the *grid file*. Think of the space of points partitioned in a grid. In each dimension, *grid lines* partition the space into *stripes.* Points that fall on a grid line will be considered to belong to the stripe for which that grid line is the lower boundary. The number of grid lines in different dimensions may vary, and there may be different spacings between adjacent grid lines, even between lines in the same dimension.

Example 27: Let us introduce a running example for multidimensional indexes: "who buys gold jewelry?" Imagine a database of customers who have bought gold jewelry. To make things simple, we assume that the only relevant attributes are the customer's age and salary. Our example database has twelve customers, which we can represent by the following age-salary pairs:

(25, 60)	(45, 60)	(50, 75)	(50, 100)
(50, 120)	(70, 110)	(85, 140)	(30, 260)
(25, 400)	(45, 350)	(50, 275)	(60, 260)

In Fig. 32 we see these twelve points located in a 2-dimensional space. We have also selected some grid lines in each dimension. For this simple example, we have chosen two lines in each dimension, dividing the space into nine rectangular regions, but there is no reason why the same number of lines must be used in each dimension. In general, a rectangle includes points on its lower and left boundaries, but not on its upper and right boundaries. For instance, the central rectangle in Fig. 32 represents points with $40 \leq age < 55$ and $90 \leq salary < 225$. □

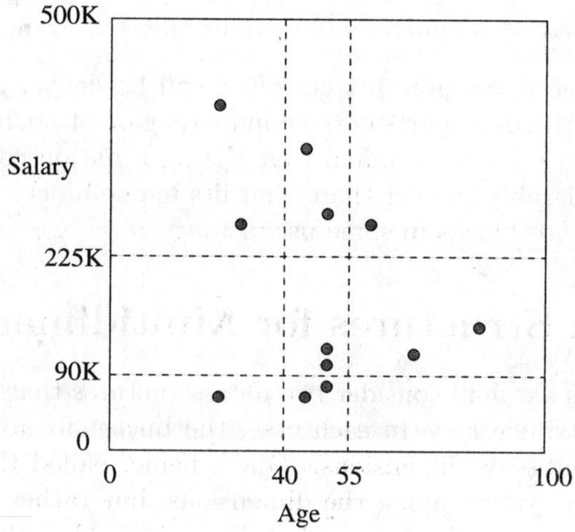

Figure 32: A grid file

5.2 Lookup in a Grid File

Each of the regions into which a space is partitioned can be thought of as a bucket of a hash table, and each of the points in that region has its record placed in a block belonging to that bucket. If needed, overflow blocks can be used to increase the size of a bucket.

Instead of a one-dimensional array of buckets, as is found in conventional hash tables, the grid file uses an array whose number of dimensions is the same as for the data file. To locate the proper bucket for a point, we need to know, for each dimension, the list of values at which the grid lines occur. Hashing a point is thus somewhat different from applying a hash function to the values of its components. Rather, we look at each component of the point and determine the position of the point in the grid for that dimension. The positions of the point in each of the dimensions together determine the bucket.

Example 28 : Figure 33 shows the data of Fig. 32 placed in buckets. Since the grids in both dimensions divide the space into three regions, the bucket array is a 3×3 matrix. Two of the buckets:

1. Salary between \$90K and \$225K and age between 0 and 40, and
2. Salary below \$90K and age above 55

are empty, and we do not show a block for that bucket. The other buckets are shown, with the artificially low maximum of two data points per block. In this simple example, no bucket has more than two members, so no overflow blocks are needed. □

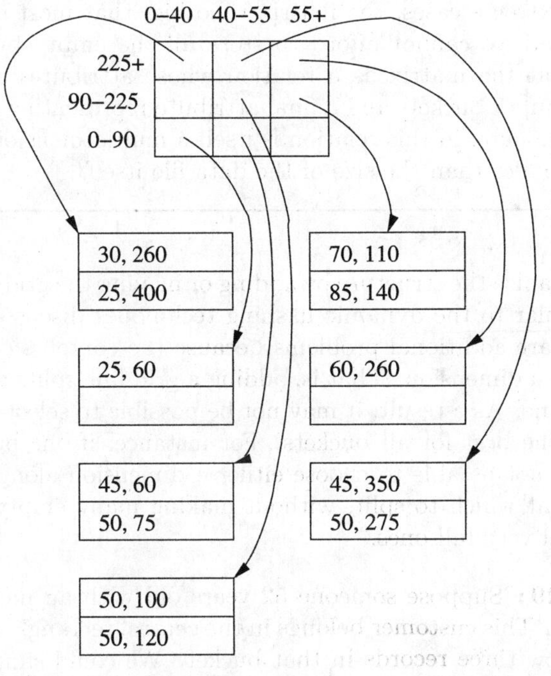

Figure 33: A grid file representing the points of Fig. 32

5.3 Insertion Into Grid Files

When we insert a record into a grid file, we follow the procedure for lookup of the record, and we place the new record in that bucket. If there is room in the block for the bucket then there is nothing more to do. The problem occurs when there is no room in the bucket. There are two general approaches:

1. Add overflow blocks to the buckets, as needed.

Accessing Buckets of a Grid File

While finding the proper coordinates for a point in a three-by-three grid like Fig. 33 is easy, we should remember that the grid file may have a very large number of stripes in each dimension. If so, then we must create an index for each dimension. The search key for an index is the set of partition values in that dimension.

Given a value v in some coordinate, we search for the greatest key value w less than or equal to v. Associated with w in that index will be the row or column of the matrix into which v falls. Given values in each dimension, we can find where in the matrix the pointer to the bucket falls. We may then retrieve the block with that pointer directly.

In extreme cases, the matrix is so big, that most of the buckets are empty and we cannot afford to store all the empty buckets. Then, we must treat the matrix as a relation whose attributes are the corners of the nonempty buckets and a final attribute representing the pointer to the bucket. Lookup in this relation is itself a multidimensional search, but its size is smaller than the size of the data file itself.

2. Reorganize the structure by adding or moving the grid lines. This approach is similar to the dynamic hashing techniques discussed in Section 3, but there are additional problems because the contents of buckets are linked across a dimension. That is, adding a grid line splits all the buckets along that line. As a result, it may not be possible to select a new grid line that does the best for all buckets. For instance, if one bucket is too big, we might not be able to choose either a dimension along which to split or a point at which to split, without making many empty buckets or leaving several very full ones.

Example 29: Suppose someone 52 years old with an income of \$200K buys gold jewelry. This customer belongs in the central rectangle of Fig. 32. However, there are now three records in that bucket. We could simply add an overflow block. If we want to split the bucket, then we need to choose either the age or salary dimension, and we need to choose a new grid line to create the division. There are only three ways to introduce a grid line that will split the central bucket so two points are on one side and one on the other, which is the most even possible split in this case.

1. A vertical line, such as age = 51, that separates the two 50's from the 52. This line does nothing to split the buckets above or below, since both points of each of the other buckets for age 40–55 are to the left of the line age = 51.

2. A horizontal line that separates the point with salary = 200 from the other two points in the central bucket. We may as well choose a number like 130, which also splits the bucket to the right (that for age 55–100 and salary 90–225).

3. A horizontal line that separates the point with salary = 100 from the other two points. Again, we would be advised to pick a number like 115 that also splits the bucket to the right.

Choice (1) is probably not advised, since it doesn't split any other bucket; we are left with more empty buckets and have not reduced the size of any occupied buckets, except for the one we had to split. Choices (2) and (3) are equally good, although we might pick (2) because it puts the horizontal grid line at salary = 130, which is closer to midway between the upper and lower limits of 90 and 225 than we get with choice (3). The resulting partition into buckets is shown in Fig. 34. □

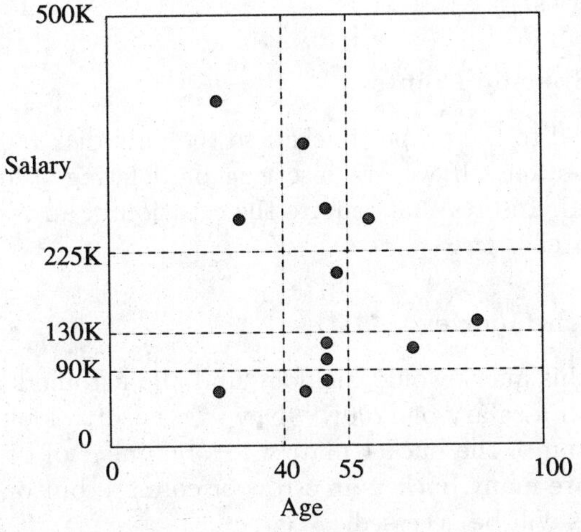

Figure 34: Insertion of the point $(52, 200)$ followed by splitting of buckets

5.4 Performance of Grid Files

Let us consider how many disk I/O's a grid file requires on various types of queries. We have been focusing on the two-dimensional version of grid files, although they can be used for any number of dimensions. One major problem in the high-dimensional case is that the number of buckets grows exponentially with the number of dimensions. If large portions of a space are empty, then there will be many empty buckets. We can envision the problem even in two dimensions. Suppose that there were a high correlation between age and salary, so all points in Fig. 32 lay along the diagonal. Then no matter where we placed the grid lines, the buckets off the diagonal would have to be empty.

However, if the data is well distributed, and the data file itself is not too large, then we can choose grid lines so that:

1. There are sufficiently few buckets that we can keep the bucket matrix in main memory, thus not incurring disk I/O to consult it, or to add rows or columns to the matrix when we introduce a new grid line.

2. We can also keep in memory indexes on the values of the grid lines in each dimension (as per the box "Accessing Buckets of a Grid File"), or we can avoid the indexes altogether and use main-memory binary search of the values defining the grid lines in each dimension.

3. The typical bucket does not have more than a few overflow blocks, so we do not incur too many disk I/O's when we search through a bucket.

Under those assumptions, here is how the grid file behaves on some important classes of queries.

Lookup of Specific Points

We are directed to the proper bucket, so the only disk I/O is what is necessary to read the bucket. If we are inserting or deleting, then an additional disk write is needed. Inserts that require the creation of an overflow block cause an additional write.

Partial-Match Queries

Examples of this query would include "find all customers aged 50," or "find all customers with a salary of $200K." Now, we need to look at all the buckets in a row or column of the bucket matrix. The number of disk I/O's can be quite high if there are many buckets in a row or column, but only a small fraction of all the buckets will be accessed.

Range Queries

A range query defines a rectangular region of the grid, and all points found in the buckets that cover that region will be answers to the query, with the exception of some of the points in buckets on the border of the search region. For example, if we want to find all customers aged 35–45 with a salary of 50–100, then we need to look in the four buckets in the lower left of Fig. 32. In this case, all buckets are on the border, so we may look at a good number of points that are not answers to the query. However, if the search region involves a large number of buckets, then most of them must be interior, and all their points are answers. For range queries, the number of disk I/O's may be large, as we may be required to examine many buckets. However, since range queries tend to produce large answer sets, we typically will examine not too many more blocks than the minimum number of blocks on which the answer could be placed by any organization whatsoever.

Nearest-Neighbor Queries

Given a point P, we start by searching the bucket in which that point belongs. If we find at least one point there, we have a candidate Q for the nearest neighbor. However, it is possible that there are points in adjacent buckets that are closer to P than Q is; the situation is like that suggested in Fig. 31. We have to consider whether the distance between P and a border of its bucket is less than the distance from P to Q. If there are such borders, then the adjacent buckets on the other side of each such border must be searched also. In fact, if buckets are severely rectangular — much longer in one dimension than the other — then it may be necessary to search even buckets that are not adjacent to the one containing point P.

Example 30: Suppose we are looking in Fig. 32 for the point nearest $P = (45, 200)$. We find that $(50, 120)$ is the closest point in the bucket, at a distance of 80.2. No point in the lower three buckets can be this close to $(45, 200)$, because their salary component is at most 90, so we can omit searching them. However, the other five buckets must be searched, and we find that there are actually two equally close points: $(30, 260)$ and $(60, 260)$, at a distance of 61.8 from P. Generally, the search for a nearest neighbor can be limited to a few buckets, and thus a few disk I/O's. However, since the buckets nearest the point P may be empty, we cannot easily put an upper bound on how costly the search is. □

5.5 Partitioned Hash Functions

Hash functions can take a list of values as arguments, although typically there is only one argument. For instance, if a is an integer-valued attribute and b is a character-string-valued attribute, then we could compute $h(a, b)$ by adding the value of a to the value of the ASCII code for each character of b, dividing by the number of buckets, and taking the remainder.

However, such a hash table could be used only in queries that specified values for both a and b. A preferable option is to design the hash function so it produces some number of bits, say k. These k bits are divided among n attributes, so that we produce k_i bits of the hash value from the ith attribute, and $\sum_{i=1}^{n} k_i = k$. More precisely, the hash function h is actually a list of hash functions $(h_1, h_2, \ldots, h_n)$, such that h_i applies to a value for the ith attribute and produces a sequence of k_i bits. The bucket in which to place a tuple with values $(v_1, v_2, \ldots, v_n)$ for the n attributes is computed by concatenating the bit sequences: $h_1(v_1)h_2(v_2)\cdots h_n(v_n)$.

Example 31: If we have a hash table with 10-bit bucket numbers (1024 buckets), we could devote four bits to attribute a and the remaining six bits to attribute b. Suppose we have a tuple with a-value A and b-value B, perhaps with other attributes that are not involved in the hash. If $h_a(A) = 0101$ and $h_b(B) = 111000$, then this tuple hashes to bucket 0101111000, the concatenation of the two bit sequences.

By partitioning the hash function this way, we get some advantage from knowing values for any one or more of the attributes that contribute to the hash function. For instance, if we are given a value A for attribute a, and we find that $h_a(A) = 0101$, then we know that the only tuples with a-value A are in the 64 buckets whose numbers are of the form $0101\cdots$, where the $\cdots$ represents any six bits. Similarly, if we are given the b-value B of a tuple, we can isolate the possible buckets of the tuple to the 16 buckets whose number ends in the six bits $h_b(B)$. □

Example 32 : Suppose we have the "gold jewelry" data of Example 27, which we want to store in a partitioned hash table with eight buckets (i.e., three bits for bucket numbers). We assume as before that two records are all that can fit in one block. We shall devote one bit to the age attribute and the remaining two bits to the salary attribute.

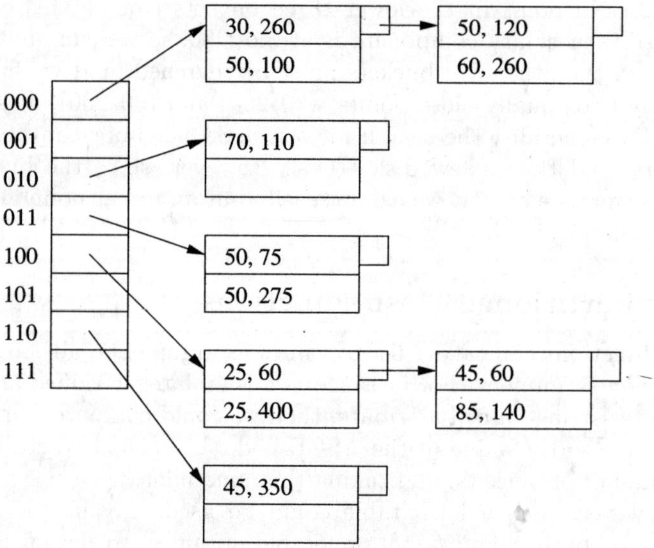

Figure 35: A partitioned hash table

For the hash function on age, we shall take the age modulo 2; that is, a record with an even age will hash into a bucket whose number is of the form $0xy$ for some bits x and y. A record with an odd age hashes to one of the buckets with a number of the form $1xy$. The hash function for salary will be the salary (in thousands) modulo 4. For example, a salary that leaves a remainder of 1 when divided by 4, such as 57K, will be in a bucket whose number is $z01$ for some bit z.

In Fig. 35 we see the data from Example 27 placed in this hash table. Notice that, because we have used mostly ages and salaries divisible by 10, the hash function does not distribute the points too well. Two of the eight buckets have four records each and need overflow blocks, while three other buckets are empty. □

5.6 Comparison of Grid Files and Partitioned Hashing

The performance of the two data structures discussed in this section are quite different. Here are the major points of comparison.

- Partitioned hash tables are actually quite useless for nearest-neighbor queries or range queries. The problem is that physical distance between points is not reflected by the closeness of bucket numbers. Of course we could design the hash function on some attribute a so the smallest values were assigned the first bit string (all 0's), the next values were assigned the next bit string ($00\cdots01$), and so on. If we do so, then we have reinvented the grid file.

- A well chosen hash function will randomize the buckets into which points fall, and thus buckets will tend to be equally occupied. However, grid files, especially when the number of dimensions is large, will tend to leave many buckets empty or nearly so. The intuitive reason is that when there are many attributes, there is likely to be some correlation among at least some of them, so large regions of the space are left empty. For instance, we mentioned in Section 5.4 that a correlation between age and salary would cause most points of Fig. 32 to lie near the diagonal, with most of the rectangle empty. As a consequence, we can use fewer buckets, and/or have fewer overflow blocks in a partitioned hash table than in a grid file.

Thus, if we are required to support only partial match queries, where we specify some attributes' values and leave the other attributes completely unspecified, then the partitioned hash function is likely to outperform the grid file. Conversely, if we need to do nearest-neighbor queries or range queries frequently, then we would prefer to use a grid file.

5.7 Exercises for Section 5

Exercise 5.1: In Fig. 36 are specifications for twelve PC's. Suppose we wish to design an index on speed and hard-disk size only.

a) Choose five grid lines (total for the two dimensions), so that there are no more than two points in any bucket.

! b) Can you separate the points with at most two per bucket if you use only four grid lines? Either show how or argue that it is not possible.

model	*speed*	*ram*	*hd*
1001	2.66	1024	250
1002	2.10	512	250
1003	1.42	512	80
1004	2.80	1024	250
1005	3.20	512	250
1006	3.20	1024	320
1007	2.20	1024	200
1008	2.20	2048	250
1009	2.00	1024	250
1010	2.80	2048	300
1011	1.86	2048	160
1012	2.80	1024	160

Figure 36: Some PC's and their characteristics

! c) Suggest a partitioned hash function that will partition these points into four buckets with at most four points per bucket.

! **Exercise 5.2:** Suppose we wish to place the data of Fig. 36 in a three-dimensional grid file, based on the speed, ram, and hard-disk attributes. Suggest a partition in each dimension that will divide the data well.

Exercise 5.3: Choose a partitioned hash function with one bit for each of the three attributes speed, ram, and hard-disk that divides the data of Fig. 36 well.

Exercise 5.4: Suppose we place the data of Fig. 36 in a grid file with dimensions for speed and ram only. The partitions are at speeds of 2.00, 2.20, and 2.80, and at ram of 1024 and 2048. Suppose also that only two points can fit in one bucket. Suggest good splits if we insert a point with speed 2.5 and ram 1536.

Exercise 5.5: Suppose we store a relation $R(x, y)$ in a grid file. Both attributes have a range of values from 0 to 1000. The partitions of this grid file happen to be uniformly spaced; for x there are partitions every 20 units, at 20, 40, 60, and so on, while for y the partitions are every 50 units, at 50, 100, 150, and so on.

a) How many buckets do we have to examine to answer the range query

```
SELECT * FROM R
WHERE 310 < x AND x < 400 AND 520 < y AND y < 730;
```

! b) We wish to perform a nearest-neighbor query for the point $(110, 205)$. We begin by searching the bucket with lower-left corner at $(100, 200)$ and upper-right corner at $(120, 250)$, and we find that the closest point in this bucket is $(115, 220)$. What other buckets must be searched to verify that this point is the closest?

!! **Exercise 5.6:** Suppose we have a hash table whose buckets are numbered 0 to $2^n - 1$; i.e., bucket addresses are n bits long. We wish to store in the table a relation with two attributes x and y. A query will specify either a value for x or y, but never both. With probability p, it is x whose value is specified.

a) Suppose we partition the hash function so that m bits are devoted to x and the remaining $n - m$ bits to y. As a function of m, n, and p, what is the expected number of buckets that must be examined to answer a random query?

b) For what value of m (as a function of n and p) is the expected number of buckets minimized? Do not worry that this m is unlikely to be an integer.

6 Tree Structures for Multidimensional Data

We shall now consider four more structures that are useful for range queries or nearest-neighbor queries on multidimensional data. In order, we shall consider:

1. Multiple-key indexes.
2. *kd*-trees.
3. Quad trees.
4. R-trees.

The first three are intended for sets of points. The R-tree is commonly used to represent sets of regions; it is also useful for points.

6.1 Multiple-Key Indexes

Suppose we have several attributes representing dimensions of our data points, and we want to support range queries or nearest-neighbor queries on these points. A simple tree scheme for accessing these points is an index of indexes, or more generally a tree in which the nodes at each level are indexes for one attribute.

The idea is suggested in Fig. 37 for the case of two attributes. The "root of the tree" is an index for the first of the two attributes. This index could be any type of conventional index, such as a B-tree or a hash table. The index associates with each of its search-key values — i.e., values for the first attribute — a pointer to another index. If V is a value of the first attribute,

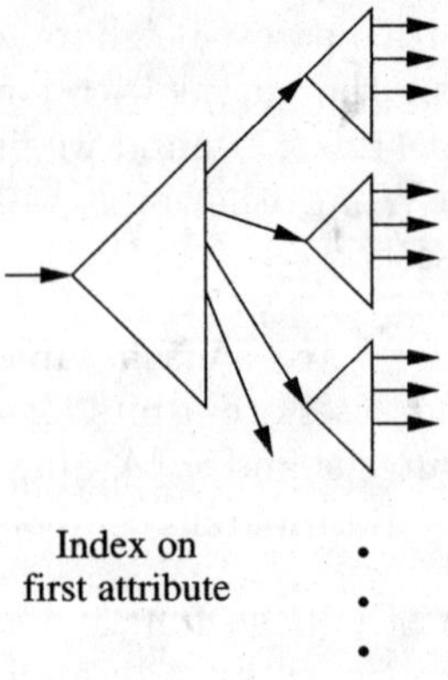

Figure 37: Using nested indexes on different keys

then the index we reach by following key V and its pointer is an index into the set of points that have V for their value in the first attribute and any value for the second attribute.

Example 33: Figure 38 shows a multiple-key index for our running "gold jewelry" example, where the first attribute is age, and the second attribute is salary. The root index, on age, is suggested at the left of Fig. 38. At the right of Fig. 38 are seven indexes that provide access to the points themselves. For example, if we follow the pointer associated with age 50 in the root index, we get to a smaller index where salary is the key, and the four key values in the index are the four salaries associated with points that have age 50: salaries 75, 100, 120, and 275. □

In a multiple-key index, some of the second- or higher-level indexes may be very small. For example, Fig 38 has four second-level indexes with but a single pair. Thus, it may be appropriate to implement these indexes as simple tables that are packed several to a block.

6.2 Performance of Multiple-Key Indexes

Let us consider how a multiple key index performs on various kinds of multidimensional queries. We shall concentrate on the case of two attributes, although the generalization to more than two attributes is unsurprising.

Partial-Match Queries

If the first attribute is specified, then the access is quite efficient. We use the root index to find the one subindex that leads to the points we want. On the

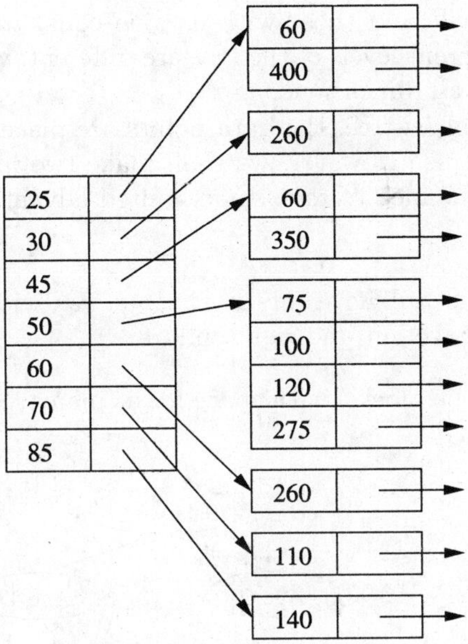

Figure 38: Multiple-key indexes for age/salary data

other hand, if the first attribute does not have a specified value, then we must search every subindex, a potentially time-consuming process.

Range Queries

The multiple-key index works quite well for a range query, provided the individual indexes themselves support range queries on their attribute — B-trees or indexed-sequential files, for instance. To answer a range query, we use the root index and the range of the first attribute to find all of the subindexes that might contain answer points. We then search each of these subindexes, using the range specified for the second attribute.

Nearest-Neighbor Queries

These queries can be answered by a series of range queries, as described in Section 4.3.

6.3 *kd*-Trees

A *kd*-tree (k-dimensional search tree) is a main-memory data structure generalizing the binary search tree to multidimensional data. We shall present the idea and then discuss how the idea has been adapted to the block model of storage. A *kd*-tree is a binary tree in which interior nodes have an associated attribute a and a value V that splits the data points into two parts: those with

a-value less than V and those with a-value equal to or greater than V. The attributes at different levels of the tree are different, with levels rotating among the attributes of all dimensions.

In the classical *kd*-tree, the data points are placed at the nodes, just as in a binary search tree. However, we shall make two modifications in our initial presentation of the idea to take some limited advantage of the block model of storage.

1. Interior nodes will have only an attribute, a dividing value for that attribute, and pointers to left and right children.

2. Leaves will be blocks, with space for as many records as a block can hold.

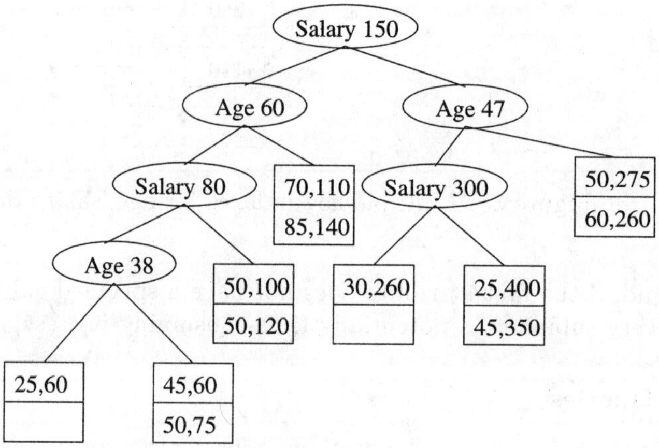

Figure 39: A *kd*-tree

Example 34: In Fig. 39 is a *kd*-tree for the twelve points of our running gold-jewelry example. We use blocks that hold only two records for simplicity; these blocks and their contents are shown as square leaves. The interior nodes are ovals with an attribute — either age or salary — and a value. For instance, the root splits by salary, with all records in the left subtree having a salary less than \$150K, and all records in the right subtree having a salary at least \$150K.

At the second level, the split is by age. The left child of the root splits at age 60, so everything in its left subtree will have age less than 60 and salary less than \$150K. Its right subtree will have age at least 60 and salary less than \$150K. Figure 40 suggests how the various interior nodes split the space of points into leaf blocks. For example, the horizontal line at salary = 150 represents the split at the root. The space below that line is split vertically at age 60, while the space above is split at age 47, corresponding to the decision at the right child of the root. □

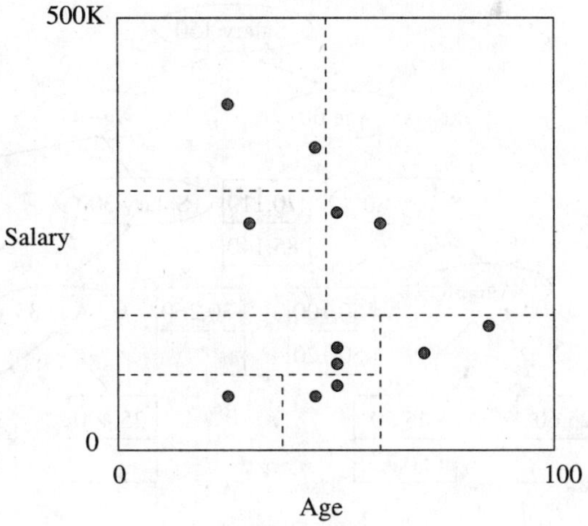

Figure 40: The partitions implied by the tree of Fig. 39

6.4 Operations on *kd*-Trees

A lookup of a tuple, given values for all dimensions, proceeds as in a binary search tree. We make a decision which way to go at each interior node and are directed to a single leaf, whose block we search.

To perform an insertion, we proceed as for a lookup. We are eventually directed to a leaf, and if its block has room we put the new data point there. If there is no room, we split the block into two, and we divide its contents according to whatever attribute is appropriate at the level of the leaf being split. We create a new interior node whose children are the two new blocks, and we install at that interior node a splitting value that is appropriate for the split we have just made.[8]

Example 35 : Suppose someone 35 years old with a salary of \$500K buys gold jewelry. Starting at the root, since the salary is at least \$150K we go to the right. There, we compare the age 35 with the age 47 at the node, which directs us to the left. At the third level, we compare salaries again, and our salary is greater than the splitting value, \$300K. We are thus directed to a leaf containing the points $(25, 400)$ and $(45, 350)$, along with the new point $(35, 500)$.

There isn't room for three records in this block, so we must split it. The fourth level splits on age, so we have to pick some age that divides the records as evenly as possible. The median value, 35, is a good choice, so we replace the leaf by an interior node that splits on age = 35. To the left of this interior node is a leaf block with only the record $(25, 400)$, while to the right is a leaf block with the other two records, as shown in Fig. 41. □

[8]One problem that might arise is a situation where there are so many points with the same value in a given dimension that the bucket has only one value in that dimension and cannot be split. We can try splitting along another dimension, or we can use an overflow block.

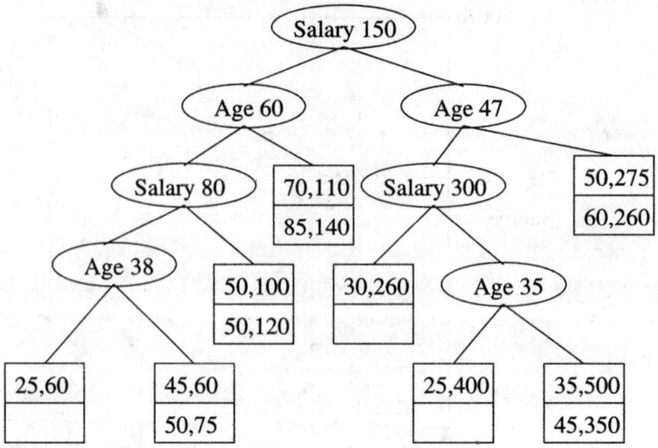

Figure 41: Tree after insertion of (35, 500)

The more complex queries discussed in this chapter are also supported by a *kd*-tree. Here are the key ideas and synopses of the algorithms:

Partial-Match Queries

If we are given values for some of the attributes, then we can go one way when we are at a level belonging to an attribute whose value we know. When we don't know the value of the attribute at a node, we must explore both of its children. For example, if we ask for all points with age = 50 in the tree of Fig. 39, we must look at both children of the root, since the root splits on salary. However, at the left child of the root, we need go only to the left, and at the right child of the root we need only explore its right subtree. For example, if the tree is perfectly balanced and the index has two dimensions, one of which is specified in the search, then we would have to explore both ways at every other level, ultimately reaching about the square root of the total number of leaves.

Range Queries

Sometimes, a range will allow us to move to only one child of a node, but if the range straddles the splitting value at the node then we must explore both children. For example, given the range of ages 35 to 55 and the range of salaries from \$100K to \$200K, we would explore the tree of Fig. 39 as follows. The salary range straddles the \$150K at the root, so we must explore both children. At the left child, the range is entirely to the left, so we move to the node with salary \$80K. Now, the range is entirely to the right, so we reach the leaf with records (50, 100) and (50, 120), both of which meet the range query. Returning to the right child of the root, the splitting value age = 47 tells us to look at both subtrees. At the node with salary \$300K, we can go only to the left, finding the point (30, 260), which is actually outside the range. At the right child of the node for age = 47, we find two other points, both of which are outside the range.

6.5 Adapting *kd*-Trees to Secondary Storage

Suppose we store a file in a *kd*-tree with n leaves. Then the average length of a path from the root to a leaf will be about $\log_2 n$, as for any binary tree. If we store each node in a block, then as we traverse a path we must do one disk I/O per node. For example, if $n = 1000$, then we need about 10 disk I/O's, much more than the 2 or 3 disk I/O's that would be typical for a B-tree, even on a much larger file. In addition, since interior nodes of a *kd*-tree have relatively little information, most of the block would be wasted space. Two approaches to the twin problems of long paths and unused space are:

1. *Multiway Branches at Interior Nodes.* Interior nodes of a *kd*-tree could look more like B-tree nodes, with many key-pointer pairs. If we had n keys at a node, we could split values of an attribute a into $n+1$ ranges. If there were $n+1$ pointers, we could follow the appropriate one to a subtree that contained only points with attribute a in that range.

2. *Group Interior Nodes Into Blocks.* We could pack many interior nodes, each with two children, into a single block. To minimize the number of blocks that we must read from disk while traveling down one path, we are best off including in one block a node and all its descendants for some number of levels. That way, once we retrieve the block with this node, we are sure to use some additional nodes on the same block, saving disk I/O's.

6.6 Quad Trees

In a *quad tree*, each interior node corresponds to a square region in two dimensions, or to a k-dimensional cube in k dimensions. As with the other data structures in this chapter, we shall consider primarily the two-dimensional case. If the number of points in a square is no larger than what will fit in a block, then we can think of this square as a leaf of the tree, and it is represented by the block that holds its points. If there are too many points to fit in one block, then we treat the square as an interior node, with children corresponding to its four quadrants.

Example 36: Figure 42 shows the gold-jewelry data points organized into regions that correspond to nodes of a quad tree. For ease of calculation, we have restricted the usual space so salary ranges between 0 and \$400K, rather than up to \$500K as in other examples of this chapter. We continue to make the assumption that only two records can fit in a block.

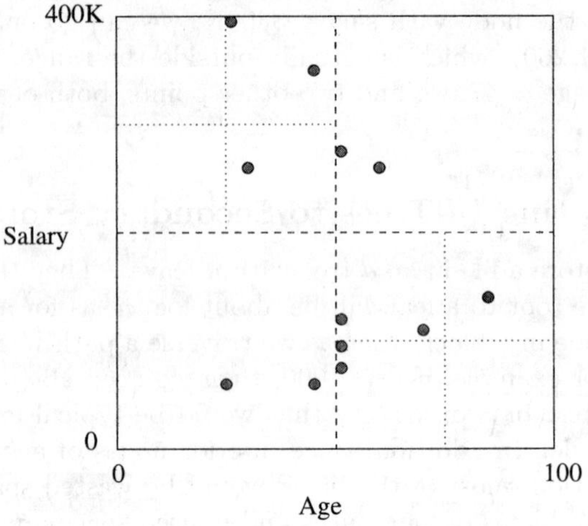

Figure 42: Data organized in a quad tree

Figure 43 shows the tree explicitly. We use the compass designations for the quadrants and for the children of a node (e.g., SW stands for the southwest quadrant — the points to the left and below the center). The order of children is always as indicated at the root. Each interior node indicates the coordinates of the center of its region.

Since the entire space has 12 points, and only two will fit in one block, we must split the space into quadrants, which we show by the dashed line in Fig. 42. Two of the resulting quadrants — the southwest and northeast — have only two points. They can be represented by leaves and need not be split further.

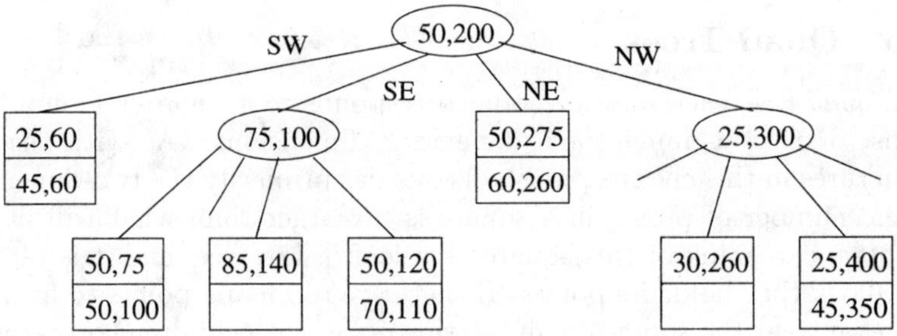

Figure 43: A quad tree

The remaining two quadrants each have more than two points. Both are split into subquadrants, as suggested by the dotted lines in Fig. 42. Each of the resulting quadrants has at most two points, so no more splitting is necessary. □

Since interior nodes of a quad tree in k dimensions have 2^k children, there is a range of k where nodes fit conveniently into blocks. For instance, if 128, or 2^7, pointers can fit in a block, then $k = 7$ is a convenient number of dimensions. However, for the 2-dimensional case, the situation is not much better than for *kd*-trees; an interior node has four children. Moreover, while we can choose the splitting point for a *kd*-tree node, we are constrained to pick the center of a quad-tree region, which may or may not divide the points in that region evenly. Especially when the number of dimensions is large, we expect to find many null pointers (corresponding to empty quadrants) in interior nodes. Of course we can be somewhat clever about how high-dimension nodes are represented, and keep only the non-null pointers and a designation of which quadrant the pointer represents, thus saving considerable space.

We shall not go into detail regarding the standard operations that we discussed in Section 6.4 for *kd*-trees. The algorithms for quad trees resemble those for *kd*-trees.

6.7 R-Trees

An *R-tree* (region tree) is a data structure that captures some of the spirit of a B-tree for multidimensional data. Recall that a B-tree node has a set of keys that divide a line into segments. Points along that line belong to only one segment, as suggested by Fig. 44. The B-tree thus makes it easy for us to find points; if we think the point is somewhere along the line represented by a B-tree node, we can determine a unique child of that node where the point could be found.

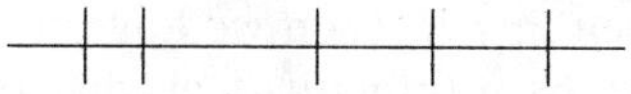

Figure 44: A B-tree node divides keys along a line into disjoint segments

An R-tree, on the other hand, represents data that consists of 2-dimensional, or higher-dimensional regions, which we call *data regions.* An interior node of an R-tree corresponds to some *interior region*, or just "region," which is not normally a data region. In principle, the region can be of any shape, although in practice it is usually a rectangle or other simple shape. The R-tree node has, in place of keys, subregions that represent the contents of its children. The subregions are allowed to overlap, although it is desirable to keep the overlap small.

Figure 45 suggests a node of an R-tree that is associated with the large solid rectangle. The dotted rectangles represent the subregions associated with four of its children. Notice that the subregions do not cover the entire region, which is satisfactory as long as each data region that lies within the large region is wholly contained within one of the small regions.

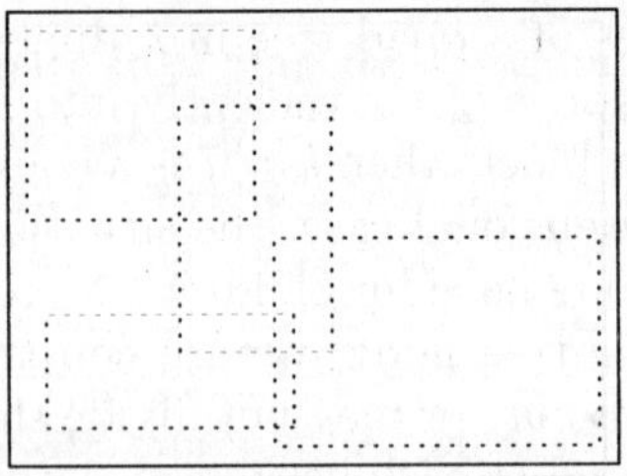

Figure 45: The region of an R-tree node and subregions of its children

6.8 Operations on R-Trees

A typical query for which an R-tree is useful is a "where-am-I" query, which specifies a point P and asks for the data region or regions in which the point lies. We start at the root, with which the entire region is associated. We examine the subregions at the root and determine which children of the root correspond to interior regions that contain point P. Note that there may be zero, one, or several such regions.

If there are zero regions, then we are done; P is not in any data region. If there is at least one interior region that contains P, then we must recursively search for P at the child corresponding to *each* such region. When we reach one or more leaves, we shall find the actual data regions, along with either the complete record for each data region or a pointer to that record.

When we insert a new region R into an R-tree, we start at the root and try to find a subregion into which R fits. If there is more than one such region, then we pick one, go to its corresponding child, and repeat the process there. If there is no subregion that contains R, then we have to expand one of the subregions. Which one to pick may be a difficult decision. Intuitively, we want to expand regions as little as possible, so we might ask which of the children's subregions would have their area increased as little as possible, change the boundary of that region to include R, and recursively insert R at the corresponding child.

Eventually, we reach a leaf, where we insert the region R. However, if there is no room for R at that leaf, then we must split the leaf. How we split the leaf is subject to some choice. We generally want the two subregions to be as small as possible, yet they must, between them, cover all the data regions of the original leaf. Having split the leaf, we replace the region and pointer for the original leaf at the node above by a pair of regions and pointers corresponding to the two new leaves. If there is room at the parent, we are done. Otherwise, as in a B-tree, we recursively split nodes going up the tree.

Example 37: Let us consider the addition of a new region to the map of Fig. 30. Suppose that leaves have room for six regions. Further suppose that the six regions of Fig. 30 are together on one leaf, whose region is represented by the outer (solid) rectangle in Fig. 46.

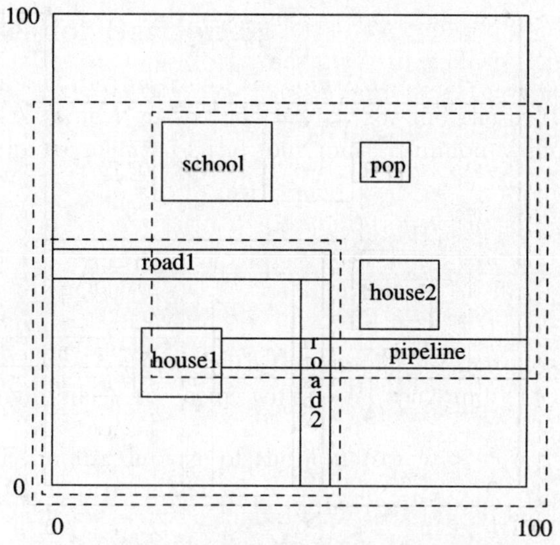

Figure 46: Splitting the set of objects

Now, suppose the local cellular phone company adds a POP (point of presence, or base station) at the position shown in Fig. 46. Since the seven data regions do not fit on one leaf, we shall split the leaf, with four in one leaf and three in the other. Our options are many; we have picked in Fig. 46 the division (indicated by the inner, dashed rectangles) that minimizes the overlap, while splitting the leaves as evenly as possible.

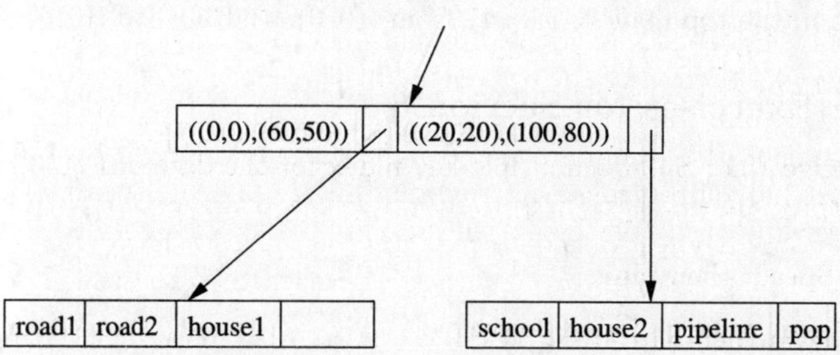

Figure 47: An R-tree

We show in Fig. 47 how the two new leaves fit into the R-tree. The parent of these nodes has pointers to both leaves, and associated with the pointers are the lower-left and upper-right corners of the rectangular regions covered by each leaf. □

Example 38: Suppose we inserted another house below house2, with lower-left coordinates $(70, 5)$ and upper-right coordinates $(80, 15)$. Since this house is

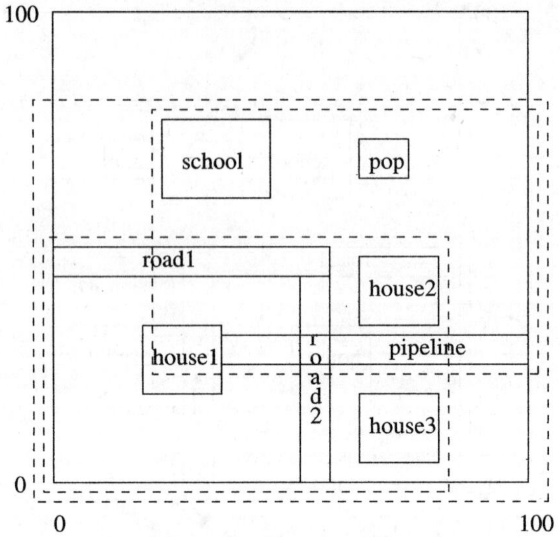

Figure 48: Extending a region to accommodate new data

not wholly contained within either of the leaves' regions, we must choose which region to expand. If we expand the lower subregion, corresponding to the first leaf in Fig. 47, then we add 1000 square units to the region, since we extend it 20 units to the right. If we extend the other subregion by lowering its bottom by 15 units, then we add 1200 square units. We prefer the first, and the new regions are changed in Fig. 48. We also must change the description of the region in the top node of Fig. 47 from $((0,0),\ (60,50))$ to $((0,0),\ (80,50))$. □

6.9 Exercises for Section 6

Exercise 6.1: Show a multiple-key index for the data of Fig. 36 if the indexes are on:

a) Speed, then ram.

b) Ram then hard-disk.

c) Speed, then ram, then hard-disk.

Exercise 6.2: Place the data of Fig. 36 in a *kd*-tree. Assume two records can fit in one block. At each level, pick a separating value that divides the data as evenly as possible. For an order of the splitting attributes choose:

a) Speed, then ram, alternating.

b) Speed, then ram, then hard-disk, alternating.

c) Whatever attribute produces the most even split at each node.

Exercise 6.3: Suppose we have a relation $R(x, y, z)$, where the pair of attributes x and y together form the key. Attribute x ranges from 1 to 100, and y ranges from 1 to 1000. For each x there are records with 100 different values of y, and for each y there are records with 10 different values of x. Note that there are thus 10,000 records in R. We wish to use a multiple-key index that will help us to answer queries of the form

```
SELECT z
FROM R
WHERE x = C AND y = D;
```

where C and D are constants. Assume that blocks can hold ten key-pointer pairs, and we wish to create dense indexes at each level, perhaps with sparse higher-level indexes above them, so that each index starts from a single block. Also assume that initially all index and data blocks are on disk.

a) How many disk I/O's are necessary to answer a query of the above form if the first index is on x?

b) How many disk I/O's are necessary to answer a query of the above form if the first index is on y?

! c) Suppose you were allowed to buffer 11 blocks in memory at all times. Which blocks would you choose, and would you make x or y the first index, if you wanted to minimize the number of additional disk I/O's needed?

Exercise 6.4: For the structure of Exercise 6.3(a), how many disk I/O's are required to answer the range query in which $20 \leq x \leq 35$ and $200 \leq y \leq 350$. Assume data is distributed uniformly; i.e., the expected number of points will be found within any given range.

Exercise 6.5: In the tree of Fig. 39, what new points would be directed to:

a) The block with point $(30, 260)$?

b) The block with points $(50, 100)$ and $(50, 120)$?

Exercise 6.6: Show a possible evolution of the tree of Fig. 41 if we insert the points $(20, 110)$ and then $(40, 400)$.

! **Exercise 6.7:** We mentioned that if a *kd*-tree were perfectly balanced, and we execute a partial-match query in which one of two attributes has a value specified, then we wind up looking at about $\sqrt{n}$ out of the n leaves.

a) Explain why.

b) If the tree split alternately in d dimensions, and we specified values for m of those dimensions, what fraction of the leaves would we expect to have to search?

c) How does the performance of (b) compare with a partitioned hash table?

Exercise 6.8: Place the data of Fig. 36 in a quad tree with dimensions speed and ram. Assume the range for speed is 1.00 to 5.00, and for ram it is 500 to 3500. No leaf of the quad tree should have more than two points.

Exercise 6.9: Repeat Exercise 6.8 with the addition of a third dimension, hard-disk, that ranges from 0 to 400.

! **Exercise 6.10:** If we are allowed to put the central point in a quadrant of a quad tree wherever we want, can we always divide a quadrant into subquadrants with an equal number of points (or as equal as possible, if the number of points in the quadrant is not divisible by 4)? Justify your answer.

! **Exercise 6.11:** Suppose we have a database of 1,000,000 regions, which may overlap. Nodes (blocks) of an R-tree can hold 100 regions and pointers. The region represented by any node has 100 subregions, and the overlap among these regions is such that the total area of the 100 subregions is 150% of the area of the region. If we perform a "where-am-I" query for a given point, how many blocks do we expect to retrieve?

7 Bitmap Indexes

Let us now turn to a type of index that is rather different from those seen so far. We begin by imagining that records of a file have permanent numbers, $1, 2, \ldots, n$. Moreover, there is some data structure for the file that lets us find the ith record easily for any i. A *bitmap index* for a field F is a collection of bit-vectors of length n, one for each possible value that may appear in the field F. The vector for value v has 1 in position i if the ith record has v in field F, and it has 0 there if not.

Example 39: Suppose a file consists of records with two fields, F and G, of type integer and string, respectively. The current file has six records, numbered 1 through 6, with the following values in order: (30, `foo`), (30, `bar`), (40, `baz`), (50, `foo`), (40, `bar`), (30, `baz`).

A bitmap index for the first field, F, would have three bit-vectors, each of length 6. The first, for value 30, is 110001, because the first, second, and sixth records have $F = 30$. The other two, for 40 and 50, respectively, are 001010 and 000100.

A bitmap index for G would also have three bit-vectors, because there are three different strings appearing there. The three bit-vectors are:

Value	Vector
`foo`	100100
`bar`	010010
`baz`	001001

In each case, 1's indicate the records in which the corresponding string appears. □

7.1 Motivation for Bitmap Indexes

It might at first appear that bitmap indexes require much too much space, especially when there are many different values for a field, since the total number of bits is the product of the number of records and the number of values. For example, if the field is a key, and there are n records, then n^2 bits are used among all the bit-vectors for that field. However, compression can be used to make the number of bits closer to n, independent of the number of different values, as we shall see in Section 7.2.

You might also suspect that there are problems managing the bitmap indexes. For example, they depend on the number of a record remaining the same throughout time. How do we find the ith record as the file adds and deletes records? Similarly, values for a field may appear or disappear. How do we find the bitmap for a value efficiently? These and related questions are discussed in Section 7.4.

The compensating advantage of bitmap indexes is that they allow us to answer partial-match queries very efficiently in many situations. In a sense they offer the advantages of buckets that we discussed in Example 7, where we found the `Movie` tuples with specified values in several attributes without first retrieving all the records that matched in each of the attributes. An example will illustrate the point.

Example 40: Recall Example 7, where we queried the `Movie` relation with the query

```
SELECT title FROM Movie
WHERE studioName = 'Disney' AND year = 2005;
```

Suppose there are bitmap indexes on both attributes `studioName` and `year`. Then we can intersect the vectors for `year` = 2005 and `studioName` = `'Disney'`; that is, we take the bitwise AND of these vectors, which will give us a vector with a 1 in position i if and only if the ith `Movie` tuple is for a movie made by Disney in 2005.

If we can retrieve tuples of `Movie` given their numbers, then we need to read only those blocks containing one or more of these tuples, just as we did in Example 7. To intersect the bit vectors, we must read them into memory, which requires a disk I/O for each block occupied by one of the two vectors. As mentioned, we shall later address both matters: accessing records given their numbers in Section 7.4 and making sure the bit-vectors do not occupy too much space in Section 7.2. □

Bitmap indexes can also help answer range queries. We shall consider an example next that both illustrates their use for range queries and shows in detail with short bit-vectors how the bitwise AND and OR of bit-vectors can be used to discover the answer to a query without looking at any records but the ones we want.

Example 41: Consider the gold-jewelry data first introduced in Example 27. Suppose that the twelve points of that example are records numbered from 1 to 12 as follows:

1:	(25, 60)	2:	(45, 60)	3:	(50, 75)	4:	(50, 100)
5:	(50, 120)	6:	(70, 110)	7:	(85, 140)	8:	(30, 260)
9:	(25, 400)	10:	(45, 350)	11:	(50, 275)	12:	(60, 260)

For the first component, age, there are seven different values, so the bitmap index for age consists of the following seven vectors:

25:	100000001000	30:	000000010000	45:	010000000100
50:	001110000010	60:	000000000001	70:	000001000000
85:	000000100000				

For the salary component, there are ten different values, so the salary bitmap index has the following ten bit-vectors:

60:	110000000000	75:	001000000000	100:	000100000000
110:	000001000000	120:	000010000000	140:	000000100000
260:	000000010001	275:	000000000010	350:	000000000100
400:	000000001000				

Suppose we want to find the jewelry buyers with an age in the range 45–55 and a salary in the range 100–200. We first find the bit-vectors for the age values in this range; in this example there are only two: 010000000100 and 001110000010, for 45 and 50, respectively. If we take their bitwise OR, we have a new bit-vector with 1 in position i if and only if the ith record has an age in the desired range. This bit-vector is 011110000110.

Next, we find the bit-vectors for the salaries between 100 and 200 thousand. There are four, corresponding to salaries 100, 110, 120, and 140; their bitwise OR is 000111100000.

The last step is to take the bitwise AND of the two bit-vectors we calculated by OR. That is:

$$011110000110 \text{ AND } 000111100000 = 000110000000$$

We thus find that only the fourth and fifth records, which are $(50, 100)$ and $(50, 120)$, are in the desired range. □

Binary Numbers Won't Serve as a Run-Length Encoding

Suppose we represented a run of i 0's followed by a 1 with the integer i in binary. Then the bit-vector 000101 consists of two runs, of lengths 3 and 1, respectively. The binary representations of these integers are 11 and 1, so the run-length encoding of 000101 is 111. However, a similar calculation shows that the bit-vector 010001 is also encoded by 111; bit-vector 010101 is a third vector encoded by 111. Thus, 111 cannot be decoded uniquely into one bit-vector.

7.2 Compressed Bitmaps

Suppose we have a bitmap index on field F of a file with n records, and there are m different values for field F that appear in the file. Then the number of bits in all the bit-vectors for this index is mn. If, say, blocks are 4096 bytes long, then we can fit 32,768 bits in one block, so the number of blocks needed is $mn/32768$. That number can be small compared to the number of blocks needed to hold the file itself, but the larger m is, the more space the bitmap index takes.

But if m is large, then 1's in a bit-vector will be very rare; precisely, the probability that any bit is 1 is $1/m$. If 1's are rare, then we have an opportunity to encode bit-vectors so that they take much less than n bits on the average. A common approach is called *run-length encoding*, where we represent a *run*, that is, a sequence of i 0's followed by a 1, by some suitable binary encoding of the integer i. We concatenate the codes for each run together, and that sequence of bits is the encoding of the entire bit-vector.

We might imagine that we could just represent integer i by expressing i as a binary number. However, that simple a scheme will not do, because it is not possible to break a sequence of codes apart to determine uniquely the lengths of the runs involved (see the box on "Binary Numbers Won't Serve as a Run-Length Encoding"). Thus, the encoding of integers i that represent a run length must be more complex than a simple binary representation.

We shall study one of many possible schemes for encoding. There are some better, more complex schemes that can improve on the amount of compression achieved here, by almost a factor of 2, but only when typical runs are very long. In our scheme, we first determine how many bits the binary representation of i has. This number j, which is approximately $\log_2 i$, is represented in "unary," by $j-1$ 1's and a single 0. Then, we can follow with i in binary.[9]

Example 42: If $i = 13$, then $j = 4$; that is, we need 4 bits in the binary

[9] Actually, except for the case that $j = 1$ (i.e., $i = 0$ or $i = 1$), we can be sure that the binary representation of i begins with 1. Thus, we can save about one bit per number if we omit this 1 and use only the remaining $j - 1$ bits.

representation of i. Thus, the encoding for i begins with 1110. We follow with i in binary, or 1101. Thus, the encoding for 13 is 11101101.

The encoding for $i = 1$ is 01, and the encoding for $i = 0$ is 00. In each case, $j = 1$, so we begin with a single 0 and follow that 0 with the one bit that represents i. □

If we concatenate a sequence of integer codes, we can always recover the sequence of run lengths and therefore recover the original bit-vector. Suppose we have scanned some of the encoded bits, and we are now at the beginning of a sequence of bits that encodes some integer i. We scan forward to the first 0, to determine the value of j. That is, j equals the number of bits we must scan until we get to the first 0 (including that 0 in the count of bits). Once we know j, we look at the next j bits; i is the integer represented there in binary. Moreover, once we have scanned the bits representing i, we know where the next code for an integer begins, so we can repeat the process.

Example 43: Let us decode the sequence 11101101001011. Starting at the beginning, we find the first 0 at the 4th bit, so $j = 4$. The next 4 bits are 1101, so we determine that the first integer is 13. We are now left with 001011 to decode.

Since the first bit is 0, we know the next bit represents the next integer by itself; this integer is 0. Thus, we have decoded the sequence 13, 0, and we must decode the remaining sequence 1011.

We find the first 0 in the second position, whereupon we conclude that the final two bits represent the last integer, 3. Our entire sequence of run-lengths is thus 13, 0, 3. From these numbers, we can reconstruct the actual bit-vector, 0000000000000110001. □

Technically, every bit-vector so decoded will end in a 1, and any trailing 0's will not be recovered. Since we presumably know the number of records in the file, the additional 0's can be added. However, since 0 in a bit-vector indicates the corresponding record is not in the described set, we don't even have to know the total number of records, and can ignore the trailing 0's.

Example 44: Let us convert some of the bit-vectors from Example 42 to our run-length code. The vectors for the first three ages, 25, 30, and 45, are 100000001000, 000000010000, and 010000000100, respectively. The first of these has the run-length sequence $(0, 7)$. The code for 0 is 00, and the code for 7 is 110111. Thus, the bit-vector for age 25 becomes 00110111.

Similarly, the bit-vector for age 30 has only one run, with seven 0's. Thus, its code is 110111. The bit-vector for age 45 has two runs, $(1, 7)$. Since 1 has the code 01, and we determined that 7 has the code 110111, the code for the third bit-vector is 01110111. □

The compression in Example 44 is not great. However, we cannot see the true benefits when n, the number of records, is small. To appreciate the value of the encoding, suppose that $m = n$, i.e., each value for the field on which the bitmap index is constructed, occurs once. Notice that the code for a run of length i has about $2\log_2 i$ bits. If each bit-vector has a single 1, then it has a single run, and the length of that run cannot be longer than n. Thus, $2\log_2 n$ bits is an upper bound on the length of a bit-vector's code in this case.

Since there are n bit-vectors in the index, the total number of bits to represent the index is at most $2n\log_2 n$. In comparison, the uncompressed bit-vectors for this data would require n^2 bits.

7.3 Operating on Run-Length-Encoded Bit-Vectors

When we need to perform bitwise AND or OR on encoded bit-vectors, we have little choice but to decode them and operate on the original bit-vectors. However, we do not have to do the decoding all at once. The compression scheme we have described lets us decode one run at a time, and we can thus determine where the next 1 is in each operand bit-vector. If we are taking the OR, we can produce a 1 at that position of the output, and if we are taking the AND we produce a 1 if and only if both operands have their next 1 at the same position. The algorithms involved are complex, but an example may make the idea adequately clear.

Example 45: Consider the encoded bit-vectors we obtained in Example 44 for ages 25 and 30: 00110111 and 110111, respectively. We can decode their first runs easily; we find they are 0 and 7, respectively. That is, the first 1 of the bit-vector for 25 occurs in position 1, while the first 1 in the bit-vector for 30 occurs at position 8. We therefore generate 1 in position 1.

Next, we must decode the next run for age 25, since that bit-vector may produce another 1 before age 30's bit-vector produces a 1 at position 8. However, the next run for age 25 is 7, which says that this bit-vector next produces a 1 at position 9. We therefore generate six 0's and the 1 at position 8 that comes from the bit-vector for age 30. The 1 at position 9 from age 25's bit-vector is produced. Neither bit-vector produces any more 1's for the output. We conclude that the OR of these bit-vectors is 100000011. Technically, we must append 000, since uncompressed bit-vectors are of length twelve in this example. □

7.4 Managing Bitmap Indexes

We have described operations on bitmap indexes without addressing three important issues:

1. When we want to find the bit-vector for a given value, or the bit-vectors corresponding to values in a given range, how do we find these efficiently?

2. When we have selected a set of records that answer our query, how do we retrieve those records efficiently?

3. When the data file changes by insertion or deletion of records, how do we adjust the bitmap index on a given field?

Finding Bit-Vectors

Think of each bit-vector as a record whose key is the value corresponding to this bit-vector (although the value itself does not appear in this "record"). Then any secondary index technique will take us efficiently from values to their bit-vectors.

We also need to store the bit-vectors somewhere. It is best to think of them as variable-length records, since they will generally grow as more records are added to the data file.

Finding Records

Now let us consider the second question: once we have determined that we need record k of the data file, how do we find it? Again, techniques we have seen already may be adapted. Think of the kth record as having search-key value k (although this key does not actually appear in the record). We may then create a secondary index on the data file, whose search key is the number of the record.

Handling Modifications to the Data File

There are two aspects to the problem of reflecting data-file modifications in a bitmap index.

1. Record numbers must remain fixed once assigned.

2. Changes to the data file require the bitmap index to change as well.

The consequence of point (1) is that when we delete record i, it is easiest to "retire" its number. Its space is replaced by a "tombstone" in the data file. The bitmap index must also be changed, since the bit-vector that had a 1 in position i must have that 1 changed to 0. Note that we can find the appropriate bit-vector, since we know what value record i had before deletion.

Next consider insertion of a new record. We keep track of the next available record number and assign it to the new record. Then, for each bitmap index, we must determine the value the new record has in the corresponding field and modify the bit-vector for that value by appending a 1 at the end. Technically, all the other bit-vectors in this index get a new 0 at the end, but if we are using a compression technique such as that of Section 7.2, then no change to the compressed values is needed.

As a special case, the new record may have a value for the indexed field that has not been seen before. In that case, we need a new bit-vector for this value, and this bit-vector and its corresponding value need to be inserted into the secondary-index structure that is used to find a bit-vector given its corresponding value.

Lastly, consider a modification to a record i of the data file that changes the value of a field that has a bitmap index, say from value v to value w. We must find the bit-vector for v and change the 1 in position i to 0. If there is a bit-vector for value w, then we change its 0 in position i to 1. If there is not yet a bit-vector for w, then we create it as discussed in the paragraph above for the case when an insertion introduces a new value.

7.5 Exercises for Section 7

Exercise 7.1: For the data of Fig. 36, show the bitmap indexes for the attributes: (a) speed (b) ram (c) hd, both in (i) uncompressed form, and (ii) compressed form using the scheme of Section 7.2.

Exercise 7.2: Using the bitmaps of Example 41, find the jewelry buyers with an age in the range 20–40 and a salary in the range 0–100.

Exercise 7.3: Consider a file of 1,000,000 records, with a field F that has m different values.

a) As a function of m, how many bytes does the bitmap index for F have?

! b) Suppose that the records numbered from 1 to 1,000,000 are given values for the field F in a round-robin fashion, so each value appears every m records. How many bytes would be consumed by a compressed index?

!! **Exercise 7.4:** We suggested in Section 7.2 that it was possible to reduce the number of bits taken to encode number i from the $2\log_2 i$ that we used in that section until it is close to $\log_2 i$. Show how to approach that limit as closely as you like, as long as i is large. *Hint*: We used a unary encoding of the length of the binary encoding that we used for i. Can you encode the length of the code in binary?

Exercise 7.5: Encode, using the scheme of Section 7.2, the following bitmaps:

a) 0110000000100000100.

b) 10000010000001001101.

c) 0001000000000001000001000O.

8 Summary

✦ *Sequential Files*: Several simple file organizations begin by sorting the data file according to some sort key and placing an index on this file.

- ✦ *Dense and Sparse Indexes*: Dense indexes have a key-pointer pair for every record in the data file, while sparse indexes have one key-pointer pair for each block of the data file.

- ✦ *Multilevel Indexes*: It is sometimes useful to put an index on the index file itself, an index file on that, and so on. Higher levels of index must be sparse.

- ✦ *Secondary Indexes*: An index on a search key K can be created even if the data file is not sorted by K. Such an index must be dense.

- ✦ *Inverted Indexes*: The relation between documents and the words they contain is often represented by an index structure with word-pointer pairs. The pointer goes to a place in a "bucket" file where is found a list of pointers to places where that word occurs.

- ✦ *B-trees*: These structures are essentially multilevel indexes, with graceful growth capabilities. Blocks with n keys and $n + 1$ pointers are organized in a tree, with the leaves pointing to records. All nonroot blocks are between half-full and completely full at all times.

- ✦ *Hash Tables*: We can create hash tables out of blocks in secondary memory, much as we can create main-memory hash tables. A hash function maps search-key values to buckets, effectively partitioning the records of a data file into many small groups (the buckets). Buckets are represented by a block and possible overflow blocks.

- ✦ *Extensible Hashing*: This method allows the number of buckets to double whenever any bucket has too many records. It uses an array of pointers to blocks that represent the buckets. To avoid having too many blocks, several buckets can be represented by the same block.

- ✦ *Linear Hashing*: This method grows the number of buckets by 1 each time the ratio of records to buckets exceeds a threshold. Since the population of a single bucket cannot cause the table to expand, overflow blocks for buckets are needed in some situations.

- ✦ *Queries Needing Multidimensional Indexes*: The sorts of queries that need to be supported on multidimensional data include partial-match (all points with specified values in a subset of the dimensions), range queries (all points within a range in each dimension), nearest-neighbor (closest point to a given point), and where-am-I (region or regions containing a given point).

- ✦ *Executing Nearest-Neighbor Queries*: Many data structures allow nearest-neighbor queries to be executed by performing a range query around the target point, and expanding the range if there is no point in that range. We must be careful, because finding a point within a rectangular range may not rule out the possibility of a closer point outside that rectangle.

- *Grid Files*: The grid file slices the space of points in each of the dimensions. The grid lines can be spaced differently, and there can be different numbers of lines for each dimension. Grid files support range queries, partial-match queries, and nearest-neighbor queries well, as long as data is fairly uniform in distribution.

- *Partitioned Hash Tables*: A partitioned hash function constructs some bits of the bucket number from each dimension. They support partial-match queries well, and are not dependent on the data being uniformly distributed.

- *Multiple-Key Indexes*: A simple multidimensional structure has a root that is an index on one attribute, leading to a collection of indexes on a second attribute, which can lead to indexes on a third attribute, and so on. They are useful for range and nearest-neighbor queries.

- kd-*Trees*: These trees are like binary search trees, but they branch on different attributes at different levels. They support partial-match, range, and nearest-neighbor queries well. Some careful packing of tree nodes into blocks must be done to make the structure suitable for secondary-storage operations.

- *Quad Trees*: The quad tree divides a multidimensional cube into quadrants, and recursively divides the quadrants the same way if they have too many points. They support partial-match, range, and nearest-neighbor queries.

- *R-Trees*: This form of tree normally represents a collection of regions by grouping them into a hierarchy of larger regions. It helps with where-am-I queries and, if the atomic regions are actually points, will support the other types of queries studied in this chapter, as well.

- *Bitmap Indexes*: Multidimensional queries are supported by a form of index that orders the points or records and represents the positions of the records with a given value in an attribute by a bit vector. These indexes support range, nearest-neighbor, and partial-match queries.

- *Compressed Bitmaps*: In order to save space, the bitmap indexes, which tend to consist of vectors with very few 1's, are compressed by using a run-length encoding.

9 References

The B-tree was the original idea of Bayer and McCreight [2]. Unlike the B+ tree described here, this formulation had pointers to records at the interior nodes as well as at the leaves. [8] is a survey of B-tree varieties.

Hashing as a data structure goes back to Peterson [19]. Extensible hashing was developed by [9], while linear hashing is from [15]. The book by Knuth [14] contains much information on data structures, including techniques for selecting hash functions and designing hash tables, as well as a number of ideas concerning B-tree variants. The B+ tree formulation (without key values at interior nodes) appeared in the 1973 edition of [14].

Secondary indexes and other techniques for retrieval of documents are covered by [23]. Also, [10] and [1] are surveys of index methods for text documents.

The *kd*-tree is from [4]. Modifications suitable for secondary storage appeared in [5] and [21]. Partitioned hashing and its use in partial-match retieval is from [20] and [7]. However, the design idea from Exercise 5.6 is from [22].

Grid files first appeared in [16] and the quad tree in [11]. The R-tree is from [13], and two extensions [24] and [3] are well known.

The bitmap index has an interesting history. There was a company called Nucleus, founded by Ted Glaser, that patented the idea and developed a DBMS in which the bitmap index was both the index structure and the data representation. The company failed in the late 1980's, but the idea has recently been incorporated into several major commercial database systems. The first published work on the subject was [17]. [18] is a recent expansion of the idea.

There are a number of surveys of multidimensional storage structures. One of the earliest is [6]. More recent surveys are found in [25] and [12]. The former also includes surveys of several other important database topics.

1. R. Baeza-Yates, "Integrating contents and structure in text retrieval," *SIGMOD Record* **25**:1 (1996), pp. 67–79.

2. R. Bayer and E. M. McCreight, "Organization and maintenance of large ordered indexes," *Acta Informatica* **1**:3 (1972), pp. 173–189.

3. N. Beckmann, H.-P. Kriegel, R. Schneider, and B. Seeger, "The R*-tree: an efficient and robust access method for points and rectangles," *Proc. ACM SIGMOD Intl. Conf. on Management of Data* (1990), pp. 322–331.

4. J. L. Bentley, "Multidimensional binary search trees used for associative searching," *Comm. ACM* **18**:9 (1975), pp. 509–517.

5. J. L. Bentley, "Multidimensional binary search trees in database applications," *IEEE Trans. on Software Engineering* **SE-5**:4 (1979), pp. 333-340.

6. J. L. Bentley and J. H. Friedman, "Data structures for range searching," *Computing Surveys* **13**:3 (1979), pp. 397–409.

7. W. A. Burkhard, "Hashing and trie algorithms for partial match retrieval," *ACM Trans. on Database Systems* **1**:2 (1976), pp. 175–187.

8. D. Comer, "The ubiquitous B-tree," *Computing Surveys* **11**:2 (1979), pp. 121–137.

9. R. Fagin, J. Nievergelt, N. Pippenger, and H. R. Strong, "Extendible hashing — a fast access method for dynamic files," *ACM Trans. on Database Systems* **4**:3 (1979), pp. 315–344.

10. C. Faloutsos, "Access methods for text," *Computing Surveys* **17**:1 (1985), pp. 49–74.

11. R. A. Finkel and J. L. Bentley, "Quad trees, a data structure for retrieval on composite keys," *Acta Informatica* **4**:1 (1974), pp. 1–9.

12. V. Gaede and O. Gunther, "Multidimensional access methods," *Computing Surveys* **30**:2 (1998), pp. 170–231.

13. A. Guttman, "R-trees: a dynamic index structure for spatial searching," *Proc. ACM SIGMOD Intl. Conf. on Management of Data* (1984), pp. 47–57.

14. D. E. Knuth, *The Art of Computer Programming, Vol. III, Sorting and Searching, Second Edition*, Addison-Wesley, Reading MA, 1998.

15. W. Litwin, "Linear hashing: a new tool for file and table addressing," *Intl. Conf. on Very Large Databases*, pp. 212–223, 1980.

16. J. Nievergelt, H. Hinterberger, and K. Sevcik, "The grid file: an adaptable, symmetric, multikey file structure," *ACM Trans. on Database Systems* **9**:1 (1984), pp. 38–71.

17. P. O'Neil, "Model 204 architecture and performance," *Proc. Second Intl. Workshop on High Performance Transaction Systems*, Springer-Verlag, Berlin, 1987.

18. P. O'Neil and D. Quass, "Improved query performance with variant indexes," *Proc. ACM SIGMOD Intl. Conf. on Management of Data* (1997), pp. 38–49.

19. W. W. Peterson, "Addressing for random access storage," *IBM J. Research and Development* **1**:2 (1957), pp. 130–146.

20. R. L. Rivest, "Partial match retrieval algorithms," *SIAM J. Computing* **5**:1 (1976), pp. 19–50.

21. J. T. Robinson, "The K-D-B-tree: a search structure for large multidimensional dynamic indexes," *Proc. ACM SIGMOD Intl. Conf. on Mamagement of Data* (1981), pp. 10–18.

22. J. B. Rothnie Jr. and T. Lozano, "Attribute based file organization in a paged memory environment, *Comm. ACM* **17**:2 (1974), pp. 63–69.

23. G. Salton, *Introduction to Modern Information Retrieval*, McGraw-Hill, New York, 1983.

24. T. K. Sellis, N. Roussopoulos, and C. Faloutsos, "The R+-tree: a dynamic index for multidimensional objects," *Intl. Conf. on Very Large Databases*, pp. 507–518, 1987.

25. C. Zaniolo, S. Ceri, C. Faloutsos, R. T. Snodgrass, V. S. Subrahmanian, and R. Zicari, *Advanced Database Systems*, Morgan-Kaufmann, San Francisco, 1997.

Query Execution

The broad topic of query processing will be covered in this chapter. The *query processor* is the group of components of a DBMS that turns user queries and data-modification commands into a sequence of database operations and executes those operations. Since SQL lets us express queries at a very high level, the query processor must supply much detail regarding how the query is to be executed. Moreover, a naive execution strategy for a query may take far more time than necessary.

Figure 1 suggests the division of topics. In this chapter, we concentrate on query execution, that is, the algorithms that manipulate the data of the database. We focus on the operations of the extended relational algebra. Because SQL uses a bag model, we also assume that relations are bags, and thus use the bag versions of the operators.

We shall cover the principal methods for execution of the operations of relational algebra. These methods differ in their basic strategy; scanning, hashing, sorting, and indexing are the major approaches. The methods also differ on their assumption as to the amount of available main memory. Some algorithms assume that enough main memory is available to hold at least one of the relations involved in an operation. Others assume that the arguments of the operation are too big to fit in memory, and these algorithms have significantly different costs and structures.

Preview of Query Compilation

To set the context for query execution, we offer a very brief outline of query compilation. Query compilation is divided into the three major steps shown in Fig. 2.

a) *Parsing.* A *parse tree* for the query is constructed.

b) *Query Rewrite.* The parse tree is converted to an initial query plan, which is usually an algebraic representation of the query. This initial plan is then

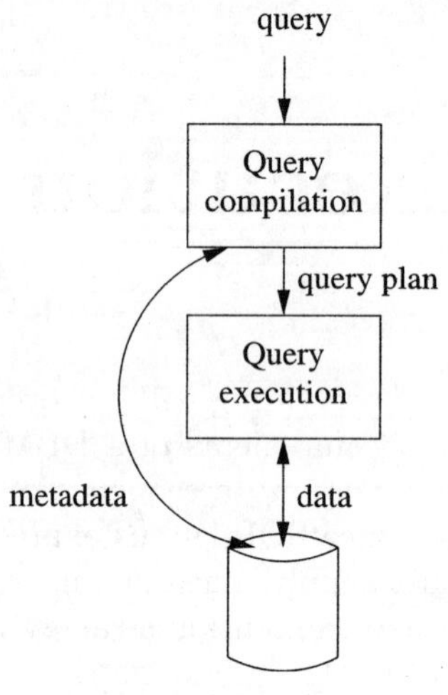

Figure 1: The major parts of the query processor

transformed into an equivalent plan that is expected to require less time to execute.

c) *Physical Plan Generation.* The abstract query plan from (b), often called a *logical query plan*, is turned into a *physical query plan* by selecting algorithms to implement each of the operators of the logical plan, and by selecting an order of execution for these operators. The physical plan, like the result of parsing and the logical plan, is represented by an expression tree. The physical plan also includes details such as how the queried relations are accessed, and when and if a relation should be sorted.

Parts (b) and (c) are often called the *query optimizer*, and these are the hard parts of query compilation. To select the best query plan we need to decide:

1. Which of the algebraically equivalent forms of a query leads to the most efficient algorithm for answering the query?

2. For each operation of the selected form, what algorithm should we use to implement that operation?

3. How should the operations pass data from one to the other, e.g., in a pipelined fashion, in main-memory buffers, or via the disk?

Each of these choices depends on the metadata about the database. Typical metadata that is available to the query optimizer includes: the size of each relation; statistics such as the approximate number and frequency of different values for an attribute; the existence of certain indexes; and the layout of data on disk.

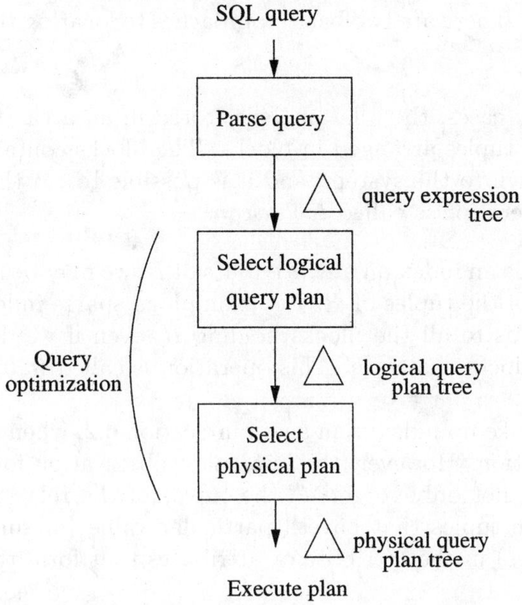

Figure 2: Outline of query compilation

1 Introduction to Physical-Query-Plan Operators

Physical query plans are built from operators, each of which implements one step of the plan. Often, the physical operators are particular implementations for one of the operations of relational algebra. However, we also need physical operators for other tasks that do not involve an operation of relational algebra. For example, we often need to "scan" a table, that is, bring into main memory each tuple of some relation. The relation is typically an operand of some other operation.

In this section, we shall introduce the basic building blocks of physical query plans. Later sections cover the more complex algorithms that implement operators of relational algebra efficiently; these algorithms also form an essential part of physical query plans. We also introduce here the "iterator" concept, which is an important method by which the operators comprising a physical query plan can pass requests for tuples and answers among themselves.

1.1 Scanning Tables

Perhaps the most basic thing we can do in a physical query plan is to read the entire contents of a relation R. A variation of this operator involves a simple predicate, where we read only those tuples of the relation R that satisfy the predicate. There are two basic approaches to locating the tuples of a relation R.

1. In many cases, the relation R is stored in an area of secondary memory, with its tuples arranged in blocks. The blocks containing the tuples of R are known to the system, and it is possible to get the blocks one by one. This operation is called *table-scan*.

2. If there is an index on any attribute of R, we may be able to use this index to get all the tuples of R. For example, a sparse index on R, can be used to lead us to all the blocks holding R, even if we don't know otherwise which blocks these are. This operation is called *index-scan*.

We shall take up index-scan again in Section 6.2, when we talk about implementing selection. However, the important observation for now is that we can use the index not only to get *all* the tuples of the relation it indexes, but to get only those tuples that have a particular value (or sometimes a particular range of values) in the attribute or attributes that form the search key for the index.

1.2 Sorting While Scanning Tables

There are a number of reasons why we might want to sort a relation as we read its tuples. For one, the query could include an `ORDER BY` clause, requiring that a relation be sorted. For another, some approaches to implementing relational-algebra operations require one or both arguments to be sorted relations. These algorithms appear in Section 4 and elsewhere.

The physical-query-plan operator *sort-scan* takes a relation R and a specification of the attributes on which the sort is to be made, and produces R in that sorted order. There are several ways that sort-scan can be implemented. If relation R must be sorted by attribute a, and there is a B-tree index on a, then a scan of the index allows us to produce R in the desired order. If R is small enough to fit in main memory, then we can retrieve its tuples using a table scan or index scan, and then use a main-memory sorting algorithm. If R is too large to fit in main memory, then we can use a multiway merge-sort, as will be discussed Section 4.1.

1.3 The Computation Model for Physical Operators

A query generally consists of several operations of relational algebra, and the corresponding physical query plan is composed of several physical operators. Since choosing physical-plan operators wisely is an essential of a good query processor, we must be able to estimate the "cost" of each operator we use. We shall use the number of disk I/O's as our measure of cost for an operation. This measure is consistent with our view that it takes longer to get data from disk than to do anything useful with it once the data is in main memory.

When comparing algorithms for the same operations, we shall make an assumption that may be surprising at first:

- We assume that the arguments of any operator are found on disk, but the result of the operator is left in main memory.

If the operator produces the final answer to a query, and that result is indeed written to disk, then the cost of doing so depends only on the size of the answer, and not on how the answer was computed. We can simply add the final write-back cost to the total cost of the query. However, in many applications, the answer is not stored on disk at all, but printed or passed to some formatting program. Then, the disk I/O cost of the output either is zero or depends upon what some unknown application program does with the data. In either case, the cost of writing the answer does not influence our choice of algorithm for executing the operator.

Similarly, the result of an operator that forms part of a query (rather than the whole query) often is not written to disk. In Section 1.6 we shall discuss "iterators," where the result of one operator O_1 is constructed in main memory, perhaps a small piece at a time, and passed as an argument to another operator O_2. In this situation, we never have to write the result of O_1 to disk, and moreover, we save the cost of reading from disk an argument of O_2.

1.4 Parameters for Measuring Costs

Now, let us introduce the parameters (sometimes called statistics) that we use to express the cost of an operator. Estimates of cost are essential if the optimizer is to determine which of the many query plans is likely to execute fastest.

We need a parameter to represent the portion of main memory that the operator uses, and we require other parameters to measure the size of its argument(s). Assume that main memory is divided into buffers, whose size is the same as the size of disk blocks. Then M will denote the number of main-memory buffers available to an execution of a particular operator.

Sometimes, we can think of M as the entire main memory, or most of the main memory. However, we shall also see situations where several operations share the main memory, so M could be much smaller than the total main memory. In fact, as we shall discuss in Section 7, the number of buffers available to an operation may not be a predictable constant, but may be decided during execution, based on what other processes are executing at the same time. If so, M is really an estimate of the number of buffers available to the operation.

Next, let us consider the parameters that measure the cost of accessing argument relations. These parameters, measuring size and distribution of data in a relation, are often computed periodically to help the query optimizer choose physical operators.

We shall make the simplifying assumption that data is accessed one block at a time from disk. In practice we might be able to speed up the algorithm if we are able to read many blocks of the relation at once, and they can be read from consecutive blocks on a track. There are three parameter families, B, T, and V:

- When describing the size of a relation R, we most often are concerned with the number of blocks that are needed to hold all the tuples of R. This number of blocks will be denoted $B(R)$, or just B if we know that relation R is meant. Usually, we assume that R is *clustered*; that is, it is stored in B blocks or in approximately B blocks.

- Sometimes, we also need to know the number of tuples in R, and we denote this quantity by $T(R)$, or just T if R is understood. If we need the number of tuples of R that can fit in one block, we can use the ratio T/B.

- Finally, we shall sometimes want to refer to the number of distinct values that appear in a column of a relation. If R is a relation, and one of its attributes is a, then $V(R, a)$ is the number of distinct values of the column for a in R. More generally, if $[a_1, a_2, \ldots, a_n]$ is a list of attributes, then $V(R, [a_1, a_2, \ldots, a_n])$ is the number of distinct n-tuples in the columns of R for attributes $a_1, a_2, \ldots, a_n$. Put formally, it is the number of tuples in $\delta(\pi_{a_1,a_2,\ldots,a_n}(R))$.

1.5 I/O Cost for Scan Operators

As a simple application of the parameters that were introduced, we can represent the number of disk I/O's needed for each of the table-scan operators discussed so far. If relation R is clustered, then the number of disk I/O's for the table-scan operator is approximately B. Likewise, if R fits in main-memory, then we can implement sort-scan by reading R into memory and performing an in-memory sort, again requiring only B disk I/O's.

However, if R is not clustered, then the number of required disk I/O's is generally much higher. If R is distributed among tuples of other relations, then a table-scan for R may require reading as many blocks as there are tuples of R; that is, the I/O cost is T. Similarly, if we want to sort R, but R fits in memory, then T disk I/O's are what we need to get all of R into memory.

Finally, let us consider the cost of an index-scan. Generally, an index on a relation R occupies many fewer than $B(R)$ blocks. Therefore, a scan of the entire R, which takes at least B disk I/O's, will require significantly more I/O's than does examining the entire index. Thus, even though index-scan requires examining both the relation and its index,

- We continue to use B or T, respectively, to estimate the cost of accessing a clustered or unclustered relation in its entirety, using an index.

However, if we only want part of R, we often are able to avoid looking at the entire index and the entire R. We shall defer analysis of these uses of indexes to Section 6.2.

1.6 Iterators for Implementation of Physical Operators

Many physical operators can be implemented as an *iterator*, which is a group of three methods that allows a consumer of the result of the physical operator to get the result one tuple at a time. The three methods forming the iterator for an operation are:

1. `Open()`. This method starts the process of getting tuples, but does not get a tuple. It initializes any data structures needed to perform the operation and calls `Open()` for any arguments of the operation.

2. `GetNext()`. This method returns the next tuple in the result and adjusts data structures as necessary to allow subsequent tuples to be obtained. In getting the next tuple of its result, it typically calls `GetNext()` one or more times on its argument(s). If there are no more tuples to return, `GetNext()` returns a special value `NotFound`, which we assume cannot be mistaken for a tuple.

3. `Close()`. This method ends the iteration after all tuples, or all tuples that the consumer wanted, have been obtained. Typically, it calls `Close()` on any arguments of the operator.

When describing iterators and their methods, we shall assume that there is a "class" for each type of iterator (i.e., for each type of physical operator implemented as an iterator), and the class defines `Open()`, `GetNext()`, and `Close()` methods on instances of the class.

Example 1: Perhaps the simplest iterator is the one that implements the table-scan operator. The iterator is implemented by a class `TableScan`, and a table-scan operator in a query plan is an instance of this class parameterized by the relation R we wish to scan. Let us assume that R is a relation clustered in some list of blocks, which we can access in a convenient way; that is, the notion of "get the next block of R" is implemented by the storage system and need not be described in detail. Further, we assume that within a block there is a directory of records (tuples), so it is easy to get the next tuple of a block or tell that the last tuple has been reached.

Figure 3 sketches the three methods for this iterator. We imagine a block pointer b and a tuple pointer t that points to a tuple within block b. We assume that both pointers can point "beyond" the last block or last tuple of a block, respectively, and that it is possible to identify when these conditions occur. Notice that `Close()` in this example does nothing. In practice, a `Close()` method for an iterator might clean up the internal structure of the DBMS in various ways. It might inform the buffer manager that certain buffers are no

```
Open() {
    b := the first block of R;
    t := the first tuple of block b;
}

GetNext() {
    IF (t is past the last tuple on block b) {
        increment b to the next block;
        IF (there is no next block)
            RETURN NotFound;
        ELSE /* b is a new block */
            t := first tuple on block b;
    } /* now we are ready to return t and increment */
    oldt := t;
    increment t to the next tuple of b;
    RETURN oldt;
}

Close() {
}
```

Figure 3: Iterator methods for the table-scan operator over relation R

longer needed, or inform the concurrency manager that the read of a relation has completed. □

Example 2: Now, let us consider an example where the iterator does most of the work in its `Open()` method. The operator is sort-scan, where we read the tuples of a relation R but return them in sorted order. We cannot return even the first tuple until we have examined each tuple of R. For simplicity, assume that R is small enough to fit in main memory.

`Open()` must read the entire R into main memory. It might also sort the tuples of R, in which case `GetNext()` needs only to return each tuple in turn, in the sorted order. Alternatively, `Open()` could leave R unsorted, and `GetNext()` could select the first of the remaining tuples, in effect performing one pass of a selection sort. □

Example 3: Finally, let us consider a simple example of how iterators can be combined by calling other iterators. The operation is the bag union $R \cup S$, in which we produce first all the tuples of R and then all the tuples of S, without regard for the existence of duplicates. Let $\mathcal{R}$ and $\mathcal{S}$ denote the iterators that produce relations R and S, and thus are the "children" of the union operator in a query plan for $R \cup S$. Iterators $\mathcal{R}$ and $\mathcal{S}$ could be table scans applied to stored relations R and S, or they could be iterators that call a network

> **Why Iterators?**
>
> Iterators support efficient execution when they are composed within query plans. They contrast with a *materialization* strategy, where the result of each operator is produced in its entirety — and either stored on disk or allowed to take up space in main memory. When iterators are used, many operations are active at once. Tuples pass between operators as needed, thus reducing the need for storage. Of course, as we shall see, not all physical operators support the iteration approach, or "pipelining," in a useful way. In some cases, almost all the work would need to be done by the `Open()` method, which is tantamount to materialization.

of other iterators to compute R and S. Regardless, all that is important is that we have available methods `R.Open()`, `R.GetNext()`, and `R.Close()`, and analogous methods for iterator S.

The iterator methods for the union are sketched in Fig. 4. One subtle point is that the methods use a shared variable `CurRel` that is either R or S, depending on which relation is being read from currently. □

2 One-Pass Algorithms

We shall now begin our study of a very important topic in query optimization: how should we execute each of the individual steps — for example, a join or selection — of a logical query plan? The choice of algorithm for each operator is an essential part of the process of transforming a logical query plan into a physical query plan. While many algorithms for operators have been proposed, they largely fall into three classes:

1. Sorting-based methods (Section 4).

2. Hash-based methods (Sections 5).

3. Index-based methods (Section 6).

In addition, we can divide algorithms for operators into three "degrees" of difficulty and cost:

a) Some methods involve reading the data only once from disk. These are the *one-pass* algorithms, and they are the topic of this section. Usually, they require at least one of the arguments to fit in main memory, although there are exceptions, especially for selection and projection as discussed in Section 2.1.

```
Open() {
    R.Open();
    CurRel := R;
}

GetNext() {
    IF (CurRel = R) {
        t := R.GetNext();
        IF (t <> NotFound) /* R is not exhausted */
            RETURN t;
        ELSE /* R is exhausted */ {
            S.Open();
            CurRel := S;
        }
    }
    /* here, we must read from S */
    RETURN S.GetNext();
    /* notice that if S is exhausted, S.GetNext()
       will return NotFound, which is the correct
       action for our GetNext as well */
}

Close() {
    R.Close();
    S.Close();
}
```

Figure 4: Building a union iterator from iterators $\mathcal{R}$ and $\mathcal{S}$

b) Some methods work for data that is too large to fit in available main memory but not for the largest imaginable data sets. These *two-pass* algorithms are characterized by reading data a first time from disk, processing it in some way, writing all, or almost all, of it to disk, and then reading it a second time for further processing during the second pass. We meet these algorithms in Sections 4 and 5.

c) Some methods work without a limit on the size of the data. These methods use three or more passes to do their jobs, and are natural, recursive generalizations of the two-pass algorithms. We shall study multipass methods in Section 8.

In this section, we shall concentrate on the one-pass methods. Here and subsequently, we shall classify operators into three broad groups:

1. *Tuple-at-a-time, unary operations.* These operations — selection and projection — do not require an entire relation, or even a large part of it, in memory at once. Thus, we can read a block at a time, use one main-memory buffer, and produce our output.

2. *Full-relation, unary operations.* These one-argument operations require seeing all or most of the tuples in memory at once, so one-pass algorithms are limited to relations that are approximately of size M (the number of main-memory buffers available) or less. The operations of this class are γ (the grouping operator) and δ (the duplicate-elimination operator).

3. *Full-relation, binary operations.* All other operations are in this class: set and bag versions of union, intersection, difference, joins, and products. Except for bag union, each of these operations requires at least one argument to be limited to size M, if we are to use a one-pass algorithm.

2.1 One-Pass Algorithms for Tuple-at-a-Time Operations

The tuple-at-a-time operations $\sigma(R)$ and $\pi(R)$ have obvious algorithms, regardless of whether the relation fits in main memory. We read the blocks of R one at a time into an input buffer, perform the operation on each tuple, and move the selected tuples or the projected tuples to the output buffer, as suggested by Fig. 5. Since the output buffer may be an input buffer of some other operator, or may be sending data to a user or application, we do not count the output buffer as needed space. Thus, we require only that $M \geq 1$ for the input buffer, regardless of B.

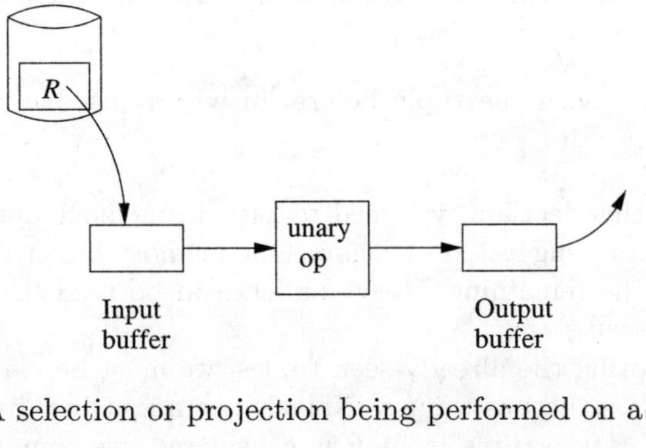

Figure 5: A selection or projection being performed on a relation R

The disk I/O requirement for this process depends only on how the argument relation R is provided. If R is initially on disk, then the cost is whatever it takes to perform a table-scan or index-scan of R. The cost was discussed in Section 1.5; typically, the cost is B if R is clustered and T if it is not clustered. However, remember the important exception where the operation being performed is a selection, and the condition compares a constant to an

> **Extra Buffers Can Speed Up Operations**
>
> Although tuple-at-a-time operations can get by with only one input buffer and one output buffer, as suggested by Fig. 5, we can often speed up processing if we allocate more input buffers. If R is stored on consecutive blocks within cylinders, then we can read an entire cylinder into buffers, while paying for the seek time and rotational latency for only one block per cylinder. Similarly, if the output of the operation can be stored on full cylinders, we waste almost no time writing.

attribute that has an index. In that case, we can use the index to retrieve only a subset of the blocks holding R, thus improving performance, often markedly.

2.2 One-Pass Algorithms for Unary, Full-Relation Operations

Now, let us consider the unary operations that apply to relations as a whole, rather than to one tuple at a time: duplicate elimination (δ) and grouping (γ).

Duplicate Elimination

To eliminate duplicates, we can read each block of R one at a time, but for each tuple we need to make a decision as to whether:

1. It is the first time we have seen this tuple, in which case we copy it to the output, or

2. We have seen the tuple before, in which case we must not output this tuple.

To support this decision, we need to keep in memory one copy of every tuple we have seen, as suggested in Fig. 6. One memory buffer holds one block of R's tuples, and the remaining $M - 1$ buffers can be used to hold a single copy of every tuple seen so far.

When storing the already-seen tuples, we must be careful about the main-memory data structure we use. Naively, we might just list the tuples we have seen. When a new tuple from R is considered, we compare it with all tuples seen so far, and if it is not equal to any of these tuples we both copy it to the output and add it to the in-memory list of tuples we have seen.

However, if there are n tuples in main memory, each new tuple takes processor time proportional to n, so the complete operation takes processor time proportional to n^2. Since n could be very large, this amount of time calls into serious question our assumption that only the disk I/O time is significant. Thus,

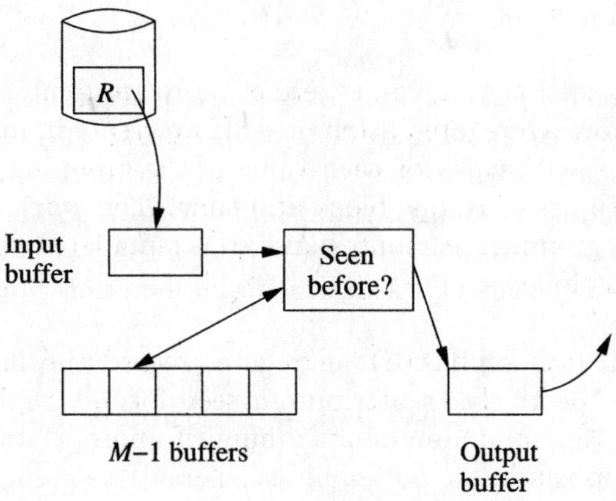

Figure 6: Managing memory for a one-pass duplicate-elimination

we need a main-memory structure that allows each us to add a new tuple and to tell whether a given tuple is already there, in time that grows slowly with n.

For example, we could use a hash table with a large number of buckets, or some form of balanced binary search tree.[1] Each of these structures has some space overhead in addition to the space needed to store the tuples; for instance, a main-memory hash table needs a bucket array and space for pointers to link the tuples in a bucket. However, the overhead tends to be small compared with the space needed to store the tuples, and we shall in this chpater neglect this overhead.

On this assumption, we may store in the $M-1$ available buffers of main memory as many tuples as will fit in $M-1$ blocks of R. If we want one copy of each distinct tuple of R to fit in main memory, then $B(\delta(R))$ must be no larger than $M-1$. Since we expect M to be much larger than 1, a simpler approximation to this rule, and the one we shall generally use, is:

- $B(\delta(R)) \leq M$

Note that we cannot in general compute the size of $\delta(R)$ without computing $\delta(R)$ itself. Should we underestimate that size, so $B(\delta(R))$ is actually larger than M, we shall pay a significant penalty due to thrashing, as the blocks holding the distinct tuples of R must be brought into and out of main memory frequently.

[1]See Aho, A. V., J. E. Hopcroft, and J. D. Ullman, *Data Structures and Algorithms*, Addison-Wesley, 1983 for discussions of suitable main-memory structures. In particular, hashing takes on average $O(n)$ time to process n items, and balanced trees take $O(n \log n)$ time; either is sufficiently close to linear for our purposes.

Grouping

A grouping operation γ_L gives us zero or more grouping attributes and presumably one or more aggregated attributes. If we create in main memory one entry for each group — that is, for each value of the grouping attributes — then we can scan the tuples of R, one block at a time. The *entry* for a group consists of values for the grouping attributes and an accumulated value or values for each aggregation, as follows:

- For a `MIN(a)` or `MAX(a)` aggregate, record the minimum or maximum value, respectively, of attribute a seen for any tuple in the group so far. Change this minimum or maximum, if appropriate, each time a tuple of the group is seen.

- For any `COUNT` aggregation, add one for each tuple of the group that is seen.

- For `SUM(a)`, add the value of attribute a to the accumulated sum for its group, provided a is not `NULL`.

- `AVG(a)` is the hard case. We must maintain two accumulations: the count of the number of tuples in the group and the sum of the a-values of these tuples. Each is computed as we would for a `COUNT` and `SUM` aggregation, respectively. After all tuples of R are seen, we take the quotient of the sum and count to obtain the average.

When all tuples of R have been read into the input buffer and contributed to the aggregation(s) for their group, we can produce the output by writing the tuple for each group. Note that until the last tuple is seen, we cannot begin to create output for a γ operation. Thus, this algorithm does not fit the iterator framework very well; the entire grouping has to be done by the `Open` method before the first tuple can be retrieved by `GetNext`.

In order that the in-memory processing of each tuple be efficient, we need to use a main-memory data structure that lets us find the entry for each group, given values for the grouping attributes. As discussed above for the δ operation, common main-memory data structures such as hash tables or balanced trees will serve well. We should remember, however, that the search key for this structure is the grouping attributes only.

The number of disk I/O's needed for this one-pass algorithm is B, as must be the case for any one-pass algorithm for a unary operator. The number of required memory buffers M is not related to B in any simple way, although typically M will be less than B. The problem is that the entries for the groups could be longer or shorter than tuples of R, and the number of groups could be anything equal to or less than the number of tuples of R. However, in most cases, group entries will be no longer than R's tuples, and there will be many fewer groups than tuples.

> **Operations on Nonclustered Data**
>
> All our calculations regarding the number of disk I/O's required for an operation are predicated on the assumption that the operand relations are clustered. In the (typically rare) event that an operand R is not clustered, then it may take us $T(R)$ disk I/O's, rather than $B(R)$ disk I/O's to read all the tuples of R. Note, however, that any relation that is the result of an operator may always be assumed clustered, since we have no reason to store a temporary relation in a nonclustered fashion.

2.3 One-Pass Algorithms for Binary Operations

Let us now take up the binary operations: union, intersection, difference, product, and join. Since in some cases we must distinguish the set- and bag-versions of these operators, we shall subscript them with B or S for "bag" and "set," respectively; e.g., $\cup_B$ for bag union or $-_S$ for set difference. To simplify the discussion of joins, we shall consider only the natural join. An equijoin can be implemented the same way, after attributes are renamed appropriately, and theta-joins can be thought of as a product or equijoin followed by a selection for those conditions that cannot be expressed in an equijoin.

Bag union can be computed by a very simple one-pass algorithm. To compute $R \cup_B S$, we copy each tuple of R to the output and then copy every tuple of S, as we did in Example 3. The number of disk I/O's is $B(R) + B(S)$, as it must be for a one-pass algorithm on operands R and S, while $M = 1$ suffices regardless of how large R and S are.

Other binary operations require reading the smaller of the operands R and S into main memory and building a suitable data structure so tuples can be both inserted quickly and found quickly, as discussed in Section 2.2. As before, a hash table or balanced tree suffices. Thus, the approximate requirement for a binary operation on relations R and S to be performed in one pass is:

- $\min\big(B(R), B(S)\big) \leq M$

More preceisely, one buffer is used to read the blocks of the larger relation, while approximately M buffers are needed to house the entire smaller relation and its main-memory data structure.

We shall now give the details of the various operations. In each case, we assume R is the larger of the relations, and we house S in main memory.

Set Union

We read S into $M - 1$ buffers of main memory and build a search structure whose search key is the entire tuple. All these tuples are also copied to the output. We then read each block of R into the Mth buffer, one at a time. For each tuple t of R, we see if t is in S, and if not, we copy t to the output. If t is also in S, we skip t.

Set Intersection

Read S into $M - 1$ buffers and build a search structure with full tuples as the search key. Read each block of R, and for each tuple t of R, see if t is also in S. If so, copy t to the output, and if not, ignore t.

Set Difference

Since difference is not commutative, we must distinguish between $R -_S S$ and $S -_S R$, continuing to assume that R is the larger relation. In each case, read S into $M - 1$ buffers and build a search structure with full tuples as the search key.

To compute $R -_S S$, we read each block of R and examine each tuple t on that block. If t is in S, then ignore t; if it is not in S then copy t to the output.

To compute $S -_S R$, we again read the blocks of R and examine each tuple t in turn. If t is in S, then we delete t from the copy of S in main memory, while if t is not in S we do nothing. After considering each tuple of R, we copy to the output those tuples of S that remain.

Bag Intersection

We read S into $M - 1$ buffers, but we associate with each distinct tuple a *count*, which initially measures the number of times this tuple occurs in S. Multiple copies of a tuple t are not stored individually. Rather we store one copy of t and associate with it a count equal to the number of times t occurs.

This structure could take slightly more space than $B(S)$ blocks if there were few duplicates, although frequently the result is that S is compacted. Thus, we shall continue to assume that $B(S) \leq M$ is sufficient for a one-pass algorithm to work, although the condition is only an approximation.

Next, we read each block of R, and for each tuple t of R we see whether t occurs in S. If not we ignore t; it cannot appear in the intersection. However, if t appears in S, and the count associated with t is still positive, then we output t and decrement the count by 1. If t appears in S, but its count has reached 0, then we do not output t; we have already produced as many copies of t in the output as there were copies in S.

Bag Difference

To compute $S -_B R$, we read the tuples of S into main memory, and count the number of occurrences of each distinct tuple, as we did for bag intersection. When we read R, for each tuple t we see whether t occurs in S, and if so, we decrement its associated count. At the end, we copy to the output each tuple in main memory whose count is positive, and the number of times we copy it equals that count.

To compute $R -_B S$, we also read the tuples of S into main memory and count the number of occurrences of distinct tuples. We may think of a tuple t with a count of c as c reasons not to copy t to the output as we read tuples of R. That is, when we read a tuple t of R, we see if t occurs in S. If not, then we copy t to the output. If t does occur in S, then we look at the current count c associated with t. If $c = 0$, then copy t to the output. If $c > 0$, do not copy t to the output, but decrement c by 1.

Product

Read S into $M-1$ buffers of main memory; no special data structure is needed. Then read each block of R, and for each tuple t of R concatenate t with each tuple of S in main memory. Output each concatenated tuple as it is formed.

This algorithm may take a considerable amount of processor time per tuple of R, because each such tuple must be matched with $M-1$ blocks full of tuples. However, the output size is also large, and the time per output tuple is small.

Natural Join

In this and other join algorithms, let us take the convention that $R(X,Y)$ is being joined with $S(Y,Z)$, where Y represents all the attributes that R and S have in common, X is all attributes of R that are not in the schema of S, and Z is all attributes of S that are not in the schema of R. We continue to assume that S is the smaller relation. To compute the natural join, do the following:

1. Read all the tuples of S and form them into a main-memory search structure with the attributes of Y as the search key. Use $M - 1$ blocks of memory for this purpose.

2. Read each block of R into the one remaining main-memory buffer. For each tuple t of R, find the tuples of S that agree with t on all attributes of Y, using the search structure. For each matching tuple of S, form a tuple by joining it with t, and move the resulting tuple to the output.

Like all the one-pass, binary algorithms, this one takes $B(R) + B(S)$ disk I/O's to read the operands. It works as long as $B(S) \leq M - 1$, or approximately, $B(S) \leq M$.

We shall not discuss joins other than the natural join. Remember that an equijoin is executed in essentially the same way as a natural join, but we must account for the fact that "equal" attributes from the two relations may have different names. A theta-join that is not an equijoin can be replaced by an equijoin or product followed by a selection.

2.4 Exercises for Section 2

Exercise 2.1: For each of the operations below, write an iterator that uses the algorithm described in this section: (a) projection (b) distinct (δ) (c) grouping (γ_L) (d) set union (e) set intersection (f) set difference (g) bag intersection (h) bag difference (i) product (j) natural join.

Exercise 2.2: For each of the operators in Exercise 2.1, tell whether the operator is *blocking*, by which we mean that the first output cannot be produced until all the input has been read. Put another way, a blocking operator is one whose only possible iterators have all the important work done by `Open`.

Exercise 2.3: Figure 9 summarizes the memory and disk-I/O requirements of the algorithms of this section and the next. However, it assumes all arguments are clustered. How would the entries change if one or both arguments were not clustered?

! **Exercise 2.4:** Give one-pass algorithms for each of the following join-like operators:

a) $R \ltimes S$, assuming R fits in memory.

b) $R \ltimes S$, assuming S fits in memory.

c) $R \overline{\ltimes} S$, assuming R fits in memory.

d) $R \overline{\ltimes} S$, assuming S fits in memory.

e) $R \stackrel{\circ}{\bowtie}_L S$, assuming R fits in memory.

f) $R \stackrel{\circ}{\bowtie}_L S$, assuming S fits in memory.

g) $R \stackrel{\circ}{\bowtie}_R S$, assuming R fits in memory.

h) $R \stackrel{\circ}{\bowtie}_R S$, assuming S fits in memory.

i) $R \stackrel{\circ}{\bowtie} S$, assuming R fits in memory.

3 Nested-Loop Joins

Before proceeding to the more complex algorithms in the next sections, we shall turn our attention to a family of algorithms for the join operator called "nested-loop" joins. These algorithms are, in a sense, "one-and-a-half" passes, since in each variation one of the two arguments has its tuples read only once, while the other argument will be read repeatedly. Nested-loop joins can be used for relations of any size; it is not necessary that one relation fit in main memory.

3.1 Tuple-Based Nested-Loop Join

The simplest variation of nested-loop join has loops that range over individual tuples of the relations involved. In this algorithm, which we call *tuple-based nested-loop join*, we compute the join $R(X, Y) \bowtie S(Y, Z)$ as follows:

```
FOR each tuple s in S DO
    FOR each tuple r in R DO
        IF r and s join to make a tuple t THEN
            output t;
```

If we are careless about how we buffer the blocks of relations R and S, then this algorithm could require as many as $T(R)T(S)$ disk I/O's. However, there are many situations where this algorithm can be modified to have much lower cost. One case is when we can use an index on the join attribute or attributes of R to find the tuples of R that match a given tuple of S, without having to read the entire relation R. We discuss index-based joins in Section 6.3. A second improvement looks much more carefully at the way tuples of R and S are divided among blocks, and uses as much of the memory as it can to reduce the number of disk I/O's as we go through the inner loop. We shall consider this block-based version of nested-loop join in Section 3.3.

3.2 An Iterator for Tuple-Based Nested-Loop Join

One advantage of a nested-loop join is that it fits well into an iterator framework, and thus allows us to avoid storing intermediate relations on disk in some situations. The iterator for $R \bowtie S$ is easy to build from the iterators for R and S, which support methods `R.Open()`, and so on, as in Section 1.6. The code for the three iterator methods for nested-loop join is in Fig. 7. It makes the assumption that neither relation R nor S is empty.

3.3 Block-Based Nested-Loop Join Algorithm

We can improve on the tuple-based nested-loop join of Section 3.1 if we compute $R \bowtie S$ by:

1. Organizing access to both argument relations by blocks, and

2. Using as much main memory as we can to store tuples belonging to the relation S, the relation of the outer loop.

Point (1) makes sure that when we run through the tuples of R in the inner loop, we use as few disk I/O's as possible to read R. Point (2) enables us to join each tuple of R that we read with not just one tuple of S, but with as many tuples of S as will fit in memory.

```
Open() {
    R.Open();
    S.Open();
    s := S.GetNext();
}

GetNext() {
    REPEAT {
        r := R.GetNext();
        IF (r = NotFound) { /* R is exhausted for
                the current s */
            R.Close();
            s := S.GetNext();
            IF (s = NotFound) RETURN NotFound;
                /* both R and S are exhausted */
            R.Open();
            r := R.GetNext();
        }
    }
    UNTIL (r and s join);
    RETURN the join of r and s;
}

Close() {
    R.Close();
    S.Close();
}
```

Figure 7: Iterator methods for tuple-based nested-loop join of R and S

As in Section 2.3, let us assume $B(S) \leq B(R)$, but now let us also assume that $B(S) > M$; i.e., neither relation fits entirely in main memory. We repeatedly read $M-1$ blocks of S into main-memory buffers. A search structure, with search key equal to the common attributes of R and S, is created for the tuples of S that are in main memory. Then we go through all the blocks of R, reading each one in turn into the last block of memory. Once there, we compare all the tuples of R's block with all the tuples in all the blocks of S that are currently in main memory. For those that join, we output the joined tuple. The nested-loop structure of this algorithm can be seen when we describe the algorithm more formally, in Fig. 8. The algorithm of Fig. 8 is sometimes called "nested-block join." We shall continue to call it simply *nested-loop join*, since it is the variant of the nested-loop idea most commonly implemented in practice.

```
FOR each chunk of M-1 blocks of S DO BEGIN
    read these blocks into main-memory buffers;
    organize their tuples into a search structure whose
        search key is the common attributes of R and S;
    FOR each block b of R DO BEGIN
        read b into main memory;
        FOR each tuple t of b DO BEGIN
            find the tuples of S in main memory that
                join with t;
            output the join of t with each of these tuples;
        END;
    END;
END;
```

Figure 8: The nested-loop join algorithm

The program of Fig. 8 appears to have three nested loops. However, there really are only two loops if we look at the code at the right level of abstraction. The first, or outer loop, runs through the tuples of S. The other two loops run through the tuples of R. However, we expressed the process as two loops to emphasize that the order in which we visit the tuples of R is not arbitrary. Rather, we need to look at these tuples a block at a time (the role of the second loop), and within one block, we look at all the tuples of that block before moving on to the next block (the role of the third loop).

Example 4: Let $B(R) = 1000$, $B(S) = 500$, and $M = 101$. We shall use 100 blocks of memory to buffer S in 100-block chunks, so the outer loop of Fig. 8 iterates five times. At each iteration, we do 100 disk I/O's to read the chunk of S, and we must read R entirely in the second loop, using 1000 disk I/O's. Thus, the total number of disk I/O's is 5500.

Notice that if we reversed the roles of R and S, the algorithm would use slightly more disk I/O's. We would iterate 10 times through the outer loop and do 600 disk I/O's at each iteration, for a total of 6000. In general, there is a slight advantage to using the smaller relation in the outer loop. □

3.4 Analysis of Nested-Loop Join

The analysis of Example 4 can be repeated for any $B(R)$, $B(S)$, and M. Assuming S is the smaller relation, the number of chunks, or iterations of the outer loop is $B(S)/(M-1)$. At each iteration, we read $M-1$ blocks of S and $B(R)$ blocks of R. The number of disk I/O's is thus $B(S)\big(M-1+B(R)\big)/(M-1)$, or $B(S)+\big(B(S)B(R)\big)/(M-1)$.

Assuming all of M, $B(S)$, and $B(R)$ are large, but M is the smallest of these, an approximation to the above formula is $B(S)B(R)/M$. That is, the cost is proportional to the product of the sizes of the two relations, divided by the amount of available main memory. We can do much better than a nested-loop join when both relations are large. But for reasonably small examples such as Example 4, the cost of the nested-loop join is not much greater than the cost of a one-pass join, which is 1500 disk I/O's for this example. In fact, if $B(S) \leq M - 1$, the nested-loop join becomes identical to the one-pass join algorithm of Section 2.3.

Although nested-loop join is generally not the most efficient join algorithm possible, we should note that in some early relational DBMS's, it was the only method available. Even today, it is needed as a subroutine in more efficient join algorithms in certain situations, such as when large numbers of tuples from each relation share a common value for the join attribute(s). For an example where nested-loop join is essential, see Section 4.6.

3.5 Summary of Algorithms so Far

The main-memory and disk I/O requirements for the algorithms we have discussed in Sections 2 and 3 are shown in Fig. 9. The memory requirements for γ and δ are actually more complex than shown, and $M = B$ is only a loose approximation. For γ, M depends on the number of groups, and for δ, M depends on the number of distinct tuples.

Operators	Approximate M required	Disk I/O	Section
σ, π	1	B	2.1
γ, δ	B	B	2.2
$\cup$, $\cap$, $-$, $\times$, $\bowtie$	$\min(B(R), B(S))$	$B(R) + B(S)$	2.3
$\bowtie$	any $M \geq 2$	$B(R)B(S)/M$	3.3

Figure 9: Main memory and disk I/O requirements for one-pass and nested-loop algorithms

3.6 Exercises for Section 3

Exercise 3.1: Give the three iterator methods for the block-based version of nested-loop join.

Exercise 3.2: Suppose $B(R) = B(S) = 10{,}000$, and $M = 1000$. Calculate the disk I/O cost of a nested-loop join.

Exercise 3.3: For the relations of Exercise 3.2, what value of M would we need to compute $R \bowtie S$ using the nested-loop algorithm with no more than (a) 100,000 ! (b) 25,000 ! (c) 15,000 disk I/O's?

! **Exercise 3.4:** If R and S are both unclustered, it seems that nested-loop join would require about $T(R)T(S)/M$ disk I/O's.

a) How can you do significantly better than this cost?

b) If only one of R and S is unclustered, how would you perform a nested-loop join? Consider both the cases that the larger is unclustered and that the smaller is unclustered.

! **Exercise 3.5:** The iterator of Fig. 7 will not work properly if either R or S is empty. Rewrite the methods so they will work, even if one or both relations are empty.

4 Two-Pass Algorithms Based on Sorting

We shall now begin the study of multipass algorithms for performing relational-algebra operations on relations that are larger than what the one-pass algorithms of Section 2 can handle. We concentrate on *two-pass algorithms*, where data from the operand relations is read into main memory, processed in some way, written out to disk again, and then reread from disk to complete the operation. We can naturally extend this idea to any number of passes, where the data is read many times into main memory. However, we concentrate on two-pass algorithms because:

a) Two passes are usually enough, even for very large relations.

b) Generalizing to more than two passes is not hard; we discuss these extensions in Section 4.1 and more generally in Section 8.

We begin with an implementation of the sorting operator τ that illustrates the general approach: divide a relation R for which $B(R) > M$ into chucks of size M, sort them, and then process the sorted sublists in some fashion that requires only one block of each sorted sublist in main memory at any one time.

4.1 Two-Phase, Multiway Merge-Sort

It is possible to sort very large relations in two passes using an algorithm called *Two-Phase, Multiway Merge-Sort* (TPMMS), Suppose we have M main-memory buffers to use for the sort. TPMMS sorts a relation R as follows:

- *Phase 1*: Repeatedly fill the M buffers with new tuples from R and sort them, using any main-memory sorting algorithm. Write out each *sorted sublist* to secondary storage.

- *Phase 2*: Merge the sorted sublists. For this phase to work, there can be at most $M - 1$ sorted sublists, which limits the size of R. We allocate one input block to each sorted sublist and one block to the output. The

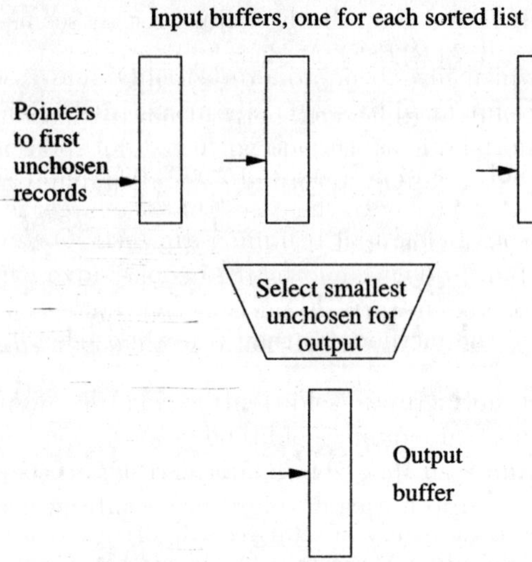

Figure 10: Main-memory organization for multiway merging

use of buffers is suggested by Fig. 10. A pointer to each input block indicates the first element in the sorted order that has not yet been moved to the output. We merge the sorted sublists into one sorted list with all the records as follows.

1. Find the smallest key among the first remaining elements of all the lists. Since this comparison is done in main memory, a linear search is sufficient, taking a number of machine instructions proportional to the number of sublists. However, if we wish, there is a method based on "priority queues"[2] that takes time proportional to the logarithm of the number of sublists to find the smallest element.
2. Move the smallest element to the first available position of the output block.
3. If the output block is full, write it to disk and reinitialize the same buffer in main memory to hold the next output block.
4. If the block from which the smallest element was just taken is now exhausted of records, read the next block from the same sorted sublist into the same buffer that was used for the block just exhausted. If no blocks remain, then leave its buffer empty and do not consider elements from that list in any further competition for smallest remaining elements.

In order for TPMMS to work, there must be no more than $M - 1$ sublists. Suppose R fits on B blocks. Since each sublist consists of M blocks, the number

[2]See Aho, A. V. and J. D. Ullman, *Foundations of Computer Science*, Computer Science Press, 1992.

of sublists is B/M. We thus require $B/M \leq M - 1$, or $B \leq M(M - 1)$ (or about $B \leq M^2$).

The algorithm requires us to read B blocks in the first pass, and another B disk I/O's to write the sorted sublists. The sorted sublists are each read again in the second pass, resulting in a total of $3B$ disk I/O's. If, as is customary, we do not count the cost of writing the result to disk (since the result may be pipelined and never written to disk), then $3B$ is all that the sorting operator τ requires. However, if we need to store the result on disk, then the requirement is $4B$.

Example 5: Suppose blocks are 64K bytes, and we have one gigabyte of main memory. Then we can afford M of 16K. Thus, a relation fitting in B blocks can be sorted as long as B is no more than $(16\text{K})^2 = 2^{28}$. Since blocks are of size $64\text{K} = 2^{14}$, a relation can be sorted as long as its size is no greater than 2^{42} bytes, or 4 terabytes. □

Example 5 shows that even on a modest machine, 2PMMS is sufficient to sort all but an incredibly large relation in two passes. However, if you have an even bigger relation, then the same idea can be applied recursively. Divide the relation into chunks of size $M(M - 1)$, use 2PMMS to sort each one, and then treat the resulting sorted lists as sublists for a third pass. The idea extends similarly to any number of passes.

4.2 Duplicate Elimination Using Sorting

To perform the $\delta(R)$ operation in two passes, we sort the tuples of R in sublists as in 2PMMS. In the second pass, we use the available main memory to hold one block from each sorted sublist and one output block, as we did for 2PMMS. However, instead of sorting on the second pass, we reapeatedly select the first (in sorted order) unconsidered tuple t among all the sorted sublists. We write one copy of t to the output and eliminate from the input blocks all occurrences of t. Thus, the output will consist of exactly one copy of any tuple in R; they will in fact be produced in sorted order. When an output block is full or an input block empty, we manage the buffers exactly as in 2PMMS.

The number of disk I/O's performed by this algorithm, as always ignoring the handling of the output, is the same as for sorting: $3B(R)$. This figure can be compared with $B(R)$ for the single-pass algorithm of Section 2.2. On the other hand, we can handle much larger files using the two-pass algorithm than with the one-pass algorithm. As for 2PMMS, approximately $B \leq M^2$ is required for the two-pass algorithm to be feasible, compared with $B \leq M$ for the one-pass algorithm. Put another way, to eliminate duplicates with the two-pass algorithm requires only $\sqrt{B(R)}$ blocks of main memory, rather than the $B(R)$ blocks required for a one-pass algorithm.

4.3 Grouping and Aggregation Using Sorting

The two-pass algorithm for $\gamma_L(R)$ is quite similar to the algorithm for $\delta(R)$ or 2PMMS. We summarize it as follows:

1. Read the tuples of R into memory, M blocks at a time. Sort the tuples in each set of M blocks, using the grouping attributes of L as the sort key. Write each sorted sublist to disk.

2. Use one main-memory buffer for each sublist, and initially load the first block of each sublist into its buffer.

3. Repeatedly find the least value of the sort key (grouping attributes) present among the first available tuples in the buffers. This value, v, becomes the next group, for which we:

   (a) Prepare to compute all the aggregates on list L for this group. As in Section 2.2, use a count and sum in place of an average.

   (b) Examine each of the tuples with sort key v, and accumulate the needed aggregates.

   (c) If a buffer becomes empty, replace it with the next block from the same sublist.

   When there are no more tuples with sort key v available, output a tuple consisting of the grouping attributes of L and the associated values of the aggregations we have computed for the group.

As for the δ algorithm, this two-pass algorithm for γ takes $3B(R)$ disk I/O's, and will work as long as $B(R) \leq M^2$.

4.4 A Sort-Based Union Algorithm

When bag-union is wanted, the one-pass algorithm of Section 2.3, where we simply copy both relations, works regardless of the size of the arguments, so there is no need to consider a two-pass algorithm for $\cup_B$. However, the one-pass algorithm for $\cup_S$ only works when at least one relation is smaller than the available main memory, so we must consider a two-pass algorithm for set union. The methodology we present works for the set and bag versions of intersection and difference as well, as we shall see in Section 4.5. To compute $R \cup_S S$, we modify 2PMMS as follows:

1. In the first phase, create sorted sublists from both R and S.

2. Use one main-memory buffer for each sublist of R and S. Initialize each with the first block from the corresponding sublist.

3. Repeatedly find the first remaining tuple t among all the buffers. Copy t to the output, and remove from the buffers all copies of t (if R and S are sets there should be at most two copies). Manage empty input buffers and a full output buffer as for 2PMMS.

We observe that each tuple of R and S is read twice into main memory, once when the sublists are being created, and the second time as part of one of the sublists. The tuple is also written to disk once, as part of a newly formed sublist. Thus, the cost in disk I/O's is $3\big(B(R) + B(S)\big)$.

The algorithm works as long as the total number of sublists among the two relations does not exceed $M - 1$, because we need one buffer for each sublist and one for the output Thus, approximately, the sum of the sizes of the two relations must not exceed M^2; that is, $B(R) + B(S) \leq M^2$.

4.5 Sort-Based Intersection and Difference

Whether the set version or the bag version is wanted, the algorithms are essentially the same as that of Section 4.4, except that the way we handle the copies of a tuple t at the fronts of the sorted sublists differs. For each algorithm, we repeatedly consider the tuple t that is least in the sorted order among all tuples remaining in the input buffers. We produce output as follows, and then remove all copies of t from the input buffers.

- For set intersection, output t if it appears in both R and S.
- For bag intersection, output t the minimum of the number of times it appears in R and in S. Note that t is not output if either of these counts is 0; that is, if t is missing from one or both of the relations.
- For set difference, $R -_S S$, output t if and only if it appears in R but not in S.
- For bag difference, $R -_B S$, output t the number of times it appears in R minus the number of times it appears in S. Of course, if t appears in S at least as many times as it appears in R, then do not output t at all.

One subtlely must be remembered for the bag operations. When counting occurrences of t, it is possible that all remaining tuples in an input buffer are t. If so, there may be more t's on the next block for that sublist. Thus, when a buffer has only t's remaining, we must load the next block for that sublist, continuing the count of t's. This process may continue for several blocks and may need to be done for several sublists.

The analysis of this family of algorithms is the same as for the set-union algorithm described in Section 4.4:

- $3\big(B(R) + B(S)\big)$ disk I/O's.
- Approximately $B(R) + B(S) \leq M^2$ for the algorithm to work.

4.6 A Simple Sort-Based Join Algorithm

There are several ways that sorting can be used to join large relations. Before examining the join algorithms, let us observe one problem that can occur when we compute a join but was not an issue for the binary operations considered so far. When taking a join, the number of tuples from the two relations that share a common value of the join attribute(s), and therefore need to be in main memory simultaneously, can exceed what fits in memory. The extreme example is when there is only one value of the join attribute(s), and every tuple of one relation joins with every tuple of the other relation. In this situation, there is really no choice but to take a nested-loop join of the two sets of tuples with a common value in the join-attribute(s).

To avoid facing this situation, we can try to reduce main-memory use for other aspects of the algorithm, and thus make available a large number of buffers to hold the tuples with a given join-attribute value. In this section we shall discuss the algorithm that makes the greatest possible number of buffers available for joining tuples with a common value. In Section 4.8 we consider another sort-based algorithm that uses fewer disk I/O's, but can present problems when there are large numbers of tuples with a common join-attribute value.

Given relations $R(X, Y)$ and $S(Y, Z)$ to join, and given M blocks of main memory for buffers, we do the following:

1. Sort R, using 2PMMS, with Y as the sort key.

2. Sort S similarly.

3. Merge the sorted R and S. We use only two buffers: one for the current block of R and the other for the current block of S. The following steps are done repeatedly:

   (a) Find the least value y of the join attributes Y that is currently at the front of the blocks for R and S.

   (b) If y does not appear at the front of the other relation, then remove the tuple(s) with sort key y.

   (c) Otherwise, identify all the tuples from both relations having sort key y. If necessary, read blocks from the sorted R and/or S, until we are sure there are no more y's in either relation. As many as M buffers are available for this purpose.

   (d) Output all the tuples that can be formed by joining tuples from R and S that have a common Y-value y.

   (e) If either relation has no more unconsidered tuples in main memory, reload the buffer for that relation.

Example 6: Let us consider the relations R and S from Example 4. Recall these relations occupy 1000 and 500 blocks, respectively, and there are $M = 101$ main-memory buffers. When we use 2PMMS on a relation and store the result on disk, we do four disk I/O's per block, two in each of the two phases. Thus, we use $4(B(R)+B(S))$ disk I/O's to sort R and S, or 6000 disk I/O's.

When we merge the sorted R and S to find the joined tuples, we read each block of R and S a fifth time, using another 1500 disk I/O's. In this merge we generally need only two of the 101 blocks of memory. However, if necessary, we could use all 101 blocks to hold the tuples of R and S that share a common Y-value y. Thus, it is sufficient that for no y do the tuples of R and S that have Y-value y together occupy more than 101 blocks.

Notice that the total number of disk I/O's performed by this algorithm is 7500, compared with 5500 for nested-loop join in Example 4. However, nested-loop join is inherently a quadratic algorithm, taking time proportional to $B(R)B(S)$, while sort-join has linear I/O cost, taking time proportional to $B(R) + B(S)$. It is only the constant factors and the small size of the example (each relation is only 5 or 10 times larger than a relation that fits entirely in the allotted buffers) that make nested-loop join preferable. □

4.7 Analysis of Simple Sort-Join

As we noted in Example 6, the algorithm of Section 4.6 performs five disk I/O's for every block of the argument relations. We also need to consider how big M needs to be in order for the simple sort-join to work. The primary constraint is that we need to be able to perform the two-phase, multiway merge sorts on R and S. As we observed in Section 4.1, we need $B(R) \leq M^2$ and $B(S) \leq M^2$ to perform these sorts. In addition, we require that all the tuples with a common Y-value must fit in M buffers. In summary:

- The simple sort-join uses $5(B(R) + B(S))$ disk I/O's.
- It requires $B(R) \leq M^2$ and $B(S) \leq M^2$ to work.
- It also requires that the tuples with a common value for the join attributes fit in M blocks.

4.8 A More Efficient Sort-Based Join

If we do not have to worry about very large numbers of tuples with a common value for the join attribute(s), then we can save two disk I/O's per block by combining the second phase of the sorts with the join itself. We call this algorithm *sort-join*; other names by which it is known include "merge-join" and "sort-merge-join." To compute $R(X,Y) \bowtie S(Y,Z)$ using M main-memory buffers:

1. Create sorted sublists of size M, using Y as the sort key, for both R and S.

2. Bring the first block of each sublist into a buffer; we assume there are no more than M sublists in all.

3. Repeatedly find the least Y-value y among the first available tuples of all the sublists. Identify all the tuples of both relations that have Y-value y, perhaps using some of the M available buffers to hold them, if there are fewer than M sublists. Output the join of all tuples from R with all tuples from S that share this common Y-value. If the buffer for one of the sublists is exhausted, then replenish it from disk.

Example 7: Let us again consider the problem of Example 4: joining relations R and S of sizes 1000 and 500 blocks, respectively, using 101 buffers. We divide R into 10 sublists and S into 5 sublists, each of length 100, and sort them.[3] We then use 15 buffers to hold the current blocks of each of the sublists. If we face a situation in which many tuples have a fixed Y-value, we can use the remaining 86 buffers to store these tuples.

We perform three disk I/O's per block of data. Two of those are to create the sorted sublists. Then, every block of every sorted sublist is read into main memory one more time in the multiway merging process. Thus, the total number of disk I/O's is 4500. □

This sort-join algorithm is more efficient than the algorithm of Section 4.6 when it can be used. As we observed in Example 7, the number of disk I/O's is $3\big(B(R) + B(S)\big)$. We can perform the algorithm on data that is almost as large as that of the previous algorithm. The sizes of the sorted sublists are M blocks, and there can be at most M of them among the two lists. Thus, $B(R) + B(S) \leq M^2$ is sufficient.

4.9 Summary of Sort-Based Algorithms

In Fig. 11 is a table of the analysis of the algorithms we have discussed in Section 4. As discussed in Sections 4.6 and 4.8, the join algorithms have limitiations on how many tuples can share a common value of the join attribute(s). If this limit is violated, we may have to use a nest-loop join instead.

4.10 Exercises for Section 4

Exercise 4.1: For each of the following operations, write an iterator that uses the algorithm described in this section: (a) distinct (δ) (b) grouping (γ_L) (c) set intersection (d) bag difference (e) natural join.

[3] Technically, we could have arranged for the sublists to have length 101 blocks each, with the last sublist of R having 91 blocks and the last sublist of S having 96 blocks, but the costs would turn out exactly the same.

Operators	Approximate M required	Disk I/O	Section
τ, γ, δ	$\sqrt{B}$	$3B$	4.1, 4.2, 4.3
$\cup$, $\cap$, $-$	$\sqrt{B(R)+B(S)}$	$3(B(R)+B(S))$	4.4, 4.5
$\bowtie$	$\sqrt{\max(B(R),B(S))}$	$5(B(R)+B(S))$	4.6
$\bowtie$	$\sqrt{B(R)+B(S)}$	$3(B(R)+B(S))$	4.8

Figure 11: Main memory and disk I/O requirements for sort-based algorithms

Exercise 4.2: If $B(R) = B(S) = 10{,}000$ and $M = 1000$, what are the disk I/O requirements of: (a) set union (b) simple sort-join (c) the more efficient sort-join of Section 4.8.

! Exercise 4.3: Suppose that the second pass of an algorithm described in this section does not need all M buffers, because there are fewer than M sublists. How might we save disk I/O's by using the extra buffers?

! Exercise 4.4: In Example 6 we discussed the join of two relations R and S, with 1000 and 500 blocks, respectively, and $M = 101$. However, we need additional additional disk I/O's if there are so many tuples with a given value that neither relation's tuples could fit in main memory. Calculate the total number of disk I/O's needed if:

a) There are only two Y-values, each appearing in half the tuples of R and half the tuples of S (recall Y is the join attribute or attributes).

b) There are five Y-values, each equally likely in each relation.

c) There are 10 Y-values, each equally likely in each relation.

! Exercise 4.5: Repeat Exercise 4.4 for the more efficient sort-join of Section 4.8.

Exercise 4.6: How much memory do we need to use a two-pass, sort-based algorithm for relations of 10,000 blocks each, if the operation is: (a) δ (b) γ (c) a binary operation such as join or union.

Exercise 4.7: Describe a two-pass, sort-based algorithm for each of the join-like operators of Exercise 2.4.

! **Exercise 4.8 :** Suppose records could be larger than blocks, i.e., we could have spanned records. How would the memory requirements of two-pass, sort-based algorithms change?

!! **Exercise 4.9 :** Sometimes, it is possible to save some disk I/O's if we leave the last sublist in memory. It may even make sense to use sublists of fewer than M blocks to take advantage of this effect. How many disk I/O's can be saved this way?

5 Two-Pass Algorithms Based on Hashing

There is a family of hash-based algorithms that attack the same problems as in Section 4. The essential idea behind all these algorithms is as follows. If the data is too big to store in main-memory buffers, hash all the tuples of the argument or arguments using an appropriate hash key. For all the common operations, there is a way to select the hash key so all the tuples that need to be considered together when we perform the operation fall into the same bucket.

We then perform the operation by working on one bucket at a time (or on a pair of buckets with the same hash value, in the case of a binary operation). In effect, we have reduced the size of the operand(s) by a factor equal to the number of buckets, which is roughly M. Notice that the sort-based algorithms of Section 4 also gain a factor of M by preprocessing, although the sorting and hashing approaches achieve their similar gains by rather different means.

5.1 Partitioning Relations by Hashing

To begin, let us review the way we would take a relation R and, using M buffers, partition R into $M - 1$ buckets of roughly equal size. We shall assume that h is the hash function, and that h takes complete tuples of R as its argument (i.e., all attributes of R are part of the hash key). We associate one buffer with each bucket. The last buffer holds blocks of R, one at a time. Each tuple t in the block is hashed to bucket $h(t)$ and copied to the appropriate buffer. If that buffer is full, we write it out to disk, and initialize another block for the same bucket. At the end, we write out the last block of each bucket if it is not empty. The algorithm is given in more detail in Fig. 12.

5.2 A Hash-Based Algorithm for Duplicate Elimination

We shall now consider the details of hash-based algorithms for the various operations of relational algebra that might need two-pass algorithms. First, consider duplicate elimination, that is, the operation $\delta(R)$. We hash R to $M - 1$ buckets, as in Fig. 12. Note that two copies of the same tuple t will hash to the same bucket. Thus, we can examine one bucket at a time, perform δ on that bucket in isolation, and take as the answer the union of $\delta(R_i)$, where

```
initialize M-1 buckets using M-1 empty buffers;
FOR each block b of relation R DO BEGIN
    read block b into the Mth buffer;
    FOR each tuple t in b DO BEGIN
        IF the buffer for bucket h(t) has no room for t THEN
            BEGIN
                copy the buffer to disk;
                initialize a new empty block in that buffer;
            END;
        copy t to the buffer for bucket h(t);
    END;
END;
FOR each bucket DO
    IF the buffer for this bucket is not empty THEN
        write the buffer to disk;
```

Figure 12: Partitioning a relation R into $M-1$ buckets

R_i is the portion of R that hashes to the ith bucket. The one-pass algorithm of Section 2.2 can be used to eliminate duplicates from each R_i in turn and write out the resulting unique tuples.

This method will work as long as the individual R_i's are sufficiently small to fit in main memory and thus allow a one-pass algorithm. Since we may assume the hash function h partitions R into equal-sized buckets, each R_i will be approximately $B(R)/(M-1)$ blocks in size. If that number of blocks is no larger than M, i.e., $B(R) \leq M(M-1)$, then the two-pass, hash-based algorithm will work. In fact, as we discussed in Section 2.2, it is only necessary that the number of distinct tuples in one bucket fit in M buffers. Thus, a conservative estimate (assuming M and $M-1$ are essentially the same) is $B(R) \leq M^2$, exactly as for the sort-based, two-pass algorithm for δ.

The number of disk I/O's is also similar to that of the sort-based algorithm. We read each block of R once as we hash its tuples, and we write each block of each bucket to disk. We then read each block of each bucket again in the one-pass algorithm that focuses on that bucket. Thus, the total number of disk I/O's is $3B(R)$.

5.3 Hash-Based Grouping and Aggregation

To perform the $\gamma_L(R)$ operation, we again start by hashing all the tuples of R to $M-1$ buckets. However, in order to make sure that all tuples of the same group wind up in the same bucket, we must choose a hash function that depends only on the grouping attributes of the list L.

Having partitioned R into buckets, we can then use the one-pass algorithm for γ from Section 2.2 to process each bucket in turn. As we discussed for δ in Section 5.2, we can process each bucket in main memory provided $B(R) \leq M^2$.

However, on the second pass, we need only one record per group as we process each bucket. Thus, even if the size of a bucket is larger than M, we can handle the bucket in one pass provided the records for all the groups in the bucket take no more than M buffers. As a consequence, if groups are large, then we may actually be able to handle much larger relations R than is indicated by the $B(R) \leq M^2$ rule. On the other hand, if M exceeds the number of groups, then we cannot fill all buckets. Thus, the actual limitation on the size of R as a function of M is complex, but $B(R) \leq M^2$ is a conservative estimate. Finally, we observe that the number of disk I/O's for γ, as for δ, is $3B(R)$.

5.4 Hash-Based Union, Intersection, and Difference

When the operation is binary, we must make sure that we use the same hash function to hash tuples of both arguments. For example, to compute $R \cup_S S$, we hash both R and S to $M - 1$ buckets each, say $R_1, R_2, \ldots, R_{M-1}$ and $S_1, S_2, \ldots, S_{M-1}$. We then take the set-union of R_i with S_i for all i, and output the result. Notice that if a tuple t appears in both R and S, then for some i we shall find t in both R_i and S_i. Thus, when we take the union of these two buckets, we shall output only one copy of t, and there is no possibility of introducing duplicates into the result. For $\cup_B$, the simple bag-union algorithm of Section 2.3 is preferable to any other approach for that operation.

To take the intersection or difference of R and S, we create the $2(M - 1)$ buckets exactly as for set-union and apply the appropriate one-pass algorithm to each pair of corresponding buckets. Notice that all these one-pass algorithms require $B(R) + B(S)$ disk I/O's. To this quantity we must add the two disk I/O's per block that are necessary to hash the tuples of the two relations and store the buckets on disk, for a total of $3\big(B(R) + B(S)\big)$ disk I/O's.

In order for the algorithms to work, we must be able to take the one-pass union, intersection, or difference of R_i and S_i, whose sizes will be approximately $B(R)/(M - 1)$ and $B(S)/(M - 1)$, respectively. Recall that the one-pass algorithms for these operations require that the smaller operand occupies at most $M - 1$ blocks. Thus, the two-pass, hash-based algorithms require that $\min\big(B(R), B(S)\big) \leq M^2$, approximately.

5.5 The Hash-Join Algorithm

To compute $R(X, Y) \bowtie S(Y, Z)$ using a two-pass, hash-based algorithm, we act almost as for the other binary operations discussed in Section 5.4. The only difference is that we must use as the hash key just the join attributes, Y. Then we can be sure that if tuples of R and S join, they will wind up in corresponding buckets R_i and S_i for some i. A one-pass join of all pairs of corresponding buckets completes this algorithm, which we call *hash-join.*[4]

Example 8: Let us renew our discussion of the two relations R and S from Example 4, whose sizes were 1000 and 500 blocks, respectively, and for which 101 main-memory buffers are made available. We may hash each relation to 100 buckets, so the average size of a bucket is 10 blocks for R and 5 blocks for S. Since the smaller number, 5, is much less than the number of available buffers, we expect to have no trouble performing a one-pass join on each pair of buckets.

The number of disk I/O's is 1500 to read each of R and S while hashing into buckets, another 1500 to write all the buckets to disk, and a third 1500 to read each pair of buckets into main memory again while taking the one-pass join of corresponding buckets. Thus, the number of disk I/O's required is 4500, just as for the efficient sort-join of Section 4.8. □

We may generalize Example 8 to conclude that:

- Hash join requires $3\big(B(R) + B(S)\big)$ disk I/O's to perform its task.
- The two-pass hash-join algorithm will work as long as approximately $\min\big(B(R), B(S)\big) \leq M^2$.

The argument for the latter point is the same as for the other binary operations: one of each pair of buckets must fit in $M - 1$ buffers.

5.6 Saving Some Disk I/O's

If there is more memory available on the first pass than we need to hold one block per bucket, then we have some opportunities to save disk I/O's. One option is to use several blocks for each bucket, and write them out as a group, in consecutive blocks of disk. Strictly speaking, this technique doesn't save disk I/O's, but it makes the I/O's go faster, since we save seek time and rotational latency when we write.

However, there are several tricks that have been used to avoid writing some of the buckets to disk and then reading them again. The most effective of them, called *hybrid hash-join*, works as follows. In general, suppose we decide that to join $R \bowtie S$, with S the smaller relation, we need to create k buckets, where k is much less than M, the available memory. When we hash S, we can choose to keep m of the k buckets entirely in main memory, while keeping only one block for each of the other $k - m$ buckets. We can manage to do so provided the expected size of the buckets in memory, plus one block for each of the other buckets, does not exceed M; that is:

$$mB(S)/k + k - m \leq M \tag{1}$$

[4]Sometimes, the term "hash-join" is reserved for the variant of the one-pass join algorithm of Section 2.3 in which a hash table is used as the main-memory search structure. Then, the two-pass hash-join algorithm described here is called "partition hash-join."

In explanation, the expected size of a bucket is $B(S)/k$, and there are m buckets in memory.

Now, when we read the tuples of the other relation, R, to hash that relation into buckets, we keep in memory:

1. The m buckets of S that were never written to disk, and

2. One block for each of the $k-m$ buckets of R whose corresponding buckets of S were written to disk.

If a tuple t of R hashes to one of the first m buckets, then we immediately join it with all the tuples of the corresponding S-bucket, as if this were a one-pass, hash-join. It is necessary to organize each of the in-memory buckets of S into an efficient search structure to facilitate this join, just as for the one-pass hash-join. If t hashes to one of the buckets whose corresponding S-bucket is on disk, then t is sent to the main-memory block for that bucket, and eventually migrates to disk, as for a two-pass, hash-based join.

On the second pass, we join the corresponding buckets of R and S as usual. However, there is no need to join the pairs of buckets for which the S-bucket was left in memory; these buckets have already been joined and their result output.

The savings in disk I/O's is equal to two for every block of the buckets of S that remain in memory, and their corresponding R-buckets. Since m/k of the buckets are in memory, the savings is $2(m/k)\big(B(R)+B(S)\big)$. We must thus ask how to maximize m/k, subject to the constraint of Equation (1). The surprising answer is: pick $m=1$, and then make k as small as possible.

The intuitive justification is that all but $k-m$ of the main-memory buffers can be used to hold tuples of S in main memory, and the more of these tuples, the fewer the disk I/O's. Thus, we want to minimize k, the total number of buckets. We do so by making each bucket about as big as can fit in main memory; that is, buckets are of size M, and therefore $k=B(S)/M$. If that is the case, then there is only room for one bucket in the extra main memory; i.e., $m=1$.

In fact, we really need to make the buckets slightly smaller than $B(S)/M$, or else we shall not quite have room for one full bucket and one block for the other $k-1$ buckets in memory at the same time. Assuming, for simplicity, that k is about $B(S)/M$ and $m=1$, the savings in disk I/O's is

$$2M\big(B(R)+B(S)\big)/B(S)$$

and the total cost is $\big(3-2M/B(S)\big)\big(B(R)+B(S)\big)$.

Example 9: Consider the problem of Example 4, where we had to join relations R and S, of 1000 and 500 blocks, respectively, using $M=101$. If we use a hybrid hash-join, then we want k, the number of buckets, to be about $500/101$. Suppose we pick $k=5$. Then the average bucket will have 100 blocks of S's tuples. If we try to fit one of these buckets and four extra blocks for the other four buckets, we need 104 blocks of main memory, and we cannot take the chance that the in-memory bucket will overflow memory.

Thus, we are advised to choose $k = 6$. Now, when hashing S on the first pass, we have five buffers for five of the buckets, and we have up to 96 buffers for the in-memory bucket, whose expected size is 500/6 or 83. The number of disk I/O's we use for S on the first pass is thus 500 to read all of S, and $500 - 83 = 417$ to write five buckets to disk. When we process R on the first pass, we need to read all of R (1000 disk I/O's) and write 5 of its 6 buckets (833 disk I/O's).

On the second pass, we read all the buckets written to disk, or $417 + 833 = 1250$ additional disk I/O's. The total number of disk I/O's is thus 1500 to read R and S, 1250 to write 5/6 of these relations, and another 1250 to read those tuples again, or 4000 disk I/O's. This figure compares with the 4500 disk I/O's needed for the straightforward hash-join or sort-join. □

5.7 Summary of Hash-Based Algorithms

Figure 13 gives the memory requirements and disk I/O's needed by each of the algorithms discussed in this section. As with other types of algorithms, we should observe that the estimates for γ and δ may be conservative, since they really depend on the number of duplicates and groups, respectively, rather than on the number of tuples in the argument relation.

Operators	Approximate M required	Disk I/O	Section
γ, δ	$\sqrt{B}$	$3B$	5.2, 5.3
$\cup$, $\cap$, $-$	$\sqrt{B(S)}$	$3(B(R) + B(S))$	5.4
$\bowtie$	$\sqrt{B(S)}$	$3(B(R) + B(S))$	5.5
$\bowtie$	$\sqrt{B(S)}$	$(3 - 2M/B(S))(B(R) + B(S))$	5.6

Figure 13: Main memory and disk I/O requirements for hash-based algorithms; for binary operations, assume $B(S) \leq B(R)$

Notice that the requirements for sort-based and the corresponding hash-based algorithms are almost the same. The significant differences between the two approaches are:

1. Hash-based algorithms for binary operations have a size requirement that depends only on the smaller of two arguments rather than on the sum of the argument sizes, that sort-based algorithms require.

2. Sort-based algorithms sometimes allow us to produce a result in sorted order and take advantage of that sort later. The result might be used in another sort-based algorithm for a subsequent operator, or it could be the answer to a query that is required to be produced in sorted order.

3. Hash-based algorithms depend on the buckets being of equal size. Since there is generally at least a small variation in size, it is not possible to use buckets that, on average, occupy M blocks; we must limit them to a slightly smaller figure. This effect is especially prominent if the number of different hash keys is small, e.g., performing a group-by on a relation with few groups or a join with very few values for the join attributes.

4. In sort-based algorithms, the sorted sublists may be written to consecutive blocks of the disk if we organize the disk properly. Thus, one of the three disk I/O's per block may require little rotational latency or seek time and therefore may be much faster than the I/O's needed for hash-based algorithms.

5. Moreover, if M is much larger than the number of sorted sublists, then we may read in several consecutive blocks at a time from a sorted sublist, again saving some latency and seek time.

6. On the other hand, if we can choose the number of buckets to be less than M in a hash-based algorithm, then we can write out several blocks of a bucket at once. We thus obtain the same benefit on the write step for hashing that the sort-based algorithms have for the second read, as we observed in (5). Similarly, we may be able to organize the disk so that a bucket eventually winds up on consecutive blocks of tracks. If so, buckets can be read with little latency or seek time, just as sorted sublists were observed in (4) to be writable efficiently.

5.8 Exercises for Section 5

Exercise 5.1: The hybrid-hash-join idea, storing one bucket in main memory, can also be applied to other operations. Show how to save the cost of storing and reading one bucket from each relation when implementing a two-pass, hash-based algorithm for: (a) δ (b) γ (c) $\cap_B$ (d) $-_S$.

Exercise 5.2: If $B(S) = B(R) = 10{,}000$ and $M = 1000$, what is the number of disk I/O's required for a hybrid hash join?

Exercise 5.3: Write iterators that implement the two-pass, hash-based algorithms for (a) δ (b) γ (c) $\cap_B$ (d) $-_S$ (e) $\bowtie$.

! **Exercise 5.4:** Suppose we are performing a two-pass, hash-based grouping operation on a relation R of the appropriate size; i.e., $B(R) \leq M^2$. However, there are so few groups, that some groups are larger than M; i.e., they will not fit in main memory at once. What modifications, if any, need to be made to the algorithm given here?

! **Exercise 5.5:** Suppose that we are using a disk where the time to move the head to a block is 100 milliseconds, and it takes 1/2 millisecond to read one block. Therefore, it takes $k/2$ milliseconds to read k consecutive blocks, once the head is positioned. Suppose we want to compute a two-pass hash-join $R \bowtie S$, where $B(R) = 1000$, $B(S) = 500$, and $M = 101$. To speed up the join, we want to use as few buckets as possible (assuming tuples distribute evenly among buckets), and read and write as many blocks as we can to consecutive positions on disk. Counting 100.5 milliseconds for a random disk I/O and $100 + k/2$ milliseconds for reading or writing k consecutive blocks from or to disk:

a) How much time does the disk I/O take?

b) How much time does the disk I/O take if we use a hybrid hash-join as described in Example 9?

c) How much time does a sort-based join take under the same conditions, assuming we write sorted sublists to consecutive blocks of disk?

6 Index-Based Algorithms

The existence of an index on one or more attributes of a relation makes available some algorithms that would not be feasible without the index. Index-based algorithms are especially useful for the selection operator, but algorithms for join and other binary operators also use indexes to very good advantage. In this section, we shall introduce these algorithms. We also continue with the discussion of the index-scan operator for accessing a stored table with an index that we began in Section 1.1. To appreciate many of the issues, we first need to digress and consider "clustering" indexes.

6.1 Clustering and Nonclustering Indexes

Recall from Section 1.3 that a relation is "clustered" if its tuples are packed into roughly as few blocks as can possibly hold those tuples. All the analyses we have done so far assume that relations are clustered.

We may also speak of *clustering indexes*, which are indexes on an attribute or attributes such that all the tuples with a fixed value for the search key of this index appear on roughly as few blocks as can hold them. Note that a relation that isn't clustered cannot have a clustering index,[5] but even a clustered relation can have nonclustering indexes.

[5]Technically, if the index is on a key for the relation, so only one tuple with a given value in the index key exists, then the index is always "clustering," even if the relation is not clustered. However, if there is only one tuple per index-key value, then there is no advantage from clustering, and the performance measure for such an index is the same as if it were considered nonclustering.

Example 10: A relation $R(a, b)$ that is sorted on attribute a and stored in that order, packed into blocks, is surely clustered. An index on a is a clustering index, since for a given a-value a_1, all the tuples with that value for a are consecutive. They thus appear packed into blocks, except possibly for the first and last blocks that contain a-value a_1, as suggested in Fig. 14. However, an index on b is unlikely to be clustering, since the tuples with a fixed b-value will be spread all over the file unless the values of a and b are very closely correlated. □

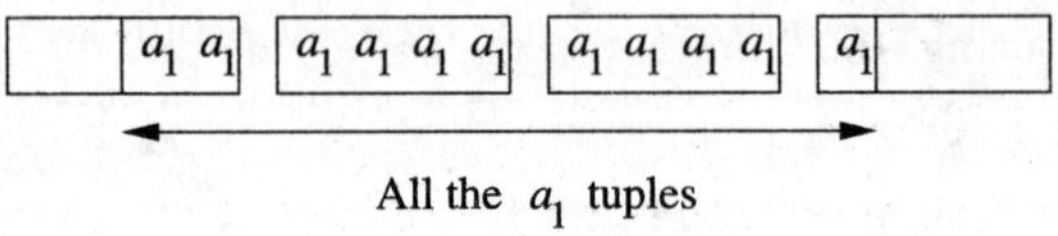

Figure 14: A clustering index has all tuples with a fixed value packed into (close to) the minimum possible number of blocks

6.2 Index-Based Selection

In Section 1.1 we discussed implementing a selection $\sigma_C(R)$ by reading all the tuples of relation R, seeing which meet the condition C, and outputting those that do. If there are no indexes on R, then that is the best we can do; the number of disk I/O's used by the operation is $B(R)$, or even $T(R)$, the number of tuples of R, should R not be a clustered relation.[6] However, suppose that the condition C is of the form $a = v$, where a is an attribute for which an index exists, and v is a value. Then one can search the index with value v and get pointers to exactly those tuples of R that have a-value v. These tuples constitute the result of $\sigma_{a=v}(R)$, so all we have to do is retrieve them.

If the index on $R.a$ is a clustering index, then the number of disk I/O's to retrieve the set $\sigma_{a=v}(R)$ will average $B(R)/V(R, a)$. The actual number may be somewhat higher for several reasons:

1. Often, the index is not kept entirely in main memory, and some disk I/O's are needed to support the index lookup.

2. Even though all the tuples with $a = v$ might fit in b blocks, they could be spread over $b + 1$ blocks because they don't start at the beginning of a block.

[6] Recall from Section 1.3 the notation we developed: $T(R)$ for the number of tuples in R, $B(R)$ for the number of blocks in which R fits, and $V(R, L)$ for the number of distinct tuples in $\pi_L(R)$.

3. Even though the tuples of R may be clustered, they may not be packed as tightly as possible into blocks. For example, there could be extra space for tuples to be inserted into R later, or R could be in a clustered file.

Moreover, we of course must round up if the ratio $B(R)/V(R,a)$ is not an integer. Most significant is that should a be a key for R, then $V(R,a) = T(R)$, which is presumably much bigger than $B(R)$, yet we surely require one disk I/O to retrieve the tuple with key value v, plus whatever disk I/O's are needed to access the index.

Now, let us consider what happens when the index on $R.a$ is nonclustering. To a first approximation, each tuple we retrieve will be on a different block, and we must access $T(R)/V(R,a)$ tuples. Thus, $T(R)/V(R,a)$ is an estimate of the number of disk I/O's we need. The number could be higher because we may also need to read some index blocks from disk; it could be lower because fortuitously some retrieved tuples appear on the same block, and that block remains buffered in memory.

Example 11: Suppose $B(R) = 1000$, and $T(R) = 20{,}000$. That is, R has 20,000 tuples, packed at most 20 to a block. Let a be one of the attributes of R, suppose there is an index on a, and consider the operation $\sigma_{a=0}(R)$. Here are some possible situations and the worst-case number of disk I/O's required. We shall ignore the cost of accessing the index blocks in all cases.

1. If R is clustered, but we do not use the index, then the cost is 1000 disk I/O's. That is, we must retrieve every block of R.

2. If R is not clustered and we do not use the index, then the cost is 20,000 disk I/O's.

3. If $V(R,a) = 100$ and the index is clustering, then the index-based algorithm uses $1000/100 = 10$ disk I/O's, plus whatever is needed to access the index.

4. If $V(R,a) = 10$ and the index is nonclustering, then the index-based algorithm uses $20{,}000/10 = 2000$ disk I/O's. Notice that this cost is higher than scanning the entire relation R, if R is clustered but the index is not.

5. If $V(R,a) = 20{,}000$, i.e., a is a key, then the index-based algorithm takes 1 disk I/O plus whatever is needed to access the index, regardless of whether the index is clustering or not.

□

Index-scan as an access method can help in several other kinds of selection operations.

a) An index such as a B-tree lets us access the search-key values in a given range efficiently. If such an index on attribute a of relation R exists, then we can use the index to retrieve just the tuples of R in the desired range for selections such as $\sigma_{a\geq 10}(R)$, or even $\sigma_{a\geq 10 \texttt{ AND } a\leq 20}(R)$.

b) A selection with a complex condition C can sometimes be implemented by an index-scan followed by another selection on only those tuples retrieved by the index-scan. If C is of the form $a = v$ AND C', where C' is any condition, then we can split the selection into a cascade of two selections, the first checking only for $a = v$, and the second checking condition C'. The first is a candidate for use of the index-scan operator. This splitting of a selection operation is one of many improvements that a query optimizer may make to a logical query plan.

6.3 Joining by Using an Index

All the binary operations we have considered, and the unary full-relation operations of γ and δ as well, can use certain indexes profitably. We shall leave most of these algorithms as exercises, while we focus on the matter of joins. In particular, let us examine the natural join $R(X,Y) \bowtie S(Y,Z)$; recall that X, Y, and Z can stand for sets of attributes, although it is sufficient to think of them as single attributes.

For our first index-based join algorithm, suppose that S has an index on the attribute(s) Y. Then one way to compute the join is to examine each block of R, and within each block consider each tuple t. Let t_Y be the component or components of t corresponding to the attribute(s) Y. Use the index to find all those tuples of S that have t_Y in their Y-component(s). These are exactly the tuples of S that join with tuple t of R, so we output the join of each of these tuples with t.

The number of disk I/O's depends on several factors. First, assuming R is clustered, we shall have to read $B(R)$ blocks to get all the tuples of R. If R is not clustered, then up to $T(R)$ disk I/O's may be required.

For each tuple t of R we must read an average of $T(S)/V(S,Y)$ tuples of S. If S has a nonclustered index on Y, then the number of disk I/O's required to read S is $T(R)T(S)/V(S,Y)$, but if the index is clustered, then only $T(R)B(S)/V(S,Y)$ disk I/O's suffice.[7] In either case, we may have to add a few disk I/O's per Y-value, to account for the reading of the index itself.

Regardless of whether or not R is clustered, the cost of accessing tuples of S dominates. Ignoring the cost of reading R, we shall take $T(R)T(S)/V(S,Y)$ or $T(R)\big(\max(1, B(S)/V(S,Y))\big)$ as the cost of this join method, for the cases of nonclustered and clustered indexes on S, respectively.

---

[7]But remember that $B(S)/V(S,Y)$ must be replaced by 1 if it is less, as discussed in Section 6.2.

Example 12: Let us consider our running example, relations $R(X,Y)$ and $S(Y,Z)$ covering 1000 and 500 blocks, respectively. Assume ten tuples of either relation fit on one block, so $T(R) = 10{,}000$ and $T(S) = 5000$. Also, assume $V(S,Y) = 100$; i.e., there are 100 different values of Y among the tuples of S.

Suppose that R is clustered, and there is a clustering index on Y for S. Then the approximate number of disk I/O's, excluding what is needed to access the index itself, is 1000 to read the blocks of R plus $10{,}000 \times 500 / 100 = 50{,}000$ disk I/O's. This number is considerably above the cost of other methods for the same data discussed previously. If either R or the index on S is not clustered, then the cost is even higher. □

While Example 12 makes it look as if an index-join is a very bad idea, there are other situations where the join $R \bowtie S$ by this method makes much more sense. Most common is the case where R is very small compared with S, and $V(S,Y)$ is large. We discuss in Exercise 6.5 a typical query in which selection before a join makes R tiny. In that case, most of S will never be examined by this algorithm, since most Y-values don't appear in R at all. However, both sort- and hash-based join methods will examine every tuple of S at least once.

6.4 Joins Using a Sorted Index

When the index is a B-tree, or any other structure from which we easily can extract the tuples of a relation in sorted order, we have a number of other opportunities to use the index. Perhaps the simplest is when we want to compute $R(X,Y) \bowtie S(Y,Z)$, and we have such an index on Y for either R or S. We can then perform an ordinary sort-join, but we do not have to perform the intermediate step of sorting one of the relations on Y.

As an extreme case, if we have sorting indexes on Y for both R and S, then we need to perform only the final step of the simple sort-based join of Section 4.6. This method is sometimes called *zig-zag join*, because we jump back and forth between the indexes finding Y-values that they share in common. Notice that tuples from R with a Y-value that does not appear in S need never be retrieved, and similarly, tuples of S whose Y-value does not appear in R need not be retrieved.

Example 13: Suppose that we have relations $R(X,Y)$ and $S(Y,Z)$ with indexes on Y for both relations. In a tiny example, let the search keys (Y-values) for the tuples of R be in order $1,3,4,4,4,5,6$, and let the search key values for S be $2,2,4,4,6,7$. We start with the first keys of R and S, which are 1 and 2, respectively. Since $1 < 2$, we skip the first key of R and look at the second key, 3. Now, the current key of S is less than the current key of R, so we skip the two 2's of S to reach 4.

At this point, the key 3 of R is less than the key of S, so we skip the key of R. Now, both current keys are 4. We follow the pointers associated with all the keys 4 from both relations, retrieve the corresponding tuples, and join them. Notice that until we met the common key 4, no tuples of the relation were retrieved.

Having dispensed with the 4's, we go to key 5 of R and key 6 of S. Since $5 < 6$, we skip to the next key of R. Now the keys are both 6, so we retrieve the corresponding tuples and join them. Since R is now exhausted, we know there are no more pairs of tuples from the two relations that join. □

If the indexes are B-trees, then we can scan the leaves of the two B-trees in order from the left, using the pointers from leaf to leaf that are built into the structure, as suggested in Fig. 15. If R and S are clustered, then retrieval of all the tuples with a given key will result in a number of disk I/O's proportional to the fractions of these two relations read. Note that in extreme cases, where there are so many tuples from R and S that neither fits in the available main memory, we shall have to use a fixup like that discussed in Section 4.6. However, in typical cases, the step of joining all tuples with a common Y-value can be carried out with only as many disk I/O's as it takes to read them.

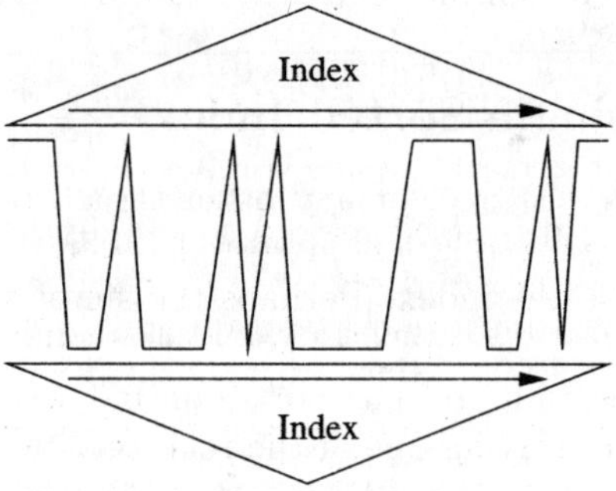

Figure 15: A zig-zag join using two indexes

Example 14: Let us continue with Example 12, to see how joins using a combination of sorting and indexing would typically perform on this data. First, assume that there is an index on Y for S that allows us to retrieve the tuples of S sorted by Y. We shall, in this example, also assume both relations and the index are clustered. For the moment, we assume there is no index on R.

Assuming 101 available blocks of main memory, we may use them to create 10 sorted sublists for the 1000-block relation R. The number of disk I/O's is 2000 to read and write all of R. We next use 11 blocks of memory — 10 for the sublists of R and one for a block of S's tuples, retrieved via the index. We neglect disk I/O's and memory buffers needed to manipulate the index, but if the index is a B-tree, these numbers will be small anyway. In this second pass, we read all the tuples of R and S, using a total of 1500 disk I/O's, plus the small amount needed for reading the index blocks once each. We thus estimate the total number of disk I/O's at 3500, which is less than that for other methods considered so far.

Now, assume that both R and S have indexes on Y. Then there is no need to sort either relation. We use just 1500 disk I/O's to read the blocks of R and S through their indexes. In fact, if we determine from the indexes alone that a large fraction of R or S cannot match tuples of the other relation, then the total cost could be considerably less than 1500 disk I/O's. However, in any event we should add the small number of disk I/O's needed to read the indexes themselves. □

6.5 Exercises for Section 6

Exercise 6.1: Suppose there is an index on attribute $R.a$. Describe how this index could be used to improve the execution of the following operations. Under what circumstances would the index-based algorithm be more efficient than sort- or hash-based algorithms?

a) $R \cup_S S$ (assume that R and S have no duplicates, although they may have tuples in common).

b) $R \cap_S S$ (again, with R and S sets).

c) $\delta(R)$.

Exercise 6.2: Suppose $B(R) = 10{,}000$ and $T(R) = 500{,}000$. Let there be an index on $R.a$, and let $V(R, a) = k$ for some number k. Give the cost of $\sigma_{a=0}(R)$, as a function of k, under the following circumstances. You may neglect disk I/O's needed to access the index itself.

a) The index is clustering.

b) The index is not clustering.

c) R is clustered, and the index is not used.

Exercise 6.3: Repeat Exercise 6.2 if the operation is the range query $\sigma_{C \leq a \texttt{ AND } a \leq D}(R)$. You may assume that C and D are constants such that $k/10$ of the values are in the range.

! **Exercise 6.4:** If R is clustered, but the index on $R.a$ is *not* clustering, then depending on k we may prefer to implement a query by performing a table-scan of R or using the index. For what values of k would we prefer to use the index if the relation and query are as in (a) Exercise 6.2 (b) Exercise 6.3.

Exercise 6.5: Consider the SQL query:

```
SELECT birthdate FROM StarsIn, MovieStar
WHERE movieTitle = 'King Kong' AND starName = name;
```

This query uses the "movie" relations:

```
StarsIn(movieTitle, movieYear, starName)
MovieStar(name, address, gender, birthdate)
```

If we translate it to relational algebra, the heart is an equijoin between

$$\sigma_{movieTitle=\texttt{'King Kong'}}(\texttt{StarsIn})$$

and MovieStar, which can be implemented much as a natural join $R \bowtie S$. Since there were only three movies named "King Kong," $T(R)$ is very small. Suppose that S, the relation MovieStar, has an index on name. Compare the cost of an index-join for this $R \bowtie S$ with the cost of a sort- or hash-based join.

! **Exercise 6.6:** In Example 14 we discussed the disk-I/O cost of a join $R \bowtie S$ in which one or both of R and S had sorting indexes on the join attribute(s). However, the methods described in that example can fail if there are too many tuples with the same value in the join attribute(s). What are the limits (in number of blocks occupied by tuples with the same value) under which the methods described will not need to do additional disk I/O's?

7 Buffer Management

We have assumed that operators on relations have available some number M of main-memory buffers that they can use to store needed data. In practice, these buffers are rarely allocated in advance to the operator, and the value of M may vary depending on system conditions. The central task of making main-memory buffers available to processes, such as queries, that act on the database is given to the *buffer manager*. It is the responsibility of the buffer manager to allow processes to get the memory they need, while minimizing the delay and unsatisfiable requests. The role of the buffer manager is illustrated in Fig. 16.

7.1 Buffer Management Architecture

There are two broad architectures for a buffer manager:

1. The buffer manager controls main memory directly, as in many relational DBMS's, or

2. The buffer manager allocates buffers in virtual memory, allowing the operating system to decide which buffers are actually in main memory at any time and which are in the "swap space" on disk that the operating system manages. Many "main-memory" DBMS's and "object-oriented" DBMS's operate this way.

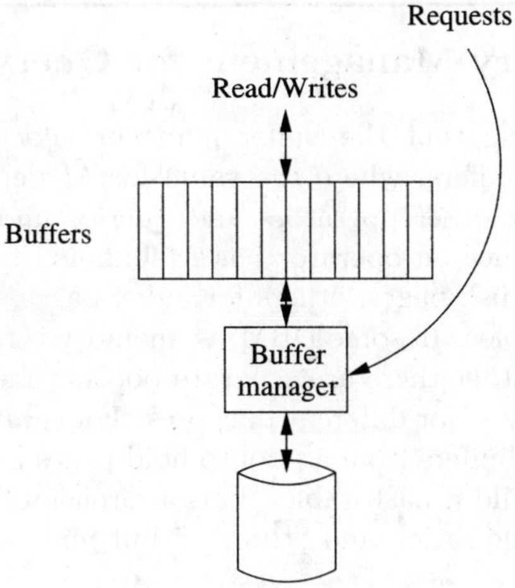

Figure 16: The buffer manager responds to requests for main-memory access to disk blocks

Whichever approach a DBMS uses, the same problem arises: the buffer manager should limit the number of buffers in use so they fit in the available main memory. When the buffer manager controls main memory directly, and requests exceed available space, it has to select a buffer to empty, by returning its contents to disk. If the buffered block has not been changed, then it may simply be erased from main memory, but if the block has changed it must be written back to its place on the disk. When the buffer manager allocates space in virtual memory, it has the option to allocate more buffers than can fit in main memory. However, if all these buffers are really in use, then there will be "thrashing," a common operating-system problem, where many blocks are moved in and out of the disk's swap space. In this situation, the system spends most of its time swapping blocks, while very little useful work gets done.

Normally, the number of buffers is a parameter set when the DBMS is initialized. We would expect that this number is set so that the buffers occupy the available main memory, regardless of whether the buffers are allocated in main or virtual memory. In what follows, we shall not concern ourselves with which mode of buffering is used, and simply assume that there is a fixed-size *buffer pool*, a set of buffers available to queries and other database actions.

7.2 Buffer Management Strategies

The critical choice that the buffer manager must make is what block to throw out of the buffer pool when a buffer is needed for a newly requested block. The *buffer-replacement strategies* in common use may be familiar to you from other applications of scheduling policies, such as in operating systems. These include:

Memory Management for Query Processing

We are assuming that the buffer manager allocates to an operator M main-memory buffers, where the value for M depends on system conditions (including other operators and queries underway), and may vary dynamically. Once an operator has M buffers, it may use some of them for bringing in disk pages, others for index pages, and still others for sort runs or hash tables. In some DBMS's, memory is not allocated from a single pool, but rather there are separate pools of memory — with separate buffer managers — for different purposes. For example, an operator might be allocated D buffers from a pool to hold pages brought in from disk and H buffers to build a hash table. This approach offers more opportunities for system configuration and "tuning," but may not make the best global use of memory.

Least-Recently Used (LRU)

The LRU rule is to throw out the block that has not been read or written for the longest time. This method requires that the buffer manager maintain a table indicating the last time the block in each buffer was accessed. It also requires that each database access make an entry in this table, so there is significant effort in maintaining this information. However, LRU is an effective strategy; intuitively, buffers that have not been used for a long time are less likely to be accessed sooner than those that have been accessed recently.

First-In-First-Out (FIFO)

When a buffer is needed, under the FIFO policy the buffer that has been occupied the longest by the same block is emptied and used for the new block. In this approach, the buffer manager needs to know only the time at which the block currently occupying a buffer was loaded into that buffer. An entry into a table can thus be made when the block is read from disk, and there is no need to modify the table when the block is accessed. FIFO requires less maintenance than LRU, but it can make more mistakes. A block that is used repeatedly, say the root block of a B-tree index, will eventually become the oldest block in a buffer. It will be written back to disk, only to be reread shortly thereafter into another buffer.

The "Clock" Algorithm ("Second Chance")

This algorithm is a commonly implemented, efficient approximation to LRU. Think of the buffers as arranged in a circle, as suggested by Fig. 17. A "hand" points to one of the buffers, and will rotate clockwise if it needs to find a buffer in which to place a disk block. Each buffer has an associated "flag," which is either 0 or 1. Buffers with a 0 flag are vulnerable to having their contents sent back to disk; buffers with a 1 are not. When a block is read into a buffer, its flag is set to 1. Likewise, when the contents of a buffer is accessed, its flag is set to 1.

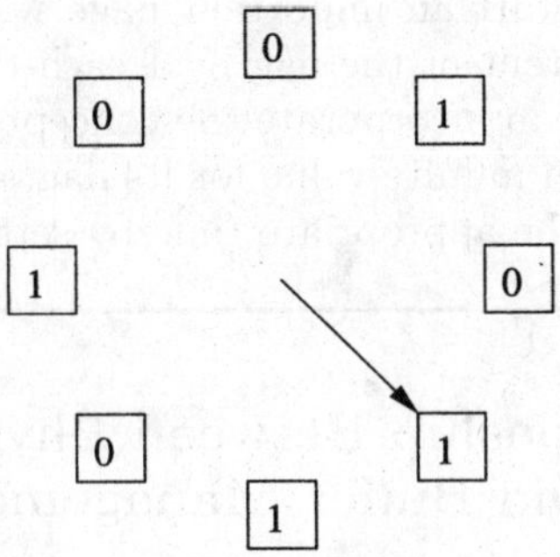

Figure 17: The clock algorithm visits buffers in a round-robin fashion and replaces $01 \cdots 1$ with $10 \cdots 0$

When the buffer manager needs a buffer for a new block, it looks for the first 0 it can find, rotating clockwise. If it passes 1's, it sets them to 0. Thus, a block is only thrown out of its buffer if it remains unaccessed for the time it takes the hand to make a complete rotation to set its flag to 0 and then make another complete rotation to find the buffer with its 0 unchanged. For instance, in Fig. 17, the hand will set to 0 the 1 in the buffer to its left, and then move clockwise to find the buffer with 0, whose block it will replace and whose flag it will set to 1.

System Control

The query processor or other components of a DBMS can give advice to the buffer manager in order to avoid some of the mistakes that would occur with a strict policy such as LRU, FIFO, or Clock. There are sometimes technical reasons why a block in main memory can *not* be moved to disk without first modifying certain other blocks that point to it. These blocks are called "pinned," and any buffer manager has to modify its buffer-replacement strategy to avoid expelling pinned blocks. This fact gives us the opportunity to force other blocks to remain in main memory by declaring them "pinned," even if there is no technical reason why they could not be written to disk. For example, a cure for the problem with FIFO mentioned above regarding the root of a B-tree is to "pin" the root, forcing it to remain in memory at all times. Similarly, for an algorithm like a one-pass hash-join, the query processor may "pin" the blocks of the smaller relation in order to assure that it will remain in main memory during the entire time.

More Tricks Using the Clock Algorithm

The "clock" algorithm for choosing buffers to free is not limited to the scheme described in Section 7.2, where flags had values 0 and 1. For instance, one can start an important page with a number higher than 1 as its flag, and decrement the flag by 1 each time the "hand" passes that page. In fact, one can incorporate the concept of pinning blocks by giving the pinned block an infinite value for its flag, and then having the system release the pin at the appropriate time by setting the flag to 0.

7.3 The Relationship Between Physical Operator Selection and Buffer Management

The query optimizer will eventually select a set of physical operators that will be used to execute a given query. This selection of operators may assume that a certain number of buffers M is available for execution of each of these operators. However, as we have seen, the buffer manager may not be willing or able to guarantee the availability of these M buffers when the query is executed. There are thus two related questions to ask about the physical operators:

1. Can the algorithm adapt to changes in the value of M, the number of main-memory buffers available?
2. When the expected M buffers are not available, and some blocks that are expected to be in memory have actually been moved to disk by the buffer manager, how does the buffer-replacement strategy used by the buffer manager impact the number of additional I/O's that must be performed?

Example 15: As an example of the issues, let us consider the block-based nested-loop join of Fig. 8. The basic algorithm does not really depend on the value of M, although its performance depends on M. Thus, it is sufficient to find out what M is just before execution begins.

It is even possible that M will change at different iterations of the outer loop. That is, each time we load main memory with a portion of the relation S (the relation of the outer loop), we can use all but one of the buffers available at that time; the remaining buffer is reserved for a block of R, the relation of the inner loop. Thus, the number of times we go around the outer loop depends on the average number of buffers available at each iteration. However, as long as M buffers are available *on average*, then the cost analysis of Section 3.4 will hold. In the extreme, we might have the good fortune to find that at the first iteration, enough buffers are available to hold all of S, in which case nested-loop join gracefully becomes the one-pass join of Section 2.3.

As another example of how nested-loop join interacts with buffering, suppose that we use an LRU buffer-replacement strategy, and there are k buffers available to hold blocks of R. As we read each block of R, in order, the blocks that remain in buffers at the end of this iteration of the outer loop will be the last k blocks of R. We next reload the $M - 1$ buffers for S with new blocks of S and start reading the blocks of R again, in the next iteration of the outer loop. However, if we start from the beginning of R again, then the k buffers for R will need to be replaced, and we do not save disk I/O's just because $k > 1$.

A better implementation of nested-loop join, when an LRU buffer-replacement strategy is used, visits the blocks of R in an order that alternates: first-to-last and then last-to-first (called *rocking*). In that way, if there are k buffers available to R, we save k disk I/O's on each iteration of the outer loop except the first. That is, the second and subsequent iterations require only $B(R) - k$ disk I/O's for R. Notice that even if $k = 1$ (i.e., no *extra* buffers are available to R), we save one disk I/O per iteration. □

Other algorithms also are impacted by the fact that M can vary and by the buffer-replacement strategy used by the buffer manager. Here are some useful observations.

- If we use a sort-based algorithm for some operator, then it is possible to adapt to changes in M. If M shrinks, we can change the size of a sublist, since the sort-based algorithms we discussed do not depend on the sublists being the same size. The major limitation is that as M shrinks, we could be forced to create so many sublists that we cannot then allocate a buffer for each sublist in the merging process.

- If the algorithm is hash-based, we can reduce the number of buckets if M shrinks, as long as the buckets do not then become so large that they do not fit in allotted main memory. However, unlike sort-based algorithms, we cannot respond to changes in M while the algorithm runs. Rather, once the number of buckets is chosen, it remains fixed throughout the first pass, and if buffers become unavailable, the blocks belonging to some of the buckets will have to be swapped out.

7.4 Exercises for Section 7

Exercise 7.1: Suppose that we wish to execute a join $R \bowtie S$, and the available memory will vary between M and $M/2$. In terms of M, $B(R)$, and $B(S)$, give the conditions under which we can guarantee that the following algorithms can be executed:

a) A one-pass join.

b) A two-pass, hash-based join.

c) A two-pass, sort-based join.

! **Exercise 7.2:** How would the number of disk I/O's taken by a nested-loop join improve if extra buffers became available and the buffer-replacement policy were:

a) First-in-first-out.

b) The clock algorithm.

!! **Exercise 7.3:** In Example 15, we suggested that it was possible to take advantage of extra buffers becoming available during the join by keeping more than one block of R buffered and visiting the blocks of R in reverse order on even-numbered iterations of the outer loop. However, we could also maintain only one buffer for R and increase the number of buffers used for S. Which strategy yields the fewest disk I/O's?

8 Algorithms Using More Than Two Passes

While two passes are enough for operations on all but the largest relations, we should observe that the principal techniques discussed in Sections 4 and 5 generalize to algorithms that, by using as many passes as necessary, can process relations of arbitrary size. In this section we shall consider the generalization of both sort- and hash-based approaches.

8.1 Multipass Sort-Based Algorithms

In Section 4.1 we alluded to how 2PMMS could be extended to a three-pass algorithm. In fact, there is a simple recursive approach to sorting that will allow us to sort a relation, however large, completely, or if we prefer, to create n sorted sublists for any desired n.

Suppose we have M main-memory buffers available to sort a relation R, which we shall assume is stored clustered. Then do the following:

BASIS: If R fits in M blocks (i.e., $B(R) \leq M$), then read R into main memory, sort it using any main-memory sorting algorithm, and write the sorted relation to disk.

INDUCTION: If R does not fit into main memory, partition the blocks holding R into M groups, which we shall call $R_1, R_2, \ldots, R_M$. Recursively sort R_i for each $i = 1, 2, \ldots, M$. Then, merge the M sorted sublists, as in Section 4.1.

If we are not merely sorting R, but performing a unary operation such as γ or δ on R, then we modify the above so that at the final merge we perform the operation on the tuples at the front of the sorted sublists. That is,

- For a δ, output one copy of each distinct tuple, and skip over copies of the tuple.

- For a γ, sort on the grouping attributes only, and combine the tuples with a given value of these grouping attributes in the appropriate manner, as discussed in Section 4.3.

When we want to perform a binary operation, such as intersection or join, we use essentially the same idea, except that the two relations are first divided into a total of M sublists. Then, each sublist is sorted by the recursive algorithm above. Finally, we read each of the M sublists, each into one buffer, and we perform the operation in the manner described by the appropriate subsection of Section 4.

We can divide the M buffers between relations R and S as we wish. However, to minimize the total number of passes, we would normally divide the buffers in proportion to the number of blocks taken by the relations. That is, R gets $M \times B(R)/\big(B(R) + B(S)\big)$ of the buffers, and S gets the rest.

8.2 Performance of Multipass, Sort-Based Algorithms

Now, let us explore the relationship between the number of disk I/O's required, the size of the relation(s) operated upon, and the size of main memory. Let $s(M, k)$ be the maximum size of a relation that we can sort using M buffers and k passes. Then we can compute $s(M, k)$ as follows:

BASIS: If $k = 1$, i.e., one pass is allowed, then we must have $B(R) \leq M$. Put another way, $s(M, 1) = M$.

INDUCTION: Suppose $k > 1$. Then we partition R into M pieces, each of which must be sortable in $k - 1$ passes. If $B(R) = s(M, k)$, then $s(M, k)/M$, which is the size of each of the M pieces of R, cannot exceed $s(M, k-1)$. That is: $s(M, k) = Ms(M, k - 1)$.

If we expand the above recursion, we find

$$s(M, k) = Ms(M, k - 1) = M^2 s(M, k - 2) = \cdots = M^{k-1} s(M, 1)$$

Since $s(M, 1) = M$, we conclude that $s(M, k) = M^k$. That is, using k passes, we can sort a relation R if $B(R) \leq M^k$. Put another way, if we want to sort R in k passes, then the minimum number of buffers we can use is $M = \big(B(R)\big)^{1/k}$.

Each pass of a sorting algorithm reads all the data from disk and writes it out again. Thus, a k-pass sorting algorithm requires $2kB(R)$ disk I/O's.

Now, let us consider the cost of a multipass join $R(X, Y) \bowtie S(Y, Z)$, as representative of a binary operation on relations. Let $j(M, k)$ be the largest number of blocks such that in k passes, using M buffers, we can join relations of $j(M, k)$ or fewer total blocks. That is, the join can be accomplished provided $B(R) + B(S) \leq j(M, k)$.

On the final pass, we merge M sorted sublists from the two relations. Each of the sublists is sorted using $k - 1$ passes, so they can be no longer than $s(M, k - 1) = M^{k-1}$ each, or a total of $Ms(M, k - 1) = M^k$. That is,

$B(R) + B(S) \leq M^k$. Reversing the role of the parameters, we can also state that to compute the join in k passes requires $\big(B(R) + B(S)\big)^{1/k}$ buffers.

To calculate the number of disk I/O's needed in the multipass algorithms, we should remember that, unlike for sorting, we do not count the cost of writing the final result to disk for joins or other relational operations. Thus, we use $2(k-1)\big(B(R)+B(S)\big)$ disk I/O's to sort the sublists, and another $B(R)+B(S)$ disk I/O's to read the sorted sublists in the final pass. The result is a total of $(2k-1)\big(B(R)+B(S)\big)$ disk I/O's.

8.3 Multipass Hash-Based Algorithms

There is a corresponding recursive approach to using hashing for operations on large relations. We hash the relation or relations into $M-1$ buckets, where M is the number of available memory buffers. We then apply the operation to each bucket individually, in the case of a unary operation. If the operation is binary, such as a join, we apply the operation to each pair of corresponding buckets, as if they were the entire relations. We can describe this approach recursively as:

BASIS: For a unary operation, if the relation fits in M buffers, read it into memory and perform the operation. For a binary operation, if either relation fits in $M-1$ buffers, perform the operation by reading this relation into main memory and then read the second relation, one block at a time, into the Mth buffer.

INDUCTION: If no relation fits in main memory, then hash each relation into $M-1$ buckets, as discussed in Section 5.1. Recursively perform the operation on each bucket or corresponding pair of buckets, and accumulate the output from each bucket or pair.

8.4 Performance of Multipass Hash-Based Algorithms

In what follows, we shall make the assumption that when we hash a relation, the tuples divide as evenly as possible among the buckets. In practice, this assumption will be met approximately if we choose a truly random hash function, but there will always be some unevenness in the distribution of tuples among buckets.

First, consider a unary operation, like γ or δ on a relation R using M buffers. Let $u(M, k)$ be the number of blocks in the largest relation that a k-pass hashing algorithm can handle. We can define u recursively by:

BASIS: $u(M, 1) = M$, since the relation R must fit in M buffers; i.e., $B(R) \leq M$.

INDUCTION: We assume that the first step divides the relation R into $M-1$ buckets of equal size. Thus, we can compute $u(M, k)$ as follows. The buckets for the next pass must be sufficiently small that they can be handled in $k-1$

passes; that is, the buckets are of size $u(M, k-1)$. Since R is divided into $M-1$ buckets, we must have $u(M, k) = (M-1)u(M, k-1)$.

If we expand the recurrence above, we find that $u(M, k) = M(M-1)^{k-1}$, or approximately, assuming M is large, $u(M, k) = M^k$. Equivalently, we can perform one of the unary relational operations on relation R in k passes with M buffers, provided $M \geq \left(B(R)\right)^{1/k}$.

We may perform a similar analysis for binary operations. As in Section 8.2, let us consider the join. Let $j(M, k)$ be an upper bound on the size of the smaller of the two relations R and S involved in $R(X, Y) \bowtie S(Y, Z)$. Here, as before, M is the number of available buffers and k is the number of passes we can use.

BASIS: $j(M, 1) = M - 1$; that is, if we use the one-pass algorithm to join, then either R or S must fit in $M - 1$ blocks, as we discussed in Section 2.3.

INDUCTION: $j(M, k) = (M-1)j(M, k-1)$; that is, on the first of k passes, we can divide each relation into $M-1$ buckets, and we may expect each bucket to be $1/(M-1)$ of its entire relation, but we must then be able to join each pair of corresponding buckets in $M - 1$ passes.

By expanding the recurrence for $j(M, k)$, we conclude that $j(M, k) = (M-1)^k$. Again assuming M is large, we can say approximately $j(M, k) = M^k$. That is, we can join $R(X, Y) \bowtie S(Y, Z)$ using k passes and M buffers provided $\min\left(B(R), B(S)\right) \leq M^k$.

8.5 Exercises for Section 8

Exercise 8.1: Suppose $B(R) = 20{,}000$, $B(S) = 50{,}000$, and $M = 101$. Describe the behavior of the following algorithms to compute $R \bowtie S$:

a) A three-pass, sort-based algorithm.

b) A three-pass, hash-based algorithm.

! Exercise 8.2: There are several "tricks" we have discussed for improving the performance of two-pass algorithms. For the following, tell whether the trick could be used in a multipass algorithm, and if so, how?

a) The hybrid-hash-join trick of Section 5.6.

b) Improving a sort-based algorithm by storing blocks consecutively on disk (Section 5.7).

c) Improving a hash-based algorithm by storing blocks consecutively on disk (Section 5.7).

9 Summary

- *Query Processing*: Queries are compiled, which involves extensive optimization, and then executed. The study of query execution involves knowing methods for executing operations of relational algebra with some extensions to match the capabilities of SQL.

- *Query Plans*: Queries are compiled first into logical query plans, which are often like expressions of relational algebra, and then converted to a physical query plan by selecting an implementation for each operator, ordering joins and making other decisions.

- *Table Scanning*: To access the tuples of a relation, there are several possible physical operators. The table-scan operator simply reads each block holding tuples of the relation. Index-scan uses an index to find tuples, and sort-scan produces the tuples in sorted order.

- *Cost Measures for Physical Operators*: Commonly, the number of disk I/O's taken to execute an operation is the dominant component of the time. In our model, we count only disk I/O time, and we charge for the time and space needed to read arguments, but not to write the result.

- *Iterators*: Several operations involved in the execution of a query can be meshed conveniently if we think of their execution as performed by an iterator. This mechanism consists of three methods, to open the construction of a relation, to produce the next tuple of the relation, and to close the construction.

- *One-Pass Algorithms*: As long as one of the arguments of a relational-algebra operator can fit in main memory, we can execute the operator by reading the smaller relation to memory, and reading the other argument one block at a time.

- *Nested-Loop Join*: This simple join algorithm works even when neither argument fits in main memory. It reads as much as it can of the smaller relation into memory, and compares that with the entire other argument; this process is repeated until all of the smaller relation has had its turn in memory.

- *Two-Pass Algorithms*: Except for nested-loop join, most algorithms for arguments that are too large to fit into memory are either sort-based, hash-based, or index-based.

- *Sort-Based Algorithms*: These partition their argument(s) into main-memory-sized, sorted sublists. The sorted sublists are then merged appropriately to produce the desired result. For instance, if we merge the tuples of all sublists in sorted order, then we have the important two-phase-multiway-merge sort.

- ✦ *Hash-Based Algorithms*: These use a hash function to partition the argument(s) into buckets. The operation is then applied to the buckets individually (for a unary operation) or in pairs (for a binary operation).

- ✦ *Hashing Versus Sorting*: Hash-based algorithms are often superior to sort-based algorithms, since they require only one of their arguments to be "small." Sort-based algorithms, on the other hand, work well when there is another reason to keep some of the data sorted.

- ✦ *Index-Based Algorithms*: The use of an index is an excellent way to speed up a selection whose condition equates the indexed attribute to a constant. Index-based joins are also excellent when one of the relations is small, and the other has an index on the join attribute(s).

- ✦ *The Buffer Manager*: The availability of blocks of memory is controlled by the buffer manager. When a new buffer is needed in memory, the buffer manager uses one of the familiar replacement policies, such as least-recently-used, to decide which buffer is returned to disk.

- ✦ *Coping With Variable Numbers of Buffers*: Often, the number of main-memory buffers available to an operation cannot be predicted in advance. If so, the algorithm used to implement an operation needs to degrade gracefully as the number of available buffers shrinks.

- ✦ *Multipass Algorithms*: The two-pass algorithms based on sorting or hashing have natural recursive analogs that take three or more passes and will work for larger amounts of data.

10 References

Two surveys of query optimization are [6] and [2]. [8] is a survey of distributed query optimization.

An early study of join methods is in [5]. Buffer-pool management was analyzed, surveyed, and improved by [3].

The use of sort-based techniques was pioneered by [1]. The advantage of hash-based algorithms for join was expressed by [7] and [4]; the latter is the origin of the hybrid hash-join.

1. M. W. Blasgen and K. P. Eswaran, "Storage access in relational databases," *IBM Systems J.* **16**:4 (1977), pp. 363–378.

2. S. Chaudhuri, "An overview of query optimization in relational systems," *Proc. Seventeenth Annual ACM Symposium on Principles of Database Systems*, pp. 34–43, June, 1998.

3. H.-T. Chou and D. J. DeWitt, "An evaluation of buffer management strategies for relational database systems," *Intl. Conf. on Very Large Databases*, pp. 127–141, 1985.

4. D. J. DeWitt, R. H. Katz, F. Olken, L. D. Shapiro, M. Stonebraker, and D. Wood, "Implementation techniques for main-memory database systems," *Proc. ACM SIGMOD Intl. Conf. on Management of Data* (1984), pp. 1–8.

5. L. R. Gotlieb, "Computing joins of relations," *Proc. ACM SIGMOD Intl. Conf. on Management of Data* (1975), pp. 55–63.

6. G. Graefe, "Query evaluation techniques for large databases," *Computing Surveys* **25**:2 (June, 1993), pp. 73–170.

7. M. Kitsuregawa, H. Tanaka, and T. Moto-oka, "Application of hash to data base machine and its architecture," *New Generation Computing* **1**:1 (1983), pp. 66–74.

8. D. Kossman, "The state of the art in distributed query processing," *Computing Surveys* **32**:4 (Dec., 2000), pp. 422–469.

The Query Compiler

We shall now take up the architecture of the query compiler and its optimizer. There are three broad steps that the query processor must take:

1. The query, written in a language like SQL, is *parsed*, that is, turned into a parse tree representing the structure of the query in a useful way.

2. The parse tree is transformed into an expression tree of relational algebra (or a similar notation), which we term a *logical query plan.*

3. The logical query plan must be turned into a *physical query plan*, which indicates not only the operations performed, but the order in which they are performed, the algorithm used to perform each step, and the ways in which stored data is obtained and data is passed from one operation to another.

The first step, parsing, is the subject of Section 1. The result of this step is a parse tree for the query. The other two steps involve a number of choices. In picking a logical query plan, we have opportunities to apply many different algebraic operations, with the goal of producing the best logical query plan. Section 2 discusses the algebraic laws for relational algebra in the abstract. Then, Section 3 discusses the conversion of parse trees to initial logical query plans and shows how the algebraic laws from Section 2 can be used in strategies to improve the initial logical plan.

When producing a physical query plan from a logical plan, we must evaluate the predicted cost of each possible option. Cost estimation is a science of its own, which we discuss in Section 4. We show how to use cost estimates to evaluate plans in Section 5, and the special problems that come up when we order the joins of several relations are the subject of Section 6. Finally, Section 7 covers additional issues and strategies for selecting the physical query plan: algorithm choice, and pipelining versus materialization.

From Chapter 16 of *Database Systems*, Second Edition. Hector Garcia-Molina, Jeffrey D. Ullman, Jennifer Widom.

1 Parsing and Preprocessing

The first stages of query compilation are illustrated in Fig. 1.

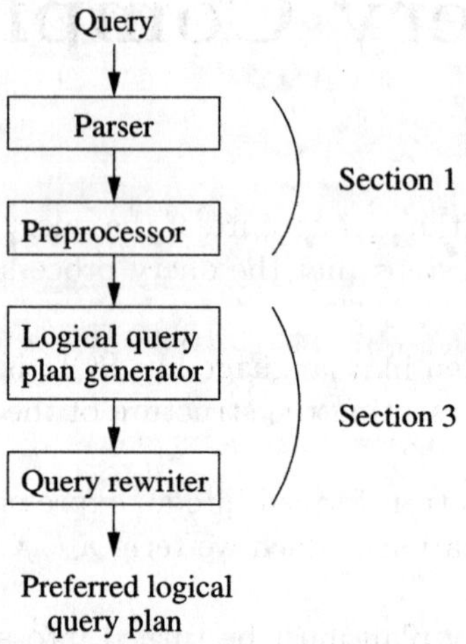

Figure 1: From a query to a logical query plan

In this section, we discuss parsing of SQL and give rudiments of a grammar that can be used for that language. We also discuss how to handle a query that involves a virtual view and other steps of preprocessing.

1.1 Syntax Analysis and Parse Trees

The job of the parser is to take text written in a language such as SQL and convert it to a *parse tree*, which is a tree whose nodes correspond to either:

1. *Atoms*, which are lexical elements such as keywords (e.g., `SELECT`), names of attributes or relations, constants, parentheses, operators such as + or <, and other schema elements, or

2. *Syntactic categories*, which are names for families of query subparts that all play a similar role in a query. We shall represent syntactic categories by triangular brackets around a descriptive name. For example, <Query> will be used to represent some queries in the common select-from-where form, and <Condition> will represent any expression that is a condition; i.e., it can follow `WHERE` in SQL.

If a node is an atom, then it has no children. However, if the node is a syntactic category, then its children are described by one of the *rules* of the grammar for the language. We shall present these ideas by example. The details of how one designs grammars for a language, and how one "parses," i.e., turns a program or query into the correct parse tree, is properly the subject of a course on compiling.[1]

1.2 A Grammar for a Simple Subset of SQL

We shall illustrate the parsing process by giving some rules that describe a small subset of SQL queries.

Queries

The syntactic category <Query> is intended to represent (some of the) queries of SQL. We give it only one rule:

```
<Query> ::= SELECT <SelList> FROM <FromList> WHERE <Condition>
```

Symbol `::=` means "can be expressed as." The syntactic categories <SelList> and <FromList> represent lists that can follow `SELECT` and `FROM`, respectively. We shall describe limited forms of such lists shortly. The syntactic category <Condition> represents SQL conditions (expressions that are either true or false); we shall give some simplified rules for this category later.

Note this rule does not provide for the various optional clauses such as `GROUP BY`, `HAVING`, or `ORDER BY`, nor for options such as `DISTINCT` after `SELECT`, nor for query expressions using `UNION`, `JOIN`, or other binary operators.

Select-Lists

```
<SelList> ::= <Attribute> , <SelList>
<SelList> ::= <Attribute>
```

These two rules say that a select-list can be any comma-separated list of attributes: either a single attribute or an attribute, a comma, and any list of one or more attributes. Note that in a full SQL grammar we would also need provision for expressions and aggregation functions in the select-list and for aliasing of attributes and expressions.

From-Lists

```
<FromList> ::= <Relation> , <FromList>
<FromList> ::= <Relation>
```

Here, a from-list is defined to be any comma-separated list of relations. For simplification, we omit the possibility that elements of a from-list can be expressionsa, such as joins or subqueries. Likewise, a full SQL grammar would have to allow tuple variables for relations.

[1]Those unfamiliar with the subject may wish to examine A. V. Aho, M. Lam, R. Sethi, and J. D. Ullman, *Compilers: Principles, Techniques, and Tools*, Addison-Wesley, 2007, although the examples of Section 1.2 should be sufficient to place parsing in the context of the query processor.

Conditions

The rules we shall use are:

```
<Condition> ::= <Condition> AND <Condition>
<Condition> ::= <Attribute> IN ( <Query> )
<Condition> ::= <Attribute> = <Attribute>
<Condition> ::= <Attribute> LIKE <Pattern>
```

Although we have listed more rules for conditions than for other categories, these rules only scratch the surface of the forms of conditions. We have omitted rules introducing operators OR, NOT, and EXISTS, comparisons other than equality and LIKE, constant operands, and a number of other structures that are needed in a full SQL grammar.

Base Syntactic Categories

Syntactic categories <Attribute>, <Relation>, and <Pattern> are special, in that they are not defined by grammatical rules, but by rules about the atoms for which they can stand. For example, in a parse tree, the one child of <Attribute> can be any string of characters that identifies an attribute of the current database schema. Similarly, <Relation> can be replaced by any string of characters that makes sense as a relation in the current schema, and <Pattern> can be replaced by any quoted string that is a legal SQL pattern.

Example 1: Recall two relations from the running movies example:

```
StarsIn(movieTitle, movieYear, starName)
MovieStar(name, address, gender, birthdate)
```

Our study of parsing and query rewriting will center around two versions of the query "find the titles of movies that have at least one star born in 1960." We identify stars born in 1960 by asking if their birthdate (a SQL string) ends in `'1960'`, using the LIKE operator.

One way to ask this query is to construct the set of names of those stars born in 1960 as a subquery, and ask about each `StarsIn` tuple whether the `starName` in that tuple is a member of the set returned by this subquery. The SQL for this variation of the query is shown in Fig. 2.

The parse tree for the query of Fig. 2, according to the grammar we have sketched, is shown in Fig. 3. At the root is the syntactic category <Query>, as must be the case for any parse tree of a query. Working down the tree, we see that this query is a select-from-where form; the select-list consists of only the attribute `movieTitle`, and the from-list is only the one relation `StarsIn`.

The condition in the outer WHERE-clause is more complex. It has the form of attribute-IN-parenthesized-query. The subquery has its own singleton select- and from-lists and a simple condition involving a LIKE operator. □

```
SELECT movieTitle
FROM StarsIn
WHERE starName IN (
    SELECT name
    FROM MovieStar
    WHERE birthdate LIKE '%1960'
);
```

Figure 2: Find the movies with stars born in 1960

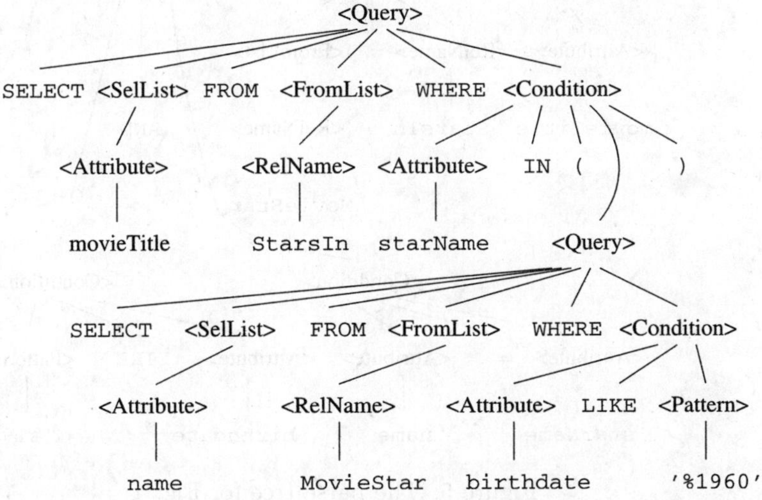

Figure 3: The parse tree for Fig. 2

Example 2: Now, let us consider another version of the query of Fig. 2, this time without using a subquery. We may instead equijoin the relations `StarsIn` and `MovieStar`, using the condition `starName = name`, to require that the star mentioned in both relations be the same. Note that `starName` is an attribute of relation `StarsIn`, while `name` is an attribute of `MovieStar`. This form of the query of Fig. 2 is shown in Fig. 4.[2]

The parse tree for Fig. 4 is seen in Fig. 5. Many of the rules used in this parse tree are the same as in Fig. 3. However, notice a from-list with more than one relation and two conditions connected by `AND`. □

[2] There is a small difference between the two queries in that Fig. 4 can produce duplicates if a movie has more than one star born in 1960. Strictly speaking, we should add `DISTINCT` to Fig. 4, but our example grammar was simplified to the extent of omitting that option.

```
SELECT movieTitle
FROM StarsIn, MovieStar
WHERE starName = name AND
    birthdate LIKE '%1960';
```

Figure 4: Another way to ask for the movies with stars born in 1960

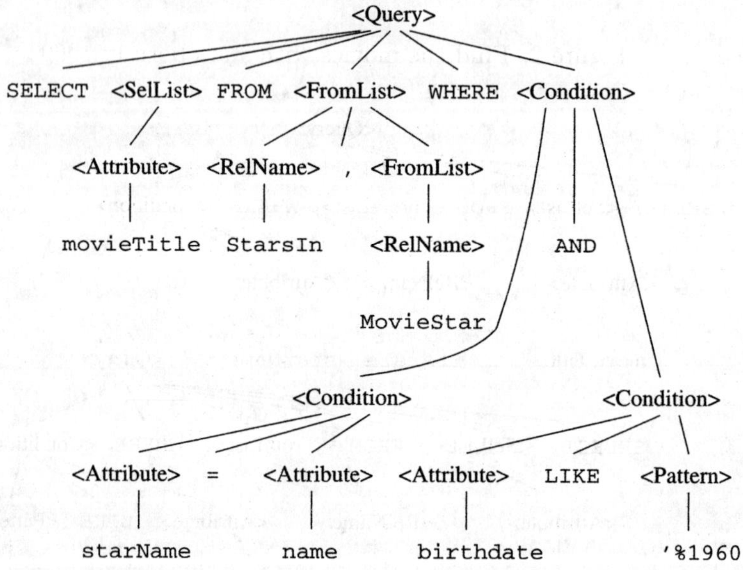

Figure 5: The parse tree for Fig. 4

1.3 The Preprocessor

The *preprocessor* has several important functions. If a relation used in the query is actually a virtual view, then each use of this relation in the from-list must be replaced by a parse tree that describes the view. This parse tree is obtained from the definition of the view, which is essentially a query. We discuss the preprocessing of view references in Section 1.4.

The preprocessor is also responsible for *semantic checking.* Even if the query is valid syntactically, it actually may violate one or more semantic rules on the use of names. For instance, the preprocessor must:

1. *Check relation uses.* Every relation mentioned in a FROM-clause must be a relation or view in the current schema.

2. *Check and resolve attribute uses.* Every attribute that is mentioned in the SELECT- or WHERE-clause must be an attribute of some relation in the current scope. For instance, attribute movieTitle in the first select-list of Fig. 3 is in the scope of only relation StarsIn. Fortunately,

movieTitle is an attribute of StarsIn, so the preprocessor validates this use of movieTitle. The typical query processor would at this point *resolve* each attribute by attaching to it the relation to which it refers, if that relation was not attached explicitly in the query (e.g., StarsIn.movieTitle). It would also check ambiguity, signaling an error if the attribute is in the scope of two or more relations with that attribute.

3. *Check types.* All attributes must be of a type appropriate to their uses. For instance, birthdate in Fig. 3 is used in a LIKE comparison, which requires that birthdate be a string or a type that can be coerced to a string. Since birthdate is a date, and dates in SQL normally can be treated as strings, this use of an attribute is validated. Likewise, operators are checked to see that they apply to values of appropriate and compatible types.

1.4 Preprocessing Queries Involving Views

When an operand in a query is a virtual view, the preprocessor needs to replace the operand by a piece of parse tree that represents how the view is constructed from base tables. The idea is illustrated in Fig. 6. A query Q is represented by its expression tree in relational algebra, and that tree may have some leaves that are views. We have suggested two such leaves, the views V and W. To interpret Q in terms of base tables, we find the definition of the views V and W. These definitions are also queries, so they can be expressed in relational algebra or as parse trees.

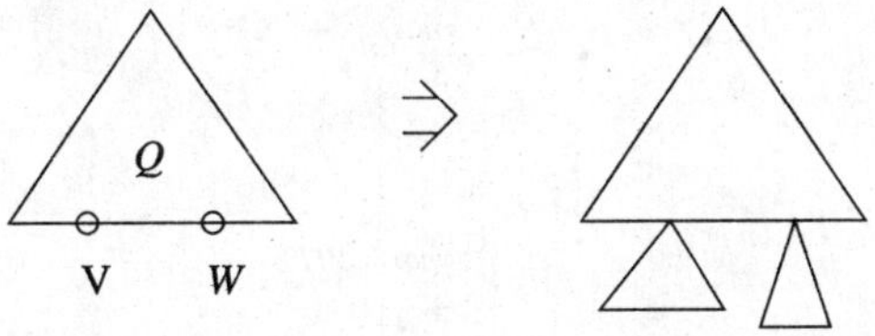

Figure 6: Substituting view definitions for view references

To form the query over base tables, we substitute, for each leaf in the tree for Q that is a view, the root of a copy of the tree that defines that view. Thus, in Fig. 6 we have shown the leaves labeled V and W replaced by the definitions of these views. The resulting tree is a query over base tables that is equivalent to the original query about views.

Example 3: Recall the definition of view ParamountMovies is:

```
CREATE VIEW ParamountMovies AS
    SELECT title, year
```

```
FROM Movies
WHERE studioName = 'Paramount';
```

The tree in Fig. 7 is a relational-algebra expression for the query; we use relational algebra here because it is more succinct than the parse trees we have been using.

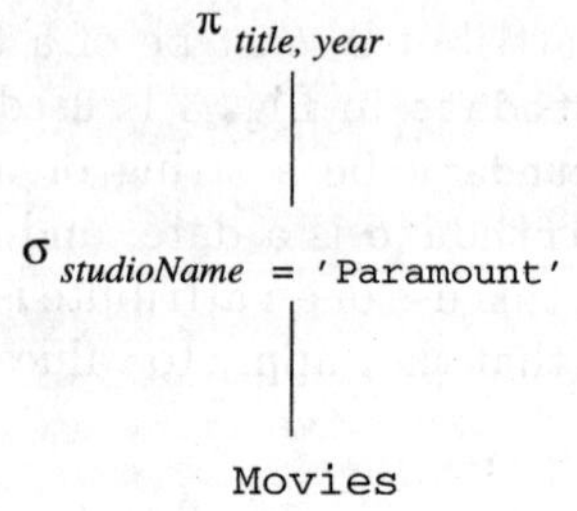

Figure 7: Expression tree for view ParamountMovies

The query is

```
SELECT title
FROM ParamountMovies
WHERE year = 1979;
```

asking for the Paramount movies made in 1979. This query has the expression tree shown in Fig. 8. Note that the one leaf of this tree represents the view ParamountMovies.

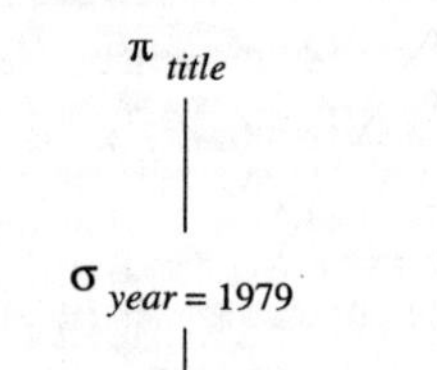

Figure 8: Expression tree for the query

We substitute the tree of Fig. 7 for the leaf ParamountMovies in Fig. 8. The resulting tree is shown in Fig. 9.

This tree, while the formal result of the view preprocessing, is not a very good way to express the query. In Section 2 we shall discuss ways to improve expression trees such as Fig. 9. In particular, we can push selections and projections down the tree, and combine them in many cases. Figure 10 is an improved representation that we can obtain by standard query-processing techniques. □

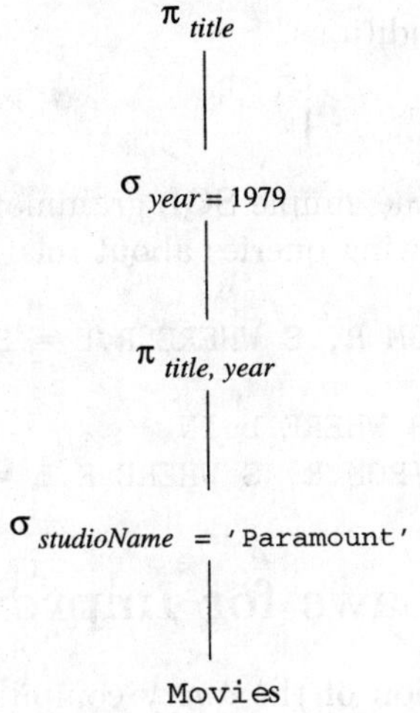

Figure 9: Expressing the query in terms of base tables

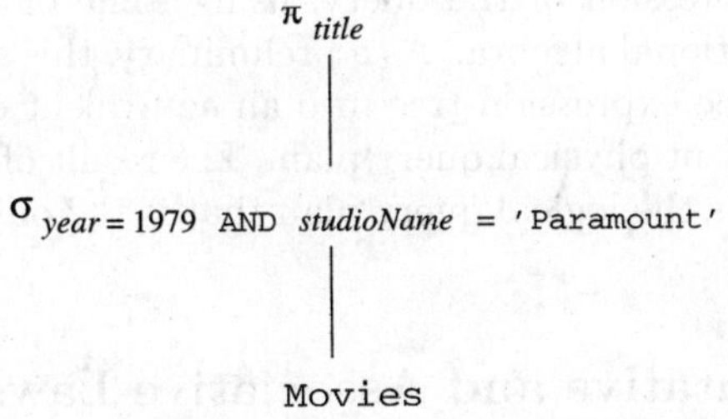

Figure 10: Simplifying the query over base tables

1.5 Exercises for Section 1

Exercise 1.1: Add to or modify the rules for <Query> to include simple versions of the following features of SQL select-from-where expressions:

a) The ability to produce a set with the `DISTINCT` keyword.

b) A `GROUP BY` clause and a `HAVING` clause.

c) Sorted output with the `ORDER BY` clause.

d) A query with no where-clause.

Exercise 1.2: Add to the rules for <Condition> to allow the following features of SQL conditionals:

a) Logical operators OR and NOT.

b) Comparisons other than =.

c) Parenthesized conditions.

d) EXISTS expressions.

Exercise 1.3: Using the simple SQL grammar exhibited in this section, give parse trees for the following queries about relations $R(a, b)$ and $S(b, c)$:

a)
```
SELECT a, c FROM R, S WHERE R.b = S.b;
```

b)
```
SELECT a FROM R WHERE b IN
    (SELECT a FROM R, S WHERE R.b = S.b);
```

2 Algebraic Laws for Improving Query Plans

We resume our discussion of the query compiler in Section 3, where we shall transform the parse tree into an expression of the extended relational algebra. Also in Section 3, we shall see how to apply heuristics that we hope will improve the algebraic expression of the query, using some of the many algebraic laws that hold for relational algebra. As a preliminary, this section catalogs algebraic laws that turn one expression tree into an equivalent expression tree that may have a more efficient physical query plan. The result of applying these algebraic transformations is the logical query plan that is the output of the query-rewrite phase.

2.1 Commutative and Associative Laws

A *commutative law* about an operator says that it does not matter in which order you present the arguments of the operator; the result will be the same. For instance, $+$ and $\times$ are commutative operators of arithmetic. More precisely, $x + y = y + x$ and $x \times y = y \times x$ for any numbers x and y. On the other hand, $-$ is not a commutative arithmetic operator: $x - y \neq y - x$.

An *associative law* about an operator says that we may group two uses of the operator either from the left or the right. For instance, $+$ and $\times$ are associative arithmetic operators, meaning that $(x + y) + z = x + (y + z)$ and $(x \times y) \times z = x \times (y \times z)$. On the other hand, $-$ is not associative: $(x - y) - z \neq x - (y - z)$. When an operator is both associative and commutative, then any number of operands connected by this operator can be grouped and ordered as we wish without changing the result. For example, $\big((w+x)+y\big)+z = (y+x)+(z+w)$.

Several of the operators of relational algebra are both associative and commutative. Particularly:

- $R \times S = S \times R$; $(R \times S) \times T = R \times (S \times T)$.
- $R \bowtie S = S \bowtie R$; $(R \bowtie S) \bowtie T = R \bowtie (S \bowtie T)$.
- $R \cup S = S \cup R$; $(R \cup S) \cup T = R \cup (S \cup T)$.

- $R \cap S = S \cap R$; $(R \cap S) \cap T = R \cap (S \cap T)$.

Note that these laws hold for both sets and bags. We shall not prove each of these laws, although we give one example of a proof, below.

Example 4: Let us verify the commutative law for $\bowtie$: $R \bowtie S = S \bowtie R$. First, suppose a tuple t is in the result of $R \bowtie S$, the expression on the left. Then there must be a tuple r in R and a tuple s in S that agree with t on every attribute that each shares with t. Thus, when we evaluate the expression on the right, $S \bowtie R$, the tuples s and r will again combine to form t.

We might imagine that the order of components of t will be different on the left and right, but formally, tuples in relational algebra have no fixed order of attributes. Rather, we are free to reorder components, as long as we carry the proper attributes along in the column headers.

We are not done yet with the proof. Since our relational algebra is an algebra of bags, not sets, we must also verify that if t appears n times on the left, then it appears n times on the right, and vice-versa. Suppose t appears n times on the left. Then it must be that the tuple r from R that agrees with t appears some number of times n_R, and the tuple s from S that agrees with t appears some n_S times, where $n_R n_S = n$. Then when we evaluate the expression $S \bowtie R$ on the right, we find that s appears n_S times, and r appears n_R times, so we get $n_S n_R$ copies of t, or n copies.

We are still not done. We have finished the half of the proof that says everything on the left appears on the right, but we must show that everything on the right appears on the left. Because of the obvious symmetry, the argument is essentially the same, and we shall not go through the details here. □

We did not include the theta-join among the associative-commutative operators. True, this operator is commutative:

- $R \bowtie_C S = S \bowtie_C R$.

Moreover, if the conditions involved make sense where they are positioned, then the theta-join is associative. However, there are examples, such as the following, where we cannot apply the associative law because the conditions do not apply to attributes of the relations being joined.

Example 5: Suppose we have three relations $R(a, b)$, $S(b, c)$, and $T(c, d)$. The expression

$$(R \bowtie_{R.b>S.b} S) \bowtie_{a<d} T$$

is transformed by a hypothetical associative law into:

$$R \bowtie_{R.b>S.b} (S \bowtie_{a<d} T)$$

However, we cannot join S and T using the condition $a < d$, because a is an attribute of neither S nor T. Thus, the associative law for theta-join cannot be applied arbitrarily. □

Laws for Bags and Sets Can Differ

Be careful about applying familiar laws about sets to relations that are bags. For instance, you may have learned set-theoretic laws such as $A \cap_S (B \cup_S C) = (A \cap_S B) \cup_S (A \cap_S C)$, which is formally the "distributive law of intersection over union." This law holds for sets, but not for bags.

As an example, suppose bags A, B, and C were each $\{x\}$. Then $A \cap_B (B \cup_B C) = \{x\} \cap_B \{x, x\} = \{x\}$. But $(A \cap_B B) \cup_B (A \cap_B C) = \{x\} \cup_B \{x\} = \{x, x\}$, which differs from the left-hand-side, $\{x\}$.

2.2 Laws Involving Selection

Since selections tend to reduce the size of relations markedly, one of the most important rules of efficient query processing is to move the selections down the tree as far as they will go without changing what the expression does. Indeed early query optimizers used variants of this transformation as their primary strategy for selecting good logical query plans. As we shall see shortly, the transformation of "push selections down the tree" is not quite general enough, but the idea of "pushing selections" is still a major tool for the query optimizer.

To start, when the condition of a selection is complex (i.e., it involves conditions connected by `AND` or `OR`), it helps to break the condition into its constituent parts. The motivation is that one part, involving fewer attributes than the whole condition, may be moved to a convenient place where the entire condition cannot be evaluated. Thus, our first two laws for σ are the *splitting laws*:

- $\sigma_{C_1 \texttt{ AND } C_2}(R) = \sigma_{C_1}\big(\sigma_{C_2}(R)\big)$.
- $\sigma_{C_1 \texttt{ OR } C_2}(R) = \big(\sigma_{C_1}(R)\big) \cup_S \big(\sigma_{C_2}(R)\big)$.

However, the second law, for OR, works only if the relation R is a set. Notice that if R were a bag, the set-union would have the effect of eliminating duplicates incorrectly.

Notice that the order of C_1 and C_2 is flexible. For example, we could just as well have written the first law above with C_2 applied after C_1, as $\sigma_{C_2}\big(\sigma_{C_1}(R)\big)$. In fact, more generally, we can swap the order of any sequence of σ operators:

- $\sigma_{C_1}\big(\sigma_{C_2}(R)\big) = \sigma_{C_2}\big(\sigma_{C_1}(R)\big)$.

Example 6: Let $R(a, b, c)$ be a relation. Then $\sigma_{(a=1 \texttt{ OR } a=3) \texttt{ AND } b<c}(R)$ can be split as $\sigma_{a=1 \texttt{ OR } a=3}\big(\sigma_{b<c}(R)\big)$. We can then split this expression at the `OR` into $\sigma_{a=1}\big(\sigma_{b<c}(R)\big) \cup \sigma_{a=3}\big(\sigma_{b<c}(R)\big)$. In this case, because it is impossible for a tuple to satisfy both $a = 1$ and $a = 3$, this transformation holds regardless

of whether or not R is a set, as long as $\cup_B$ is used for the union. However, in general the splitting of an OR requires that the argument be a set and that $\cup_S$ be used.

Alternatively, we could have started to split by making $\sigma_{b<c}$ the outer operation, as $\sigma_{b<c}\big(\sigma_{a=1 \texttt{ OR } a=3}(R)\big)$. When we then split the OR, we would get $\sigma_{b<c}\big(\sigma_{a=1}(R) \cup \sigma_{a=3}(R)\big)$, an expression that is equivalent to, but somewhat different from the first expression we derived. □

The next family of laws involving σ allow us to push selections through the binary operators: product, union, intersection, difference, and join. There are three types of laws, depending on whether it is optional or required to push the selection to each of the arguments:

1. For a union, the selection *must* be pushed to both arguments.

2. For a difference, the selection must be pushed to the first argument and optionally may be pushed to the second.

3. For the other operators it is only required that the selection be pushed to one argument. For joins and products, it may not make sense to push the selection to both arguments, since an argument may or may not have the attributes that the selection requires. When it is possible to push to both, it may or may not improve the plan to do so; see Exercise 2.1.

Thus, the law for union is:

- $\sigma_C(R \cup S) = \sigma_C(R) \cup \sigma_C(S)$.

Here, it is mandatory to move the selection down both branches of the tree.

For difference, one version of the law is:

- $\sigma_C(R - S) = \sigma_C(R) - S$.

However, it is also permissible to push the selection to both arguments, as:

- $\sigma_C(R - S) = \sigma_C(R) - \sigma_C(S)$.

The next laws allow the selection to be pushed to one or both arguments. If the selection is σ_C, then we can only push this selection to a relation that has all the attributes mentioned in C, if there is one. We shall show the laws below assuming that the relation R has all the attributes mentioned in C.

- $\sigma_C(R \times S) = \sigma_C(R) \times S$.
- $\sigma_C(R \bowtie S) = \sigma_C(R) \bowtie S$.
- $\sigma_C(R \bowtie_D S) = \sigma_C(R) \bowtie_D S$.
- $\sigma_C(R \cap S) = \sigma_C(R) \cap S$.

If C has only attributes of S, then we can instead write:

- $\sigma_C(R \times S) = R \times \sigma_C(S)$.

and similarly for the other three operators $\bowtie$, $\bowtie_D$, and $\cap$. Should relations R and S both happen to have all attributes of C, then we can use laws such as:

- $\sigma_C(R \bowtie S) = \sigma_C(R) \bowtie \sigma_C(S)$.

Note that it is impossible for this variant to apply if the operator is $\times$ or $\bowtie_D$, since in those cases R and S have no shared attributes. On the other hand, for $\cap$ this form of law always applies, since the schemas of R and S must then be the same.

Example 7: Consider relations $R(a, b)$ and $S(b, c)$ and the expression

$$\sigma_{(a=1 \texttt{ OR } a=3) \texttt{ AND } b<c}(R \bowtie S)$$

The condition $b < c$ applies only to to S, and the condition $a = 1$ OR $a = 3$ applies only to R. We thus begin by splitting the AND of the two conditions as we did in the first alternative of Example 6:

$$\sigma_{a=1 \texttt{ OR } a=3}\big(\sigma_{b<c}(R \bowtie S)\big)$$

Next, we can push the selection $\sigma_{b<c}$ to S, giving us the expression:

$$\sigma_{a=1 \texttt{ OR } a=3}\big(R \bowtie \sigma_{b<c}(S)\big)$$

Finally, push the first condition to R, yielding: $\sigma_{a=1 \texttt{ OR } a=3}(R) \bowtie \sigma_{b<c}(S)$. □

2.3 Pushing Selections

As was illustrated in Example 3, pushing a selection down an expression tree — that is, replacing the left side of one of the rules in Section 2.2 by its right side — is one of the most powerful tools of the query optimizer. However, when queries involve virtual views, it is sometimes necessary first to move a selection as far *up* the tree as it can go, and then push the selections down all possible branches. An example will illustrate the proper selection-pushing approach.

Example 8: Suppose we have the relations

```
StarsIn(title, year, starName)
Movies(title, year, length, genre, studioName, producerC#)
```

Note that we have altered the first two attributes of `StarsIn` from the usual `movieTitle` and `movieYear` to make this example simpler to follow. Define view `MoviesOf1996` by:

> **Some Trivial Laws**
>
> We are not going to state every true law for the relational algebra. The reader should be alert, in particular, for laws about extreme cases: a relation that is empty, a selection or theta-join whose condition is always true or always false, or a projection onto the list of all attributes, for example. A few of the many possible special-case laws:
>
> - Any selection on an empty relation is empty.
> - If C is an always-true condition (e.g., $x > 10$ OR $x \leq 10$ on a relation that forbids $x =$ NULL), then $\sigma_C(R) = R$.
> - If R is empty, then $R \cup S = S$.

```
CREATE VIEW MoviesOf1996 AS
    SELECT *
    FROM Movies
    WHERE year = 1996;
```

We can ask the query "which stars worked for which studios in 1996?" by the SQL query:

```
SELECT starName, studioName
FROM MoviesOf1996 NATURAL JOIN StarsIn;
```

The view MoviesOf1996 is defined by the relational-algebra expression

$$\sigma_{year=1996}(\texttt{Movies})$$

Thus, the query, which is the natural join of this expression with StarsIn, followed by a projection onto attributes starName and studioName, has the expression shown in Fig. 11.

Here, the selection is already as far down the tree as it will go, so there is no way to "push selections down the tree." However, the rule $\sigma_C(R \bowtie S) = \sigma_C(R) \bowtie S$ can be applied "backwards," to bring the selection $\sigma_{year=1996}$ above the join in Fig. 11. Then, since *year* is an attribute of both Movies and StarsIn, we may push the selection down to *both* children of the join node. The resulting logical query plan is shown in Fig. 12. It is likely to be an improvement, since we reduce the size of the relation StarsIn before we join it with the movies of 1996. □

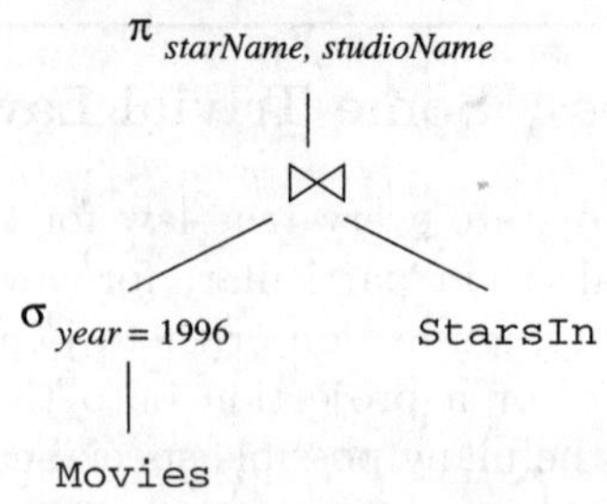

Figure 11: Logical query plan constructed from definition of a query and view

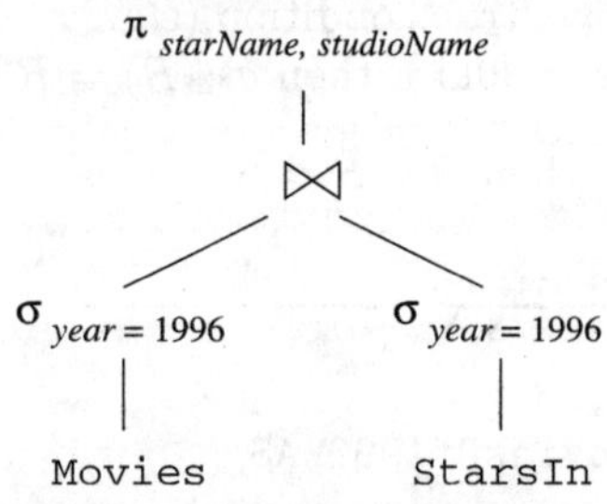

Figure 12: Improving the query plan by moving selections up and down the tree

2.4 Laws Involving Projection

Projections, like selections, can be "pushed down" through many other operators. Pushing projections differs from pushing selections in that when we push projections, it is quite usual for the projection also to remain where it is. Put another way, "pushing" projections really involves introducing a new projection somewhere below an existing projection.

Pushing projections is useful, but generally less so than pushing selections. The reason is that while selections often reduce the size of a relation by a large factor, projection keeps the number of tuples the same and only reduces the length of tuples. In fact, the extended projection operator can actually increase the length of tuples.

To describe the transformations of extended projection, we need to introduce some terminology. Consider a term $E \rightarrow x$ on the list for a projection, where E is an attribute or an expression involving attributes and constants. We say all attributes mentioned in E are *input* attributes of the projection, and x is an *output* attribute. If a term is a single attribute, then it is both an input and output attribute. If a projection list consists only of attributes, with no renaming or expressions other than a single attribute, then we say the projection is *simple.*

Example 9: Projection $\pi_{a,b,c}(R)$ is simple; a, b, and c are both its input attributes and its output attributes. On the other hand, $\pi_{a+b \to x,\ c}(R)$ is not simple. It has input attributes a, b, and c, and its output attributes are x and c. □

The principle behind laws for projection is that:

- We may introduce a projection anywhere in an expression tree, as long as it eliminates only attributes that are neither used by an operator above nor are in the result of the entire expression.

In the most basic form of these laws, the introduced projections are always simple, although the pre-existing projections, such as L below, need not be.

- $\pi_L(R \bowtie S) = \pi_L\big(\pi_M(R) \bowtie \pi_N(S)\big)$, where M and N are the join attributes and the input attributes if L that are found among the attributes of R and S, respectively.
- $\pi_L(R \bowtie_C S) = \pi_L\big(\pi_M(R) \bowtie_C \pi_N(S)\big)$, where M and N are the join attributes (i.e., those mentioned in condition C) and the input attributes of L that are found among the attributes of R and S respectively.
- $\pi_L(R \times S) = \pi_L\big(\pi_M(R) \times \pi_N(S)\big)$, where M and N are the lists of all attributes of R and S, respectively, that are input attributes of L.

Example 10: Let $R(a, b, c)$ and $S(c, d, e)$ be two relations. Consider the expression $\pi_{a+e \to x,\ b \to y}(R \bowtie S)$. The input attributes of the projection are a, b, and e, and c is the only join attribute. We may apply the law for pushing projections below joins to get the equivalent expression:

$$\pi_{a+e \to x,\ b \to y}\big(\pi_{a,b,c}(R) \bowtie \pi_{c,e}(S)\big)$$

Notice that the projection $\pi_{a,b,c}(R)$ is trivial; it projects onto all the attributes of R. We may thus eliminate this projection and get a third equivalent expression: $\pi_{a+e \to x,\ b \to y}\big(R \bowtie \pi_{c,e}(S)\big)$. That is, the only change from the original is that we remove the attribute d from S before the join. □

We can perform a projection entirely before a bag union. That is:

- $\pi_L(R \cup_B S) = \pi_L(R) \cup_B \pi_L(S)$.

On the other hand, projections cannot be pushed below set unions or either the set or bag versions of intersection or difference at all.

Example 11: Let $R(a, b)$ consist of the one tuple $\{(1, 2)\}$ and $S(a, b)$ consist of the one tuple $\{(1, 3)\}$. Then $\pi_a(R \cap S) = \pi_a(\emptyset) = \emptyset$. However, $\pi_a(R) \cap \pi_a(S) = \{(1)\} \cap \{(1)\} = \{(1)\}$. □

If the projection involves some computations, and the input attributes of a term on the projection list belong entirely to one of the arguments of a join or product below the projection, then we have the option, although not the obligation, to perform the computation directly on that argument. An example should help illustrate the point.

Example 12: Again let $R(a, b, c)$ and $S(c, d, e)$ be relations, and consider the join and projection $\pi_{a+b \rightarrow x,\ d+e \rightarrow y}(R \bowtie S)$. We can move the sum $a + b$ and its renaming to x directly onto the relation R, and move the sum $d + e$ to S similarly. The resulting equivalent expression is

$$\pi_{x,y}\big(\pi_{a+b \rightarrow x,\ c}(R) \bowtie \pi_{d+e \rightarrow y,\ c}(S)\big)$$

One special case to handle is if x or y were c. Then, we could not rename a sum to c, because a relation cannot have two attributes named c. Thus, we would have to invent a temporary name and do another renaming in the projection above the join. For example, $\pi_{a+b \rightarrow c,\ d+e \rightarrow y}(R \bowtie S)$ could become $\pi_{z \rightarrow c,\ y}\big(\pi_{a+b \rightarrow z,\ c}(R) \bowtie \pi_{d+e \rightarrow y,\ c}(S)\big)$. □

It is also possible to push a projection below a selection.

- $\pi_L\big(\sigma_C(R)\big) = \pi_L\Big(\sigma_C\big(\pi_M(R)\big)\Big)$, where M is the list of all attributes that are either input attributes of L or mentioned in condition C.

As in Example 12, we have the option of performing computations on the list L in the list M instead, provided the condition C does not need the input attributes of L that are involved in a computation.

2.5 Laws About Joins and Products

We saw in Section 2.1 many of the important laws involving joins and products: their commutative and associative laws. However, there are a few additional laws that follow directly from the definition of the join.

- $R \bowtie_C S = \sigma_C(R \times S)$.

- $R \bowtie S = \pi_L\big(\sigma_C(R \times S)\big)$, where C is the condition that equates each pair of attributes from R and S with the same name, and L is a list that includes one attribute from each equated pair and all the other attributes of R and S.

In practice, we usually want to apply these rules from right to left. That is, we identify a product followed by a selection as a join of some kind. The reason for doing so is that the algorithms for computing joins are generally much faster than algorithms that compute a product followed by a selection on the (very large) result of the product.

2.6 Laws Involving Duplicate Elimination

The operator δ, which eliminates duplicates from a bag, can be pushed through many, but not all operators. In general, moving a δ down the tree reduces the size of intermediate relations and may therefore be beneficial. Moreover, we can sometimes move the δ to a position where it can be eliminated altogether, because it is applied to a relation that is known not to possess duplicates:

- $\delta(R) = R$ if R has no duplicates. Important cases of such a relation R include

  a) A stored relation with a declared primary key, and

  b) The result of a γ operation, since grouping creates a relation with no duplicates.

  c) The result of a set union, intersection, or difference.

Several laws that "push" δ through other operators are:

- $\delta(R \times S) = \delta(R) \times \delta(S)$.
- $\delta(R \bowtie S) = \delta(R) \bowtie \delta(S)$.
- $\delta(R \bowtie_C S) = \delta(R) \bowtie_C \delta(S)$.
- $\delta\big(\sigma_C(R)\big) = \sigma_C\big(\delta(R)\big)$.

We can also move the δ to either or both of the arguments of an intersection:

- $\delta(R \cap_B S) = \delta(R) \cap_B S = R \cap_B \delta(S) = \delta(R) \cap_B \delta(S)$.

On the other hand, δ generally cannot be pushed through the operators $\cup_B$, $-_B$, or π.

Example 13: Let R have two copies of the tuple t and S have one copy of t. Then $\delta(R \cup_B S)$ has one copy of t, while $\delta(R) \cup_B \delta(S)$ has two copies of t. Also, $\delta(R -_B S)$ has one copy of t, while $\delta(R) -_B \delta(S)$ has no copy of t.

Now, consider relation $T(a, b)$ with one copy each of the tuples $(1, 2)$ and $(1, 3)$, and no other tuples. Then $\delta\big(\pi_a(T)\big)$ has one copy of the tuple (1), while $\pi_a\big(\delta(T)\big)$ has two copies of (1). □

2.7 Laws Involving Grouping and Aggregation

When we consider the operator γ, we find that the applicability of many transformations depends on the details of the aggregate operators used. Thus, we cannot state laws in the generality that we used for the other operators. One exception is the law, mentioned in Section 2.6, that a γ absorbs a δ. Precisely:

- $\delta(\gamma_L(R)) = \gamma_L(R)$.

Another general rule is that we may project useless attributes from the argument should we wish, prior to applying the γ operation. This law can be written:

- $\gamma_L(R) = \gamma_L(\pi_M(R))$ if M is a list containing at least all those attributes of R that are mentioned in L.

The reason that other transformations depend on the aggregation(s) involved in a γ is that some aggregations — MIN and MAX in particular — are not affected by the presence or absence of duplicates. The other aggregations — SUM, COUNT, and AVG — generally produce different values if duplicates are eliminated prior to application of the aggregation.

Thus, let us call an operator γ_L *duplicate-impervious* if the only aggregations in L are MIN and/or MAX. Then:

- $\gamma_L(R) = \gamma_L(\delta(R))$ provided γ_L is duplicate-impervious.

Example 14: Suppose we have the relations

```
MovieStar(name, addr, gender, birthdate)
StarsIn(movieTitle, movieYear, starName)
```

and we want to know for each year the birthdate of the youngest star to appear in a movie that year. We can express this query as

```
SELECT movieYear, MAX(birthdate)
FROM MovieStar, StarsIn
WHERE name = starName
GROUP BY movieYear;
```

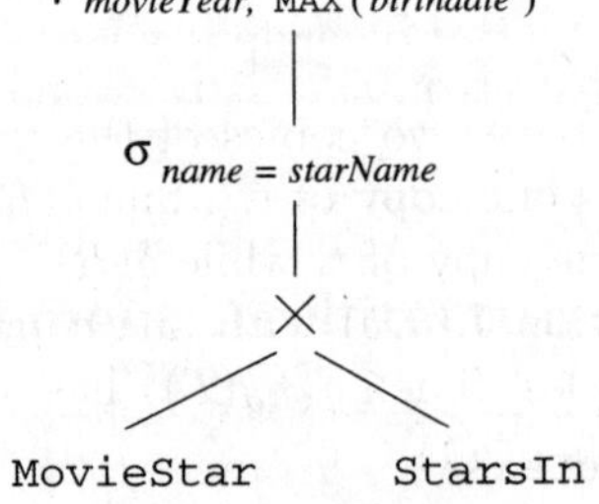

Figure 13: Initial logical query plan for the query of Example 14

An initial logical query plan constructed directly from the query is shown in Fig. 13. The FROM list is expressed by a product, and the WHERE clause by a selection above it. The grouping and aggregation are expressed by the γ operator above those. Some transformations that we could apply to Fig. 13 if we wished are:

1. Combine the selection and product into an equijoin.

2. Generate a δ below the γ, since the γ is duplicate-impervious.

3. Generate a π between the γ and the introduced δ to project onto `movieYear` and `birthdate`, the only attributes relevant to the γ.

The resulting plan is shown in Fig. 14.

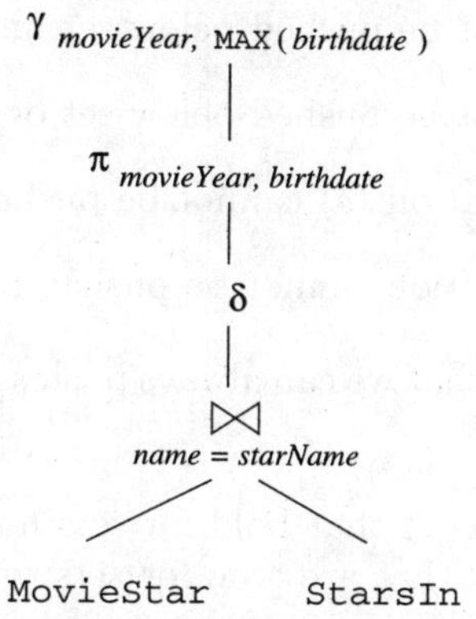

Figure 14: Another query plan for the query of Example 14

We can now push the δ below the $\bowtie$ and introduce π's below that if we wish. This new query plan is shown in Fig. 15. If `name` is a key for `MovieStar`, the δ can be eliminated along the branch leading to that relation. □

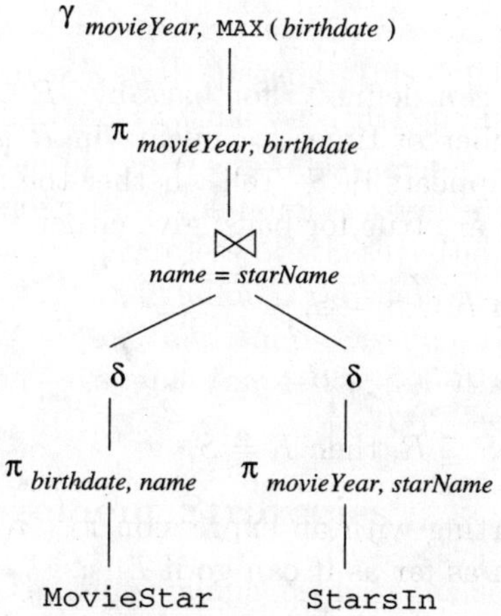

Figure 15: A third query plan for Example 14

2.8 Exercises for Section 2

Exercise 2.1: When it is possible to push a selection to both arguments of a binary operator, we need to decide whether or not to do so. How would the existence of indexes on one of the arguments affect our choice? Consider, for instance, an expression $\sigma_C(R \cap S)$, where there is an index on S.

Exercise 2.2: Give examples to show that:

a) Projection cannot be pushed below set union.

b) Projection cannot be pushed below set or bag difference.

c) Duplicate elimination (δ) cannot be pushed below projection.

d) Duplicate elimination cannot be pushed below bag union or difference.

! **Exercise 2.3:** Prove that we can always push a projection below both branches of a bag union.

! **Exercise 2.4:** Some laws that hold for sets hold for bags; others do not. For each of the laws below that are true for sets, tell whether or not it is true for bags. Either give a proof the law for bags is true, or give a counterexample.

a) $R \cup R = R$ (the idempotent law for union).

b) $R \cap R = R$ (the idempotent law for intersection).

c) $R - R = \emptyset$.

d) $R \cup (S \cap T) = (R \cup S) \cap (R \cup T)$ (distribution of union over intersection).

! **Exercise 2.5:** We can define $\subseteq$ for bags by: $R \subseteq S$ if and only if for every element x, the number of times x appears in R is less than or equal to the number of times it appears in S. Tell whether the following statements (which are all true for sets) are true for bags; give either a proof or a counterexample:

a) If $R \subseteq S$, then $R \cup S = S$.

b) If $R \subseteq S$, then $R \cap S = R$.

c) If $R \subseteq S$ and $S \subseteq R$, then $R = S$.

Exercise 2.6: Starting with an expression $\pi_L\big(R(a, b, c) \bowtie S(b, c, d, e)\big)$, push the projection down as far as it can go if L is:

a) $b + c \rightarrow x,\ c + d \rightarrow y$.

b) $a,\ b,\ a + d \rightarrow z$.

! Exercise 2.7: We mentioned in Example 14 that none of the plans we showed is necessarily the best plan. Can you think of a better plan?

! Exercise 2.8: The following are possible equalities involving operations on a relation $R(a, b)$. Tell whether or not they are true; give either a proof or a counterexample.

a) $\gamma_{MIN(a)\rightarrow y,\ x}\big(\gamma_{a,\ SUM(b)\rightarrow x}(R)\big) = \gamma_{y,SUM(b)\rightarrow x}\big(\gamma_{MIN(a)\rightarrow y,\ b}(R)\big)$.

b) $\gamma_{MIN(a)\rightarrow y,\ x}\big(\gamma_{a,\ MAX(b)\rightarrow x}(R)\big) = \gamma_{y,MAX(b)\rightarrow x}\big(\gamma_{MIN(a)\rightarrow y,\ b}(R)\big)$.

!! Exercise 2.9: The join-like operators obey some of the familiar laws, and others do not. Tell whether each of the following is or is not true. Give either a proof that the law holds or a counterexample.

a) $\sigma_C(R \ltimes S) = \sigma_C(R) \ltimes S$.

b) $\sigma_C(R \overset{\circ}{\bowtie} S) = \sigma_C(R) \overset{\circ}{\bowtie} S$.

c) $\sigma_C(R \overset{\circ}{\bowtie}_L S) = \sigma_C(R) \overset{\circ}{\bowtie}_L S$, where C involves only attributes of R.

d) $\sigma_C(R \overset{\circ}{\bowtie}_L S) = R \overset{\circ}{\bowtie}_L \sigma_C(S)$, where C involves only attributes of S.

e) $\pi_L(R \overline{\ltimes} S) = \pi_L(R) \overline{\ltimes} S$.

f) $(R \overset{\circ}{\bowtie} S) \overset{\circ}{\bowtie} T = R \overset{\circ}{\bowtie} (S \overset{\circ}{\bowtie} T)$.

g) $R \overset{\circ}{\bowtie} S = S \overset{\circ}{\bowtie} R$.

h) $R \overset{\circ}{\bowtie}_L S = S \overset{\circ}{\bowtie}_L R$.

i) $R \ltimes S = S \ltimes R$.

!! Exercise 2.10: While it is not precisely an algebraic law, because it involves an indeterminate number of operands, it is generally true that

$$\texttt{SUM}(a_1, a_2, \ldots, a_n) = a_1 + a_2 + \cdots + a_n$$

SQL has both a `SUM` operator and addition for integers and reals. Considering the possibility that one or more of the a_i's could be `NULL`, rather than an integer or real, does this "law" hold in SQL?

3 From Parse Trees to Logical Query Plans

We now resume our discussion of the query compiler. Having constructed a parse tree for a query in Section 1, we next need to turn the parse tree into the preferred logical query plan. There are two steps, as was suggested in Fig. 1.

The first step is to replace the nodes and structures of the parse tree, in appropriate groups, by an operator or operators of relational algebra. We shall suggest some of these rules and leave some others for exercises. The second step is to take the relational-algebra expression produced by the first step and to turn it into an expression that we expect can be converted to the most efficient physical query plan.

3.1 Conversion to Relational Algebra

We shall now describe informally some rules for transforming SQL parse trees to algebraic logical query plans. The first rule, perhaps the most important, allows us to convert all "simple" select-from-where constructs to relational algebra directly. Its informal statement:

- If we have a <Query> with a <Condition> that has no subqueries, then we may replace the entire construct — the select-list, from-list, and condition — by a relational-algebra expression consisting, from bottom to top, of:

  1. The product of all the relations mentioned in the <FromList>, which is the argument of:
  2. A selection σ_C, where C is the <Condition> expression in the construct being replaced, which in turn is the argument of:
  3. A projection π_L, where L is the list of attributes in the <SelList>.

Example 15: Let us consider the parse tree of Fig. 5. The select-from-where transformation applies to the entire tree of Fig. 5. We take the product of the two relations `StarsIn` and `MovieStar` of the from-list, select for the condition in the subtree rooted at <Condition>, and project onto the select-list, `movieTitle`. The resulting relational-algebra expression is Fig. 16.

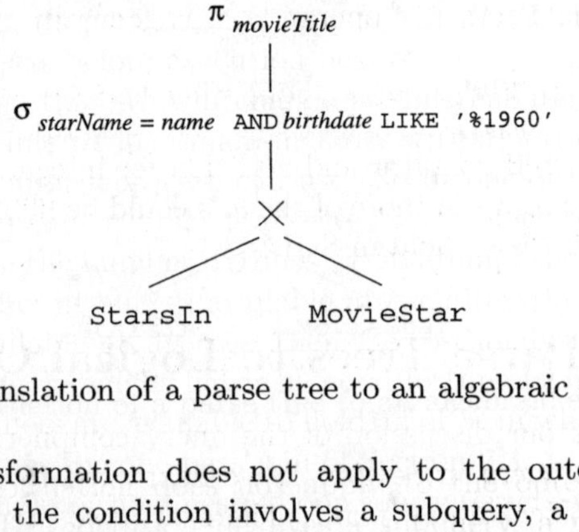

Figure 16: Translation of a parse tree to an algebraic expression tree

The same transformation does not apply to the outer query of Fig. 3. The reason is that the condition involves a subquery, a matter we defer to Section 3.2. However, we can apply the transformation to the subquery in

Limitations on Selection Conditions

One might wonder why we do not allow C, in a selection operator σ_C, to involve a subquery. It is conventional in relational algebra for the *arguments* of an operator — the elements that do not appear in subscripts — to be expressions that yield relations. On the other hand, *parameters* — the elements that appear in subscripts — have a type other than relations. For instance, parameter C in σ_C is a boolean-valued condition, and parameter L in π_L is a list of attributes or formulas.

If we follow this convention, then whatever calculation is implied by a parameter can be applied to each tuple of the relation argument(s). That limitation on the use of parameters simplifies query optimization. Suppose, in contrast, that we allowed an operator like $\sigma_C(R)$, where C involves a subquery. Then the application of C to each tuple of R involves computing the subquery. Do we compute it anew for every tuple of R? That would be unnecessarily expensive, unless the subquery were *correlated*, i.e., its value depends on something defined outside the query, as the subquery of Fig. 3 depends on the value of `starName`. Even correlated subqueries can be evaluated without recomputation for each tuple, in most cases, provided we organize the computation correctly.

Fig. 3. The expression of relational algebra that we get from the subquery is $\pi_{name}\big(\sigma_{birthdate\ \texttt{LIKE '\%1960'}}(\texttt{MovieStar})\big)$. □

3.2 Removing Subqueries From Conditions

For parse trees with a <Condition> that has a subquery, we shall introduce an intermediate form of operator, between the syntactic categories of the parse tree and the relational-algebra operators that apply to relations. This operator is often called *two-argument selection.* We shall represent a two-argument selection in a transformed parse tree by a node labeled σ, with no parameter. Below this node is a left child that represents the relation R upon which the selection is being performed, and a right child that is an expression for the condition applied to each tuple of R. Both arguments may be represented as parse trees, as expression trees, or as a mixture of the two.

Example 16: In Fig. 17 is a rewriting of the parse tree of Fig. 3 that uses a two-argument selection. Several transformations have been made to construct Fig. 17 from Fig. 3:

1. The subquery in Fig. 3 has been replaced by an expression of relational algebra, as discussed at the end of Example 15.

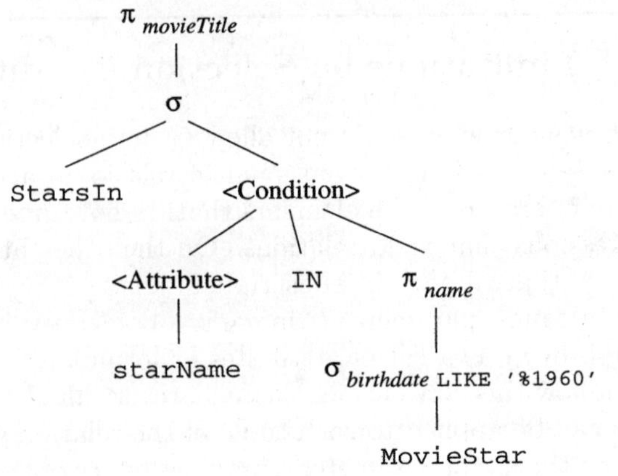

Figure 17: An expression using a two-argument σ, midway between a parse tree and relational algebra

2. The outer query has also been replaced, using the rule for select-from-where expressions from Section 3.1. However, we have expressed the necessary selection as a two-argument selection, rather than by the conventional σ operator of relational algebra. As a result, the upper node of the parse tree labeled <Condition> has not been replaced, but remains as an argument of the selection, with its parentheses and <Query> replaced by relational algebra, per point (1).

This tree needs further transformation, which we discuss next. □

We need rules that allow us to replace a two-argument selection by a one-argument selection and other operators of relational algebra. Each form of condition may require its own rule. In common situations, it is possible to remove the two-argument selection and reach an expression that is pure relational algebra. However, in extreme cases, the two-argument selection can be left in place and considered part of the logical query plan.

We shall give, as an example, the rule that lets us deal with the condition in Fig. 17 involving the `IN` operator. Note that the subquery in this condition is uncorrelated; that is, the subquery's relation can be computed once and for all, independent of the tuple being tested. The rule for eliminating such a condition is stated informally as follows:

- Suppose we have a two-argument selection in which the first argument represents some relation R and the second argument is a <Condition> of the form t `IN` S, where expression S is an uncorrelated subquery, and t is a tuple composed of (some) attributes of R. We transform the tree as follows:

  a) Replace the <Condition> by the tree that is the expression for S. If S may have duplicates, then it is necessary to include a δ operation at the root of the expression for S, so the expression being formed does not produce more copies of tuples than the original query does.

b) Replace the two-argument selection by a one-argument selection σ_C, where C is the condition that equates each component of the tuple t to the corresponding attribute of the relation S.

c) Give σ_C an argument that is the product of R and S.

Figure 18 illustrates this transformation.

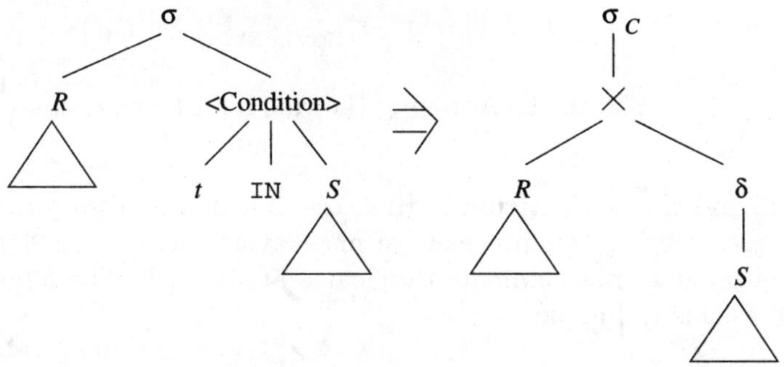

Figure 18: This rule handles a two-argument selection with a condition involving `IN`

Example 17: Consider the tree of Fig. 17, to which we shall apply the rule for `IN` conditions described above. In this figure, relation R is `StarsIn`, and relation S is the result of the relational-algebra expression consisting of the subtree rooted at π_{name}. The tuple t has one component, the attribute `starName`.

The two-argument selection is replaced by $\sigma_{starName=name}$; its condition C equates the one component of tuple t to the attribute of the result of query S. The child of the σ node is a $\times$ node, and the arguments of the $\times$ node are the node labeled `StarsIn` and the root of the expression for S. Notice that, because `name` is the key for `MovieStar`, there is no need to introduce a duplicate-eliminating δ in the expression for S. The new expression is shown in Fig. 19. It is completely in relational algebra, and is equivalent to the expression of Fig. 16, although its structure is quite different. □

The strategy for translating subqueries to relational algebra is more complex when the subquery is correlated. Since correlated subqueries involve unknown values defined outside themselves, they cannot be translated in isolation. Rather, we need to translate the subquery so that it produces a relation in which certain extra attributes appear — the attributes that must later be compared with the externally defined attributes. The conditions that relate attributes from the subquery to attributes outside are then applied to this

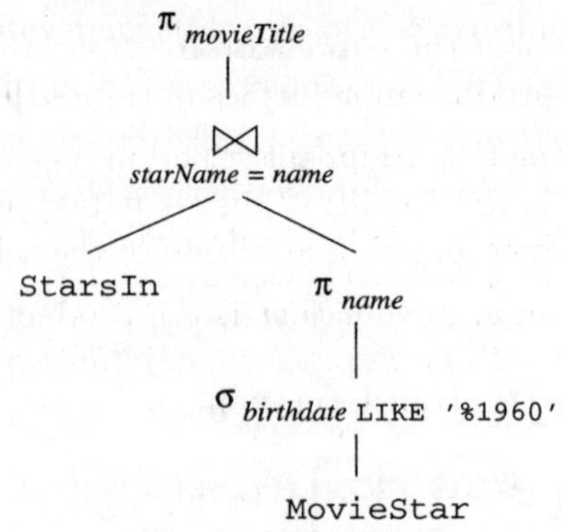

Figure 19: Applying the rule for IN conditions

relation, and the extra attributes that are no longer necessary can then be projected out. During this process, we must avoid introducing duplicate tuples, if the query does not eliminate duplicates at the end. The following example illustrates this technique.

```
SELECT DISTINCT m1.movieTitle, m1.movieYear
FROM StarsIn m1
WHERE m1.movieYear - 40 <= (
    SELECT AVG(birthdate)
    FROM StarsIn m2, MovieStar s
    WHERE m2.starName = s.name AND
        m1.movieTitle = m2.movieTitle AND
        m1.movieYear = m2.movieYear
);
```

Figure 20: Finding movies with high average star age

Example 18: Figure 20 is a SQL rendition of the query: "find the movies where the average age of the stars was at most 40 when the movie was made." To simplify, we treat `birthdate` as a birth year, so we can take its average and get a value that can be compared with the `movieYear` attribute of `StarsIn`. We have also written the query so that each of the three references to relations has its own tuple variable, in order to help remind us where the various attributes come from.

Fig. 21 shows the result of parsing the query and performing a partial translation to relational algebra. During this initial translation, we split the `WHERE`-clause of the subquery in two, and used part of it to convert the product of relations to an equijoin. We have retained the aliases `m1`, `m2`, and `s` in the nodes of this tree, in order to make clearer the origin of each attribute.

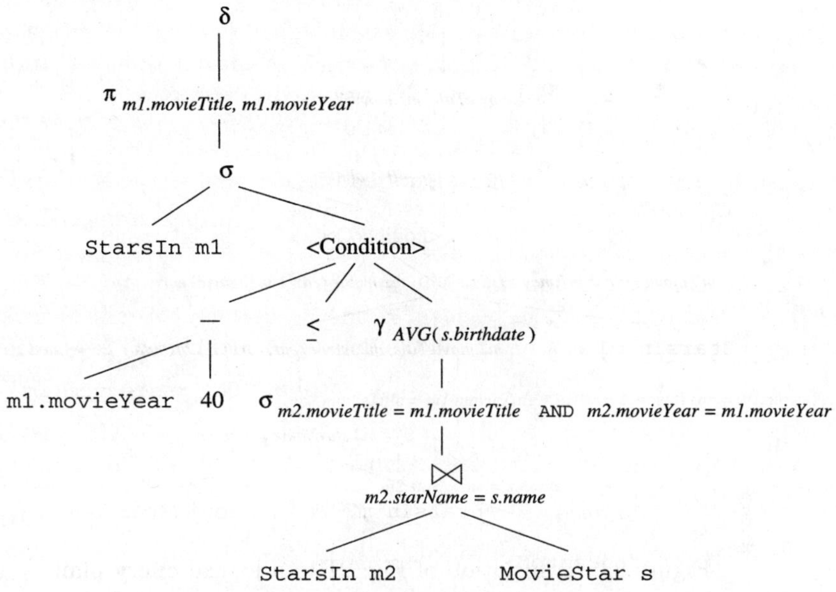

Figure 21: Partially transformed parse tree for Fig. 20

Alternatively, we could have used projections to rename attributes and thus avoid conflicting attribute names, but the result would be harder to follow.

In order to remove the <Condition> node and eliminate the two-argument σ, we need to create an expression that describes the relation in the right branch of the <Condition>. However, because the subquery is correlated, there is no way to obtain the attributes `m1.movieTitle` or `m1.movieYear` from the relations mentioned in the subquery, which are `StarsIn` (with alias `m2`) and `MovieStar`. Thus, we need to defer the selection

$$\sigma_{m2.movieTitle=m1.movieTitle \text{ AND } m2.movieYear=m1.movieYear}$$

until after the relation from the subquery is combined with the copy of `StarsIn` from the outer query (the copy aliased `m1`). To transform the logical query plan in this way, we need to modify the γ to group by the attributes `m2.movieTitle` and `m2.movieYear`, so these attributes will be available when needed by the selection. The net effect is that we compute for the subquery a relation consisting of movies, each represented by its title and year, and the average star birth year for that movie.

The modified group-by operator appears in Fig. 22; in addition to the two grouping attributes, we need to rename the average `abd` (average birthdate) so we can refer to it later. Figure 22 also shows the complete translation to relational algebra. Above the γ, the `StarsIn` from the outer query is joined with the result of the subquery. The selection from the subquery is then applied to the product of `StarsIn` and the result of the subquery; we show this selection as

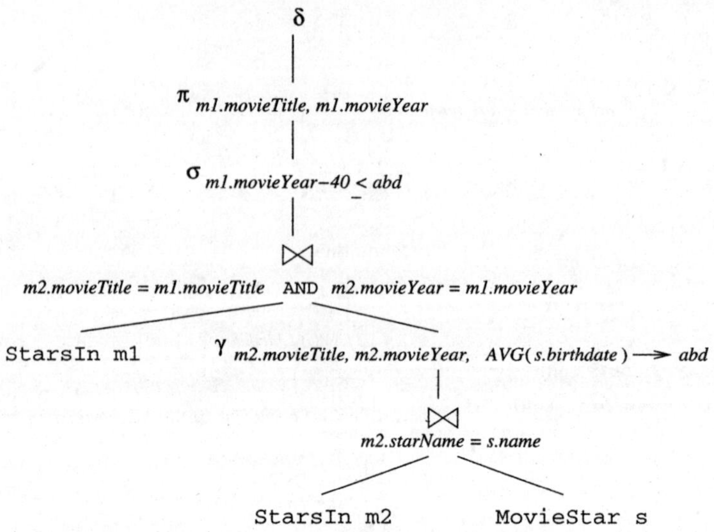

Figure 22: Translation of Fig. 21 to a logical query plan

a theta-join, which it would become after normal application of algebraic laws. Above the theta-join is another selection, this one corresponding to the selection of the outer query, in which we compare the movie's year to the average birth year of its stars. The algebraic expression finishes at the top like the expression of Fig. 21, with the projection onto the desired attributes and the elimination of duplicates.

As we shall see in Section 3.3, there is much more that a query optimizer can do to improve the query plan. This particular example satisfies three conditions that let us improve the plan considerably. The conditions are:

1. Duplicates are eliminated at the end,

2. Star names from `StarsIn m1` are projected out, and

3. The join between `StarsIn m1` and the rest of the expression equates the title and year attributes from `StarsIn m1` and `StarsIn m2`.

Because these conditions hold, we can replace all uses of `m1.movieTitle` and `m1.movieYear` by `m2.movieTitle` and `m2.movieYear`, respectively. Thus, the upper join in Fig. 22 is unnecessary, as is the argument `StarsIn m1`. This logical query plan is shown in Fig. 23. □

3.3 Improving the Logical Query Plan

When we convert our query to relational algebra we obtain one possible logical query plan. The next step is to rewrite the plan using the algebraic laws outlined

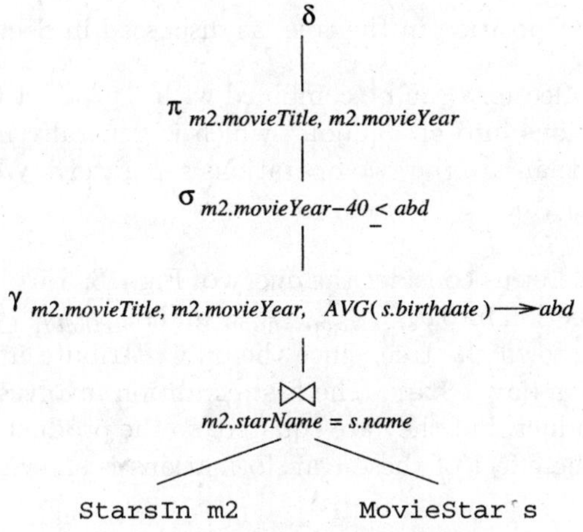

Figure 23: Simplification of Fig. 22

in Section 2. Alternatively, we could generate more than one logical plan, representing different orders or combinations of operators. But in this chapter we shall assume that the query rewriter chooses a single logical query plan that it believes is "best," meaning that it is likely to result ultimately in the cheapest physical plan.

We do, however, leave open the matter of what is known as "join ordering," so a logical query plan that involves joining relations can be thought of as a family of plans, corresponding to the different ways a join could be ordered and grouped. We discuss choosing a join order in Section 6. Similarly, a query plan involving three or more relations that are arguments to the other associative and commutative operators, such as union, should be assumed to allow reordering and regrouping as we convert the logical plan to a physical plan. We begin discussing the issues regarding ordering and physical plan selection in Section 4.

There are a number of algebraic laws from Section 2 that tend to improve logical query plans. The following are most commonly used in optimizers:

- Selections can be pushed down the expression tree as far as they can go. If a selection condition is the AND of several conditions, then we can split the condition and push each piece down the tree separately. This strategy is probably the most effective improvement technique, but we should recall the discussion in Section 2.3, where we saw that in some circumstances it was necessary to push the selection up the tree first.

- Similarly, projections can be pushed down the tree, or new projections can be added. As with selections, the pushing of projections should be done with care, as discussed in Section 2.4.

- Duplicate eliminations can sometimes be removed, or moved to a more convenient position in the tree, as discussed in Section 2.6.

- Certain selections can be combined with a product below to turn the pair of operations into an equijoin, which is generally much more efficient to evaluate than are the two operations separately. We discussed these laws in Section 2.5.

Example 19: Let us consider the query of Fig. 16. First, we may split the two parts of the selection into $\sigma_{starName=name}$ and $\sigma_{birthdate \texttt{ LIKE '\%1960'}}$. The latter can be pushed down the tree, since the only attribute involved, `birthdate`, is from the relation `MovieStar`. The first condition involves attributes from both sides of the product, but they are equated, so the product and selection is really an equijoin. The effect of these transformations is shown in Fig. 24. □

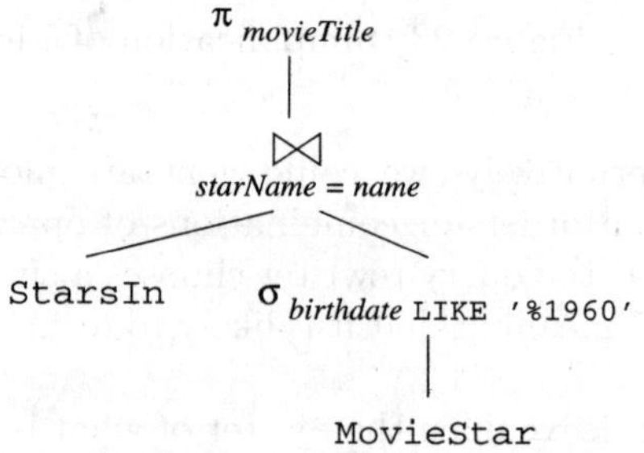

Figure 24: The effect of query rewriting

3.4 Grouping Associative/Commutative Operators

An operator that is associative and commutative operators may be thought of as having any number of operands. Thinking of an operator such as join as having any number of operands lets us reorder those operands so that when the multiway join is executed as a sequence of binary joins, they take less time than if we had executed the joins in the order implied by the parse tree. We discuss ordering multiway joins in Section 6.

Thus, we shall perform a last step before producing the final logical query plan: for each portion of the subtree that consists of nodes with the same associative and commutative operator, we group the nodes with these operators into a single node with many children. Recall that the usual associative/commutative operators are natural join, union, and intersection. Natural joins and theta-joins can also be combined with each other under certain circumstances:

1. We must replace the natural joins with theta-joins that equate the attributes of the same name.

2. We must add a projection to eliminate duplicate copies of attributes involved in a natural join that has become a theta-join.

3. The theta-join conditions must be associative. Recall there are cases, as discussed in Section 2.1, where theta-joins are not associative.

In addition, products can be considered as a special case of natural join and combined with joins if they are adjacent in the tree. Figure 25 illustrates this transformation in a situation where the logical query plan has a cluster of two union operators and a cluster of three natural join operators. Note that the letters R through W stand for any expressions, not necessarily for stored relations.

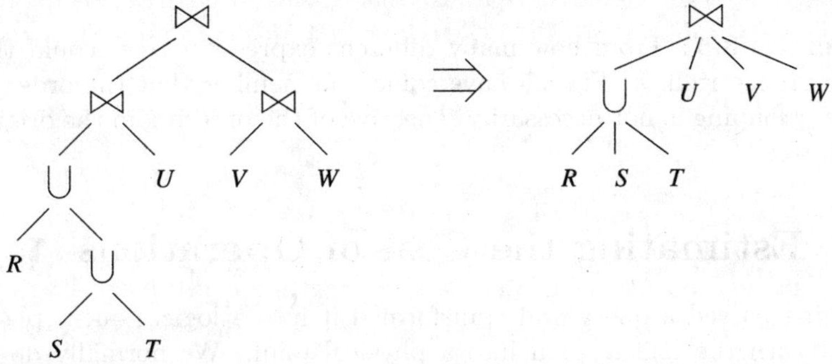

Figure 25: Final step in producing the logical query plan: group the associative and commutative operators

3.5 Exercises for Section 3

Exercise 3.1: Replace the natural joins in the following expressions by equivalent theta-joins and projections. Tell whether the resulting theta-joins form a commutative and associative group.

a) $\big(R(a,b) \bowtie S(b,c)\big) \bowtie_{S.c>T.c} T(c,d)$.

b) $\big(R(a,b) \bowtie S(b,c)\big) \bowtie \big(T(c,d) \bowtie U(d,e)\big)$.

c) $\big(R(a,b) \bowtie S(b,c)\big) \bowtie \big(T(c,d) \bowtie U(a,d)\big)$.

Exercise 3.2: Convert to relational algebra your parse trees from Exercise 1.3(a) and (b). For (b), show both the form with a two-argument selection and its eventual conversion to a one-argument (conventional σ_C) selection.

! **Exercise 3.3:** Give a rule for converting each of the following forms of <Condition> to relational algebra. All conditions may be assumed to be applied (by a two-argument selection) to a relation R. You may assume that the subquery is not correlated with R. Be careful that you do not introduce or eliminate duplicates in opposition to the formal definition of SQL.

a) A condition of the form `EXISTS`(<Query>).

b) A condition of the form a = `ANY` <Query>, where a is an attribute of R.

c) A condition of the form a = `ALL` <Query>, where a is an attribute of R.

!! **Exercise 3.4:** Repeat Exercise 3.3, but allow the subquery to be corollated with R. For simplicity, you may assume that the subquery has the simple form of select-from-where expression described in this section, with *no* further subqueries.

!! **Exercise 3.5:** From how many different expression trees could the grouped tree on the right of Fig. 25 have come? Remember that the order of children after grouping is not necessarily reflective of the ordering in the original expression tree.

4 Estimating the Cost of Operations

Having parsed a query and transformed it into a logical query plan, we must next turn the logical plan into a physical plan. We normally do so by considering many different physical plans that are derived from the logical plan, and evaluating or estimating the cost of each. After this evaluation, often called *cost-based enumeration*, we pick the physical query plan with the least estimated cost; that plan is the one passed to the query-execution engine. When enumerating possible physical plans derivable from a given logical plan, we select for each physical plan:

1. An order and grouping for associative-and-commutative operations like joins, unions, and intersections.

2. An algorithm for each operator in the logical plan, for instance, deciding whether a nested-loop join or a hash-join should be used.

3. Additional operators — scanning, sorting, and so on — that are needed for the physical plan but that were not present explicitly in the logical plan.

4. The way in which arguments are passed from one operator to the next, for instance, by storing the intermediate result on disk or by using iterators and passing an argument one tuple or one main-memory buffer at a time.

To make each of these choices, we need to understand what the costs of the various physical plans are. We cannot know these costs exactly without executing the plan. But almost always, the cost of executing a query plan is

Review of Notation

Recall the following size parameters:

- $B(R)$ is the number of blocks needed to hold relation R.
- $T(R)$ is the number of tuples of relation R.
- $V(R, a)$ is the *value count* for attribute a of relation R, that is, the number of distinct values relation R has in attribute a. Also, $V(R, [a_1, a_2, \ldots, a_n])$ is the number of distinct values R has when all of attributes $a_1, a_2, \ldots, a_n$ are considered together, that is, the number of tuples in $\delta(\pi_{a_1,a_2,\ldots,a_n}(R))$.

significantly greater than all the work done by the query compiler in selecting a plan. Thus, we do not want to execute more than one plan for one query, and we are forced to estimate the cost of any plan without executing it.

Therefore, our first problem is how to estimate costs of plans accurately. Such estimates are based on parameters of the data (see the box on "Review of Notation") that must be either computed exactly from the data or estimated by a process of "statistics gathering" that we discuss in Section 5.1. Given values for these parameters, we may make a number of reasonable estimates of relation sizes that can be used to predict the cost of a complete physical plan.

4.1 Estimating Sizes of Intermediate Relations

The physical plan is selected to minimize the estimated cost of evaluating the query. No matter what method is used for executing query plans, and no matter how costs of query plans are estimated, the sizes of intermediate relations of the plan have a profound influence on costs. Ideally, we want rules for estimating the number of tuples in an intermediate relation so that the rules:

1. Give accurate estimates.
2. Are easy to compute.
3. Are logically consistent; that is, the size estimate for an intermediate relation should not depend on how that relation is computed. For instance, the size estimate for a join of several relations should not depend on the order in which we join the relations.

There is no universally agreed-upon way to meet these three conditions. We shall give some simple rules that serve in most situations. Fortunately, the goal of size estimation is not to predict the exact size; it is to help select a physical query plan. Even an inaccurate size-estimation method will serve that purpose well if it errs consistently, that is, if the size estimator assigns the least cost to the best physical query plan, even if the actual cost of that plan turns out to be different from what was predicted.

4.2 Estimating the Size of a Projection

We shall treat a clasical, duplicate-eliminating projection as a bag-projection followed by a δ. The extended projection of bags is different from the other operators, in that the size of the result is computable exactly. Normally, tuples shrink during a projection, as some components are eliminated. However, the extended projection allows the creation of new components that are combinations of attributes, and so there are situations where a π operator actually increases the size of the relation.

Example 20: Suppose $R(a, b, c)$ is a relation, where a and b are integers of four bytes each, and c is a string of 100 bytes. Let tuple headers require 12 bytes. Then each tuple of R requires 120 bytes. Let blocks be 1024 bytes long, with block headers of 24 bytes. We can thus fit 8 tuples in one block. Suppose $T(R) = 10{,}000$; i.e., there are 10,000 tuples in R. Then $B(R) = 1250$.

Consider $S = \pi_{a+b \to x, c}(R)$; that is, we replace a and b by their sum. Tuples of S require 116 bytes: 12 for header, 4 for the sum, and 100 for the string. Although tuples of S are slightly smaller than tuples of R, we can still fit only 8 tuples in a block. Thus, $T(S) = 10{,}000$ and $B(S) = 1250$.

Now consider $U = \pi_{a,b}(R)$, where we eliminate the string component. Tuples of U are only 20 bytes long. $T(U)$ is still 10,000. However, we can now pack 50 tuples of U into one block, so $B(U) = 200$. This projection thus shrinks the relation by a factor slightly more than 6. □

4.3 Estimating the Size of a Selection

When we perform a selection, we generally reduce the number of tuples, although the sizes of tuples remain the same. In the simplest kind of selection, where an attribute is equated to a constant, there is an easy way to estimate the size of the result, provided we know, or can estimate, the number of different values the attribute has. Let $S = \sigma_{A=c}(R)$, where A is an attribute of R and c is a constant. Then we recommend as an estimate:

- $T(S) = T(R)/V(R, A)$

This rule surely holds if the value of A is chosen randomly from among all the possible values.

The size estimate is more problematic when the selection involves an inequality comparison, for instance, $S = \sigma_{a<10}(R)$. One might think that on the average, half the tuples would satisfy the comparison and half not, so $T(R)/2$

The Zipfian Distribution

In estimating the size of a selection $\sigma_{A=c}$ it is not necessary to assume that values of A appear equally often. In fact, many attributes have values whose occurrences follow a *Zipfian distribution*, where the frequencies of the ith most common values are in proportion to $1/\sqrt{i}$. For example, if the most common value appears 1000 times, then the second most common value would be expected to appear about $1000/\sqrt{2}$ times, or 707 times, and the third most common value would appear about $1000/\sqrt{3}$ times, or 577 times. Originally postulated as a way to describe the relative frequencies of words in English sentences, this distribution has been found to appear in many sorts of data. For example, in the US, state populations follow an approximate Zipfian distribution. The three most populous states, California, Texas, and New York, have populations in ratio approximately 1:0.62:0.56, compared with the Zipfian ideal of 1:0.71:0.58. Thus, if `state` were an attribute of a relation describing US people, say a list of magazine subscribers, we would expect the values of `state` to distribute in the Zipfian, rather than uniform manner.

As long as the constant in the selection condition is chosen randomly, it doesn't matter whether the values of the attribute involved have a uniform, Zipfian, or other distribution; the *average* size of the matching set will still be $T(R)/V(R,a)$. However, if the constants are also chosen with a Zipfian distribution, then we would expect the average size of the selected set to be somewhat larger than $T(R)/V(R,a)$.

would estimate the size of S. However, there is an intuition that queries involving an inequality tend to retrieve a small fraction of the possible tuples.[3] Thus, we propose a rule that acknowledges this tendency, and assumes the typical inequality will return about one third of the tuples, rather than half the tuples. If $S = \sigma_{a<c}(R)$, then our estimate for $T(S)$ is:

- $T(S) = T(R)/3$

The case of a "not equals" comparison is rare. However, should we encounter a selection like $S = \sigma_{a\neq 10}(R)$, we recommend assuming that essentially all tuples will satisfy the condition. That is, take $T(S) = T(R)$ as an estimate. Alternatively, we may use $T(S) = T(R)\big(V(R,a)-1\big)/V(R,a)$, which is slightly less, as an estimate, acknowledging that about fraction $1/V(R,a)$ tuples of R will fail to meet the condition because their a-value *does* equal the constant.

When the selection condition C is the `AND` of several equalities and inequalities, we can treat the selection $\sigma_C(R)$ as a cascade of simple selections, each of

[3]For instance, if you had data about faculty salaries, would you be more likely to query for those faculty who made *less* than \$200,000 or *more* than \$200,000?

which checks for one of the conditions. Note that the order in which we place these selections doesn't matter. The effect will be that the size estimate for the result is the size of the original relation multiplied by the *selectivity* factor for each condition. That factor is 1/3 for any inequality, 1 for $\neq$, and $1/V(R, A)$ for any attribute A that is compared to a constant in the condition C.

Example 21: Let $R(a, b, c)$ be a relation, and $S = \sigma_{a=10 \texttt{ AND } b<20}(R)$. Also, let $T(R)$ = 10,000, and $V(R, a) = 50$. Then our best estimate of $T(S)$ is $T(R)/(50 \times 3)$, or 67. That is, 1/50th of the tuples of R will survive the $a = 10$ filter, and 1/3 of those will survive the $b < 20$ filter.

An interesting special case where our analysis breaks down is when the condition is contradictory. For instance, consider $S = \sigma_{a=10 \texttt{ AND } a>20}(R)$. According to our rule, $T(S) = T(R)/3V(R, a)$, or 67 tuples. However, it should be clear that no tuple can have both $a = 10$ and $a > 20$, so the correct answer is $T(S) = 0$. When rewriting the logical query plan, the query optimizer can look for instances of many special-case rules. In the above instance, the optimizer can apply a rule that finds the selection condition logically equivalent to FALSE and replaces the expression for S by the empty set. □

When a selection involves an OR of conditions, say $S = \sigma_{C_1 \texttt{ OR } C_2}(R)$, then we have less certainty about the size of the result. One simple assumption is that no tuple will satisfy both conditions, so the size of the result is the sum of the number of tuples that satisfy each. That measure is generally an overestimate, and in fact can sometimes lead us to the absurd conclusion that there are more tuples in S than in the original relation R.

A less simple, but possibly more accurate estimate of the size of

$$S = \sigma_{C_1 \texttt{ OR } C_2}(R)$$

is to assume that C_1 and C_2 are independent. Then, if R has n tuples, m_1 of which satisfy C_1 and m_2 of which satisfy C_2, we would estimate the number of tuples in S as $n\big(1 - (1 - m_1/n)(1 - m_2/n)\big)$. In explanation, $1 - m_1/n$ is the fraction of tuples that do not satisfy C_1, and $1 - m_2/n$ is the fraction that do not satisfy C_2. The product of these numbers is the fraction of R's tuples that are *not* in S, and 1 minus this product is the fraction that are in S.

Example 22: Suppose $R(a, b)$ has $T(R)$ = 10,000 tuples, and

$$S = \sigma_{a=10 \texttt{ OR } b<20}(R)$$

Let $V(R, a) = 50$. Then the number of tuples that satisfy $a = 10$ we estimate at 200, i.e., $T(R)/V(R, a)$. The number of tuples that satisfy $b < 20$ we estimate at $T(R)/3$, or 3333.

The simplest estimate for the size of S is the sum of these numbers, or 3533. The more complex estimate based on independence of the conditions $a = 10$ and $b < 20$ gives $10000\big(1 - (1 - 200/10000)(1 - 3333/10000)\big)$, or 3466. In this case, there is little difference between the two estimates, and it is very unlikely that choosing one over the other would change our estimate of the best physical query plan. □

The final operator that could appear in a selection condition is `NOT`. The estimated number of tuples of R that satisfy condition `NOT` C is $T(R)$ minus the estimated number that satisfy C.

4.4 Estimating the Size of a Join

We shall consider here only the natural join. Other joins can be handled according to the following outline:

1. The number of tuples in the result of an equijoin can be computed exactly as for a natural join, after accounting for the change in variable names. Example 24 will illustrate this point.

2. Other theta-joins can be estimated as if they were a selection following a product. Note that the number of tuples in a product is the product of the number of tuples in the relations involved.

We shall begin our study with the assumption that the natural join of two relations involves only the equality of two attributes. That is, we study the join $R(X, Y) \bowtie S(Y, Z)$, but initially we assume that Y is a single attribute although X and Z can represent any set of attributes.

The problem is that we don't know how the Y-values in R and S relate. For instance:

1. The two relations could have disjoint sets of Y-values, in which case the join is empty and $T(R \bowtie S) = 0$.

2. Y might be the key of S and the corresponding foreign key of R, so each tuple of R joins with exactly one tuple of S, and $T(R \bowtie S) = T(R)$.

3. Almost all the tuples of R and S could have the same Y-value, in which case $T(R \bowtie S)$ is about $T(R)T(S)$.

To focus on the most common situations, we shall make two simplifying assumptions:

- *Containment of Value Sets.* If Y is an attribute appearing in several relations, then each relation chooses its values from the front of a fixed list of values $y_1, y_2, y_3, \ldots$ and has all the values in that prefix. As a consequence, if R and S are two relations with an attribute Y, and $V(R, Y) \leq V(S, Y)$, then every Y-value of R will be a Y-value of S.

- *Preservation of Value Sets.* If we join a relation R with another relation, then an attribute A that is not a join attribute (i.e., not present in both relations) does not lose values from its set of possible values. More precisely, if A is an attribute of R but not of S, then $V(R \bowtie S, A) = V(R, A)$.

Assumption (1), containment of value sets, clearly might be violated, but it *is* satisfied when Y is a key in S and the corresponding foreign key in R. It also is approximately true in many other cases, since we would intuitively expect that if S has many Y-values, then a given Y-value that appears in R has a good chance of appearing in S.

Assumption (2), preservation of value sets, also might be violated, but it is true when the join attribute(s) of $R \bowtie S$ are a key for S and the corresponding foreign key of R. In fact, (2) can only be violated when there are "dangling tuples" in R, that is, tuples of R that join with no tuple of S; and even if there *are* dangling tuples in R, the assumption might still hold.

Under these assumptions, we can estimate the size of $R(X, Y) \bowtie S(Y, Z)$ as follows. Suppose r is a tuple in R, and S is a tuple in S. What is the probability that r and s agree on attribute Y? Suppose that $V(R, Y) \geq V(S, Y)$. Then the Y-value of s is surely one of the Y values that appear in R, by the containment-of-value-sets assumption. Hence, the chance that r has the same Y-value as s is $1/V(R, Y)$. Similarly, if $V(R, Y) < V(S, Y)$, then the value of Y in r will appear in S, and the probability is $1/V(S, Y)$ that r and s will share the same Y-value. In general, we see that the probability of agreement on the Y value is $1/\max\big(V(R, Y), V(S, Y)\big)$. Thus:

- $T(R \bowtie S) = T(R)T(S)/\max\big(V(R, Y), V(S, Y)\big)$

That is, the estimated number of tuples in $T(R \bowtie S)$ is the number of pairs of tuples — one from R and one from S, times the probability that such a pair shares a common Y value.

Example 23 : Let us consider the following three relations and their important statistics:

$R(a, b)$	$S(b, c)$	$U(c, d)$
$T(R) = 1000$	$T(S) = 2000$	$T(U) = 5000$
$V(R, b) = 20$	$V(S, b) = 50$	
	$V(S, c) = 100$	$V(U, c) = 500$

Suppose we want to compute the natural join $R \bowtie S \bowtie U$. One way is to group R and S first, as $(R \bowtie S) \bowtie U$. Our estimate for $T(R \bowtie S)$ is $T(R)T(S)/\max\big(V(R, b), V(S, b)\big)$, which is $1000 \times 2000/50$, or 40,000.

We then need to join $R \bowtie S$ with U. Our estimate for the size of the result is $T(R \bowtie S)T(U)/\max\big(V(R \bowtie S, c), V(U, c)\big)$. By our assumption that value sets are preserved, $V(R \bowtie S, c)$ is the same as $V(S, c)$, or 100; that is no values of attribute c disappeared when we performed the join. In that case, we get as our estimate for the number of tuples in $R \bowtie S \bowtie U$ the value $40{,}000 \times 5000/\max(100, 500)$, or 400,000.

We could also start by joining S and U. If we do, then we get the estimate $T(S \bowtie U) = T(S)T(U)/\max\big(V(S, c), V(U, c)\big) = 2000 \times 5000/500 = 20{,}000$.

By our assumption that value sets are preserved, $V(S \bowtie U, b) = V(S, b) = 50$, so the estimated size of the result is

$$T(R)T(S \bowtie U) / \max\big(V(R, b), V(S \bowtie U, b)\big)$$

which is $1000 \times 20{,}000/50$, or 400,000. □

4.5 Natural Joins With Multiple Join Attributes

When the set of attributes Y in the join $R(X, Y) \bowtie S(Y, Z)$ consists of more than one attribute, the same argument as we used for a single attribute Y applies to each attribute in Y. That is:

- The estimate of the size of $R \bowtie S$ is computed by multiplying $T(R)$ by $T(S)$ and dividing by the larger of $V(R, y)$ and $V(S, y)$ for each attribute y that is common to R and S.

Example 24: The following example uses the rule above. It also illustrates that the analysis we have been doing for natural joins applies to any equijoin. Consider the join

$$R(a, b, c) \bowtie_{R.b=S.d \text{ AND } R.c=S.e} S(d, e, f)$$

Suppose we have the following size parameters:

$R(a, b, c)$	$S(d, e, f)$
$T(R) = 1000$	$T(S) = 2000$
$V(R, b) = 20$	$V(S, d) = 50$
$V(R, c) = 100$	$V(S, e) = 50$

We can think of this join as a natural join if we regard $R.b$ and $S.d$ as the same attribute and also regard $R.c$ and $S.e$ as the same attribute. Then the rule given above tells us the estimate for the size of $R \bowtie S$ is the product 1000×2000 divided by the larger of 20 and 50 and also divided by the larger of 100 and 50. Thus, the size estimate for the join is $1000 \times 2000/(50 \times 100) = 400$ tuples. □

Example 25: Let us reconsider Example 23, but consider the third possible order for the joins, where we first take $R(a, b) \bowtie U(c, d)$. This join is actually a product, and the number of tuples in the result is $T(R)T(U) = 1000 \times 5000 =$ 5,000,000. Note that the number of different b's in the product is $V(R, b) = 20$, and the number of different c's is $V(U, c) = 500$.

When we join this product with $S(b, c)$, we multiply the numbers of tuples and divide by both $\max\big(V(R, b), V(S, b)\big)$ and $\max\big(V(U, c), V(S, c)\big)$. This quantity is $2000 \times 5{,}000{,}000/(50 \times 500) = 400{,}000$. Note that this third way of joining gives the same estimate for the size of the result that we found in Example 23. □

4.6 Joins of Many Relations

Finally, let us consider the general case of a natural join:

$$S = R_1 \bowtie R_2 \bowtie \cdots \bowtie R_n$$

Suppose that attribute A appears in k of the R_i's, and the numbers of its sets of values in these k relations — that is, the various values of $V(R_i, A)$ for $i = 1, 2, \ldots, k$ — are $v_1 \leq v_2 \leq \cdots \leq v_k$, in order from smallest to largest. Suppose we pick a tuple from each relation. What is the probability that all tuples selected agree on attribute A?

In answer, consider the tuple t_1 chosen from the relation that has the smallest number of A-values, v_1. By the containment-of-value-sets assumption, each of these v_1 values is among the A-values found in the other relations that have attribute A. Consider the relation that has v_i values in attribute A. Its selected tuple t_i has probability $1/v_i$ of agreeing with t_1 on A. Since this claim is true for all $i = 2, 3, \ldots, k$, the probability that all k tuples agree on A is the product $1/v_2 v_3 \cdots v_k$. This analysis gives us the rule for estimating the size of any join.

- Start with the product of the number of tuples in each relation. Then, for each attribute A appearing at least twice, divide by all but the least of the $V(R, A)$'s.

Likewise, we can estimate the number of values that will remain for attribute A after the join. By the preservation-of-value-sets assumption, it is the least of these $V(R, A)$'s.

Example 26: Consider the join $R(a, b, c) \bowtie S(b, c, d) \bowtie U(b, e)$, and suppose the important statistics are as given in Fig. 26. To estimate the size of this join, we begin by multiplying the relation sizes; $1000 \times 2000 \times 5000$. Next, we look at the attributes that appear more than once; these are b, which appears three times, and c, which appears twice. We divide by the two largest of $V(R, b)$, $V(S, b)$, and $V(U, b)$; these are 50 and 200. Finally, we divide by the larger of $V(R, c)$ and $V(S, c)$, which is 200. The resulting estimate is

$$1000 \times 2000 \times 5000/(50 \times 200 \times 200) = 5000$$

We can also estimate the number of values for each of the attributes in the join. Each estimate is the least value count for the attribute among all the relations in which it appears. These numbers are, for a, b, c, d, e respectively: 100, 20, 100, 400, and 500. □

Based on the two assumptions we have made — containment and preservation of value sets — we have a surprising and convenient property of the estimating rule given above.

- No matter how we group and order the terms in a natural join of n relations, the estimation rules, applied to each join individually, yield the

$R(a,b,c)$	$S(b,c,d)$	$U(b,e)$
$T(R) = 1000$	$T(S) = 2000$	$T(U) = 5000$
$V(R,a) = 100$		
$V(R,b) = 20$	$V(S,b) = 50$	$V(U,b) = 200$
$V(R,c) = 200$	$V(S,c) = 100$	
	$V(S,d) = 400$	
		$V(U,e) = 500$

Figure 26: Parameters for Example 26

same estimate for the size of the result. Moreover, this estimate is the same that we get if we apply the rule for the join of all n relations as a whole.

Examples 23 and 25 form an illustration of this rule for the three groupings of a three-relation join, including the grouping where one of the "joins" is actually a product.

4.7 Estimating Sizes for Other Operations

We have seen two operations — selection and join — with reasonable estimating techniques. In addition, projections do not change the number of tuples in a relation, and products multiply the numbers of tuples in the argument relations. However, for the remaining operations, the size of the result is not easy to determine. We shall review the other relational-algebra operators and give some suggestions as to how this estimation could be done.

Union

If the bag union is taken, then the size is exactly the sum of the sizes of the arguments. A set union can be as large as the sum of the sizes or as small as the larger of the two arguments. We suggest that something in the middle be chosen, e.g., the larger plus half the smaller.

Intersection

The result can have as few as 0 tuples or as many as the smaller of the two arguments, regardless of whether set- or bag-intersection is taken. One approach is to take the average of the extremes, which is half the smaller.

Difference

When we compute $R - S$, the result can have between $T(R)$ and $T(R) - T(S)$ tuples. We suggest the average as an estimate: $T(R) - T(S)/2$.

Duplicate Elimination

If $R(a_1, a_2, \ldots, a_n)$ is a relation, then $V(R, [a_1, a_2, \ldots, a_n])$ is the size of $\delta(R)$. However, often we shall not have this statistic available, so it must be approximated. In the extremes, the size of $\delta(R)$ could be the same as the size of R (no duplicates) or as small as 1 (all tuples in R are the same).[4] Another upper limit on the number of tuples in $\delta(R)$ is the maximum number of distinct tuples that could exist: the product of $V(R, a_i)$ for $i = 1, 2, \ldots, n$. That number could be smaller than other estimates of $T\big(\delta(R)\big)$. There are several rules that could be used to estimate $T\big(\delta(R)\big)$. One reasonable one is to take the smaller of $T(R)/2$ and the product of all the $V(R, a_i)$'s.

Grouping and Aggregation

Suppose we have an expression $\gamma_L(R)$, the size of whose result we need to estimate. If the statistic $V(R, [g_1, g_2, \ldots, g_k])$, where the g_i's are the grouping attributes in L, is available, then that is our answer. However, that statistic may well not be obtainable, so we need another way to estimate the size of $\gamma_L(R)$. The number of tuples in $\gamma_L(R)$ is the same as the number of groups. There could be as few as one group in the result or as many groups as there are tuples in R. As with δ, we can also upper-bound the number of groups by a product of $V(R, A)$'s, but here attribute A ranges over only the grouping attributes of L. We again suggest an estimate that is the smaller of $T(R)/2$ and this product.

4.8 Exercises for Section 4

Exercise 4.1: Below are the vital statistics for four relations, W, X, Y, and Z:

$W(a,b)$	$X(b,c)$	$Y(c,d)$	$Z(d,e)$
$T(W) = 100$	$T(X) = 200$	$T(Y) = 300$	$T(Z) = 400$
$V(W,a) = 20$	$V(X,b) = 50$	$V(Y,c) = 50$	$V(Z,d) = 40$
$V(W,b) = 60$	$V(X,c) = 100$	$V(Y,d) = 50$	$V(Z,e) = 100$

Estimate the sizes of relations that are the results of the following expressions:

(a) $W \bowtie X \bowtie Y \bowtie Z$ (b) $\sigma_{a=10}(W)$ (c) $\sigma_{c=20}(Y)$
(d) $\sigma_{c=20}(Y) \bowtie Z$ (e) $W \times Y$ (f) $\sigma_{d>10}(Z)$
(g) $\sigma_{a=1 \texttt{ AND } b=2}(W)$ (h) $\sigma_{a=1 \texttt{ AND } b>2}(W)$ (i) $X \bowtie_{X.c<Y.c} Y$

Exercise 4.2: Here are the statistics for four relations E, F, G, and H:

---

[4]Strictly speaking, if R is empty there are no tuples in either R or $\delta(R)$, so the lower bound is 0. However, we are rarely interested in this special case.

$E(a,b,c)$	$F(a,b,d)$	$G(a,c,d)$	$H(b,c,d)$
$T(E) = 1000$	$T(F) = 2000$	$T(G) = 3000$	$T(H) = 4000$
$V(E,a) = 1000$	$V(F,a) = 50$	$V(G,a) = 50$	$V(H,b) = 40$
$V(E,b) = 50$	$V(F,b) = 100$	$V(G,c) = 300$	$V(H,c) = 100$
$V(E,c) = 20$	$V(F,d) = 200$	$V(G,d) = 500$	$V(H,d) = 400$

How many tuples does the join of these tuples have, using the techniques for estimation from this section?

! **Exercise 4.3:** How would you estimate the size of a semijoin?

!! **Exercise 4.4:** Suppose we compute $R(a,b) \bowtie S(a,c)$, where R and S each have 1000 tuples. The a attribute of each relation has 100 different values, and they are the *same* 100 values. If the distribution of values was uniform; i.e., each a-value appeared in exactly 10 tuples of each relation, then there would be 10,000 tuples in the join. Suppose instead that the 100 a-values have the same Zipfian distribution in each relation. Precisely, let the values be $a_1, a_2, \ldots, a_{100}$. Then the number of tuples of both R and S that have a-value a_i is proportional to $1/\sqrt{i}$. Under these circumstances, how many tuples does the join have? You should ignore the fact that the number of tuples with a given a-value may not be an integer.

5 Introduction to Cost-Based Plan Selection

Whether selecting a logical query plan or constructing a physical query plan from a logical plan, the query optimizer needs to estimate the cost of evaluating certain expressions. We study the issues involved in cost-based plan selection here, and in Section 6 we consider in detail one of the most important and difficult problems in cost-based plan selection: the selection of a join order for several relations.

As before, we shall assume that the "cost" of evaluating an expression is approximated well by the number of disk I/O's performed. The number of disk I/O's, in turn, is influenced by:

1. The particular logical operators chosen to implement the query, a matter decided when we choose the logical query plan.

2. The sizes of intermediate results, whose estimation we discussed in Section 4.

3. The physical operators used to implement logical operators, e.g., the choice of a one-pass or two-pass join, or the choice to sort or not sort a given relation; this matter is discussed in Section 7.

4. The ordering of similar operations, especially joins as discussed in Section 6.

5. The method of passing arguments from one physical operator to the next, which is also discussed in Section 7.

Many issues need to be resolved in order to perform effective cost-based plan selection. In this section, we first consider how the size parameters, which were so essential for estimating relation sizes in Section 4, can be obtained from the database efficiently. We then revisit the algebraic laws we introduced to find the preferred logical query plan. Cost-based analysis justifies the use of many of the common heuristics for transforming logical query plans, such as pushing selections down the tree. Finally, we consider the various approaches to enumerating all the physical query plans that can be derived from the selected logical plan. Especially important are methods for reducing the number of plans that need to be evaluated, while making it likely that the least-cost plan is still considered.

5.1 Obtaining Estimates for Size Parameters

The formulas of Section 4 were predicated on knowing certain important parameters, especially $T(R)$, the number of tuples in a relation R, and $V(R, a)$, the number of different values in the column of relation R for attribute a. A modern DBMS generally allows the user or administrator explicitly to request the gathering of statistics, such as $T(R)$ and $V(R, a)$. These statistics are then used in query optimization, unchanged until the next command to gather statistics.

By scanning an entire relation R, it is straightforward to count the number of tuples $T(R)$ and also to discover the number of different values $V(R, a)$ for each attribute a. The number of blocks in which R can fit, $B(R)$, can be estimated either by counting the actual number of blocks used (if R is clustered), or by dividing $T(R)$ by the number of R's tuples that can fit in one block.

In addition, a DBMS may compute a *histogram* of the values for a given attribute. If $V(R, A)$ is not too large, then the histogram may consist of the number (or fraction) of the tuples having each of the values of attribute A. If there are many values of this attribute, then only the most frequent values may be recorded individually, while other values are counted in groups. The most common types of histograms are:

1. *Equal-width.* A width w is chosen, along with a constant v_0. Counts are provided of the number of tuples with values v in the ranges $v_0 \le v < v_0 + w$, $v_0 + w \le v < v_0 + 2w$, and so on. The value v_0 may be the lowest possible value or a lower bound on values seen so far. In the latter case, should a new, lower value be seen, we can lower the value of v_0 by w and add a new count to the histogram.

2. *Equal-height.* These are the common "percentiles." We pick some fraction p, and list the lowest value, the value that is fraction p from the lowest, the fraction $2p$ from the lowest, and so on, up to the highest value.

3. *Most-frequent-values.* We may list the most common values and their numbers of occurrences. This information may be provided along with a count of occurrences for all the other values as a group, or we may record frequent values in addition to an equal-width or equal-height histogram for the other values.

One advantage of keeping a histogram is that the sizes of joins can be estimated more accurately than by the simplified methods of Section 4. In particular, if a value of the join attribute appears explicitly in the histograms of both relations being joined, then we know exactly how many tuples of the result will have this value. For those values of the join attribute that do not appear explicitly in the histogram of one or both relations, we estimate their effect on the join as in Section 4. However, if we use an equal-width histogram, with the same bands for the join attributes of both relations, then we can estimate the size of the joins of corresponding bands, and sum those estimates. The result will be a good estimate, because only tuples in corresponding bands can join. The following examples will suggest how to carry out histogram-based estimation; we shall not use histograms in estimates subsequently.

Example 27: Consider histograms that mention the three most frequent values and their counts, and group the remaining values. Suppose we want to compute the join $R(a,b) \bowtie S(b,c)$. Let the histogram for $R.b$ be:

1: 200, 0: 150, 5: 100, others: 550

That is, of the 1000 tuples in R, 200 of them have b-value 1, 150 have b-value 0, and 100 have b-value 5. In addition, 550 tuples have b-values other than 0, 1, or 5, and none of these other values appears more than 100 times.

Let the histogram for $S.b$ be:

0: 100, 1: 80, 2: 70, others: 250

Suppose also that $V(R,b) = 14$ and $V(S,b) = 13$. That is, the 550 tuples of R with unknown b-values are divided among eleven values, for an average of 50 tuples each, and the 250 tuples of S with unknown b-values are divided among ten values, each with an average of 25 tuples each.

Values 0 and 1 appear explicitly in both histograms, so we can calculate that the 150 tuples of R with $b = 0$ join with the 100 tuples of S having the same b-value, to yield 15,000 tuples in the result. Likewise, the 200 tuples of R with $b = 1$ join with the 80 tuples of S having $b = 1$ to yield 16,000 more tuples in the result.

The estimate of the effect of the remaining tuples is more complex. We shall continue to make the assumption that every value appearing in the relation with the smaller set of values (S in this case) will also appear in the set of values of the other relation. Thus, among the eleven remaining b-values of S, we know one of those values is 2, and we shall assume another of the values is 5, since that is one of the most frequent values in R. We estimate that 2 appears 50 times in R, and 5 appears 25 times in S. These estimates are each obtained by assuming that the value is one of the "other" values for its relation's histogram. The number of additional tuples from b-value 2 is thus $70 \times 50 = 3500$, and the number of additional tuples from b-value 5 is $100 \times 25 = 2500$.

Finally, there are nine other b-values that appear in both relations, and we estimate that each of them appears in 50 tuples of R and 25 tuples of S. Each of the nine values thus contributes $50 \times 25 = 1250$ tuples to the result. The estimate of the output size is thus:

$$15000 + 16000 + 3500 + 2500 + 9 \times 1250$$

or 48,250 tuples. Note that the simpler estimate from Section 4 would be $1000 \times 500/14$, or 35,714, based on the assumptions of equal numbers of occurrences of each value in each relation. □

Example 28: In this example, we shall assume an equal-width histogram, and we shall demonstrate how knowing that values of two relations are almost disjoint can impact the estimate of a join size. Our relations are:

```
Jan(day, temp)
July(day, temp)
```

and the query is:

```
SELECT Jan.day, July.day
FROM Jan, July
WHERE Jan.temp = July.temp;
```

That is, find pairs of days in January and July that had the same temperature. The query plan is to equijoin `Jan` and `July` on the temperature, and project onto the two `day` attributes.

Suppose the histogram of temperatures for the relations `Jan` and `July` are as given in the table of Fig. 27.[5] In general, if both join attributes have equal-width histograms with the same set of bands, then we can estimate the size of the join by considering each pair of corresponding bands and summing.

If two corresponding bands have T_1 and T_2 tuples, respectively, and the number of values in a band is V, then the estimate for the number of tuples in the join of those bands is T_1T_2/V, following the principles laid out in Section 4.4. For the histograms of Fig. 27, many of these products are 0, because one or the other of T_1 and T_2 is 0. The only bands for which neither is 0 are 40–49 and 50–59. Since $V = 10$ is the width of a band, the 40–49 band contributes $10 \times 5/10 = 5$ tuples, and the 50–59 band contributes $5 \times 20/10 = 10$ tuples.

[5] Our friends south of the equator should reverse the columns for January and July, and convert to centigrade as well.

Range	Jan	July
0–9	40	0
10–19	60	0
20–29	80	0
30–39	50	0
40–49	10	5
50–59	5	20
60–69	0	50
70–79	0	100
80–89	0	60
90–99	0	10

Figure 27: Histograms of temperature

Thus our estimate for the size of this join is $5 + 10 = 15$ tuples. If we had no histogram, and knew only that each relation had 245 tuples distributed among 100 values from 0 to 99, then our estimate of the join size would be $245 \times 245/100 = 600$ tuples. □

5.2 Computation of Statistics

Statistics normally are computed only periodically, for several reasons. First, statistics tend not to change radically in a short time. Second, even somewhat inaccurate statistics are useful as long as they are applied consistently to all the plans. Third, the alternative of keeping statistics up-to-date can make the statistics themselves into a "hot-spot" in the database; because statistics are read frequently, we prefer not to update them frequently too.

The recomputation of statistics might be triggered automatically after some period of time, or after some number of updates. However, a database administrator, noticing that poor-performing query plans are being selected by the query optimizer on a regular basis, might request the recomputation of statistics in an attempt to rectify the problem.

Computing statistics for an entire relation R can be very expensive, particularly if we compute $V(R, a)$ for each attribute a in the relation (or even worse, compute histograms for each a). One common approach is to compute approximate statistics by sampling only a fraction of the data. For example, let us suppose we want to sample a small fraction of the tuples to obtain an estimate for $V(R, a)$. A statistically reliable calculation can be complex, depending on a number of assumptions, such as whether values for a are distributed uniformly, according to a Zipfian distribution, or according to some other distribution. However, the intuition is as follows. If we look at a small sample of R, say 1% of its tuples, and we find that most of the a-values we see are different, then it is likely that $V(R, a)$ is close to $T(R)$. If we find that the sample has very few different values of a, then it is likely that we have seen most of the a-values that exist in the current relation.

5.3 Heuristics for Reducing the Cost of Logical Query Plans

One important use of cost estimates for queries or subqueries is in the application of heuristic transformations of the query. We already have observed in Section 3.3 how certain heuristics, such as pushing selections down the tree, can be expected almost certainly to improve the cost of a logical query plan, regardless of relation sizes. However, there are other points in the query optimization process where estimating the cost both before and after a transformation will allow us to apply a transformation where it appears to reduce cost and avoid the transformation otherwise. In particular, when the preferred logical query plan is being generated, we may consider a number of optional transformations and the costs before and after.

Because we are estimating the cost of a *logical* query plan, and so we have not yet made decisions about the physical operators that will be used to implement the operators of relational algebra, our cost estimate cannot be based on disk I/O's. Rather, we estimate the sizes of all intermediate results using the techniques of Section 4, and their sum is our heuristic estimate for the cost of the entire logical plan. One example will serve to illustrate the issues and process.

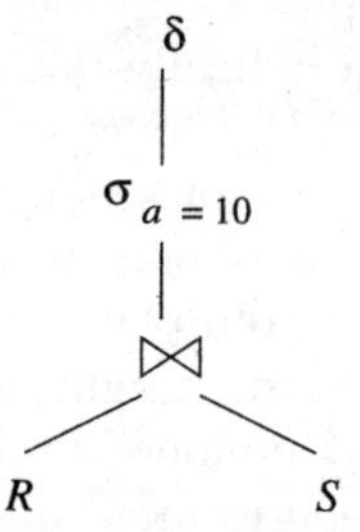

Figure 28: Logical query plan for Example 29

Example 29: Consider the initial logical query plan of Fig. 28, and let the statistics for the relations R and S be as follows:

$R(a,b)$	$S(b,c)$
$T(R) = 5000$	$T(S) = 2000$
$V(R,a) = 50$	
$V(R,b) = 100$	$V(S,b) = 200$
	$V(S,c) = 100$

To generate a final logical query plan from Fig. 28, we shall insist that the selection be pushed down as far as possible. However, we are not sure whether it makes sense to push the δ below the join or not. Thus, we generate from Fig. 28 the two query plans shown in Fig. 29; they differ in whether we have chosen to eliminate duplicates before or after the join. Notice that in plan (a) the δ is pushed down both branches of the tree. If R and/or S is known to have no duplicates, then the δ along its branch could be eliminated.

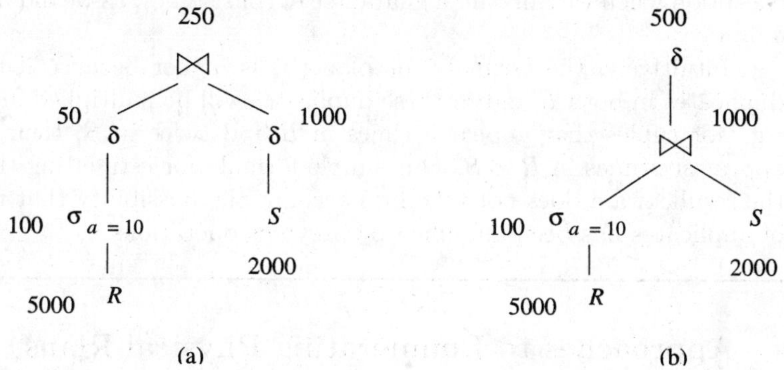

Figure 29: Two candidates for the best logical query plan

We know how to estimate the size of the result of the selections, from Section 4.3; we divide $T(R)$ by $V(R,a) = 50$. We also know how to estimate the size of the joins; we multiply the sizes of the arguments and divide by $\max\big(V(R,b), V(S,b)\big)$, which is 200. What we don't know is how to estimate the size of the relations with duplicates eliminated.

First, consider the size estimate for $\delta\big(\sigma_{a=10}(R)\big)$. Since $\sigma_{a=10}(R)$ has only one value for a and up to 100 values for b, and there are an estimated 100 tuples in this relation, the rule from Section 4.7 tells us that the product of the value counts for each of the attributes is not a limiting factor. Thus, we estimate the size of the result of δ as half the tuples in $\sigma_{a=10}(R)$, and Fig. 29(a) shows an estimate of 50 tuples for $\delta\big(\sigma_{a=10}(R)\big)$.

Now, consider the estimate of the result of the δ in Fig. 29(b). The join has one value for a, an estimated $\min\big(V(R,b), V(S,b)\big) = 100$ values for b, and an estimated $V(S,c) = 100$ values for c. Thus again the product of the value counts does not limit how big the result of the δ can be. We estimate this result as 500 tuples, or half the number of tuples in the join.

To compare the two plans of Fig. 29, we add the estimated sizes for all the nodes except the root and the leaves. We exclude the root and leaves, because these sizes are not dependent on the plan chosen. For plan (a) this cost, the sum of the estimated sizes of the interior nodes, is $100 + 50 + 1000 = 1150$, while for plan (b) the sum is $100 + 1000 = 1100$. Thus, by a small margin we conclude that deferring the duplicate elimination to the end is a better plan. We would come to the opposite conclusion if, say, R or S had fewer b-values. Then the join size would be greater, making the cost of plan (b) greater. □

Estimates for Result Sizes Need Not Be the Same

Notice that in Fig. 29 the estimates at the roots of the two trees are different: 250 in one case and 500 in the other. Because estimation is an inexact science, these sorts of anomalies will occur. In fact, it is the exception when we can offer a guarantee of consistency, as we did in Section 4.6.

Intuitively, the estimate for plan (b) is higher because if there are duplicates in both R and S, these duplicates will be multiplied in the join; e.g., for tuples that appear 3 times in R and twice in S, their join will appear six times in $R \bowtie S$. Our simple formula for estimating the size of the result of a δ does not take into account the possibility that the effect of duplicates has been amplified by previous operations.

5.4 Approaches to Enumerating Physical Plans

Now, let us consider the use of cost estimates in the conversion of a logical query plan to a physical query plan. The baseline approach, called *exhaustive*, is to consider all combinations of choices for each of the issues outlined at the beginning of Section 4 (order of joins, physical implementation of operators, and so on). Each possible physical plan is assigned an estimated cost, and the one with the smallest cost is selected.

However, there are a number of other approaches to selection of a physical plan. In this section, we shall outline various approaches that have been used, while Section 6 focuses on selecting a join order. Before proceeding, let us comment that there are two broad approaches to exploring the space of possible physical plans:

- *Top-down*: Here, we work down the tree of the logical query plan from the root. For each possible implementation of the operation at the root, we consider each possible way to evaluate its argument(s), and compute the cost of each combination, taking the best.[6]
- *Bottom-up*: For each subexpression of the logical-query-plan tree, we compute the costs of all possible ways to compute that subexpression. The possibilities and costs for a subexpression E are computed by considering the options for the subexpressions of E, and combining them in all possible ways with implementations for the root operator of E.

There is actually not much difference between the two approaches in their broadest interpretations, since either way, all possible combinations of ways to

[6]Remember from Section 3.4 that a single node of the logical-query-plan tree may represent many uses of a single commutative and associative operator, such as join. Thus, the consideration of all possible plans for a single node may itself involve enumeration of very many choices.

implement each operator in the query tree are considered. We shall concentrate on bottom-up methods in what follows.

You may, in fact, have noticed that there is an apparent simplification of the bottom-up method, where we consider only the *best* plan for each subexpression when we compute the plans for a larger subexpression. This approach, called *dynamic programming* in the list of methods below, is not guaranteed to yield the best overall plan, although often it does. The approach called *Selinger-style* (or *System-R-style*) optimization, also listed below, exploits additional properties that some of the plans for a subexpression may have, in order to produce optimal overall plans from plans that are not optimal for certain subexpressions.

Heuristic Selection

One option is to use the same approach to selecting a physical plan that is generally used for selecting a logical plan: make a sequence of choices based on heuristics. In Section 6.6, we shall discuss a "greedy" heuristic for join ordering, where we start by joining the pair of relations whose result has the smallest estimated size, then repeat the process for the result of that join and the other relations in the set to be joined. There are many other heuristics that may be applied; here are some of the most commonly used ones:

1. If the logical plan calls for a selection $\sigma_{A=c}(R)$, and stored relation R has an index on attribute A, then perform an index-scan to obtain only the tuples of R with A-value equal to c.

2. More generally, if the selection involves one condition like $A = c$ above, and other conditions as well, we can implement the selection by an index-scan followed by a further selection on the tuples, which we shall represent by the physical operator *filter*. This matter is discussed further in Section 7.1.

3. If an argument of a join has an index on the join attribute(s), then use an index-join with that relation in the inner loop.

4. If one argument of a join is sorted on the join attribute(s), then prefer a sort-join to a hash-join, although not necessarily to an index-join if one is possible.

5. When computing the union or intersection of three or more relations, group the smallest relations first.

Branch-and-Bound Plan Enumeration

This approach, often used in practice, begins by using heuristics to find a good physical plan for the entire logical query plan. Let the cost of this plan be C. Then as we consider other plans for subqueries, we can eliminate any plan for a subquery that has a cost greater than C, since that plan for the subquery could not possibly participate in a plan for the complete query that is better than what we already know. Likewise, if we construct a plan for the complete query that has cost less than C, we replace C by the cost of this better plan in subsequent exploration of the space of physical query plans.

An important advantage of this approach is that we can choose when to cut off the search and take the best plan found so far. For instance, if the cost C is small, then even if there are much better plans to be found, the time spent finding them may exceed C, so it does not make sense to continue the search. However, if C is large, then investing time in the hope of finding a faster plan is wise.

Hill Climbing

This approach, in which we really search for a "valley" in the space of physical plans and their costs, starts with a heuristically selected physical plan. We can then make small changes to the plan, e.g., replacing one method for executing an operator by another, or reordering joins by using the associative and/or commutative laws, to find "nearby" plans that have lower cost. When we find a plan such that no small modification yields a plan of lower cost, we make that plan our chosen physical query plan.

Dynamic Programming

In this variation of the general bottom-up strategy, we keep for each subexpression only the plan of least cost. As we work up the tree, we consider possible implementations of each node, assuming the best plan for each subexpression is also used. We examine this approach extensively in Section 6.

Selinger-Style Optimization

This approach improves upon the dynamic-programming approach by keeping for each subexpression not only the plan of least cost, but certain other plans that have higher cost, yet produce a result that is sorted in an order that may be useful higher up in the expression tree. Examples of such *interesting* orders are when the result of the subexpression is sorted on one of:

1. The attribute(s) specified in a sort (τ) operator at the root.

2. The grouping attribute(s) of a later group-by (γ) operator.

3. The join attribute(s) of a later join.

If we take the cost of a plan to be the sum of the sizes of the intermediate relations, then there appears to be no advantage to having an argument sorted. However, if we use the more accurate measure, disk I/O's, as the cost, then the advantage of having an argument sorted becomes clear if we can use one of the sort-based algorithms, and save the work of the first pass for the argument that is sorted already.

5.5 Exercises for Section 5

Exercise 5.1: Estimate the size of the join $R(a, b) \bowtie S(b, c)$ using histograms for $R.b$ and $S.b$. Assume $V(R, b) = V(S, b) = 20$, and the histograms for both attributes give the frequency of the four most common values, as tabulated below:

	0	1	2	3	4	others
$R.b$	5	6	4	5		32
$S.b$	10	8	5		7	48

How does this estimate compare with the simpler estimate, assuming that all 20 values are equally likely to occur, with $T(R) = 52$ and $T(S) = 78$?

Exercise 5.2: Estimate the size of the join $R(a, b) \bowtie S(b, c)$ if we have the following histogram information:

	$b < 0$	$b = 0$	$b > 0$
R	500	100	400
S	300	200	500

! **Exercise 5.3:** In Example 29 we suggested that reducing the number of values that either attribute named b had could make plan (a) better than plan (b) of Fig. 29. For what values of:

a) $V(R, b)$

b) $V(S, b)$

will plan (a) have a lower estimated cost than plan (b)?

! **Exercise 5.4:** Consider four relations R, S, T, and V. Respectively, they have 200, 300, 400, and 500 tuples, chosen randomly and independently from the same pool of 1000 tuples (e.g., the probabilities of a given tuple being in R is 1/5, in S is 3/10, and in both is 3/50).

a) What is the expected size of $R \cup S \cup T \cup V$?

b) What is the expected size of $R \cap S \cap T \cap V$?

c) What order of unions gives the least cost (estimated sum of the sizes of the intermediate relations)?

d) What order of intersections gives the least cost (estimated sum of the sizes of the intermediate relations)?

! **Exercise 5.5:** Repeat Exercise 5.4 if all four relations have 500 of the 1000 tuples, at random.

!! **Exercise 5.6:** Suppose we wish to compute the expression

$$\tau_b\big(R(a,b) \bowtie S(b,c) \bowtie T(c,d)\big)$$

That is, we join the three relations and produce the result sorted on attribute b. Let us make the simplifying assumptions:

i. We shall not "join" R and T first, because that is a product.

ii. Any other join can be performed with a two-pass sort-join or hash-join, but in no other way.

iii. Any relation, or the result of any expression, can be sorted by a two-phase, multiway merge-sort, but in no other way.

iv. The result of the first join will be passed as an argument to the last join one block at a time and not stored temporarily on disk.

v. Each relation occupies 1000 blocks, and the result of either join of two relations occupies 5000 blocks.

Answer the following based on these assumptions:

a) What are all the subexpressions and orders that a Selinger-style optimization would consider?

b) Which query plan uses the fewest disk I/O's?[7]

!! **Exercise 5.7:** Give an example of a logical query plan of the form $E \bowtie F$, for some expressions E and F (which you may choose), where using the best plans to evaluate E and F does not allow any choice of algorithm for the final join that minimizes the total cost of evaluating the entire expression. Make whatever assumptions you wish about the number of available main-memory buffers and the sizes of relations mentioned in E and F.

6 Choosing an Order for Joins

In this section we focus on a critical problem in cost-based optimization: selecting an order for the (natural) join of three or more relations. Similar ideas can be applied to other binary operations like union or intersection, but these operations are less important in practice, because they typically take less time to execute than joins, and they more rarely appear in clusters of three or more.

[7]Notice that, because we have made some very specific assumptions about the join methods to be used, we can estimate disk I/O's, instead of relying on the simpler, but less accurate, counts of tuples as our cost measure.

6.1 Significance of Left and Right Join Arguments

When ordering a join, we should remember that many join methods are asymmetric. That is, the roles played by the two argument relations are different, and the cost of the join depends on which relation plays which role. Perhaps most important, the one-pass join reads one relation — preferably the smaller — into main memory, creating a structure such as a hash table to facilitate matching of tuples from the other relation. It then reads the other relation, one block at a time, to join its tuples with the tuples stored in memory.

For instance, suppose that when we select a physical plan we decide to use a one-pass join. Then we shall assume the left argument of the join is the smaller relation and store it in a main-memory data structure. This relation is called the *build relation.* The right argument of the join, called the *probe relation*, is read a block at a time and its tuples are matched in main memory with those of the build relation. Other join algorithms that distinguish between their arguments include:

1. Nested-loop join, where we assume the left argument is the relation of the outer loop.

2. Index-join, where we assume the right argument has the index.

6.2 Join Trees

When we have the join of two relations, we need to order the arguments. We shall conventionally select the one whose estimated size is the smaller as the left argument. It is quite common for there to be a significant and discernible difference in the sizes of arguments, because a query involving joins often also involves a selection on at least one attribute, and that selection reduces the estimated size of one of the relations greatly.

Example 30: Recall the query

```
SELECT movieTitle
FROM StarsIn, MovieStar
WHERE starName = name AND
    birthdate LIKE '%1960';
```

from Fig. 4, which leads to the preferred logical query plan of Fig. 24, in which we take the join of relation `StarsIn` and the result of a selection on relation `MovieStar`. We have not given estimates for the sizes of relations `StarsIn` or `MovieStar`, but we can assume that selecting for stars born in a single year will produce about 1/50th of the tuples in `MovieStar`. Since there are generally several stars per movie, we expect `StarsIn` to be larger than `MovieStar` to begin with, so the second argument of the join, $\sigma_{birthdate\ \texttt{LIKE}\ \texttt{'\%1960'}}$(`MovieStar`), is much smaller than the first argument `StarsIn`. We conclude that the order of arguments in Fig. 24 should be reversed, so that the selection on `MovieStar` is the left argument. □

There are only two choices for a join tree when there are two relations — take either of the two relations to be the left argument. When the join involves more than two relations, the number of possible join trees grows rapidly. For example, Fig. 30 shows three of the five shapes of trees in which four relations R, S, T, and U, are joined. However, each of these trees has the four relations in alphabetical order from the left. Since order of arguments matters, and there are $n!$ ways to order n things, each tree represents $4! = 24$ different trees when the possible labelings of the leaves are considered.

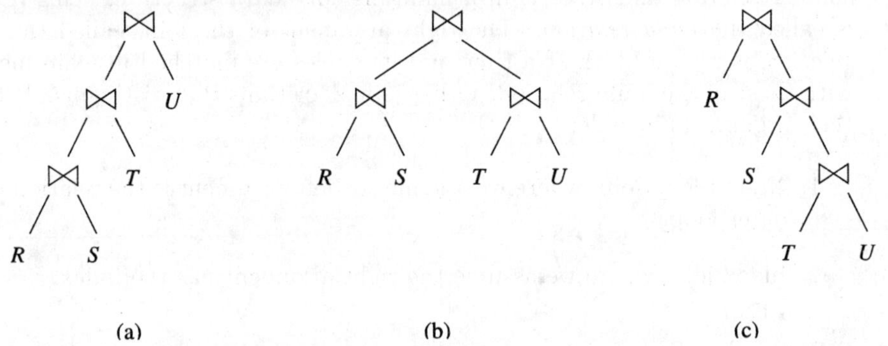

Figure 30: Ways to join four relations

6.3 Left-Deep Join Trees

Figure 30(a) is an example of what is called a *left-deep* tree. In general, a binary tree is left-deep if all right children are leaves. Similarly, a tree like Fig. 30(c), all of whose left children are leaves, is called a *right-deep* tree. A tree such as Fig. 30(b), that is neither left-deep nor right-deep, is called *bushy*. We shall argue below that there is a two-fold advantage to considering only left-deep trees as possible join orders.

1. The number of possible left-deep trees with a given number of leaves is large, but not nearly as large as the number of all trees. Thus, searches for query plans can be used for larger queries if we limit the search to left-deep trees.

2. Left-deep trees for joins interact well with common join algorithms — nested-loop joins and one-pass joins in particular. Query plans based on left-deep trees plus these join implementations will tend to be more efficient than the same algorithms used with non-left-deep trees.

The "leaves" in a left- or right-deep join tree can actually be interior nodes, with operators other than a join. Thus, for instance, Fig. 24 is technically a left-deep join tree with one join operator. The fact that a selection is applied to the right operand of the join does not take the tree out of the left-deep join class.

The number of left-deep trees does not grow nearly as fast as the number of all trees for the multiway join of a given number of relations. For n relations, there is only one left-deep tree shape, to which we may assign the relations in $n!$ ways. There are the same number of right-deep trees for n relations. However, the total number of tree shapes $T(n)$ for n relations is given by the recurrence:

$$\begin{aligned} T(1) &= 1 \\ T(n) &= \sum_{i=1}^{n-1} T(i)T(n-i) \end{aligned}$$

The explanation for the second equation is that we may pick any number i between 1 and $n-1$ to be the number of leaves in the left subtree of the root, and those leaves may be arranged in any of the $T(i)$ ways that trees with i leaves can be arranged. Similarly, the remaining $n-i$ leaves in the right subtree can be arranged in any of $T(n-i)$ ways.

The first few values of $T(n)$ are:

n	1	2	3	4	5	6
$T(n)$	1	1	2	5	14	42

To get the total number of trees once relations are assigned to the leaves, we multiply $T(n)$ by $n!$. Thus, for instance, the number of leaf-labeled trees of 6 leaves is $42 \times 6!$ or 30,240, of which 6!, or 720, are left-deep trees and another 720 are right-deep trees.

Now, let us consider the second advantage mentioned for left-deep join trees: their tendency to produce efficient plans. We shall give two examples:

1. If one-pass joins are used, and the build relation is on the left, then the amount of memory needed at any one time tends to be smaller than if we used a right-deep tree or a bushy tree for the same relations.

2. If we use nested-loop joins, with the relation of the outer loop on the left, then we avoid constructing any intermediate relation more than once.

Example 31 : Consider the left-deep tree in Fig. 30(a), and suppose that we use a simple one-pass join for each of the three $\bowtie$ operators. As always, the left argument is the build relation; i.e., it will be held in main memory. To compute $R \bowtie S$, we need to keep R in main memory, and as we compute $R \bowtie S$ we need to keep the result in main memory as well. Thus, we need $B(R) + B(R \bowtie S)$ main-memory buffers. If we pick R to be the smallest of the relations, and a selection has made R be rather small, then there is likely to be no problem making this number of buffers available.

Having computed $R \bowtie S$, we must join this relation with T. However, the buffers used for R are no longer needed and can be reused to hold (some of) the result of $(R \bowtie S) \bowtie T$. Similarly, when we join this relation with U, the relation $R \bowtie S$ is no longer needed, and its buffers can be reused for the result of the final join. In general, a left-deep join tree that is computed by one-pass joins requires main-memory space for at most two of the temporary relations any time.

Now, let us consider a similar implementation of the right-deep tree of Fig. 30(c). The first thing we need to do is load R into main-memory buffers, since left arguments are always the build relation. Then, we need to construct $S \bowtie (T \bowtie U)$ and use that as the probe relation for the join at the root. To compute $S \bowtie (T \bowtie U)$ we need to bring S into buffers and then compute $T \bowtie U$ as the probe relation for S. But $T \bowtie U$ requires that we first bring T into buffers. Now we have all three of R, S, and T in memory at the same time. In general, if we try to compute a right-deep join tree with n leaves, we shall have to bring $n-1$ relations into memory simultaneously.

Of course it is possible that the total size $B(R) + B(S) + B(T)$ is less than the amount of space we need at either of the two intermediate stages of the computation of the left-deep tree, which are $B(R) + B(R \bowtie S)$ and $B(R \bowtie S) + B\big((R \bowtie S) \bowtie T\big)$, respectively. However, as we pointed out in Example 30, queries with several joins often will have a small relation with which we can start as the leftmost argument in a left-deep tree. If R is small, we might expect $R \bowtie S$ to be significantly smaller than S and $(R \bowtie S) \bowtie T$ to be smaller than T, further justifying the use of a left-deep tree. □

Example 32: Now, let us suppose we are going to implement the four-way join of Fig. 30 by nested-loop joins, and that we use an iterator for each of the three joins involved. Also, assume for simplicity that each of the relations R, S, T, and U are stored relations, rather than expressions. If we use the left-deep tree of Fig. 30(a), then the iterator at the root gets a main-memory-sized chunk of its left argument $(R \bowtie S) \bowtie T$. It then joins the chunk with all of U, but as long as U is a stored relation, it is only necessary to scan U, not to construct it. When the next chunk of the left argument is obtained and put in memory, U will be read again, but nested-loop join requires that repetition, which cannot be avoided if both arguments are large.

Similarly, to get a chunk of $(R \bowtie S) \bowtie T$, we get a chunk of $R \bowtie S$ into memory and scan T. Several scans of T may eventually be necessary, but cannot be avoided. Finally, to get a chunk of $R \bowtie S$ requires reading a chunk of R and comparing it with S, perhaps several times. However, in all this action, only stored relations are read multiple times, and this repeated reading is an artifact of the way nested-loop join works when the main memory is insufficient to hold an entire relation.

Now, compare the behavior of iterators on the left-deep tree with the behavior of iterators on the right-deep tree of Fig. 30(c). The iterator at the root starts by reading a chunk of R. It must then construct the entire relation $S \bowtie (T \bowtie U)$ and compare it with that chunk of R. When we read the next chunk of R into memory, $S \bowtie (T \bowtie U)$ must be constructed again. Each subsequent chunk of R likewise requires constructing this same relation.

Of course, we could construct $S \bowtie (T \bowtie U)$ once and store it, either in memory or on disk. If we store it on disk, we are using extra disk I/O's compared with the left-deep tree's plan, and if we store it in memory, then we run into the same problem with overuse of memory that we discussed in Example 31. □

6.4 Dynamic Programming to Select a Join Order and Grouping

To pick an order for the join of many relations we have three choices:

1. Consider them all.
2. Consider a subset.
3. Use a heuristic to pick one.

We shall here consider a sensible approach to enumeration called *dynamic programming.* It can be used either to consider all orders, or to consider certain subsets only, such as orders restricted to left-deep trees. In Section 6.6 we consider a heuristic for selecting a single ordering. Dynamic programming is a common algorithmic paradigm.[8] The idea behind dynamic programming is that we fill in a table of costs, remembering only the minimum information we need to proceed to a conclusion.

Suppose we want to join $R_1 \bowtie R_2 \bowtie \cdots \bowtie R_n$. In a dynamic programming algorithm, we construct a table with an entry for each subset of one or more of the n relations. In that table we put:

1. The estimated size of the join of these relations. For this quantity we may use the formula of Section 4.6.

[8] See Aho, Hopcroft and Ullman, *Data Structures and Algorithms*, Addison-Wesley, 1983, for a general treatment of dynamic programming.

2. The least cost of computing the join of these relations. We shall use in our examples the sum of the sizes of the intermediate relations (not including the R_i's themselves or the join of the full set of relations associated with this table entry).

3. The expression that yields the least cost. This expression joins the set of relations in question, with some grouping. We can optionally restrict ourselves to left-deep expressions, in which case the expression is just an ordering of the relations.

The construction of this table is an induction on the subset size. There are two variations, depending on whether we wish to consider all possible tree shapes or only left-deep trees. We explain the difference when we discuss the inductive step of table construction.

BASIS: The entry for a single relation R consists of the size of R, a cost of 0, and an expression that is just R itself. The entry for a pair of relations $\{R_i, R_j\}$ is also easy to compute. The cost is 0, since there are no intermediate relations involved, and the size estimate is given by the rule of Section 4.6; it is the product of the sizes of R_i and R_j divided by the larger value-set size for each attribute shared by R_i and R_j, if any. The expression is either $R_i \bowtie R_j$ or $R_j \bowtie R_i$. Following the idea introduced in Section 6.1, we pick the smaller of R_i and R_j as the left argument.

INDUCTION: Now, we can build the table, computing entries for all subsets of size 3, 4, and so on, until we get an entry for the one subset of size n. That entry tells us the best way to compute the join of all the relations; it also gives us the estimated cost of that method, which is needed as we compute later entries. We need to see how to compute the entry for a set of k relations $\mathcal{R}$.

If we wish to consider only left-deep trees, then for each of the k relations R in $\mathcal{R}$ we consider the possibility that we compute the join for $\mathcal{R}$ by first computing the join of $\mathcal{R} - \{R\}$ and then joining it with R. The cost of the join for $\mathcal{R}$ is the cost of $\mathcal{R} - \{R\}$ plus the size of the result for $\mathcal{R} - \{R\}$. We pick whichever R yields the least cost. The expression for $\mathcal{R}$ has the best join expression for $\mathcal{R} - \{R\}$ as the left argument of a final join, and R as the right argument. The size for $\mathcal{R}$ is whatever the formula from Section 4.6 gives.

If we wish to consider all trees, then computing the entry for a set of relations $\mathcal{R}$ is somewhat more complex. We need to consider all ways to partition $\mathcal{R}$ into disjoint sets $\mathcal{R}_1$ and $\mathcal{R}_2$. For each such subset, we consider the sum of:

1. The best costs of $\mathcal{R}_1$ and $\mathcal{R}_2$.

2. The sizes of the results for $\mathcal{R}_1$ and $\mathcal{R}_2$.

For whichever partition gives the best cost, we use this sum as the cost for $\mathcal{R}$, and the expression for $\mathcal{R}$ is the join of the best join orders for $\mathcal{R}_1$ and $\mathcal{R}_2$.

Example 33: Consider the join of four relations R, S, T, and U. For simplicity, we shall assume they each have 1000 tuples. Their attributes and the estimated sizes of values sets for the attributes in each relation are summarized in Fig. 31.

$R(a,b)$	$S(b,c)$	$T(c,d)$	$U(d,a)$
$V(R,a) = 100$			$V(U,a) = 50$
$V(R,b) = 200$	$V(S,b) = 100$		
	$V(S,c) = 500$	$V(T,c) = 20$	
		$V(T,d) = 50$	$V(U,d) = 1000$

Figure 31: Parameters for Example 33

For the singleton sets, the sizes, costs, and best plans are as in the table of Fig. 32. That is, for each single relation, the size is as given, 1000 for each, the cost is 0 since there are no intermediate relations needed, and the best (and only) expression is the relation itself.

	$\{R\}$	$\{S\}$	$\{T\}$	$\{U\}$
Size	1000	1000	1000	1000
Cost	0	0	0	0
Best plan	R	S	T	U

Figure 32: The table for singleton sets

Now, consider the pairs of relations. The cost for each is 0, since there are still no intermediate relations in a join of two. There are two possible plans, since either of the two relations can be the left argument, but since the sizes happen to be the same for each relation we have no basis on which to choose between the plans. We shall take the first, in alphabetical order, to be the left argument in each case. The sizes of the resulting relations are computed by the usual formula. The results are summarized in Fig. 33.

	$\{R,S\}$	$\{R,T\}$	$\{R,U\}$	$\{S,T\}$	$\{S,U\}$	$\{T,U\}$
Size	5000	1,000,000	10,000	2000	1,000,000	1000
Cost	0	0	0	0	0	0
Best plan	$R \bowtie S$	$R \bowtie T$	$R \bowtie U$	$S \bowtie T$	$S \bowtie U$	$T \bowtie U$

Figure 33: The table for pairs of relations

Now, consider the table for joins of three out of the four relations. The only way to compute a join of three relations is to pick two to join first. The size estimate for the result is computed by the standard formula, and we omit the details of this calculation; remember that we'll get the same size regardless of which way we compute the join.

The cost estimate for each triple of relations is the size of the one intermediate relation — the join of the first two chosen. Since we want this cost to be as small as possible, we consider each pair of two out of the three relations and take the pair with the smallest size.

For the expression, we group the two chosen relations first, but these could be either the left or right argument. Let us suppose that we are only interested in left-deep trees, so we always use the join of the first two relations as the left argument. Since in all cases the estimated size for the join of two of our relations is at least 1000 (the size of each individual relation), were we to allow non-left-deep trees we would always select the single relation as the left argument in this example. The summary table for the triples is shown in Fig. 34.

	$\{R, S, T\}$	$\{R, S, U\}$	$\{R, T, U\}$	$\{S, T, U\}$
Size	10,000	50,000	10,000	2,000
Cost	2,000	5,000	1,000	1,000
Best plan	$(S \bowtie T) \bowtie R$	$(R \bowtie S) \bowtie U$	$(T \bowtie U) \bowtie R$	$(T \bowtie U) \bowtie S$

Figure 34: The table for triples of relations

Let us consider $\{R, S, T\}$ as an example of the calculation. We must consider each of the three pairs in turn. If we start with $R \bowtie S$, then the cost is the size of this relation, which is 5000 (see Fig. 33). Starting with $R \bowtie T$ gives us a cost of 1,000,000 for the intermediate relation, and starting with $S \bowtie T$ has a cost of 2000. Since the latter is the smallest cost of the three options, we choose that plan. The choice is reflected not only in the cost entry of the $\{R, S, T\}$ column, but in the best-plan row, where the plan that groups S and T first appears.

Now, we must consider the situation for the join of all four relations. There are two general ways we can compute the join of all four:

1. Pick three to join in the best possible way, and then join in the fourth.

2. Divide the four relations into two pairs of two, join the pairs and then join the results.

Of course, if we consider only left-deep trees then the second type of plan is excluded, because it yields bushy trees. The table of Fig. 35 summarizes the seven possible ways to group the joins, based on the preferred groupings from Figs. 33 and 34.

For instance, consider the first expression in Fig. 35. It represents joining R, S, and T first, and then joining that result with U. From Fig. 34, we know that the best way to join R, S, and T is to join S and T first. We have used the left-deep form of this expression, and joined U on the right to continue

Grouping	Cost
$((S \bowtie T) \bowtie R) \bowtie U$	12,000
$((R \bowtie S) \bowtie U) \bowtie T$	55,000
$((T \bowtie U) \bowtie R) \bowtie S$	11,000
$((T \bowtie U) \bowtie S) \bowtie R$	3,000
$(T \bowtie U) \bowtie (R \bowtie S)$	6,000
$(R \bowtie T) \bowtie (S \bowtie U)$	2,000,000
$(S \bowtie T) \bowtie (R \bowtie U)$	12,000

Figure 35: Join groupings and their costs

the left-deep form. If we consider only left-deep trees, then this expression and relation order is the only option. If we allowed bushy trees, we would join U on the left, since it is smaller than the join of the other three. The cost of this join is 12,000, which is the sum of the cost and size of $(S \bowtie T) \bowtie R$, which are 2000 and 10,000, respectively.

The last three expressions in Fig. 35 represent additional options if we include bushy trees. These are formed by joining relations first in two pairs. For example, the last line represents the strategy of joining $R \bowtie U$ and $S \bowtie T$, and then joining the result. The cost of this expression is the sum of the sizes and costs of the two pairs. The costs are 0, as must be the case for any pair, and the sizes are 10,000 and 2000, respectively. Since we generally select the smaller relation to be the left argument, we show the expression as $(S \bowtie T) \bowtie (R \bowtie U)$.

In this example, we see that the least of all costs is associated with the fourth expression: $((T \bowtie U) \bowtie S) \bowtie R$. This expression is the one we select for computing the join; its cost is 3000. Since it is a left-deep tree, it is the selected logical query plan regardless of whether our dynamic-programming strategy considers all plans or just left-deep plans. □

6.5 Dynamic Programming With More Detailed Cost Functions

Using relation sizes as the cost estimate simplifies the calculations in a dynamic-programming algorithm. However, a disadvantage of this simplification is that it does not involve the actual costs of the joins in the calculation. As an extreme example, if one possible join $R(a, b) \bowtie S(b, c)$ involves a relation R with one tuple and another relation S that has an index on the join attribute b, then the join takes almost no time. On the other hand, if S has no index, then we must scan it, taking $B(S)$ disk I/O's, even when R is a singleton. A cost measure that only involved the sizes of R, S, and $R \bowtie S$ cannot distinguish these two cases, so the cost of using $R \bowtie S$ in the grouping will be either overestimated or underestimated.

However, modifying the dynamic programming algorithm to take join algorithms into account is not hard. First, the cost measure we use becomes disk

I/O's. When computing the cost of $\mathcal{R}_1 \bowtie \mathcal{R}_2$, we sum the cost of $\mathcal{R}_1$, the cost of $\mathcal{R}_2$, and the least cost of joining these two relations using the best available algorithm. Since the latter cost usually depends on the sizes of $\mathcal{R}_1$ and $\mathcal{R}_2$, we must also compute estimates for these sizes as we did in Example 33.

An even more powerful version of dynamic programming is based on the Selinger-style optimization mentioned in Section 5.4. Now, for each set of relations that might be joined, we keep not only one cost, but several costs. Recall that Selinger-style optimization considers not only the least cost of producing the result of the join, but also the least cost of producing that relation sorted in any of a number of "interesting" orders. These interesting sorts include any that might be used to advantage in a later sort-join or that could be used to produce the output of the entire query in the sorted order desired by the user. When sorted relations must be produced, the use of sort-join, either one-pass or multipass, must be considered as an option, while without considering the value of sorting a result, hash-joins are always at least as good as the corresponding sort-join.

6.6 A Greedy Algorithm for Selecting a Join Order

As Example 33 suggests, even the carefully limited search of dynamic programming leads to a number of calculations that is exponential in the number of relations joined. It is reasonable to use an exhaustive method like dynamic programming or branch-and-bound search to find optimal join orders of five or six relations. However, when the number of joins grows beyond that, or if we choose not to invest the time necessary for an exhaustive search, then we can use a join-order heuristic in our query optimizer.

The most common choice of heuristic is a *greedy* algorithm, where we make one decision at a time about the order of joins and never backtrack or reconsider decisions once made. We shall consider a greedy algorithm that only selects a left-deep tree. The "greediness" is based on the idea that we want to keep the intermediate relations as small as possible at each level of the tree.

BASIS: Start with the pair of relations whose estimated join size is smallest. The join of these relations becomes the *current tree*.

INDUCTION: Find, among all those relations not yet included in the current tree, the relation that, when joined with the current tree, yields the relation of smallest estimated size. The new current tree has the old current tree as its left argument and the selected relation as its right argument.

Example 34: Let us apply the greedy algorithm to the relations of Example 33. The basis step is to find the pair of relations that have the smallest join. Consulting Fig. 33, we see that this honor goes to the join $T \bowtie U$, with a cost of 1000. Thus, $T \bowtie U$ is the "current tree."

We now consider whether to join R or S into the tree next. Thus we compare the sizes of $(T \bowtie U) \bowtie R$ and $(T \bowtie U) \bowtie S$. Figure 34 tells us that the

Join Selectivity

A useful way to view heuristics such as the greedy algorithm for selecting a left-deep join tree is that each relation R, when joined with the current tree, has a *selectivity*, which is the ratio of the size of the join result to size of the current tree's result. Since we usually do not have the exact sizes of either relation, we estimate these sizes as we have done previously. A greedy approach to join ordering is to pick that relation with the smallest selectivity.

For example, if a join attribute is a key for R, then the selectivity is at most 1, which is usually a favorable situation. Notice that, judging from the statistics of Fig. 31, attribute d is a key for U, and there are no keys for other relations, which suggests why joining T with U is the best way to start the join.

latter, with a size of 2000 is better than the former, with a size of 10,000. Thus, we pick as the new current tree $(T \bowtie U) \bowtie S$.

Now there is no choice; we must join R at the last step, leaving us with a total cost of 3000, the sum of the sizes of the two intermediate relations. Note that the tree resulting from the greedy algorithm is the same as that selected by the dynamic-programming algorithm in Example 33. However, there are examples where the greedy algorithm fails to find the best solution, while the dynamic-programming algorithm guarantees to find the best; see Exercise 6.4. □

6.7 Exercises for Section 6

Exercise 6.1: For the relations of Exercise 4.1, give the dynamic-programming table entries that evaluates all possible join orders allowing: a) All trees b) Left-deep trees only. What is the best choice in each case?

Exercise 6.2: Repeat Exercise 6.1 with the following modifications:

i. The schema for Z is changed to $Z(d, a)$.

ii. $V(Z, a) = 100$.

Exercise 6.3: Repeat Exercise 6.1 with the relations of Exercise 4.2.

Exercise 6.4: Consider the join of relations $R(a, b)$, $S(b, c)$, $T(c, d)$, and $U(a, d)$, where R and U each have 1000 tuples, while S and T each have 100 tuples. Further, there are 100 values of all attributes of all relations, except for attribute c, where $V(S, c) = V(T, c) = 10$.

a) What is the order selected by the greedy algorithm? What is its cost?

b) What is the optimum join ordering and its cost?

Exercise 6.5: How many trees are there for the join of (a) seven (b) eight relations? How many of these are neither left-deep nor right-deep?

! **Exercise 6.6:** Suppose we wish to join the relations R, S, T, and U in one of the tree structures of Fig. 30, and we want to keep all intermediate relations in memory until they are no longer needed. Following our usual assumption, the result of the join of all four will be consumed by some other process as it is generated, so no memory is needed for that relation. In terms of the number of blocks required for the stored relations and the intermediate relations [e.g., $B(R)$ or $B(R \bowtie S)$], give a lower bound on M, the number of blocks of memory needed, for each of the trees in Fig. 30? What assumptions let us conclude that one tree is certain to use less memory than another?

! **Exercise 6.7:** If we use dynamic programming to select an order for the join of k relations, how many entries of the table do we have to fill?

7 Completing the Physical-Query-Plan

We have parsed the query, converted it to an initial logical query plan, and improved that logical query plan with transformations described in Section 3. Part of the process of selecting the physical query plan is enumeration and cost-estimation for all of our options, which we discussed in Section 5. Section 6 focused on the question of enumeration, cost estimation, and ordering for joins of several relations. By extension, we can use similar techniques to order groups of unions, intersections, or any associative/commutative operation.

There are still several steps needed to turn the logical plan into a complete physical query plan. The principal issues that we must yet cover are:

1. Selection of algorithms to implement the operations of the query plan, when algorithm-selection was not done as part of some earlier step such as selection of a join order by dynamic programming.

2. Decisions regarding when intermediate results will be *materialized* (created whole and stored on disk), and when they will be *pipelined* (created only in main memory, and not necessarily kept in their entirety at any one time).

3. Notation for physical-query-plan operators, which must include details regarding access methods for stored relations and algorithms for implementation of relational-algebra operators.

We shall not discuss the subject of selection of algorithms for operators in its entirety. Rather, we sample the issues by discussing two of the most important operators: selection in Section 7.1 and joins in Section 7.2.

Then, we consider the choice between pipelining and materialization in Sections 7.3 through 7.5. A notation for physical query plans is presented in Section 7.6.

7.1 Choosing a Selection Method

One of the important steps in choosing a physical query plan is to pick algorithms for each selection operator. You may recall the obvious implementation of a $\sigma_C(R)$ operator, where we access the entire relation R and see which tuples satisfy condition C. We also considered the possibility that C was of the form "attribute equals constant," and we had an index on that attribute. If so, then we can find the tuples that satisfy condition C without looking at all of R. Now, let us consider the generalization of this problem, where we have a selection condition that is the `AND` of several conditions. Assume at least one condition is of the form $A\theta c$, where A is an attribute with an index, c is a constant, and θ is a comparison operator such as $=$ or $<$.

Each physical plan uses some number of attributes that each:

a) Have an index, and

b) Are compared to a constant in one of the terms of the selection.

We then use these indexes to identify the sets of tuples that satisfy each of the conditions. You may recall that we discussed how we could use pointers obtained from these indexes to find only the tuples that satisfied all the conditions before we read these tuples from disk.

For simplicity, we shall not consider the use of several indexes in this way. Rather, we limit our discussion to physical plans that:

1. Retrieve all tuples that satisfy a comparison for which an index exists, using the index-scan physical operator.

2. Consider each tuple selected in (1) to decide whether it satisfies the rest of the selection condition. The physical operator that performs this step is callled `Filter`.

In addition to physical plans of this form, we must also consider the plan that uses no index but reads the entire relation (using the table-scan physical operator) and passes each tuple to the `Filter` operator to check for satisfaction of the selection condition.

We decide among the possible physical plans for a selection by estimating the cost of reading data with each plan. To compare costs of alternative plans we cannot continue using the simplified cost estimate of intermediate-relation size. The reason is that we are now considering implementations of a single step of the logical query plan, and intermediate relations are independent of implementation.

Thus, we shall refocus our attention and resume counting disk I/O's. To simplify as before, we shall count only the cost of accessing the data blocks, not the index blocks. Recall that the number of index blocks needed is generally much smaller than the number of data blocks needed, so this approximation to disk I/O cost is usually accurate enough.

The following is an outline of how costs for the various plans are estimated. We assume that the operation is $\sigma_C(R)$, where condition C is the AND of one or more terms.

1. The cost of the table-scan algorithm coupled with a filter step is:
   (a) $B(R)$ if R is clustered, and
   (b) $T(R)$ if R is not clustered.
2. The cost of a plan that picks an equality term such as $a = 10$ for which an index on attribute a exists, uses index-scan to find the matching tuples, and then filters the retrieved tuples to see if they satisfy the full condition C is:
   (a) $B(R)/V(R, a)$ if the index is clustering, and
   (b) $T(R)/V(R, a)$ if the index is not clustering.
3. The cost of a plan that picks an inequality term such as $b < 20$ for which an index on attribute b exists, uses index-scan to retrieve the matching tuples, and then filters the retrieved tuples to see if they satisfy the full condition C is:
   (a) $B(R)/3$ if the index is clustering,[9] and
   (b) $T(R)/3$ if the index is not clustering.

Example 35: Consider selection $\sigma_{x=1 \texttt{ AND } y=2 \texttt{ AND } z<5}(R)$, where $R(x, y, z)$ has the following parameters: $T(R) = 5000$, $B(R) = 200$, $V(R, x) = 100$, and $V(R, y) = 500$. Further, suppose R is clustered, and there are indexes on all of x, y, and z, but only the index on z is clustering. The following are the options for implementing this selection:

1. Table-scan followed by filter. The cost is $B(R)$, or 200 disk I/O's, since R is clustered.
2. Use the index on x and the index-scan operator to find those tuples with $x = 1$, then use the filter operator to check that $y = 2$ and $z < 5$. Since there are about $T(R)/V(R, x) = 50$ tuples with $x = 1$, and the index is not clustering, we require about 50 disk I/O's.

[9] Recall that we assume the typical inequality retrieves only 1/3 the tuples, for reasons discussed in Section 4.3.

3. Use the index on y and index-scan to find those tuples with $y = 2$, then filter these tuples to see that $x = 1$ and $z < 5$. The cost for using this nonclustering index is about $T(R)/V(R, y)$, or 10 disk I/O's.

4. Use the clustering index on z and index-scan to find those tuples with $z < 5$, then filter these tuples to see that $x = 1$ and $y = 2$. The number of disk I/O's is about $B(R)/3 = 67$.

We see that the least cost plan is the third, with an estimated cost of 10 disk I/O's. Thus, the preferred physical plan for this selection retrieves all tuples with $y = 2$ and then filters for the other two conditions. □

7.2 Choosing a Join Method

If we are not sure of, or cannot know, the number of buffers that will be available during the execution of this query (because we do not know what else the DBMS is doing at the same time), or if we do not have estimates of important size parameters such as the $V(R, a)$'s, then there are still some principles we can apply to choosing a join method. Similar ideas apply to other binary operations such as unions, and to the full-relation, unary operators, γ and δ.

- One approach is to call for the one-pass join, hoping that the buffer manager can devote enough buffers to the join, or that the buffer manager can come close, so thrashing is not a major cost. An alternative (for joins only, not for other binary operators) is to choose a nested-loop join, hoping that if the left argument cannot be granted enough buffers to fit in memory at once, then that argument will not have to be divided into too many pieces, and the resulting join will still be reasonably efficient.

- A sort-join is a good choice when either:

    1. One or both arguments are already sorted on their join attribute(s), or

    2. There are two or more joins on the same attribute, such as

    $$\big(R(a, b) \bowtie S(a, c)\big) \bowtie T(a, d)$$

    where sorting R and S on a will cause the result of $R \bowtie S$ to be sorted on a and used directly in a second sort-join.

- If there is an index opportunity such as a join $R(a, b) \bowtie S(b, c)$, where R is expected to be small (perhaps the result of a selection on a key that must yield only one tuple), and there is an index on the join attribute $S.b$, then we should choose an index-join.

- If there is no opportunity to use already-sorted relations or indexes, and a multipass join is needed, then hashing is probably the best choice, because the number of passes it requires depends on the size of the smaller argument rather than on both arguments.

7.3 Pipelining Versus Materialization

The last major issue we shall discuss in connection with choice of a physical query plan is pipelining of results. The naive way to execute a query plan is to order the operations appropriately (so an operation is not performed until the argument(s) below it have been performed), and store the result of each operation on disk until it is needed by another operation. This strategy is called *materialization*, since each intermediate relation is materialized on disk.

A more subtle, and generally more efficient, way to execute a query plan is to interleave the execution of several operations. The tuples produced by one operation are passed directly to the operation that uses it, without ever storing the intermediate tuples on disk. This approach is called *pipelining*, and it typically is implemented by a network of iterators, whose methods call each other at appropriate times. Since it saves disk I/O's, there is an obvious advantage to pipelining, but there is a corresponding disadvantage. Since several operations must share main memory at any time, there is a chance that algorithms with higher disk-I/O requirements must be chosen, or thrashing will occur, thus giving back all the disk-I/O savings that were gained by pipelining, and possibly more.

7.4 Pipelining Unary Operations

Unary operations — selection and projection — are excellent candidates for pipelining. Since these operations are tuple-at-a-time, we never need to have more than one block for input, and one block for the output.

We may implement a pipelined unary operation by iterators. The consumer of the pipelined result calls `GetNext()` each time another tuple is needed. In the case of a projection, it is only necessary to call `GetNext()` once on the source of tuples, project that tuple appropriately, and return the result to the consumer. For a selection σ_C (technically, the physical operator `Filter(`C`)`), it may be necessary to call `GetNext()` several times at the source, until one tuple that satisfies condition C is found. Figure 36 illustrates this process.

7.5 Pipelining Binary Operations

The results of binary operations can also be pipelined. We use one buffer to pass the result to its consumer, one block at a time. However, the number of other buffers needed to compute the result and to consume the result varies,

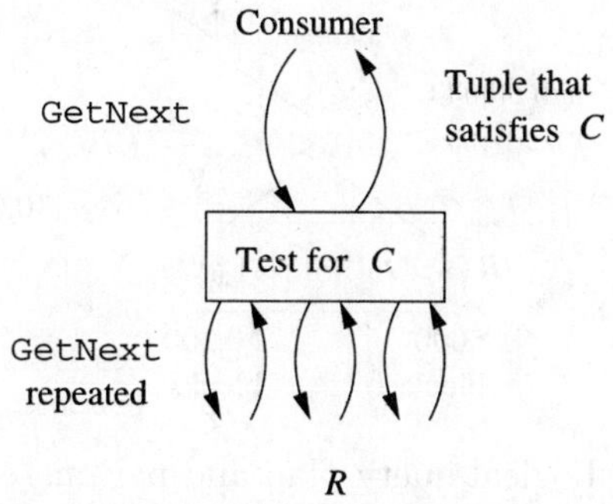

Figure 36: Execution of a pipelined selection using iterators

Materialization in Memory

One might imagine that there is an intermediate approach, between pipelining and materialization, where the entire result of one operation is stored in main-memory buffers (not on disk) before being passed to the consuming operation. We regard this possible mode of operation as pipelining, where the first thing that the consuming operation does is organize the entire relation, or a large portion of it, in memory. An example of this sort of behavior is a selection whose result becomes the left (build) argument to one of several join algorithms, including the simple one-pass join, multipass hash-join, or sort-join.

depending on the size of the result and the sizes of the arguments. We shall use an extended example to illustrate the tradeoffs and opportunities.

Example 36: Let us consider physical query plans for the expression

$$\big(R(w,x) \bowtie S(x,y)\big) \bowtie U(y,z)$$

We make the following assumptions:

1. R occupies 5000 blocks; S and U each occupy 10,000 blocks.

2. The intermediate result $R \bowtie S$ occupies k blocks for some k.

3. Both joins will be implemented as hash-joins, either one-pass or two-pass, depending on k.

4. There are 101 buffers available. This number, as usual, is set artificially low.

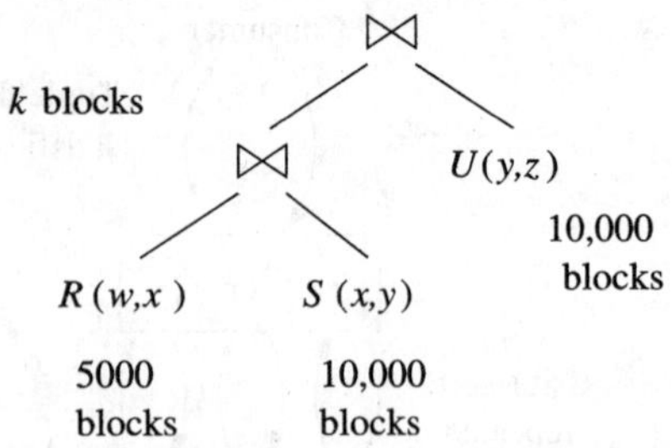

Figure 37: Logical query plan and parameters for Example 36

A sketch of the expression with key parameters is in Fig. 37.

First, consider the join $R \bowtie S$. Neither relation fits in main memory, so we need a two-pass hash-join. If the smaller relation R is partitioned into the maximum-possible 100 buckets on the first pass, then each bucket for R occupies 50 blocks.[10] If R's buckets have 50 blocks, then the second pass of the hash-join $R \bowtie S$ uses 51 buffers, leaving 50 buffers to use for the join of the result of $R \bowtie S$ with U.

Now, suppose that $k \leq 49$; that is, the result of $R \bowtie S$ occupies at most 49 blocks. Then we can pipeline the result of $R \bowtie S$ into 49 buffers, organize them for lookup as a hash table, and we have one buffer left to read each block of U in turn. We may thus execute the second join as a one-pass join. The total number of disk I/O's is:

a) 45,000 to perform the two-pass hash join of R and S.

b) 10,000 to read U in the one-pass hash-join of $(R \bowtie S) \bowtie U$.

The total is 55,000 disk I/O's.

Now, suppose $k > 49$, but $k \leq 5000$. We can still pipeline the result of $R \bowtie S$, but we need to use another strategy, in which this relation is joined with U in a 50-bucket, two-pass hash-join.

1. Before we start on $R \bowtie S$, we hash U into 50 buckets of 200 blocks each.

2. Next, we perform a two-pass hash join of R and S using 51 buckets as before, but as each tuple of $R \bowtie S$ is generated, we place it in one of the 50 remaining buffers that is used to help form the 50 buckets for the join of $R \bowtie S$ with U. These buffers are written to disk when they get full, as is normal for a two-pass hash-join.

3. Finally, we join $R \bowtie S$ with U bucket by bucket. Since $k \leq 5000$, the buckets of $R \bowtie S$ will be of size at most 100 blocks, so this join is feasible. The fact that buckets of U are of size 200 blocks is not a problem, since

[10]We shall assume for convenience that all buckets wind up with exactly their fair share of tuples.

we are using buckets of $R \bowtie S$ as the build relation and buckets of U as the probe relation in the one-pass joins of buckets.

The number of disk I/O's for this pipelined join is:

a) 20,000 to read U and write its tuples into buckets.

b) 45,000 to perform the two-pass hash-join $R \bowtie S$.

c) k to write out the buckets of $R \bowtie S$.

d) k + 10,000 to read the buckets of $R \bowtie S$ and U in the final join.

The total cost is thus 75,000 + $2k$. Note that there is an apparent discontinuity as k grows from 49 to 50, since we had to change the final join from one-pass to two-pass. In practice, the cost would not change so precipitously, since we could use the one-pass join even if there were not enough buffers and a small amount of thrashing occurred.

Last, let us consider what happens when $k > 5000$. Now, we cannot perform a two-pass join in the 50 buffers available if the result of $R \bowtie S$ is pipelined. We could use a three-pass join, but that would require an extra 2 disk I/O's per block of either argument, or 20,000 + $2k$ more disk I/O's. We can do better if we instead decline to pipeline $R \bowtie S$. Now, an outline of the computation of the joins is:

1. Compute $R \bowtie S$ using a two-pass hash join and store the result on disk.

2. Join $R \bowtie S$ with U, also using a two-pass hash-join. Note that since $B(U)$ = 10,000, we can perform a two-pass hash-join using 100 buckets, regardless of how large k is. Technically, U should appear as the left argument of its join in Fig. 37 if we decide to make U the build relation for the hash join.

The number of disk I/O's for this plan is:

a) 45,000 for the two-pass join of R and S.

b) k to store $R \bowtie S$ on disk.

c) 30,000 + $3k$ for the two-pass hash-join of U with $R \bowtie S$.

The total cost is thus 75,000 + $4k$, which is less than the cost of going to a three-pass join at the final step. The three complete plans are summarized in the table of Fig. 38. □

Range of k	Pipeline or Materialize	Algorithm for final join	Total Disk I/O's
$k \leq 49$	Pipeline	one-pass	55,000
$50 \leq k \leq 5000$	Pipeline	50-bucket, two-pass	$75{,}000 + 2k$
$5000 < k$	Materialize	100-bucket, two-pass	$75{,}000 + 4k$

Figure 38: Costs of physical plans as a function of the size of $R \bowtie S$

7.6 Notation for Physical Query Plans

We have seen many examples of the operators that can be used to form a physical query plan. In general, each operator of the logical plan becomes one or more operators of the physical plan, and leaves (stored relations) of the logical plan become, in the physical plan, one of the scan operators applied to that relation. In addition, materialization would be indicated by a `Store` operator applied to the intermediate result that is to be materialized, followed by a suitable scan operator (usually `TableScan`, since there is no index on the intermediate relation unless one is constructed explicitly) when the materialized result is accessed by its consumer. However, for simplicity, in our physical-query-plan trees we shall indicate that a certain intermediate relation is materialized by a double line crossing the edge between that relation and its consumer. All other edges are assumed to represent pipelining between the supplier and consumer of tuples.

We shall now catalog the various operators that are typically found in physical query plans. Unlike the relational algebra, whose notation is fairly standard, each DBMS will use its own internal notation for physical query plans.

Operators for Leaves

Each relation R that is a leaf operand of the logical-query-plan tree will be replaced by a scan operator. The options are:

1. `TableScan(R)`: All blocks holding tuples of R are read in arbitrary order.

2. `SortScan(R,L)`: Tuples of R are read in order, sorted according to the attribute(s) on list L.

3. `IndexScan(R,C)`: Here, C is a condition of the form $A\theta c$, where A is an attribute of R, θ is a comparison such as $=$ or $<$, and c is a constant. Tuples of R are accessed through an index on attribute A. If the comparison θ is not $=$, then the index must be one, such as a B-tree, that supports range queries.

4. `IndexScan(R,A)`: Here A is an attribute of R. The entire relation R is retrieved via an index on $R.A$. This operator behaves like `TableScan`,

but may be more efficient if R is not clustered.

Physical Operators for Selection

A logical operator $\sigma_C(R)$ is often combined, or partially combined, with the access method for relation R, when R is a stored relation. Other selections, where the argument is not a stored relation or an appropriate index is not available, will be replaced by the corresponding physical operator we have called `Filter`. Recall the strategy for choosing a selection implementation, which we discussed in Section 7.1. The notation we shall use for the various selection implementations are:

1. We may simply replace $\sigma_C(R)$ by the operator `Filter(C)`. This choice makes sense if there is no index on R, or no index on an attribute that condition C mentions. If R, the argument of the selection, is actually an intermediate relation being pipelined to the selection, then no other operator besides `Filter` is needed. If R is a stored or materialized relation, then we must use an operator, `TableScan` or `SortScan(R,L)`, to access R. We prefer sort-scan if the result of $\sigma_C(R)$ will later be passed to an operator that requires its argument sorted.

2. If condition C can be expressed as $A\theta c$ `AND` D for some other condition D, and there is an index on $R.A$, then we may:

   (a) Use the operator `IndexScan(R,Aθc)` to access R, and

   (b) Use `Filter(D)` in place of the selection $\sigma_C(R)$.

Physical Sort Operators

Sorting of a relation can occur at any point in the physical query plan. We have already introduced the `SortScan(R,L)` operator, which reads a stored relation R and produces it sorted according to the list of attributes L. When we apply a sort-based algorithm for operations such as join or grouping, there is an initial phase in which we sort the argument according to some list of attributes. It is common to use an explicit physical operator `Sort(L)` to perform this sort on an operand relation that is not stored. This operator can also be used at the top of the physical-query-plan tree if the result needs to be sorted because of an `ORDER BY` clause in the original query, thus playing the same role as the τ operator.

Other Relational-Algebra Operations

All other operations are replaced by a suitable physical operator. These operators can be given designations that indicate:

1. The operation being performed, e.g., join or grouping.

2. Necessary parameters, e.g., the condition in a theta-join or the list of elements in a grouping.

3. A general strategy for the algorithm: sort-based, hash-based, or index-based, e.g.

4. A decision about the number of passes to be used: one-pass, two-pass, or multipass (recursive, using as many passes as necessary for the data at hand). Alternatively, this choice may be left until run-time.

5. An anticipated number of buffers the operation will require.

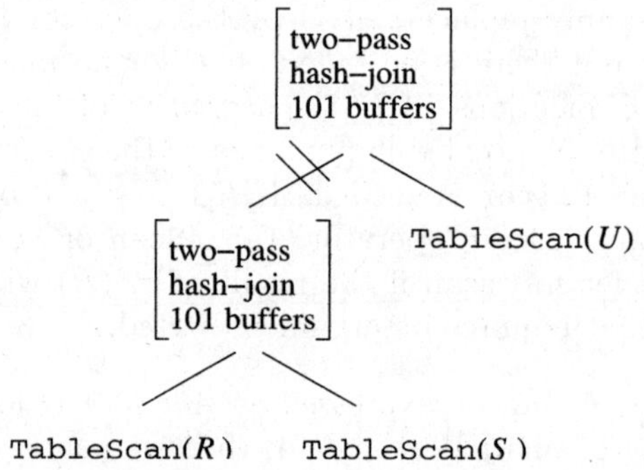

Figure 39: A physical plan from Example 36

Example 37: Figure 39 shows the physical plan developed in Example 36 for the case $k > 5000$. In this plan, we access each of the three relations by a table-scan. We use a two-pass hash-join for the first join, materialize it, and use a two-pass hash-join for the second join. By implication of the double-line symbol for materialization, the left argument of the top join is also obtained by a table-scan, and the result of the first join is stored using the `Store` operator.

In contrast, if $k \leq 49$, then the physical plan developed in Example 36 is that shown in Fig. 40. Notice that the second join uses a different number of passes, a different number of buffers, and a left argument that is pipelined, not materialized. □

Example 38: Consider the selection operation in Example 35, where we decided that the best of options was to use the index on y to find those tuples with $y = 2$, then check these tuples for the other conditions $x = 1$ and $z < 5$. Figure 41 shows the physical query plan. The leaf indicates that R will be accessed through its index on y, retrieving only those tuples with $y = 2$. The filter operator says that we complete the selection by further selecting those of the retrieved tuples that have both $x = 1$ and $z < 5$. □

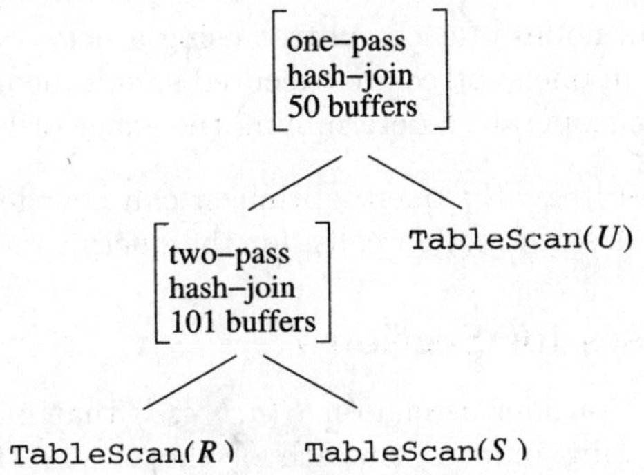

Figure 40: Another physical plan for the case where $R \bowtie S$ is expected to be very small

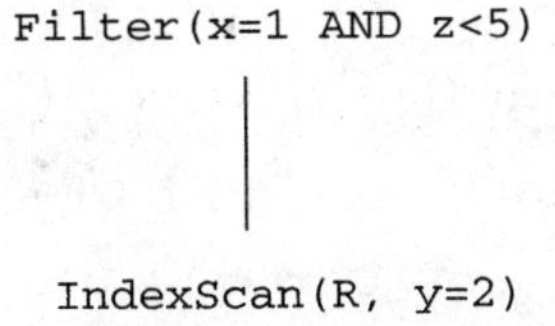

Figure 41: Annotating a selection to use the most appropriate index

7.7 Ordering of Physical Operations

Our final topic regarding physical query plans is the matter of order of operations. The physical query plan is generally represented as a tree, and trees imply something about order of operations, since data must flow up the tree. However, since bushy trees may have interior nodes that are neither ancestors nor descendants of one another, the order of evaluation of interior nodes may not always be clear. Moreover, since iterators can be used to implement operations in a pipelined manner, it is possible that the times of execution for various nodes overlap, and the notion of "ordering" nodes makes no sense.

If materialization is implemented in the obvious store-and-later-retrieve way, and pipelining is implemented by iterators, then we may establish a fixed sequence of events whereby each operation of a physical query plan is executed. The following rules summarize the ordering of events implicit in a physical-query-plan tree:

1. Break the tree into subtrees at each edge that represents materialization. The subtrees will be executed one-at-a-time.

2. Order the execution of the subtrees in a bottom-up, left-to-right manner. To be precise, perform a preorder traversal of the entire tree. Order the subtrees in the order in which the preorder traversal exits from the subtrees.

3. Execute all nodes of each subtree using a network of iterators. Thus, all the nodes in one subtree are executed simultaneously, with `GetNext` calls among their operators determining the exact order of events.

Following this strategy, the query optimizer can now generate executable code, perhaps a sequence of function calls, for the query.

7.8 Exercises for Section 7

Exercise 7.1: Consider a relation $R(a, b, c, d)$ that has a clustering index on a and nonclustering indexes on each of the other attributes. The relevant parameters are: $B(R) = 1000$, $T(R) = 5000$, $V(R, a) = 20$, $V(R, b) = 1000$, $V(R, c) = 5000$, and $V(R, d) = 500$. Give the best query plan (index-scan or table-scan followed by a filter step) and the disk-I/O cost for each of the following selections:

a) $\sigma_{a=1 \text{ AND } b=2 \text{ AND } d=3}(R)$.

b) $\sigma_{a=1 \text{ AND } b=2 \text{ AND } c\geq 3}(R)$.

c) $\sigma_{a=1 \text{ AND } b\leq 2 \text{ AND } c\geq 3}(R)$.

! **Exercise 7.2:** In terms of $B(R)$, $T(R)$, $V(R, x)$, and $V(R, y)$, express the following conditions about the cost of implementing a selection on R:

a) It is better to use index-scan with a nonclustering index on x and a term that equates x to a constant than a nonclustering index on y and a term that equates y to a constant.

b) It is better to use index-scan with a nonclustering index on x and a term that equates x to a constant than a clustering index on y and a term that equates y to a constant.

c) It is better to use index-scan with a nonclustering index on x and a term that equates x to a constant than a clustering index on y and a term of the form $y > C$ for some constant C.

Exercise 7.3: How would the conclusions about when to pipeline in Example 36 change if the size of relation R were not 5000 blocks, but: (a) 2000 blocks ! (b) 10,000 blocks ! (c) 100 blocks?

! **Exercise 7.4:** Suppose we want to compute $(R(a, b) \bowtie S(a, c)) \bowtie T(a, d)$ in the order indicated. We have $M = 101$ main-memory buffers, and $B(R) = B(S) = 2000$. Because the join attribute a is the same for both joins, we decide to implement the first join $R \bowtie S$ by a two-pass sort-join, and we shall use the appropriate number of passes for the second join, first dividing T into some number of sublists sorted on a, and merging them with the sorted and pipelined stream of tuples from the join $R \bowtie S$. For what values of $B(T)$ should we choose for the join of T with $R \bowtie S$:

a) A one-pass join; i.e., we read T into memory, and compare its tuples with the tuples of $R \bowtie S$ as they are generated.

b) A two-pass join; i.e., we create sorted sublists for T and keep one buffer in memory for each sorted sublist, while we generate tuples of $R \bowtie S$.

8 Summary

✦ *Compilation of Queries*: Compilation turns a query into a physical query plan, which is a sequence of operations that can be implemented by the query-execution engine. The principal steps of query compilation are parsing, semantic checking, selection of the preferred logical query plan (algebraic expression), and generation from that of the best physical plan.

✦ *The Parser*: The first step in processing a SQL query is to parse it, as one would for code in any programming language. The result of parsing is a parse tree with nodes corresponding to SQL constructs.

✦ *View Expansion*: Queries that refer to virtual views must have these references in the parse tree replaced by the tree for the expression that defines the view. This expansion often introduces several opportunities to optimize the complete query.

✦ *Semantic Checking*: A preprocessor examines the parse tree, checks that the attributes, relation names, and types make sense, and resolves attribute references.

✦ *Conversion to a Logical Query Plan*: The query processor must convert the semantically checked parse tree to an algebraic expression. Much of the conversion to relational algebra is straightforward, but subqueries present a problem. One approach is to introduce a two-argument selection that puts the subquery in the condition of the selection, and then apply appropriate transformations for the common special cases.

✦ *Algebraic Transformations*: There are many ways that a logical query plan can be transformed to a better plan by using algebraic transformations. Section 2 enumerates the principal ones.

✦ *Choosing a Logical Query Plan*: The query processor must select that query plan that is most likely to lead to an efficient physical plan. In addition to applying algebraic transformations, it is useful to group associative and commutative operators, especially joins, so the physical query plan can choose the best order and grouping for these operations.

✦ *Estimating Sizes of Relations*: When selecting the best logical plan, or when ordering joins or other associative-commutative operations, we use the estimated size of intermediate relations as a surrogate for the true running time. Knowing, or estimating, both the size (number of tuples) of relations and the number of distinct values for each attribute of each relation helps us get good estimates of the sizes of intermediate relations.

- *Histograms*: Some systems keep histograms of the values for a given attribute. This information can be used to obtain better estimates of intermediate-relation sizes than the simple methods stressed here.

- *Cost-Based Optimization*: When selecting the best physical plan, we need to estimate the cost of each possible plan. Various strategies are used to generate all or some of the possible physical plans that implement a given logical plan.

- *Plan-Enumeration Strategies*: The common approaches to searching the space of physical plans for the best include dynamic programming (tabularizing the best plan for each subexpression of the given logical plan), Selinger-style dynamic programming (which includes the sort-order of results as part of the table, giving best plans for each sort-order and for an unsorted result), greedy approaches (making a series of locally optimal decisions, given the choices for the physical plan that have been made so far), and branch-and-bound (enumerating only plans that are not immediately known to be worse than the best plan found so far).

- *Left-Deep Join Trees*: When picking a grouping and order for the join of several relations, it is common to restrict the search to left-deep trees, which are binary trees with a single spine down the left edge, with only leaves as right children. This form of join expression tends to yield efficient plans and also limits significantly the number of physical plans that need to be considered.

- *Physical Plans for Selection*: If possible, a selection should be broken into an index-scan of the relation to which the selection is applied (typically using a condition in which the indexed attribute is equated to a constant), followed by a filter operation. The filter examines the tuples retrieved by the index-scan and passes through only those that meet the portions of the selection condition other than that on which the index scan is based.

- *Pipelining Versus Materialization*: Ideally, the result of each physical operator is consumed by another operator, with the result being passed between the two in main memory ("pipelining"), perhaps using an iterator to control the flow of data from one to the other. However, sometimes there is an advantage to storing ("materializing") the result of one operator to save space in main memory for other operators. Thus, the physical-query-plan generator should consider both pipelining and materialization of intermediates.

9 References

We recommend the survey [1], which contains material on the query optimizers of commercial systems.

Three of the earliest studies of query optimization are [4], [5], and [3]. Paper [6], another early study, incorporates the idea of pushing selections down the tree with the greedy algorithm for join-order choice. [2] is the source for "Selinger-style optimization" as well as describing the System R optimizer, which was one of the most ambitious attempts at query optimization of its day.

1. G. Graefe (ed.), *Data Engineering* **16**:4 (1993), special issue on query processing in commercial database management systems, IEEE.

2. P. Griffiths-Selinger, M. M. Astrahan, D. D. Chamberlin, R. A. Lorie, and T. G. Price, "Access path selection in a relational database system," *Proc. ACM SIGMOD Intl. Conf. on Management of Data* (1979), pp. 23–34.

3. P. A. V. Hall, "Optimization of a single relational expression in a relational database system," *IBM J. Research and Development* **20**:3 (1976), pp. 244–257.

4. F. P. Palermo, "A database search problem," in: J. T. Tou (ed.) *Information Systems COINS IV*, Plenum, New York, 1974.

5. J. M. Smith and P. Y. Chang, "Optimizing the performance of a relational algebra database interface," *Comm. ACM* **18**:10 (1975), pp. 568–579.

6. E. Wong and K. Youssefi, "Decomposition — a strategy for query processing," *ACM Trans. on Database Systems* **1**:3 (1976), pp. 223–241.

Coping With System Failures

Starting with this chapter, we focus our attention on those parts of a DBMS that control access to data. There are two major issues to address:

1. Data must be protected in the face of a system failure. This chapter deals with techniques for supporting the goal of *resilience*, that is, integrity of the data when the system fails in some way.

2. Data must not be corrupted simply because several error-free queries or database modifications are being done at once.

The principal technique for supporting resilience is a *log*, which records securely the history of database changes. We shall discuss three different styles of logging, called "undo," "redo," and "undo/redo." We also discuss *recovery*, the process whereby the log is used to reconstruct what has happened to the database when there has been a failure. An important aspect of logging and recovery is avoidance of the situation where the log must be examined into the distant past. Thus, we shall learn about "checkpointing," which limits the length of log that must be examined during recovery.

In a final section, we discuss "archiving," which allows the database to survive not only temporary system failures, but situations where the entire database is lost. Then, we must rely on a recent copy of the database (the archive) plus whatever log information survives, to reconstruct the database as it existed at some point in the recent past.

1 Issues and Models for Resilient Operation

We begin our discussion of coping with failures by reviewing the kinds of things that can go wrong, and what a DBMS can and should do about them. We

From Chapter 17 of *Database Systems*, Second Edition. Hector Garcia-Molina, Jeffrey D. Ullman, Jennifer Widom.

initially focus on "system failures" or "crashes," the kinds of errors that the logging and recovery methods are designed to fix. We also introduce in Section 1.4 the model for buffer management that underlies all discussions of recovery from system errors.

1.1 Failure Modes

There are many things that can go wrong as a database is queried and modified. Problems range from the keyboard entry of incorrect data to an explosion in the room where the database is stored on disk. The following items are a catalog of the most important failure modes and what the DBMS can do about them.

Erroneous Data Entry

Some data errors are impossible to detect. For example, if a clerk mistypes one digit of your phone number, the data will still look like a phone number that *could* be yours. On the other hand, if the clerk omits a digit from your phone number, then the data is evidently in error, since it does not have the form of a phone number. The principal technique for addressing data-entry errors is to write constraints and triggers that detect data believed to be erroneous.

Media Failures

A local failure of a disk, one that changes only a bit or a few bits, can normally be detected by parity checks associated with the sectors of the disk. Head crashes, where the entire disk becomes unreadable, are generally handled by one or both of the following approaches:

1. Use a RAID scheme, so the lost disk can be restored.

2. Maintain an *archive*, a copy of the database on a medium such as tape or optical disk. The archive is periodically created, either fully or incrementally, and stored at a safe distance from the database itself. We shall discuss archiving in Section 5.

3. Instead of an archive, one could keep redundant copies of the database on-line, distributed among several sites.

Catastrophic Failure

In this category are a number of situations in which the media holding the database is completely destroyed. Examples include explosions, fires, or vandalism at the site of the database. RAID will not help, since all the data disks and their parity check disks become useless simultaneously. However, the other approaches that can be used to protect against media failure — archiving and redundant, distributed copies — will also protect against a catastrophic failure.

System Failures

The processes that query and modify the database are called *transactions.* A transaction, like any program, executes a number of steps in sequence; often, several of these steps will modify the database. Each transaction has a *state*, which represents what has happened so far in the transaction. The state includes the current place in the transaction's code being executed and the values of any local variables of the transaction that will be needed later on.

System failures are problems that cause the state of a transaction to be lost. Typical system failures are power loss and software errors. Since main memory is "volatile," a power failure will cause the contents of main memory to disappear, along with the result of any transaction step that was kept only in main memory, rather than on (nonvolatile) disk. Similarly, a software error may overwrite part of main memory, possibly including values that were part of the state of the program.

When main memory is lost, the transaction state is lost; that is, we can no longer tell what parts of the transaction, including its database modifications, were made. Running the transaction again may not fix the problem. For example, if the transaction must add 1 to a value in the database, we do not know whether to repeat the addition of 1 or not. The principal remedy for the problems that arise due to a system error is logging of all database changes in a separate, nonvolatile log, coupled with recovery when necessary. However, the mechanisms whereby such logging can be done in a fail-safe manner are surprisingly intricate, as we shall see starting in Section 2.

1.2 More About Transactions

We introduced the idea of transactions from the point of view of the SQL programmer. Before proceeding to our study of database resilience and recovery from failures, we need to discuss the fundamental notion of a transaction in more detail.

The transaction is the unit of execution of database operations. For example, if we are issuing ad-hoc commands to a SQL system, then each query or database modification statement (plus any resulting trigger actions) is a transaction. When using an embedded SQL interface, the programmer controls the extent of a transaction, which may include several queries or modifications, as well as operations performed in the host language. In the typical embedded SQL system, transactions begin as soon as operations on the database are executed and end with an explicit `COMMIT` or `ROLLBACK` ("abort") command.

As we shall discuss in Section 1.3, a transaction must execute atomically, that is, all-or-nothing and as if it were executed at an instant in time. Assuring that transactions are executed correctly is the job of a *transaction manager*, a subsystem that performs several functions, including:

1. Issuing signals to the log manager (described below) so that necessary information in the form of "log records" can be stored on the log.

2. Assuring that concurrently executing transactions do not interfere with each other in ways that introduce errors ("scheduling").

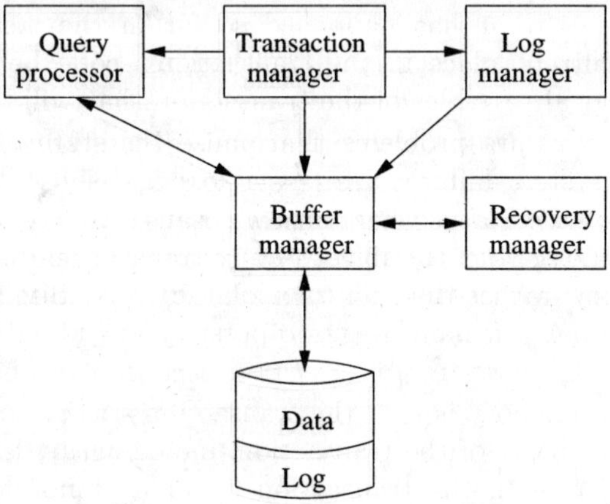

Figure 1: The log manager and transaction manager

The transaction manager and its interactions are suggested by Fig. 1. The transaction manager will send messages about actions of transactions to the log manager, to the buffer manager about when it is possible or necessary to copy the buffer back to disk, and to the query processor to execute the queries and other database operations that comprise the transaction.

The log manager maintains the log. It must deal with the buffer manager, since space for the log initially appears in main-memory buffers, and at certain times these buffers must be copied to disk. The log, as well as the data, occupies space on the disk, as we suggest in Fig. 1.

Finally, we show a recovery manager in Fig. 1. When there is a crash, the recovery manager is activated. It examines the log and uses it to repair the data, if necessary. As always, access to the disk is through the buffer manager.

1.3 Correct Execution of Transactions

Before we can deal with correcting system errors, we need to understand what it means for a transaction to be executed "correctly." To begin, we assume that the database is composed of "elements." We shall not specify precisely what an "element" is, except to say it has a value and can be accessed or modified by transactions. Different database systems use different notions of elements, but they are usually chosen from one or more of the following:

1. Relations.

2. Disk blocks or pages.

3. Individual tuples or objects.

In examples to follow, one can imagine that database elements are tuples, or in many examples, simply integers. However, there are several good reasons in practice to use choice (2) — disk blocks or pages — as the database element. In this way, buffer-contents become single elements, allowing us to avoid some serious problems with logging and transactions that we shall explore periodically as we learn various techniques. Avoiding database elements that are bigger than disk blocks also prevents a situation where part but not all of an element has been placed in nonvolatile storage when a crash occurs.

A database has a *state*, which is a value for each of its elements.[1] Intuitively, we regard certain states as *consistent*, and others as inconsistent. Consistent states satisfy all constraints of the database schema, such as key constraints and constraints on values. However, consistent states must also satisfy implicit constraints that are in the mind of the database designer. The implicit constraints may be maintained by triggers that are part of the database schema, but they might also be maintained only by policy statements concerning the database, or warnings associated with the user interface through which updates are made.

A fundamental assumption about transactions is:

- *The Correctness Principle*: If a transaction executes in the absence of any other transactions or system errors, and it starts with the database in a consistent state, then the database is also in a consistent state when the transaction ends.

There is a converse to the correctness principle that forms the motivation for both the logging techniques discussed in this chapter and concurrency control mechanisms. This converse involves two points:

1. A transaction is *atomic*; that is, it must be executed as a whole or not at all. If only part of a transaction executes, then the resulting database state may not be consistent.

2. Transactions that execute simultaneously are likely to lead to an inconsistent state unless we take steps to control their interactions.

[1]We should not confuse the database state with the state of a transaction; the latter is values for the transaction's local variables, not database elements.

Is the Correctness Principle Believable?

Given that a database transaction could be an ad-hoc modification command issued at a terminal, perhaps by someone who doesn't understand the implicit constraints in the mind of the database designer, is it plausible to assume all transactions take the database from a consistent state to another consistent state? Explicit constraints are enforced by the database, so any transaction that violates them will be rejected by the system and not change the database at all. As for implicit constraints, one cannot characterize them exactly under any circumstances. Our position, justifying the correctness principle, is that if someone is given authority to modify the database, then they also have the authority to judge what the implicit constraints are.

1.4 The Primitive Operations of Transactions

Let us now consider in detail how transactions interact with the database. There are three address spaces that interact in important ways:

1. The space of disk blocks holding the database elements.

2. The virtual or main memory address space that is managed by the buffer manager.

3. The local address space of the transaction.

For a transaction to read a database element, that element must first be brought to a main-memory buffer or buffers, if it is not already there. Then, the contents of the buffer(s) can be read by the transaction into its own address space. Writing a new value for a database element by a transaction follows the reverse route. The new value is first created by the transaction in its own space. Then, this value is copied to the appropriate buffer(s).

The buffer may or may not be copied to disk immediately; that decision is the responsibility of the buffer manager in general. As we shall soon see, one of the principal tools for assuring resilience is forcing the buffer manager to write the block in a buffer back to disk at appropriate times. However, in order to reduce the number of disk I/O's, database systems can and will allow a change to exist only in volatile main-memory storage, at least for certain periods of time and under the proper set of conditions.

In order to study the details of logging algorithms and other transaction-management algorithms, we need a notation that describes all the operations that move data between address spaces. The primitives we shall use are:

1. `INPUT(X)`: Copy the disk block containing database element X to a memory buffer.

2. `READ(X,t)`: Copy the database element X to the transaction's local variable t. More precisely, if the block containing database element X is not in a memory buffer then first execute `INPUT(X)`. Next, assign the value of X to local variable t.

3. `WRITE(X,t)`: Copy the value of local variable t to database element X in a memory buffer. More precisely, if the block containing database element X is not in a memory buffer then execute `INPUT(X)`. Next, copy the value of t to X in the buffer.

4. `OUTPUT(X)`: Copy the block containing X from its buffer to disk.

The above operations make sense as long as database elements reside within a single disk block, and therefore within a single buffer. If a database element occupies several blocks, we shall imagine that each block-sized portion of the element is an element by itself. The logging mechanism to be used will assure that the transaction cannot complete without the write of X being atomic; i.e., either all blocks of X are written to disk, or none are. Thus, we shall assume for the entire discussion of logging that

- A database element is no larger than a single block.

Different DBMS components issue the various commands we just introduced. `READ` and `WRITE` are issued by transactions. `INPUT` and `OUTPUT` are normally issued by the buffer manager. `OUTPUT` can also be initiated by the log manager under certain conditions, as we shall see.

Example 1 : To see how the above primitive operations relate to what a transaction might do, let us consider a database that has two elements, A and B, with the constraint that they must be equal in all consistent states.[2]

Transaction T consists logically of the following two steps:

[2]One reasonably might ask why we should bother to have two different elements that are constrained to be equal, rather than maintaining only one element. However, this simple numerical constraint captures the spirit of many more realistic constraints, e.g., the number of seats sold on a flight must not exceed the number of seats on the plane by more than 10%, or the sum of the loan balances at a bank must equal the total debt of the bank.

```
A := A*2;
B := B*2;
```

If T starts in a consistent state (i.e., $A = B$) and completes its activities without interference from another transaction or system error, then the final state must also be consistent. That is, T doubles two equal elements to get new, equal elements.

Execution of T involves reading A and B from disk, performing arithmetic in the local address space of T, and writing the new values of A and B to their buffers. The relevant steps of T are thus:

```
READ(A,t); t := t*2; WRITE(A,t); READ(B,t); t := t*2; WRITE(B,t);
```

In addition, the buffer manager will eventually execute the `OUTPUT` steps to write these buffers back to disk. Figure 2 shows the primitive steps of T, followed by the two `OUTPUT` commands from the buffer manager. We assume that initially $A = B = 8$. The values of the memory and disk copies of A and B and the local variable t in the address space of transaction T are indicated for each step.

Action	t	Mem A	Mem B	Disk A	Disk B
`READ(A,t)`	8	8		8	8
`t := t*2`	16	8		8	8
`WRITE(A,t)`	16	16		8	8
`READ(B,t)`	8	16	8	8	8
`t := t*2`	16	16	8	8	8
`WRITE(B,t)`	16	16	16	8	8
`OUTPUT(A)`	16	16	16	16	8
`OUTPUT(B)`	16	16	16	16	16

Figure 2: Steps of a transaction and its effect on memory and disk

At the first step, T reads A, which generates an `INPUT(A)` command for the buffer manager if A's block is not already in a buffer. The value of A is also copied by the `READ` command into local variable t of T's address space. The second step doubles t; it has no affect on A, either in a buffer or on disk. The third step writes t into A of the buffer; it does not affect A on disk. The next three steps do the same for B, and the last two steps copy A and B to disk.

Observe that as long as all these steps execute, consistency of the database is preserved. If a system error occurs before `OUTPUT(A)` is executed, then there is no effect to the database stored on disk; it is as if T never ran, and consistency is preserved. However,if there is a system error after `OUTPUT(A)` but before `OUTPUT(B)`, then the database is left in an inconsistent state. We cannot prevent this situation from ever occurring, but we can arrange that when it does occur, the problem can be repaired — either both A and B will be reset to 8, or both will be advanced to 16. □

1.5 Exercises for Section 1

Exercise 1.1: Suppose that the consistency constraint on the database is $0 \leq A \leq B$. Tell whether each of the following transactions preserves consistency.

a) `A := A+B; B := A+B;`

b) `B := A+B; A := A+B;`

c) `A := B+1; B := A+1;`

Exercise 1.2: For each of the transactions of Exercise 1.1, add the read- and write-actions to the computation and show the effect of the steps on main memory and disk. Assume that initially $A = 5$ and $B = 10$. Also, tell whether it is possible, with the appropriate order of `OUTPUT` actions, to assure that consistency is preserved even if there is a crash while the transaction is executing.

2 Undo Logging

A *log* is a file of *log records*, each telling something about what some transaction has done. If log records appear in nonvolatile storage, we can use them to restore the database to a consistent state after a system crash. Our first style of logging — *undo logging* — makes repairs to the database state by undoing the effects of transactions that may not have completed before the crash.

Additionally, in this section we introduce the basic idea of log records, including the *commit* (successful completion of a transaction) action and its effect on the database state and log. We shall also consider how the log itself is created in main memory and copied to disk by a "flush-log" operation. Finally, we examine the undo log specifically, and learn how to use it in recovery from a crash. In order to avoid having to examine the entire log during recovery, we introduce the idea of "checkpointing," which allows old portions of the log to be thrown away.

2.1 Log Records

Imagine the log as a file opened for appending only. As transactions execute, the *log manager* has the job of recording in the log each important event. One block of the log at a time is filled with log records, each representing one of these events. Log blocks are initially created in main memory and are allocated

> **Why Might a Transaction Abort?**
>
> One might wonder why a transaction would abort rather than commit. There are actually several reasons. The simplest is when there is some error condition in the code of the transaction itself, e.g., an attempted division by zero. The DBMS may also abort a transaction for one of several reasons. For instance, a transaction may be involved in a deadlock, where it and one or more other transactions each hold some resource that the other needs. Then, one or more transactions must be forced by the system to abort.

by the buffer manager like any other blocks that the DBMS needs. The log blocks are written to nonvolatile storage on disk as soon as is feasible; we shall have more to say about this matter in Section 2.2.

There are several forms of log record that are used with each of the types of logging we discuss in this chapter. These are:

1. <`START` T>: This record indicates that transaction T has begun.

2. <`COMMIT` T>: Transaction T has completed successfully and will make no more changes to database elements. Any changes to the database made by T should appear on disk. However, because we cannot control when the buffer manager chooses to copy blocks from memory to disk, we cannot in general be sure that the changes are already on disk when we see the <`COMMIT` T> log record. If we insist that the changes already be on disk, this requirement must be enforced by the log manager (as is the case for undo logging).

3. <`ABORT` T>: Transaction T could not complete successfully. If transaction T aborts, no changes it made can have been copied to disk, and it is the job of the transaction manager to make sure that such changes never appear on disk, or that their effect on disk is cancelled if they do.

For an undo log, the only other kind of log record we need is an *update record*, which is a triple $<T, X, v>$. The meaning of this record is: transaction T has changed database element X, and its former value was v. The change reflected by an update record normally occurs in memory, not disk; i.e., the log record is a response to a `WRITE` action into memory, not an `OUTPUT` action to disk. Notice also that an undo log does not record the new value of a database element, only the old value. As we shall see, should recovery be necessary in a system using undo logging, the only thing the recovery manager will do is cancel the possible effect of a transaction on disk by restoring the old value.

Preview of Other Logging Methods

In "redo logging" (Section 3), on recovery we redo any transaction that has a COMMIT record, and we ignore all others. Rules for redo logging assure that we may ignore transactions whose COMMIT records never reached the log on disk. "Undo/redo logging" (Section 4) will, on recovery, undo any transaction that has not committed, and will redo those transactions that have committed. Again, log-management and buffering rules will assure that these steps successfully repair any damage to the database.

2.2 The Undo-Logging Rules

An undo log is sufficient to allow recovery from a system failure, provided transactions and the buffer manager obey two rules:

U_1: If transaction T modifies database element X, then the log record of the form $<T, X, v>$ must be written to disk *before* the new value of X is written to disk.

U_2: If a transaction commits, then its COMMIT log record must be written to disk only *after* all database elements changed by the transaction have been written to disk, but as soon thereafter as possible.

To summarize rules U_1 and U_2, material associated with one transaction must be written to disk in the following order:

a) The log records indicating changed database elements.

b) The changed database elements themselves.

c) The COMMIT log record.

However, the order of (a) and (b) applies to each database element individually, not to the group of update records for a transaction as a whole.

In order to force log records to disk, the log manager needs a *flush-log* command that tells the buffer manager to copy to disk any log blocks that have not previously been copied to disk or that have been changed since they were last copied. In sequences of actions, we shall show FLUSH LOG explicitly. The transaction manager also needs to have a way to tell the buffer manager to perform an OUTPUT action on a database element. We shall continue to show the OUTPUT action in sequences of transaction steps.

Example 2: Let us reconsider the transaction of Example 1 in the light of undo logging. Figure 3 expands on Fig. 2 to show the log entries and flush-log actions that have to take place along with the actions of the transaction T.

Step	Action	t	M-A	M-B	D-A	D-B	Log
1)							<START T>
2)	READ(A,t)	8	8		8	8	
3)	t := t*2	16	8		8	8	
4)	WRITE(A,t)	16	16		8	8	$<T, A, 8>$
5)	READ(B,t)	8	16	8	8	8	
6)	t := t*2	16	16	8	8	8	
7)	WRITE(B,t)	16	16	16	8	8	$<T, B, 8>$
8)	FLUSH LOG						
9)	OUTPUT(A)	16	16	16	16	8	
10)	OUTPUT(B)	16	16	16	16	16	
11)							<COMMIT T>
12)	FLUSH LOG						

Figure 3: Actions and their log entries

Note we have shortened the headers to M-A for "the copy of A in a memory buffer" or D-B for "the copy of B on disk," and so on.

In line (1) of Fig. 3, transaction T begins. The first thing that happens is that the <START T> record is written to the log. Line (2) represents the read of A by T. Line (3) is the local change to t, which affects neither the database stored on disk nor any portion of the database in a memory buffer. Neither lines (2) nor (3) require any log entry, since they have no affect on the database.

Line (4) is the write of the new value of A to the buffer. This modification to A is reflected by the log entry $<T, A, 8>$ which says that A was changed by T and its former value was 8. Note that the new value, 16, is not mentioned in an undo log.

Lines (5) through (7) perform the same three steps with B instead of A. At this point, T has completed and must commit. The changed A and B must migrate to disk, but in order to follow the two rules for undo logging, there is a fixed sequence of events that must happen.

First, A and B cannot be copied to disk until the log records for the changes are on disk. Thus, at step (8) the log is flushed, assuring that these records appear on disk. Then, steps (9) and (10) copy A and B to disk. The transaction manager requests these steps from the buffer manager in order to commit T.

Now, it is possible to commit T, and the <COMMIT T> record is written to the log, which is step (11). Finally, we must flush the log again at step (12) to make sure that the <COMMIT T> record of the log appears on disk. Notice that without writing this record to disk, we could have a situation where a transaction has committed, but for a long time a review of the log does not tell us that it has committed. That situation could cause strange behavior if there were a crash, because, as we shall see in Section 2.3, a transaction that appeared to the user to have completed long ago would then be undone and effectively aborted. □

Background Activity Affects the Log and Buffers

As we look at a sequence of actions and log entries like Fig. 3, it is tempting to imagine that these actions occur in isolation. However, the DBMS may be processing many transactions simultaneously. Thus, the four log records for transaction T may be interleaved on the log with records for other transactions. Moreover, if one of these transactions flushes the log, then the log records from T may appear on disk earlier than is implied by the flush-log actions of Fig. 3. There is no harm if log records reflecting a database modification appear earlier than necessary. The essential policy for undo logging is that we don't write the <COMMIT T> record until the OUTPUT actions for T are completed.

A trickier situation occurs if two database elements A and B share a block. Then, writing one of them to disk writes the other as well. In the worst case, we can violate rule U_1 by writing one of these elements prematurely. It may be necessary to adopt additional constraints on transactions in order to make undo logging work. For instance, we might use a locking scheme where database elements are disk blocks to prevent two transactions from accessing the same block at the same time. This and other problems that appear when database elements are fractions of a block motivate our suggestion that blocks *be* the database elements.

2.3 Recovery Using Undo Logging

Suppose now that a system failure occurs. It is possible that certain database changes made by a given transaction were written to disk, while other changes made by the same transaction never reached the disk. If so, the transaction was not executed atomically, and there may be an inconsistent database state. The *recovery manager* must use the log to restore the database to some consistent state.

In this section we consider only the simplest form of recovery manager, one that looks at the entire log, no matter how long, and makes database changes as a result of its examination. In Section 2.4 we consider a more sensible approach, where the log is periodically "checkpointed," to limit the distance back in history that the recovery manager must go.

The first task of the recovery manager is to divide the transactions into committed and uncommitted transactions. If there is a log record <COMMIT T>, then by undo rule U_2 all changes made by transaction T were previously written to disk. Thus, T by itself could not have left the database in an inconsistent state when the system failure occurred.

However, suppose that we find a <START T> record on the log but no <COMMIT T> record. Then there could have been some changes to the database made by T that were written to disk before the crash, while other changes by T either were not made, or were made in the main-memory buffers but not copied to disk. In this case, T is an *incomplete transaction* and must be *undone*. That is, whatever changes T made must be reset to their previous value. Fortunately, rule U_1 assures us that if T changed X on disk before the crash, then there will be a $<T, X, v>$ record on the log, and that record will have been copied to disk before the crash. Thus, during the recovery, we must write the value v for database element X. Note that this rule begs the question whether X had value v in the database anyway; we don't even bother to check.

Since there may be several uncommitted transactions in the log, and there may even be several uncommitted transactions that modified X, we have to be systematic about the order in which we restore values. Thus, the recovery manager must scan the log from the end (i.e., from the most recently written record to the earliest written). As it travels, it remembers all those transactions T for which it has seen a <`COMMIT` T> record or an <`ABORT` T> record. Also as it travels backward, if it sees a record $<T, X, v>$, then:

1. If T is a transaction whose `COMMIT` record has been seen, then do nothing. T is committed and must not be undone.

2. Otherwise, T is an incomplete transaction, or an aborted transaction. The recovery manager must change the value of X in the database to v, in case X had been altered just before the crash.

After making these changes, the recovery manager must write a log record <`ABORT` T> for each incomplete transaction T that was not previously aborted, and then flush the log. Now, normal operation of the database may resume, and new transactions may begin executing.

Example 3: Let us consider the sequence of actions from Fig. 3 and Example 2. There are several different times that the system crash could have occurred; let us consider each significantly different one.

1. The crash occurs after step (12). Then the <`COMMIT` T> record reached disk before the crash. When we recover, we do not undo the results of T, and all log records concerning T are ignored by the recovery manager.

2. The crash occurs between steps (11) and (12). It is possible that the log record containing the `COMMIT` got flushed to disk; for instance, the buffer manager may have needed the buffer containing the end of the log for another transaction, or some other transaction may have asked for a log flush. If so, then the recovery is the same as in case (1) as far as T is concerned. However, if the `COMMIT` record never reached disk, then the recovery manager considers T incomplete. When it scans the log backward, it comes first to the record $<T, B, 8>$. It therefore stores 8 as the value of B on disk. It then comes to the record $<T, A, 8>$ and makes A have value 8 on disk. Finally, the record <`ABORT` T> is written to the log, and the log is flushed.

Crashes During Recovery

Suppose the system again crashes while we are recovering from a previous crash. Because of the way undo-log records are designed, giving the old value rather than, say, the change in the value of a database element, the recovery steps are *idempotent*; that is, repeating them many times has exactly the same effect as performing them once. We already observed that if we find a record $<T, X, v>$, it does not matter whether the value of X is already v — we may write v for X regardless. Similarly, if we repeat the recovery process, it does not matter whether the first recovery attempt restored some old values; we simply restore them again. The same reasoning holds for the other logging methods we discuss in this chapter. Since the recovery operations are idempotent, we can recover a second time without worrying about changes made the first time.

3. The crash occurs between steps (10) and (11). Now, the `COMMIT` record surely was not written, so T is incomplete and is undone as in case (2).

4. The crash occurs between steps (8) and (10). Again, T is undone. In this case the change to A and/or B may not have reached disk. Nevertheless, the proper value, 8, is restored for each of these database elements.

5. The crash occurs prior to step (8). Now, it is not certain whether any of the log records concerning T have reached disk. However, we know by rule U_1 that if the change to A and/or B reached disk, then the corresponding log record reached disk. Therefore if there were changes to A and/or B made on disk by T, then the corresponding log record will cause the recovery manager to undo those changes.

□

2.4 Checkpointing

As we observed, recovery requires that the entire log be examined, in principle. When logging follows the undo style, once a transaction has its `COMMIT` log record written to disk, the log records of that transaction are no longer needed during recovery. We might imagine that we could delete the log prior to a `COMMIT`, but sometimes we cannot. The reason is that often many transactions execute at once. If we truncated the log after one transaction committed, log records pertaining to some other active transaction T might be lost and could not be used to undo T if recovery were necessary.

The simplest way to untangle potential problems is to *checkpoint* the log periodically. In a simple checkpoint, we:

1. Stop accepting new transactions.

2. Wait until all currently active transactions commit or abort and have written a `COMMIT` or `ABORT` record on the log.

3. Flush the log to disk.

4. Write a log record <CKPT>, and flush the log again.

5. Resume accepting transactions.

Any transaction that executed prior to the checkpoint will have finished, and by rule U_2 its changes will have reached the disk. Thus, there will be no need to undo any of these transactions during recovery. During a recovery, we scan the log backwards from the end, identifying incomplete transactions as in Section 2.3. However, when we find a <CKPT> record, we know that we have seen all the incomplete transactions. Since no transactions may begin until the checkpoint ends, we must have seen every log record pertaining to the incomplete transactions already. Thus, there is no need to scan prior to the <CKPT>, and in fact the log before that point can be deleted or overwritten safely.

Example 4: Suppose the log begins:

$$<\texttt{START } T_1>$$
$$<T_1, A, 5>$$
$$<\texttt{START } T_2>$$
$$<T_2, B, 10>$$

At this time, we decide to do a checkpoint. Since T_1 and T_2 are the active (incomplete) transactions, we shall have to wait until they complete before writing the <CKPT> record on the log.

A possible extension of the log is shown in Fig. 4. Suppose a crash occurs at this point. Scanning the log from the end, we identify T_3 as the only incomplete transaction, and restore E and F to their former values 25 and 30, respectively. When we reach the <CKPT> record, we know there is no need to examine prior log records and the restoration of the database state is complete. □

2.5 Nonquiescent Checkpointing

A problem with the checkpointing technique described in Section 2.4 is that effectively we must shut down the system while the checkpoint is being made. Since the active transactions may take a long time to commit or abort, the system may appear to users to be stalled. Thus, a more complex technique known as *nonquiescent checkpointing*, which allows new transactions to enter the system during the checkpoint, is usually preferred. The steps in a nonquiescent checkpoint are:

<START T_1>
<$T_1, A, 5$>
<START T_2>
<$T_2, B, 10$>
<$T_2, C, 15$>
<$T_1, D, 20$>
<COMMIT T_1>
<COMMIT T_2>
<CKPT>
<START T_3>
<$T_3, E, 25$>
<$T_3, F, 30$>

Figure 4: An undo log

1. Write a log record <START CKPT ($T_1, \ldots, T_k$)> and flush the log. Here, $T_1, \ldots, T_k$ are the names or identifiers for all the *active* transactions (i.e., transactions that have not yet committed and written their changes to disk).

2. Wait until all of $T_1, \ldots, T_k$ commit or abort, but do not prohibit other transactions from starting.

3. When all of $T_1, \ldots, T_k$ have completed, write a log record <END CKPT> and flush the log.

With a log of this type, we can recover from a system crash as follows. As usual, we scan the log from the end, finding all incomplete transactions as we go, and restoring old values for database elements changed by these transactions. There are two cases, depending on whether, scanning backwards, we first meet an <END CKPT> record or a <START CKPT ($T_1, \ldots, T_k$)> record.

- If we first meet an <END CKPT> record, then we know that all incomplete transactions began after the previous <START CKPT ($T_1, \ldots, T_k$)> record. We may thus scan backwards as far as the next START CKPT, and then stop; previous log is useless and may as well have been discarded.

- If we first meet a record <START CKPT ($T_1, \ldots, T_k$)>, then the crash occurred during the checkpoint. However, the only incomplete transactions are those we met scanning backwards before we reached the START CKPT and those of $T_1, \ldots, T_k$ that did not complete before the crash. Thus, we need scan no further back than the start of the earliest of these incomplete transactions. The previous START CKPT record is certainly prior to any of these transaction starts, but often we shall find the starts of the

Finding the Last Log Record

It is common to recycle blocks of the log file on disk, since checkpoints allow us to drop old portions of the log. However, if we overwrite old log records, then we need to keep a serial number, which may only increase, as suggested by:

~~1~~ 9	~~2~~ 10	~~3~~ 11	4	5	6	7	8

Then, we can find the record whose serial number is greater than that of the next record; the latter record will be the current end of the log, and the entire log is found by ordering the current records by their present serial numbers.

In practice, a large log may be composed of many files, with a "top" file whose records indicate the files that comprise the log. Then, to recover, we find the last record of the top file, go to the file indicated, and find the last record there.

incomplete transactions long before we reach the previous checkpoint.[3] Moreover, if we use pointers to chain together the log records that belong to the same transaction, then we need not search the whole log for records belonging to active transactions; we just follow their chains back through the log.

As a general rule, once an <END CKPT> record has been written to disk, we can delete the log prior to the previous START CKPT record.

Example 5: Suppose that, as in Example 4, the log begins:

<START T_1>
<$T_1, A, 5$>
<START T_2>
<$T_2, B, 10$>

Now, we decide to do a nonquiescent checkpoint. Since T_1 and T_2 are the active (incomplete) transactions at this time, we write a log record

<START CKPT (T_1, T_2)>

Suppose that while waiting for T_1 and T_2 to complete, another transaction, T_3, initiates. A possible continuation of the log is shown in Fig. 5.

Suppose that at this point there is a system crash. Examining the log from the end, we find that T_3 is an incomplete transaction and must be undone.

[3]Notice, however, that because the checkpoint is nonquiescent, one of the incomplete transactions could have begun between the start and end of the previous checkpoint.

<START T_1>
<$T_1, A, 5$>
<START T_2>
<$T_2, B, 10$>
<START CKPT (T_1, T_2)>
<$T_2, C, 15$>
<START T_3>
<$T_1, D, 20$>
<COMMIT T_1>
<$T_3, E, 25$>
<COMMIT T_2>
<END CKPT>
<$T_3, F, 30$>

Figure 5: An undo log using nonquiescent checkpointing

The final log record tells us to restore database element F to the value 30. When we find the <END CKPT> record, we know that all incomplete transactions began after the previous START CKPT. Scanning further back, we find the record <$T_3, E, 25$>, which tells us to restore E to value 25. Between that record, and the START CKPT there are no other transactions that started but did not commit, so no further changes to the database are made.

<START T_1>
<$T_1, A, 5$>
<START T_2>
<$T_2, B, 10$>
<START CKPT (T_1, T_2)>
<$T_2, C, 15$>
<START T_3>
<$T_1, D, 20$>
<COMMIT T_1>
<$T_3, E, 25$>

Figure 6: Undo log with a system crash during checkpointing

Now suppose the crash occurs during the checkpoint, and the end of the log after the crash is as shown in Fig. 6. Scanning backwards, we identify T_3 and then T_2 as incomplete transactions and undo changes they have made. When we find the <START CKPT (T_1, T_2)> record, we know that the only other possible incomplete transaction is T_1. However, we have already scanned the <COMMIT T_1> record, so we know that T_1 is *not* incomplete. Also, we have already seen the <START T_3> record. Thus, we need only to continue backwards until we meet the START record for T_2, restoring database element B to value

10 as we go. □

2.6 Exercises for Section 2

Exercise 2.1: Show the undo-log records for each of the transactions (call each T) of Exercise 1.1, assuming that initially $A = 5$ and $B = 10$.

Exercise 2.2: For each of the sequences of log records representing the actions of one transaction T, tell all the sequences of events that are legal according to the rules of undo logging, where the events of interest are the writing to disk of the blocks containing database elements, and the blocks of the log containing the update and commit records. You may assume that log records are written to disk in the order shown; i.e., it is not possible to write one log record to disk while a previous record is not written to disk.

a) <START T>; <$T, A, 10$>; <$T, B, 20$>; <COMMIT T>;

b) <START T>; <$T, A, 10$>; <$T, B, 20$>; <$T, C, 30$><COMMIT T>;

! **Exercise 2.3:** The pattern introduced in Exercise 2.2 can be extended to a transaction that writes new values for n database elements. How many legal sequences of events are there for such a transaction, if the undo-logging rules are obeyed?

Exercise 2.4: The following is a sequence of undo-log records written by two transactions T and U: <START T>; <$T, A, 10$>; <START U>; <$U, B, 20$>; <$T, C, 30$>; <$U, D, 40$>; <COMMIT U>; <$T, E, 50$>; <COMMIT T>. Describe the action of the recovery manager, including changes to both disk and the log, if there is a crash and the last log record to appear on disk is:

(a) <START U> (b) <COMMIT U> (c) <$T, E, 50$> (d) <COMMIT T>.

Exercise 2.5: For each of the situations described in Exercise 2.4, what values written by T and U *must* appear on disk? Which values *might* appear on disk?

! **Exercise 2.6:** Suppose that the transaction U in Exercise 2.4 is changed so that the record <$U, D, 40$> becomes <$U, A, 40$>. What is the effect on the disk value of A if there is a crash at some point during the sequence of events? What does this example say about the ability of logging by itself to preserve atomicity of transactions?

Exercise 2.7: Consider the following sequence of log records: <START S>; <$S, A, 60$>; <COMMIT S>; <START T>; <$T, A, 10$>; <START U>; <$U, B, 20$>; <$T, C, 30$>; <START V>; <$U, D, 40$>; <$V, F, 70$>; <COMMIT U>; <$T, E, 50$>; <COMMIT T>; <$V, B, 80$>; <COMMIT V>. Suppose that we begin a nonquiescent checkpoint immediately after one of the following log records has been written (in memory):

(a) $<S, A, 60>$ (b) $<T, A, 10>$ (c) $<U, B, 20>$
(d) $<U, D, 40>$ (e) $<T, E, 50>$

For each, tell:

i. When the <END CKPT> record is written, and

ii. For each possible point at which a crash could occur, how far back in the log we must look to find all possible incomplete transactions.

3 Redo Logging

Undo logging has a potential problem that we cannot commit a transaction without first writing all its changed data to disk. Sometimes, we can save disk I/O's if we let changes to the database reside only in main memory for a while. As long as there is a log to fix things up in the event of a crash, it is safe to do so.

The requirement for immediate backup of database elements to disk can be avoided if we use a logging mechanism called *redo logging*. The principal differences between redo and undo logging are:

1. While undo logging cancels the effect of incomplete transactions and ignores committed ones during recovery, redo logging ignores incomplete transactions and repeats the changes made by committed transactions.

2. While undo logging requires us to write changed database elements to disk before the COMMIT log record reaches disk, redo logging requires that the COMMIT record appear on disk before any changed values reach disk.

3. While the old values of changed database elements are exactly what we need to recover when the undo rules U_1 and U_2 are followed, to recover using redo logging, we need the new values instead.

3.1 The Redo-Logging Rule

In redo logging the meaning of a log record $<T, X, v>$ is "transaction T wrote new value v for database element X." There is no indication of the old value of X in this record. Every time a transaction T modifies a database element X, a record of the form $<T, X, v>$ must be written to the log.

For redo logging, the order in which data and log entries reach disk can be described by a single "redo rule," called the *write-ahead logging rule.*

R_1: Before modifying any database element X on disk, it is necessary that all log records pertaining to this modification of X, including both the update record $<T, X, v>$ and the <COMMIT T> record, must appear on disk.

The COMMIT record for a transaction can only be written to the log when the transaction completes, so the commit record must follow all the update log records. Thus, when redo logging is in use, the order in which material associated with one transaction gets written to disk is:

1. The log records indicating changed database elements.

2. The COMMIT log record.

3. The changed database elements themselves.

Example 6: Let us consider the same transaction T as in Example 2. Figure 7 shows a possible sequence of events for this transaction.

Step	Action	t	M-A	M-B	D-A	D-B	Log
1)							<START T>
2)	READ(A,t)	8	8		8	8	
3)	t := t*2	16	8		8	8	
4)	WRITE(A,t)	16	16		8	8	<$T, A, 16$>
5)	READ(B,t)	8	16	8	8	8	
6)	t := t*2	16	16	8	8	8	
7)	WRITE(B,t)	16	16	16	8	8	<$T, B, 16$>
8)							<COMMIT T>
9)	FLUSH LOG						
10)	OUTPUT(A)	16	16	16	16	8	
11)	OUTPUT(B)	16	16	16	16	16	

Figure 7: Actions and their log entries using redo logging

The major differences between Figs. 7 and 3 are as follows. First, we note in lines (4) and (7) of Fig. 7 that the log records reflecting the changes have the new values of A and B, rather than the old values. Second, we see that the <COMMIT T> record comes earlier, at step (8). Then, the log is flushed, so all log records involving the changes of transaction T appear on disk. Only then can the new values of A and B be written to disk. We show these values written immediately, at steps (10) and (11), although in practice they might occur later. □

3.2 Recovery With Redo Logging

An important consequence of the redo rule R_1 is that unless the log has a <COMMIT T> record, we know that no changes to the database made by transaction T have been written to disk. Thus, incomplete transactions may be treated during recovery as if they had never occurred. However, the committed transactions present a problem, since we do not know which of their database changes have been written to disk. Fortunately, the redo log has exactly the

Order of Redo Matters

Since several committed transactions may have written new values for the same database element X, we have required that during a redo recovery, we scan the log from earliest to latest. Thus, the final value of X in the database will be the one written last, as it should be. Similarly, when describing undo recovery, we required that the log be scanned from latest to earliest. Thus, the final value of X will be the value that it had before any of the incomplete transactions changed it.

However, if the DBMS enforces atomicity, then we would not expect to find, in an undo log, two uncommitted transactions, each of which had written the same database element. In contrast, with redo logging we focus on the committed transactions, as these need to be redone. It is quite normal for there to be two *committed* transactions, each of which changed the same database element at different times. Thus, order of redo is always important, while order of undo might not be if the right kind of concurrency control were in effect.

information we need: the new values, which we may write to disk regardless of whether they were already there. To recover, using a redo log, after a system crash, we do the following.

1. Identify the committed transactions.
2. Scan the log forward from the beginning. For each log record $<T, X, v>$ encountered:
   (a) If T is not a committed transaction, do nothing.
   (b) If T is committed, write value v for database element X.
3. For each incomplete transaction T, write an <`ABORT` T> record to the log and flush the log.

Example 7: Let us consider the log written in Fig. 7 and see how recovery would be performed if the crash occurred after different steps in that sequence of actions.

1. If the crash occurs any time after step (9), then the <`COMMIT` T> record has been flushed to disk. The recovery system identifies T as a committed transaction. When scanning the log forward, the log records $<T, A, 16>$ and $<T, B, 16>$ cause the recovery manager to write values 16 for A and B. Notice that if the crash occurred between steps (10) and (11), then the write of A is redundant, but the write of B had not occurred and

changing B to 16 is essential to restore the database state to consistency. If the crash occurred after step (11), then both writes are redundant but harmless.

2. If the crash occurs between steps (8) and (9), then although the record <COMMIT T> was written to the log, it may not have gotten to disk (depending on whether the log was flushed for some other reason). If it did get to disk, then the recovery proceeds as in case (1), and if it did not get to disk, then recovery is as in case (3), below.

3. If the crash occurs prior to step (8), then <COMMIT T> surely has not reached disk. Thus, T is treated as an incomplete transaction. No changes to A or B on disk are made on behalf of T, and eventually an <ABORT T> record is written to the log.

□

3.3 Checkpointing a Redo Log

Redo logs present a checkpointing problem that we do not see with undo logs. Since the database changes made by a committed transaction can be copied to disk much later than the time at which the transaction commits, we cannot limit our concern to transactions that are active at the time we decide to create a checkpoint. Regardless of whether the checkpoint is quiescent or nonquiescent, between the start and end of the checkpoint we must write to disk all database elements that have been modified by committed transactions. To do so requires that the buffer manager keep track of which buffers are *dirty*, that is, they have been changed but not written to disk. It is also required to know which transactions modified which buffers.

On the other hand, we can complete the checkpoint without waiting for the active transactions to commit or abort, since they are not allowed to write their pages to disk at that time anyway. The steps to perform a nonquiescent checkpoint of a redo log are as follows:

1. Write a log record <START CKPT $(T_1, \ldots, T_k)$>, where $T_1, \ldots, T_k$ are all the active (uncommitted) transactions, and flush the log.

2. Write to disk all database elements that were written to buffers but not yet to disk by transactions that had already committed when the START CKPT record was written to the log.

3. Write an <END CKPT> record to the log and flush the log.

Example 8: Figure 8 shows a possible redo log, in the middle of which a checkpoint occurs. When we start the checkpoint, only T_2 is active, but the value of A written by T_1 may have reached disk. If not, then we must copy A

<START T_1>
<$T_1, A, 5$>
<START T_2>
<COMMIT T_1>
<$T_2, B, 10$>
<START CKPT (T_2)>
<$T_2, C, 15$>
<START T_3>
<$T_3, D, 20$>
<END CKPT>
<COMMIT T_2>
<COMMIT T_3>

Figure 8: A redo log

to disk before the checkpoint can end. We suggest the end of the checkpoint occurring after several other events have occurred: T_2 wrote a value for database element C, and a new transaction T_3 started and wrote a value of D. After the end of the checkpoint, the only things that happen are that T_2 and T_3 commit. □

3.4 Recovery With a Checkpointed Redo Log

As for an undo log, the insertion of records to mark the start and end of a checkpoint helps us limit our examination of the log when a recovery is necessary. Also as with undo logging, there are two cases, depending on whether the last checkpoint record is START or END.

Suppose first that the last checkpoint record on the log before a crash is <END CKPT>. Now, we know that every value written by a transaction that committed before the corresponding <START CKPT $(T_1, \ldots, T_k)$> has had its changes written to disk, so we need not concern ourselves with recovering the effects of these transactions. However, any transaction that is either among the T_i's or that started after the beginning of the checkpoint can still have changes it made not yet migrated to disk, even though the transaction has committed. Thus, we must perform recovery as described in Section 3.2, but may limit our attention to the transactions that are either one of the T_i's mentioned in the last <START CKPT $(T_1, \ldots, T_k)$> or that started after that log record appeared in the log. In searching the log, we do not have to look further back than the earliest of the <START T_i> records. Notice, however, that these START records could appear prior to any number of checkpoints. Linking backwards all the log records for a given transaction helps us to find the necessary records, as it did for undo logging.

Now, suppose the last checkpoint record on the log is

<START CKPT $(T_1, \ldots, T_k)$>

We cannot be sure that committed transactions prior to the start of this checkpoint had their changes written to disk. Thus, we must search back to the previous <END CKPT> record, find its matching <START CKPT $(S_1, \ldots, S_m)$> record,[4] and redo all those committed transactions that either started after that START CKPT or are among the S_i's.

Example 9: Consider again the log of Fig. 8. If a crash occurs at the end, we search backwards, finding the <END CKPT> record. We thus know that it is sufficient to consider as candidates to redo all those transactions that either started after the <START CKPT (T_2)> record was written or that are on its list (i.e., T_2). Thus, our candidate set is $\{T_2, T_3\}$. We find the records <COMMIT T_2> and <COMMIT T_3>, so we know that each must be redone. We search the log as far back as the <START T_2> record, and find the update records <$T_2, B, 10$>, <$T_2, C, 15$>, and <$T_3, D, 20$> for the committed transactions. Since we don't know whether these changes reached disk, we rewrite the values 10, 15, and 20 for B, C, and D, respectively.

Now, suppose the crash occurred between the records <COMMIT T_2> and <COMMIT T_3>. The recovery is similar to the above, except that T_3 is no longer a committed transaction. Thus, its change <$T_3, D, 20$> must *not* be redone, and no change is made to D during recovery, even though that log record is in the range of records that is examined. Also, we write an <ABORT T_3> record to the log after recovery.

Finally, suppose that the crash occurs just prior to the <END CKPT> record. In principal, we must search back to the next-to-last START CKPT record and get its list of active transactions. However, in this case there is no previous checkpoint, and we must go all the way to the beginning of the log. Thus, we identify T_1 as the only committed transaction, redo its action <$T_1, A, 5$>, and write records <ABORT T_2> and <ABORT T_3> to the log after recovery. □

Since transactions may be active during several checkpoints, it is convenient to include in the <START CKPT $(T_1, \ldots, T_k)$> records not only the names of the active transactions, but pointers to the place on the log where they started. By doing so, we know when it is safe to delete early portions of the log. When we write an <END CKPT>, we know that we shall never need to look back further than the earliest of the <START T_i> records for the active transactions T_i. Thus, anything prior to that START record may be deleted.

3.5 Exercises for Section 3

Exercise 3.1: Show the redo-log records for each of the transactions (call each T) of Exercise 1.1, assuming that initially $A = 5$ and $B = 10$.

[4]There is a small technicality that there could be a START CKPT record that, because of a previous crash, has no matching <END CKPT> record. Therefore, we must look not just for the previous START CKPT, but first for an <END CKPT> and then the previous START CKPT.

Exercise 3.2: Repeat Exercise 2.2 for redo logging.

Exercise 3.3: Repeat Exercise 2.4 for redo logging.

Exercise 3.4: Repeat Exercise 2.5 for redo logging.

Exercise 3.5: Using the data of Exercise 2.7, answer for each of the positions (a) through (e) of that exercise:

i. At what points could the <END CKPT> record be written, and

ii. For each possible point at which a crash could occur, how far back in the log we must look to find all possible incomplete transactions. Consider both the case that the <END CKPT> record was or was not written prior to the crash.

4 Undo/Redo Logging

We have seen two different approaches to logging, differentiated by whether the log holds old values or new values when a database element is updated. Each has certain drawbacks:

- Undo logging requires that data be written to disk immediately after a transaction finishes, perhaps increasing the number of disk I/O's that need to be performed.
- On the other hand, redo logging requires us to keep all modified blocks in buffers until the transaction commits and the log records have been flushed, perhaps increasing the average number of buffers required by transactions.
- Both undo and redo logs may put contradictory requirements on how buffers are handled during a checkpoint, unless the database elements are complete blocks or sets of blocks. For instance, if a buffer contains one database element A that was changed by a committed transaction and another database element B that was changed in the same buffer by a transaction that has not yet had its COMMIT record written to disk, then we are required to copy the buffer to disk because of A but also forbidden to do so, because rule R_1 applies to B.

We shall now see a kind of logging called *undo/redo logging*, that provides increased flexibility to order actions, at the expense of maintaining more information on the log.

4.1 The Undo/Redo Rules

An undo/redo log has the same sorts of log records as the other kinds of log, with one exception. The update log record that we write when a database element changes value has four components. Record $<T, X, v, w>$ means that transaction T changed the value of database element X; its former value was v, and its new value is w. The constraints that an undo/redo logging system must follow are summarized by the following rule:

UR_1 Before modifying any database element X on disk because of changes made by some transaction T, it is necessary that the update record $<T, X, v, w>$ appear on disk.

Rule UR_1 for undo/redo logging thus enforces only the constraints enforced by *both* undo logging and redo logging. In particular, the <COMMIT T> log record can precede or follow any of the changes to the database elements on disk.

Example 10: Figure 9 is a variation in the order of the actions associated with the transaction T that we last saw in Example 6. Notice that the log records for updates now have both the old and the new values of A and B. In this sequence, we have written the <COMMIT T> log record in the middle of the output of database elements A and B to disk. Step (10) could also have appeared before step (8) or step (9), or after step (11). □

Step	Action	t	M-A	M-B	D-A	D-B	Log
1)							<START T>
2)	`READ(A,t)`	8	8		8	8	
3)	`t := t*2`	16	8		8	8	
4)	`WRITE(A,t)`	16	16		8	8	$<T, A, 8, 16>$
5)	`READ(B,t)`	8	16	8	8	8	
6)	`t := t*2`	16	16	8	8	8	
7)	`WRITE(B,t)`	16	16	16	8	8	$<T, B, 8, 16>$
8)	`FLUSH LOG`						
9)	`OUTPUT(A)`	16	16	16	16	8	
10)							<COMMIT T>
11)	`OUTPUT(B)`	16	16	16	16	16	

Figure 9: A possible sequence of actions and their log entries using undo/redo logging

4.2 Recovery With Undo/Redo Logging

When we need to recover using an undo/redo log, we have the information in the update records either to undo a transaction T by restoring the old values of

A Problem With Delayed Commitment

Like undo logging, a system using undo/redo logging can exhibit a behavior where a transaction appears to the user to have been completed (e.g., they booked an airline seat over the Web and disconnected), and yet because the <`COMMIT` T> record was not flushed to disk, a subsequent crash causes the transaction to be undone rather than redone. If this possibility is a problem, we suggest the use of an additional rule for undo/redo logging:

UR_2 A <`COMMIT` T> record must be flushed to disk as soon as it appears in the log.

For instance, we would add `FLUSH LOG` after step (10) of Fig. 9.

the database elements that T changed, or to redo T by repeating the changes it has made. The undo/redo recovery policy is:

1. Redo all the committed transactions in the order earliest-first, and

2. Undo all the incomplete transactions in the order latest-first.

Notice that it is necessary for us to do both. Because of the flexibility allowed by undo/redo logging regarding the relative order in which `COMMIT` log records and the database changes themselves are copied to disk, we could have either a committed transaction with some or all of its changes not on disk, or an uncommitted transaction with some or all of its changes on disk.

Example 11 : Consider the sequence of actions in Fig. 9. Here are the different ways that recovery would take place on the assumption that there is a crash at various points in the sequence.

1. Suppose the crash occurs after the <`COMMIT` T> record is flushed to disk. Then T is identified as a committed transaction. We write the value 16 for both A and B to the disk. Because of the actual order of events, A already has the value 16, but B may not, depending on whether the crash occurred before or after step (11).

2. If the crash occurs prior to the <`COMMIT` T> record reaching disk, then T is treated as an incomplete transaction. The previous values of A and B, 8 in each case, are written to disk. If the crash occurs between steps (9) and (10), then the value of A was 16 on disk, and the restoration to value 8 is necessary. In this example, the value of B does not need to be undone, and if the crash occurs before step (9) then neither does the value of A. However, in general we cannot be sure whether restoration is necessary, so we always perform the undo operation.

□

Strange Behavior of Transactions During Recovery

You may have noticed that we did not specify whether undo's or redo's are done first during recovery using an undo/redo log. In fact, whether we perform the redo's or undo's first, we are open to the following situation: a transaction T has committed and is redone. However, T read a value X written by some transaction U that has not committed and is undone. The problem is not whether we redo first, and leave X with its value prior to U, or we undo first and leave X with its value written by T. The situation makes no sense either way, because the final database state does not correspond to the effect of any sequence of atomic transactions.

4.3 Checkpointing an Undo/Redo Log

A nonquiescent checkpoint is somewhat simpler for undo/redo logging than for the other logging methods. We have only to do the following:

1. Write a <`START CKPT` $(T_1, \ldots, T_k)$> record to the log, where $T_1, \ldots, T_k$ are all the active transactions, and flush the log.

2. Write to disk all the buffers that are *dirty*; i.e., they contain one or more changed database elements. Unlike redo logging, we flush all dirty buffers, not just those written by committed transactions.

3. Write an <`END CKPT`> record to the log, and flush the log.

Notice in connection with point (2) that, because of the flexibility undo/redo logging offers regarding when data reaches disk, we can tolerate the writing to disk of data written by incomplete transactions. Therefore we can tolerate database elements that are smaller than complete blocks and thus may share buffers. The only requirement we must make on transactions is:

- A transaction must not write any values (even to memory buffers) until it is certain not to abort.

This constraint is almost certainly needed anyway, in order to avoid inconsistent interactions between transactions. Notice that under redo logging, the above condition is not sufficient, since even if the transaction that wrote B is certain to commit, rule R_1 requires that the transaction's `COMMIT` record be written to disk before B is written to disk.

Example 12: Figure 10 shows an undo/redo log analogous to the redo log of Fig. 8. We have changed only the update records, giving them an old value as well as a new value. For simplicity, we have assumed that in each case the old value is one less than the new value.

$$
\begin{array}{l}
\texttt{<START } T_1\texttt{>} \\
\texttt{<}T_1, A, 4, 5\texttt{>} \\
\texttt{<START } T_2\texttt{>} \\
\texttt{<COMMIT } T_1\texttt{>} \\
\texttt{<}T_2, B, 9, 10\texttt{>} \\
\texttt{<START CKPT } (T_2)\texttt{>} \\
\texttt{<}T_2, C, 14, 15\texttt{>} \\
\texttt{<START } T_3\texttt{>} \\
\texttt{<}T_3, D, 19, 20\texttt{>} \\
\texttt{<END CKPT>} \\
\texttt{<COMMIT } T_2\texttt{>} \\
\texttt{<COMMIT } T_3\texttt{>}
\end{array}
$$

Figure 10: An undo/redo log

As in Example 8, T_2 is identified as the only active transaction when the checkpoint begins. Since this log is an undo/redo log, it is possible that T_2's new B-value 10 has been written to disk, which was not possible under redo logging. However, it is irrelevant whether or not that disk write has occurred. During the checkpoint, we shall surely flush B to disk if it is not already there, since we flush all dirty buffers. Likewise, we shall flush A, written by the committed transaction T_1, if it is not already on disk.

If the crash occurs at the end of this sequence of events, then T_2 and T_3 are identified as committed transactions. Transaction T_1 is prior to the checkpoint. Since we find the <END CKPT> record on the log, T_1 is correctly assumed to have both completed and had its changes written to disk. We therefore redo both T_2 and T_3, as in Example 8, and ignore T_1. However, when we redo a transaction such as T_2, we do not need to look prior to the <START CKPT (T_2)> record, even though T_2 was active at that time, because we know that T_2's changes prior to the start of the checkpoint were flushed to disk during the checkpoint.

For another instance, suppose the crash occurs just before the <COMMIT T_3> record is written to disk. Then we identify T_2 as committed but T_3 as incomplete. We redo T_2 by setting C to 15 on disk; it is not necessary to set B to 10 since we know that change reached disk before the <END CKPT>. However, unlike the situation with a redo log, we also undo T_3; that is, we set D to 19 on disk. If T_3 had been active at the start of the checkpoint, we would have had to look prior to the START-CKPT record to find if there were more actions by T_3 that may have reached disk and need to be undone. □

4.4 Exercises for Section 4

Exercise 4.1: Show the undo/redo-log records for each of the transactions (call each T) of Exercise 1.1, assuming that initially $A = 5$ and $B = 10$.

Exercise 4.2: For each of the sequences of log records representing the actions of one transaction T, tell all the sequences of events that are legal according to the rules of undo/redo logging, where the events of interest are the writing to disk of the blocks containing database elements, and the blocks of the log containing the update and commit records. You may assume that log records are written to disk in the order shown; i.e., it is not possible to write one log record to disk while a previous record is not written to disk.

a) <`START` T>; <$T, A, 10, 11$>; <$T, B, 20, 21$>; <`COMMIT` T>;

b) <`START` T>; <$T, A, 10, 21$>; <$T, B, 20, 21$>; <$T, C, 30, 31$>; <`COMMIT` T>;

Exercise 4.3: The following is a sequence of undo/redo-log records written by two transactions T and U: <`START` T>; <$T, A, 10, 11$>; <`START` U>; <$U, B, 20, 21$>; <$T, C, 30, 31$>; <$U, D, 40, 41$>; <`COMMIT` U>; <$T, E, 50, 51$>; <`COMMIT` T>. Describe the action of the recovery manager, including changes to both disk and the log, if there is a crash and the last log record to appear on disk is:

(a) <`START` U> (b) <`COMMIT` U> (c) <$T, E, 50, 51$> (d) <`COMMIT` T>.

Exercise 4.4: For each of the situations described in Exercise 4.3, what values written by T and U *must* appear on disk? Which values *might* appear on disk?

Exercise 4.5: Consider the following sequence of log records: <`START` S>; <$S, A, 60, 61$>; <`COMMIT` S>; <`START` T>; <$T, A, 61, 62$>; <`START` U>; <$U, B, 20, 21$>; <$T, C, 30, 31$>; <`START` V>; <$U, D, 40, 41$>; <$V, F, 70, 71$>; <`COMMIT` U>; <$T, E, 50, 51$>; <`COMMIT` T>; <$V, B, 21, 22$>; <`COMMIT` V>. Suppose that we begin a nonquiescent checkpoint immediately after one of the following log records has been written (in memory):

(a) <$S, A, 60, 61$> (b) <$T, A, 61, 62$> (c) <$U, B, 20, 21$>
(d) <$U, D, 40, 41$> (e) <$T, E, 50, 51$>

For each, tell:

i. At what points could the <`END CKPT`> record be written, and

ii. For each possible point at which a crash could occur, how far back in the log we must look to find all possible incomplete transactions. Consider both the case that the <`END CKPT`> record was or was not written prior to the crash.

5 Protecting Against Media Failures

The log can protect us against system failures, where nothing is lost from disk, but temporary data in main memory is lost. However, as we discussed in Section 1.1, more serious failures involve the loss of one or more disks. An archiving system, which we cover next, is needed to enable a database to survive losses involving disk-resident data.

5.1 The Archive

To protect against media failures, we are thus led to a solution involving *archiving* — maintaining a copy of the database separate from the database itself. If it were possible to shut down the database for a while, we could make a backup copy on some storage medium such as tape or optical disk, and store the copy remote from the database, in some secure location. The backup would preserve the database state as it existed at the time of the backup, and if there were a media failure, the database could be restored to this state.

To advance to a more recent state, we could use the log, provided the log had been preserved since the archive copy was made, and the log itself survived the failure. In order to protect against losing the log, we could transmit a copy of the log, almost as soon as it is created, to the same remote site as the archive. Then, if the log as well as the data is lost, we can use the archive plus remotely stored log to recover, at least up to the point that the log was last transmitted to the remote site.

Since writing an archive is a lengthy process, we try to avoid copying the entire database at each archiving step. Thus, we distinguish between two levels of archiving:

1. A *full dump*, in which the entire database is copied.

2. An *incremental dump*, in which only those database elements changed since the previous full or incremental dump are copied.

It is also possible to have several levels of dump, with a full dump thought of as a "level 0" dump, and a "level i" dump copying everything changed since the last dump at a level less than or equal to i.

We can restore the database from a full dump and its subsequent incremental dumps, in a process much like the way a redo or undo/redo log can be used to repair damage due to a system failure. We copy the full dump back to the database, and then in an earliest-first order, make the changes recorded by the later incremental dumps.

5.2 Nonquiescent Archiving

The problem with the simple view of archiving in Section 5.1 is that most databases cannot be shut down for the period of time (possibly hours) needed

Why Not Just Back Up the Log?

We might question the need for an archive, since we have to back up the log in a secure place anyway if we are not to be stuck at the state the database was in when the previous archive was made. While it may not be obvious, the answer lies in the typical rate of change of a large database. While only a small fraction of the database may change in a day, the changes, each of which must be logged, will over the course of a year become much larger than the database itself. If we never archived, then the log could never be truncated, and the cost of storing the log would soon exceed the cost of storing a copy of the database.

to make a backup copy. We thus need to consider *nonquiescent archiving*, which is analogous to nonquiescent checkpointing. Recall that a nonquiescent checkpoint attempts to make a copy on the disk of the (approximate) database state that existed when the checkpoint started. We can rely on a small portion of the log around the time of the checkpoint to fix up any deviations from that database state, due to the fact that during the checkpoint, new transactions may have started and written to disk.

Similarly, a nonquiescent dump tries to make a copy of the database that existed when the dump began, but database activity may change many database elements on disk during the minutes or hours that the dump takes. If it is necessary to restore the database from the archive, the log entries made during the dump can be used to sort things out and get the database to a consistent state. The analogy is suggested by Fig. 11.

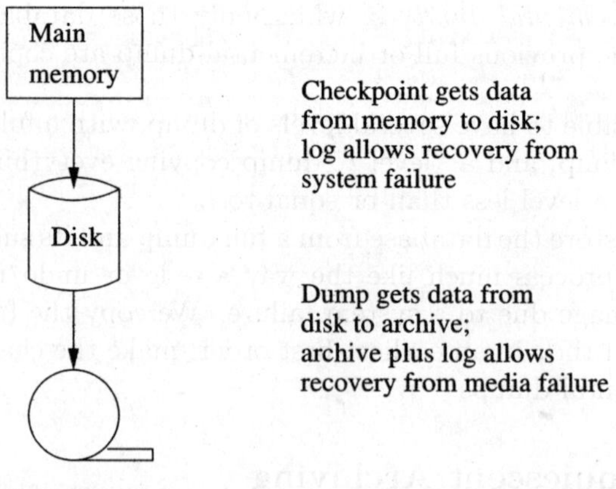

Figure 11: The analogy between checkpoints and dumps

A nonquiescent dump copies the database elements in some fixed order, possibly while those elements are being changed by executing transactions. As a result, the value of a database element that is copied to the archive may or may not be the value that existed when the dump began. As long as the log for the duration of the dump is preserved, the discrepancies can be corrected from the log.

Example 13: For a very simple example, suppose that our database consists of four elements, A, B, C, and D, which have the values 1 through 4, respectively, when the dump begins. During the dump, A is changed to 5, C is changed to 6, and B is changed to 7. However, the database elements are copied in order, and the sequence of events shown in Fig. 12 occurs. Then although the database at the beginning of the dump has values $(1, 2, 3, 4)$, and the database at the end of the dump has values $(5, 7, 6, 4)$, the copy of the database in the archive has values $(1, 2, 6, 4)$, a database state that existed at no time during the dump. □

Disk	Archive
	Copy A
`A := 5`	
	Copy B
`C := 6`	
	Copy C
`B := 7`	
	Copy D

Figure 12: Events during a nonquiescent dump

In more detail, the process of making an archive can be broken into the following steps. We assume that the logging method is either redo or undo/redo; an undo log is not suitable for use with archiving.

1. Write a log record `<START DUMP>`.

2. Perform a checkpoint appropriate for whichever logging method is being used.

3. Perform a full or incremental dump of the data disk(s), as desired, making sure that the copy of the data has reached the secure, remote site.

4. Make sure that enough of the log has been copied to the secure, remote site that at least the prefix of the log up to and including the checkpoint in item (2) will survive a media failure of the database.

5. Write a log record `<END DUMP>`.

At the completion of the dump, it is safe to throw away log prior to the beginning of the checkpoint *previous* to the one performed in item (2) above.

Example 14: Suppose that the changes to the simple database in Example 13 were caused by two transactions T_1 (which writes A and B) and T_2 (which writes C) that were active when the dump began. Figure 13 shows a possible undo/redo log of the events during the dump.

<START DUMP>
<START CKPT (T_1, T_2)>
<$T_1, A, 1, 5$>
<$T_2, C, 3, 6$>
<COMMIT T_2>
<$T_1, B, 2, 7$>
<END CKPT>
Dump completes
<END DUMP>

Figure 13: Log taken during a dump

Notice that we did not show T_1 committing. It would be unusual that a transaction remained active during the entire time a full dump was in progress, but that possibility doesn't affect the correctness of the recovery method that we discuss next. □

5.3 Recovery Using an Archive and Log

Suppose that a media failure occurs, and we must reconstruct the database from the most recent archive and whatever prefix of the log has reached the remote site and has not been lost in the crash. We perform the following steps:

1. Restore the database from the archive.

   (a) Find the most recent full dump and reconstruct the database from it (i.e., copy the archive into the database).

   (b) If there are later incremental dumps, modify the database according to each, earliest first.

2. Modify the database using the surviving log. Use the method of recovery appropriate to the log method being used.

Example 15: Suppose there is a media failure after the dump of Example 14 completes, and the log shown in Fig. 13 survives. Assume, to make the process interesting, that the surviving portion of the log does not include a <COMMIT T_1> record, although it does include the <COMMIT T_2> record shown in that figure.

The database is first restored to the values in the archive, which is, for database elements A, B, C, and D, respectively, $(1, 2, 6, 4)$.

Now, we must look at the log. Since T_2 has completed, we redo the step that sets C to 6. In this example, C already had the value 6, but it might be that:

a) The archive for C was made before T_2 changed C, or

b) The archive actually captured a later value of C, which may or may not have been written by a transaction whose commit record survived. Later in the recovery, C will be restored to the value found in the archive *if* the transaction was committed.

Since T_1 does not have a `COMMIT` record, we must undo T_1. We use the log records for T_1 to determine that A must be restored to value 1 and B to 2. It happens that they had these values in the archive, but the actual archive value could have been different because the modified A and/or B had been included in the archive. □

5.4 Exercises for Section 5

Exercise 5.1: If a redo log, rather than an undo/redo log, were used in Examples 14 and 15:

a) What would the log look like?

! b) If we had to recover using the archive and this log, what would be the consequence of T_1 not having committed?

c) What would be the state of the database after recovery?

6 Summary

✦ *Transaction Management*: The two principal tasks of the transaction manager are assuring recoverability of database actions through logging, and assuring correct, concurrent behavior of transactions through the scheduler (discussed in the next chapter).

✦ *Database Elements*: The database is divided into elements, which are typically disk blocks, but could be tuples or relations, for instance. Database elements are the units for both logging and scheduling.

✦ *Logging*: A record of every important action of a transaction — beginning, changing a database element, committing, or aborting — is stored on a log. The log must be backed up on disk at a time that is related to when the corresponding database changes migrate to disk, but that time depends on the particular logging method used.

- *Recovery*: When a system crash occurs, the log is used to repair the database, restoring it to a consistent state.

- *Logging Methods*: The three principal methods for logging are undo, redo, and undo/redo, named for the way(s) that they are allowed to fix the database during recovery.

- *Undo Logging*: This method logs the old value, each time a database element is changed. With undo logging, a new value of a database element can be written to disk only after the log record for the change has reached disk, but before the commit record for the transaction performing the change reaches disk. Recovery is done by restoring the old value for every uncommitted transaction.

- *Redo Logging*: Here, only the new value of database elements is logged. With this form of logging, values of a database element can be written to disk only after both the log record of its change and the commit record for its transaction have reached disk. Recovery involves rewriting the new value for every committed transaction.

- *Undo/Redo Logging*: In this method, both old and new values are logged. Undo/redo logging is more flexible than the other methods, since it requires only that the log record of a change appear on the disk before the change itself does. There is no requirement about when the commit record appears. Recovery is effected by redoing committed transactions and undoing the uncommitted transactions.

- *Checkpointing*: Since all recovery methods require, in principle, looking at the entire log, the DBMS must occasionally checkpoint the log, to assure that no log records prior to the checkpoint will be needed during a recovery. Thus, old log records can eventually be thrown away and their disk space reused.

- *Nonquiescent Checkpointing*: To avoid shutting down the system while a checkpoint is made, techniques associated with each logging method allow the checkpoint to be made while the system is in operation and database changes are occurring. The only cost is that some log records prior to the nonquiescent checkpoint may need to be examined during recovery.

- *Archiving*: While logging protects against system failures involving only the loss of main memory, archiving is necessary to protect against failures where the contents of disk are lost. Archives are copies of the database stored in a safe place.

- *Incremental Backups*: Instead of copying the entire database to an archive periodically, a single complete backup can be followed by several incremental backups, where only the changed data is copied to the archive.

- ✦ *Nonquiescent Archiving*: We can create a backup of the data while the database is in operation. The necessary techniques involve making log records of the beginning and end of the archiving, as well as performing a checkpoint for the log during the archiving.

- ✦ *Recovery From Media Failures*: When a disk is lost, it may be restored by starting with a full backup of the database, modifying it according to any later incremental backups, and finally recovering to a consistent database state by using an archived copy of the log.

7 References

The major textbook on all aspects of transaction processing, including logging and recovery, is by Gray and Reuter [5]. This book was partially fed by some informal notes on transaction processing by Jim Gray [3] that were widely circulated; the latter, along with [4] and [8] are the primary sources for much of the logging and recovery technology.

[2] is an earlier, more concise description of transaction-processing technology. [7] is a recent treatment of recovery.

Two early surveys, [1] and [6] both represent much of the fundamental work in recovery and organized the subject in the undo-redo-undo/redo tricotomy that we followed here.

1. P. A. Bernstein, N. Goodman, and V. Hadzilacos, "Recovery algorithms for database systems," *Proc. 1983 IFIP Congress*, North Holland, Amsterdam, pp. 799–807.

2. P. A. Bernstein, V. Hadzilacos, and N. Goodman, *Concurrency Control and Recovery in Database Systems*, Addison-Wesley, Reading MA, 1987.

3. J. N. Gray, "Notes on database operating systems," in *Operating Systems: an Advanced Course*, pp. 393–481, Springer-Verlag, 1978.

4. J. N. Gray, P. R. McJones, and M. Blasgen, "The recovery manager of the System R database manager," *Computing Surveys* **13**:2 (1981), pp. 223–242.

5. J. N. Gray and A. Reuter, *Transaction Processing: Concepts and Techniques*, Morgan-Kaufmann, San Francisco, 1993.

6. T. Haerder and A. Reuter, "Principles of transaction-oriented database recovery — a taxonomy," *Computing Surveys* **15**:4 (1983), pp. 287–317.

7. V. Kumar and M. Hsu, *Recovery Mechanisms in Database Systems*, Prentice-Hall, Englewood Cliffs NJ, 1998.

8. C. Mohan, D. J. Haderle, B. G. Lindsay, H. Pirahesh, and P. Schwarz, "ARIES: a transaction recovery method supporting fine-granularity locking and partial rollbacks using write-ahead logging," *ACM Trans. on Database Systems* **17**:1 (1992), pp. 94–162.

Concurrency Control

Interactions among concurrently executing transactions can cause the database state to become inconsistent, even when the transactions individually preserve correctness of the state, and there is no system failure. Thus, the timing of individual steps of different transactions needs to be regulated in some manner. This regulation is the job of the *scheduler* component of the DBMS, and the general process of assuring that transactions preserve consistency when executing simultaneously is called *concurrency control.* The role of the scheduler is suggested by Fig. 1.

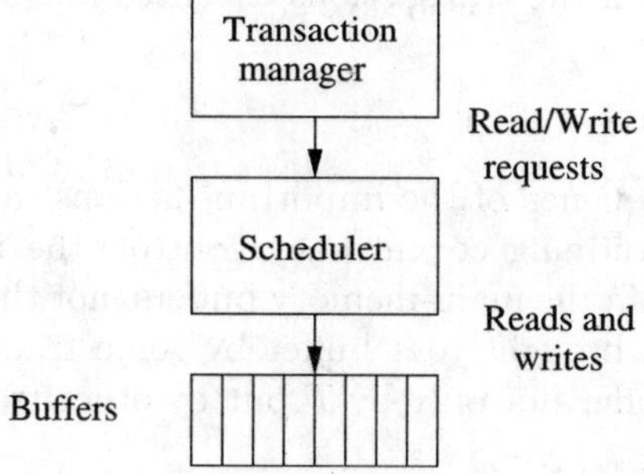

Figure 1: The scheduler takes read/write requests from transactions and either executes them in buffers or delays them

As transactions request reads and writes of database elements, these requests are passed to the scheduler. In most situations, the scheduler will execute the reads and writes directly, first calling on the buffer manager if the desired database element is not in a buffer. However, in some situations, it is not safe for the request to be executed immediately. The scheduler must delay the request; in some concurrency-control techniques, the scheduler may even abort the transaction that issued the request.

From Chapter 18 of *Database Systems*, Second Edition. Hector Garcia-Molina, Jeffrey D. Ullman, Jennifer Widom.

We begin by studying how to assure that concurrently executing transactions preserve correctness of the database state. The abstract requirement is called *serializability*, and there is an important, stronger condition called *conflict-serializability* that most schedulers actually enforce. We consider the most important techniques for implementing schedulers: locking, timestamping, and validation. Our study of lock-based schedulers includes the important concept of "two-phase locking," which is a requirement widely used to assure serializability of schedules.

1 Serial and Serializable Schedules

Recall the "correctness principle" every transaction, if executed in isolation (without any other transactions running concurrently), will transform any consistent state to another consistent state. In practice, transactions often run concurrently with other transactions, so the correctness principle doesn't apply directly. This section introduces the notion of "schedules," the sequence of actions performed by transactions and "serializable schedules," which produce the same result as if the transactions executed one-at-a-time.

1.1 Schedules

A *schedule* is a sequence of the important actions taken by one or more transactions. When studying concurrency control, the important read and write actions take place in the main-memory buffers, not the disk. That is, a database element A that is brought to a buffer by some transaction T may be read or written in that buffer not only by T but by other transactions that access A.

T_1	T_2
`READ(A,t)`	`READ(A,s)`
`t := t+100`	`s := s*2`
`WRITE(A,t)`	`WRITE(A,s)`
`READ(B,t)`	`READ(B,s)`
`t := t+100`	`s := s*2`
`WRITE(B,t)`	`WRITE(B,s)`

Figure 2: Two transactions

Example 1: Let us consider two transactions and the effect on the database when their actions are executed in certain orders. The important actions of the transactions T_1 and T_2 are shown in Fig. 2. The variables t and s are local variables of T_1 and T_2, respectively; they are *not* database elements.

We shall assume that the only consistency constraint on the database state is that $A = B$. Since T_1 adds 100 to both A and B, and T_2 multiplies both

A and B by 2, we know that each transaction, run in isolation, will preserve consistency. □

1.2 Serial Schedules

A schedule is *serial* if its actions consist of all the actions of one transaction, then all the actions of another transaction, and so on. No mixing of the actions is allowed.

T_1	T_2	A	B
		25	25
`READ(A,t)`			
`t := t+100`			
`WRITE(A,t)`		125	
`READ(B,t)`			
`t := t+100`			
`WRITE(B,t)`			125
	`READ(A,s)`		
	`s := s*2`		
	`WRITE(A,s)`	250	
	`READ(B,s)`		
	`s := s*2`		
	`WRITE(B,s)`		250

Figure 3: Serial schedule in which T_1 precedes T_2

Example 2: For the transactions of Fig. 2, there are two serial schedules, one in which T_1 precedes T_2 and the other in which T_2 precedes T_1. Figure 3 shows the sequence of events when T_1 precedes T_2, and the initial state is $A = B = 25$. We shall take the convention that when displayed vertically, time proceeds down the page. Also, the values of A and B shown refer to their values in main-memory buffers, not necessarily to their values on disk.

Figure 4 shows another serial schedule in which T_2 precedes T_1; the initial state is again assumed to be $A = B = 25$. Notice that the final values of A and B are different for the two schedules; they both have value 250 when T_1 goes first and 150 when T_2 goes first. In general, we would not expect the final state of a database to be independent of the order of transactions. □

We can represent a serial schedule as in Fig. 3 or Fig. 4, listing each of the actions in the order they occur. However, since the order of actions in a serial schedule depends only on the order of the transactions themselves, we shall sometimes represent a serial schedule by the list of transactions. Thus, the schedule of Fig. 3 is represented (T_1, T_2), and that of Fig. 4 is (T_2, T_1).

T_1	T_2	A	B
		25	25
	`READ(A,s)`		
	`s := s*2`		
	`WRITE(A,s)`	50	
	`READ(B,s)`		
	`s := s*2`		
	`WRITE(B,s)`		50
`READ(A,t)`			
`t := t+100`			
`WRITE(A,t)`		150	
`READ(B,t)`			
`t := t+100`			
`WRITE(B,t)`			150

Figure 4: Serial schedule in which T_2 precedes T_1

1.3 Serializable Schedules

The correctness principle for transactions tells us that every serial schedule will preserve consistency of the database state. But are there any other schedules that also are guaranteed to preserve consistency? There are, as the following example shows. In general, we say a schedule S is *serializable* if there is a serial schedule S' such that for every initial database state, the effects of S and S' are the same.

T_1	T_2	A	B
		25	25
`READ(A,t)`			
`t := t+100`			
`WRITE(A,t)`		125	
	`READ(A,s)`		
	`s := s*2`		
	`WRITE(A,s)`	250	
`READ(B,t)`			
`t := t+100`			
`WRITE(B,t)`			125
	`READ(B,s)`		
	`s := s*2`		
	`WRITE(B,s)`		250

Figure 5: A serializable, but not serial, schedule

Example 3: Figure 5 shows a schedule of the transactions from Example 1 that is serializable but not serial. In this schedule, T_2 acts on A after T_1 does, but before T_1 acts on B. However, we see that the effect of the two transactions scheduled in this manner is the same as for the serial schedule (T_1, T_2) from Fig. 3. To convince ourselves of the truth of this statement, we must consider not only the effect from the database state $A = B = 25$, which we show in Fig. 5, but from any consistent database state. Since all consistent database states have $A = B = c$ for some constant c, it is not hard to deduce that in the schedule of Fig. 5, both A and B will be left with the value $2(c + 100)$, and thus consistency is preserved from any consistent state.

T_1	T_2	A	B
		25	25
`READ(A,t)`			
`t := t+100`			
`WRITE(A,t)`		125	
	`READ(A,s)`		
	`s := s*2`		
	`WRITE(A,s)`	250	
	`READ(B,s)`		
	`s := s*2`		
	`WRITE(B,s)`		50
`READ(B,t)`			
`t := t+100`			
`WRITE(B,t)`			150

Figure 6: A nonserializable schedule

On the other hand, consider the schedule of Fig. 6, which is not serializable. The reason we can be sure it is not serializable is that it takes the consistent state $A = B = 25$ and leaves the database in an inconsistent state, where $A = 250$ and $B = 150$. Notice that in this order of actions, where T_1 operates on A first, but T_2 operates on B first, we have in effect applied different computations to A and B, that is $A := 2(A + 100)$ versus $B := 2B + 100$. The schedule of Fig. 6 is the sort of behavior that concurrency control mechanisms must avoid. □

1.4 The Effect of Transaction Semantics

In our study of serializability so far, we have considered in detail the operations performed by the transactions, to determine whether or not a schedule is serializable. The details of the transactions do matter, as we can see from the following example.

T_1	T_2	A	B
		25	25
`READ(A,t)`			
`t := t+100`			
`WRITE(A,t)`		125	
	`READ(A,s)`		
	`s := s+200`		
	`WRITE(A,s)`	325	
	`READ(B,s)`		
	`s := s+200`		
	`WRITE(B,s)`		225
`READ(B,t)`			
`t := t+100`			
`WRITE(B,t)`			325

Figure 7: A schedule that is serializable only because of the detailed behavior of the transactions

Example 4: Consider the schedule of Fig. 7, which differs from Fig. 6 only in the computation that T_2 performs. That is, instead of multiplying A and B by 2, T_2 adds 200 to each. One can easily check that regardless of the consistent initial state, the final state is the one that results from the serial schedule (T_1, T_2). Coincidentally, it also results from the other serial schedule, (T_2, T_1). □

Unfortunately, it is not realistic for the scheduler to concern itself with the details of computation undertaken by transactions. Since transactions often involve code written in a general-purpose programming language as well as SQL or other high-level-language statements, it is impossible to say for certain what a transaction is doing. However, the scheduler does get to see the read and write requests from the transactions, so it can know what database elements each transaction reads, and what elements it *might* change. To simplify the job of the scheduler, it is conventional to assume that:

- Any database element A that a transaction T writes is given a value that depends on the database state in such a way that no arithmetic coincidences occur.

An example of a "coincidence" is that in Example 4, where $A + 100 + 200 = B + 200 + 100$ whenever $A = B$, even though the two operations are carried out in different orders on the two variables. Put another way, if there is something that T could do to a database element to make the database state inconsistent, then T will do that.

1.5 A Notation for Transactions and Schedules

If we assume "no coincidences," then only the reads and writes performed by the transaction matter, not the actual values involved. Thus, we shall represent transactions and schedules by a shorthand notation, in which the actions are $r_T(X)$ and $w_T(X)$, meaning that transaction T reads, or respectively writes, database element X. Moreover, since we shall usually name our transactions $T_1, T_2, \ldots$, we adopt the convention that $r_i(X)$ and $w_i(X)$ are synonyms for $r_{T_i}(X)$ and $w_{T_i}(X)$, respectively.

Example 5: The transactions of Fig. 2 can be written:

$$T_1\text{: } r_1(A);\ w_1(A);\ r_1(B);\ w_1(B);$$
$$T_2\text{: } r_2(A);\ w_2(A);\ r_2(B);\ w_2(B);$$

As another example,

$$r_1(A);\ w_1(A);\ r_2(A);\ w_2(A);\ r_1(B);\ w_1(B);\ r_2(B);\ w_2(B);$$

is the serializable schedule from Fig. 5. □

To make the notation precise:

1. An *action* is an expression of the form $r_i(X)$ or $w_i(X)$, meaning that transaction T_i reads or writes, respectively, the database element X.

2. A *transaction* T_i is a sequence of actions with subscript i.

3. A *schedule* S of a set of transactions $\mathcal{T}$ is a sequence of actions, in which for each transaction T_i in $\mathcal{T}$, the actions of T_i appear in S in the same order that they appear in the definition of T_i itself. We say that S is an *interleaving* of the actions of the transactions of which it is composed.

For instance, the schedule of Example 5 has all the actions with subscript 1 appearing in the same order that they have in the definition of T_1, and the actions with subscript 2 appear in the same order that they appear in the definition of T_2.

1.6 Exercises for Section 1

Exercise 1.1: A transaction T_1, executed by an airline-reservation system, performs the following steps:

i. The customer is queried for a desired flight time and cities. Information about the desired flights is located in database elements (perhaps disk blocks) A and B, which the system retrieves from disk.

ii. The customer is told about the options, and selects a flight whose data, including the number of reservations for that flight is in B. A reservation on that flight is made for the customer.

iii. The customer selects a seat for the flight; seat data for the flight is in database element C.

iv. The system gets the customer's credit-card number and appends the bill for the flight to a list of bills in database element D.

v. The customer's phone and flight data is added to another list on database element E for a fax to be sent confirming the flight.

Express transaction T_1 as a sequence of r and w actions.

! **Exercise 1.2:** If two transactions consist of 4 and 6 actions, respectively, how many interleavings of these transactions are there?

2 Conflict-Serializability

Schedulers in commercial systems generally enforce a condition, called "conflict-serializability," that is stronger than the general notion of serializability introduced in Section 1.3. It is based on the idea of a *conflict*: a pair of consecutive actions in a schedule such that, if their order is interchanged, then the behavior of at least one of the transactions involved can change.

2.1 Conflicts

To begin, let us observe that most pairs of actions do *not* conflict. In what follows, we assume that T_i and T_j are different transactions; i.e., $i \neq j$.

1. $r_i(X)$; $r_j(Y)$ is never a conflict, even if $X = Y$. The reason is that neither of these steps change the value of any database element.

2. $r_i(X)$; $w_j(Y)$ is not a conflict provided $X \neq Y$. The reason is that should T_j write Y before T_i reads X, the value of X is not changed. Also, the read of X by T_i has no effect on T_j, so it does not affect the value T_j writes for Y.

3. $w_i(X)$; $r_j(Y)$ is not a conflict if $X \neq Y$, for the same reason as (2).

4. Similarly, $w_i(X)$; $w_j(Y)$ is not a conflict as long as $X \neq Y$.

On the other hand, there are three situations where we may not swap the order of actions:

a) Two actions of the same transaction, e.g., $r_i(X)$; $w_i(Y)$, always conflict. The reason is that the order of actions of a single transaction are fixed and may not be reordered.

b) Two writes of the same database element by different transactions conflict. That is, $w_i(X)$; $w_j(X)$ is a conflict. The reason is that as written, the value of X remains afterward as whatever T_j computed it to be. If we swap the order, as $w_j(X)$; $w_i(X)$, then we leave X with the value computed by T_i. Our assumption of "no coincidences" tells us that the values written by T_i and T_j will be different, at least for some initial states of the database.

c) A read and a write of the same database element by different transactions also conflict. That is, $r_i(X)$; $w_j(X)$ is a conflict, and so is $w_i(X)$; $r_j(X)$. If we move $w_j(X)$ ahead of $r_i(X)$, then the value of X read by T_i will be that written by T_j, which we assume is not necessarily the same as the previous value of X. Thus, swapping the order of $r_i(X)$ and $w_j(X)$ affects the value T_i reads for X and could therefore affect what T_i does.

The conclusion we draw is that any two actions of different transactions may be swapped unless:

1. They involve the same database element, and

2. At least one is a write.

Extending this idea, we may take any schedule and make as many nonconflicting swaps as we wish, with the goal of turning the schedule into a serial schedule. If we can do so, then the original schedule is serializable, because its effect on the database state remains the same as we perform each of the nonconflicting swaps.

We say that two schedules are *conflict-equivalent* if they can be turned one into the other by a sequence of nonconflicting swaps of adjacent actions. We shall call a schedule *conflict-serializable* if it is conflict-equivalent to a serial schedule. Note that conflict-serializability is a sufficient condition for serializability; i.e., a conflict-serializable schedule is a serializable schedule. Conflict-serializability is not required for a schedule to be serializable, but it is the condition that the schedulers in commercial systems generally use when they need to guarantee serializability.

Example 6: Consider the schedule

$$r_1(A);\ w_1(A);\ r_2(A);\ w_2(A);\ r_1(B);\ w_1(B);\ r_2(B);\ w_2(B);$$

from Example 5. We claim this schedule is conflict-serializable. Figure 8 shows the sequence of swaps in which this schedule is converted to the serial schedule (T_1, T_2), where all of T_1's actions precede all those of T_2. We have underlined the pair of adjacent actions about to be swapped at each step. □

$$r_1(A);\ w_1(A);\ r_2(A);\ \underline{w_2(A)};\ r_1(B);\ w_1(B);\ r_2(B);\ w_2(B);$$
$$r_1(A);\ w_1(A);\ r_2(A);\ \underline{r_1(B)};\ w_2(A);\ w_1(B);\ r_2(B);\ w_2(B);$$
$$r_1(A);\ w_1(A);\ r_1(B);\ r_2(A);\ \underline{w_2(A)};\ \underline{w_1(B)};\ r_2(B);\ w_2(B);$$
$$r_1(A);\ w_1(A);\ r_1(B);\ \underline{r_2(A)};\ \underline{w_1(B)};\ w_2(A);\ r_2(B);\ w_2(B);$$
$$r_1(A);\ w_1(A);\ r_1(B);\ w_1(B);\ r_2(A);\ w_2(A);\ r_2(B);\ w_2(B);$$

Figure 8: Converting a conflict-serializable schedule to a serial schedule by swaps of adjacent actions

2.2 Precedence Graphs and a Test for Conflict-Serializability

It is relatively simple to examine a schedule S and decide whether or not it is conflict-serializable. When a pair of conflicting actions appears anywhere in S, the transactions performing those actions must appear in the same order in any conflict-equivalent serial schedule as the actions appear in S. Thus, conflicting pairs of actions put constraints on the order of transactions in the hypothetical, conflict-equivalent serial schedule. If these constraints are not contradictory, we can find a conflict-equivalent serial schedule. If they are contradictory, we know that no such serial schedule exists.

Given a schedule S, involving transactions T_1 and T_2, perhaps among other transactions, we say that T_1 *takes precedence over* T_2, written $T_1 <_S T_2$, if there are actions A_1 of T_1 and A_2 of T_2, such that:

1. A_1 is ahead of A_2 in S,

2. Both A_1 and A_2 involve the same database element, and

3. At least one of A_1 and A_2 is a write action.

Notice that these are exactly the conditions under which we cannot swap the order of A_1 and A_2. Thus, A_1 will appear before A_2 in any schedule that is conflict-equivalent to S. As a result, a conflict-equivalent serial schedule must have T_1 before T_2.

We can summarize these precedences in a *precedence graph*. The nodes of the precedence graph are the transactions of a schedule S. When the transactions are T_i for various i, we shall label the node for T_i by only the integer i. There is an arc from node i to node j if $T_i <_S T_j$.

Example 7: The following schedule S involves three transactions, T_1, T_2, and T_3.

$$S\colon r_2(A);\ r_1(B);\ w_2(A);\ r_3(A);\ w_1(B);\ w_3(A);\ r_2(B);\ w_2(B);$$

If we look at the actions involving A, we find several reasons why $T_2 <_S T_3$. For example, $r_2(A)$ comes ahead of $w_3(A)$ in S, and $w_2(A)$ comes ahead of both

Why Conflict-Serializability is not Necessary for Serializability

Consider three transactions T_1, T_2, and T_3 that each write a value for X. T_1 and T_2 also write values for Y before they write values for X. One possible schedule, which happens to be serial, is

$$S_1\text{: } w_1(Y);\ w_1(X);\ w_2(Y);\ w_2(X);\ w_3(X);$$

S_1 leaves X with the value written by T_3 and Y with the value written by T_2. However, so does the schedule

$$S_2\text{: } w_1(Y);\ w_2(Y);\ w_2(X);\ w_1(X);\ w_3(X);$$

Intuitively, the values of X written by T_1 and T_2 have no effect, since T_3 overwrites their values. Thus, X has the same value after either S_1 or S_2, and likewise Y has the same value after either S_1 or S_2. Since S_1 is serial, and S_2 has the same effect as S_1 on any database state, we know that S_2 is serializable. However, since we cannot swap $w_1(Y)$ with $w_2(Y)$, and we cannot swap $w_1(X)$ with $w_2(X)$, therefore we cannot convert S_2 to any serial schedule by swaps. That is, S_2 is serializable, but not conflict-serializable.

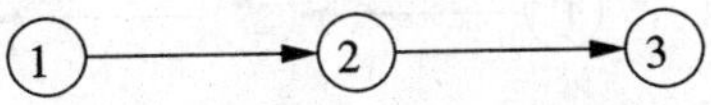

Figure 9: The precedence graph for the schedule S of Example 7

$r_3(A)$ and $w_3(A)$. Any one of these three observations is sufficient to justify the arc in the precedence graph of Fig. 9 from 2 to 3.

Similarly, if we look at the actions involving B, we find that there are several reasons why $T_1 <_S T_2$. For instance, the action $r_1(B)$ comes before $w_2(B)$. Thus, the precedence graph for S also has an arc from 1 to 2. However, these are the only arcs we can justify from the order of actions in schedule S. □

To tell whether a schedule S is conflict-serializable, construct the precedence graph for S and ask if there are any cycles. If so, then S is not conflict-serializable. But if the graph is acyclic, then S is conflict-serializable, and moreover, any topological order of the nodes[1] is a conflict-equivalent serial order.

[1] A *topological order* of an acyclic graph is any order of the nodes such that for every arc $a \rightarrow b$, node a precedes node b in the topological order. We can find a topological order for any acyclic graph by repeatedly removing nodes that have no predecessors among the remaining nodes.

Example 8: Figure 9 is acyclic, so the schedule S of Example 7 is conflict-serializable. There is only one order of the nodes or transactions consistent with the arcs of that graph: (T_1, T_2, T_3). Notice that it is indeed possible to convert S into the schedule in which all actions of each of the three transactions occur in this order; this serial schedule is:

$$S'\text{: } r_1(B);\ w_1(B);\ r_2(A);\ w_2(A);\ r_2(B);\ w_2(B);\ r_3(A);\ w_3(A);$$

To see that we can get from S to S' by swaps of adjacent elements, first notice we can move $r_1(B)$ ahead of $r_2(A)$ without conflict. Then, by three swaps we can move $w_1(B)$ just after $r_1(B)$, because each of the intervening actions involves A and not B. We can then move $r_2(B)$ and $w_2(B)$ to a position just after $w_2(A)$, moving through only actions involving A; the result is S'. □

Example 9: Consider the schedule

$$S_1\text{: } r_2(A);\ r_1(B);\ w_2(A);\ r_2(B);\ r_3(A);\ w_1(B);\ w_3(A);\ w_2(B);$$

which differs from S only in that action $r_2(B)$ has been moved forward three positions. Examination of the actions involving A still give us only the precedence $T_2 <_{S_1} T_3$. However, when we examine B we get not only $T_1 <_{S_1} T_2$ [because $r_1(B)$ and $w_1(B)$ appear before $w_2(B)$], but also $T_2 <_{S_1} T_1$ [because $r_2(B)$ appears before $w_1(B)$]. Thus, we have the precedence graph of Fig. 10 for schedule S_1.

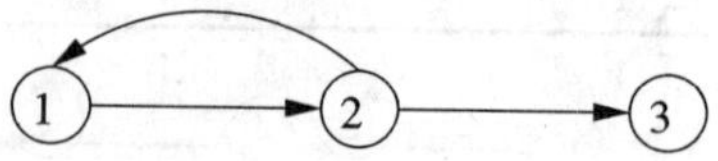

Figure 10: A cyclic precedence graph; its schedule is not conflict-serializable

This graph evidently has a cycle. We conclude that S_1 is not conflict-serializable. Intuitively, any conflict-equivalent serial schedule would have to have T_1 both ahead of and behind T_2, so therefore no such schedule exists. □

2.3 Why the Precedence-Graph Test Works

If there is a cycle involving n transactions $T_1 \rightarrow T_2 \rightarrow \ldots \rightarrow T_n \rightarrow T_1$, then in the hypothetical serial order, the actions of T_1 must precede those of T_2, which precede those of T_3, and so on, up to T_n. But the actions of T_n, which therefore come after those of T_1, are also required to precede those of T_1 because of the arc $T_n \rightarrow T_1$. Thus, if there is a cycle in the precedence graph, then the schedule is not conflict-serializable.

The converse is a bit harder. We must show that if the precedence graph has no cycles, then we can reorder the schedule's actions using legal swaps of adjacent actions, until the schedule becomes a serial schedule. If we can do so, then we have our proof that every schedule with an acyclic precedence graph is conflict-serializable. The proof is an induction on the number of transactions involved in the schedule.

BASIS: If $n = 1$, i.e., there is only one transaction in the schedule, then the schedule is already serial, and therefore surely conflict-serializable.

INDUCTION: Let the schedule S consist of the actions of n transactions

$$T_1, T_2, \ldots, T_n$$

We suppose that S has an acyclic precedence graph. If a finite graph is acyclic, then there is at least one node that has no arcs in; let the node i corresponding to transaction T_i be such a node. Since there are no arcs into node i, there can be no action A in S that:

1. Involves any transaction T_j other than T_i,
2. Precedes some action of T_i, and
3. Conflicts with that action.

For if there were, we should have put an arc from node j to node i in the precedence graph.

It is thus possible to swap all the actions of T_i, keeping them in order, but moving them to the front of S. The schedule has now taken the form

$$\text{(Actions of } T_i\text{)(Actions of the other } n-1 \text{ transactions)}$$

Let us now consider the tail of S — the actions of all transactions other than T_i. Since these actions maintain the same relative order that they did in S, the precedence graph for the tail is the same as the precedence graph for S, except that the node for T_i and any arcs out of that node are missing.

Since the original precedence graph was acyclic, and deleting nodes and arcs cannot make it cyclic, we conclude that the tail's precedence graph is acyclic. Moreover, since the tail involves $n-1$ transactions, the inductive hypothesis applies to it. Thus, we know we can reorder the actions of the tail using legal swaps of adjacent actions to turn it into a serial schedule. Now, S itself has been turned into a serial schedule, with the actions of T_i first and the actions of the other transactions following in some serial order. The induction is complete, and we conclude that every schedule with an acyclic precedence graph is conflict-serializable.

2.4 Exercises for Section 2

Exercise 2.1: Below are two transactions, described in terms of their effect on two database elements A and B, which we may assume are integers.

T_1: `READ(A,t); t:=t+2; WRITE(A,t); READ(B,t); t:=t*3; WRITE(B,t);`
T_2: `READ(B,s); s:=s*2; WRITE(B,s); READ(A,s); s:=s+3; WRITE(A,s);`

We assume that, whatever consistency constraints there are on the database, these transactions preserve them in isolation. Note that $A = B$ is *not* the consistency constraint.

a) It turns out that both serial orders have the same effect on the database; that is, (T_1, T_2) and (T_2, T_1) are equivalent. Demonstrate this fact by showing the effect of the two transactions on an arbitrary initial database state.

b) Give examples of a serializable schedule and a nonserializable schedule of the 12 actions above.

c) How many serial schedules of the 12 actions are there?

!! d) How many serializable schedules of the 12 actions are there?

Exercise 2.2: The two transactions of Exercise 2.1 can be written in our notation that shows read- and write-actions only, as:

$$T_1\colon\ r_1(A);\ w_1(A);\ r_1(B);\ w_1(B);$$
$$T_2\colon\ r_2(B);\ w_2(B);\ r_2(A);\ w_2(A);$$

Answer the following:

! a) Among the possible schedules of the eight actions above, how many are conflict-equivalent to the serial order (T_1, T_2)?

b) How many schedules of the eight actions are equivalent to the serial order (T_2, T_1)?

!! c) How many schedules of the eight actions are equivalent (not necessarily conflict-equivalent) to the serial schedule (T_1, T_2), assuming the transactions have the effect on the database described in Exercise 2.1?

! d) Why are the answers to (c) above and Exercise 2.1(d) different?

! **Exercise 2.3:** Suppose the transactions of Exercise 2.2 are changed to be:

$$T_1\colon\ r_1(A);\ w_1(A);\ r_1(B);\ w_1(B);$$
$$T_2\colon\ r_2(A);\ w_2(A);\ r_2(B);\ w_2(B);$$

That is, the transactions retain their semantics from Exercise 2.1, but T_2 has been changed so A is processed before B. Give:

a) The number of conflict-serializable schedules.

b) The number of serializable schedules, assuming the transactions have the same effect on the database state as in Exercise 2.1.

Exercise 2.4: For each of the following schedules:

a) $r_1(A); r_2(A); r_3(B); w_1(A); r_2(C); r_2(B); w_2(B); w_1(C);$

b) $r_1(A); w_1(B); r_2(B): w_2(C); r_3(C); w_3(A);$

c) $w_3(A); r_1(A); w_1(B); r_2(B): w_2(C); r_3(C);$

d) $r_1(A); r_2(A); w_1(B); w_2(B); r_1(B); r_2(B); w_2(C); w_1(D);$

e) $r_1(A); r_2(A); r_1(B); r_2(B); r_3(A); r_4(B); w_1(A); w_2(B);$

Answer the following questions:

i. What is the precedence graph for the schedule?

ii. Is the schedule conflict-serializable? If so, what are all the equivalent serial schedules?

! *iii.* Are there any serial schedules that must be equivalent (regardless of what the transactions do to the data), but are not conflict-equivalent?

!! **Exercise 2.5:** Say that a transaction T *precedes* a transaction U in a schedule S if every action of T precedes every action of U in S. Note that if T and U are the only transactions in S, then saying T precedes U is the same as saying that S is the serial schedule (T, U). However, if S involves transactions other than T and U, then S might not be serializable, and in fact, because of the effect of other transactions, S might not even be conflict-serializable. Give an example of a schedule S such that:

i. In S, T_1 precedes T_2, and

ii. S is conflict-serializable, but

iii. In every serial schedule conflict-equivalent to S, T_2 precedes T_1.

! **Exercise 2.6:** Explain how, for any $n > 1$, one can find a schedule whose precedence graph has a cycle of length n, but no smaller cycle.

3 Enforcing Serializability by Locks

In this section we consider the most common architecture for a scheduler, one in which "locks" are maintained on database elements to prevent unserializable behavior. Intuitively, a transaction obtains locks on the database elements it accesses to prevent other transactions from accessing these elements at roughly the same time and thereby incurring the risk of unserializability.

In this section, we introduce the concept of locking with an (overly) simple locking scheme. In this scheme, there is only one kind of lock, which transactions must obtain on a database element if they want to perform any operation whatsoever on that element. In Section 4, we shall learn more realistic locking schemes, with several kinds of lock, including the common shared/exclusive locks that correspond to the privileges of reading and writing, respectively.

3.1 Locks

In Fig. 11 we see a scheduler that uses a lock table to help perform its job. Recall from the chapter introduction that the responsibility of the scheduler is to take requests from transactions and either allow them to operate on the database or block the transaction until such time as it is safe to allow it to continue. A lock table will be used to guide this decision in a manner that we shall discuss at length.

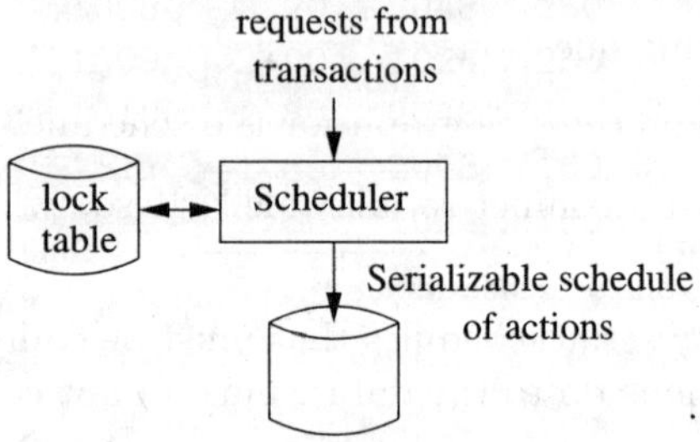

Figure 11: A scheduler that uses a lock table to guide decisions

Ideally, a scheduler would forward a request if and only if its execution cannot possibly lead to an inconsistent database state after all active transactions commit or abort. A locking scheduler, like most types of scheduler, instead enforces conflict-serializability, which as we learned is a more stringent condition than correctness, or even than serializability.

When a scheduler uses locks, transactions must request and release locks, in addition to reading and writing database elements. The use of locks must be proper in two senses, one applying to the structure of transactions, and the other to the structure of schedules.

- *Consistency of Transactions*: Actions and locks must relate in the expected ways:

  1. A transaction can only read or write an element if it previously was granted a lock on that element and hasn't yet released the lock.

  2. If a transaction locks an element, it must later unlock that element.

- *Legality of Schedules*: Locks must have their intended meaning: no two transactions may have locked the same element without one having first released the lock.

We shall extend our notation for actions to include locking and unlocking actions:

$l_i(X)$: Transaction T_i requests a lock on database element X.

$u_i(X)$: Transaction T_i releases ("unlocks") its lock on database element X.

Thus, the consistency condition for transactions can be stated as: "Whenever a transaction T_i has an action $r_i(X)$ or $w_i(X)$, then there is a previous action $l_i(X)$ with no intervening action $u_i(X)$, and there is a subsequent $u_i(X)$." The legality of schedules is stated: "If there are actions $l_i(X)$ followed by $l_j(X)$ in a schedule, then somewhere between these actions there must be an action $u_i(X)$."

Example 10: Let us consider the two transactions T_1 and T_2 that we introduced in Example 1. Recall that T_1 adds 100 to database elements A and B, while T_2 doubles them. Here are specifications for these transactions, in which we have included lock actions as well as arithmetic actions to help us remember what the transactions are doing.[2]

T_1: $l_1(A)$; $r_1(A)$; `A := A+100`; $w_1(A)$; $u_1(A)$; $l_1(B)$; $r_1(B)$; `B := B+100`; $w_1(B)$; $u_1(B)$;

T_2: $l_2(A)$; $r_2(A)$; `A := A*2`; $w_2(A)$; $u_2(A)$; $l_2(B)$; $r_2(B)$; `B := B*2`; $w_2(B)$; $u_2(B)$;

Each of these transactions is consistent. They each release the locks on A and B that they take. Moreover, they each operate on A and B only at steps where they have previously requested a lock on that element and have not yet released the lock.

T_1	T_2	A	B
		25	25
$l_1(A)$; $r_1(A)$;			
`A := A+100;`			
$w_1(A)$; $u_1(A)$;		125	
	$l_2(A)$; $r_2(A)$;		
	`A := A*2;`		
	$w_2(A)$; $u_2(A)$;	250	
	$l_2(B)$; $r_2(B)$;		
	`B := B*2;`		
	$w_2(B)$; $u_2(B)$;		50
$l_1(B)$; $r_1(B)$;			
`B := B+100;`			
$w_1(B)$; $u_1(B)$;			150

Figure 12: A legal schedule of consistent transactions; unfortunately it is not serializable

Figure 12 shows one legal schedule of these two transactions. To save space we have put several actions on one line. The schedule is legal because

[2]Remember that the actual computations of the transaction usually are not represented in our current notation, since they are not considered by the scheduler when deciding whether to grant or deny transaction requests.

the two transactions never hold a lock on A at the same time, and likewise for B. Specifically, T_2 does not execute $l_2(A)$ until after T_1 executes $u_1(A)$, and T_1 does not execute $l_1(B)$ until after T_2 executes $u_2(B)$. As we see from the trace of the values computed, the schedule, although legal, is not serializable. We shall see in Section 3.3 the additional condition, "two-phase locking," that we need to assure that legal schedules are conflict-serializable. □

3.2 The Locking Scheduler

It is the job of a scheduler based on locking to grant requests if and only if the request will result in a legal schedule. If a request is not granted, the requesting transaction is delayed; it waits until the scheduler grants its request at a later time. To aid its decisions, the scheduler has a *lock table* that tells, for every database element, the transaction (if any) that currently holds a lock on that element. We shall discuss the structure of a lock table in more detail in Section 5.2. However, when there is only one kind of lock, as we have assumed so far, the table may be thought of as a relation `Locks(element, transaction)`, consisting of pairs (X, T) such that transaction T currently has a lock on database element X. The scheduler has only to query and modify this relation.

Example 11: The schedule of Fig. 12 is legal, as we mentioned, so the locking scheduler would grant every request in the order of arrival shown. However, sometimes it is not possible to grant requests. Here are T_1 and T_2 from Example 10, with simple but important changes, in which T_1 and T_2 each lock B before releasing the lock on A.

T_1: $l_1(A)$; $r_1(A)$; `A := A+100`; $w_1(A)$; $l_1(B)$; $u_1(A)$; $r_1(B)$; `B := B+100`; $w_1(B)$; $u_1(B)$;

T_2: $l_2(A)$; $r_2(A)$; `A := A*2`; $w_2(A)$; $l_2(B)$; $u_2(A)$; $r_2(B)$; `B := B*2`; $w_2(B)$; $u_2(B)$;

In Fig. 13, when T_2 requests a lock on B, the scheduler must deny the lock, because T_1 still holds a lock on B. Thus, T_2 is delayed, and the next actions are from T_1. Eventually, T_1 executes $u_1(B)$, which unlocks B. Now, T_2 can get its lock on B, which is executed at the next step. Notice that because T_2 was forced to wait, it wound up multiplying B by 2 after T_1 added 100, resulting in a consistent database state. □

3.3 Two-Phase Locking

There is a surprising condition, called *two-phase locking* (or *2PL*) under which we can guarantee that a legal schedule of consistent transactions is conflict-serializable:

- In every transaction, all lock actions precede all unlock actions.

T_1	T_2	A	B
		25	25
$l_1(A)$; $r_1(A)$;			
`A := A+100;`			
$w_1(A)$; $l_1(B)$; $u_1(A)$;		125	
	$l_2(A)$; $r_2(A)$;		
	`A := A*2;`		
	$w_2(A)$;	250	
	$l_2(B)$ **Denied**		
$r_1(B)$; `B := B+100;`			
$w_1(B)$; $u_1(B)$;			125
	$l_2(B)$; $u_2(A)$; $r_2(B)$;		
	`B := B*2;`		
	$w_2(B)$; $u_2(B)$;		250

Figure 13: The locking scheduler delays requests that would result in an illegal schedule

The "two phases" referred to by 2PL are thus the first phase, where locks are obtained, and the second phase, where locks are relinquished. Two-phase locking is a condition, like consistency, on the order of actions in a transaction. A transaction that obeys the 2PL condition is said to be a *two-phase-locked transaction*, or 2PL transaction.

Example 12: In Example 10, the transactions do not obey the two-phase locking rule. For instance, T_1 unlocks A before it locks B. However, the versions of the transactions found in Example 11 *do* obey the 2PL condition. Notice that T_1 locks both A and B within the first five actions and unlocks them within the next five actions; T_2 behaves similarly. If we compare Figs. 12 and 13, we see how the 2PL transactions interact properly with the scheduler to assure consistency, while the non-2PL transactions allow non-conflict-serializable behavior. □

3.4 Why Two-Phase Locking Works

Intuitively, each two-phase-locked transaction may be thought to execute in its entirety at the instant it issues its first unlock request, as suggested by Fig. 14. Thus, there is always at least one conflict-equivalent serial schedule for a schedule S of 2PL transactions: the one in which the transactions appear in the same order as their first unlocks.

We shall show how to convert any legal schedule S of consistent, two-phase-locked transactions to a conflict-equivalent serial schedule. The conversion is best described as an induction on n, the number of transactions in S. In what follows, it is important to remember that the issue of conflict-equivalence refers

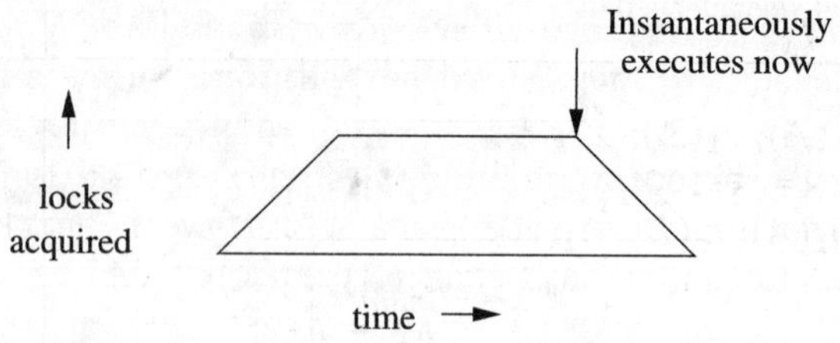

Figure 14: Every two-phase-locked transaction has a point at which it may be thought to execute instantaneously

to the read and write actions only. As we swap the order of reads and writes, we ignore the lock and unlock actions. Once we have the read and write actions ordered serially, we can place the lock and unlock actions around them as the various transactions require. Since each transaction releases all locks before its end, we know that the serial schedule is legal.

BASIS: If $n = 1$, there is nothing to do; S is already a serial schedule.

INDUCTION: Suppose S involves n transactions $T_1, T_2, \ldots, T_n$, and let T_i be the transaction with the first unlock action in the entire schedule S, say $u_i(X)$. We claim it is possible to move all the read and write actions of T_i forward to the beginning of the schedule without passing any conflicting reads or writes.

Consider some action of T_i, say $w_i(Y)$. Could it be preceded in S by some conflicting action, say $w_j(Y)$? If so, then in schedule S, actions $u_j(Y)$ and $l_i(Y)$ must intervene, in a sequence of actions

$$\cdots w_j(Y); \cdots ;\ u_j(Y); \cdots ;\ l_i(Y); \cdots ;\ w_i(Y); \cdots$$

Since T_i is the first to unlock, $u_i(X)$ precedes $u_j(Y)$ in S; that is, S might look like:

$$\cdots ;\ w_j(Y); \cdots ;\ u_i(X); \cdots ;\ u_j(Y); \cdots ;\ l_i(Y); \cdots ;\ w_i(Y); \cdots$$

or $u_i(X)$ could even appear before $w_j(Y)$. In any case, $u_i(X)$ appears before $l_i(Y)$, which means that T_i is *not* two-phase-locked, as we assumed. While we have only argued the nonexistence of conflicting pairs of writes, the same argument applies to any pair of potentially conflicting actions, one from T_i and the other from another T_j.

We conclude that it is indeed possible to move all the actions of T_i forward to the beginning of S, using swaps of nonconflicting read and write actions, followed by restoration of the lock and unlock actions of T_i. That is, S can be written in the form

$$\text{(Actions of } T_i\text{)(Actions of the other } n-1 \text{ transactions)}$$

The tail of $n-1$ transactions is still a legal schedule of consistent, 2PL transactions, so the inductive hypothesis applies to it. We convert the tail to a

A Risk of Deadlock

One problem that is not solved by two-phase locking is the potential for deadlocks, where several transactions are forced by the scheduler to wait forever for a lock held by another transaction. For instance, consider the 2PL transactions from Example 11, but with T_2 changed to work on B first:

T_1: $l_1(A)$; $r_1(A)$; `A := A+100`; $w_1(A)$; $l_1(B)$; $u_1(A)$; $r_1(B)$; `B := B+100`; $w_1(B)$; $u_1(B)$;

T_2: $l_2(B)$; $r_2(B)$; `B := B*2`; $w_2(B)$; $l_2(A)$; $u_2(B)$; $r_2(A)$; `A := A*2`; $w_2(A)$; $u_2(A)$;

A possible interleaving of the actions of these transactions is:

T_1	T_2	A	B
		25	25
$l_1(A)$; $r_1(A)$;			
	$l_2(B)$; $r_2(B)$;		
`A := A+100;`			
	`B := B*2;`		
$w_1(A)$;		125	
	$w_2(B)$;		50
$l_1(B)$ **Denied**	$l_2(A)$ **Denied**		

Now, neither transaction can proceed, and they wait forever. Observe that it is not possible to allow both transactions to proceed, since if we do so the final database state cannot possibly have $A = B$.

conflict-equivalent serial schedule, and now all of S has been shown conflict-serializable.

3.5 Exercises for Section 3

Exercise 3.1: Below are two transactions, with lock requests and the semantics of the transactions indicated. Recall from Exercise 2.1 that these transactions have the unusual property that they can be scheduled in ways that are not conflict-serializable, but, because of the semantics, are serializable.

T_1: $l_1(A)$; $r_1(A)$; `A := A+2`; $w_1(A)$; $u_1(A)$; $l_1(B)$; $r_1(B)$; `B := B*3`; $w_1(B)$; $u_1(B)$;

T_2: $l_2(B)$; $r_2(B)$; B := B*2; $w_2(B)$; $u_2(B)$; $l_2(A)$; $r_2(A)$; A := A+3; $w_2(A)$; $u_2(A)$;

In the questions below, consider only schedules of the read and write actions, not the lock, unlock, or assignment steps.

a) Give an example of a schedule that is prohibited by the locks.

! b) Of the $\binom{8}{4} = 70$ orders of the eight read and write actions, how many are legal schedules (i.e., they are permitted by the locks)?

! c) Of the legal schedules, how many are serializable (according to the semantics of the transactions given)?

! d) Of those schedules that are legal and serializable, how many are conflict-serializable?

!! e) Since T_1 and T_2 are not two-phase-locked, we would expect that some nonserializable behaviors would occur. Are there any legal schedules that are unserializable? If so, give an example, and if not, explain why.

! **Exercise 3.2:** Here are the transactions of Exercise 3.1, with all unlocks moved to the end so they are two-phase-locked.

T_1: $l_1(A)$; $r_1(A)$; A := A+2; $w_1(A)$; $l_1(B)$; $r_1(B)$; B := B*3; $w_1(B)$; $u_1(A)$; $u_1(B)$;

T_2: $l_2(B)$; $r_2(B)$; B := B*2; $w_2(B)$; $l_2(A)$; $r_2(A)$; A := A+3; $w_2(A)$; $u_2(B)$; $u_2(A)$;

How many legal schedules of all the read and write actions of these transactions are there?

Exercise 3.3: For each of the schedules of Exercise 2.4, assume that each transaction takes a lock on each database element immediately before it reads or writes the element, and that each transaction releases its locks immediately after the last time it accesses an element. Tell what the locking scheduler would do with each of these schedules; i.e., what requests would get delayed, and when would they be allowed to resume?

! **Exercise 3.4:** For each of the transactions described below, suppose that we insert one lock and one unlock action for each database element that is accessed.

a) $r_1(A)$; $w_1(B)$;

b) $r_2(A)$; $w_2(A)$; $w_2(B)$;

Tell how many orders of the lock, unlock, read, and write actions are:

i. Consistent and two-phase locked.

ii. Consistent, but not two-phase locked.

iii. Inconsistent, but two-phase locked.

iv. Neither consistent nor two-phase locked.

4 Locking Systems With Several Lock Modes

The locking scheme of Section 3 illustrates the important ideas behind locking, but it is too simple to be a practical scheme. The main problem is that a transaction T must take a lock on a database element X even if it only wants to read X and not write it. We cannot avoid taking the lock, because if we didn't, then another transaction might write a new value for X while T was active and cause unserializable behavior. On the other hand, there is no reason why several transactions could not read X at the same time, as long as none is allowed to write X.

We are thus motivated to introduce the most common locking scheme, where there are two different kinds of locks, one for reading (called a "shared lock" or "read lock"), and one for writing (called an "exclusive lock" or "write lock"). We then examine an improved scheme where transactions are allowed to take a shared lock and "upgrade" it to an exclusive lock later. We also consider "increment locks," which treat specially write actions that increment a database element; the important distinction is that increment operations commute, while general writes do not. These examples lead us to the general notion of a lock scheme described by a "compatibility matrix" that indicates what locks on a database element may be granted when other locks are held.

4.1 Shared and Exclusive Locks

The lock we need for writing is "stronger" than the lock we need to read, since it must prevent both reads and writes. Let us therefore consider a locking scheduler that uses two different kinds of locks: *shared locks* and *exclusive locks.* For any database element X there can be either one exclusive lock on X, or no exclusive locks but any number of shared locks. If we want to write X, we need to have an exclusive lock on X, but if we wish only to read X we may have either a shared or exclusive lock on X. If we want to read X but not write it, it is better to take only a shared lock.

We shall use $sl_i(X)$ to mean "transaction T_i requests a shared lock on database element X" and $xl_i(X)$ for "T_i requests an exclusive lock on X." We continue to use $u_i(X)$ to mean that T_i unlocks X; i.e., it relinquishes whatever lock(s) it has on X.

The three kinds of requirements — consistency and 2PL for transactions, and legality for schedules — each have their counterpart for a shared/exclusive lock system. We summarize these requirements here:

1. *Consistency of transactions*: A transaction may not write without holding an exclusive lock, and you may not read without holding some lock. More precisely, in any transaction T_i,

   (a) A read action $r_i(X)$ must be preceded by $sl_i(X)$ or $xl_i(X)$, with no intervening $u_i(X)$.

   (b) A write action $w_i(X)$ must be preceded by $xl_i(X)$, with no intervening $u_i(X)$.

   All locks must be followed by an unlock of the same element.

2. *Two-phase locking of transactions*: Locking must precede unlocking. To be more precise, in any two-phase locked transaction T_i, no action $sl_i(X)$ or $xl_i(X)$ can be preceded by an action $u_i(Y)$, for any Y.

3. *Legality of schedules*: An element may either be locked exclusively by one transaction or by several in shared mode, but not both. More precisely:

   (a) If $xl_i(X)$ appears in a schedule, then there cannot be a following $xl_j(X)$ or $sl_j(X)$, for some j other than i, without an intervening $u_i(X)$.

   (b) If $sl_i(X)$ appears in a schedule, then there cannot be a following $xl_j(X)$, for $j \neq i$, without an intervening $u_i(X)$.

   Note that we *do* allow one transaction to request and hold both shared and exclusive locks on the same element, provided its doing so does not conflict with the lock(s) of other transactions. If transactions know in advance their needs for locks, then only the exclusive lock would have to be requested, but if lock needs are unpredictable, then it is possible that one transaction would request both shared and exclusive locks at different times.

Example 13: Let us examine a possible schedule of the following two transactions, using shared and exclusive locks:

$$T_1\text{: } sl_1(A);\ r_1(A);\ xl_1(B);\ r_1(B);\ w_1(B);\ u_1(A);\ u_1(B);$$
$$T_2\text{: } sl_2(A);\ r_2(A);\ sl_2(B);\ r_2(B);\ u_2(A);\ u_2(B);$$

Both T_1 and T_2 read A and B, but only T_1 writes B. Neither writes A.

In Fig. 15 is an interleaving of the actions of T_1 and T_2 in which T_1 begins by getting a shared lock on A. Then, T_2 follows by getting shared locks on both A and B. Now, T_1 needs an exclusive lock on B, since it will both read and write B. However, it cannot get the exclusive lock because T_2 already has a shared lock on B. Thus, the scheduler forces T_1 to wait. Eventually, T_2 releases the lock on B. At that time, T_1 may complete. □

T_1	T_2
$sl_1(A);\ r_1(A);$	
	$sl_2(A);\ r_2(A);$
	$sl_2(B);\ r_2(B);$
$xl_1(B)$ **Denied**	
	$u_2(A);\ u_2(B)$
$xl_1(B);\ r_1(B);\ w_1(B);$	
$u_1(A);\ u_1(B);$	

Figure 15: A schedule using shared and exclusive locks

Notice that the resulting schedule in Fig 15 is conflict-serializable. The conflict-equivalent serial order is (T_2, T_1), even though T_1 started first. The argument we gave in Section 3.4 to show that legal schedules of consistent, 2PL transactions are conflict-serializable applies to systems with shared and exclusive locks as well. In Fig. 15, T_2 unlocks before T_1, so we would expect T_2 to precede T_1 in the serial order.

4.2 Compatibility Matrices

If we use several lock modes, then the scheduler needs a policy about when it can grant a lock request, given the other locks that may already be held on the same database element. A *compatibility matrix* is a convenient way to describe lock-management policies. It has a row and column for each lock mode. The rows correspond to a lock that is already held on an element X by another transaction, and the columns correspond to the mode of a lock on X that is requested. The rule for using a compatibility matrix for lock-granting decisions is:

- We can grant the lock on X in mode C if and only if for every row R such that there is already a lock on X in mode R by some other transaction, there is a "Yes" in column C.

		Lock requested	
		S	X
Lock held	S	Yes	No
in mode	X	No	No

Figure 16: The compatibility matrix for shared and exclusive locks

Example 14: Figure 16 is the compatibility matrix for shared (S) and exclusive (X) locks. The column for S says that we can grant a shared lock on an element if the only locks held on that element currently are shared locks. The column for X says that we can grant an exclusive lock only if there are no other locks held currently. □

4.3 Upgrading Locks

A transaction T that takes a shared lock on X is being "friendly" toward other transactions, since they are allowed to read X at the same time T is. Thus, we might wonder whether it would be friendlier still if a transaction T that wants to read and write a new value of X were first to take a shared lock on X, and only later, when T was ready to write the new value, *upgrade* the lock to exclusive (i.e., request an exclusive lock on X in addition to its already held shared lock on X). There is nothing that prevents a transaction from issuing requests for locks on the same database element in different modes. We adopt the convention that $u_i(X)$ releases all locks on X held by transaction T_i, although we could introduce mode-specific unlock actions if there were a use for them.

Example 15: In the following example, transaction T_1 is able to perform its computation concurrently with T_2, which would not be possible had T_1 taken an exclusive lock on B initially. The two transactions are:

$$T_1\text{: } sl_1(A);\ r_1(A);\ sl_1(B);\ r_1(B);\ xl_1(B);\ w_1(B);\ u_1(A);\ u_1(B);$$
$$T_2\text{: } sl_2(A);\ r_2(A);\ sl_2(B);\ r_2(B);\ u_2(A);\ u_2(B);$$

Here, T_1 reads A and B and performs some (possibly lengthy) calculation with them, eventually using the result to write a new value of B. Notice that T_1 takes a shared lock on B first, and later, after its calculation involving A and B is finished, requests an exclusive lock on B. Transaction T_2 only reads A and B, and does not write.

T_1	T_2
$sl_1(A);\ r_1(A);$	
	$sl_2(A);\ r_2(A);$
	$sl_2(B);\ r_2(B);$
$sl_1(B);\ r_1(B);$	
$xl_1(B)$ **Denied**	
	$u_2(A);\ u_2(B)$
$xl_1(B);\ w_1(B);$	
$u_1(A);\ u_2(B);$	

Figure 17: Upgrading locks allows more concurrent operation

Figure 17 shows a possible schedule of actions. T_2 gets a shared lock on B before T_1 does, but on the fourth line, T_1 is also able to lock B in shared mode.

Thus, T_1 has both A and B and can perform its computation using their values. It is not until T_1 tries to upgrade its lock on B to exclusive that the scheduler must deny the request and force T_1 to wait until T_2 releases its lock on B. At that time, T_1 gets its exclusive lock on B, writes B, and finishes.

Notice that had T_1 asked for an exclusive lock on B initially, before reading B, then the request would have been denied, because T_2 already had a shared lock on B. T_1 could not perform its computation without reading B, and so T_1 would have more to do after T_2 releases its locks. As a result, T_1 finishes later using only an exclusive lock on B than it would if it used the upgrading strategy. □

Example 16 : Unfortunately, indiscriminate use of upgrading introduces a new and potentially serious source of deadlocks. Suppose, that T_1 and T_2 each read database element A and write a new value for A. If both transactions use an upgrading approach, first getting a shared lock on A and then upgrading it to exclusive, the sequence of events suggested in Fig. 18 will happen whenever T_1 and T_2 initiate at approximately the same time.

T_1	T_2
$sl_1(A)$	
	$sl_2(A)$
$xl_1(A)$ **Denied**	
	$xl_2(A)$ **Denied**

Figure 18: Upgrading by two transactions can cause a deadlock

T_1 and T_2 are both able to get shared locks on A. Then, they each try to upgrade to exclusive, but the scheduler forces each to wait because the other has a shared lock on A. Thus, neither can make progress, and they will each wait forever, or until the system discovers that there is a deadlock, aborts one of the two transactions, and gives the other the exclusive lock on A. □

4.4 Update Locks

We can avoid the deadlock problem of Example 16 with a third lock mode, called *update locks.* An update lock $ul_i(X)$ gives transaction T_i only the privilege to read X, not to write X. However, only the update lock can be upgraded to a write lock later; a read lock cannot be upgraded. We can grant an update lock on X when there are already shared locks on X, but once there is an update lock on X we prevent additional locks of any kind — shared, update, or exclusive — from being taken on X. The reason is that if we don't deny such locks, then the updater might never get a chance to upgrade to exclusive, since there would always be other locks on X.

This rule leads to an asymmetric compatibility matrix, because the update (U) lock looks like a shared lock when we are requesting it and looks like an exclusive lock when we already have it. Thus, the columns for U and S locks are the same, and the rows for U and X locks are the same. The matrix is shown in Fig. 19.[3]

	S	X	U
S	Yes	No	Yes
X	No	No	No
U	No	No	No

Figure 19: Compatibility matrix for shared, exclusive, and update locks

Example 17: The use of update locks would have no effect on Example 15. As its third action, T_1 would take an update lock on B, rather than a shared lock. But the update lock would be granted, since only shared locks are held on B, and the same sequence of actions shown in Fig. 17 would occur.

However, update locks fix the problem shown in Example 16. Now, both T_1 and T_2 first request update locks on A and only later take exclusive locks. Possible descriptions of T_1 and T_2 are:

$$T_1\text{: } ul_1(A);\ r_1(A);\ xl_1(A);\ w_1(A);\ u_1(A);$$
$$T_2\text{: } ul_2(A);\ r_2(A);\ xl_2(A);\ w_2(A);\ u_2(A);$$

The sequence of events corresponding to Fig. 18 is shown in Fig. 20. Now, T_2, the second to request an update lock on A, is denied. T_1 is allowed to finish, and then T_2 may proceed. The lock system has effectively prevented concurrent execution of T_1 and T_2, but in this example, any significant amount of concurrent execution will result in either a deadlock or an inconsistent database state. □

T_1	T_2
$ul_1(A);\ r_1(A);$	
	$ul_2(A)$ **Denied**
$xl_1(A);\ w_1(A);\ u_1(A);$	
	$ul_2(A);\ r_2(A);$
	$xl_2(A);\ w_2(A);\ u_2(A);$

Figure 20: Correct execution using update locks

[3]Remember, however, that there is an additional condition regarding legality of schedules that is not reflected by this matrix: a transaction holding a shared lock but not an update lock on an element X cannot be given an exclusive lock on X, even though we do not in general prohibit a transaction from holding multiple locks on an element.

4.5 Increment Locks

Another interesting kind of lock that is useful in some situations is an "increment lock." Many transactions operate on the database only by incrementing or decrementing stored values. For example, consider a transaction that transfers money from one bank account to another.

The useful property of increment actions is that they commute with each other, since if two transactions add constants to the same database element, it does not matter which goes first, as the diagram of database state transitions in Fig. 21 suggests. On the other hand, incrementation commutes with neither reading nor writing; If you read A before or after it is incremented, you leave different values, and if you increment A before or after some other transaction writes a new value for A, you get different values of A in the database.

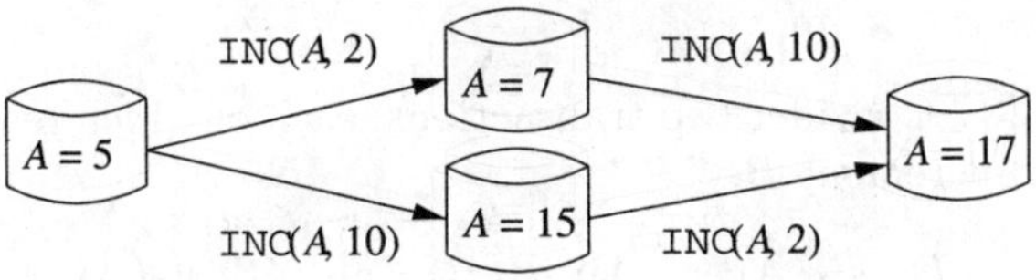

Figure 21: Two increment actions commute, since the final database state does not depend on which went first

Let us introduce as a possible action in transactions the *increment* action, written `INC(A,c)`. Informally, this action adds constant c to database element A, which we assume is a single number. Note that c could be negative, in which case we are really decrementing A. In practice, we might apply `INC` to a component of a tuple, while the tuple itself, rather than one of its components, is the lockable element. More formally, we use `INC(A,c)` to stand for the atomic execution of the following steps: `READ(A,t); t := t+c; WRITE(A,t);`.

Corresponding to the increment action, we need an *increment lock.* We shall denote the action of T_i requesting an increment lock on X by $il_i(X)$. We also use shorthand $inc_i(X)$ for the action in which transaction T_i increments database element X by some constant; the exact constant doesn't matter.

The existence of increment actions and locks requires us to make several modifications to our definitions of consistent transactions, conflicts, and legal schedules. These changes are:

a) A consistent transaction can only have an increment action on X if it holds an increment lock on X at the time. An increment lock does not enable either read or write actions, however.

b) In a legal schedule, any number of transactions can hold an increment lock on X at any time. However, if an increment lock on X is held by some transaction, then no other transaction can hold either a shared or exclusive lock on X at the same time. These requirements are expressed by the compatibility matrix of Fig. 22, where I represents a lock in increment mode.

c) The action $inc_i(X)$ conflicts with both $r_j(X)$ and $w_j(X)$, for $j \neq i$, but does not conflict with $inc_j(X)$.

	S	X	I
S	Yes	No	No
X	No	No	No
I	No	No	Yes

Figure 22: Compatibility matrix for shared, exclusive, and increment locks

Example 18: Consider two transactions, each of which read database element A and then increment B.

$$T_1\text{: } sl_1(A);\ r_1(A);\ il_1(B);\ inc_1(B);\ u_1(A);\ u_1(B);$$
$$T_2\text{: } sl_2(A);\ r_2(A);\ il_2(B);\ inc_2(B);\ u_2(A);\ u_2(B);$$

Notice that the transactions are consistent, since they only perform an incrementation while they have an increment lock, and they only read while they have a shared lock. Figure 23 shows a possible interleaving of T_1 and T_2. T_1 reads A first, but then T_2 both reads A and increments B. However, T_1 is then allowed to get its increment lock on B and proceed.

T_1	T_2
$sl_1(A);\ r_1(A);$	
	$sl_2(A);\ r_2(A);$
	$il_2(B);\ inc_2(B);$
$il_1(B);\ inc_1(B);$	
	$u_2(A);\ u_2(B);$
$u_1(A);\ u_1(B);$	

Figure 23: A schedule of transactions with increment actions and locks

Notice that the scheduler did not have to delay any requests in Fig. 23. Suppose, for instance, that T_1 increments B by A, and T_2 increments B by $2A$. They can execute in either order, since the value of A does not change, and the incrementations may also be performed in either order.

Put another way, we may look at the sequence of non-lock actions in the schedule of Fig. 23; they are:

$$S\text{: } r_1(A);\ r_2(A);\ inc_2(B);\ inc_1(B);$$

We may move the last action, $inc_1(B)$, to the second position, since it does not conflict with another increment of the same element, and surely does not conflict with a read of a different element. This sequence of swaps shows that S is conflict-equivalent to the serial schedule $r_1(A)$; $inc_1(B)$; $r_2(A)$; $inc_2(B)$;. Similarly, we can move the first action, $r_1(A)$ to the third position by swaps, giving a serial schedule in which T_2 precedes T_1. □

4.6 Exercises for Section 4

Exercise 4.1: For each of the schedules of transactions T_1, T_2, and T_3 below:

a) $r_1(A)$; $r_2(B)$; $r_3(C)$; $w_1(B)$; $w_2(C)$; $w_3(D)$;

b) $r_1(A)$; $r_2(B)$; $r_3(C)$; $w_1(B)$; $w_2(C)$; $w_3(A)$;

c) $r_1(A)$; $r_2(B)$; $r_3(C)$; $r_1(B)$; $r_2(C)$; $r_3(D)$; $w_1(C)$; $w_2(D)$; $w_3(E)$;

d) $r_1(A)$; $r_2(B)$; $r_3(C)$; $r_1(B)$; $r_2(C)$; $r_3(D)$; $w_1(A)$; $w_2(B)$; $w_3(C)$;

e) $r_1(A)$; $r_2(B)$; $r_3(C)$; $r_1(B)$; $r_2(C)$; $r_3(A)$; $w_1(A)$; $w_2(B)$; $w_3(C)$;

do each of the following:

i. Insert shared and exclusive locks, and insert unlock actions. Place a shared lock immediately in front of each read action that is not followed by a write action of the same element by the same transaction. Place an exclusive lock in front of every other read or write action. Place the necessary unlocks at the end of every transaction.

ii. Tell what happens when each schedule is run by a scheduler that supports shared and exclusive locks.

iii. Insert shared and exclusive locks in a way that allows upgrading. Place a shared lock in front of every read, an exclusive lock in front of every write, and place the necessary unlocks at the ends of the transactions.

iv. Tell what happens when each schedule from (*iii*) is run by a scheduler that supports shared locks, exclusive locks, and upgrading.

v. Insert shared, exclusive, and update locks, along with unlock actions. Place a shared lock in front of every read action that is not going to be upgraded, place an update lock in front of every read action that will be upgraded, and place an exclusive lock in front of every write action. Place unlocks at the ends of transactions, as usual.

vi. Tell what happens when each schedule from (*v*) is run by a scheduler that supports shared, exclusive, and update locks.

! **Exercise 4.2:** Consider the two transactions:

$$T_1\text{: } r_1(A);\ r_1(B);\ inc_1(A);\ inc_1(B);$$
$$T_2\text{: } r_2(A);\ r_2(B);\ inc_2(A);\ inc_2(B);$$

Answer the following:

a) How many interleavings of these transactions are serializable?

b) If the order of incrementation in T_2 were reversed [i.e., $inc_2(B)$ followed by $inc_2(A)$], how many serializable interleavings would there be?

Exercise 4.3: For each of the following schedules, insert appropriate locks (read, write, or increment) before each action, and unlocks at the ends of transactions. Then tell what happens when the schedule is run by a scheduler that supports these three types of locks.

a) $r_1(A);\ r_2(B);\ inc_1(B);\ inc_2(C);\ w_1(C);\ w_2(D);$

b) $r_1(A);\ r_2(B);\ inc_1(B);\ inc_2(A);\ w_1(C);\ w_2(D);$

c) $inc_1(A);\ inc_2(B);\ inc_1(B);\ inc_2(C);\ w_1(C);\ w_2(D);$

Exercise 4.4: In Exercise 1.1, we discussed a hypothetical transaction involving an airline reservation. If the transaction manager had available to it shared, exclusive, update, and increment locks, what lock would you recommend for each of the steps of the transaction?

Exercise 4.5: The action of multiplication by a constant factor can be modeled by an action of its own. Suppose `MC(X,c)` stands for an atomic execution of the steps `READ(X,t); t := c*t; WRITE(X,t);`. We can also introduce a lock mode that allows only multiplication by a constant factor.

a) Show the compatibility matrix for read, write, and multiplication-by-a-constant locks.

! b) Show the compatibility matrix for read, write, incrementation, and multiplication-by-a-constant locks.

! **Exercise 4.6:** Suppose for sake of argument that database elements are two-dimensional vectors. There are four operations we can perform on vectors, and each will have its own type of lock.

i. Change the value along the x-axis (an X-lock).

ii. Change the value along the y-axis (a Y-lock).

iii. Change the angle of the vector (an A-lock).

iv. Change the magnitude of the vector (an M-lock).

Answer the following questions.

a) Which pairs of operations commute? For example, if we rotate the vector so its angle is 120° and then change the x-coordinate to be 10, is that the same as first changing the x-coordinate to 10 and then changing the angle to 120°?

b) Based on your answer to (a), what is the compatibility matrix for the four types of locks?

!! c) Suppose we changed the four operations so that instead of giving new values for a measure, the operations incremented the measure (e.g., "add 10 to the x-coordinate," or "rotate the vector 30° clockwise"). What would the compatibility matrix then be?

! **Exercise 4.7:** Here is a schedule with one action missing:

$$r_1(A);\ r_2(B);\ ???;\ w_1(C);\ w_2(A);$$

Your problem is to figure out what actions of certain types could replace the ??? and make the schedule not be serializable. Tell all possible nonserializable replacements for each of the following types of action: (a) Read (b) Write (c) Update (d) Increment.

5 An Architecture for a Locking Scheduler

Having seen a number of different locking schemes, we next consider how a scheduler that uses one of these schemes operates. We shall consider here only a simple scheduler architecture based on several principles:

1. The transactions themselves do not request locks, or cannot be relied upon to do so. It is the job of the scheduler to insert lock actions into the stream of reads, writes, and other actions that access data.

2. Transactions do not release locks. Rather, the scheduler releases the locks when the transaction manager tells it that the transaction will commit or abort.

5.1 A Scheduler That Inserts Lock Actions

Figure 24 shows a two-part scheduler that accepts requests such as read, write, commit, and abort, from transactions. The scheduler maintains a lock table, which, although it is shown as secondary-storage data, may be partially or completely in main memory. Normally, the main memory used by the lock table is not part of the buffer pool that is used for query execution and logging. Rather, the lock table is just another component of the DBMS, and will be

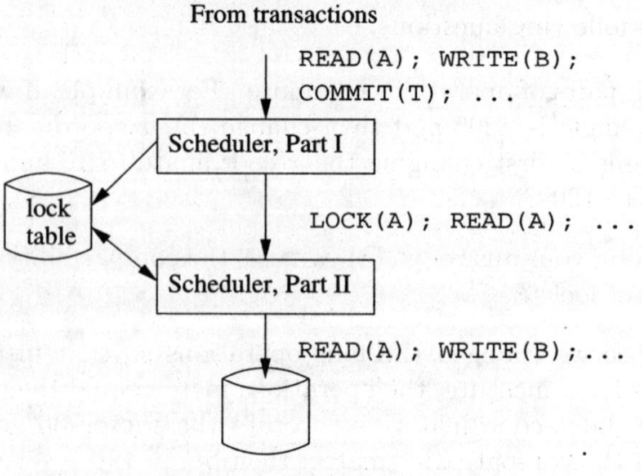

Figure 24: A scheduler that inserts lock requests into the transactions' request stream

allocated space by the operating system like other code and internal data of the DBMS.

Actions requested by a transaction are generally transmitted through the scheduler and executed on the database. However, under some circumstances a transaction is *delayed*, waiting for a lock, and its requests are not (yet) transmitted to the database. The two parts of the scheduler perform the following actions:

1. Part I takes the stream of requests generated by the transactions and inserts appropriate lock actions ahead of all database-access operations, such as read, write, increment, or update. The database access actions are then transmitted to Part II. Part I of the scheduler must select an appropriate lock mode from whatever set of lock modes the scheduler is using.

2. Part II takes the sequence of lock and database-access actions passed to it by Part I, and executes each appropriately. If a lock or database-access request is received by Part II, it determines whether the issuing transaction T is already delayed, because a lock has not been granted. If so, then the action is itself delayed and added to a list of actions that must eventually be performed for transaction T. If T is *not* delayed (i.e., all locks it previously requested have been granted already), then

   (a) If the action is a database access, it is transmitted to the database and executed.

   (b) If a lock action is received by Part II, it examines the lock table to see if the lock can be granted.

      i. If so, the lock table is modified to include the lock just granted.

   ii. If not, then an entry must be made in the lock table to indicate that the lock has been requested. Part II of the scheduler then delays transaction T until such time as the lock is granted.

3. When a transaction T commits or aborts, Part I is notified by the transaction manager, and releases all locks held by T. If any transactions are waiting for any of these locks, Part I notifies Part II.

4. When Part II is notified that a lock on some database element X is available, it determines the next transaction or transactions that can now be given a lock on X. The transaction(s) that receive a lock are allowed to execute as many of their delayed actions as can execute, until they either complete or reach another lock request that cannot be granted.

Example 19: If there is only one kind of lock, as in Section 3, then the task of Part I of the scheduler is simple. If it sees any action on database element X, and it has not already inserted a lock request on X for that transaction, then it inserts the request. When a transaction commits or aborts, Part I can forget about that transaction after releasing its locks, so the memory required for Part I does not grow indefinitely.

When there are several kinds of locks, the scheduler may require advance notice of what future actions on the same database element will occur. Let us reconsider the case of shared-exclusive-update locks, using the transactions of Example 15, which we now write without any locks at all:

$$T_1\text{: } r_1(A);\ r_1(B);\ w_1(B);$$
$$T_2\text{: } r_2(A);\ r_2(B);$$

The messages sent to Part I of the scheduler must include not only the read or write request, but an indication of future actions on the same element. In particular, when $r_1(B)$ is sent, the scheduler needs to know that there will be a later $w_1(B)$ action (or might be such an action). There are several ways the information might be made available. For example, if the transaction is a query, we know it will not write anything. If the transaction is a SQL database modification command, then the query processor can determine in advance the database elements that might be both read and written. If the transaction is a program with embedded SQL, then the compiler has access to all the SQL statements (which are the only ones that can access the database) and can determine the potential database elements written.

In our example, suppose that events occur in the order suggested by Fig. 17. Then T_1 first issues $r_1(A)$. Since there will be no future upgrading of this lock, the scheduler inserts $sl_1(A)$ ahead of $r_1(A)$. Next, the requests from T_2 — $r_2(A)$ and $r_2(B)$ — arrive at the scheduler. Again there is no future upgrade, so the sequence of actions $sl_2(A)$; $r_2(A)$; $sl_2(B)$; $r_2(B)$ are issued by Part I.

Then, the action $r_1(B)$ arrives at the scheduler, along with a warning that this lock may be upgraded. The scheduler Part I thus emits $ul_1(B)$; $r_1(B)$ to

Part II. The latter consults the lock table and finds that it can grant the update lock on B to T_1, because there are only shared locks on B.

When the action $w_1(B)$ arrives at the scheduler, Part I emits $xl_1(B); w_1(B)$. However, Part II cannot grant the $xl_1(B)$ request, because there is a shared lock on B for T_2. This and any subsequent actions from T_1 are delayed, stored by Part II for future execution. Eventually, T_2 commits, and Part I releases the locks on A and B that T_2 held. At that time, it is found that T_1 is waiting for a lock on B. Part II of the scheduler is notified, and it finds the lock $xl_1(B)$ is now available. It enters this lock into the lock table and proceeds to execute stored actions from T_1 to the extent possible. In this case, T_1 completes. □

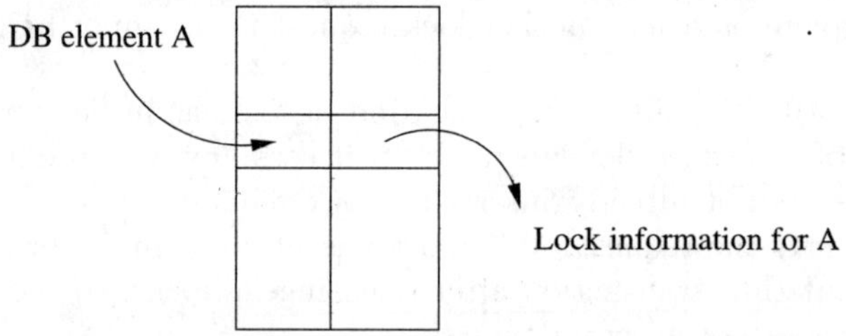

Figure 25: A lock table is a mapping from database elements to their lock information

5.2 The Lock Table

Abstractly, the lock table is a relation that associates database elements with locking information about that element, as suggested by Fig. 25. The table might, for instance, be implemented with a hash table, using (addresses of) database elements as the hash key. Any element that is not locked does not appear in the table, so the size is proportional to the number of locked elements only, not to the size of the entire database.

In Fig. 26 is an example of the sort of information we would find in a lock-table entry. This example structure assumes that the shared-exclusive-update lock scheme of Section 4.4 is used by the scheduler. The entry shown for a typical database element A is a tuple with the following components:

1. The *group mode* is a summary of the most stringent conditions that a transaction requesting a new lock on A faces. Rather than comparing the lock request with every lock held by another transaction on the same element, we can simplify the grant/deny decision by comparing the request with only the group mode.[4] For the shared-exclusive-update (SXU) lock scheme, the rule is simple: the group mode:

[4]The lock manager must, however, deal with the possibility that the requesting transaction already has a lock in another mode on the same element. For instance, in the SXU lock system discussed, the lock manager may be able to grant an X-lock request if the requesting

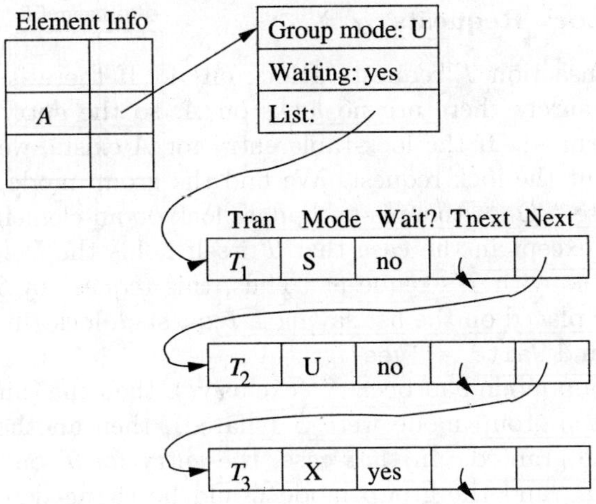

Figure 26: Structure of lock-table entries

(a) S means that only shared locks are held.

(b) U means that there is one update lock and perhaps one or more shared locks.

(c) X means there is one exclusive lock and no other locks.

For other lock schemes, there is usually an appropriate system of summaries by a group mode; we leave examples as exercises.

2. The *waiting* bit tells that there is at least one transaction waiting for a lock on A.

3. A list describing all those transactions that either currently hold locks on A or are waiting for a lock on A. Useful information that each list entry has might include:

   (a) The name of the transaction holding or waiting for a lock.

   (b) The mode of this lock.

   (c) Whether the transaction is holding or waiting for the lock.

   We also show in Fig. 26 two links for each entry. One links the entries themselves, and the other links all entries for a particular transaction (`Tnext` in the figure). The latter link would be used when a transaction commits or aborts, so that we can easily find all the locks that must be released.

---

transaction is the one that holds a U lock on the same element. For systems that do not support multiple locks held by one transaction on one element, the group mode always tells what the lock manager needs to know.

Handling Lock Requests

Suppose transaction T requests a lock on A. If there is no lock-table entry for A, then surely there are no locks on A, so the entry is created and the request is granted. If the lock-table entry for A exists, we use it to guide the decision about the lock request. We find the group mode, which in Fig. 26 is U, or "update." Once there is an update lock on an element, no other lock can be granted (except in the case that T itself holds the U lock and other locks are compatible with T's request). Thus, this request by T is denied, and an entry will be placed on the list saying T requests a lock (in whatever mode was requested), and `Wait? = 'yes'`.

If the group mode had been X (exclusive), then the same thing would happen, but if the group mode were S (shared), then another shared or update lock could be granted. In that case, the entry for T on the list would have `Wait? = 'no'`, and the group mode would be changed to U if the new lock were an update lock; otherwise, the group mode would remain S. Whether or not the lock is granted, the new list entry is linked properly, through its `Tnext` and `Next` fields. Notice that whether or not the lock is granted, the entry in the lock table tells the scheduler what it needs to know without having to examine the list of locks.

Handling Unlocks

Now suppose transaction T unlocks A. T's entry on the list for A is deleted. If the lock held by T is not the same as the group mode (e.g., T held an S lock, while the group mode was U), then there is no reason to change the group mode. On the other hand, if T's lock is in the group mode, we may have to examine the entire list to find the new group mode. In the example of Fig. 26, we know there can be only one U lock on an element, so if that lock is released, the new group mode could be only S (if there are shared locks remaining) or nothing (if no other locks are currently held).[5] If the group mode is X, we know there are no other locks, and if the group mode is S, we need to determine whether there are other shared locks.

If the value of `Waiting` is `'yes'`, then we need to grant one or more locks from the list of requested locks. There are several different approaches, each with its advantages:

1. *First-come-first-served*: Grant the lock request that has been waiting the longest. This strategy guarantees no *starvation*, the situation where a transaction can wait forever for a lock.
2. *Priority to shared locks*: First grant all the shared locks waiting. Then, grant one update lock, if there are any waiting. Only grant an exclusive lock if no others are waiting. This strategy can allow starvation, if a transaction is waiting for a U or X lock.

---

[5]We would never actually see a group mode of "nothing," since if there are no locks and no lock requests on an element, then there is no lock-table entry for that element.

3. *Priority to upgrading*: If there is a transaction with a U lock waiting to upgrade it to an X lock, grant that first. Otherwise, follow one of the other strategies mentioned.

5.3 Exercises for Section 5

Exercise 5.1: What are suitable group modes for a lock table if the lock modes used are:

a) Shared and exclusive locks.

! b) Shared, exclusive, and increment locks.

!! c) The lock modes of Exercise 4.6.

Exercise 5.2: For each of the schedules of Exercise 2.4, tell the steps that the locking scheduler described in this section would execute.

6 Hierarchies of Database Elements

Let us now return to the exploration of different locking schemes that we began in Section 4. In particular, we shall focus on two problems that come up when there is a tree structure to our data.

1. The first kind of tree structure we encounter is a hierarchy of lockable elements. We shall discuss in this section how to allow locks on both large elements, e.g., relations, and smaller elements contained within these, such as blocks holding several tuples of the relation, or individual tuples.

2. The second kind of hierarchy that is important in concurrency-control systems is data that is itself organized in a tree. A major example is B-tree indexes. We may view nodes of the B-tree as database elements, but if we do, then as we shall see in Section 7, the locking schemes studied so far perform poorly, and we need to use a new approach.

6.1 Locks With Multiple Granularity

Recall that the term "database element" was purposely left undefined, because different systems use different sizes of database elements to lock, such as tuples, pages or blocks, and relations. Some applications benefit from small database elements, such as tuples, while others are best off with large elements.

Example 20: Consider a database for a bank. If we treated relations as database elements, and therefore had only one lock for an entire relation such as the one giving account balances, then the system would allow very little concurrency. Since most transactions will change an account balance either positively or negatively, most transactions would need an exclusive lock on the accounts relation. Thus, only one deposit or withdrawal could take place at any time, no matter how many processors we had available to execute these transactions. A better approach is to lock individual pages or data blocks. Thus, two accounts whose tuples are on different blocks can be updated at the same time, offering almost all the concurrency that is possible in the system. The extreme would be to provide a lock for every tuple, so any set of accounts whatsoever could be updated at once, but this fine a grain of locks is probably not worth the extra effort.

In contrast, consider a database of documents. These documents may be edited from time to time, but most transactions will retrieve whole documents. The sensible choice of database element is a complete document. Since most transactions are *read-only* (i.e., they do not perform any write actions), locking is only necessary to avoid the reading of a document that is in the middle of being edited. Were we to use smaller-granularity locks, such as paragraphs, sentences, or words, there would be essentially no benefit but added expense. The only activity a smaller-granularity lock would support is the ability for two people to edit different parts of a document simultaneously. □

Some applications could use both large- and small-grained locks. For instance, the bank database discussed in Example 20 clearly needs block- or tuple-level locking, but might also at some time need a lock on the entire accounts relation in order to audit accounts (e.g., check that the sum of the accounts is correct). However, permitting a shared lock on the accounts relation, in order to compute some aggregation on the relation, while at the same time there are exclusive locks on individual account tuples, can lead easily to unserializable behavior. The reason is that the relation is actually changing while a supposedly frozen copy of it is being read by the aggregation query.

6.2 Warning Locks

The solution to the problem of managing locks at different granularities involves a new kind of lock called a "warning." These locks are useful when the database elements form a nested or hierarchical structure, as suggested in Fig. 27. There, we see three levels of database elements:

1. Relations are the largest lockable elements.
2. Each relation is composed of one or more block or pages, on which its tuples are stored.
3. Each block contains one or more tuples.

The rules for managing locks on a hierarchy of database elements constitute the *warning protocol*, which involves both "ordinary" locks and "warning" locks. We shall describe the lock scheme where the ordinary locks are S and X (shared and exclusive). The warning locks will be denoted by prefixing I (for "intention

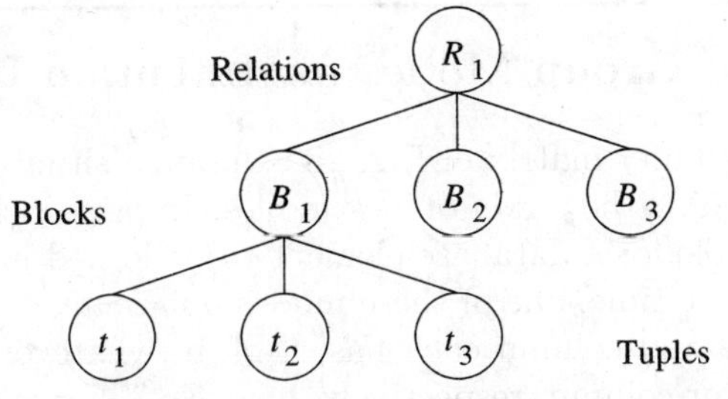

Figure 27: Database elements organized in a hierarchy

to") to the ordinary locks; for example IS represents the intention to obtain a shared lock on a subelement. The rules of the warning protocol are:

1. To place an ordinary S or X lock on any element, we must begin at the root of the hierarchy.

2. If we are at the element that we want to lock, we need look no further. We request an S or X lock on that element.

3. If the element we wish to lock is further down the hierarchy, then we place a warning at this node; that is, if we want to get a shared lock on a subelement we request an IS lock at this node, and if we want an exclusive lock on a subelement, we request an IX lock on this node. When the lock on the current node is granted, we proceed to the appropriate child (the one whose subtree contains the node we wish to lock). We then repeat step (2) or step (3), as appropriate, until we reach the desired node.

	IS	IX	S	X
IS	Yes	Yes	Yes	No
IX	Yes	Yes	No	No
S	Yes	No	Yes	No
X	No	No	No	No

Figure 28: Compatibility matrix for shared, exclusive, and intention locks

In order to decide whether or not one of these locks can be granted, we use the compatibility matrix of Fig. 28. To see why this matrix makes sense, consider first the IS column. When we request an IS lock on a node N, we intend to read a descendant of N. The only time this intent could create a problem is if some other transaction has already claimed the right to write a new copy of the entire database element represented by N; thus we see "No" in the row for X. Notice that if some other transaction plans to write only a subelement, indicated by an IX lock at N, then we can afford to grant the IS

Group Modes for Intention Locks

The compatibility matrix of Fig. 28 exhibits a situation we have not seen before regarding the power of lock modes. In prior lock schemes, whenever it was possible for a database element to be locked in both modes M and N at the same time, one of these modes *dominates* the other, in the sense that its row and column each has "No" in whatever positions the other mode's row or column, respectively, has "No." For example, in Fig. 19 we see that U dominates S, and X dominates both S and U. An advantage of knowing that there is always one dominant lock on an element is that we can summarize the effect of many locks with a "group mode," as discussed in Section 5.2.

As we see from Fig. 28, neither of modes S and IX dominate the other. Moreover, it is possible for an element to be locked in both modes S and IX at the same time, provided the locks are requested by the same transaction (recall that the "No" entries in a compatibility matrix only apply to locks held by some *other* transaction). A transaction might request both locks if it wanted to read an entire element and then write a few of its subelements. If a transaction has both S and IX locks on an element, then it restricts other transactions to the extent that either lock does. That is, we can imagine another lock mode SIX, whose row and column have "No" everywhere except in the entry for IS. The lock mode SIX serves as the group mode if there is a transaction with locks in S and IX modes, but not X mode.

Incidentally, we might imagine that the same situation occurs in the matrix of Fig 22 for increment locks. That is, one transaction could hold locks in both S and I modes. However, this situation is equivalent to holding a lock in X mode, so we could use X as the group mode in that situation.

lock at N, and allow the conflict to be resolved at a lower level, if indeed the intent to write and the intent to read happen to involve a common element.

Now consider the column for IX. If we intend to write a subelement of node N, then we must prevent either reading or writing of the entire element represented by N. Thus, we see "No" in the entries for lock modes S and X. However, per our discussion of the IS column, another transaction that reads or writes a subelement can have potential conflicts dealt with at that level, so IX does not conflict with another IX at N or with an IS at N.

Next, consider the column for S. Reading the element corresponding to node N cannot conflict with either another read lock on N or a read lock on some subelement of N, represented by IS at N. Thus, we see "Yes" in the rows for both S and IS. However, either an X or an IX means that some other transaction will write at least a part of the element represented by N. Thus, we cannot grant the right to read all of N, which explains the "No" entries in the column for S.

Finally, the column for X has only "No" entries. We cannot allow writing of all of node N if any other transaction already has the right to read or write N, or to acquire that right on a subelement.

Example 21: Consider the relation

```
Movie(title, year, length, studioName)
```

Let us postulate a lock on the entire relation and locks on individual tuples. Then transaction T_1, which consists of the query

```
SELECT *
FROM Movie
WHERE title = 'King Kong';
```

starts by getting an IS lock on the entire relation. It then moves to the individual tuples (there are three movies with the title *King Kong*), and gets S locks on each of them.

Now, suppose that while we are executing the first query, transaction T_2, which changes the year component of a tuple, begins:

```
UPDATE Movie
SET year = 1939
WHERE title = 'Gone With the Wind';
```

T_2 needs an IX lock on the relation, since it plans to write a new value for one of the tuples. T_1's IS lock on the relation is compatible, so the lock is granted. When T_2 goes to the tuple for *Gone With the Wind*, it finds no lock there, and so gets its X lock and rewrites the tuple. Had T_2 tried to write a new value in the tuple for one of the *King Kong* movies, it would have had to wait until T_1 released its S lock, since S and X are not compatible. The collection of locks is suggested by Fig. 29. □

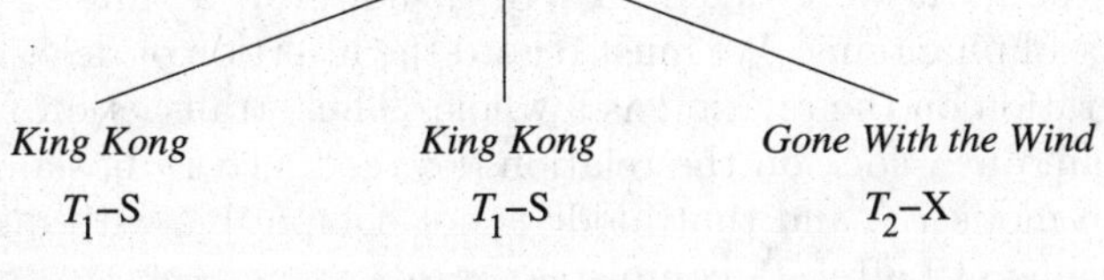

Figure 29: Locks granted to two transactions accessing `Movie` tuples

6.3 Phantoms and Handling Insertions Correctly

When transactions create new subelements of a lockable element, there are some opportunities to go wrong. The problem is that we can only lock existing items; there is no easy way to lock database elements that do not exist but might later be inserted. The following example illustrates the point.

Example 22: Suppose we have the same `Movie` relation as in Example 21, and the first transaction to execute is T_3, which is the query

```
SELECT SUM(length)
FROM Movie
WHERE studioName = 'Disney';
```

T_3 needs to read the tuples of all the Disney movies, so it might start by getting an IS lock on the `Movie` relation and S locks on each of the tuples for Disney movies.[6]

Now, a transaction T_4 comes along and inserts a new Disney movie. It seems that T_4 needs no locks, but it has made the result of T_3 incorrect. That fact by itself is not a concurrency problem, since the serial order (T_3, T_4) is equivalent to what actually happened. However, there could also be some other element X that both T_3 and T_4 write, with T_4 writing first, so there *could* be an unserializable behavior of more complex transactions.

To be more precise, suppose that D_1 and D_2 are pre-existing Disney movies, and D_3 is the new Disney movie inserted by T_4. Let L be the sum of the lengths of the Disney movies computed by T_3, and assume the consistency constraint on the database is that L should be equal to the sum of all the lengths of the Disney movies that existed the last time L was computed. Then the following is a sequence of events that is legal under the warning protocol:

$$r_3(D_1);\ r_3(D_2);\ w_4(D_3);\ w_4(X);\ w_3(L);\ w_3(X);$$

Here, we have used $w_4(D_3)$ to represent the creation of D_3 by transaction T_4. The schedule above is not serializable. In particular, the value of L is not the sum of the lengths of D_1, D_2, and D_3, which are the current Disney movies. Moreover, the fact that X has the value written by T_3 and not T_4 rules out the possibility that T_3 was ahead of T_4 in a supposed equivalent serial order. □

The problem in Example 22 is that the new Disney movie has a *phantom* tuple, one that should have been locked but wasn't, because it didn't exist at the time the locks were taken. There is, however, a simple way to avoid the occurrence of phantoms. We must regard the insertion or deletion of a tuple as a write operation on the relation as a whole. Thus, transaction T_4 in Example 22 must obtain an X lock on the relation `Movie`. Since T_3 has already locked this relation in mode IS, and that mode is not compatible with mode X, T_4 would have to wait until after T_3 completes.

---

[6]However, if there were many Disney movies, it might be more efficient just to get an S lock on the entire relation.

6.4 Exercises for Section 6

Exercise 6.1: Consider, for variety, an object-oriented database. The objects of class C are stored on two blocks, B_1 and B_2. Block B_1 contains objects O_1 and O_2, while block B_2 contains objects O_3, O_4, and O_5. The entire set of objects of class C, the blocks, and the individual objects form a hierarchy of lockable database elements. Tell the sequence of lock requests and the response of a warning-protocol-based scheduler to the following sequences of requests. You may assume all requests occur just before they are needed, and all unlocks occur at the end of the transaction.

a) $r_1(O_1)$; $w_2(O_2)$; $r_2(O_3)$; $w_1(O_4)$;

b) $r_1(O_5)$; $w_2(O_5)$; $r_2(O_3)$; $w_1(O_4)$;

c) $r_1(O_1)$; $r_1(O_3)$; $r_2(O_1)$; $w_2(O_4)$; $w_2(O_5)$;

d) $r_1(O_1)$; $r_2(O_2)$; $r_3(O_1)$; $w_1(O_3)$; $w_2(O_4)$; $w_3(O_5)$; $w_1(O_2)$;

Exercise 6.2: Change the sequence of actions in Example 22 so that the $w_4(D_3)$ action becomes a write by T_4 of the entire relation `Movie`. Then, show the action of a warning-protocol-based scheduler on this sequence of requests.

!! **Exercise 6.3:** Show how to add increment locks to a warning-protocol-based scheduler.

7 The Tree Protocol

Like Section 6, this section deals with data in the form of a tree. However, here, the nodes of the tree do not form a hierarchy based on containment. Rather, database elements are disjoint pieces of data, but the only way to get to a node is through its parent; B-trees are an important example of this sort of data. Knowing that we must traverse a particular path to an element gives us some important freedom to manage locks differently from the two-phase locking approaches we have seen so far.

7.1 Motivation for Tree-Based Locking

Let us consider a B-tree index in a system that treats individual nodes (i.e., blocks) as lockable database elements. The node is the right level of lock granularity, because treating smaller pieces as elements offers no benefit, and treating the entire B-tree as one database element prevents the sort of concurrent use of the index that can be achieved via the mechanisms that form the subject of this section.

If we use a standard set of lock modes, like shared, exclusive, and update locks, and we use two-phase locking, then concurrent use of the B-tree is almost impossible. The reason is that every transaction using the index must begin by locking the root node of the B-tree. If the transaction is 2PL, then it cannot unlock the root until it has acquired all the locks it needs, both on B-tree nodes and other database elements.[7] Moreover, since in principle any transaction that inserts or deletes could wind up rewriting the root of the B-tree, the transaction needs at least an update lock on the root node, or an exclusive lock if update mode is not available. Thus, only one transaction that is not read-only can access the B-tree at any time.

However, in most situations, we can deduce almost immediately that a B-tree node will not be rewritten, even if the transaction inserts or deletes a tuple. For example, if the transaction inserts a tuple, but the child of the root that we visit is not completely full, then we know the insertion cannot propagate up to the root. Similarly, if the transaction deletes a single tuple, and the child of the root we visit has more than the minimum number of keys and pointers, then we can be sure the root will not change.

Thus, as soon as a transaction moves to a child of the root and observes the (quite usual) situation that rules out a rewrite of the root, we would like to release the lock on the root. The same observation applies to the lock on any interior node of the B-tree. Unfortunately, releasing the lock on the root early will violate 2PL, so we cannot be sure that the schedule of several transactions accessing the B-tree will be serializable. The solution is a specialized protocol for transactions that access tree-structured data such as B-trees. The protocol violates 2PL, but uses the fact that accesses to elements must proceed down the tree to assure serializability.

7.2 Rules for Access to Tree-Structured Data

The following restrictions on locks form the *tree protocol*. We assume that there is only one kind of lock, represented by lock requests of the form $l_i(X)$, but the idea generalizes to any set of lock modes. We assume that transactions are consistent, and schedules must be legal (i.e., the scheduler will enforce the expected restrictions by granting locks on a node only when they do not conflict with locks already on that node), but there is no two-phase locking requirement on transactions.

1. A transaction's first lock may be at any node of the tree.[8]

2. Subsequent locks may only be acquired if the transaction currently has a lock on the parent node.

3. Nodes may be unlocked at any time.

4. A transaction may not relock a node on which it has released a lock, even if it still holds a lock on the node's parent.

---

[7] Additionally, there are good reasons why a transaction will hold all its locks until it is ready to commit.

[8] In the B-tree example of Section 7.1, the first lock would always be at the root.

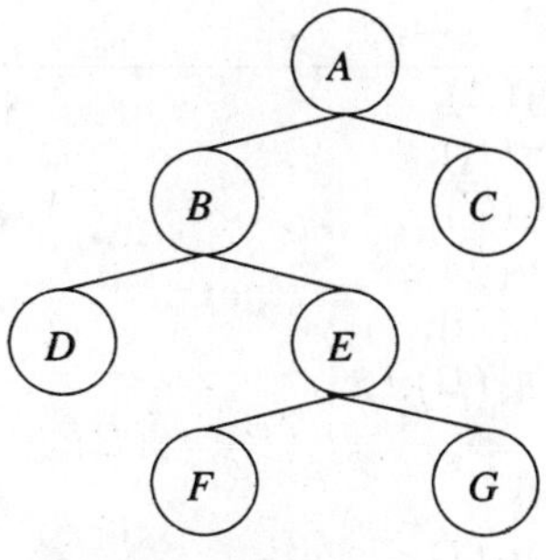

Figure 30: A tree of lockable elements

Example 23: Figure 30 shows a hierarchy of nodes, and Fig. 31 indicates the action of three transactions on this data. T_1 starts at the root A, and proceeds downward to B, C, and D. T_2 starts at B and tries to move to E, but its move is initially denied because of the lock by T_3 on E. Transaction T_3 starts at E and moves to F and G. Notice that T_1 is not a 2PL transaction, because the lock on A is relinquished before the lock on D is acquired. Similarly, T_3 is not a 2PL transaction, although T_2 happens to be 2PL. □

7.3 Why the Tree Protocol Works

The tree protocol implies a serial order on the transactions involved in a schedule. We can define an order of precedence as follows. Say that $T_i <_S T_j$ if in schedule S, the transactions T_i and T_j lock a node in common, and T_i locks the node first.

Example 24: In the schedule S of Fig. 31, we find T_1 and T_2 lock B in common, and T_1 locks it first. Thus, $T_1 <_S T_2$. We also find that T_2 and T_3 lock E in common, and T_3 locks it first; thus $T_3 <_S T_2$. However, there is no precedence between T_1 and T_3, because they lock no node in common. Thus, the precedence graph derived from these precedence relations is as shown in Fig. 32. □

If the precedence graph drawn from the precedence relations that we defined above has no cycles, then we claim that any topological order of the transactions is an equivalent serial schedule. For example, either (T_1, T_3, T_2) or (T_3, T_1, T_2) is an equivalent serial schedule for Fig. 31. The reason is that in such a serial schedule, all nodes are touched in the same order as they are in the original schedule.

To understand why the precedence graph described above must always be acyclic if the tree protocol is obeyed, observe the following:

- If two transactions lock several elements in common, then they are all locked in the same order.

T_1	T_2	T_3
$l_1(A);\ r_1(A);$		
$l_1(B);\ r_1(B);$		
$l_1(C);\ r_1(C);$		
$w_1(A);\ u_1(A);$		
$l_1(D);\ r_1(D);$		
$w_1(B);\ u_1(B);$		
	$l_2(B);\ r_2(B);$	
		$l_3(E);\ r_3(E);$
$w_1(D);\ u_1(D);$		
$w_1(C);\ u_1(C);$		
	$l_2(E)$ **Denied**	
		$l_3(F);\ r_3(F);$
		$w_3(F);\ u_3(F);$
		$l_3(G);\ r_3(G)$
		$w_3(E);\ u_3(E);$
	$l_2(E);\ r_2(E);$	
		$w_3(G);\ u_3(G)$
	$w_2(B);\ u_2(B);$	
	$w_2(E);\ u_2(E);$	

Figure 31: Three transactions following the tree protocol

To see why, consider some transactions T and U, which lock two or more items in common. First, notice that each transaction locks a set of elements that form a tree, and the intersection of two trees is itself a tree. Thus, there is some one highest element X that both T and U lock. Suppose that T locks X first, but that there is some other element Y that U locks before T. Then there is a path in the tree of elements from X to Y, and both T and U must lock each element along the path, because neither can lock a node without having a lock on its parent.

Consider the first element along this path, say Z, that U locks first, as suggested by Fig. 33. Then T locks the parent P of Z before U does. But then T is still holding the lock on P when it locks Z, so U has not yet locked P when

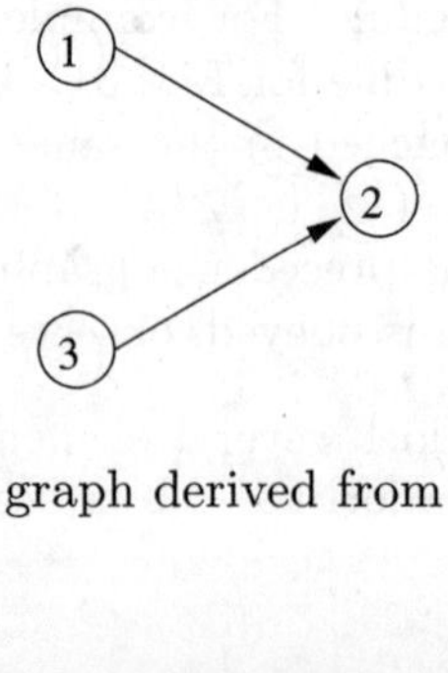

Figure 32: Precedence graph derived from the schedule of Fig. 31

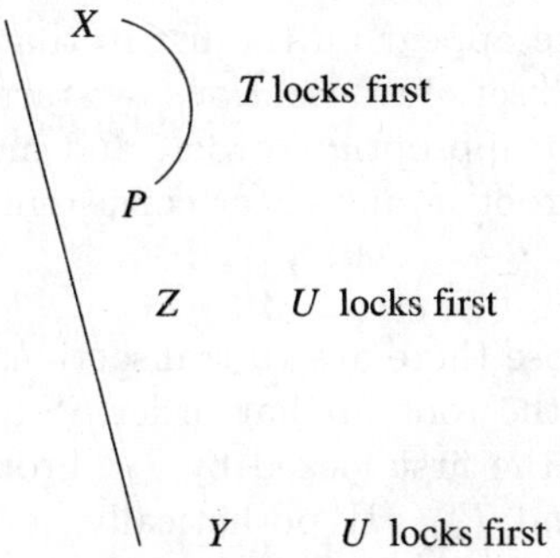

Figure 33: A path of elements locked by two transactions

it locks Z. It cannot be that Z is the first element U locks in common with T, since they both lock ancestor X (which could also be P, but not Z). Thus, U cannot lock Z until after it has acquired a lock on P, which is after T locks Z. We conclude that T precedes U at every node they lock in common.

Now, consider an arbitrary set of transactions $T_1, T_2, \ldots, T_n$ that obey the tree protocol and lock some of the nodes of a tree according to schedule S. First, among those that lock the root, they do so in some order, and by the rule just observed:

- If T_i locks the root before T_j, then T_i locks every node in common with T_j before T_j does. That is, $T_i <_S T_j$, but not $T_j <_S T_i$.

We can show by induction on the number of nodes of the tree that there is some serial order equivalent to S for the complete set of transactions.

BASIS: If there is only one node, the root, then as we just observed, the order in which the transactions lock the root serves.

INDUCTION: If there is more than one node in the tree, consider for each subtree of the root the set of transactions that lock one or more nodes in that subtree. Note that transactions locking the root may belong to more than one subtree, but a transaction that does not lock the root will belong to only one subtree. For instance, among the transactions of Fig. 31, only T_1 locks the root, and it belongs to both subtrees — the tree rooted at B and the tree rooted at C. However, T_2 and T_3 belong only to the tree rooted at B.

By the inductive hypothesis, there is a serial order for all the transactions that lock nodes in any one subtree. We have only to blend the serial orders for the various subtrees. Since the only transactions these lists of transactions have in common are the transactions that lock the root, and we established that these transactions lock every node in common in the same order that they lock the root, it is not possible that two transactions locking the root appear in different orders in two of the sublists. Specifically, if T_i and T_j appear on the list for some child C of the root, then they lock C in the same order as they lock the root and therefore appear on the list in that order. Thus, we can build a serial order for the full set of transactions by starting with the transactions that lock the root, in their appropriate order, and interspersing those transactions that do not lock the root in any order consistent with the serial order of their subtrees.

Example 25: Suppose there are 10 transactions $T_1, T_2, \ldots, T_{10}$, and of these, T_1, T_2, and T_3 lock the root in that order. Suppose also that there are two children of the root, the first locked by T_1 through T_7 and the second locked by T_2, T_3, T_8, T_9, and T_{10}. Hypothetically, let the serial order for the first subtree be $(T_4, T_1, T_5, T_2, T_6, T_3, T_7)$; note that this order must include T_1, T_2, and T_3 in that order. Also, let the serial order for the second subtree be $(T_8, T_2, T_9, T_{10}, T_3)$. As must be the case, the transactions T_2 and T_3, which locked the root, appear in this sequence in the order in which they locked the root.

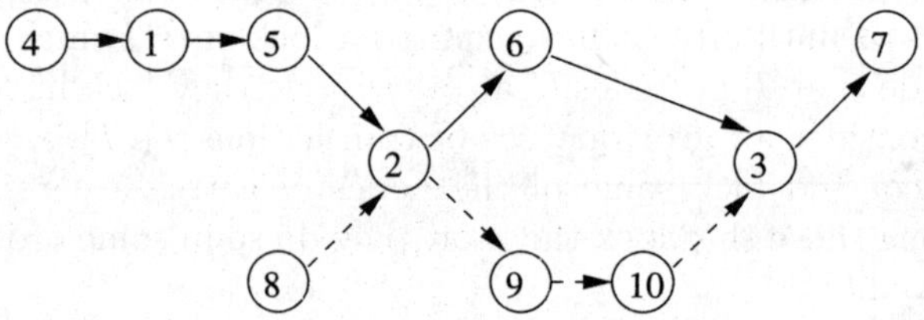

Figure 34: Combining serial orders for the subtrees into a serial order for all transactions

The constraints imposed on the serial order of these transactions are as shown in Fig. 34. Solid lines represent constraints due to the order at the first child of the root, while dashed lines represent the order at the second child. $(T_4, T_8, T_1, T_5, T_2, T_9, T_6, T_{10}, T_3, T_7)$ is one of the many topological sorts of this graph. □

7.4 Exercises for Section 7

! Exercise 7.1: Consider the following transactions that operate on the tree of Fig. 30.

$$T_1\text{: } r_1(A);\ r_1(B);\ r_1(E);$$
$$T_2\text{: } r_2(A);\ r_2(C);\ r_2(B);$$
$$T_3\text{: } r_3(B);\ r_3(E);\ r_3(F);$$

If schedules follow the tree protocol, in how many ways can we interleave: (a) T_1 and T_2 (b) T_1 and T_3 !! (c) all three?

! **Exercise 7.2:** Suppose there are eight transactions $T_1, T_2, \ldots, T_8$, of which the odd-numbered transactions, T_1, T_3, T_5, and T_7, lock the root of a tree, in that order. There are three children of the root, the first locked by T_1, T_2, T_3, and T_4 in that order. The second child is locked by T_3, T_6, and T_5, in that order, and the third child is locked by T_8 and T_7, in that order. How many serial orders of the transactions are consistent with these statements?

!! **Exercise 7.3:** Suppose we use the tree protocol with shared and exclusive locks for reading and writing, respectively. Rule (2), which requires a lock on the parent to get a lock on a node, must be changed to prevent unserializable behavior. What is the proper rule (2) for shared and exclusive locks? *Hint*: Does the lock on the parent have to be of the same type as the lock on the child?

8 Concurrency Control by Timestamps

Next, we shall consider two methods other than locking that are used in some systems to assure serializability of transactions:

1. *Timestamping.* Assign a "timestamp" to each transaction. Record the timestamps of the transactions that last read and write each database element, and compare these values with the transactions timestamps, to assure that the serial schedule according to the transactions' timestamps is equivalent to the actual schedule of the transactions. This approach is the subject of the present section.

2. *Validation.* Examine timestamps of the transaction and the database elements when a transaction is about to commit; this process is called "validation" of the transaction. The serial schedule that orders transactions according to their validation time must be equivalent to the actual schedule. The validation approach is discussed in Section 9.

Both these approaches are *optimistic*, in the sense that they assume that no unserializable behavior will occur and only fix things up when a violation is apparent. In contrast, all locking methods assume that things will go wrong unless transactions are prevented in advance from engaging in nonserializable behavior. The optimistic approaches differ from locking in that the only remedy when something does go wrong is to abort and restart a transaction that tries to engage in unserializable behavior. In contrast, locking schedulers delay transactions, but do not abort them.[9] Generally, optimistic schedulers are better than

[9]That is not to say that a system using a locking scheduler will never abort a transaction. However, a locking scheduler never uses a transaction abort simply as a response to a lock request that it cannot grant.

locking when many of the transactions are read-only, since those transactions can never, by themselves, cause unserializable behavior.

8.1 Timestamps

To use timestamping as a concurrency-control method, the scheduler needs to assign to each transaction T a unique number, its *timestamp* $\text{TS}(T)$. Timestamps must be issued in ascending order, at the time that a transaction first notifies the scheduler that it is beginning. Two approaches to generating timestamps are:

a) We can use the system clock as the timestamp, provided the scheduler does not operate so fast that it could assign timestamps to two transactions on one tick of the clock.

b) The scheduler can maintain a counter. Each time a transaction starts, the counter is incremented by 1, and the new value becomes the timestamp of the transaction. In this approach, timestamps have nothing to do with "time," but they have the important property that we need for any timestamp-generating system: a transaction that starts later has a higher timestamp than a transaction that starts earlier.

Whatever method of generating timestamps is used, the scheduler must maintain a table of currently active transactions and their timestamps.

To use timestamps as a concurrency-control method, we need to associate with each database element X two timestamps and an additional bit:

1. $\text{RT}(X)$, the *read time* of X, which is the highest timestamp of a transaction that has read X.

2. $\text{WT}(X)$, the *write time* of X, which is the highest timestamp of a transaction that has written X.

3. $\text{C}(X)$, the *commit bit* for X, which is true if and only if the most recent transaction to write X has already committed. The purpose of this bit is to avoid a situation where one transaction T reads data written by another transaction U, and U then aborts. This problem, where T makes a "dirty read" of uncommitted data, certainly can cause the database state to become inconsistent, and any scheduler needs a mechanism to prevent dirty reads.[10]

8.2 Physically Unrealizable Behaviors

In order to understand the architecture and rules of a timestamp scheduler, we need to remember that the scheduler assumes the timestamp order of transactions is also the serial order in which they must appear to execute. Thus,

[10] Although commercial systems generally give the user an option to allow dirty reads, as suggested by the SQL isolation level `READ UNCOMMITTED`.

the job of the scheduler, in addition to assigning timestamps and updating RT, WT, and C for the database elements, is to check that whenever a read or write occurs, what happens in real time *could* have happened if each transaction had executed instantaneously at the moment of its timestamp. If not, we say the behavior is *physically unrealizable.* There are two kinds of problems that can occur:

1. *Read too late*: Transaction T tries to read database element X, but the write time of X indicates that the current value of X was written after T theoretically executed; that is, $\text{TS}(T) < \text{WT}(X)$. Figure 35 illustrates the problem. The horizontal axis represents the real time at which events occur. Dotted lines link the actual events to the times at which they theoretically occur — the timestamp of the transaction that performs the event. Thus, we see a transaction U that started after transaction T, but wrote a value for X before T reads X. T should not be able to read the value written by U, because theoretically, U executed after T did. However, T has no choice, because U's value of X is the one that T now sees. The solution is to abort T when the problem is encountered.

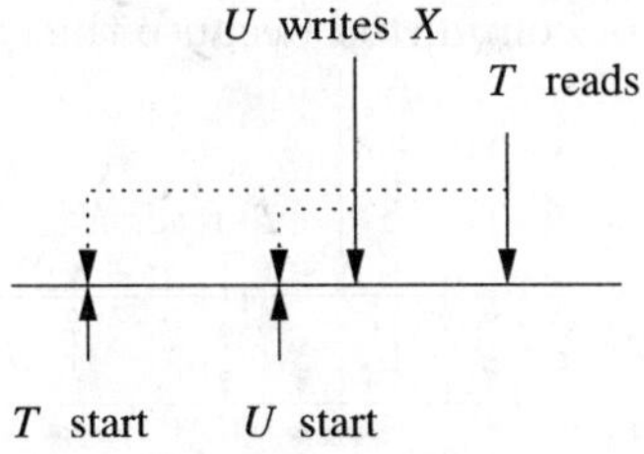

Figure 35: Transaction T tries to read too late

2. *Write too late*: Transaction T tries to write database element X. However, the read time of X indicates that some other transaction should have read the value written by T, but read some other value instead. That is, $\text{WT}(X) < \text{TS}(T) < \text{RT}(X)$. The problem is shown in Fig. 36. There we see a transaction U that started after T, but read X before T got a chance to write X. When T tries to write X, we find $\text{RT}(X) > \text{TS}(T)$, meaning that X has already been read by a transaction U that theoretically executed later than T. We also find $\text{WT}(X) < \text{TS}(T)$, which means that no other transaction wrote into X a value that would have overwritten T's value, thus, negating T's responsibility to get its value into X so transaction U could read it.

8.3 Problems With Dirty Data

There is a class of problems that the commit bit is designed to solve. One of these problems, a "dirty read," is suggested in Fig. 37. There, transaction

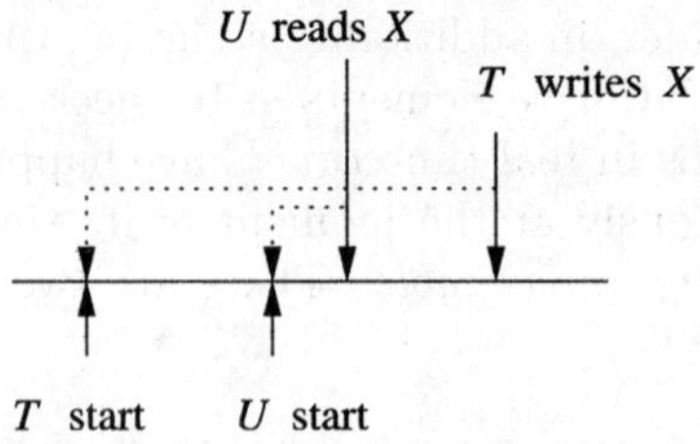

Figure 36: Transaction T tries to write too late

T reads X, and X was last written by U. The timestamp of U is less than that of T, and the read by T occurs after the write by U in real time, so the event seems to be physically realizable. However, it is possible that after T reads the value of X written by U, transaction U will abort; perhaps U encounters an error condition in its own data, such as a division by 0, or as we shall see in Section 8.4, the scheduler forces U to abort because it tries to do something physically unrealizable. Thus, although there is nothing physically unrealizable about T reading X, it is better to delay T's read until U commits or aborts. We can tell that U is not committed because the commit bit $\mathrm{C}(X)$ will be false.

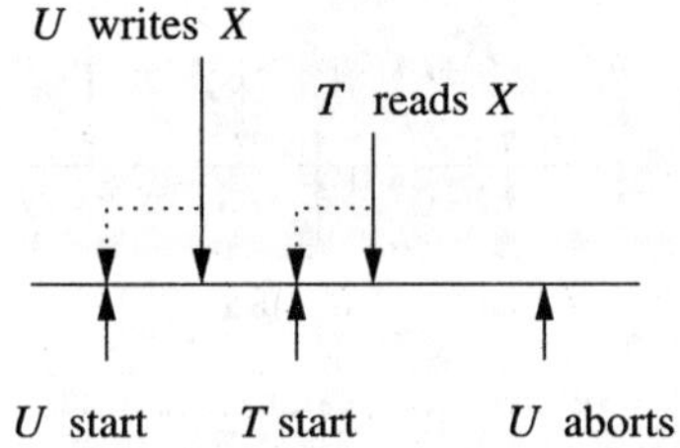

Figure 37: T could perform a dirty read if it reads X when shown

A second potential problem is suggested by Fig. 38. Here, U, a transaction with a later timestamp than T, has written X first. When T tries to write, the appropriate action is to do nothing. Evidently no other transaction V that should have read T's value of X got U's value instead, because if V tried to read X it would have aborted because of a too-late read. Future reads of X will want U's value or a later value of X, not T's value. This idea, that writes can be skipped when a write with a later write-time is already in place, is called the *Thomas write rule*.

There is a potential problem with the Thomas write rule, however. If U later aborts, as is suggested in Fig. 38, then its value of X should be removed and the previous value and write-time restored. Since T is committed, it would seem that the value of X should be the one written by T for future reading. However, we already skipped the write by T and it is too late to repair the damage.

While there are many ways to deal with the problems just described, we

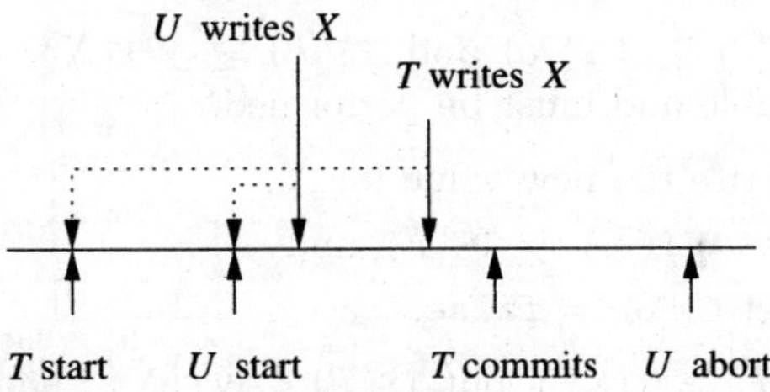

Figure 38: A write is cancelled because of a write with a later timestamp, but the writer then aborts

shall adopt a relatively simple policy based on the following assumed capability of the timestamp-based scheduler.

- When a transaction T writes a database element X, the write is "tentative" and may be undone if T aborts. The commit bit $C(X)$ is set to false, and the scheduler makes a copy of the old value of X and its previous $\text{WT}(X)$.

8.4 The Rules for Timestamp-Based Scheduling

We can now summarize the rules that a scheduler using timestamps must follow to make sure that nothing physically unrealizable may occur. The scheduler, in response to a read or write request from a transaction T has the choice of:

a) Granting the request,

b) Aborting T (if T would violate physical reality) and restarting T with a new timestamp (abort followed by restart is often called *rollback*), or

c) Delaying T and later deciding whether to abort T or to grant the request (if the request is a read, and the read might be dirty, as in Section 8.3).

The rules are as follows:

1. Suppose the scheduler receives a request $r_T(X)$.

   (a) If $\text{TS}(T) \geq \text{WT}(X)$, the read is physically realizable.

      i. If $\text{C}(X)$ is true, grant the request. If $\text{TS}(T) > \text{RT}(X)$, set $\text{RT}(X) := \text{TS}(T)$; otherwise do not change $\text{RT}(X)$.

      ii. If $\text{C}(X)$ is false, delay T until $\text{C}(X)$ becomes true, or the transaction that wrote X aborts.

   (b) If $\text{TS}(T) < \text{WT}(X)$, the read is physically unrealizable. Rollback T; that is, abort T and restart it with a new, larger timestamp.

2. Suppose the scheduler receives a request $w_T(X)$.

(a) If $\text{TS}(T) \geq \text{RT}(X)$ and $\text{TS}(T) \geq \text{WT}(X)$, the write is physically realizable and must be performed.

i. Write the new value for X,

ii. Set $\text{WT}(X) := \text{TS}(T)$, and

iii. Set $\text{C}(X) :=$ `false`.

(b) If $\text{TS}(T) \geq \text{RT}(X)$, but $\text{TS}(T) < \text{WT}(X)$, then the write is physically realizable, but there is already a later value in X. If $C(X)$ is true, then the previous writer of X is committed, and we simply ignore the write by T; we allow T to proceed and make no change to the database. However, if $C(X)$ is false, then we must delay T as in point 1(a)ii.

(c) If $\text{TS}(T) < \text{RT}(X)$, then the write is physically unrealizable, and T must be rolled back.

3. Suppose the scheduler receives a request to commit T. It must find (using a list the scheduler maintains) all the database elements X written by T, and set $\text{C}(X) :=$ `true`. If any transactions are waiting for X to be committed (found from another scheduler-maintained list), these transactions are allowed to proceed.

4. Suppose the scheduler receives a request to abort T or decides to rollback T as in 1b or 2c. Then any transaction that was waiting on an element X that T wrote must repeat its attempt to read or write, and see whether the action is now legal after T's writes are cancelled.

Example 26: Figure 39 shows a schedule of three transactions, T_1, T_2, and T_3 that access three database elements, A, B, and C. The real time at which events occur increases down the page, as usual. We have also indicated the timestamps of the transactions and the read and write times of the elements. At the beginning, each of the database elements has both a read and write time of 0. The timestamps of the transactions are acquired when they notify the scheduler that they are beginning. Notice that even though T_1 executes the first data access, it does not have the least timestamp. Presumably T_2 was the first to notify the scheduler of its start, and T_3 did so next, with T_1 last to start.

In the first action, T_1 reads B. Since the write time of B is less than the timestamp of T_1, this read is physically realizable and allowed to happen. The read time of B is set to 200, the timestamp of T_1. The second and third read actions similarly are legal and result in the read time of each database element being set to the timestamp of the transaction that read it.

At the fourth step, T_1 writes B. Since the read time of B is not bigger than the timestamp of T_1, the write is physically realizable. Since the write time of B is no larger than the timestamp of T_1, we must actually perform the write. When we do, the write time of B is raised to 200, the timestamp of the writing transaction T_1.

T_1	T_2	T_3	A	B	C
200	150	175	RT=0 WT=0	RT=0 WT=0	RT=0 WT=0
$r_1(B)$;				RT=200	
	$r_2(A)$;		RT=150		
		$r_3(C)$;			RT=175
$w_1(B)$;				WT=200	
$w_1(A)$;			WT=200		
	$w_2(C)$; **Abort**;				
		$w_3(A)$;			

Figure 39: Three transactions executing under a timestamp-based scheduler

Next, T_2 tries to write C. However, C was already read by transaction T_3, which theoretically executed at time 175, while T_2 would have written its value at time 150. Thus, T_2 is trying to do something that s physically unrealizable, and T_2 must be rolled back.

The last step is the write of A by T_3. Since the read time of A, 150, is less than the timestamp of T_3, 175, the write is legal. However, there is already a later value of A stored in that database element, namely the value written by T_1, theoretically at time 200. Thus, T_3 is not rolled back, but neither does it write its value. □

8.5 Multiversion Timestamps

An important variation of timestamping maintains old versions of database elements in addition to the current version that is stored in the database itself. The purpose is to allow reads $r_T(X)$ that otherwise would cause transaction T to abort (because the current version of X was written in T's future) to proceed by reading the version of X that is appropriate for a transaction with T's timestamp. The method is especially useful if database elements are disk blocks or pages, since then all that must be done is for the buffer manager to keep in memory certain blocks that might be useful for some currently active transaction.

Example 27: Consider the set of transactions accessing database element A shown in Fig. 40. These transactions are operating under an ordinary timestamp-based scheduler, and when T_3 tries to read A, it finds WT(A) to be greater than its own timestamp, and must abort. However, there is an old value of A written by T_1 and overwritten by T_2 that would have been suitable for T_3 to read; this version of A had a write time of 150, which is less than T_3's timestamp of 175. If this old value of A were available, T_3 could be allowed to read it, even though it is not the "current" value of A. □

T_1	T_2	T_3	T_4	A
150	200	175	225	RT=0
				WT=0
$r_1(A)$				RT=150
$w_1(A)$				WT=150
	$r_2(A)$			RT=200
	$w_2(A)$			WT=200
		$r_3(A)$		
		Abort		
			$r_4(A)$	RT=225

Figure 40: T_3 must abort because it cannot access an old value of A

A multiversion-timestamp scheduler differs from the scheduler described in Section 8.4 in the following ways:

1. When a new write $w_T(X)$ occurs, if it is legal, then a new version of database element X is created. Its write time is $\text{TS}(T)$, and we shall refer to it as X_t, where $t = \text{TS}(T)$.
2. When a read $r_T(X)$ occurs, the scheduler finds the version X_t of X such that $t \leq \text{TS}(T)$, but there is no other version $X_{t'}$ with $t < t' \leq \text{TS}(T)$. That is, the version of X written immediately before T theoretically executed is the version that T reads.
3. Write times are associated with *versions* of an element, and they never change.
4. Read times are also associated with versions. They are used to reject certain writes, namely one whose time is less than the read time of the previous version. Figure 41 suggests the problem, where X has versions X_{50} and X_{100}, the former was read by a transaction with timestamp 80, and a new write by a transaction T whose timestamp is 60 occurs. This write must cause T to abort, because its value of X should have been read by the transaction with timestamp 80, had T been allowed to execute.
5. When a version X_t has a write time t such that no active transaction has a timestamp less than t, then we may delete any version of X *previous* to X_t.

Example 28: Let us reconsider the actions of Fig. 40 if multiversion timestamping is used. First, there are three versions of A: A_0, which exists before these transactions start, A_{150}, written by T_1, and A_{200}, written by T_2. Figure 42 shows the sequence of events, when the versions are created, and when they are read. Notice in particular that T_3 does not have to abort, because it can read an earlier version of A. □

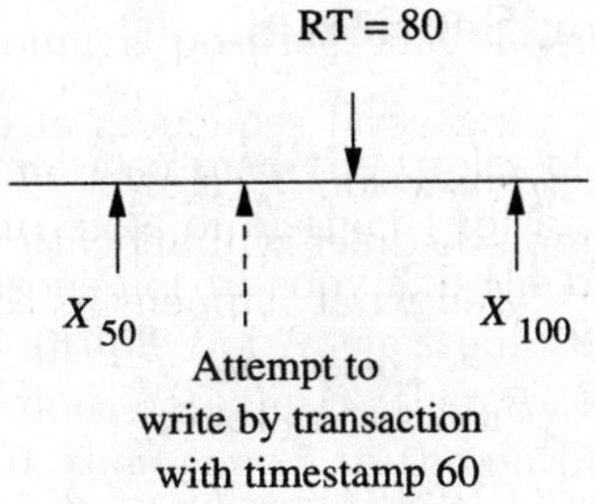

Figure 41: A transaction tries to write a version of X that would make events physically unrealizable

T_1	T_2	T_3	T_4	A_0	A_{150}	A_{200}
150	200	175	225			
$r_1(A)$				Read		
$w_1(A)$					Create	
	$r_2(A)$				Read	
	$w_2(A)$					Create
		$r_3(A)$			Read	
			$r_4(A)$			Read

Figure 42: Execution of transactions using multiversion concurrency control

8.6 Timestamps Versus Locking

Generally, timestamping is superior in situations where either most transactions are read-only, or it is rare that concurrent transactions will try to read and write the same element. In high-conflict situations, locking performs better. The argument for this rule-of-thumb is:

- Locking will frequently delay transactions as they wait for locks.
- But if concurrent transactions frequently read and write elements in common, then rollbacks will be frequent in a timestamp scheduler, introducing even more delay than a locking system.

There is an interesting compromise used in several commercial systems. The scheduler divides the transactions into read-only transactions and read/write transactions. Read/write transactions are executed using two-phase locking, to keep all transactions from accessing the elements they lock.

Read-only transactions are executed using multiversion timestamping. As the read/write transactions create new versions of a database element, those versions are managed as in Section 8.5. A read-only transaction is allowed to read whatever version of a database element is appropriate for its timestamp. A read-only transaction thus never has to abort, and will only rarely be delayed.

8.7 Exercises for Section 8

Exercise 8.1: Below are several sequences of events, including *start* events, where st_i means that transaction T_i starts. These sequences represent real time, and the timestamp scheduler will allocate timestamps to transactions in the order of their starts. Tell what happens as each executes.

a) st_1; st_2; $r_1(A)$; $r_2(B)$; $w_2(A)$; $w_1(B)$;

b) st_1; $r_1(A)$; st_2; $w_2(B)$; $r_2(A)$; $w_1(B)$;

c) st_1; st_2; st_3; $r_1(A)$; $r_2(B)$; $w_1(C)$; $r_3(B)$; $r_3(C)$; $w_2(B)$; $w_3(A)$;

d) st_1; st_3; st_2; $r_1(A)$; $r_2(B)$; $w_1(C)$; $r_3(B)$; $r_3(C)$; $w_2(B)$; $w_3(A)$;

Exercise 8.2: Tell what happens during the following sequences of events if a multiversion, timestamp scheduler is used. What happens instead, if the scheduler does not maintain multiple versions?

a) st_1; st_2; st_3; st_4; $w_1(A)$; $w_2(A)$; $w_3(A)$; $r_2(A)$; $r_4(A)$;

b) st_1; st_2; st_3; st_4; $w_1(A)$; $w_3(A)$; $r_4(A)$; $r_2(A)$;

c) st_1; st_2; st_3; st_4; $w_1(A)$; $w_4(A)$; $r_3(A)$; $w_2(A)$;

!! **Exercise 8.3:** We observed in our study of lock-based schedulers that there are several reasons why transactions that obtain locks could deadlock. Can a timestamp scheduler using the commit bit $C(X)$ have a deadlock?

9 Concurrency Control by Validation

Validation is another type of optimistic concurrency control, where we allow transactions to access data without locks, and at the appropriate time we check that the transaction has behaved in a serializable manner. Validation differs from timestamping principally in that the scheduler maintains a record of what active transactions are doing, rather than keeping read and write times for all database elements. Just before a transaction starts to write values of database elements, it goes through a "validation phase," where the sets of elements it has read and will write are compared with the write sets of other active transactions. Should there be a risk of physically unrealizable behavior, the transaction is rolled back.

9.1 Architecture of a Validation-Based Scheduler

When validation is used as the concurrency-control mechanism, the scheduler must be told for each transaction T the sets of database elements T reads and writes, the *read set*, RS(T), and the *write set*, WS(T), respectively. Transactions are executed in three phases:

1. *Read.* In the first phase, the transaction reads from the database all the elements in its read set. The transaction also computes in its local address space all the results it is going to write.

2. *Validate.* In the second phase, the scheduler validates the transaction by comparing its read and write sets with those of other transactions. We shall describe the validation process in Section 9.2. If validation fails, then the transaction is rolled back; otherwise it proceeds to the third phase.

3. *Write.* In the third phase, the transaction writes to the database its values for the elements in its write set.

Intuitively, we may think of each transaction that successfully validates as executing at the moment that it validates. Thus, the validation-based scheduler has an assumed serial order of the transactions to work with, and it bases its decision to validate or not on whether the transactions' behaviors are consistent with this serial order.

To support the decision whether to validate a transaction, the scheduler maintains three sets:

1. *START*, the set of transactions that have started, but not yet completed validation. For each transaction T in this set, the scheduler maintains START(T), the time at which T started.

2. *VAL*, the set of transactions that have been validated but not yet finished the writing of phase 3. For each transaction T in this set, the scheduler maintains both START(T) and VAL(T), the time at which T validated. Note that VAL(T) is also the time at which T is imagined to execute in the hypothetical serial order of execution.

3. *FIN*, the set of transactions that have completed phase 3. For these transactions T, the scheduler records START(T), VAL(T), and FIN(T), the time at which T finished. In principle this set grows, but as we shall see, we do not have to remember transaction T if FIN(T) $<$ START(U) for any active transaction U (i.e., for any U in *START* or *VAL*). The scheduler may thus periodically purge the *FIN* set to keep its size from growing beyond bounds.

9.2 The Validation Rules

The information of Section 9.1 is enough for the scheduler to detect any potential violation of the assumed serial order of the transactions — the order in which the transactions validate. To understand the rules, let us first consider what can be wrong when we try to validate a transaction T.

1. Suppose there is a transaction U such that:

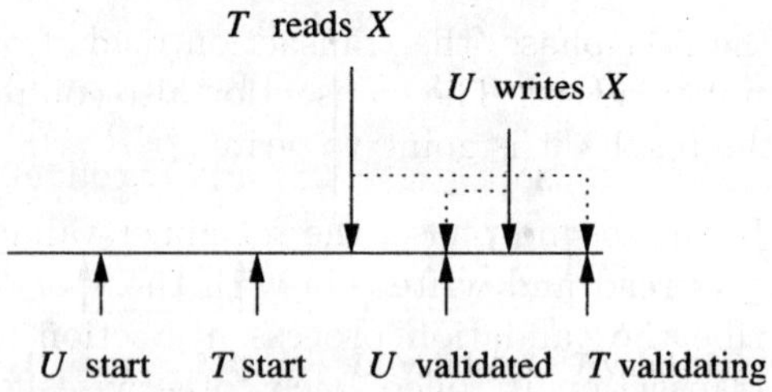

Figure 43: T cannot validate if an earlier transaction is now writing something that T should have read

(a) U is in *VAL* or *FIN*; that is, U has validated.

(b) FIN(U) > START(T); that is, U did not finish before T started.[11]

(c) RS(T) $\cap$ WS(U) is not empty; in particular, let it contain database element X.

Then it is possible that U wrote X after T read X. In fact, U may not even have written X yet. A situation where U wrote X, but not in time is shown in Fig. 43. To interpret the figure, note that the dotted lines connect the events in real time with the time at which they would have occurred had transactions been executed at the moment they validated. Since we don't know whether or not T got to read U's value, we must rollback T to avoid a risk that the actions of T and U will not be consistent with the assumed serial order.

2. Suppose there is a transaction U such that:

(a) U is in *VAL*; i.e., U has successfully validated.

(b) FIN(U) > VAL(T); that is, U did not finish before T entered its validation phase.

(c) WS(T) $\cap$ WS(U) $\neq \emptyset$; in particular, let X be in both write sets.

Then the potential problem is as shown in Fig. 44. T and U must both write values of X, and if we let T validate, it is possible that it will write X before U does. Since we cannot be sure, we rollback T to make sure it does not violate the assumed serial order in which it follows U.

The two problems described above are the only situations in which a write by T could be physically unrealizable. In Fig. 43, if U finished before T started, then surely T would read the value of X that either U or some later transaction wrote. In Fig. 44, if U finished before T validated, then surely U wrote X before

[11]Note that if U is in *VAL*, then U has not yet finished when T validates. In that case, FIN(U) is technically undefined. However, we know it must be larger than START(T) in this case.

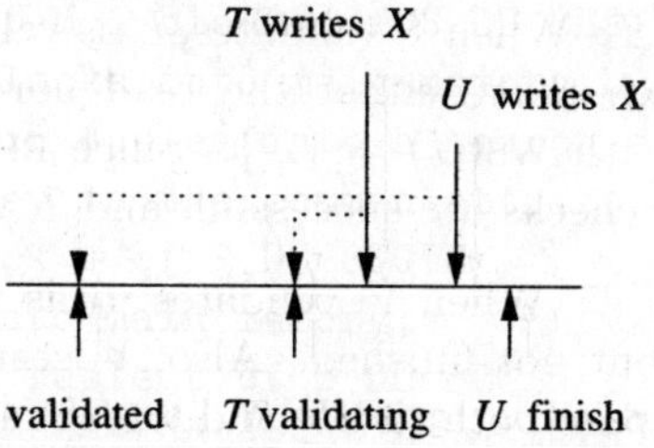

Figure 44: T cannot validate if it could then write something ahead of an earlier transaction

T did. We may thus summarize these observations with the following rule for validating a transaction T:

- Check that $\text{RS}(T) \cap \text{WS}(U) = \emptyset$ for any previously validated U that did not finish before T started, i.e., if $\text{FIN}(U) > \text{START}(T)$.
- Check that $\text{WS}(T) \cap \text{WS}(U) = \emptyset$ for any previously validated U that did not finish before T validated, i.e., if $\text{FIN}(U) > \text{VAL}(T)$.

Example 29: Figure 45 shows a time line during which four transactions T, U, V, and W attempt to execute and validate. The read and write sets for each transaction are indicated on the diagram. T starts first, although U is the first to validate.

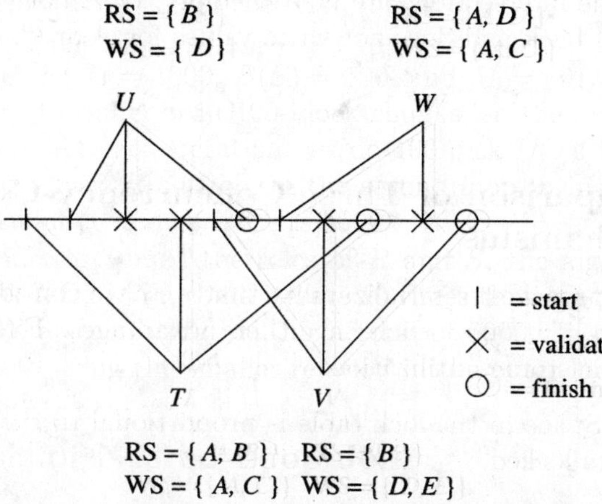

Figure 45: Four transactions and their validation

1. Validation of U: When U validates there are no other validated transactions, so there is nothing to check. U validates successfully and writes a value for database element D.

2. Validation of T: When T validates, U is validated but not finished. Thus, we must check that neither the read nor write set of T has anything in common with $\text{WS}(U) = \{D\}$. Since $\text{RS}(T) = \{A, B\}$, and $\text{WS}(T) = \{A, C\}$, both checks are successful, and T validates.

3. Validation of V: When V validates, U is validated and finished, and T is validated but not finished. Also, V started before U finished. Thus, we must compare both $\text{RS}(V)$ and $\text{WS}(V)$ against $\text{WS}(T)$, but only $\text{RS}(V)$ needs to be compared against $\text{WS}(U)$. we find:
   - $\text{RS}(V) \cap \text{WS}(T) = \{B\} \cap \{A, C\} = \emptyset$.
   - $\text{WS}(V) \cap \text{WS}(T) = \{D, E\} \cap \{A, C\} = \emptyset$.
   - $\text{RS}(V) \cap \text{WS}(U) = \{B\} \cap \{D\} = \emptyset$.

   Thus, V also validates successfully.

4. Validation of W: When W validates, we find that U finished before W started, so no comparison between W and U is performed. T is finished before W validates but did not finish before W started, so we compare only $\text{RS}(W)$ with $\text{WS}(T)$. V is validated but not finished, so we need to compare both $\text{RS}(W)$ and $\text{WS}(W)$ with $\text{WS}(V)$. These tests are:
   - $\text{RS}(W) \cap \text{WS}(T) = \{A, D\} \cap \{A, C\} = \{A\}$.
   - $\text{RS}(W) \cap \text{WS}(V) = \{A, D\} \cap \{D, E\} = \{D\}$.
   - $\text{WS}(W) \cap \text{WS}(V) = \{A, C\} \cap \{D, E\} = \emptyset$.

   Since the intersections are not all empty, W is not validated. Rather, W is rolled back and does not write values for A or C.

□

9.3 Comparison of Three Concurrency-Control Mechanisms

The three approaches to serializability that we have considered — locks, timestamps, and validation — each have their advantages. First, they can be compared for their storage utilization:

- *Locks*: Space in the lock table is proportional to the number of database elements locked.
- *Timestamps*: In a naive implementation, space is needed for read- and write-times with every database element, whether or not it is currently accessed. However, a more careful implementation will treat all timestamps that are prior to the earliest active transaction as "minus infinity" and not record them. In that case, we can store read- and write-times in a table analogous to a lock table, in which only those database elements that have been accessed recently are mentioned at all.

Just a Moment

You may have been concerned with a tacit notion that validation takes place in a moment, or indivisible instant of time. For example, we imagine that we can decide whether a transaction U has already validated before we start to validate transaction T. Could U perhaps finish validating while we are validating T?

If we are running on a uniprocessor system, and there is only one scheduler process, we can indeed think of validation and other actions of the scheduler as taking place in an instant of time. The reason is that if the scheduler is validating T, then it cannot also be validating U, so all during the validation of T, the validation status of U cannot change.

If we are running on a multiprocessor, and there are several scheduler processes, then it might be that one is validating T while the other is validating U. If so, then we need to rely on whatever synchronization mechanism the multiprocessor system provides to make validation an atomic action.

- *Validation*: Space is used for timestamps and read/write sets for each currently active transaction, plus a few more transactions that finished after some currently active transaction began.

Thus, the amounts of space used by each approach is approximately proportional to the sum over all active transactions of the number of database elements the transaction accesses. Timestamping and validation may use slightly more space because they keep track of certain accesses by recently committed transactions that a lock table would not record. A potential problem with validation is that the write set for a transaction must be known before the writes occur (but after the transaction's local computation has been completed).

We can also compare the methods for their effect on the ability of transactions to complete without delay. The performance of the three methods depends on whether *interaction* among transactions (the likelihood that a transaction will access an element that is also being accessed by a concurrent transaction) is high or low.

- Locking delays transactions but avoids rollbacks, even when interaction is high. Timestamps and validation do not delay transactions, but can cause them to rollback, which is a more serious form of delay and also wastes resources.

- If interference is low, then neither timestamps nor validation will cause many rollbacks, and may be preferable to locking because they generally have lower overhead than a locking scheduler.

- When a rollback is necessary, timestamps catch some problems earlier than validation, which always lets a transaction do all its internal work before considering whether the transaction must rollback.

9.4 Exercises for Section 9

Exercise 9.1: In the following sequences of events, we use $R_i(X)$ to mean "transaction T_i starts, and its read set is the list of database elements X." Also, V_i means "T_i attempts to validate," and $W_i(X)$ means that "T_i finishes, and its write set was X." Tell what happens when each sequence is processed by a validation-based scheduler.

a) $R_1(A, B)$; $R_2(B, C)$; V_1; $R_3(C, D)$; V_3; $W_1(A)$; V_2; $W_2(A)$; $W_3(B)$;

b) $R_1(A, B)$; $R_2(B, C)$; V_1; $R_3(C, D)$; V_3; $W_1(A)$; V_2; $W_2(A)$; $W_3(D)$;

c) $R_1(A, B)$; $R_2(B, C)$; V_1; $R_3(C, D)$; V_3; $W_1(C)$; V_2; $W_2(A)$; $W_3(D)$;

d) $R_1(A, B)$; $R_2(B, C)$; $R_3(C)$; V_1; V_2; V_3; $W_1(A)$; $W_2(B)$; $W_3(C)$;

e) $R_1(A, B)$; $R_2(B, C)$; $R_3(C)$; V_1; V_2; V_3; $W_1(C)$; $W_2(B)$; $W_3(A)$;

f) $R_1(A, B)$; $R_2(B, C)$; $R_3(C)$; V_1; V_2; V_3; $W_1(A)$; $W_2(C)$; $W_3(B)$;

10 Summary

- ✦ *Consistent Database States*: Database states that obey whatever implied or declared constraints the designers intended are called consistent. It is essential that operations on the database preserve consistency, that is, they turn one consistent database state into another.

- ✦ *Consistency of Concurrent Transactions*: It is normal for several transactions to have access to a database at the same time. Transactions, run in isolation, are assumed to preserve consistency of the database. It is the job of the scheduler to assure that concurrently operating transactions also preserve the consistency of the database.

- ✦ *Schedules*: Transactions are broken into actions, mainly reading and writing from the database. A sequence of these actions from one or more transactions is called a schedule.

- ✦ *Serial Schedules*: If transactions execute one at a time, the schedule is said to be serial.

- ✦ *Serializable Schedules*: A schedule that is equivalent in its effect on the database to some serial schedule is said to be serializable. Interleaving of actions from several transactions is possible in a serializable schedule that is not itself serial, but we must be very careful what sequences of actions we allow, or an interleaving will leave the database in an inconsistent state.

- ✦ *Conflict-Serializability*: A simple-to-test, sufficient condition for serializability is that the schedule can be made serial by a sequence of swaps of adjacent actions without conflicts. Such a schedule is called conflict-serializable. A conflict occurs if we try to swap two actions of the same transaction, or to swap two actions that access the same database element, at least one of which actions is a write.

- ✦ *Precedence Graphs*: An easy test for conflict-serializability is to construct a precedence graph for the schedule. Nodes correspond to transactions, and there is an arc $T \rightarrow U$ if some action of T in the schedule conflicts with a later action of U. A schedule is conflict-serializable if and only if the precedence graph is acyclic.

- ✦ *Locking*: The most common approach to assuring serializable schedules is to lock database elements before accessing them, and to release the lock after finishing access to the element. Locks on an element prevent other transactions from accessing the element.

- ✦ *Two-Phase Locking*: Locking by itself does not assure serializability. However, two-phase locking, in which all transactions first enter a phase where they only acquire locks, and then enter a phase where they only release locks, will guarantee serializability.

- ✦ *Lock Modes*: To avoid locking out transactions unnecessarily, systems usually use several lock modes, with different rules for each mode about when a lock can be granted. Most common is the system with shared locks for read-only access and exclusive locks for accesses that include writing.

- ✦ *Compatibility Matrices*: A compatibility matrix is a useful summary of when it is legal to grant a lock in a certain lock mode, given that there may be other locks, in the same or other modes, on the same element.

- ✦ *Update Locks*: A scheduler can allow a transaction that plans to read and then write an element first to take an update lock, and later to upgrade the lock to exclusive. Update locks can be granted when there are already shared locks on the element, but once there, an update lock prevents other locks from being granted on that element.

- ✦ *Increment Locks*: For the common case where a transaction wants only to add or subtract a constant from an element, an increment lock is suitable. Increment locks on the same element do not conflict with each other, although they conflict with shared and exclusive locks.

✦ *Locking Elements With a Granularity Hierarchy*: When both large and small elements — relations, disk blocks, and tuples, perhaps — may need to be locked, a warning system of locks enforces serializability. Transactions place intention locks on large elements to warn other transactions that they plan to access one or more of its subelements.

✦ *Locking Elements Arranged in a Tree*: If database elements are only accessed by moving down a tree, as in a B-tree index, then a non-two-phase locking strategy can enforce serializability. The rules require a lock to be held on the parent while obtaining a lock on the child, although the lock on the parent can then be released and additional locks taken later.

✦ *Optimistic Concurrency Control*: Instead of locking, a scheduler can assume transactions will be serializable, and abort a transaction if some potentially nonserializable behavior is seen. This approach, called optimistic, is divided into timestamp-based, and validation-based scheduling.

✦ *Timestamp-Based Schedulers*: This type of scheduler assigns timestamps to transactions as they begin. Database elements have associated read- and write-times, which are the timestamps of the transactions that most recently performed those actions. If an impossible situation, such as a read by one transaction of a value that was written in that transaction's future is detected, the violating transaction is rolled back, i.e., aborted and restarted.

✦ *Multiversion Timestamps*: A common technique in practice is for read-only transactions to be scheduled by timestamps, but with multiple versions, where a write of an element does not overwrite earlier values of that element until all transactions that could possibly need the earlier value have finished. Writing transactions are scheduled by conventional locks.

✦ *Validation-Based Schedulers*: These schedulers validate transactions after they have read everything they need, but before they write. Transactions that have read, or will write, an element that some other transaction is in the process of writing, will have an ambiguous result, so the transaction is not validated. A transaction that fails to validate is rolled back.

11 References

The book [6] is an important source for material on scheduling, as well as locking. [3] is another important source. Two recent surveys of concurrency control are [12] and [11].

Probably the most significant paper in the field of transaction processing is [4] on two-phase locking. The warning protocol for hierarchies of granularity is from [5]. Non-two-phase locking for trees is from [10]. The compatibility matrix was introduced to study behavior of lock modes in [7].

Timestamps as a concurrency control method appeared in [2] and [1]. Scheduling by validation is from [8]. The use of multiple versions was studied by [9].

1. P. A. Bernstein and N. Goodman, "Timestamp-based algorithms for concurrency control in distributed database systems," *Intl. Conf. on Very Large Databases*, pp. 285–300, 1980.

2. P. A. Bernstein, N. Goodman, J. B. Rothnie, Jr., and C. H. Papadimitriou, "Analysis of serializability in SDD-1: a system of distributed databases (the fully redundant case)," *IEEE Trans. on Software Engineering* **SE-4**:3 (1978), pp. 154–168.

3. P. A. Bernstein, V. Hadzilacos, and N. Goodman, *Concurrency Control and Recovery in Database Systems*, Addison-Wesley, Reading MA, 1987.

4. K. P. Eswaran, J. N. Gray, R. A. Lorie, and I. L. Traiger, "The notions of consistency and predicate locks in a database system," *Comm. ACM* **19**:11 (1976), pp. 624–633.

5. J. N. Gray, F. Putzolo, and I. L. Traiger, "Granularity of locks and degrees of consistency in a shared data base," in G. M. Nijssen (ed.), *Modeling in Data Base Management Systems*, North Holland, Amsterdam, 1976.

6. J. N. Gray and A. Reuter, *Transaction Processing: Concepts and Techniques*, Morgan-Kaufmann, San Francisco, 1993.

7. H. F. Korth, "Locking primitives in a database system," *J. ACM* **30**:1 (1983), pp. 55–79.

8. H.-T. Kung and J. T. Robinson, "Optimistic concurrency control," *ACM Trans. on Database Systems* **6**:2 (1981), pp. 312–326.

9. C. H. Papadimitriou and P. C. Kanellakis, "On concurrency control by multiple versions," *ACM Trans. on Database Systems* **9**:1 (1984), pp. 89–99.

10. A. Silberschatz and Z. Kedem, "Consistency in hierarchical database systems," *J. ACM* **27**:1 (1980), pp. 72–80.

11. A. Thomasian, "Concurrency control: methods, performance, and analysis," *Computing Surveys* **30**:1 (1998), pp. 70–119.

12. B. Thuraisingham and H.-P. Ko, "Concurrency control in trusted database management systems: a survey," *SIGMOD Record* **22**:4 (1993), pp. 52–60.

The [illegible] approach to concurrency control is from [1] and [2]. Scheduling by validation is from [8]. The use of multiple versions is from [illegible].

1. P. A. Bernstein and N. Goodman, "Timestamp-based algorithms for concurrency control in distributed database systems," *Proc. Intl. Conf. on Very Large Data Bases* (1980), pp. 285–300.

2. P. A. Bernstein, N. Goodman, J. B. Rothnie, Jr., and C. H. Papadimitriou, "Analysis of serializability in SDD-1: a system of distributed databases (the fully redundant case)," *IEEE Trans. on Software Engineering* SE-4:3 (1978), pp. 154–168.

3. P. A. Bernstein, V. Hadzilacos, and N. Goodman, *Concurrency Control and Recovery in Database Systems*, Addison-Wesley, Reading MA, 1987.

4. K. P. Eswaran, J. N. Gray, R. A. Lorie, and I. L. Traiger, "The notions of consistency and predicate locks in a database system," *Comm. ACM* 19:11 (1976), pp. 624–633.

5. J. N. Gray, F. Putzolo, and I. L. Traiger, "Granularity of locks and degrees of consistency in a shared data base," in G. M. Nijssen (ed.), *Modeling in Data Base Management Systems*, North Holland, Amsterdam, 1976.

6. J. N. Gray and A. Reuter, *Transaction Processing: Concepts and Techniques*, Morgan-Kaufmann, San Francisco, 1993.

7. H. F. Korth, "Locking primitives in a database system," *J. ACM* 30:1 (1983), pp. 55–79.

8. H.-T. Kung and J. T. Robinson, "Optimistic concurrency control," *ACM Trans. on Database Systems* 6:2 (1981), pp. 312–326.

9. C. H. Papadimitriou, P. A. Bernstein, and J. B. Rothnie, Jr., "Some computational problems related to database concurrency control," *Proc. Conf. on Theoretical Computer Science*, Univ. of Waterloo, 1977.

10. A. Silberschatz and Z. Kedem, "Consistency in hierarchical database systems," *J. ACM* 27:1 (1980), pp. 72–80.

11. A. Thomasian, "Concurrency control: methods, performance, and analysis," *Computing Surveys* 30:1 (1998), pp. 70–119.

12. B. Thuraisingham and H.-P. Ko, "Concurrency control in trusted database management systems," *SIGMOD Record* 22:4 (1993), pp. 52–60.

More About Transaction Management

In this chapter we cover several issues about transaction management. How do the needs to recover from errors, to allow transactions to abort, and to maintain serializability interact? Then, we discuss the management of deadlocks among transactions, which typically result from several transactions each having to wait for a resource, such as a lock, that is held by another transaction.

Finally, we consider the problems that arise due to "long transactions." There are applications, such as CAD systems or "workflow" systems, in which human and computer processes interact, perhaps over a period of days. These systems, like short-transaction systems such as banking or airline reservations, need to preserve consistency of the database state.

1 Serializability and Recoverability

You may recall that we discussed the creation of a log and its use to recover the database state when a system crash occurs. We introduced the view of database computation in which values move between nonvolatile disk, volatile main-memory, and the local address space of transactions. The guarantee the various logging methods give is that, should a crash occur, it will be able to reconstruct the actions of the committed transactions on the disk copy of the database. A logging system makes no attempt to support serializability; it will blindly reconstruct a database state, even if it is the result of a nonserializable schedule of actions. In fact, commercial database systems do not always insist on serializability, and in some systems, serializability is enforced only on explicit

From Chapter 19 of *Database Systems*, Second Edition. Hector Garcia-Molina, Jeffrey D. Ullman, Jennifer Widom.

request of the user.

Schedulers designed according to the principles of serializability may do things that the log manager cannot tolerate. For instance, there is nothing in the serializability definition that forbids a transaction with a lock on an element A from writing a new value of A into the database before committing, and thus violating a rule of the logging policy. Worse, a transaction might write into the database and then abort without undoing the write, which could easily result in an inconsistent database state, even though there is no system crash and the scheduler theoretically maintains serializability.

1.1 The Dirty-Data Problem

Recall that data is "dirty" if it has been written by a transaction that is not yet committed. The dirty data could appear either in the buffers, or on disk, or both; either can cause trouble.

T_1	T_2	A	B
		25	25
$l_1(A)$; $r_1(A)$;			
`A := A+100;`			
$w_1(A)$; $l_1(B)$; $u_1(A)$;		125	
	$l_2(A)$; $r_2(A)$;		
	`A := A*2;`		
	$w_2(A)$;	250	
	$l_2(B)$ **Denied**		
$r_1(B)$;			
Abort; $u_1(B)$;			
	$l_2(B)$; $u_2(A)$; $r_2(B)$;		
	`B := B*2;`		
	$w_2(B)$; $u_2(B)$;		50

Figure 1: T_1 writes dirty data and then aborts

Example 1: Let us reconsider the serializable schedule in Fig. 1. After T_1 aborts, the scheduler releases the lock on B that T_1 obtained; that step is essential, or else the lock on B would be unavailable to any other transaction, forever.

However, T_2 has now read data that does not represent a consistent state of the database. That is, T_2 read the value of A that T_1 changed, but read the value of B that existed prior to T_1's actions. It doesn't matter in this case whether or not the value 125 for A that T_1 created was written to disk or not; T_2

gets that value from a buffer, regardless. Because it read an inconsistent state, T_2 leaves the database (on disk) with an inconsistent state, where $A \neq B$.

The problem in Fig. 1 is that A written by T_1 is dirty data, whether it is in a buffer or on disk. The fact that T_2 read A and used it in its own calculation makes T_2's actions questionable. As we shall see in Section 1.2, it is necessary, if such a situation is allowed to occur, to abort and roll back T_2 as well as T_1. □

T_1	T_2	T_3	A	B	C
200	150	175	RT=0 WT=0	RT=0 WT=0	RT=0 WT=0
	$w_2(B);$			WT=150	
$r_1(B);$					
	$r_2(A);$		RT=150		
		$r_3(C);$			RT=175
	$w_2(C);$				
	Abort;			WT=0	
		$w_3(A);$	WT=175		

Figure 2: T_1 has read dirty data from T_2 and must abort when T_2 does

Example 2: Now, consider Fig. 2, which shows a sequence of actions under a timestamp-based scheduler. However, we imagine that this scheduler does not use the commit bit. Recall that the purpose of this bit is to prevent a value that was written by an uncommitted transaction to be read by another transaction. Thus, when T_1 reads B at the second step, there is no commit-bit check to tell T_1 to delay. T_1 can proceed and could even write to disk and commit; we have not shown further details of what T_1 does.

Eventually, T_2 tries to write C in a physically unrealizable way, and T_2 aborts. The effect of T_2's prior write of B is cancelled; the value and write-time of B is reset to what it was before T_2 wrote. Yet T_1 has been allowed to use this cancelled value of B and can do anything with it, such as using it to compute new values of A, B, and/or C and writing them to disk. Thus, T_1, having read a dirty value of B, can cause an inconsistent database state. Note that, had the commit bit been recorded and used, the read $r_1(B)$ at step (2) would have been delayed, and not allowed to occur until after T_2 aborted and the value of B had been restored to its previous (presumably committed) value. □

1.2 Cascading Rollback

As we see from the examples above, if dirty data is available to transactions, then we sometimes have to perform a *cascading rollback*. That is, when a transaction T aborts, we must determine which transactions have read data written by T, abort them, and recursively abort any transactions that have read data written by an aborted transaction. To cancel the effect of an aborted transaction, we can use the log, if it is one of the types (undo or undo/redo) that provides former values. We may also be able to restore the data from the disk copy of the database, if the effect of the dirty data has not migrated to disk.

As we have noted, a timestamp-based scheduler with a commit bit prevents a transaction that may have read dirty data from proceeding, so there is no possibility of cascading rollback with such a scheduler. A validation-based scheduler avoids cascading rollback, because writing to the database (even in buffers) occurs only after it is determined that the transaction will commit.

1.3 Recoverable Schedules

For any of the logging methods we have discussed to allow recovery, the set of transactions that are regarded as committed *after* recovery must be consistent. That is, if a transaction T_1 is, after recovery, regarded as committed, and T_1 used a value written by T_2, then T_2 must also remain committed, after recovery. Thus, we define:

- A schedule is *recoverable* if each transaction commits only after each transaction from which it has read has committed.

Example 3: In this and several subsequent examples of schedules with read- and write-actions, we shall use c_i for the action "transaction T_i commits." Here is an example of a recoverable schedule:

$$S_1\text{: } w_1(A);\ w_1(B);\ w_2(A);\ r_2(B);\ c_1;\ c_2;$$

Note that T_2 reads a value (B) written by T_1, so T_2 must commit after T_1 for the schedule to be recoverable.

Schedule S_1 above is evidently serial (and therefore serializable) as well as recoverable, but the two concepts are orthogonal. For instance, the following variation on S_1 is still recoverable, but not serializable.

$$S_2\text{: } w_2(A);\ w_1(B);\ w_1(A);\ r_2(B);\ c_1;\ c_2;$$

In schedule S_2, T_2 must precede T_1 in a serial order because of the writing of A, but T_1 must precede T_2 because of the writing and reading of B.

Finally, observe the following variation on S_1, which is serializable but not recoverable:

$$S_3\text{: } w_1(A);\ w_1(B);\ w_2(A);\ r_2(B);\ c_2;\ c_1;$$

In schedule S_3, T_1 precedes T_2, but their commitments occur in the wrong order. If before a crash, the commit record for T_2 reached disk, but the commit record for T_1 did not, then regardless of whether undo, redo, or undo/redo logging were used, T_2 would be committed after recovery, but T_1 would not. □

In order for recoverable schedules to be truly recoverable under any of the three logging methods, there is one additional assumption we must make regarding schedules:

- The log's commit records reach disk in the order in which they are written.

As we observed in Example 3 concerning schedule S_3, should it be possible for commit records to reach disk in the wrong order, then consistent recovery might be impossible. We shall return to and exploit this principle in Section 1.6.

1.4 Schedules That Avoid Cascading Rollback

Recoverable schedules sometimes require cascading rollback. For instance, if after the first four steps of schedule S_1 in Example 3 T_1 had to roll back, it would be necessary to roll back T_2 as well. To guarantee the absence of cascading rollback, we need a stronger condition than recoverability. We say that:

- A schedule *avoids cascading rollback* (or "is an *ACR schedule*") if transactions may read only values written by committed transactions.

Put another way, an ACR schedule forbids the reading of dirty data. As for recoverable schedules, we assume that "committed" means that the log's commit record has reached disk.

Example 4: The schedules of Example 3 are not ACR. In each case, T_2 reads B from the uncommitted transaction T_1. However, consider:

$$S_4\text{: } w_1(A);\ w_1(B);\ w_2(A);\ c_1;\ r_2(B);\ c_2;$$

Now, T_2 reads B only after T_1, the transaction that last wrote B, has committed, and its log record written to disk. Thus, schedule S_4 is ACR, as well as recoverable. □

Notice that should a transaction such as T_2 read a value written by T_1 after T_1 commits, then surely T_2 either commits or aborts after T_1 commits. Thus:

- Every ACR schedule is recoverable.

1.5 Managing Rollbacks Using Locking

Our prior discussion applies to schedules that are generated by any kind of scheduler. In the common case that the scheduler is lock-based, there is a simple and commonly used way to guarantee that there are no cascading rollbacks:

- *Strict Locking*: A transaction must not release any exclusive locks (or other locks, such as increment locks that allow values to be changed) until the transaction has either committed or aborted, and the commit or abort log record has been flushed to disk.

A schedule of transactions that follow the strict-locking rule is called a *strict schedule.* Two important properties of these schedules are:

1. *Every strict schedule is ACR.* The reason is that a transaction T_2 cannot read a value of element X written by T_1 until T_1 releases any exclusive lock (or similar lock that allows X to be changed). Under strict locking, the release does not occur until after commit.

2. *Every strict schedule is serializable.* To see why, observe that a strict schedule is equivalent to the serial schedule in which each transaction runs instantaneously at the time it commits.

With these observations, we can now picture the relationships among the different kinds of schedules we have seen so far. The containments are suggested in Fig. 3.

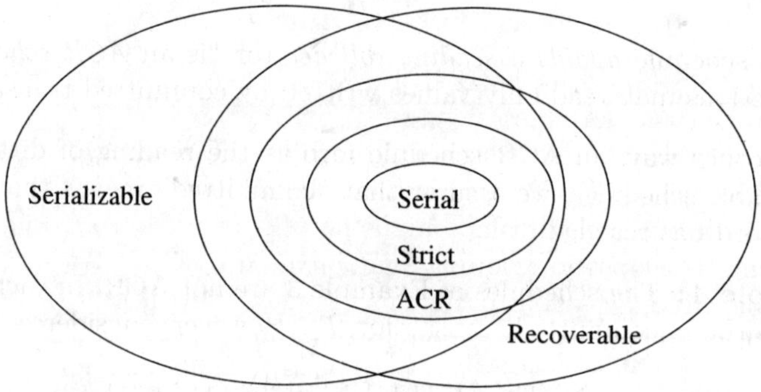

Figure 3: Containments and noncontainments among classes of schedules

Clearly, in a strict schedule, it is not possible for a transaction to read dirty data, since data written to a buffer by an uncommitted transaction remains locked until the transaction commits. However, we still have the problem of fixing the data in buffers when a transaction aborts, since these changes must have their effects cancelled. How difficult it is to fix buffered data depends on whether database elements are blocks or something smaller. We shall consider each.

Rollback for Blocks

If the lockable database elements are blocks, then there is a simple rollback method that never requires us to use the log. Suppose that a transaction T has obtained an exclusive lock on block A, written a new value for A in a buffer, and then had to abort. Since A has been locked since T wrote its value, no other transaction has read A. It is easy to restore the old value of A provided the following rule is followed:

- Blocks written by uncommitted transactions are pinned in main memory; that is, their buffers are not allowed to be written to disk.

In this case, we "roll back" T when it aborts by telling the buffer manager to ignore the value of A. That is, the buffer occupied by A is not written anywhere, and its buffer is added to the pool of available buffers. We can be sure that the value of A on disk is the most recent value written by a committed transaction, which is exactly the value we want A to have.

There is also a simple rollback method if we are using a multiversion system. We must again assume that blocks written by uncommitted transactions are pinned in memory. Then, we simply remove the value of A that was written by T from the list of available values of A. Note that because T was a writing transaction, its value of A was locked from the time the value was written to the time it aborted (assuming the timestamp/lock scheme).

Rollback for Small Database Elements

When lockable database elements are fractions of a block (e.g., tuples or objects), then the simple approach to restoring buffers that have been modified by aborted transactions will not work. The problem is that a buffer may contain data changed by two or more transactions; if one of them aborts, we still must preserve the changes made by the other. We have several choices when we must restore the old value of a small database element A that was written by the transaction that has aborted:

1. We can read the original value of A from the database stored on disk and modify the buffer contents appropriately.

2. If the log is an undo or undo/redo log, then we can obtain the former value from the log itself. The same code used to recover from crashes may be used for "voluntary" rollbacks as well.

3. We can keep a separate main-memory log of the changes made by each transaction, preserved for only the time that transaction is active. The old value can be found from this "log."

None of these approaches is ideal. The first surely involves a disk access. The second (examining the log) might not involve a disk access, if the relevant portion of the log is still in a buffer. However, it could also involve extensive examination of portions of the log on disk, searching for the update record that tells the correct former value. The last approach does not require disk accesses, but may consume a large fraction of memory for the main-memory "logs."

1.6 Group Commit

Under some circumstances, we can avoid reading dirty data even if we do not flush every commit record on the log to disk immediately. As long as we flush log records in the order that they are written, we can release locks as soon as the commit record is written to the log in a buffer.

Example 5: Suppose transaction T_1 writes X, finishes, writes its COMMIT record on the log, but the log record remains in a buffer. Even though T_1 has not committed in the sense that its commit record can survive a crash, we shall release T_1's locks. Then T_2 reads X and "commits," but its commit record, which follows that of T_1, also remains in a buffer. Since we are flushing log records in the order written, T_2 cannot be perceived as committed by a recovery manager (because its commit record reached disk) unless T_1 is also perceived as committed. Thus, the recovery manager will find either one of two things:

1. T_1 is committed on disk. Then regardless of whether or not T_2 is committed on disk, we know T_2 did not read X from an uncommitted transaction.

2. T_1 is not committed on disk. Then neither is T_2, and both are aborted by the recovery manager. In this case, the fact that T_2 read X from an uncommitted transaction has no effect on the database.

On the other hand, suppose that the buffer containing T_2's commit record got flushed to disk (say because the buffer manager decided to use the buffer for something else), but the buffer containing T_1's commit record did not. If there is a crash at that point, it will look to the recovery manager that T_1 did not commit, but T_2 did. The effect of T_2 will be permanently reflected in the database, but this effect was based on the dirty read of X by T_2. □

Our conclusion from Example 5 is that we can release locks earlier than the time that the transaction's commit record is flushed to disk. This policy, often called *group commit*, is:

- Do not release locks until the transaction finishes, and the commit log record at least appears in a buffer.

- Flush log blocks in the order that they were created.

Group commit, like the policy of requiring "recoverable schedules" as discussed in Section 1.3, guarantees that there is never a read of dirty data.

1.7 Logical Logging

We saw in Section 1.5 that dirty reads are easier to fix up when the unit of locking is the block or page. However, there are at least two problems presented when database elements are blocks.

1. All logging methods require either the old or new value of a database element, or both, to be recorded in the log. When the change to a block

When is a Transaction Really Committed?

The subtlety of group commit reminds us that a completed transaction can be in several different states between when it finishes its work and when it is truly "committed," in the sense that under no circumstances, including the occurrence of a system failure, will the effect of that transaction be lost. It is possible for a transaction to finish its work and even write its `COMMIT` record to the log in a main-memory buffer, yet have the effect of that transaction lost if there is a system crash and the `COMMIT` record has not yet reached disk. Moreover, even if the `COMMIT` record is on disk but not yet backed up in the archive, a media failure can cause the transaction to be undone and its effect to be lost.

In the absence of failure, all these states are equivalent, in the sense that each transaction will surely advance from being finished to having its effects survive even a media failure. However, when we need to take failures and recovery into account, it is important to recognize the differences among these states, which otherwise could all be referred to informally as "committed."

is small, e.g., a rewritten attribute of one tuple, or an inserted or deleted tuple, then there is a great deal of redundant information written on the log.

2. The requirement that the schedule be recoverable, releasing its locks only after commit, can inhibit concurrency severely. For example, recall the advantage of early lock release as we access data through a B-tree index. If we require that locks be held until commit, then this advantage cannot be obtained, and we effectively allow only one writing transaction to access a B-tree at any time.

Both these concerns motivate the use of *logical logging*, where only the changes to the blocks are described. There are several degrees of complexity, depending on the nature of the change.

1. A small number of bytes of the database element are changed, e.g., the update of a fixed-length field. This situation can be handled in a straightforward way, where we record only the changed bytes and their positions. Example 6 will show this situation and an appropriate form of update record.

2. The change to the database element is simply described, and easily restored, but it has the effect of changing most or all of the bytes in the database element. One common situation, discussed in Example 7, is

when a variable-length field is changed and much of its record, and even other records, must slide within the block. The new and old values of the block look very different unless we realize and indicate the simple cause of the change.

3. The change affects many bytes of a database element, and further changes can prevent this change from ever being undone. This situation is true "logical" logging, since we cannot even see the undo/redo process as occurring on the database elements themselves, but rather on some higher-level "logical" structure that the database elements represent. We shall, in Example 8, take up the matter of B-trees, a logical structure represented by database elements that are disk blocks, to illustrate this complex form of logical logging.

Example 6: Suppose database elements are blocks that each contain a set of tuples from some relation. We can express the update of an attribute by a log record that says something like "tuple t had its attribute a changed from value v_1 to v_2." An insertion of a new tuple into empty space on the block can be expressed as "a tuple t with value $(a_1, a_2, \ldots, a_k)$ was inserted beginning at offset position p." Unless the attribute changed or the tuple inserted are comparable in size to a block, the amount of space taken by these records will be much smaller than the entire block. Moreover, they serve for both undo and redo operations.

Notice that both these operations are idempotent; if you perform them several times on a block, the result is the same as performing them once. Likewise, their implied inverses, where the value of $t[a]$ is restored from v_2 back to v_1, or the tuple t is removed, are also idempotent. □

Example 7: Again assume database elements are blocks holding tuples, but the tuples have some variable-length fields. If a change to a field such as was described in Example 6 occurs, we may have to slide large portions of the block to make room for a longer field, or to preserve space if a field becomes smaller. In extreme cases, we could have to create an overflow block to hold part of the contents of the original block, or we could remove an overflow block if a shorter field allows us to combine the contents of two blocks into one.

As long as the block and its overflow block(s) are considered part of one database element, then it is straightforward to use the old and/or new value of the changed field to undo or redo the change. However, the block-plus-overflow-block(s) must be thought of as holding certain tuples at a "logical" level. We may not even be able to restore the bytes of these blocks to their original state after an undo or redo, because there may have been reorganization of the blocks due to other changes that varied the length of other fields. Yet if we think of a database element as being a collection of blocks that together represent certain tuples, then a redo or undo can indeed restore the logical "state" of the element. □

However, it may not be possible, as we suggested in Example 7, to treat blocks as expandable through the mechanism of overflow blocks. We may thus be able to undo or redo actions only at a level higher than blocks. The next example discusses the important case of B-tree indexes, where the management of blocks does not permit overflow blocks, and we must think of undo and redo as occurring at the "logical" level of the B-tree itself, rather than the blocks.

Example 8: Let us consider the problem of logical logging for B-tree nodes. Instead of writing the old and/or new value of an entire node (block) on the log, we write a short record that describes the change. These changes include:

1. Insertion or deletion of a key/pointer pair for a child.
2. Change of the key associated with a pointer.
3. Splitting or merging of nodes.

Each of these changes can be indicated with a short log record. Even the splitting operation requires only telling where the split occurs, and where the new nodes are. Likewise, merging requires only a reference to the nodes involved, since the manner of merging is determined by the B-tree management algorithms used.

Using logical update records of these types allows us to release locks earlier than would otherwise be required for a recoverable schedule. The reason is that dirty reads of B-tree blocks are never a problem for the transaction that reads them, provided its only purpose is to use the B-tree to locate the data the transaction needs to access.

For instance, suppose that transaction T reads a leaf node N, but the transaction U that last wrote N later aborts, and some change made to N (e.g., the insertion of a new key/pointer pair into N due to an insertion of a tuple by U) needs to be undone. If T has also inserted a key/pointer pair into N, then it is not possible to restore N to the way it was before U modified it. However, the effect of U on N can be undone; in this example we would delete the key/pointer pair that U had inserted. The resulting N is not the same as that which existed before U operated; it has the insertion made by T. However, there is no database inconsistency, since the B-tree as a whole continues to reflect only the changes made by committed transactions. That is, we have restored the B-tree at a logical level, but not at the physical level. □

1.8 Recovery From Logical Logs

If the logical actions are idempotent — i.e., they can be repeated any number of times without harm — then we can recover easily using a logical log. For instance, we discussed in Example 6 how a tuple insertion could be represented in the logical log by the tuple and the place within a block where the tuple was placed. If we write that tuple in the same place two or more times, then it is as if we had written it once. Thus, when recovering, should we need to redo a transaction that inserted a tuple, we can repeat the insertion into the proper block at the proper place, without worrying whether we had already inserted that tuple.

In contrast, consider a situation where tuples can move around within blocks or between blocks, as in Examples 7 and 8. Now, we cannot associate a particular place into which a tuple is to be inserted; the best we can do is place in the log an action such as "the tuple t was inserted somewhere on block B." If we need to redo the insertion of t during recovery, we may wind up with two copies of t in block B. Worse, we may not know whether the block B with the first copy of t made it to disk. Another transaction writing to another database element on block B may have caused a copy of B to be written to disk, for example.

To disambiguate situations such as this when we recover using a logical log, a technique called *log sequence numbers* has been developed.

- Each log record is given a number one greater than that of the previous log record.[1] Thus, a typical logical log record has the form $<L, T, A, B>$, where:
  - L is the log sequence number, an integer.
  - T is the transaction involved.
  - A is the action performed by T, e.g., "insert of tuple t."
  - B is the block on which the action was performed.
- For each action, there is a *compensating action* that logically undoes the action. As discussed in Example 8, the compensating action may not restore the database to exactly the same state S it would have been in had the action never occurred, but it restores the database to a state that is logically equivalent to S. For instance, the compensating action for "insert tuple t" is "delete tuple t."
- If a transaction T aborts, then for each action performed on the database by T, the compensating action is performed, and the fact that this action was performed is also recorded in the log.
- Each block maintains, in its header, the log sequence number of the last action that affected that block.

Suppose now that we need to use the logical log to recover after a crash. Here is an outline of the steps to take.

[1] Eventually the log sequence numbers must restart at 0, but the time between restarts of the sequence is so large that no ambiguity can occur.

1. Our first step is to reconstruct the state of the database at the time of the crash, including blocks whose current values were in buffers and therefore got lost. To do so:

   (a) Find the most recent checkpoint on the log, and determine from it the set of transactions that were active at that time.

   (b) For each log entry $<L, T, A, B>$, compare the log sequence number N on block B with the log sequence number L for this log record. If $N < L$, then redo action A; that action was never performed on block B. However, if $N \geq L$, then do nothing; the effect of A was already felt by B.

   (c) For each log entry that informs us that a transaction T started, committed, or aborted, adjust the set of active transactions accordingly.

2. The set of transactions that remain active when we reach the end of the log must be aborted. To do so:

   (a) Scan the log again, this time from the end back to the previous checkpoint. Each time we encounter a record $<L, T, A, B>$ for a transaction T that must be aborted, perform the compensating action for A on block B and record in the log the fact that that compensating action was performed.

   (b) If we must abort a transaction that began prior to the most recent checkpoint (i.e., that transaction was on the active list for the checkpoint), then continue back in the log until the start-records for all such transactions have been found.

   (c) Write abort-records in the log for each of the transactions we had to abort.

1.9 Exercises for Section 1

Exercise 1.1: What are all the ways to insert locks (of a single type only) into the sequence of actions

$$r_1(A); r_1(B); w_1(A); w_1(B);$$

so that the transaction T_1 is:

a) Two-phase locked, and strict.

b) Two-phase locked, but not strict.

Exercise 1.2: Suppose that each of the sequences of actions below is followed by an abort action for transaction T_1. Tell which transactions need to be rolled back.

a) $r_1(A); r_2(B); w_1(B); w_2(C); r_3(B); r_3(C); w_3(D);$

b) $r_1(A)$; $w_1(B)$; $r_2(B)$; $w_2(C)$; $r_3(C)$; $w_3(D)$;

c) $r_2(A)$; $r_3(A)$; $r_1(A)$; $w_1(B)$; $r_2(B)$; $r_3(B)$; $w_2(C)$; $r_3(C)$;

d) $r_2(A)$; $r_3(A)$; $r_1(A)$; $w_1(B)$; $r_3(B)$; $w_2(C)$; $r_3(C)$;

Exercise 1.3: Consider each of the sequences of actions in Exercise 1.2, but now suppose that all three transactions commit and write their commit record on the log immediately after their last action. However, a crash occurs, and a tail of the log was not written to disk before the crash and is therefore lost. Tell, depending on where the lost tail of the log begins:

i. What transactions could be considered uncommitted?

ii. Are any dirty reads created during the recovery process? If so, what transactions need to be rolled back?

iii. What additional dirty reads could have been created if the portion of the log lost was not a tail, but rather some portions in the middle?

! **Exercise 1.4:** Consider the following two transactions:

$$T_1\text{: } w_1(A);\ w_1(B);\ r_1(C);\ c_1;$$
$$T_2\text{: } w_2(A);\ r_2(B);\ w_2(C);\ c_2;$$

a) How many schedules of T_1 and T_2 are recoverable?

b) Of these, how many are ACR schedules?

c) How many are both recoverable and serializable?

d) How many are both ACR and serializable?

Exercise 1.5: Give an example of an ACR schedule with shared and exclusive locks that is not strict.

2 Deadlocks

Several times we have observed that concurrently executing transactions can compete for resources and thereby reach a state where there is a *deadlock*: each of several transactions is waiting for a resource held by one of the others, and none can make progress.

- Ordinary operation of two-phase-locked transactions can still lead to a deadlock, because each has locked something that another transaction also needs to lock.

- The ability to upgrade locks from shared to exclusive can cause a deadlock because each transaction holds a shared lock on the same element and wants to upgrade the lock.

There are two broad approaches to dealing with deadlock. We can detect deadlocks and fix them, or we can manage transactions in such a way that deadlocks are never able to form.

2.1 Deadlock Detection by Timeout

When a deadlock exists, it is generally impossible to repair the situation so that all transactions involved can proceed. Thus, at least one of the transactions will have to be aborted and restarted.

The simplest way to detect and resolve deadlocks is with a *timeout.* Put a limit on how long a transaction may be active, and if a transaction exceeds this time, roll it back. For example, in a simple transaction system, where typical transactions execute in milliseconds, a timeout of one minute would affect only transactions that are caught in a deadlock.

Notice that when one deadlocked transaction times out and rolls back, it releases its locks or other resources. Thus, there is a chance that the other transactions involved in the deadlock will complete before reaching their timeout limits. However, since transactions involved in a deadlock are likely to have started at approximately the same time (or else, one would have completed before another started), it is also possible that spurious timeouts of transactions that are no longer involved in a deadlock will occur.

2.2 The Waits-For Graph

Deadlocks that are caused by transactions waiting for locks held by another can be detected by a *waits-for graph*, indicating which transactions are waiting for locks held by another transaction. This graph can be used either to detect deadlocks after they have formed or to prevent deadlocks from ever forming. We shall assume the latter, which requires us to maintain the waits-for graph at all times, refusing to allow an action that creates a cycle in the graph.

A lock table maintains for each database element X a list of the transactions that are waiting for locks on X, as well as transactions that currently hold locks on X. The waits-for graph has a node for each transaction that currently holds any lock or is waiting for one. There is an arc from node (transaction) T to node U if there is some database element A such that:

1. U holds a lock on A,

2. T is waiting for a lock on A, and

3. T cannot get a lock on A in its desired mode unless U first releases its lock on A.[2].

[2]In common situations, such as shared and exclusive locks, every waiting transaction will have to wait until *all* current lock holders release their locks, but there are examples of systems of lock modes where a transaction can get its lock after only some of the current locks are released.

If there are no cycles in the waits-for graph, then each transaction can complete eventually. There will be at least one transaction waiting for no other transaction, and this transaction surely can complete. At that time, there will be at least one other transaction that is not waiting, which can complete, and so on.

However, if there is a cycle, then no transaction in the cycle can ever make progress, so there is a deadlock. Thus, a strategy for deadlock avoidance is to roll back any transaction that makes a request that would cause a cycle in the waits-for graph.

Example 9: Suppose we have the following four transactions, each of which reads one element and writes another:

T_1: $l_1(A)$; $r_1(A)$; $l_1(B)$; $w_1(B)$; $u_1(A)$; $u_1(B)$;

T_2: $l_2(C)$; $r_2(C)$; $l_2(A)$; $w_2(A)$; $u_2(C)$; $u_2(A)$;

T_3: $l_3(B)$; $r_3(B)$; $l_3(C)$; $w_3(C)$; $u_3(B)$; $u_3(C)$;

T_4: $l_4(D)$; $r_4(D)$; $l_4(A)$; $w_4(A)$; $u_4(D)$; $u_4(A)$;

	T_1	T_2	T_3	T_4
1)	$l_1(A)$; $r_1(A)$;			
2)		$l_2(C)$; $r_2(C)$;		
3)			$l_3(B)$; $r_3(B)$;	
4)				$l_4(D)$; $r_4(D)$;
5)		$l_2(A)$; **Denied**		
6)			$l_3(C)$; **Denied**	
7)				$l_4(A)$; **Denied**
8)	$l_1(B)$; **Denied**			

Figure 4: Beginning of a schedule with a deadlock

We use a simple locking system with only one lock mode, although the same effect would be noted if we were to use a shared/exclusive system. In Fig. 4 is the beginning of a schedule of these four transactions. In the first four steps, each transaction obtains a lock on the element it wants to read. At step (5), T_2 tries to lock A, but the request is denied because T_1 already has a lock on A. Thus, T_2 waits for T_1, and we draw an arc from the node for T_2 to the node for T_1.

Similarly, at step (6) T_3 is denied a lock on C because of T_2, and at step (7), T_4 is denied a lock on A because of T_1. The waits-for graph at this point is as shown in Fig. 5. There is no cycle in this graph.

At step (8), T_1 must wait for the lock on B held by T_3. If we allow T_1 to wait, there is a cycle in the waits-for graph involving T_1, T_2, and T_3, as seen

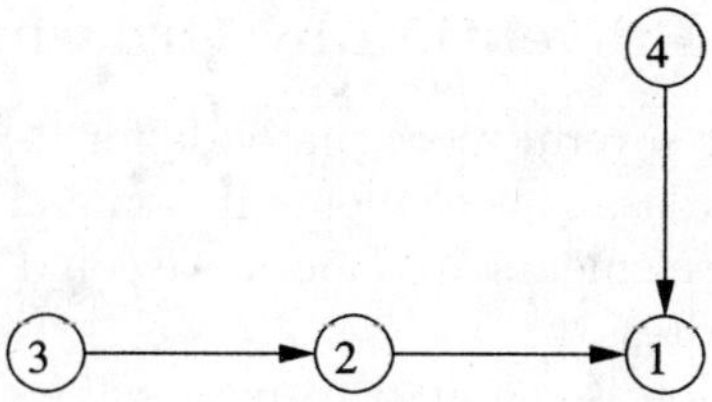

Figure 5: Waits-for graph after step (7) of Fig. 4

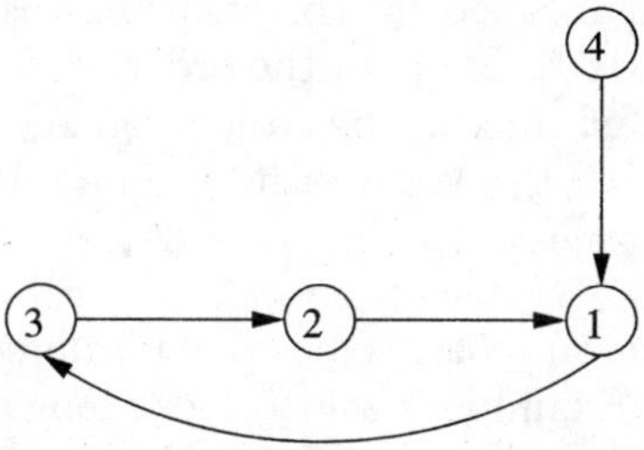

Figure 6: Waits-for graph with a cycle caused by step (8) of Fig. 4

in Fig. 6. Since each of these transactions is waiting for another to finish, none can make progress, and therefore there is a deadlock involving these three transactions. Incidentally, T_4 can not finish either, although it is not in the cycle, because T_4's progress depends on T_1 making progress.

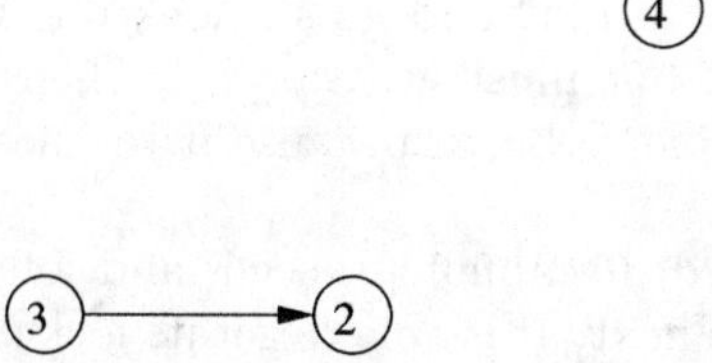

Figure 7: Waits-for graph after T_1 is rolled back

Since we roll back any transaction that causes a cycle, T_1 must be rolled back, yielding the waits-for graph of Fig. 7. T_1 relinquishes its lock on A, which may be given to either T_2 or T_4. Suppose it is given to T_2. Then T_2 can complete, whereupon it relinquishes its locks on A and C. Now T_3, which needs a lock on C, and T_4, which needs a lock on A, can both complete. At some time, T_1 is restarted, but it cannot get locks on A and B until T_2, T_3, and T_4 have completed. □

2.3 Deadlock Prevention by Ordering Elements

Now, let us consider several more methods for deadlock prevention. The first requires us to order database elements in some arbitrary but fixed order. For instance, if database elements are blocks, we could order them lexicographically by their physical address.

If every transaction is required to request locks on elements in order, then there can be no deadlock due to transactions waiting for locks. For suppose T_2 is waiting for a lock on A_1 held by T_1; T_3 is waiting for a lock on A_2 held by T_2, and so on, while T_n is waiting for a lock on A_{n-1} held by T_{n-1}, and T_1 is waiting for a lock on A_n held by T_n. Since T_2 has a lock on A_2 but is waiting for A_1, it must be that $A_2 < A_1$ in the order of elements. Similarly, $A_i < A_{i-1}$ for $i = 3, 4, \ldots, n$. But since T_1 has a lock on A_1 while it is waiting for A_n, it also follows that $A_1 < A_n$. We now have $A_1 < A_n < A_{n-1} < \cdots < A_2 < A_1$, which is impossible, since it implies $A_1 < A_1$.

Example 10: Let us suppose elements are ordered alphabetically. Then if the four transactions of Example 9 are to lock elements in alphabetical order, T_2 and T_4 must be rewritten to lock elements in the opposite order. Thus, the four transactions are now:

T_1: $l_1(A)$; $r_1(A)$; $l_1(B)$; $w_1(B)$; $u_1(A)$; $u_1(B)$;

T_2: $l_2(A)$; $l_2(C)$; $r_2(C)$; $w_2(A)$; $u_2(C)$; $u_2(A)$;

T_3: $l_3(B)$; $r_3(B)$; $l_3(C)$; $w_3(C)$; $u_3(B)$; $u_3(C)$;

T_4: $l_4(A)$; $l_4(D)$; $r_4(D)$; $w_4(A)$; $u_4(D)$; $u_4(A)$;

Figure 8 shows what happens if the transactions execute with the same timing as Fig. 4. T_1 begins and gets a lock on A. T_2 tries to begin next by getting a lock on A, but must wait for T_1. Then, T_3 begins by getting a lock on B, but T_4 is unable to begin because it too needs a lock on A, for which it must wait.

Since T_2 is stalled, it cannot proceed, and following the order of events in Fig. 4, T_3 gets a turn next. It is able to get its lock on C, whereupon it completes at step (6). Now, with T_3's locks on B and C released, T_1 is able to complete, which it does at step (8). At this point, the lock on A becomes available, and we suppose that it is given on a first-come-first-served basis to T_2. Then, T_2 can get both locks that it needs and completes at step (11). Finally, T_4 can get its locks and completes. □

2.4 Detecting Deadlocks by Timestamps

We can detect deadlocks by maintaining the waits-for graph, as we discussed in Section 2.2. However, this graph can be large, and analyzing it for cycles each time a transaction has to wait for a lock can be time-consuming. An

	T_1	T_2	T_3	T_4
1)	$l_1(A)$; $r_1(A)$;			
2)		$l_2(A)$; **Denied**		
3)			$l_3(B)$; $r_3(B)$;	
4)				$l_4(A)$; **Denied**
5)			$l_3(C)$; $w_3(C)$;	
6)			$u_3(B)$; $u_3(C)$;	
7)	$l_1(B)$; $w_1(B)$;			
8)	$u_1(A)$; $u_1(B)$;			
9)		$l_2(A)$; $l_2(C)$;		
10)		$r_2(C)$; $w_2(A)$;		
11)		$u_2(A)$; $u_2(C)$;		
12)				$l_4(A)$; $l_4(D)$;
13)				$r_4(D)$; $w_4(A)$;
14)				$u_4(A)$; $u_4(D)$;

Figure 8: Locking elements in alphabetical order prevents deadlock

alternative to maintaining the waits-for graph is to associate with each transaction a timestamp. This timestamp is for deadlock detection only. In particular, if a transaction is rolled back, it restarts with a new, later concurrency timestamp, but its timestamp for deadlock detection never changes.

The timestamp is used when a transaction T has to wait for a lock that is held by another transaction U. Two different things happen, depending on whether T or U is *older* (has the earlier timestamp). There are two different policies that can be used to manage transactions and detect deadlocks.

1. The *Wait-Die Scheme*:

   (a) If T is older than U (i.e., the timestamp of T is smaller than U's timestamp), then T is allowed to wait for the lock(s) held by U.

   (b) If U is older than T, then T "dies"; it is rolled back.

2. The *Wound-Wait Scheme*:

   (a) If T is older than U, it "wounds" U. Usually, the "wound" is fatal: U must roll back and relinquish to T the lock(s) that T needs from U. There is an exception if, by the time the "wound" takes effect, U has already finished and released its locks. In that case, U survives and need not be rolled back.

   (b) If U is older than T, then T waits for the lock(s) held by U.

Example 11: Let us consider the wait-die scheme, using the transactions of Example 10. We shall assume that T_1, T_2, T_3, T_4 is the order of times; i.e., T_1 is the oldest transaction. We also assume that when a transaction rolls back, it does not restart soon enough to become active before the other transactions finish.

Figure 9 shows a possible sequence of events under the wait-die scheme. T_1 gets the lock on A first. When T_2 asks for a lock on A, it dies, because T_1 is older than T_2. In step (3), T_3 gets a lock on B, but in step (4), T_4 asks for a lock on A and dies because T_1, the holder of the lock on A, is older than T_4. Next, T_3 gets its lock on C and completes. When T_1 continues, it finds the lock on B available and also completes at step (8).

Now, the two transactions that rolled back — T_2 and T_4 — start again. Their timestamps, as far as deadlock is concerned, do not change; T_2 is still older than T_4. However, we assume that T_4 restarts first, at step (9), and when the older transaction T_2 requests a lock on A at step (10), it is forced to wait, but does not abort. T_4 completes at step (12), and then T_2 is allowed to run to completion, as shown in the last three steps. □

Example 12: Next, let us consider the same transactions running under the wound-wait policy, as shown in Fig. 10. As in Fig. 9, T_1 begins by locking A. When T_2 requests a lock on A at step (2), it waits, since T_1 is older than T_2. After T_3 gets its lock on B at step (3), T_4 is also made to wait for the lock on A.

Then, suppose that T_1 continues at step (5) with its request for the lock on B. That lock is already held by T_3, but T_1 is older than T_3. Thus, T_1 "wounds" T_3. Since T_3 is not yet finished, the wound is fatal: T_3 relinquishes its lock and rolls back. Thus, T_1 is able to complete.

When T_1 makes the lock on A available, suppose it is given to T_2, which is then able to proceed. After T_2, the lock is given to T_4, which proceeds to completion. Finally, T_3 restarts and completes without interference. □

2.5 Comparison of Deadlock-Management Methods

In both the wait-die and wound-wait schemes, older transactions kill off newer transactions. Since transactions restart with their old timestamp, eventually each transaction becomes the oldest in the system and is sure to complete. This guarantee, that every transaction eventually completes, is called *no starvation.* Notice that other schemes described in this section do not necessarily prevent starvation; if extra measures are not taken, a transaction could repeatedly start, get involved in a deadlock, and be rolled back. (see Exercise 2.6).

There is, however, a subtle difference in the way wait-die and wound-wait behave. In wound-wait, a newer transaction is killed whenever an old transaction asks for a lock held by the newer transaction. If we assume that transactions take their locks near the time that they begin, it will be rare that an old transaction was beaten to a lock by a new transaction. Thus, we expect rollback to be rare in wound-wait.

	T_1	T_2	T_3	T_4
1)	$l_1(A)$; $r_1(A)$;			
2)		$l_2(A)$; **Dies**		
3)			$l_3(B)$; $r_3(B)$;	
4)				$l_4(A)$; **Dies**
5)			$l_3(C)$; $w_3(C)$;	
6)			$u_3(B)$; $u_3(C)$;	
7)	$l_1(B)$; $w_1(B)$;			
8)	$u_1(A)$; $u_1(B)$;			
9)				$l_4(A)$; $l_4(D)$;
10)		$l_2(A)$; **Waits**		
11)				$r_4(D)$; $w_4(A)$;
12)				$u_4(A)$; $u_4(D)$;
13)		$l_2(A)$; $l_2(C)$;		
14)		$r_2(C)$; $w_2(A)$;		
15)		$u_2(A)$; $u_2(C)$;		

Figure 9: Actions of transactions detecting deadlock under the wait-die scheme

	T_1	T_2	T_3	T_4
1)	$l_1(A)$; $r_1(A)$;			
2)		$l_2(A)$; **Waits**		
3)			$l_3(B)$; $r_3(B)$;	
4)				$l_4(A)$; **Waits**
5)	$l_1(B)$; $w_1(B)$;		**Wounded**	
6)	$u_1(A)$; $u_1(B)$;			
7)		$l_2(A)$; $l_2(C)$;		
8)		$r_2(C)$; $w_2(A)$;		
9)		$u_2(A)$; $u_2(C)$;		
10)				$l_4(A)$; $l_4(D)$;
11)				$r_4(D)$; $w_4(A)$;
12)				$u_4(A)$; $u_4(D)$;
13)			$l_3(B)$; $r_3(B)$;	
14)			$l_3(C)$; $w_3(C)$;	
15)			$u_3(B)$; $u_3(C)$;	

Figure 10: Actions of transactions detecting deadlock under the wound-wait scheme

Why Timestamp-Based Deadlock Detection Works

We claim that in either the wait-die or wound-wait scheme, there can be no cycle in the waits-for graph, and hence no deadlock. Suppose there is a cycle such as $T_1 \rightarrow T_2 \rightarrow T_3 \rightarrow T_1$. One of the transactions is the oldest, say T_2.

In the wait-die scheme, you can only wait for younger transactions. Thus, it is not possible that T_1 is waiting for T_2, since T_2 is surely older than T_1. In the wound-wait scheme, you can only wait for older transactions. Thus, there is no way T_2 could be waiting for the younger T_3. We conclude that the cycle cannot exist, and therefore there is no deadlock.

On the other hand, when a rollback does occur, wait-die rolls back a transaction that is still in the stage of gathering locks, presumably the earliest phase of the transaction. Thus, although wait-die may roll back more transactions than wound-wait, these transactions tend to have done little work. In contrast, when wound-wait does roll back a transaction, it is likely to have acquired its locks and for substantial processor time to have been invested in its activity. Thus, either scheme may turn out to cause more wasted work, depending on the population of transactions processed.

We should also consider the advantages and disadvantages of both wound-wait and wait-die when compared with a straightforward construction and use of the waits-for graph. The important points are:

- Both wound-wait and wait-die are easier to implement than a system that maintains or periodically constructs the waits-for graph.

- Using the waits-for graph minimizes the number of times we must abort a transaction because of deadlock. If we abort a transaction, there really is a deadlock. On the other hand, either wound-wait or wait-die will sometimes roll back a transaction when there really is no deadlock.

2.6 Exercises for Section 2

Exercise 2.1: For each of the sequences of actions below, assume that shared locks are requested immediately before each read action, and exclusive locks are requested immediately before every write action. Also, unlocks occur immediately after the final action that a transaction executes. Tell what actions are denied, and whether deadlock occurs. Also tell how the waits-for graph evolves during the execution of the actions. If there are deadlocks, pick a transaction to abort, and show how the sequence of actions continues.

a) $r_1(A)$; $r_2(B)$; $w_1(C)$; $r_3(D)$; $r_4(E)$; $w_3(B)$; $w_2(C)$; $w_4(A)$; $w_1(D)$;

b) $r_1(A); r_2(B); r_3(C); w_1(B); w_2(C); w_3(D);$

c) $r_1(A); r_2(B); r_3(C); w_1(B); w_2(C); w_3(A);$

d) $r_1(A); r_2(B); w_1(C); w_2(D); r_3(C); w_1(B); w_4(D); w_2(A);$

Exercise 2.2: For each of the action sequences in Exercise 2.1, tell what happens under the wound-wait deadlock avoidance system. Assume the order of deadlock-timestamps is the same as the order of subscripts for the transactions, that is, T_1, T_2, T_3, T_4. Also assume that transactions that need to restart do so in the order that they were rolled back.

Exercise 2.3: For each of the action sequences in Exercise 2.1, tell what happens under the wait-die deadlock avoidance system. Make the same assumptions as in Exercise 2.2.

! **Exercise 2.4:** Can one have a waits-for graph with a cycle of length n, but no smaller cycle, for any integer $n > 1$? What about $n = 1$, i.e., a loop on a node?

!! **Exercise 2.5:** One approach to avoiding deadlocks is to require each transaction to announce all the locks it wants at the beginning, and to either grant all those locks or deny them all and make the transaction wait. Does this approach avoid deadlocks due to locking? Either explain why, or give an example of a deadlock that can arise.

! **Exercise 2.6:** In Section 2.5 we pointed out that deadlock-detection methods other than wound-wait and wait-die do not necessarily prevent starvation, where a transaction is repeatedly rolled back and never gets to finish. Give an example of how using the policy of rolling back any transaction that would cause a cycle can lead to starvation. Does requiring that transactions request locks on elements in a fixed order necessarily prevent starvation? What about timeouts as a deadlock-resolution mechanism?

3 Long-Duration Transactions

There is a family of applications for which a database system is suitable for maintaining data, but the model of many short transactions on which database concurrency-control mechanisms are predicated, is inappropriate. In this section we shall examine some examples of these applications and the problems that arise. We then discuss a solution based on "compensating transactions" that negate the effects of transactions that were committed, but shouldn't have been.

3.1 Problems of Long Transactions

Roughly, a *long transaction* is one that takes too long to be allowed to hold locks that another transaction needs. Depending on the environment, "too long" could mean seconds, minutes, or hours. Three broad classes of applications that involve long transactions are:

1. *Conventional DBMS Applications.* While common database applications run mostly short transactions, many applications require occasional long transactions. For example, one transaction might examine all of a bank's accounts to verify that the total balance is correct. Another application may require that an index be reconstructed occasionally to keep performance at its peak.

2. *Design Systems.* Whether the thing being designed is mechanical like an automobile, electronic like a microprocessor, or a software system, the common element of design systems is that the design is broken into a set of components (e.g., files of a software project), and different designers work on different components simultaneously. We do not want two designers taking a copy of a file, editing it to make design changes, and then writing the new file versions back, because then one set of changes would overwrite the other. Thus, a *check-out-check-in* system allows a designer to "check out" a file and check it in when the changes are finished, perhaps hours or days later. Even if the first designer is changing the file, another designer might want to look at the file to learn something about its contents. If the check-out operation were tantamount to an exclusive lock, then some reasonable and sensible actions would be delayed, possibly for days.

3. *Workflow Systems.* These systems involve collections of processes, some executed by software alone, some involving human interaction, and perhaps some involving human action alone. We shall give shortly an example of office paperwork involving the payment of a bill. Such applications may take days to perform, and during that entire time, some database elements may be subject to change. Were the system to grant an exclusive lock on data involved in a transaction, other transactions could be locked out for days.

Example 13 : Consider the problem of an employee vouchering travel expenses. The intent of the traveler is to be reimbursed from account A123, and the process whereby the payment is made is shown in Fig. 11. The process begins with action A_1, where the traveler's secretary fills out an on-line form describing the travel, the account to be charged, and the amount. We assume in this example that the account is A123, and the amount is \$1000.

The traveler's receipts are sent physically to the departmental authorization office, while the form is sent on-line to an automated action A_2. This process checks that there is enough money in the charged account (A123) and reserves the money for expenditure; i.e., it tentatively deducts \$1000 from the account

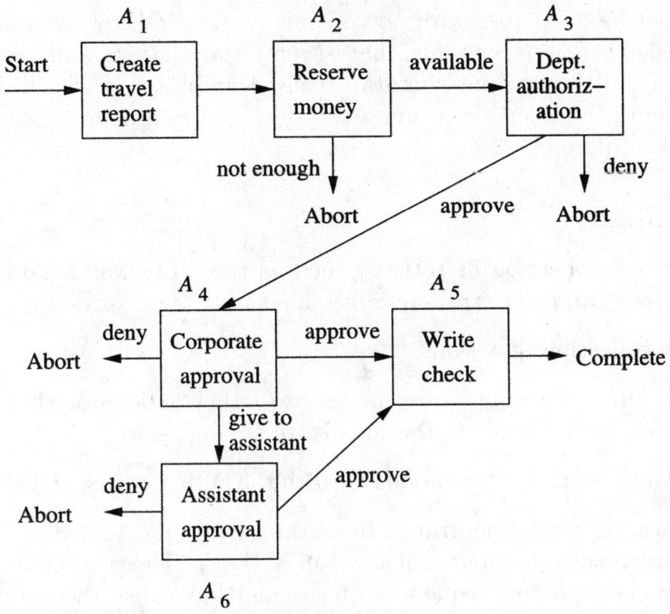

Figure 11: Workflow for a traveler requesting expense reimbursement

but does not issue a check for that amount. If there is not enough money in the account, the transaction aborts, and presumably it will restart when either enough money is in the account or after changing the account to be charged.

Action A_3 is performed by the departmental administrator, who examines the receipts and the on-line form. This action might take place the next day. If everything is in order, the form is approved and sent to the corporate administrator, along with the physical receipts. If not, the transaction is aborted. Presumably the traveler will be required to modify the request in some way and resubmit the form.

In action A_4, which may take place several days later, the corporate administrator either approves or denies the request, or passes the form to an assistant, who will then make the decision in action A_5. If the form is denied, the transaction again aborts and the form must be resubmitted. If the form is approved, then at action A_6 the check is written, and the deduction of \$1000 from account A123 is finalized.

However, suppose that the only way we could implement this workflow is by conventional locking. In particular, since the balance of account A123 may be changed by the complete transaction, it has to be locked exclusively at action A_2 and not unlocked until either the transaction aborts or action A_6 completes. This lock may have to be held for days, while the people charged with authorizing the payment get a chance to look at the matter. If so, then there can be no other charges made to account A123, even tentatively. On the other hand, if there are no controls at all over how account A123 can be accessed, then it is possible that several transactions will reserve or deduct money from the account simultaneously, leading to an overdraft. Thus, some compromise between rigid, long-term locks on one hand, and anarchy on the other, is required. □

3.2 Sagas

A *saga* is a collection of actions, such as those of Example 13, that together form a long-duration "transaction." That is, a saga consists of:

1. A collection of actions.
2. A directed graph whose nodes are either actions or the *terminal* nodes *Abort* and *Complete.* No arcs leave the terminal nodes.
3. An indication of the node at which the action starts, called the *start node.*

The paths through the graph, from the start node to either of the terminal nodes, represent possible sequences of actions. Those paths that lead to the *Abort* node represent sequences of actions that cause the overall transaction to be rolled back, and these sequences of actions should leave the database unchanged. Paths to the *Complete* node represent successful sequences of actions, and all the changes to the database system that these actions perform will remain in the database.

Example 14: The paths in the graph of Fig. 11 that lead to the *Abort* node are: A_1A_2, $A_1A_2A_3$, $A_1A_2A_3A_4$, and $A_1A_2A_3A_4A_5$. The paths that lead to the *Complete* node are $A_1A_2A_3A_4A_6$, and $A_1A_2A_3A_4A_5A_6$. Notice that in this case the graph has no cycles, so there are a finite number of paths leading to a terminal node. However, in general, a graph can have cycles and an infinite number of paths. □

Concurrency control for sagas is managed by two facilities:

1. Each action may be considered itself a (short) transaction, that when executed uses a conventional concurrency-control mechanism, such as locking. For instance, A_2 may be implemented to (briefly) obtain a lock on account A123, decrement the amount indicated on the travel voucher, and release the lock. This locking prevents two transactions from trying to write new values of the account balance at the same time, thereby losing the effect of the first to write and making money "appear by magic."
2. The overall transaction, which can be any of the paths to a terminal node, is managed through the mechanism of "compensating transactions," which are inverses to the transactions at the nodes of the saga. Their job is to roll back the effect of a committed action in a way that does not depend on what has happened to the database between the time the action was executed and the time the compensating transaction is executed.

When are Database States "The Same"?

When discussing compensating transactions, we should be careful about what it means to return the database to "the same" state that it had before. We had a taste of the problem when we discussed logical logging for B-trees in Example 8. There we saw that if we "undid" an operation, the state of the B-tree might not be identical to the state before the operation, but would be equivalent to it as far as access operations on the B-tree were concerned. More generally, executing an action and its compensating transaction might not restore the database to a state literally identical to what existed before, but the differences must not be detectable by whatever application programs the database supports.

3.3 Compensating Transactions

In a saga, each action A has a *compensating transaction*, which we denote A^{-1}. Intuitively, if we execute A, and later execute A^{-1}, then the resulting database state is the same as if neither A nor A^{-1} had executed. More formally:

- If D is any database state, and $B_1B_2 \cdots B_n$ is any sequence of actions and compensating transactions (whether from the saga in question or any other saga or transaction that may legally execute on the database) then the same database states result from running the sequences $B_1B_2 \cdots B_n$ and $AB_1B_2 \cdots B_nA^{-1}$ starting in database state D.

If a saga execution leads to the *Abort* node, then we roll back the saga by executing the compensating transactions for each executed action, in the reverse order of those actions. By the property of compensating transactions stated above, the effect of the saga is negated, and the database state is the same as if it had never happened. An explanation of why the effect is guaranteed to be negated is given in Section 3.4.

Example 15: Let us consider the actions in Fig. 11 and see what the compensating transactions for A_1 through A_6 might be. First, A_1 creates an on-line document. If the document is stored in the database, then A_1^{-1} must remove it from the database. Notice that this compensation obeys the fundamental property for compensating transactions: If we create the document, do any sequence of actions α (including deletion of the document if we wish), then the effect of $A_1\alpha A_1^{-1}$ is the same as the effect of α.

A_2 must be implemented carefully. We "reserve" the money by deducting it from the account. The money will stay removed unless restored by the compensating transaction A_2^{-1}. We claim that this A_2^{-1} is a correct compensating transaction if the usual rules for how accounts may be managed are followed. To appreciate the point, it is useful to consider a similar transaction where the obvious compensation will not work; we consider such a case in Example 16, next.

The actions A_3, A_4, and A_6 each involve adding an approval to a form. Thus, their compensating transactions can remove that approval.[3]

Finally, A_5, which writes the check, does not have an obvious compensating transaction. In practice none is needed, because once A_5 is executed, this saga cannot be rolled back. However, technically A_5 does not affect the database anyway, since the money for the check was deducted by A_2. Should we need to consider the "database" as the larger world, where effects such as cashing a check affected the database, then we would have to design A_5^{-1} to first try to cancel the check, next write a letter to the payee demanding the money back, and if all remedies failed, restoring the money to the account by declaring a loss due to a bad debt. □

Next, let us take up the example, alluded to in Example 15, where a change to an account cannot be compensated by an inverse change. The problem is that accounts normally are not allowed to go negative.

Example 16: Suppose B is a transaction that adds \$1000 to an account that has \$2000 in it initially, and B^{-1} is the compensating transaction that removes the same amount of money. Also, it is reasonable to assume that transactions may fail if they try to delete money from an account and the balance would thereby become negative. Let C be a transaction that deletes \$2500 from the same account. Then $BCB^{-1} \not\equiv C$. The reason is that C by itself fails, and leaves the account with \$2000, while if we execute B then C, the account is left with \$500, whereupon B^{-1} fails.

Our conclusion that a saga with arbitrary transfers among accounts and a rule about accounts never being allowed to go negative cannot be supported simply by compensating transactions. Some modification to the system must be done, e.g., allowing negative balances in accounts. □

3.4 Why Compensating Transactions Work

Let us say that two sequences of actions are *equivalent* ($\equiv$) if they take any database state D to the same state. The fundamental assumption about compensating transactions can be stated:

- If A is any action and α is any sequence of legal actions and compensating transactions, then $A\alpha A^{-1} \equiv \alpha$.

Now, we need to show that if a saga execution $A_1A_2 \cdots A_n$ is followed by its compensating transactions in reverse order, $A_n^{-1} \cdots A_2^{-1}A_1^{-1}$, with any intervening actions whatsoever, then the effect is as if neither the actions nor the compensating transactions executed. The proof is an induction on n.

[3] In the saga of Fig. 11, the only time these actions are compensated is when we are going to delete the form anyway, but the definition of compensating transactions require that they work in isolation, regardless of whether some other compensating transaction was going to make their changes irrelevant.

BASIS: If $n = 1$, then the sequence of all actions between A_1 and its compensating transaction A_1^{-1} looks like $A_1 \alpha A_1^{-1}$. By the fundamental assumption about compensating transactions, $A_1 \alpha A_1^{-1} \equiv \alpha$.

INDUCTION: Assume the statement for paths of up to $n - 1$ actions, and consider a path of n actions, followed by its compensating transactions in reverse order, with any other transactions intervening. The sequence looks like

$$A_1 \alpha_1 A_2 \alpha_2 \cdots \alpha_{n-1} A_n \beta A_n^{-1} \gamma_{n-1} \cdots \gamma_2 A_2^{-1} \gamma_1 A_1^{-1} \tag{1}$$

where all Greek letters represent sequences of zero or more actions. By the definition of compensating transaction, $A_n \beta A_n^{-1} \equiv \beta$. Thus, (1) is equivalent to

$$A_1 \alpha_1 A_2 \alpha_2 \cdots A_{n-1} \alpha_{n-1} \beta \gamma_{n-1} A_{n-1}^{-1} \gamma_{n-2} \cdots \gamma_2 A_2^{-1} \gamma_1 A_1^{-1} \tag{2}$$

By the inductive hypothesis, expression (2) is equivalent to

$$\alpha_1 \alpha_2 \cdots \alpha_{n-1} \beta \gamma_{n-1} \cdots \gamma_2 \gamma_1$$

since there are only $n-1$ actions in (2). That is, the saga and its compensation leave the database state the same as if the saga had never occurred.

3.5 Exercises for Section 3

! **Exercise 3.1:** The process of "uninstalling" software can be thought of as a compensating transaction for the action of installing the same software. In a simple model of installing and uninstalling, suppose that an action consists of *loading* one or more files from the source (e.g., a CD-ROM) onto the hard disk of the machine. To load a file f, we copy f from CD-ROM. If there was a file f' with the same path name, we back up f' before replacement. To distinguish files with the same path name, we may assume each file has a timestamp.

a) What is the compensating transaction for the action that loads file f? Consider both the case where no file with that path name existed, and where there was a file f' with the same path name.

b) Explain why your answer to (a) is guaranteed to compensate. *Hint*: Consider carefully the case where after replacing f' by f, a later action replaces f by another file with the same path name.

! **Exercise 3.2:** Describe the process of booking an airline seat as a saga. Consider the possibility that the customer will query about a seat but not book it. The customer may book the seat, but cancel it, or not pay for the seat within the required time limit. The customer may or may not show up for the flight. For each action, describe the corresponding compensating transaction.

4 Summary

✦ *Dirty Data*: Data that has been written, either into main-memory buffers or on disk, by a transaction that has not yet committed is called "dirty."

✦ *Cascading Rollback*: A combination of logging and concurrency control that allows a transaction to read dirty data may have to roll back transactions that read such data from a transaction that later aborts.

✦ *Strict Locking*: The strict locking policy requires transactions to hold their locks (except for shared-locks) until not only have they committed, but the commit record on the log has been flushed to disk. Strict locking guarantees that no transaction can read dirty data, even retrospectively after a crash and recovery.

✦ *Group Commit*: We can relax the strict-locking condition that requires commit records to reach disk if we assure that log records are written to disk in the order that they are written. There is still then a guarantee of no dirty reads, even if a crash and recovery occurs.

✦ *Restoring Database State After an Abort*: If a transaction aborts but has written values to buffers, then we can restore old values either from the log or from the disk copy of the database. If the new values have reached disk, then the log may still be used to restore the old value.

✦ *Logical Logging*: For large database elements such as disk blocks, it saves much space if we record old and new values on the log incrementally, that is, by indicating only the changes. In some cases, recording changes logically, that is, in terms of an abstraction of what blocks contain, allows us to restore state logically after a transaction abort, even if it is impossible to restore the state literally.

✦ *Deadlocks*: These occur when each of a set of transactions is waiting for a resource, such as a lock, currently held by another transaction in the set.

✦ *Waits-For Graphs*: Create a node for each waiting transaction, with an arc to the transaction it is waiting for. The existence of a deadlock is the same as the existence of one or more cycles in the waits-for graph. We can avoid deadlocks if we maintain the waits-for graph and abort any transaction whose waiting would cause a cycle.

✦ *Deadlock Avoidance by Ordering Resources*: Requiring transactions to acquire resources according to some lexicographic order of the resources will prevent a deadlock from arising.

✦ *Timestamp-Based Deadlock Avoidance*: Other schemes maintain a timestamp and base their abort/wait decision on whether the requesting transaction is newer or older than the one with the resource it wants. In the wait-die scheme, an older requesting transaction waits, and a newer one is rolled back with the same timestamp. In the wound-wait scheme, a newer transaction waits and an older one forces the transaction with the resource to roll back and give up the resource.

- *Sagas*: When transactions involve long-duration steps that may take hours or days, conventional locking mechanisms may limit concurrency too much. A saga consists of a network of actions, each of which may lead to one or more other actions, to the completion of the entire saga, or to a requirement that the saga abort.

- *Compensating Transactions*: For a saga to make sense, each action must have a compensating action that will undo the effects of the first action on the database state, while leaving intact any other actions that have been made by other sagas that have completed or are currently in operation. If a saga aborts, the appropriate sequence of compensating actions is executed.

5 References

Some useful general sources for topics covered here are [2], [1], and [7]. The material on logical logging follows [6].

Deadlock prevention was surveyed in [5]; the waits-for graph is from there. The wait-die and wound-wait schemes are from [8].

Long transactions were introduced by [4]. Sagas were described in [3].

1. N. S. Barghouti and G. E. Kaiser, "Concurrency control in advanced database applications," *Computing Surveys* **23**:3 (Sept., 1991), pp. 269–318.

2. S. Ceri and G. Pelagatti, *Distributed Databases: Principles and Systems*, McGraw-Hill, New York, 1984.

3. H. Garcia-Molina and K. Salem, "Sagas," *Proc. ACM SIGMOD Intl. Conf. on Management of Data* (1987), pp. 249–259.

4. J. N. Gray, "The transaction concept: virtues and limitations," *Intl. Conf. on Very Large Databases* (1981), pp. 144–154.

5. R. C. Holt, "Some deadlock properties of computer systems," *Computing Surveys* **4**:3 (1972), pp. 179–196.

6. C. Mohan, D. J. Haderle, B. G. Lindsay, H. Pirahesh, and P. Schwarz, "ARIES: a transaction recovery method supporting fine-granularity locking and partial rollbacks using write-ahead logging," *ACM Trans. on Database Systems* **17**:1 (1992), pp. 94–162.

7. M. T. Ozsu and P. Valduriez, *Principles of Distributed Database Systems*, Prentice-Hall, Englewood Cliffs NJ, 1999.

8. D. J. Rosenkrantz, R. E. Stearns, and P. M. Lewis II, "System-level concurrency control for distributed database systems," *ACM Trans. on Database Systems* **3**:2 (1978), pp. 178–198.

Parallel and Distributed Databases

While many databases sit at a single machine, a database can also be distributed over many machines. There are other databases that reside at a single highly parallel machine. When computation is either parallel or distributed, there are many database-implementation issues that need to be reconsidered.

In this chapter, we first look at the different kinds of parallel architectures that have been used. On a parallel machine it is important that the most expensive operations take advantage of parallelism, and for databases, these operations are the full-relation operations such as join. We then discuss the map-reduce paradigm for expressing large-scale computations. This formulation of algorithms is especially amenable to execution on large-scale parallel machines, and it is simple to express important database processes in this manner.

We then turn to distributed architectures. These include grids and networks of workstations, as well as corporate databases that are distributed around the world. Now, we must worry not only about exploiting the many available processors for query execution, but some database operations become much harder to perform correctly in a distributed environment. Notable among these are distributed commitment of transactions and distributed locking.

The extreme case of a distributed architecture is a collection of independent machines, often called "peer-to-peer" networks, In these networks, even data lookup becomes problematic. We shall therefore discuss distributed hash tables and distributed search in peer-to-peer networks.

1 Parallel Algorithms on Relations

Database operations, frequently being time-consuming and involving a lot of data, can generally profit from parallel processing. In this section, we shall review the principal architectures for parallel machines. We then concentrate on the "shared-nothing" architecture, which appears to be the most cost effective for database operations, although it may not be superior for other parallel applications. There are simple modifications of the standard algorithms for most relational operations that will exploit parallelism almost perfectly. That is, the time to complete an operation on a p-processor machine is about $1/p$ of the time it takes to complete the operation on a uniprocessor.

1.1 Models of Parallelism

At the heart of all parallel machines is a collection of processors. Often the number of processors p is large, in the hundreds or thousands. We shall assume that each processor has its own local cache, which we do not show explicitly in our diagrams. In most organizations, each processor also has local memory, which we do show. Of great importance to database processing is the fact that along with these processors are many disks, perhaps one or more per processor, or in some architectures a large collection of disks accessible to all processors directly.

Additionally, parallel computers all have some communications facility for passing information among processors. In our diagrams, we show the communication as if there were a shared bus for all the elements of the machine. However, in practice a bus cannot interconnect as many processors or other elements as are found in the largest machines, so the interconnection system in many architectures is a powerful switch, perhaps augmented by busses that connect subsets of the processors in local clusters. For example, the processors in a single rack are typically connected.

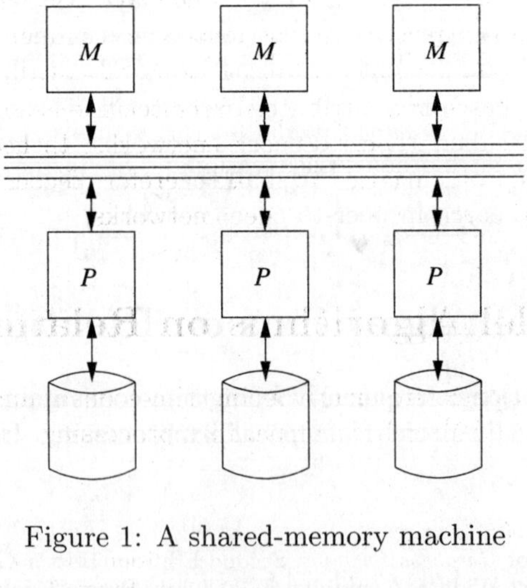

Figure 1: A shared-memory machine

We can classify parallel architectures into three broad groups. The most tightly coupled architectures share their main memory. A less tightly coupled architecture shares disk but not memory. Architectures that are often used for databases do not even share disk; these are called "shared nothing" architectures, although the processors are in fact interconnected and share data through message passing.

Shared-Memory Machines

In this architecture, illustrated in Fig. 1, each processor has access to all the memory of all the processors. That is, there is a single physical address space for the entire machine, rather than one address space for each processor. The diagram of Fig. 1 is actually too extreme, suggesting that processors have no private memory at all. Rather, each processor has some local main memory, which it typically uses whenever it can. However, it has direct access to the memory of other processors when it needs to. Large machines of this class are of the *NUMA* (nonuniform memory access) type, meaning that it takes somewhat more time for a processor to access data in a memory that "belongs" to some other processor than it does to access its "own" memory, or the memory of processors in its local cluster. However, the difference in memory-access times are not great in current architectures. Rather, all memory accesses, no matter where the data is, take much more time than a cache access, so the critical issue is whether or not the data a processor needs is in its own cache.

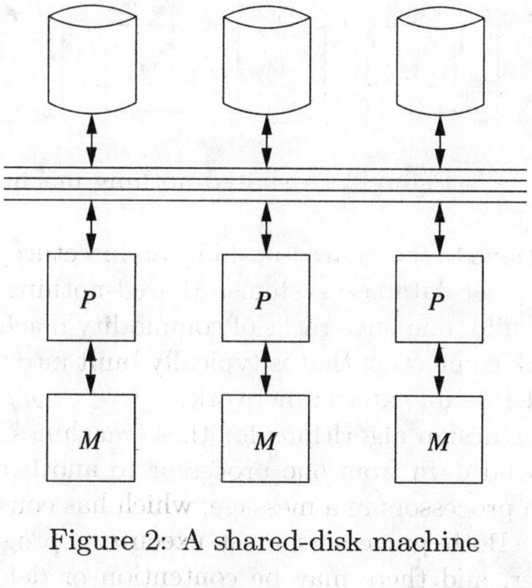

Figure 2: A shared-disk machine

Shared-Disk Machines

In this architecture, suggested by Fig. 2, every processor has its own memory, which is not accessible directly from other processors. However, the disks are accessible from any of the processors through the communication network. Disk controllers manage the potentially competing requests from different processors.

The number of disks and processors need not be identical, as it might appear from Fig. 2.

This architecture today appears in two forms, depending on the units of transfer between the disks and processors. Disk farms called *network attached storage* (NAS) store and transfer files. The alternative, *storage area networks* (SAN) transfer disk blocks to and from the processors.

Shared-Nothing Machines

Here, all processors have their own memory and their own disk or disks, as in Fig. 3. All communication is via the network, from processor to processor. For example, if one processor P wants to read tuples from the disk of another processor Q, then processor P sends a message to Q asking for the data. Q obtains the tuples from its disk and ships them over the network in another message, which is received by P.

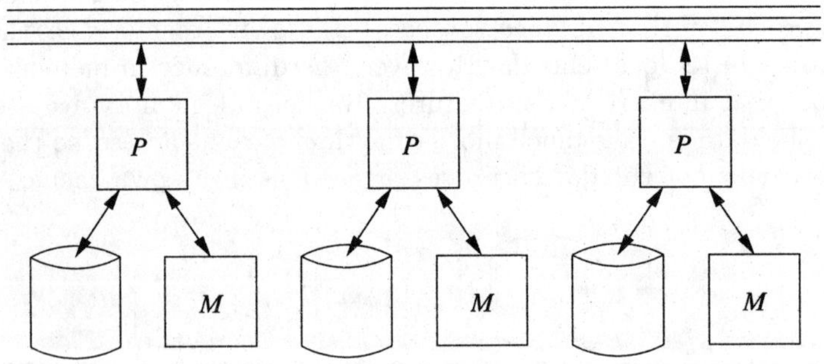

Figure 3: A shared-nothing machine

As we mentioned, the shared-nothing architecture is the most commonly used architecture for database systems. Shared-nothing machines are relatively inexpensive to build; one buys racks of commodity machines and connects them with the network connection that is typically built into the rack. Multiple racks can be connected by an external network.

But when we design algorithms for these machines we must be aware that it is costly to send data from one processor to another. Normally, data must be sent between processors in a message, which has considerable overhead associated with it. Both processors must execute a program that supports the message transfer, and there may be contention or delays associated with the communication network as well. Typically, the cost of a message can be broken into a large fixed overhead plus a small amount of time per byte transmitted. Thus, there is a significant advantage to designing a parallel algorithm so that communications between processors involve large amounts of data sent at once. For instance, we might buffer several blocks of data at processor P, all bound for processor Q. If Q does not need the data immediately, it may be much more efficient to wait until we have a long message at P and then send it to

Q. Fortunately, the best known parallel algorithms for database operations can use long messages effectively.

1.2 Tuple-at-a-Time Operations in Parallel

Let us begin our discussion of parallel algorithms for a shared-nothing machine by considering the selection operator. First, we must consider how data is best stored. It is useful to distribute our data across as many disks as possible. For convenience, we shall assume there is one disk per processor. Then if there are p processors, divide any relation R's tuples evenly among the p processor's disks.

To compute $\sigma_C(R)$, we may use each processor to examine the tuples of R on its own disk. For each, it finds those tuples satisfying condition C and copies those to the output. To avoid communication among processors, we store those tuples t in $\sigma_C(R)$ at the same processor that has t on its disk. Thus, the result relation $\sigma_C(R)$ is divided among the processors, just like R is.

Since $\sigma_C(R)$ may be the input relation to another operation, and since we want to minimize the elapsed time and keep all the processors busy all the time, we would like $\sigma_C(R)$ to be divided evenly among the processors. If we were doing a projection, rather than a selection, then the number of tuples in $\pi_L(R)$ at each processor would be the same as the number of tuples of R at that processor. Thus, if R is distributed evenly, so would be its projection. However, a selection could radically change the distribution of tuples in the result, compared to the distribution of R.

Example 1: Suppose the selection is $\sigma_{a=10}(R)$, that is, find all the tuples of R whose value in the attribute a is 10. Suppose also that we have divided R according to the value of the attribute a. Then all the tuples of R with $a = 10$ are at one processor, and the entire relation $\sigma_{a=10}(R)$ is at one processor. □

To avoid the problem suggested by Example 1, we need to think carefully about the policy for partitioning our stored relations among the processors. Probably the best we can do is to use a hash function h that involves all the components of a tuple in such a way that changing one component of a tuple t can change $h(t)$ to be any possible bucket number. For example, if we want B buckets, we might convert each component somehow to an integer between 0 and $B - 1$, add the integers for each component, divide the result by B, and take the remainder as the bucket number. If B is also the number of processors, then we can associate each processor with a bucket and give that processor the contents of its bucket.

1.3 Parallel Algorithms for Full-Relation Operations

First, let us consider the operation $\delta(R)$. If we use a hash function to distribute the tuples of R as in Section 1.2, then we shall place duplicate tuples of R at the same processor. We can produce $\delta(R)$ in parallel by applying a standard, uniprocessor algorithm to the portion of R at each processor. Likewise, if we use the same hash function to distribute the tuples of both R and S, then we can take the union, intersection, or difference of R and S by working in parallel on the portions of R and S at each processor.

However, suppose that R and S are not distributed using the same hash function, and we wish to take their union.[1] In this case, we first must make copies of all the tuples of R and S and distribute them according to a single hash function h.[2]

In parallel, we hash the tuples of R and S at each processor, using hash function h. The hashing proceeds normally, but when the buffer corresponding to a bucket i at one processor j is filled, instead of moving it to the disk at j, we ship the contents of the buffer to processor i. If we have room for several blocks per bucket in main memory, then we may wait to fill several buffers with tuples of bucket i before shipping them to processor i.

Thus, processor i receives all the tuples of R and S that belong in bucket i. In the second stage, each processor performs the union of the tuples from R and S belonging to its bucket. As a result, the relation $R \cup S$ will be distributed over all the processors. If hash function h truly randomizes the placement of tuples in buckets, then we expect approximately the same number of tuples of $R \cup S$ to be at each processor.

The operations of intersection and difference may be performed just like a union; it does not matter whether these are set or bag versions of these operations. Moreover:

- To take a join $R(X,Y) \bowtie S(Y,Z)$, we hash the tuples of R and S to a number of buckets equal to the number of processors. However, the hash function h we use must depend only on the attributes of Y, not all the attributes, so that joining tuples are always sent to the same bucket. As with union, we ship tuples of bucket i to processor i. We may then perform the join at each processor using any uniprocessor join algorithm.

- To perform grouping and aggregation $\gamma_L(R)$, we distribute the tuples of R using a hash function h that depends only on the grouping attributes in list L. If each processor has all the tuples corresponding to one of the buckets of h, then we can perform the γ_L operation on these tuples locally, using any uniprocessor γ algorithm.

1.4 Performance of Parallel Algorithms

Now, let us consider how the running time of a parallel algorithm on a p-processor machine compares with the time to execute an algorithm for the

[1]In principle, this union could be either a set- or bag-union. But the simple bag-union technique of copying all the tuples from both arguments works in parallel, so we probably would not want to use the algorithm described here for a bag-union.

[2]If the hash function used to distribute tuples of R or S is known, we can use that hash function for the other and not distribute both relations.

same operation on the same data, using a uniprocessor. The total work — disk I/O's and processor cycles — cannot be smaller for a parallel machine than for a uniprocessor. However, because there are p processors working with p disks, we can expect the elapsed, or wall-clock, time to be much smaller for the multiprocessor than for the uniprocessor.

A unary operation such as $\sigma_C(R)$ can be completed in $1/p$th of the time it would take to perform the operation at a single processor, provided relation R is distributed evenly, as was supposed in Section 1.2. The number of disk I/O's is essentially the same as for a uniprocessor selection. The only difference is that there will, on average, be p half-full blocks of R, one at each processor, rather than a single half-full block of R had we stored all of R on one processor's disk.

Now, consider a binary operation, such as join. We use a hash function on the join attributes that sends each tuple to one of p buckets, where p is the number of processors. To distribute the tuples belonging to one processor, we must read each tuple from disk to memory, compute the hash function, and ship all tuples except the one out of p tuples that happens to belong to the bucket at its own processor.

If we are computing $R(X,Y) \bowtie S(Y,Z)$, then we need to do $B(R) + B(S)$ disk I/O's to read all the tuples of R and S and determine their buckets. We then must ship $\big((p-1)/p\big)\big(B(R) + B(S)\big)$ blocks of data across the machine's internal interconnection network to their proper processors; only the $(1/p)$th of the tuples already at the right processor need not be shipped. The cost of shipment can be greater or less than the cost of the same number of disk I/O's, depending on the architecture of the machine. However, we shall assume that shipment across the internal network is significantly cheaper than movement of data between disk and memory, because no physical motion is involved in shipment among processors, while it is for disk I/O.

In principle, we might suppose that the receiving processor has to store the data on its own disk, then execute a local join on the tuples received. For example, if we used a two-pass sort-join at each processor, a naive parallel algorithm would use $3\big(B(R) + B(S)\big)/p$ disk I/O's at each processor, since the sizes of the relations in each bucket would be approximately $B(R)/p$ and $B(S)/p$, and this type of join takes three disk I/O's per block occupied by each of the argument relations. To this cost we would add another $2\big(B(R) + B(S)\big)/p$ disk I/O's per processor, to account for the first read of each tuple and the storing away of each tuple by the processor receiving the tuple during the hash and distribution of tuples. We should also add the cost of shipping the data, but we have elected to consider that cost negligible compared with the cost of disk I/O for the same data.

The above comparison demonstrates the value of the multiprocessor. While we do more disk I/O in total — five disk I/O's per block of data, rather than three — the elapsed time, as measured by the number of disk I/O's performed at each processor has gone down from $3\big(B(R) + B(S)\big)$ to $5\big(B(R) + B(S)\big)/p$, a significant win for large p.

Biiig Mistake

When using hash-based algorithms to distribute relations among processors and to execute operations, as in Example 2, we must be careful not to overuse one hash function. For instance, suppose we used a hash function h to hash the tuples of relations R and S among processors, in order to take their join. We might be tempted to use h to hash the tuples of S locally into buckets as we perform a one-pass hash-join at each processor. But if we do so, all those tuples will go to the same bucket, and the main-memory join suggested in Example 2 will be extremely inefficient.

Moreover, there are ways to improve the speed of the parallel algorithm so that the total number of disk I/O's is not greater than what is required for a uniprocessor algorithm. In fact, since we operate on smaller relations at each processor, we may be able to use a local join algorithm that uses fewer disk I/O's per block of data. For instance, even if R and S were so large that we need a two-pass algorithm on a uniprocessor, we may be able to use a one-pass algorithm on $(1/p)$th of the data.

We can avoid two disk I/O's per block if, when we ship a block to the processor of its bucket, that processor can use the block immediately as part of its join algorithm. Many algorithms known for join and the other relational operators allow this use, in which case the parallel algorithm looks just like a multipass algorithm in which the first pass uses a hashing technique.

Example 2: Consider our running example of the join $R(X,Y) \bowtie S(Y,Z)$, where R and S occupy 1000 and 500 blocks, respectively. Now, let there be 101 buffers at each processor of a 10-processor machine. Also, assume that R and S are distributed uniformly among these 10 processors.

We begin by hashing each tuple of R and S to one of 10 "buckets," using a hash function h that depends only on the join attributes Y. These 10 "buckets" represent the 10 processors, and tuples are shipped to the processor corresponding to their "bucket." The total number of disk I/O's needed to read the tuples of R and S is 1500, or 150 per processor. Each processor will have about 15 blocks worth of data for each other processor, so it ships 135 blocks to the other nine processors. The total communication is thus 1350 blocks.

We shall arrange that the processors ship the tuples of S before the tuples of R. Since each processor receives about 50 blocks of tuples from S, it can store those tuples in a main-memory data structure, using 50 of its 101 buffers. Then, when processors start sending R-tuples, each one is compared with the local S-tuples, and any resulting joined tuples are output.

In this way, the only cost of the join is 1500 disk I/O's. Moreover, the elapsed time is primarily the 150 disk I/O's performed at each processor, plus the time to ship tuples between processors and perform the main-memory computations. Note that 150 disk I/O's is less than 1/10th of the time to perform the same algorithm on a uniprocessor; we have not only gained because we had 10 processors working for us, but the fact that there are a total of 1010 buffers among those 10 processors gives us additional efficiency. □

1.5 Exercises for Section 1

Exercise 1.1: Suppose that a disk I/O takes 100 milliseconds. Let $B(R) = 100$, so the disk I/O's for computing $\sigma_C(R)$ on a uniprocessor machine will take about 10 seconds. What is the speedup if this selection is executed on a parallel machine with p processors, where: (a) $p = 8$ (b) $p = 100$ (c) $p = 1000$.

! **Exercise 1.2:** In Example 2 we described an algorithm that computed the join $R \bowtie S$ in parallel by first hash-distributing the tuples among the processors and then performing a one-pass join at the processors. In terms of $B(R)$ and $B(S)$, the sizes of the relations involved, p (the number of processors), and M (the number of blocks of main memory at each processor), give the condition under which this algorithm can be executed successfully.

2 The Map-Reduce Parallelism Framework

Map-reduce is a high-level programming system that allows many important database processes to be written simply. The user writes code for two functions, map and reduce. A master controller divides the input data into chunks, and assigns different processors to execute the map function on each chunk. Other processors, perhaps the same ones, are then assigned to perform the reduce function on pieces of the output from the map function.

2.1 The Storage Model

For the map-reduce framework to make sense, we should assume a massively parallel machine, most likely shared-nothing. Typically, the processors are commodity computers, mounted in racks with a simple communication network among the processors on a rank. If there is more than one rack, the racks are also connected by a simple network.

Data is assumed stored in files. Typically, the files are very large compared with the files found in conventional systems. For example, one file might be all the tuples of a very large relation. Or, the file might be a terabyte of "market-baskets." For another example of a single file, you may see the "transition matrix of the Web," which is a representation of the graph with all Web pages as nodes and hyperlinks as edges.

Files are divided into *chunks*, which might be complete cylinders of a disk, and are typically many megabytes. For resiliency, each chunk is replicated several times, so it will not be lost if the disk holding it crashes.

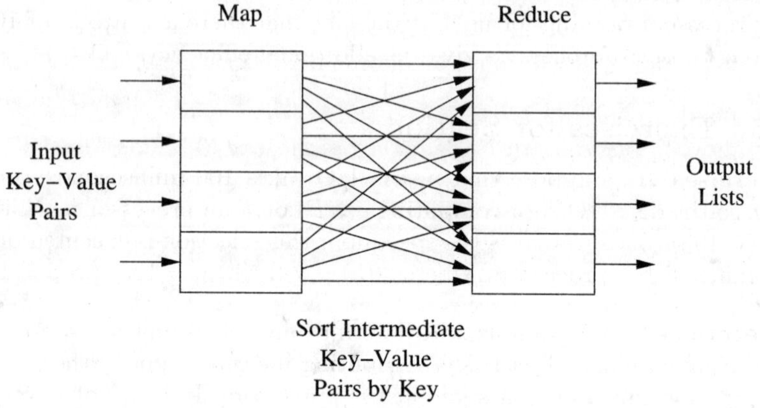

Figure 4: Execution of map and reduce functions

2.2 The Map Function

The outline of what user-defined map and reduce functions do is suggested in Fig. 4. The input is generally thought of as a set of key-value records, although in fact the input could be objects of any type.[3] The function *map* is executed by one or more processes, located at any number of processors. Each map process is given a chunk of the entire input data on which to work.

The map function is designed to take one key-value pair as input and to produce a list of key-value pairs as output. However:

- The types of keys and values for the output of the map function need not be the same as the types of input keys and values.
- The "keys" that are output from the map function are not true keys in the database sense. That is, there can be many pairs with the same key value. However, the key field of output pairs plays a special role in the reduce process to be explained next.

The result of executing all the *map* processes is a collection of key-value pairs called the *intermediate result.* These key-value pairs are the outputs of the map function applied to every input pair. Each pair appears at the processor that generated it. Remember that there may be many *map* processes executing the same algorithm on a different part of the input file at different processors.

[3]As we shall see, the output of a map-reduce algorithm is always a set of key-value pairs. Since it is useful in some applications to compose two or more map-reduce operations, it is conventional to assume that both input and output are sets of key-value pairs.

Example 3: We shall consider as an example, constructing an inverted index for words in documents. That is, our input is a collection of documents, and we desire to construct as the final output (not as the output of *map*) a list for each word of the documents that contain that word at least once. The input is a set of pairs each of whose keys are document ID's and whose values are the corresponding documents.

The map function takes a pair consisting of a document ID i and a document d. This function scans d character by character, and for each word w it finds, it emits the pair (w, i). Notice that in the output, the word is the key and the document ID is the associated value. The output of *map* for a single ID-document pair is a list of word-ID pairs. It is not necessary to catch duplicate words in the document; the elimination of duplicates can be done later, at the reduce phase. The intermediate result is the collection of all word-ID pairs created from all the documents in the input database. □

2.3 The Reduce Function

The second user-defined function, *reduce*, is also executed by one or more processes, located at any number of processors. The input to *reduce* is a single key value from the intermediate result, together with the list of all values that appear with this key in the intermediate result. Duplicate values are not eliminated.

In Fig. 4, we suggest that the output of *map* at each of four processors is distributed to four processors, each of which will execute *reduce* for a subset of the intermediate keys. However, there are a number of ways in which this distribution could be managed. For example, Each *map* process could leave its output on its local disk, and a *reduce* process could retrieve the portion of the intermediate result that it needed, over whatever network or bus interconnects the processors.

The reduce function itself combines the list of values associated with a given key k. The result is k paired with a value of some type. In many simple cases, the reduce function is associative and commutative, and the entire list of values is reduced to a single value of the same type as the list elements. For instance, if *reduce* is addition, the result is the some of a list of numbers.

When *reduce* is associative and commutative, it is possible to speed up the execution of *reduce* by starting to apply its operation to the pairs produced by the *map* processes, even before they finish. Moreover, if a given *map* process produces more than one intermediate pair with the same key, then the reduce operation can be applied on the spot to combine the pairs, without waiting for them to be passed to the *reduce* process for that key.

Example 4: Let us consider the reduce function that lets us complete Example 3 to produce inverted indexes. The intermediate result consists of pairs of the form $(w, [i_1, i_2, \ldots, i_n])$, where the i's are a list of document ID's, one for each occurrence of word w. The reduce function we need takes a list of ID's, eliminates duplicates, and sorts the list of unique ID's.

Notice how this organization of the computation makes excellent use of whatever parallelism is available. The map function works on a single document, so we could have as many processes and processors as there are documents in the database. The reduce function works on a single word, so we could have as many processes and processors as there are words in the database. Of course, it is unlikely that we would use so many processors in practice. □

Example 5: Suppose rather than constructing an inverted index, we want to construct a word count. That is, for each word w that appears at least once in our database of documents, we want our output to have the pair (w, c), where c is the number of times w appears among all the documents. The map function takes an input document, goes through the document character by character, and each time it encounters another word w, it emits the pair $(w, 1)$. The intermediate result is a list of pairs $(w_1, 1), (w_2, 1), \ldots$.

In this example, the reduce function is addition of integers. That is, the input to *reduce* is a pair $(w, [1, 1, \ldots, 1])$, with a 1 for each occurrence of the word w. The reduce function sums the 1's, producing the count. □

Example 6: It is a little trickier to express the join of relations in the map-reduce framework. In this simple special case, we shall take the natural join of relations $R(A, B)$ and $S(B, C)$. First, the input to the map function is key-value pairs (x, t), where x is either R or S, and t is a tuple of the relation named by x. The output is a single pair consisting of the join value B taken from the tuple t and a pair consisting of x (to let us remember which relation this tuple came from) and the other component of t, either A (if $x = R$) or C (if $x = S$). All these records of the form $\big(b, (R, a)\big)$ or $\big(b, (S, c)\big)$ form the intermediate result.

The reduce function takes a B-value b, the key, together with a list that consists of pairs of the form (R, a) or (S, c). The result of the join will have as many tuples with B-value b as we can form by pairing an a from an (R, a) element on the list with a c from an (S, c) element on the list. Thus, *reduce* must extract from the list all the A-values associated with R and the list of all C-values associated with S. These are paired in all possible ways, with the b in the middle to form a tuple of the result. □

2.4 Exercises for Section 2

Exercise 2.1: Modify Example 5 to count the number of documents in which each word w appears.

Exercise 2.2: Express, in the map-reduce framework, the following operations on relations: (a) σ_C (b) π_L (c) $R \bowtie_C S$ (d) $R \cup S$ (e) $R \cap S$.

3 Distributed Databases

We shall now consider the elements of distributed database systems. In a distributed system, there are many, relatively autonomous processors that may participate in database operations. The difference between a distributed system and a shared-nothing parallel system is in the assumption about the cost of communication. Shared-nothing parallel systems usually have a message-passing cost that is small compared with disk accesses and other costs. In a distributed system, the processors are typically physically distant, rather than in the same room. The network connecting processors may have much less capacity than the network in a shared-nothing system.

Distributed databases offer significant advantages. Like parallel systems, a distributed system can use many processors and thereby accelerate the response to queries. Further, since the processors are widely separated, we can increase resilience in the face of failures by replicating data at several sites.

On the other hand, distributed processing increases the complexity of every aspect of a database system, so we need to rethink how even the most basic components of a DBMS are designed. Since the cost of communicating may dominate the cost of processing in main memory, a critical issue is how many messages are sent between sites. In this section we shall introduce the principal issues, while the next sections concentrate on solutions to two important problems that come up in distributed databases: distributed commit and distributed locking.

3.1 Distribution of Data

One important reason to distribute data is that the organization is itself distributed among many sites, and the sites each have data that is germane primarily to that site. Some examples are:

1. A bank may have many branches. Each branch (or the group of branches in a given city) will keep a database of accounts maintained at that branch (or city). Customers can choose to bank at any branch, but will normally bank at "their" branch, where their account data is stored. The bank may also have data that is kept in the central office, such as employee records and policies such as current interest rates. Of course, a backup of the records at each branch is also stored, probably in a site that is neither a branch office nor the central office.

2. A chain of department stores may have many individual stores. Each store (or a group of stores in one city) has a database of sales at that store and inventory at that store. There may also be a central office with data about employees, a chain-wide inventory, data about credit-card customers, and information about suppliers such as unfilled orders, and what each is owed. In addition, there may be a copy of all the stores'

sales data in a data warehouse that is used to analyze and predict sales through ad-hoc queries issued by analysts.

3. A digital library may consist of a consortium of universities that each hold on-line books and other documents. Search at any site will examine the catalog of documents available at all sites and deliver an electronic copy of the document to the user if any site holds it.

In some cases, what we might think of logically as a single relation has been partitioned among many sites. For example, the chain of stores might be imagined to have a single sales relation, such as

```
Sales(item, date, price, purchaser)
```

However, this relation does not exist physically. Rather, it is the union of a number of relations with the same schema, one at each of the stores in the chain. These local relations are called *fragments*, and the partitioning of a logical relation into physical fragments is called *horizontal decomposition* of the relation `Sales`. We regard the partition as "horizontal" because we may visualize a single `Sales` relation with its tuples separated, by horizontal lines, into the sets of tuples at each store.

In other situations, a distributed database appears to have partitioned a relation "vertically," by decomposing what might be one logical relation into two or more, each with a subset of the attributes, and with each relation at a different site. For instance, if we want to find out which sales at the Boston store were made to customers who are more than 90 days in arrears on their credit-card payments, it would be useful to have a relation (or view) that included the item, date, and purchaser information from `Sales`, along with the date of the last credit-card payment by that purchaser. However, in the scenario we are describing, this relation is decomposed vertically, and we would have to join the credit-card-customer relation at the central headquarters with the fragment of `Sales` at the Boston store.

3.2 Distributed Transactions

A consequence of the distribution of data is that a transaction may involve processes at several sites. Thus, our model of what a transaction is must change. No longer is a transaction a piece of code executed by a single processor communicating with a single scheduler and a single log manager at a single site. Rather, a transaction consists of communicating *transaction components*, each at a different site and communicating with the local scheduler and logger. Two important issues that must thus be looked at anew are:

1. How do we manage the commit/abort decision when a transaction is distributed? What happens if one component of the transaction wants to abort the whole transaction, while others encountered no problem and

want to commit? We discuss a technique called "two-phase commit" in Section 5; it allows the decision to be made properly and also frequently allows sites that are up to operate even if some other site(s) have failed.

2. How do we assure serializability of transactions that involve components at several sites? We look at locking in particular, in Section 6 and see how local lock tables can be used to support global locks on database elements and thus support serializability of transactions in a distributed environment.

3.3 Data Replication

One important advantage of a distributed system is the ability to *replicate* data, that is, to make copies of the data at different sites. One motivation is that if a site fails, there may be other sites that can provide the same data that was at the failed site. A second use is in improving the speed of query answering by making a copy of needed data available at the sites where queries are initiated. For example:

1. A bank may make copies of current interest-rate policy available at each branch, so a query about rates does not have to be sent to the central office.

2. A chain store may keep copies of information about suppliers at each store, so local requests for information about suppliers (e.g., the manager needs the phone number of a supplier to check on a shipment) can be handled without sending messages to the central office.

3. A digital library may temporarily cache a copy of a popular document at a school where students have been assigned to read the document.

However, there are several problems that must be faced when data is replicated.

a) How do we keep copies identical? In essence, an update to a replicated data element becomes a distributed transaction that updates all copies.

b) How do we decide where and how many copies to keep? The more copies, the more effort is required to update, but the easier queries become. For example, a relation that is rarely updated might have copies everywhere for maximum efficiency, while a frequently updated relation might have only one copy and a backup.

c) What happens when there is a communication failure in the network, and different copies of the same data have the opportunity to evolve separately and must then be reconciled when the network reconnects?

3.4 Exercises for Section 3

!! **Exercise 3.1:** The following exercise will allow you to address some of the problems that come up when deciding on a replication strategy for data. Suppose there is a relation R that is accessed from n sites. The ith site issues q_i queries about R and u_i updates to R per second, for $i = 1, 2, \ldots, n$. The cost of executing a query if there is a copy of R at the site issuing the query is c, while if there is no copy there, and the query must be sent to some remote site, then the cost is $10c$. The cost of executing an update is d for the copy of R at the issuing site and $10d$ for every copy of R that is not at the issuing site. As a function of these parameters, how would you choose, for large n, a set of sites at which to replicate R.

4 Distributed Query Processing

We now turn to optimizing queries on a network of distributed machines. When communication among processors is a significant cost, there are some query plans that can be more efficient than the ones we developed in Section 1 for processors that could communicate locally. Our principal objective is a new way of computing joins, using the semijoin operator.

4.1 The Distributed Join Problem

Suppose we want to compute $R(A, B) \bowtie S(B, C)$. However, R and S reside at different nodes of a network, as suggested in Fig. 5. There are two obvious ways to compute the join.

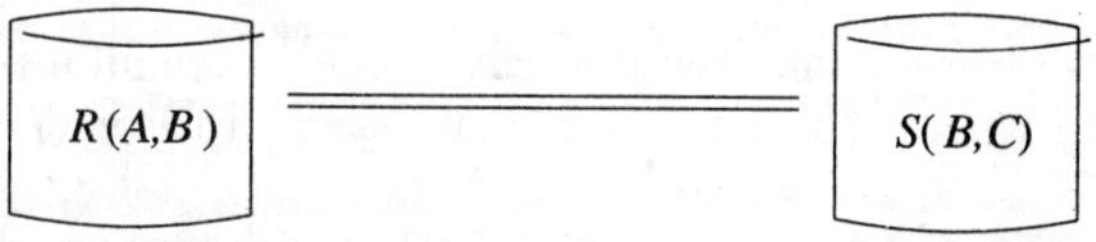

Figure 5: Joining relations at different nodes of a network

1. Send a copy of R to the site of S, and compute the join there.

2. Send a copy of S to the site of R and compute the join there.

In many situations, either of these methods is fine. However, problems can arise, such as:

a) What happens if the channel between the sites has low-capacity, e.g., a phone line or wireless link? Then, the cost of the join is primarily the time it takes to copy one of the relations, so we need to design our query plan to minimize communication.

b) Even if communication is fast, there may be a better query plan if the shared attribute B has values that are much smaller than the values of A and C. For example, B could be an identifier for documents or videos, while A and C are the documents or videos themselves.

4.2 Semijoin Reductions

Both these problems can be dealt with using the same type of query plan, in which only the relevant part of each relation is shipped to the site of the other. Recall that the semijoin of relations $R(X,Y)$ and $S(Y,Z)$, where X, Y, and Z are sets of attributes, is $R \ltimes S = R \bowtie \big(\pi_Y(S)\big)$. That is, we project S onto the common attributes, and then take the natural join of that projection with R. $\pi_Y(S)$ is a set-projection, so duplicates are eliminated. It is unusual to take a natural join where the attributes of one argument are a subset of the attributes of the other, but the definition of the join covers this case. The effect is that $R \ltimes S$ contains all those tuples of R that join with at least one tuple of S. Put another way, the semijoin $R \ltimes S$ eliminates the dangling tuples of R.

Having sent $\pi_Y(S)$ to the site of R, we can compute $R \ltimes S$ there. We know those tuples of R that are not in $R \ltimes S$ cannot participate in $R \bowtie S$. Therefore it is sufficient to send $R \ltimes S$, rather than all of R, to the site of S and to compute the join there. This plan is suggested by Fig. 6 for the relations $R(A,B)$ and $S(B,C)$. Of course there is a symmetric plan where the roles of R and S are interchanged.

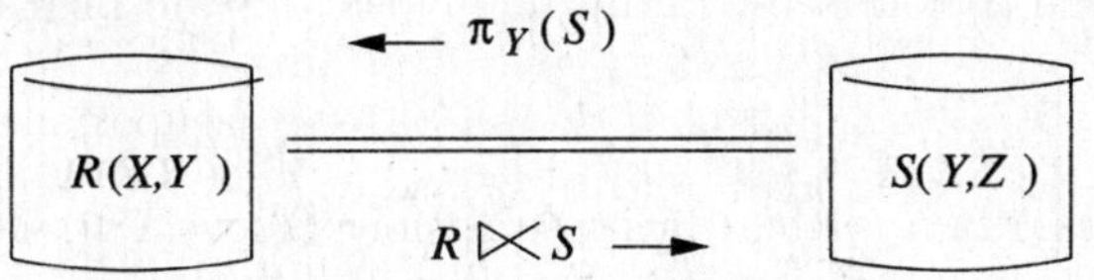

Figure 6: Exploiting the semijoin to minimize communication

Whether this semijoin plan, or the plan with R and S interchanged is more efficient than one of the obvious plans depends on several factors. First, if the projection of S onto Y results in a relation much smaller than S, then it is cheaper to send $\pi_Y(S)$ to the site of R, rather than S itself. $\pi_Y(S)$ will be small compared with S if either or both of the following hold:

1. There are many duplicates to be eliminated; i.e., many tuples of S share Y-values.

2. The components for the attributes of Z are large compared with the components of Y; e.g., Z includes attributes whose values are audios, videos, or documents.

In order for the semijoin plan to be superior, we also need to know that the size of $R \ltimes S$ is smaller than R. That is, R must contain many dangling tuples in its join with S.

4.3 Joins of Many Relations

When we want to take the natural join of two relations, only one semijoin is useful. The same holds for an equijoin, since we can act as if the equated pairs of attributes had the same name and treat the equijoin as if it were a natural join. However, when we take the natural join or equijoin of three or more relations at different sites, several surprising things happen.

- We may need several semijoins to eliminate all the dangling tuples from the relations before shipping them to other sites for joining.
- There are sets of relation schemas such that no finite sequence of semijoins eliminates all dangling tuples.
- It is possible to identify those sets of relation schemas such that there is a finite way to eliminate dangling tuples by semijoins.

Example 7: To see what can go wrong when we take the natural join of more than two relations, consider $R(A,B)$, $S(B,C)$, and $T(C,A)$. Suppose R and S have exactly the same n tuples: $\{(1,1),\ (2,2),\dots,(n,n)\}$. T has $n-1$ tuples: $\{(1,2),\ (2,3),\dots,(n-1,n)\}$. The relations are shown in Fig. 7.

A	B
1	1
2	2
.	.
.	.
.	.
n	n

R

B	C
1	1
2	2
.	.
.	.
.	.
n	n

S

C	A
1	2
2	3
.	.
.	.
.	.
$n-1$	n

T

Figure 7: Three relations for which elimination of dangling tuples by semijoins is very slow

Notice that while R and S join to produce the n tuples

$$\{(1,1,1),\ (2,2,2),\dots,(n,n,n)\}$$

none of these tuples can join with any tuple of T. The reason is that all tuples of $R \bowtie S$ agree in their A and C components, while the tuples of T disagree in their A and C components. That is, $R \bowtie S \bowtie T$ is empty, and *all* tuples of each relation are dangling.

However, no one semijoin can eliminate more than one tuple from any relation. For example, $S \ltimes T$ eliminates only (n,n) from S, because $\pi_C(T) = \{1,2,\dots,n-1\}$. Similarly, $R \ltimes T$ eliminates only $(1,1)$ from R, because $\pi_A(T) = \{2,3,\dots,n\}$. We can then continue, say, with $R \ltimes S$, which eliminates (n,n) from R, and $T \ltimes R$, which eliminates $(n-1,n)$ from T. Now we can compute $S \ltimes T$ again and eliminate $(n-1, n-1)$ from S, and so on. While we shall not prove it, we in fact need $3n-1$ semijoins to make all three relations empty. □

Since n in Example 7 is arbitrary, we see that for the particular relations discussed there, no fixed, finite sequence of semijoins is guaranteed to eliminate all dangling tuples, regardless of the data currently held in the relations. On the other hand, as we shall see, many typical joins of three or more relations do have fixed, finite sequences of semijoins that are guaranteed to eliminate all the dangling tuples. We call such a sequence of semijoins a *full reducer* for the relations in question.

4.4 Acyclic Hypergraphs

Let us assume that we are taking a natural join of several relations, although as mentioned, we can also handle equijoins by pretending the names of equated attributes from different relations are the same, and renaming attributes to make that pretense a reality. If we do, then we can draw a useful picture of every natural join as a *hypergraph*, that is a set of nodes with *hyperedges* that are sets of nodes. A traditional graph is then a hypergraph all of whose hyperedges are sets of size two.

The hypergraph for a natural join is formed by creating one node for each attribute name. Each relation is represented by a hyperedge containing all of its attributes.

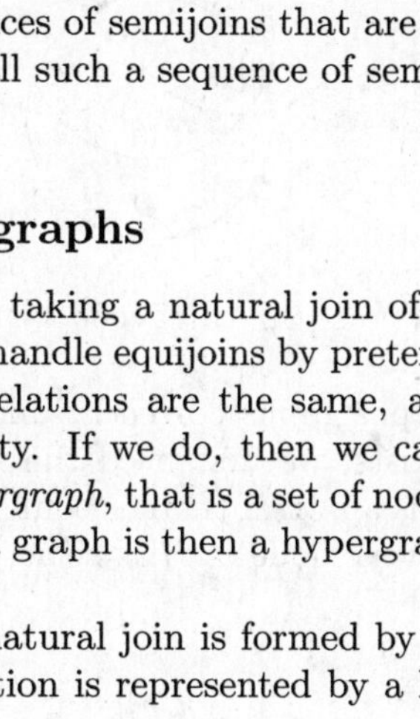

Figure 8: The hypergraph for Example 7

Example 8: Figure 8 is the hypergraph for the three relations from Example 7. The relation $R(A, B)$ is represented by the hyperedge $\{A, B\}$; S is represented by the hyperedge $\{B, C\}$, and T is the hyperedge $\{A, C\}$. Notice that this hypergraph is actually a graph, since the hyperedges are each pairs of nodes. Also observe that the three hyperedges form a cycle in the graph. As we shall see, it is this cyclicity that causes there to be no full reducer.

However, the question of when a hypergraph is cyclic has a somewhat unintuitive answer. In Fig. 9 is another hypergraph, which could be used, for instance, to represent the join of the relations $R(A, E, F)$, $S(A, B, C)$,

$T(C, D, E)$, and $U(A, C, E)$. This hypergraph is a true hypergraph, since it has hyperedges with more than two nodes. It also happens to be an "acyclic" hypergraph, even though it appears to have cycles. □

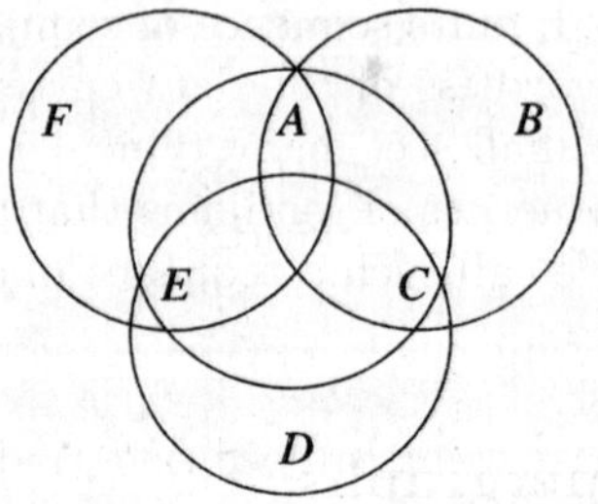

Figure 9: An acyclic hypergraph

To define acyclic hypergraphs correctly, and thus get the condition under which a full reducer exists, we first need the notion of an "ear" in a hypergraph. A hyperedge H is an *ear* if there is some other hyperedge G in the same hypergraph such that every node of H is either:

1. Found only in H, or

2. Also found in G.

We shall say that G *consumes* H, for a reason that will become apparent when we discuss reduction of the hypergraph.

Example 9: In Fig. 9, hyperedge $H = \{A, E, F\}$ is an ear. The role of G is played by $\{A, C, E\}$. Node F is unique to H; it appears in no other hyperedge. The other two nodes of H (A and E) are also members of G. □

A hypergraph is *acyclic* if it can be reduced to a single hyperedge by a sequence of *ear reductions.* An ear reduction is simply the elimination of one ear from the hypergraph, along with any nodes that appear only in that ear. Note that an ear, if not eliminated at one step, remains an ear after another ear is eliminated. However, it is possible that a hyperedge that was not an ear, becomes an ear after another hyperedge is eliminated.

Example 10: Figure 8 is not acyclic. No hyperedge is an ear, so we cannot get started with any ear reduction. For example, $\{A, B\}$ is not an ear because neither A nor B is unique to this hyperedge, and no other hyperedge contains both A and B.

On the other hand, Fig. 9 is acyclic. As we mentioned in Example 9, $\{A, E, F\}$ is an ear; so are $\{A, B, C\}$ and $\{C, D, E\}$. We can therefore eliminate hyperedge $\{A, E, F\}$ from the hypergraph. When we eliminate this ear, node F

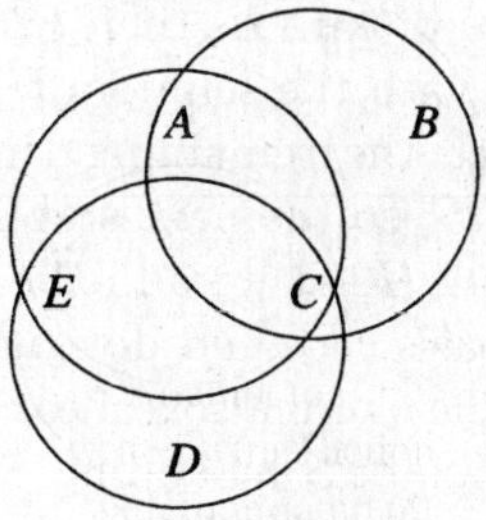

Figure 10: After one ear reduction

disappears, but the other five nodes and three hyperedges remain, as suggested in Fig. 10.

Since $\{A, B, C\}$ is an ear in Fig. 10, we may eliminate it and node B in a second ear reduction. Now, we are left with only hyperedges $\{A, C, E\}$ and $\{C, D, E\}$. Each is now an ear; notice that $\{A, C, E\}$ was not an ear until now. We can eliminate either, leaving a single hyperedge and proving that Fig. 9 is an acyclic hypergraph. □

4.5 Full Reducers for Acyclic Hypergraphs

We can construct a full reducer for any acyclic hypergraph by following the sequence of ear reductions. We construct the sequence of semijoins as follows, by induction on the number of hyperedges in an acyclic hypergraph.

BASIS: If there is only one hyperedge, do nothing. The "join" of one relation is the relation itself, and there are surely no dangling tuples.

INDUCTION: If the acyclic hypergraph has more than one hyperedge, then it must have at least one ear. Pick one, say H, and suppose it is consumed by hyperedge G.

1. Execute the semijoin $G := G \ltimes H$; that is, eliminate from G any of its tuples that do not join with H.[4]

2. Recursively, find a semijoin sequence for the hypergraph with ear H eliminated.

3. Execute the semijoin $H := H \ltimes G$.

Example 11: Let us construct the full reducer for the relations $R(A, E, F)$, $S(A, B, C)$, $T(C, D, E)$, and $U(A, C, E)$, whose hypergraph we saw in Fig. 9.

[4]We are identifying hyperedges with the relations that they represent for convenience in notation. Moreover, if the sets of tuples corresponding to a hyperedge are stored tables, rather than temporary relations, we do not actually replace a relation by a semijoin, as would be suggested by a step like $G := G \ltimes H$, but instead we store the result in a new temporary, G'.

We shall use the sequence of ears R, then S, then U, as in Example 10. Since U consumes R, we begin with the semijoin $U := U \ltimes R$.

Recursively, we reduce the remaining three hyperedges. That reduction starts with U consuming S, so the next step is $U := U \ltimes S$. Another level of recursion has T consuming U, so we add the step $T := T \ltimes U$. With only T remaining, we have the basis case and do nothing.

Finally, we complete the elimination of ear U by adding $U := U \ltimes T$. Then, we complete the elimination of S by adding $S := S \ltimes U$, and we complete the elimination of R with $R := R \ltimes U$. The entire sequence of semijoins that forms a full reducer for Fig. 9 is shown in Fig. 11. □

$$
\begin{aligned}
U &:= U \ltimes R \\
U &:= U \ltimes S \\
T &:= T \ltimes U \\
U &:= U \ltimes T \\
S &:= S \ltimes U \\
R &:= R \ltimes U
\end{aligned}
$$

Figure 11: A full reducer for Fig. 9

Once we have executed all the semijoins in the full reducer, we can copy all the reduced relations to the site of one of them, knowing that the relations to be shipped contain no dangling tuples and therefore are as small as can be. In fact, if we know at which site the join will be performed, then we do not have to eliminate all dangling tuples for relations at that site. We can stop applying semijoins to a relation as soon as that relation will no longer be used to reduce other relations.

Example 12: If the full reducer of Fig. 11 will be followed by a join at the site of S, then we do not have to do the step $S := S \ltimes U$. However, if the join is to be conducted at the site of T, then we still have to do the reduction $T := T \ltimes U$, because T is used to reduce other relations at later steps. □

4.6 Why the Full-Reducer Algorithm Works

We can show that the algorithm produces a full reducer for any acyclic hypergraph by induction on the number of hyperedges.

BASIS: One hyperedge. There are no dangling tuples, so nothing needs to be done.

INDUCTION: When we eliminate the ear H, we eliminate, from the hyperedge G that consumes H, all tuples that will not join with at least one tuple of H. Thus, whatever further reductions are done, the join of the relations for all the hyperedges besides H cannot contain a tuple that will not join with H.

Note that this statement is true because G is the only link between H and the remaining relations.

By induction, all tuples that are dangling in the join of the remaining relations are eliminated. When we do the final semijoin $H := H \ltimes G$ to eliminate dangling tuples from H, we know that no relation has dangling tuples.

4.7 Exercises for Section 4

! **Exercise 4.1:** Suppose we want to take the natural join of $R(A,B)$ and $S(B,C)$, where R and S are at different sites, and the size of the data communicated is the dominant cost of the join. Suppose the sizes of R and S are s_R and s_S, respectively. Suppose that the size of $\pi_B(R)$ is fraction p_R of the size of R and $\pi_B(S)$ is fraction p_S of the size of S. Finally, suppose that fractions d_R and d_S of relations R and S, respectively, are dangling. Write expressions, in terms of these six parameters, for the costs of the four strategies for evaluating $R \bowtie S$, and determine the conditions under which each is the best strategy. The four strategies are:

i) Ship R to the site of S.

ii) Ship S to the site of R.

iii) Ship $\pi_B(S)$ to the site of R, and then $R \ltimes S$ to the site of S.

iv) Ship $\pi_B(R)$ to the site of S, and then $S \ltimes R$ to the site of R.

Exercise 4.2: Determine which of the following hypergraphs are acyclic. Each hypergraph is represented by a list of its hyperedges.

a) $\{A,B\}$, $\{B,C,D\}$, $\{B,E,F\}$, $\{F,G,H\}$, $\{G,I\}$, $\{H,J\}$.

b) $\{A,B\}$, $\{B,C,D\}$, $\{B,E,F\}$, $\{F,G,H\}$, $\{G,I\}$, $\{B,H\}$.

c) $\{A,B,C,D\}$, $\{A,B,E\}$, $\{B,D,F\}$, $\{C,D,G\}$, $\{A,C,H\}$.

Exercise 4.3: For those hypergraphs of Exercise 4.2 that are acyclic, construct a full reducer.

! **Exercise 4.4:** Besides the full reducer of Example 11, how many other full reducers of six steps can be constructed for the hypergraph of Fig. 9 by choosing other orders for the elimination of ears?

! **Exercise 4.5:** A well known property of acyclic graphs is that if you delete an edge from an acyclic graph it remains acyclic. Is the analogous statement true for hypergraphs? That is, if you eliminate a hyperedge from an acyclic hypergraph, is the remaining hypergraph always acyclic? *Hint*: consider the acyclic hypergraph of Fig. 9.

!! **Exercise 4.6:** Not all binary operations on relations located at different nodes of a network can have their execution time reduced by preliminary operations like the semijoin. Is it possible to improve on the obvious algorithm (ship one of the relations to the other site) when the operation is (a) union (b) intersection (c) difference?

5 Distributed Commit

In this section, we shall address the problem of how a distributed transaction that has components at several sites can execute atomically. The next section discusses another important property of distributed transactions: executing them serializably.

5.1 Supporting Distributed Atomicity

We shall begin with an example that illustrates the problems that might arise.

Example 13: Consider our example of a chain of stores mentioned in Section 3. Suppose a manager of the chain wants to query all the stores, find the inventory of toothbrushes at each, and issue instructions to move toothbrushes from store to store in order to balance the inventory. The operation is done by a single global transaction T that has component T_i at the ith store and a component T_0 at the office where the manager is located. The sequence of activities performed by T are summarized below:

1. Component T_0 is created at the site of the manager.

2. T_0 sends messages to all the stores instructing them to create components T_i.

3. Each T_i executes a query at store i to discover the number of toothbrushes in inventory and reports this number to T_0.

4. T_0 takes these numbers and determines, by some algorithm we do not need to discuss, what shipments of toothbrushes are desired. T_0 then sends messages such as "store 10 should ship 500 toothbrushes to store 7" to the appropriate stores (stores 7 and 10 in this instance).

5. Stores receiving instructions update their inventory and perform the shipments.

□

There are a number of things that could go wrong in Example 13, and many of these result in violations of the atomicity of T. That is, some of the actions comprising T get executed, but others do not. Mechanisms such as logging and recovery, which we assume are present at each site, will assure that each T_i is executed atomically, but do not assure that T itself is atomic.

Example 14: Suppose a bug in the algorithm to redistribute toothbrushes might cause store 10 to be instructed to ship more toothbrushes than it has. T_{10} will therefore abort, and no toothbrushes will be shipped from store 10; neither will the inventory at store 10 be changed. However, T_7 detects no problems and commits at store 7, updating its inventory to reflect the supposedly shipped toothbrushes. Now, not only has T failed to execute atomically (since T_{10} never completes), but it has left the distributed database in an inconsistent state. □

Another source of problems is the possibility that a site will fail or be disconnected from the network while the distributed transaction is running.

Example 15: Suppose T_{10} replies to T_0's first message by telling its inventory of toothbrushes. However, the machine at store 10 then crashes, and the instructions from T_0 are never received by T_{10}. Can distributed transaction T ever commit? What should T_{10} do when its site recovers? □

5.2 Two-Phase Commit

In order to avoid the problems suggested in Section 5.1, distributed DBMS's use a complex protocol for deciding whether or not to commit a distributed transaction. In this section, we shall describe the basic idea behind these protocols, called *two-phase commit.*[5] By making a global decision about committing, each component of the transaction will commit, or none will. As usual, we assume that the atomicity mechanisms at each site assure that either the local component commits or it has no effect on the database state at that site; i.e., components of the transaction are atomic. Thus, by enforcing the rule that either all components of a distributed transaction commit or none does, we make the distributed transaction itself atomic.

Several salient points about the two-phase commit protocol follow:

- In a two-phase commit, we assume that each site logs actions at that site, but there is no global log.
- We also assume that one site, called the *coordinator*, plays a special role in deciding whether or not the distributed transaction can commit. For example, the coordinator might be the site at which the transaction originates, such as the site of T_0 in the examples of Section 5.1.
- The two-phase commit protocol involves sending certain messages between the coordinator and the other sites. As each message is sent, it is logged at the sending site, to aid in recovery should it be necessary.

With these points in mind, we can describe the two phases in terms of the messages sent between sites.

[5] Do not confuse two-phase commit with two-phase locking. They are independent ideas, designed to solve different problems.

Phase I

In phase 1 of the two-phase commit, the coordinator for a distributed transaction T decides when to attempt to commit T. Presumably the attempt to commit occurs after the component of T at the coordinator site is ready to commit, but in principle the steps must be carried out even if the coordinator's component wants to abort (but with obvious simplifications as we shall see). The coordinator polls the sites of all components of the transaction T to determine their wishes regarding the commit/abort decision, as follows:

1. The coordinator places a log record <`Prepare` T> on the log at its site.

2. The coordinator sends to each component's site (in principle including itself) the message `prepare` T.

3. Each site receiving the message `prepare` T decides whether to commit or abort its component of T. The site can delay if the component has not yet completed its activity, but must eventually send a response.

4. If a site wants to commit its component, it must enter a state called *precommitted.* Once in the precommitted state, the site cannot abort its component of T without a directive to do so from the coordinator. The following steps are done to become precommitted:

   (a) Perform whatever steps are necessary to be sure the local component of T will not have to abort, even if there is a system failure followed by recovery at the site. Thus, not only must all actions associated with the local T be performed, but the appropriate actions regarding the log must be taken so that T will be redone rather than undone in a recovery. The actions depend on the logging method, but surely the log records associated with actions of the local T must be flushed to disk.

   (b) Place the record <`Ready` T> on the local log and flush the log to disk.

   (c) Send to the coordinator the message `ready` T.

   However, the site does not commit its component of T at this time; it must wait for phase 2.

5. If, instead, the site wants to abort its component of T, then it logs the record <`Don't commit` T> and sends the message `don't commit` T to the coordinator. It is safe to abort the component at this time, since T will surely abort if even one component wants to abort.

The messages of phase 1 are summarized in Fig. 12.

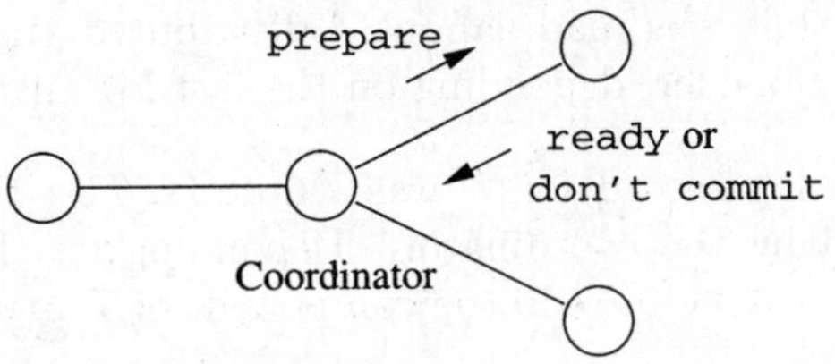

Figure 12: Messages in phase 1 of two-phase commit

Phase II

The second phase begins when responses **ready** or **don't commit** are received from each site by the coordinator. However, it is possible that some site fails to respond; it may be down, or it has been disconnected by the network. In that case, after a suitable timeout period, the coordinator will treat the site as if it had sent **don't commit**.

1. If the coordinator has received **ready** T from all components of T, then it decides to commit T. The coordinator logs <**Commit** T> at its site and then sends message **commit** T to all sites involved in T.

2. However, if the coordinator has received **don't commit** T from one or more sites, it logs <**Abort** T> at its site and then sends **abort** T messages to all sites involved in T.

3. If a site receives a **commit** T message, it commits the component of T at that site, logging <**Commit** T> as it does.

4. If a site receives the message **abort** T, it aborts T and writes the log record <**Abort** T>.

The messages of phase 2 are summarized in Fig. 13.

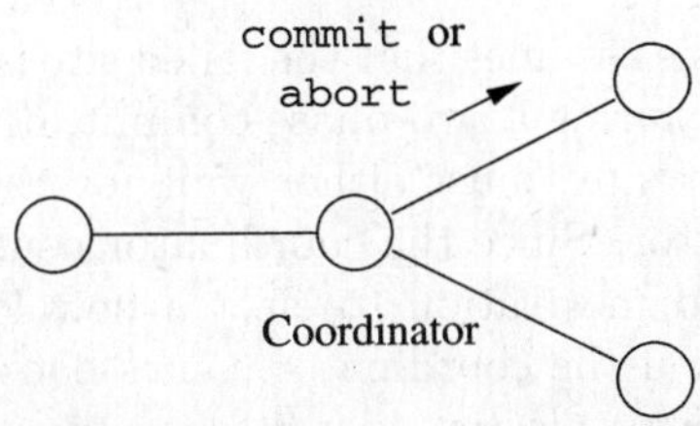

Figure 13: Messages in phase 2 of two-phase commit

5.3 Recovery of Distributed Transactions

At any time during the two-phase commit process, a site may fail. We need to make sure that what happens when the site recovers is consistent with the global decision that was made about a distributed transaction T. There are several cases to consider, depending on the last log entry for T.

1. If the last log record for T was <Commit T>, then T must have been committed by the coordinator. Depending on the log method used, it may be necessary to redo the component of T at the recovering site.

2. If the last log record is <Abort T>, then similarly we know that the global decision was to abort T. If the log method requires it, we undo the component of T at the recovering site.

3. If the last log record is <Don't commit T>, then the site knows that the global decision must have been to abort T. If necessary, effects of T on the local database are undone.

4. The hard case is when the last log record for T is <Ready T>. Now, the recovering site does not know whether the global decision was to commit or abort T. This site must communicate with at least one other site to find out the global decision for T. If the coordinator is up, the site can ask the coordinator. If the coordinator is not up at this time, some other site may be asked to consult its log to find out what happened to T. In the worst case, no other site can be contacted, and the local component of T must be kept active until the commit/abort decision is determined.

5. It may also be the case that the local log has no records about T that come from the actions of the two-phase commit protocol. If so, then the recovering site may unilaterally decide to abort its component of T, which is consistent with all logging methods. It is possible that the coordinator already detected a timeout from the failed site and decided to abort T. If the failure was brief, T may still be active at other sites, but it will never be inconsistent if the recovering site decides to abort its component of T and responds with don't commit T if later polled in phase 1.

The above analysis assumes that the failed site is not the coordinator. When the coordinator fails during a two-phase commit, new problems arise. First, the surviving participant sites must either wait for the coordinator to recover or elect a new coordinator. Since the coordinator could be down for an indefinite period, there is good motivation to elect a new leader, at least after a brief waiting period to see if the coordinator comes back up.

The matter of *leader election* is in its own right a complex problem of distributed systems, beyond the scope of this book. However, a simple method will work in most situations. For instance, we may assume that all participant sites have unique identifying numbers, e.g., IP addresses. Each participant sends messages announcing its availability as leader to all the other sites, giving its identifying number. After a suitable length of time, each participant acknowledges as the new coordinator the lowest-numbered site from which it has heard, and sends messages to that effect to all the other sites. If all sites receive consistent messages, then there is a unique choice for new coordinator, and everyone knows about it. If there is inconsistency, or a surviving site has failed to respond, that too will be universally known, and the election starts over.

Now, the new leader polls the sites for information about each distributed transaction T. Each site reports the last record on its log concerning T, if there is one. The possible cases are:

1. Some site has `<Commit` T`>` on its log. Then the original coordinator must have wanted to send `commit` T messages everywhere, and it is safe to commit T.

2. Similarly, if some site has `<Abort` T`>` on its log, then the original coordinator must have decided to abort T, and it is safe for the new coordinator to order that action.

3. Suppose now that no site has `<Commit` T`>` or `<Abort` T`>` on its log, but at least one site does *not* have `<Ready` T`>` on its log. Then since actions are logged before the corresponding messages are sent, we know that the old coordinator never received `ready` T from this site and therefore could not have decided to commit. It is safe for the new coordinator to decide to abort T.

4. The most problematic situation is when there is no `<Commit` T`>` or `<Abort` T`>` to be found, but every surviving site has `<Ready` T`>`. Now, we cannot be sure whether the old coordinator found some reason to abort T or not; it could have decided to do so because of actions at its own site, or because of a `don't commit` T message from another failed site, for example. Or the old coordinator may have decided to commit T and already committed its local component of T. Thus, the new coordinator is not able to decide whether to commit or abort T and must wait until the original coordinator recovers. In real systems, the database administrator has the ability to intervene and manually force the waiting transaction components to finish. The result is a possible loss of atomicity, but the person executing the blocked transaction will be notified to take some appropriate compensating action.

5.4 Exercises for Section 5

! **Exercise 5.1:** Consider a transaction T initiated at a home computer that asks bank B to transfer \$10,000 from an account at B to an account at another bank C.

a) What are the components of distributed transaction T? What should the components at B and C do?

b) What can go wrong if there is not \$10,000 in the account at B?

c) What can go wrong if one or both banks' computers crash, or if the network is disconnected?

d) If one of the problems suggested in (c) occurs, how could the transaction resume correctly when the computers and network resume operation?

Exercise 5.2: In this exercise, we need a notation for describing sequences of messages that can take place during a two-phase commit. Let (i, j, M) mean that site i sends the message M to site j, where the value of M and its meaning can be P (prepare), R (ready), D (don't commit), C (commit), or A (abort). We shall discuss a simple situation in which site 0 is the coordinator, but not otherwise part of the transaction, and sites 1 and 2 are the components. For instance, the following is one possible sequence of messages that could take place during a successful commit of the transaction:

$$(0, 1, P),\ (0, 2, P),\ (2, 0, R),\ (1, 0, R),\ (0, 2, C),\ (0, 1, C)$$

a) Give an example of a sequence of messages that could occur if site 1 wants to commit and site 2 wants to abort.

! b) How many possible sequences of messages such as the above are there, if the transaction successfully commits?

! c) If site 1 wants to commit, but site 2 does not, how many sequences of messages are there, assuming no failures occur?

! d) If site 1 wants to commit, but site 2 is down and does not respond to messages, how many sequences are there?

!! **Exercise 5.3:** Using the notation of Exercise 5.2, suppose the sites are a coordinator and n other sites that are the transaction components. As a function of n, how many sequences of messages are there if the transaction successfully commits?

6 Distributed Locking

In this section we shall see how to extend a locking scheduler to an environment where transactions are distributed and consist of components at several sites. We assume that lock tables are managed by individual sites, and that the component of a transaction at a site can request locks on the data elements only at that site.

When data is replicated, we must arrange that the copies of a single element X are changed in the same way by each transaction. This requirement introduces a distinction between locking the *logical* database element X and locking one or more of the copies of X. In this section, we shall offer a cost model for distributed locking algorithms that applies to both replicated and nonreplicated data. However, before introducing the model, let us consider an obvious (and sometimes adequate) solution to the problem of maintaining locks in a distributed database — centralized locking.

6.1 Centralized Lock Systems

Perhaps the simplest approach is to designate one site, the *lock site*, to maintain a lock table for logical elements, whether or not they have copies at that site. When a transaction wants a lock on logical element X, it sends a request to the lock site, which grants or denies the lock, as appropriate. Since obtaining a global lock on X is the same as obtaining a local lock on X at the lock site, we can be sure that global locks behave correctly as long as the lock site administers locks conventionally. The usual cost is three messages per lock (request, grant, and release), unless the transaction happens to be running at the lock site.

The use of a single lock site can be adequate in some situations, but if there are many sites and many simultaneous transactions, the lock site could become a bottleneck. Further, if the lock site crashes, no transaction at any site can obtain locks. Because of these problems with centralized locking, there are a number of other approaches to maintaining distributed locks, which we shall introduce after discussing how to estimate the cost of locking.

6.2 A Cost Model for Distributed Locking Algorithms

Suppose that each data element exists at exactly one site (i.e., there is no data replication) and that the lock manager at each site stores locks and lock requests for the elements at its site. Transactions may be distributed, and each transaction consists of components at one or more sites.

While there are several costs associated with managing locks, many of them are fixed, independent of the way transactions request locks over a network. The one cost factor over which we have control is the number of messages sent between sites when a transaction obtains and releases its locks. We shall thus count the number of messages required for various locking schemes on the assumption that all locks are granted when requested. Of course, a lock request may be denied, resulting in an additional message to deny the request and a later message when the lock is granted. However, since we cannot predict the rate of lock denials, and this rate is not something we can control anyway, we shall ignore this additional requirement for messages in our comparisons.

Example 16: As we mentioned in Section 6.1, in the central locking method, the typical lock request uses three messages, one to request the lock, one from the central site to grant the lock, and a third to release the lock. The exceptions are:

1. The messages are unnecessary when the requesting site is the central lock site, and
2. Additional messages must be sent when the initial request cannot be granted.

However, we assume that both these situations are relatively rare; i.e., most lock requests are from sites other than the central lock site, and most lock requests can be granted. Thus, three messages per lock is a good estimate of the cost of the centralized lock method. □

Now, consider a situation more flexible than central locking, where there is no replication, but each database element X can maintain its locks at its own site. It might seem that, since a transaction wanting to lock X will have a component at the site of X, there are no messages between sites needed. The local component simply negotiates with the lock manager at that site for the lock on X. However, if the distributed transaction needs locks on several elements, say X, Y, and Z, then the transaction cannot complete its computation until it has locks on all three elements. If X, Y, and Z are at different sites, then the components of the transactions at those sites must at least exchange synchronization messages to prevent the transaction from proceeding before it has all the locks it needs.

Rather than deal with all the possible variations, we shall take a simple model of how transactions gather locks. We assume that one component of each transaction, the *lock coordinator* for that transaction, has the responsibility to gather all the locks that all components of the transaction require. The lock coordinator locks elements at its own site without messages, but locking an element X at any other site requires three messages:

1. A message to the site of X requesting the lock.
2. A reply message granting the lock (recall we assume all locks are granted immediately; if not, a denial message followed by a granting message later will be sent).
3. A message to the site of X releasing the lock.

If we pick as the lock coordinator the site where the most locks are needed by the transaction, then we minimize the requirement for messages. The number of messages required is three times the number of database elements at the other sites.

6.3 Locking Replicated Elements

When an element X has replicas at several sites, we must be careful how we interpret the locking of X.

Example 17: Suppose there are two copies, X_1 and X_2, of a database element X. Suppose also that a transaction T gets a shared lock on the copy X_1 at the site of that copy, while transaction U gets an exclusive lock on the copy X_2 at its site. Now, U can change X_2 but cannot change X_1, resulting in the two copies of the element X becoming different. Moreover, since T and U may lock other elements as well, and the order in which they read and write X is not forced by the locks they hold on the copies of X, there is also an opportunity for T and U to engage in unserializable behavior. □

The problem illustrated by Example 17 is that when data is replicated, we must distinguish between getting a shared or exclusive lock on the logical element X and getting a local lock on a copy of X. That is, in order to assure serializability, we need for transactions to take global locks on the logical elements. But the logical elements don't exist physically — only their copies do — and there is no global lock table. Thus, the only way that a transaction can obtain a global lock on X is to obtain local locks on one or more copies of X at the site(s) of those copies. We shall now consider methods for turning local locks into global locks that have the required property:

- A logical element X can have either one exclusive lock and no shared lock, or any number of shared locks and no exclusive locks.

6.4 Primary-Copy Locking

An improvement on the centralized locking approach, one which also allows replicated data, is to distribute the function of the lock site, but still maintain the principle that each logical element has a single site responsible for its global lock. This distributed-lock method, called *primary copy*, avoids the possibility that the central lock site will become a bottleneck, while still maintaining the simplicity of the centralized method.

In the primary copy lock method, each logical element X has one of its copies designated the "primary copy." In order to get a lock on logical element X, a transaction sends a request to the site of the primary copy of X. The site of the primary copy maintains an entry for X in its lock table and grants or denies the request as appropriate. Again, global (logical) locks will be administered correctly as long as each site administers the locks for the primary copies correctly.

Also as with a centralized lock site, most lock requests require three messages, except for those where the transaction and the primary copy are at the same site. However, if we choose primary copies wisely, then we expect that these sites will frequently be the same.

Example 18: In the chain-of-stores example, we should make each store's sales data have its primary copy at the store. Other copies of this data, such as at the central office or at a data warehouse used by sales analysts, are not primary copies. Probably, the typical transaction is executed at a store and updates only sales data for that store. No messages are needed when this type of transaction takes its locks. Only if the transaction examined or modified data at another store would lock-related messages be sent. □

6.5 Global Locks From Local Locks

Another approach is to synthesize global locks from collections of local locks. In these schemes, no copy of a database element X is "primary"; rather they are symmetric, and local shared or exclusive locks can be requested on any of these

Distributed Deadlocks

There are many opportunities for transactions to get deadlocked as they try to acquire global locks on replicated data. There are also many ways to construct a global waits-for graph and thus detect deadlocks. However, in a distributed environment, it is often simplest and also most effective to use a timeout. Any transaction that has not completed after an appropriate amount of time is assumed to have gotten deadlocked and is rolled back.

copies. The key to a successful global locking scheme is to require transactions to obtain a certain number of local locks on copies of X before the transaction can assume it has a global lock on X.

Suppose database element A has n copies. We pick two numbers:

1. s is the number of copies of A that must be locked in shared mode in order for a transaction to have a global shared lock on A.

2. x is the number of copies of A that must be locked in exclusive mode in order for a transaction to have an exclusive lock on A.

As long as $2x > n$ and $s + x > n$, we have the desired properties: there can be only one global exclusive lock on A, and there cannot be both a global shared and global exclusive lock on A. The explanation is as follows. Since $2x > n$, if two transactions had global exclusive locks on A, there would be at least one copy that had granted local exclusive locks to both (because there are more local exclusive locks granted than there are copies of A). However, then the local locking method would be incorrect. Similarly, since $s + x > n$, if one transaction had a global shared lock on A and another had a global exclusive lock on A, then some copy granted both local shared and exclusive locks at the same time.

In general, the number of messages needed to obtain a global shared lock is $3s$, and the number to obtain a global exclusive lock is $3x$. That number seems excessive, compared with centralized methods that require 3 or fewer messages per lock on the average. However, there are compensating arguments, as the following two examples of specific (s, x) choices shows.

Read-Locks-One; Write-Locks-All

Here, $s = 1$ and $x = n$. Obtaining a global exclusive lock is very expensive, but a global shared lock requires three messages at the most. Moreover, this scheme has an advantage over the primary-copy method: while the latter allows us to avoid messages when we read the primary copy, the read-locks-one scheme allows us to avoid messages whenever the transaction is at the site of *any copy* of the database element we desire to read. Thus, this scheme can be superior when most transactions are read-only, but transactions to read an element X initiate at different sites. An example would be a distributed digital library that caches copies of documents where they are most frequently read.

Majority Locking

Here, $s = x = \lceil (n+1)/2 \rceil$. It seems that this system requires many messages no matter where the transaction is. However, there are several other factors that may make this scheme acceptable. First, many network systems support *broadcast*, where it is possible for a transaction to send out one general request for local locks on an element X, which will be received by all sites. Similarly, the release of locks may be achieved by a single message.

Moreover, this selection of s and x provides an advantage others do not: it allows partial operation even when the network is disconnected. As long as there is one component of the network that contains a majority of the sites with copies of X, then it is possible for a transaction to obtain a lock on X. Even if other sites are active while disconnected, we know that they cannot even get a shared lock on X, and thus there is no risk that transactions running in different components of the network will engage in behavior that is not serializable.

6.6 Exercises for Section 6

! Exercise 6.1 : We showed how to create global shared and exclusive locks from local locks of that type. How would you create:

a) Global shared, exclusive, and increment locks

b) Global shared, exclusive, and update locks

!! c) Global shared, exclusive, and intention locks for each type

from local locks of the same types?

Exercise 6.2 : Suppose there are five sites, each with a copy of a database element X. One of these sites P is the dominant site for X and will be used as X's primary site in a primary-copy distributed-lock system. The statistics regarding accesses to X are:

i. 50% of all accesses are read-only accesses originating at P.

ii. Each of the other four sites originates 10% of the accesses, and these are read-only.

iii. The remaining 10% of accesses require exclusive access and may originate at any of the five sites with equal probability (i.e., 2% originate at each).

For each of the lock methods below, give the average number of messages needed to obtain a lock. Assume that all requests are granted, so no denial messages are needed.

Grid Computing

Grid computing is a term that means almost the same as peer-to-peer computing. However, the applications of grids usually involve sharing of computing resources rather than data, and there is often a master node that controls what the others do. Popular examples include SETI, which attempts to distribute the analysis of signals for signs of extraterrestrial intelligence among participating nodes, and Folding-at-Home, which attempts to do the same for protein-folding.

a) Read-locks-one; write-locks-all.

b) Majority locking.

c) Primary-copy locking, with the primary copy at P.

7 Peer-to-Peer Distributed Search

In this section, we examine peer-to-peer distributed systems. When these systems are used to store and deliver data, the problem of search becomes surprisingly hard. That is, each node in the peer-to-peer network has a subset of the data elements, but there is no centralized index that says where something is located. The method called "distributed hashing" allows peer-to-peer networks to grow and shrink, yet allows us to find available data much more efficiently than sending messages to every node.

7.1 Peer-to-Peer Networks

A *peer-to-peer* network is a collection of *nodes* or *peers* (participating machines) that:

1. Are *autonomous*: participants do not respect any central control and can join or leave the network at will.

2. Are *loosely coupled*; they communicate over a general-purpose network such as the Internet, rather than being hard-wired together like the processors in a parallel machine.

3. Are equal in functionality; there is no leader or controlling node.

4. Share resources with one another.

Peer-to-peer networks initially received a bad name, because their first popular use was in sharing copyrighted files such as music. However, they have many

Copyright Issues in Digital Libraries

In order for a distributed world-wide digital library to become a reality, there will have to be some resolution of the severe copyright issues that arise. Current, small-scale versions of this network have partial solutions. For example, on-line university libraries often pass accesses to the ACM digital library only from IP addresses in the university's domain. Other arrangements are based on the idea that only one user at a time can access a particular copyrighted document. The digital library can "loan" the right to another library, but then users of the first library cannot access the document. The world awaits a solution that is easily implementable and fair to all interests.

legitimate uses. For example, as libraries replace books by digital images, it becomes feasible for all the world's libraries to share what they have. It should not be necessary for each library to store a copy of every book or document in the world. But then, when you request a book from your local library, that library's node needs to find a peer library that does have a copy of what you want.

As another example, we might imagine a peer-to-peer network for the sharing of personal collections of photographs or videos, that is, a peer-to-peer version of Flickr or YouTube. The images are housed on participants' personal computers, so they will be turned on and off periodically. There can be millions of participants, and each has only a small fraction of the resources of the entire network.

7.2 The Distributed-Hashing Problem

Early peer-to-peer networks such as Napster used a centralized table that told where data elements could be found. Later systems distributed the function of locating elements, either by replication or division of the task among the peers. When the database is truly large, such as a shared worldwide library or photo-sharing network, there is no choice but to share the task in some way.

We shall abstract the problem to one of lookup of records in a (very large) set of key-value pairs. Associated with each key K is a value V. For example, K might be the identifier of a document. V could be the document itself, or it could be the set of nodes at which the document can be found.

If the size of the key-value data is small, there are several simple solutions. We could use a central node that holds the entire key-value table. All nodes would query the central node when they wanted the value V associated with a given key K. In that case, a pair of query-response messages would answer any lookup question for any node. Alternatively, we could replicate the entire table at each node, so there would be no messages needed at all.

The problem becomes more interesting when the key-value table is too large to be handled by a single node. We shall consider this problem, using the following constraints:

1. At any time, only one node among the peers knows the value associated with any given key K.

2. The key-value pairs are distributed roughly equally among the peers.

3. Any node can ask the peers for the value V associated with a chosen key K. The value of V should be obtained in a way such that the number of messages sent among the peers grows much more slowly than the number of peers.

4. The amount of routing information needed at each node to help locate keys must also grow much more slowly than the number of nodes.

7.3 Centralized Solutions for Distributed Hashing

If the set of participants in the network is fixed once and for all, or the set of participants changes slowly, then there are straightforward ways to manage lookup of keys. For example, we could use a hash function h that hashes keys into node numbers. We place the key-value pair (K, V) at the node $h(K)$.

In fact, Google and similar search engines effectively maintain a centralized index of the entire Web and manage huge numbers of requests. They do so by behaving logically as if there were a centralized index, when in fact the index is replicated at a very large number of nodes. Each node consists of many machines that together share the index of the Web.

However, machines at Google are not really "peers." They cannot decide to leave the network, and they each have a specific function to perform. While machines can fail, their load is simply assumed by a node of similar machines until the failed machine is replaced. In the balance of this section, we shall consider the more complex solution that is needed when the data is maintained by a true collection of peer nodes.

7.4 Chord Circles

We shall now describe one of several possible algorithms for distributed hashing, an algorithm with the desirable property that it uses a number of messages that is logarithmic in the number of peers. In addition, the amount of information other than key-value peers needed at each node grows logarithmically in the number of nodes.

In this algorithm, we arrange the peers in a "chord circle." Each node knows its predecessor and successor around the circle, and nodes also have links to nodes located at an exponentially growing set of distances around the circle (these links are the "chords"). Figure 14 suggests what the chord circle looks like.

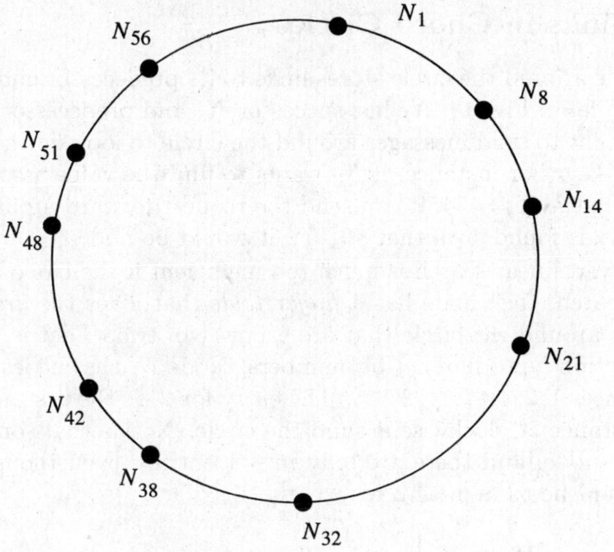

Figure 14: A chord circle

To place a node in the circle, we hash its ID i, and place it at position $h(i)$. We shall henceforth refer to this node as $N_{h(i)}$. Thus, for example, in Fig. 14, N_{21} is a node whose ID i has $h(i) = 21$. The successor of each node is the next higher one clockwise around the circle. For example, the successor of N_{21} is N_{32}, and N_1 is the successor of N_{56}. Likewise, N_{21} is the predecessor of N_{32}, and N_{56} is the predecessor of N_1.

The nodes are located around the circle using a hash function h that is capable of mapping both keys and node ID's (e.g., IP-addresses) to m-bit numbers, for some m. In Fig. 14, we suppose that $m = 6$, so there are 64 different possible locations for nodes around the circle. In a real application, m would be much larger.

Key-value pairs are also distributed around the circle using the hash function h. If (K, V) is a key-value pair, then we compute $h(K)$ and place (K, V) at the lowest numbered node N_j such that $h(K) \leq j$. As a special case, if $h(K)$ is above the highest-numbered node, then it is assigned to the lowest-numbered node. That is, key K goes to the first node at or clockwise of the position $h(K)$ in the circle.

Example 19: In Fig. 14, any (K, V) pair such that $42 < h(K) \leq 48$ would be stored at N_{48}. If $h(K)$ is any of $57, 58, \ldots, 63, 0, 1$, then (K, V) would be placed at N_1. □

7.5 Links in Chord Circles

Each node around the circle stores links to its predecessor and successor. Thus, for example, in Fig. 14, N_1 has successor N_8 and predecessor N_{56}. These links are sufficient to send messages around the circle to look up the value associated with any key. For instance, if N_8 wants to find the value associated with a key K such that $h(K) = 54$, it can send the request forward around the circle until a node N_j is found such that $j \geq 54$; it would be node N_{56} in Fig. 14.

However, linear search is much too inefficient if the circle is large. To speed up the search, each node has a *finger table* that gives the first nodes found at distances around the circle that are a power of two. That is, suppose that the hash function h produces m-bit numbers. Node N_i has entries in its finger table for distances $1, 2, 4, 8, \ldots, 2^{m-1}$. The entry for 2^j is the first node we meet after going distance 2^j clockwise around the circle. Notice that some entries may be the same node, and there are only $m - 1$ entries, even though the number of nodes could be as high as 2^m.

Distance	1	2	4	8	16	32
Node	N_{14}	N_{14}	N_{14}	N_{21}	N_{32}	N_{42}

Figure 15: Finger table for N_8

Example 20: Referring to Fig. 14, let us construct the finger table for N_8; this table is shown in Fig. 15. For distance 1, we ask what is the lowest numbered node whose number is at least $8 + 1 = 9$. That node is N_{14}, since there are no nodes numbered $9, 10, \ldots, 13$. For distance 2, we ask for the lowest node that is at least $8 + 2 = 10$; the answer is N_{14} again. Likewise, for distance 4, N_{14} is is lowest-numbered node that is at least $8 + 4 = 12$.

For distance 8, we look for the lowest-numbered node that is at least $8+8 = 16$. Now, N_{14} is too low. The lowest-numbered node that is at least 16 is N_{21}, so that is the entry in the finger table for 8. For 16, we need a node numbered at least 24, so the entry for 16 is N_{32}. For 32, we need a node numbered at least 40, and the proper entry is N_{42}. Figure 16 shows the four links that are in the finger table for N_8. □

7.6 Search Using Finger Tables

Suppose we are at node N_i and we want to find the key-value pair (K, V) where $h(K) = j$. We know that (K, V), if it exists, will be at the lowest-numbered node that is at least j.[6] We can use the finger table and knowledge of successors

[6] As always, "lowest" must be taken in the circular sense, as the first node you meet traveling clockwise around the circle, after reaching the point j.

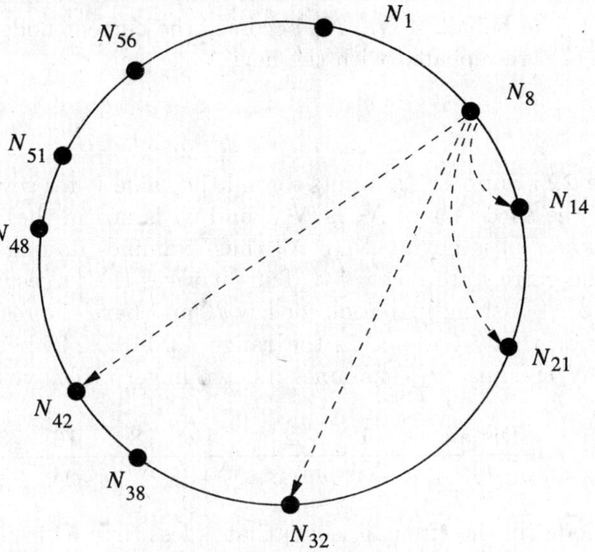

Figure 16: Links in the finger table for N_8

to find (K, V), if it exists, using at most $m+1$ messages, where m is the number of bits in the hash values produced by hash function h. Note that messages do not have to follow the entries of the finger table, which is needed only to help each node find out what other nodes exist.

Algorithm 21: Lookup in a Chord Circle.

INPUT: An initial request by a node N_i for the value associated with key value K, where $h(K) = j$.

OUTPUT: A sequence of messages sent by various nodes, resulting in a message to N_i with either the value of V in the key-value pair (K, V), or a statement that such a pair does not exist.

METHOD: The steps of the algorithm are actually executed by different nodes. At any time, activity is at some "current" node N_c, and initially N_c is N_i. Steps (1) and (2) below are done repeatedly. Note that N_i is a part of each request message, so the current node always knows that N_i is the node to which the answer must be sent.

1. End the search if $c < j \leq s$, where N_s is the successor of N_c, around the circle. Then, N_c sends a message to N_s asking for (K, V) and informing N_s that the originator of the request is N_i. N_s will send a message to N_i with either the value V or a statement that (K, V) does not exist.

2. Otherwise, N_c consults its finger table to find the highest-numbered node N_h that is less than j. N_c sends N_h a message asking it to search for

(K, V) on behalf of N_i. N_h becomes the current node N_c, and steps (1) and (2) are repeated with the new N_c.

□

Example 22: Suppose N_8 wants to find the value V for key K, where $h(K) = 54$. Since the successor of N_8 is N_{14}, and 54 is not in the range $9, 10, \ldots, 14$, N_8 knows (K, V) is not at N_{14}. N_8 thus examines its finger table, and finds that all the entries are below 54. Thus it takes the largest, N_{42}, and sends a message to N_{42} asking it to look for key K and have the result sent to N_8.

N_{42} finds that 54 is not in the range $43, 44, \ldots, 48$ between N_{42} and its successor N_{48}. Thus, N_{42} examines its own finger table, which is:

Distance	1	2	4	8	16	32
Node	N_{48}	N_{48}	N_{48}	N_{51}	N_1	N_{14}

The last node (in the circular sense) that is less than 54 is N_{51}, so N_{42} sends a message to N_{51}, asking it to search for (K, V) on behalf of N_8.

N_{51} finds that 54 is no greater than its successor, N_{56}. Thus, if (K, V) exists, it is at N_{56}. N_{51} sends a request to N_{56}, which replies to N_8. The sequence of messages is shown in Fig. 17. □

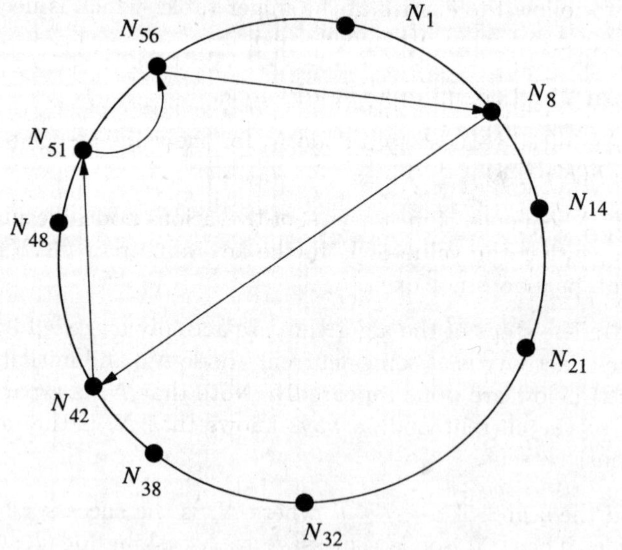

Figure 17: Message sequence in the search for (K, V)

In general, this recursive algorithm sends no more than m request messages. The reason is that whenever a node N_c has to consult its finger table, it messages

Dealing with Hash Collisions

Occasionally, when we insert a node, the hash value of its ID will be the same as that of some node already in the circle. The actual position of a particular node doesn't matter, as long as it knows its position and acts as if that position was the hash value of its ID. Thus, we can adjust the position of the new node up or down, until we find a position around the circle that is unoccupied.

a node that is no more than half the distance (measured clockwise around the circle) from the node holding (K, V) as N_c is. One response message is sent in all cases.

7.7 Adding New Nodes

Suppose a new node N_i (i.e., a node whose ID hashes to i) wants to join the network of peers. If N_i does not know how to communicate with any peer, it is not possible for N_i to join. However, if N_i knows even one peer, N_i can ask that peer what node would be N_i's successor around the circle. To answer, the known peer performs Algorithm 21 as if it were looking for a key that hashed to i. The node at which this hypothetical key would reside is the successor of N_i. Suppose that the successor of N_i is N_j.

We need to do two things:

1. Change predecessor and successor links, so N_i is properly linked into the circle.

2. Rearrange data so N_i gets all the data at N_j that belongs to N_i, that is, key-value pairs whose key hashes to something i or less.

We could link N into the circle at once, although it is difficult to do so correctly, because of concurrency problems. That is, several nodes whose successor would be N_j may be adding themselves at once. To avoid concurrency problems, we proceed in two steps. The first step is to set the successor of N to N_j and its predecessor to nil. N has no data at this time, and it has an empty finger table.

Example 23: Suppose we add to the circle of Fig. 14 a node N_{26}, i.e., a node whose ID hashes to 26. Whatever peer N_{26} contacted will be told that N_{26}'s successor is N_{32}. N_{26} sets its successor to N_{32} and its predecessor to nil. The predecessor of N_{32} remains N_{21} for the moment. The situation is suggested by Fig. 18. There, solid lines are successor links and dashed lines are predecessor links. □

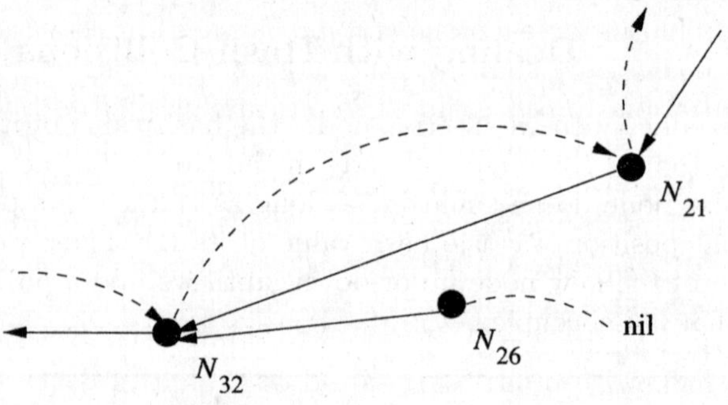

Figure 18: Adding node N_{26} to the network of peers

The second step is done automatically by all nodes, and is not a direct response to the insertion of N_i. All nodes must periodically perform a *stabilization* check, during which time predecessors and successors are updated, and if necessary, data is shared between a new node and its successor. Surely, N_{26} in Fig. 18 will have to perform a stabilization to get N_{32} to accept N_{26} as its predecessor, but N_{21} also needs to perform a stabilization in order to realize that N_{26} is its new successor. Note that N_{21} has not been informed of the existence of N_{26}, and will not be informed until N_{21} discovers this fact for itself during its own stabilization. The stabilization process at any node N is as follows.

1. Let S be the successor of N. N sends a message to S asking for P, the predecessor of S, and S replies. In normal cases, $P = N$, and if so, skip to step (4).

2. If P lies strictly between N and S, then N records that P is its successor.

3. Let S' be the current successor of N; S' could be either S or P, depending on what step (2) decided. If the predecessor of S' is nil or N lies strictly between S' and its predecessor, then N sends a message to S' telling S' that N is the predecessor of S'. S' sets its predecessor to N.

4. S' shares its data with N. That is, all (K, V) pairs at S' such that $h(K) \leq N$ are moved to N.

Example 24: Following the events of Example 23, with the predecessor and successor links in the state of Fig. 18, node N_{26} will perform a stabilization. For this stabilization, $N = N_{26}$, $S = N_{32}$, and $P = N_{21}$. Since P does not lie between N and S, step (2) makes no change, so $S' = S = N_{32}$ at step (3). Since $N = N_{26}$ lies strictly between $S' = N_{32}$ and its predecessor N_{21}, we make N_{26} the predecessor of N_{32}. The state of the links is shown in Fig. 19. At step (4), all key-value pairs whose keys hash to 22 through 26 are moved from N_{32} to N_{26}.

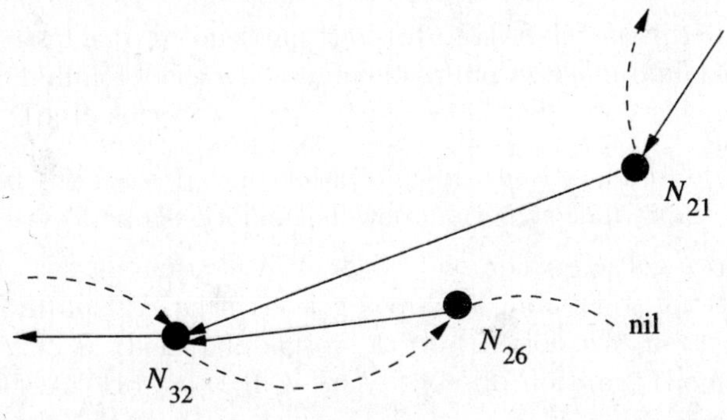

Figure 19: After making N_{26} the predecessor of N_{32}

The circle has still not stabilized, since N_{21} and many other nodes do not know about N_{26}. Searches for keys in the 22–26 range will still wind up at N_{32}. However, N_{32} knows that it no longer has keys in this range. N_{32}, which is N_c in Algorithm 21, simply continues the search according to this algorithm, which in effect causes the search to go around the circle again, possibly several times.

Eventually, N_{21} runs the stabilization operation, which it, like all nodes, does periodically. Now, $N = N_{21}$, $S = N_{32}$, and $P = N_{26}$. The test of step (2) is satisfied, so N_{26} becomes the successor of N_{21}. At step (3), $S' = N_{26}$. Since the predecessor of N_{26} is nil, we make N_{21} the predecessor of N_{26}. No data is shared at step (4), since all data at N_{26} belongs there. The final state of the predecessor and successor links is shown in Fig. 20.

At this time, the search for a key in the range 22–26 will reach N_{26} and be answered properly. It is possible, under rare circumstances, that insertion of many new nodes will keep the network from becoming completely stable for a long time. In that case, the search for a key in the range 22–26 could continue running until the network finally does stabilize. However, as soon as the network does stablize, the search comes to an end. □

There is still more to do, however. In terms of the running example, the finger table for N_{26} needs to be constructed, and other finger tables may now be wrong because they will link to N_{32} in some cases when they should link to N_{26}. Thus, it is necessary that every node N periodically checks its finger table. For each $i = 1, 2, 4, 8, \ldots$, node N must execute Algorithm 21 with $j = N + i \bmod 2^m$. When it gets back the node at which the network thinks such a key would be located, N sets its finger-table entry for distance i to that value.

Notice that a new node, such as N_{26} in our running example, can construct its initial finger table this way, since the construction of any entry requires only entries that have already been constructed. That is, the entry for distance 1 is always the successor. For distance $2i$, either the successor is the correct entry, or we can find the correct entry by calling upon whatever node is the finger-table

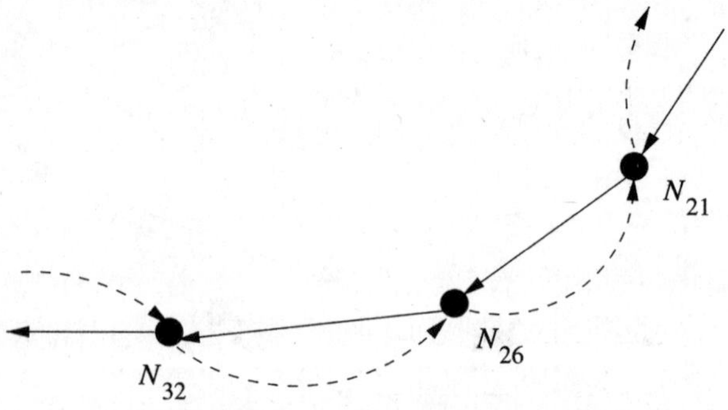

Figure 20: After N_{21} runs the stabilization algorithm

entry for distance i.

7.8 When a Peer Leaves the Network

A central tenet of peer-to-peer systems is that a node cannot be compelled to participate. Thus, a node can leave the circle at any time. The simple case is when a node leaves "gracefully," that is, cooperating with other nodes to keep the data available. To leave gracefully, a node:

1. Notifies its predecessor and successor that it is leaving, so they can become each other's predecessor and successor.

2. Transfers its data to its successor.

The network is still in a state that has errors; in particular the node that left may still appear in the finger tables of some nodes. These nodes will discover the error, either when they periodically update their finger tables, as discussed in Section 7.7, or when they try to communicate with the node that has disappeared. In the latter case, they can recompute the erroneous finger-table entry exactly as they would during periodic update.

7.9 When a Peer Fails

A harder problem occurs when a node fails, is turned off, or decides to leave without doing the "graceful" steps of Section 7.8. If the data is not replicated, then data at the failed node is now unavailable to the network. To avoid total unavailability of data, we can replicate it at several nodes. For example, we can place each (K, V) pair at three nodes: the correct node, its predecessor in the circle, and its successor.

To reestablish the circle when a node leaves, we can have each node record not only its predecessor and successor, but the predecessor of its predecessor and the successor of its successor. An alternative approach is to cluster nodes into groups of (say) three or more. Nodes in a cluster replicate their data and can substitute for one another, if one leaves or fails. When clusters get too large, they can be split into two clusters that are adjacent on the circle, using an algorithm similar to that described in Section 7.7 for node insertion. Similarly, clusters that get too small can be combined with a neighbor, a process similar to graceful leaving as in Section 7.8. Insertion of a new node is executed by having the node join its nearest cluster.

7.10 Exercises for Section 7

Exercise 7.1: Given the circle of nodes of Fig. 14, where do key-value pairs reside if the key hashes to: (a) 24 (b) 60?

Exercise 7.2: Given the circle of nodes of Fig. 14, construct the finger tables for: (a) N_1 (b) N_{48} (c) N_{56}.

Exercise 7.3: Given the circle of nodes of Fig. 14, what is the sequence of messages sent if:

a) N_1 searches for a key that hashes to 27.

b) N_1 searches for a key that hashes to 0.

c) N_{51} searches for a key that hashes to 45.

Exercise 7.4: Show the sequence of steps that adjust successor and predecessor pointers and share data, for the circle of Fig. 14 when nodes are added that hash to: (a) 41 (b) 62.

! **Exercise 7.5:** Suppose we want to guard against node failures by having each node maintain the predecessor information, successor information, and data of its predecessor and successor, as well as its own, as discussed in Section 7.9. How would you modify the node-insertion algorithm described in Section 7.7?

8 Summary

- ✦ *Parallel Machines*: Parallel machines can be characterized as shared-memory, shared-disk, or shared-nothing. For database applications, the shared-nothing architecture is generally the most cost-effective.

- ✦ *Parallel Algorithms*: The operations of relational algebra can generally be sped up on a parallel machine by a factor close to the number of processors. The preferred algorithms start by hashing the data to buckets that correspond to the processors, and shipping data to the appropriate processor. Each processor then performs the operation on its local data.

- *The Map-Reduce Framework*: Often, highly parallel algorithms on massive files can be expressed by a map function and a reduce function. Many *map* processes execute on parts of the file in parallel, to produce key-value pairs. These pairs are then distributed so each key's pairs can be handled by one *reduce* process.

- *Distributed Data*: In a distributed database, data may be partitioned horizontally (one relation has its tuples spread over several sites) or vertically (a relation's schema is decomposed into several schemas whose relations are at different sites). It is also possible to replicate data, so presumably identical copies of a relation exist at several sites.

- *Distributed Joins*: In an environment with expensive communication, semijoins can speed up the join of two relations that are located at different sites. We project one relation onto the join attributes, send it to the other site, and return only the tuples of the second relation that are not dangling tuples.

- *Full Reducers*: When joining more than two relations at different sites, it may or may not be possible to eliminate all dangling tuples by performing semijoins. A finite sequence of semijoins that is guaranteed to eliminate all dangling tuples, no matter how large the relations are, is called a full reducer.

- *Hypergraphs*: A natural join of several relations can be represented by a hypergraph, which has a node for each attribute name and a hyperedge for each relation, which contains the nodes for all the attributes of that relation.

- *Acyclic Hypergraphs*: These are the hypergraphs that can be reduced to a single hyperedge by a series of ear-reductions — elimination of hyperedges all of whose nodes are either in no other hyperedge, or in one particular other hyperedge. Full reducers exist for all and only the hypergraphs that are acyclic.

- *Distributed Transactions*: In a distributed database, one logical transaction may consist of components, each executing at a different site. To preserve consistency, these components must all agree on whether to commit or abort the logical transaction.

- *Two-Phase Commit*: This algorithm enables transaction components to decide whether to commit or abort, often allowing a resolution even in the face of a system crash. In the first phase, a coordinator component polls the components whether they want to commit or abort. In the second phase, the coordinator tells the components to commit if and only if all have expressed a willingness to commit.

✦ *Distributed Locks*: If transactions must lock database elements found at several sites, a method must be found to coordinate these locks. In the centralized-site method, one site maintains locks on all elements. In the primary-copy method, the home site for an element maintains its locks.

✦ *Locking Replicated Data*: When database elements are replicated at several sites, global locks on an element must be obtained through locks on one or more replicas. The majority locking method requires a read- or write-lock on a majority of the replicas to obtain a global lock. Alternatively, we may allow a global read lock by obtaining a read lock on any copy, while allowing a global write lock only through write locks on every copy.

✦ *Peer-to-Peer Networks*: These networks consist of independent, autonomous nodes that all play the same role in the network. Such networks are generally used to share data among the peer nodes.

✦ *Distributed Hashing*: Distributed hashing is a central database problem in peer-to-peer networks. We are given a set of key-value pairs to distribute among the peers, and we must find the value associated with a given key without sending messages to all, or a large fraction of the peers, and without relying on any one peer that has all the key-value pairs.

✦ *Chord Circles*: A solution to the distributed hashing problem begins by using a hash function that hashes both node ID's and keys into the same m-bit values, which we perceive as forming a circle with 2^m positions. Keys are placed at the node at the position immediately clockwise of the position to which the key hashes. By use of a finger-table, which gives the nodes at distances $1, 2, 4, 8, \ldots$ around the circle from a given node, key lookup can be accomplished in time that is logarithmic in the number of nodes.

9 References

The use of hashing in parallel join and other operations has been proposed several times. The earliest source we know of is [8]. The map-reduce framework for parallelism was expressed in [2]. There is an open-souce implementation available [6].

The relationship between full reducers and acyclic hypergraphs is from [1]. The test for whether a hypergraph is acyclic was discovered by [5] and [13].

The two-phase commit protocol was proposed in [7]. A more powerful scheme (not covered here) called three-phase commit is from [9]. The leader-election aspect of recovery was examined in [4].

Distributed locking methods have been proposed by [3] (the centralized locking method) [11] (primary-copy) and [12] (global locks from locks on copies).

The chord algorithm for distributed hashing is from [10].

1. P. A. Bernstein and N. Goodman, "The power of natural semijoins," *SIAM J. Computing* **10**:4 (1981), pp. 751–771.

2. J. Dean and S. Ghemawat, "MapReduce: simplified processing on large clusters," *Sixth Symp. on Operating System Design and Implementation*, 2004.

3. H. Garcia-Molina, "Performance comparison of update algorithms for distributed databases," TR Nos. 143 and 146, Computer Systems Laboratory, Stanford Univ., 1979.

4. H. Garcia-Molina, "Elections in a distributed computer system," *IEEE Trans. on Computers* **C-31**:1 (1982), pp. 48–59.

5. M. H. Graham, "On the universal relation," Technical report, Dept. of CS, Univ. of Toronto, 1979.

6. Hadoop home page `lucene.apache.org/hadoop`.

7. B. Lampson and H. Sturgis, "Crash recovery in a distributed data storage system," Technical report, Xerox Palo Alto Research Center, 1976.

8. D. E. Shaw, "Knowledge-based retrieval on a relational database machine," Ph. D. thesis, Dept. of CS, Stanford Univ. (1980).

9. D. Skeen, "Nonblocking commit protocols," *Proc. ACM SIGMOD Intl. Conf. on Management of Data* (1981), pp. 133–142.

10. I. Stoica, R. Morris, D. Karger, M. Kaashoek, and H. Balakrishnan, "Chord: A scalabale peer-to-peer lookup service for Internet applications," *Proc. ACM SIGCOMM* (2001) pp. 149–160.

11. M. Stonebraker, "Retrospection on a database system," *ACM Trans. on Database Systems* **5**:2 (1980), pp. 225–240.

12. R. H. Thomas, "A majority consensus approach to concurrency control," *ACM Trans. on Database Systems* **4**:2 (1979), pp. 180–219.

13. C. T. Yu and M. Z. Ozsoyoglu, "An algorithm for tree-query membership of a distributed query," *Proc. IEEE COMPSAC* (1979), pp. 306–312.

Information Integration

Information integration is the process of taking several databases or other information sources and making the data in these sources work together as if they were a single database. The integrated database may be physical (a "warehouse") or virtual (a "mediator" or "middleware" that may be queried even though its does not exist physically). The sources may be conventional databases or other types of information, such as collections of Web pages.

We begin by exploring the ways in which seemingly similar databases can actually embody conflicts that are hard to resolve correctly. The solution lies in the design of "wrappers" — translators between the schema and data values at a source and the schema and data values at the integrated database.

Information-integration systems require special kinds of query-optimization techniques for their efficient operation. Mediator systems can be divided into two classes: "global-as-view" (the data at the integrated database is defined by how it is constructed from the sources) and "local-as-view" (the content of the sources is defined in terms of the schema that the integrated database supports). We examine capability-based optimization for global-as-view mediators. We also consider local-as-view mediation, which requires effort even to figure out how to compose the answer to a query from defined views, but which offers advantages in flexibility of operation.

In the last section, we examine another important issue in information integration, called "entity resolution." Different information sources may talk about the same entities (e.g., people) but contain discrepancies such as misspelled names or out-of-date addresses. We need to make a best estimate of which data elements at the different sources actually refer to the same entity.

1 Introduction to Information Integration

In this section, we discuss the ways in which information-integration is essential for many database applications. We then sample some of the problems that make information integration difficult.

1.1 Why Information Integration?

If we could start anew with an architecture and schema for all the data in the world, and we could put that data in a single database, there would be no need for information integration. However, in the real world, matters are rather different.

- Databases are created independently, even if they later need to work together.

- The use of databases evolves, so we cannot design a database to support every possible future use.

To see the need for information integration, we shall consider two typical scenarios: building applications for a university and integrating employee databases. In both scenarios, a key problem is that the overall data-management system must make use of *legacy* data sources — databases that were created independently of any other data source. Each legacy source is used by applications that expect the structure of "their" database not to change, so modification of the schema or data of legacy sources is not an option.

University Databases

As databases came into common use, each university started using them for several functions that were once done by hand. Here is a typical scenario. The Registrar builds a database of courses, and uses it to record the courses each student took and their grades. Applications are built using this database, such as a transcript generator.

The Bursar builds another database for recording tuition payments by students. The Human Resources Department builds a database for recording employees, including those students with teaching-assistant or research-assistant jobs. Applications include generation of payroll checks, calculation of taxes and social-security payments to the government, and many others. The Grants Office builds a database to keep track of expenditures on grants, which includes salaries to certain faculty, students, and staff. It may also include information about biohazards, use of human subjects, and many other matters related to research projects.

Pretty soon, the university realizes that all these databases are not helping nearly as much as they could, and are sometimes getting in the way. For example, suppose we want to make sure that the Registrar does not record grades for students that the Bursar says did not pay tuition. Someone has to get a list of students who paid tuition from the Bursar's database and compare that with a list of students from the Registrar's database. As another example, when Sally is appointed on grant 123 as a research assistant, someone needs to tell the Grants Office that her salary should be charged to grant 123. Someone also needs to tell Human Resources that they should pay her salary. And the salaries in the two databases had better be exactly the same.

So at some point, the university decides that it needs one database for all functions. The first thought might be: start over. Build one database that contains all the information of all the legacy databases and rewrite all the applications to use the new database. This approach has been tried, with great pain resulting. In addition to paying for a very expensive software-architecture task, the university has to run both the old and new systems in parallel for a long time to see that the new system actually works. And when they cut over to the new system, the users find that the applications do not work in the accustomed way, and turmoil results.

A better way is to build a layer of abstraction, called *middleware*, on top of all the legacy databases and allow the legacy databases to continue serving their current applications. The layer of abstraction could be relational views — either virtual or materialized. Then, SQL can be used to "query" the middleware layer. Often, this layer is defined by a collection of classes and queried in an object-oriented language. Or the middleware layer could use XML documents, which are queried using XQuery. This middleware may be an important component of the application tier in a 3-tier architecture.

Once the middleware layer is built, new applications can be written to access this layer for data, while the legacy applications continue to run using the legacy databases. For example, we can write a new application that enters grades for students only if they have paid their tuition. Another new application could appoint a research assistant by getting their name, grant, and salary from the user. This application would then enter the name and salary into the Human-Resources database and the name, salary, and grant into the Grants-Office database.

Integrating Employee Databases

Compaq bought DEC and Tandem, and then Hewlett-Packard bought Compaq. Each company had a database of employees. Because the companies were previously independent, the schemas and architecture of their databases naturally differed. Moreover, each company actually had many databases about employees, and these databases probably differed on matters as basic as who is an employee. For example, the Payroll Department would not include retirees, but might include contractors. The Benefits Department would include retirees but not contractors. The Safety Office would include not only regular employees and contractors, but the employees of the company that runs the cafeteria.

For reasons we discussed in connection with the university database, it may not be practical to shut down these legacy databases and with them all the applications that run on them. However, it is possible to create a middleware layer that holds — virtually or physically — all information available for each employee.

1.2 The Heterogeneity Problem

When we try to connect information sources that were developed independently, we invariably find that the sources differ in many ways, even if they are intended to store the same kinds of data. Such sources are called *heterogeneous*, and the problem of integrating them is referred to as the *heterogeneity problem.* We shall introduce a running example of an automobile database and then discuss examples of the different levels at which heterogeneity can make integration difficult.

Example 1 : The Aardvark Automobile Co. has 1000 dealers, each of which maintains a database of their cars in stock. Aardvark wants to create an integrated database containing the information of all 1000 sources.[1] The integrated database will help dealers locate a particular model at another dealer, if they don't have one in stock. It also can be used by corporate analysts to predict the market and adjust production to provide the models most likely to sell.

However, the dealers' databases may differ in a great number of ways. We shall enumerate below the most important ways and give some examples in terms of the Aardvark database. □

Communication Heterogeneity

Today, it is common to allow access to your information using the HTTP protocol that drives the Web. However, some dealers may not make their databases available on the Web, but instead accept remote accesses via remote procedure calls or anonymous FTP, for instance.

Query-Language Heterogeneity

The manner in which we query or modify a dealer's database may vary. It would be nice if the database accepted SQL queries and modifications, but not all do. Of those that do, each accepts a dialect of SQL — the version supported by the vendor of the dealer's DBMS. Another dealer may not have a relational database at all. They could use an Excel Spreadsheet, or an object-oriented database, or an XML database using XQuery as the language.

Schema Heterogeneity

Even assuming that all the dealers use a relational DBMS supporting SQL as the query language, we can find many sources of heterogeneity. At the highest level, the schemas can differ. For example, one dealer might store cars in a single relation that looks like:

[1]Most real automobile companies have similar facilities in place, and the history of their development may be different from our example; e.g., the centralized database may have come first, with dealers later able to download relevant portions to their own database. However, this scenario serves as an example of what companies in many industries are attempting today.

```
Cars(serialNo, model, color, autoTrans, navi,...)
```

with one boolean-valued attribute for every possible option. Another dealer might use a schema in which options are separated out into a second relation, such as:

```
Autos(serial, model, color)
Options(serial, option)
```

Notice that not only is the schema different, but apparently equivalent relation or attribute names have changed: `Cars` becomes `Autos`, and `serialNo` becomes `serial`.

Moreover, one dealer's schema might not record information that most of the other dealers provide. For instance, one dealer might not record colors at all. To deal with missing values, sometimes we can use `NULL`'s or default values. However, because missing schema elements are a common problem, there is a trend toward using semistructured data such as XML as the data model for integrating middleware.

Data type differences

Serial numbers might be represented by character strings of varying length at one source and fixed length at another. The fixed lengths could differ, and some sources might use integers rather than character strings.

Value Heterogeneity

The same concept might be represented by different constants at different sources. The color black might be represented by an integer code at one source, the string `BLACK` at another, and the code `BL` at a third. The code `BL` might stand for "blue" at yet another source.

Semantic Heterogeneity

Terms may be given different interpretations at different sources. One dealer might include trucks in the `Cars` relation, while another puts only automobile data in the `Cars` relation. One dealer might distinguish station wagons from minivans, while another doesn't.

2 Modes of Information Integration

There are several ways that databases or other distributed information sources can be made to work together. In this section, we consider the three most common approaches:

1. *Federated databases.* The sources are independent, but one source can call on others to supply information.

2. *Warehousing.* Copies of data from several sources are stored in a single database, called a *(data) warehouse.* Possibly, the data stored at the warehouse is first processed in some way before storage; e.g., data may be filtered, and relations may be joined or aggregated. The warehouse is updated periodically, perhaps overnight. As the data is copied from the sources, it may need to be transformed in certain ways to make all data conform to the schema at the warehouse.

3. *Mediation.* A mediator is a software component that supports a *virtual database*, which the user may query as if it were *materialized* (physically constructed, like a warehouse). The mediator stores no data of its own. Rather, it translates the user's query into one or more queries to its sources. The mediator then synthesizes the answer to the user's query from the responses of those sources, and returns the answer to the user.

We shall introduce each of these approaches in turn. One of the key issues for all approaches is the way that data is transformed when it is extracted from an information source. We discuss the architecture of such transformers — called *wrappers*, *adapters*, or *extractors* — in Section 3.

2.1 Federated Database Systems

Perhaps the simplest architecture for integrating several databases is to implement one-to-one connections between all pairs of databases that need to talk to one another. These connections allow one database system D_1 to query another D_2 in terms that D_2 can understand. The problem with this architecture is that if n databases each need to talk to the $n-1$ other databases, then we must write $n(n-1)$ pieces of code to support queries between systems. The situation is suggested in Fig. 1. There, we see four databases in a federation. Each of the four needs three components, one to access each of the other three databases.

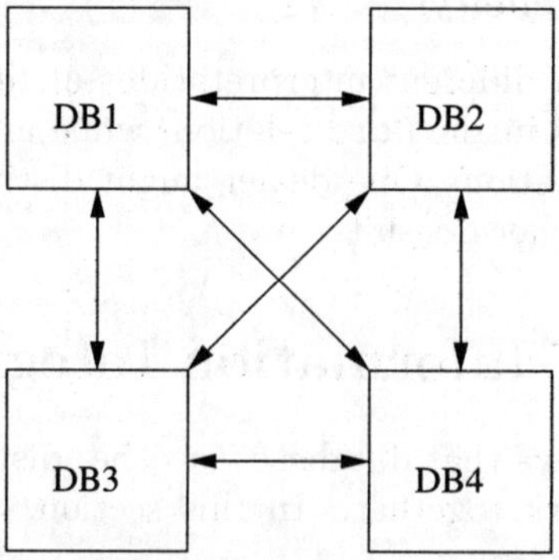

Figure 1: A federated collection of four databases needs 12 components to translate queries from one to another

Nevertheless, a federated system may be the easiest to build in some circumstances, especially when the communications between databases are limited in nature. An example will show how the translation components might work.

Example 2: Suppose the Aardvark Automobile dealers want to share inventory, but each dealer only needs to query the database of a few local dealers to see if they have a needed car. To be specific, consider Dealer 1, who has a relation

```
NeededCars(model, color, autoTrans)
```

whose tuples represent cars that customers have requested, by model, color, and whether or not they want an automatic transmission (`'yes'` or `'no'` are the possible values). Dealer 2 stores inventory in the two-relation schema discussed in Example 1:

```
Autos(serial, model, color)
Options(serial, option)
```

Dealer 1 writes an application program that queries Dealer 2 remotely for cars that match each of the cars described in `NeededCars`. Figure 2 is a sketch of a program with embedded SQL that would find the desired cars. The intent is that the embedded SQL represents remote queries to the Dealer 2 database, with results returned to Dealer 1. We use the convention from standard SQL of prefixing a colon to variables that represent constants retrieved from a database.

These queries address the schema of Dealer 2. If Dealer 1 also wants to ask the same question of Dealer 3, who uses the first schema discussed in Example 1, with a single relation

```
Cars(serialNo, model, color, autoTrans,...)
```

the query would look quite different. But each query works properly for the database to which it is addressed. □

2.2 Data Warehouses

In the *data warehouse* integration architecture, data from several sources is extracted and combined into a *global* schema. The data is then stored at the warehouse, which looks to the user like an ordinary database. The arrangement is suggested by Fig. 3, although there may be many more than the two sources shown.

Once the data is in the warehouse, queries may be issued by the user exactly as they would be issued to any database. There are at least three approaches to constructing the data in the warehouse:

1. The warehouse is periodically closed to queries and reconstructed from the current data in the sources. This approach is the most common, with reconstruction occurring once a night or at even longer intervals.

```
for(each tuple (:m, :c, :a) in NeededCars) {
    if(:a = TRUE) { /* automatic transmission wanted */
        SELECT serial FROM Autos, Options
        WHERE Autos.serial = Options.serial AND
              Options.option = 'autoTrans' AND
              Autos.model = :m AND Autos.color = :c;
    }
    else { /* automatic transmission not wanted */
        SELECT serial
        FROM Autos
        WHERE Autos.model = :m AND Autos.color = :c AND
              NOT EXISTS (
                  SELECT * FROM Options
                  WHERE serial = Autos.serial AND
                        option = 'autoTrans'
              );
    }
}
```

Figure 2: Dealer 1 queries Dealer 2 for needed cars

2. The warehouse is updated periodically (e.g., each night), based on the changes that have been made to the sources since the last time the warehouse was modified. This approach can involve smaller amounts of data, which is very important if the warehouse needs to be modified in a short period of time, and the warehouse is large (multiterabyte warehouses are in common use). The disadvantage is that calculating changes to the warehouse, a process called *incremental update*, is complex, compared with algorithms that simply construct the warehouse from scratch.

Note that either of these approaches allow the warehouse to get out of date. However, it is generally too expensive to reflect immediately, at the warehouse, every change to the underlying databases.

Example 3: Suppose for simplicity that there are only two dealers in the Aardvark system, and they respectively use the schemas

```
Cars(serialNo, model, color, autoTrans, navi,...)
```

and

```
Autos(serial, model, color)
Options(serial, option)
```

We wish to create a warehouse with the schema

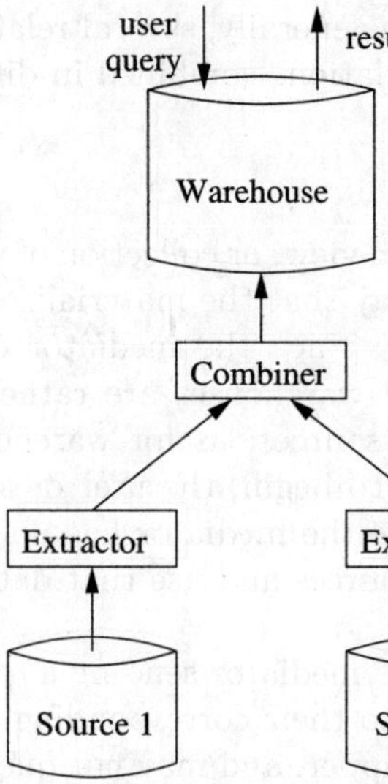

Figure 3: A data warehouse stores integrated information in a separate database

```
AutosWhse(serialNo, model, color, autoTrans, dealer)
```

That is, the global schema is like that of the first dealer, but we record only the option of having an automatic transmission, and we include an attribute that tells which dealer has the car.

The software that extracts data from the two dealers' databases and populates the global schema can be written as SQL queries. The query for the first dealer is simple:

```
INSERT INTO AutosWhse(serialNo, model, color,
        autoTrans, dealer)
    SELECT serialNo, model, color, autoTrans, 'dealer1'
    FROM Cars;
```

The extractor for the second dealer is more complex, since we have to decide whether or not a given car has an automatic transmission. We leave this SQL code as an exercise.

In this simple example, the combiner, shown in Fig. 3, for the data extracted from the sources is not needed. Since the warehouse is the union of the relations extracted from each source, the data may be loaded directly into the warehouse. However, many warehouses perform operations on the relations that they extract from each source. For instance relations extracted from two sources might be joined, and the result put at the warehouse. Or we might take the union of relations extracted from several sources and then aggregate the data of this union. More generally, several relations may be extracted from each source, and different relations combined in different ways. □

2.3 Mediators

A mediator supports a virtual view, or collection of views, that integrates several sources in much the same way that the materialized relation(s) in a warehouse integrate sources. However, since the mediator doesn't store any data, the mechanics of mediators and warehouses are rather different. Figure 4 shows a mediator integrating two sources; as for warehouses, there would typically be more than two sources. To begin, the user or application program issues a query to the mediator. Since the mediator has no data of its own, it must get the relevant data from its sources and use that data to form the answer to the user's query.

Thus, we see in Fig. 4 the mediator sending a query to each of its wrappers, which in turn send queries to their corresponding sources. The mediator may send several queries to a wrapper, and may not query all wrappers. The results come back and are combined at the mediator; we do not show an explicit combiner component as we did in the warehouse diagram, Fig. 3, because in the case of the mediator, the combining of results from the sources is one of the tasks performed by the mediator.

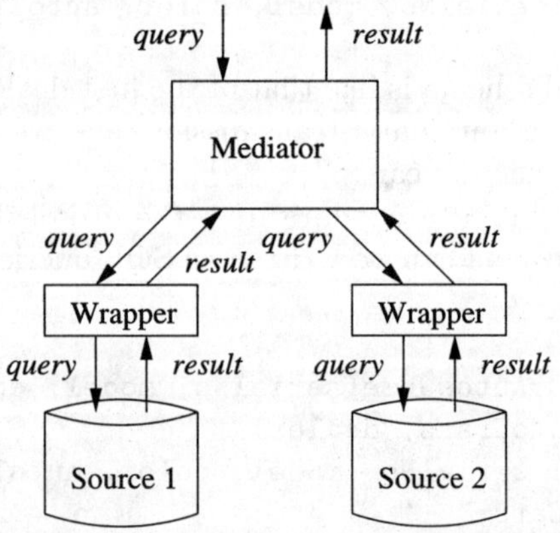

Figure 4: A mediator and wrappers translate queries into the terms of the sources and combine the answers

Example 4: Let us consider a scenario similar to that of Example 3, but use a mediator. That is, the mediator integrates the same two automobile sources into a view that is a single relation with schema:

```
AutosMed(serialNo, model, color, autoTrans, dealer)
```

Suppose the user asks the mediator about red cars, with the query:

```
SELECT serialNo, model
FROM AutosMed
WHERE color = 'red';
```

The mediator, in response to this user query, can forward the same query to each of the two wrappers. The way that wrappers can be designed and implemented to handle queries like this one is the subject of Section 3. In more complex scenarios, the mediator would first have to break the query into pieces, each of which is sent to a subset of the wrappers. However, in this case, the translation work can be done by the wrappers alone.

The wrapper for Dealer 1 translates the query into the terms of that dealer's schema, which we recall is

```
Cars(serialNo, model, color, autoTrans, navi,...)
```

A suitable translation is:

```
SELECT serialNo, model
FROM Cars
WHERE color = 'red';
```

An answer, which is a set of `serialNo-model` pairs, will be returned to the mediator by the first wrapper.

At the same time, the wrapper for Dealer 2 translates the same query into the schema of that dealer, which is:

```
Autos(serial, model, color)
Options(serial, option)
```

A suitable translated query for Dealer 2 is almost the same:

```
SELECT serial, model
FROM Autos
WHERE color = 'red';
```

It differs from the query at Dealer 1 only in the name of the relation queried, and in one attribute. The second wrapper returns to the mediator a set of `serial-model` pairs, which the mediator interprets as `serialNo-model` pairs. The mediator takes the union of these sets and returns the result to the user. □

There are several options, not illustrated by Example 4, that a mediator may use to answer queries. For instance, the mediator may issue one query to one source, look at the result, and based on what is returned, decide on the next query or queries to issue. This method would be appropriate, for instance, if the user query asked whether there were any Aardvark "Gobi" model sport-utility vehicles available in blue. The first query could ask Dealer 1, and only if the result was an empty set of tuples would a query be sent to Dealer 2.

2.4 Exercises for Section 2

! **Exercise 2.1:** Computer company A keeps data about the PC models it sells in the schema:

```
Computers(number, proc, speed, memory, hd)
Monitors(number, screen, maxResX, maxResY)
```

For instance, the tuple (123, **Athlon64**, 3.1, 512, 120) in `Computers` means that model 123 has an Athlon 64 processor running at 3.1 gigahertz, with 512M of memory and a 120G hard disk. The tuple (456, 19, 1600, 1050) in `Monitors` means that model 456 has a 19-inch screen with a maximum resolution of 1600×1050.

Computer company B only sells complete systems, consisting of a computer and monitor. Its schema is

```
Systems(id, processor, mem, disk, screenSize)
```

The attribute `processor` is the speed in gigahertz; the type of processor (e.g., Athlon 64) is not recorded. Neither is the maximum resolution of the monitor recorded. Attributes `id`, `mem`, and `disk` are analogous to `number`, `memory`, and `hd` from company A, but the disk size is measured in megabytes instead of gigabytes.

a) If company A wants to insert into its relations information about the corresponding items from B, what SQL insert statements should it use?

b) If Company B wants to insert into `Systems` as much information about the systems that can be built from computers and monitors made by A, what SQL statements best allow this information to be obtained?

! **Exercise 2.2:** Suggest a global schema that would allow us to maintain as much information as we could about the products sold by companies A and B of Exercise 2.1.

Exercise 2.3: Write SQL queries to gather the information from the data at companies A and B and put it in a warehouse with your global schema of Exercise 2.2.

Exercise 2.4: Suppose your global schema from Exercise 2.2 is used at a mediator. How would the mediator process the query that asks for the maximum amount of hard-disk available with any computer with a 3 gigahertz processor speed?

! **Exercise 2.5:** Suggest two other schemas that computer companies might use to hold data like that of Exercise 2.1. How would you integrate your schemas into your global schema from Exercise 2.2?

Exercise 2.6: In Example 3 we talked about a relation `Cars` at Dealer 1 that conveniently had an attribute `autoTrans` with only the values `'yes'` and `'no'`. Since these were the same values used for that attribute in the global schema, the construction of relation `AutosWhse` was especially easy. Suppose instead that the attribute `Cars.autoTrans` has values that are integers, with 0 meaning no automatic transmission, and $i > 0$ meaning that the car has an i-speed automatic transmission. Show how the translation from `Cars` to `AutosWhse` could be done by a SQL query.

Exercise 2.7: Write the insert-statements for the second dealer in Example 3. You may assume the values of `autoTrans` are `'yes'` and `'no'`.

Exercise 2.8: How would the mediator of Example 4 translate the following queries?

a) Find the serial numbers of cars with automatic transmission.

b) Find the serial numbers of cars without automatic transmission.

! c) Find the serial numbers of the blue cars from Dealer 1.

Exercise 2.9: Go to the Web pages of several on-line booksellers, and see what information about this book you can find. How would you combine this information into a global schema suitable for a warehouse or mediator?

3 Wrappers in Mediator-Based Systems

In a data warehouse system like Fig. 3, the source extractors consist of:

1. One or more predefined queries that are executed at the source to produce data for the warehouse.

2. Suitable communication mechanisms, so the wrapper (extractor) can:

   (a) Pass ad-hoc queries to the source,

   (b) Receive responses from the source, and

   (c) Pass information to the warehouse.

The predefined queries to the source could be SQL queries if the source is a SQL database as in our examples of Section 2. Queries could also be operations in whatever language was appropriate for a source that was not a database system; e.g., the wrapper could fill out an on-line form at a Web page, issue a query to an on-line bibliography service in that system's own, specialized language, or use myriad other notations to pose the queries.

However, mediator systems require more complex wrappers than do most warehouse systems. The wrapper must be able to accept a variety of queries from the mediator and translate any of them to the terms of the source. Of course, the wrapper must then communicate the result to the mediator, just as a wrapper in a warehouse system communicates with the warehouse. In the balance of this section, we study the construction of flexible wrappers that are suitable for use with a mediator.

3.1 Templates for Query Patterns

A systematic way to design a wrapper that connects a mediator to a source is to classify the possible queries that the mediator can ask into *templates*, which are queries with parameters that represent constants. The mediator can provide the constants, and the wrapper executes the query with the given constants. An example should illustrate the idea; it uses the notation T => S to express the idea that the template T is turned by the wrapper into the source query S.

Example 5: Suppose we want to build a wrapper for the source of Dealer 1, which has the schema

```
Cars(serialNo, model, color, autoTrans, navi,...)
```

for use by a mediator with schema

```
AutosMed(serialNo, model, color, autoTrans, dealer)
```

Consider how the mediator could ask the wrapper for cars of a given color. If we denote the code representing that color by the parameter `$c`, then we can use the template shown in Fig. 5.

```
SELECT *
FROM AutosMed
WHERE color = '$c';
    =>
SELECT serialNo, model, color, autoTrans, 'dealer1'
FROM Cars
WHERE color = '$c';
```

Figure 5: A wrapper template describing queries for cars of a given color

Similarly, the wrapper could have another template that specified only the parameter `$m` representing a model, yet another template in which it was only specified whether an automatic transmission was wanted, and so on. In this case, there are eight choices, if queries are allowed to specify any of three attributes: `model`, `color`, and `autoTrans`. In general, there would be 2^n templates if we have the option of specifying n attributes.[2] Other templates would

[2]If the source is a database that can be queried in SQL, as in our example, you would rightly expect that one template could handle any number of attributes equated to constants,

be needed to deal with queries that asked for the total number of cars of certain types, or whether there exists a car of a certain type. The number of templates could grow unreasonably large, but some simplifications are possible by adding more sophistication to the wrapper, as we shall discuss starting in Section 3.3. □

3.2 Wrapper Generators

The templates defining a wrapper must be turned into code for the wrapper itself. The software that creates the wrapper is called a *wrapper generator*; it is similar in spirit to the parser generators (e.g., YACC) that produce components of a compiler from high-level specifications. The process, suggested in Fig. 6, begins when a specification, that is, a collection of templates, is given to the wrapper generator.

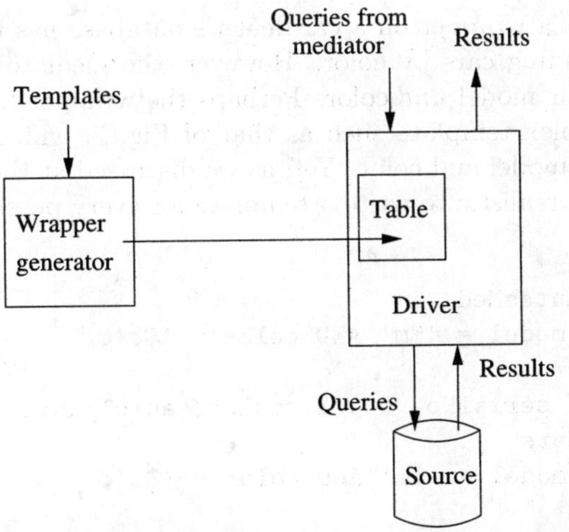

Figure 6: A wrapper generator produces tables for a driver; the driver and tables constitute the wrapper

The wrapper generator creates a table that holds the various query patterns contained in the templates, and the source queries that are associated with each. A *driver* is used in each wrapper; in general the driver can be the same for each generated wrapper. The task of the driver is to:

1. Accept a query from the mediator. The communication mechanism may be mediator-specific and is given to the driver as a "plug-in," so the same

simply by making the **WHERE** clause a parameter. While that approach will work for SQL sources and queries that only bind attributes to constants, we could not necessarily use the same idea with an arbitrary source, such as a Web site that allowed only certain forms as an interface. In the general case, we cannot assume that the way we translate one query resembles at all the way similar queries are translated.

driver can be used in systems that communicate differently.

2. Search the table for a template that matches the query. If one is found, then the parameter values from the query are used to instantiate a source query. If there is no matching template, the wrapper responds negatively to the mediator.

3. The source query is sent to the source, again using a "plug-in" communication mechanism. The response is collected by the wrapper.

4. The response is processed by the wrapper, if necessary, and then returned to the mediator. The next sections discuss how wrappers can support a larger class of queries by processing results.

3.3 Filters

Suppose that a wrapper on a car dealer's database has the template shown in Fig. 5 for finding cars by color. However, the mediator is asked to find cars of a particular model *and* color. Perhaps the wrapper has been designed with a more complex template such as that of Fig. 7, which handles queries that specify both model and color. Yet, as we discussed at the end of Example 5, it is not always realistic to write a template for every possible form of query.

```
SELECT *
FROM AutosMed
WHERE model = '$m' AND color = '$c';
    =>
SELECT serialNo, model, color, autoTrans, 'dealer1'
FROM Cars
WHERE model = '$m' AND color = '$c';
```

Figure 7: A wrapper template that gets cars of a given model and color

Another approach to supporting more queries is to have the wrapper *filter* the results of queries that it poses to the source. As long as the wrapper has a template that (after proper substitution for the parameters) returns a superset of what the query wants, then it is possible to filter the returned tuples at the wrapper and pass only the desired tuples to the mediator.

Example 6: Suppose the only template we have is the one in Fig. 5 that finds cars given a color. However, the wrapper is asked by the mediator to find blue Gobi model cars. A possible way to answer the query is to use the template of Fig. 5 with `$c = 'blue'` to find all the blue cars and store them in a temporary relation

```
TempAutos(serialNo, model, color, autoTrans, dealer)
```

Position of the Filter Component

We have, in our examples, supposed that the filtering operations take place at the wrapper. It is also possible that the wrapper passes raw data to the mediator, and the mediator filters the data. However, if most of the data returned by the template does not match the mediator's query, then it is best to filter at the wrapper and avoid the cost of shipping unneeded tuples.

The wrapper may then return to the mediator the desired set of automobiles by executing the local query:

```
SELECT *
FROM TempAutos
WHERE model = 'Gobi';
```

In practice, the tuples of `TempAutos` could be produced one-at-a-time and filtered one-at-a-time, in a pipelined fashion, rather than having the entire relation `TempAutos` materialized at the wrapper and then filtered. □

3.4 Other Operations at the Wrapper

It is possible to transform data in other ways at the wrapper, as long as we are sure that the source-query part of the template returns to the wrapper all the data needed in the transformation. For instance, columns may be projected out of the tuples before transmission to the mediator. It is even possible to take aggregations or joins at the wrapper and transmit the result to the mediator.

Example 7: Suppose the mediator wants to know about blue Gobis at the various dealers, but only asks for the serial number, dealer, and whether or not there is an automatic transmission, since the value of the `model` and `color` attributes are obvious from the query. The wrapper could proceed as in Example 6, but at the last step, when the result is to be returned to the mediator, the wrapper performs a projection in the `SELECT` clause as well as the filtering for the Gobi model in the `WHERE clause`. The query

```
SELECT serialNo, autoTrans, dealer
FROM TempAutos
WHERE model = 'Gobi';
```

does this additional filtering, although as in Example 6 relation `TempAutos` would probably be pipelined into the projection operator, rather than materialized at the wrapper. □

Example 8: For a more complex example, suppose the mediator is asked to find dealers and models such that the dealer has two red cars, of the same model, one with and one without an automatic transmission. Suppose also that the only useful template for Dealer 1 is the one about colors from Fig. 5. That is, the mediator asks the wrapper for the answer to the query of Fig. 8. Note that we do not have to specify a dealer for either `A1` or `A2`, because this wrapper can only access data belonging to Dealer 1. The wrappers for all the other dealers will be asked the same query by the mediator.

```
SELECT A1.model A1.dealer
FROM AutosMed A1, AutosMed A2
WHERE A1.model = A2.model AND
      A1.color = 'red' AND
      A2.color = 'red' AND
      A1.autoTrans = 'no' AND
      A2.autoTrans = 'yes';
```

Figure 8: Query from mediator to wrapper

A cleverly designed wrapper could discover that it is possible to answer the mediator's query by first obtaining from the Dealer-1 source a relation with all the red cars at that dealer:

```
RedAutos(serialNo, model, color, autoTrans, dealer)
```

To get this relation, the wrapper uses its template from Fig. 5, which handles queries that specify a color only. In effect, the wrapper acts as if it were given the query:

```
SELECT *
FROM AutosMed
WHERE color = 'red';
```

The wrapper can then create the relation `RedAutos` from Dealer 1's database by using the template of Fig. 5 with `$c` = `'red'`. Next, the wrapper joins `RedAutos` with itself, and performs the necessary selection, to get the relation asked for by the query of Fig. 8. The work performed by the wrapper for this step is shown in Fig. 9. □

3.5 Exercises for Section 3

Exercise 3.1: In Fig. 5 we saw a simple wrapper template that translated queries from the mediator for cars of a given color into queries at the dealer with relation `Cars`. Suppose that the color codes used by the mediator in its schema were different from the color codes used at this dealer, and there was

```
SELECT DISTINCT A1.model, A1.dealer
FROM RedAutos A1, RedAutos A2
WHERE A1.model = A2.model AND
      A1.autoTrans = 'no' AND
      A2.autoTrans = 'yes';
```

Figure 9: Query performed at the wrapper (or mediator) to complete the answer to the query of Fig. 8

a relation `GtoL(globalColor, localColor)` that translated between the two sets of codes. Rewrite the template so the correct query would be generated.

Exercise 3.2: In Exercise 2.1 we spoke of two computer companies, A and B, that used different schemas for information about their products. Suppose we have a mediator with schema

```
PCMed(manf, speed, mem, disk, screen)
```

with the intuitive meaning that a tuple gives the manufacturer (A or B), processor speed, main-memory size, hard-disk size, and screen size for one of the systems you could buy from that company. Write wrapper templates for the following types of queries. Note that you need to write two templates for each query, one for each of the manufacturers.

a) Given a speed, find the tuples with that speed.

b) Given a screen size, find the tuples with that size.

c) Given memory and disk sizes, find the matching tuples.

Exercise 3.3: Suppose you had the wrapper templates described in Exercise 3.2 available in the wrappers at each of the two sources (computer manufacturers). How could the mediator use these capabilities of the wrappers to answer the following queries?

a) Find the manufacturer, memory size, and screen size of all systems with a 3.1 gigahertz speed and a 120 gigabyte disk.

! b) Find the maximum amount of hard disk available on a system with a 2.8 gigahertz processor.

c) Find all the systems with 512M memory and a screen size (in inches) that exceeds the disk size (in gigabytes).

4 Capability-Based Optimization

Recall the idea of cost-based query optimization. A typical DBMS estimates the cost of each query plan and picks what it believes to be the best. When a mediator is given a query to answer, it often has little knowledge of how long its sources will take to answer the queries it sends them. Furthermore, many sources are not SQL databases, and often they will answer only a small subset of the kinds of queries that the mediator might like to pose. As a result, optimization of mediator queries cannot rely on cost measures alone to select a query plan.

Optimization by a mediator usually follows the simpler strategy known as *capability-based optimization.* The central issue is not what a query plan costs, but whether the plan can be executed at all. Only among plans found to be executable ("feasible") do we try to estimate costs.

4.1 The Problem of Limited Source Capabilities

Today, many useful sources have only Web-based interfaces, even if they are, behind the scenes, an ordinary database. Web sources usually permit querying only through a query form, which does not accept arbitrary SQL queries. Rather, we are invited to enter values for certain attributes and can receive a response that gives values for other attributes.

Example 9: The Amazon.com interface allows us to query about books in many different ways. We can specify an author and get all their books, or we can specify a book title and receive information about that book. We can specify keywords and get books that match the keywords. However, there is also information we can receive in answers but cannot specify. For instance, Amazon ranks books by sales, but we cannot ask "give me the top 10 sellers." Moreover, we cannot ask questions that are too general. For instance, the query:

```
SELECT * FROM Books;
```

"tell me everything you know about books," cannot be asked or answered through the Amazon Web interface, although it could be answered behind the scenes if we were able to access the Amazon database directly. □

There are a number of other reasons why a source may limit the ways in which queries can be asked. Among them are:

1. Many of the earliest data sources did not use a DBMS, surely not a relational DBMS that supports SQL queries. These systems were designed to be queried in certain very specific ways only.

2. For reasons of security, a source may limit the kinds of queries that it will accept. Amazon's unwillingness to answer the query "tell me about all

your books" is a rudimentary example; it protects against a rival exploiting the Amazon database. As another instance, a medical database may answer queries about averages, but won't disclose the details of a particular patient's medical history.

3. Indexes on large databases may make certain kinds of queries feasible, while others are too expensive to execute. For instance, if a books database were relational, and one of the attributes were `author`, then without an index on that attribute, it would be infeasible to answer queries that specified only an author.[3]

4.2 A Notation for Describing Source Capabilities

If data is relational, or may be thought of as relational, then we can describe the legal forms of queries by *adornments.* These are sequences of codes that represent the requirements for the attributes of the relation, in their standard order. The codes we shall use for adornments reflect the most common capabilities of sources. They are:

1. f (free) means that the attribute can be specified or not, as we choose.

2. b (bound) means that we must specify a value for the attribute, but any value is allowed.

3. u (unspecified) means that we are not permitted to specify a value for the attribute.

4. $c[S]$ (choice from set S) means that a value must be specified, and that value must be one of the values in the finite set S. This option corresponds, for instance, to values that are specified from a pulldown menu in a Web interface.

5. $o[S]$ (optional, from set S) means that we either do not specify a value, or we specify one of the values in the finite set S.

In addition, we place a prime (e.g., f') on a code to indicate that the attribute is not part of the output of the query.

A *capabilities specification* for a source is a set of adornments. The intent is that in order to query the source successfully, the query must match one of the adornments in its capabilities specification. Note that, if an adornment has free or optional components, then queries with different sets of attributes specified may match that adornment.

---

[3]We should be aware, however, that information like Amazon's about products is not accessed as if it were a relational database. Rather, the information about books is stored as text, with an inverted index. Thus, queries about any aspect of books — authors, titles, words in titles, and perhaps words in descriptions of the book — are supported by this index.

Example 10: Suppose we have two sources like those of the two dealers in Example 4. Dealer 1 is a source of data in the form:

```
Cars(serialNo, model, color, autoTrans, navi)
```

Note that in the original, we suggested relation `Cars` could have additional attributes representing options, but for simplicity in this example, let us limit our thinking to automatic transmissions and navigation systems only. Here are two possible ways that Dealer 1 might allow this data to be queried:

1. The user specifies a serial number. All the information about the car with that serial number (i.e., the other four attributes) is produced as output. The adornment for this query form is *b′uuuu*. That is, the first attribute, `serialNo` must be specified and is not part of the output. The other attributes must *not* be specified and *are* part of the output.

2. The user specifies a model and color, and perhaps whether or not automatic transmission and navigation system are wanted. All five attributes are printed for all matching cars. An appropriate adornment is

   ubbo[yes, no]*o*[yes, no]

   This adornment says we must not specify the serial number; we must specify a model and color, but are allowed to give any possible value in these fields. Also, we may, if we wish, specify whether we want automatic transmission and/or a navigation system, but must do so by using only the values "yes" and "no" in those fields.

□

4.3 Capability-Based Query-Plan Selection

Given a query at the mediator, a capability-based query optimizer first considers what queries it can ask at the sources to help answer the query. If we imagine those queries asked and answered, then we have bindings for some more attributes, and these bindings may make some more queries at the sources possible. We repeat this process until either:

1. We have asked enough queries at the sources to resolve all the conditions of the mediator query, and therefore we may answer that query. Such a plan is called *feasible.*

2. We can construct no more valid forms of source queries, yet we still cannot answer the mediator query, in which case the mediator must give up; it has been given an impossible query.

What Do Adornments Guarantee?

It would be wonderful if a source that supported queries matching a given adornment would return all possible answers to the query. However, sources normally have only a subset of the possible answers to a query. For instance, Amazon does not stock every book that has ever been written, and the two dealers of our running automobiles example each have distinct sets of cars in their database. Thus, a more proper interpretation of an adornment is: "I will answer a query in the form described by this adornment, and every answer I give will be a true answer, but I do not guarantee to provide all true answers." An important consequence of this state of affairs is that if we want all available tuples for a relation R, then we must query every source that might contribute such tuples.

The simplest form of mediator query for which we need to apply the above strategy is a join of relations, each of which is available, with certain adornments, at one or more sources. If so, then the search strategy is to try to get tuples for each relation in the join, by providing enough argument bindings that some source allows a query about that relation to be asked and answered. A simple example will illustrate the point.

Example 11: Let us suppose we have sources like the relations of Dealer 2 in Example 4:

```
Autos(serial, model, color)
Options(serial, option)
```

Suppose that *ubf* is the sole adornment for `Autos`, while `Options` has two adornments, *bu* and *uc*[autoTrans, navi], representing two different kinds of queries that we can ask at that source. Let the query be "find the serial numbers and colors of Gobi models with a navigation system."

Here are three different query plans that the mediator must consider:

1. Specifying that the model is Gobi, query `Autos` and get the serial numbers and colors of all Gobis. Then, using the *bu* adornment for `Options`, for each such serial number, find the options for that car and filter to make sure it has a navigation system.

2. Specifying the navigation-system option, query `Options` using the

   uc[autoTrans, navi]

   adornment and get all the serial numbers for cars with a navigation system. Then query `Autos` as in (1), to get all the serial numbers and colors of Gobis, and intersect the two sets of serial numbers.

3. Query `Options` as in (2) to get the serial numbers for cars with a navigation system. Then use these serial numbers to query `Autos` and see which of these cars are Gobis.

Either of the first two plans are acceptable. However, the third plan is one of several plans that will not work; the system does not have the capability to execute this plan because the second part — the query to `Autos` — does not have a matching adornment. □

4.4 Adding Cost-Based Optimization

The mediator's query optimizer is not done when the capabilities of the sources are examined. Having found the feasible plans, it must choose among them. Making an intelligent, cost-based optimization requires that the mediator know a great deal about the costs of the queries involved. Since the sources are usually independent of the mediator, it is difficult to estimate the cost. For instance, a source may take less time during periods when it is lightly loaded, but when are those periods? Long-term observation by the mediator is necessary for the mediator even to guess what the response time might be.

In Example 11, we might simply count the number of queries to sources that must be issued. Plan (2) uses only two source queries, while plan (1) uses one plus the number of Gobis found in the `Autos` relation. Thus, it appears that plan (2) has lower cost. On the other hand, if the queries of `Options`, one with each serial number, could be combined into one query, then plan (1) might turn out to be the superior choice.

4.5 Exercises for Section 4

Exercise 4.1: Suppose each relation from Exercise 2.1:

```
Computers(number, proc, speed, memory, hd)
Monitors(number, screen, maxResX, maxResY)
```

is an information source. Using the notation from Section 4.2, write one or more adornments that express the following capabilities:

a) We can query for computers having a given processor, which must be one of "P-IV," "G5," or "Athlon," a given speed, and (optionally) a given amount of memory.

b) We can query for computers having any specified hard-disk size and/or any given memory size.

c) We can query for monitors if we specify either the number of the monitor, the screen size, or the maximum resolution in both dimensions.

d) We can query for monitors if we specify the screen size, which must be either 19, 22, 24, or 30 inches. All attributes except the screen size are returned.

! e) We can query for computers if we specify any two of the processor type, processor speed, memory size, or disk size.

Exercise 4.2: Suppose we have the two sources of Exercise 4.1, but understand the attribute `number` of both relations to refer to the number of a complete system, some of whose attributes are found in one source and some in the other. Suppose also that the adornments describing access to the `Computers` relation are *buuuu*, *ubbff*, and *uuubb*, while the adornments for `Monitors` are *bfff* and *ubbb*. Tell what plans are feasible for the following queries (exclude any plans that are obviously more expensive than other plans on your list):

a) Find the systems with 512 megabytes of memory, an 80-gigabyte hard disk, and a 22-inch monitor.

b) Find the systems with a Pentium-IV processor running at 3.0 gigahertz with a 22-inch monitor and a maximum resolution of 1600-by-1050.

! c) Find all systems with a G5 processor running at 1.8 gigahertz, with 2 gigabytes of memory, a 300 gigabyte disk, and a 19-inch monitor.

5 Optimizing Mediator Queries

In this section, we shall give a greedy algorithm for answering queries at a mediator. This algorithm, called *chain*, always finds a way to answer the query by sending a sequence of requests to its sources, provided at least one solution exists. The class of queries that can be handled is those that involve joins of relations that come from the sources, followed by an optional selection and optional projection onto output attributes. This class of queries is exactly what can be expressed as Datalog rules.

5.1 Simplified Adornment Notation

The Chain Algorithm concerns itself with Datalog rules and with whether prior source requests have provided bindings for any of the variables in the body of the rule. Since we care only about whether we have found all possible constants for a variable, we can limit ourselves, in the query at the mediator (although not at the sources), to the b (bound) and f (free) adornments. That is, a $c[S]$ adornment for an attribute of a source relation can be used as soon as we know all possible values of interest for that attribute (i.e., the corresponding position in the mediator query has a b adornment). Note that the source will not provide matches for the values outside S, so there is no point in asking questions about these values. The optional adornment $o[S]$ can be treated as free, since there is no need to have a binding for the corresponding attribute in the query at the mediator (although we could). Likewise, adornment u can be treated as free, since although we cannot then specify a value for the attribute at the source, we can have, or not have, a binding for the corresponding variable at the mediator.

Example 12: Let us use the same query and source relations as in Example 11, but with different capabilities at the sources. In what follows we shall use superscripts on the predicate or relation names to show the adornment or permitted set of adornments. In this example, the permitted adornments for the two source relations are:

$$\texttt{Autos}^{buu}\texttt{(serial, model, color)}$$
$$\texttt{Options}^{uc[\texttt{autoTrans, navi}]}\texttt{(serial, option)}$$

That is, we can only access `Options` by providing a binding "autoTrans" or "navi" for the `option` attribute, and we can only access `Autos` by providing a binding for the `serial` attribute.

The query "find the serial numbers and colors of Gobi models with a navigation system" is expressed in Datalog by:

$$\texttt{Answer(s,c)} \leftarrow \texttt{Autos}^{fbf}\texttt{(s,"Gobi",c) AND Options}^{fb}\texttt{(s,"navi")}$$

Here, notice the adornments on the subgoals of the body. These, at the moment, are commentaries on what arguments of each subgoal are bound to a set of constants. Initially, only the middle argument of the `Autos` subgoal is bound (to the set containing only the constant "Gobi") and the second argument of the `Options` subgoal is bound to the set containing only "navi." We shall see shortly that as we use the sources to find tuples that match one or another subgoal, we get bindings for some of the variables in the Datalog rule, and thus change some of the f's to b's in the adornments. □

5.2 Obtaining Answers for Subgoals

We now need to formalize the comments made at the beginning of Section 5.1 about when a subgoal with some of its arguments bound can be answered by a source query. Suppose we have a subgoal $R^{x_1x_2\cdots x_n}(a_1, a_2, \ldots, a_n)$, where each x_i is either b or f. R is a relation that can be queried at some source, and which has some set of adornments.

Suppose $y_1y_2\cdots y_n$ is one of the adornments for R at its source. Each y_i can be any of b, f, u, $c[S]$ or $o[S]$ for any set S. Then it is possible to obtain a relation for the subgoal provided, for each $i = 1, 2, \ldots, n$, provided:

- If y_i is b or of the form $c[S]$, then $x_i = b$.
- If $x_i = f$, then y_i is not output restricted (i.e., not primed).

Note that if y_i is any of f, u, or $o[S]$, then x_i can be either b or f. We say that the adornment on the subgoal *matches* the adornment at the source.

Example 13: Suppose the subgoal in question is $R^{bbff}(p,q,r,s)$, and the adornments for R at its source are $\alpha_1 = fc[S_1]uo[S_2]$ and $\alpha_2 = c[S_3]bfc[S_4]$. Then *bbff* matches adornment α_1, so we may use α_1 to get the relation for subgoal $R(p,q,r,s)$. That is, α_1 has no b's and only one c, in the second position. Since the adornment of the subgoal has b in the second position, we know that there is a set of constants to which the variable q (the variable in the second argument of the subgoal) has been bound. For each of those constants that are a member of the set S_1 we can issue a query to the source for R, using that constant as the binding for the second argument. We do not provide bindings for any other argument, even though α_1 allows us to provide a binding for the first and/or fourth argument as well.

However, *bbff* does not match α_2. The reason is that α_2 has $c[S_4]$ in the fourth position, while *bbff* has f in that position. If we were to try to obtain R using α_2, we would have to provide a binding for the fourth argument, which means that variable s in $R(p,q,r,s)$ would have to be bound to a set of constants. But we know that is not the case, or else the adornment on the subgoal would have had b in the fourth position. □

5.3 The Chain Algorithm

The *Chain Algorithm* is a greedy approach to selecting an order in which we obtain relations for each of the subgoals of a Datalog rule. It is not guaranteed to provide the most efficient solution, but it will provide a solution whenever one exists, and in practice, it is very likely to obtain the most efficient solution. The algorithm maintains two kinds of information:

- An adornment is maintained for each subgoal. Initially, the adornment for a subgoal has b if and only if the mediator query provides a constant binding for the corresponding argument of that subgoal, as for instance, the query in Example 12 provided bindings for the second arguments of both the `Autos` and `Options` subgoals. In all other places, the adornment has f's.

- A relation X that is (a projection of) the join of the relations for all the subgoals that have been *resolved.* We resolve a subgoal when the adornment for the subgoal matches one of the adornments at the source for this subgoal, and we have extracted from the source all possible tuples for that subgoal. Initially, since no subgoals have been resolved, X is a relation over no attributes, containing just the empty tuple (i.e., the tuple with zero components). Note that for empty X and any relation R, $X \bowtie R = R$; i.e., X is initially the identity relation for the natural-join operation. As the algorithm progresses, X will have attributes that are variables of the rule — those variables that correspond to b's in the adornments of the subgoals in which they appear.

The core of the Chain Algorithm is as follows. After initializing relation X and the adornments of the subgoals as above, we repeatedly select a subgoal that can be resolved. Let $R^{\alpha}(a_1, a_2, \ldots, a_n)$ be the subgoal to be resolved. We do so by:

1. Wherever α has a b, we shall find that either the corresponding argument of R is a constant rather than a variable, or it is one of the variables in the schema of the relation X. Project X onto those of its variables that appear in subgoal R. Each tuple in the projection, together with constants in the subgoal R, if any, provide sufficient bindings to use one of the adornments for the source relation R — whichever adornment α matches.

2. Issue a query to the source for each tuple t in the projection of X. We construct the query as follows, depending on the source adornment β that α matches.

   (a) If a component of β is b, then the corresponding component of α is too, and we can use the corresponding component of t (or a constant in the subgoal) to provide the necessary binding for the source query.

   (b) If a component of β is $c[S]$, then again the corresponding component of α will be b, and we can obtain a constant from the subgoal or the tuple t. However, if that constant is not in S, then there is no chance the source can produce any tuples that match t, so we do not generate any source query for t.

   (c) If a component of β is f, then produce a constant value for this component in the source query if we can; otherwise do not provide a value for this component in the source query. Note that we can provide a constant exactly when the corresponding component of α is b.

   (d) If a component of β is u, provide no binding for this component, even if the corresponding component of α is b.

   (e) If a component of β is $o[S]$, treat this component as if it were f in the case that the corresponding component of α is f, and as $c[S]$ if the corresponding component of α is b.

   For each tuple returned, extend the tuple so it has one component for each argument of the subgoal (i.e., n components). Note that the source will return every component of R that is not output restricted, so the only components that are not present have b in the adornment α. Thus, the returned tuples can be padded by using either the constant from the subgoal, or the constant from the tuple in the projection of X. The union of all the responses is the relation R for the subgoal $R(a_1, a_2, \ldots, a_n)$.

3. Every variable among $a_1, a_2, \ldots, a_n$ is now bound. For each subgoal that has not yet been resolved, change its adornment so any position holding one of these variables is now bound (b).

4. Replace X by $X \bowtie \pi_S(R)$, where S is all the variables among

$$a_1, a_2, \ldots, a_n$$

5. Project out of X all components that correspond to variables that do not appear in the head or in any unresolved subgoal. These components can never be useful in what follows.

The complete Chain Algorithm, then, consists of the initialization described above, followed by as many subgoal-resolution steps as we can manage. If we succeed in resolving every subgoal, then relation X will be the answer to the query. If at some point, there are unresolved subgoals, yet none can be resolved, then the algorithm fails. In that case, there can be no other sequence of resolution steps that answers the query.

Example 14: Consider the mediator query

Q: `Answer(c)` ← `R`^{bf}`(1,a) AND S`^{ff}`(a,b) AND T`^{ff}`(b,c)`

There are three sources that provide answers to queries about R, S, and T, respectively. The contents of these relations at the sources and the only adornments supported by these sources are shown in Fig. 10.

Relation	R		S		T	
	w	x	x	y	y	z
Data	1	2	2	4	4	6
	1	3	3	5	5	7
	1	4			5	8
Adornment	bf		$c'[2,3,5]f$		bu	

Figure 10: Data for Example 14

Initially, the adornments on the subgoals are as shown in the query Q, and the relation X that we construct initially contains only the empty tuple. Since subgoals S and T have *ff* adornments, but the adornments at the corresponding sources each have a component with b or c, neither of these subgoals can be resolved. Fortunately, the first subgoal, $R(1, a)$, can be resolved, since the bf adornment at the corresponding source is matched by the adornment of the subgoal. Thus, we send the source for $R(w, x)$ a query with $w = 1$, and the response is the set of three tuples shown in the first column of Fig. 10.

We next project the subgoal's relation onto its second component, since only the second component of $R(1, a)$ is a variable. That gives us the relation

a
2
3
4

This relation is joined with X, which currently has no attributes and only the empty tuple. The result is that X becomes the relation above. Since a is now bound, we change the adornment on the S subgoal from ff to bf.

At this point, the second subgoal, $S^{bf}(a, b)$, can be resolved. We obtain bindings for the first component by projecting X onto a; the result is X itself. That is, we can go to the source for $S(x, y)$ with bindings 2, 3, and 4 for x. We do not need bindings for y, since the second component of the adornment for the source is f. The $c'[2, 3, 5]$ code for x says that we can give the source the value 2, 3, or 5 for the first argument. Since there is a prime on the c, we know that only the corresponding y value(s) will be returned, not the value of x that we supplied in the request. We care about values 2, 3, and 4, but 4 is not a possible value at the source for S, so we never ask about it.

When we ask about $x = 2$, we get one response: $y = 4$. We pad this response with the value 2 we supplied to conclude that $(2, 4)$ is a tuple in the relation for the S subgoal. Similarly, when we ask about $x = 3$, we get $y = 5$ as the only response and we add $(3, 5)$ to the set of tuples constructed for the S subgoal. There are no more requests to ask at the source for S, so we conclude that the relation for the S subgoal is

a	b
2	4
3	5

When we join this relation with the previous value of X, the result is just the relation above. However, variable a now appears neither in the head nor in any unresolved subgoal. Thus, we project it out, so X becomes

b
4
5

Since b is now bound, we change the adornment on the T subgoal, so it becomes $T^{bf}(b, c)$. Now this last subgoal can be resolved, which we do by sending requests to the source for $T(y, z)$ with $y = 4$ and $y = 5$. The responses we get back give us the following relation for the T subgoal:

b	c
4	6
5	7
5	8

We join it with the relation for X above, and then project onto the c attribute to get the relation for the head. That is, the answer to the query at the mediator is $\{(6), (7), (8)\}$. □

5.4 Incorporating Union Views at the Mediator

In our description of the Chain Algorithm, we assumed that each predicate in the Datalog query at the mediator was a "view" of data at one particular source. However, it is common for there to be several sources that can contribute tuples to the relation for the predicate. How we construct the relation for such a predicate depends on how we expect the sources for the predicate to interact.

The easy case is where we expect the sources for a predicate to contain replicated information. In that case, we can turn to any one of the sources to get the relation for a predicate. This case thus looks exactly like the case where there is a single source for a predicate, but there may be several adornments that allows us to query that source.

The more complex case is when the sources each contribute some tuples to the predicate that the other sources may not contribute. In that case, we should consult all the sources for the predicate. However, there is still a policy choice to be made. Either we can refuse to answer the query unless we can consult all the sources, or we can make best efforts to return all the answers to the query that we can obtain by combinations of sources.

Consult All Sources

If we must consult all sources to consider a subgoal resolved, then we can only resolve a subgoal when each source for its relation has an adornment matched by the current adornment of the subgoal. This rule is a small modification of the Chain Algorithm. However, not only does it make queries harder to answer, it makes queries impossible to answer when any source is "down," even if the Chain Algorithm provides a feasible ordering in which to resolve the subgoals. Thus, as the number of sources grows, this policy becomes progressively less practical.

Best Efforts

Under this assumption, we only need one source with a matching adornment to resolve a subgoal. However, we need to modify the chain algorithm to revisit each subgoal when that subgoal has new bound arguments. We may find that some source that could not be matched is now matched by the subgoal with its new adornment.

Example 15: Consider the mediator query

$$\texttt{answer(a,c)} \leftarrow \texttt{R}^{ff}\texttt{(a,b) AND S}^{ff}\texttt{(b,c)}$$

Suppose also that R has two sources, one described by adornment *ff* and the other by fb. Likewise, S has two sources, described by *ff* and bf. We could start by using either source with adornment *ff*; suppose we start with R's source. We query this source and get some tuples for R.

Now, we have some bindings, but perhaps not all, for the variable b. We can now use both sources for S to obtain tuples and the relation for S can be set to their union. At this point, we can project the relation for S onto variable b and get some b-values. These can be used to query the second source for R, the one with adornment fb. In this manner, we can get some additional R-tuples. It is only at this point that we can join the relations for R and S, and project onto a and c to get the best-effort answer to the query. □

5.5 Exercises for Section 5

Exercise 5.1: Apply the Chain Algorithm to the mediator query

```
Answer(a,e) ← R(a,b,c) AND S(c,d) AND T(b,d,e)
```

with the following adornments at the sources for R, S, and T. If there is more than one adornment for a predicate, either may be used.

a) R^{fff}, S^{bf}, T^{bff}, T^{fbf}.

b) R^{ffb}, S^{fb}, T^{fbf}, T^{bff}.

c) R^{fbf}, S^{fb}, S^{bf}, T^{fff}.

In each case:

i. Indicate all possible orders in which the subgoals can be resolved.

ii. Does the Chain Algorithm produce an answer to the query?

iii. Give the sequence of relational-algebra operations needed to compute the intermediate relation X at each step and the result of the query.

! **Exercise 5.2:** Suppose that for the mediator query of Exercise 5.1, each predicate is a view defined by the union of two sources. For each predicate, one of the sources has an all-f adornment. The other sources have the following adornments: R^{fbb}, S^{bf}, and T^{bff}. Find a best-effort sequence of source requests that will produce all the answers to the mediator query that can be obtained from these sources.

Exercise 5.3: Describe all the source adornments that are matched by a subgoal with adornment R^{bf}.

!! **Exercise 5.4:** Prove that if there is any sequence of subgoal resolutions that will resolve all subgoals, then the Chain Algorithm will find one. *Hint*: Notice that if a subgoal can be resolved at a certain step, then if it is not selected for resolution, it can still be resolved at the next step.

6 Local-as-View Mediators

The mediators discussed so far are called *global-as-view* (GAV) mediators. The global data (i.e., the data available for querying at the mediator) is like a view; it doesn't exist physically, but pieces of it are constructed by the mediator, as needed, by asking queries of the sources.

In this section, we introduce another approach to connecting sources with a mediator. In a *local-as-view* (LAV) mediator, we define global predicates at the mediator, but we do not define these predicates as views of the source data. Rather, we define, for each source, one or more expressions involving the global predicates that describe the tuples that the source is able to produce. Queries are answered at the mediator by discovering all possible ways to construct the query using the views provided by the sources.

6.1 Motivation for LAV Mediators

In many applications, GAV mediators are easy to construct. You decide on the global predicates or relations that the mediator will support, and for each source, you consider which predicates it can support, and how it can be queried. That is, you determine the set of adornments for each predicate at each source. For instance, in our Aardvark Automobiles example, if we decide we want `Autos` and `Options` predicates at the mediator, we find a way to query each dealer's source for those concepts and let the `Autos` and `Options` predicates at the mediator represent the union of what the sources provide. Whenever we need one or both of those predicates to answer a mediator query, we make requests of each of the sources to obtain their data.

However, there are situations where the relationship between what we want to provide to users of the mediator and what the sources provide is more subtle. We shall look at an example where the mediator is intended to provide a single predicate $Par(c, p)$, meaning that p is a parent of c. As with all mediators, this predicate represents an abstract concept — in this case, the set of all child-parent facts that could ever exist — and the sources will provide information about whatever child-parent facts they know. Even put together, the sources probably do not know about everyone in the world, let along everyone who ever lived.

Life would be simple if each source held some child-parent information and nothing else that was relevant to the mediator. Then, all we would have to do is determine how to query each one for whatever facts they could provide. However, suppose we have a database maintained by the Association of Grandparents that doesn't provide any child-parent facts at all, but provides child-grandparent facts. We can never use this source to help answer a query about someone's parents or children, but we can use it to help answer a mediator query that uses the `Par` predicate several times to ask for the grandparents of an individual, or their great-grandparents, or another complex relationship among people.

GAV mediators do not allow us to use a grandparents source at all, if our goal is to produce a Par relation. Producing both a parent and a grandparent predicate at the mediator is possible, but it might be confusing to the user and would require us to figure out how to extract grandparents from all sources, including those that only allow queries for child-parent facts. However, LAV mediators allow us to say that a certain source provides grandparent facts. Moreover, the technology associated with LAV mediators lets us discover how and when to use that source in a given query.

6.2 Terminology for LAV Mediation

LAV mediators are always defined using a form of logic that serves as the language for defining views. In our presentation, we shall use Datalog. Both the queries at the mediator and the queries (view definitions) that describe the sources will be single Datalog rules. A query that is a single Datalog rule is often called a *conjunctive query*, and we shall use the term here.

A LAV mediator has a set of *global predicates*, which are used as the subgoals of mediator queries. There are other conjunctive queries that define *views*; i.e., their heads each have a unique view predicate that is the name of a view. Each view definition has a body consisting of global predicates and is associated with a particular source, from which that view can be constructed. We assume that each view can be constructed with an all-free adornment. If capabilities are limited, we can use the chain algorithm to decide whether solutions using the views are feasible.

Suppose we are given a conjunctive query Q whose subgoals are predicates defined at the mediator. We need to find all *solutions* — conjunctive queries whose bodies are composed of view predicates, but that can be "expanded" to produce a conjunctive query involving the global predicates. Moreover, this conjunctive query must produce only tuples that are also produced by Q. We say such expansions are *contained* in Q. An example may help with these tricky concepts, after which we shall define "expansion" formally.

Example 16: Suppose there is one global predicate $Par(c, p)$ meaning that p is a parent of c. There is one source that produces some of the possible parent facts; its view is defined by the conjunctive query

$$\texttt{V}_1\texttt{(c,p)} \leftarrow \texttt{Par(c,p)}$$

There is another source that produces some grandparent facts; its view is defined by the conjunctive query

$$\texttt{V}_2\texttt{(c,g)} \leftarrow \texttt{Par(c,p) AND Par(p,g)}$$

Our query at the mediator will ask for great-grandparent facts that can be obtained from the sources. That is, the mediator query is

$$\texttt{Q(w,z)} \leftarrow \texttt{Par(w,x) AND Par(x,y) AND Par(y,z)}$$

How might we answer this query? The source view V_1 contributes to the parent predicate directly, so we can use it three times in the obvious solution

$$\texttt{Q(w,z)} \leftarrow \texttt{V}_1\texttt{(w,x) AND V}_1\texttt{(x,y) AND V}_1\texttt{(y,z)}$$

There are, however, other solutions that may produce additional answers, and thus must be part of the logical query plan for answering the query. In particular, we can use the view V_2 to get grandparent facts, some of which may not be inferrable by using two parent facts from V_1. We can use V_1 to make a step of one generation, and then use V_2 to make a step of two generations, as in the solution

$$\texttt{Q(w,z)} \leftarrow \texttt{V}_1\texttt{(w,x) AND V}_2\texttt{(x,z)}$$

Or, we can use V_2 first, followed by V_1, as

$$\texttt{Q(w,z)} \leftarrow \texttt{V}_2\texttt{(w,y) AND V}_1\texttt{(y,z)}$$

It turns out these are the only solutions we need; their union is all the great-grandparent facts that we can produce from the sources V_1 and V_2. There is still a great deal to explain. Why are these solutions guaranteed to produce only answers to the query? How do we tell whether a solution is part of the answer to a query? How do we find all the useful solutions to a query? We shall answer each of these questions in the next sections. □

6.3 Expanding Solutions

Given a query Q, a solution S has a body whose subgoals are views, and each view V is defined by a conjunctive query with that view as the head. We can substitute the body of V's conjunctive query for a subgoal in S that uses predicate V, as long as we are careful not to confuse variable names from one body with those of another. Once we substitute rule bodies for the views that are in S, we have a body that consists of global predicates only. The expanded solution can be compared with Q, to see if the results produced by the solution S are guaranteed to be answers to the query Q, in a manner we shall discuss later.

However, first we must be clear about the expansion algorithm. Suppose that there is a solution S that has a subgoal $V(a_1, a_2, \ldots, a_n)$. Here the a_i's can be any variables or constants, and it is possible that two or more of the a_i's are actually the same variable. Let the definition of view V be of the form

$$V(b_1, b_2, \ldots, b_n) \leftarrow B$$

where B represents the entire body. We may assume that the b_i's are distinct variables, since there is no need to have two identical components in a view, nor is there a need for components that are constant. We can replace $V(a_1, a_2, \ldots, a_n)$ in solution S by a version of body B that has all the subgoals of B, but with variables possibly altered. The rules for altering the variables of B are:

1. First, identify the *local variables* of B — those variables that appear in the body, but not in the head. Note that, within a conjunctive query, a local variable can be replaced by any other variable, as long as the replacing variable does not appear elsewhere in the conjunctive query. The idea is the same as substituting different names for local variables in a program.

2. If there are any local variables of B that appear in B or in S, replace each one by a distinct new variable that appears nowhere in the rule for V or in S.

3. In the body B, replace each b_i by a_i, for $i = 1, 2, \ldots, n$.

Example 17: Suppose we have the view definition

```
V(a,b,c,d) ← E(a,b,x,y) AND F(x,y,c,d)
```

Suppose further that some solution S has in its body a subgoal $V(x, y, 1, x)$.

The local variables in the definition of V are x and y, since these do not appear in the head. We need to change them both, because they appear in the subgoal for which we are substituting. Suppose e and f are variable names that appear nowhere in S. We can rewrite the body of the rule for V as

```
V(a,b,c,d) ← E(a,b,e,f) AND F(e,f,c,d)
```

Next, we must substitute the arguments of the V subgoal for a, b, c, and d. The correspondence is that a and d become x, b becomes y, and c becomes the constant 1. We therefore substitute for $V(x, y, 1, x)$ the two subgoals $E(x, y, e, f)$ and $F(e, f, 1, x)$. □

The expansion process is essentially the substitution described above for each subgoal of the solution S. There is one extra caution of which we must be aware, however. Since we may be substituting for the local variables of several view definitions, and may in fact need to create several versions of one view definition (if S has several subgoals with the same view predicate), we must make sure that in the substitution for each subgoal of S, we use unique local variables — ones that do not appear in any other substitution or in S itself. Only then can we be sure that when we do the expansion we do not use the same name for two variables that should be distinct.

Example 18: Let us resume the discussion we began in Example 16, where we had view definitions

```
V1(c,p) ← Par(c,p)
V2(c,g) ← Par(c,p) AND Par(p,g)
```

One of the proposed solutions S is

```
Q(w,z) ← V1(w,x) AND V2(x,z)
```

Let us expand this solution. The first subgoal, with predicate V_1 is easy to expand, because the rule for V_1 has no local variables. We substitute w and x for c and p respectively, so the body of the rule for V_1 becomes $Par(w, x)$. This subgoal will be substituted in S for $V_1(w, x)$.

We must also substitute for the V_2 subgoal. Its rule has local variable p. However, since p does not appear in S, nor has it been used as a local variable in another substitution, we are free to leave p as it is. We therefore have only to substitute x and z for the variables c and g, respectively. The two subgoals in the rule for V_2 become $Par(x, p)$ and $Par(p, z)$. When we substitute these two subgoals for $V_2(x, z)$ in S, we have constructed the complete expansion of S:

```
Q(w,z) ← Par(w,x) AND Par(x,p) AND Par(p,z)
```

Notice that this expansion is practically identical to the query in Example 16. The only difference is that the query uses local variable y where the expansion uses p. Since the names of local variables do not affect the result, it appears that the solution S is the answer to the query. However, that is not quite right. The query is looking for all great-grandparent facts, and all the expansion says is that the solution S provides only facts that answer the query. S might not produce all possible answers. For example, the source of V_2 might even be empty, in which case nothing is produced by solution S, even though another solution might produce some answers. □

6.4 Containment of Conjunctive Queries

In order for a conjunctive query S to be a solution to the given mediator query Q, the expansion of S, say E, must produce only answers that Q produces, regardless of what relations are represented by the predicates in the bodies of E and Q. If so, we say that $E \subseteq Q$.

There is an algorithm to tell whether $E \subseteq Q$; we shall see this test after introducing the following important concept. A *containment mapping* from Q to E is a function τ from the variables of Q to the variables and constants of E, such that:

1. If x is the ith argument of the head of Q, then $\tau(x)$ is the ith argument of the head of E.

2. Add to τ the rule that $\tau(c) = c$ for any constant c. If $P(x_1, x_2, \ldots, x_n)$ is a subgoal of Q, then $P\big(\tau(x_1), \tau(x_2), \ldots, \tau(x_n)\big)$ is a subgoal of E.

Example 19: Consider the following two conjunctive queries:

Q_1: `H(x,y) ← A(x,z) AND B(z,y)`
Q_2: `H(a,b) ← A(a,c) AND B(d,b) AND A(a,d)`

We claim that $Q_2 \subseteq Q_1$. In proof, we offer the following containment mapping: $\tau(x) = a$, $\tau(y) = b$, and $\tau(z) = d$. Notice that when we apply this substitution, the head of Q_1 becomes $H(a, b)$, which is the head of Q_2. The first subgoal of Q_1 becomes $A(a, d)$, which is the third subgoal of Q_2. Likewise, the second subgoal of Q_1 becomes the second subgoal of Q_2. That proves there is a containment mapping from Q_1 to Q_2, and therefore $Q_2 \subseteq Q_1$. Notice that no subgoal of Q_1 maps to the first subgoal of Q_2, but the containment-mapping definition does not require that there be one.

Surprisingly, there is also a containment mapping from Q_2 to Q_1, so the two conjunctive queries are in fact equivalent. That is, not only is one contained in the other, but on any relations A and B, they produce exactly the same set of tuples for the relation H. The containment mapping from Q_2 to Q_1 is $\rho(a) = x$, $\rho(b) = y$, and $\rho(c) = \rho(d) = z$. Under this mapping, the head of Q_2 becomes the head of Q_1, the first and third subgoals of Q_2 become the first subgoal of Q_1, and the second subgoal of Q_2 becomes the second subgoal of Q_1.

While it may appear strange that two such different looking conjunctive queries are equivalent, the following is the intuition. Think of A and B as two different colored edges on a graph. Then Q_1 asks for the pairs of nodes x and y such that there is an A-edge from x to some z and a B-edge from z to y. Q_2 asks for the same thing, using its second and third subgoals respectively, although it calls x, y, and z by the names a, b, and d respectively. In addition, Q_2 seems to have the added condition expressed by the first subgoal that there is an edge from node a to somewhere (node c). But we already know that there is an edge from a to somewhere, namely d. That is, we are always free to use the same node for c as we did for d, because there are no other constraints on c. □

Example 20: Here are two queries similar, but not identical, to those of Example 19:

P_1: `H(x,y) ← A(x,z) AND A(z,y)`
P_2: `H(a,b) ← A(a,c) AND A(c,d) AND A(d,b)`

Intuitively, if we think of A as representing edges in a graph, then P_1 asks for paths of length 2 and P_2 asks for paths of length 3. We do not expect either to be contained in the other, and indeed the containment-mapping test confirms that fact.

Consider a possible containment mapping τ from P_1 to P_2. Because of the conditions on heads, we know $\tau(x) = a$ and $\tau(y) = b$. To what does z map? Since we already know $\tau(x) = a$, the first subgoal $A(x, z)$ can only map to $A(a, c)$ of P_2. That means $\tau(z)$ must be c. However, since $\tau(y) = b$, the subgoal $A(z, y)$ of P_1 can only become $A(d, b)$ in P_2. That means $\tau(z)$ must be d. But z can only map to one value; it cannot map to both c and d. We conclude that no containment mapping from P_1 to P_2 exists.

A similar argument shows that there is no containment mapping from P_2 to P_1. We leave it as an exercise. □

Complexity of the Containment-Mapping Test

It is NP-complete to decide whether there is a containment mapping from one conjunctive query to another. However, in practice, it is usually quite easy to decide whether a containment mapping exists. Conjunctive queries in practice have few subgoals and few variables. Moreover, for the class of conjunctive queries that have no more than two subgoals with the same predicate — a very common condition — there is a linear-time test for the existence of a containment mapping.

The importance of containment mappings is expressed by the following theorem:

- If Q_1 and Q_2 are conjunctive queries, then $Q_2 \subseteq Q_1$ if and only if there is a containment mapping from Q_1 to Q_2.

Notice that the containment mapping goes in the opposite direction from the containment; that is, the containment mapping is from the conjunctive query that produces the larger set of answers to the one that produces the smaller, contained set.

6.5 Why the Containment-Mapping Test Works

We need to argue two points. First, if there is a containment mapping, why must there be a containment of conjunctive queries? Second, if there is containment, why must there be a containment mapping? We shall not give formal proofs, but will sketch the arguments.

First, suppose there is a containment mapping τ from Q_1 to Q_2. When we apply Q_2 to a database, we look for substitutions σ for all the variables of Q_2 that make all its relational subgoals be tuples of the corresponding relation of the database. The substitution for the head becomes a tuple t that is returned by Q_2. If we compose τ and then σ, we have a mapping from the variables of Q_1 to tuples of the database that produces the same tuple t for the head of Q_1. Thus, on any given database, everything that Q_2 produces is also produced by Q_1.

Conversely, suppose that $Q_2 \subseteq Q_1$. That is, on any database D, everything that Q_2 produces is also produced by Q_1. Construct a particular database D that has only the subgoals of Q_2. That is, pretend the variables of Q_2 are distinct constants, and for each subgoal $P(a_1, a_2, \ldots, a_n)$, put the tuple $(a_1, a_2, \ldots, a_n)$ in the relation for P. There are no other tuples in the relations of D.

When Q_2 is applied to database D, surely the tuple whose components are the arguments of the head of Q_2 is produced. Since $Q_2 \subseteq Q_1$, it must be that

Q_1 applied to D also produces the head of Q_2. Again, we use the definition of how a conjunctive query is applied to a database. That definition tells us that there is a substitution of constants of D for the variables of Q_1 that turns each subgoal of Q_1 into a tuple in D and turns the head of Q_1 into the tuple that is the head of Q_2. But remember that the constants of D are the variables of Q_2. Thus, this substitution is actually a containment mapping.

6.6 Finding Solutions to a Mediator Query

We have one more issue to resolve. We are given a mediator query Q, and we need to find all solutions S such that the expansion E of S is contained in Q. But there could be an infinite number of S built from the views using any number of subgoals and variables. The following theorem limits our search.

- If a query Q has n subgoals, then any answer produced by any solution is also produced by a solution that has at most n subgoals.

This theorem, often called the LMSS Theorem,[4] gives us a finite, although exponential task to find a sufficient set of solutions. There has been considerable work on making the test much more efficient in typical situations.

Example 21 : Recall the query

Q_1: `Q(w,z)` ← `Par(w,x) AND Par(x,y) AND Par(y,z)`

from Example 16. This query has three subgoals, so we don't have to look at solutions with more than three subgoals. One of the solutions we proposed was

S_1: `Q(w,z)` ← V_1`(w,x) AND `V_2`(x,z)`

This solution has only two subgoals, and its expansion is contained in the query. Thus, it needs to be included among the set of solutions that we evaluate to answer the query.

However, consider the following solution:

S_2: `Q(w,z)` ← V_1`(w,x) AND `V_2`(x,z) AND `V_1`(t,u) AND `V_2`(u,v)`

It has four subgoals, so we know by the LMSS Theorem that it does not need to be considered. However, it is truly a solution, since its expansion

E_2: `Q(w,z)` ← `Par(w,x) AND Par(x,p) AND Par(p,z) AND Par(t,u)`
`AND Par(u,q) AND Par(q,v)`

[4]For the authors, A. Y. Levy, A. O. Mendelzon, Y. Sagiv, and D. Srivastava.

is contained in the query Q_1. To see why, use the containment mapping that maps w, x, and z to themselves and y to p.

However, E_2 is also contained in the expansion E_1 of the smaller solution S_1. Recall from Example 18 that the expansion of S_1 is

E_1: `Q(w,z)` $\leftarrow$ `Par(w,x) AND Par(x,p) AND Par(p,z)`

We can see immediately that $E_2 \subseteq E_1$, using the containment mapping that sends each variable of E_1 to the same variable in E_2. Thus, every answer to Q_1 produced by S_2 is also produced by S_1. Notice, incidentally, that S_2 is really S_1 with the two subgoals of S_1 repeated with different variables. □

In principle, to apply the LMSS Theorem, we must consider a number of possible solutions that is exponential in the query size. We must consider not only the choices of predicates for the subgoals, but which arguments of which subgoals hold the same variable. Note that within a conjunctive query, the names of the variables do not matter, but it matters which sets of arguments have the same variable. Most query processing is worst-case exponential in the query size anyway. Moreover, there are some powerful techniques known for limiting the search for solutions by looking at the structure of the conjunctive queries that define the views. We shall not go into depth here, but one easy but powerful idea is the following.

- If the conjunctive query that defines a view V has in its body a predicate P that does not appear in the body of the mediator query, then we need not consider any solution that uses V.

6.7 Why the LMSS Theorem Holds

Suppose we have a query Q with n subgoals, and there is a solution S with more than n subgoals. The expansion E of S must be contained in query Q, which means that there is a containment mapping from Q to the expansion E, as suggested in Fig. 11. If there are n subgoals ($n = 2$ in Fig. 11) in Q, then the containment mapping turns Q's subgoals into at most n of the subgoals of the expansion E. Moreover, these subgoals of E come from at most n of the subgoals of the solution S.

Suppose we removed from S all subgoals whose expansion was not the target of one of Q's subgoals under the containment mapping. We would have a new conjunctive query S' with at most n subgoals. Now S' must also be a solution to Q, because the same containment mapping that showed $E \subseteq Q$ in Fig. 11 also shows that $E' \subseteq Q$, where E' is the expansion of S'.

We must show one more thing: that any answer provided by S is also provided by S'. That is, $S \subseteq S'$. But there is an obvious containment mapping from S' to S: the identity mapping. Thus, there is no need for solution S among the solutions to query Q.

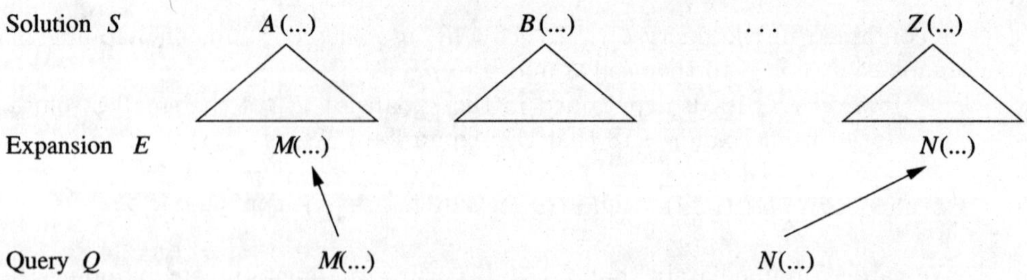

Figure 11: Why a query with n subgoals cannot need a solution with more than n subgoals

6.8 Exercises for Section 6

Exercise 6.1: Find all the containments among the following four conjunctive queries:

Q_1: `P(x,y) ← Q(x,a) AND Q(a,b) AND Q(b,y)`
Q_2: `P(x,y) ← Q(x,a) AND Q(a,b) AND Q(b,c) AND Q(c,y)`
Q_3: `P(x,y) ← Q(x,a) AND Q(b,c) AND Q(d,y) AND Q(x,b) AND Q(a,c) AND Q(c,y)`
Q_4: `P(x,y) ← Q(x,a) AND Q(a,1) AND Q(1,b) AND Q(b,y)`

! **Exercise 6.2:** For the mediator and views of Example 16, find all the needed solutions to the great-great-grandparent query:

`Q(x,y) ← Par(x,a) AND Par(a,b) AND Par(b,c) AND Par(c,y)`

! **Exercise 6.3:** Show that there is no containment mapping from P_2 to P_1 in Example 20.

! **Exercise 6.4:** Show that if conjunctive query Q_2 is constructed from conjunctive query Q_1 by removing one or more subgoals of Q_1, then $Q_1 \subseteq Q_2$.

7 Entity Resolution

We shall now take up a problem that must be solved in many information-integration scenarios. We have tacitly assumed that sources agree on the representation of entities or values, or at least that it is possible to perform a translation of data as we go through a wrapper. Thus, we are not afraid of two sources that report temperatures, one in Fahrenheit and one in Centigrade. Neither are we afraid of sources that support a concept like "employee" but have somewhat different sets of employees.

What happens, however, if two sources not only have different sets of employees, but it is unclear whether records at the two sources represent the same individual or not? Discrepancies can occur for many reasons, such as misspellings.

In this section, we shall begin by discussing some of the reasons why *entity resolution* — determining whether two records or tuples do or do not represent the same person, organization, place, or other entity — is a hard problem. We then look at the process of comparing records and merging those that we believe represent the same entity. Under some fairly reasonable conditions, there is an algorithm for finding a unique way to group all sets of records that represent a common entity and to perform this grouping efficiently.

7.1 Deciding Whether Records Represent a Common Entity

Imagine we have a collection of records that represent members of an entity set. These records may be tuples derived from several different sources, or even from one source. We only need to know that the records each have the same fields (although some records may have null in some fields). We hope to compare the values in corresponding fields to decide whether or not two records represent the same entity.

To be concrete, suppose that the entities are people, and the records have three fields: name, address, and phone. Intuitively, we want to say that two records represent the same individual if the two records have similar values for each of the three fields. It is not sufficient to insist that the values of corresponding fields be identical for a number of reasons. Among them:

1. *Misspellings.* Often, data is entered by a clerk who hears something over the phone, or who copies a written form carelessly. Thus, "Smythe" may appear as "Smith," or "Jones" may appear as "Jomes" ("m" and "n" are adjacent on the keyboard). Two phone numbers or street addresses may differ in a digit, yet really represent the same phone or house.

2. *Variant Names.* A person may supply their middle initial or not. They may use their complete first name or just their initial, or a nickname. Thus, "Susan Williams" may appear as "Susan B. Williams," "S. Williams," or "Sue Williams" in different records.

3. *Misunderstanding of Names.* There are many different systems of names used throughout the world. In the US, it is sometimes not understood that Asian names generally begin with the family name. Thus, "Chen Li" and "Li Chen" may or may not turn out to be the same person. The first author of this book has been referred to as "Hector Garcia-Molina," "Hector Garcia," and even "Hector G. Molina."

4. *Evolution of Values.* Sometimes, two different records that represent the same entity were created at different times. A person may have moved in the interrim, so the address fields in the two records are completely different. Or they may have started using a cell phone, so the phone fields are completely different. Area codes are sometimes changed. For

example, every (650) number used to be a (415) number, so an old record may have (415) 555-1212 and a newer record (650) 555-1212, and yet these numbers refer to the same phone.

5. *Abbreviations.* Sometimes words in an address are spelled out; other times an abbreviation may be used. Thus, "Sesame St." and "Sesame Street" may be the same street.

Thus, when deciding whether two records represent the same entity, we need to look carefully at the kinds of discrepancies that occur and devise a scoring system or other test that measures the similarity of records. Ultimately, we must turn the score into a yes/no decision: do the records represent the same entity or not? We shall mention below two useful approaches to measuring the similarity of records.

Edit Distance

Values that are strings can be compared by counting the number of insertions and/or deletions of characters it takes to turn one string into another. Thus, `Smythe` and `Smith` are at distance 3 (delete the "y" and "e," then insert the "i").

An alternative edit distance counts 1 for a *mutation*, that is, a replacement of one letter by another. In this measure, `Smythe` and `Smith` are at distance 2 (mutate "y" to "i" and delete "e"). This edit distance makes mistyped characters "cost" less, and therefore may be appropriate if typing errors are common in the data.

Finally, we may devise a specialized distance that takes into account the way the data was constructed. For instance, if we decide that changes of area codes are a major source of errors, we might charge only 1 for changing the entire area code from one to another. We might decide that the problem of misinterpreted family names was severe and allow two components of a name to be swapped at low cost, so `Chen Li` and `Li Chen` are at distance 1.

Once we have decided on the appropriate edit distance for each field, we can define a similarity measure for records. For example, we could sum the edit distances of each of the pairs of corresponding fields in the two records, or we could compute the sum of the squares of those distances. Whatever formula we use, we have then to say that records represent the same entity if their similarity measure is below a given threshold.

Normalization

Before applying an edit distance, we might wish to "normalize" records by replacing certain substrings by others. The goal is that substrings representing the same "thing" will become identical. For instance, it may make sense to use a table of abbreviations and replace abbreviations by what they normally stand for. Thus, `St.` would be replaced by `Street` in street addresses and by `Saint` in town names. Also, we could use a table of nicknames and variant spellings, so `Sue` would become `Susan` and `Jeffery` would become `Geoffrey`.

One could even use the *Soundex* encoding of names, so names that sound the same are represented by the same string. This system, used by telephone information services, for example, would represent `Smith` and `Smythe` identically. Once we have normalized values in the records, we could base our similarity test on identical values only (e.g., a majority of fields have identical values in the two records), or we could further use an edit distance to measure the difference between normalized values in the fields.

7.2 Merging Similar Records

In many applications, when we find two records that are similar enough to merge, we would like to replace them by a single record that, in some sense, contains the information of both. For instance, if we want to compile a "dossier" on the entity represented, we might take the union of all the values in each field. Or we might somehow combine the values in corresponding fields to make a single value. If we try to combine values, there are many rules that we might follow, with no obvious best approach. For example, we might assume that a full name should replace a nickname or initials, and a middle initial should be used in place of no middle initial. Thus, "Susan Williams" and "S. B. Williams" would be combined into "Susan B. Williams."

It is less clear how to deal with misspellings. For instance, how would we combine the addresses "123 Oak St." and "123 Yak St."? Perhaps we could look at the town or zip-code and determine that there was an Oak St. there and no Yak St. But if both existed and had 123 in their range of addresses, there is no right answer.

Another problem that arises if we use certain combinations of a similarity test and a merging rule is that our decision to merge one pair of records may preclude our merging another pair. An example may help illustrate the risk.

	name	*address*	*phone*
(1)	`Susan Williams`	`123 Oak St.`	`818-555-1234`
(2)	`Susan Williams`	`456 Maple St.`	`818-555-1234`
(3)	`Susan Williams`	`456 Maple St.`	`213-555-5678`

Figure 12: Three records to be merged

Example 22: Suppose that we have the three name-address-phone records in Fig. 12. and our similarity rule is: "must agree exactly in at least two out of the three fields." Suppose also that our merge rule is: "set the field in which the records disagree to the empty string."

Then records (1) and (2) are similar; so are records (2) and (3). Note that records (1) and (3) are not similar to each other, which serves to remind us that "similarity" is not normally a transitive relationship. If we decide to replace (1) and (2) by their merger, we are left with the two tuples:

	name	*address*	*phone*
(1-2)	Susan Williams		818-555-1234
(3)	Susan Williams	456 Maple St.	213-555-5678

These records disagree in two fields, so they cannot be merged. Had we merged (1) and (3) first, we would again have a situation where the remaining record cannot be merged with the result.

Another choice for similarity and merge rules is:

1. Merge by taking the union of the values in each field, and
2. Declare two records similar if at least two of the three fields have a nonempty intersection.

Consider the three records in Fig. 12. Again, (1) is similar to (2) and (2) is similar to (3), but (1) is not similar to (3). If we choose to merge (1) and (2) first, we get:

	name	*address*	*phone*
(1-2)	Susan Williams	{123 Oak St. 456 Maple St.}	818-555-1234
(3)	Susan Williams	456 Maple St.	213-555-5678

Now, the remaining two tuples are similar, because `456 Maple St.` is a member of both address sets and `Susan Williams` is a member of both name sets. The result is a single tuple:

	name	*address*	*phone*
(1-2-3)	Susan Williams	{123 Oak St., 456 Maple St.}	{818-555-1234, 213-555-5678}

□

7.3 Useful Properties of Similarity and Merge Functions

Any choice of similarity and merge functions allows us to test pairs of records for similarity and merge them if so. As we saw in the first part of Example 22, the result we get when no more records can be merged may depend on which pairs of mergeable records we consider first. Whether or not different ending configurations can result depends on properties of similarity and merger.

There are several properties that we would expect any merge function to satisfy. If $\wedge$ is the operation that produces the merge of two records, it is reasonable to expect:

1. $r \wedge r = r$ (*Idempotence*). That is, the merge of a record with itself should surely be that record.

2. $r \wedge s = s \wedge r$ (*Commutativity*). If we merge two records, the order in which we list them should not matter.

3. $(r \wedge s) \wedge t = r \wedge (s \wedge t)$ (*Associativity*). The order in which we group records for a merger should not matter.

These three properties say that the merge operation is a semilattice. Note that both merger functions in Example 22 have these properties. The only tricky point is that we must remember that $r \wedge s$ need not defined for all records r and s. We do, however, assume that:

- If r and s are similar, then $r \wedge s$ is defined.

There are also some properties that we expect the similarity relationship to have, and ways that we expect similarity and merging to interact. We shall use $r \approx s$ to say that records r and s are similar.

a) $r \approx r$ (*Idempotence* for similarity). A record is always similar to itself.

b) $r \approx s$ if and only if $s \approx r$ (*Commutativity* of similarity). That is, in deciding whether two records are similar, it does not matter in which order we list them.

c) If $r \approx s$, then $r \approx (s \wedge t)$ (*Representability*). This rule requires that if r is similar to some other record s (and thus could be merged with s), but s is instead merged with some other record t, then r remains similar to the merger of s and t and can be merged with that record.

Note that representability is the property most likely to fail. In particular, it fails for the first merger rule in Example 22, where we merge by setting disagreeing fields to the empty string. In particular, representability fails when r is record (3) of Fig. 12, s is (2), and t is (1). On the other hand, the second merger rule of Example 22 satisfies the representability rule. If r and s have nonempty intersections in at least two fields, those shared values will still be present if we replace s by $s \wedge t$.

The collection of properties above are called the *ICAR properties.* The letters stand for Idempotence, Commutativity, Associativity, and Representability, respectively.

7.4 The R-Swoosh Algorithm for ICAR Records

When the similarity and merge functions satisfy the ICAR properties, there is a simple algorithm that merges all possible records. The representability property guarantees that if two records are similar, then as they are merged with other records, the resulting records are also similar and will eventually be merged. Thus, if we repeatedly replace any pair of similar records by their merger, until no more pairs of similar records remain, then we reach a unique set of records that is independent of the order in which we merge.

A useful way to think of the merger process is to imagine a graph whose nodes are the records. There is an edge between nodes r and s if $r \approx s$. Since similarity need not be transitive, it is possible that there are edges between r and s and between s and t, yet there is no edge between r and t. For instance, the records of Fig. 12 have the graph of Fig. 13.

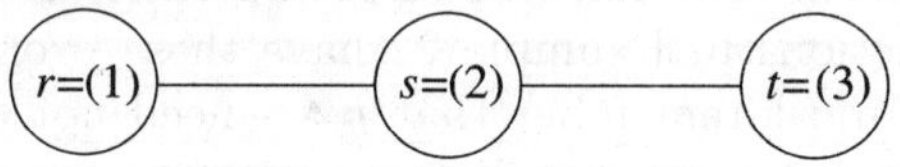

Figure 13: Similarity graph from Fig. 12

However, representability tells us that if we merge s and t, then because r is similar to s, it will be similar to $s \wedge t$. Thus, we can merge all three of r, s, and t. Likewise, if we merge r and s first, representability says that because $s \approx t$, we also have $(r \wedge s) \approx t$, so we can merge t with $r \wedge s$. Associativity tells us that the resulting record will be the same, regardless of the order in which we do the merge.

The idea described above extends to any set of ICAR nodes (records) that are connected in any way. That is, regardless of the order in which we do the merges, the result is that every connected component of the graph becomes a single record. This record is the merger of all the records in that component. Commutativity and associativity are enough to tell us that the order in which we perform the mergers does not matter.

Although computing connected components of a graph is simple in principle, when we have millions of records or more, it is not feasible to construct the graph. To do so would require us to test similarity of every pair of records. The "R-Swoosh" algorithm is an implementation of this idea that organizes the comparisons so we avoid, in many cases, comparing all pairs of records. Unfortunately, if no records at all are similar, then there is no algorithm that can avoid comparing all pairs of records to determine this fact.

Algorithm 23: R-Swoosh.

INPUT: A set of records I, a similarity function $\approx$, and a merge function $\wedge$. We assume that $\approx$ and $\wedge$ satisfy the ICAR properties. If they do not, then the algorithm will still merge some records, but the result may not be the maximum or best possible merging.

OUTPUT: A set of merged records O.

METHOD: Execute the steps of Fig. 14. The value of O at the end is the output. □

```
O := emptyset;
WHILE I is not empty DO BEGIN
    let r be any record in I;
    find, if possible, some record s in O that is similar to r;
    IF no record s exists THEN
        move r from I to O
    ELSE BEGIN
        delete r from I;
        delete s from O;
        add the merger of r and s to I;
    END;
END;
```

Figure 14: The R-Swoosh Algorithm

Example 24: Suppose that I is the three records of Fig. 12, and that we use the ICAR similarity and merge functions from Example 22, where we take the union of possible values for a field to produce the corresponding field in the merged record. Initially, O is empty. We pick one of the records from I, say record (1) to be the record r in Fig. 14. Since O is empty, there is no possible record s, so we move record (1) from I to O.

We next pick a new record r. Suppose we pick record (3). Since record (3) is not similar to record (1), which is the only record in O, we again have no value of s, so we move record (3) from I to O. The third choice of r must be record (2). That record is similar to both of the records in O, so we must pick one to be s; say we pick record (1). Then we merge records (1) and (2) to get the record

	name	*address*	*phone*
(1-2)	Susan Williams	{123 Oak St., 456 Maple St.}	818-555-1234

We remove record (2) from I, remove record (1) from O, and insert the above record into I. At this point, I consists of only the record (1-2) and O consists of only the record (3).

The execution of the R-Swoosh Algorithm ends after we pick record (1-2) as r — the only choice — and pick record (3) as s — again the only choice. These records are merged, to produce

	name	*address*	*phone*
(1-2-3)	Susan Williams	{123 Oak St., 456 Maple St.}	{818-555-1234, 213-555-5678}

and deleted from I and O, respectively. The record (1-2-3) is put in I, at which point it is the only record in I, and O is empty. At the last step, this record is moved from I to O, and we are done. □

7.5 Why R-Swoosh Works

Recall that for ICAR similarity and merge functions, the goal is to merge records that form connected components. There is a loop invariant that holds for the while-loop of Fig. 14:

- If a connected component C is not completely merged into one record, then there is at least one record in I that is either in C or was formed by the merger of some records from C.

To see why this invariant must hold, suppose that the selected record r in some iteration of the loop is the last record in I from its connected component C. If r is the only record that is the merger of one or more records from C, then it may be moved to O without violating the loop invariant.

However, if there are other records that are the merger of one or more records from C, they are in O. Let r be the merger of the set of records $R \subseteq C$. Note that R could be only one record, or could be many records. However, since R is not all of C, there must be an original record r_1 in R that is similar to another original record r_2 that is in $C - R$. Suppose r_2 is currently merged into a record r' in O. By representability, perhaps applied several times, we can start with the known $r_1 \approx r_2$ and deduce that $r \approx r'$. Thus, r' can be s in Fig. 14. As a result, r will surely be merged with some record from O. The resulting merged record will be placed in I and is the merger of some or all records from C. Thus, the loop invariant continues to hold.

7.6 Other Approaches to Entity Resolution

There are many other algorithms known to discover and (optionally) merge similar records. We shall outline some of them briefly here.

Non-ICAR Datasets

First, suppose the ICAR properties do not hold, but we want to find all possible mergers of records, including cases where one record r_1 is merged with a record r_2, but later, r_1 (not the merger $r_1 \wedge r_2$) is also merged with r_3. If so, we need to systematically compare all records, including those we constructed by merger, with all other records, again including those constructed by merger.

To help control the proliferation of records, we can define a *dominance* relation $r \leq s$ that means record s contains all the information contained in record r. If so, we can eliminate record r from further consideration. If the merge function is a semilattice, then the only reasonable choice for $\leq$ is $a \leq b$ if and only if $a \wedge b = b$. This dominance function is always a partial order, regardless of what semilattice is used. If the merge operation is not even a semilattice, then the dominance function must be constructed in an ad-hoc manner.

Clustering

In some entity-resolution applications, we do not want to merge at all, but will instead group records into *clusters* such that members of a cluster are in some sense similar to each other and members of different clusters are not similar. For example, if we are looking for similar products sold on eBay, we might want the result to be not a single record for each kind of product, but rather a list of the records that represent a common product for sale. Clustering of large-scale data involves a complex set of options.

Partitioning

Since any algorithm for doing a complete merger of similar records may be forced to examine each pair of records, it may be infeasible to get an exact answer to a large entity-resolution problem. One solution is to group the records, perhaps several times, into groups that are likely to contain similar records, and look only within each group for pairs of similar records.

Example 25: Suppose we have millions of name-address-phone records, and our measure of similarity is that the total edit distance of the values in the three fields must be at most 5. We could partition the records into groups such that each group has the same name field. We could also partition the records according to the value in their address field, and a third time according to their phone numbers. Thus, each record appears in three groups and is compared only with the members of those groups. This method will not notice a pair of similar records that have edit distance 2 in their phone fields, 2 in their name fields, and 1 in their address fields. However, in practice, it will catch almost all similar pairs. □

The idea in Example 25 is actually a special case of an important idea: "locality-sensitive hashing."

7.7 Exercises for Section 7

Exercise 7.1: A string s is a *subsequence* of a string t if s is formed from t by deleting 0 or more positions of t. For example, if $t =$ `"abcab"`, then substrings of t include `"aba"` (delete positions 3 and 5), `"bc"` (delete positions 1, 4, and 5), and the empty string (delete all positions).

a) What are all the other subsequences of `"abcab"`?

b) What are the subsequences of `"aabb"`?

! c) If a string consists of n distinct characters, how many subsequences does it have?

Exercise 7.2: A *longest common subsequence* of two strings s and t is any string r that is a subsequence of both s and t and is as long as any other string that is a substring of both. For example, the longest common subsequences of "aba" and "bab" are "ab" and "ba". Give a the longest common subsequence for each pair of the following strings: "she", "hers", "they", and "theirs"?

Exercise 7.3: A *shortest common supersequence* of two strings s and t is any string r of which both s and t are subsequences, such that no string shorter than r has both s and t as subsequences. For example, the some of the shortest common supersequences of "abc" and "cb" are "abcb" and "acbc".

a) What are the shortest common supersequences of each pair of strings in Exercise 7.2?

! b) What are all the other shortest common supersequences of "abc" and "cb"?

!! c) If two strings have no characters in common, and are of lengths m and n, respectively, how many shortest common supersequences do the two strings have?

!! **Exercise 7.4:** Suppose we merge records (whose fields are strings) by taking, for each field, the lexicographically first longest common subsequence of the strings in the corresponding fields.

a) Does this definition of merge satisfy the idempotent, commutative, and associative laws?

b) Repeat (a) if instead corresponding fields are merged by taking the lexicographically first shortest common supersequence.

! **Exercise 7.5:** Suppose we define the similarity and merge functions by:

i. Records are similar if in all fields, or in all but one field, either both records have the same value or one has NULL.

ii. Merge records by letting each field have the common value if both records agree in that field or have value NULL if the records disagree in that field. Note that NULL disagrees with any nonnull value.

Show that these similarity and merge functions have the ICAR properties.

! **Exercise 7.6:** In Section 7.6 we suggested that if $\wedge$ is a semilattice, then the dominance relationship defined by $a \leq b$ if and only if $a \wedge b = b$ is a partial order. That is, $a \leq b$ and $b \leq c$ imply $a \leq c$ (transitivity) and $a \leq b$ and $b \leq a$ if and only if $a = b$ (antisymmetry). Prove that $\leq$ is a partial order, using the reflexivity, commutativity, and associativity properties of a semilattice.

8 Summary

- *Integration of Information*: When many databases or other information sources contain related information, we have the opportunity to combine these sources into one. However, heterogeneities in the schemas often exist; these incompatibilities include differing types, codes or conventions for values, interpretations of concepts, and different sets of concepts represented in different schemas.

- *Approaches to Information Integration*: Early approaches involved "federation," where each database would query the others in the terms understood by the second. A more recent approach is warehousing, where data is translated to a global schema and copied to the warehouse. An alternative is mediation, where a virtual warehouse is created to allow queries to a global schema; the queries are then translated to the terms of the data sources.

- *Extractors and Wrappers*: Warehousing and mediation require components at each source, called extractors and wrappers, respectively. A major function of either is to translate queries and results between the global schema and the local schema at the source.

- *Wrapper Generators*: One approach to designing wrappers is to use templates, which describe how a query of a specific form is translated from the global schema to the local schema. These templates are tabulated and interpreted by a driver that tries to match queries to templates. The driver may also have the ability to combine templates in various ways, and/or perform additional work such as filtering, to answer more complex queries.

- *Capability-Based Optimization*: The sources for a mediator often are able or willing to answer only limited forms of queries. Thus, the mediator must select a query plan based on the capabilities of its sources, before it can even think about optimizing the cost of query plans as conventional DBMS's do.

- *Adornments*: These provide a convenient notation in which to describe the capabilities of sources. Each adornment tells, for each attribute of a relation, whether, in queries matching that adornment, this attribute requires or permits a contant value, and whether constants must be chosen from a menu.

- *Conjunctive Queries*: A single Datalog rule, used as a query, is a convenient representation for queries involving joins, possibly followed by selection and/or projection.

- *The Chain Algorithm*: This algorithm is a greedy approach to answering mediator queries that are in the form of a conjunctive query. Repeatedly look for a subgoal that matches one of the adornments at a source, and obtain the relation for that subgoal from the source. Doing so may provide a set of constant bindings for some variables of the query, so repeat the process, looking for additional subgoals that can be resolved.

- *Local-as-View Mediators*: These mediators have a set of global, virtual predicates or relations at the mediator, and each source is described by views, which are conjunctive queries whose subgoals use the global predicates. A query at the mediator is also a conjunctive query using the global predicates.

- *Answering Queries Using Views*: A local-as-view mediator searches for solutions to a query, which are conjunctive queries whose subgoals use the views as predicates. Each such subgoal of a proposed solution is expanded using the conjunctive query that defines the view, and it is checked that the expansion is contained in the query. If so, the proposed solution does indeed provide (some of the) answers to the query.

- *Containment of Conjunctive Queries*: We test for containment of conjunctive queries by looking for a containment mapping from the containing query to the contained query. A containment mapping is a substitution for variables that turns the head of the first into the head of the second and turns each subgoal of the first into some subgoal of the second.

- *Limiting the Search for Solutions*: The LMSS Theorem says that when seaching for solutions to a query at a local-as-view mediator, it is sufficient to consider solutions that have no more subgoals than the query does.

- *Entity Resolution*: The problem is to take records with a common schema, find pairs or groups of records that are likely to represent the same entity (e.g., a person) and merge these records into a single record that represents the information of the entire group.

- *ICAR Similarity and Merge Functions*: Certain choices of similarity and merge functions satisfy the properties of idempotence, commutativity, associativity, and representability. The latter is the key to efficient algorithms for merging, since it guarantees that if two records are similar, their successors will also be similar even as they are merged into records that represent progressively larger sets of original records.

- *The R-Swoosh Algorithm*: If similarity and merge functions have the ICAR properties, then the complete merger of similar records will group all records that are in a connected component of the graph formed from the similarity relation on the original records. The R-Swoosh algorithm is an efficient way to make all necessary mergers without determining similarity for every pair of records.

9 References

Federated systems are surveyed in [11]. The concept of the mediator comes from [12]. Implementation of mediators and wrappers, especially the wrapper-generator approach, is covered in [4]. Capability-based optimization for mediators was explored in [10, 13]; the latter describes the Chain Algorithm.

Local-as-view mediators come from [7]. The LMSS Theorem is from [6], and the idea of containment mappings to decide containment of conjunctive queries is from [2]. [8] extends the idea to sources with limited capabilities. [5] is a survey of logical information-integration techniques.

Entity resolution was first studied informally by [9] and formally by [3]. The theory presented here, the R-Swoosh Algorithm, and related algorithms are from [1].

1. O. Benjelloun, H. Garcia-Molina, J. Jonas, Q. Su, S. E. Whang, and J. Widom, "Swoosh: a generic approach to entity resolution." Available as `http://dbpubs.stanford.edu:8090/pub/2005-5`.

2. A. K. Chandra and P. M. Merlin, "Optimal implementation of conjunctive queries in relational databases," *Proc. Ninth Annual Symposium on Theory of Computing*, pp. 77–90, 1977.

3. I. P. Fellegi and A. B. Sunter, "A theory for record linkage," *J. American Statistical Assn.* **64**, pp. 1183–1210, 1969.

4. H. Garcia-Molina, Y. Papakonstantinou, D. Quass, A. Rajaraman, Y. Sagiv, V. Vassalos, J. D. Ullman, and J. Widom, "The TSIMMIS approach to mediation: data models and languages," *J. Intelligent Information Systems* **8**:2 (1997), pp. 117–132.

5. A. Y. Levy, "Logic-based techniques in data integration," *Logic-Based Artificial Intelligence* (J. Minker, ed.), pp. 575–595, Kluwer, Norwell, MA, 2000.

6. A. Y. Levy, A. O. Mendelzon, Y. Sagiv, and D. Srivastava, "Answering queries using views," *Proc. 25th Annual Symposium on Principles of Database Systems*, pp. 95–104, 1995.

7. A. Y. Levy, A. Rajaraman, and J. J. Ordille, "Querying heterogeneous information sources using source descriptions," *Intl. Conf. on Very Large Databases*, pp. 251–262, 1996.

8. A. Y. Levy, A. Rajaraman, and J. D. Ullman, "Answering queries using limited external query processors," *Proc. Fifteenth Annual Symposium on Principles of Database Systems*, pp. 227–237, 1996.

9. H. B. Newcombe, J. M. Kennedy, S. J. Axford, and A. P. James, "Automatic linkage of vital records," *Science* **130**, pp. 954–959, 1959.

10. Y. Papakonstantinou, A. Gupta, and L. Haas, "Capabilities-base query rewriting in mediator systems," *Conference on Parallel and Distributed Information Systems* (1996). Available as `http://dbpubs.stanford.edu/pub/1995-2`.

11. A. P. Sheth and J. A. Larson, "Federated databases for managing distributed, heterogeneous, and autonomous databases," *Computing Surveys* **22**:3 (1990), pp. 183–236.

12. G. Wiederhold, "Mediators in the architecture of future information systems," *IEEE Computer* **C-25**:1 (1992), pp. 38–49.

13. R. Yerneni, C. Li, H. Garcia-Molina, and J. D. Ullman, "Optimizing large joins in mediation systems," *Proc. Seventh Intl. Conf. on Database Theory*, pp. 348–364, 1999.

Database Systems and the Internet

The age of the World-Wide Web has had a profound effect on database technology. Conventional relational databases sit behind, and power, many of the most important Web applications. But Web applications have also forced databases to assume new forms. Often, massive databases are not found inside a relational DBMS, but in complex, ad-hoc file structures. One of the most important examples of this phenomenon is the way search engines manage their data. Thus, in this chapter we shall examine algorithms for crawling the Web and for answering search-engine queries.

Other sources of data are dynamic in nature. Rather than existing in a database, the data is a stream of information that must either be processed and stored as it arrives, or thrown away. One example is the click streams (sequence of URL requests) received at major Web sites. Non-Web-related streams of data also exist, such as the "call-detail records" generated by all the telephone calls traveling through a network, and data generated by satellites and networks of sensors. Thus, the second part of this chapter addresses the stream data model and the technology needed to manage massive data in the form of streams.

1 The Architecture of a Search Engine

The search engine has become one of the most important tools of the 21st century. The repositories managed by the major search engines are among the largest databases on the planet, and surely no other database is accessed so frequently and by so many users. In this section, we shall examine the key components of a search engine, which are suggested schematically in Fig. 1.

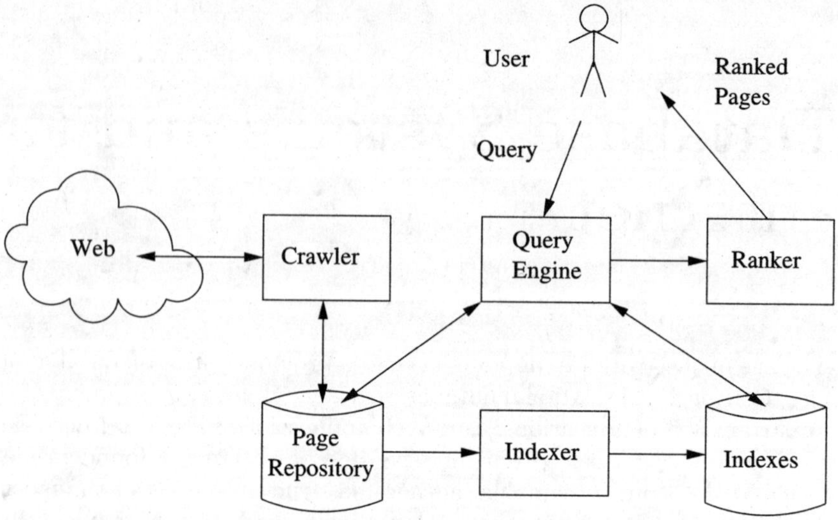

Figure 1: The components of a search engine

1.1 Components of a Search Engine

There are two main functions that a search engine must perform.

1. The Web must be *crawled.* That is, copies of many of the pages on the Web must be brought to the search engine and processed.

2. Queries must be answered, based on the material gathered from the Web. Usually, the query is in the form of a word or words that the desired Web pages should contain, and the answer to a query is a ranked list of the pages that contain all those words, or at least some of them.

Thus, in Fig. 1, we see the *crawler* interacting with the Web and with the *page repository*, a database of pages that the crawler has found. We shall discuss crawling in more detail in Section 1.2.

The pages in the page repository are indexed. Typically, these indexes are inverted indexes. That is, for each word, there is a list of the pages that contain that word. Additional information in the index for the word may include its location(s) within the page or its role, e.g., whether the word is in the header.

We also see in Fig. 1 a user issuing a query that consists of one or more words. A *query engine* takes those words and interacts with the indexes, to determine which pages satisfy the query. These pages are then ordered by a *ranker*, and presented to the user, typically 10 at a time, in ranked order. We shall have more to say about the query process in Section 1.3.

1.2 Web Crawlers

A crawler can be a single machine that is started with a set S, containing the URL's of one or more Web pages to crawl. There is a repository R of pages, with the URL's that have already been crawled; initially R is empty.

Algorithm 1: A Simple Web Crawler.

INPUT: An initial set of URL's S.

OUTPUT: A repository R of Web pages.

METHOD: Repeatedly, the crawler does the following steps.

1. If S is empty, end.
2. Select a page p from the set S to "crawl" and delete p from S.
3. Obtain a copy of p, using its URL. If p is already in repository R, return to step (1) to select another page.
4. If p is not already in R:
   (a) Add p to R.
   (b) Examine p for links to other pages. Insert into S the URL of each page q that p links to, but that is not already in R or S.
5. Go to step (1).

□

Algorithm 1 raises several questions.

a) How do we terminate the search if we do not want to search the entire Web?

b) How do we check efficiently whether a page is already in repository R?

c) How do we select a page p from S to search next?

d) How do we speed up the search, e.g., by exploiting parallelism?

Terminating Search

Even if we wanted to search the "entire Web," we must limit the search somehow. The reason is that some pages are generated dynamically, so when the crawler asks a site for a URL, the site itself constructs the page. Worse, that page may have URL's that also refer to dynamically constructed pages, and this process could go on forever.

As a consequence, it is generally necessary to cut off the search at some point. For example, we could put a limit on the number of pages to crawl, and stop when that limit is reached. The limit could be either on each site or on the total number of pages. Alternatively, we could limit the *depth* of the crawl. That is, say that the pages initially in set S have depth 1. If the page p selected for crawling at step (2) of Algorithm 1 has depth i, then any page q that we add to S at step (4b) is given depth $i+1$. However, if p has depth equal to the limit, then we do not examine links out of p at all. Rather we simply add p to R, if it is not already there.

Managing the Repository

There are two points where we must avoid duplication of effort. First, when we add a new URL for a page q to the set S, we should check that it is not already there or among the URL's of pages in R. There may be billions of URL's in R and/or S, so this job requires an efficient index structure.

Second, when we decide to add a new page p to R at step (4a) of Algorithm 1, we should be sure the page is not already there. How could it be, since we make sure to search each URL only once? Unfortunately, the same page can have several different URL's, so our crawler may indeed encounter the same page via different routes. Moreover, the Web contains mirror sites, where large collection of pages are duplicated, or nearly duplicated (e.g., each may have different internal links within the site, and each may refer to the other mirror sites). Comparing a page p with all the pages in R can be much too time-consuming. However, we can make this comparison efficient as follows:

1. If we only want to detect exact duplicates, hash each Web page to a signature of, say, 64 bits. The signatures themselves are stored in a hash table T; i.e., they are further hashed into a smaller number of buckets, say one million buckets. If we are considering inserting p into R, compute the 64-bit signature $h(p)$, and see whether $h(p)$ is already in the hash table T. If so, do not store p; otherwise, store p in R. Note that we could get some false positives; it could be that $h(p)$ is in T, yet some page other than p produced the same signature. However, by making signatures sufficiently long, we can reduce the probability of a false positive essentially to zero.

2. If we want to detect near duplicates of p, then we can store minhash signatures in place of the simple hash-signatures mentioned in (1). Further, we need to use locality-sensitive hashing in place of the simple hash table T of option (1).

Selecting the Next Page

We could use a completely random choice of next page. A better strategy is to manage S as a queue, and thus do a breadth-first search of the Web from the starting point or points with which we initialized S. Since we presumably start the search from places in the Web that have "important" pages, we thus are assured of visiting preferentially those portions of the Web that the authors of these "important" pages thought were also important.

An alternative is to try to estimate the importance of pages in the set S, and to favor those pages we estimate to be most important. We shall take up in Section 2 the idea of PageRank as a measure of the importance that the Web attributes to certain pages. It is impossible to compute PageRank exactly while the crawl is in progress. However, a simple approximation is to count the number of known in-links for each page in set S. That is, each time we examine a link to a page q at step (4b) of Algorithm 1, we add one to the count of in-links for q. Then, when selecting the next page p to crawl at step (2), we always pick one of the pages with the highest number of in-links.

Speeding Up the Crawl

We do not need to limit ourselves to one crawling machine, and we do not need to limit ourselves to one process per machine. Each process that acts on the set of available URL's (what we called S in Algorithm 1) must lock the set, so we do not find two processes obtaining the same URL to crawl, or two processes writing the same URL into the set at the same time. If there are so many processes that the lock on S becomes a bottleneck, there are several options.

We can assign processes to entire hosts or sites to be crawled, rather than to individual URL's. If so, a process does not have to access the set of URL's S so often, since it knows no other process will be accessing the same site while it does.

There is a disadvantage to this approach. A crawler gathering pages at a site can issue page requests at a very rapid rate. This behavior is essentially a denial-of-service attack, where the site can do no useful work while it strives to answer all the crawler's requests. Thus, a responsible crawler does not issue frequent requests to a single site; it might limit itself to one every several seconds. If a crawling process is visiting a single site, then it must slow down its rate of requests to the point that it is often idle. That in itself is not a problem, since we can run many crawling processes at a single machine. However, operating-system software has limits on how many processes can be alive at any time.

An alternative way to avoid bottlenecks is to partition the set S, say by hashing URL's into several buckets. Each process is assigned to select new URL's to crawl from a particular one of the buckets. When a process follows a link to find a new URL, it hashes that URL to determine which bucket it belongs in. That bucket is the only one that needs to be examined to see if the new URL is already there, and if it is not, that is the bucket into which the new URL is placed.

The same bottleneck issues that arise for the set S of active URL's also come up in managing the page repository R and its set of URL's. The same two techniques — assigning processes to sites or partitioning the set of URL's by hashing — serve to avoid bottlenecks in the accessing of R as well.

1.3 Query Processing in Search Engines

Search engine queries are not like SQL queries. Rather they are typically a set of words, for which the search engine must find and rank all pages containing all, or perhaps a subset of, those words. In some cases, the query can be a boolean combination of words, e.g., all pages that contain the word "data" or the word "base." Possibly, the query may require that two words appear consecutively, or appear near each other, say within 5 words.

Answering queries such as these requires the use of inverted indexes. Recall from our discussion of Fig. 1 that once the crawl is complete, the indexer constructs an inverted index for all the words on the Web. Note that there will be hundreds of millions of words, since any sequence of letters and digits surrounded by punctuation or whitespace is an indexable word. Thus, "words" on the Web include not only the words in any of the world's natural languages, but all misspellings of these words, error codes for all sorts of systems, acronyms, names, and jargon of many kinds.

The first step of query processing is to use the inverted index to determine those pages that contain the words in the query. To offer the user acceptable response time, this step must involve few, if any, disk accesses. Search engines today give responses in fractions of a second, an amount of time so small that it amounts to only a few disk-access times.

On the other hand, the vectors that represent occurrences of a single word have components for each of the pages indexed by the search engine, perhaps tens of billions of pages. Very rare words might be represented by listing their occurrences, but for common, or even reasonably rare words, it is more efficient to represent by a bit vector the pages in which they occur. The AND of bit vectors gives the pages containing both words, and the OR of bit vectors gives the pages containing one or both. To speed up the selection of pages, it is essential to keep as many vectors as possible in main memory, since we cannot afford disk accesses. Teams of machines may partition the job, say each managing the portion of bit vectors corresponding to a subset of the Web pages.

1.4 Ranking Pages

Once the set of pages that match the query is determined, these pages are ranked, and only the highest-ranked pages are shown to the user. The exact way that pages are ranked is a secret formula, as closely guarded by search engines as the formula for Coca Cola. One important component is the "PageRank," a measure of how important the Web itself believes the page to be. This measure is based on links to the page in question, but is significantly more complex than that. We discuss PageRank in detail in Section 2.

Some of the other measures of how likely a page is to be a relevant response to the query are fairly easy to reason out. The following is a list of typical components of a relevance measure for pages.

1. The presence of all the query words. While search engines will return

pages with only a proper subset of the query words, these pages are generally ranked lower than pages having all the words.

2. The presence of query words in important positions in the page. For example, we would expect that a query word appearing in a title of the page would indicate more strongly that the page was relevant to that word than its mere occurrence in the middle of a paragraph. Likewise, appearance of the word in a header cell of a table would be a more favorable indication than its appearance in a data cell of the same table.

3. Presence of several query words near each other would be a more favorable indication than if the words appeared in the page, but widely separated. For example, if the query consists of the words "sally" and "jones," we are probably looking for pages that mention a certain person. Many pages have lists of names in them. If "sally" and "jones" appear adjacent, or perhaps separated by a middle initial, then there is a better chance the page is about the person we want than if "sally" appeared, but nowhere near "jones." In that case, there are probably two different people, one with first name Sally, and the other with last name Jones.

4. Presence of the query words in or near the anchor text in links leading to the page in question. This insight was one of the two key ideas that made the Google search engine the standard for the field (the other is PageRank, to be discussed next). A page may lie about itself, by using words designed to make it appear to be a good answer to a query, but it is hard to make other people confirm your lie in their own pages.

2 PageRank for Identifying Important Pages

One of the key technological advances in search is the PageRank[1] algorithm for identifying the "importance" of Web pages. In this section, we shall explain how the algorithm works, and show how to compute PageRank for very large collections of Web pages.

2.1 The Intuition Behind PageRank

The insight that makes Google and other search engines able to return the "important" pages on a topic is that the Web itself points out the important pages. When you create a page, you tend to link that page to others that you think are important or valuable, rather than pages you think are useless. Of course others may differ in their opinions, but on balance, the more ways one can get to a page by following links, the more likely the page is to be important.

We can formalize this intuition by imagining a random walker on the Web. At each step, the random walker is at one particular page p and randomly

[1] After Larry Page, who first proposed the algorithm.

picks one of the pages that p links to. At the next step, the walker is at the chosen successor of p. The structure of the Web links determines the long-run probability that the walker is at each individual page. This probability is termed the *PageRank* of the page.

Intuitively, pages that a lot of other pages point to are more likely to be the location of the walker than pages with few in-links. But all in-links are not equal. It is better for a page to have a few links from pages that themselves are likely places for the walker to be than to have many links from pages that the walker visits infrequently or not at all. Thus, it is not sufficient to count the in-links to compute the PageRank. Rather, we must solve a recursive equation that formalizes the idea:

- A Web page is important if many important pages link to it.

2.2 Recursive Formulation of PageRank — First Try

To describe how the random walker moves, we can use the *transition matrix of the Web.* Number the pages $1, 2, \ldots, n$. The matrix $\mathbf{M}$, the transition matrix of the Web has element m_{ij} in row i and column j, where:

1. $m_{ij} = 1/r$ if page j has a link to page i, and there are a total of $r \geq 1$ pages that j links to.

2. $m_{ij} = 0$ otherwise.

If every page has at least one link out, then the transition matrix will be (*left*) *stochastic* — elements are nonnegative, and its columns each sum to exactly 1. If there are pages with no links out, then the column for that page will be all 0's, and the transition matrix is said to be *substochastic* (all columns sum to at most 1).

Example 2: As we all know, the Web has been growing exponentially, so if you extrapolate back to 1839, you find that the Web consisted of only three pages. Figure 2 shows what the Web looked like in 1839.

We have numbered the pages 1, 2, and 3, so the transition matrix for this graph is:

$$\mathbf{M} = \begin{bmatrix} 1/2 & 1/2 & 0 \\ 1/2 & 0 & 1 \\ 0 & 1/2 & 0 \end{bmatrix}$$

For example, node 3, the page for Microsoft, links only to node 2, the page for Amazon. Thus, in column 3, only row 2 is nonzero, and its value is 1 divided by the number of out-links of node 3, which is 1. As another example, node 1, Yahoo!, links to itself and to Amazon (node 2). Thus, in column 1, row 3 is 0, and rows 1 and 2 are each 1 divided by the number of out-links from node 1, i.e., 1/2. □

PageRank Combats Spam

Before Google and PageRank, search engines had a great deal of trouble recognizing important pages on the Web. It was common for unscrupulous Web sites ("spammers") to put bogus content on their pages, often in ways that could not be seen by users, but that search engines would see in the text of the page (e.g., by making the writing have the same color as the background). If Google had simply counted in-links to measure the importance of pages, then the spammers could have created massive numbers of other bogus pages that linked to the page they wanted the search engines to think was important. However, simply creating a page doesn't give it much PageRank, since truly important pages are unlikely to link to it. Thus, PageRank defeated the spammers of the day.

Interestingly, the war between spammers and search engines continues. The spammers eventually learned how to increase the PageRank of bogus pages, which led to techniques for combating new forms of spam, often called "link spam." We shall address link spam in Section 3.3.

Suppose y, a, and m represent the fractions of the time the random walker spends at the three pages of Fig. 2. Then multiplying the column-vector of these three values by $\mathbf{M}$ will not change their values. The reason is that, after a large number of moves, the walker's distribution of possible locations is the same at each step, regardless where the walker started. That is, the unknowns y, a, and m must satisfy:

$$\begin{bmatrix} y \\ a \\ m \end{bmatrix} = \begin{bmatrix} 1/2 & 1/2 & 0 \\ 1/2 & 0 & 1 \\ 0 & 1/2 & 0 \end{bmatrix} \begin{bmatrix} y \\ a \\ m \end{bmatrix}$$

Although there are three equations in three unknowns, you cannot solve these equations for more than the ratios of y, a, and m. That is, if $[y, a, m]$ is a solution to the equations, then $[cy, ca, cm]$ is also a solution, for any constant c. However, since y, a, and m form a probability distribution, we also know $y + a + m = 1$.

While we could solve the resulting equations without too much trouble, solving large numbers of simultaneous linear equations takes time $O(n^3)$, where n is the number of variables or equations. If n is in the billions, as it would be for the Web of today, it is utterly infeasible to solve for the distribution of the walker's location by Gaussian elimination or another direct solution method. However, we can get a good approximation by the method of *relaxation*, where we start with some estimate of the solution and repeatedly multiply the estimate by the matrix $\mathbf{M}$. As long as the columns of $\mathbf{M}$ each add up to 1, then the sum of the values of the variables will not change, and eventually they converge to

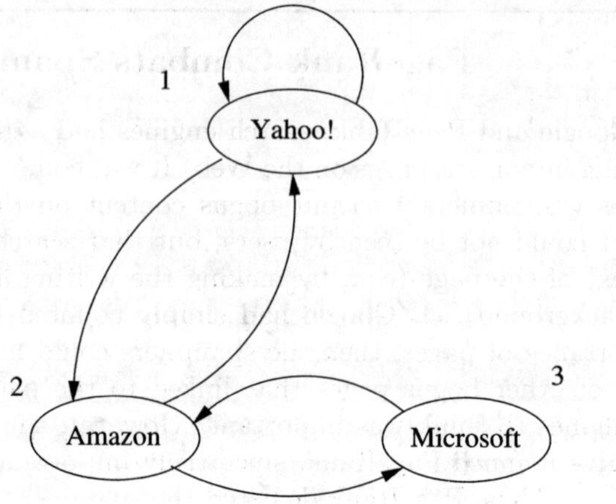

Figure 2: The Web in 1839

the distribution of the walker's location. In practice, 50 to 100 iterations of this process suffice to get very close to the exact solution.

Example 3: Suppose we start with $[y, a, m] = [1/3, 1/3, 1/3]$. Multiply this vector by $\mathbf{M}$ to get

$$\begin{bmatrix} 2/6 \\ 3/6 \\ 1/6 \end{bmatrix} = \begin{bmatrix} 1/2 & 1/2 & 0 \\ 1/2 & 0 & 1 \\ 0 & 1/2 & 0 \end{bmatrix} \begin{bmatrix} 1/3 \\ 1/3 \\ 1/3 \end{bmatrix}$$

At the next iteration, we multiply the new estimate [2/6,3/6,1/6] by $\mathbf{M}$, as:

$$\begin{bmatrix} 5/12 \\ 4/12 \\ 3/12 \end{bmatrix} = \begin{bmatrix} 1/2 & 1/2 & 0 \\ 1/2 & 0 & 1 \\ 0 & 1/2 & 0 \end{bmatrix} \begin{bmatrix} 2/6 \\ 3/6 \\ 1/6 \end{bmatrix}$$

If we repeat this process, we get the following sequence of vectors:

$$\begin{bmatrix} 9/24 \\ 11/24 \\ 4/24 \end{bmatrix}, \begin{bmatrix} 20/48 \\ 17/48 \\ 11/48 \end{bmatrix}, \ldots, \begin{bmatrix} 2/5 \\ 2/5 \\ 1/5 \end{bmatrix}$$

That is, asymptotically, the walker is equally likely to be at Yahoo! or Amazon, and only half as likely to be at Microsoft as either one of the other pages. □

2.3 Spider Traps and Dead Ends

The graph of Fig. 2 is atypical of the Web, not only because of its size, but for two structural reasons:

1. Some Web pages (called *dead ends*) have no out-links. If the random walker arrives at such a page, there is no place to go next, and the walk ends.

2. There are sets of Web pages (called *spider traps*) with the property that if you enter that set of pages, you can never leave, because there are no links from any page in the set to any page outside the set.

Any dead end is, by itself, a spider trap. However, one also finds on the Web spider traps all of whose pages have out-links. For example, any page that links only to itself is a spider trap.

If a spider trap can be reached from outside, then the random walker may wind up there eventually, and never leave. Put another way, applying relaxation to the matrix of the Web with spider traps can result in a limiting distribution where all probabilities outside a spider trap are 0.

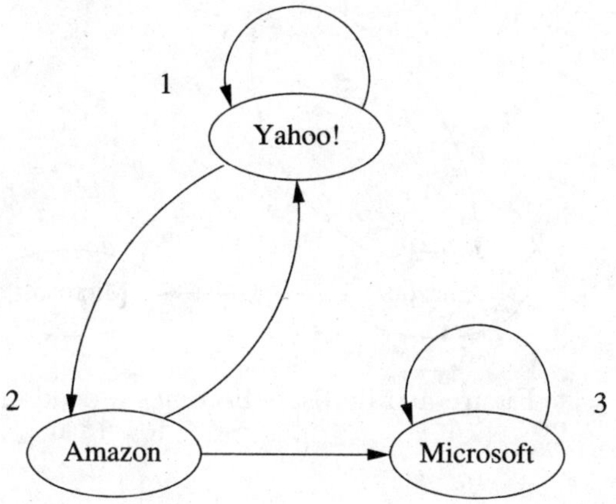

Figure 3: The Web, if Microsoft becomes a spider trap

Example 4: Suppose Microsoft decides to link only to itself, rather than Amazon, resulting in the Web of Fig. 3. Then the set of pages consisting of Microsoft alone is a spider trap, and that trap can be reached from either of the other pages. The matrix **M** for this Web graph is

$$\mathbf{M} = \begin{bmatrix} 1/2 & 1/2 & 0 \\ 1/2 & 0 & 0 \\ 0 & 1/2 & 1 \end{bmatrix}$$

Here is the sequence of approximate distributions that is obtained if we start, as we did in Example 3, with $[y, a, m] = [1/3, 1/3, 1/3]$ and repeatedly multiply by the matrix **M** for Fig. 3:

$$\begin{bmatrix} 1/3 \\ 1/3 \\ 1/3 \end{bmatrix}, \begin{bmatrix} 2/6 \\ 1/6 \\ 3/6 \end{bmatrix}, \begin{bmatrix} 3/12 \\ 2/12 \\ 7/12 \end{bmatrix}, \begin{bmatrix} 5/24 \\ 3/24 \\ 16/24 \end{bmatrix}, \begin{bmatrix} 8/48 \\ 5/48 \\ 35/48 \end{bmatrix}, \ldots, \begin{bmatrix} 0 \\ 0 \\ 1 \end{bmatrix}$$

That is, with probability 1, the walker will eventually wind up at the Microsoft page and stay there. □

If we interpret these PageRank probabilities as "importance" of pages, then the Microsoft page has gathered all importance to itself simply by choosing not to link outside. That situation intuitively violates the principle that other pages, not you yourself, should determine your importance on the Web. The other problem we mentioned — dead ends — also cause the PageRank not to reflect importance of pages, as we shall see in the next example.

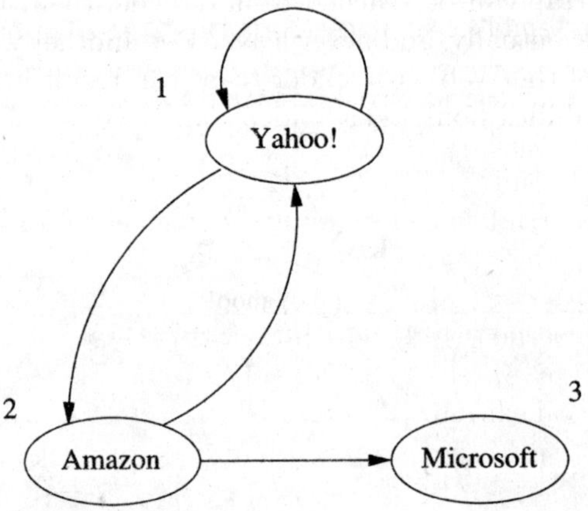

Figure 4: Microsoft becomes a dead end

Example 5: Suppose that instead of linking to itself, Microsoft links nowhere, as suggested in Fig. 4. The matrix **M** for this Web graph is

$$\mathbf{M} = \begin{bmatrix} 1/2 & 1/2 & 0 \\ 1/2 & 0 & 0 \\ 0 & 1/2 & 0 \end{bmatrix}$$

Notice that this matrix is not stochastic, because its columns do not all add up to 1. If we try to apply the method of relaxation to this matrix, with initial vector $[1/3, 1/3, 1/3]$, we get the sequence:

$$\begin{bmatrix} 1/3 \\ 1/3 \\ 1/3 \end{bmatrix}, \begin{bmatrix} 2/6 \\ 1/6 \\ 1/6 \end{bmatrix}, \begin{bmatrix} 3/12 \\ 2/12 \\ 1/12 \end{bmatrix}, \begin{bmatrix} 5/24 \\ 3/24 \\ 2/24 \end{bmatrix}, \begin{bmatrix} 8/48 \\ 5/48 \\ 3/48 \end{bmatrix}, \ldots, \begin{bmatrix} 0 \\ 0 \\ 0 \end{bmatrix}$$

That is, the walker will eventually arrive at Microsoft, and at the next step has nowhere to go. Eventually, the walker disappears. □

2.4 PageRank Accounting for Spider Traps and Dead Ends

The solution to both spider traps and dead ends is to limit the time the random walker is allowed to wander at random. We pick a constant $\beta < 1$, typically in the range 0.8 to 0.9, and at each step, we let the walker follow a random out-link, if there is one, with probability β. With probability $1 - \beta$ (called the *taxation rate*), we remove that walker and deposit a new walker at a randomly chosen Web page. This modification solves both problems.

- If the walker gets stuck in a spider trap, it doesn't matter, because after a few time steps, that walker will disappear and be replaced by a new walker.

- If the walker reaches a dead end and disappears, a new walker will take over shortly.

Example 6: Let us use $\beta = 0.8$ and reformulate the calculation of PageRank for the Web of Fig. 3. If $\mathbf{p}_{new}$ and $\mathbf{p}_{old}$ are the new and old distributions of the location of the walker after one iteration, the relationship between these two can be expressed as:

$$\mathbf{p}_{new} = 0.8 \begin{bmatrix} 1/2 & 1/2 & 0 \\ 1/2 & 0 & 0 \\ 0 & 1/2 & 1 \end{bmatrix} \mathbf{p}_{old} + 0.2 \begin{bmatrix} 1/3 \\ 1/3 \\ 1/3 \end{bmatrix}$$

That is, with probability 0.8, we multiply $\mathbf{p}_{old}$ by the matrix of the Web to get the new location of the walker, and with probability 0.2 we start with a new walker at a random place. If we start with $\mathbf{p}_{old} = [1/3, 1/3, 1/3]$ and repeatedly compute $\mathbf{p}_{new}$ and then replace $\mathbf{p}_{old}$ by $\mathbf{p}_{new}$, we get the following sequence of approximations to the asymptotic distribution of the walker:

$$\begin{bmatrix} .333 \\ .333 \\ .333 \end{bmatrix}, \begin{bmatrix} .333 \\ .200 \\ .467 \end{bmatrix}, \begin{bmatrix} .280 \\ .200 \\ .520 \end{bmatrix}, \begin{bmatrix} .259 \\ .179 \\ .563 \end{bmatrix}, \ldots, \begin{bmatrix} 7/33 \\ 5/33 \\ 21/33 \end{bmatrix}$$

Notice that Microsoft, because it is a spider trap, gets a large share of the importance. However, the effect of the spider trap has been mitigated considerably by the policy of redistributing the walker with probability 0.2. □

The same idea fixes dead ends as well as spider traps. The resulting matrix that describes transitions is substochastic, since a column will sum to 0 if there are no out-links. Thus, there will be a small probability that the walker is "nowhere" at any given time. That is, the sums of the probabilities of the walker being at each of the pages will be less than one. However, the relative sizes of the probabilities will still be a good measure of the importance of the page.

Teleportation of Walkers

Another view of the random-walking process is that there are no "new" walkers, but rather the walker *teleports* to a random page with probability $1-\beta$. For this view to make sense, we have to assume that if the walker is at a dead end, then the probability of teleport is 100%. Equivalently, we can scale up the probabilities to sum to one at each step of the iteration. Doing so does not affect the ratios of the probabilities, and therefore the relative PageRank of pages remains the same. For instance, in Example 7, the final pageRank vector would be $[35/81, 25/81, 21/81]$.

Example 7: Let us reconsider Example 5, using $\beta = 0.8$. The formula for iteration is now:

$$\mathbf{p}_{new} = 0.8 \begin{bmatrix} 1/2 & 1/2 & 0 \\ 1/2 & 0 & 0 \\ 0 & 1/2 & 0 \end{bmatrix} \mathbf{p}_{old} + 0.2 \begin{bmatrix} 1/3 \\ 1/3 \\ 1/3 \end{bmatrix}$$

Starting with $\mathbf{p}_{old} = [1/3, 1/3, 1/3]$, we get the following sequence of approximations to the asymptotic distribution of the walker:

$$\begin{bmatrix} .333 \\ .333 \\ .333 \end{bmatrix}, \begin{bmatrix} .333 \\ .200 \\ .200 \end{bmatrix}, \begin{bmatrix} .280 \\ .200 \\ .147 \end{bmatrix}, \begin{bmatrix} .259 \\ .179 \\ .147 \end{bmatrix}, \ldots, \begin{bmatrix} 35/165 \\ 25/165 \\ 21/165 \end{bmatrix}$$

Notice that these probabilities do not sum to one, and there is slightly more than 50% probability that the walker is "lost" at any given time. However, the ratio of the importances of Yahoo!, and Amazon are the same as in Example 6. That makes sense, because in neither Fig. 3 nor Fig. 4 are there links from the Microsoft page to influence the importance of Yahoo! or Amazon. □

2.5 Exercises for Section 2

Exercise 2.1: Compute the PageRank of the four nodes in Fig. 5, assuming no "taxation."

Exercise 2.2: Compute the PageRank of the four nodes in Fig. 5, assuming a taxation rate of: (a) 10% (b) 20%.

Exercise 2.3: Repeat Exercise 2.2 for the Web graph of

i. Fig. 6.

ii. Fig. 7.

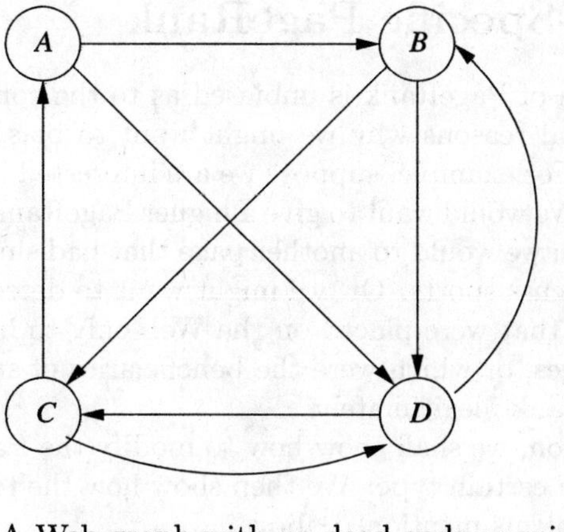

Figure 5: A Web graph with no dead-ends or spider traps

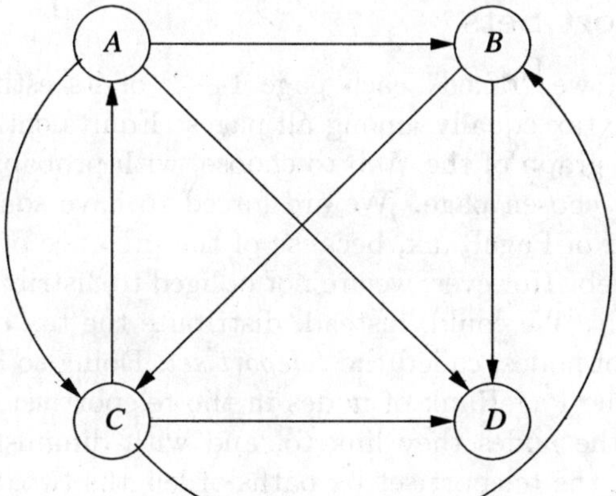

Figure 6: A Web graph with a dead end

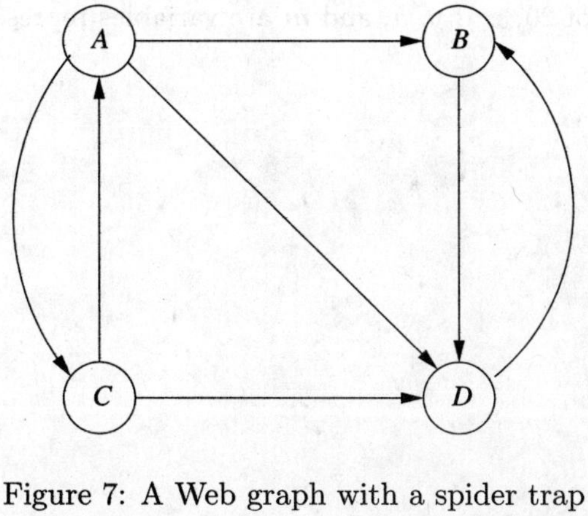

Figure 7: A Web graph with a spider trap

3 Topic-Specific PageRank

The calculation of PageRank is unbiased as to the content of pages. However, there are several reasons why we might want to bias the calculation to favor certain pages. For example, suppose we are interested in answering queries only about sports. We would want to give a higher PageRank to a page that discusses some sport than we would to another page that had similar links from the Web, but did not discuss sports. Or, we might want to detect and eliminate "spam" pages — those that were placed on the Web only to increase the PageRank of some other pages, or which were the beneficiaries of such planned attempts to increase PageRank illegitimately.

In this section, we shall show how to modify the PageRank computation to favor pages of a certain type. We then show how the technique yields solutions to the two problems mentioned above.

3.1 Teleport Sets

In Section 2.4, we "taxed" each page $1 - \beta$ of its estimated PageRank and distributed the tax equally among all pages. Equivalently, we allowed random walkers on the graph of the Web to choose, with probability $1 - \beta$, to teleport to a randomly chosen page. We are forced to have some taxation scheme in any calculation of PageRank, because of the presence of dead-ends and spider traps on the Web. However, we are not obliged to distribute the tax (or random walkers) equally. We could, instead, distribute the tax or walkers only among a selected set of nodes, called the *teleport set.* Doing so has the effect not only of increasing the PageRank of nodes in the teleport set, but of increasing the PageRank of the nodes they link to, and with diminishing effect, the nodes reachable from the teleport set by paths of lengths two, three, and so on.

Example 8: Let us reconsider the original Web graph of Fig. 2, which we reproduce here as Fig. 8. Assume we are interested only in retail sales, so we chose a teleport set that consists of Amazon alone. We shall use $\beta = 0.8$, i.e., a taxation rate of 20%. If y, a, and m are variables representing the PageRanks

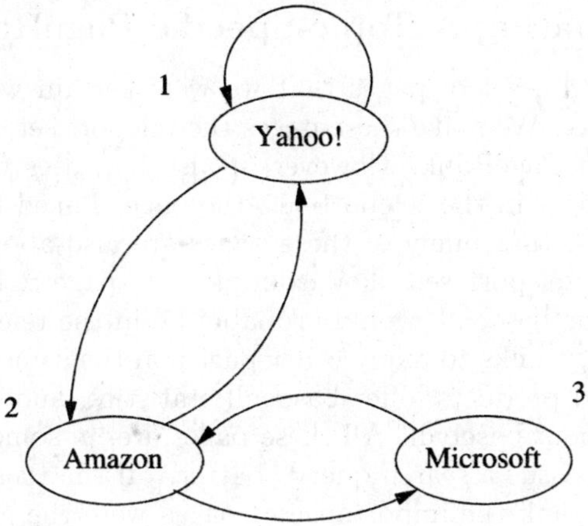

Figure 8: Web graph for Example 8

of Yahoo!, Amazon, and Microsoft, respectively, then the equations we need to solve are:

$$\begin{bmatrix} y \\ a \\ m \end{bmatrix} = 0.8 \begin{bmatrix} 1/2 & 1/2 & 0 \\ 1/2 & 0 & 1 \\ 0 & 1/2 & 0 \end{bmatrix} \begin{bmatrix} y \\ a \\ m \end{bmatrix} + 0.2 \begin{bmatrix} 0 \\ 1 \\ 0 \end{bmatrix}$$

The vector $[0, 1, 0]$ added at the end represents the fact that all the tax is distributed equally among the members of the teleport set. In this case, there is only one member of the teleport set, so the vector has 1 for that member (Amazon) and 0's elsewhere. We can solve the equations by relaxation, as we have done before. However, the example is small enough to apply Gaussian elimination and get the exact solution; it is $y = 10/31$, $a = 15/31$, and $m = 6/31$. The expected thing has happened; the PageRank of Amazon is elevated, because it is a member of the teleport set. □

The general rule for setting up the equations in a topic-specific PageRank problem is as follows. Suppose there are k pages in the teleport set. Let $\mathbf{t}$ be a column-vector that has $1/k$ in the positions corresponding to members of the teleport set and 0 elsewhere. Let $1 - \beta$ be the taxation rate, and let $\mathbf{M}$ be the transition matrix of the Web. Then we must solve by relaxation the following iterative rule:

$$\mathbf{p}_{new} = \beta \mathbf{M} \mathbf{p}_{old} + (1 - \beta)\mathbf{t}$$

Example 8 was an illustration of this process, although we set both $\mathbf{p}_{new}$ and $\mathbf{p}_{old}$ to $[y, a, m]$ and solved for the fixedpoint of the equations, rather than iterating to converge to the solution.

3.2 Calculating A Topic-Specific PageRank

Suppose we had a set of pages that we were certain were about a particular topic, say sports. We make these pages the teleport set, which has the effect of increasing their PageRank. However, it also increases the PageRank of pages linked to by pages in the teleport set, the pages linked to by those pages, and so on. We hope that many of these pages are also about sports, even if they are not in the teleport set. For example, the page `mlb.com`, the home page for major-league baseball, would probably be in the teleport set for the sports topic. That page links to many other pages on the same site — pages that sell baseball-related products, offer baseball statistics, and so on. It also links to news stories about baseball. All these pages are, in some sense, about sports.

Suppose we issue a search query "batter." If the PageRank that the search engine uses to rank the importance of pages were the general PageRank (i.e., the version where all pages are in the teleport set), then we would expect to find pages about baseball batters, but also cupcake recipes. If we used the PageRank that is specific to sports, i.e., one where only sports pages are in the teleport set, then we would expect to find, among the top-ranked pages, nothing about cupcakes, but only pages about baseball or cricket.

It is not hard to reason that the home page for a major-league sport will be a good page to use in the teleport set for sports. However, we might want to be sure we got a good sample of pages that were about sports into our teleport set, including pages we might not think of, even if we were an expert on the subject. For example, starting at major-league baseball might not get us to pages for the Springfield Little League, even though parents in Springfield would want that page in response to a search involving the words "baseball" and "Springfield." To get a larger and wider selection of pages on sports to serve as our teleport set, some approaches are:

1. Start with a curated selection of pages. For example, the Open Directory (`www.dmoz.org`) has human-selected pages on sixteen topics, including sports, as well as many subtopics.

2. Learn the keywords that appear, with unusually high frequency, in a small set of pages on a topic. For instance if the topic were sports, we would expect words like "ball," "player," and "goal" to be among the selected keywords. Then, examine the entire Web, or a larger subset thereof, to identify other pages that also have unusually high concentrations of some of these keywords.

The next problem we have to solve, in order to use a topic-specific PageRank effectively, is determining which topic the user is interested in. Several possibilities exist.

a) The easiest way is to ask the user to select a topic.

b) If we have keywords associated with different topics, as described in (2) above, we can try to discover the likely topic on the user's mind. We can examine pages that we think are important to the user, and find, in these pages, the frequency of keywords that are associated with each of the topics. Topics whose keywords occur frequently in the pages of interest are assumed to be the preference(s) of the user. To find these "pages of interest," we might:

i. Look at the pages the user has bookmarked.

ii. Look at the pages the user has recently searched.

3.3 Link Spam

Another application of topic-specific PageRank is in combating "link spam." Because it is known that many search engines use PageRank as part of the formula to rank pages by importance, it has become financially advantageous to invest in mechanisms to increase the PageRank of your pages. This observation spawned an industry: *spam farming.* Unscrupulous individuals create networks of millions of Web pages, whose sole purpose is to accumulate and concentrate PageRank on a few pages.

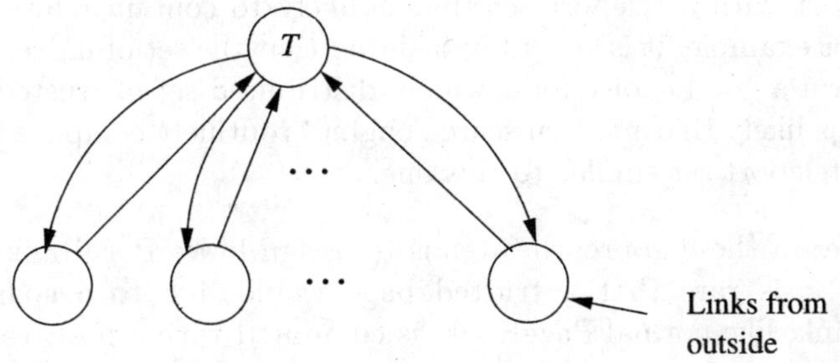

Figure 9: A spam farm concentrates PageRank in page T

A simple structure that accumulates PageRank in a target page T is shown in Fig. 9. Suppose that, in a PageRank calculation with taxation $1 - \beta$, the pages shown in the bottom row of Fig. 9 get, from the outside, a total PageRank of r, and let the total PageRank of these pages be x. Also, let the PageRank of page T be t. Then, in the limit, $t = \beta x$, because T gets all the PageRank of the other pages, except for the tax. Also, $x = r + \beta t$, because the other pages collectively get r from the outside and a total of βt from T. If we solve these equations for t, we get $t = \beta r/(1 - \beta^2)$. For instance, if $\beta = .85$, then we have amplified the external PageRank by factor $0.85/\big(1-(0.85)^2\big) = 3.06$. Moreover, we have concentrated this PageRank in a single page, T.

Of course, if $r = 0$ then T still gets no PageRank at all. In fact, it is cut off from the rest of the Web and would be invisible to search engines. However, it is not hard for spam farmers to get a reasonable value for r. As one example, they create links to the spam farm from publicly accessible blogs, with messages like "I agree with you. See x123456.mySpamFarm.com." Moreover, if the number of pages in the bottom row is large, and the "tax" is distributed among all pages, then r will include the share of the tax that is given to these pages. That is why spam farmers use many pages in their structure, rather than just one or two.

3.4 Topic-Specific PageRank and Link Spam

A search engine needs to detect pages that are on the Web for the purpose of creating link spam. A useful tool is to compute the *TrustRank* of pages. Although the original definition is somewhat different, we may take the TrustRank to be the topic-specific PageRank computed with a teleport set consisting of only "trusted" pages. Two possible methods for selecting the set of trusted pages are:

1. Examine pages by hand and do an evaluation of their role on the Web. It is hard to automate this process, because spam farmers often copy the text of perfectly legitimate pages and populate their spam farm with pages containing that text plus the necessary links.

2. Start with a teleport set that is likely to contain relatively little spam. For example, it is generally believed that the set of university home pages form a good choice for a widely distributed set of trusted pages. In fact, it is likely that modern search engines routinely compute PageRank using a teleport set similar to this one.

Either of these approaches tends to assign lower PageRank to spam pages, because it is rare that a trusted page would link to a spam page. Since TrustRank, like normal PageRank, is computed with a positive taxation factor $1-\beta$, the trust imparted by a trusted page attenuates, the further we get from that trusted page. The TrustRank of pages may substitute for PageRank, when the search engine chooses pages in response to a query. So doing reduces the likelihood that spam pages will be offered to the queryer.

Another approach to detecting link-spam pages is to compute the *spam mass* of pages as follows:

a) Compute the ordinary PageRank, that is, using all pages as the teleport set.

b) Compute the TrustRank of all pages, using some reasonable set of trusted pages.

c) Compute the difference between the PageRank and TrustRank for each page. This difference is the *negative TrustRank*.

d) The spam mass of a page is the ratio of its negative TrustRank to its ordinary PageRank, that is, the fraction of its PageRank that appears to come from spam farms.

While TrustRank alone can bias the PageRank to minimize the effect of link spam, computing the spam mass also allows us to see where the link spam is coming from. Sites that have many pages with high spam mass may be owned by spam farmers, and a search engine can eliminate from its database all pages from such sites.

3.5 Exercises for Section 3

Exercise 3.1: Compute the topic-specific PageRank for Fig. 5, assuming

a) Only A is in the teleport set.

b) The teleport set is $\{A, B\}$.

Assume a taxation rate of 20%.

Exercise 3.2: Repeat Exercise 3.1 for the graph of Fig. 6.

Exercise 3.3: Repeat Exercise 3.1 for the graph of Fig. 7.

!! **Exercise 3.4:** Suppose we fix the taxation rate and compute the topic-specific PageRank for a graph G, using only node a as the teleport set. We then do the same using only another node b as the teleport set. Prove that the average of these PageRanks is the same as what we get if we repeated the calculation with $\{a, b\}$ as the teleport set.

!! **Exercise 3.5:** What is the generalization of Exercise 3.4 to a situation where there are two disjoint teleport sets S_1 and S_2, perhaps with different numbers of elements? That is, suppose we compute the PageRanks with just S_1 and then just S_2 as the teleport sets. How could we use these results to compute the PageRank with $S_1 \cup S_2$ as the teleport set?

4 Data Streams

We now turn to an extension of the ideas contained in the traditional DBMS to deal with *data streams*. As the Internet has made communication among machines routine, a class of applications has developed that stress the traditional model of a database system. Recall that a typical database system is primarily a repository of data. Input of data is done as part of the query language or a special data-load utility, and is assumed to occur at a rate controlled by the DBMS.

However, in some applications, the inputs arrive at a rate the DBMS cannot control. For example, Yahoo! may wish to record every "click," that is, every page request made by any user anywhere. The sequence of URL's representing these requests arrive at a very high rate that is determined only by the desires of Yahoo!'s customers.

4.1 Data-Stream-Management Systems

If we are to allow queries on such streams of data, we need some new mechanisms. While we may be able to store the data on high-rate streams, we cannot do so in a way that allows instantaneous queries using a language like SQL. Further, it is not even clear what some queries mean; for instance, how can we take the join of two streams, when we never can see the completed streams? The rough structure of a data-stream-management system (*DSMS*) is shown in Fig. 10.

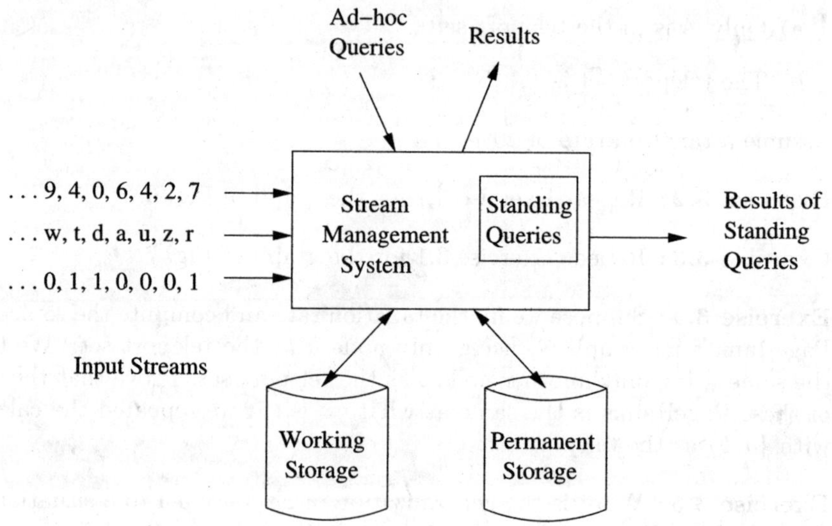

Figure 10: A data-stream-management system

The system accepts data streams as input, and also accepts queries. These queries may be of two kinds:

1. Conventional ad-hoc queries.

2. *Standing queries* that are stored by the system and run on the input stream(s) at all times.

Example 9: Whether ad-hoc or standing, queries in a DSMS need to be expressed so they can be answered using limited portions of the streams. As an example, suppose we are receiving streams of radiation levels from sensors around the world. While the DSMS cannot store and query streams from arbitrarily far back in time, it can store a *sliding window* of each input stream. It might be able to keep on disk, in the "working storage" referred to in Fig. 10, all readings from all sensors for the past 24 hours. Data from further back in time could be dropped, could be summarized (e.g., replaced by the daily average), or copied in its entirety to the permanent store (*archive*).

An ad-hoc query might ask for the average radiation level over the past hour for all locations in North Korea. We can answer this query, because we have all data from all streams over the past 24 hours in our working store. A standing query might ask for a notification if any reading on any stream exceeds a certain limit. As each data element of each stream enters the system, it is compared with the threshold, and an output is made if the entering value exceeds the threshold. This sort of query can be answered from the streams themselves, although we would need to examine the working store if, say, we asked to be alerted if the average over the past 5 minutes for any one stream exceeded the threshold. □

4.2 Stream Applications

Before addressing the mechanics of data-stream-management systems, let us look at some of the applications where the data is in the form of a stream or streams.

1. *Click Streams.* As we mentioned, a common source of streams is the clicks by users of a large Web site. A Web site might wish to analyze the clicks it receives for a number of reasons; an increase in clicks on a link may indicate that link is broken, or that it has become of much more interest recently. A search engine may want to analyze clicks on the links to ads that it shows, to determine which ads are most attractive.

2. *Packet Streams.* We may wish to analyze the sources and destinations of IP packets that pass through a switch. An unusual increase in packets for a destination may warn of a denial-of-service attack. Examination of the recent history of destinations may allow us to predict congestion in the network and to reroute packets accordingly.

3. *Sensor Data.* We also mentioned a hypothetical example of a network of radiation sensors. There are many kinds of sensors whose outputs need to be read and considered collectively, e.g., tsunami warning sensors that record ocean levels at subsecond frequencies or the signals that come from seismometers around the world, recording the shaking of the earth. Cities that have networks of security cameras can have the video from these cameras read and analyzed for threats.

4. *Satellite Data.* Satellites send back to earth incredible streams of data, often petabytes per day. Because scientists are reluctant to throw any of this data away, it is often stored in raw form in archival memory systems. These are half-jokingly referred to as "write-only memory." Useful products are extracted from the streams as they arrive and stored in more accessible storage places or distributed to scientists who have made standing requests for certain kinds of data.

5. *Financial Data.* Trades of stocks, commodities, and other financial instruments are reported as a stream of tuples, each representing one financial transaction. These streams are analyzed by software that looks for events or patterns that trigger actions by traders. The most successful traders have access to the largest amount of data and process it most quickly, because opportunities involving stock trades often last for only fractions of a second.

4.3 A Data-Stream Data Model

We shall now offer a data model useful for discussing algorithms on data streams. First, we shall assume the following about the streams themselves:

- Each stream consists of a sequence of tuples. The tuples have a fixed relation schema (list of attributes), just as the tuples of relations do. However, unlike relations, the sequence of tuples in a stream may be unbounded.

- Each tuple has an associated *arrival time*, at which time it becomes available to the data-stream-management system for processing. The DSMS has the option of placing it in the working storage or in the permanent storage, or of dropping the tuple from memory altogether. The tuple may also be processed in simple ways before storing it.

For any stream, we can define a *sliding window* (or just "window"), which is a set consisting of the most recent tuples to arrive. A window can be *time-based* with a constant τ, in which case it consists of the tuples whose arrival time is between the current time t and $t-\tau$. Or, a window can be *tuple-based*, in which case it consists of the most recent n tuples to arrive, for some fixed n.

We shall describe windows on a stream S by the notation $S\ [W]$, where W is the window description, either:

1. `Rows` n, meaning the most recent n tuples of the stream, or

2. `Range` τ, meaning all tuples that arrived within the previous amount of time τ.

Example 10: Let `Sensors(sensID, temp, time)` be a stream, each of whose tuples represent a temperature reading of `temp` at a certain `time` by the sensor named `sensID`. It might be more common for each sensor to produce its own stream, but all readings could also be merged into one stream if the data were accumulated outside the data-stream-management system. The expression

```
Sensors [Rows 1000]
```

describes a window on the `Sensors` stream consisting of the most recent 1000 tuples. The expression

```
Sensors [Range 10 Seconds]
```

describes a window on the same stream consisting of all tuples that arrived in the past 10 seconds. □

4.4 Converting Streams Into Relations

Windows allow us to convert streams into relations. That is, the window expressions as in Example 10 describe a relation at any time. The contents of the relation typically changes rapidly. For example, consider the expression `Sensors [Rows 1000]`. Each time a new tuple of `Sensors` arrives, it is inserted into the described relation, and the oldest of the tuples is deleted. For the expression `Sensors [Range 10 Seconds]`, we must insert tuples of the stream when they arrive and delete tuples 10 seconds after they arrive.

Window expressions can be used like relations in an extended SQL for streams. The following example suggests what such an extended SQL looks like.

Example 11: Suppose we would like to know, for each sensor, the highest recorded temperature to arrive at the DSMS in the past hour. We form the appropriate time-based window and query it as if it were an ordinary relation. The query looks like:

```
SELECT sensID, MAX(temp)
FROM Sensors [Range 1 Hour]
GROUP BY sensID;
```

This query can be issued as an ad-hoc query, in which case it is executed once, based on the window that exists at the instant the query is issued. Of course the DSMS must have made available to the query processor a window on `Sensors` of at least one hour's length.[2] The same query could be a standing query, in which case the current result relation should be maintained as if it were a materialized view that changes from time to time. In Section 4.5 we shall consider an alternative way to represent the result of this query as a standing query. □

Window relations can be combined with other window relations, or with "ordinary" relations — those that do not come from streams. An example will suggest what is possible.

Example 12: Suppose that our DSMS has the stream `Sensors` as an input stream and also maintains in its working storage an ordinary relation

```
Calibrate(sensID, mult, add)
```

[2]Strictly speaking, the DSMS only needs to have retained enough information to answer the query. For example, it could still answer the query at any time if it threw away every tuple for which there was a later reading from the same sensor with a higher temperature.

which gives a multiplicative factor and additive term that are used to correct the reading from each sensor. The query

```
SELECT MAX(mult*temp + add)
FROM Sensors [Range 1 Hour], Calibrate
WHERE Sensors.sensID = Calibrate.sensID;
```

finds the highest, properly calibrated temperature reported by any sensor in the past hour. Here, we have joined a window relation from `Sensors` with the ordinary relation `Calibrate`. □

We can also compute joins of window-relations. The following query illustrates a self-join by means of a subquery, but all the SQL tools for expressing joins are available.

Example 13: Suppose we wanted to give, for each sensor, its maximum temperature over the past hour (as in Example 11), but we also wanted the resulting tuples to give the most recent time at which that maximum temperature was recorded. Figure 11 is one way to write the query using window relations.

```
SELECT s.sensID, s.temp, s.time
FROM Sensors [Range 1 Hour] s
WHERE NOT EXISTS (
    SELECT * FROM Sensors [Range 1 Hour]
    WHERE sensID = s.sensID AND (
        temp > s.temp OR
            (temp = s.temp AND time > s.time)
    )
);
```

Figure 11: Including time with the maximum temperature readings of sensors

That is, the subquery checks if there is not another tuple in the window-relation `Sensors [Range 1 Hour]` that refers to the same sensor as the tuple s, and has either a higher temperature or has the same temperature but a more recent time. If no such tuple exists, then the tuple s is part of the result. □

4.5 Converting Relations Into Streams

When we issue queries such as that of Example 11 as standing queries, the resulting relations change frequently. Maintaining these relations as materialized views may result in a lot of effort making insertions and deletions that no one ever looks at. An alternative is to convert the relation that is the result of the query back into streams, which may be processed like any other streams.

For example, we can issue an ad-hoc query to construct the query result at a particular time when we are interested in its value.

If R is a relation, define `Istream(`R`)` to be the stream consisting of each tuple that is inserted into R. This tuple appears in the stream at the time the insertion occurs. Similarly, define `Dstream(`R`)` to be the stream of tuples deleted from R; each tuple appears in this stream at the moment it is deleted. An update to a tuple can be represented by an insertion and deletion at the same time.

Example 14: Let R be the relation constructed by the query of Example 13, that is, the relation that has, for each sensor, the maximum temperature it recorded in any tuple that arrived in the past hour, and the time at which that temperature was most recently recorded. Then `Istream(`R`)` has a tuple for every event in which a new tuple is added to R. Note that there are two events that add tuples to R:

1. A `Sensors` tuple arrives with a temperature that is at least as high as any tuple currently in R with the same sensor ID. This tuple is inserted into R and becomes an element of `Istream(`R`)` at that time.

2. The current maximum temperature for a sensor i was recorded an hour ago, and there has been at least one tuple for sensor i in the `Sensors` stream in the past hour. In that case, the new tuple for R and for `Istream(`R`)` is the `Sensors` tuple for sensor i that arrived in the past hour, but no other tuple for i that also arrived in the past hour has:

   (a) A higher temperature, or

   (b) The same temperature and a more recent time.

The same two events may generate tuples for the stream `Dstream(`R`)` as well. In (1) above, if there was any other tuple in R for the same sensor, then that tuple is deleted from R and becomes an element of `Dstream(`R`)`. In (2), the hour-old tuple of R for sensor i is deleted from R and becomes an element of `Dstream(`R`)`. □

If we compute the Istream and Dstream for a relation like that constructed by the query of Fig. 11, then we do not have to maintain that relation as a materialized view. Rather, we can query its Istream and Dstream to answer queries about the relation when we wish.

Example 15: Suppose we form the Istream I and the Dstream D for the relation R of Fig. 11. When we wish, we can issue an ad-hoc query to these streams. For instance, suppose we want to find the maximum temperature recorded by sensor 100 that arrived over the past hour. That will be the temperature in the tuple in I for sensor 100 that:

1. Has a `time` in the past hour.

2. Was not deleted from R (i.e., is not in D restricted to the past hour).

This query can be written as shown in Fig. 12. The keyword `Now` represents the current time.

Note that we must check that a tuple of I both arrived in the past hour and that it has a timestamp within the past hour. To see why these conditions are not the same, consider the case of a tuple of I that arrived in the past hour, because it became the maximum temperature t for sensor 100 thirty minutes ago. However, that temperature itself has an associated `time` that is eighty minutes ago. The reason is that a temperature higher than t was recorded by sensor 100 ninety minutes ago. It wasn't until 30 minutes ago that t became the highest temperature for sensor 100 in the sixty minutes preceding. □

```
(SELECT * FROM I [Range 1 Hour]
 WHERE sensID = 100 AND
       time >= [Now - 1 Hour])
     EXCEPT
(SELECT * FROM D [Range 1 Hour]
 WHERE sensID = 100);
```

Figure 12: Querying an Istream and a Dstream

4.6 Exercises for Section 4

Exercise 4.1: Using the `Sensors` stream from Example 11, write the following queries:

a) Find the oldest tuple (lowest `time`) among the last 1000 tuples to arrive.

b) Find those sensors for which at least two readings have arrived in the past minute.

! c) Find those sensors for which more readings arrived in the past minute than arrived between one and two minutes ago.

Exercise 4.2: Following the example of sensor data from this section, suppose that the following temperature-time readings are generated by sensor 100, and each arrives at the DSMS at the time generated: $(80,0)$, $(70,50)$, $(60,70)$, $(65,100)$. Times are in minutes. If R is the query of Fig. 11, What are the tuples of `Istream(`R`)` and `Dstream(`R`)`, and at what time is each of these tuples generated?

5 Data Mining of Streams

When processing streams, there are a number of problems that become quite hard, even though the analogous problems for relations are easy. In this section, we shall concentrate on representing the contents of windows more succinctly than by listing the current set of tuples in the window. Surely, we are not then able to answer all possible queries about the window, but if we know what kinds of queries we are expected to support, we might be able to compress the window and answer those queries. Another possibility is that we cannot compress the window and answer our selected queries exactly, but we can guarantee to be able to answer them within a fixed error bound.

We shall consider two fundamental problems of this type. First, we consider binary streams (streams of 0's and 1's), and ask whether we can answer queries about the number of 1's in any time range contained within the window. Obviously, if we keep the exact sequence of bits and their timestamps, we can manage to answer those questions exactly. However, it is possible to compress the data significantly and still answer this family of queries within a fixed error bound. Second, we address the problem of counting the number of different values within a sliding window. Here is another family of problems that cannot be answered exactly without keeping the data in the window exactly. However, we shall see that a good approximation is possible using much less space than the size of the window.

5.1 Motivation

Suppose we wish to have a stream with a window of a billion integers. Such a window could fit in a large main memory of four gigabytes, and it would have no trouble fitting on disk. Surely, if we are only interested in recent data from the stream, a billion tuples should suffice. But what if there are a million such streams?

For example, we might be trying to integrate the data from a million sensors placed around a city. Or we might be given a stream of market baskets, and try to compute the frequency, over any time range, of all sets of items contained in those baskets. In that case, we need a window for each set, with bits indicating whether or not that set was contained in each of the baskets.

In situations such as these, the amount of space needed to store all the windows exceeds what is available using disk storage. Moreover, for efficient response, we might want to keep all windows in main memory. Then, a few windows of length a billion, or a few thousand windows of length a million exceed what even a large main memory can hold. We are thus led to consider compressing the data in windows. Unfortunately, even some very simple queries cannot be answered if we compress the window, as the next example suggests.

Example 16: Suppose we have a sliding window that stores stream elements that are integers, and we have a standing query that asks for an alert any time the sum of the integers in the window exceeds a certain threshold t. We thus only need to maintain the sum of the integers in the window in order to answer this query. When a new integer comes in, we can add it to the sum.

However, at certain times, integers leave the window and must be subtracted from the sum. If the window is tuple-based, then we must subtract the last integer from the sum each time a new integer arrives. If the window is time-based, then when the time of an integer in the window expires, it must be subtracted from the sum.

Unfortunately, if we don't know exactly what integers are in the window, or we don't know their order of arrival (for tuple-based windows) or their time of arrival (for time-based windows), then we cannot maintain the sum properly. To see why we cannot compress, observe the following. If there is any compression at all, then two different window-contents, W_1 and W_2, must have the same compressed value. Since $W_1 \neq W_2$, there is some time t at which the integers for time t are different in W_1 and W_2. Consider what happens when t is the oldest time in the window, and another integer arrives. We must have to do different subtractions from the sum, to maintain the sums for W_1 and W_2. But since the compressed representation does not tell us which of W_1 and W_2 is the true contents of the window, we cannot maintain the proper sum in both cases. □

Example 16 tells us that we cannot compress the sum of a sliding window if we are to get exact answers for the sum at all times. However, suppose we are willing to accept an approximate sum. Then there are many options, and we shall look at a very simple one here. We can group the stream elements into groups of 100; say the first hundred elements of the stream ever to arrive, then the next hundred, and so on. Each group is represented by the sum of elements in that group. Thus, we have a compression factor of 100; i.e., the window is represented by $1/100^{\text{th}}$ of the number of integers that are theoretically "in" in window.

Suppose for simplicity that we have a tuple-based window, and the number of tuples in the window is a multiple of 100. When the number of stream elements that have arrived is also a multiple of 100, then we can get the sum of the elements in the window exactly, just by summing the sums of the groups.

Suppose another integer arrives. That integer starts another group, so we keep it as the sum of that group. Now, we can only estimate the sum of all the integers in the window. The reason is that the last group has only 99 of its 100 members in the window, and we don't know the value of the integer, from the last group, that is no longer in the window.

The best estimate of the deleted integer is 1% of the sum of the last group. That is, we estimate the sum of all the integers in the window by taking 0.99 times the recorded sum of the last group, plus the recorded sums of all the other groups.

Forty-nine arrivals later, there are fifty integers in the group formed from the most recent arrivals, and the sum of the window includes exactly half of the last group. Our best estimate of the sum of the fifty integers of the last group that remain in the window is half the group's sum. After another fifty arrivals, the most recent group is complete, and the last group has left the window entirely. We therefore can drop the recorded sum of the last group and prepare to start another group with the next arrival.

Intuitively, this method gives a "good" approximation to the sum. If integers are nonnegative, and there is not too much variance in the values of the integers, then assuming that the missing integers are average for their group is a close estimate. Unfortunately, if the variance is high, or integers can be both positive and negative, there is no worst-case bound on how bad the estimate of the sum can be. Consider what happens if integers can range from minus infinity to plus infinity, and the last group consists of fifty large negative numbers followed by fifty large positive numbers, such that the sum for the group is 0. Then the estimate of the contribution of the last group, when only half of it is in the window is zero, but in fact the true sum is very large — perhaps much larger than the sum of all the integers that followed them in the stream.

One can modify this compression approach in various ways. For example, we can increase the size of the groups to reduce the amount of space taken by the representation. Doing so increases the error in the estimate, however. In the next section, we shall see how to get a bounded error rate, while getting significant compression, for the binary version of this problem, where stream elements are either 0 or 1. The same method extends to streams of positive integers with an upper bound, if we treat each position in the binary representation of the integers as a bit stream (see Exercise 5.3).

5.2 Counting Bits

In this section, we shall examine the following problem. Assume that the length of the sliding window is N, and the stream consists of bits, 0 or 1. We assume that the stream began at some time in the past, and we associate a *time* with each arriving bit that is its position in the stream; i.e., the first to arrive is at time 1, the next at time 2, and so on.

Our queries, which may be asked at any time, are of the form "how many 1's are there in the most recent k bits?" where k is any integer between 1 and

N. Obviously, if we stored the window with no compression, we could answer any such query exactly, although we would have to sum the last k bits to do so. Since k could be very large, the time needed to answer queries could itself be large. Suppose, however, that along with the bits themselves we stored the sums of certain groups of consecutive bits — groups of size 2, 4, 8,.... We could then decrease the time needed to answer the queries exactly to $O(\log N)$. However, if we also stored sums of these groups, then even more space would be needed than what we use to store the window elements themselves.

An attractive alternative is to keep an amount of information about the window that is logarithmic in N, and yet be able to answer any query of the type described above, with a fractional error that is as low as we like. Formally, for any $\epsilon > 0$, we can produce an estimate that is in the range of $1 - \epsilon$ to $1 + \epsilon$ times the true result. We shall give the method for $\epsilon = 1/2$, and we leave the generalization to any $\epsilon > 0$ as an exercise with hints (see Exercise 5.4).

Buckets

To describe the algorithm for approximate counting of 1's, we need to define a *bucket* of size m; it is a section of the window that contains exactly m 1's. The window will be partitioned completely into such buckets, except possibly for some 0's that are not part of any bucket. Thus, we can represent any such bucket by (m, t), where m is the size of the bucket, and t is the time of the most recent 1 belonging to that bucket. There are a number of rules that we shall follow in determining the buckets that represent the current window:

1. The size of every bucket is a power of 2.
2. As we look back in time, the sizes of the buckets never decrease.
3. For $m = 1, 2, 4, 8, \ldots$ up to some largest-size bucket, there are one or two buckets of each size, never zero and never more than two.
4. Each bucket begins somewhere within the current window, although the last (largest) bucket maybe partially outside the window.

Figure 13 suggests what a window partitioned into buckets might look like.

Representing Buckets

We shall see that under these assumptions, a bucket can be represented by $O(\log N)$ bits. Further, there are at most $O(\log N)$ buckets that must be represented. Thus, a window of length N can be represented in space $O(\log^2 N)$, rather than $O(N)$ bits. To see why only $O(\log^2 N)$ bits are needed, observe the following:

- A bucket (m, t) can be represented in $O(\log N)$ bits. First, m, the size of a bucket, can never get above N. Moreover, m is always a power of 2, so

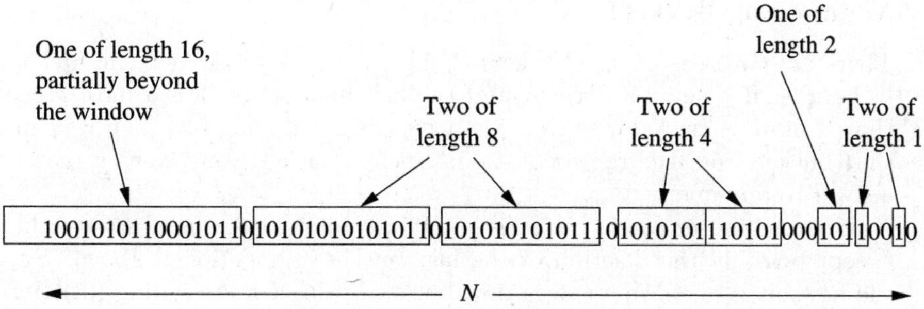

Figure 13: Bucketizing a sliding window

we don't have to represent m itself; rather we can represent $\log_2 m$. That requires $O(\log\log N)$ bits. However, we also need to represent t, the time of the most recent 1 in the bucket. In principle, t can be an arbitrarily large integer, but it is sufficient to represent t modulo N, since we know t has to be in the window of length N. Thus, $O(\log N)$ bits suffice to represent both m and t. So that we can know the time of newly arriving 1's, we maintain the current time, but also represent it modulo N, so $O(\log N)$ bits suffice for this count.

- There can be only $O(\log N)$ buckets. The sum of the sizes of the buckets is at most N, and there can be at most two of any size. If there are more than $2 + 2\log_2 N$ buckets, then the largest one is of size at least $2 \times 2^{\log_2 N}$, which is $2N$. There must be a smaller bucket of half that size, so the supposed largest bucket is certainly completely outside the window.

Answering Queries Approximately, Using Buckets

Notice that we can answer a query to count the 1's in the most recent k bits approximately, as follows. Find the least recent bucket B whose most recent bit arrived within the last k time units. All later buckets are entirely within the range of k time units. We know exactly how many 1's are in each of these buckets; it is their size. The bucket B is partially in the query's range, and partially outside it. We cannot tell how much is in and how much is out, so we choose half its size as the best guess.

Example 17: Suppose $k = N$ and the window is represented by the buckets of Fig. 13. We see two buckets of size 1 and one of size 2, which implies four 1's. Then, there are two buckets of size 4, giving another eight 1's, and two buckets of size 4, implying another sixteen 1's. Finally, the last bucket, of size 16, is partially in the window, so we add another 8 to the estimate. The approximate answer is thus $2 \times 1 + 1 \times 2 + 2 \times 4 + 2 \times 8 + 8 = 36$. □

Maintaining Buckets

There are two reasons the buckets change as new bits arrive. The first is easy to handle: if a new bit arrives, and the last bucket now has a most recent bit that is more than N lower than the time of the arriving bit, then we can drop that bucket from the representation. Such a bucket can never be part of the answer to any query.

Now, suppose a new bit arrives. If the bit is a 0, there are no changes, except possibly the deletion of the last bucket as mentioned above. Suppose the new bit is a 1. We create a new bucket of size 1 representing just that bit. However, we may now have three buckets of size 1, which violates the rule that there can be only one or two buckets of each size. Thus, we enter a recursive combining-buckets phase.

Suppose we have three consecutive buckets of size m, say (m, t_1), (m, t_2), and (m, t_3), where $t_1 < t_2 < t_3$. We combine the two least recent of the buckets, (m, t_1) and (m, t_2), into one bucket of size $2m$. The time of the most recent bit for the combined bucket is that of the most recent bit for the more recent of the two combined buckets. That is, (m, t_1) and (m, t_2) are replaced by a bucket $(2m, t_2)$.

This combination may cause there to be three consecutive buckets of size $2m$, if there were two of that size previously. Thus, we apply the combination algorithm recursively, with the size now $2m$. It can take no more than $O(\log N)$ time to do all the necessary combinations.

Example 18: Suppose we have the list of bucket sizes implied by Fig. 13, that is, $16, 8, 8, 4, 4, 2, 1, 1$. If a 1 arrives, we have three buckets of size 1, so we combine the two earlier 1's, to get the list $16, 8, 8, 4, 4, 2, 2, 1$. As this combination gives us only two buckets of size 2, no recursive combining is needed. If another 1 arrives, no combining at all is needed, and we get sequence of bucket sizes $16, 8, 8, 4, 4, 2, 2, 1, 1$. When the next 1 arrives, we must combine 1's, leaving $16, 8, 8, 4, 4, 2, 2, 2, 1$. Now we have three 2's, so we recursively combine the least recent of them, leaving $16, 8, 8, 4, 4, 4, 2, 1$. Now there are three 4's, and the least recent of them are combined to give $16, 8, 8, 8, 4, 2, 1$. Again, we must combine the least recent of the three 8's, giving us the final list of bucket sizes $16, 16, 8, 4, 2, 1$. □

A Bound on the Error

Suppose that in answer to a query the last bucket whose represented 1's are in the range of the query has size m. Since we estimate $m/2$ for its contribution to the count, we cannot be off by more than $m/2$. The correct answer is at least the sum of all the smaller buckets, and there is at least one bucket of each size $m/2, m/4, m/8, \ldots, 1$. This sum is $m - 1$. Thus, the fractional error is at most $(m/2)/(m - 1)$, or approximately 50%. In fact, if we look more carefully, 50% is an exact upper bound. The reason is that when we underestimate (i.e., all m 1's from the last bucket are in the query range), the error is no more than 1/3.

When we overestimate, we can really only overestimate by $(m/2) - 1$, not $m/2$, since we know that at least one 1 contributes to the query. Since $(m/2) - 1$ is less than half $m - 1$, the error is truly upper bounded by 50%.

5.3 Counting the Number of Distinct Elements

We now turn to another important problem: counting the distinct elements in a (window on) a stream. The problem has a number of applications, such as the following:

1. The popularity of a Web site is often measured by unique visitors per month or similar statistics. Think of the logins at a site like Yahoo! as a stream. Using a window of size one month, we want to know how many different logins there are.

2. Suppose a crawler is examining sites. We can think of the words encountered on the pages as forming a stream. If a site is legitimate, the number of distinct words will fall in a range that is neither too high (few repetitions of words) nor too low (excessive repetition of words). Falling outside that range suggests that the site could be artificial, e.g., a spam site.

To get an exact answer to the question, we must store the entire window and apply the δ operator to it, in order to find the distinct elements. However, we don't want to *see* the distinct elements; we just want to know how many there are. Even getting this count requires that we maintain the window in its entirety, but we can get an approximation to the count by several different methods. The following technique actually computes the number of distinct elements in the entire stream, rather than in a finite window. However, we can, if we like, restart the process periodically, e.g., once a month to count unique visitors or each time we visit a new site (to count distinct words).

The necessary tools are a number N that is certain to be at least as large as the number of distinct values in the stream, and a hash function h that maps values to $\log_2 N$ bits. We maintain a number R that is initially 0. As each stream value v arrives, do the following:

1. Compute $h(v)$.

2. Let r be the number of trailing 0's in $h(v)$.

3. If $r > R$, set R to be r.

Then, the estimate of the number of distinct values seen so far is 2^R. To see why this estimate makes sense, note the following.

a) The probability that $h(v)$ ends in at least i 0's is 2^{-i}.

b) If there are m distinct elements in the stream so far, the probability that $R > i$ is $(1 - 2^{-i})^m$.

c) If i is much less than $\log_2 m$, then this probability is close to 1, and if i is much greater than $\log_2 m$, then this probability is close to 0.

d) Thus, R will frequently be near $\log_2 m$, and 2^R, our estimate, will frequently be near m.

While the above reasoning is comforting, it is actually inaccurate, to say the least. The reason is that the expected value of 2^R is infinite, or at least it is as large as possible given that N is finite. The intuitive reason is that, for large R, when R increases by 1, the probability of R being that large halves, but the value of R doubles, so each possible value of R contributes the same to the expected value.

It is therefore necessary to get around the fact that there will occasionally be a value of R that is so large it biases the estimate of m upwards. While we shall not go into the exact justification, we can avoid this bias by:

1. Take many estimates of R, using different hash functions.

2. Group these estimates into small groups and take the median of each group. Doing so eliminates the effect of occasional large R's.

3. Take the average of the medians of the groups.

5.4 Exercises for Section 5

Exercise 5.1: Starting with the window of Fig. 13, suppose that the next ten bits to arrive are all 1's. What will be the sequence of buckets at that time?

Exercise 5.2: What buckets are used in Fig. 13 to answer queries of the form "how many 1's in the most recent k bits?" if k is (a) 10 (b) 15 (c) 20? What are the estimates for each of these queries? How close are the estimates?

! **Exercise 5.3:** Suppose that we have a stream of integers in the range 0 to 1023. How can you adapt the method of Section 5.2 to estimate the sum of the integers in a window of size N, keeping the error to 50%? *Hint*: treat each of the ten bits that represent an integer as a separate stream.

! **Exercise 5.4:** We can modify the algorithm of Section 5.2 to use buckets whose sizes are powers of 2, but there are between p and $p+1$ buckets of each size, for a chosen integer $p \geq 1$. As before, sizes do not decrease as we go further back in time.

a) Give the recursive rule for combining buckets when there are too many buckets of a given size.

b) Show that the fractional error of this scheme is at most $1/2p$.

Exercise 5.5: Suppose that we wish to estimate the number of distinct values in a stream of integers. The integers are in the range 0 to 1023. We'll use the following hash functions, each of which hashes to a 9-bit integer:

a) $h_1(v) = v$ modulo 512.

b) $h_2(v) = v + 159$ modulo 512.

c) $h_3(v) = v + 341$ modulo 512.

Compute the estimate of the number of distinct values in the following stream, using each of these hash functions:

$$24, 45, 102, 24, 78, 222, 45, 24, 670, 78, 999, 576, 222, 24$$

Exercise 5.6: In Example 11 we observed that if all we wanted was the maximum of N temperature readings in a sliding window of time-temperature tuples, then when a reading of t arrives, we can delete immediately any earlier reading that is smaller than t.

! a) Does this rule always compress the data in the window?

!! b) Suppose temperatures are real numbers chosen uniformly and at random from some fixed range of values. On average, how many tuples will be retained, as a function of N?

6 Summary

- *Search Engines*: A search engine requires a crawler to gather information about pages and a query engine to answer search queries.

- *Crawlers*: A crawler consists of one or more processes that visit Web pages and follow links found in those pages. The crawler must maintain a repository of pages already visited, so it does not revisit the same page too frequently. Shingling and minhashing can be used to detect duplicate pages with different URL's.

- *Limiting the Crawl*: Crawlers normally limit the depth to which they will search, declining to follow links from pages that are too far from their root page or pages. They also can prioritize the search to visit preferentially pages that are estimated to be popular.

- *Preparing Crawled Pages to Be Searched*: The search engine creates an inverted index on the words of the crawled pages. The index may also include information about the role of the word (e.g., is it part of a header?), and the index for each word may be represented by a bit-vector indicating on which pages the word appears.

- *Answering Search Queries*: A search query normally consists of a set of words. The query engine uses the inverted index to find the Web pages containing all these words. The pages are then ranked, using a formula that is determined by each search engine, but typically favors pages with close occurrences of the words, use of the words in important places (e.g., headers), and favors important pages using a measure such as PageRank.

- *The Transition Matrix of the Web*: This matrix is an important analytic tool for estimating the importance of Web pages. There is a row and column for each page, and the column for page j has $1/r$ in the ith row if page i is one of r pages with links from page j, and 0 otherwise.

- *PageRank*: The PageRank of Web pages is the principal eigenvector of the transition matrix of the Web. If there are n pages, we can compute the PageRank vector by starting with a vector of length n, and repeatedly multiplying the current vector by the transition matrix of the Web.

- *Taxation of PageRank*: Because of Web artifacts such as dead ends (pages without out-links) and spider traps (sections of the Web that cannot be exited), it is normal to introduce a small tax, say 15%, and redistribute that fraction of a page's PageRank equally among all pages, after each matrix-vector multiplication.

- *Teleport Sets*: Instead of redistributing the tax equally among all pages during an iteration of the PageRank computation, we can distribute the tax only among a subset of the pages, called the teleport set. Then, the computation of PageRank simulates a walker on the graph of the Web who normally follows a randomly chosen out-link from their current page, but with a small probability instead jumps to a random member of the teleport set.

- *Topic-Specific PageRank*: One application of the teleport-set idea is to pick a teleport set consisting of a set of pages known to be about a certain topic. Then, the PageRank will measure not only the importance of the page in general, but to what extent it is relevant to the selected topic.

- *Link Spam*: Spam farmers create large collections of Web pages whose sole purpose is to increase the PageRank of certain target pages, and thus make them more likely to be displayed by a search engine. One way to combat such spam farms is to compute PageRank using a teleport set consisting of known, trusted pages — those that are unlikely to be spam.

- *Data Streams*: A data stream is a sequence of tuples arriving at a fixed place, typically at a rate so fast as to make processing and storage in its entirety difficult. Examples include streams of data from satellites and click streams of requests at a Web site.

✦ *Data-Stream-Management Systems*: A DSMS accepts data in the form of streams. It maintains working storage and permanent (archival) storage. Working storage is limited, although it may involve disks. The DSMS accepts both ad-hoc and standing queries about the streams.

✦ *Sliding Windows*: To query a stream, it helps to be able to talk about portions of the stream as a relation. A sliding window is the most recent portion of the stream. A window can be time-based, in which case it consists of all tuples arriving over some fixed time interval, or tuple-based, in which case it is a fixed number of the most recently arrived tuples.

✦ *Compressing Windows*: If the DSMS must maintain large windows on many streams, it can run out of main memory, or even disk space. Depending on the family of queries that will be asked about the window, it may be possible to compress the window so it uses significantly less space. However, in many cases, we can compress a window only if we are willing to accept approximate answers to queries.

✦ *Counting Bits*: A fundamental problem that allows a space/accuracy trade-off is that of counting the number of 1's in a window of a bit-stream. We partition the window into buckets representing exponentially increasing numbers of 1's. The last bucket may be partially outside the window, leading to inaccuracy in the count of 1's, but the error is limited to a fixed fraction of the count and can be any $\epsilon > 0$.

✦ *Counting Distinct Elements*: Another important stream problem is counting the number of distinct elements in the stream without keeping a table of all the distinct elements ever seen. An unbiased estimate of this number can be made by picking a hash function, hashing elements to bit strings, and estimating the number of distinct elements to be 2 raised to the power that is the largest number of consecutive 0's ever seen at the end of the hash function of any stream element.

7 References

References [3] and [8] summarize issues in crawling, based on the Stanford WebBase system. An analysis of the degree to which crawlers reach the entire Web was given in [15].

PageRank and the Google search engine are described in [6] and [16]. An alternative formulation of Web structure, often referred to as "hubs and authorities," is in [14].

Topic-specific PageRank, as described here, is from [12]. TrustRank and combating link spam are discussed in [11].

Two on-line histories of search engines are [17] and [18].

The study of data streams as a data model can be said to begin with the "chronicle data model" of [13]. References [7] and [2] describe the architecture of early data-stream management systems. Reference [5] surveys data-stream systems.

The algorithm described here for approximate counting of 1's in a sliding window is from [9].

The problem of estimating the number of distinct elements in a stream originated with [10] and [4]. The method described here is from [1], which also generalizes the technique to estimate higher moments of the data, e.g., the sum of the squares of the number of occurrences of each element.

1. N. Alon, Y. Matias, and M. Szegedy, "The space complexity of approximating frequency moments," *Twenty-Eighth ACM Symp. on Theory of Computing* (1996), pp. 20–29.

2. A. Arasu, S. Babu, and J. Widom, "The CQL continuous query language: semantic foundations and query execution,"

   `http://dbpubs.stanford.edu/pub/2003-67`

   Dept. of Computer Science, Stanford Univ., Stanford CA, 2003.

3. A. Arasu, J. Cho, H. Garcia-Molina, A. Paepcke, and S. Raghavan, "Searching the Web," *ACM Trans. on Internet Technologies* **1**:1 (2001), pp. 2–43.

4. M. M. Astrahan, M. Schkolnick, and K.-Y. Whang, "Approximating the number of unique values of an attribute without sorting," *Information Systems* **12**:1 (1987), pp. 11-15.

5. B. Babcock, S. Babu, M. Datar, R. Motwani, and J. Widom, "Models and issues in data stream systems," *Twenty-First ACM Symp. on Principles of Database Systems* (2002), pp. 261–272.

6. S. Brin and L. Page, "Anatomy of a large-scale hypertextual Web search engine," *Proc. Seventh Intl. World-Wide Web Conference*, 1998.

7. D. Carney, U. Cetintemel, M. Cherniack, C. Convey, S. Lee, G. Seidman, M. Stonebraker, N. Tatbul, and S. Zdonik, "Monitoring streams — a new class of data management applications," *Proc. Intl. Conf. on Very Large Database Systems* (2002), pp. 215–226.

8. J. Cho, H. Garcia-Molina, T. Haveliwala, W. Lam, A. Paepcke, S. Raghavan, and G. Wesley, "Stanford WebBase components and applications," *ACM Trans. on Internet Technologies* **6**:2 (2006), pp. 153–186.

9. M. Datar, A. Gionis, P. Indyk, and R. Motwani, "Maintaining stream statistics over sliding windows," *SIAM J. Computing* **31** (2002), pp. 1794–1813.

10. P. Flagolet and G. N. Martin, "Probabilistic counting for database applications," *J. Computer and System Sciences* **31**:2 (1985), pp. 182–209.

11. Z. Gyongyi, H. Garcia-Molina, and J. Pedersen, "Combating Web spam with TrustRank," *Proc. Intl. Conf. on Very Large Database Systems* (2004), pp. 576–587.

12. T. Haveliwala, "Topic-sensitive PageRank," *Proc. Eleventh Intl. World-Wide Web Conference* (2002).

13. H. V. Jagadish, I. S. Mumick, and A Silberschatz, "View maintenance issues for the chronicle data model," *Fourteenth ACM Symp. on Principles of Database Systems* (1995), pp. 113–124.

14. J. Kleinberg, "Authoritative sources in a hyperlinked environment," *J. ACM* **46**:5 (1999), pp. 604–632.

15. S. Lawrence and C. L. Giles, "Searching the World-Wide Web," *Science* **280**(5360):98, 1998.

16. L. Page, S. Brin, R. Motwani, and T. Winograd, "The PageRank citation ranking: bringing order to the Web," unpublished manuscript, Dept. of CS, Stanford Univ., Stanford CA, 1998.

17. L. Underwood, "A brief history of search engines," `www.webreference.com/authoring/search_history`

18. A. Wall, "Search engine history," `www.searchenginehistory.com`.

Index

Page references followed by "f" indicate illustrated figures or photographs; followed by "t" indicates a table.

B

C

D

E

F

J

K

L

M

N

O

P

Q

R

S

T

U

V

W

X

Y

Z